M000305155

MISSION:
POSSIBLE

Ship To:
Shelly Chen
1030 Columbia Ave
227
Claremont, CA 91711-3905
Order ID 104-9335023-4110656

Shipping Address
1030 Columbia Ave #227
Claremont, CA 91711-3905

Order Date
Jan 19, 2012
Standard

Lutheran
Community
Services

www.lcsnw.org

Handbook of
ASIAN AMERICAN
PSYCHOLOGY

SECOND EDITION

EDITORS

Frederick T. L. Leong
Michigan State University

Arpana G. Inman
Lehigh University

Angela Ebreo
University of Illinois, Chicago

Lawrence Hsin Yang
Columbia University

Lisa Kinoshita
Stanford University School of Medicine

Michi Fu
Asian Pacific Family Center of Pacific Clinics

SAGE Publications
Thousand Oaks ▪ London ▪ New Delhi

Copyright © 2007 by Sage Publications, Inc.

All rights reserved. No part of this book may be reproduced or utilized in any form or by any means, electronic or mechanical, including photocopying, recording, or by any information storage and retrieval system, without permission in writing from the publisher.

For information:

Sage Publications, Inc.
2455 Teller Road
Thousand Oaks, California 91320
E-mail: order@sagepub.com

Sage Publications Ltd.
1 Oliver's Yard
55 City Road
London EC1Y 1SP
United Kingdom

Sage Publications India Pvt. Ltd.
B-42, Panchsheel Enclave
Post Box 4109
New Delhi 110 017 India

Printed in the United States of America on acid-free paper

Library of Congress Cataloging-in-Publication Data

Handbook of Asian American psychology / editors, Frederick T. L. Leong . . . [et al.].—2nd ed.
    p. cm.
Rev. ed. of: Handbook of Asian American psychology / Lee C. Lee, Nolan W.S. Zane, editors.
Includes bibliographical references and index.
ISBN 1–4129–4133–4 (cloth)—ISBN 1–4129–2467–7 (pbk.)
    1. Asian Americans—Psychology. 2. Asian Americans—Social conditions.
I. Leong, Frederick T. L. II. Title.
E184.A75H36 2006
155.8'495073—dc22

                                                        2006004935

07   08   09   10   11   10   10   9   8   7   6   5   4   3   2   1

Acquiring Editor:	Cheri Dellelo
Editorial Assistant:	Karen Ehrmann
Production Editor:	Sanford Robinson
Copy Editor:	Colleen Brennan
Typesetter:	C&M Digitals (P) Ltd.
Indexer:	Kathleen Paparchontis
Cover Designer:	Edgar Abarca

CONTENTS

Foreword   ix
Richard M. Suinn

1. Introduction and Overview   1
Frederick T. L. Leong, Arpana Inman, Angela Ebreo,
Lawrence Hsin Yang, Lisa M. Kinoshita, and Michi Fu

PART I: HISTORICAL, CONCEPTUAL,
AND METHODOLOGICAL ISSUES   **9**

2. History and Future of Asian American Psychology   11
Frederick T. L. Leong, Sumie Okazaki, and E. J. R. David

3. Theoretical and Conceptual Models: Toward
Asian Americanist Psychology   29
Sumie Okazaki, Richard M. Lee, and Stanley Sue

4. Conducting Research With Diverse Asian American Groups   47
Kevin M. Chun, Osvaldo F. Morera, Jolynne D. Andal,
and Monica C. Skewes

PART II: LIFE COURSE DEVELOPMENT   **67**

5. Asian American and Pacific Islander Families: Resiliency
and Life-Span Socialization in a Cultural Context   69
Barbara W. K. Yee, Barbara D. DeBaryshe, Sylvia Yuen,
Su Yeong Kim, and Hamilton I. McCubbin

6. Understanding Asian American Youth Development:
A Social Ecological Perspective   87
Ly Nguyen and Larke Nahme Huang

7. Asian Americans' Educational Experiences   105
Vivian Tseng, Ruth K. Chao, and Inna Artati Padmawidjaja

8. Ethnic Identity   125
Sapna Cheryan and Jeanne L. Tsai

9. Acculturation and Enculturation 141
Bryan S. K. Kim

10. Career Development and Vocational Behaviors of Asian Americans 159
Frederick T. L. Leong and Arpana Gupta

PART III: SPECIFIC POPULATIONS **179**

11. The Psychology and Mental Health of Asian American Women 181
Debra M. Kawahara and Michi Fu

12. Asian American Masculinities 197
William Ming Liu and Tai Chang

13. The Psychology of Asian American Older Adults 213
Gayle Y. Iwamasa and Kristen H. Sorocco

14. Asian Immigrants and Refugees 227
Rita Chi-Ying Chung and Fred Bemak

15. International Students From Asia 245
*Yu-Wei Wang, Jun-chih Gisela Lin, Lan-Sze Pang,
and Frances C. Shen*

PART IV: SOCIAL AND PERSONAL ADJUSTMENT **263**

16. In Search of Personality in Asian Americans: What We
Know and What We Don't Know 265
Edward C. Chang, Rita Chang, and Joyce P. Chu

17. Interpersonal Effectiveness Among Asian Americans: Issues
of Leadership, Career Advancement, and Social Competence 283
Nolan Zane and Anna Song

18. Health Psychology and Asian Pacific Islanders:
Learning From Cardiovascular Disease 303
Angela Ebreo, Yukiko Shiraishi, Paul Leung, and Jenny Kisuk Yi

19. Asian American Stress and Coping 323
Arpana G. Inman and Christine J. Yeh

20. Racism Against Asian/Pacific Island Americans 341
*Jeffery Scott Mio, Donna K. Nagata, Amy H. Tsai,
and Nita Tewari*

21. Family Violence Among Asian Americans 363
Irene J. Kim, Anna S. Lau, and Doris F. Chang

22. Psychopathology Among Asian Americans 379
Lawrence Hsin Yang and Ahtoy J. WonPat-Borja

PART V: ASSESSMENT AND INTERVENTIONS   **407**

23.   Assessment of Asian Americans: Fundamental
       Issues and Clinical Applications   409
       Lisa M. Kinoshita and Jeanette Hsu

24.   Counseling and Psychotherapy With Asian Americans:
       Process and Outcomes   429
       Frederick T. L. Leong, Doris F. Chang, and Szu-Hui Lee

25.   Empirically Supported Therapies for Asian Americans   449
       Gordon C. Nagayama Hall and Sopagna Eap

Author Index   **469**

Subject Index   **489**

About the Editors   **501**

About the Contributors   **505**

FOREWORD

This is a simply remarkable new edition of an excellent book. Although based upon the success of the history-making first volume, the second edition is in many ways a new endeavor. Unlike other approaches to new editions, the editorial team did a systematic evaluation of each chapter in the first edition. The result involves ten new chapters, deletion of five prior chapters, extended coverage within two chapters, and expansion of the Handbook by nearly 50 percent. The editors have achieved their goals of producing a volume that not only covers the sociohistorical background and demographics of Asian Americans and reviews core research and cultural principles, but also updates the discussions with literature from the new generation of Asian American scholars.

More so today, there is a need for such a scholarly review and presentation of what we know about Asian American psychology. This book is of value for several important reasons. First, Asian Americans are the fastest-growing ethnic minority group in the United States (Reeves & Bennett, 2004). In 1980, Asian Americans made up 1.5 percent of the U.S. population. Between 1980 and 2000, although European Americans increased by only 8 percent, in contrast Asian Americans increased by 190 percent compared with a Latino/Latinas increase of 143 percent, African Americans of 30 percent, and American Indians/Alaska Natives of 46 percent (Social Science Data Analysis Network, 2004). As Asian American populations increase in size, visibility, and influence, they bring cultural beliefs, language systems, traditions, customs, worldviews, and values. These special characteristics need to be acknowledged and understood by all who will ultimately interact with Asian Americans.

The second value of the book is that it meets the growing interest and awareness among science disciplines of the importance of cultural variables. Psychology is defined as the discipline and profession that engages in the systematic study of human behavior. However, the history of American psychology has previously defined the study of human behavior as the study of the behavior of White persons. More and more attention is being directed toward appreciating that knowledge only about the Euro-American or White population is insufficient and frequently not relevant for understanding ethnic populations such as Asian Americans. This volume fills the knowledge gap by providing a much-needed substantive knowledge base.

This volume is of great importance for bringing together recent advances in the field of Asian American psychology. From the seeds of scholarship in the 1980s, much new research has been released. More important than the sheer amount is the content of such scholarship. Applying new and more sophisticated methodologies and conceptualizations based upon a cultural perspective and analyses, a modern field of Asian American psychology has evolved and is captured in this volume. In this way the scholarly writings within the Handbook represent the first steps of a mature ethnic minority psychology.

The authors and editors are a perfect blend of senior scholars and new-generation researchers. They draw upon the empirical literature as well as their own personal experiences to share insights, issues, critiques, and formulations. Where the literature is sparse, they rely upon well-thought-through theoretical positions and knowledge of Asian American culture, beliefs, behaviors and core values. As Asian Americans themselves, their voices exhibit pride in their commitment to a psychology of Asian Americans, and also sometimes uneasiness as they review and confront the history of American racism and its current consequences.

The chapters introduce the reader to conceptual models, research reviews, critical epistemology, views of the future, and practical advice. Where relevant, demographic data are provided as well as core definitions. Often, theories from other perspectives are introduced and integrated as explanatory visions into Asian American issues. Discussions never permit the reader to forget that understanding Asian American populations demands continuous attention to the sociocultural background, the cultural individuality of the approximately 28 Asian group identities, and the familial/community/workplace context, all of which interact with each Asian American person's unique personal characteristics.

From chapter to chapter, readers are introduced to a comprehensive set of findings and discourse, beginning with Part I's coverage of historical information, a critique of conceptual models regarding ethnic minority psychology, and a detailed orientation to research methods. The decision to summarize the history of the Asian American Psychological Association is an implicit statement that this group's history reflects the growth of the field of Asian American psychology from being nonexistent in American psychology to being a recognizable and valid entity. Part II reviews what is known about the various developmental tasks facing Asian American youth, families, and adults, including the important areas of educational experiences, self-identity/acculturation, and career development. Special populations then receive attention in Part III— Asian American women, Asian American men, older Asian Americans, Asian immigrants and refugees, and an often overlooked group, international students. Part IV presents a unique but valuable coverage of topics such as personality characteristics, leadership and interpersonal effectiveness, as well as health behaviors, psychological coping styles, family violence, racism, and psychopathology. Finally, Part V completes the volume with concrete recommendations for appropriate assessment methods, a scholarly review of psychotherapy/counseling process and outcome research, and considerations regarding empirically supported interventions for Asian Americans.

It is my belief that readers of all levels and backgrounds will discover valuable insights and information in the second edition of the *Handbook of Asian American Psychology.* For scholars, practitioners, educators, students, and indeed anyone wishing to encounter the latest findings on this extremely important population, this volume serves as essential reading.

Richard M. Suinn, Ph.D.
Emeritus Professor of Psychology
Colorado State University

REFERENCES

Reeves, T. & Bennett, C. (2004). We the people: Asians in the United States (CENSR-17), Census 2000 Special Reports. Washington D.C.: U.S. Census Bureau.

Social Science Data Analysis Network, (2004). *United States population by race.* Retrieved October, 2004, from www.censuscope.org/us/chart_race.html

1

INTRODUCTION AND OVERVIEW

FREDERICK T. L. LEONG

ARPANA INMAN

ANGELA EBREO

LAWRENCE HSIN YANG

LISA M. KINOSHITA

MICHI FU

The first edition of the *Handbook of Asian American Psychology*, which was edited by L. C. Lee and N. W. S. Zane, was published in 1998 (Lee & Zane, 1998). Since the publication of the first edition seven years ago, Asian American psychology has seen considerable growth not only in its theoretical and research focus but in its demographic representation as well. Asian Americans have been the fastest-growing racial/ethnic group in the United States (Hobbs & Stoops, 2002). From the 1980s to the 1990s, the Asian American population increased from 3,726,440 to 7,273,662 (U.S. Census Bureau, 1995). Currently, 10.2 million Asian Americans reside in the United States, constituting 3.6% of the total population (U.S. Census Bureau, 2000).

With this rapid population growth, there has been an increase in attention to Asian Americans as an ethnic and racial minority. Whereas 155 articles addressing Asian American psychology were published in the 1980s, the 1990s saw an increase in publications by almost 500% (i.e., 769 articles and dissertations). Furthermore, between 2000 and 2004, there were 652 articles and dissertations addressing Asian American issues. These trends suggest that Asian Americans have established themselves as an important minority within the American landscape. Moreover, whereas research in the 1980s began addressing aspects such as Asian American assessment and intervention, employment and vocational issues, help-seeking behaviors, and mental health issues, thus identifying Asians Americans as distinct from other ethnic and racial groups, the 1990s saw a greater focus on Asian American identities and self-construal through research studies focusing on ethnicity, race, gender, and the intersection of various identities within an acculturative context. This emerging literature highlighted the need to integrate Asian collectivistic cultural values and attend to generational issues while noting the diversity among Asian ethnic groups. Although this focus has continued into the 21st century, there also has been a proliferation of research by a new generation of Asian American scholars who have begun to focus attention on life-span developmental issues, multiracial-multiple identities, health psychology, and the impact of stereotyping and discrimination within the Asian American community. Asian American psychological research has also included more high-risk (e.g., Southeast Asian refugee) and recently immigrated Asian American groups in addition to more established, acculturated groups, which has broadened the depth of research and focused attention on populations who are most vulnerable and at risk for developing mental disorders.

In keeping with these trends, Frederick Leong selected, as one of his presidential initiatives during his two-year term as president of the Asian American Psychological Association, the publication of the second edition of the *Handbook of Asian American Psychology*. With selected members of his executive committee joining him as coeditors, they proposed the second edition as an important scholarly contribution by this new generation of researchers and scholars who will address the shifts in contemporary issues for Asians and Asian Americans in the United States. To provide a salient and comprehensive coverage of Asian American psychology, the new editorial team critically reviewed the first edition to assess how it may meet the current needs of the field. In reviewing the contents of the first edition, a decision was made to retain 12 chapters/topics. Additionally, two chapters were expanded from their initial focus. Specifically, the concept of acculturation was added to the chapter on ethnic identity, and the chapter on racism included a focus on intergroup relations. Additionally, five chapters were discarded due to their narrow focus (e.g., the chapter titled "Internment and Intergenerational Relations" was discarded because of its focus on Japanese Americans), and 10 new chapters were added to the handbook. We believe that these 10 new chapters will achieve two important goals. First, the new

chapters will broaden the scope of the topic. For example, we added a chapter on health psychology to cover an area that was not previously covered. Second, the new chapters will provide a more balanced coverage. For instance, we have included chapters on both men and women and on personality and psychopathology.

The second edition of the *Handbook of Asian American Psychology* is divided into five parts. In **Part I**, historical, conceptual, and methodological issues that serve as the foundation of the field are addressed in three chapters. In Chapter 2, Frederick Leong, Sumie Okazaki, and E. J. R. David provide an overview of the history of Asian American psychology by examining the history of the Asian American Psychological Association, recent developments in the Asian American Psychological Association, and substantive areas of Asian American psychological research. Additionally, they forecast the future of Asian American psychology by surveying experts in the field regarding important areas for future development in Asian American psychology.

Sumie Okazaki, Richard Lee, and Stanley Sue, in Chapter 3, consider constructs that appear to be the most fundamental to research on Asian Americans: (a) race, ethnicity, and culture; (b) acculturation; and (c) racial and ethnic identity. In the course of their discussion, they examine challenges to Asian American psychology's current conceptualizations, particularly those presented in the study of immigrant, multiethnic, and transculturally adopted populations. Okazaki et al. end the chapter with thought-provoking recommendations concerning the relation between Asian American psychology and Asian American studies and the promise of breakthroughs coming through interdisciplinary and multidisciplinary collaboration.

In Chapter 4, Kevin Chun, Osvaldo Morera, Jolynne Andal, and Monica Skewes focus on research methods as they relate to the study of diverse Asian American populations. Building on previous discussions of the methodological challenges in Asian American psychology, Chun et al. present some promising qualitative and quantitative approaches to describing and examining Asian Americans' experiences. Using the authors' own experiences in conducting community-based research, the chapter illustrates cultural and practical considerations for conducting culturally appropriate investigations. Chun et al. end the chapter by discussing traditional biases against qualitative methods in the field and the need to more fully explore qualitative and quantitative approaches that uncover the heterogeneity of Asian American groups.

Part II of the handbook is concerned with a life-course developmental perspective. In the first chapter of this section, Chapter 5, Barbara Yee, Barbara DeBaryshe, Sylvia Yuen, Su Yeong Kim, and Hamilton McCubbin adopt a resiliency conceptual framework for understanding how Asian American and Pacific Islander families face life-span developmental challenges in the United States. In particular, the authors highlight specific socioeconomic status, familial and cultural variables, and external factors that serve as protective and risk factors for Asian American families as they traverse developmental milestones and cope with life challenges over the life course. The chapter concludes by highlighting directions for future Asian American and Pacific Islander family research and federal family research funding policies.

Ly Nguyen and Larke Nahme Huang, in Chapter 6, recognize the importance of understanding Asian American child development within a conceptual framework that best captures the experience of being an ethnic minority. Using an integrative model developed by Garcia Coll et al. (1996), the authors critically examine the extant literature on Asian Americans to determine what we know about the role of social ecological contexts in youth development. Of particular interest is the authors' discussion of linguistic capabilities, biculturalism, and racial socialization as important developmental competencies. Overall, the authors argue for an increase in researcher attention to the broad range of contextual variables that can influence developmental outcomes and competencies.

In Chapter 7, Vivian Tseng, Ruth Chao, and Inna Padmawidjaja examine Asian American educational experience within a sociohistorical context of the "model minority" stereotype and the "yellow peril." The authors take a life-span perspective of Asian American academic experiences from early childhood through college, highlighting significant areas of strengths and barriers among ethnic groups. Finally, the emphasis on racial, social, and economic contexts of instruction, peer experiences, schools, teacher and peer-related attitudes, and bullying and violence highlight important elements in the lives of Asian Americans.

In Chapter 8, Sapna Cheryan and Jeanne Tsai address the topic of ethnic identity of Asian Americans. They discuss three kinds of ethnic identities that pertain to this population: the Asian ethnic identities, the American identities, and the Asian American identities. For each kind of identity, research studies on its concept and significance are reviewed. The authors also review Asian Americans' ethnic identity through two approaches: the individual level and the contextual level. The three identity types are said to form part of Asian Americans' worlds by directing their understanding of situations, foretelling their social milieu, picking their ways to adapt to the environments, and comprehending others' reactions toward them.

Bryan Kim reviews the models and research on acculturation among Asian Americans in Chapter 9. According to Kim, adaptation to a cultural or social group's shared values and agreed-on principles that are viewed in rituals, expressed in symbols, and observed in its group members' psychological and social functioning are encompassed by the constructs of acculturation and enculturation. After introducing these concepts, Kim reviews the psychometric properties of the measures that have been developed to assess these two constructs, progressing from a unilinear (i.e., single continuum) to a bilinear (i.e., measuring acculturation and enculturation separately) perspective. Kim further reviews how acculturation and enculturation impact important mental health outcomes such as psychological and vocational functioning, attitudes toward seeking mental health services, and the short-term therapy process among Asian Americans. The chapter concludes by summarizing the current state of research and recommending future areas of study.

In the final chapter of Part 2, Chapter 10, Frederick Leong and Arpana Gupta review the state of the current literature on career development and vocational behaviors of Asian Americans. By conducting (a) individual-level analysis related to Asian American career inter-est, occupational values, career development, career choice, professions, personality vari-ables, and work adjustment and (b) group-level analysis related to family influences, occupa-tional stereotyping, discrimination, and segrega-tion, the authors provide a broad overview of the specific issues pertinent to Asian American communities. In addressing these issues, the authors highlight historical patterns and shifts reflected in the career literature and propose an integrative multidimensional model to cross-cultural counseling and psychotherapy with Asian Americans.

Part 3 of the handbook moves us into the con-sideration of specific populations. In Chapter 11, Debra Kawahara and Michi Fu emphasize the historical and political experiences of Asian American women and thus set an important framework for understanding the experiences of these women. Their focus on clinical issues that manifest from the different experiences provide some important insights into Asian American women's lives. Specifically, the negotiation and creation of Asian American identities within this context highlight the specific cultural and contextual nuances that need to be considered in understanding Asian American women's experiences. Finally, in discussing help-seeking patterns, the nature of Asian American female client–therapist dyads, and clinical considera-tions in therapy, the authors provide some important recommendations for practice.

In Chapter 12, William Ming Liu and Tai Chang recognize the importance of understand-ing the experience of Asian American men against a U.S.-based historical background and cultural constructions of masculinity. The dis-cussion of current theories of masculinity pro-vides important theoretical and practical foundations as well as biases inherent in con-ceptualizing Asian American masculinities. Finally, the proposal of social identity theory in understanding how Asian American men might negotiate and create positive identities highlights the specific cultural, contextual nuances that need to be considered in under-standing Asian American conceptualizations of masculinity.

Gayle Iwamasa and Kristen Sorocco summa-rize the existing psychological research on Asian American older adults in Chapter 13. The chapter begins with a discussion on the increase in the population of Asian American older adults and the variability among them in terms of country of origin, generational status, use of language, acculturation level, religiosity/spirituality, edu-cation, socioeconomic status, and age. Like other areas of Asian American psychology, there is an overall lack of empirical research on Asian American older adults. Iwamasa and Sorocco explore specific methodological issues related to conducting research with Asian American older adults and review the aging process in terms of *physical aging* and *psychological aging.* Next, the authors focus on the different ways Asian American older adults conceptualize psychiatric problems, and they provide a review of prevalent mental health issues that Asian American older adults experience. The various risk factors for mental health problems among Asian American older adults are explored. The authors review treatment issues faced by Asian American older adults, including general barriers to treatment and culturally appropriate treatment interventions. The chapter concludes with a discussion on gen-eral guidelines for working with Asian American older adults.

The special experiences and unique chal-lenges faced by immigrants and refugees are covered by Rita Chi-Ying Chung and Fred Bemak in Chapter 14. Given that the explosion in the Asian American population is driven, in part, by immigration from Asia, it is essential to understand how Asian Americans' premigration and postmigration experiences affect their mental health. According to Chung and Bemak, these immigrants negotiate universal stages of the migration process and face common psy-chosocial adjustment challenges. A clear dis-tinction exists between immigrant and refugee status; whereas immigrants voluntarily migrate to other countries to seek better opportunities, refugees involuntarily migrate to avoid war or persecution. Premigration trauma has been found to predict subsequent adaptation to the United States. Such premigration trauma may also result in loss, grief, and psychological problems such as post-traumatic stress disorder, depression, and suicide. Lastly, both immigrants and refugees retain indigenous beliefs that result in barriers to mental health service use and require the use of culturally responsive techniques in treatment.

In Chapter 15, Yu-Wei Wang, Jun-chih Gisela Lin, Lan-Sze Pang, and Frances Shen provide a review of the literature on the adaptation experiences of international students from Asia and outline recommendations for mental health professionals who work and conduct research with this population. In particular, they define and offer a profile of international students from Asia, present the cross-cultural adjustment processes and outcomes for international students, outline implications for counseling with this population, and suggest directions for future research.

The social and personal adjustment issues of Asian Americans are covered in **Part 4**. Edward C. Chang, Rita Chung, and Joyce P. Chu review, in Chapter 16, the current state of the literature on individual differences in Asian American populations. Strikingly, the chapter draws readers' attention to the lack of existing research in this area. The authors review literature on six individual difference variables (i.e., risk taking, cognitive style, sexuality, locus of control, empathy, and self-control) that generated the greatest number of empirical articles since 1990 and contained information about Asian Americans. The authors generally conclude that more research is needed to understand the nature and function of these individual differences and their relation with mental health. The chapter ends with some ideas about future directions for research on Asian American personalities.

In Chapter 17, Nolan Zane and Anna Song address the interpersonal effectiveness dimension of Asian Americans' adjustment. They focus on the importance of understanding the difficulties and challenges Asian Americans encounter in career advancement opportunities and interpersonal relations within the "agency/communion" conceptual framework. *Agency* and *communion skills* are terms given to help the reader better understand Asian American issues in career advancement and opportunities for attaining leadership positions. Three hypotheses are examined as possible explanations for Asian American challenges in interpersonal effectiveness: interpersonal skill deficit difficulties, social marginalization, and

culturally reinforced incompatible behaviors. The authors consider LaFromboise, Coleman, and Gerton's (1993) alternation model of biculturalism to be one adaptive answer to these sociocultural issues.

In Chapter 18, Angela Ebreo, Yukiko Shiraishi, Paul Leung, and Jenny Kisuk Yi present the current explanations of the links between psychological characteristics and disease, which are primarily viewed as being culturally universal in nature; describe models of health disparities as being complementary to these existing biopsychosocial models by their inclusion of culturally specific factors; and illustrate the application of these models to Asian Pacific Islander populations using cardiovascular disease as an example of chronic illness, which they specifically chose because of its being among the leading, largely preventable causes of death globally. They present issues that health psychologists might consider in understanding the health of specific racial or ethnic populations. They also offer recommendations for future research on Asian Pacific Islanders.

In Chapter 19, Arpana Inman and Christine Yeh focus on the idea that stress and coping have to be viewed from a cultural perspective and a sociocultural context. They review the growing body of literature on Asian American stress and coping. After a general discussion on culture, stress, and Asian American cultural values, the authors discuss various stressors, including familial and generational stress, cultural conflicts, "model minority" stress, and stress related to racism and discrimination. Specific coping perspectives are discussed with reference to indigenous healers, familial support, social support, and religious and spiritual support. In the concluding remarks, the authors note that the Asian priority of interconnectedness is a common thread among the various coping perspectives.

Racism against Asian/Pacific Island Americans (APIAs) is covered in Chapter 20, which is authored by Jeffery Mio, Donna Nagata, Amy Tsai, and Nita Tewari. Overall, the authors provide a thorough history lesson on racism against APIAs in the United States from its beginnings to the present. The authors begin by reviewing the four major APIA groups, namely East Asians, Southeast Asians, South

Asians, and Pacific Islanders. Then, they explore terms of categorization that are sometimes confused: stereotypes, prejudice, discrimination, and racism. The "model minority" stereotype also is discussed. The authors offer a comprehensive review of anti-Asian laws and of the history of racism against APIAs in the United States. They next discuss the history of Hawaii and the associated political struggles since it became part of the United States. The authors also provide a discussion on the injustices that occurred during World War II to Japanese Americans living in the United States when the government decided to intern these individuals following the Japanese attack on Pearl Harbor. The authors discuss racism in the 1980s and 1990s and the associated hate crimes against APIAs during this time, and they explore the anti-Indian attitudes in the 1990s, which surfaced with the technology boom. Mio et al. review the post-9/11 backlash toward the South Asian community with direct acts of racism against South Asians as part of the aftermath. They conclude the chapter with a review of the recent trend toward globalization and outsourcing to foreign countries.

Irene Kim, Anna Lau, and Doris Chang, in Chapter 21, aim specifically to name many of the challenging issues involved in family violence—namely, intimate partner violence and child abuse—among Asian Americans. They examine the scope and significance of these problems, factors that may be especially salient for Asian Americans, and empirical research on variables that increase the risk for these two types of family violence. In addition to discussing emerging research on intimate partner violence and child physical abuse among Asian Americans, they also provide implications for clinical practice as well as directions for future research.

In Chapter 22, Lawrence Yang and Ahtoy WonPat-Borja focus on the cultural processes that shape psychopathology within Asian Americans. Previous research is discussed in terms of ways in which Asian Americans employ various aspects of somatization as an expression of distress. Certain culture-bound syndromes are briefly mentioned and explained. The authors synthesize studies that examine the prevalence and manifestation of psychopathology among Asian Americans. Specific attention is given to disorders such as anxiety disorders, schizophrenia-spectrum disorders, major depressive disorders, and suicide. Of particular interest is the authors' exploration of psychopathology in reference to issues of immigration and acculturation. The authors highlight and synthesize potential problems associated with the lack of attention of this subject to Asian American subgroups, inadequate cross-cultural assessment procedures or instruments of psychopathology with Asian Americans, and the underutilization of mental health services found within this population. The chapter ends with some suggestions, conclusions, and ideas about future directions for research on issues of psychopathology with Asian Americans.

In **Part V,** the final part of the handbook, clinical assessment and intervention issues are addressed. Chapter 23, authored by Lisa Kinoshita and Jeanette Hsu, focuses on clinical assessment. According to Kinoshita and Hsu, culturally competent assessment approaches are necessary for practitioners working with Asian American individuals who come from diverse cultural, immigration, ethnic, and linguistic backgrounds. Cultural competence begins with practitioners' developing self-awareness of their own cultural heritages, particularly in domains that may influence their worldviews and lead to privilege in everyday social encounters. Further, gaining knowledge of historical and sociocultural factors concerning Asian American groups, and utilizing this knowledge to form potential cultural explanations, is critical. It is essential to understand the client's problem in the context of his or her whole person, which necessitates a multidimensional perspective (including consideration of race, gender, ethnicity, acculturation, disability, religion, socioeconomic status, sexual orientation, and familial influences). To establish rapport with Asian American clients, psychologists, especially during initial assessment sessions, should be sensitive to the possibility that clients will be unfamiliar with the therapeutic situation. Because many standardized assessment scales have been designed and validated using a European American population, it is difficult to know whether elevated scores among Asian Americans demonstrate actual psychopathology or normative cultural differences. It is the responsibility of culturally competent mental health professionals to choose assessments that are appropriate to the specific Asian American individual by evaluating the match between the measure's normative sample and the individual's characteristics. Further, evaluation of the reliability, validity, and cross-cultural equivalence of translated measures for use with Asian Americans is essential. The chapter concludes with a review of some commonly used assessment measures that have been adapted for Asian and Asian American groups, including acculturation, personality, psychopathology, intelligence, and neuropsychological assessments.

In Chapter 24, Frederick Leong, Doris Chang, and Szu-Hui Lee review the growing literature on psychotherapy process and outcome with Asian Americans published since the last major review (Leong, 1986). They provide a review organized by empirical studies, culture-specific treatment models, general treatment strategies and recommendations, and clinical case studies. They conclude that although more research has been conducted since the last major review, further research is still needed. Furthermore, they applaud the efforts of those who represent the realities of cross-cultural counseling encounters by utilizing transactional and interactional models to guide research in this area.

In the final chapter of the handbook, Gordon Hall and Sopagna Eap cover the topic of empirically supported therapies for Asian Americans. This chapter reviews treatment research with Asian Americans with a focus on Asian American client cultural values that may moderate treatment outcome. The authors address the fact that there is a growing body of evidence of the general effectiveness of treatments for psychological disorders but limited evidence of such treatment effectiveness for Asian Americans. The authors define the criterion for well-established, empirically supported treatments and explore the criticisms involved in such research. They argue that there is a need for clinical research to determine the effectiveness of empirically supported therapies with groups such as Asian Americans, who have not been adequately represented in clinical trials.

Treatment outcome studies on cognitive-behavioral interventions, pharmacotherapy, play therapy, acupuncture, and meditation are reviewed in this chapter. The authors suggest that individual differences may offer clues to what might constitute the most effective treatments for particular patients. An important individual difference is *patient ethnicity.* Thus, they review available research on therapist-client ethnic match. The authors also discuss variables that may moderate the effects of treatment, namely *somatization* and *loss of face,* which may interfere with some Asian Americans seeking Western forms of psychiatric treatment. The authors conclude by reviewing research recommendations to modify cognitive therapy so that it is more culturally sensitive. They suggest that federal funding priorities need to be altered to fund empirical research and other large-scale randomized clinical trials with Asian Americans.

REFERENCES

Garcia Coll, C., Laberty, G., Jenkins, R., McAdoo, H. P., Crnic, K., Wasik, B. H., et al. (1996). An integrative model for the study of developmental competencies in minority children. *Child Development, 67*, 1891–1914.

Hobbs, F., & Stoops, N. (2002). *Demographic trends in the 20th century* (Census 2000 Special Report No. CENSR-4). Washington, DC: U.S. Government Printing Office.

LaFromboise, T., Coleman, H. L., & Gerton, J. (1993). Psychological impact of biculturalism: Evidence and theory. *Psychological Bulletin, 114*, 395–412.

Lee, L. C., & Zane, N. W. S. (Eds.). (1998). *Handbook of Asian American psychology.* Thousand Oaks, CA: Sage.

Leong, F. T. (1986). Counseling and psychotherapy with Asian Americans: Review of the literature. *Journal of Counseling Psychology, 33*, 196–206.

U.S. Census (1995). *The nation's Asian and Pacific Islander population: 1994* (Statistical brief). Washington DC: U.S. Department of Commerce. Retrieved October 21, 2005, from http://www.census.gov/apsd/www/statbrief/sb95_24.pdf

U.S. Census (2001). *Table DP-1: Profile of general demographic characteristics: 2000.* Washington DC: U.S. Department of Commerce.

PART I

HISTORICAL, CONCEPTUAL, AND METHODOLOGICAL ISSUES

2

History and Future of Asian American Psychology

Frederick T. L. Leong

Sumie Okazaki

E. J. R. David

The primary purpose of this chapter is to provide an overview of the history of Asian American psychology by examining (a) the history of the Asian American Psychological Association (AAPA), (b) recent developments in the AAPA, and (c) substantive areas of Asian American psychological research. The second purpose of this chapter is to engage in a forecasting of the future of Asian American psychology by using the Delphi method, and this constitutes the last section of the chapter.

History of the Asian American Psychological Association

The AAPA, founded in 1972, has played a central role in defining Asian American psychology as a scholarly field of its own, in serving as a key advocate in multicultural and ethnic minority psychology, and in collaborating with allied disciplines to define and implement culturally competent mental health services to Asian

American populations. Of course, Asian American psychology, as a field, encompasses figures and activities beyond the organization and the membership of the AAPA. However, a historical review of the association—particularly its activities in the early years—provides insight into the hallmark of Asian American psychology, notably the intersection of science, practice, and advocacy.

Founding of the Association

The AAPA was founded on December 10, 1972, by a group of Asian American psychologists and other mental health professionals in the San Francisco Bay area. The new organization was initially referred to as the Association of Asian American Psychologists. Interviews with the founders, Derald W. Sue and Stanley Sue, were conducted for the AAPA history monograph (Leong, 1995) by Frederick Leong and Diane Fujino, respectively. Here, we summarize the key points made by the Sue brothers as they recalled the founding of the organization. Derald Sue served as the AAPA's first president. He recalled, with humor, that because the organization was so small when founded, there were no formal elections for the leadership positions. He was appointed by the group to take on the presidency because he was the older of the Sue brothers.

Around the time that the association was being formed, Derald Sue had been working as a psychologist at the University of California, Berkeley, counseling center. He described in the interview that many Chinese American students were using counseling services and that many of their presenting concerns revolved around identity issues and the conflicts they felt between traditional Asian values and Western values. Derald Sue also felt that his graduate training had not prepared him adequately for working with Asian American clients and clients of other minority backgrounds.

Both Stanley Sue and Derald Sue recalled that the sense of isolation among Asian American mental health professionals and scholars served as a primary impetus for forming the AAPA. The Sue brothers began meeting and discussing their common concerns with other Asian American mental health professionals in the San Francisco Bay area (master's-level counselors, social workers, educators, and psychologists). The organization started out locally. Stanley Sue and his graduate students, Rod Kazama and Davis Ja, decided to start the process of forming a national organization by going through the American Psychological Association (APA) directory and using the surnames to identifying psychologists of possible Asian ancestry, then sending letters to assess their interests in joining a new organization. The organization of AAPA was modeled after the Association of Black Psychologists. They were also aware that Latinos were planning to form their own organization.

Stanley Sue recalled in the interview (Leong, 1995) that in the early 1970s, Asian Americans lacked visibility within the APA and that African American psychologists were the primary forces in articulating the concerns of ethnic minorities within the larger APA. Between 1969 and 1970, Robert Chin—one of the early members of the AAPA— was serving as the president of the Society for the Psychological Study of Social Issues (SPSSI), an international group of psychologists, allied scientists, students, and others who share a common interest in research on the psychological aspects of important societal problems. Stanley Sue also became active in SPSSI (and went on to serve as its president in 1990–1991). At Chin's suggestion, Stanley Sue requested a grant (in the amount of $250) from SPSSI to support the newsletter mailings for the new organization (noted in the January 1974 newsletter).

Advocacy and Alliance Building

In the next developmental stage of the AAPA, the leaders aimed to increase their visibility at the national level through the APA. The initial goals of the AAPA, according to Stanley Sue, were to promote knowledge about Asian American psychology and to influence public policies and programs. The interviews with the Sue brothers (Leong, 1995) and the archival records of the AAPA, such as the newsletters and early communications among its members, reveal the critical significance of the relationship between the AAPA and the APA. Thus, we first review the climate of the APA at the time as a backdrop against which the AAPA's advocacy on behalf of Asian American psychology took place.

The late 1960s to early 1970s was a time when the APA, as a national organization, was beginning to grapple with the diversification of psychology. Pallak (1992) characterized the period from 1970 to 1975 for the APA as rife with internal political conflicts that derived partly from growth and diversity in its membership, with the resulting conflict dominating the APA's resources. In 1968 (according to Smith, 1992), the board of directors asked George Albee to head a conference on the recruitment of minority students into psychology. In 1970, the APA Council of Representatives authorized a three-year loan (later forgiven) to assist the Black Students' Psychological Association and the Association of Black Psychologists to develop a headquarters office. In 1971, the ad hoc Committee on Social and Ethical Responsibility was established, and in 1972, this ad hoc committee was institutionalized as the Board on Social and Ethical Responsibility for Psychology (BSERP).[1] Smith (1992) characterized these movements as a legacy of Kenneth B. Clark's APA presidential term of 1971. In 1974, the APA Minority Fellowship Program was established through funding from the National Institute of Mental Health (NIMH).

In the formative years of the AAPA, its leadership identified the APA boards and standing committees that were seen as allies in articulating the concerns of Asian Americans and ethnic minorities within the APA. In his interview (Leong, 1995), Derald Sue described the Committee on Equal Opportunity in Psychology (CEOP), established in 1963, as the "ethnic/racial minority conscience" of APA (p. 15). Derald Sue also recalled that when he presented the argument for a greater representation of Asian Americans in the APA governance, members of BSERP grilled him with questions concerning why Asians should be considered a minority group. Derald Sue's letter to the BSERP, in which he advocated in detailed and forceful manner the need for Asian American representation on this important board, was reproduced in its entirety in the July 1974 issue of the AAPA's newsletter. Eventually, Derald Sue was asked to join the CEOP of the APA. The CEOP had representatives from Asian American, African American, Latino, and American Indian psychology organizations or groups.

In the interview (Leong, 1995), Derald Sue recalled how he and Stanley Sue learned to advocate in such a way as to create the perception of power and influence. As representatives of the AAPA, Derald and Stanley Sue, as well as other AAPA board members, articulated to the APA that Asian Americans had concerns that were similar to those of African Americans (e.g., underrepresentation on journal editorial boards, on APA boards and committees, and on the APA Council of Representatives, which was the policy-setting body of the APA). In retrospect, Derald Sue acknowledged that he and Stanley Sue, at various times, acted as if they had a great deal of influence (e.g., by presenting themselves as members of the AAPA), thereby giving both themselves and the AAPA more legitimacy. The AAPA became an institution to which other psychology bodies (e.g., APA, Association for Psychological Science) turned to for guidance and input regarding Asian American psychological issues.

In 1978, under the helm of Brewster Smith, the APA convened the National Conference for Increasing Roles of Culturally Diverse People in Psychology, held near Washington Dulles International Airport and more informally known as the Dulles Conference. At this three-day conference, a number of ethnic minority psychologists met with APA officials to discuss ways to restructure the APA to enhance participation of ethnic minority psychologists. Stanley Sue recalled that, initially, representatives of various ethnic minority groups could not agree on how to accomplish better representation of ethnic minority voices in the APA, but after some heated debates, a compromise was forged and all groups agreed to be sensitive to one another's concerns. That Dulles Conference resulted in the formation of the ad hoc Committee on Cultural and Ethnic Affairs. Reiko True and Robert Chin, representing the AAPA, were appointed to this committee and advocated for the formation of the Board of Minority Affairs (BEMA). BEMA was established by the bylaw amendment voted by the general membership of the APA and began its activities in 1981 (Smith, 1992).

Going beyond the APA, the AAPA leadership also sought to influence public policy on a national stage. Stanley Sue discussed that the AAPA became aware that a President's Commission on Mental Health had been formed (circa 1977–1978) by President Jimmy Carter. Because the commission did not initially solicit participation of the AAPA or its members, the AAPA leadership mobilized their allies to protest the absence of Asian American representation on the commission. The AAPA obtained the help of Senator Daniel Inouye of Hawaii, who then nominated an Asian American psychologist to be appointed to the commission in case of vacancy. Herbert Z. Wong (who was, at the time, the director of the Richmond Maxi Center, an NIMH-funded outpatient mental health facility in San Francisco) was appointed by the president of the AAPA to make a presentation on behalf of the organization and the Asian American community regarding the mental health needs of this population. Robert Chin and Stanley Sue were eventually asked to serve on that subpanel on the President's Commission on Mental Health.

Advocacy Through Scholarship

Paralleling the founding of the AAPA was the development of the pioneering scholarship of Stanley Sue, who was not only active as an advocate of Asian American issues in the field but also the major figure in building the scholarly foundation for Asian American psychology research. Stanley Sue recalled that at his first faculty position at the University of Washington, Ned Wagner, who was a full professor and the director of clinical training, strongly encouraged him to conduct research on Asian Americans. In addition, there were several key publications in the early to mid-1970s that the AAPA organizers authored in order to articulate the unique psychological issues facing Asian Americans to the field at large. In 1973, the *Journal of Social Issues* (the journal of the SPSSI) published a special issue of the journal, guest-edited by Stanley Sue and Harry Kitanao and titled "Asian Americans: A Success Story?" In the same year, Derald Sue edited a special issue of the *Personnel and Guidance Journal* titled "Understanding Asian-Americans: The Neglected Minority." Stanley Sue credited Fred Strasburger, who was a member of the APA BSERP and also on the editorial board of the *American Psychologist*, for publishing a paper by Stanley Sue, Derald Sue, and David Sue (1975) on psychological issues facing Asian Americans. Stanley Sue believed because of the journal's prominence and wide circulation, the publication of this article resulted in tremendous publicity to Asian American issues in psychology.

Key People in the Organization

Since its establishment, the AAPA has seen the leadership and involvement of a number of Asian American psychologists (and in its early days, Asian American psychiatrists, social workers, and other mental health professionals), who have been committed to the advancement of Asian American welfare and concerns. Table 2.1 lists the AAPA presidents and their terms of service. Notably, Christine Hall was the first woman elected (in 1995) to serve as AAPA president. Her presidential term was followed successively by three other women in this leadership role.

Although it is beyond the scope of the present article to list all the AAPA members who served in various leadership capacities throughout its first three decades, there are a few key figures whose work and activities in service of the association are particularly noteworthy. Table 2.2 displays the recipients of the Asian American Psychological Association Outstanding Contributions Awards. These are the individuals who have made a significant contribution to the

Table 2.1 Asian American Psychological Association Presidents (1972–2005)

Term	President
1972–1975	Derald Sue
1975–1979	Robert Chin
1979–1982	Albert H. Yee
1982–1984	Harry Yamaguchi
1984–1988[a]	Herbert Z. Wong
1988–1990	Katsuyuki Sakamoto
1990–1991	David S. Goh
1991–1993	Nolan W. S. Zane
1993–1995	S. Andrew Chen
1995–1997	Christine C. Iijima Hall
1997–1999	Reiko Homma True
1999–2001	Gayle Y. Iwamasa
2001–2003	J.-C. Gisela Lin
2003–2005	Frederick Leong
2005–	Alvin Alvarez

a. Due to incomplete archival records, the start and end dates of Wong's presidential term are uncertain. There are records that indicate that Yamaguchi finished his term in summer 1984, that Wong was serving as the president in 1985 and 1986, and that Sakamoto's term was 1988–1990.

science and practice of Asian American psychology as well as the education and training of Asian American psychologists.

Publications of the Asian American Psychology Association

The archival records of the AAPA indicate that from 1972 to 1979, the association produced newsletters consisting primarily of the news of the association and its activities, editorials, and occasional publications of research or conceptual articles. Derald Sue edited the newsletters between 1972 and 1975, followed by Roger Lum. In 1979, the association renamed its communication the *Journal of the Asian American Psychological Association*. The inaugural journal issue listed a team of editors (Robert Chin, Tim Dong, Roger Lum, Stanley Sue), and the reason for the change from the newsletter to the journal format is cited as arising from a newly elected board of directors who "felt that a journal would not only attract more articles of high quality and interest but that it would be a better reflection of the actual content" (Asian American Psychological Association, p. 2). The journal was published by the organization and

Table 2.2   Asian American Psychological Association Outstanding Contributions Awards

Year	Recipients (Awards)
1985	Robert Chin (Distinguished Contribution)
1987	Patrick Okura & Richard M. Suinn (Distinguished Contribution)
1989	Derald Sue (Distinguished Contribution)
1990	Stanley Sue & Reiko Homma True (Distinguished Contribution)
1991	Bertram Brown & Chalsa Loo (Distinguished Contribution)
1992	S. Andrew Chen (Distinguished Contribution) Derald W. Sue & Stanley Sue (Lifetime Achievement)
1993	Harry Yamaguchi (Distinguished Contribution)
1994	Nolan W. S. Zane (Distinguished Contribution)
1995	Alice F. Chang (Distinguished Contribution)
1996	Maria P. P. Root (Distinguished Contribution)
1997	Yoshito Kawahara (Distinguished Contribution)
1998	Frederick Leong & Katsuyuki Sakamoto (Distinguished Contribution)
1999	Gayle Iwamasa (Early Career) Gordon C. N. Hall (Distinguished Contribution) Richard M. Suinn (Lifetime Contribution)
2000	Sumie Okazaki (Early Career) Christine Iijima Hall (Distinguished Contribution)
2001	Christine J. Yeh & Jeannette Hsu (Early Career) Jean Lau Chin (Distinguished Contribution)
2002	Richard M. Lee (Early Career) George Hong (Distinguished Contribution) Reiko Homma True (Okura Community Leadership) Ford Kuramoto (Friend of AAPA) Patrick Okura (Presidential Award)
2003	Bryan S. K. Kim & Jeanne Tsai (Early Career) John Moritsugu (Distinguished Contribution) Reiko Homma True (Lifetime Achievement) Luke Kim (Friend of AAPA) Allen Ivey (Presidential Award)
2004	Alvin Alvarez (Early Career) Larke N. Huang & Jeffrey S. Mio (Distinguished Contribution) Alice F. Chang (Lifetime Achievement) Barbara W. K. Yee (Okura Community Leadership) Paul B. Pedersen (Friend of AAPA) Anthony Marsella & James Jones (Presidential Award)
2005	Kevin Chun and Barry Chung (Early Career) Yu-Wen Ying (Distinguished Contribution) Richard Suinn (Okura Community Leadership) Norman Anderson (Friend of AAPA) Daniel Inouye and Ruby Takanishi (Presidential Award)

Note: The AAPA awards began in 1985 with Robert Chin as the first recipient. No awards were given during some years because the AAPA conference was not held annually during the early 1980s, and the awards were given during the conference.

contained some original pieces as well as reprints of papers by association members that had appeared in other publications. Albert Yee assumed the editorship of the journal during his presidency (1979–1982). Between 1983 and 1989, Martin R. Wong assumed the editorship of the journal and began soliciting and publishing original pieces, including brief articles by Senators Daniel Inouye and Spark Matsunaga (of Hawaii), in the 1984 issue, calling for greater political action in Asian American communities.

In 1990, the association once again changed the format of its regular communication with its members. In resuming the regular publication of the association newsletter (now titled *Asian American Psychologist*), the association leadership planned to use the newsletter to communicate the association's news and to use the journal and monograph format to publish research and theory pieces. Jeffrey S. Tanaka was appointed as the journal's editor at the time, but no issues were published between 1990 and 1992, at the time of Tanaka's untimely death, or subsequently. The history monograph written by Frederick Leong in 1995 is the only monograph published by the AAPA to date.

Significant Conferences for the Field

For Asian American psychologists, one of the key conferences that helped coalesce the field was the San Francisco conference on Asian American mental health. In 1971, as a result of contacts among K. Patrick Okura (then executive assistant director of NIMH), James Ralph (chief of the Center for Minority Mental Health Programs), and the Asian American Social Workers Organization, NIMH agreed to fund the first national conference on Asian American mental health. This 1972 conference, which was held in San Francisco, was intended to convene 81 delegates from throughout the nation to examine the mental health needs and priorities of Asian Americans. Conference organizers expected another 300 to 400 persons as participants/observers. However, more than 600 individuals attended, giving rise to much conflict and tension. Demands emerged for giving all participants voices as delegates, and tensions developed between different factions, for example, grassroots constituency versus agency

professional groups. The more-militant versus the less-militant approaches to confronting the governmental agencies were discussed. Underlying the tension were feelings of frustration and anger over years of inadequate services and programs for Asian and Pacific American communities. Details concerning some of the problems and tensions of that conference were documented in Sue and Chin (1976) and also briefly reviewed by Sue and Morishima (1982).

Another landmark conference was the 1976 National Asian American Psychology Training Conference. With encouragement from Patrick Okura, who was the executive assistant to the NIMH director as well as on the board of the AAPA, Stanley Sue wrote a conference grant proposal to the NIMH to convene a national conference on the training of mental health service providers to serve Asian American communities. After two years of planning, the conference was held in Long Beach, California, on July 31–August 1, 1976. Albert H. Yee, Dean of Graduate Studies and Research at California State University, Long Beach, and on the AAPA board, was instrumental in securing the conference site. The report of the conference (Sue & Chin, 1976) details both the process and the substantive content of the conference. The report contains a number of recommendations for training of psychologists to deliver mental health services to Asian Americans (e.g., increase the number of bilingual, bicultural trainees; establish a training center specific to meeting the needs of Asian American clients; explore alternative models of psychological treatments for Asian Americans rather than rely solely on Western models of psychotherapy).

More than a quarter of a century after the first Asian American mental health conference was held in San Francisco in 1972, the Center for Mental Health Services (CMHS) of the Substance Abuse and Mental Health Services Administration (SAMHSA) convened an Asian American Pacific Islander Mental Health Summit on July 10–12, 1999, in Washington, D.C. This conference was the brainchild of a Vietnamese American psychiatrist, Tiffany Ho, who worked at CMHS. Leaders from government, academia, and the community were invited to this summit to discuss the mental health needs of Asian Americans and Pacific

Islanders across the country. A strategic planning committee was formed, and in July 2000, the National Asian American Pacific Islander Mental Health Association (NAAPIMHA) was formed with D. J. Ida as its executive director.

Finally, at the 2005 AAPA annual convention in Washington, D.C., the association celebrated 20 years of consecutive annual conventions. The 1985 convention was chaired by Nolan Zane, with Herbert Wong as president. Before 1985, the AAPA had held sporadic conventions according to where APA was holding its annual convention. Whenever APA had chosen to hold their conference in a city with significant numbers of Asian Americans (e.g., San Francisco, Los Angeles, or New York), AAPA was able to get sufficient turnout to hold their conference. Ironically, the decision in 1985 to hold an annual AAPA convention, regardless of which city was hosting the APA convention, resulted in a certain level of continuity and stability that led to considerable growth in the association which, in turn, led to a sufficient turnout at each convention.

Recent Developments in the Asian American Psychological Association

With the move to an annual convention format, as well as a tremendous increase in the number of younger members, the AAPA became a very stable organization that saw considerable growth during the past two decades. The membership of AAPA grew from 229 members in 1984 to close to 500 members in 2005. Within this shift toward a younger membership, a variety of activities were developed to meet the needs of these members, including the establishment of a book sale at the annual convention that provides the funds to support scholarships that enable selected students to attend and present at the annual convention. This was followed by the establishment of the mentor-mentee lunch at the annual convention, the dissertation awards, and presentations of the student awards at the annual awards banquet. At the same time, K. Patrick Okura and his wife, Lily Okura, established the Okura Mental Health Leadership Foundation, which funded a fellowship that enabled many younger AAPA members to learn about advocacy and public policy issues in Washington, D.C.

At the same time, the awards program of the Asian American Psychological Association also witnessed a parallel growth and expansion. As shown in Table 2.2, the AAPA award program began with the presentation of the Distinguished Contributions Award to Robert Chin in 1985. Before then, awards were not given consistently because the association was not yet holding conventions on an annual basis. From 1985 to 1998, the major award given out by the association was that of the Distinguished Contributions Award. In 1991, during the presidency of Nolan Zane, Frederick Leong had noted that the association would be celebrating its 20th anniversary at the 1992 convention, and the decision was made to give a Special Presidential Award to Derald Sue and Stanley Sue. It had been a tradition within AAPA that the winner of the Distinguished Contribution Awards would become chair of the Awards Committee the following year. In 1998, Leong was appointed as chair of the Awards Committee and with the support of President Reiko True, he decided to expand the awards program by instituting the Early Career Award and the Lifetime Achievement Award. In 1999, the first Early Career Award was given to Gayle Iwamasa and the first Lifetime Achievement Award was presented to Richard Suinn. After some discussion, it was also decided that the Special Presidential Awards given to our AAPA founders, Derald Sue and Stanley Sue, be redesignated as Lifetime Achievement Awards. The awards program continued to grow with the addition of the Friend of AAPA Award, the Okura Award, and the Presidential Awards.

In 1995, Christine Hall was elected as the first female president of the Asian American Psychological Association. This was followed by three consecutive female presidents: Reiko True (1997–1999), Gayle Iwamasa (1999–2001), and J.-C. Gisela Lin (2001–2003). During Hall's presidency (1995–1997), she made it her presidential goal to improve the structure and functioning of the association. Many of her initiatives have helped stabilize the association. These initiatives included establishing a headquarters for AAPA in Phoeniz, Arizona, with a permanent mailing address and voice mail;

creating the secretary/historian position, which was filled first by Sumie Okazaki; and regulating the renewal of membership more closely. In addition, Christine Hall, with the help of Richard Kim, launched the Web site of the AAPA in April 1996. Until that point, the association newsletter had been the primary form of communication and news for the membership. The AAPA Web site has continued to grow and has become a focal point of communication for the association. A couple of years earlier, the association had also established a Listserv as another forum for member communication. This Listserv was first hosted by Richard Suinn at Colorado State University and eventually transferred to Alvin Alvarez at San Francisco State University.

In 1997, Reiko True became the president of the AAPA and brought financial stability to the association with several significant financial contributions to the annual convention (which was the biggest budget item). At that same time, the AAPA Executive Committee also voted to formally recognize the Division on Women. This was also the time when the association lent its support for the appointment of Bill Lann Lee to the U.S. Civil Rights Commission. Other association activities spearheaded by True included supporting (a) the formation of regional and networking groups, (b) the National Multicultural Summit and Conference, and (c) publication of *Guidelines for Research with Ethnic Minority Communities* (Council of National Psychological Association for the Advancement of Ethnic Minority Interests, 2000) (with Stanley and Derald Sue writing the lead article), a monograph in the series published by the APA and by the Council of National Psychological Association for the Advancement of Ethnic Minority Interests of which AAPA is a member.

Reiko True was succeeded by Gayle Iwamasa as president of AAPA in 1999 in an election whereby Iwamasa (president) and Kawahara (vice president) ran as a joint-slate. Iwamasa took the initiative during her presidency to further improve the structure and functioning of the association. This included consulting with an attorney and getting the association incorporated, as well as obtaining tax-exempt status. At the same time, she firmly established the procedures for offering continuing education credits as part of the annual convention while continuing with the tradition of organizing regional conferences, including one in San Diego. Iwamasa also undertook some significant changes to the association bylaws.

J.-C. Gisela Lin became the president of AAPA in 2001 and oversaw the 30th anniversary celebration of the AAPA's founding with a major celebration at the 2002 annual convention in Chicago. This celebration included a reception and a symposium during the APA's annual convention. During her presidency, Lin established the K. Patrick Okura Community Leadership Award and the Dissertation Award. She also supported the trial run for a special discussion forum for student members, moderated by Tai Chang. Lin's major presidential initiative was the commissioning of the association's comprehensive needs assessment in 2001–2002 to aid in long-term and strategic planning for the AAPA. The results of this needs assessment is reported in the winter 2003 issue of the *Asian American Psychologist*, the AAPA newsletter. The results of the needs assessment were also presented and discussed at a town hall meeting at the 2002 AAPA convention in Chicago.

During his presidency from 2003 to 2005, Frederick Leong had the primary goal of improving the structure and functioning of the association. This was accomplished by the passage of several important bylaw changes. The first bylaw change involved establishing a new category of membership of fellows, which recognizes distinguished members for outstanding and unusual contributions to Asian American psychology. As part of that process, AAPA also grandfathered in some members as fellows of the association. The decision was made to automatically grant fellow status to the most distinguished members of our association, namely our Lifetime Achievement Award winners, Distinguished Contributions Award winners, as well as past presidents of the association (see Tables 2.1 and 2.2). At the 2005 AAPA convention, with Gordon Hall as chair of the Fellows Committee, D. J. Ida and Allen Ivey were inducted as the new fellows of the association.

The second major bylaw change that was passed involved the formation of the Council of Past Presidents (COPP). Together with the fellows category, the COPP was established to recognize the important contributions that these "senior" members of our association can make. It was envisioned that future presidents and executive committees of the AAPA could benefit from the advice and wisdom of the COPP. The third and final bylaw change was to create a mechanism for formation of new divisions. With the leadership of Alice Chang and others, the Division on Women was formed in 1996. The Division on Women has been an important and integral part of AAPA. In addition, there are plans under way for the formation of a student division under the leadership of Szu-Hui Lee. It is hoped that with the passage of these bylaws, some group of like-minded members who would like to organize themselves to share information, resources, and support can take advantage of this new mechanism. Although this did not require a bylaw change, a fourth and equally important structural change that Fred Leong made during his term of office was to initiate the association's policies and procedures manual.

Leong's other accomplishments during his presidency included the launching of this book, the second edition of the *Handbook of Asian American Psychology,* with several members of the executive committee as coeditors (Inman, Ebreo, Yang, Kinoshita, and Fu) and many AAPA members as contributing authors. The royalties from this handbook will be donated to AAPA. Another significant development during this particular administration of the AAPA was the production and distribution of the Digital History Project (DHP). Leong initiated the DHP when he began to notice that some of the historical documents of the association were gradually being lost. With the help of the secretary/historian, Irene Kim, Leong had all of the documents within the AAPA historical archives scanned and digitized onto CD. The DHP CD was then distributed to all members of the executive committee and made available to both members and nonmembers for a nominal price.

SUBSTANTIVE AREAS OF ASIAN AMERICAN PSYCHOLOGICAL RESEARCH

A historical review of Asian American psychology would not be complete without an analysis of the substantive content areas of the field. Referring again to the history monograph by Leong (1995), we find that he had used the bibliography by Leong and Wittfield (1992), titled *Asians in the United States: Abstracts of the Psychological and Behavior Literature 1967–1991,* as the basis for identifying the content areas that have been most heavily researched with regard to Asian American psychology for that period. Using the topic classification provided by PsycINFO, Leong (1995) found that the most frequently researched area written about in journal articles was social processes and social issues, which constituted 22.9% of the journal articles on Asians published between 1967 and 1991. This, in turn, was followed by health and mental health treatment and prevention (19.3%), educational psychology (11.5%), and psychological and physical disorders (10.6%).

To examine possible convergences in this pattern, Leong (1995) also analyzed the dissertation literature on Asians in the United States between the years 1967 and 1991. Consistent with the findings for the journal articles, the primary area covered by dissertations was also that of social processes and social issues, which constituted 28.7% of that literature. However, this was closely followed by educational psychology (25.8%), which was double that of the journal articles. In addition, unlike the journal articles, 13.4% of the dissertations focused on developmental psychology, as opposed to only 9.5% of the journal articles. In summary, it appeared that social processes and social issues were the most heavily researched areas of Asian American psychology during that period. On the other hand, considerably more attention was focused on health and mental health treatment and prevention within the journal articles than within the dissertation studies. Dissertation topics tended to focus more on developmental psychology and educational psychology. The journal articles tended to focus on treatment and prevention, psychological and physiological disorders, and, to a lesser extent, educational psychology.

The relative amount of attention devoted to treatment, prevention, and psychological disorders is important in light of continuing criticism that the AAPA, like the APA, has been dominated by clinical and counseling psychologists. Thus, it appears that the journal literature from 1967 to 1991 mirrors the specialty training and background of the AAPA membership. However, it should be noted that this is a complex problem, and we cannot assume a direct linkage between these two trends. For example, the lower level of coverage of the "clinical" topics among dissertations may be due to the fact that those studies (which require access to clinical populations) may be more difficult for doctoral students to undertake.

Leong (1995) proposed that another way of obtaining an overview of the research content of Asian American psychology was to identify the leading contributors to the Asian American psychological literature from the years 1967–1991. He suggested that in examining these individuals for their primary areas of research and contribution, we might identify the more popular specialty areas within the field. In examining the citation at the end of the Leong and Wittfield volume (1992), it was discovered that the leading contributors to the Asian American psychological literature were Ronald C. Johnson (22 articles), Joseph Westermeyer (19), Stanley Sue (18), David Kinsey (18), Craig T. Nagoshi (13), Anthony Marsella (11), Harry H. Kitano (11), Donald Atkinson (10), Jacquelyn H. Flaskerud (10), Frederick T. L. Leong (10), Kay Midlan (10), and Joe Yamamoto (10).

Leong (1995) noted that, with few exceptions, most of these researchers focused on mental health issues of Asian Americans. For example, Joseph Westermeyer's work was primarily focused on immigrant and refugee mental health, whereas Stanley Sue's work was focused on Asian American mental health, community issues, and mental health treatment. David Kinsey also researched immigrant and refugee issues, and Anthony Marsella researched issues related to mental disorders among Asian Americans.

Before the formation of the AAPA and the pioneering work of Stanley Sue, Derald Sue, and their colleagues, much of the psychological research on Asian Americans was conducted by a handful of social scientists, such as Abe Arkoff at the University of Hawaii, Harry Kitano at UCLA, and Stanley Fong at San Francisco State University. Most of this early research was published in the 1960s and is reviewed in Sue and Morishima's (1982) book on the mental health of Asian Americans.

Moving to a higher level of analysis, another perspective on substantive content within Asian American psychology would be to analyze the PsycINFO coverage of the topic over the past decade and a half. Using 1991 as the starting point, as Leong and Whitfield (1992) covered literature until that period, we find 1,834 entries on Asians from 1967 to 1991. Incidentally, Asians, rather than Asian Americans, is the preferred indexing term in PsycINFO because there are Asians in the United States, Canada, United Kingdom, Brazil, and many other countries. We could then plot the growth of the field by various time periods from 1991. Using the time periods established by the PsycINFO database, we found that the number of entries devoted to Asians grew from 1,834 in 1967–1991 to 2,739 in 1994, which was a 49% increase. It continued to grow from 2,739 entries in 1994 to 3,558 entries in 1997 (another 29% increase), from 3,558 to 4,147 in 1999 (16% increase), from 4,147 to 5,148 in 2002 (24% increase), and finally from 5,148 to 6,045 in 2005 (17% increase). Put differently, the coverage of Asians in the psychological literature as represented in PsycINFO grew 229% in the 14 years from 1991 to 2005.

Another perspective on the coverage of substantive areas is to review the various books that have been published on this topic. Although there have been numerous books published on Asian Americans from the perspective of Asian American Studies (e.g., Kitano and Daniels's *Asian Americans: Emerging Minorities,* first published in 1988 with subsequent editions published in 1995 and 2000), our present focus is on books with a psychological focus. The first two volumes on this topic were published by Stanley Sue and his colleagues: (a) *Asian Americans: Psychological Perspectives,* coedited by Stanley Sue and Nathaniel Wagner in 1973; and (b) *Asian Americans: Social and Psychological Perspectives, Volume 2,* coedited by Russell Endo, Stanley Sue, and Nathaniel Wagner in 1980. With the increasing attention paid to this population and the growing literature, Stanley Sue obtained a grant with James Morishima from the NIMH to provide an overview to the Asian American mental health literature. The *Handbook of Asian American/Pacific Islander Mental Health, Volume 1* (1980) was published by NIMH with Morishima, Sue, Teng, Zane, and Cram as coeditors. This volume was essentially an annotated bibliography, with Volume 2 providing the critical analysis of the literature. Volume 2 was later published as the now classic *Mental Health of Asian Americans* by Stanley Sue and James Morishima (1982). An updated annotated bibliography titled *Asians in the United States: Abstracts of the Psychological and Behavioral Literature, 1967–1991* was later coedited by Leong and Whitfield (1992) and published by APA as part of the bibliography series on racial and ethnic minority groups. Incidentally, the Morishima et al. NIMH bibliography contained 401 entries, whereas the Leong and Whitfield bibliography covered 1,750 entries. As mentioned earlier in this chapter, a recent search of the PsycINFO database found 6,045 entries on Asians as of October 2005. This tremendous growth in the literature probably parallels the fact that Asian Americans have been one of the fastest-growing ethnic minority groups in the United States, with projections that they will move from 10.9 million in 2002 to 37 million in 2050.

While the Sue and Morishima (1982) volume on the mental health of Asian Americans has remained a classic in the field, other volumes had also begun to emerge. For example, Laura Uba published her *Asian Americans: Personality Patterns, Identity, and Mental Health* in 1994, which many have considered to be an update and successor to the Sue and Morishima (1982) volume. Some years later, Uba (2002) published *A Postmodern Psychology of Asian Americans: Creating Knowledge of a Racial Minority*, a volume in which she suggested that Asian American psychology can move in a new direction by incorporating a postmodern perspective into our scholarship and teaching. Other volumes were devoted to specialty topics within Asian American psychology, for example, Zane, Takeuchi, and Young's (1994) volume on health psychology, titled *Confronting Critical Health Issues of Asian and Pacific Islander Americans* (Sage). Other examples of specialty books include Kurasaki, Okasaki, and Sue's (2002)

Asian American Mental Health: Assessment Theories and Methods, which focused on assessment, and Evelyn Lee's (1997) *Working With Asian Americans: A Guide for Clinicians*, which focused on therapy and treatment. One of the most recent additions to the book literature is *Asian American Psychology: The Science of Lives in Context*, coedited by Gordon C. Nagayama Hall and Sumie Okazaki (2002). The chapters for this book were presented at a one-day "think-tank" meeting during the 2000 AAPA convention, and the feedback and comments from the think-tank participants were incorporated into the final versions of the chapters. Of course, one knows that most fields of inquiry have actually matured when they launch a handbook, and this occurred with the publication of the first edition of the *Handbook of Asian American Psychology* (Lee & Zane, 1998). The second edition of the *Handbook of Asian American Psychology*, in which this present chapter appears, was an AAPA presidential initiative of Frederick Leong with several members of his executive committee (Arpana Inman, Angela Ebreo, Lawrence Yang, Lisa Kinoshita, and Michi Fu).

FORECASTING THE FUTURE

Despite the tremendous advances and accomplishments of Asian American psychology in its first three decades, there are many areas in Asian American psychology that need further research and clinical attention. In this section, we describe the results of a survey of the experts in the field regarding important areas for future development in Asian American psychology.

Method

As the forecasting tool, we used the Delphi polling method (Linstone & Turoff, 1975; Turoff & Linstone, 2002). Consistent with the first step of the Delphi method, a pool of identified experts (23 AAPA charter fellows) was contacted by e-mail, telephone, or both[2] to ask for their participation. On agreement, a telephone interview was scheduled and conducted with each of the respondents. Participants were also given the option of responding to the interview questions in writing instead of through the phone interview. Respondents were asked their opinions regarding the future of Asian American psychology, the field's progress in important research topics, service availability and delivery, education and training of psychologists, and understudied populations, among many other topics. The interviews were recorded for later analyses.

Based on an analysis and synthesis of the initial interviews, items were generated to create a three-part questionnaire. Part 1 (40 items) asked about the experts' thoughts regarding the field's progress and interest in the next 10 years in various topics, issues, or areas pertaining to theory, research, and practice. For example, "Within the next 10 years, how much progress (in terms of research, publications, knowledge base, approved grant applications, approved research funding, community programs, services, interest) do you think the field of Asian American psychology WILL have regarding lesbian, gay, bisexual, and transgender Asians?" Part 2 (17 items) is divided into two sections and asked the experts about (Section 1) their thoughts regarding how much the field will increase or decrease the number of various training opportunities and (Section 2) their thoughts regarding the field's progress and interest in the next 10 years in various topics, issues, or areas pertaining to the training and preparation of psychologists. For example, (Section 1) "Within the next 10 years, how much do you think the field of Asian American psychology WILL increase or decrease the number of training workshops on Asian American psychology?" and (Section 2) "Regarding the training and preparation of psychologists within the next 10 years, how much progress (in terms of workshops, seminars, classes, doctoral programs, internships, etc.) do you think the field of Asian American psychology WILL have addressing culturally appropriate research methods?" Part 3 (26 items) asked about participants' thoughts regarding AAPA's progress and interest in the next 10 years in various topics, issues, or areas that are of concern to the organization. For example, "Within the next 10 years, how much progress do you think the Asian American Psychological Association (AAPA) WILL have in its efforts to bring Asian American psychology into mainstream psychology?"

Except for the items in Section 1 of Part 2, the respondents were given five answer choices for all items: No progress, with significant decrease in interest and activity; No progress, with slight decrease in interest and activity; Very little to no change; Good progress, with continued interest and activity; and Significant progress, with increased interest and activity.

For Section 1 of Part 2 (Training and Preparation), the answer choices were Significant decrease, Slight decrease, No change, Slight increase, and Significant increase.

Immediately following each of the three parts, the respondents were asked to rate the top five most important topics, issues, or areas they think *SHOULD* be given more attention by the field or by the AAPA (for Part 3).

Results and Discussion

Nineteen AAPA charter fellows agreed to respond to the interview questions, either through the telephone or by writing. After analysis and synthesis of their responses and development of the questionnaire items, the survey was sent to all of the charter fellows regardless of whether they participated in the interview round. The survey round yielded 19 respondents (11 males and 8 females), the majority of them being Chinese American descent ($n = 12$).[2]

Overall, the predictions of the panel were optimistic, suggesting that they viewed Asian American psychology as continuing its progress across all of its endeavors. To identify the aggregate ranking of all the topics, issues, or areas that the experts believe will experience significant progress and are the most important, we gave numerical weights to the experts' predictions. Specifically, a response of "No progress, with significant decrease in interest and activity" was weighted as 1, "No progress, with slight decrease in interest and activity" was weighted as 2, "Very little to no change" was weighted as 3, "Good progress, with continued interest and activity" was weighted as 4, and "Significant progress, with increased interest and activity" was weighted as 5. (Note: The same weighting system was also used for Part 2, Section 1, with "Significant decrease" = 1, "Slight decrease" = 2, etc.). This coding system was also used for the parts of the questionnaire in which the panel was asked to select and rank-order the top five topics, issues, or areas they think *SHOULD* be given more attention, with a first place vote = 5 points, second place = 4 points, third place = 3 points, fourth place = 2 points, and fifth place = 1 point.

Part 1. Theory, Research, and Practice

According to the panel, the topic, issue, or area that they predicted would experience the greatest amount of progress within the next 10 years is cultural competence (see Table 2.3). Fifty-two percent of the experts believed that cultural competence will experience "Significant progress, with increased interest and activity." An additional 37% predicted "Good progress, with continued interest and activity" on cultural competence in the next 10 years. Rounding out the top five topics, issues, or areas in terms of Asian American psychological theory, research, and practice were multiracial Asian Americans; multiethnic Asian Americans; biculturalism/bicultural competence, and cultural identity. Also shown in Table 2.3 are the topics, issues, or areas that need the most attention. According to the panel, cultural competence was the most important topic, issue, or area that needs to be addressed, followed by empirically supported treatments, culture-specific constructs (e.g., neurasthenia, loss of face), Asian coping styles, and cultural identity.

Part 2. Training and Preparation of Psychologists

The panel predicted that the number of doctoral students specializing in Asian American psychology will increase significantly within the next 10 years. They also predicted that the number of training workshops in Asian American psychology, seminars or classes in Asian American psychology, doctoral programs with faculty specializing in Asian American psychology, and pre-doctoral internships specifically tailored for Asian American psychology will increase within 10 years. On Section 2, the panel predicted that the training and preparation topic, issue, or area that will experience the most amount of progress is cultural competence in service delivery, receiving a "Significant progress, with increased

interest and activity" prediction from 26% of the panel and a "Good progress, with continued interest and activity" prediction from an additional 68%. Ranked second through fifth were ethnic-specific competence, culturally appropriate research methods, clinical skills development, and empirically supported treatments. Table 2.4 presents the training opportunities (Section 1) and topics, issues, or areas (Section 2) that the panel believed deserve more attention. Cultural competence in service delivery topped the list, followed by culturally appropriate research methods, empirically supported treatments, clinical skills development, and ethnic-specific competence.

One major theme that arises from these results is the relative importance that the panel of experts placed on the need for current and future psychologists to become more culturally competent in all aspects of their professional careers. More specifically, these results indicate that current and future psychologists need to learn and utilize Asian-specific and culturally appropriate techniques and strategies in both research and service settings.

Part 3. Social/Organizational

According to the panel, within the next 10 years, AAPA will have the most progress in its efforts to attract new members into the organization, receiving a "Significant progress, with increased interest and activity" prediction from 26% of the panel and a "Good progress, with continued interest and activity" prediction from an additional 63%. Completing the top five were to become more inclusive of other Asian groups, become more sensitive to women's issues, attract young people into the discipline, and improve the scientific basis of Asian American psychology. Table 2.5 displays the topics, issues, or areas that the panel believed deserve more AAPA attention. The top five are to improve the political basis of Asian American psychology, improve the scientific basis of Asian American psychology, become more inclusive of other Asian ethnic groups, bring Asian American psychology into mainstream psychology, and politically advocate for issues affecting Asian American communities.

Table 2.3   Rankings of Topics, Issues, or Areas in Terms of Theory, Research, and Practice

	Predictions Within the Next 10 Years			*Topics, Issues, Areas Needing Attention*	
Rank	*Topic, Issue, or Area*	*Total Points*	*Rank*	*Topic, Issue, or Area*	*Total Points*
1	Cultural Competence	84	1	Cultural Competence	44
2	Multiracial AA	78	2	Empirically Supported Treatments	24
2	Multiethnic AA	78	3	Culture-Specific Constructs	19
2	Biculturalism	78	4	Asian Coping Styles	17
5	Cultural Identity	77	4	Cultural Identity	17
6	Multiracial Marriages	76	6	Multiethnic AA	12
7	Family Issues	75	6	Family Issues	12
8	The Elderly	74	6	Domestic Violence	12
9	Immigrant Populations	73	9	Multiracial Marriages	11
10	AA Females	71	10	Multiracial AA	10
11	LGBT	71	10	Immigrant Populations	10
12	South Asians	71	10	Development of Culture-Specific Assessment Instruments	10
12	Expressions of Cultural Values	71	13	The Elderly	9
12	Domestic Violence	71	13	Expressions of Cultural Values	9
15	Acculturation	70	13	Acculturation	9
16	Empirically Supported Treatments	69	16	Racism	8
16	Parenting Issues	69	17	Youths and Gangs	7
16	Substance Abuse	69	18	AA Males	6
19	Youths and Gangs	68	19	AA Females	5
19	Development of Culture-Specific Assessment Instruments	68	19	Substance Abuse	5
21	Vietnamese Americans	67	21	Contemporary Oppression	4
21	Asian Coping Styles	67	21	Parenting Issues	4
21	Culture-Specific Constructs	67	21	Media Portrayal of Asians	4
21	Generation Gaps	67	21	Stigma of Mental Disorders	4
25	Racism	66	25	Biculturalism	3
25	Contemporary Oppression	66	25	Underutilization & Termination	3
25	Stigma of Mental Disorders	66	27	LGBT	2
28	Filipino Americans	65	27	Racialization	2
28	Media Portrayal of Asians	65	27	How AA Communities Function	2
28	Sexual Risk Behaviors	65	30	Generation Gaps	1
31	Underutilization & Termination	64	31	Extended Families	0
32	AA Males	63	32	Asian Refugees	0
33	Asian Refugees	62	32	Filipino Americans	0
33	Racialization	62	32	South Asians	0
33	How AA Communities Function	62	32	Vietnamese Americans	0
36	Transnationalism	61	32	Lao	0
37	Extended Families	60	32	Transnationalism	0
38	Lao	58	32	Historical Oppression	0
39	Historical Oppression	54	32	Colonization	0
40	Colonization	49	32	Sexual Risk Behaviors	0

Note: AA, Asian Americans; LGBT, lesbian, gay, bisexual, transgender.

Table 2.4   Rankings of Opportunities, Topics, Issues, or Areas in Terms of Training and Preparation

	Predictions Within the Next 10 Years			*Opportunities, Topics, Issues, or Areas Needing Attention*	
Rank	*Training Opportunities (Section 1)*	*Total Points*	*Rank*	*Opportunities, Topic, Issue, or Area*	*Total Points*
1	Doctoral Students Specializing in AA	77	1	Cultural Competence in Service Delivery	60
2	Training Workshops on AA Psychology	75	2	Culturally Appropriate Research Methods	55
2	Seminars or Classes in AA Psychology	75	3	Empirically Supported Treatments	29
4	Doctoral Programs With Faculty Specializing in AA Psychology	67	4	Clinical Skills Development	26
4	Predoctoral Internships Tailored for AA	67	5	Developing Ethnic-Specific Competence	20
6	Postdoctoral Internships Tailored for AA	66	6	Seminars or Classes in AA Psychology	19
6	Predoctoral Training Grants for AA Research	66	6	Doctoral Programs With Faculty Specializing in AA Psychology	19
8	Postdoctoral Training Grants for AA Research	64	8	Training Workshops on AA Psychology	16
Rank	*Topic, Issue, or Area (Section 2)*	*Total Points*	9	Experimental Research Paradigms	10
1	Cultural Competence in Service Delivery	80	10	Indigenous Psychology Research Paradigms	9
2	Developing Ethnic-Specific Competence	76	11	Postdoctoral Training Grants for AA Research	7
3	Culturally Appropriate Research Methods	74	12	Predoctoral Training Grants for AA Research	4
4	Clinical Skills Development	73	12	Self-Examination of Prejudice	4
5	Empirically Supported Treatments	71	14	Predoctoral Internships Tailored for AA	3
6	Consciousness Raising	69	14	Postdoctoral Internships Tailored for AA	3
6	Experimental Research Paradigms	69	16	Consciousness Raising	1
8	Indigenous Psychology Research Paradigms	67	17	Doctoral Students Specializing in AA	0
9	Self-Examination of Prejudice	60			

Note: AA, Asian Americans.

Table 2.5   Rankings of Social/Organizational Topics, Issues, or Areas

	Predictions Within the Next 10 Years			Topics, Issues, Areas Needing Attention	
Rank	Topic, Issue, or Area	Total Points	Rank	Topic, Issue, or Area	Total Points
1	Attract New Members	79	1	Improve the Political Basis	38
2	Be More Inclusive of Other Asians	76	2	Improve the Scientific Basis	36
2	Be More Sensitive to Women's Issues	76	3	Be More Inclusive of Other Asians	28
2	Attract Young People Into AA Psychology	76	4	Bring AA Psychology Into Mainstream Psychology	25
5	Improve the Scientific Basis	74	5	Politically Advocate for AA Community	21
6	Create Systematic Mentoring	73	6	Have Research Influence Policy	19
7	Improve the Political Basis	72	6	Attract New Members	19
7	Politically Advocate for AA Community	72	8	Create Systematic Mentoring	17
7	Have Research Influence Policy	72	9	Reestablish a Scientific Journal	13
10	Pay More Attention to Asians and Asian Issues	71	10	Collaborate and Make Alliances With AA Community Organizations	12
10	Bring AA Psychology Into Mainstream Psychology	71	11	Educate the Mainstream About Variability in AA Population	10
10	Collaborate and Make Alliances With Other Ethnic Minority Organizations	71	12	Attract Young People Into AA Psychology	9
13	Be More Inclusive of Pacific Islanders	70	13	Be More Inclusive of Pacific Islanders	6
13	Increase Representation Outside of California	70	14	Collaborate and Make Alliances With Other Ethnic Minority Organizations	4
15	Increase the Visibility of AAPA in the Media	69	14	Improve AA Community's Perception of Psychology	4
16	Collaborate and Make Alliances With AA Community Organizations	68	16	Pay More Attention to Asians and Asian Issues	3
16	Make Information More Easily Accessible to AA	68	16	Be More Sensitive to Women's Issues	3
16	Improve AA Community's Perception of Psychology	68	16	Reach AA in Areas With Low Concentration of AA	3
19	Educate the Mainstream About Variability Within AA Population	67	16	Make Information More Easily Accessible to AA	3
19	Educate AA About Variability Within AA Population	67	16	Make Better Connections With the Younger Generations	3

19	Make Better Connections With the Younger Generations	67	22	Increase the Visibility of AAPA in the Media	2
23	Integrate Multiple Disciplines Into the Field of AA Psychology	66	22	Clearly Disseminate Knowledge to AA Communities	2
23	Reestablish a Scientific Journal	66	24	Collaborate and Make Alliances With Organizations in Asia	1
25	Reach AA in Areas With Low Concentration of AA	62	24	Increase Representation Outside of California	1
26	Collaborate and Make Alliances With Organizations in Asia	60	26	Educate AA About Variability Within AA Population	0

Note: AA, Asian American; AAPA, Asian American Psychological Association.

Three major themes arise from these results: (a) AAPA, as an organization, needs to increase the number of its members and address the needs of its current members; (b) AAPA needs to solidify its political influence through several strategies; and (c) AAPA needs to become more responsive to the needs of the Asian American community. Based on the initial interviews, an overwhelming majority of the experts believe that although attracting new and younger members into the organization or Asian American psychology is important, AAPA also needs to address the concerns of its current members. For instance, many fellows pointed out that many non-Chinese or non-Japanese members feel neglected in both social (e.g., conference activities) and academic (e.g., research activities) settings. It was also a common sentiment among the fellows that the AAPA needs to further strengthen its political influence by increasing collaboration with other ethnic organizations, having research play a more influential role in public policy, and further legitimizing the status of Asian American psychology by increasing the scientific sophistication of its research activities. Finally, the experts also believe that it is important for AAPA, in terms of its activities (e.g., research, service), to become more connected and responsive to issues that Asian American communities perceive as important. Becoming more culturally attuned to the issues and concerns of the community may facilitate an improvement in how Asian American communities perceive psychology and psychologists.

CONCLUSION

Our review of the history of Asian American psychology has shown that AAPA has been at the center of this movement. From a small group of Asian psychologists who met informally in California back in the early 1970s, AAPA has grown to an association with close to 500 members. Some of the leading members of AAPA have played significant roles in advancing the welfare of Americans at the national level. For example, Stanley Sue was involved in President Carter's Mental Health Commission and more recently authored a chapter for the Surgeon General's Report on Culture, Race, and Ethnicity. Larke Nahme Huang served on the current President's New Freedom Commission on Mental Health. We even had one of our members serve as a president of APA (Richard Suinn, 1999). Our Delphi poll also confirmed that AAPA will remain an active and vibrant association concerned with advancing the welfare of Asian Americans through psychology for the foreseeable future.

NOTES

1. In 1991, the Board for the Advancement of the Public Interest in Psychology (BAPIP) replaced BSERP and BEMA. This merger was accomplished by James M. Jones, the executive director of the Public Interest Directorate (Smith, 1992).

2. We gratefully acknowledge the following AAPA charter members who participated in the Delphi poll in the interview (I) and survey (S) rounds: Alice Chang (I, S), S. Andrew Chen (I, S), Jean Lau Chin (I, S), David Goh (I, S), Christine Iijima Hall (I, S), Gordon C. N. Hall (I, S), George Hong (S), Larke Nahme Huang (I), Gayle Y. Iwamasa (S), Yoshito Kawahara (I, S), Frederick Leong (I, S), J.-C. Gisela Lin (I, S), Chalsa Loo (I, S), Jeffrey S. Mio (I, S), John Moritsugu (I, S), Maria P. P. Root (I), Derald W. Sue (I, S), Stanley Sue (I, S), Reiko Homma True (I, S), Herbert Z. Wong (I, S), and Nolan W. S. Zane (I, S).

REFERENCES

Asian American Psychological Association. (1979, October–December). New journal format. *Journal of the Asian American Psychological Association, 5*(1).

Council of National Psychological Association for the Advancement of Ethnic Minority Interests. (2000). *Guidelines for research with ethnic minority communities.* Washington, DC: American Psychological Association. Available at http://www.apa.org/pi/oema/programs/ cnpaaemi_pubs.html

Endo, R., Sue, S., & Wagner, N. N. (Eds.). (1980). *Asian-Americans: Social and psychological perspectives* (Vol. 2). Palo Alto, CA: Science & Behavior Books.

Hall, G. C. N., & Okazaki, S. (2002). *Asian American psychology: The science of lives in context.* Washington, DC: American Psychological Association.

Kurasaki, K. S., Okazaki, S., & Sue, S. (2002). *Asian American mental health: Assessment theories and methods.* New York: Kluwer Academic/ Plenum.

Lee, E. (1997). *Working with Asian Americans: A guide for clinicians.* New York: Guilford Press.

Lee, L. C., & Zane, N. W. S. (1998). *Handbook of Asian American psychology.* Thousand Oaks, CA: Sage.

Leong, F. T. L. (1995). History of Asian American psychology. *Asian American Psychological Association Monograph Series, 1.*

Leong, F. T. L., & Whitfield, J. R. (Eds.). (1992). *Asians in the United States: Abstracts of the psychological and behavioral literature, 1967–1991.* Washington, DC: American Psychological Association.

Linstone, H. A., & Turoff, M. (1975). *The Delphi method: Techniques and applications.* Reading, MA: Addison-Wesley.

Morishima, J. K., Sue, S., Teng, L. N., Zane, N. W. S., & Cram, J. R. (1980). *Handbook of Asian American/Pacific Islander mental health* (Vol. 1). Rockville, MD: National Institute of Mental Health.

Pallak, M. S. (1992). Growth, conflict, and public policy: The American Psychological Association from 1970 to 1985. In R. B. Evans, V. S. Sexton, & T. C. Cadwallader (Eds.), *The American Psychological Association: A historical perspective* (pp. 233–262). Washington, DC: American Psychological Association.

Smith, M. B. (1992). The American Psychological Association and social responsibility. In R. B. Evans, V. S. Sexton, & T. C. Cadwallader (Eds.), *The American Psychological Association: A historical perspective* (pp. 327–345). Washington, DC: American Psychological Association.

Sue, S., & Chin, R. (1976). *The National Asian American Psychology Training Conference: The report of the conference, 1976, Long Beach, California.* Phoenix, AZ: Asian American Psychological Association.

Sue, S., Sue, D. W., & Sue, D. (1975). Asian Americans as a minority group. *American Psychologist, 30,* 906–910.

Sue, S., & Morishima, J. (1982). *The mental health of Asian Americans: Contemporary issues in identifying and treating mental health problems.* San Francisco: Jossey-Bass.

Sue, S., & Wagner, N. N. (1973). *Asian-Americans: Psychological perspectives.* Palo Alto, CA: Science & Behavior Books.

Turoff, M., & Linstone, H. A. (2002). The Delphi method: Techniques and applications [Electronic version]. Retrieved August 5, 2005, from http://www.is.njit.edu/pubs/delphibook/ index.html

Uba, L. (1994). *Asian Americans: Personality patterns, identity, and mental health.* New York: Guilford Press.

Uba, L. (2002). *A postmodern psychology of Asian Americans: Creating knowledge of a racial minority.* Buffalo, NY: SUNY Press.

Zane, N. W. S., Takeuchi, D. T., & Young, K. N. J. (1994). *Confronting critical health issues of Asian and Pacific Islander Americans.* Thousand Oaks, CA: Sage.

3

Theoretical and Conceptual Models: Toward Asian Americanist Psychology

Sumie Okazaki

Richard M. Lee

Stanley Sue

What theoretical and conceptual models do we employ in Asian American psychology? The literature in Asian American psychology to date has raised many questions about whether all or most theories and principles in psychology are sufficient. However, there has not been a clear explication to date on which, if any, theories are best suited in psychological research and practice with Asian Americans. Moreover, the intellectual relationship between Asian American psychology and major theoretical movements that have been associated with ethnic and gender scholarship—such as critical theory, feminist theory, queer theory, postcolonial theory, indigenous psychology, and so on—have not been extensively discussed. This is not to say that Asian American psychology is atheoretical. Far from it, scholars and practitioners of Asian American psychology have contributed to the development of conceptual models relevant to multiple aspects of the Asian American psychological experience and

ethnic minority psychology. In this chapter, we discuss some of the major theories and concepts that have been produced or employed to better understand the psychology of Asian Americans. We then build on these considerations to suggest a reformulation of Asian American psychology that would bring the field of Asian American psychology full circle back to its roots in ethnic studies scholarship.

Before we proceed, a brief explanation of the scope of our discussion is needed. In considering what theoretical and conceptual issues are relevant to Asian American psychology, we discuss both specific theories (e.g., cultural competence) as well as the underlying epistemological and ontological questions that frame the questions we may ask in Asian American psychology. At a first glance, ontological questions (e.g., What is the nature of the world and people?) and epistemological questions (e.g., What can we know about the world and people?) may seem to be in the realm of philosophy far removed from theoretical and conceptual questions we typically ask in Asian American psychology. However, as articulated by critical psychologists (e.g., Nightingale & Neilands, 1997), these ontological and episte-mological issues are inextricably tied to the methodology used to carry out the project of psy-chology. Consequently, although this chapter's focus is on the theoretical and conceptual issues, we discuss methodological issues in Asian American psychology to the extent that there are relevant consequences of particular theoretical approaches in Asian American psychology.

MAJOR AREAS OF CONCEPTUAL DEVELOPMENT

Scholars in Asian American psychology have contributed to the development of theories and conceptual models, particularly in the applied areas of psychology. These substantive content areas include acculturation (e.g., Suinn, Rickard-Figueroa, Lew, & Vigil, 1987; Tsai, Ying, & Lee, 2000), identity development (e.g., D.W. Sue & D. Sue, 1990), academic achieve-ment and career development (e.g., Leong & Hardin, 2002; S. Sue & Okazaki, 1990), parent-ing and family dynamics (e.g., Chao, 1994), biracial identity (e.g., Root, 1998), multicultural psychology (e.g., D. W. Sue et al., 1999), psy-chopathology (e.g., Hall, 2003), and cultural competence in psychotherapy and mental health services (e.g., Hall, 2001; S. Sue, 1999; S. Sue & Zane, 1987). Because this space does not allow for a comprehensive review of all theories and concepts in Asian American psychology, we have elected to discuss the theoretical bases of the constructs that appear most fundamental to the premise of Asian American psychology— and Asian American Studies in general—that form the basis for all else that follows. These constructs are (a) race, culture, and ethnicity; (b) acculturation; and (c) ethnicity and identity.

Race and Culture

Are Asian Americans an ethnic group, a cul-tural group, or a racial group? As a term used to designate those who reside in the United States (and sometimes inclusive of Canada) of full-or part-Asian descent, *Asian American* has become a catch-all phrase to designate all of the above. In fact, the notions of Asian America as a race, culture, and ethnicity permeate the research questions asked in Asian American psychology. To be sure, there has been an active dialogue in psychology (primarily initiated by ethnic minor-ity psychology researchers) concerning exactly what we are referring to with respect to the ques-tions of race, culture, and ethnicity (e.g., Betancourt & Lopez, 1993; Helms, 1994; Phinney, 1996; Pope-Davis & Liu, 1998; Yee, Fairchild, Weizmann, & Wyatt, 1993), and Asian American psychologists have taken an active part in this discussion. Notwithstanding the des-ignation of Asians as a "race" by the U.S. Census Bureau, Asian American psychology has, for the most part, focused on the notion of Asian Americans as a cultural group rather than as a racial group. This may be, in part, because Asian American psychology has followed the intellec-tual tradition of cross-cultural psychology and, in part, because the notion of race as a biological construct has been debunked (see e.g., Smedley & Smedley, 2005; Yee et al., 1993).

Asian America as culture. Asian American psychology research has borrowed heavily from cross-cultural psychology with respect to both methodological and intellectual approaches. The de facto paradigm in cross-cultural psy-chology is a comparative framework in which psychological constructs developed in the West are examined across two or more cultural groups, with the resulting differences explained in terms of cultural differences between the West and the other culture. Perhaps it is because so much of cross-cultural psychology has flour-ished with the East-West comparisons (typically comparisons between the United States and East Asian nations) that the extension of both the methodological and theoretical paradigms to Asian American psychology has been an easy one. In both cross-cultural American–East Asian comparisons and cross-ethnic European American–Asian American comparisons, some aspect of Asian culture is invoked either post hoc or as a measured variable. In fact, there has been a notable trend within cross-cultural social psychological research to use the within-U.S. cross-ethnic comparisons of European Americans and Asian Americans as a replication of cross-national comparisons of Americans and East Asians (e.g., Oishi & Diener, 2003).

So what are the theorized elements of Asian culture that have been used to explain these cross-national and cross-ethnic differences? By far, the most dominant cultural theories for both cross-cultural psychology and Asian American psychology are the constructs of individualism-collectivism (Triandis, 1989) and independent-interdependent self-construal (Markus & Kitayama, 1991). The invocation of these theories to explain Asian American behavior are evident in discussions of a wide range of phenomena from depression and anxiety (e.g., Okazaki, 1997), psychopathology and psycho-therapy (e.g., Hall, 2003), child-rearing beliefs (Chao, 1995), academic achievement (U. Kim & Chun, 1994), career development (Leong & Hardin, 2002), to violence (Hall, 2002).

Secondary to the use of individualism-collectivism as a cultural explanation, there is a set of specific Asian cultural constructs that have been invoked. Most frequently, the cultural explanations include some references to Confucianism and its derivatives (e.g., filial piety and obligations, prescriptions of roles, etc.) and face and its derivatives (loss of face, shame). For example, Chao (1994) has argued that concepts of authoritative and authoritarian parenting (and the associated differential out-comes for children's achievement) are ethno-centric to the West and that the parenting styles of immigrant Chinese American mothers can be better described using the Chinese notions of *chiao shun* and *guan,* which are referenced to the role relationships described by Confucius.

B. S. K. Kim and colleagues (2005) have attempted to identify (via scale development) the core Asian cultural values that are salient to all Asian Americans but would be endorsed most strongly by those who are highly encultur-ated. Included in the resulting measure, the Asian American Values Scale, are the following five value dimensions: collectivism, conformity to norms, emotional self-control, family recog-nition through achievement, and humility. Kim et al.'s scale was developed to engender more specificity—that is, which aspects of Asian cultural values are associated with various psychological phenomena—and consequently, the value dimensions were empirically and

theoretically conceptualized as separable dimensions. However, each cultural dimension identified by Kim et al. can be viewed as a refrain on the familiar theme of collectivism-individualism or Confucian moral code.

On the one hand, these attempts to identify and examine non-Western concepts to under-stand the mentality and behavior of Asian Americans make significant contributions. There is an implicit, and sometimes explicit, argument made by Asian American researchers that Asian American behaviors are not always best understood using Western theories and that some practices (e.g., parenting practices that appear "authoritarian") are actually normative rather than pathological within this non-Western perspective.

On the other hand, several critiques are also leveled against these attempts to provide cul-tural explanations for Asian American behavior. First, the "culture" in question most often does not refer to Asian American culture (i.e., culture that is distinct from Asian culture or American culture). In most cases, the culture invoked to explain the mental life and behavior of Asian American individuals (even those who are Southeast Asian American or South Asian American) refers to primarily East Asian cul-ture. In fact, there has been very little conceptu-alization and research regarding the nature and impact of the hybrid, diasporic *Asian American* culture in Asian American psychology. One descriptive example of a hybrid culture in Asian American psychology can be seen in the work of Miyamoto (1986–1987). Miyamoto has hypothesized that Japanese American Nisei (children of immigrants) developed a unique personality and interactional style. Based on Japanese and American cultural values, the product of the two for the Nisei resulted in a hybrid. For example, spontaneity and directness in communication styles among Americans can be contrasted with self-restraint and inhibition among Japanese. The Nisei had to find means to spontaneously express themselves and yet show self-restraint. To adapt to both cultures, many Nisei developed a joking style. Miyamoto argues that joking implies that what is being said is not to be taken seriously. It therefore tends to neutralize interpersonal sensitivities, and it allows the Nisei to express themselves more spontaneously. Strictly speaking, this style is culturally neither Japanese nor American.

Second, the East Asian cultural values that are often used to explain Asian American behavior are often portrayed in an essentialized manner, divorced from other cultural sources that influence values and behavior (such as religion, urban vs. rural setting, contemporary societal changes in Asia, etc.) In a recent report in a major national newspaper about extremely long lines for attractions at the newly opened Hong Kong Disneyland, a former Disney theme park designer who, at one time, was involved in the Tokyo Disneyland gave the following explanation for why he thought the Japanese patrons were more patient about waiting in long lines than were Western patrons: "They are very Eastern mystical in their ignoring everyone else, and that's why they are able to deal with long lines" (Fountain, 2005). As scholars and practitioners, we cringe at such a broad and unabashedly exotic characterization of the behavior of Japanese patrons at a theme park. However cast in the academic language, there is a similar danger in Asian American psychology that explaining contemporary Asian American behavior using Confucianism results in the perpetuation of homogenized and stereotyped characterization of Asian Americans.

Third, cross-cultural psychology researchers themselves have begun to question the utility of broad constructs such as individualism-collectivism. For example, Matsumoto (1999) criticized Markus and Kitayama's (1991) theory of independent and interdependent self-construal on the basis of inconsistent results of various cross-cultural studies of individualism-collectivism measures. Similarly, Oyserman, Coon, and Kemmelmeier's (2002) meta-analysis of cross-cultural differences on individualism-collectivism measures found that overall, European Americans were not more individualistic than African Americans or Latino Americans in the within-U.S. comparisons and not less collectivistic than Japanese or Koreans in cross-national studies (but see Schimmack, Oishi, & Diener, 2005). Hermans and Kempen (1998) have argued that cultural dichotomies (e.g., individualistic vs. collectivistic cultures) also do not reflect the increasingly complex, hybrid, and interconnected nature of cultures in the era of globalization.

Asian America as race. Modern psychology's treatment of race is aptly summarized by the title of a recent paper by Smedley and Smedley (2005) published in the *American Psychologist:* "Race as Biology Is Fiction, Racism as a Social Problem Is Real." It is now widely accepted that race is a social construction rather than a fixed entity that is based in biology. Some have used this debunking of race as a biological entity, and the lack of consensual scientific or theoretical meaning of race in psychology, as bases for recommending that psychology researchers avoid using the term *race* to refer to ethnic groups in the United States (Phinney, 1996; Yee et al., 1993; Zuckerman, 1990), and the American Psychological Association's Council of Representatives has passed a resolution opposing the use of race as an explanatory construct in psychology (Yee, 1983). More recently, theorists such as Helms, Jernigan, and Mascher (2005), as well as Smedley and Smedley (2005), have articulated the way in which psychological research can shed light on the impact of race, as a socially constructed but lived experience, on human behavior. Specifically, these authors call attention to the effects of society's racial categorization, including both the meanings attached to race (e.g., racial identity) and the real-life and public policy consequences of historical and contemporary racism (e.g., health disparities, poverty).

It appears clear that the use of race (to imply innate biological differences) as an explanation for group differences in behavior is not scientifically defensible, and studies of Asian American–White American comparisons have tended to favor cultural explanations. Whereas Black psychology has continued to interrogate the questions of racial identity and effects of racism, Asian American psychology has not engaged as rigorously in the theoretical and empirical work surrounding race. This relative lack of attention to racialized experience of Asian Americans in psychology is puzzling given the history of Asian immigrants and their descendants in the United States as racialized "others" against whom various discriminatory legislations and executive orders have been enacted.

Perhaps the most forceful empirical documentation of the psychological legacy of historical oppression has been Donna Nagata's (1990) work with the children of Japanese American internment camp survivors. In her work, Nagata has employed theoretical models of transgenerational transmission of trauma developed with the survivors of the Nazi Holocaust as well as the Japanese cultural values of modesty and shame to explain the intergenerational silence surrounding this historical act of injustice.

There have also been some efforts in recent years to begin identifying and assessing racial identity and its effects on Asian Americans. For example, Alvarez and Helms (2001) extended Helms's racial identity model to Asian Americans. Loo et al. (2001) developed the Race-Related Stressor Scale to assess exposure to race-related stressors among Asian American Vietnam War veterans. Liang, Li, and Kim (2004) developed the Asian American Racism-Related Stress Inventory to assess awareness of sociohistorical racism, general racism, and the "perpetual foreigner" racism among Asian American university students. Another way in which the effects of racialization on Asian Americans have been discussed within Asian American psychology has been the examination of the effects of the "model minority" stereotype on Asian Americans (e.g., Cheryan & Bodenhausen, 2000; Oyserman & Sakamoto, 1997; Ying et al., 2001). However, in our view, there is much room for theoretical and conceptual development surrounding the experience and the consequences of racialization among Asian Americans.

Acculturation

One of the central constructs in both cross-cultural psychology and ethnic minority psychology is acculturation, and Asian American psychologists have participated actively in the refinement of theories and measurement. For example, Kevin Chun, along with Pamela Balls Organista and Gerardo Marín (2002), edited a volume compiling the most recent theories and research on acculturation, to which a number of Asian American researchers contributed chapters. In addition, research with Asian Americans (and Asian Canadians) has contributed to empirical advances in acculturation research (e.g., Flannery, Reise, & Yu, 2001; Ryder, Alden, & Paulhus, 2000) as well as in related constructs such as ethnic identity and cultural orientation

(e.g., Tsai, Chentsova-Dutton, & Wong, 2002; Tsai et al., 2000).

One of the earliest empirical works on acculturation among Asian Americans was conducted by Richard Suinn and colleagues (Suinn et al., 1987), in which the researchers developed a self-report measure of acculturation for Asian Americans. Their conceptualization and measurement approach were modeled after similar efforts in Latino/a psychology. Acculturation was conceptualized and assessed as a unidimensional (and implicitly unidirectional) continuum anchored by high identification and practices of Asian culture on the one end and high identification and practices of mainstream American culture on the other end.

A significant trend in contemporary acculturation theories in the past two decades has been the widespread acceptance of the bidimensional model of acculturation. With the acknowledgment that acculturation does not happen in a linear, unidimensional, unidirectional fashion that always results in full assimilation, the fourfold theory of acculturation (Berry, 1980), sometimes called the bidirectional model or bidimensional model, has become the most widely adopted conceptual model of acculturation in Asian American psychology. Berry's fourfold model posits that a person can identify with, and become competent with, two different cultures and that the degree of such acculturation to each culture can be independent of one another. Cross-cultural psychologists Ryder, Alden, and Paulhus's (2000) study of "a head-to-head comparison" of unidimensional versus bidimensional models of acculturation among Chinese Canadians claimed that the empirical evidence points toward the bidimensional model as the more valid and useful conceptualization.

It should be noted that Berry's fourfold paradigm of acculturation has also come under increasing scrutiny within cross-cultural psychology. Berry's (2003) own review of acculturation theories acknowledged the roles that researchers' as well as the society's political ideology play in the formulation of acculturation theory and research. Rudmin (2003) has criticized the typological model of acculturation for its lack of effectiveness in explaining differences between groups or between individuals, its poor validity, and its lack of logic.

Research with Asian Americans has contributed to the advancement in acculturation research. For example, the universal applicability of the bidimensional model of acculturation for Asian Americans has also been subject to critiques and empirical challenges. For example, Tsai et al. (2000) showed that there is not one model that fits the patterns of cultural orientation for Asian Americans. In examining the acculturation patterns for Chinese Americans who were born in the United States versus those who immigrated before age 12 versus those immigrated after age 12, Tsai and colleagues showed that the unidimensional model represented the experiences of recently immigrated Chinese Americans whereas the bidimensional model was a better fit for later-generation Asian Americans.

However, current theories and research on acculturation among Asian Americans continue to reflect underlying assumptions about the acculturative process, namely, that acculturation among Asian Americans is being researched and theorized from a middle-class, upwardly mobile, voluntary immigrant perspective. Bhatia (2003), a cultural psychologist who studies the development of self and identity in global and transnational contexts, has argued that acculturation researchers have implicitly privileged a specific developmental trajectory for immigrants. In most contemporary theories of acculturation (e.g., LaFromboise, Coleman, & Gerton, 1993), there is a presumption that immigrants should strive toward what Berry called the "integration strategy" (to be highly acculturated to the dominant culture while retaining a high level of ethnic or heritage culture) and that those who develop high bicultural competence are psychologically the best adjusted, although there appears to be no conclusive evidence that biculturalism is consistently associated with positive outcomes (Rudmin, 2003). Bhatia (2003) also noted that acculturation models seldom take into account the power and status asymmetry between the dominant host culture and the immigrant culture. Such lack of acknowledgment of the political realities in current theories implies that every immigrant is free to choose to pursue an integration strategy. However, evidence from studies of Asian American immigrants has pointed to the multiple ways in which such presumptions are not supported.

Identity

Stanley Sue and Derald W. Sue published a paper titled "Chinese-American Personality and Mental Health" in the *Amerasia* journal in 1971, which was in its inaugural year of publication as the first Asian American studies journal.[1] In this paper, Sue and Sue put forth a conceptual scheme of the development of ethnic identity among Chinese Americans. They argued that three typological characters of the Traditionalist, the Marginal Man, and the Asian American develop differentially as a Chinese American individual struggles to negotiate the clash between Chinese and Western values and racism. Ethnic identity has continued to receive much empirical and theoretical attention in Asian American psychology since then. A thorough review of the research and theory on ethnic identity, as well as the articulation of the relationship between ethnic identity and acculturation, can be found elsewhere (D. Sue, Mak, & D. W. Sue, 1998; Chapters 8 & 9, this volume). Here, we note the strengths as well as critiques of the major conceptual models that have been put forth.

As suggested by the early work on typology of Chinese American identity, theories of Asian American ethnic identity (as well as those of various ethnic minority and racial identity theories) are based on a developmental model. Noting the various ways in which Asian American individuals define their ethnic identity, theorists have been eager to explain how such identities develop in interaction within various micro and macro contexts (e.g., familial environment, societal contexts, etc.) The early S. Sue & D. W. Sue (1971) work conceptualized a differential type of ethnic identification according to how an individual manages the conflict with parents. Later, D. W. Sue and D. Sue (1990) put forth the Racial/Cultural Identity Development (R/CID) model, which articulated a five-stage developmental model. The five stages involved conformity stage (similar to the earlier Marginal type in which the individual accepts the dominant culture's values and norms), dissonance stage (in which the individual begins to question the dominant hegemony), resistance and immersion stage (in which the individual actively rejects the dominant culture's values and becomes immersed in the ethnic culture), the introspection stage (in which the individual reevaluates his or her total immersion in the ethnic culture), and the final stage of integrative awareness (in which the individual has worked through the conflicts and arrives at a secure ethnic identity).

Some critiques have been leveled against the R/CID and typological approaches to the conceptualization of ethnic identity, such as the assumed linear unidirectional progression of identity development, its questionable applicability to immigrants, and its conceptual origin during the civil rights movement of the late 1960s (D. Sue et al., 1998). Other theorists have written thoughtfully regarding the epistemological and methodological questions implicated by our exploration of what it means to be Asian American. In a thoughtful piece on research methods in Asian American psychology, Tanaka, Ebreo, Linn, and Morera (1998) articulated the critical importance for the field to establish a solid conceptual framework in Asian American identity as a starting point for all other research in Asian American psychology. Tanaka et al. argued that for psychological research to be able to claim that membership in the social category of "Asian American" has behavioral correlates and consequences (e.g., academic achievement, help-seeking attitudes), there needs to be a theory about conditions under which we would expect ethnicity to guide behavior. Importantly, Tanaka et al. advocated for more contextualized theories (and methods) of ethnic identity that correspond to our understanding of ethnic identity as a nonstatic construct that is situated within the immediate and proximal social contexts (e.g., ethnic backgrounds of others in that particular setting, research participant or client's understanding of the demand characteristics of ethnic identification questions). Tsai, Chentsova-Dutton, and Wong (2002) also posed the critical question regarding whether researchers' notion of ethnic identity and the meaning of group membership are constructed according to Western theories of the self and identity.

Another way in which the earlier models of Asian American ethnic identity have been challenged is through the work on biracial, multiracial, and transculturally adopted Asian Americans. Maria Root (1992) edited the first empirically based text on multiracial identity and has conducted seminal work in this area. Root (1998) identified the ways in which multiracial Asian Americans challenge definitions and assumptions of Asian American ethnic identity that have been centered on monoracial assumptions. Root (1998) and other Asian Americanists (e.g., Bradshaw, 1992; Williams, 1996) have called attention to the critical question of the body (i.e., ambiguity in phenotypical features) as a dimension of identity for multiracial individuals. Root (2002) has also articulated the particularity of Asian American mixed race identity that is distinct from the discourse in Black-White multiracial identity because of the differences in which the questions of race were historically treated in the United States. Departing from stage models of identity development, Root (1998) conceptualized an ecological framework for racial identity development to accommodate both monoracial and multiracial identity solutions. This ecological model places gender, class, and regional history of race as the larger contexts through which the meanings of everyday experiences and situations are understood by Asian Americans. In addition, Root identified a set of "inherited" influences (e.g., given name, languages spoken at home, cultural values, phenotype, parents' identity), individual traits (e.g., temperament, coping skills), and social environments (e.g., home, school, work) that filter the meaning of daily experiences to contribute to the racial and ethnic identification of Asian Americans.

Although the literature on the ethnic and racial identity of transracially adopted children is not large, existing data appear to point to the inadequacy of monoracial identity models to capture the experiences of this growing segment of Asian Americans. For example, as with multiracial Asian Americans, Korean American adoptees have less freedom to choose to immerse themselves in the minority culture (Mullen, 1995). A qualitative family study of internationally adopted children of color (Friedlander et al., 2000), half of whom were adopted from Korea, found that the children reported little confusion over their identity or the pressure to choose a specific identity.

Summary

The foregoing review of the current status of theories on race and culture, acculturation, and identity point to the significant strides that Asian American psychology has made in the past three decades. At the same time, there are multiple ways in which the existing theories and conceptual models are not able to capture the complex and dynamic experiences of Asian American individuals and communities. In the next section, we build on these previous critiques by discussing the larger theoretical discourses and dialogues in and out of Asian American psychology.

EXPANDING THE CRITICAL DIALOGUE

Why Reformulate?

Given that Asian American psychology has enjoyed an exponential growth in the number of researchers, practitioners, and products (e.g., books, articles) in the past three decades, given the growing sophistication of research being produced, and given the increased participation of senior Asian American psychologists in leadership positions, why should the field consider a reformulation of its conceptual approaches? We can think of four major reasons.

First, the field's dominant reliance on modernist scientific approaches will always short-change Asian American psychology scholarship as well as the Asian American communities whose voices and experiences we profess to represent. As argued by Uba (2002) specifically about Asian American psychology and as pointed out by other scholars who study Asian American (or more broadly, ethnic minority) populations (e.g., Verkuyten & de Wolf, 2002), many aspects of Asian Americans' psychological experiences should not be reduced to a single index.

Second, as has been long recognized, the nature of the Asian American population is quite dynamic and subject to larger global forces that

are moving at a fast pace. Some Asian American communities often intersect geographically, economically, and politically not only with White middle-class communities but also with other ethnic minority communities, particularly in urban settings (e.g., Abelmann & Lie, 1997). To describe and explain the central phenomenological experiences of Asian Americans (such as acculturation, ethnic identity) within the context of ever-changing communities and the world, Asian American psychologists must not only be attuned to the changes within the United States, but also we must span the boundaries of our conceptual model to encompass a more global perspective and to be more responsive to the changes in context. A continued focus by the field only on variables that are internal to the individual (e.g., level of acculturation, ethnic identity) is to miss the critical roles of ideologically driven contextual factors (e.g., political climate toward Mexican immigrants in a particular town) or geopolitical circumstances (e.g., a climate of pervasive national economic anxiety in South Korea following the International Monetary Fund crisis in Asia) that may better explain the behavior.

Third, Asian American psychology has been dominated by a particular prototype, and some may say stereotype, of Asian American individuals and families. These prototypical features include monoracial individuals from monoracial families, often from East Asia (China, Korea, Japan), who are highly educated and upwardly mobile in their socioeconomic status. However, the demographics of the population of Asian Americans are shifting quite rapidly. For example, a nontrivial proportion of Asians immigrating to the United States in recent years were infants or children who were being adopted by American families. As indicated by the 2000 Census, which for the first time allowed respondents to identify themselves as being of more than one race, a sizable segment of the Asian American population is biracial or multiracial.

Fourth, the field of Asian American psychology has been dominated by those trained in applied fields such as clinical and counseling psychology. Although this has been the case from the start, there are clear conceptual implications for the field to have this disciplinary bias. Uba (2002) also argues that to the extent that most Asian American psychologists continue to be educated and trained based on mainstream approaches to understanding and treating psychopathology and other problems of living, they may perpetuate the modernist conceptualization of psychological problems (and the solution) as being centered within the individual.

Critical Discourses Within Psychology

In reformulating Asian American psychology to be more responsive to the complex realities of Asian Americans' lives, there exists a tension over the extent to which our theoretical and conceptual framework and dialogue should stay within or go beyond the bounds of scientific psychology. Here we contrast S. Sue's (1999) critique of mainstream psychology's reliance on internal validity with Uba's (2002) critique of Asian American psychology's reliance on modernist epistemology.

Taking scientific psychology to task. S. Sue (1999) took a critical stance toward the practice of scientific psychology and its failure to be inclusive of ethnic minority psychology, but his critiques were communicated using the principles of the modernist scientific approach. Sue framed the problem of mainstream psychology as privileging internal validity over external validity, which he argued has hindered progress in ethnic minority research. Sue argued that because many of the psychological principles and measures have not been examined with respect to their reliability and validity with ethnic minorities, ethnic minority research that attempts to use mainstream measures or provide descriptive data are often faulted for lacking internal validity and rigor.

Postmodern perspective. In her book, *A Postmodern Psychology of Asian Americans: Creating Knowledge of a Racial Minority,* Uba (2002) used a deconstructionist, postmodernist view to contend that the shortcomings of Asian American psychology lie in its epistemological allegiance to mainstream psychology's modernist scientific principles. She argued that these modern scientific principles were historically developed by Europeans and European Americans, with the presumption of neutrality and objectivity. The postmodernist approach, which is closely allied with similar intellectual endeavors such as critical theory and postcolonial theory, is concerned with disrupting the status quo. One of Uba's challenges to mainstream psychology—and, to some extent, the current practices of Asian American psychology—is its rejection of race as a valid scientific concept and its consequent lack of attention to racial narratives.

Another of Uba's challenges to cross-cultural and Asian American psychology is the comparative paradigm in which nonwhites' behavior (within the United States as well as the rest of the world) is indexed against those of European Americans. In such a comparative framework, whenever Asian Americans' behaviors are found to differ from those of the norm, it is the Asian American behaviors that are presumed to be in the need of explanation. Like colonialists who saw themselves as naturally entitled to dominate, speak for, and understand the colonized (often people of color) better than the colonized themselves, the postcolonial scholars see modern researchers, with their privileging of positivistic scientific methods, as presuming that they know more about their human research participants than the participants know about themselves. Uba called for a postmodern approach to Asian American psychological research and argued that "to continue to use the lexicon of American psychology implies that the limited texts (used by students of psychology) institutionally considered relevant to psychology are adequate for studying minorities. They are not" (p. 146).

Critical psychology. Uba's (2002) postmodern argument appears thus far to have had little impact on Asian American psychology as a whole. However, her arguments are consistent with other voices within psychology that are beginning to challenge some of the basic theoretical and methodological assumptions in mainstream psychology. "Critical psychology" in the United States is a loosely organized movement whose central project is to critique and challenge the status quo in mainstream psychology, namely the discipline's assumptions and practices that reify and institutionalize societal power structure in a discipline that has been dominated by white middle-class male psychologists and white middle-class male subjects

(Prilleltensky & Fox, 1997). Critical psychology contends that this has resulted in the dominant majority psychologists presuming the normative behavior of members of their culture as the universal norm representative of all humans. Critical psychology advocates for theory and practice of psychology that disrupts this status quo in its ontology, epistemology, and methods. In essence, it "asks us to understand and change the ritual practices of our discipline" (Rappaport & Stewart, 1997, p. 303).

Although cross-cultural psychology, in theory, has the potential to challenge mainstream psychology's assumptions and institutions, critical psychologists have critiqued cross-cultural psychology as participating in the continued reification and legitimization of white middle-class culture and people as both the producers of knowledge and as the normative "subjects" of the discipline. For example, Moghaddam and Studer (1997) note that cross-cultural psychology's cognitive and laboratory approaches to the understanding of culture neglect the societal, historical, and political contexts in which human behavior occurs. They further argue that a neglect of ideology, power disparities, and other social justice–related issues in both mainstream psychology and cross-cultural psychology is manifested in reductionism, wherein researchers attempt to explain complex sociocultural behavior by identifying causal relationships among few variables internal to individuals. Critical psychology's challenges to the assumptions and practices of psychology, while far from offering easy solutions to Asian American psychology, are worth noting.

Asian Americanist Perspective

Our discussion thus far has centered primarily on discourse and dialogues within psychology, and we have pointed to the limitations of the normative ontological, epistemological, and methodological practices of psychology for Asian American psychology. In the following sections, we argue that theories and conceptual approaches to Asian American psychology would be enriched by a greater incorporation of theoretical models from Asian American Studies. Historically, Asian American psychology can trace its roots to the formation of Asian

American Studies in the late 1960s and early 1970s. We reiterate that S. Sue and D. W. Sue's (1971) classic work on Chinese American personality and identity was published in an Asian American Studies journal and made ample references to racism and the influence of civil rights activism in their formulation of what it means to be a Chinese American. We suggest that the time is ripe for Asian American psychology to revisit its roots in ethnic studies. However, this is not to say that Asian American psychology should return to where Asian American Studies was in its founding circa the civil rights era. Asian American Studies, as an interdisciplinary project, has evolved and become institutionalized in many top universities around the nation, and it has developed its own set of theoretical practices in response to the changing faces of its practitioners, its "objects" of study, and the U.S. and international contexts.

Asian American Studies traditionally has examined the Asian American experience in terms of shared and unique immigration histories; legal, economic, and social contributions to American society; the cultural production of ethnicity and race; and political resistances against discrimination and racism (Chan, 1991; Okihiro, 1994; Ong, 1999; Takaki, 1989). At the same time, Asian American Studies has continued to revisit, contest, and subsequently broaden its understanding of what is the Asian American experience (Hune, 1995; Lowe, 1991; Okihiro, 1994). Today, Asian American Studies embraces transnationalism, globalization, and diaspora as critical entry points into the field (Anderson & Lee, 2005; Ong, 1999). Asian American Studies also acknowledges and emphasizes the intersections of race, ethnicity, class, gender, sexuality, and religion in the context of different migration and settlement histories (see Mahalingam & Haritatos, in press, as an example of psychology informed by these intersections). Lowe (1991) best described this shift in Asian American Studies as a move toward the heterogeneity, hybridity, and multiplicity of the Asian American experience.

The practice of Asian Americanist psychology, as we envision it, would draw from this broader and continually updated Asian American literature across disciplinary boundaries. Table 3.1 outlines some of the major characteristics of

Table 3.1 Major Characteristics of Asian Americanist Psychology

Philosophical antecedents

- Academic-scientific psychology, cross-cultural psychology
- Multicultural psychology, cultural psychology, indigenous psychology
- Postmodern theory, postcolonial theory, critical race theory
- Asian American Studies

Principal emphasis in psychology

- Heterogeneity, hybridity, and multiplicity of Asian American experiences
- Racial and ethnic identity, racism and racialization, minority status
- Intersections of race, ethnicity, gender, class, sexuality, religion
- Acculturation and enculturation, biculturalism, transnationalism
- Mental health and public policy (help-seeking, access to services, service use, outcomes, cultural competence)

Principal methods of investigation

- Interdisciplinarity
- Multimethod (surveys, laboratory-based paradigms, focus groups, interviews, ethnography)
- Quantitative and qualitative

Primary areas of protest

- Against a psychology that perpetuates the model minority stereotype and that Orientalizes Asian Americans as the "other"
- Against essentialized view of cultures as an East-West binary
- Against a psychology that views deviation from the White norm as deficient
- Against the imposition of a narrow view of scientific psychology

Position on psychological practice

- Advocates for a greater cultural competence by mainstream systems
- Advocates for a development of theories and models that acknowledge fluidity and heterogeneity among Asian American individuals and communities
- Advocates for a development of more community-based, strength-based models

---

Asian Americanist psychology. Such practice would involve questioning and deconstructing dominant paradigms and reconstructing, redefining, and reformulating the psychological experiences of Asian Americans. Asian Americanist psychology also would strive to understand that the contemporary mentality and behavior of Asian American individuals and community are inextricably tied to what happens inside, outside, and across U.S. borders.

Put another way, we propose the Asian American experience as a multifaceted (or prismatic) lens through which to understand psychological processes and phenomena, rather than the more traditional converse relationship that employs psychological theory as the dominant lens to understand the Asian American experience. For example, we should consider the ways in which different segments and subgroups of the Asian American community define, configure, and locate ethnic identity, along with more traditional approaches that test the fit of contemporary psychological theories of ethnic identity on Asian American populations. From this perspective, it becomes evident that Asian Americanist psychology requires a contextualized and comparative approach to understanding human development and behavior that contests dominant psychology paradigms.

Toward this end, we have identified three critical points of entry or streams of psychological experience—namely, migration histories, population trends, and internal processes—that expand the boundaries of the Asian American experience and concurrently help to define

Asian Americanist psychology. The examples provided within each entry point, however, are not fixed or static variables. We raise this cautionary note because, as already noted, the past and present psychology on Asian Americans has tended to essentialize group differences (e.g., generation status), privilege certain constructs (e.g., acculturation), and evoke master narratives (e.g., filial loyalty) that obscure and minimize the complexities of human development. Instead, these examples simply reflect the ever-shifting nature and diversity of the Asian American experience.

Migration histories. Modern-day migration of Asians to the United States bears many similarities to the historical Asian migration patterns of the 19th and 20th centuries, but there are some distinctive qualities to 21st-century migration that directly relate to the psychological study of Asian Americans. These fluid, multiple, and forced migrations, and the reasons that underlie them, significantly challenge and alter traditional conceptualizations of acculturation/enculturation and ethnic identity. For instance, economic and political globalization, along with the expansion of transportation, communications, and information networks, has led to transnationalism and the fluidity of migration. The United States is no longer viewed as the final destination for many immigrants. Ong (1999) described a new class of affluent migrants with "flexible citizenship" who, because of their wealth and mobility, situate their identity, culture, and sense of home on multiple continents. Globalization also has led to new waves of working-class migrants, such as the Filipina nannies and nurses, who are redefining the sojourner motif and conceptions of family by financially supporting their families from abroad (Parreñas, 2001).

There also is a growing trend toward multiple migration patterns for new immigrants. Historically, Asian immigrants came directly to the United States through West and East coast ports and remained in these coastal regions. Today, immigrants may migrate initially to a more proximal country, such as Brazil, Ecuador, Mexico, or Canada, and make secondary or tertiary migrations to the United States. Consequently, their acculturation experience

may be an amalgamation of these different cultures and contexts. Additionally, internal migration away from the East and West coasts occurs more frequently, resulting in Asian ethnic groups establishing communities in America's "heartland" (e.g., the Hmong in Minnesota, Indians in rural Tennessee, and Pakistani in Detroit) and developing regionally inflected identities that differentiate them from their counterparts in Los Angeles or New York City.

It also is important to remember that not all Asian Americans voluntarily chose to settle in the United States. There is an increased recognition of the displacement and diaspora experiences of numerous Asian ethnic groups, especially those from Southeast Asia (e.g., Hmong, Laotian, Burmese). Diaspora scholars, such as Cohen (1997), note that there is a unique sense of loss, trauma, and yearning for the homeland that afflicts individuals and families who are dislocated due to war, oppression, and persecution. The psychology of diaspora, then, must take into account the historical and current contexts in which ethnic identity and perceived discrimination may operate differently for a diasporic population than a nativistic population (Lee, Noh, Yoo, & Doh, in press).

Population trends. Whereas historical definitions of Asian Americans were often restricted to those of Chinese and Japanese descent, the notion of who is Asian American is now, more than ever before, being contested and reformulated with the new waves and patterns of immigration and increasing rates of U.S. nativity and outmarriage. Importantly, the visibility and viability of these emergent Asian ethnic groups need to be recognized and incorporated into the psychological study of Asian Americans. For example, South Asian and Southeast Asian immigrant and refugee populations are among the fastest-growing ethnic populations in the country, and their distinctive cultures and religions, as well as contrasting pre- and postmigration experiences, are redefining the Asian American landscape. By contrast, the Japanese American population is decreasing due to low rates of immigration and high outmarriage among this predominantly U.S.-born population. We expect that this demographic shift eventually will alter the operational definitions of collectivistism, Asian values, and other cultural tropes used in psychology that are largely derived from perceived characteristics of East Asian cultures (e.g., Confucianism).

Demographers have reported on the dramatic increase in outmarriages and other forms of interracial/interethnic relationships among all Asian ethnic groups, resulting in the rise of multiracial/multiethnic families and children who identify, in varying degrees, with their racial and ethnic heritages. The social and political significance of this population was most evident with the 2000 U.S. Census, which included a multiracial category for the first time. In the field of psychology, it will be important for researchers to determine a priori whether to include a multiracial individual who identifies as Korean in a study on Korean Americans. Certain assumptions are made when researchers elect to study a specific ethnic group (e.g., a shared cultural socialization history or similar experiences with discrimination), but these assumptions may be violated with the inclusion of multiracial participants who have had a very different history of cultural socialization and have the ability to "pass" as White or another race. The omission of this large segment of the Asian American community, however, also poses serious problems for the field, as it privileges notions of "pure blood" and simultaneously perpetuates the invisibility of multiracial/multiethnic individuals.

Asian children adopted internationally into predominantly White families represent another overlooked Asian American population. The annual number of international adoptions has increased threefold over the past 15 years, and Asian adoptees now constitute nearly 10% of Chinese and Koreans who are issued immigrant visas each year. Moreover, the majority of Korean adoptees are now coming of age as adults and many are reexamining the meaning of ethnicity and race in their lives. Hubinette (2005) has discussed the importance of Korean adoptees creating a third space that situates them between immigrant and U.S.-raised Korean Americans. This third space, in turn, serves as a context in which to establish one's ethnic identity as a Korean and as an adoptee. Clearly, the study of Korean adoptees alters the way in which we historically have construed ethnic identity development.

Internal processes. Theory and research on cultural constructs that reflect the internal processes of individuals and families, such as acculturation/enculturation and ethnic identity, have advanced tremendously over the past decade. At the same time, many of the theoretical assumptions and propositions associated with these constructs have not been thoroughly tested, yet they have become reified and therefore uncontestable. Moreover, there is a tendency to view Asian Americans as passive recipients or victims of history and context. Yet it remains critically important to view Asian Americans as active contributors, resistors, and transformers in their lives and in their communities.

Acculturation/enculturation theory, despite significant measurement advances, still rests on the assumption of upward mobility and consequently perpetuates a middle-class mythology (Lee & Dean, 2004). However, Asian Americanist scholars have recognized that the lived experiences of many immigrants and refugees, particularly those living in poor urban centers, are in stark contrast to the linearity and verticality of traditional acculturation/enculturation theory. Zhou (1997) specifically proposed segmented assimilation as an alternative way to understand the multiplicity of ways in which Asian immigrants and refugees may acculturate vertically in some life domains but horizontally in other life domains. Third-culture identification, for example, occurs when Asian Americans identify with another minority group (e.g., African Americans) due to discrimination by White society and proximity to African American culture. In other words, segmented assimilation recognizes the societal constraints that can hinder vertical acculturation and the active efforts of immigrants and refugees to adapt to their given life circumstances.

Social identity theory and its corollary rejection-identification model serve as the theoretical framework to understand discrimination and ethnic identity development. This approach, however, fails to take into consideration the racial dynamics that often situate Asian Americans as intermediaries between African Americans and Whites. Claire Jean Kim's (1999) theory of racial triangulation contrasts and positions Asian Americans along two dimensions of valorization and insider-outsider to better explain the racial realities of Asian Americans. According to Kim, Asian Americans are more valorized than Blacks by Whites, but they are perceived as foreigners by both Whites and Blacks. Extending this idea of racial triangulation, Asian Americans themselves may offset their experiences of discrimination and treatment as foreigners by disparaging and making downward comparisons with African Americans.

CONCLUSIONS

In this chapter, we have reviewed theoretical and conceptual contributions to Asian American psychology. Several points are apparent. First, important and rich conceptual and theoretical advances have been made. However, they have developed largely without reference to perspectives found in Asian American and ethnic studies, such as critical theory, feminist theory, queer theory, and indigenous psychology. Second, popular constructs such as race/culture/ ethnicity, acculturation, and identity have emerged, but their theoretical base has been criticized for reflecting Western thought and orientation. Third, the world is confronted with emerging issues such as globalization, migration, transnationalism, diaspora, population and demographic changes, and social identity. These criticisms of current perspectives in Asian American psychology (e.g., lack of integration with other theories and Western orientation), as well as the emerging issues, have pressed desires for theoretical reformulations in Asian American psychology. Reformulation would involve the integration of other approaches in Asian American studies and the newly emerging issues.

Where should the field of Asian American psychology head? At this point, more has been written on the failures of Western approaches to research and theory than in an actual reformulation. The field is now in need of articulated theories and approaches that are more contextually based and that address these criticisms. Strengths and limitations of reformulations should be delineated. Finally, more integrated approaches should not be viewed as simply a means of better capturing the experiences of Asian Americans. Rather, theories that are able to deal with contemporary issues and with limitations found in Western approaches are probably good for everyone. In the context of universities increasingly moving toward interdisciplinary scholarship and teaching (Lattuca, 2001), an emergence of Asian Americanist psychology represents contemporary and future trends for our field.

NOTE

1. Interestingly, because the S. Sue & D. W. Sue (1971) paper appeared in an ethnic studies journal, it was not included in the bibliographic compendium (Leong & Whitfield, 1992) published by the American Psychological Association that compiled abstracts of the psychological and behavioral literature on Asians in the United States published between 1967 and 1991. *Amerasia,* although it occasionally publishes papers in psychology or related social science disciplines, is not included in PsycINFO database.

REFERENCES

Abelmann, N., & Lie, J. (1997). *Blue dreams: Korean Americans and the Los Angeles riots.* Cambridge, MA: Harvard University Press.

Alvarez, A. N., & Helms, J. E. (2001). Racial identity and reflected appraisals as influences on Asian Americans' racial adjustment. *Cultural Diversity & Ethnic Minority Psychology, 7,* 217–231.

Anderson, W. W., & Lee, R. G. (2005). Asian American displacements. In W. W. Anderson & R. G. Lee (Eds.), *Displacements and diasporas: Asians in the Americas* (pp. 3–22). New Brunswick, NJ: Rutgers University Press.

Berry, J. W. (1980). Acculturation as varieties of adaptation. In A. Padilla (Ed.), *Acculturation: Theory, models, and findings* (pp. 9–25). Boulder, CO: Westview Press.

Berry, J. W. (2002). Conceptual approaches to acculturation. In K. M. Chun, P. B. Organista, & G. Marín (Eds.), *Acculturation: Advances in theory, measurement, and applied research* (pp. 17–37). Washington, DC: American Psychological Association.

Betancourt, H., & Lopez, S. R. (1993). The study of culture, ethnicity, and race in American psychology. *American Psychologist, 48,* 629–637.

Bhatia, S. (2003). Is "integration" the developmental end goal for all immigrants? Redefining "acculturation strategies" from a genetic-dramatistic perspective. In I. E. Josephs (Ed.), *Dialogicality in development* (pp. 198–216). Westport, CT: Praeger/Greenwood.

Bradshaw, C. K. (1992). Beauty and the beast: On racial ambiguity. In M. P. P. Root (Ed.), *Racially mixed people in America* (pp. 77–88). Thousand Oaks, CA: Sage.

Chan, S. (1991). *Asian Americans: An interpretive history.* New York: Twayne.

Chao, R. K. (1994). Beyond parental control and authoritarian parenting style: Understanding Chinese parenting through the cultural notion of training. *Child Development, 65,* 1111–1119.

Chao, R. K. (1995). Chinese and European American cultural models of the self reflected in mothers' childrearing beliefs. *Ethos, 23,* 328–354.

Cheryan, S., & Bodenhausen, G. V. (2000). When positive stereotypes threaten intellectual performance: The psychological hazards of "model minority" status. *Psychological Science, 11,* 399–402.

Chun, K. M., Organista, P. B., & Marín, G. (Eds.). (2002). *Acculturation: Advances in theory, measurement, and applied research.* Washington, DC: American Psychological Association.

Cohen, R. (1997). *Global diasporas: An introduction.* Seattle: University of Washington Press.

Flannery, W. P., Reise, S. P., & Yu, J. (2001). An empirical comparison of acculturation models. *Personality and Social Psychology Bulletin, 27,* 1035–1045.

Fountain, H. (2005, September 18). The ultimate body language: How you line up for Mickey. *The New York Times,* Section 4, p. 4.

Friedlander, M. L., Larney, L. C., Skau, M., Hotaling, M., Cutting, M. L., & Schwam, M. (2000). Bicultural identification: Experiences of internationally adopted children and their parents. *Journal of Counseling Psychology, 47,* 187–198.

Hall, G. C. N. (2001). Psychotherapy research with ethnic minorities: Empirical, ethical, and conceptual issues. *Journal of Consulting and Clinical Psychology, 69,* 502–510.

Hall, G. C. N. (2002). Culture-specific ecological models of Asian American violence. In G. C. N. Hall & S. Okazaki (Eds.), *Asian American psychology: The science of lives in context* (pp. 153–170). Washington, DC: American Psychological Association.

Hall, G. C. N. (2003). The self in context: Implications for psychopathology and psychotherapy. *Journal of Psychotherapy Integration, 13,* 66–82.

Helms, J. E. (1994). The conceptualization of racial identity and other "racial" constructs. In E. J. Trickett, R. J. Watts, & D. Birman (Eds.), *Human diversity: Perspectives on people in context* (pp. 285–311). San Francisco: Jossey-Bass.

Helms, J. E., Jernigan, M., & Mascher, J. (2005). The meaning of race in psychology and how to change it: A methodological perspective. *American Psychologist, 60,* 27–36.

Hermans, H. J. M., & Kempen, H. J. G. (1998). Moving cultures: The perilous problems of cultural dichotomies in a globalizing society. *American Psychologist, 53,* 1111–1120.

Hubinette, T. (2005). *Comforting an orphaned nation: Representations of international adoption and adopted Koreans in Korean popular culture.* Unpublished doctoral dissertation, Stockholm University, Sweden.

Hune, S. (1995). Rethinking race: Paradigms and policy formation. *Amerasia, 21,* 29–40.

Kim, B. S. K., Li, L. C., & Ng, G. F. (2005). The Asian American Values Scale—Multidimensional: Development, reliability, and validity. *Cultural Diversity & Ethnic Minority Psychology, 11,* 187–201.

Kim, C. J. (1999). The racial triangulation of Asian Americans. *Politics & Society, 27,* 105–138.

Kim, U., & Chun, M. B. J. (1994). Educational "success" of Asian Americans: An indigenous perspective. *Journal of Applied Developmental Psychology, 15,* 329–339.

LaFromboise, T., Coleman, H. L., & Gerton, J. (1993). Psychological impact of biculturalism: Evidence and theory. *Psychological Bulletin, 114,* 395–412.

Lattuca, L. R. (2001). *Creating interdisciplinarity: Interdisciplinary research and teaching among college and university faculty.* Nashville, TN: Vanderbilt University Press.

Lee, R. M., & Dean, B. L. (2004). Middle-class mythology in an age of immigration and segmented assimilation: Implication for counseling psychology. *Journal of Counseling Psychology, 51,* 19–24.

Lee, R. M., Noh, C.-Y., Yoo, H. C., & Doh, H.-S. (in press). The psychology of diaspora experiences: Intergroup contact, perceived discrimination, and the ethnic identity of Koreans in China. *Cultural Diversity & Ethnic Minority Psychology.*

Leong, F. T. L., & Hardin, E. (2002). Career psychology of Asian Americans: Cultural validity and cultural specificity. In G. C. N. Hall & S. Okazaki (Eds.), *Asian American psychology: The science of lives in context* (pp. 131–152). Washington, DC: American Psychological Association.

Leong, F. T. L., & Whitfield, J. R. (Eds.). (1992). *Asians in the United States: Abstracts of the psychological and behavioral literature, 1967–1991.* Washington, DC: American Psychological Association.

Liang, C. T. H, Li, L. C., & Kim, B. S. K. (2004). The Asian American Racism-Related Stress Inventory: Development, factor analysis, reliability, and validity. *Journal of Counseling Psychology, 51,* 103–114.

Loo, C. M., Fairbank, J. A., Scurfield, R. M., Ruch, L. O., King, D. W., Adams, L. J., et al. (2001). Measuring exposure to racism: Development and validation of a Race-Related Stressor Scale (RRSS) for Asian American Vietnam veterans. *Psychological Assessment, 13,* 503–520.

Lowe, L. (1991). Heterogeneity, hybridity, multiplicity: Marking Asian American differences. *Diaspora, 1,* 24–44.

Mahalingam, R., & Haritatos, J. (in press). Cultural psychology of gender and immigration. In R. Mahalingam (Ed.), *Cultural psychology of immigrants.* Mahwah, NJ.: Lawrence Erlbaum.

Markus, H. R., & Kitayama, S. (1991). Culture and the self: Implications for cognition, emotion, and motivation. *Psychological Review, 98,* 224–253.

Matsumoto, D. (1999). Culture and self: An empirical assessment of Markus and Kitayama's theory of independent and interdependent self-construal. *Asian Journal of Social Psychology, 2,* 289–310.

Miyamoto, S. F. (1986–1987). Problems of interpersonal style among the Nisei. *Amerasia, 13,* 29–45.

Moghaddam, F. M., & Studer, C. (1997). Cross-cultural psychology: The frustrated gadfly's promises, potentialities, and failures. In D. Fox & I. Prilleltensky (Eds.), *Critical psychology: An introduction* (pp. 185–201). Thousand Oaks, CA: Sage.

Mullen, M. (1995). Identity development of Korean adoptees. In W. L. Ng, S. Chin, J. S. Moy, & G. Y. Okihiro (Eds.), *Reviewing Asian America: Locating diversity* (pp. 61–74). Pullman: Washington State University Press.

Nagata, D. K. (1990). The Japanese American internment: Exploring the transgenerational consequences of traumatic stress. *Journal of Traumatic Stress, 3*(1), 47–69.

Nightingale, D., & Neilands, T. (1997). Understanding and practicing critical psychology. In D. Fox & I. Prilleltensky (Eds.), *Critical psychology: An introduction* (pp. 68–84). Thousand Oaks, CA: Sage.

Oishi, S., & Diener, E. (2003). Culture and well-being: The cycle of action, evaluation and decision. *Personality and Social Psychology Bulletin, 29,* 939–949.

Okazaki, S. (1997). Sources of ethnic differences between Asian American and White American college students on measures of depression and social anxiety. *Journal of Abnormal Psychology, 106,* 52–60.

Okihiro, G. Y. (1994). *Margins and mainstreams: Asians in American history and culture.* Seattle: University of Washington Press.

Ong, A. (1999). *Flexible citizenship: The cultural logics of transnationality.* Durham, NC: Duke University Press.

Oyserman, D., Coon, H. M., & Kemmelmeier, M. (2002). Rethinking individualism and collectivism: Evaluation of theoretical assumptions and meta-analyses. *Psychological Bulletin, 128,* 3–72.

Oyserman, D., & Sakamoto, I. (1997). Being Asian American: Identity, cultural constructs, and stereotype perception. *Journal of Applied Behavioral Science, 33,* 435–453.

Parreñas, R. S. (2001). *Servants of globalization: Women, migration, and domestic work.* Palo Alto, CA: Stanford University Press.

Phinney, J. S. (1996). When we talk about American ethnic groups, what do we mean? *American Psychologist, 51,* 918–927.

Pope-Davis, D. B., & Liu, W. M. (1998). The social construction of race: Implications for counselling psychology. *Counselling Psychology Quarterly, 11*(2), 151–161.

Prilleltensky, I., & Fox, D. (1997). Introducing critical psychology: Values, assumptions, and the status quo. In D. Fox & I. Prilleltensky (Eds.), *Critical psychology: An introduction* (pp. 3–20). Thousand Oaks, CA: Sage.

Rappaport, J., & Stewart, E. (1997). A critical look at critical psychology: Elaborating the questions. In D. Fox & I. Prilleltensky (Eds.), *Critical psychology: An introduction* (pp. 301–317). Thousand Oaks, CA: Sage.

Root, M. P. P. (Ed.). (1992). *Racially mixed people in America.* Thousand Oaks, CA: Sage.

Root, M. P. P. (1998). Experiences and processes affecting racial identity development: Preliminary results from the Biracial Sibling Project. *Cultural Diversity & Ethnic Minority Psychology, 4,* 237–247.

Root, M. P. P. (2002). Methodological issues in multiracial research. In G. C. N. Hall & S. Okazaki (Eds.), *Asian American psychology: The science of lives in context* (pp. 171–193). Washington, DC: American Psychological Association.

Rudmin, F. W. (2003). Critical history of the acculturation psychology of assimilation, separation, integration, and marginalization. *Review of General Psychology, 7,* 3–37.

Ryder, A. G., Alden, L. E., & Paulhus, D. L. (2000). Is acculturation unidimensional or bidimensional? A head-to-head comparison in the prediction of personality, self-identity, and adjustment. *Journal of Personality and Social Psychology, 79,* 49–65.

Schimmack, U., Oishi, S., & Diener, E. (2005). Individualism: A valid and important dimension of cultural differences between nations. *Personality and Social Psychology Review, 9,* 17–31.

Smedley, A., & Smedley, B. D. (2005). Race as biology is fiction, racism as a social problem is real: Anthropological and historical perspectives on the social construction of race. *American Psychologist, 60,* 16–26.

Sue, D., Mak, W., & Sue, D. W. (1998). Ethnic identity. In L. C. Lee & N. W. S. Zane (Eds.), *Handbook of Asian American psychology* (pp. 289–323). Thousand Oaks, CA: Sage.

Sue, D. W., Bingham, R. P., Porche-Burke, L., & Vasquez, M. (1999). The diversification of psychology: A multicultural revolution. *American Psychologist, 54,* 1061–1069.

Sue, D. W., & Sue, D. (1990). *Counseling the culturally different: Theory and practice* (2nd ed.). New York: Wiley.

Sue, S. (1999). Science, ethnicity, and bias: Where have we gone wrong? *American Psychologist, 54,* 1070–1077.

Sue, S., & Okazaki, S. (1990). Asian-American educational achievements: A phenomenon in search of an explanation. *American Psychologist, 45,* 913–920.

Sue, S., & Sue, D. W. (1971). Chinese-American personality and mental health. *Amerasia, 1*(2), 36–50.

Sue, S., & Zane, N. (1987). The role of culture and cultural techniques in psychotherapy: A critique and reformulation. *American Psychologist, 42,* 37–45.

Suinn, R. M., Rickard-Figueroa, K., Lew, S., & Vigil, P. (1987). The Suinn-Lew Asian Self-Identity Acculturation Scale: An initial report. *Educational and Psychological Measurement, 47,* 401–407.

Takaki, R. (1989). *Strangers from a different shore: A history of Asian Americans.* New York: Penguin Books.

Tanaka, J. S., Ebreo, A., Linn, N., & Morera, O. F. (1998). Research methods: The construct validity of self-identity and its psychological implications. In L. C. Lee & N. W. S. Zane (Eds.), *Handbook of Asian American psychology* (pp. 21–79). Thousand Oaks, CA: Sage.

Triandis, H. C. (1989). The self and social behavior in differing cultural contexts. *Psychological Review, 96*(3), 506–520.

Tsai, J. L., Chentsova-Dutton, Y., & Wong, Y. (2002). Why and how researchers should study ethnic identity, acculturation, and cultural orientation. In G. C. N. Hall & S. Okazaki (Eds.), *Asian American psychology: The science of lives in context* (pp. 41–65). Washington, DC: American Psychological Association.

Tsai, J. L., Ying, Y., & Lee, P. A. (2000). The meaning of "being Chinese" and "being American": Variation among Chinese American young adults. *Journal of Cross-Cultural Psychology, 31*(3), 302–332.

Uba, L. (2002). *A postmodern psychology of Asian Americans: Creating knowledge of a racial minority.* Albany, NY: State University of New York Press.

Verkuyten, M., & de Wolf, A. (2002). Being, feeling and doing: Discourses and ethnic self-definitions among minority group members. *Culture & Psychology, 8,* 371–399.

Williams, T. K. (1996). Race as process: Reassessing the "what are you?" Encounters of biracial individuals. In M. P. P. Root (Ed.), *The multiracial experience: Racial borders as the new frontier* (pp. 191–210). Thousand Oaks, CA: Sage.

Yee, A. H. (1983). Ethnicity and race: Psychological perspectives. *Educational Psychologist, 18,* 14–24.

Yee, A. H., Fairchild, H. H., Weizmann, F., & Wyatt, G. E. (1993). Addressing psychology's problem with race. *American Psychologist, 48,* 1132–1140.

Ying, Y., Lee, P. A., Tsai, J. L., Hung, Y., Lin, M., & Wan, C. T. (2001). Asian American college students as model minorities: An examination of their overall competence. *Cultural Diversity & Ethnic Minority Psychology, 7,* 59–74.

Zhou, M. (1997). Segmented assimilation: Issues, controversies, and recent research on the new second generation. *International Migration Review, 31,* 975–1008.

Zuckerman, M. (1990). Some dubious premises in research and theory on racial differences: Scientific, social, and ethical issues. *American Psychologist, 45,* 1297–1303.

4

Conducting Research With Diverse Asian American Groups

Kevin M. Chun

Osvaldo F. Morera

Jolynne D. Andal

Monica C. Skewes

Over the past two decades, the field of Asian American psychology has generated more extensive and sophisticated research methods for studying diverse Asian American groups. Of particular note are the introduction of new, culturally appropriate self-report instruments (e.g., the Asian American Values Scale–Multidimensional, Loss of Face Scale, Asian American Family Conflicts Scale), the development of innovative assessment methods (e.g., psychophysiological measures), and growing attention to comprehensive multimethod evaluation strategies (e.g., combined qualitative-quantitative methods). These advances in measurement and evaluation have been accompanied by greater in-depth discussion and analyses of complex conceptual and theoretical issues. Much of this discussion centers on the limitations of ethnic and racial classifications and the continuing need for sampling and analytic strategies for

Authors' Note: The work of the first author was supported by the National Institute of Nursing Research, National Institutes of Health grant #1 R01 NR009111–01 (Principal Investigator: Catherine A. Chesla).

The work of the second and the fourth authors was supported by grants from the National Institutes of Health/National Center for Minority Health and Health Disparities, grant #1 R24MD00520–03 (Principal Investigator: Osvaldo F. Morera) and the National Institute of Mental Health, grant #2 R24 MH47167–11 (Principal Investigator: Michael Zárate).

heterogeneous Asian American populations (Okazaki, 2002). Researchers also have focused tremendous attention on clarifying operational definitions of culture and the nature of cultural and ethnic group differences (Tanaka, Ebreo, Linn, & Morera, 1998). All of these research developments in Asian American psychology clearly indicate that the field has moved well beyond simplistic notions of ethnic group "difference" to a new, albeit more nuanced, understanding of what difference actually means and how it is experienced by individuals.

Not surprisingly, however, studies involving diverse Asian American groups have not uniformly moved forward in this direction, possibly due to a number of obstacles. First, researchers face practical constraints that can leave them wondering how to actually implement or follow past methodological recommendations. For example, the significance of trust and rapport building to working with diverse Asian American communities has been well established, but practical advice on how to accomplish this is often lacking. Likewise, when qualitative research is highlighted as a viable investigative approach, its specific applications and methodological challenges are not always presented. The same holds true for new and innovative statistical models that are often noted in research texts without detailed explanation or instruction.

Potential methodological advancements in the field might also be stymied by a narrow range of study illustrations and examples. To date, much of the research methods literature is rooted in the fields of clinical and counseling psychology. Consequently, investigators outside of these fields—including the sizeable number of developmental, social, and health psychologists—may have difficulties comprehending the relevance or conceptual basis of certain research recommendations. Lastly, matters are complicated when research recommendations only focus on specific phases of an investigation (e.g., data collection or data analyses) and do not fully address the myriad conceptual and methodological considerations throughout a study.

As a primary goal of this chapter, we aim to offer practical research advice for a number of conceptual and methodological challenges to studying diverse Asian American groups.

Applied research illustrations from our diverse investigative experiences are presented to illuminate the nature of these challenges and possible resolution strategies. This chapter is thus structured as a research guide that offers "working details" that are often overlooked in broader discussions on methodological concepts and theory. Chapter topics are organized sequentially, beginning with building culturally competent teams, moving on to analyzing data, and next to highlighting the methodological challenges and issues that can arise at different phases of an investigation. At the end of this chapter, we revisit the relative merits of utilizing qualitative and quantitative methods in Asian American psychology.

BUILDING CULTURALLY COMPETENT RESEARCH TEAMS

More researchers are acknowledging the need to study diverse Asian American communities in order to improve the ecological validity and generalizability of research findings. Often missing from this discussion, however, are guidelines on assembling a research team that can effectively and meaningfully work in Asian American communities. A research team's effectiveness in this regard can easily be overlooked or assumed when its members possess "facial" or "linguistic" diversity. These two superficial aspects of diversity assume cultural competence by virtue of one's ethnic group membership, physical appearance, or language skills and preferences. However, given the tremendous heterogeneity in Asian America, research teams and community members may share the same ethnic heritage but differ in gender, age, sexual orientation, socioeconomic status (SES), linguistic dialects, generational status, acculturation and enculturation levels, and other facets of identity. Thus, assembling a research team of Asian Americans is beneficial, but it does not guarantee cultural competence and success in the community. What then defines cultural competence beyond language skills and ethnic background? The counseling and clinical psychology literature provides helpful referents on this issue. D. W. Sue (2001) outlines three specific components of cultural competence: (a) *attitudes and beliefs,* which refer to understanding one's own cultural history or background and how it shapes personal beliefs, values, and attitudes; (b) *knowledge,* or comprehension of different worldviews across individuals and groups; and (c) *skills,* or the use of culturally appropriate communication and intervention. Although there is little information on how researchers should evaluate their teams on these three components, cultural competence questionnaires created for therapists might serve as helpful resources (e.g., the Multicultural Awareness-Knowledge-Skills Survey, D'Andrea, Daniels, & Heck, 1991; Multicultural Counseling Inventory, Sodowsky, Taffe, Gutkin, & Wise, 1994), and these components can guide open team discussion and reflection. Outside experts who work directly with the community under investigation should be recruited for these discussions and for educational and training purposes.

ENTERING THE COMMUNITY

The third author (Andal) participated in a community needs assessment project, named Operation Mango (Avrushin, Azada, & Andal, 2005), which illustrates some cultural considerations when entering diverse Asian American communities. In this project, Andal and her fellow Filipino American researchers set out to identify social and health services needs of the Filipino American community in Chicago, Illinois, and its surrounding suburbs. The researchers acknowledged that their professional roles and diverse individual backgrounds potentially situated them as "outsiders" vis-à-vis the community despite their shared ethnicity. Their first task thus involved identifying key civic leaders who could help legitimize their research project in the community. Civic leaders also can serve as important gatekeepers to study sites, and provide important "insider" knowledge that can inform culturally competent research methods. Once respected civic leaders were identified in Operation Mango with the assistance of community members, the researchers were faced with assuaging some leaders' concerns about the project. Although this appeared to be a straightforward task, the researchers again

faced the issue of insider versus outsider status. A researcher's status along these dimensions can constantly change depending on the salience of certain identity traits or characteristics and changing social or interpersonal contexts (Manalansan, 2000). For instance, the third author, Andal, found that her status as a second-generation Filipina American required her to negotiate differences in age, gender, generational status, and educational background with some leaders. Managing these differences is complicated by the context of research, which creates artificial or impersonal conditions for building interpersonal relations (Vo, 2000). Andal overcame these differences by sharing personal stories about how her family helped Filipino immigrant relatives in the United States. These stories strengthened the salience of her ethnic background, knowledge of immigrant experiences, and commitment to serving the community in her interactions with the civic leaders, which eventually helped her to secure their trust and support.

Researchers also may have to negotiate competing agendas among different groups or organizations when entering the community. Community agencies often compete for the same funding sources and possess distinct organizational cultures, political agendas, and institutional histories that can make collaboration difficult. Researchers must therefore map the different organizational structures and features of community partners, and their historical and contemporary relations with one another before research collaborations are proposed. As noted in the ethnography section of this chapter, "mapping" community agencies can involve making detailed field observations and notes and soliciting assistance from community informants.

RECRUITING STUDY PARTICIPANTS

There are a number of cultural and logistical considerations for recruiting Asian American study participants. In particular, lack of familiarity with research and cultural mistrust have been widely documented as potential cultural barriers to research participation (S. Sue & Sue, 2003). In Operation Mango, first-generation

Filipino American immigrants were less familiar with research and tended to feel that it was a waste of time and without any immediate or direct benefits. Asian American immigrants may also avoid participation out of fear of jeopardizing their immigration or residency status, or due to past experiences of persecution in their home countries. Support from trusted community leaders and describing a study's potential benefits to the community can help ease some of these concerns.

In Operation Mango, the study was framed in a culturally meaningful way (e.g., helping others and serving the community) that appealed to new immigrants' collectivistic social orientation. This paralleled past recommendations to speak to cultural notions of kinship or interdependence during participant recruitment (Nemoto, Huang, & Aoki, 1999). Finally, safeguards for protecting confidentiality should be highlighted. This was particularly important for first-generation immigrants in Operation Mango. In Filipino culture, discussion of personal matters is often restricted to one's immediate family, trusted family friends, or a parish priest. Operation Mango researchers took this into consideration when selecting an anonymous survey format which helped to alleviate some loss of face concerns. These researchers also selected a nonjudgmental project name ("Operation Mango" versus "social service needs assessment study") to minimize possible social or cultural stigma with participation. Concerns over confidentiality and loss of face were less pronounced, however, for their second-generation Filipino American participants. Thus, information about confidentiality and study goals must be tailored to the respective acculturation levels of different Asian American participants.

Lastly, logistical challenges may complicate participant recruitment. Extended work hours in immigrant households require researchers to offer flexible interview or meeting times during evening hours and weekends. In Operation Mango, the survey format was helpful because they could be completed at any time. Asian American immigrants may also avoid research participation due to a lack of transportation, child care, or elder care. In such instances, taxis can be hired to transport participants to study sites, or community agencies that are centrally located in immigrant neighborhoods can be used as interview sites. Other solutions to logistical challenges that are mentioned in the literature include offering monetary incentives, collecting data in a setting that is familiar to participants (e.g., conducting home interviews), and making follow-up calls to keep immigrant participants engaged in the research process (Burlew, 2003). In all cases, researchers must be mindful of certain cultural norms (e.g., reciprocity and perceived loss of face with refusal to participate) that may inadvertently coerce some to participate. Such situations again underscore the importance of assembling a culturally competent research team at the very outset of investigation.

DATA COLLECTION AND ANALYSES

Once researchers have successfully established working relationships in the community, a number of qualitative and quantitative strategies can be used to gather and analyze data. The following sections spotlight some promising qualitative and quantitative methods that can advance the state of research in Asian American psychology. These methods were selected because they are relatively overlooked in the field although they represent innovative and culturally appropriate ways to gather and analyze data.

Promising Qualitative Methods: Focus Groups and Ethnography

Defining Qualitative Methods

Qualitative methods are difficult to define because they encompass a broad spectrum of investigative approaches that span across diverse disciplines. Furthermore, some scholars assert that qualitative methods are more aptly framed as a "qualitative stance" or "qualitative inquiry" because they cannot be reduced to a definitive set of tools and techniques as implied by "methods" (Marecek, 2003). The characteristics and nature of qualitative research also vary by the theoretical stance of the researcher as reflected by her or his perceived relationship with study participants, views about how data should be interpreted, and beliefs about how the world operates. Nonetheless, qualitative research generally aims to comprehend the meaning and nature of human activities in context through the use of interpretive activities (Denzin & Lincoln, 2003). In the field of Asian American psychology, investigators are beginning to recognize the benefits of qualitative research for theory development and investigating unique or relatively unexplored phenomena. However, it appears that the many other strengths of qualitative research are often overlooked in psychology. One in particular, lies in its ability to contextualize behavior unlike traditional self-report paper and pencil methods that tend to focus on isolated data points. This emphasis on contextual analysis potentially strengthens the ecological validity of study findings, which, as S. Sue (1999) noted, deserves added attention in the field.

Qualitative research also extends beyond traditional notions of naturalistic observation in psychology. Most notably, qualitative research holds that the basic premise of naturalistic observation—whereby researchers generate "objective" observations by assuming a distanced or removed stance from the phenomena under study—is founded on tenuous or false assumptions. Qualitative frameworks treat an investigator's subjectivity, frames of reference or cultural lenses, biases, and opinions as fodder for open critical examination and self-reflection in data analyses and interpretation. Furthermore, qualitative research begins with the premise that investigators invariably affect the persons and the contexts under study; therefore, it is unrealistic to control an investigator's "contaminating effects" given the human context of research (Hammersley & Atkinson, 1995). Qualitative investigators are encouraged to detail their experiences and interactions with study participants, which potentially elicits important information on the nature of interpersonal relationships and behaviors in a specified cultural milieu.

Finally, qualitative research attempts to gain insight into the subjective experiences of study participants (Camic, Rhodes, & Yardley, 2003). This counters logical-positivistic approaches in which researchers impose a prescribed theory or worldview on a given study population to test its relevance or "truth." Qualitative researchers are more inclined to explore how people understand and experience particular psychological phenomena and how they construct meaning around these phenomena in their daily lives. As such, this approach strives to anchor study observations and findings in the daily practices, belief systems, and lives of the study participants. This feature of qualitative research promotes "culturally anchored" data that support more accurate and complete portraits of Asian Americans' psychological experiences. Two forms of qualitative inquiry—focus groups and ethnography—speak to these aforementioned strengths and have the potential to advance the state of research in the field.

Focus Groups

Although psychologists have traditionally used focus groups to gather preliminary information for quantitative projects, the focus group format lends itself as a primary method to study psychological phenomena. This is especially true when considering a social constructionist perspective of focus groups. According to this perspective, focus groups research examines how meaning is constructed collectively as group members develop, present, defend, and modify their views through their social interactions and exchanges (Wilkinson, 2003). Focus groups, therefore, create novel opportunities to examine the dynamic characteristics of psychological phenomena (e.g., acculturation processes, ethnic identity formation) that are often overlooked by quantitative self-report data.

Focus groups have been used with Asian American populations to explore such topics as women's perceptions of health care, cancer screening, and illness (Liang, Yuan, Mandelblatt, & Pasick, 2004); effects of Asian American media representations on self-concepts of college students (Sun, 2003); and perceived social support among new immigrants (Wong, Yoo, & Stewart, 2005). Still, specific cultural considerations for Asian American focus groups have yet to be fully explored in the field. The primary text on focus group research, *Focus Groups: A Practical Guide for Applied Research* by Krueger and Casey (2000), makes general recommendations for ethnically diverse populations (i.e., establish rapport, use a familiar language and a moderator that is similar to the participants) but falls short in this respect as well. A number of questions thus remain open to speculation: How do Asian Americans experience the focus group process? Can moderators who are ethnically dissimilar from group members successfully conduct a group? One of the few studies that examined the utility of focus groups for Asian Americans (Iwamasa & Hilliard, 1998) provides some preliminary insights into these questions. Also, the Asian American clinical and counseling literature, although not directed toward focus group methods, can offer some perspective on these questions.

Iwamasa and Hilliard (1998) evaluated the appropriateness of focus group methodology for older Japanese Americans in their study of successful aging. These older adult participants generally reported feeling comfortable with the focus group format and reported enjoying their group participation immediately after the study and three months later during follow-up. Iwamasa and Sorocco (2002) asserted that the effectiveness of focus groups lay in their (a) consistency with Asian values (e.g., cooperation and group harmony), (b) provision of in-depth data for formulating hypotheses and research questions, (c) ability to assess the value of topics to Asian Americans, and (d) opportunities for researchers to convey their interest in group members as "real people." The idea that focus groups can potentially validate and affirm Asian Americans and other ethnic minorities has been echoed by scholars from other disciplines. Feminist scholars have noted that focus groups provide a unique forum for ethnic minority women to break silence and to confront and endure their marginality together in meaningful ways (Madriz, 2003).

One critical question concerning the use of focus groups is whether moderators can be of a different ethnicity from group members. A similar question has been previously raised in the psychotherapy literature on client-therapist ethnic match (e.g., Maramba & Hall, 2002; S. Sue, Fujino, Hu, Takeuchi, & Zane, 1991). Although this literature does not speak directly to the focus group process, it suggests that having an Asian American moderator might benefit Asian American group members, particularly those with low acculturation levels, although ethnic matching does not guarantee success. Based on new findings on client-therapist "cognitive match" (Zane et al., 2005), it is plausible that moderators who share similar cultural attitudes and beliefs with group members, regardless of their ethnicity, may appear more credible in their roles, which in turn may improve the likelihood of successful group process. Again, these assertions are somewhat tenuous given the complexities of the focus group process and the distinctiveness of the therapeutic context in which these studies are based. Nonetheless, studies on ethnic and cognitive match might stimulate new ideas for future focus group research with Asian Americans.

Lastly, the clinical and counseling literature highlights a number of cultural issues in interpersonal and group dynamics that are relevant to focus groups with Asian Americans (e.g., Lee, 1997; D. W. Sue & Sue, 1999). Specifically, loss of face concerns, cultural notions of the public versus private self, collectivistic attitudes, and an interdependent self-construal may inhibit self-disclosure and the expression of negative emotions for some Asian American group members. Likewise, culturally prescribed gender and age-related roles may complicate the relationship between moderators and group members. All of these considerations, however, vary by the acculturation levels of group members. Also, these considerations, although important, are sometimes overgeneralized and, in the worst case scenario, stereotype Asian Americans as being withholding, unemotional, and avoidant in group situations. In a study of Chinese Americans with type 2 diabetes and their families (Chun & Chesla, 2004), new immigrants openly discussed personal information, including experiences of marital and family conflict, and expressed anger and sadness in group interviews. These same immigrants reported overall positive reactions to the group interview format. In particular, they noted that the interview groups offered a rare opportunity to publicly share their illness experiences and that the groups compelled them to pay closer attention to their health. The success of these group interviews appeared to be directly related to the cultural competencies of the interviewers and also the group interview format. The Chinese American interviewers in this study were not only fluent in Cantonese but also possessed the aforementioned cultural competency components.

Additionally, group sharing and support were facilitated by holding separate group sessions for spouses and patients.

Ethnography

Ethnography is another form of qualitative inquiry that has yet to be fully explored in psychology, with perhaps the exception of cross-cultural, cultural, and developmental areas where its utility and strengths have been discussed (e.g., Camic et al., 2003; Greenfield, 1997). To date, discussion of ethnography in Asian American psychology is conspicuously absent despite growing interest in this investigative method. This section introduces some basic principles of ethnography and methodological considerations for participant-observation in Asian American communities. Research examples from the first author's three-year ethnographic study in San Francisco's Chinatown (Chun, 2005) are presented to illustrate the nature of these methodological considerations and how they can be addressed. A bilingual afterschool program for Chinese American students (elementary through middle school) served as one of the field sites in this study of youth acculturation processes.

What is ethnography? Ethnography basically involves studying groups and individuals as they attend to the activities and relationships of their day-to-day lives (LeCompte & Schensul, 1999). This typically entails entering a particular ecological niche or social setting, often one that is relatively new or unfamiliar, to observe and experience a particular phenomenon. It also typically involves developing ongoing relations with the people in the study setting in order to better understand their activities, interactions, relationships, and experiences (Emerson, Fretz, & Shaw, 1995). This type of ethnographic work, called "participant-observation," involves systematically recording and interpreting observations in the field while participating in the daily lives of the study participants. Data-gathering techniques revolve around field notes, individual and group interviews, visual and audio recordings, and examination of archival materials. Participant-observation thus provides rich, contextual, dynamic and multilayered portraits of psychological phenomena that are often obscured or only partially captured by traditional self-report paper and pencil measures. For this reason, the first author selected participant-observation to more fully comprehend the nature and process of acculturation as it unfolded in the natural environments of inner-city Chinese American youth. During his study, he encountered a number of methodological considerations that revolved around levels of immersion in the field, the scope and focus of one's observational lens, and writing field notes.

Levels of immersion. How involved should a researcher be in the activities and interpersonal relationships in a study setting? How much personal information should be disclosed to study participants? Qualitative investigators have varying responses to these questions depending on their theoretical training; some follow a participatory-action stance by fully immersing themselves in a study setting (e.g., living, working, establishing close relationships with study participants) and collaborating with community members on social-action projects, including political or social movements. Others opt for a more limited approach in which they participate in communities in a more cautious or narrow fashion, often in the form of limited social interactions and casual conversation. In short, there is a broad continuum of immersion in ethnographic research that relies on a researcher's thoughtful deliberation and training, the purpose of a study, and the nature of study settings. Nonetheless, determining an "appropriate" level of immersion in the field often requires continuous evaluation and reflection due to changing situational demands and contexts.

The first author faced some challenges around immersion at the very outset of his participant-observation study. He was initially inclined to limit his immersion, but staff and youth at the bilingual afterschool program routinely asked him for assistance with activities and inquired about his personal background. There were a number of cultural and practical issues that the first author had to consider in deciding how to respond to these situations. Namely, a generation gap between the staff (mostly local Chinese American high-school and college students) and first author created some interpersonal distance between them. Also, the staff's limited experience with research fueled their wariness and skepticism about the project. Lastly, the bilingual afterschool program was built around a culture of service; therefore, all able-bodied individuals were expected to assist with activities. This expectation was reinforced by observed collectivistic attitudes and behaviors and the cultural norms of reciprocity and interdependence. Thus, the proposition that an older stranger would idly observe program activities like "a fly on the wall"—as prescribed by naturalistic observation—was culturally inappropriate in this setting and could have jeopardized relationships with the staff and youth. These considerations compelled the first author to participate more in program activities and initiate more social interactions with staff and youth. As a result, the staff and youth gradually became more at ease with his presence, shared more personal information, and exhibited a greater range of behaviors.

Determining the scope of one's observational lens. What should be the researcher's focus of attention in the field? How should researchers begin their observations? Initial observations of a site can feel overwhelming, especially when it is filled with activity, numerous personages, and myriad perceptual qualities. Under such circumstances, discerning when to narrow one's observational focus (e.g., observing a particular conversation or interaction between two people) and when to broaden it (e.g., observing group dynamics or the characteristics of the social setting) becomes a challenge. Ethnographers recommend "casting a broad net" when entering a site for the first time. This entails recording a broad and diverse range of events and interactions and characteristics of a site (Hammersley & Atkinson, 1995). This initial data-gathering approach then leads to more focused observations of patterns in activities and behaviors that can point to specific cultural norms, beliefs, and attitudes. Also, researchers can focus on specific contextual or environmental factors that are associated with the phenomena under investigation. As field observations progress, researchers should likewise search for activities and behaviors that may be nonnormative or unique in order to

comprehend variations or exceptions to observed patterns. This search for disconfirming evidence or data leads to modification or expansion of interpretations, more refined analyses of possible causes and circumstances for observed variations and differences, and a deeper understanding of the observed phenomena (Emerson et al., 1995). When the first author initially entered the bilingual afterschool program, various tutorial and recreational activities were occurring simultaneously, overlapping English and Cantonese conversations between staff and youth were overheard, and numerous parents and family members were coming and going. The first author felt pulled in different directions, struggling to observe important details about these activities without losing sight of the broader context in which they occurred. He thus decided to initially cast a broad net by describing the look and feel of the setting, as well as any sign of acculturation processes across a broad range of domains (e.g., language and dialect preferences, cultural behaviors, dress and foods, and the exchange of cultural elements). On subsequent visits, he narrowed his observational lens to certain program activities and contexts that permitted analyses of specific developmental patterns in youth acculturation processes.

Writing field notes. How should an observed phenomenon be described in field notes? How much detail should be included? Ethnographers should strive for "thick description" or highly detailed descriptions of behaviors, interpersonal exchanges, events and settings. This entails recording (a) initial impressions of the "look and feel" of the site, including sounds, sights, and smells; (b) activities and social exchanges that provide insights to what is deemed significant and meaningful to those who inhabit the ecological niche; and (c) key events or incidents that, from the researcher's perspective, counter or support expectations or elicit emotional reactions (Emerson et al., 1995). Thick descriptions also include noting the actual phrases and everyday speech of study participants. For instance, the first author focused on thick description of conversations between immigrant Chinese youth in his study. This entailed recording the content of their dialogue, conversational style, and the nature and context of their social interactions. This type of thick description made it possible to identify specific cultural elements that were being exchanged (e.g., knowledge of popular music and fashion), the nature of this exchange (e.g., building new friendships and joining new peer groups), and its overall significance to their acculturation and psychosocial adjustment (e.g., developing bicultural self-efficacy and fulfilling developmental tasks). Such analyses would not have been possible if the youths' conversations were summarized into general statements or summary impressions that omitted specific details and the actual content of their conversations.

Field notes also should emphasize study participants' perspectives and experiences. Making an active effort to understand how a phenomenon is actually experienced and understood by study participants forms the basis for "grounded theory." Theoretical frameworks for a particular phenomenon become "grounded" in the daily lives and ecological niche(s) of study participants when their perspectives are emphasized. In contrast, traditional empirical methods in psychology involve formulating hypotheses and theories mostly outside of study participants' day-to-day realities and settings. As previously noted, this traditional method of hypothesis generation potentially undermines the ecological validity of findings because it is too far removed from the lived experiences of the individuals and groups under investigation.

Lastly, the complexities of recording field notes require extensive practice and training. The first author found it beneficial to solicit expert ethnographers from other disciplines to make a joint visit at a site, record simultaneous observations, and compare field notes on content, style, and focus. Alternatively, more convenient settings can be selected (e.g., a university setting) for observation. Feedback can revolve around why certain words or descriptors were selected, why certain aspects of an activity were focal points for observation, and whether other important aspects of an activity were overlooked or elicited divergent interpretations.

Analyzing Qualitative Data

The number of texts on data-analytic strategies in qualitative research is increasing (e.g., Denzin & Lincoln, 2003; Emerson, Fritz, & Shaw, 1995; Grills, 1998; LeCompte & Schensul, 1999), especially for qualitative psychological studies (e.g., Camic et al., 2003; Smith, 2003). One method for analyzing focus group data is thematic analysis and interpretation of narratives. The content and presentation of narratives reflect individuals' cultural belief systems and worldviews, the significance of persons, objects, and events within their culture; and what might be termed a "background understanding" of their lives and experiences (Chesla, 1995). In a study of Chinese Americans with type 2 diabetes and their families (Chun & Chesla, 2004), group interviews were analyzed from a holistic and thematic perspective. This entailed reviewing the entire interview texts across groups to track holistic themes (e.g., "traditional Chinese medicine practices"), selecting themes and issues that were discussed within a specific group (e.g., "brewing corn silk or bitter melon soup to remedy diabetes"), detailing interpretations of each interview (e.g., "foods have medicinal as well as nutritional value that affects internal 'chi' or energy"), and marking text that addressed each of the identified themes. Furthermore, concrete narratives of diabetes care were analyzed for individual families so that the family context of diabetes care could be identified. This type of narrative analysis was beneficial because it provided a holistic, rather than an isolated, perspective on Asian American patients' illness experiences.

Analyses of ethnographic data can include both deductive (top-down) and inductive (bottom-up) strategies. Deductive analyses involve dividing data into predetermined categories or concepts that are based on the theoretical framework or questions of a study (LeCompte & Schensul, 1999). In contrast, inductive analyses begin with identifying individual cases, incidents, or experiences and then gradually creating more abstract conceptual categories that explain a particular phenomenon (Charmaz, 2003). Researchers often speak of codes emerging from their field notes during inductive analyses. These codes (which should stay close to the concepts that they describe) are then assembled into patterns or groups based on some shared property or relationship. Larger groups of patterns or relationships are then organized into structures leading to "grounded theory," as previously described.

Psychological researchers are often skeptical about the validity and reliability of qualitative data and interpretative strategies. In their seminal article on this issue, Henwood and Pidgeon (1992) recommend a number of practices that can improve the evaluation and rigor of qualitative psychological research:

1. To ensure that conceptual units and categories accurately reflect the data, their definitions and relation to the phenomenon under examination should be clearly explicated.

2. To develop a theory that is meaningfully related to the phenomenon under investigation, its "structure" should be complex and multi-layered. Researchers should illustrate how different levels of data are synthesized, integrated, and linked to form a theory. This should include drafting detailed analytic memoranda on the conceptual basis for data categories, connections between different levels of data, and the rationale for interpretations.

3. To account for the potential effects of researchers' roles and activities on observed phenomena, analyses and interpretation should incorporate "reflexive" observations from the field. Researchers should document their own emotional and cognitive responses to their field observations and their possible effects on study participants for consideration during data analysis and interpretation.

4. To allow for external audit of findings, researchers should extensively document other activities, including their initial concerns about the study, impressions on the quality of the data gathered, and observations about the context of data generation.

5. To add to the robustness of interpretations, researchers should use "negative case analysis" in their field observations. In this case, researchers should routinely seek disconfirming data that challenge initial assumptions and conceptualizations of the phenomena under investigation.

6. To evaluate "goodness of fit" between theory and the experiences and perspectives of study participants, researchers can compare their interpretations of the data with those of the study participants. This type of dialogue between researchers and study participants can generate additional data (including differences of opinion and interpretation) and potentially improve an emergent theory.

7. To comprehend the "transferability" or applicability of study findings to other contexts, researchers should fully describe contextual details and features from which the findings were generated. For instance, researchers should fully report on specific social or environmental conditions associated with a particular psychological phenomenon.

Extended discussion on the theoretical underpinnings and crafting of field notes and qualitative data analyses can be found in a number of widely referenced texts (e.g., Denzin & Lincoln, 2003; Emerson et al., 1995; Grills, 1998; LeCompte & Schensul, 1999; Smith, 2003; Strauss & Corbin, 1998).

PROMISING QUANTITATIVE METHODS: HIERARCHICAL LINEAR MODELS, GROWTH CURVE MODELS, AND EVALUATING MEASUREMENT INVARIANCE

Significant advances in quantitative methods for the social and behavioral sciences have tremendous implications for Asian American psychology research. In this section, we highlight the utility of (a) hierarchical linear models to evaluate the effectiveness of clinical interventions and (b) growth curve models to comprehend behavioral changes over time in longitudinal research designs. Lastly, we discuss the benefits of means and covariance structure analysis, and we examine item response theory in relation to measurement invariance issues.

Random Effects Regression Models

Let us assume that a health psychologist is interested in implementing an intervention targeting cardiovascular disease among Asian Americans in one clinic. The clinic has several physicians, where several physicians have a number of patients being randomly assigned to one of the two study conditions. Patients are randomly assigned to either a control condition or an intervention condition. In assessing the effectiveness of this intervention, a researcher might be tempted to perform an analysis of covariance to assess differences in self-reported exercise behavior across groups while controlling for SES. However, random-effects regression models (or hierarchical linear models) may be more effective when data are nested in this way. An assumption of analysis of covariance is independence of error terms. However, patients who see the same physician have something in common. This degree of similarity among patients who are nested within physicians is known as an intraclass correlation and is measured by an intraclass correlation coefficient (ICC). In other words, persons within their own cluster (physician) tend to be more similar than they are between clusters (physicians). Approaches like ANOVA and regression ignore the impact of the ICC. As the ICC increases, standard errors from the resulting analysis of covariance become more biased, making it easier to reject the null hypothesis.

Hierarchical linear models (HLMs) account for the ICC. To use an HLM in this example concerning cardiovascular disease, we would perform a series of regressions. Within each physician, we would regress self-reported exercise behavior on SES, patient gender, and experimental condition. This is typically referred to as the first level of a hierarchical model. In the second level of a hierarchical model, we are trying to predict the slopes and the intercepts from the first level with explanatory variables that describe the physician (e.g., physician gender, whether the physician is a resident or faculty member, etc.). This example can be much more complex, as physicians may be nested within clinic, requiring a third level of analysis that involves the prediction of slopes and intercepts from the second level using data that describe clinics (e.g., university hospital vs. community clinic). HLMs allow for modeling to occur at the level of the patient and at the level of the physician. Because a discussion of hierarchical linear models is well beyond the scope of this chapter,

see Raudenbush and Bryk (2002) for a more detailed discussion. For a nontechnical discussion of issues related to statistical power to determine the adequate number of respondents per cluster and the adequate number of clusters, see Raudenbush (1997) and Raudenbush and Liu (2000).

Growth Curve Models

Researchers in the social and behavioral sciences also are becoming interested in the analysis of change over time (Collins & Sayer, 2001). Earlier research in the assessment of change over time involved repeated analysis of variance (Moskowitz & Hershberger, 2002). The repeated measures analysis of variance model has several limitations, including the requirement that there are no missing data at each of the assessment points and the assumption of compound symmetry. As a result, repeated measures ANOVA may not be an accurate tool for evaluating longitudinal treatment programs.

For example, a repeated measures design may be used to examine how Asian American community members utilize a smoking cessation program sponsored by a local hospital. Some community members may not consistently attend this program, thus yielding missing data. Moreover, analysis on the remaining data may be biased, as missing participants may differ from non-missing participants on several important variables.

Growth curve models are applicable and extremely useful for research in a community setting, where the exogeneous variables are not as controlled as in a laboratory setting. Due to the limited control over variables, it is more likely to have missing data in a community setting. Growth curve models are also conceptually similar to hierarchical linear models, in that the repeated observations can be thought of as being nested within individuals.

In the first level of a growth curve model, each person has a number of equally spaced repeated assessments. The researcher attempts to fit a regression line to those data points. Unlike in a repeated measures ANOVA, it is not necessary for someone to have complete data at all repeated assessments to perform these regressions. The intercept would represent the value at the first time point, and the slope would represent rate of change across the repeated assessments. The simplest growth curve model posits linear growth, but nonlinear growth models also may be modeled. Linear growth is typically an example of something that grows in similar amounts over equal periods of time. A disciplined person who quits smoking on a consistent schedule for 12 weeks, such as smoking two fewer cigarettes a day, illustrates linear growth. A person who is less consistent may illustrate nonlinear growth. Alternatively, another person may quit smoking two cigarettes consecutively for the first 6 weeks of a program, but then begin smoking more cigarettes during the last 6 weeks of the program. Growth curves modeling allows for assessment of variability in growth patterns, thus permitting researchers to determine whether everyone follows the same growth trajectory or whether different people have different trajectories.

The resulting intercepts and slopes for each regression at the individual level would be used as outcome variables in the second level of the model, where person-level predictors like gender, race, and treatment effects between persons would be used to predict the intercepts and slopes from the first level. Latent growth curve modeling is an extension of growth curve modeling, in that it uses means and covariance structures to obtain estimates of latent variables that reflect the slope and intercept. An excellent tutorial on latent growth curve modeling can be found in Byrne and Crombie (2003) and Curran and Hussong (2002). Current versions of SPSS (Statistical Package for the Social Sciences) and SAS (Statistical Analysis Software) allows for the estimation of linear hierarchical models.

Evaluating Measurement Invariance

Researchers often assume that mean differences on a measure of interest between two populations are indicative of "true" differences between those groups. However, measurement invariance must hold across populations for those mean differences to be commensurate (Thissen, Steinberg, & Gerrard, 1986). Formal definitions of measurement invariance have been established by psychometricians (Byrne, Shavelson, &

Muthén, 1989; Meredith, 1993; Reise, Widamin, & Pugh, 1993), but this research has not been fully appreciated outside the domain of psychological measurement. According to Meredith (1993), measurement invariance holds when the likelihood of endorsing an item depends only on the level of the latent trait that is being measured and is independent of group membership. Under measurement invariance, individuals who are matched on the latent trait being measured, but who are from different groups, will have equal probabilities of endorsing an item. For example, a researcher may be interested in determining whether an English version and a Korean version of a smoking self-efficacy measure are invariant across language versions. Individuals with the same latent level of self-efficacy should be equally likely to endorse the item, regardless of the language of the measure. In this example, group membership would be defined by whether the respondent answered the questionnaire in English or Korean.

There are a variety of procedures to ensure that measures are commensurable across populations (Millsap & Everson, 1993). Two popular methods that are used in the assessment of measurement invariance are means and covariance structure analysis and item response theory.

Means and covariance structure analysis. Means and covariance structure analysis (Chan, 2000; Panter, Swygert, Dahlstrom, & Tanaka, 1997; Widaman & Reise, 1997) has also been referred to as multigroup confirmatory factor analysis (Jöreskog, 1971; Meredith, 1993). Meredith (1993) and Horn, McArdle, and Mason (1983) indicate that the first step in making group comparisons is establishing a baseline model that has the same pattern of factor loadings across groups. The baseline model is called the *configural invariance model.* This model is minimally necessary but is not sufficient in establishing invariance. For example, a researcher who is interested in assessing the language invariance of the self-efficacy measure has to determine that configural invariance holds before proceeding with any invariance assessment.

Meredith (1993) delineated several forms of factorial invariance. *Weak factorial invariance* occurs when the factor loadings of language versions are constrained to invariance across groups. This form of measurement invariance has also been referred to as metric invariance (Hong, Malik, & Lee, 2003; Steenkamp & Baumgartner, 1998). In the assessment of language invariance, metric invariance is a necessary, but not sufficient, condition for comparing means on the measures across groups.

Strong factorial invariance requires an additional set of constraints on the confirmatory factor model. Strong factorial invariance is said to occur when both the factor pattern coefficients and item intercepts in a factor model are equivalent across groups. This condition is also referred to as scalar invariance (Hong et al., 2003; Steenkamp & Baumgartner, 1998). Should strong factorial invariance hold, it is then possible to assess whether the mean of the latent variable differs across language versions.

Often, however, one subset of the factor loadings and/or intercepts will not statistically differ across groups, while another subset of factor loadings and/or intercepts will statistically differ across groups. If a researcher is interested in making mean comparisons among latent constructs, latent means can be meaningfully interpreted under conditions of partial metric invariance. This finding is important, as it allows for some of the factor loadings and intercepts to differ across groups. For example, etic items may be invariant across groups, whereas emic items may have different slopes or intercepts.

In assessing various forms of invariance, one must determine whether the model adequately describes the data. Although no model will perfectly explain the complexities of any data set (MacCallum, 2003), fit indices can be used to evaluate whether the various forms of invariance provide adequate descriptions of the data set. A summary of these fit indices can be found in Hu and Bentler (1999). In addition to using fit indices, researchers can also use the chi-square difference test to assess the parsimony of the weak, strong, and strict invariance models. Such comparisons are possible, as the more restrictive forms of invariance are nested within the lesser-restrictive invariance models.

Researchers who are interested in performing these invariance assessments are well advised to perform an a priori power analysis. For example, a researcher may conclude that a hypothesized factor model does not provide an adequate description of one's data. Even though it may be the case that the items do not function equivalently across language versions, model misfit across populations may be the function of inadequate sample size. Previously, researchers followed heuristic rules such as multiplying the number of items on the inventory by 10 to determine sample size. Research by MacCallum and colleagues has shown that such heuristic rules may be problematic. As a result, power analysis for factor analytic models and structural equation modeling have been discussed extensively by MacCallum, Browne, and Sugawara (1996) and MacCallum, Widaman, Zhang, and Hong (1999). Software is also available that can perform these power calculations (Steiger, 1999).

Item response theory. Imagine that a researcher who works at a federal prison wants to use the Minnesota Multiphasic Personality Inventory (MMPI) as a screening tool to determine whether an inmate is eligible to participate in an educational program. This educational program, if successfully completed, will reduce the length of a prisoner's sentence. Previous research shows that some ethnic groups tend to have elevated L scale scores on the MMPI when compared to Anglo participants (Plemons, 1977). To ensure that the MMPI does not function differentially across populations, this researcher believes that the measurement invariance of the MMPI must be assessed. Clearly, the use of the MMPI as a screening tool has practical policy implications for Asian American and other ethnic minority groups.

According to Panter et al. (1997), a specific problem with factor analysis when used on personality data is that the data are assumed to be continuously measured on an interval scale. Item scores from ordered categories may not meet the strict assumptions of linearity in a linear confirmatory factor analysis model (McDonald, 1999; Panter et al., 1997). For example, a researcher may want to perform a confirmatory factor analysis on a measure that consists of items that are either scored dichotomously (e.g., MMPI items) or items that are scored on a 3- or 4-point Likert scale. In this situation, the linear factor model would not be an appropriate measurement technique to assess measurement invariance.

In situations where the linear factor model is not appropriate, item response theory (IRT) can be used to assess measurement invariance. The use of IRT in personality assessment, for example, is increasingly common (Waller, 1999; Waller, Thompson, & Wenk, 2000). Recent books have made a convincing case that IRT is a valuable tool for researchers in the social and behavioral sciences (Embretson & Hershberger, 1999; Embretson & Reise, 2000).

IRT posits that the relationship between the probability of an item response ($P_i(\theta)$) and the latent trait (θ) is nonlinear (Hambleton, Swaminathan, & Rogers, 1991). This nonlinear relationship between ($P_i(\theta)$) and (θ) is called an item response function (IRF). In an IRF, the X-axis represents the examinee's trait level, and the Y-axis represents the examinee's response probability. The latent trait is assumed to have a mean equal to zero and a standard deviation equal to 1. In other words, θ is scaled on the z-score metric.

The IRF is a monotonic increasing function, such that individuals with more of the latent trait are more likely to endorse the item. Several parameters influence the relationship between probability of item endorsement and ability. The most popular models that describe this relationship are the 1-parameter logistic model, the 2-parameter logistic model, and the 3-parameter logistic model.

Expressed mathematically, the 1-parameter logistic model is

$$P_i(\theta) = 1/\{1 + \exp[-1.7(\theta - b)]\}$$

The 1-parameter model estimates the b parameter, which represents the difficulty of each test item and is typically measured in the same metric as the ability (θ) parameter. The b parameter can also be thought of as an "item threshold" (Waller, 2000), or the level of ability where the person has a 50% probability of endorsing the item. Difficult items have higher threshold values and thus require greater levels of the latent trait to answer the item correctly.

Expressed mathematically, the 2-parameter logistic model is

$$P_i(\theta) = 1/\{1 + \exp[-1.7a(\theta - b)]\}$$

The 2-parameter model estimates both the difficulty parameter and the a parameter, which represents the discrimination of a test item. The discrimination parameter determines how efficient a test item is in distinguishing examinees with low ability from those with high ability. The a parameter is related to the slope of the ICC (Waller, 2000). A steep slope indicates the ability of the item to discriminate within a small range of ability continuum.

Expressed mathematically, the 3-parameter logistic model is

$$P\theta = \frac{c + 1 - c}{1 + \exp[-1.7a(\theta - b)]}$$

The 3-parameter model allows for the estimation of the a, b, and c parameters. In the 3-parameter model, the c parameter represents the probability that an examinee with low ability will correctly answer the test item by guessing. This pseudo-guessing parameter is typically evaluated in educational tests. For personality tests, it is not intuitive to model a pseudo-guessing parameter, as examinees do not have a clear incentive to guess at personality items. Respondents don't have an incentive to "guess," but they might have an incentive to not be truthful with their responses, particularly on some personality tests.

It should be noted that group membership was not mentioned in any of the preceding equations and is not involved in the estimation of an IRF. In other words, the probability of endorsing an item is independent of group membership. This implies that all groups should therefore have identical IRFs. Nonequivalence of IRFs would be indicative of differential item functioning across language versions.

Suggestions on which IRT model should be estimated can be found in Suen (1990) or Camilli and Shepard (1994). For most personality inventories, we believe a researcher should assess the reasonableness of the assumption that items have equivalent discriminability. If this is not a reasonable assumption, the researcher should estimate the 2-parameter logistic model. There are some limitations in using IRT. First, large sample sizes are required to obtain stable parameter estimates for these item response models. For the 2- and 3-parameter logistic models, Nandakumar, Glutting, and Oakland (1993) recommend that at least 1,000 examinees and 20 items are necessary to obtain stable parameter estimates. For the 1-parameter logistic model, Nandakumar et al. (1993) indicate that 200 subjects per group are needed to obtain stable estimates of difficulty. While obtaining such sample sizes may not be problematic in the area of educational testing, social scientists interested in studying Asian American populations may not ordinarily obtain samples that large.

Another potential shortcoming of IRT involves the assessment of model fit. Because an item response model is a model of categorical data (Agresti, 1994), the G^2 or χ^2 statistic can be used to assess model fit. Taking the 15 items from the L-scale from the MMPI-2 as an example, item response models would be fitted to a contingency table consisting of 32,768 cells. In most cases, the use of the G^2 or χ^2 statistic in this example would be meaningless, as an insufficient number of data will be collected. Recent research by Maydeu-Olivares and Joe (2005) has begun to look at developing measures of model fit for contingency tables with sparse data.

Summary

IRT and means and covariance structure analysis have been presented as distinct statistical models; however, recent work by Maydeu-Olivares (2005) has unified the two approaches. Researchers who are interested in exploring ethnic group differences must be aware that the probability of endorsing an item ideally should be dependent on the level of latent trait being measured. Furthermore, differences across groups can be meaningfully assessed if the measure is invariant.

CONCLUSION

As we illustrated in this chapter, there are important cultural and practical considerations for working with diverse Asian American groups at each phase of an investigation. All of these considerations point to a growing movement in Asian American psychology to acknowledge and embrace the human context of our research endeavors. Even in the case of technical statistical models, there is a fundamental aim to more accurately and fully comprehend psychological phenomena for Asian Americans. As

such, a growing chorus of scholars in the field are calling for combined qualitative-quantitative research designs. However, this recommendation often presumes that qualitative inquiry facilitates theory development whereas quantitative inquiry establishes or confirms causal relationships. Although this can be an effective investigative strategy, it is often rooted in a prevailing myth that qualitative methods are a "softer" ancillary to "rigorous" quantitative methods. As we discussed in this chapter, such assumptions are problematic in light of the distinct strengths and benefits of qualitative methods in psychological research. In particular, qualitative investigation strives to comprehend and contextualize the diverse range of behaviors and experiences that are associated with psychological phenomena. This contrasts with a historical trend in the field to identify and quantify normative behaviors, which has inadvertently perpetuated limited or essentialized representations of Asian Americans in some cases.

Historical debates over the relative merits of qualitative and quantitative methods continue, and opinions on the "best" approach rest on the nature of the study question and ultimately on researchers' training and philosophical views. Regardless of which investigative approach is favored, this chapter attempts to illustrate that both have their rightful place in Asian American psychology. Our field is uniquely situated to help dismantle the historical divide between qualitative and quantitative research that continues to plague psychology as a whole. As noted by Okazaki, Lee, and Sue in Chapter 3 of this handbook, Asian American psychology has historical linkages to Asian American Studies, which is less beholden to logical positivism in its overarching conceptual and investigative frameworks. Asian American psychology also is a relatively new discipline with significant degrees of freedom for growth and evolution. In this context, perhaps the future of Asian American psychology lies in rediscovering our past and critically examining where we have gone and where we are headed. This most certainly includes taking stock of our current investigative methods and asking ourselves whether we have unknowingly constricted our disciplinary perspective and knowledge base by continuing to privilege some over others. In doing so, the field stands to make a paradigm shift by more fully exploring how qualitative and quantitative methods can equally shed new light on the diversity and complexities of Asian Americans' psychological experiences.

REFERENCES

Agretsi, A. (1994). *Analysis of ordinal categorical data.* New York: Wiley.

Avrushin, M. F., Azada, J., & Andal, J. (2005). *Are we empowered yet? A community report on the needs assessment survey of the Chicago Filipino American community.* Unpublished manuscript.

Burlew, A. K. (2003). Research with ethnic minorities: conceptual, methodological, and analytical issues. In G. Bernal, J. E. Trimble, A. K. Burlew, & F. T. L. Leong (Eds.), *Handbook of racial and ethnic minority psychology* (pp. 179–197). Thousand Oaks, CA: Sage.

Byrne, B., & Crombie, G. (2003). Modeling and testing change: An introduction to the latent growth curve model. *Understanding Statistics, 2,* 177–203.

Byrne, B. M., Shavelson, R. J., & Muthén, B. (1989). Testing for the equivalence of factor covariance and mean structures: The issue of partial measurement invariance. *Psychological Bulletin, 105,* 456–466.

Camic, P. M., Rhodes, J. E., & Yardley, L. (Eds). (2003). *Qualitative research in psychology: Expanding perspectives in methodology and design.* Washington, DC: American Psychological Association.

Camilli, G., & Shepard, L. A. (1994). *Methods for identifying biased test items.* Thousand Oaks: Sage.

Chan, D. (2000). Detection of differential item functioning on the Kirton Adaption-Innovation Inventory using multi-group mean and covariance structure analyses. *Multivariate Behavioral Research, 35,* 169–199.

Charmaz, K. (2003). Grounded theory. In J. A. Smith (Ed.), *Qualitative psychology: A practical guide to research methods* (pp. 184–204). Thousand Oaks, CA: Sage.

Chesla, C. A. (1995). Hermeneutic phenomenology: An approach to understanding families. *Journal of Family Nursing, 1*(1), 63–78.

Chun, K. M. (2005). Religious organizations in San Francisco Chinatown: Sites of acculturation and adaptation for Chinese immigrants. In

L. Lorentzen, K. M. Chun, J. Gonzalez, & H. D. Do (Eds.), *On the corner of bliss and nirvana: The religious lives of new immigrants in San Francisco.* Manuscript submitted for publication.

Chun, K. M., & Chesla, C. A. (2004). Cultural issues in disease management for Chinese Americans with type 2 diabetes. *Psychology and Health, 19*(6), 767–785.

Collins, L. M., & Sayer, A. G. (2001). *New methods for the analysis of change.* Washington, DC: American Psychological Association.

Curran, P. J., & Hussong, A. M. (2002). Structural equation modeling of repeated measures data: Latent curve analysis. In D. S. Moskowitz & S. L. Hershberger (Eds.), *Modeling intraindividual variability with repeated measures data: Methods and applications.* Mahwah, NJ: Lawrence Erlbaum.

D'Andrea, M., Daniels, J., & Heck, R. (1991). Evaluating the impact of multicultural counseling training. *Journal of Counseling and Development, 70,* 143–150.

Denzin, N. K., & Lincoln, Y. S. (Eds.). (2003). *Collecting and interpreting qualitative materials* (2nd ed.). Thousand Oaks, CA: Sage.

Embretson, S. E., & Hershberger, S. L. (1999). *The new rules of measurement: What every psychologist and educator should know.* Mahwah, NJ: Lawrence Erlbaum.

Embretson, S. E., & Reise, S. P. (2000) *Item response theory for psychologists.* Mahwah, NJ: Lawrence Erlbaum.

Emerson, R. M., Fretz, R. I., & Shaw, L. L. (1995). *Writing ethnographic field notes.* Chicago: University of Chicago Press.

Greenfield, P. M. (1997). Culture as process: Empirical methods for cultural psychology. In J. W. Berry (Series Ed.) & Y. H. Poortinga & J. Pandey (Vol. Eds.), *Handbook of cross-cultural psychology: Vol. 1. Theory and method* (2nd ed., pp. 301–346). Boston: Allyn & Bacon.

Grills, S. (Ed.). (1998). *Doing ethnographic research: Fieldwork settings.* Thousand Oaks, CA: Sage.

Hambleton, R. K., Swaminathan, H., & Rogers, H. J. (1991). *Fundamentals of item response theory.* Thousand Oaks, CA: Sage.

Hammersley, M., & Atkinson, P. (1995). *Ethnography: Principles in practice* (2nd ed.). New York: Routledge.

Henwood, K., & Pidgeon, N. (1992). Qualitative research and psychological theorizing. *British Journal of Psychology, 83,* 97–111.

Hong, S. H., Malik, M. L., & Lee, M. K. (2003). Testing configural, metric, scalar and latent mean invariance across genders in sociotropy and autonomy using a non-Western sample. *Educational and Psychological Measurement, 63,* 636–654.

Horn, J. L., McArdle, J. J., & Mason, R. (1983). When is invariance not invariant: A practical scientist's look at the ethereal concept of factor invariance. *Southern Psychologist, 1,* 179–188.

Hu, L., & Bentler, P. M. (1999). Cutoff criteria for fit indexes in covariance structure analysis: Conventional criteria versus new alternatives. *Structural Equation Modeling, 6,* 1–55.

Iwamasa, G. Y., & Hilliard, K. M. (1998). *Are focus groups effective with Japanese American older adults?* Poster presented at the annual meeting of the Association for the Advancement of Behavior Therapy, Washington, DC.

Iwamasa, G. Y., & Sorocco, K. H. (2002). Aging and Asian Americans: Developing culturally-appropriate research methodology. In G. Nagayama-Hall & S. Okazaki (Eds.), *Asian American psychology: The science of lives in context* (pp. 105–130). Washington, DC: American Psychological Association.

Jöreskog, K. G. (1971). Simultaneous factor analysis in several populations. *Psychometrika, 36,* 409–426.

Krueger, R. A., & Casey, M. A. (2000). *Focus groups: A practical guide for applied research* (3rd ed.). Thousand Oaks, CA: Sage.

LeCompte, M. D., & Schensul, J. J. (1999). *Designing and conducting ethnographic research.* Walnut Creek, CA: AltaMira Press.

Lee, E. (Ed.). (1997). *Working with Asian Americans: A guide for clinicians.* New York: Guilford Press.

Liang, W., Yuan, E., Mandelblatt, J. S., & Pasick, R. J. (2004). How do older Chinese Women view health and cancer screening? Results from focus groups and implications for interventions. *Ethnicity and Health, 9,* 283–304.

MacCallum, R. C. (2003). 2001 Presidential Address: Working with imperfect models. *Multivariate Behavioral Research, 38,* 113–139.

MacCallum, R. C., Browne, M. W., & Sugawara, H. M. (1996). Power analysis and determination of sample size for covariance structure modeling. *Psychological Methods, 1,* 130–149.

MacCallum, R. C., Widaman, K. F., Zhang, S., & Hong, S. (1999). Sample size in factor analysis. *Psychological Methods, 4,* 84–99.

Madriz, E. (2003). Focus groups in feminist research. In N. K. Denzin & Y. S. Lincoln (Eds.), *Collecting and interpreting qualitative materials* (2nd ed., pp. 363–388). Thousand Oaks, CA: Sage.

Manalansan, M. F. (Ed.). (2000). *Cultural compass: Ethnographic exploration of Asian America.* Philadelphia: Temple University Press.

Maramba, G. G., & Hall, G. N. (2002). Meta-analysis of ethnic match as a predictor of dropout, utilization, and level of functioning. *Cultural Diversity & Ethnic Minority Psychology, 8,* 290–297.

Marecek, J. (2003). Dancing through minefields: Towards a qualitative stance in psychology. In P. M. Camic, J. E. Rhodes, & L. Yardley (Eds.), *Qualitative research in psychology: Expanding perspectives in methodology and design* (pp. 49–69). Washington DC: American Psychological Association.

Maydeu-Olivares, A. (2005). Linear IRT, nonlinear IRT, and factor analysis: A unified framework. In A. Maydeu-Olivares & J. J. McArdle (Eds.), *Contemporary psychometrics. A Festschrift to Roderick P. McDonald* (pp. 73–100). Mahwah, NJ: Lawrence Erlbaum.

Maydeu-Olivares, A., & Joe, H. (2005). Limited and full information estimation and testing in 2^n contingency tables: A unified framework. *Journal of the American Statistical Association, 100,* 1009–1020.

McDonald, R. P. (1999). *Test theory: A unified treatment.* Mahwah, NJ: Lawrence Erlbaum.

Meredith, W. (1993). Measurement invariance, factor analysis and factorial invariance. *Psychometrika, 58,* 525–543.

Millsap, R. E., & Everson, H. T. (1993). Methodology review: Statistical approaches for assessing measurement bias. *Applied Psychological Measurement, 17,* 297–334.

Moskowitz, D. S., & Hershberger, S. L. (2002). *Modeling intraindividual variability with repeated measures data: Methods and applications.* Mahwah, NJ: Lawrence Erlbaum.

Nandakumar, R., Glutting, J. J., & Oakland, T. (1993). Mantel-Haenszel methodology for detecting item bias: An introduction and example using the guide to the assessment of test session behavior. *Journal of Psychoeducational Assessment, 11,* 108–119.

Nemoto, T., Huang, K., & Aoki, B. (1999). Strategies for accessing and retaining Asian drug users in research studies. *Drugs & Society, 14*(1/2), 151–165.

Okazaki, S. (2002). Beyond questionnaires: Conceptual and methodological innovations in Asian American psychology. In G. Nagayama-Hall & S. Okazaki (Eds.), *Asian American psychology: The science of lives in context* (pp. 13–40). Washington, DC: American Psychological Association.

Panter, A. T., Swygert, K. A., Dahlstrom, W. G., & Tanaka, J. S. (1997). Factor analytic approaches to personality item-level data. *Journal of Personality Assessment, 68,* 561–589.

Plemons, G. (1977). A comparison of MMPI scores of Anglo- and Mexican-American psychiatric patients. *Journal of Consulting and Clinical Psychology, 45,* 149–150.

Raudenbush, S. W. (1997). Statistical analysis and optimal design for cluster randomized trials. *Psychological Methods, 2,* 173–185.

Raudenbush, S. W., & Bryk, A. S. (2002). *Hierarchical linear models: Applications and data analysis methods.* Thousand Oaks: Sage.

Raudenbush, S. W., & Liu, X. (2000). Statistical power and optimal design for multisite randomized trials. *Psychological Methods, 5,* 199–213.

Reise, S. P., Widamin, K. F., & Pugh, R. H. (1993). Confirmatory factor analysis and item response theory: Two approaches for exploring measurement invariance. *Psychological Bulletin, 114,* 552–566.

Root, M. P. P (2002). Methodological issues in multiracial research. In G. Nagayama-Hall & S. Okazaki (Eds.), *Asian American psychology: The science of lives in context* (pp. 171–194). Washington, DC: American Psychological Association.

Smith, J. A. (Ed.). (2003). *Qualitative psychology: A practical guide to research methods.* London: Sage.

Sodowsky, G. R., Taffe, R. C., Gutkin, T. B., & Wise, S. L. (1994). Development of the Multicultural Counseling Inventory: A self-report measure of multicultural competencies. *Journal of Counseling Psychology, 41,* 137–148.

Steiger, J. H. (1997). STATISTICA Power Analysis [Computer software]. Tulsa, OK: StatSoft.

Steenkamp, J., & Baumgartner, H. (1998). Assessing measurement invariance in cross-national consumer research. *Journal of Consumer Research, 25,* 580–591.

Strauss, A., & Corbin, J. (1998). *Basics of qualitative research: Grounded theory procedures and techniques* (2nd ed.). Thousand Oaks, CA: Sage.

Sue, D. W. (2001). Multidimensional facets of cultural competence. *The Counseling Psychologist, 29*(6), 790–821.

Sue, D. W., & Sue, D. (1999). *Counseling the culturally different: Theory and practice* (3rd ed.). New York: Wiley.

Sue, S. (1999). Science, ethnicity, and bias: Where have we gone wrong? *American Psychologist, 54,* 1070–1077.

Sue, S., Fujino, D. C., Hu, L., Takeuchi, D. T., & Zane, N. W. S. (1991). Community mental health services for ethnic minority groups: A test of the cultural responsiveness hypothesis. *Journal of Consulting and Clinical Psychology, 59,* 533–540.

Sue, S., & Sue, L. (2003). Ethnic research is good science. In G. Bernal, J. E. Trimble, A. K. Burlew, & F. T. L. Leong (Eds.), *Handbook of racial and ethnic minority psychology* (pp. 198–207). Thousand Oaks, CA: Sage.

Sun, C. (2003). *Stories matter: Media influence on Asian American identities and interracial relationships.* Unpublished doctoral dissertation, University of Massachusetts, Amherst.

Suen, H. K. (1990). *Principles of test theory.* Hillsdale, NJ: Lawrence Erlbaum.

Tanaka, J. S., Ebreo, A., Linn, N., & Morera, O. F. (1998). Research methods: The construct validity of self-identity and its psychological implications. In N. Zane & L. C. Lee (Eds.), *Handbook of Asian American psychology* (pp. 21–79). Thousand Oaks, CA: Sage.

Thissen, D., Steinberg, L., & Gerrard, M. (1986). Beyond group-mean differences: The concept of item bias. *Psychological Bulletin, 99,* 118–128.

Vo, L. T. (2000). Performing ethnography in Asian American communities: Beyond the insider-versus-outsider perspective. In M. F. Manalansan (Ed.), *Cultural compass: Ethnographic explorations of Asian America* (pp. 17–37). Philadelphia: Temple University Press.

Waller, N. G. (1999) Searching for structure in the MMPI. In S. E. Embretson & S. Hershberger (Eds.), *The new rules of measurement: What every psychologist and educator should know* (pp. 185–217). Mahwah, NJ: Lawrence Erlbaum.

Waller, N. G., Thompson, J. S., & Wenk, E. (2000). Using IRT to separate measurement bias from true group differences on homogeneous and heterogeneous scales: An illustration with the MMPI. *Psychological Methods, 5,* 125–146.

Widaman, K. F., & Reise, S. P. (1997). Exploring the measurement invariance of psychological instruments: Applications in the substance use domain. In K. J. Bryant, M. Windle, & S. G. West (Eds.), *The science of prevention: Methodological advances from alcohol and drug abuse research* (pp. 281–324). Washington, DC: American Psychological Association.

Wilkinson, S. (2003). Focus groups. In J. A. Smith (Ed.), *Qualitative psychology: A practical guide to research methods* (pp. 184–204). Thousand Oaks, CA: Sage.

Wong, S. T., Yoo, G. J., & Stewart, A. L. (2005). Examining the types of social support and the actual sources of social support in older Chinese and Koreans. *International Journal of Aging and Human Development, 61,* 105–121.

Zane, N., Sue, S., Chang, J., Huang, L., Huang, J., Lowe, S., et al. (2005). Beyond ethnic match: Effects of client-therapist cognitive match in problem perception, coping orientation, and therapy goals on treatment outcome. *Journal of Community Psychology, 33*(5), 569–585.

PART II

LIFE COURSE DEVELOPMENT

5

Asian American and Pacific Islander Families: Resiliency and Life-Span Socialization in a Cultural Context

Barbara W. K. Yee

Barbara D. DeBaryshe

Sylvia Yuen

Su Yeong Kim

Hamilton I. McCubbin

Asian American and Pacific Islanders (AAPIs) are often portrayed as a resilient "model minority." AAPI individuals have been described as being well educated and financially stable; valuing hard work and family ties; and exhibiting positive social behaviors. This positive characterization overlooks the difficult life circumstances that some AAPI individuals experience and downplays the very real needs of those who are vulnerable to experiences of discrimination, trauma, or poverty. An examination of the evidence reveals great variation in the prevalence of risk and protective factors and resiliency processes across AAPI ethnic groups (Yee, Huang, & Lew, 1998). In this chapter, we highlight how AAPI families provide protection and diminish risk for family members as they traverse developmental milestones and cope with challenges over the life course. Specifically, we (a) provide a family resilience conceptual framework for understanding risk and protective factors in AAPI families, (b) discuss how AAPI cultures promote family interdependence as a basis for family protective or risk factors, (c) outline key demographic variables that serve as risk and protective factors for

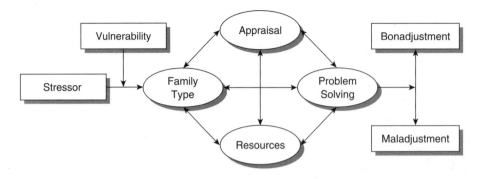

Source: Adapted from the Resiliency Model of Family Stress, Adjustment, and Adaptation (McCubbin, McCubbin, Thompson, & Thompson, 1998).

AAPI families, (d) address family life-cycle issues for AAPI families, and (e) conclude by highlighting directions for future AAPI family research opportunities and federal family research funding policies.

ASIAN AMERICAN AND PACIFIC ISLANDER FAMILIES: CONCEPTUAL FRAMEWORK

Family Resilience: Risk Factors and Protective Factors

In this chapter, we rely on the Resiliency Model of Family Stress, Adjustment, and Adaptation (McCubbin, McCubbin, Thompson, & Thompson, 1998) to provide a framework for explaining variability across Asian American and Pacific Islander families in response to both normative and nonnormative life changes, and stressful life events (see figure). This model highlights developmental stages, culture, values, interpersonal skills, and family system properties as critical resources on which the family unit may draw as it negotiates change and adaptation over the life course.

Every family has a blend of risk factors and protective factors, and these proportions may change over time. Risk factors are characteristics of the family in a particular situational context that tend to be associated with nonoptimal outcomes (e.g., poverty, chronic illness, or disability, divorce, exposure to community violence). Protective factors are internal or external characteristics that are associated with well-being and optimal development (e.g., financial security, education, social support, strong family communication, spirituality). Resiliency is a process through which families exposed to objectively high levels of risk are able to mobilize resources and maintain healthy outcomes. Resilient families succeed in overcoming the odds that would usually be expected to cause lasting harm to the family unit or its individual members (Luthar & Zelazo, 2003).

From time to time, all families face *stressors,* or demands, that potentially lead to changes in the existing family system. More severe stressors pose greater threats to the family system (e.g., bankruptcy, divorce). The impact of a stressor is also dependent on the existing *vulnerability,* or pile-up of demands, that the family already faces. Two ecological challenges commonly faced by AAPI families are minority status and acculturation. Minority status confers a subordinate position and restricted range of opportunities for mobility and success. In addition to the normative tasks of development, AAPIs must master the stress of "being different" and overcome the labels of being "inferior" or "not belonging." Another ecological challenge for Asian and Pacific Islander families is the tension associated with acculturation. AAPI families must bridge two, sometimes conflicting, cultures, and some family members (typically children and adolescents) acculturate more quickly than others.

Families differ widely in how they react to stressors and vulnerability and whether their reaction has positive or negative consequences for long-term family adaptation. Family outcomes depend on the interaction between four key family characteristics: family type, resistance resources, appraisal, and problem-solving/coping strategies. *Family type* is the predictable pattern of overall functioning. For example, "balanced" families show strong instead of extreme levels of both coherence and flexibility, whereas "rhythmic families" are characterized by their reliance on routines and shared family time. Compared to other family types, both balanced and rhythmic families are more successful in weathering change. Family *resistance resources* are the capabilities and strengths that family members may potentially call on. These resources are highly varied and include economic or material assets, social network support, intellectual capital, family traditions, role clarity, cooperation, and communication. Family *appraisal* functions at several levels. At the simplest level, appraisal is the subjective assessment of the stressful event, that is, the family's definition of the stressor as an overwhelming versus a manageable challenge. But how the family interprets a single stressful situation depends on broader and more fundamental patterns of (a) family paradigms (e.g., shared beliefs about family functions such as child rearing and balancing work and family responsibilities); (b) the family's sense of coherence (e.g., a sense of agency vs. acceptance of external circumstances); and (c) family schema (i.e, the general worldview that guides the family's sense of spirituality and deeper purpose). Ethnicity and culture may be especially operative at the level of family appraisal. Finally, *problem solving and coping* refer to the specific behavioral, cognitive, and emotional strategies that families use to address the stressful situation. Problem solving refers to the plans that families make to alleviate or ameliorate the stressor itself. For example, does the family organize the stressful situation into smaller, more manageable parts? Coping refers to the concrete steps that families take to either remove the threatening situation or maintain and strengthen the families' emotional state and ongoing well-being.

The interaction of these four components (family type, resources, appraisal, and problem solving and coping) determines the outcome, or family *adaptation process*. When families are able to change their rules, routines, and/or appraisals in ways that respond to change and still maintain family well-being, then positive adaptation has occurred. Families that cannot change in a positive manner will remain in a maladaptive state of crisis until a new level or reorganization can be achieved.

The resiliency model draws attention to the central role that family strengths, ethnicity, and culture play, as families deal with developmental tasks, adapt to change, and overcome adversity. The resiliency framework reinforces the notion that a sole focus on the negative repercussions of trauma loses sight of the tremendous resilience demonstrated by some families even under deplorable conditions. This concept is reflected in the Chinese ideogram for crisis, which is composed of the symbols meaning danger and opportunity—two possible outcomes of a crisis. Adversity can be an insurmountable barrier or a worthy challenge despite the odds. The following section outlines how AAPI cultural values promote family interdependence, a foundation for protective factors and possible risk factors for AAPI families living in the United States.

ASIAN AMERICAN AND PACIFIC ISLANDER CULTURAL VALUES PROMOTE FAMILY INTERDEPENDENCE

Although there is much diversity within the broad AAPI ethnic category, certain pan-AAPI values underlie similarities in family practices across AAPI subgroups. Cross-national examinations have identified four cultural themes that are common to Chinese, Japanese, Filipino, Southeast Asian, South Asian, Hawaiian, and Samoan cultures:

1. *Collectivism* is the tendency to place group needs and goals above the goals and desires of the individual (Hofstede, 1980).

2. A *relational orientation* is a cultural frame in which the self is defined in terms of its essential

and continuing interdependence with others (Enriquez, 1993; Markus & Kitayama, 1991).

3. *Familism* defines a hierarchically organized extended family system as the basic social unit (Fugita, Ito, Abe, & Takeuchi, 1991).

4. *Family obligation* includes both attitudinal and behavioral responsibilities in which children are expected to: show respect and affection for older family members; seek their advice and accept their decisions; and maintain propinquity, instrumental assistance, and emotional ties with parents across the life span (Chao & Tseng, 2002; Phinney, Ong, & Madden, 2000).

The common thread uniting these four culturally relevant values is the theme of family interdependence.

In light of the strong emphasis on family obligation and filial piety, family interdependence is a core issue for AAPI families. A strong kinship system with high levels of mutual obligation provides family members with a clearly defined group that can be counted on to provide assistance and aid (Tseng & Hsu, 1991). Family interdependence can be a powerful resource, but it can also be a source of stress.

AAPI adolescents demonstrate a strong sense of obligation to the family (Chao & Tseng, 2002; DeBaryshe, Yuen, & Stern, 2001). Paradoxically, while a strong sense of obligation can provide motivation to succeed for the good of one's family, strong family demands can also reduce the amount of time that youths can devote to school, thus undermining their academic success (Tseng, 2004). Another feature of family interdependence during adolescence is the delayed autonomy of AAPI adolescents from their parents compared to other ethnic groups (Kwak, 2003). When there is a match between parents and their adolescent children in autonomy expectations (i.e., delayed autonomy), this may foster positive adjustment in Asian American adolescents (Juang, Lerner, McKinney, & von Eye, 1999).

Family interdependence creates ecological challenges in the context of acculturation in AAPI families where individualistic goals may be subsumed by goals chosen by family elders. With increasing years of living in the United States, children quickly adopt American language, values, and behaviors, whereas parents retain their traditional values (Nguyen & Williams, 1989). Discrepant levels of acculturation between parents and adolescents can have negative consequences for family functioning and adolescent well-being (Crane, Ngai, Larson, & Hafen, 2005; Farver, Narang, & Bhadha, 2002).

Interdependence issues are salient also for the older generations. Asians (42%) are more likely to assist in caring for or financially supporting parents, in-laws, or other older relatives than are Whites (19%), Blacks (28%), or Hispanics (34%) (American Association of Retired Persons, 2003). Of course, not all elders are in a dependent relationship with their adult children; grandparents and other coresiding relatives often fulfill important functions for the family unit, such as child care and housework. Using extended family members as unpaid or underpaid domestic workers is a practice common among AAPI families (Barringer, Gardner, & Levin, 1993). Thus, intergenerational living appears to benefit the overall family unit, although individual family members often make personal sacrifices for the common good.

A corollary of family interdependence is the need to maintain harmonious relationships among family members. AAPI families avoid displays of strong emotion, including both negative and positive emotions (Uba, 1994). The tempering of negative emotional expression may enhance the stability and socially supportive nature of AAPI family interaction. However, suppression of positive emotional expression, such as verbal praise for successes, may result in AAPIs who lack confidence in their abilities or lowered self-esteem (Stevenson & Stigler, 1992). Asian Americans report experiencing elevated levels of emotional distress and symptoms indicative of high anxiety or depression (Wei, Russel, Mallinckrodt, & Zakalik, 2004). The suppression of negative emotions may be a protective factor, but suppression of positive emotions may be a risk factor for AAPI families. Family resilience also depends on the constellation of important family demographic characteristics that describe the vulnerabilities or resources that are available to facilitate positive family adaptation. The following section highlights important AAPI demographic factors that illustrate the diversity of risk and protective factors seen across different AAPI ethnic subgroups.

ASIAN AMERICAN AND PACIFIC ISLANDER FAMILY DEMOGRAPHICS

By 2020, the AAPI population is projected to constitute 6% of the total U.S. population (Ong & Leung, 2003). In 2000, 11.9 million Americans (4.2%) were Asian, and 861,000 (0.3%) were Pacific Islanders (Harris & Jones, 2005; Reeves & Bennett, 2004). Persons of Chinese, Filipino, Asian Indian, Vietnamese, and Korean heritage comprise 80% of the U.S. Asian population, while Native Hawaiians comprise 45% of the Pacific Islander group. The majority of Pacific Islanders are of mixed racial ancestry (55%) as compared to 16% of Asian Americans.

Of all racial groups in the United States, AAPI families have the highest percentage of immigrants: 69% of Asians and 20% of Pacific Islanders are foreign-born, as compared to 10% of the overall population (Harris & Jones, 2005; Reeves & Bennett, 2004). The majority of AAPI immigrants living in the United States in the year 2000 entered the country in the 1980s and 1990s, which indicates a pattern of relatively recent migration. In addition to being a small demographic group, AAPI individuals are also geographically concentrated in coastal urban areas; the majority of AAPIs live in only three states—California, New York, and Hawai'i (Barnes & Bennett, 2002; Grieco, 2001).

In terms of socioeconomic status (SES), Asians are relatively advantaged, whereas Pacific Islanders are more likely to be disadvantaged (Harris & Jones, 2005; Reeves & Bennett, 2004). Compared to the overall population, Asians are more likely to hold a bachelor's or graduate degree (44% vs. 24%), have higher median household incomes ($59,300 vs. $50,000), work in managerial or professional occupations (45% vs. 34%), and earn higher wages than the national mean (9% greater for Asian men and 14% higher for Asian women). On the other hand, Pacific Islanders are less likely to hold a bachelor's degree or higher (14%); have lower median household incomes of $45,915; tend to hold jobs in the sales, office, and service sectors; and earn lower wages (16% lower than the national average for men and 6% lower for women). Although Pacific Islander women are more likely than other women to be in the workforce, Pacific Islanders are overrepresented among those living in poverty (18% vs. 12% nationally). There is considerable diversity within the AAPI population, and SES tends to be associated with national origin. That is, South Asian and East Asians are most likely to be more advantaged, whereas Cambodians, Laotians, and Hmong tend to have lower educational and occupational status. Among the Pacific Islander groups, Marshallese have the highest poverty rate.

The AAPI population is relatively young (Harris & Jones, 2005; Reeves & Bennett, 2004). Compared to the U.S. population as a whole, the Pacific Islander population has larger proportions of both children and young adults (ages 0–34 years). The Asian population has proportionately more young adults (ages 20–39), and fewer children (those younger than age 14) and older adults (those 55 and older). However, certain Asian subgroups are quite young. The Cambodian, Laotian, and especially the Hmong populations have very high proportions of children (e.g., 55% of the Hmong population is younger than age 18).

AAPIs are especially likely to live with family members, with relatively low rates of residing alone or with roommates (Harris & Jones, 2005; Reeves & Bennett, 2004). Compared to the population overall, both Asian and Pacific Islander households are more likely to include a married couple (62% and 56%, respectively, vs. 53% for all households). Asians show low rates of single-mother households (9% vs. 12% nationally), whereas Pacific Islanders show relatively high rates of both single-mother (15%) and single-father (7%) living arrangements. AAPI children are more likely to live with both parents than are children of other ethnic groups. Over three-quarters (78%) of Asian children and 58% of Pacific Islander children live in a home with both of their parents (U.S. Census Bureau, 2003a).

Multigenerational and multifamily households also are more common among AAPI families. Compared to their Caucasian counterparts, Asian elders who are 60 years and older are three times as likely to live in a household with a spouse and other kin present (34% vs. 11%) and one-third as likely to be institutionalized (1% vs. 3%) (Himes, Hogan, & Eggebeen, 1996). Only 2% of non–Hispanic Whites, but 6% of Asians and 10% of Pacific Islanders, live with their grandchildren (Simmons & Dye, 2003). Intergenerational living arrangements are more common among recently arrived Asian immigrants than among U.S.-born Asians (30% vs. 4%) (Glick & Hook, 2002). Although coresidence is most common among financially dependent immigrants, at all levels of income and generational status, Asian households are more likely to be intergenerational when compared with non–Hispanic Whites. This suggests that cultural, as well as economic, factors explain the high rates of intergenerational AAPI households.

This review of AAPI family demographics reveals the presence of protective factors (e.g., two parent families with children, intergenerational living, higher SES levels, lower divorce rates, etc.) for many, but not all, AAPI groups. Other AAPI groups (typically recent immigrants and Southeast Asian and Pacific Islander families) are at risk for poverty, underemployment, and refugee status (Braun, Yee, Brown, & Mokuau, 2004; Yee et al., 1998).

The following section highlights how AAPI families traverse normative family transitions (such as marriage, parenting, intergenerational relationships, and care for frail elders) and deal with the challenges of minority status and acculturation.

FAMILY LIFE CYCLE ISSUES

Asian American and Pacific Islander Marriage and Marital Satisfaction

Marital satisfaction is an important protective factor for both spouses and their children (Gottman, 1998). Cultural scripts and acculturation processes shape who may be considered an eligible marriage partner, what may be the marital role expectations, or whether marriage is based on romance or other factors such as family or financial status of the potential marital partner. An examination of marriage and divorce in AAPI families reveals extensive cultural variations and commonalities in contemporary society.

Romantic attachment is the primary goal in the selection of a marital partner in contemporary U.S. society. This provides a dilemma for recent immigrants whose cultural values may consider other factors as being more important (e.g.,

financial situation, family status, or as a means to ensure continuity of family lineage). For example, second-generation female Muslim Pakistanis felt conflicted because in America, one was free to choose a marriage partner, but more traditional family members wanted to screen and make the final selection of marriage partners for their adult children based on approval by the family as in the South Asian homeland of family elders (Zaidi & Shuraydi, 2002). Interracial mate selection has been used as an indicator of racial discrimination and acculturation; it also is influenced by the availability of potential mates in the community (Fujino, 2000). In the period following contact with Westerners, interethnic marriages were encouraged and fostered in the Native Hawaiian community; this was done to slow the alarming decline in the Hawaiian population caused by introduced diseases, as well as for political reasons (McCubbin & McCubbin, 2005). In contemporary society, more acculturated AAPIs may choose marital partners outside their own race (non-Asian) or among other AAPI groups. (Aguirre, Saenz, & Hwang, 1995).

Marital satisfaction is largely a function of agreement on gender roles and marital expectations, both of which are highly influenced by culture (Lebra, 1976), family schemas (McCubbin & McCubbin, 2005), and family boundaries and structure (e.g., nuclear vs. extended family) (Tseng & Hsu, 1991). Marital conflicts and tensions may arise as a result of differing culture, gender and marital role expectations; disapproval of the marriage from the family of origin; and intrusiveness of in-laws in the family unit (Inman, Altman, & Kaduvettoor, 2004).

Information on marital violence in AAPI families is both scant and contradictory (Malley-Morrison & Hines, 2004). National and statewide studies of victimization and domestic violence rarely report statistics for AAPI. National self-reported rates in domestic violence were lowest for both AAPI women (15%) and AAPI men (3%). By contrast, studies with smaller AAPI subgroup community samples show rates as high as 80% and suggest that Japanese, Vietnamese, and South Asian women are most at risk for domestic violence. Many AAPI groups define abuse in a way that excludes emotional maltreatment. The lingering effects of patriarchy, values related to forbearance and saving face, linguistic isolation, and refugee status have been offered as explanations for widely disparate reported rates or poor detection of domestic violence in AAPI families. To date, no studies have examined whether family interdependence tends to reduce the risk of violence in AAPI families (e.g., closely connected family members may intervene when abuse is threatened) or increase the risk (e.g., family members avoid seeking help from outsiders). Thus, AAPI families can be an important source of protection or a risk factor in domestic violence. The following section describes how AAPI parenting and parental practices may function as protective or risk factors.

Parenting Styles and Practices in AAPI Families

An important issue in understanding parenting in AAPI populations is the extent to which the more traditional aspects of Asian and Pacific Island cultures operate within contemporary family life. Asian American parents have been described as more hierarchical, less democratic, and more controlling than parents from other ethnic backgrounds, particularly when compared to Caucasian families (Chao & Tseng, 2002; Uba, 1994). AAPI parents tend to exhibit less physical affection, praise, and personal disclosure and to hold greater expectations for instrumental assistance and shared family time.

Information on Pacific Islander family interaction is scant. Ethnographic work suggests that Native Hawaiian parents are affectionate and indulgent with infants but are less demonstrative toward older children (Howard, 1974). Children spend much time with their extended family, and caregiving by grandparents, siblings, and other relatives is common; thus, Pacific Islander children have multiple parent figures (Howard, 1974; Korbin, 1990). The explicit use of parental praise or rewards is uncommon in Pacific Islander families (Howard, 1974). Children are also expected to be sensitive to social cues and attend to others' needs and expectations without prompting or acknowledgment (Shook, 1985). Although cultural historians suggest that severe punishment was not part of traditional Pacific child-rearing practices

(Korbin, 1990), Pacific Islander children are overrepresented among the ranks of confirmed abuse cases in Hawai'i (Furoto, 1991). Pacific Island parents appear to set a relatively high threshold for distinguishing appropriate punishment from harsh discipline and view parental responses to transgressions as an obligation and expression of concern for the child (Furoto, 1991; Korbin, 1990).

Overall, the literature presents a contradictory picture of AAPI child rearing. On one hand, parents are described as strict, undemonstrative, and demanding. If parents place excessive demands on their children, this may generate resentment and interfere with children's ability to form peer relationships and develop independent interests outside the family sphere. On the other hand, parental control and high expectations for children also are given as explanations for the academic success and low rates of risk behavior evidenced by many AAPI youth. It is unclear which picture is more accurate. Do AAPI parenting practices serve as risk or protective factors for different aspects of children's socioemotional and intellectual development?

A large literature on parent-child relations indicates that child-rearing practices are robustly associated with children's psychosocial adjustment (Lamborn, Mounts, Steinberg, Dornbusch, 1991; Maccoby & Martin, 1983). Within this literature, much attention has been paid to identifying the consequences of different parenting styles (e.g., authoritative, authoritarian, permissive, and neglectful). In general, when families within North America and Europe are considered, findings most often indicate that an authoritative parenting style (one that balances warm parental involvement, the granting of psychological autonomy, and nonpunitive, reason-oriented control) is beneficial to children across age, SES, and ethnic group (Mason, Cauce, Gonzales, Hiraga, & Grove, 1994; Mistry, Vandewater, Huston, & McLoyd, 2002; Parker & Benson, 2004; Steinberg, Mounts, Lamborn, & Dornbusch, 1991) However, there has been controversy as to whether the authoritative parenting style is a universal construct or is more specific to Western and/or Caucasian families (e.g., Chao & Tseng, 2002). Studies of child rearing in East Asia suggest that Chinese and Korean parents exert high levels of control over many aspects of their children's lives and show more muted expressions of physical and emotional affection (Lau, Lew, Hau, Cheung, & Berndt, 1990; Rohner & Pettengill, 1985) with no adverse effects on child outcomes. Chao and Tseng (2002) argue that it is a misnomer to label Asian parents as authoritarian or controlling. Rather, in these family systems, intensive guidance and training of one's children is both given and received as an expression of parental concern, duty, and love. They argue that parental control has a different, more positive meaning in Asian families.

By extension, one might predict that AAPI parents in the United States may be less likely to use a prototypically authoritative parenting style and more likely to use an authoritarian style. If Chao and Tseng's (2002) cultural compatibility argument is accurate, then AAPI youth should benefit from (or at least not be harmed by) an authoritarian parenting style. Results in this regard are mixed. Some researchers suggest that an authoritative parenting style is indeed less common among Asian American families, especially in comparison to Caucasian families (Dornbusch, Ritter, Leiderman, Roberts, & Fraleigh, 1987). Consistent with Chao and Tseng's (2002) predictions, unilateral parental decision making is associated with worse levels of behavioral, emotional, and academic adjustment among Caucasian adolescents but is not related to adjustment among Asian American adolescents. In contrast, one study of multiethnic AAPI families found that an authoritative parenting style was positively associated with adolescent self-concept and school performance (DeBaryshe et al., 2005). Differences across studies may be related to diversity within the AAPI population. Acculturated families or families living in the United States for several generations may show parenting styles that are closer to the authoritative prototype, and the correlation between child outcomes and parenting styles may differ as a function of family acculturation.

Sibling Relationships in Asian American and Pacific Islander Families

Parents play a central role in the socialization of life skills and family support network of AAPI families. Siblings may have a vital role in the socialization of younger siblings because siblings or older family members, such as cousins, are the first peers that children encounter. Although siblings provide a source of conflict and sibling rivalry, they can be a great source of support and comfort over a lifetime. For instance, sibling relationships allow younger siblings to practice and sharpen social skills, while nurturing the emotional relationships between family members. These skills and role modeling enhance younger siblings' ability to adapt and function in important social spheres to successfully traverse developmental transitions over the life course.

Cicirelli (1994) found cross-cultural differences in both the definition of sibling roles and the cultural norms regulating sibling role responsibilities and behaviors. For instance, Seymour (1993) found that older South Asian siblings care for younger siblings and teach them survival skills such as personal self-care, domestic skills, or occupational skills. Older siblings were provided parent training skills and served as insurance against early parental death. Sibling caregiving may also have adaptive value in single-parent households and dual-career households, in families that cannot afford babysitting expenses, or in families that do not have adult extended family members to provide these services. Sibling caregiving has been brought by AAPI families to the United States, but it has not been systematically examined.

In a study of acculturative differences across Vietnamese and Korean American siblings, birth order appears to influence the acculturation level of first born versus younger siblings (Pyke, 2005). This acculturation birth order effect was independent of years living in the United States First-born and older siblings were likely to have been afforded higher status, were disciplinarians to younger siblings, and had more traditional viewpoints and behaviors closer to those of their parents and not their own generation in the family. Pyke (2005) described first-born and older siblings as traditionalists because they differed from more acculturated younger siblings who were described as "generational deserters and black sheep." The author argued that diversity in acculturative pathways across siblings may enhance a family's ability to adapt in new cultural environments. For example, younger acculturated siblings expressed relief when older siblings relieved them of family obligations, felt that both parents and older siblings provided help when needed, felt that older siblings served as mediators between their traditional parents and themselves (acculturated younger siblings), and appreciated when family traditions were maintained by older siblings. Younger, more acculturated siblings served as an effective bridge to the mainstream American culture. Although the different acculturation levels within and across generations may be a source of family tension, it appears that it may also serve an adaptive function for immigrant families. Given that sibling relationships may be one of the longest family relationships that humans may have, more research must be done to examine this important family relationship and source of social support. The following section will describe how AAPI families nurture and shape identity (including gender identity and gender roles) among its younger family members to successfully traverse normative developmental tasks and cope with life crises.

Family Socialization of Identity and Gender Roles

AAPI families play a central role in the socialization of younger family members. During this family socialization process, risk and protective factors play a central role in guiding the development of ethnic and gender identity, autonomy and dependence, language acquisition, and attainment of education and occupational goals. Parents play an important role in the ethnic socialization process of their children. For example, Sikh parents socialize their children by providing messages about the importance of maintaining strong ties to the heritage culture while also encouraging their children to accommodate to the American environment. The adolescents' accommodation of the dominant culture, while resisting complete assimilation, is linked to adolescents' school success (Gibson, 1988).

Families also play an important role in the socialization of gender identity and gender roles. Immigrant AAPI families often experience a disruption in traditional gender roles after migration. Typically, men experience economic and social loss while women become either co-providers or the sole providers for their families (Espiritu, 2001); positive adaptation to such changes requires families to flexibly redefine gender roles. As a strategy for maintaining traditional patriarchal family structures, AAPI families often socialize their children toward traditional gender roles. This is reflected in Asian American girls reporting conflicts with parents about traditional gender roles (Tang & Dion, 1999), dating, and marriage (Chung, 2001). Moreover, Filipino and Asian Indian parents closely monitor their daughter's sexuality as a way to protect their daughters from the "corruption" of American society (Espiritu, 2001; Gupta, 1997). The girls themselves often resent the gender inequality in their families, as daughters recognize that they have less autonomy and mobility than even their younger male siblings (Espiritu, 2001). One way that Asian American daughters respond to gender oppression is to express preference for White mainstream culture, which is perceived to be more egalitarian in gender roles than in their own families (Pyke & Johnson, 2003).

Asian American and Pacific Islander Families and Language Acquisition

Nationally, 82% of Americans speak only English in their homes (U.S. Census Bureau, 2003). In contrast, 44% of Pacific Islanders and 79% of Asian Americans have knowledge of both English and a heritage language. Two-thirds of those who speak a Pacific Island language and half of those who speak an Asian language also speak English "very well" (Harris & Jones, 2005; Reeves & Bennett, 2004), and bilingual fluency is even higher for AAPI school-age children, at 95% (U.S. Department of Education, National Center for Education Statistics, 2005). Thus, many AAPI individuals benefit from the cognitive and social advantages of being bilingual or multilingual. These advantages include enhanced metalinguistic awareness, or knowledge of the properties of languages; divergent thinking and problem-solving abilities; intercultural awareness and interaction skills; and more employment opportunities (Cloud, Genesee, & Hamayan, 2000).

Loss of one's heritage language is an important issue for immigrant and minority families.

If parents and children do not share a common language in which both are fluent, family communication problems can arise and possibly threaten the quality of parent-child relationships (Fillmore, 1991). When children acquire English proficiency sooner than adults, they may play the role of "language brokers," translating and speaking for their parents when interacting with persons outside of the family circle. A role reversal may occur through this brokering and can be a significant source of stress (Tse & McQuillan, 1996). In the course of brokering, children may be exposed to medical, financial, and other personal information that is not usually shared with youngsters. Children may also feel pressure to make decisions about what kind of information is shared, how to alter the tone of what is said, or whether to even bring school documents to their parents' attention. However, brokering can have positive consequences (Weisskirch, 2005). Youths may take pride in being able to assist their parents, and brokering can improve bicultural and bilingual skills and support the development of a positive ethnic identity. Children who broker may also benefit from the early mastery of practical skills, such as negotiation and advocacy, record keeping, and completing job and loan applications. Overall, it appears that positive individual and family outcomes occur when AAPI families are able to promote strong bilingual skills in their children.

Asian American and Pacific Islander Families, Education, and Occupational Pathways

A commonly held belief among the American public is that Asian nationals and Asian Americans are uniquely driven and successful in academic pursuits. Indeed, as an undifferentiated group, Asian American adults ages 25 and older are almost twice as likely to have graduated from college (44.1%) than the overall U.S. adult population (24.4%) (Reeves & Bennett, 2004). Among school-age children, Asian Americans show either the strongest academic performance of all ethnic groups or are comparable to Caucasian children on outcomes such as grade point average; national assessments of reading, writing, and mathematics achievement; and success in obtaining prestigious science scholarships (Chao & Tseng, 2002; Chen & Stevenson, 1995; Kao & Thompson, 2003; U.S. Department of Education, 2005). Furthermore, Asian American children of immigrants have higher grade point averages and show better reading and math performance than native-born Asians of third-generation or higher status (Kao & Thompson, 2003). These achievements have been described as "remarkable" (Chen & Stevenson, 1995, p. 1215) and "exceptional" (Sue & Okazaki, 1990, p. 913) and are cited as one of the main factors supporting the stereotype of the Asian American model minority (Chao & Tseng, 2002).

Although there is support for remarkable academic achievements of some Asian Americans, not all AAPI subgroups show equal levels of academic success, nor do all subgroups start from a level playing field. For instance, South Asians are much more likely to attain a college degree as compared to Southeast Asians (Reeves & Bennett, 2004). Furthermore, the U.S. Census (Harris & Jones, 2005) shows Pacific Island adults to be underrepresented in the population of college graduates (13.8% of Pacific Island adults hold a college degree). National educational surveys (e.g., NELS:88, NAEP) include too few AAPI youth to report results by specific ethnicities; however, data from the state of Hawai'i suggests that Native Hawaiian children show lower levels of performance on school achievement tests than non-Hawaiians (Kana'iapuni, Malone, & Ishibashi, 2005), and Native Hawaiians enrolled in the University of Hawai'i system are less likely to remain in college and graduate in a timely manner than are their peers of Chinese, Japanese, and Filipino ancestry (University of Hawai'i, 1997).

Many Asian American children and parents exhibit values and behaviors that may promote academic competence. Compared to youths from other ethnic groups, Asian American high school students are more likely to enroll in a college preparatory track and take more credits of advanced math, science, and foreign languages (Chen & Stevenson, 1995; Kao & Thompson, 2003). These behaviors appear to be strategies for attaining longer-term goals; Asian American youths hold the highest aspirations for their eventual educational achievement (Kao & Tienda, 1998). Asian American parents are most likely to expect that their own children will complete a college or graduate degree program (Kao & Tienda, 1995; Mau, 1997; Peng & Wright, 1994). In comparison to native-born Whites, Asian American parents tend to use different educational socialization strategies (Chao & Tseng, 2002). Asian and immigrant parents are more likely to ensure that their child has a place to study, tutor younger children on academic skills, limit television viewing, and specifically discuss college enrollment and college entrance exams with their children (Chao & Tseng; Kao & Tienda, 1995; Mau, 1997). Compared to Caucasian parents, Asian American parents are less likely to help children with their homework, have contact with teachers, or participate directly in the school setting (Mau, 1997). It is interesting that these latter, "hands-on" strategies are associated with better academic performance for Caucasian children but not for Asian American children.

Overall, the generally positive educational outlook for Asian American youth seems best explained by two circumstances. First, Asian American youth from families who have long resided in the United States tend to come from advantaged backgrounds; they come from wealthier homes, are more likely to attend high-performing schools, have parents who are more highly educated, and are more likely to live in intact families than are children from any other ethnic group (Chen & Stevenson, 1995; Peng & Wright, 1994). It is not surprising, then, that these children show educational trajectories that are similar to those of middle- and upper-middle-class Whites. Second, children of immigrants share their parents' belief in education as path to self-betterment; this motivates first- and second-generation youth to work especially hard, even in the face of obstacles such as low English proficiency, family poverty, or substandard schooling. Most often, when family socioeconomic advantage, youth educational motivation, and study behavior variables are controlled, the Asian achievement advantage is reduced or eliminated (Chen & Stevenson, 1995; Kao & Thompson, 2003; Kao & Tienda, 1995, 1998; Peng & Wright, 1994); this suggests that these variables are of causal status. In the future, more attention should be paid to the educational progress of Pacific Islander and Southeast Asian children and youth. Because these groups are small in number, it is easy to overlook their needs and focus on the over-simplified characterization of monolithic Asian American academic success.

The empirical literature suggests that the family plays a significant role in helping AAPI youths and young adults choose certain occupational pathways; this is especially true among less acculturated families. Immigrant families have perceptions about which occupations will more effectively ensure economic viability of the family and strongly encourage pursuit of these occupational careers by younger family members (Castelino, 2005). Tang, Fouad, and Smith (1999) found that Asian American career choices are influenced primarily by acculturation, family influences, self-efficacy, and interest. Leong and Hardin (2002) found that less acculturated Asian Americans, with stronger collective and interdependent self-construals, were more influenced by family input, whereas personal interests and individual strengths more strongly influenced career decisions among more acculturated Asian Americans. Among immigrants with limited education, job skills, and English fluency, there are greater employment options for women (e.g., garment, micro-electronics, social service industries) than for men (e.g., production, distribution of goods). This produces a shift in status, power, and control between the sexes and increases the potential for family conflict (Clement & Myles, 1994; Espiritu, 1999; Kibria, 1993; Ui, 1991; Williams, 1989). Although AAPI women are still seen as holding primary responsibility for the care of home and children, there is evidence that men are assuming greater family responsibilities.

AAPI families influence occupational choices of younger family members; however, acculturation tempers the strength of that influence. Strong AAPI family influence over career choices could be a risk factor by limiting possible career choices to those careers that may not match the interests or talents of the family member. AAPI families may be protective by steering younger family members to careers that will enhance the financial success of the family. AAPI families influence decisions regarding marital, parenting, educational, and occupational choices of younger family members, and they also have a central role making family decisions regarding the lives of older family members.

Asian American and Pacific Islander Families and Elders

Traditional Asian and Pacific Island cultures endorse filial piety values and behavior. With acculturation, however, there may be an ambivalent endorsement of filial piety (Antonucci, Akiyama, & Landsford, 1998). AAPI elders serve as a family resource while they are healthy, but they may be a source of burden or family risk when their health fails. Providing care to a frail family member is a very stressful time in family life. Takamura, Nitz, and Haruki (1991) found that 20% of Hawai'i government employees provided help to an older frail family member, and AAPIs were overrepresented in the caregiver group as compared to Caucasians. Although AAPI caregivers felt overwhelmed and confined, they also regarded this responsibility as an opportunity to fulfill family obligations and demonstrate filial piety.

Conditions in the near social context (i.e., household and community) influence how long elders are able to function independently as their health declines. Ikels (1983) found that healthy Chinese elders in Hong Kong and Boston ran the household so that younger household members were free to engage in money-making activities. When their health started to fail, the Chinese elderly in Hong Kong could function by themselves or through neighborhood supports (i.e., ready access to shopping, medical treatments of choice, and speaking a common language) to a greater degree than Chinese American elders in Boston. Yu, Kim, Liu, and Wong (1993) found that more traditional desires among Chinese and Korean American elders (i.e., living with one's family) increased as the elder's health declined. Although Asian American families have become more accepting of the institutionalization of their elderly relatives, they are still more reluctant to do so than the general population (Watari & Gatz, 2004). This reluctance is overcome when behaviors such as violence or emotional outbursts, wandering, incontinence, or secondary illnesses overwhelm the family's ability to manage everyday functions (Morton, Stanford, Happersett, & Molgaard, 1992).

While most of our current notions about AAPI family caregiving come from a few studies on Chinese and Japanese American families, our conclusions may not generalize to other AAPI families. For instance, after years of caring for their grandchildren, South Asian elderly women found it difficult to ask for their family's help in dealing with chronic illnesses or financial assistance. A fear of isolation was expressed by the South Asian elderly women with limited English proficiency and financial resources as they became less mobile due to poor health (National Asian Women's Health Organization, 1996). A high incidence of independent living among this South Asian sample suggested that appropriate aging services must be established because their families may not be willing or able to provide these services.

More traditional AAPI families may consider it their responsibility to care for their elderly relatives and may be less likely to seek professional caregiver respite and supportive services. Elder abuse may occur when immigrant families' resources are stretched beyond their capacity to care for frail and vulnerable family elders. In a rare study of elder abuse, Moon and Williams (1993) found that when presented with hypothetical situations, Korean American elders perceived less abuse and defined it more narrowly than either African or Caucasian American samples. Moon and Williams suggested that Korean American elders were not only less likely to seek help but were also reluctant to reveal "family shame" to others and feared creating family conflict as a consequence of divulging an abusive family situation to outsiders.

AAPI families struggle with advanced directives and life support decisions when a family member is dying. Lifesaving techniques may be considered violent or inhumane interventions that disrupt the natural dying process. Life support decisions may be influenced by cultural beliefs regarding WHO (i.e., God, patient, patient's family, the doctor), WHEN, and HOW (active or passive) interventions are to be used to prolong or end life (Klessig, 1992). Culture also prescribes the rules for disclosure (truth telling) of terminal health diagnosis and prognosis and the role of the family in making medical decisions. The Asian family imperative of filial obligation is to protect the patient (Orona,

Koenig, & Davis, 1994), maintain hope, and ensure a "good death" (i.e., dying peacefully in old age surrounded by family) because "bad deaths" create shame for the entire family (Muller & Desmond, 1992). These decisions are complicated by cultural, linguistic, and communication barriers between AAPI families and medical personnel.

Der-McLeod (1995) found that culturally competent requests for advanced directives and life support decisions can be made with frail Chinese elders and their families within an established trusting relationship prior to development of a health crisis. These investigators found that family members were often relieved that their elderly relative made a decision, because they no longer had that responsibility. Nishimura and Yeo (1992) found that more highly acculturated Japanese Americans expressed a desire to have control over their own health care decisions. In contrast, McLaughlin and Braun's (1998) study, AAPI elders believed in the collective wisdom of their family and health professionals to make the correct decision.

ASIAN AND PACIFIC ISLANDER FAMILY RESEARCH OPPORTUNITIES AND POLICY CHALLENGES

There are many research opportunities to explore the diversity of AAPI family processes and outcomes over the life cycle. First, advancement in the study of AAPI families has been misdirected and curtailed by the bundling of Asians and Pacific Islanders into a single ethnic category. As this chapter demonstrates, findings that hold for one particular AAPI ethnic group do not necessarily apply to other ethnic groups. Research on multiethnic AAPI families (i.e., families of mixed racial or ethnic heritages) is especially scant.

Second, we must examine how AAPI families cope with normative and nonnormative lifespan developmental hurdles that expend the resources of even the most resilient families. In terms of family life-cycle issues, little is known about how parenting practices in AAPI families may vary as a function of national origin, immigration status, and acculturation level, and whether specific parenting strategies have

different functional effects for different AAPI subgroups. We note an almost complete absence of research on normative sibling and marital relationships in AAPI families. At the later end of the life cycle, we need more information on the ways in which AAPI elders make contributions to their families and communities. In addition, we need to better understand the factors that influence AAPI family decision making concerning the care of frail elderly family members. We need to know how professional services can become culturally responsive and can successfully support AAPI families in their efforts to care for dependent family members.

More attention needs to be paid to those AAPI families that do not fit the model minority stereotype—families characterized by low academic achievement, marital distress, or youth delinquent involvement. We also need to know more about linkages between different contexts of development in families. For example, how do school-family contexts or work-family contexts interact to influence the development of AAPI families? Finally, room remains for additional studies of the AAPI acculturation process. We need to better understand how acculturation to the American cultural context, through socialization and enculturation, produces adaptive strategies that enable immigrant AAPI families to succeed. In addition, there is too little work on how these same processes operate across second-, third-, and fourth-generation AAPI families and families of mixed heritage.

Third, more progress can be made by psychologists in the development of culturally competent and responsive family measurement and research methodologies for AAPI families (e.g., Whitborne, Bringle, Yee, Chiriboga, & Whitfield, 2006). There is an absence of family assessment or measurement tools to conduct AAPI family research, with a few notable exceptions (e.g., Inman, Ladany, Constantine, & Morano, 2001; Lee, Choe, Kim, & Ngo, 2000). Cultural and shared beliefs of AAPI populations have not been examined. Cross-sectional research designs allow a narrow glimpse of family processes, but much can be gained by examining family processes over time. "Gold standard" family methodologies (i.e., videotaping family interactions) may be problematic because cultural factors (i.e., saving face and shame in public) may confound and call into question the validity of these data for AAPI families. Qualitative methods may be undertaken to understand how families construct meaning in their lives and make causal attributions and decisions in their lives. The basic AAPI family development research has lagged far behind, and we cannot move forward until these family research infrastructure steps have been taken (Yee et al., 1998).

Fourth, we must examine federal research policies that have created the lack of an AAPI family research infrastructure in the United States. The model minority myth and an over-representation of Asian American investigators conducting basic research in the biomedical and physical sciences (which has led to an exclusion of Asian American trainees in the National Science Foundation portfolio) have reinforced the mistaken notion that there is a sufficient AAPI family research infrastructure. Targeted AAPI research center grants would promote the formation of a critical mass of investigators working on AAPI family research tools and expand AAPI research resources such as the training of students and postdoctoral researchers from underrepresented AAPI groups.

We cannot be discouraged by the size of the gaps in AAPI family theory, research, and measurement, because this situation cannot and will not be remedied overnight. However, psychology can make major contributions to answering this question: How do AAPI families provide protection and diminish risk for their family members as they traverse developmental milestones and cope with life challenges over the life course?

REFERENCES

Aguirre, B. E., Saenz, R., & Hwang, S. (1995). Remarriage and intermarriage of Asians in the United States of America. *Journal of Comparative Family Studies, 26,* 207–215.

American Association of Retired Persons (AARP). (2001). *In the middle: A report on multicultural boomers coping with family and aging issues.* Retrieved August 23, 2003, fromhttp://www.aarp.org/research/housing-mobility/caregiving/aresearch-import-789-D17446.html

Antonucci, T. C., Akiyama, H., & Landsford, J. E. (1998). The negative effects of close social relations among older adults. *Family Relations, 47,* 379–384.

Barnes, J. S., & Bennett, C. E. (2002). *The Asian population: 2000* (Census 2000 Brief No. C2KBR-01–16).Washington, DC: U.S. Census Bureau.

Barringer, H. R., Gardner, R. W., & Levin, M. J. (1993). *Asians and Pacific Islanders in the United States.* New York: Russell Sage.

Braun, K., Yee, B. W. K., Brown, C. V., & Mokuau, N. (2004). Native Hawaiian and Pacific Islander Elders. In K. E. Whitfield (Ed.), *Closing the gap: Improving the health of minority elders in the new millennium* (pp. 55–67). Washington, DC: Gerontological Society of America.

Castelino, P. (2005). Factors influencing career choices of South Asian Americans: A path analysis. *Dissertation Abstracts International, 65*(8A), 2906.

Chao, R., & Tseng, V. (2002). Parenting of Asians. In M. H. Bornstein (Ed.), *Handbook of parenting: Vol. 4. Social conditions and applied parenting* (2nd ed., pp. 59–93). Mahwah, NJ: Lawrence Erlbaum.

Chen, C., & Stevenson, H. W. (1995). Motivation and mathematics achievement: A comparative study of Asian-American, Caucasian-American and East Asian high school students. *Child Development, 66,* 1215–1234.

Chung, R. H. G. (2001). Gender, ethnicity, and acculturation in intergenerational conflict of Asian American college students. *Cultural Diversity & Ethnic Minority Psychology, 7,* 376–386.

Clement, W., & Myles, J. (1994). *Relations of ruling: Class and gender in postindustrial societies.* Montreal, Canada: McGill-Queen's University Press.

Cloud, N., Genesee, F., & Hamayan, E. (2000). *Dual language instruction: A handbook for enriched education.* Boston: Heinle & Heinle.

Cicirelli, V. G. (1994). Sibling relationships in cross-cultural perspective. *Journal of Marriage and the Family, 56,* 7–20.

Crane, D. R., Ngai, S. W., Larson, J. H., & Hafen, M. (2005). The influence of family functioning and parent-adolescent acculturation on North American Chinese adolescent outcomes. *Family Relations: Interdisciplinary Journal of Applied Family Studies, 54,* 400–410.

DeBaryshe, B. D., Yuen, S., & Stern, I. R. (2001). Psychosocial adjustment in Asian Pacific Islander youth: The role of coping strategies, parenting practices, and community social support. *Journal of Adolescent & Family Health, 2,* 63–71.

Der-McLeod, D. (1995). *Alternative ways of talking with elderly Chinese concerning end-of-life choices.* Paper presented at the Gerontological Society of America meeting, Los Angeles, CA.

Dornbusch, S. M., Ritter, P. L., Leiderman, P., Roberts, D., & Fraleigh, M. (1987). The relationship of parenting style to adolescent school performance. *Child Development, 58,* 1244–1257.

Enriquez, V. G. (1993). Developing a Filipino psychology. In U. Kim & J. W. Berry (Eds.), *Indigenous psychologies: Research and experience in cultural context* (pp. 152–220). Newbury Park, CA: Sage.

Espiritu, Y. L. (1999). Gender and labor in Asian immigrant families. *American Behavioral Scientist, 42,* 628–647.

Espiritu, Y. L. (2001). "We don't sleep around like White girls do": Family, culture and gender in Filipino American lives. *Signs, 26,* 415–440.

Farver, J. A. M., Narang, S. K., & Bhadha, B. R. (2002). East meets West: Ethnic identity, acculturation, and conflict in Asian Indian families. *Journal of Family Psychology, 16,* 338–350.

Fillmore, L. W. (1991). When learning a second language means losing the first. *Early Childhood Research Quarterly, 6,* 323–346.

Fugita, S., Ito, K. L., Abe, J., & Takeuchi, D. T. (1991). Japanese Americans. In N. Mokuau (Ed.), *Handbook of social services for Asian and Pacific Islanders* (pp. 61–77). New York: Greenwood Press.

Fujino, D. (2000). Structural and individual influences affecting racialized dating relationships. In J. L. Chin (Ed.), *Relationships among Asian American women* (pp. 181–209). Washington, DC: American Psychological Association.

Furoto, S. M. (1991). Family violence among Pacific Islanders. In N. Mokuau (Ed.), *Handbook of social services for Asian and Pacific Islanders* (pp. 203 - 216). New York: Greenwood.

Gibson, M. A. (1988). *Accommodation without assimilation: Sikh immigrants in an American High School.* New York: Cornell University Press.

Glick, J. E., & Hook, J. V. (2002). Parents' coresidence with adult children: Can immigration explain racial and ethnic variation? *Journal of Marriage and Family, 64*(1), 240–253.

Gottman, J. M. (1998). Psychology and the study of marital processes. *Annual Review of Psychology, 49,* 169–197.

Grieco, E. M. (2001). *The native Hawaiian and other Pacific Islander population: 2000.* Washington, DC: U.S. Census Bureau.

Gupta, M. D. (1997). "What is Indian about you?" A gendered, transnational approach to ethnicity. *Gender and Society, 11,* 572–596.

Harris, P. M., & Jones, N. A. (2005). *We the people: Pacific Islanders in the United States* (Census 2000 Special Report No. CENSR-26). Washington, DC: U.S. Census Bureau.

Himes, C. L., Hogan, D. P., & Eggebeen, D. J. (1996). Living arrangements of minority elders. *Journal of Gerontology: Social Sciences* (Vol. 51B, pp. S42–S48).

Hofstede, G. (1980). *Culture's consequences: International differences in work-related values.* Newbury Park, CA: Sage.

Howard, A. (1974). *Ain't no big thing: Coping strategies in a Hawaiian-American community.* Honolulu: University of Hawaii Press.

Ikels, C. (1983). *Aging and adaptation: Chinese in Hong Kong and the United States.* Hamden, CT: Archon Books.

Inman, A. G., Altman, A., & Kaduvettoor, A. (2004, April). *South Asian interracial marriages and marital satisfaction.* Poster session presented at the annual meeting of the American Counseling Association, Kansas City, MO.

Inman, A. G., Ladany, N., Constantine, M. G., & Morano, C. K. (2001). Development and preliminary validation of the cultural values conflict scale for South Asian women. *Journal of Counseling Psychology, 48,* 17–27.

Juang, L. P., Lerner, J. V., McKinney, J. P., & von Eye, A. (1999). The goodness of fit in autonomy timetable expectations between Asian-American late adolescents and their parents. *International Journal of Behavioral Development, 23,* 1023–1048.

Kana'iapuni, S. M., Malone, N, J., & Ishibashi, K. (2005). *Ka huaka'i imua:* Findings from the 2005 Native Hawaiian educational assessment. Honolulu HI: Kamehameha Schools–PASE.

Kao, G., & Thompson, J. S. (2003). Racial and ethnic stratification in educational achievement and attainment. *American Review of Sociology, 29,* 417–442.

Kao, G., & Tienda, M. (1995). Optimism and achievement: The educational performance of immigrant youth. *Social Science Quarterly, 76,* 1–19.

Kao, G., & Tienda, M. (1998). Educational aspirations of minority youth. *American Journal of Education, 106,* 349–384.

Kibria, N. (1993). *Family tightrope: The changing lives of Vietnamese Americans.* Princeton, NJ: Princeton University Press.

Kitayama, S., & Markus, H. R. (1994). The cultural shaping of emotion: A conceptual framework. In S. Kitayama & H. R. Markus (Eds.), *Emotion and culture: Empirical studies of mutual influence* (pp. 339–351). Washington, DC: American Psychological Association.

Klessig, J. (1992). The effect of values and culture on life-support decisions. *Western Journal of Medicine, 157,* 316–322.

Korbin, J. E. (1990). *Hana'ino:* Child maltreatment in a Hawaiian-American community. *Pacific Studies, 13*(3), 7–22.

Kwak, K. (2003). Adolescents and their parents: A review of intergenerational family relations of immigrant and non-immigrant families, *Human Development 46* (2–3): 15–136.

Lamborn, S. D., Mounts, N. S., Steinberg, L., & Dornbusch, S. M. (1991). Patterns of competence and adjustment among adolescents from authoritative, authoritarian, indulgent, and neglectful families. *Child Development, 62,* 1049–1065.

Lau, S., Lew, W. J., Hau, K., Cheung, P. C., & Berndt, T. J. (1990). Relations among perceived parental control, warmth, indulgence, and family harmony of Chinese in Mainland China. *Developmental Psychology, 26,* 674–677.

Lebra, T. S. (1976). *Japanese patterns of behavior.* Honolulu: University of Hawaii Press.

Lee, R. M., Choe, J., Kim, G., & Ngo, V. (2000). Construction of the Asian American family conflicts scale. *Journal of Counseling Psychology, 47*(2), 211–222.

Leong, F., & Hardin, E. (2002). Career psychology of Asian Americans: Cultural validity and cultural specificity. In G. Nagayama & S. Okazaki (Eds.), *Asian American psychology: The science of lives in context* (pp. 131–152). Washington, DC: American Psychological Association.

Luthar, S. S., & Zelazo, L. B. (2003). Research on resilience: An integrative review. In S. S. Luthar (Ed.), *Resilience and vulnerability: Adaptation in the context of childhood adversities* (pp. 510–549). New York: Cambridge University Press.

Maccoby, E., & Martin, J. (1983). Socialization in the context of the family: Parent-child interaction. In E. M. Hetherington (Ed.), *Handbook of child psychology: Socialization, personality, and social development* (Vol. 4, pp. 1–101). New York: Wiley.

Malley-Morison, K., & Hines, D.A. (2004) *Family violence in cultural perspective: Defining understanding and combating abuse.* Thousand Oaks, CA: Sage.

Markus, H. R., & Kitayama, S. (1991). Culture and the self: Implications for cognition, emotion, and motivation. *Psychological Review, 98*(2), 224–253.

Mason, C. A., Cauce, A. M., Gonzales, N., Hiraga, Y., & Grove, K. (1994). An ecological model of externalizing behaviors in African-American adolescents: No family is an island. *Journal of Research on Adolescence, 4*(4), 639–655.

Mau, W. (1997). Parental influences on the high school students' academic achievement: A comparison of Asian immigrants, Asian-Americans, and white Americans. *Psychology in the Schools, 34,* 267–277.

McCubbin, L., & McCubbin, H. (2005). Culture and ethnic identity in family resilience: Dynamic processes in trauma and transformation of indigenous people. In M. Unger (Ed.), *Pathways to resilience* (pp. 27–44). Thousand Oaks, CA: Sage.

McCubbin, H. I., McCubbin, M. A., Thompson, A. I., & Thompson, E. A. (1998). Resilience in ethnic families: A conceptual model for predicting family adjustment and adaptation. In H. I. McCubbin, E. A. Thompson, A. I. Thompson, & J. E. Fromer (Eds.), *Resiliency in Native American and immigrant families* (pp. 3–48). Thousand Oaks, CA: Sage.

McLaughlin, L. A., & Braun, K. L. (1998). Asian and Pacific Islander cultural values: Consideration for health care decision making. *Health Care and Social Work, 23,* 116–126.

Mistry, R. S., Vandewater, E. A., Huston, A. C., & McLoyd, V. C. (2002). Economic well-being and children's social adjustment: The role of family process in an ethnically diverse low-income sample. *Child Development, 73,* 935–951.

Moon, A., & Williams, O. (1993), Perceptions of elder abuse and help-seeking patterns among

African-American, Caucasian American, and Korean-American elderly women. *The Gerontologist, 33,* 386–395.

Morton, D. J., Stanford, E. P., Happersett, C. J., & Molgaard, C. A. (1992). Acculturation and functional impairment among older Chinese and Vietnamese in San Diego County, California. *Journal of Cross-cultural Gerontology, 7,* 151–176.

Muller, J. H., & Desmond, B. (1992). Ethical dilemmas in a cross-cultural context: A Chinese example. *Western Journal of Medicine, 157,* 323–327.

National Asian Women's Health Organization. (1996). *A health needs assessment of South Asian women in 3 California counties: Alameda, Santa Clara, Sutter.* San Francisco: Author. Retrieved February 5, 2006, from http://www.nawho.org/pubs/NAWHOEmerg.pdf

Nguyen, N. A., & Williams, H. L. (1989). Transition from East to West: Vietnamese adolescents and their parents. *Journal of the American Academy of Child Adolescent Psychiatry, 28,* 505–515.

Nishimura, M., & Yeo, G. (1992). *Ethnicity, medical decisions, and the care of Japanese American elders.* Poster presented at the American Geriatric Society meeting in Washington, DC.

Ong, P. M., & Leung, L.-S. (2003). Diversified growth. In E. Lai & D. Arguelles (Eds.), *The new face of Asian Pacific America: Numbers, diversity and change in the 21st century* (pp. 7–16). San Francisco: AsianWeek Books.

Orona, C. J., Koenig, B. A., & Davis, A. J. (1994). Cultural aspects of nondisclosure. *Cambridge Quarterly of Healthcare Ethics, 3,* 338–346.

Parker, J. S., & Benson, M. J. (2004). Parent-adolescent relations and adolescent functioning: Self-esteem, substance abuse, and delinquency. *Adolescence, 39,* 519–530.

Peng, S. S., & Wright, D. (1994). Explanation of academic achievement of Asian American students. *Journal of Educational Research, 87,* 346–352.

Phinney, J. S., Ong, A., & Madden, T. (2000). Cultural values and intergenerational value discrepancies in immigrant and non-immigrant families. *Child Development, 71,* 528–539.

Pyke, K. (2005). "Generational deserters" and "black sheep": Acculturative differences among siblings in Asian immigrant families. *Journal of Family Issues, 26,* 491–517.

Pyke, K., & Johnson, D. L. (2003). Asian American women and racialized femininities: "Doing" gender across cultural worlds. *Gender and Society, 17,* 33–53.

Reeves, T. J., & Bennett, C. E. (2004). *We the people: Asians in the United States* (Census 2000 Special Report No. CENSR–17). Washington, DC: U.S. Census Bureau.

Rohner, R. P., & Pettengill, S. M. (1985). Perceived parental acceptance-rejection and parental control among Korean adolescents. *Child Development, 56,* 524–528.

Seymour, S. (1993). Sociocultural contexts: Examining sibling roles in South Asia. In C. W. Nuckolls (Ed.), *Siblings in South Asia: Brothers and sisters in cultural context* (pp. 45–69). New York: Guilford Press.

Shook, E. V. (1985). *Ho'oponopono: Contemporary uses of a Hawaiian problem-solving process.* Honolulu: University of Hawaii Press.

Simmons, T., & Dye, J. L. (2003). *Grandparents living with grandchildren: 2000.* Washington, DC: U.S. Census Bureau.

Steinberg L., Mounts, N. S., Lamborn, S. D., & Dornbusch, S. M. (1991). Authoritative parenting and adolescent adjustment across varied ecological niches. *Journal of Research on Adolescence, 1,* 19–36.

Stevenson, H. W., & Stigler, J. W. (1992). *The learning gap: Why our schools are failing and what we can learn from Japanese and Chinese education.* New York: Simon & Schuster.

Sue, S., & Okazaki, S. (1990). Asian-American educational achievements: A phenomenon in search of an explanation. *American Psychologist, 45,* 913–920.

Takamura, J. C., Nitz, K., & Haruki, G. (1991, March 17). *Ethnicity and caregiving: Developing research-based support programs for multigenerational caregivers from diverse ethnocultural groups.* Paper presented at the 37th annual meeting of the American Society on Aging, New Orleans, LA.

Tang, M., Fouad, N. A., & Smith, P. L. (1999). Asian American's career choices: A path model to examine factors influencing their career choices. *Journal of Vocational Behavior, 54,* 142–157.

Tang, T. N., & Dion, K. L. (1999). Gender and acculturation in relation to traditionalism: Perceptions of self and parents among Chinese students. *Sex Roles, 41,* 17–29.

Tse, L., & McQuillan, J. (1996). *Culture, language, and literacy: The effects of child brokering in language minority education.* (ERIC Document Reproduction Service No. ED394357)

Tseng, V. (2004). Family interdependence and academic adjustment in college: Youth from immigrant and U.S.-born families. *Child Development, 75,* 966–983.

Tseng, W.-S., & Hsu, J. (1991). *Culture and family: Problems and therapy.* New York: Haworth Press.

Uba, L. (1994). *Asian Americans: Personality patterns, identity, and mental health.* New York: Guilford Press.

Ui, S. (1991). "Unlikely heroes": The evolution of female leadership in a Cambodian ethnic enclave. In M. Burawoy (Ed.), *Ethnography unbound* (pp. 161–177). Berkeley: University of California Press.

University of Hawai'i, Institutional Research Office. (1997). *Graduation and persistence rates. University of Hawai'i at Mânoa fall 1987–fall 1995 cohorts.* Honolulu: University of Hawai'i.

U.S. Census Bureau. (2003a). *Asian Pacific American Heritage Month: May 2003.* Retrieved June 7, 2005, from http://www.census.gov/Press-Release/www/2003/cb03-ff05. html

U.S. Census Bureau. (2003b). *Language use and English-speaking ability: 2000* (Census 2000 Brief No. C2KBR-29). Washington DC: Author.

U.S. Department of Education, National Center for Education Statistics. (2005). *The condition of education, 2005* (NCES Publication No. 2005–094). Washington, DC: Author.

Watari, K. F., & Gatz, M. (2004). Pathways to care for Alzheimer's disease among Korean Americans. *Cultural Diversity & Ethnic Minority Psychology, 10,* 23–38.

Wei, M., Russel, D. W., Mallinckrodt, B., & Zakalik R. A. (2004). Cultural equivalence of adult attachment across four ethnic groups: Factor structure, structured means, and associations with negative mood. *Journal of Counseling Psychology, 51,* 408–417.

Weisskirch, R. S. (2005). The relationship of language brokering to ethnic identity for Latino early adolescents. *Hispanic Journal of Behavioral Sciences, 27,* 286–299.

Whitborne, S. K., Bringle, J. R., Yee, B. W. K., Chiriboga, D. A., & Whitfield, K. (2006). Ethical research dilemmas with minority elders. In J. E. Trimble & C. B. Fisher (Eds.), *Handbook of ethical research with ethnocultural populations and communities* (pp. 217–241). Thousand Oaks, CA: Sage.

Williams, M. (1989). Ladies on the line: Punjabi cannery workers in central California. In Asian Women United of California (Ed.), *Making waves: An anthology of writings by and about Asian American women* (pp. 148–159). Boston: Beacon Press.

Yee, B. W. K., Huang, L. N., & Lew, A. (1998). Families: Life-span socialization in a cultural context. In L. C. Lee & N. W. S. Zane (Eds.), *Handbook of Asian American psychology* (pp. 73–124). Thousand Oaks, CA: Sage.

Yu, E. S., Kim, K., Liu, W. T., & Wong, S. C. (1993). Functional abilities of Chinese and Korean elder in congregate housing. In D. Barressi & D. Stull (Eds.), *Ethnic elderly and long term care* (pp. 87–100). New York: Springer.

Zaidi, A.U., & Shuraydi, M. (2002). Perceptions of arranged marriages by young Pakistani Muslim women living in a Western Society. *Journal of Comparative Family Studies, 33,* 495–514.

6

UNDERSTANDING ASIAN AMERICAN YOUTH DEVELOPMENT: A SOCIAL ECOLOGICAL PERSPECTIVE

LY NGUYEN

LARKE NAHME HUANG

Asian American youth are the fastest-growing segment of the population in the United States. Over one-third of the Asian American population in the United States is younger than 19 years of age, with 7.1% of its population younger than 5 years; 6.9%, 5 to 9 years; 7.2%, 10 to 14 years; and 7.7%, 15 to 19 years (Reeves & Bennett, 2003). The projected rate of growth of the Asian American youth population exceeds that of any other group. Between 1995 and 2015, Asian American youth are expected to increase 74%, compared to 19% for African American, 17% for American Indian, and 59% for Hispanic juveniles. In contrast, the number of White, non-Hispanic juveniles is expected to decrease by 3% (Office of Juvenile Justice and Delinquency Prevention, 1999).

A closer look at the demographic characteristics of this population shows a tremendous diversity within the population. For example, Asian Americans represent some 28 ethnic groups, including persons of Chinese, Japanese, Filipino, Asian Indian, Korean, and Vietnamese descent. There is diversity in terms of generational and acculturation status. The term *Asian American* encompasses the Hmong, who are more recent immigrants, as well as the Japanese, many of whom are now into their fifth generation and beyond. Asian American groups have entered the United States with varying status. Some, such as the Vietnamese, entered as political refugees; others entered as immigrants and still others as "sojourners" who planned to return to their countries of origin. This diversity is further reflected in significant cultural, linguistic, and socioeconomic differences. Although there are some shared values across different Asian groups, there are vast differences in their traditions, cultural practices, and languages. This also extends to parenting and child-rearing practices, which represent different belief systems and family role relationships and have important implications for offspring being raised in the United States and within American culture. The rapid growth and rich diversity in the Asian American youth population underscores the demographic imperative to better understand Asian American youth. The rapidly growing and evolving population challenges our usual notions of youth development and reveals a need to identify relevant frameworks for culturally diverse youth. The research and theory regarding this population of youth has not grown commensurate with the growth in this population. Clearly, there is a need to accelerate the research on this population and improve our understanding of the developmental process for Asian American children in the United States.

The purpose of this chapter is to examine the current research on Asian American child development using an organizational framework that best captures the experience of a minority group in America. Whereas most theories of child and youth development focus on the individual person, understanding the developmental process for a child of color in the United States needs to be embedded in critical contextual issues. The integrative model of child development proposed by Garcia Coll and colleagues (1996) is a social ecological perspective that provides face validity for understanding Asian American child development. Garcia Coll's model represents a significant advancement in child development theory, and as such, it is used here to frame the discussion of existing research on Asian American children.

SOCIAL ECOLOGICAL FRAMEWORKS FOR UNDERSTANDING CHILD DEVELOPMENT

Until recently, developmental theories have not fully considered the role of culture, context, and socioenvironmental processes on the developing child. Child development has been viewed predominantly as a universal process, advancing through epigenetic stages with stage-determined developmental tasks. Historically, this approach is represented by theories focusing on predetermined organismic bases of development, such as attachment theory (Bowlby, 1969), psychoanalytic theory (Freud, 1954), and neo-analytic theory (Erikson, 1968). Few theories emphasized the interaction between organismic and environmental sources of development.

Current work uses more dynamic, systems models that consider contextual influences on development (e.g., Bronfenbrenner, 1979; Garcia Coll et al., 1996; Harrison, Wilson, Pine, Chan, & Buriel, 1990; Lerner & Castellino, 1998; Ogbu, 1981). These frameworks are relevant to the development of ethnically and racially diverse youth in that they emphasize sociocultural factors and their impact on youth development. For studying Asian American youth, this would mean a closer examination of factors such as socioeconomic, minority, immigration, and acculturation status, as well as cultural and linguistic influences.

Previous developmental theory had minimal focus on racial and ethnic minority children and the specific sociocultural factors contributing to their development (e.g., physiological status, cognition, personality, and temperament). Understanding healthy development requires examining the effects of maternal employment, single parenting, child temperament, school structure, and neighborhood resources, in addition to individual-level factors. This chapter focuses on Garcia Coll's model because it offers the most comprehensive view, to date, of child development from a social ecological perspective.

Garcia Coll's model identifies eight major interconnected constructs that influence the development of children of color (see Figure 6.1). The model assumes that development in children of color must be understood in the children's social ecological context. This conceptual framework posits that aspects unique to children of color, such as racism and segregation, are an integral aspect of child development for youth of color and must be addressed in understanding developmental pathways and outcomes. The model also examines the importance of culture and expounds on the role of family and extended kinship networks. Each of the model's components has implications for how researchers and practitioners view youth of color. Additionally, attention to children's ecological contexts has the potential to advance our understanding of developmental processes and outcomes in all children.

Garcia Coll's model focuses on individual and self-regulatory aspects of child development. However, of primary importance, and its significant contribution, is the integration of the macro or distal constructs and their influence on development. This includes, for example, social stratification, or "the attributes of individuals that societies use to stratify or place individuals

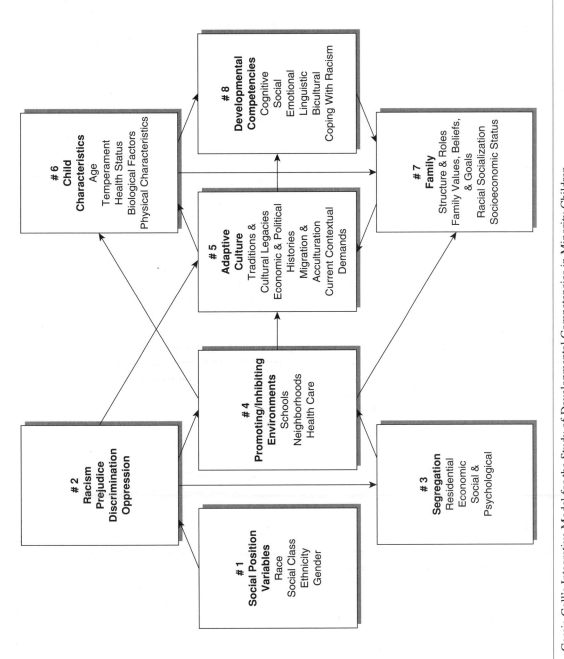

Figure 6.1   Garcia Coll's Integrative Model for the Study of Developmental Competencies in Minority Children.

Source: Garcia Coll, et al. (1996). Reprinted with permission from the Society for Research in Child Development.

in the social hierarchy" (Garcia Coll et al., 1996, p. 1895). These factors include, but are not limited to, race, social class, ethnicity, and gender. These social position factors represent social "addresses" that influence or create alternative developmental pathways in children and often lead to inflexible social stratification. Social position itself is not viewed as directly affecting developmental outcomes but as a mediating variable in that social strata are differentially associated with the racism, prejudice, discrimination, and oppression that are so prevalent in society. These, in turn, create segregated environments in which youth of color live, including Asian American children. Segregation is described as a residential, economic, social, and psychological phenomenon. The results of the interaction of social position, racism, and segregation create the unique experiences of children of color.

Across cultures, children are exposed to similar social settings, including schools, neighborhoods, and child-serving and -supporting systems such as health care, child care, or child welfare. For racially and ethnically diverse children, however, racism, prejudice, discrimination, oppression, and segregation directly affect children's experiences in these environments. Because it is in these settings that social stratification variables and processes become operationalized in the lives of minority families and children (Bronfenbrenner & Crouter, 1983), it is necessary to evaluate how these environments can promote and/or inhibit their development. Promoting and inhibiting environments then directly influence the adaptive cultures that are created in response to children's and families' experiences. An adaptive culture involves "a social system defined by sets of goals, values, and attitudes that differ from the dominant culture" and evolves from historical forces and present-day demands (Garcia Coll et al., 1996, p. 1896).

The model's micro, or proximal, constructs deal with child and family components. Child characteristics include the biological, constitutional, and psychological attributes that are affected by inhibiting and promoting environments as well as the adaptive culture. Children, in turn, are viewed as influencing their family processes and thus contributing to their own socialization. Likewise, family characteristics are influenced by promoting and inhibiting environments and adaptive culture, but they are also affected by child characteristics. Family characteristics include the family's structure, roles, values, beliefs, goals, socioeconomic status, and racial socialization of its children. In addition to the more commonly studied outcomes, such as cognitive and social skills, more culture-specific skills—for example, emotional, linguistic, and bicultural competencies and coping with racism—also are included as outcomes in the integrative conceptual model. Children's developmental competencies emerge as a direct function of the interplay of the factors described previously.

Garcia Coll's model has been discussed in the context of African American, Latino American, and American Indian child development (Garcia Coll et al., 1996). The model has been applied also to the provision of early child care for families of color (Johnson, Cauce, Jaeger, Suzanne, & Ward, 2003). Here, we offer Garcia Coll's integrative conceptual model as a way to present and better understand the current research on Asian American child development.

GARCIA COLL'S INTEGRATIVE CONCEPTUAL MODEL AS A FRAMEWORK FOR ASIAN AMERICAN CHILD DEVELOPMENT

In order to illustrate the concepts in Garcia Coll's model as they apply to Asian Americans, we often make reference to a particular Asian American subgroup. As discussed earlier, however, Asian Americans are a richly diverse population in terms of cultural, socioeconomic, immigration, acculturation, and linguistic backgrounds. It is not our intention to oversimplify the experiences of this diverse group or generalize to all Asian Americans the experiences of any one group in any discussion of the model. Due to limited space, however, it is not possible to describe the heterogeneity within the Asian American population for each component of the model. Our goal is to illustrate, using specific examples from the Asian American population, how the different components could be applied in order to better understand Asian American child development from a social ecological perspective.

Not A NEGATIVE IMPACT?

As a further cautionary note, it is also not possible in this limited space to describe in detail all of the current research on Asian American child development as it pertains to this complex model. We are able to present only research summaries in the major domains of interest. Although we could have written a more detailed review of established domains in child developmental research, more extensive reviews have been written elsewhere (Gibbs & Huang, 2003; Johnson-Powell, Yamamoto, Wyatt, & Arroyo, 1997; S. Y. Kim & Wong, 2002; Okagaki & Bojczyk, 2002). Moreover, we want to go beyond traditional concepts to focus more on the understudied socioecological concepts so as to broaden the discussion of child developmental processes and outcomes and make it more relevant to Asian American youth.

Social Stratification

A basic assumption of Garcia Coll's model is that child development is significantly affected by social stratification and the associated constructs of social position, racism, prejudice, discrimination, oppression, and segregation. U.S. history is replete with incidents of social disadvantage for Asian Americans, due to racism, prejudice, discrimination, and oppression. Asian Americans have been subject to discriminatory immigration and naturalization policies; discriminatory federal, state, and local laws; and discriminatory governmental treatment. Asian American communities have been the target of significant prejudice and outright violence from the larger public (U.S. Commission on Civil Rights, 1992).

Discrimination and prejudice have also contributed to residential, economic, and social and psychological segregation among Asian Americans. It is important to consider residential segregation, because where a family lives often determines whether the environment will promote or inhibit a child's development, mainly through access to resources or through exposure to risk or protective factors. However, there is little research on residential segregation among Asian Americans (Acevedo-Garcia, Lochner, Osypuk, & Subramanian, 2003), and some researchers have questioned whether residential segregation and housing discrimination

in the Asian American community have the same negative impact that they do in the African American community (Gee, 2002). Of course, although residential segregation may be due to personal preferences, the historical role of racism and discrimination in establishing such enclaves to begin with cannot be ignored.

Economic segregation involves persistent employment discrimination in salary and hiring practices. As with residential segregation, these practices are likely to lower the economic status of parents and result in diminished access to developmental opportunities for their children (Williams & Jackson, 2005). One example of economic segregation and its impact on child development can be found in the area of child care. Unable to speak English and lacking an American education, many Asian American immigrants must work in low-paying industries such as the garment, restaurant, domestic work, and day labor trades. Some studies show that many are compelled to work 70 to 100 hours a week, without receiving minimum wage or overtime pay (Asian American Legal Defense Fund, n.d.). In this context, access to quality child care is likely to be limited. Because child care in the United States is not affordable and parents work long hours, some families have even been known to send their infants to family in Asia until they reach school age. Even where child care is available, perceived or institutional racism also may affect parents' choices and limit their options (Coalition for Asian American Children and Families, 2001).

Social and psychological segregation are viewed as the marginalization and social isolation of Asian Americans. This kind of segregation occurs when families of color are denied access to social and emotional resources based on social position, prejudice, racism, and discrimination. For instance, the devaluation of Asian American ethnic cultures by mainstream society may contribute to cultural alienation and diminished self-concept among Asian American youth. Racism, an important social stratification variable, has been cited frequently by youth as a contributing factor for getting involved with gangs or other delinquent behavior (Ida & Yang, 2002). These dynamics impact on self-esteem and sense of belonging, often resulting in negative self-image or group identity (Yamamoto,

Silva, Ferrari, & Nukariya, 1997). Real or perceived prejudice and discrimination can isolate and discourage Asian American youth and their families from interacting with key institutions, other families, and other youth. In one study, many Seattle youth reported feeling that they were treated unfairly by school personnel, police, security personnel, and the larger community (Asian/Pacific Islander Task Force on Youth, 1993).

As noted earlier in this chapter, residential, economic, social, and psychological segregation may not apply equally to all Asian Americans, given that they are a diverse group economically and otherwise. However, the influence of social stratification on the lives of people of color is a constant, despite variations in its expression.

Promoting and Inhibiting Environments

Because of the significance of socioenvironmental factors such as social stratification, the settings in which Asian American children live must be evaluated on the extent to which they promote or inhibit their developmental competencies. Promoting and inhibiting environments are viewed as the direct consequence of the degree to which social stratification variables have an influence on access to resources.

Promoting environments can result not only from an appropriate number and quality of resources to children but also from settings that are consistent with family culture and supportive of developmental outcomes for children. For example, ethnic enclaves may serve as promoting environments in the sense that they allow community members access to key resources (Garcia Coll et al., 1996). The voluntary mutual aid organizations found in many Asian American immigrant communities are often a source of economic assistance and a social safety net. These mutual aid associations also provide an opportunity for social connectedness and a sense of belonging. In this sense, residential segregation in Asian American communities may represent a set of resources as opposed to externally imposed restrictions and limitations on choice. Internal community resources, such as sense of community and belonging, have been shown to contribute to a child's developmental competencies and filter out the harmful effects of mainstream society (Barnes, 1991). A study of Vietnamese youth, for instance, showed that involvement in their community had a strong negative correlation with drug and alcohol abuse (Bankston, 1995).

In a review of research on schooling and achievement, researchers point to the important role of the family in the school achievement of Asian American children (Slaughter-Defoe, Nakagawa, Takanishi, & Johnson, 1990). Japanese Americans' academic and occupational successes have been attributed to a value system that stresses a need for achievement and the need for affiliation. Given this cultural conditioning, first- and second-generation Japanese Americans hold values such as politeness, respect for authority, diligence, and setting and achieving long-term goals. The associated attitudes and behaviors are highly compatible with the values of the dominant American middle-class culture and are seen as necessary for obtaining access to resources and achieving upward mobility.

However, researchers have noted also that research predicting educational achievement for Asian American students reflects a pervasive stereotype in theory and research design (Slaughter-Defoe et al., 1990). Little differentiation has been made among Asian Americans of various cultural, linguistic, immigration, and economic backgrounds. Indeed, as argued by Garcia Coll et al. (1996), there is a need to examine educational achievement while considering all of these contextual factors. What appears as a promoting environment for some may, in fact, represent an inhibiting environment for others. For example, there is little research on the underachievement found among certain Asian subgroups such as the Khmer and Laotian (Lee & Zhan, 1998). These children are more likely than other Asian Americans to live in poverty, and they may show underachievement in school because of limited English skills and lack of familiarity with mainstream American culture and formal school systems. Traditional vehicles for promoting parental involvement may feel bewildering and unwelcoming to some Asian American families (Huang & Gibbs, 1992). The mismatch between the family and mainstream school settings for many Asian Americans may represent inhibiting environments for their children.

Likewise, some child care settings may be viewed as inhibiting environments for Asian American children. As discussed previously, the availability of affordable child care is a challenge for many Asian American families. However, some localities have looked beyond the issue of affordability to question the adequacy of existing child care standards and their relevance for Asian American children. The Asian and Pacific Islander Task Force in King County, Washington, for example, has noted some of the following challenges to achieving quality child care for Asian American children: Eurocentric practices by providers, gaps between provider and parent perspectives, lack of training for working with Asian American families, and lack of written and translated information in the parents' first language. One of the task force goals was to eliminate the "institutional racism of systems connected to early childhood education and out-of-school time care" (Asian and Pacific Islander Child Care Task Force, 2000).

Adaptive Culture

In response to social stratification, families and children create adaptive cultures that reflect the goals, values, attitudes, and behaviors consistent with their collective history (cultural, political, and economic) as well as with the current contextual demands stemming from promoting and inhibiting environments. An important example of adaptive culture among Asian American families is the development and use of kinship and extended social networks. The traditional Asian American family has been characterized by well-defined, unilaterally organized, hierarchical, and highly interdependent roles within a patriarchal, vertical, extended family structure. Although kinship and extended social networks reflect traditional Asian cultural patterns, they are also an adaptation to a socially stratified American society that provides additional resources promoting the survival and well-being of the community, family, and individual. Kinship and extended social networks may provide material support, such as income, child care, household assistance, and intangible help, such as emotional support, counseling, instruction, and social regulation (Harrison et al., 1990).

A survey of 490 second- and third-generation Japanese Americans found a persistence of traditional social relationships across the generations that served as a buffer against assaults from the outside community and strengthened ethnic solidarity and cultural values (Fugita & O'Brien, 1991).

Kinship and extended social networks are an integral part of Asian American adaptive culture, and they permeate the child developmental processes of Asian American children. With increased acculturation, however, extended family may be experienced as strength for some members and as restriction on autonomy for others. Asian American parents must decide which traditional aspects of parenting they wish to keep and which to relinquish in the face of the dominant culture's influence on parenting styles and practices. Parental acculturation levels might affect parenting style by influencing developmental expectations, mother-infant interactions, feeding and caregiving practices, and the role of extended family (Garcia Coll, Meyer, & Brillon, 1995). Garcia Coll's model argues that adaptive culture, perhaps as embodied in the form of extended family and related parenting practices in Asian American families, impacts characteristics of families and children and, ultimately, child developmental outcomes.

Family

The family's characteristics can be defined in terms of its structure and roles, values, beliefs, goals, racial socialization, and socioeconomic status. It is a function of adaptive culture as well as child characteristics. Many Asian Americans tend to use extended family for material and emotional support. As such, extended family is more likely to co-reside in the family and become part of the family structure and roles. These extended family relationships may have a positive effect on child development. Interaction with kin may reinforce a cultural continuity that contributes to healthy ethnic identity development. Research on child care has found that children who are exposed to multiple caregivers are more independent and adaptable to change (Scarr & Eisenberg, 1993). As discussed previously, Asian American family

AAPI children must be very independent then...

values, beliefs, and goals reflect cultural and religious traditions as well as adaptive culture, and they affect child rearing as well.

Racial socialization, described in greater detail later in this chapter, describes how families of color cope with social stratification variables and how they socialize their children and protect them from the negative effects of racism and discrimination. For Asian American parents, this may mean that they must teach their children that their ethnic identity may not be respected in the larger society and that it may be the target of hostility, antagonism, or exclusion. Asian American parents have the task of protecting their children from real and perceived racism that has been demonstrated to diminish psychological well-being among people of color (Serafica, 1990).

Finally, the socioeconomic resources available to families of color also influence the developmental competencies of their children. To the extent that families experience poverty, the effects tend to be more extreme and long lasting for families of color (U.S. Bureau of the Census, 1991). Although the median family income for Asian Americans is higher than the national average, this statistic obfuscates two critical factors: First, many Asian American households consist of extended family members and have multiple adult workers contributing to this family income and, second, there is wide income variability among distinct Asian American groups with some of the more recent immigrants and refugees living in poverty and more established groups in the upper-middle-class range. Asian Americans continue to have a lower per capita income and higher rate of poverty than non-Hispanic White Americans (DeNavas-Walt, Cleveland, & Webster, 2003; Proctor & Dalaker, 2003).

Socioeconomic disadvantage has been shown to be directly related to poor child developmental outcomes. In particular, family poverty can have significant negative effects on children's health and development. Children living in poverty are more likely to be of low birth weight, are less likely to receive recommended immunizations, are more likely to be sick and underweight as toddlers, and may not receive adequate nutrition. They are less likely to have access to adequate health care and more likely to suffer from lead poisoning, iron deficiency, and exposure to parental tobacco smoke. As a result, poor children between the ages of 2 and 5 years, on average, have significantly lower scores on intelligence and verbal tests than other children and are more likely to have behavior problems. Some of the consequences are directly caused by poverty, whereas others reflect the many factors correlated with poverty, such as low parental education and limited access to quality child care and early childhood education (Brown et al., 2004).

Child Characteristics

Child characteristics such as age, temperament, health status, physical characteristics, and biological factors are important in mediating the relationship of adaptive culture and family characteristics to developmental outcomes. While research on Asian American child temperament is limited, temperament is generally viewed as a behavioral style that may be a result of genetic endowment and parenting style. One study found that Chinese American newborns tended to be less changeable and less perturbable than European American newborns (Freedman & Freedman, 1969). Chinese infants have been found to be significantly less active, irritable, and vocal than Irish or American infants, even at 4 months of age (Kagan et al., 1994). X. Chen et al. (1998) also reported similar levels of reactiveness by Chinese infants at 2 years of age.

Other studies have found Asian American parenting practices to influence the temperament of their children. For example, one study showed that Chinese American infants vocalized less, were less likely to smile at external stimuli, and exhibited more social inhibition than European American infants. Researchers attributed this difference to Asian American parenting styles that provided less reinforcement of verbal and affective displays (Kagan, Kearsley, & Zelazo, 1978). There is little research on the connection between extended family/kinship networks and child temperament.

A child's health status is a function of adaptive culture and family characteristics, but it also serves as a mediator between family characteristics, adaptive culture, and developmental outcomes. Children are not just passive actors in their environment but may also contribute to their own socialization and development. Low birth weight and prematurity represent "at-risk" factors, which may contribute to poorer developmental outcomes. For example, Filipinos have been shown to be at increased risk for poor outcomes due to low birth weight (Fuentes-Afflick & Hessol, 1997). Southeast Asians have shown a higher prevalence of iron deficiency (Sargent, Stukel, Dalton, Freeman, & Brown, 1996), and low iron has been associated with fatigue, decreased attentiveness, and impaired cognitive and behavioral functioning in general (Grantham-McGregor & Ani, 2001). To the extent that a child is affected by physical problems such as low birth weight and low iron, and to the extent that a child exhibits a particular temperament, caregivers may respond differently than they might to other children.

Developmental Competencies

Cognitive, social, and emotional outcomes have been the most widely studied developmental competencies. Developmental outcomes or competencies must be considered within the context of the specific ecological circumstances in which children of color exist. In contexts where children must adapt to the effects of racism and its concomitant processes, they must also develop another set of competencies. In addition to cognitive, social, and emotional competencies, these other competencies include linguistic competencies, biculturalism, and the ability to cope with racism.

Cognitive development. The research on the development of cognitive competencies in Asian American children has been narrowly focused on academic achievement and the cultural factors that influence positive outcomes experienced by Asian American children in this domain. Although underachieving Asian American youth are an understudied group, Asian American youth, on the whole, are the subject of much attention because they consistently demonstrate higher achievement scores than White or other American students (S. Sue & Okazaki, 1990).

Some researchers have suggested a biological or genetic basis for seemingly superior cognitive abilities among Asians as a whole (Rushton & Jensen, 2005), but the majority of empirical research studies emphasize cultural explanations for this phenomenon. Existing research supports the following cultural explanations. First, Asian American parental expectations are high, and children also share these expectations (Okagaki & Frensch, 1998). Second, there is an underlying belief in Asian culture that effort, rather than inherent ability, is the determining factor in educational attainment (Chen & Stevenson, 1995). Third, Asian American children are socialized toward educational success, taking a more serious approach to schoolwork and spending more time on schoolwork and extracurricular classes. Asian American parents use indirect strategies to encourage achievement, such as structuring their home environments to facilitate learning, checking homework, attending school functions, and generally accepting "managerial parental involvement" as it relates to their children's education (Okagaki & Bojczyk, 2002).

Although there has been much interest in Asian American school achievement, research on cognitive competencies must broaden its scope. As discussed previously, the research on school achievement is narrowly focused on the Asian students who are doing well in school rather than on those who may be struggling. The research on cognitive development is also too narrowly focused on school achievement rather than other areas of cognitive development (Okagaki & Bojczyk, 2002).

In sum, there has been much emphasis on culture and parenting style as major determinants of cognitive achievement in Asian American youth. Research should be expanded to include other potential sociocultural determinants of cognitive outcomes. For instance, much research has explored the relationship between economic disadvantage and cognitive outcomes, but there is little research focusing specifically on the effects of such disadvantage on Asian American children. It is possible to extrapolate from research showing that some Asian American subgroups may experience significant socioeconomic disadvantage and that socioeconomic disadvantage has been associated with prematurity, low birth weight, nutritional deficits, and subsequent cognitive deficits in children. However, more research is needed to better understand the interaction of socioeconomic variables, race and ethnicity, and cognitive outcomes.

Social development. Much of the research on the social development of Asian American youth pertains to parenting styles and parent-child relationships. A widely used model for understanding parenting styles presents a parenting typology that includes authoritarian and authoritative styles (Baumrind, 1971). Authoritative parenting is characterized by responsive and nurturing parenting that, at the same time, sets clear expectations considering the child's perspective in decision making. Authoritarian parenting, on the other hand, is typified not by warmth and nurturance but by valuing obedience to, and respect for, authority; having high expectations for the child's behaviors; and not considering the child's perspective in decision making. Authoritative parenting generally has been associated with positive psychosocial and cognitive child outcomes (Baumrind, 1991); however, it has not been found to be associated with the academic achievement of Asian American students, whose parents tend to have more authoritarian parenting styles. Chao (1994) has suggested that such parenting constructs may not fully capture parenting in Asian families. In this cultural context, parents must "train" children in the appropriate behaviors, and this training is not equated with harsh overcontrol, as it might be in American culture, but as parental concern, caring, and involvement. Within such a model, underlying cultural differences in child developmental outcomes cannot be captured in a concept such as authoritarianism.

Attachment theory, an influential theory of relatedness, indicates that children who are securely attached tend to be more autonomous, less dependent, better able to regulate negative affect, less likely to have behavior problems, and more likely to form close, stable peer relationships than those who are insecurely attached (Cassidy & Shaver, 1999). However, it has been argued that attachment theory is inherently Western in its values and meaning and neglects important cultural differences. For example, social competence, having been defined in attachment theory as individuation and self-reliance, does not fit with what is known about Japanese cultures, in which reliance on others is often favored and essential to broader goals of social harmony. The indigenous Japanese concept of "amae" refers to the loving indulgence characterized by the relationship of attachment and dependence between mother and child. Whereas such relationships would lead to insecure-ambivalent attachments as defined in Western culture, such outcomes are regarded as normal and adaptive in Japan (Rothbaum, Weisz, Pott, Miyake, & Morelli, 2000).

With regard to parent-child relationships, research suggests that parent-child conflict may arise from the family's immigration experiences and acculturation differences between parents and their children. Difficulties arising from immigration may include the reversal of child and parenting roles and strained relationships between parents and their children (James, 1997). Although moral development, autonomy, and peer relationships are established areas of study, such research, as it pertains to Asian American children, is lacking. The concept of moral development of Asian American families may differ from that of mainstream American society and may lead to differences in moral development of Asian American children. Asian cultures, having been described as more collectivistic, might appear to hinder the development of autonomy and self-reliance. However, as the studies of amae suggest, development of autonomy must be viewed within the appropriate cultural context. Ho and Chiu (1994) also note that both collectivistic and individualistic orientations coexist in Chinese culture. Asian American parents have been found to encourage independent, as well as interdependent, behavior in children. Whereas Asian American parents tend to be more restrictive of their children's independence in social activities and occupational choices, they foster greater early independence in the academic area as compared to White parents (Lin & Fu, 1990). Differences in acculturation exist also, with more acculturated Asian Americans less restrictive and more encouraging of behavioral autonomy than less acculturated parents (Uba, 1994).

Finally, there is relatively little research on the development of normative peer relationships. Existing research shows that many Asian American students tend to socialize with and have friends of different races (Wang, Sedlacek, & Westbrook, 1992). Research has also found that for Asian American youth, other academically oriented peers may play an important role in supporting their academic success. Academically oriented Asian Americans are more likely to have friends who shared a similar academic orientation (Hamm, 2000). With regard to social support, it has been hypothesized that Asian American youth may turn to peers rather than parents and that delinquent peers may have a stronger influence than parental support in predicting delinquency (T. E. Kim & Goto, 2000).

While parenting styles, peer relationships, moral development, and other social developmental outcomes are likely to be related to the more macro level variables, such as social stratification and adaptive culture, we know of no studies that deal explicitly with such relationships. As with cognitive development, more research is needed to examine how social development is shaped by sociocultural factors.

Emotional development. Emotion has been defined universally as a set of largely pre-wired internal processes of self-maintenance and self-regulation (Buck, 1988). Emotional development among Asian American children is not well understood, but there is evidence that normative emotional development is regarded differently in different cultures. Among the Japanese, for example, there is a concern with avoiding anger and disruption of harmony in social situations (Markus & Kitayama, 1991). Other emotions, such as pride or guilt, may also differ according to the nature of the mediating self-system. As with anger, these expressions may be avoided, or they will assume a somewhat different form. Other researchers have noted that in Confucian cultures, children are socialized early on to master impulse control. Japanese mothers have been found to expect emotional maturity in terms of self-control, compliance, and social courtesy in their children, whereas mothers in the United States expect verbal assertiveness and social skills (Hess, Kashiwagi, Azuma, Price, & Dickson, 1980). Similarly, qualitative studies have found that Asian parents tend to exercise high impulse control over their children, training them to behave with self-control and discouraging them from showing emotions (S. Y. Kim & Wong, 2002). Again, as with social and cognitive

development, future research should explore the relationship of emotional developmental competencies to sociocultural factors in children's development.

In addition to the cognitive, social, and emotional domains, Asian American children must acquire another set of competencies. Because of the role of social stratification and cultural background in influencing developmental processes for Asian American and other children of color, it is important to consider linguistic competence, biculturalism, and the capacity to cope with racism.

Linguistic development. Many Asian American children grow up in monolingual, non-English speaking households and in environments where more than one language is spoken. As a result, they often must attain a greater degree of linguistic competence than their monolingual peers. According to the U.S. Bureau of the Census (2000), in approximately 25% of households in which an Asian language is spoken, adults reported that they speak English "not well" or "not at all." When looking at specific subgroups, this percentage ranges from 19% of households where Japanese is spoken to 39.4% of households where Mien or Hmong is spoken.

The linguistic origins of Asian languages are considerably diverse, and they contrast markedly with the English language. The psycholinguistic characteristics of these languages, that is, how they influence thought, and their associated verbal and nonverbal communication patterns also serve to reinforce traditional cultural values. As such, recent research shows that bilingualism represents a developmental asset that should be preserved and nurtured (Chiocca, 1998; Fierro-Cobas & Chan, 2001). Some research has demonstrated that bilingualism can contribute to cognitive complexity and attentional control (Bialystok, 1999). Studies also show that bilingual children, as compared to monolingual children, exhibit more cognitive flexibility and metalinguistic awareness, that is, the ability to attend to language as an object of thoughts rather than just for the content or idea (Diaz, 1983). Additionally, speaking the language of parents and grandparents offers a way for the child to better understand the family's heritage and culture.

Conversely, with such marked contrasts in language structure and function, gaining English proficiency can be especially difficult for many Asian American refugees and immigrants. Lack of English skills places them at continued risk of marginality, and it is not uncommon for children of all ages to serve as interpreters. Although this can serve an important function by helping parents communicate outside the family, it also can have negative consequences for both parties. Such role reversals may exacerbate an already tenuous situation where there has been a shift in status, placing the parents in a position of less power and authority. It also places an undue burden on the youth to translate information that may be beyond his or her cognitive abilities. In other instances, critical information is not passed on, leaving the parents unaware of the emotional, behavioral, legal, or academic problems of their children (James, 1997). Additionally, research has found that the preference of children for speaking English rather than the language of their parents is a significant predictor of parent-child conflict (Rumbaut, 1994). In short, bilingualism represents opportunities as well as challenges for developmental outcomes in Asian American children. As such, it is important to include linguistics as central to any notions of developmental competence in Asian American children and youth.

Biculturalism. A central task in childhood and adolescence is achieving a sense of identity, or a sense of continuity that provides a foundation for adulthood. Failure to establish a coherent and stable identity may lead to confusion and psychological distress (Erikson, 1968). For Asian American youth, identity development may prove problematic because they straddle multiple cultures including mainstream and ethnic cultures. Acculturation and ethnic identity development have been discussed extensively (D. Sue, Mak, & Sue, 1998; Tsai, Chentsova-Dutton, & Wong, 2002); these are important constructs to consider because they significantly influence Asian American child development.

In general, studies have shown a relationship between successful acculturation and ethnic identity formation as measures of psychological adjustment and self-esteem (Huang, 1997). However, research has demonstrated that many Asian American families suffer from intergenerational conflict caused by generational differences in acculturation and cultural orientation (Tsai, Chentsova-Dutton, & Wong, 2002). Acculturation and ethnic identity development often can become more problematic in the context of forces of social stratification and the devaluing of their ethnic culture by the dominant culture.

One strategy for adapting to conflicts arising from acculturation and ethnic identity development has been for Asian American youth to adapt a bicultural orientation. Biculturalism has been defined as the ability to negotiate successfully two or more distinct cultures, valuing various aspects of each culture, and experiencing positive outcomes and a core sense of coherence. The bicultural person learns to function optimally in more than one cultural context and to switch repertoires of behavior appropriately and adaptively, as indicated by the situation (Huang & Ida, 2004).

Because Asian American children live in at least two distinct cultures, an important developmental task is learning to negotiate their desire to affiliate and be independent of Asian and European American cultures. In most models of acculturation and ethnic identity, biculturalism is the desired adaptation. A review of the literature on the adaptation of minority individuals to the majority culture suggests that individuals who can effectively function in both the indigenous and dominant cultures may exhibit increased cognitive functioning and mental health (LaFromboise, Coleman, & Gerton, 1993). Other studies show benefits of biculturalism to include lower school dropout rates among Vietnamese, Koreans, Chinese, Filipinos, and Japanese immigrants (Feliciano, 2001). Lacking a sense of belonging to either culture has been associated with feelings of hopelessness, low self-esteem, depression, and suicide (Phinney, Lochner, & Murphy, 1990).

Coping with racism. Real or perceived racism may be a significant developmental risk factor for Asian American children. Measures of peer discrimination have found that Southeast Asian youth experience more discriminatory acts from schoolmates than do other groups and that these experiences are related to increased levels of psychological distress (Fisher, Wallace, & Fenton, 2000). Discrimination in educational contexts has been associated with depressed academic performance and self-esteem (Steele, 1997). Unlike their majority peers, Asian American children and youth must acquire coping with racism as a developmental competency.

To date, much of what is known about coping with racism in Asian American children comes from the research on racial socialization, which is viewed as a set of adaptive and protective practices that ethnic minority parents use to promote children's functioning in a world that is stratified by ethnicity and race (Hughes, 2003). Whereas some parents prepare children for racial barriers (Hughes & Chen, 1999), recent data indicate that, as compared to other racial and ethnic minorities, Asian American parents are more likely to convey messages about racial pride rather than racial bias and to tell their children how to respond to racial bias (Buriel & DeMent, 1997; Phinney & Chavira, 1995).

Research focusing on how Asian American youth experience and cope with racism is limited. However, research on other children of color has shown that teenagers socialized to be aware of, and respond proactively to, racism have a greater sense of personal efficacy and self-esteem, increased academic success, and fewer behavioral problems (Bowman & Howard, 1985; Caughy, O'Campo, Randolph, & Nickerson, 2002; Phinney & Chavira, 1995). In contrast, other studies have shown that parents' overemphasis on racial barriers may undermine youth's efficacy and prompt them to withdraw from activities that are essential for access to opportunity and reward structures in the dominant society (Marshall, 1995). The net effect of racial socialization remains unclear and may depend on the nature of the messages transmitted.

SUMMARY AND CONCLUSION

We have attempted in this chapter to provide a summary of the research on Asian American child development to date, using Garcia Coll's integrative conceptual model to both frame the discussion and offer a more comprehensive view for understanding child development. According to this framework, Asian American children are influenced by societal forces such as racism, prejudice, discrimination, and segregation. They are nested in a context encompassing various promoting and inhibiting environments, their adaptive cultures, and their families. As a result of these processes and as a result of their own characteristics, Asian American children acquire developmental competencies that are not necessarily universally determined but are influenced by these same processes.

Garcia Coll's social ecological perspective emphasizes the contextual variables that are relevant to the lives of Asian American children; these are variables that traditional developmental models do not consider. The existing research on child development has primarily focused on intraindividual variables, whereas the social ecological view requires a shift to a broader view of the world to include social stratification and cultural variables.

The adoption of this model as a heuristic guide to research can lead to increased research on Asian American child development. Where there is research on developmental competencies, most research on Asian American child development is focused narrowly on cognitive, social, and emotional development of Asian American children, with only limited attention to bicultural adaptation and coping with racism. More research is needed to better understand the role of broader contextual variables in mediating child developmental outcomes as well as the broad range of developmental competencies and how some may be unique to Asian American children.

As related to practice, this model can help to identify and describe the developmental competencies in Asian American children that are not captured in standard assessment instruments. This is true for developmental outcomes, such as cognition and emotion, and for biculturalism, linguistic development, and coping with racism. Interventions could prove more effective if emphasis were moved beyond characteristics of the youth to the youth in their settings. For example, prevention programs that aim to reduce risk and enhance protective factors in Asian American children are likely to be more effective if they address ethnic heritage, devalued ethnic identity, and the development of bicultural skills.

On the whole, the Garcia Coll integrative conceptual model offers a comprehensive view of child development for Asian American children. A model that places social class, culture, ethnicity, and race at the core of child development theory represents a timely and important advance given the increasing diversity of childhood and the multiplicity of factors that may influence developmental outcomes for Asian American children and youth.

REFERENCES

Acevedo-Garcia, D., Lochner, K. A., Osypuk, T. L., & Subramanian, S. V. (2003). Future directions in residential segregation and health research: A multilevel approach. *American Journal of Public Health, 93,* 215–221.

Asian American Legal Defense and Education Fund. (n.d.). *Economic justice.* Retrieved June 15, 2005, from http://www.aaldef.org/economic.html

Asian and Pacific Islander Child Care Task Force. (2000). *Taking steps to improve the quality of care for Asian and Pacific Islander children, youth and families.* King County, WA: Author.

Asian/Pacific Islander Task Force on Youth. (1993). *Executive summary of a framework for meeting the needs of at-risk Asian/Pacific Islander youth.* King County, WA: Author.

Bankston, C. (1995). Vietnamese ethnicity and adolescent substance abuse: Evidence for a community level approach. *Deviant Behavior, 16,* 59–80.

Barnes, E. J. (1991). The black community as the source of positive self-concept for black children: A theoretical perspective. In L. Jones (Ed.), *Black psychology* (pp. 667–692). Berkeley, CA: Cobb & Henry.

Baumrind, D. (1971). Current patterns of parental authority. *Developmental Psychology Monographs, 4*(1, Pt. 2).

Baumrind, D. (1991). The influence of parenting styles and adolescent development. In J. Brooks-Gunn, R. Lerner, & A. C. Petersen (Eds.), *The encyclopedia of adolescence* (pp. 746–758).

Bialystok, E. (1999). Cognitive complexity and attentional control in the bilingual mind. *Child Development, 70*(3), 636–644.

Bowlby, J. (1969). *Attachment and loss: Vol. 1. Attachment.* New York: Basic Books.

Bowman, P. J., & Howard, C. (1985). Race-related socialization, motivation, and academic achievement: A study of black youths in three-generation families. *Journal of the American Academy of Child Psychiatry, 24,* 134–141.

Bronfenbrenner, U. (1979). *The ecology of human development: Experiments by nature and design.* Cambridge, MA: Harvard University Press.

Bronfenbrenner, U., & Crouter, A. C. (1983). The evolution of environmental models in developmental research. In P. H. Mussen (Series Ed.) & W. Kessen (Vol. Ed.), *Handbook of child psychology: Vol. 1. History, theory, and methods* (4th ed., pp. 357–414). New York: Wiley.

Brown, B., Weitzman, M., Bzostek, S., Kavanaugh, M., Aufseeser, D., Bagley, S., et al. (2004). Early child development in social context: A chartbook. New York: Commonwealth Fund.

Buck, R. (1988). *Human motivation and emotion* (2nd ed.). New York: Wiley.

Buriel, R., & DeMent, T. (1997). Immigration and sociocultural change in Mexican, Chinese, and Vietnamese American families. In A. Booth, A. C. Crouter, & N. Landale (Eds.), *Immigration and the family: Research and policy on U.S. immigration* (pp. 165–200). Mahwah, NJ: Erlbaum.

Cassidy, J., & Shaver, P. R. (1999). *Handbook of attachment: Theory, research and clinical application.* New York: Guilford Press.

Caughy, M. O., O'Campo, P. J., Randolph, S. M., & Nickerson, K. (2002). The influence of racial socialization practices on the cognitive and behavioral competence of African American preschoolers. *Child Development, 73,* 1611–1625.

Chao, R. K. (1994). Beyond parental control and authoritarian parenting style: Understanding Chinese parenting through the cultural notion of training. *Child Development, 65,* 111–119.

Chen, C., & Stevenson, H. W. (1995). Motivation and mathematics achievement: A comparative study of Asian-American, Caucasian-American, and East Asian high school students. *Child Development, 66,* 1215–1234.

Chen, X., Hastings, P. D., Rubin, K. H., Chen, H., Cen, G., & Stewart, S. L. (1998). Child-rearing attitudes and behavioral inhibition in Chinese and Canadian toddlers: A cross-cultural study. *Developmental Psychology, 34*(4), 1097–1104.

Chiocca, E. M. (1998). Language development in bilingual children. *Pediatric Nursing, 24,* 43–47.

Coalition for Asian American Children and Families. (2001). *Crossing the divide: Asian American families and the child welfare system.* New York: Author.

DeNavas-Walt, C., Cleveland, B., & Webster, B. H. (2003). *Income in the United States: 2002* (U.S. Census Bureau Current Population Report No. P60–221). Washington, DC: US Government Printing Office.

Diaz, R. M. (1983). The impact of bilingualism on cognitive development. In E. W. Gordon (Ed.), *Review of research in education* (Vol. 10, pp. 23–54). Washington, DC: American Educational Research Association.

Erikson, E. (1968). *Identity: Youth and crisis.* New York: Norton.

Feliciano, C. (2001). The benefits of biculturalism: Exposure to immigrant culture and dropping out of school among Asian and Latino youths. *Social Science Quarterly, 82,* 865–879.

Fierro-Cobas, V., & Chan, E. (2001). Language development in bilingual children: A primer for pediatricians. *Contemporary Pediatrics, 18,* 79–98.

Fisher, C. B., Wallace, S. A., & Fenton, R. E. (2000). Discrimination distress during adolescence. *Journal of Youth and Adolescence, 29,* 679–695.

Freedman, D. G., & Freedman, N. (1969). Behavioral differences between Chinese-Americans and European American newborns. *Nature, 224,* 1127.

Freud, S. (1954). *Collected works* (Standard ed.). London: Hogarth Press.

Fuentes-Afflick, E., & Hessol, N. A. (1997). Impact of Asian ethnicity and national origin on infant birth weight. *American Journal of Epidemiology, 145,* 148–155.

Fugita, S. S., & O'Brien, D. J. (1991). *Japanese American ethnicity: The persistence of community.* Seattle: University of Washington Press.

Garcia Coll, C. T., Meyer, E. C., & Brillon, L. (1995). Ethnic and minority parenting. In M. Bronstein (Ed.), *Handbook of parenting: Vol. 2. Biology and ecology of parenting* (pp. 180–209). Mahwah, NJ: Lawrence Erlbaum.

Garcia Coll, C. T., Crnic, K., Lamberty, G., Wasik, B. H., Jenkins, R., Garcia, H. V., et al. (1996). An integrative model for the study of developmental competencies in minority children. *Child Development, 67,* 1891–1914.

Gee, G. C. (2002). A multilevel analysis of the relationship between institutional and individual racial discrimination and health status. *American Journal of Public Health, 92,* 615–624.

Gibbs, J. T., & Huang, L. N. (2003). *Children of color: Psychological interventions with culturally diverse youth.* San Francisco: Jossey-Bass.

Grantham-MacGregor, S., & Ani, C. (2001). A review of studies on the effect of iron deficiency on cognitive development in children. *Journal of Nutrition, 13,* 649–668.

Hamm, J. V. (2000). Do birds of a feather flock together? The variable bases for African American, Asian American, and European American adolescents' selection of similar friends. *Developmental Psychology, 36,* 209–219.

Harrison, A. O., Wilson, M. N., Pine, C. J., Chan, S. Q., & Buriel, R. (1990). Family ecologies of ethnic minority children. *Child Development, 61,* 347–362.

Hess, R., Kashiwagi, K., Azuma, H., Price, G., & Dickson, W. (1980). Maternal expectations for mastery of developmental tasks in Japan and the United States. *International Journal of Psychology, 15,* 259–271.

Ho, D., & Chiu, C. Y. (1994). Component ideas of individualism, collectivism, and social organization. In U. Kim, H. C. Triandis, C. Kagitchibasi, S. C. Choi, & G. Yoon (Eds.), *Individualism and collectivism: Theory, method and applications* (pp. 137–156). Thousand Oaks, CA: Sage.

Huang, L. N. (1997). Asian American adolescents. In E. Lee (Ed.), *Working with Asian Americans: A guide for clinicians* (pp. 175–195). New York: Guilford Press.

Huang, L. N., & Gibbs, J. T. (1992). Partners or adversaries? Home-school collaboration across culture, race, and ethnicity. In S. Christenson & J. Conoley (Eds.), *Home school collaboration: Enhancing children's academic and social competence* (pp. 19–52). Silver Spring, MD: National Association of School Psychologists.

Huang, L. N., & Ida, D. J. (2004). *Promoting positive development and preventing youth violence and high-risk behaviors in Asian American/Pacific Islander communities: A social ecology perspective.* Manuscript submitted for publication.

Hughes, D. (2003). Correlates of African American and Latino parents' messages to children about ethnicity and race: A comparative study of racial socialization. *American Journal of Community Psychology, 31,* 15–33.

Hughes, D., & Chen, L. (1999). The nature of parents' race-related communications to children: A developmental perspective. In L. Balter & C. S. Tamis-LeMonda (Eds.), *Child psychology: A handbook of contemporary issues* (pp. 467–490). Philadelphia: Taylor & Francis.

Ida, D. J., & Yang, P. (2002). Working with Southeast Asian children and families. In J. Gibbs & L. Huang (Eds.), *Children of color: Psychological interventions with culturally diverse youth.* San Francisco: Jossey-Bass.

James, D. C. S. (1997). Coping with a new society: The unique psychosocial problems of immigrant youth. *Journal of School Health, 67,* 98–102.

Johnson, D. J., Jaeger, E., Suzanne, S. M., Cauce, A. M., & Ward, J. (2003). Studying the effects of early child care experiences on the development of children of color in the United States. *Child Development, 74,* 1227–1244.

Johnson-Powell, G., Yamamoto, J., Wyatt, G., & Arroyo, W. (1997). *Transcultural child development.* New York: Wiley.

Kagan, J., Archus, D., Snidman, N., Feng, W. Y., Hender, J., & Greene, S. (1994). Reactivity in infants: A cross-national comparison. *Developmental Psychology, 30,* 342–345.

Kagan, J., Kearsley, R. B., & Zelazo, P. R. (1978). *Infancy: Its place in human development.* Cambridge, MA: Harvard University Press.

Kim, S. Y., & Wong, V. Y. (2002). Assessing Asian and Asian American parenting: A review of the literature. In K. S. Kurasaki, S. Okazaki, & S. Sue (Eds.), *Asian American mental health: Assessment theories and methods.* New York: Kluwer Academic/Plenum.

Kim, T. E., & Goto, S. G. (2000). Peer delinquency and parental social support as predictors of Asian American adolescent delinquency. *Deviant Behavior: An Interdisciplinary Journal, 21,* 331–347.

LaFromboise, T., Coleman, H. L., & Gerton, J. (1993). Psychological impact of biculturalism: Evidence and theory. *Psychological Bulletin, 114,* 395–412.

Lee, L. C., & Zhan, G. (1998). Psychosocial status of children and youths. In L. C. Lee & N. W. S. Zane (Eds.), *Handbook of Asian American psychology* (pp. 137–163). Thousand Oaks, CA: Sage.

Lerner, R., & Castellino, D. (1998). *Contemporary developmental theory and adolescence: Developmental systems and applied developmental science.* Paper prepared for Health Future of Youth II: Pathways to Adolescent Health. Maternal and Child Health Bureau, Annapolis, MD.

Lin, C. C., & Fu, V. R. (1990). A comparison of child-rearing practices among Chinese, immigrant Chinese, and Caucasian-American parents. *Child Development, 61,* 429–433.

Markus, H., & Kitayama, S. (1991). Culture and the self: Implications for cognition, emotion, and motivation. *Psychological Review, 98,* 224–253.

Marshall, S. (1995). Ethnic socialization of African American children: Implications for parenting, identity development, and academic achievement. *Journal of Youth and Adolescence, 24,* 377–396.

Office of Juvenile Justice and Delinquency Prevention, U.S. Department of Justice. (1999). *Juvenile offenders and victims: 1999 national report.* (H. Snyder & M. Sickmund, Compilers), National Center for Juvenile Justice. Washington, DC: Author.

Ogbu, J. V. (1981). Origins of human competence: A cultural-ecological perspective. *Child Development, 52,* 413–429.

Okagaki, L., & Bojczyk, K. E. (2002). Perspectives on Asian American development. In G. C. Nagayama Hall & S. Okazaki (Eds.), *Asian American psychology: The science of lives in context.* Washington, DC: American Psychological Association.

Okagaki, L., & Frensch, P. A. (1998). Parenting and children's school achievement: A multi-ethnic perspective. *American Educational Research Journal, 35,* 123–144.

Phinney, J. S., & Chavira, V. (1995). Parental ethnic socialization and adolescent coping with problems related to ethnicity. *Journal of Research on Adolescence, 5,* 31–54.

Phinney, J. S., Lochner, B. T., & Murphy, R. (1990). Ethnic identity development and psychological adjustment in adolescence. In A. R. Stiffman & L. E. Davis (Eds.), *Ethnic issues in adolescent mental health* (pp. 53–72). Newbury Park, CA: Sage.

Piaget, J. (1950). *The psychology of intelligence.* New York: Harcourt Brace.

Proctor, B. D., & Dalaker, J. (2003). *Poverty in the United States: 2002* (U.S. Census Bureau Current Population Report No. P60–222). Washington, DC: U.S. Government Printing Office.

Reeves, T., & Bennett, C. (2003). *The Asian and Pacific Islander Population in the United States: March 2002* (U.S. Census Bureau Current Population Report No. P20–540). Washington, DC: Government Printing Office.

Rothbaum, F. Weisz, J., Pott, M., Miyake, K., & Morelli, G. (2000). Attachment and culture: Security in the United States and Japan. *American Psychologist, 55,* 1093–1104.

Rumbaut, R. (1994). The crucible within: Ethnic identity, self-esteem, and segmented assimilation among children of immigrants. *International Migration Review, 28,* 748–794.

Rushton, J. P., & Jensen, A. R. (2005). Thirty years of research on race differences in cognitive ability. *Psychology, Public Policy, and Law, 11,* 235–294.

Sargent, J. D., Stukel, T. A., Dalton, M. A., Freeman, J. L., & Brown, M. J. (1996). Iron deficiency in Massachusetts communities: Socioeconomic and demographic risk factors among children. *American Journal of Public Health, 86,* 544–550,

Scarr, S., & Eisenberg, M. (1993). Child care research: Issues, perspectives, and results. *Annual Review of Psychology, 44,* 613–644.

Serafica, F. (1990). Counseling Asian-American parents: A cultural-developmental approach. In F. Serafica, A. Schwebel, R. Russell, P. Isaac, & L. Myers (Eds.), *Mental health of ethnic minorities.* New York: Praeger.

Slaughter-Defoe, D. T., Nakagawa, K., Takanishi, R., & Johnson, D. J. (1990). Toward cultural/ecological perspectives on schooling and achievement in African- and Asian-American children. *Child Development, 61,* 363–83.

Steele, C. M. (1997). A threat in the air: How stereotypes shape intellectual identity and performance. *American Psychologist, 52,* 613–629.

Sue, D., Mak, W. S., & Sue, D. W. (1998). Ethnic identity. In L. C. Lee & N. W. S. Zane (Eds.), *Handbook of Asian American psychology.* Thousand Oaks, CA: Sage.

Sue, S., & Okazaki, S. (1990). Asian-American educational achievements: A phenomenon in search of an explanation. *American Psychologist, 45,* 913–920.

Tsai, J. L., Chentsova-Dutton, Y., & Wong, Y. (2002). Why and how researchers should study ethnic identity, acculturation and cultural orientation. In G. C. Nagayama Hall & S. Okazaki (Eds.), *Asian American psychology: The science of lives in context.* Washington, DC: American Psychological Association.

Uba, L. (1994). *Asian Americans: Personality patterns, identity, and mental health.* New York: Guilford Press.

U.S. Bureau of the Census. (1991). *Poverty in the United States* (U.S. Census Bureau Current Population Reports: Consumer Income, Series P-60, No. 175). Washington, DC: Government Printing Office.

U.S. Bureau of the Census. (2000). *Ability to speak English by language spoken at home for the population 18 years and older: 2000.* Retrieved June 14, 2005, from http://www.census.gov/population/cen2000/phc-t37/tab01b.pdf

U.S. Commission on Civil Rights. (1992). *Civil rights issues facing Asian Americans in the 1990s: A report of the United States Commission on Civil Rights, February 1992.* Washington, DC: Author.

Wang, Y., Sedlacek, W. E., & Westbrook, F. D. (1992). Asian Americans and student organization: Attitudes and participation. *Journal of College Student Development, 33,* 214–221.

Williams, D. R., & Jackson, P. B. (2005). Social sources of racial disparities in health. *Health Affairs, 24,* 325–334.

Yamamoto, J., Silva, J., Ferrari, M., & Nukariya, K. (1997). Culture and psychopathology. In G. Johnson-Powell, J. Yamamoto, G. Wyatt, & W. Arroyo (Eds.), *Transcultural child development.* New York: Wiley.

7

Asian Americans' Educational Experiences

Vivian Tseng

Ruth K. Chao

Inna Artati Padmawidjaja

By almost every educational gauge, young Asian Americans are soaring. They are finishing way above the mean on the math section of the Scholastic Aptitude Test . . . and outscoring their peers of other races in high school grade-point averages. They spend more time on their homework . . . take more advanced high school courses and graduate with more credits than other American students. A higher percentage of these young people complete high school and finish college than do White American students. Trying to explain why so many Asian-American students are superachievers, Harvard Psychology Professor Jerome Kagan comes up with this simple answer: "To put it plainly, they work harder."

Brand (*Time Magazine*, 1987)

[At] Lafayette High in Brooklyn, Chinese immigrant students . . . are harassed and bullied so routinely that school officials in June agreed to a Department of Justice consent decree to curb alleged "severe and pervasive harassment directed at Asian-American students by their classmates." Since then, the Justice Department credits Lafayette officials with addressing the problem but the case is far from isolated. Nationwide, Asian students say they're often beaten, threatened and called ethnic slurs by other young people, and school safety data suggest that the problem may be worsening. Youth advocates say these Asian teens, stereotyped as high-achieving students who rarely fight back, have for years borne the brunt of ethnic tension as Asian communities expand and neighborhoods become more racially diverse.

Texeira (*The Washington Post*, 2005)

There are two prevailing images of Asian American students. The first popular image casts Asian Americans as "model minority" students, outperforming other students and unencumbered by their status as racial minorities. The second, contrasting image casts Asian Americans as the targets of racial bias, violence, and stereotyping in schools. In this chapter, we examine what research findings bring to bear about both these images: Asian Americans' achievement from elementary school through college and their experiences with racism in schools.

We begin by placing Asian Americans' educational experiences within a sociohistorical context, illustrating the progression of public images of Asian Americans from a "yellow peril" threatening race mixing in public schools to "model minority" students, succeeding in schools through the virtues of hard work and uncomplaining perseverance. Second, we review research on Asian Americans' academic performance from elementary school through college. Where possible, we report ethnic, generational, and socioeconomic variations in academic performance among Asian Americans. Third, we examine Asian Americans' experiences of racism and intergroup relations within schools, particularly in instructional and peer settings. We end the chapter by discussing the broader implications of the model minority stereotype for Asian American students and other students of color.

SOCIOHISTORICAL CONTEXT: FROM YELLOW PERIL TO MODEL MINORITY

Today, the predominant image of Asian American youth is that of the model minority; but this image belies a long history of Asian American struggles over integration and access to public schools. In the mid to late 1800s in San Francisco, Chinese American parents sought public education for their children but were rebuffed by racist stereotypes of Chinese immigrants as invading "yellow hordes" and a "yellow peril" threatening race mixing, immorality, and debauchery (Wollenberg, 1978). In 1885, Mamie Tape and her parents brought a suit against San Francisco schools in Tape v. Hurley and won the legal standing for Chinese Americans to be served by public schools. While significant, the case largely resulted in the establishment of segregated public schools for Chinese Americans. In the early 1900s, Chinese Americans in San Francisco began challenging the doctrine of "separate but equal" schools, and eventually rigid segregation policy began to break down (Wollenberg, 1978). Almost a century later, in 1974, immigrant Chinese students filed a class action lawsuit in the landmark case of *Lau v. Nichols,* arguing that schools needed to pay attention to the educational needs of limited-English proficient students. They won their case in front of the U.S. Supreme Court, bolstering support for bilingual education for the growing tide of immigrant Asian and non-Asian students in the latter part of the 20th century (Chang, 2003; Wang, 1976).

In the 1960s, the image of Chinese and Japanese Americans as a yellow peril in schools gave way to the image of them as a model minority success story (Suzuki, 1977). Despite nearly a century of political and legal struggles against racial exclusion, Asian Americans were cast as model minorities that had obtained success without the need for public services. In the press, Asian Americans were hailed as successful minorities, compared to other racial minorities and even to White Americans. Under the headline, "Success Story of One Minority Group in the U.S.," *U.S. News and World Report* reported,

> At a time when Americans are awash in worry over the plight of racial minorities . . . At a time when it is being proposed that hundreds of billions be spent to uplift Negroes and other minorities, the nation's 300,000 Chinese-Americans are moving ahead on their own—with no help from anyone else. . . . The large majority are moving ahead by applying the virtues of hard work, thrift, and morality. ("Success Story," 1966, pp. 73–74)

Earlier that year, sociologist William Petersen (1966) had written similarly in the *New York Times* about a "Success Story, Japanese-American Style":

> Japanese-Americans are better than any other group in our society, including native-born whites.

They have established this remarkable record . . . by their own almost totally unaided effort. . . . Even in a country whose patron saint is the Horatio Alger hero, there is no parallel to this success story. (p. 21)

This shift from yellow peril to model minority images of Asian Americans gained prominence during the civil rights and Black Power movements, a time when communities of color—most visibly, African Americans–were demanding structural changes in U.S. society. The propagation of the model minority image challenged sociopolitical demands to address racism in schools and other public institutions (Chun, 1980). Specifically, the model minority thesis implied that societal structures could be preserved because minorities can achieve wealth, respect, and success through their own hard work (Suzuki, 1977; Wollenberg, 1978).

The model minority image pits Asian Americans against other racial minorities (Leong, Chao, & Hardin, 2000). The image casts Asian Americans in terms of hard work, uncomplaining perseverance, and quiet accommodation while implying that other racial minorities are lazy, complaining, and disruptive (Suzuki, 1977). Propagating the model minority image ignores the historical and contemporary roles of Asian Americans as political actors who challenged racism in public education, at times alongside African Americans, Latinos, and Native Americans. As the model minority image took firmer root in the late 1960s, it contrasted sharply with growing racial consciousness and political activism among Asian American youth (Suzuki, 1977). It was young Asian American activists on college campuses who first came together and forged a pan-Asian identity (Espiritu, 1992). In the 1970s and 1980s, these students joined with community members to create "Asian American" panethnic unity, building pan-Asian civil rights groups, community organizations, and social services (Nakanishi, 2001).

Since the 1960s, the demographic profile of Asian Americans has shifted dramatically. The fight against Nazism during World War II had fostered greater attention to domestic racism (Takaki, 1989). Racially discriminatory immigration quotas were repealed and replaced with the 1965 Hart-Cellar Act. Prior to World War II, the majority of Asian Americans were of Chinese, Japanese, and Filipino backgrounds, with smaller populations of Indians and Koreans. After passage of the 1965 Act and the wars in Southeast Asia, larger populations of Southeast Asian refugees, South Asian immigrants, and Pacific Islanders joined new immigrants from East Asia and the Philippines. Chinese and Japanese Americans had been the predominant foci of early yellow peril and model minority images, but over time, the success stories of Asian American students have been generalized to include the influx of new Asian and Pacific Islander groups. As we discuss in the ensuing sections, studying Asian American achievement obliges a consideration of the increasing diversity of Asian American populations, including immigration and refugee experiences, and ethnic, cultural, and socioeconomic diversity.

ACADEMIC ACHIEVEMENT

Next, we review research findings on Asian Americans' academic achievement from elementary school through college. We have chosen to focus on findings from large-scale, nationally representative data sets because of the importance of representative sampling in making group comparisons. Too often racial/panethnic and ethnic comparisons are based on convenience sampling, which complicates the interpretation of observed differences between groups. Data for these national studies are collected primarily through the U.S. Department of Education's National Center for Educational Statistics (NCES) and include the Early Childhood Longitudinal Study, Kindergarten Class of 1998–1999 (ECLS-K), National Assessment of Educational Progress (NAEP), National Educational Longitudinal Study of 1988 (NELS:88), High School and Beyond Study (HS&B), and Beginning Postsecondary Students Longitudinal Study (BPS: 96/01). We supplement review of these large-scale nationally representative studies with smaller-scale, local studies that examine ethnic and generational differences in achievement and include additional academic outcomes.

Before presenting the review, we offer a few cautionary notes for interpreting the findings, particularly those focused on panethnic differences. Panethnic comparisons are based on the *mean* or *average* achievement of Asian Americans. These averages, however, can mask significant variation in achievement across individuals and subgroups of Asian Americans. Studies do not consistently examine differences among Asian Pacific subgroups by ethnicity or generational/immigrant status, but when they do so, we present these subgroup differences.

Second, we discuss various indicators of achievement across stages of schooling and domains of study (i.e., math, reading, science, etc.). In early elementary school, research focuses on acquisition of particular skills such as recognition of letters, numbers, and shapes; in middle and high school, the focus is on grades, dropout rates, and course selection; and in college, the focus is on grades, persistence, and graduation rates. Across all stages of schooling, standardized test scores are examined. Regrettably, reports often present average test scores for panethnic groups but no additional information (e.g., standard deviations) for interpreting the size and significance of group differences.

Third, space limits prohibit extensive discussion of why there are achievement differences between groups. Readers are referred to other publications that examine structural (see Sue & Okazaki, 1990; Suzuki, 1977; Xie & Goyette, 2003) as well as cultural and immigration influences (see Chao, 1996, 2000; Chao & Tseng, 2002) on achievement. Leong et al. (2000) provide a comprehensive review exploring all three sets of influences.

Elementary School

Although scholarly and political interest in early childhood education is growing, very little research has examined this stage of schooling for Asian Americans. Here, we review findings from ECLS-K, NAEP, and smaller-scale studies during elementary school. Given that studies of early elementary education only recently have included Asian Americans, it is perhaps unsurprising that most studies do not examine differences between Asian subgroups.

Nationally representative studies. The ECLS-K is the first study by the NCES that focuses nationally on the educational progress of children in early elementary school. It includes a nationally representative sample of 22,782 kindergartners who attended 1,277 kindergarten programs during the 1998–1999 school year. Of these children, only 3% (660) were Asian American, a sample size with limited power to examine ethnic or generational differences. Children were followed through the fifth grade, but findings for the later years are not yet available. ECLS-K findings indicate that Asian American children entered kindergarten with greater math and reading skills than did White, Black, and Latino children, and Asian American children maintained that advantage through the end of the kindergarten year (West, Denton, & Reaney, 2000). By the third grade, however, White children were similar to Asian American children on reading and math scores, and both groups had higher scores than Black and Latino children (Rathbun, West, & Germino-Hausken, 2004). In the third grade, ECLS-K also began assessing science skills; as with reading and math, Asian American children had similar levels of science skills as White children, and both groups had higher skills than Latino and Black children. Demographic factors, such as socioeconomic status, primary home language, and type of kindergarten program and schools attended, fully accounted for differences between White and Latino children in reading and math scores, but not science; these demographic factors did not fully account for differences between White and Black children. In their analyses of ECLS-K data, Lee and Burkham (2002) also found that much of the achievement differences between Latinos and Whites, and between Blacks and Whites, were associated with family structure, human capital, socioeconomic status, and other demographic variables. These factors, however, did not explain differences between Asians and Whites.

The NAEP conducted math and reading assessments of 187,581 fourth graders attending approximately 7,500 schools (NCES, 2004a, 2004b). Nationally representative samples of students attending private and public schools were assessed on math and reading abilities. On *math* tests, in Grade 4, Asian/Pacific Islanders had slightly higher test scores (246 out of 500) than Whites (243) and both groups had higher scores than Native Americans (223), Latinos (222), and Blacks (216). On *reading* tests, however, Whites had the highest average scores (229 out of 300), followed very closely by Asian/Pacific Islanders (226), and then by Native Americans (202), Latinos (200), and Blacks (198).

Smaller-scale local studies. Huntsinger and colleagues (1997, 2000) studied the math skills of middle-class White American and second-generation Chinese American children during preschool and kindergarten and, again, 2 and 4 years later. For math, Chinese American children scored higher than did White American children on every subtest of the Sequential Assessment of Mathematics Inventory and at each of the three time points. For receptive English vocabulary, White children had higher scores than Chinese children at both time 1 and time 2, but at time 3, Chinese children had caught up to the White children. This catch-up in English skills by Chinese American children was remarkable given that they were children of immigrants.

Other studies have compared Asian ethnic groups on less traditional indicators of school performance, specifically qualification for gifted and talented education (GATE) services. Based on data from a large urban school district in 1998–1999, Kitano and DiJiosia (2000) found that although Asian Americans comprised 18% of the total enrollment, 21% of them qualified for GATE. Rates of GATE qualification varied by ethnicity: 40% to 50% of Chinese, Koreans, Asian Indians, and Japanese qualified, compared to 20% to 30% of Guamanian, Hawaiian, Filipino, Vietnamese; 13% to 16% of Laotians, Hmongs, and Cambodians; and 7% of Samoans.

Middle School

Findings from NAEP, NELS:88, and the smaller-scale Children of Immigrants Longitudinal Study (CILS) suggest that Asian Americans' achievement differs according to achievement indicator (i.e., grades, test scores, etc.) and domain of study (i.e., math, reading, etc.). These studies suggest that Asian Americans tend to achieve similar or higher grade point averages (GPAs) than Whites. Panethnic differences on standardized tests vary according to domain of study: Asian Americans achieve slightly higher scores on math, but slightly lower scores on reading and writing, than Whites. The NELS:88 and CILS studies also reveal ethnic differences among Asian Americans, with Chinese and Koreans having higher achievement than Filipinos, Japanese, and Southeast Asians, who sometimes have higher achievement than Pacific Islanders.

Nationally representative studies. The NAEP assessments of math and reading performance included 155,183 students in the eighth grade who were attending about 6,100 schools (NCES, 2004a, 2004b). The results at eighth grade paralleled those at fourth grade. On standardized math tests, Asian American children had the highest average scores (291 out of a possible 500 points), followed very closely by Whites (288), and then Native Americans (263), Latinos (259), and Blacks (252), in each year that math was assessed (1990, 1992, 2000, and 2003). On standardized reading tests, however, White children had the highest average scores (272), followed very closely by Asian Americans (270), and then Native Americans (246), Latinos (245), and Blacks (244).

NELS:88 also has yielded analyses on Asian American achievement. The original sample consisted of 24,599 eighth graders from 1,035 public and private schools. Achievement was assessed in terms of standardized test scores in math, science, reading, and social studies; and grades in English, math, science, and social studies. Based on these data, Kao, Tienda, and Schneider (1996) found that Asian Americans had higher GPAs than the other panethnic groups in Grades 6 and 8. In analyses of *composite* test scores in reading and math, studies also found that Asian Americans had similar scores as Whites and higher scores than Blacks, Latinos, and Native Americans (Kao et al., 1996; Peng & Wright, 1994).

Based on NELS:88 data, Kao (1995) examined standardized test scores among Whites and specific Asian Pacific ethnic groups: Chinese, Filipino, Japanese, Korean, Southeast Asian, Pacific Islander, South Asian, and West Asian. For both *reading* and *math* tests, Pacific

Islanders had lower scores than all the Asian groups. Chinese, Koreans, and Southeast Asians had higher math scores, but similar reading scores, as Whites. Filipinos, Japanese, South Asians, and West Asians had comparable math and reading scores as Whites. Pacific Islanders had lower math and reading scores than Whites. As for *grades*, Chinese, Koreans, Southeast Asians, and South Asians earned higher grades than Whites, whereas Filipinos, Japanese, Pacific Islanders, and West Asians earned similar grades as Whites. All these differences remained significant after controlling for socioeconomic status, gender, mother's immigrant status, and material and other educational resources.

Smaller-scale studies. Using their CILS data, Portes and Rumbaut (2001) compared the math and reading test scores and GPAs of Asian and Latino children of immigrants enrolled in 49 schools in the metropolitan areas of Miami–Ft. Lauderdale (Florida) and San Diego (California). Their analyses indicated differing patterns across standardized tests versus GPAs. For reading and math test scores, Chinese, Koreans, and Cubans in private schools scored the highest, followed by Filipino, Vietnamese, Nicaraguans, Colombians, West Indians, and Cubans in public schools; Laotian, Cambodian, Mexican, and Haitian students had the lowest test scores. Examination of GPAs indicated different ethnic patterns than those for standardized tests. GPAs were highest for Chinese and Koreans, followed by Filipinos, Vietnamese, Laotians and Cambodians, then Cubans in private schools, and then the other Latino and Caribbean groups. Portes and Rumbaut speculate grades may reveal different ethnic patterns because, unlike test scores, grades are influenced by teachers' evaluations of proper student conduct, demeanor, and work habits. Perhaps, as we discuss later, differences in grades are influenced partly by teachers' racially biased expectations of Asian American as compared to Latino and African American students.

High School

Research on Asian Americans' academic achievement has focused most often on high school students. Findings from the 12th-grade assessments of NAEP in 2000, follow-ups to NELS:88, and smaller-scale local studies suggest that the pattern of high grades during middle school extends into high school. Test score differences are more ambiguous, in part because studies do not consistently report test scores separately by domain of study. The large-scale national studies and smaller-scale local studies continue to indicate ethnic differences similar to those found in middle school; they also indicate generational differences.

Nationally representative studies. Similar to 4th- and 8th-grade assessments, the 12th-grade 2000 and 2002 NAEP assessments (NCES, 2001, 2002, 2003a, 2003b) revealed differences in achievement patterns depending on domain of study. For math, Asian Americans achieved the highest scores (319 out of a possible 500 points), followed by Whites (308), Native Americans (293), Latinos (283), and Blacks (274). For reading and writing, Whites had the highest average scores in both areas (292 and 154, respectively), followed by Asian Americans (286 and 151), Latinos (273 and 136) and Blacks (267 and 130). The NAEP 12th-grade assessment also included science; and in this domain, Whites (154) achieved similar scores as Asian Americans (153); both had higher scores than Native Americans (139), Latinos (128), and Blacks (123).

In the NELS:88 study, 8th-grade students were followed up when most of the cohort was in the 10th and then 12th grades. Studies examining GPAs (self-reported grades in four subject areas) found that Asian Americans had higher GPAs in 10th grade than did Whites, Blacks, and Latinos (Kao, 1995; Kao & Thompson, 2003; Kao et al., 1996). By the 12th grade, however, Broh (2002) found that White students had similar math grades as Asian Americans, after controlling for achievement in the 10th grade, socioeconomic factors, gender, participation in interscholastic sports, and school characteristics. Both groups' math grades remained higher than those of African Americans, Latinos, and Native Americans.

NELS:88 studies examining *composite* test scores suggest that Asian Americans' achievement might be rising, relative to Whites, as they move through high school. Recall that Peng and

Wright (1994) found that Asian Americans in 8th grade had similar *composite* reading and math scores as Whites. By the 10th grade, however, Mau (1997) found that Asian Americans were higher than Whites in their composite test scores. By the 12th grade, Asian Americans still had higher test scores than Whites, Blacks, Latinos, and Native Americans, after controlling for 10th-grade test scores and socioeconomic and other demographic factors (Broh, 2002).

Blair and Qian (1998) compared the GPAs of 12th graders across different Asian American ethnic groups using NELS:88 data. They found that Chinese received the highest GPAs, followed closely by Koreans and South Asians, and then Japanese and Filipinos. Also relying on NELS data, Zhang (2003) examined generational differences among Asian Americans on standardized tests of math, reading, science, and social studies. At each grade level (10th, 11th, and 12th), there were no significant differences between first- and second-generation students on any of the tests, except reading, even after accounting for socioeconomic status, ethnicity, and language factors. These first- and second-generation students, however, outperformed third-generation students in math and science, after controlling for the same factors. In addition, Zhang examined generational differences in the rates of *change* in test scores. First- and second-generation students had similar growth rates in math, reading, and science, and their growth rates in math and science were significantly greater than that for third-generation students.

Smaller-scale, local studies. As part of a longitudinal study of over 4,000 9th graders from eight southern California high schools, Kanatsu and Chao (2005) examined the achievement of first- and second-generation students of Chinese, Korean, Filipino, and Mexican backgrounds, as well as that of third- and higher-generation European Americans. They found that first- and second-generation Chinese were comparable to each other in overall GPAs and grades in English/history and math/science. They also had higher GPAs and subject area grades than first- and second-generation Korean, Filipino, and Mexican Americans. Both generations of Chinese and Korean Americans had higher GPAs and grades than later-generation European Americans. First- and second-generation Filipino Americans had comparable GPAs and grades as European Americans, whereas both generations of Mexican Americans had lower grades than European Americans. For standardized math tests, both generations of Chinese and Korean Americans had higher scores than all other groups. Both generations of Filipino Americans were comparable to later-generation European Americans, and these groups were higher than both generations of Mexican Americans. For reading and language tests, both generations of Chinese, second-generation Koreans, and later-generation European Americans achieved similar scores; first-generation Koreans and both generations of Filipinos had somewhat lower scores, followed by both generations of Mexican Americans. Other studies also report higher math scores and grades for Chinese and East Asians than for other Asian ethnic groups, even after accounting for socioeconomic and generational status, and language fluency (Fuligni, 1997; Fuligni & Witkow, 2004; Mouw & Xie, 1999).

Studies have not found consistent differences between first- and second-generation students. Kanatsu and Chao (2005) found differences only among Korean Americans, such that first-generation Korean students had higher grades in *math/science* than did second-generation Korean students. However, second-generation Korean students had higher *reading* and *language* test scores than did first-generation Korean students. In another study of high school students by Chao (2001), first-generation Chinese Americans had higher overall GPAs than did the second generation.

ADDITIONAL OUTCOMES: DROPOUTS AND COURSE SELECTION

The HS&B study provided base-year information on about 28,000 students who were high school seniors in 1980. About 12,000 students were followed up in 1982, 1984, and 1986. Based on these data, Kao and Thompson (2003) reported that Asian Americans had the lowest percentage of dropouts (14%), compared to Whites (17%), Native Americans (29%), Mexican Americans (28%), and Puerto Ricans (26%). These findings were replicated using the NELS:88 data and in a smaller study of northern California high schools (Kao et al., 1996; Rumberger, Ghatak, Poulos, Ritter, & Dornbusch, 1990).

Using HS&B data, Kao and Thompson (2003) also found that a greater proportion of Asian American high school seniors (51%) were likely to be in college preparatory courses, as compared to White (46%), Black (36%), Latino (31%), and Native American (23%) seniors. In a study of two high schools in northern California, Fuligni (1997) found that a greater proportion of East Asian 10th graders (40%) were taking advanced math classes than Filipinos (20%), Whites (20%), and Latinos (7%). East Asians (over 80%) were also more likely to be in college placement English classes than were Filipinos (58%), Whites (48%), and Latinos (24%).

College

Although the studies discussed in the previous paragraphs found that Asian Americans have the same or higher grades than Whites in elementary, middle, and high school, this is not the case in college. In this next section, we review achievement according to grades, college entrance exams, and college persistence and graduation using studies based on nationally representative data sets (i.e., HS&B, BPS: 96/01), as well as studies of specific universities and the University of California system.

Grades. Sue and Abe (1988) reported on the high school and college GPAs of Asian American and White students enrolled in the eight University of California campuses in 1984. Although Asian American freshmen had higher high school GPAs than did White freshmen, the two groups had similar GPAs in their first year of college (2.74 and 2.72, respectively). Other studies also report similar college GPAs for Asian Americans and Whites, and higher college GPAs for Asian Americans compared to other students of color (Castro & Rice, 2003; Tan, 1994).

Additional studies have reported lower college GPAs for Asian Americans than Whites or non-Asians (Ahn Toupin & Son, 1991; Tseng, 2005; Ying et al., 2001). Research only on

students at the University of California, Berkeley, found that Whites had higher GPAs (3.18) than Asian Americans (3.05) who had higher GPAs than Latinos (2.86) and African Americans (2.71) (Ying et al., 2001). A study by Ahn Toupin and Son (1991) of all Asian American students in the College of Arts and Science at a small, private, highly selective university in the Northeast in 1984, 1985, and 1986 found that Asian Americans had lower GPAs than non-Asians (matched on socioeconomic background and SAT scores). Asian Americans also were more likely to be placed on academic probation and less likely to ever appear on the dean's list. A study by Tseng (2005), based on a sample of 1,200 students who entered a large urban university in the Northeast in 1996 and 1998, found that Whites had higher college GPAs than Asian Americans, who had similar GPAs to Latinos and Blacks. The lower college GPAs of Asian Americans was particularly stark when set against the fact that they began college with higher GPAs and SAT scores than Whites.

Tseng (2005) examined whether lower college GPAs among Asian Americans was due to their greater likelihood of being enrolled in math and science majors where, on average, students receive lower grades than in other majors. Other studies have confirmed that a greater proportion of Asian Americans than other panethnic groups enroll in math and science majors and courses (Ahn Toupin & Son, 1991; Tan, 1994; Tseng, 2005; Xie & Goyette, 2003). Tseng found that even after accounting for majors, there remained a significant difference in GPAs between Asian American and White American students. Moreover, part of this difference was associated with Asian Americans' greater perceptions of prejudice and discrimination on campus.

College entrance exams. In their report of all freshmen enrolled in the eight University of California campuses, Sue and Abe (1988) found that Asian Americans had higher math scores and lower verbal scores than Whites, on both the SAT and College Board Achievement Tests. More current data on incoming freshmen, compiled by institutional research offices at the University of California campuses in Los Angeles (Office of Analysis and Information

Management, 2004) and Berkeley (Office of Student Research, 2000), also indicated that incoming Asian Americans had lower SAT verbal scores than Whites but higher math scores. However, Asian American and White differences in verbal scores diminished from 47 to 17 points between 1991 and 2004 among UCLA students, and from 50 to 10 points between 1983 and 2000 among UC Berkeley students. It is important to note that these differences pertain to students admitted to and enrolled in these universities, and may not be generalizable to students who did not apply to the university or who applied and were not accepted.

In their analyses of the University of California campuses, Sue and Abe (1988) reported on the high school GPAs and SAT scores of different Asian Pacific ethnic groups. In high school, Indians and Pakistanis had the highest GPAs (3.8), followed by Japanese (3.75) and Chinese (3.73), and then Filipinos (3.56). All Asian Pacific groups, except Filipinos, had higher mean GPAs than Whites (3.59). For SAT scores, Indians and Pakistanis had the highest verbal scores (520), followed by Japanese (511), Chinese (473), and Koreans (418), whereas Chinese had the highest math scores (612), followed by Indians and Pakistanis (606), Japanese (604), and Koreans (594). Only Indians and Pakistanis had higher verbal scores than Whites (512), whereas all the Asian Pacific ethnic groups except Filipinos had higher math scores than Whites (577).

College persistence and graduation. Based on the third follow-up of HS&B, Porter (1990) reported on undergraduate graduation rates for students who attended a 4-year baccalaureate-granting institution at some point between 1980 and 1986. Asian Americans (42%) and European Americans (44%) were more likely to have graduated or completed college within 6 years after high school than were Latinos (20%) and Blacks (24%). Also, Asian Americans were least likely to leave school in the critical first semester or first year of college, especially those who attended public institutions. Less than 10% of Asian Americans dropped out in their first year of college, compared to approximately 20% of Whites, 25% of Blacks, and 27% of Latinos.

In 1996 through 2001, the BPS: 96/01 collected data on student persistence, progress, and attainment. The sample included traditional and nontraditional (older) students and was representative of all beginning students in postsecondary education. Based on these data, Snyder, Tan, and Hoffman (2004) found that 58% of all students who enrolled in a 4-year college in 1995–1996 had completed a bachelor's degree by 2001. Asian Americans had the highest rates of completion (69%), followed by Whites (62%), Native Americans (53%), Latinos (44%), and Blacks (43%).

Thomson (1998) also reported the graduation rates of entering students in 1983 to 1992 at the University of California, Berkeley: 91% of Asian American freshman completed their undergraduate degree within six years or less, compared to 86% of European Americans, 79% of Native Americans, 78% of Latinos, and 72% of African Americans. Among Asian Americans, Thompson (1998) found the highest completion rates among Pacific Islanders, Chinese, and Japanese (93%), followed by Indians and Pakistanis (90%), Koreans (88%), and Filipinos (87%).

On the other hand, Ahn Toupin and Son's (1991) study of Asian American students at a private, highly selective university in the Northeast found that they were less likely to graduate than were their matched non-Asian counterparts. It is possible that Asian Americans attending private universities in the Northeast may be more likely to leave college than those in public universities on the West Coast. Porter (1990) found that the greatest proportion of students who remained on track in their education are Asian Americans at public universities (89%) and that a much larger proportion of Asian Americans attended universities on the West coast than in other areas of the country. Perhaps the high representation of Asian Americans in many California public universities fosters a welcoming atmosphere that promotes Asian American retention.

FUTURE RESEARCH ON ACADEMIC ACHIEVEMENT

Our review suggests several directions for the next generation of research. First, findings indicate that Asian Americans, as a whole, are doing well in school, but there is significant variability across subgroups of Asian Americans that warrants further study. The next generation of studies should include more routine data collection and analysis of ethnic, immigrant/refugee, and socioeconomic diversity among Asian Americans. Studies should focus on the achievement of Southeast Asians and Pacific Islanders, low-income Asians, and the children of refugees and immigrants. Ethnicity, migration, and social class are confounded, but not completely so. Whereas Cambodians and Hmongs are often children of war refugees and are more likely to live in poverty, Chinese are economically bifurcated with 40% of immigrants from mainland China not having high school degrees compared to 8% of those from Taiwan and 18% of those from Hong Kong (Reeves & Bennett, 2004; Zhou, 2003).

National studies might need to include additional factors that can explain achievement differences between Asian Americans, or subgroups of them, and Whites. The demographic factors assessed in national studies are more useful for explaining differences between Whites and Latinos or Whites and Blacks, but they do not explain differences between Asians and Whites. In addition to national data sets, data collection at the level of school districts and entire schools may be fruitful given that Asian Americans are concentrated in select metropolitan areas. Studies such as Portes and Rumbaut (2001) and Chao (2005) uniquely allow for comparisons of diverse ethnic groups (i.e., Chinese, Filipino, Laotian, Mexican, Cuban, Haitian, etc.) that constitute panethnic labels.

Overall, Asian Americans tend to score lower than, or similar to, Whites in reading and verbal tests but higher in overall GPAs and math tests. Differences in grades are found in later elementary, middle, and high school but disappear in college. Future research should empirically investigate why achievement differs across domains of study (i.e., reading, math, etc.), and why Asian Americans' achievement seems to drop off, relative to Whites, in college. Future studies may benefit from closer examination of how immigration affects achievement given that 88% of Asian Americans, compared to 11% of European Americans, are children of foreign-born parents (Schmidley, 2001). Concentrating on math rather than reading skills might be associated more closely with being an immigrant than with being Asian per se. In addition, longitudinal studies following students from high school to college can illuminate the features of the college transition that impinge on Asian Americans' achievement.

RACISM AND INTERGROUP RELATIONS IN SCHOOLS

Academic success among Asian American students often has been interpreted to signify that they are unencumbered by racism and discrimination—either it does not impact them or they do not experience it. Instead, it has been argued that Asian Americans' cultural values regarding hard work, family, and the importance of education are responsible for their success (Lee, 1996). In arguing against a purely cultural explanation, Sue and Okazaki (1990) propose a theory of "relative functionalism," suggesting that academic pursuits do not signify lack of racism but are a reaction to racial, cultural, and political barriers. Asian Americans, they argue, pursue education because they perceive blocked mobility in non-educational endeavors. Xie and Goyette (2003) build on this theory, arguing that Asian Americans respond to these barriers not simply by pursuing formal education but by pursuing particular fields of study that are in high demand in the economy. Xie and Goyette provide empirical evidence for this favoring of particular fields of study, but little empirical work has directly examined the influence of racial barriers on Asian Americans' educational pursuits.

In contrast to the voluminous body of work on Asian Americans' academic achievement, fewer studies have examined Asian Americans' racial experiences with school staff and peers. This work is critically important, given alarming reports of race-related bullying and violence against Asian American students (Texeira, 2005) and findings that peer harassment is associated with school absenteeism, depression, and loneliness (Juvonen, Nishina, & Graham, 2000). Findings from qualitative and ethnographic studies resonate with reports by civil rights groups and community organizations. The Asian American Legal Defense and Education Fund, for example, has filed complaints charging school officials in New York City with ignoring peer harassment of Chinese and Pakistani students and racial profiling of South Asian and Muslim students following September 11, 2001, and in Lowell, Massachusetts, of "pushing out" low-achieving Southeast Asian students by encouraging them to drop out or enter a GED program (Aung, personal communication, November 23, 2005). In California, the Services and Advocacy for Asian Youth Consortium (2004) and Asian and Pacific Islander Youth Violence Prevention Center (2003) have identified school-based, race-related violence, as a critical issue confronting Asian American youth. Following high profile cases of anti-Asian violence, the New York City Council passed legislation to track bullying and train educators in its prevention, and the California State Assembly extended the time limit for hate crime victims to file civil suits (Texeira, 2005).

In the next section, we review research on Asian American students' experiences with racism in schools and their potential implications for bullying, violence, and teasing. Whereas the previous section on academic achievement drew on a large literature of quantitative findings from nationally representative data sets, the following review draws predominantly on ethnographic and qualitative research in local schools. These studies are conducted primarily in urban high schools and provide in-depth analyses of students' lived experiences in these schools. Before reviewing that work, we discuss the broader social and economic context of schools.

SOCIAL AND ECONOMIC CONTEXT OF SCHOOLS

Resegregation of schools since the 1970s has meant that large numbers of low-income Asian Americans and other children of color are concentrated in poor, often urban, schools in a handful of states (Suarez-Orozco & Suarez-Orozco, 2001; Zhou & Bankston, 1998). Very often, these Asian American students are immigrants, refugees, or the U.S-born children of immigrants or refugees (Schmidley, 2001). The 2000 Census reveals that 60% of Asian immigrants reside in

only six states: California, New York, Hawai'i, New Jersey, Texas, and Washington (Modarres, 2003; Ong & Leung, 2003). Within these states, newer Asian immigrants often are concentrated within metropolitan areas that have also witnessed a large influx of other immigrant groups (Modarres, 2003). Among groups such as Chinese in San Francisco and New York, there is a socioeconomic bifurcation, with some ethnic Chinese attending middle-class schools and others attending poor schools in and around Chinatowns (Orfield et al., 1999, in Suarez-Orozco & Suarez-Orozco, 2001). Southeast Asians have the highest poverty rates among Asian Americans (i.e., 40% among Hmongs, 30% among Cambodians, and 20% among Laotians), and they often are concentrated in smaller cities, such as Fresno, Sacramento, and Minneapolis–St. Paul for Hmongs; Long Beach, Stockton, Seattle, Boston, Philadelphia, and Providence for Cambodians; and the San Francisco Bay Area, Seattle, Minneapolis–St. Paul, Dallas–Ft. Worth, and Boston for Laotians (Reeves & Bennett, 2004; Thongthiraj, 2003).

Substantial numbers of Asian Americans also attend suburban middle-class schools, but low-income Asian American children, many of them immigrants and refugees, attend schools in large urban school districts confronting major fiscal challenges (McDonnell & Hill, 1993). Together with low-income Latino and African American students, low-income Asian immigrants and refugees find themselves contending with dilapidated buildings, overcrowded classrooms, and underfunded schools, left behind by "White flight" from urban school districts and economic restructuring (Ong & Wing, 1996; Zhou & Bankston, 1998).

Some research suggests that Asian Americans, often Southeast Asian refugees, attending large urban schools feel unsafe in their school environments. In San Diego schools, Portes and Rumbaut (2001) found that Laotian and Cambodian refugees perceived their schools to be less safe and to include more race-related fights than did Chinese, Filipino, Mexican, and Central American students. Vietnamese youths' perceptions of school unsafety fell in the middle. These ethnic differences are important to document, but more clarity is needed on whether Southeast Asian students are concentrated in more dangerous schools than are other Asians or whether they are exposed to (or perceive) greater danger in the same schools as other Asians.

In analyses of NELS:88, Kao (1999) found that children of Asian immigrants, like their Latino counterparts, felt more alienated from their school peers than did later-generation White students. Part of the difference in Latino and White students' feelings of alienation was related to their socioeconomic status, but SES accounted for little of the difference between Asian American and White students. Kao also analyzed ethnic group differences and found that Chinese felt more alienated than did Whites, but Filipinos did not differ from Whites. Again, these differences in students' sense of alienation are important to document, but research needs to replicate these findings and to examine why Asian Americans, or subgroups of them, feel alienated from their school peers. As suggested below, Asian youths' feelings of unsafety and alienation in school might be partly related to racial stereotypes, bullying, and teasing.

Experiences With Teachers and Peers

Research on teacher expectations has focused more often on teachers' perceptions of African American and Latino students than of Asian American students. A number of studies, however, suggest that teachers conjointly construct their expectations for racial groups, particularly in mixed-race schools. That is, teachers' expectations of African American and Latino students as academically unsuccessful are often constructed in contrast to their expectations of Asian American students as academically successful (Gibson, 1988). Rosenbloom and Way (2004) argue that these racial constructions of students within classrooms affect students' interactions as they step out of classes and into peer-dominated spaces such as hallways, lunchrooms, and school buses. Specifically, they suggest that teachers' preferences for Asian American students in the classroom become a source of resentment that is channeled, at times, into verbal and physical harassment of Asian American students outside the classroom.

In interviews with students about their discrimination experiences, Rosenbloom and Way (2004) found that Asian American students most often described discriminatory incidents involving their peers. In contrast, African American and Latino adolescents more often described discriminatory incidents involving adults: teachers, storekeepers, and police officers. From the perspective of African American and Latino students, teachers favored and had higher academic expectations for Asian American students than they did for African American and Latino students. This favoring of Asian Americans by teachers contributed to interracial tensions between Asian American students and their African American and Latino peers.

In interviews, teachers frequently describe their perceptions of Asian American students as respectful, well behaved, and unquestioning of teacher authority (Gibson, 1988; Lee, 1996; Schneider & Lee, 1990). In her ethnographic study, Lee (1996) quotes a science teacher who says that "he liked Asian American students because they were 'easy to teach and don't cause any trouble'" (p. 62). The teacher later adds, "Of course, some Asians aren't as good. But even those who cut class—at least they don't flaunt it in your face. They are even respectful about that. Anyway, most of my Asians are good, hard-working students" (p. 66).

Peers, like teachers, express contrasting race-related attitudes about Asian American students as compared to African American and Latino students (Kao, 2000; Lee, 1996). In focus groups, African American, Latino, and White high school students described the group image of Asian Americans as "smart," "incredibly brilliant in math and science," and "quiet" (pp. 417–418). Youths' group image of Latinos focused on manual labor: "cleaning floors" and "cutting grass" (p. 419). Group images of African Americans were constructed in contrast to Whites: "acting Black" was seen as "not as intelligent as white people," "ghetto," and "don't know how to behave" (Kao, 2000, p. 416). As with teacher expectations, students' predominant images of Asian American, Latino, and African American students were as unitary groups, constructed in contrasting terms to one another.

In describing themselves, Asian American youth make sharp distinctions regarding their peer groups, perhaps partly in reaction to the stereotypes and discrimination they experience. In Lee's (1996) interviews, Asian American students used the markers of ethnicity, language, class, acculturation, dress, and sociopolitical beliefs to create their separate peer groups of "Koreans," "Asians," "New Wavers," and "Asian Americans." Asians, Koreans, and Asian Americans all distinguished themselves from the New Wavers who tended to be recent immigrants and refugees from working-class families. Pyke and Dang (2003) examined the ways that Asian Americans also internalize anti-Asian racism and derogatory racial stereotypes. Their use of derogatory terms for recent immigrants as "FOBs" (fresh-off-the-boat) and for U.S.-born youth as "white-washed" ("acting White") reflects the racial stereotypes perpetuated in the larger, White-dominated society.

BULLYING, VIOLENCE, AND TEASING

Scholars working in a number of urban high schools note that Asian American students are often the targets of verbal and physical harassment by their peers from other racial groups (Gibson, 1988; Ima, 1995; Lee, 1996; Rosenbloom & Way, 2004; Tuan, 1995). Often concentrated in poor, racially mixed urban settings, Asian American, African American, Latino, and working-class White students experience intergroup tensions within the U.S. racial and social class hierarchy. In interviews in a poor urban high school (Rosenbloom & Way, 2004), Asian American students described "slappings"—quick strikes to the head or body—by male and female peers as they walked through hallways. Students also reported being pushed, punched, teased, and mocked, at times with slurs such as "chino" or "geek." Asian American students described being viewed as weaker and smaller than other students, and robbed in school by their peers. Gibson (1988), too, found that Punjabi students in an agricultural community were abused physically and verbally, with students refusing to sit next to Punjabis in class, crowding ahead of them in lines, throwing food at them, sticking them with pins, telling them they stink, and harassing boys for wearing turbans.

Harassment also takes the form of verbal taunting, teasing, and ethnic slurs. In their narratives, new Asian groups such as Hmongs report being called "Chink" and "Jap" (Chan, 1994). Verbal harassment sometimes centers on students' immigrant status, being told to "go back to where you came from" and teased for having Asian accents and Asian names. Asian American Studies scholars Chan (1994) and Espiritu (1995) note that racism against Asian Americans often involves ridiculing language, such as using singsong pidgin English to represent the speech of Asian immigrants.

Less research has examined intergroup relations in middle-class schools that have substantial populations of Asian American and White students. Lee's (1996) study within a competitive, special-admit urban high school suggests that discrimination might take the form of racial teasing and jokes (e.g., "busting") of Asian American and other students of color by White students. Many of the Asian American students reported discomfort with the jokes but did not challenge them; others refused to participate in the jokes but were then considered humorless by White students. Still other Asian Americans joined in or initiated the racial jokes, and Lee observed that it was this latter group who were often befriended by White students. On college campuses, Asian American students also have been the targets of more extreme forms of racial harassment. Higher-education scholar, Chang (2003), describes

> an email message sent to Asian American students and staff members at the University of California at Irvine, warning them to leave the campus, and threatening that if they did not, "I personally will make it my life career to find and kill every one of you personally" (October, 1996); and explicit pornography depicting Asian females printed on the front page of the student newspaper at the University of Massachusetts Boston (November, 1997). (p. 207)

At the University of Michigan (September, 2005), a White student was accused of urinating on two Asian American students walking below his apartment balcony, and shouting "you need to learn English" (George, 2005). Interracial tensions within schools may reflect those relationships in the broader community context. In cities such as Los Angeles and New York, where African American and Latino neighborhood residents and Korean American storeowners have experienced conflict, community tensions may manifest themselves among youth in schools. Lee (1996), for example, argues that intergroup tension between Korean American and African American students parallels the tensions involving Korean-owned businesses in African American neighborhoods, with some African American students describing Asian American students' success as being at the expense of African Americans. For example, Lee quotes an African American informant who explains, "a lot of people I know don't like Asian people. . . . They say, they came over here and they bought up everything and now look at them in school" (p. 99). Interracial tensions and violence also have increased in newer Asian immigrant destinations, such as Fresno, California, where many Hmong and other Southeast Asian refugees have settled (Chan, 1994).

FUTURE RESEARCH ON RACISM AND INTERGROUP RELATIONS IN SCHOOLS

Our review of research suggests that the model minority stereotype of Asian Americans is evident in teachers' and peers' attitudes in U.S. high schools. While this may not be surprising or novel, scholars theorize that these stereotyped expectations for Asian American success contribute to peer harassment (Gibson, 1988; Rosenbloom & Way, 2004). They argue that school staff's stereotyped expectations of Asian American, Latino, and African American students can become channeled into acts of peer aggression as students move from the classroom into the peer-dominated spaces of lunchrooms, hallways, and school buses. In some instances, peer aggression takes the form of physical violence and, in other instances, teasing and racial jokes. Moreover, interracial tensions among students are situated within broader community contexts, in which Asian immigrants move into under-resourced urban and rural communities in which other communities of color also are concentrated.

Although it may be tempting as psychologists to focus on the attitudes and behaviors of teachers and students, we also need to study schools and classrooms in an effort to identify the features of these settings that create and/or maintain racism and intergroup tensions. While individuals can express racist attitudes and behaviors, schools vary greatly in the social practices, policies, and processes that support or counter individuals' attitudes and behaviors. Ethnographic research is well suited for identifying the social practices, policies, and processes within classrooms and schools that contribute to interracial tensions and can aid in the development of quantitative and standardized observational measures of those setting features. Such mixed-method approaches are valuable for examining the dynamics and course of intergroup tensions. For example, what are the characteristics of teacher-student interactions that communicate stereotypes about Asian American, African American, and Latino students? What are schools' official and unofficial policies that support or counter race-related bullying, violence, and teasing? And how can interventions alter these setting-level aspects of school racism?

BROADER CONTEXT OF EDUCATION RESEARCH ON ASIAN AMERICANS AND IMPLICATIONS OF THE MODEL MINORITY STEREOTYPE

We began this chapter with a sociohistorical context for the model minority stereotype. Although the stereotype is less blatantly invoked by scholars and the media today than a few decades ago, it is still reflected in contemporary classroom and school experiences (Suzuki, 2002). Depictions and examinations of Asian Americans' educational experiences have tended to focus only on their academic achievement. This overemphasis on academic achievement obscures attention to interracial tensions and race-related violence directed at Asian Americans in schools, and ignores the harmful consequences of those experiences.

The model minority stereotype first gained prominence in the late 1960s, a time of visible political struggle against racial and class inequality. Then, and now, stereotypes of Asian Americans' ability to succeed based solely on hard work, smarts, and uncomplaining persever-ance obfuscate the structural challenges plaguing public schools. It also serves to pit the academic achievement of Asian Americans against that of their African American and Latino peers. Propagation of the model minority thesis for Asian Americans deflects attention away from the impact of societal forces, such as resegrega-tion and economic restructuring, on poor urban schools. In 1987, an article in *Time* magazine reported that

> the largely successful Asian-American experience is a challenging counterpoint to the charges that U.S. schools are now producing less-educated mainstream students and failing to help underclass Blacks and Latinos. One old lesson apparently still holds. "It doesn't really matter where you come from or what your language is," observes Educational Historian Diane Ravitch. "If you arrive with high aspirations and self-discipline, schools are a path to upward mobility." (Brand, 1987, p. 49)

Another problem with the model minority stereotype is that it is used to overgeneralize to all members of a group, including some who are struggling academically. We have little under-standing of how lower-performing Asian Americans are affected by the burden of the stereotype, but scholars suggest that the stereo-type may make it difficult for teachers and school staff to identify Asian American students who need assistance (Lee, 1996; Rosenbloom & Way, 2004; Suzuki, 2002). Even among those Asian Americans who succeed through high school, initial studies indicate that they may experience challenges in the transition to col-lege, perhaps particularly at elite Northeast uni-versities where Asians may feel more alienation, competition, and discrimination.

More broadly, the model minority stereotype may affect the ways in which students view themselves and understand their community's history. Educational curriculum rarely acknowl-edges Asian Americans as political actors who challenged inequality in schools through legal advocacy and collective action. The model minority image of Asian Americans' uncom-plaining perseverance in the face of adversity may further obscure Asian American youths'

knowledge and sense of connection with their predecessors who led struggles for justice in the U.S. education system (Omatsu, 1994; Rhoads, Lee, & Yamada, 2002; Wollenberg, 1978).

REFERENCES

Ahn Toupin, E. S. W., & Son, L. (1991). Preliminary findings on Asian Americans: The model minor-ity in a small private East Coast College. *Journal of Cross-Cultural Psychology, 22*(3), 403–417.

Asian Pacific Islander Youth Violence Prevention Center. (2003). *Under the microscope: Asian and Pacific Islander youth in Oakland* (Executive summary). Retrieved February 9, 2005, from www.api-center.org

Blair, S. L., & Qian, Z. (1998). Family and Asian students' educational performance: A considera-tion of diversity. *Journal of Family Issues, 19*(4), 355–374.

Brand, D. (1987, August 31). Those Asian-American whiz kids. *Time, 130*(9), 42–49.

Broh, B. A. (2002). Linking extracurricular program-ming to academic achievement: Who benefits and why? *Sociology of Education, 75*(1), 69–95.

Castro, J. R., & Rice, K. G. (2003). Perfectionism and ethnicity implications for depressive symptoms and self-reported academic achievement. *Cultural Diversity & Ethnic Minority Psychology, 9,* 64–78.

Chan, S. (1994). *Hmong means free: Life in Laos and America.* Philadelphia: Temple University Press.

Chang, M. (2003). Education. In E. Lai & D. Arguelles (Eds.), *The new face of Asian Pacific America* (pp. 203–208). San Francisco: AsianWeek Books.

Chao, R. K. (1996). Chinese and European-American mothers' beliefs about the role of parenting in children's school success. *Journal of Cross-Cultural Psychology, 27,* 403–423.

Chao, R. K. (2000). Cultural explanations for the role of parenting in the school success of Asian American children. In R. W. Taylor & M. C. Wang (Eds.), *Resilience across contexts* (pp. 333–363). Mahwah, NJ: Lawrence Erlbaum.

Chao, R. K. (2001). Extending research on the conse-quences of parenting style for Chinese Americans and European Americans. *Child Development, 72*(6), 1832–1843.

Chao, R. K. (2005, April). The importance of guan in describing the parental control of immigrant

Chinese. In R. Chao & H. Fung (Chairs), *Cultural perspectives of Chinese socialization.* Symposium conducted at the biennial meeting of the Society for Research in Child Development, Atlanta, GA.

Chao, R. K., & Tseng, V. (2002). Parenting of Asians. In M. H. Bornstein (Ed.), *Handbook of parenting: Vol. 4. Social conditions and applied parenting* (2nd ed., pp. 59–93). Mahwah, NJ: Lawrence Erlbaum.

Espiritu, Y. L. (1992). *Asian American panethnicity.* Philadelphia: Temple University Press.

Espiritu, Y. L. (1995). *Filipino American lives.* Philadelphia: Temple University Press.

Fuligni, A. J. (1997). The academic achievement of adolescences from immigrant families: The roles of family background, attitudes, and behavior. *Child Development, 68,* 351–363.

Fuligni, A. J., & Witkow, M. (2004). The post-secondary educational progress of youth from immigrant families. *Journal of Research on Adolescence, 14,* 159–183.

George, M. (2005, September 23). University officials asked to step in. *Detroit Free Press.* Retrieved November 23, 2005, from http://umichstopthehate.blogspot.com/2005/09/story-hits-detroit-free-press.html

Gibson, M. A. (1988). *Accommodation without assimilation.* Ithaca, NY: Cornell University Press.

Huntsinger, C. S., Jose, P. E., Larson, S. L., Balsink Krieg, D., & Shaligram, C. (2000). Mathematics, vocabulary, and reading development in Chinese American and European American children over the primary school years. *Journal of Educational Psychology, 92,* 745–760.

Huntsinger, C. S., Jose, P. E., Liaw, F., & Ching, W. (1997). Cultural differences in early mathematics learning: A comparison of Euro-American, Chinese-American, and Taiwan-Chinese families. *International Journal of Behavioral Development, 21,* 371–387.

Ima, K. (1995). Testing the American dream: Case studies of at-risk Southeast Asian refugee students in secondary schools. In R. G. Rumbaut & W. A. Cornelius (Eds.), *California's immigrant children* (pp. 191–208). San Diego: University of California, San Diego, Center for U.S.-Mexican Studies.

Juvonen, J., Nishina, A., & Graham, S. (2000). Peer harassment, psychological adjustment, and school functioning in early adolescence. *Journal of Educational Psychology, 92,* 349–359.

Kanatsu, A., & Chao, R. K. (2005, April). The influence of parental involvement in school on the academic achievement of Asian immigrant high school students. In J. Rodriguez (Chair), *Parental involvement in school for ethnic minority and immigrant students.* Symposium conducted at the biennial meeting of the Society for Research in Child Development, Atlanta, GA.

Kao, G. (1995). Asian Americans as model minorities? A look at their academic performance. *American Journal of Education, 103,* 121–159.

Kao, G. (1999). Psychological well-being and educational achievement among immigrant youth. In D. J. Hernandez (Ed.), *Children of immigrants: Health, adjustment, and public assistance.* Washington, DC: National Academy Press.

Kao, G. (2000). Group images and possible selves among adolescents: Linking students to expectations by race and ethnicity. *Sociological Forum, 15*(3), p. 407–430.

Kao, G., & Thompson, J. S. (2003). Racial and ethnic stratification in educational achievement and attainment. *Annual Review of Sociology, 29,* 417–442.

Kao, G., Tienda, M., & Schneider, B. (1996). Racial and ethnic variation in academic performance. In A. M. Pallas (Ed.), *Research in sociology of education and socialization, 11,* 263–297.

Kitano, M. K., & DiJiosia, M. (2000). Are Asian and Pacific Americans over represented in programs for the gifted? *Roeper Review: A Journal on Gifted Education, 24,* 76–80.

Lee, S. J. (1996). *Unraveling the "model minority" stereotype: Listening to Asian American youth.* New York: Teachers College Press.

Lee, V. E., & Burkham, D. T. (2002). *Inequality at the starting gate: Social background differences in achievement as children begin school.* New York: Economic Policy Institute.

Leong, F. T. L., Chao, R. K., & Hardin, E. (2000). Asian American adolescents: A research review to dispel the model minority myth. In R. Montemayor (Ed.), *Advances in adolescent development: Vol. 10. Adolescent experiences: Cultural and economic diversity in adolescent development* (pp. 179–207). Thousand Oaks, CA: Sage.

Mau, W. (1997). Parental influences on the high school students' academic achievement: A comparison of Asian immigrants, Asian Americans, and white Americans. *Psychology in the Schools, 34,* 267–277.

McDonnell, L. M., & Hill, P. T. (1993). *Newcomers in American schools.* Santa Monica, CA: Institute on Education and Training, Center for Research on Immigration Policy, RAND.

Modarres, A. (2003). Immigration. In E. Lai & D. Arguelles (Eds.), *The new face of Asian Pacific America* (pp. 23–26). San Francisco: AsianWeek Books.

Mouw, T., & Xie, Y. (1999). Bilingualism and the academic achievement of first and second generation Asian Americans: Accommodation with or without assimilation? *American Sociological Review, 64,* 232–252.

Nakanishi, D. (2001). Moving the historical movement forward. In S. Louie & G. Omatsu (Eds.), *Asian Americans: The movement and the moment* (pp. viii–x). Los Angeles: UCLA Asian American Studies Center Press.

National Center for Education Statistics. (2001). *The National Assessment of Educational Progress (NAEP). The Nation's Report Card. Mathematics 2000.* U.S. Department of Education, Office of Educational Research and Improvement. Washington, DC: Author.

National Center for Education Statistics. (2002). *The National Assessment of Educational Progress (NAEP). Science Highlights. The Nation's Report Card 2000.* U.S. Department of Education, Office of Educational Research and Improvement. Washington, DC: Author.

National Center for Education Statistics. (2003a). *The National Assessment of Educational Progress (NAEP). The Nation's Report Card. Reading Highlights 2002. 2002 reading trends differ by grade.* U.S. Department of Education, Institute of Education Sciences. Washington, DC: Author.

National Center for Education Statistics. (2003b). *The National Assessment of Educational Progress (NAEP). The Nation's Report Card. Writing Highlights 2002. Fourth- and eighth-grade students make gains in writing since 1998.* U.S. Department of Education, Institute of Education Sciences. Washington, DC: Author.

National Center for Education Statistics. (2004a). *The National Assessment of Educational Progress (NAEP). The Nation's Report Card. Mathematics Highlights 2003. Fourth- and eighth-graders' average mathematics scores increase.* U.S. Department of Education, Institute of Education Sciences. Washington, DC: Author.

National Center for Education Statistics. (2004b). *The National Assessment of Educational Progress (NAEP). The Nation's Report Card. Reading Highlights 2003. Average fourth- and eighth-grade reading scores show little change.* U.S. Department of Education, Institute of Education Sciences. Washington, DC: Author.

Office of Analysis and Information Management. (2004). *UCLA new freshmen GPA and SAT scores: Fall 1991 through fall 2004* (APB Admission Report No. GPASAT 03–1, Sect. 17). Los Angeles: University of California, Office of Analysis and Information Management.

Office of Student Research. (2000). *SAT percentile scores by ethnicity, Fall 1983–fall 2000, for new from high school (NFHS) freshmen, excluding accelerated high school students.* Berkeley: University of California, Office of Student Research.

Omatsu, G. (1994). The "four prisons" and the movements of liberation. In K. Aguilar-San Juan (Ed.), *The state of Asian America: Activism and resistance in the 1990s* (pp. 19–69). Boston: South End Press.

Ong, P., & Leung, L. (2003). Asian Pacific American demographics in 2000: Past, present and future. In E. Lai & D. Arguelles (Eds.), *The new face of Asian Pacific America* (pp. 7–16). San Francisco: AsianWeek Books.

Ong, P., & Wing, L.C. (1996). The social contract to educate all children. In B. O. Hing & R. Lee (Eds.), *Reframing the immigration debate* (pp. 223–266). Los Angeles: LEAP APA Public Policy Institute & UCLA Asian American Studies Center.

Peng, S. S., & Wright, D. (1994). Explanation of academic achievement of Asian students. *Journal of Educational Research, 87,* 346–352.

Petersen, W. (1966, January 9). Success story, Japanese-American style. *New York Times,* 21.

Porter, O. F. (1990). *Undergraduate completion and persistence at four year colleges and universities: Detailed findings.* Washington, DC: National Institute of Independent Colleges and Universities.

Portes, A., & Rumbaut, R. (2001). *Legacies: The story of the immigrant second generation.* Berkeley: University of California Press.

Pyke, K., & Dang, T. (2003). "FOB" and "whitewashed": Identity and internalized racism among second generation Asian Americans. *Qualitative Sociology, 26,* 147–172.

Rathbun, A., West, J., & Germino-Hausken, E. (2004). *From kindergarten through third grade* (NCES Report No. 2004–007). Washington, DC: National Center for Education Statistics.

Reeves, T. J., & Bennett, C. E. (2004). *We the people: Asians in the United States* (Census 2000 Special Report No. CENSR–17). Washington, DC: U.S. Census Bureau.

Rhoads, R. A., Lee, J. J., & Yamada, M. (2002). Panethnicity and collective action among Asian American students: A qualitative case study. *Journal of College Student Development, 43*(6), 876–891.

Rosenbloom, S. R., & Way, N. (2004). Experiences of discrimination among African American, Asian American, and Latino Adolescents in an urban school. *Youth & Society, 35*(4), 420–451.

Rumberger, R. W., Ghatak, R., Poulos, G., Ritter, P. L., & Dornbusch, S. M. (1990). Family influences on dropout behavior in one California high school. *Sociology of Education, 63,* 283–299.

Services and Advocacy for Asian Youth Consortium. (2004, March). *Moving beyond exclusion.* Retrieved February 10, 2005, from www.jcyc.org

Schmidley, A. D. (2001). *Profile of the foreign-born population in the United States: 2000* (U.S. Census Bureau Current Population Report No. P23–206). Washington, DC: U.S. Government Printing Office.

Schneider, B., & Lee, Y. (1990). A model for academic success: the school and home environment of Asian students. *Anthropology and Education Quarterly, 21*(4), 358–377.

Snyder, T. D., Tan, A. G., & Hoffman, C. M. (2004). *Digest of education statistics 2003* (NCES Report No. 2005–025). U.S. Department of Education, National Center for Education Statistics. Washington, DC: Government Printing Office.

Suarez-Orozco, C., & Suarez-Orozco, M. (2001). *Children of immigration.* Cambridge, MA: Harvard University Press.

The success story of one minority group in the U.S. (1966, December 26). *U.S. News & World Report,* pp. 73–76.

Sue, S., & Abe, J. (1988). Predictors of academic achievement among Asian American and White students. In D. T. Nakanishi & T. Y. Nishida (Eds.), *The Asian American educational experience* (pp. 303–321). New York: Routledge.

Sue, S., & Okazaki, S. (1990). Asian American educational achievements: A phenomenon in search of an explanation. *American Psychologist, 45,* 913–920.

Suzuki, B. H. (1977). Education and the socialization of Asian Americans: A revisionist analysis of the "model minority" thesis. In D. T. Nakanishi & T. Y. Nishida (Eds.), *The Asian American educational experience* (pp. 113–132). New York: Routledge.

Suzuki, B. H. (2002). Revisiting the model minority stereotype: Implications for student affairs practice and higher education. *New Directions for Student Services, 97,* 21–32.

Takaki, R. (1989). *A different mirror: A history of multicultural America.* Boston: Little, Brown.

Tan, D. L. (1994). Uniqueness of the Asian-American experience in higher education. *College Student Journal, 28,* 412–421.

Texeira, E. (2005, November 13). Asian youths suffer harassment in schools. *The Washington Post.* Retrieved November 14, 2005, from http://www.washingtonpost.com

Thomson, G. (1998). *Six-year graduation rates at UC Berkeley: New fall freshman entering 1983–1992 by ethnicity.* Berkeley: University of California, Office of Student Research.

Thongthiraj, R. (2003). Southeast Asians. In E. Lai & D. Arguelles (Eds.), *The new face of Asian Pacific America* (pp. 93–104). San Francisco: AsianWeek Books.

Tseng, V. (2005, April). *Racial climate and adjustment to college.* In R. K. Chao's (Chair) *Race/intergroup relations.* Symposium conducted at the biennial meeting of the Society for Research in Child Development, Atlanta, GA.

Tuan, M. (1995). Korean and Russian students in a Los Angeles high school: Exploring the alternative strategies of two high-achieving groups. In R. G. Rumbaut & W. A. Cornelius (Eds.), *California's immigrant children* (pp. 107–130). San Diego: University of California, San Diego, Center for U.S.-Mexican Studies.

Wang, L. L.-C. (1976). Lau v. Nichols: *History of a struggle for equal and quality education* (Excerpt). Berkeley: Berkeley Unified School District, California Asian American Bilingual Center. (ERIC Document Reproduction Service No. ED1288521)

West, J., Denton, K., & Reaney, L. M. (2000). *The kindergarten year: Findings from the early childhood longitudinal study, kindergarten class of 1998–99* (Publication No. 2000–12–00). Washington, DC: National Center for Education Statistics. (ERIC Document Reproduction Service No. ED447933)

Wollenberg, C. M. (1978). "Yellow peril" in the schools (I and II). In D. T. Nakanishi & T. Y. Nishida (Eds.), *The Asian American educational experience* (pp. 3–29). New York: Routledge.

Ying, Y., Lee, P. A., Tsai, J. L., Hung, Y., Lin, M., & Wan, C. T. (2001). Asian American college students as model minorities: An examination of their overall competence. *Cultural Diversity & Ethnic Minority Psychology, 7,* 59–74.

Xie, Y., & Goyette, K. (2003). Social mobility and the educational choices of Asian Americans. *Social Science Research, 32,* 467–498.

Zhang, Y. (2003). Immigrant generational differences in academic achievements. In C. Park, A. Lin, & S. Lee (Eds.), *Asian American identities, families, and schooling* (pp. 201–224). Greenwich, CT: Information Age.

Zhou, M. (2003). Chinese. In E. Lai & D. Arguelles (Eds.), *The new face of Asian Pacific America* (pp. 37–44). San Francisco: AsianWeek Books.

Zhou, M., & Bankston, C. L. (1998). *Growing up American: How Vietnamese children adapt to life in the United States.* New York: Russell Sage.

8

ETHNIC IDENTITY

SAPNA CHERYAN

JEANNE L. TSAI

Ethnic identity in Asian Americans is often understood as the degree to which individuals identify with their country of ancestral origin (e.g., China, Japan). Accordingly, much of the research on ethnic identity among Asian Americans has related various psychological outcomes (e.g., well-being) to attachment to an Asian country (e.g., identification as Chinese). Focusing only on identification with one's country of ancestral origin, however, overlooks the other ways in which Asian Americans can be ethnically identified. As we explain in this chapter, ethnic identity can be understood more broadly as the attachment one feels to one's cultural *heritages,* including those not based specifically on one's country of origin. In this chapter, we review research on three ethnic identities—Asian, American, and Asian American—and contend that all must be taken into account in order to achieve a comprehensive understanding of Asian American ethnic identity. After looking at each identity, we examine the ways in which these identities relate to each other within an individual. We conclude the chapter with what

we see as an emerging theme in Asian American psychology: the contextual and dynamic nature of identity.

Ethnic identity, which is the degree to which one feels part of a group, must be distinguished from acculturation, which is the degree to which one has adapted to a certain culture (Laroche, Kim, Hui, & Tomiak, 1998; Tsai & Chentsova-Dutton, 2002; Tsai, Chentsova-Dutton, & Wong, 2002).[1] Ethnic identity involves one's subjective sense of attachment whereas acculturation focuses on actual practices and behaviors (e.g., speaking English) that are adopted when arriving in a new culture. Although concepts of identity and acculturation can be extended to Asian, American, and Asian American domains, most research on Asian Americans in our field has examined identification with an Asian ethnic identity (e.g., Chinese) and acculturation to American society. This can be contrasted to research on African Americans, which focuses more on African American ethnic identity (see Rowley, Sellers, Chavous, & Smith, 1998; Sellers & Shelton, 2003; Wong, Eccles, & Sameroff, 2003) than on acculturation

Authors' Note: The authors would like to thank Yu-Wen Ying and I-Chant Chiang for their comments on an earlier version of this chapter and Pam Sawyer for her assistance in collecting the data.

to American society. This difference can be attributed to the proportion of foreign-born individuals in the two groups. Whereas the majority of Asian Americans are foreign-born, the majority of African Americans are American-born (Malone, Baluja, Costanzo, & Davis, 2003), making questions of acculturation and identification with one's ancestral country more relevant for Asian Americans than for African Americans. However, the steady rise in the number of U.S.-born Asian Americans, for whom acculturation concerns are relatively low (Tsai & Chentsova-Dutton, 2002; Ying, Lee, & Tsai, 2000), will likely increase the presence and importance of research on Asian American identity.[2] In this chapter, we focus on Asian, American, and Asian American identities. (For further discussion of acculturation, see Chapter 9, this volume.)

ASIAN ETHNIC IDENTITIES

Although ethnic identity for Asian Americans involves more than just a sense of attachment to their Asian cultural heritage, we begin our chapter with a section on Asian ethnic identities because it is an important concept for the Asian American population. In part, this is because two-thirds (68.9%) of Asian Americans in the United States are foreign-born (Malone et al., 2003). First, we define the Asian ethnic identity, and then we review research on the links between Asian ethnic identities and various psychosocial outcomes, including mental health and achievement.

What Is an Asian Ethnic Identity?

Identification with one's Asian ethnicity is the degree to which individuals view themselves as members of a particular Asian cultural group (Phinney, 1996; Tsai, Chentsova-Dutton, et al., 2002) and incorporate specific Asian cultural ideas and practices into their self-concepts (Phinney, 1996). Measures of Asian ethnic identities instruct respondents to rate their feelings and sense of attachment to their Asian heritages. Popular measures of Asian ethnic identities include the General Ethnicity Questionnaire (Tsai, Ying, & Lee, 2000), the

Suinn-Lew Asian Self-Identity Acculturation Rating Scale (Suinn, Rickard-Figueroa, Lew, & Vigil, 1987), and the Multigroup Ethnic Identity Measures (Phinney, 1992). Some researchers also use the Collective Self-Esteem Scale (Crocker, Luhtanen, Blaine, & Broadnax, 1994) to measure ethnic identity (see Lay & Verkuyten, 1999; Verkuyten & Lay, 1998) because it not only requires respondents to evaluate their ethnic group (*private collective self-esteem*) and how important that group is to their self-concept (*identity collective self-esteem*) but also asks them how they perceive their membership (*membership collective self-esteem*) and how they think their ethnic group is viewed by others (*public collective self-esteem*).

Why Is the Asian Ethnic Identity Important?

To assess whether Asian Americans feel their Asian ethnic identities are important to them, relative to White Americans, we collected data from 98 Asian American Stanford University students (72.3% of whom were born in the United States) on their Asian ethnic identities and 143 White American Stanford students (94.7% of whom were born in the United States) on their European ethnic identities.[3] Participants indicated their level of agreement to 40 statements on a scale of 1 (strongly disagree) to 7 (strongly agree). The statements included measures of ethnic identity (e.g., "I am proud of Chinese/ German culture") and were adapted from the General Ethnicity Questionnaire (Tsai et al., 2000), the National Attachment Scale (Sidanius, Feshbach, Levin, & Pratto, 1997), and the General Social Survey (J. A. Davis, Smith, & Marsden, 2002). As predicted, Asian Americans identified more strongly with their Asian ethnicities ($M = 3.82$, $SD = .82$) than White Americans identified with their European ethnicities ($M = 3.11$, $SD = 1.09$), $t(218.0) = 5.55$, $p < .001$, reflecting the importance of the Asian ethnic identity to Asian Americans.[4]

Past research demonstrates that a strong ethnic identity has positive effects on a variety of psychosocial outcomes for Asian Americans, such as mental health (Mossakowski, 2003;

Williams et al., 2005), personal self-esteem (Phinney & Alipuria, 1990; Tsai et al., 2001; Yip & Fuligni, 2002), and well-being (Crocker et al., 1994; Yip & Fuligni, 2002). The mediators of these positive effects are thought to be greater social connectedness (Tajfel, 1978) and ethnic pride (Mossakowski, 2003; Sellers & Shelton, 2003; Wong et al., 2003; Yasui, Dorham, & Dishion, 2004).

Although most studies have observed that higher Asian ethnic identification is associated with more positive psychological outcomes, other studies have not found a positive effect of Asian ethnic identity on mental health (Noh, Beiser, Kaspar, Hou, & Rummens, 1999) or self-esteem (Yip & Cross, 2004). R. M. Lee (2003) did find a positive relationship between Asian ethnic identity and self-esteem among Asian American college students, but further analyses revealed that Asian ethnic identity did not mediate or moderate the effect of perceived discrimination on well-being. These inconsistencies in the findings that relate high Asian ethnic identification to psychological outcomes might be explained by the generation status of the study participants. Maintaining a connection to one's Asian heritage may be a buffer against stress in foreign-born individuals who are adjusting to a new cultural environment. However, Asian ethnic identity may have no such effect on U.S.-born Asian Americans who have a significant amount of competence with the majority culture and may rely on another identity (e.g., their American identity) for their well-being. In line with this prediction, Ying et al. (2000) found that pride in China predicted greater agreement that one's life was meaningful and manageable for foreign-born, but not U.S.-born, Chinese Americans. Williams et al. (2005) also observed that for Japanese Americans who led a primarily American lifestyle, Japanese ethnic identity and depressive symptoms were not related; however, for Japanese Americans who led a more Japanese lifestyle, a higher Japanese ethnic identification protected them against depressive symptoms. Discrepancies in the literature regarding the relationship between Asian ethnic identification and mental health might also be due to differences in how researchers measure Asian ethnic identification. For instance, R. M. Lee (2005) found that while the Asian ethnic

pride component was related to fewer depressive symptoms, clarity about one's Asian ethnicity or commitment to learning more about one's Asian ethnicity did not offer the same benefit. More research is needed on how methodological differences may account for different relationships between Asian ethnic identification and mental health.

Ethnic identities are also important because they organize and guide information processing (Fiske & Taylor, 1991). As a result, many studies have linked level of ethnic identification to attitudes and behaviors (Rotherman & Phinney, 1987). Studies have found that a higher ethnic identity predicts more support for increasing diversity in organizations (Linnehan, Konrad, Reitman, & Greenhalgh, & London, 2003) and more positive attitudes toward organizations that explicitly value diversity (S. S. Kim & Gelfand, 2003). Finally, level of ethnic identity predicts certain behaviors, such as consumer choices (Xu, Shim, Lotz, & Almeida, 2004) and community involvement (Mitchell & Dell, 1992; Sidanius, Van Laar, Levin, & Sinclair, 2004; Taylor & Howard-Hamilton, 1995; Yip & Cross, 2004).

What Can We Conclude About the Asian Ethnic Identity?

A large body of research exists examining the presence and consequences of Asian ethnic identities in Asian Americans. These identities provide Asian Americans with a sense of self and guide their daily behaviors. One theme that clearly emerges from this literature is the different ways the Asian ethnic identities may function in foreign-born versus U.S.-born Asian Americans. The research on generation status and mental health suggests that Asian ethnic identification is salient and more protective for foreign-born than American-born Asian Americans. Clearly, future research will need to examine the relationship between generation status and Asian ethnic identification further. Rather than suggesting that U.S.-born Asian Americans are less ethnically identified than their foreign-born counterparts, we suggest that U.S.-born Asian Americans are more oriented to other ethnic identities, such as their American and Asian American identities. We discuss these identities next.

AMERICAN IDENTITY

Asian Americans' relationship to America has been studied primarily in terms of acculturation, or how much Asian Americans have adapted to being in the United States. However, Asian Americans also have a sense of national identity, or feelings of attachment to the United States. In this section, we examine how Asian Americans understand their American identity and how this relates to the way they are seen by others.

What Is the American Identity for Asian Americans?

How do Asian Americans define being American, and does this differ from how other Americans define it? Devos and Banaji (2005) asked Asian Americans, White Americans, and African Americans about the degree to which they define being American in terms of civic values, patriotism, and native status and found that all three groups ranked the belief in civic values as primary, followed by patriotism, and finally native status, suggesting that there is some common understanding of what it means to be an American. However, other studies have found variation between ethnic groups. Tsai, Morstensen, Wong, and Hess (2002) found that there were significant differences between Asian Americans and White Americans in how they spontaneously defined being American. Asian Americans tended to define American culture and being American more in terms of customs and traditions (e.g., holidays, food) than did White Americans. Interestingly, the longer the Asian American participants had been in the United States, the more they differed from White Americans in their definition. These findings suggest that even among Americans, what it means to be a citizen is not widely agreed on and may differ by ethnicity and years spent engaging with American culture.

Why Is American Identity Important?

One reason we know that the American identity is a factor in the lives of Asian Americans is because Asian Americans say it is. In the study described in the Asian identities section of this chapter, we also included measures of America identity (e.g., "I am proud of American culture") and level of acculturation (e.g., "I listen to American music"). A repeated-measures ANOVA with Group (Asian American, White American) × Subscale (American Identity, Acculturation) revealed no main effect of Group, $F(1, 234) < 1$, ns. Both Asian Americans ($M = 5.14$, $SD = .82$) and White Americans ($M = 5.23$, $SD = .87$) reported being American to the same extent. Interestingly, this main effect was qualified by a significant interaction, $F(1, 234) = 17.35$, $p < .001$ (see Figure 8.1). Although Asian Americans ($M = 5.62$, $SD = .82$) reported being less acculturated than White Americans ($M = 5.91$, $SD = .86$), $F(1, 234) = 7.32$, $p < .01$, they did not differ from White Americans in their identification with American culture (Asian Americans: $M = 4.67$, $SD = .82$, White Americans: $M = 4.54$, $SD = .88$), $F(1, 234) = 1.31$, ns. Although Asian American college students may be less acculturated on average than their European American peers, they do not differ in their levels of attachment to being American.

However, just because Asian Americans may report feeling American does not mean they are seen that way by others. Assumptions about who is American affect Asian Americans as they are forced to contend with and dispel stereotypes. The exclusion of Asian Americans from being considered American can be seen throughout American history from the Chinese Exclusion Act of 1882, to Japanese internment during World War II (Chan & Hune, 1995), to the case of Dr. Wen Ho Lee who was falsely accused of spying for China (W. H. Lee, 2001), to the post-9/11 hate crimes against Asian Americans (Federal Bureau of Investigation, 2002). In a large phone survey asking Americans to imagine voting for a candidate from different minority groups for the presidency, 23% reported that they would be uncomfortable voting for an Asian American for president of the United States. This percentage is significantly greater than the 15% of respondents who said that they would feel uncomfortable voting for an African American candidate (Yankelovich Partners, 2001). For Asian Americans, the struggle to be included as full members of American society continues today.

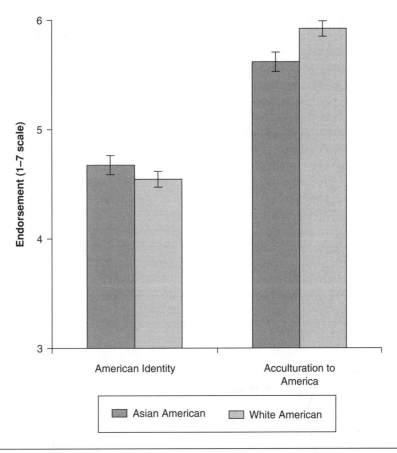

Figure 8.1   Reported Level of Identification With America and Acculturation to American Practices by Asian Americans (*n* = 98) and White Americans (*n* = 143).

Research in social psychology has begun to look closely at the incidence and consequence of this exclusion from the American ingroup. In line with the historical data, researchers have found that Asian American faces (Cheryan & Monin, 2005) and Asian Americans in general (Devos & Banaji, 2005) are perceived to be less American than White Americans. In one particularly clever study, Devos and Banaji (2005) demonstrated that White American participants had a stronger implicit association between American symbols and White *European* celebrity faces (e.g., Gerard Depardieu) than between the same symbols and Asian *American* celebrity faces (e.g., Connie Chung), despite the fact that they knew the nationalities of the celebrities when explicitly asked. Among African Americans, Asian Americans, White Americans, and Hispanic Americans, Asian

Americans appear to be perceived as the *least* American (Cheryan & Monin, 2005; Devos & Banaji, 2005), demonstrating that this bias is more than simply being non-White (as is the case of African Americans) or being part of a recently immigrated group (as is the case of Hispanic Americans). Asian Americans themselves appear to be aware that they are perceived as less American than their White American counterparts. They report being misperceived as foreigners more often than White Americans, and they report a discrepancy between how much they believe they belong in America and how much they think others believe they belong in America (Cheryan & Monin, 2005).

How do Asian Americans react to being seen as less American than their White American peers? Cheryan and Monin (2005) showed that Asian Americans found statements alleging they were not American to be offensive and disliked those who made such statements. In addition, when denied their American identity, Asian Americans reacted by increasing their reports of their participation in American practices, presumably as a way of proving their American identity to those who doubted it. For example, in one study, a White American experimenter attempted to deny the American identities of Asian Americans and White Americans by stopping them on campus and asking if they spoke English, implying that they were foreigners. Asian Americans who were asked, "Do you speak English?" spent more time recalling American television shows from the 1980s as a way of proving they were American (and perhaps lived in America in the 1980s) than did Asian Americans who were not asked. In contrast, there was no difference between White Americans who were asked if they spoke English and those who were not.

Although the impact of identity on psychosocial variables such as mental health has been studied most often with Asian ethnic identities, some research indicates that being oriented to American culture increases feelings of efficacy and competence for foreign-born Asian Americans (Ying et al., 2000). In addition, having a strong national identity appears to promote social and psychological adjustment because it enables individuals to relate to the dominant culture in an effective way (Phinney, Horenczyk, Liebkind, & Vedder, 2001; Ying, 1995). For Asian immigrants, their ability to learn the ways of a new culture predicts how well they fit into their new environments.

National identity is important to consider not only from the point of view of Asian Americans but also with regard to how to best construct a multicultural society. Research on the Common Ingroup Identity model (Gaertner & Dovidio, 2000) and superordinate identity (Huo, 2003; Huo, Smith, Tyler, & Lind, 1996) find that having a strong national identity encourages cohesion between ethnic groups and minimizes strife. Hong et al. (2004) found that among Asian Americans who believed human character was malleable, those who were encouraged to think about their American identity were less prejudiced against African Americans than those who were primed with their Asian American identity. Therefore, it appears that having a strong superordinate identity may be beneficial for Asian Americans and for society in general.

What Can We Conclude About the American Identity?

Although the American identity is not always thought of as an ethnic identity, the research described in the previous paragraphs demonstrates that it is an important identity for both foreign-born and U.S.-born Asian Americans. Because being American is tied to positive outcomes in America (i.e., inclusion, civic rights, feelings of belonging), understanding the ways in which Asian Americans relate to their American identity and the ways in which they are prevented from doing so becomes an important aspect of understanding Asian American psychology. Taken together, the research makes it clear that American national identity is of importance to Asian Americans and that whether or not others view Asian Americans as American has important social, political, and economic consequences.

RELATIONSHIPS BETWEEN ASIAN AND AMERICAN IDENTITIES

The findings described in the previous section seem to suggest that having both a strong Asian ethnic identity and a strong American identity is desirable for psychological protection and positive ethnic group relations. But can one successfully have two strong ethnic identities? The dominant discourse in America during the wave of 19th-century immigration was that having an Irish, Chinese, or some other ethnic identity precluded immigrants from having a strong American identity, as reflected in Theodore Roosevelt's statement that "a hyphenated American is not an American at all" (P. Davis, 1920, p. 648). However, research on U.S.-born Asian Americans supports the bidimensionality of identity: The Asian ethnic and American identities are orthogonal (LaFromboise, Coleman, & Gerton, 1993; Tsai et al., 2000). In other words, having a strong Asian ethnic identity does *not* preclude individuals from having a strong American identity (Huo, 2003).

Other research suggests that the relationship between Asian ethnic and American identities might vary by component of identity. Cheryan and Monin (2005) found that reports of participation in American and ethnic practices, such as listening to American/Asian music, were marginally negatively correlated, whereas reports of pride in America or Asian country of origin were marginally positively correlated. Dimensionality also appears to depend on generation status: Whereas ethnic and national orientation did not correlate for U.S.-born Asian Americans, the two were negatively correlated for foreign-born Asian Americans (Tsai, Ying, & Lee, 2000).

The ability for some to identify strongly with two cultures does not mean that belonging to two cultures, or having a "double-consciousness" (Du Bois, 1903), is easy or painless. Being forced to learn two modes of functioning can be stressful, particularly for immigrants who must learn such skills in a short amount of time (Berry, 1990; Yeh et al., 2003). However, other research demonstrates that there might also be benefits to successfully learning to integrate two cultures. Specifically, being bicultural—high on both ethnic and national identity—appears to have a positive impact on mental health (Phinney et al., 2001; LaFromboise et al., 1993; Ying, 1995; Ying et al., 2000).

Researchers have recognized the interplay between national and ethnic identities and the role both identities play in psychosocial adjustment. Indeed, for Asians in America, both identities provide a frame with which to view the world. One important caveat to keep in mind while interpreting research on ethnic and national identity in Asian Americans is that living in two cultures is more than simply internalizing the two cultures. Bringing together two cultures results in creating a new culture (Garcia & Hurtado, 1995). This necessitates studying a third type of identity—the Asian American identity.

ASIAN AMERICAN IDENTITY

In psychological research, Asian Americans are often used as a proxy for Asians to study East-West cultural differences. Although this strategy is a useful way to test cultural psychology hypotheses and has successfully yielded important insight into East-West cultural differences (see Ji, Peng, & Nisbett, 2000; H. S. Kim, 2002; H. S. Kim & Markus, 1999), many other studies attest to the fact that Asian Americans are not identical to Asians in the psychological data they generate. In some studies, Asian Americans are somewhere in between Asians and White Americans (Iyengar & Lepper, 1999). Other studies have found that Asian Americans act even more "American" than White Americans (Cheryan & Monin, 2005; see also Triandis, Kashima, Shimada, & Villareal, 1986, for a discussion of "cultural overshooting") and in yet other studies, Asian Americans act even more "Asian" than their Asian counterparts (Tsai, Knutson, & Fung, in press). Why does this happen, and how do Asian Americans themselves view their group? Do they distinguish themselves from their Asian forebears or from their White American peers? To answer these questions, we need to examine Asian American identity.

What Is the Asian American Identity?

The Asian American identity is the extent to which individuals identify with other Asian Americans and see themselves as part of a larger pan-ethnic group. (This identity is sometimes termed *racial identity,* see Alvarez & Helms, 2001.) Before the mid–20th century, individuals from one Asian country did not think of themselves as connected to individuals from other Asian countries because they perceived their cultures to be dissimilar, and there were feelings of animosity due to previous wars and political tensions between their countries. However, in the 1970s, the Asian groups were lumped together by the dominant society and assigned the label "Asian American." In time, these Asian groups, which had previously been opposed to one another, began to construct a shared sense of history and discrimination. This process was facilitated by Asian Americans who fought alongside African Americans in their struggle for civil rights in the 1960s, making Asian Americans even more aware of the injustices experienced by their own group. Embracing the Asian American identity, therefore, became a way to fight for political rights and representation (Chan & Hune, 1995). Whereas the Asian ethnic identity is often based on one's home context and one's adherence to specific cultural traditions (Tsai & Chentsova-Dutton, 2002; Ying, Coombs, & Lee, 1999), the Asian American identity was constructed as a way for individuals of different Asian backgrounds to jointly gain political access and representation (Chan & Hune, 1995; Kibria, 1998).

As we suggested earlier, one of the original functions of Asian American identity was to organize against discrimination and encourage greater political participation by Asian Americans. Interestingly, although foreign-born Asian Americans experience more race-based discrimination than their U.S.-born counterparts, U.S.-born Asian Americans participate more in Asian American political and social organizations (Espiritu & Ong, 1994). This may be because discrimination has a greater negative impact on psychological well-being for U.S.-born Asian Americans than for their foreign-born counterparts (Ying et al., 2000). It may also be that U.S.-born Asian Americans feel they have more of a right to contest discrimination than foreign-born Asian Americans, who may feel that their immigrant status prevents them from having the right to object.

Why Is the Asian American Identity Important?

Today, many Asian American organizations continue to educate others about a shared history of exclusion and continue to fight for representation (Kibria, 1998). Those who identify as Asian American are more likely to be politically involved in Asian American causes than those who do not (Lien et al., 2003). However, the Asian American identity today has become more than just a political identity. Many Asian Americans have a sense of belonging to a pan-Asian race and of having pan-Asian values, which they construct to stand in opposition to dominant White America (Kibria, 1997). More than 50% of Asian Americans responding to a large-scale phone survey in 2000–2001 stated that the Asian American identity was part of their ethnic identification, although only one in six preferred it as their primary ethnic identification (Lien et al., 2003). The notion of a pan-Asian race has extended into the daily lives and customs of Asian Americans, including creating new

patterns of marriage between people of differing Asian ethnicities (Kibria, 1997). Thus, although the Asian American identity is a relatively new identity, it has been embraced by Asian Americans themselves as a political tool while at the same time generating a new cultural group and identity. However, the formation of an Asian American identity is by no means complete. Some Asian American groups, such as South Asian Americans, report feeling marginalized and excluded by the Asian American community (Doshi, 1996). It remains to be seen whether the Asian American identity will become more inclusive or will dissolve into separate identities as the number of Asian Americans increases.

What Can We Conclude About the Asian American Identity?

The history of the Asian American identity makes evident the political nature of identity. This identity was imposed on Asian Americans, who have since come to embrace it as a political and social tool. However, the fact that the Asian American identity might not be embraced to the same degree by foreign-born immigrants, who still have strong ties to their home country, is one reason this identity has not been studied in the field as much as the Asian ethnic identities. However, we expect that this tendency will change as the Asian American population increases and as Asian Americans strengthen their sense of ingroup identity in the face of discrimination (Jetten, Branscombe, Schmitt, & Spears, 2001). Future research will need to assess the impact of the Asian American ethnic identity on mental health outcomes.

ETHNIC IDENTITY ACROSS INDIVIDUALS AND SITUATIONS

Identity researchers often assign each person an "ethnic identity score," based on their responses to a series of questions, that represents how attached that individual is to his or her ethnicity. These identity scores have predictive value for Asian Americans. However, seeing ethnic identity purely as a fixed entity within an individual ignores its contextual aspect. Ethnic identity is also a dynamic concept that depends on one's immediate environment. Therefore, in addition to the personality component, there is a situational component to ethnic identity. We address both aspects of ethnic identity in this section, starting with identity across individuals and moving on to identity across situations.

Individual Differences

Ethnic identity on an individual level depends on various factors. Many researchers have examined the interactions between ethnic identity and other identities, such as gender (Gonzales & Cauce, 1995; Oyserman, Harrison, & Bybee, 2001; Tsai et al., 2001). Research on Asian Americans finds that, in general, female Asian Americans are more oriented toward their ethnicity than are their male counterparts (Ting-Toomey, 1981; Yip & Fuligni, 2002), perhaps because they have more social attachments to family and friends (Gilligan, 1993) and consequently internalize their ethnicity to a greater degree. Differences between individuals also develop over one's lifetime. Typical phases of ethnic identity development generally begin with a period of conforming to the majority culture, followed by a period of embracing one's cultural heritage, and finally, a successful integration of both identities (Alvarez & Yeh, 1999; Gonzales & Cauce, 1995; Helms, 1995; J. Kim, 2001; Phinney, 1990; Ying & Lee, 1999). Demographic variables such as religion (Kurien, 2001), socioeconomic status (Dhingra, 2003; Espiritu & Ong, 1994), birth order (Manaster, Rhodes, Marcus, & Chan, 1998), terms of immigration (Ying & Han, in press), and Asian country of origin (Lien et al., 2003) are also important in constructing one's ethnic identity.

As we have mentioned previously in this chapter, generation status also matters in determining how much Asian Americans identify with their Asian ethnic and American identities. Foreign-born Asian Americans are more likely to espouse traditional Asian values whereas U.S.-born Asian Americans are more likely to integrate Asian and American values (Weisman, Snadowsky, & Gannon, 1972; Ting-Toomey, 1981; Ying et al., 1999). In addition, U.S.-born Asian Americans are much more likely to identify themselves as "American" than are their foreign-born counterparts (Lien et al.,

2003). Does this mean that Asian Americans will eventually be diffused into the mainstream to the point where their ethnic identity is subsumed by their national identity? In fact, research suggests the opposite. Third- and fourth-generation Asian Americans are actually no lower in their levels of ethnic identification than second-generation Asian Americans (Wooden, Leon, & Toshima, 1988), and in some cases their levels of identification are actually higher than those of second-generation Asian Americans (Ting-Toomey, 1981). Asian Americans' distinctive features, the continued flow of immigrants from Asia, and the discrimination they face may ensure a certain level of Asian ethnic identification among Asian Americans (Kibria, 1998). This experience can be contrasted to the Irish and Italians who also arrived in America during the 19th century and "became White" in the eyes of mainstream Americans (Ignatiev, 1995).

Individuals can also vary in the degree to which they integrate their identities. Benet-Martinez, Leu, Lee, and Morris (2002) examined Bicultural Identity Integration (BII), or the extent to which biculturals perceive that their ethnic and national identities are at odds. They found that some Chinese American biculturals perceived their dual cultures to be compatible and integrated (high BII), whereas others perceived their cultures to be conflicting and hard to integrate (low BII). These two groups responded differently to cultural primes that made their Chinese ethnicity salient (e.g., pictures of the Great Wall) than to cultural primes that made their American identity salient (e.g., pictures of the U.S. Capitol). High BII individuals responded in a culturally congruent manner by making more external attributions (a typically Chinese behavior), whereas low BII individuals responded in an oppositional fashion and increased their internal attributions (a typically American behavior).

Contextual Nature of Identity

Although much of the research on identity among Asian Americans has treated identity as an individual difference variable that varies across people, overlooking the contextual nature of identity would be short-sighted. Identity is a dynamic construction that is defined by individuals

(Phinney, 1990) within a larger system of power (Kibria, 1998). Societal constraints, such as the meaning assigned to various skin colors and features, limit one's ability to claim a particular ethnic identity (Espiritu, 1992; Phinney, 1990; Phinney et al., 2001). Furthermore, ethnic identity varies depending on the immediate social cues (Cheryan & Bodenhausen, 2000; Hong et al., 2004; Shih, Pittinsky, & Ambady, 1999; Yip & Fuligni, 2002). Rather than being merely a static entity, identity is fluid and process-driven.

The dynamic and contextual nature of identity is apparent in research on Asian Americans, which demonstrates that certain contexts can activate ethnic identity. Kim-Ju and Liem (2003) found that imagining interacting with a group of White American strangers made Asian ethnic identity more salient for Asian Americans than imagining interacting with an ethnically diverse group of strangers. Interestingly, Asian ethnic identity was also more salient for Asian Americans when they imagined interacting with strangers of the same race, whereas the same was not true for White Americans, perhaps because for White Americans, the event of interacting with other White Americans is common and not thought of along ethnic lines. Ethnic and national identities can also be separately activated in the presence of objects or other reminders that cue their identities. These cues can be images, such as famous landmarks in China or the United States (Benet-Martinez et al., 2002; Hong, Morris, Chiu, & Benet-Martinez, 2000), questionnaires or tasks that ask about one identity in particular (Cheryan & Bodenhausen, 2000; Shih et al., 1999), or even a statement that encourages participants to see themselves as members of a particular group (Hong et al., 2004). Hong et al. (2000) use the term "cultural frame switching" to refer to this tendency for biculturals to (often automatically) alternate identities based on the situational demands. Another factor that may play a role in determining how much one identifies as Asian, American, or Asian American is exposure to Asian culture. Asian Americans who visit Asia or spend more time there may experience a higher level of identification with their home countries, whereas those who spend more time in America may identify more strongly as American or Asian American.

In addition to being a reactive construct that varies based on one's context, identity can also be a strategic choice made in order to maximize a positive social identity (Tajfel & Turner, 1979). Cheryan and Monin (2005) found that Asian Americans responded to an accusation that they were not American by increasing their level of reported participation in American practices as a way of proving their American identity to others. People also choose contexts that allow them to enhance a rewarding social identity or to distance themselves from a threatening social identity (Ethier & Deaux, 2001; & Deaux, 2001; Jackson, Sullivan, Harnish, & Hodge, 1996). Thus, identity negotiation is an ongoing process based on one's larger sociocultural and immediate context that involves responding to social cues, selecting certain environments, and presenting relevant information to others.

CONCLUSION

In this chapter, we reviewed research on three types of ethnic identities for Asian Americans: the Asian ethnic identities, the American identity, and the Asian American identity. The importance of these ethnic identities can be seen both in people's own reports and in the outcomes related to ethnic identification. All three identities construct the worlds of Asian Americans by guiding their interpretations of situations (Cheryan & Monin, 2005; Kibria, 1997), predicting with whom they associate (Sidanius et al., 2004), choosing how they adapt to their environments (Oyserman & Sakamoto, 1997), and understanding how others react to them (Cheryan & Monin, 2005; Oyserman & Sakamoto, 1997).

Individuals vary in the ways in which their ethnic identities are constructed and displayed. A first-generation Chinese immigrant who speaks Chinese at home and has warm feelings toward China can be identified as having a high ethnic identity, but so can a fourth-generation Japanese American whose home life is highly American but who is an ardent activist for Asian American causes. Asian ethnic identities continue to be important due to the recency of immigration (Malone et al., 2003), but an understanding of ethnic identity in Asian Americans is not complete without an examination of the American and Asian American identities. The American identity is a goal and a reality as Asian Americans engage with American culture in their daily lives. And the Asian American identity persists due to its power as an organizing tool, both politically and socially. For Asian Americans, the notion of ethnic identity is clearly complex, involving multiple interrelating identities. Allowing this complexity to guide our research in the coming years will be even more crucial as the Asian American population increases in the years to come.

NOTES

1. Because identity refers to an individual's subjective experience whereas acculturation refers to a set of behaviors (Tsai, Chentsova-Dutton, et al., 2002), Asian Americans can both participate heavily in American activities (i.e., be highly acculturated) yet feel disconnected from their American identity (i.e., not identify with American culture). Furthermore, one's level of acculturation is independent of one's Asian ethnic or Asian American identities: Asian Americans can be highly acculturated to American culture and simultaneously be highly identified with their Asian ethnic and Asian American identities (Laroche et al., 1988; Liebkind, Jasinskaja-Lahti, & Solheim, 2004).

2. We do not predict a decrease in the importance of acculturation research due to the continuous influx of Asian immigrants to the United States.

3. Ethnic heritages listed by Asian Americans were: Chinese (46), Taiwanese (10), Japanese (9), Filipino (8), Korean (9), Vietnamese (6), Indian (5), South East Asian (1) and 4 did not indicate a response. Ethnic heritages listed by White Americans were: German (26), English (17), Irish (11), Italian (11), Scottish (7), European (8), Swedish (7), Polish (6), Russian (5), Jewish (5), American (4), White (2), French (3), Scandinavian (2), Slavic (2), Hungarian (2), Albanian (1), Danish (1), Finnish (1), Israeli (1), Lithuanian (1), Welsh (2), Hawaiian (1), Japanese (1), Serbian (1), Portuguese (1), Norwegian (3), and 11 did not indicate a response. Eight White Americans listed non-European ethnicities; removing these individuals from the analyses did not change the results.

4. We also included measures of participation in cultural practices (e.g., "I listen to Chinese/German

music"). A repeated-measures analysis of variance (ANOVA) with Subscale (Pride, Practices) × Group (Asian American, White American) revealed a two-way Group × Subscale interaction, $F(1, 218) = 36.62$, $p < .001$. Asian Americans reported engaging in more Asian ethnic practices ($M = 4.25$, $SD = 1.00$) than having pride in their Asian heritage ($M = 3.82$, $SD = .82$), $F(1, 218) = 23.65$, $p < .001$. In contrast, White Americans reported more pride in their European heritage ($M = 3.11$, $SD = 1.09$) than participation in European practices ($M = 2.83$, $SD = 1.29$), $F(1, 238) = 13.16$, $p < .001$. This difference may be explained by the fact that as a group, Asian Americans are more recent immigrants to the United States than White Americans and, therefore, may engage in traditional Asian practices to a greater degree at home than White Americans. White Americans, however, may continue to feel some attachment to their European heritages, even if they no longer engage in traditionally European practices at home.

REFERENCES

Alvarez, A. N., & Helms, J. E. (2001). Racial identity and reflected appraisals as influences on Asian Americans' racial adjustment. *Cultural Diversity & Ethnic Minority Psychology, 7*(3), 217–231.

Alvarez, A. N., & Yeh, T. L. (1999). Asian Americans in college: A racial identity perspective. In D. Sandhu (Ed.), *Asian and Pacific Islander Americans: Issues and concerns for counseling and psychotherapy* (pp. 105–120). Huntington, NY: Nova Science.

Benet-Martínez, V., Leu, J., Lee, F., & Morris, M. W. (2002). Negotiating biculturalism: Cultural frame switching in biculturals with oppositional versus compatible cultural identities. *Journal of Cross-Cultural Psychology, 33*(5), 492–516.

Berry, J. W. (1990). Psychology of acculturation. In J. Berman (Ed.), *Nebraska Symposium on Motivation, 1989: Cross-cultural perspectives* (pp. 201–234). Lincoln: Nebraska University Press.

Chan, K. S., & Hune, S. (1995). Racialization and panethnicity: From Asians in America to Asian Americans. In W. D. Hawley & A. W. Jackson (Eds.), *Toward a common destiny: Improving race and ethnic relations in America* (pp. 205–233). San Francisco: Jossey-Bass.

Cheryan, S., & Bodenhausen, G. V. (2000). When positive stereotypes threaten intellectual performance: The psychological hazards of "model minority" status. *Psychological Science, 11*(5), 399–402.

Cheryan, S., & Monin, B. M. (2005). Where are you *really* from? Asian Americans and identity denial. *Journal of Personality and Social Psychology. 89*(5), 717–730.

Crocker, J., Luhtanen, R., Blaine, B., & Broadnax, S. (1994). Collective self-esteem and psychological well-being among White, Black, and Asian college students. *Personality and Social Psychology Bulletin, 20,* 503–513.

Davis, J. A, Smith, T. A., & Marsden, P. V. (2002). General Social Surveys, 1972–2002: Cumulative Codebook. National Roper Center for Public Opinion Research, Chicago, IL.

Davis, P. (1920). *Immigration and Americanization.* Boston: Ginn.

Devos, T., & Banaji, M. R. (2005). American = white? *Journal of Personality & Social Psychology, 88*(3), 447–466.

Dhingra, P. (2003). The second generation in "big D": Korean American and Indian American organizations in Dallas, Texas. *Sociological Spectrum, 23*(2), 247–278.

Doshi, S. J. (1996). Divided consciousness amidst a new Orientalism: South Asian American identity formation on campus. In S. Maira & R. Srikanth (Eds.), *Contours of the heart: South Asians map North America.* New York: Asian American Writers' Workshop.

Du Bois, W. E. B. (1903). *The souls of black folk: Essays and sketches.* Chicago: A. C. McClurg.

Ethier, K. A., & Deaux, K. (2001). Negotiating social identity when contexts change: Maintaining identification and responding to threat. In M. A. Hogg & D. Abrams (Eds.), *Intergroup relations: Essential readings* (pp. 254–265). New York: Psychology Press.

Espiritu, Y. L. (1992). *Asian American panethnicity: Bridging institutions and identities.* Philadelphia: Temple University Press.

Espiritu, Y. L., & Ong, P. (1994). Class constraints on racial solidarity among Asian Americans. In P. Ong, E. Bonacich, & L. Cheng (Eds.), *The New Asian immigration in Los Angeles and global restructuring* (pp. 295–321). Philadelphia: Temple University Press.

Federal Bureau of Investigation. (2002). *Hate crimes statistics.* Retrieved May 29, 2005, from http://www.fbi.gov/ucr/01hate.pdf

Fiske, S. T., & Taylor, S. E. (1991). *Social cognition* (2nd ed.). New York: McGraw-Hill.

Garcia, E. E., & Hurtado, A. (1995). Becoming American: A review of current research on the development of racial and ethnic identity in children. In W. D. Hawley & A. W. Jackson (Eds.), *Toward a common destiny: Improving race and ethnic relations in America* (pp. 163–184). San Francisco: Jossey-Bass.

Gaertner, S. L., & Dovidio, J. F. (2000). *Reducing intergroup bias: The common ingroup identity model.* New York: Psychology Press.

Gilligan, C. (1993). *In a different voice: Psychological theory and women's development.* Cambridge: Harvard University Press.

Gonzales, N. A., & Cauce, A. M. (1995). Ethnic identity and multicultural competence: Dilemmas and challenges for minority youth. In W. D. Hawley & A. W. Jackson (Eds.), *Toward a common destiny: Improving race and ethnic relations in America* (pp. 131–162). San Francisco: Jossey-Bass.

Helms, J. E. (1995). An update of Helms' white and people of color racial identity models. In J. G. Ponterotto & J. M. Casas (Eds.), *Handbook of multicultural counseling* (pp. 181–198). Thousand Oaks, CA: Sage.

Hong, Y., Coleman, J., Chan, G., Wong, R. Y. M., Chiu, C., & Hansen, I. G., et al. (2004). Predicting intergroup bias: The interactive effects of implicit theory and social identity. *Personality and Social Psychology Bulletin, 30*(8), 1035–1047.

Hong, Y., Morris, M. W., Chiu, C., & Benet-Martínez, V. (2000). Multicultural minds: A dynamic constructivist approach to culture and cognition. *American Psychologist, 55*(7), 709–720.

Huo, Y. J., Smith, H. J., Tyler, T. R., & Lind, E. A. (1996). Superordinate identification, subgroup identification, and justice concerns: Is separatism the problem; is assimilation the answer? *Psychological Science, 7*(1), 40–45.

Huo, Y. J. (2003). Procedural justice and social regulation across group boundaries: Does subgroup identity undermine relationship-based governance? *Personality and Social Psychology Bulletin, 29*(3), 336–348.

Ignatiev, N. (1995). *How the Irish became white.* New York: Routledge.

Iyengar, S. S., & Lepper, M. R. (1999). Rethinking the value of choice: A cultural perspective on intrinsic motivation. *Journal of Personality and Social Psychology, 76*(3), 349–366.

Jackson, L. A., Sullivan, L. A., Harnish, R., & Hodge, C. N. (1996). Achieving positive social identity: Social mobility, social creativity, and permeability of group boundaries. *Journal of Personality and Social Psychology, 70,* 241–254.

Jetten, J., Branscombe, N. R., Schmitt, M. T., & Spears, R. (2001). Rebels with a cause: Group identification as a response to perceived discrimination from the mainstream. *Personality and Social Psychology Bulletin, 27*(9), 1204–1213.

Ji, L., Peng, K., & Nisbett, R. E. (2000). Culture, control, and perception of relationships in the environment. *Journal of Personality and Social Psychology, 78*(5), 943–955.

Kibria, N. (1997). The construction of "Asian American": Reflections on intermarriage and ethnic identity among second-generation Chinese and Korean Americans. *Ethnic and Racial Studies, 20*(3), 523–544.

Kibria, N. (1998). The contested meanings of "Asian American": Racial dilemmas in the contemporary U.S. *Ethnic and Racial Studies, 21*(5), 939–958.

Kim, H. S. (2002). We talk, therefore we think? A cultural analysis of the effect of talking on thinking. *Journal of Personality and Social Psychology, 83*(4), 828–842.

Kim, H. S, & Markus, H. R. (1999). Deviance or uniqueness, harmony or conformity? A cultural analysis. *Journal of Personality and Social Psychology, 77*(4), 785–800.

Kim, J. (2001). Asian American identity development theory. In B. W. Jackson, III, & C. L. Wijeyesinghe (Eds.), *New perspectives on racial identity development: A theoretical and practical anthology* (pp. 67–90). New York: New York University Press.

Kim, S. S., & Gelfand, M. J. (2003). The influence of ethnic identity on perceptions of organizational recruitment. *Journal of Vocational Behavior, 63*(3), 396–116.

Kim-Ju, G. M., & Liem, R. (2003). Ethnic self-awareness as a function of ethnic group status, group composition, and ethnic identity orientation. *Cultural Diversity & Ethnic Minority Psychology, 9*(3), 289–302.

Kurien, P. (2001). Religion, ethnicity and politics: Hindu and Muslim Indian immigrants in the United States. *Ethnic and Racial Studies, 24*(2), 263–293.

LaFromboise, T., Coleman, H. L., & Gerton, J. (1993). Psychological impact of biculturalism:

Evidence and theory. *Psychological Bulletin, 114,* 395–412.

Lay, C., & Verkuyten, M. (1999). Ethnic identity and its relation to personal self-esteem: A comparison of Canadian-born and foreign-born Chinese adolescents: Personal self-esteem, collective self-esteem, and identity. *Journal of Social Psychology, 139,* 288–199.

Laroche, M., Kim, C., Hui, M. K., & Tomiuk, M. A. (1998). Test of a nonlinear relationship between linguistic acculturation and ethnic identification. *Journal of Cross-Cultural Psychology, 29*(3), 418–433.

Lee, R. M. (2003). Do ethnic identity and other-group orientation protect against discrimination for Asian Americans. *Journal of Counseling Psychology, 50*(2), 133–141.

Lee, R. M. (2005). Resilience against discrimination: Ethnic identity and other-group orientation as protective factors for Korean Americans. *Journal of Counseling Psychology, 52*(1), 36–44.

Lee, W. H. (2001). *My country versus me: The first-hand account by the Los Alamos scientist who was falsely accused of being a spy.* New York: Hyperion.

Liebkind, K., Jasinskaja-Lahti, I., & Solheim, E. (2004). Cultural identity, perceived discrimination, and parental support as determinants of immigrants' school adjustments: Vietnamese youth in Finland. *Journal of Adolescent Research, 19*(6), 635–656.

Lien, P., Conway, M. M., & Wong, J. (2003). The contours and sources of ethnic identity choices among Asian Americans. *Social Science Quarterly, 84*(2), 461–481.

Linnehan, F., Konrad, A. M., Reitman, F., Greenhalgh, A., & London, M. (2003). Behavioral goals for a diverse organization: The effects of attitudes, social norms, and racial identity for Asian Americans and whites. *Journal of Applied Social Psychology, 33*(7), 1331–1359.

Malone, N., Baluja, K. F., Costanzo, J. M., & Davis, C. J. (2003). *The foreign-born population: 2000* (Census 2000 Brief No. C2KBR-34). Retrieved May 29, 2005, from http://www.census.gov/prod/2003pubs/c2kbr-34.pdf

Manaster, G. J., Rhodes, C., Marcus, M. B. & Chan, J. C. (1998). The role of birth order in the acculturation of Japanese Americans. *Psychologia, 41*(3), 155–170.

Mitchell, S. L., & Dell, D. M. (1992). The relationship between black students' racial identity attitude and participation in campus organizations. *Journal of College Student Development, 33*(1), 39–43.

Mossakowski, K. N. (2003). Coping with perceived discrimination: Does ethnic identity protect mental health? *Journal of Health and Social Behavior, 44*(3), 318–331.

Noh, S., Beiser, M., Kaspar, V., Hou, F., & Rummens, J. (1999). Perceived racial discrimination, depression, and coping: A study of southeast Asian refugees in Canada. *Journal of Health and Social Behavior, 40*(3), 193–207.

Oyserman, D., Harrison, K., & Bybee, D. (2001). Can racial identity be promotive of academic efficacy? *International Journal of Behavioral Development, 25*(4), 379–385.

Oyserman, D., & Sakamoto, I. (1997). Being Asian American: Identity, cultural constructs, and stereotype perception. *Journal of Applied Behavioral Science, 33*(4), 435–453.

Phinney, J. S. (1990). Ethnic identity in adolescents and adults: Review of research. *Psychological Bulletin, 108*(3), 499–514.

Phinney, J. S. (1992). The multigroup ethnic identity measure: A new scale for use with diverse groups. *Journal of Adolescent Research, 7*(2), 156–176.

Phinney, J. S. (1996). When we talk about American ethnic groups, what do we mean? *American Psychologist, 51*(9), 918–927.

Phinney, J. S., & Alipuria, L. L. (1990). Ethnic identity in college students from four ethnic groups. *Journal of Adolescence, 13*(2), 171–183.

Phinney, J. S., Horenczyk, G., Liebkind, K., & Vedder, P. (2001). Ethnic identity, immigration, and well-being: An interactional perspective. *Journal of Social Issues, 57*(3), 493–510.

Rotherman, M. J., & Phinney, J. S. (1987). Ethnic behavior patterns as an aspect of identity. In J. S. Phinney & M. J. Rotherman (Eds.), *Children's ethnic socialization: Pluralism and development* (pp. 210–218). Beverly Hills, CA: Sage.

Rowley, S. J., Sellers, R. M., Chavous, T. M., & Smith, M. A. (1998). The relationship between racial identity and self-esteem in African American college and high school students. *Journal of Personality and Social Psychology, 74*(3), 715–724.

Sellers, R. M., & Shelton, J. N. (2003). The role of racial identity in perceived racial discrimination. *Journal of Personality and Social Psychology, 84*(5), 1079–1092.

Shih, M., Pittinsky, T. L., & Ambady, N. (1999). Stereotype susceptibility: Identity salience and shifts in quantitative performance. *Psychological Science, 10*(1), 80–83.

Sidanius, J., Feshbach, S., Levin, S., & Pratto, F. (1997). The interface between ethnic and national attachment: Ethnic pluralism or ethnic dominance? *Public Opinion Quarterly, 61*(1), 102–133.

Sidanius, J., Van Laar, C., Levin, S., & Sinclair, S. (2004). Ethnic enclaves and the dynamics of social identity on the college campus: The good, the bad, and the ugly. *Journal of Personality and Social Psychology, 87*, 96–110.

Suinn, R. M., Rickard-Figueroa, K., Lew, S., & Vigil, P. (1987). The Suinn-Lew Asian self-identity acculturation scale: An initial report. *Educational and Psychological Measurement, 47*(2), 401–407.

Tajfel, H. (1978). *Differentiation between social groups: Studies in the social psychology of intergroup relations.* Oxford, UK: Academic Press.

Tajfel, H., & Turner, J. (2001). An integrative theory of intergroup conflict. In M. A. Hogg & D. Abrams (Eds.), *Intergroup relations: Essential readings* (pp. 94–109). New York: Psychology Press.

Taylor, C. M., & Howard-Hamilton, M. F. (1995). Student involvement and racial identity attitudes among African American males. *Journal of College Student Development, 36*(4), 330–336.

Ting-Toomey, S. (1981). Ethnic identity and close friendship in Chinese-American college students. *International Journal of Intercultural Relations, 5*, 383–406.

Triandis, H. C., Kashima, Y., Shimada, E., & Villareal, M. (1986). Acculturation indices as a means of confirming cultural differences. *International Journal of Psychology, 21*(1), 43–70.

Tsai, J. L., & Chentsova-Dutton, Y. (2002). Models of cultural orientation: Differences between American-born and overseas-born Asians. In K. S. Kurasaki & S. Okazaki (Eds.), *Asian American mental health: Assessment theories and methods* (pp. 95–106). New York: Kluwer Academic/Plenum.

Tsai, J. L., Chentsova-Dutton, Y., & Wong, Y. (2002). Why and how we should study ethnic identity, acculturation, and cultural orientation. In

G. Hall & S. Okazaki (Eds.), *Asian American psychology: The science of lives in context* (pp. 41–65). Washington, DC: American Psychological Association.

Tsai, J. L., Knutson, B., & Fung, H. H. (2006). Cultural variation in affect valuation. *Journal of Personality and Social Psychology, 90,* 288–307.

Tsai, J. L., Morstensen, H., Wong, Y., & Hess, D. (2002). What does "being American" mean? A comparison of Asian American and European American young adults. *Cultural Diversity & Ethnic Minority Psychology, 8*(3), 257–273.

Tsai, J. L., Ying, Y., & Lee, P. A. (2000). The meaning of "being Chinese" and "being American": Variation among Chinese American young adults. *Journal of Cross-Cultural Psychology, 31*(3), 302–322.

Tsai, J. L., Ying, Y., & Lee, P. A. (2001). Cultural predictors of self-esteem: A study of Chinese American female and male young adults. *Cultural Diversity & Ethnic Minority Psychology, 7*(3), 284–297.

Verkuyten, M., & Lay, C. (1998). Ethnic minority identity and psychological well-being: The mediating role of collective self-esteem, *Journal of Applied Social Psychology, 28,* 1969–1986.

Weisman, S., Snadomsky, A., & Gannon, M. (1972). Chinese college students perceive their cultural identity. *Education, 92*(4), 116–118.

Williams, J. K. Y., Else, R. N., Hishinuma, E. S., Goebert, D. A., Chang, J. Y., & Andrade, N. N., et al. (2005). A confirmatory model for depression among Japanese American and part-Japanese American adolescents. *Cultural Diversity & Ethnic Minority Psychology, 11*(1), 41–56.

Wong, C. A., Eccles, J. S., & Sameroff, A. (2003). The influence of ethnic discrimination and ethnic identification on African American adolescents' school and socioemotional adjustment. *Journal of Personality, 71*(6), 1197–1232.

Wooden, W. S., Leon, J. J., & Toshima, M. T. (1988). Ethnic identity among sansei and yonsei church-affiliated youth in Los Angeles and Honolulu. *Psychological Reports, 62*(1), 268–270.

Xu, J., Shim, S., Lotz, S., & Almeida, D. (2004). Ethnic identity, socialization factors, and culture-specific consumption behavior. *Psychology & Marketing, 21*(2), 93–112.

Yankelovich Partners. (2001). *American attitudes towards Chinese Americans and Asian Americans.* Retrieved March 14, 2003, from http://www.committee100.org/Published/C100survey.pdf

Yasui, M., Dorham, C. L., & Dishion, T. J. (2004). Ethnic identity and psychological adjustment: A validity analysis for European American and African American adolescents. *Journal of Adolescent Research, 19*(6), 807–825.

Yeh, C. J., Arora, A. K., Inose, M., Okubo, Y., Li, R. H., & Greene, P. (2003). The cultural adjustment and mental health of Japanese immigrant youth. *Adolescence, 38*(151), 481–500.

Ying, Y. (1995). Cultural orientation and psychological well-being in Chinese Americans. *American Journal of Community Psychology, 23*(6), 893–911.

Ying, Y., Coombs, M., & Lee, P. A. (1999). Family intergenerational relationship of Asian American adolescents. *Cultural Diversity & Ethnic Minority Psychology, 5*(4), 350–363.

Ying, Y., & Han, M. (in press). Familism and mental health: Variation between Asian American children of refugees and immigrants. *Journal of Applied Psychoanalytic Studies.*

Ying, Y., & Lee, P. A. (1999). The development of ethnic identity in Asian American adolescents: Status and outcome. *American Journal of Orthopsychiatry, 69*(2), 194–208.

Ying, Y., Lee, P. A., & Tsai, J. L. (2000). Cultural orientation and racial discrimination: Predictors of coherence in Chinese American young adults. *Journal of Community Psychology, 28*(4), 427–442.

Yip, T., & Cross, W. E. J. (2004). A daily diary study of mental health and community involvement outcomes for three Chinese American social identities. *Cultural Diversity & Ethnic Minority Psychology, 10*(4), 394–408.

Yip, T., & Fuligni, A. J. (2002). Daily variation in ethnic identity, ethnic behaviors, and psychological well-being among American adolescents of Chinese descent. *Child Development, 73*(5), 1557–1572.

9

ACCULTURATION AND ENCULTURATION

BRYAN S. K. KIM

Asian Americans comprise individuals with diverse immigration histories. Many of these persons are five and six generations removed from immigration, whose ancestors entered the United States between the mid 1800s and early 1900s during the gold rush and transcontinental railroad eras in California and the sugar plantation period in Hawaii. Others are third- and fourth-generation Americans whose Asian ancestors entered the United States during World War II and the Korean War. There are also Asian Americans who entered the United States after the passing of the Immigration Act of 1965 or after the U.S. military forces pulled out of Southeast Asia in 1975, as well as their second- and third-generation progenies. Furthermore, Asian Americans consist of individuals who arrived from various Asian countries as recently as yesterday. The diversity of the length of residence in the United States suggests that Asian Americans represent a dramatic range on the degrees to which they have adapted to the norms of the dominant U.S. culture and to which they have retained the norms of the Asian culture.

In attempting to understand the adaptation experiences of Asian Americans and their psychological implications, many researchers, in the past 15 years, have focused on the construct of acculturation. For example, at the time of this writing, a search of the PsycINFO database using "acculturation" and "Asian American" as keywords yielded 263 citations, with all but 13 references having the publication date of 1990 or later. This finding is consistent with the results of a Delphi survey of researchers in the field of cross-cultural counseling (Heath, Neimeyer, & Pedersen, 1988). The results revealed a consensus among these experts in predicting that the construct of acculturation would play an increasingly important role in psychological theory and research during the 1990s, as the numbers of ethnic minorities in the United States, especially Asian Americans, continue to rise rapidly. Given this attention to acculturation in the psychological literature, this chapter explores psychological theories related to this construct, measurement of this and closely related constructs, and research findings bearing on the relations between these constructs and psychological functioning among Asian Americans.

THEORIES OF ACCULTURATION AND ENCULTURATION

Construct Definitions

In defining acculturation and enculturation, it is helpful to first describe the broader construct of culture because they are integrally intertwined with each other. An underlying definition of culture has included the presence of shared characteristics among a group of people. Culture has been referred to as a multidimensional construct that can be defined as a social group's shared values, traditions, norms, behaviors, and rituals (Triandis, 1994). Hofstede (2001) defined culture as "the collective programming of the mind that distinguished the members of one group of people from another" (p. 9). This "programming" can encompass shared values and agreed-on practices that are observed as rituals, characterized in heroes, and expressed in symbols. In a further elaboration, Atkinson (2004) described culture as consisting of "values and behaviors that are learned and transmitted within an identifiable community. It also includes the symbols, artifacts, and products of that community. . . . Thus, people commonly associate specific food, language, music, art, and rituals with particular cultures" (p. 10). Hence, a culture can be observed in the various aspects of psychological and social functioning that are shared among a group of people. Culture also is a fluid construct that can undergo reconstruction over a period of time. It follows, then, that the processes of change in these aspects of functioning can be represented by the constructs of acculturation and enculturation.

Acculturation was first defined by Redfield, Linton, and Herskovits (1936) as follows:

Acculturation comprehends those phenomena which result when groups of individuals sharing different cultures come into continuous first-hand contact, with subsequent changes in the original culture patterns of either or both groups. . . . Under this definition acculturation is to be distinguished from culture change, of which it is but one aspect, and assimilation, which is at times a phase of acculturation. It is also to be differentiated from diffusion, which while occurring in all instances of acculturation, is not only a phenomenon which

frequently takes place without the occurrence of the types of contact between peoples specified in the definition above, but also constitutes only one aspect of the process of acculturation. (pp. 149–152)

Three decades later, Graves (1967) coined the term *psychological acculturation* to describe the effects of acculturation at the individual level of study. Graves described this type of acculturation as the changes that an individual experiences in terms of his or her attitudes, values, and identity as a result of being in contact with other cultures. More recently, John Berry and his colleagues (e.g., Berry, 1980; Segall, Dasen, Berry, & Poortinga, 1999) developed a two-continua model of acculturation in which one continuum represents "*contact and participation* (to what extent should [people] become involved in other cultural groups, or remain primarily among themselves)" and the other continuum representing "*cultural maintenance* (to what extent are cultural identity and characteristics considered to be important, and their maintenance striven for)" (Segall et al., 1999, p. 305).

Associated with the concept of acculturation is the concept of *enculturation*. Herskovits (1948) described enculturation as the process of socialization to, and maintenance of, the norms of one's indigenous culture, including the salient values, ideas, and concepts. Based on this description, it can be explained that the "cultural maintenance" process that is described as a part of acculturation may be better represented within this broader concept of enculturation. Although Segall et al.'s (1999) characterization of acculturation in terms of cultural maintenance may work well for immigrant Asian Americans who have been socialized into their Asian cultural norms before arriving in the United States, it may not accurately describe the experiences of Asian Americans who were born in the United States These Asian Americans, particularly individuals who are several generations removed from immigration, may never have been fully enculturated into the Asian ethnic group's cultural norms by their parents and family who also may be U.S.-born. For these persons, the application of "cultural maintenance" process may not be appropriate because they might have never been completely socialized in their Asian ethnic cultural norms in the first place. In addition, these persons may be socialized to their Asian heritage more fully later in life and hence engage in the process of enculturation during this time. For these reasons, the term enculturation offers a more comprehensive description of incorporating and maintaining one's ethnic cultural norms, in comparison to the "cultural maintenance" concept within the acculturation construct. Furthermore, an additional benefit of using the term enculturation is that it places an equal level of focus on the process of socializing into and retaining one's Asian cultural norms as compared to the process of adapting to the norms of the U.S. culture.

Consistent with this explanation is Kim and Abreu's (2001) proposal that (a) enculturation be used to describe the process of (re)socializing into and maintaining the norms of the indigenous culture and (b) acculturation be used to describe the process of adapting to the norms of the dominant culture. For Asian Americans, therefore, acculturation refers to the process of adapting to the norms of the U.S. culture, and enculturation refers to the process of becoming socialized into and maintaining the norms of the Asian culture. Current theories of acculturation and enculturation suggest that Asian Americans who are further removed from immigration will adhere to the mainstream U.S. cultural norms more strongly than Asian Americans who are recent immigrants (Kim, Atkinson, & Umemoto, 2001). On the other hand, Asian Americans who are closer to immigration will adhere to Asian cultural norms more strongly than their counterparts who are several generations removed from immigration.

PSYCHOLOGICAL EFFECTS OF ACCULTURATION AND ENCULTURATION

To understand the psychological experiences of Asian Americans as they engage in the process of adaptation to the mainstream U.S. culture and retention of traditional Asian culture, it is helpful to consider a model proposed by John Berry and his colleagues (Berry, 1980; Segall et al., 1999). These authors theorized the following four acculturation "attitudes" based on combining either high or low levels

of acculturation and enculturation: *integration, assimilation, separation,* and *marginalization.* Integration occurs when individuals are proficient in the culture of the dominant group while retaining proficiency in the indigenous culture. Hence, people in this status are both highly acculturated and strongly enculturated. Asian Americans in this status may be most psychologically healthy because it allows them to hold cultural norms that are functional in both U.S. and Asian cultures while being able to reconcile any conflicts that arise between the two cultural systems. Assimilation, on the other hand, occurs when an individual absorbs the culture of the dominant group while rejecting the indigenous culture. Hence, individuals in this status are highly acculturated but not enculturated. Asian Americans in this status typically maintain cultural norms that are important in the mainstream U.S. culture but have no interest in adhering to Asian cultural norms. Separation occurs when an individual does not absorb the culture of the dominant group and maintains and perpetuates the culture of origin. Hence, individuals in this status are strongly enculturated but not acculturated. Asian Americans in this status typically maintain Asian cultural norms but have no interest in adhering to the mainstream U.S. cultural norms. Finally, marginalization represents the attitude of an individual with no interest in maintaining or acquiring proficiency in any culture, dominant or indigenous. Hence, individuals in this status are neither acculturated nor enculturated. Marginalization is perhaps the most problematic of the four statuses because marginalized Asian Americans will tend to reject both sets of norms.

As noted in the previous paragraph, the integration (or biculturalism) status may be the psychologically healthiest status for Asian Americans. The literature on biculturalism suggests that individuals who can effectively function in both indigenous and dominant cultures may exhibit increased cognitive functioning and better mental health (LaFromboise, Coleman, and Gerton, 1993). LaFromboise et al. (1993) used the term *bicultural competence* to describe the process in which individuals are able to successfully meet the demands of two distinct cultures. They described bicultural competence as including (a) knowledge of cultural beliefs and values of both cultures, (b) positive attitudes toward both groups, (c) bicultural efficacy, or belief that one can live in a satisfying manner within both cultures without sacrificing one's cultural identity, (d) communication ability in both cultures, (e) role repertoire, or the range of culturally appropriate behaviors, and (f) a sense of being grounded in both cultures. LaFromboise et al. noted that individuals may experience difficulties adjusting to the different and sometimes opposing demands, but when they are able to obtain these skills, they may be able to increase their performance in vocational and academic endeavors.

Another possible psychological outcome during the processes of adaptation is acculturative stress. Berry and Annis (1974) noted that members of immigrant ethnic minority groups, including Asian Americans, are vulnerable to stresses arising out of the acculturation process and have labeled this phenomenon "acculturative stress." For example, a highly enculturated Asian American might experience acculturative stress when the person attempts to juggle the competing demands of two cultures as the person acculturates into the dominant U.S. culture; if the stress is successfully overcome, the person typically would enter either the integration or assimilation status. Psychological symptoms of acculturative stress include lowered mental health status (e.g., confusion, anxiety, depression), feelings of marginality and alienation from the dominant culture, heightened psychosomatic symptom level, and identity confusion (Berry & Annis, 1974). Smart and Smart (1995) explained that people with acculturative stress tend to narrow the range of options that they perceive as viable and experience decreased abilities to make decisions with clarity and to carry them out effectively. Acculturative stress impairs occupational functioning because it tends to cause heightened emotional stress and a sense of hopelessness. A meta-analysis of 49 acculturation studies by Moyerman and Forman (1992) found that stress and anxiety may be acute at the very beginning of the acculturation process but gradually become less pronounced. The authors also found that acculturative stress is positively correlated with psychosocial and health problems.

ASSESSMENT OF ACCULTURATION AND ENCULTURATION

Several psychological instruments have been developed to assess acculturation and enculturation among Asian Americans. What follows are descriptions of these instruments, the measurement models on which they are based, and the type of construct dimensions assessed by these measures.

Instruments Based on the Unilinear Measurement Model

Early acculturation theorists (Berry & Annis, 1974; Szapocznik, Scopetta, Kurtines, & Aranalde, 1978) conceptualized acculturation and enculturation as a process that takes place along a single, or unilinear, continuum. According to this model, adaptation occurs when a person moves from one end of a continuum, reflecting involvement in the culture of origin (i.e., enculturation), to the other end of the same continuum, reflecting involvement in the host culture (i.e., acculturation). Szapocznik, Kurtines, and Fernandez (1980) noted that these theories

> conceptualized immigrants as adopting host-culture behavior and values while simultaneously discarding those attributes of their culture of origin. Thus, acculturation has been viewed as a process in which there is an inverse linear relationship between an individual's involvement with his/her original and host cultures. (p. 353)

An early instrument that was based on this unilinear model of measurement is the Acculturation Scale for Chinese Americans (ASCA) (Yao, 1979). The ASCA comprises two scales, designated by the author as Instruments A and B, with high scores on both scales representing high acculturation and low scores representing high enculturation. The 24-item Instrument A measures beliefs and attitudes about family relations, interpersonal relations, sex education, women's status, social/economic/ political issues, and America and its people. Instrument B, which has 16 items, measures an individual's feelings about social isolation, English proficiency, adaptation to the American lifestyle, and future life prospective. All 24 items were generated by the author based on intrinsic and extrinsic cultural traits of Chinese Americans (Yao, 1979). The internal reliabilities for Instruments A and B were reported to be .58 and .75, respectively (Yao, 1979). The author did not report any evidence of construct validity.

An instrument that also is based on the unilinear model but with greater psychometric strength is the Suinn-Lew Asian Self-Identity Acculturation Scale (SL-ASIA) (Suinn, Rickard-Figueroa, Lew, & Vigil, 1987; Suinn, Ahuna, & Khoo, 1992). The 21-item SL-ASIA was modeled after the Acculturation Rating Scale for Mexican Americans (Cuellar, Harris, & Jasso, 1980) and has been the most widely used acculturation scale for Asian Americans. Respondents rate the items on a scale of 1 to 5; low scores are reflective of high Asian identification, and high scores are reflective of high acculturation to Western culture. The SL-ASIA items reflect language use, friendship choice, food preference, media preference, participation in cultural activity, generation and geographic history of life experiences, and ethnic/racial identity. Internal consistency for the SL-ASIA ranges from .68 to .91, with a modal range in the .80s (Ponterotto, Baluch, & Carielli, 1998). Correlations between SL-ASIA scores and generation status, length of residence in the United States, self-rating of ethnic identity, and country of residence have been reported as evidence of criterion-related validity (Ponterotto et al., 1998). Also, evidence for concurrent validity was observed in the correlation between SL-ASIA scores and attitudes toward mental health services, preferred source of help, scores on the Brief Symptom Inventory, Holland career codes, and locus of control orientation (Ponterotto et al., 1998). Exploratory factor analysis has provided further evidence of construct validity, but the exact factor structure underlying SL-ASIA has not been confirmed (Ponterotto et al., 1998).

Instruments Based on the Bilinear Measurement Model

Despite the psychometric strength of the SL-ASIA and its wide utility, a number of scholars (e.g., Ramirez, 1984; Szapocznik et al., 1980) have pointed out the limitations of using this unilinear model, specifically noting its inability to represent true biculturalism. Szapocznik et al. (1980) noted that biculturalism would be an important aspect of acculturation (and enculturation) because the preexistence of a minority community would lead to the process of an individual retaining the culture of origin while accommodating to the host culture. Given that there are already large communities of Asian Americans across the country and new immigrants who continue to join these ethnic enclaves, the concept of biculturalism is particularly relevant. In support of these ideas, Abe-Kim, Okazaki, and Goto (2001), based on data from 355 Asian American college students, found that the bilinear model better described Asian Americans' cultural orientation, including the bicultural orientation. Also, in a study with 588 Asian Canadians, Ryder, Alden, and Paulhus (2000) compared unilinear and bilinear models of assessing acculturation and enculturation and found stronger support for the bilinear model.

Consistent with this current trend toward the bilinear measurement model, several authors have made changes on existing instruments or have developed new instruments that are designed to assess acculturation and enculturation on separate scales among Asian Americans. Based on the original SL-ASIA, Mallinkrodt, Shigeoka, and Suzuki (2005) created the Western Cultural Identification (WCI) index by summing only the responses at points 4 and 5 on the scale while ignoring the responses at the midpoint or below for each item. Conversely, Traditional Culture Identification (TCI) index was created by summing the responses on points 1 and 2 on the scale, with reverse scoring so that higher scores indicate greater identification with the traditional culture, while ignoring the responses at the midpoint and above. Similarly, Abe-Kim et al. (2001) simply counted the responses at points 1 and 2 on the scale to represent adherence to the culture of origin and the responses at points 4 and 5 on the scale to reflect adherence to the dominant culture. In sum, both of these strategies allow researchers to have separate indices of acculturation and enculturation. It should also be mentioned that Suinn (1998) added five additional items to the original 21-item SL-ASIA.

Four of these items separately assess the degree to which respondents adhere to traditional Asian values and American (Western) values, and the extent to which they feel they fit with other Asians of the same ethnicity and Americans who are non-Asians. Hence, these four items attempt to separately assess acculturation and enculturation. As for the fifth item, respondents are asked to indicate one of the following five identities: Asian self-identified, Western self-identified, bicultural–Asian self-identified, bicultural–Western self-identified, and bicultural–bicultural self-identified. Although these scoring changes and addition of new items represent important advances to the original SL-ASIA, more research is needed to examine the psychometric properties of the scores resulting from these revisions.

A recently published new instrument that utilized the multilinear measurement model is the Asian American Multidimensional Acculturation Scale (AAMAS) (Chung, Kim, & Abreu, 2004). The AAMAS is a 15-item measure of Asian Americans' engagement in the norms of one's Asian culture-of-origin, other Asian American cultures, and the European American culture. It contains three subscales: Culture of Origin (AAMAS-CO), Other Asian American Cultures (AAMAS-AA), and European American Culture (AAMAS-EA). The first and the third subscales represent enculturation and acculturation, respectively. As for the second subscale, it represents the possibility of Asian Americans adhering to the norms of a pan-ethnic Asian American culture. For each item in these scales, respondents indicate on a 6-point scale (1 = *not very well*; 6 = *very well*) the extent to which they engage in a particular cultural norm with respect to each of the three cultural groups; the responses for each cultural group are summed to calculate each subscale score. Largely adapted from the SL-ASIA, most of the items in the AAMAS are behavioral in nature and describe activities such as language usage, food consumption, practice of traditions, and association with people. In support of the behavioral nature of the items, Chung et al. (2004) reported low correlation coefficients of .37, .18, and −.25 between the Asian Values Scale (AVS) (Kim, Atkinson, & Yang, 1999), a measure of adherence to Asian cultural values, and the AAMAS-CO, AAMAS-AA, and AAMAS-EA, respectively. In terms of reliability, Chung et al. reported coefficient alphas ranging from .76 to .91 for the three subscales across three studies. In addition, the authors reported 2-week test-retest coefficients ranging from .75 to .89 for the subscales. In terms of validity, Chung et al. reported evidence of factorial validity via exploratory and confirmatory factor analyses. In addition, Chung et al. reported evidence of concurrent, criterion-related, and discriminant validity for the AAMAS's subscale scores based on comparisons with measures of cultural identity, other acculturation measures, generation status, intergenerational conflict, and self-esteem.

Instruments Based on the Bilinear Measurement Model and Single Construct Dimension

In examining levels of acculturation and enculturation, it is also important to consider the construct dimensions on which the two types of adherence can be assessed. Szapocznik et al. (1978) first elaborated on ways of assessing acculturation (and enculturation) by proposing that it involved changes in two personal dimensions: behaviors and values. The behavioral dimension of acculturation includes language use and participation in various cultural activities (e.g., food consumption), while the values dimension reflects relational style, person-nature relationships, beliefs about human nature, and time orientation. Definitions of acculturation (and enculturation) have continued to grow progressively more comprehensive and integrative (e.g., Berry, 1980; Cuellar, Arnold, & Maldonado, 1995). Berry (1980), for example, identified six dimensions of psychological functioning directly affected by acculturation: language, cognitive styles, personality, identity, attitudes, and acculturative stress. Berry posited that, as an individual moves through the acculturation process, changes occur in each of these areas. More recently, Cuellar et al. (1995) defined acculturation in terms of changes at three levels of functioning: behavioral, affective, and cognitive.

The behavioral level includes many types of behaviors, including verbal behavior or language.

Language development obviously includes aspects beyond the behavioral and is understood to include cognitive aspects and related processes. Also at the behavioral level are customs, foods, and such cultural expressions as the music one chooses to listen to or dance to. At the affective level are the emotions that have cultural connections. For example, the way a person feels about important aspects of identity, the symbols one loves or hates, and the meaning one attaches to life itself are all culturally based. At the cognitive level are beliefs about male/female roles, ideas about illness, attitudes toward illness, and fundamental values. (p. 281)

Recently, Kim and Abreu (2001) reviewed the item contents of 33 instruments designed to measure acculturation and enculturation and proposed a set of dimensions along the conceptual framework of Cuellar et al. (1995). Kim and Abreu proposed that acculturation and enculturation consist of the following four dimensions: behavior, values, knowledge, and identity. Behavior is a dimension along the Cuellar et al.'s behavioral level of functioning and refers to friendship choice, preferences for television program and reading, participation in cultural activities, contact with indigenous culture (e.g., time spent in the country of origin), language use, food choice, and music preference. Along the cognitive level of functioning, Kim and Abreu proposed two dimensions: values and knowledge. The value dimension of acculturation and enculturation refers to attitudes and beliefs about social relations, cultural customs, and cultural traditions, along with gender roles and attitudes and ideas about health and illness. The knowledge dimension of acculturation and enculturation refers to culturally specific information such as names of historical leaders in the culture of origin and the dominant culture, and significance of culturally specific activities. Along the affective level of functioning, Kim and Abreu proposed the inclusion of identity as a dimension of acculturation and enculturation. Cultural identify refers to attitudes toward one's cultural identification (e.g., preferred name is in Mandarin), attitudes toward indigenous and dominant groups (e.g., feelings of pride toward the indigenous group), and level of comfort toward people of indigenous and dominant

groups. In classifying identity as one of these four dimensions, Kim and Abreu pointed out that this concept largely overlaps with the construct of "ethnic and racial identity"; indeed, "acculturation" and "ethnic and racial identity" are constructs that are not well differentiated in the literature (Sodowsky & Maestas, 2000). Also, Kim and Abreu pointed out that the four dimensions of acculturation and enculturation are not orthogonal to each other. For example, the behavioral and knowledge dimensions may be correlated, as behavior is likely to be preceded by knowledge, a principle that also applies to other pairs of dimensions.

Unfortunately for both the SL-ASIA and the AAMAS, the items in the instruments represent a mixture of dimensions such as behavior and identity. For example, 76% of the items on the SL-ASIA are designed to measure behavior and 24% reflect cultural identity. Consequently, it is not clear whether a high score on either of the scales is due to one's behavioral acculturation or acculturation along the identity dimension. The importance of assessing these construct dimensions separately was evidenced in a research study, which revealed that although there were no differences between first-, second-, and third-generation (and beyond) Asian Americans on their adherence to Asian cultural values, there were significant differences on their adherence to behaviors and identity norms (Kim et al., 1999). In this study, Asian values adherence was assessed using the AVS, and behavioral and identity adherence were assessed using the SL-ASIA. This finding suggests that behavioral and identity norms tend to change more rapidly than do values norms and, hence, suggest the need for these dimensions to be assessed separately.

An instrument that is designed to assess solely the cultural values dimension and based on the bilinear measurement model is the AVS. The AVS is designed to assess the enculturation linearity of the bilinear model and contains 36 items reflecting several dimensions of Asian values such as collectivism, conformity to norms, emotional self-control, family recognition through achievement, filial piety, and humility. The items utilize a 7-point scale (1 = *strongly disagree;* 7 = *strongly agree*). Kim et al. (1999) reported coefficient alphas of .81 and .82 and a 2-week test-retest reliability of .83 for the 36-item scale. Support for construct validity was obtained through exploratory factor analysis that identified a six-factor solution (Kim et al., 1999) and confirmatory factor analyses (Kim, Yang, Atkinson, Wolfe, & Hong, 2001) that supported a hierarchical factor structure with one second-degree factor and six first-degree factors; however, based on the low coefficient alphas of the factors, Kim et al. recommended against using the six factors as subscales. Evidence of concurrent validity was obtained through a confirmatory factor analysis, in which a two-factor structure comprising a values adaptation construct (with the AVS and two measures of individualism and collectivism serving as its indicators) and a behavioral adaptation construct (with three parcels of the SL-ASIA serving as its indicators) was confirmed. Discriminant validity was evidenced in the low correlation between the AVS, a values-focused measure, and the SL-ASIA, a behavior-focused measure.

Parenthetically, the availability of the AVS led to a study examining the similarities and differences among Asian American ethnic groups on their adherence to Asian cultural values. Given the extensive cultural diversity among Asian Americans, Kim, Yang, et al. (2001) investigated whether Asian American ethnic groups might differ in their adherence to the values assessed by the AVS. Using data on 570 Chinese, Filipino, Korean, and Japanese American college students, the six value dimensions of the AVS were subjected to the following structural equation modeling procedures: confirmatory factor analysis, factorial invariance analysis, and structured means analysis. The combined results of the confirmatory factor analysis and factorial invariance analysis showed that these cultural values are commonly observed across the four ethnic groups and that the members of these groups perceived and defined the values in a similar manner. Furthermore, the results showed that Filipino Americans indicated (a) less adherence to emotional self-control than the other three groups, (b) less adherence to family recognition through achievement and filial piety than Japanese and Korean Americans, (c) less adherence to conformity to norms than Chinese and Japanese Americans, and (d) less adherence to collectivism than Japanese Americans. Japanese Americans had higher adherence to conformity to norms than did Chinese Americans, and Japanese and Korean Americans had higher adherence to family recognition through achievement than did Chinese Americans. These findings are important because they suggest that although these value dimensions are commonly observed across the four groups, they tend to endorse them to different degrees.

Notwithstanding these findings, the psychometric limitations inherent in the AVS have led to its revision. Using the Rasch model (Rasch, 1960), the AVS was revised to establish the 25-item Asian Values Scale–Revised (AVS-R) (Kim & Hong, 2004). To develop the AVS-R, the original 7-point anchor was changed to a 4-point scale (1 = *strongly disagree,* 2 = *disagree,* 3 = *agree,* 4 = *strongly agree*) because three categories of the original anchor were found to give inadequate representation of the responses. Second, the infit and outfit statistics were used to identify and delete 11 items, 7 of which were found to contribute to a decrease in the measure's construct homogeneity and 4 items that were redundant with other items. Despite the removal of nearly one-third of the items, the AVS-R retained the same level of internal consistency as the AVS, with a person-separation reliability (a Rasch model analogue of the Cronbach's alpha) of .80. The AVS-R also well represented the full range of *person trait level* and *item difficulty level.* Person trait level (also known as "person ability" or "agreeability") refers to the degree to which a person has the trait of interest, and in our case, Asian values. Item difficulty level (also known as "difficult to endorse") refers to the degree to which an item is difficult to endorse in comparison to other items.

While the AVS-R was being developed, Kim, Li, and Ng (2005) developed the Asian American Values Scale–Multidimensional (AAVS-M). Recognizing the importance of assessing various dimensions of Asian cultural values separately (i.e., subscales), the authors developed the 42-item AAVS-M. Based on principal components and confirmatory factor analyses, five subscales were established: Collectivism (7 items), Conformity to Norms (7 items), Emotional Self-Control (8 items), Family Recognition Through Achievement (14 items), and Humility (6 items); recall that the factors underlying the AVS could not be used as subscales due to their inadequate internal consistency. Like the AVS, the items utilize a 7-point scale (1 = *strongly disagree;* 7 = *strongly agree*). The total and subscale scores yielded coefficient alphas ranging from .75 to .95 across three samples from the East Coast and the West Coast. In addition, two-week test-retest reliability coefficients ranging from .73 to .92 were observed based on a sample from the East Coast. Evidence of concurrent validity was observed in the significant correlations between the AAVS-M scores and the AVS score, as well as the measure of loss of face (the instrument for this construct is described in the next paragraph), self-construal, cultural identification, attitudes toward seeking professional psychological help, and willingness to see a counselor. Evidence of discriminant validity was observed in the lack of significant correlations between the AAVS-M scores and the scores on measures of self-esteem and social desirability. The samples for the construct validity also were obtained from the East and West Coasts.

Another instrument that is based on the bilinear measurement model and that focuses on the assessment of the values enculturation is the Loss of Face (LOF) (Zane & Yeh, 2002). The LOF contains 21 items designed to assess the extent to which participants were concerned for loss of face. "Face" represents the person's moral reputation or social integrity that is gained and maintained by the performance of specific social roles that are well recognized by others. As such, face has esteem implications that extend beyond the individual to that individual's reference group. For each item on the LOF, respondents give an endorsement rating on a 7-point Likert-type scale (1 = *strongly disagree;* 7 = *strongly agree*). Zane and Yeh (2002) reported a coefficient alpha of .83, suggesting the score's internal reliability. In terms of validity, the LOF score correlated in the expected directions with measures of other-directedness, private self-consciousness, public self-consciousness, social anxiety, extraversion, and behavioral acculturation, indicating the score's concurrent validity. In terms of discriminant validity, the LOF score was not correlated with psychological maladjustment.

Complementing the assessment of Asian values enculturation by the AVS, AVS-R, AAVS-M,

and LOF, Wolfe, Yang, Wong, and Atkinson (2001) developed the 18-item European American Values Scale for Asian Americans (EAVS-AA) to empirically examine the construct of values acculturation. The items reflect mainstream U.S. values in various situations including self-confidence, autonomy, marital behavior, and child-rearing practices. The EAVS-AA utilizes a 7-point Likert-type scale (1 = *strongly disagree;* 7 = *strongly agree*). Similar to the development of the AVS, Wolfe et al. selected items based on *t* tests of the mean scores of 180 preliminary items that were generated based on a review of the literature describing European American culture; items that were scored significantly higher by European Americans than by first-generation Asian Americans were retained. This process led to 26 items, but the authors determined that these items, as a whole, did not have adequate internal consistency. As a result, the authors removed 8 items based on item score-total score statistics, leading to the 18-item measure and an alpha coefficient of .69. In a further analysis, the authors reported that an exploratory factor analysis did not converge after 200 iterations, and hence the dimensionality of this scale is unknown. Therefore, to conclude, despite a strong theoretical grounding and methodological sophistication in developing the EAVS-AA, this instrument had limitations in terms of low reliability, unclear factor structure, and items not fully representing the entire range of the construct.

Recently, an effort was made to improve the EAVS-AA with the publication of the European American Values Scale for Asian Americans–Revised (EAVS-AA-R) (Hong, Kim, & Wolfe, 2005). Hong et al. (2005) used the Rasch model (Rasch, 1960) to select 25 items from the original pool of items in the Wolfe et al. (2001) study that reflected the full range of the person trait level and item difficulty level. As explained earlier in this section, a combination of person trait and item difficulty levels indicates how well the items in an instrument are representative of the full range of the construct. Also, Hong et al. changed the scale anchor to a 4-point Likert scale (1 = *strongly disagree;* 4 = *strongly agree*). The results of subsequent Rasch analysis using the final 25 EAVS-AA-R items indicated that the new instrument has a unidimensional factor structure (an evidence of construct validity) and a person-separation reliability (the Rasch analogue to the coefficient alpha) of .78. Furthermore, the results of the Rasch analysis indicated that the 4-point scale used in the EAVS-AA-R was psychometrically better than the original 7-point scale.

RESEARCH FINDINGS ON ACCULTURATION AND ENCULTURATION

Reflecting the popular interest in the constructs of acculturation and enculturation, there has been a growing body of research studies on the psychological correlates of these constructs among Asian Americans. In general, the results from these studies suggest that acculturation and enculturation have important implications for psychological functioning, vocational functioning (education and occupation), attitudes toward seeking mental health services, and therapy process.

Psychological Functioning

Based on the largely theoretical literature on the psychological effects of acculturation and enculturation that were described in the previous section, a small number of studies have examined relations between acculturation and enculturation on psychological outcomes among Asian Americans. One study (Kim & Omizo, in press) examined the behavioral dimension of these adaptation processes, and another study (Kim & Omizo, 2005) focused on the values dimension. For the behavioral dimension, Kim and Omizo (in press) examined the behavioral acculturation to U.S. cultural norms and behavioral enculturation to Asian cultural norms among 156 Asian American college students, and their relationships to ratings on measures of cognitive flexibility, general self-efficacy, collective self-esteem, acculturative stress, and attitudes toward seeking professional psychological help. The behavioral acculturation was assessed using the AAMAS-EA, and behavioral enculturation was measured using the AAMAS-CO. Based on the theory of biculturalism, Kim and Omizo hypothesized that

scoring high on both behavioral acculturation and enculturation would be positively associated with positive psychological outcomes. The results indicated support for this hypothesis for the membership dimension of collective self-esteem, suggesting that bicultural Asian Americans tend to feel good about their membership in the Asian American group. The results also indicated that behavioral acculturation was positively related to cognitive flexibility, general self-efficacy, and the public dimension of collective self-esteem. In addition, behavioral enculturation was positively related to the private dimension and the importance of identity dimension of collective self-esteem.

The study examining values acculturation and enculturation was identical to the Kim and Omizo (in press) study, except that the EAVS-AA-R was used to assess values acculturation and the AVS was used to assess values enculturation (Kim & Omizo, 2005). Based on the data from the same participants, the biculturalism hypothesis was supported in that adherence to both Asian and mainstream U.S. values were associated with membership and private dimensions of collective self-esteem. The results also indicated that adherence to Asian values was positively correlated with the importance-to-identity dimension of collective self-esteem. Adherence to U.S. values was positively correlated with cognitive flexibility and general self-efficacy.

The combined results of these two studies provide some support for LaFromboise et al.'s (1993) description of the positive benefits of biculturalism. The results also support the idea from John Berry and colleagues (e.g., Berry, 1980; Segall et al., 1999) that the integration attitude may be most beneficial psychologically. Interestingly, on the dependent variable (membership domain of collective self-esteem) on which biculturalism was found to have a significant relation in both studies, the results showed that behavioral biculturalism accounted for greater variance (25%) than did values biculturalism (10%). These findings suggest the differences in the relative importance between values and behavior with respect to membership self-esteem. However, more study is needed, particularly given that the studies do not go beyond college-based samples.

Vocational Functioning

In terms of career development, including educational and occupational issues, six studies were found on the relations between acculturation and vocational experiences among Asian Americans. All of these studies assessed acculturation using the SL-ASIA. In an early acculturation study, Leong and Tata (1990) examined the occupational values among 5th- and 6th-grade Chinese American students. To assess acculturation, some of the items in the SL-ASIA were reworded so that they could be easily understood by these elementary school children. Based on data from 177 respondents, the results indicated that acculturation was positively related to the valuing of self-realization (i.e., using one's skills and talents) in that this value tended to be more important among higher acculturated children.

Park and Harrison (1995) examined the relation between acculturation and career interests. Based on data from 184 Asian American college students, the authors found that acculturation was positively correlated with perceived control in the personal and interpersonal spheres (i.e., socializing with others in large groups) and with the enterprising type of occupations (e.g., insurance agent, retailer, realtor). Also, acculturation was negatively correlated with interests in investigative (e.g., scientist, physician) and conventional (e.g., bank cashier, book keeper) types of occupations.

Tang, Fouad, and Smith (1999) investigated the relations between acculturation and occupational interests. Based on data from 187 Asian American college students, Tang et al. found that lower acculturated Asian Americans tended to choose more typical occupations (e.g., mechanic, computer operator, paralegal) than their high acculturated counterparts. In addition, the results showed that family background was influential on their choices and that interest may not necessarily be related to their occupational choices.

In a study examining the relation between acculturation and ability to make mature career decisions, Hardin, Leong, and Osipow (2002) surveyed 182 Asian American and 235 European American college students. The results indicated that, although as a group Asian Americans exhibited less mature career choice attitudes than European Americans, the high acculturated Asian Americans did not differ from European Americans in maturity of career choice attitudes.

Chung (2001) examined the relation between acculturation and child-parent intergeneration conflicts, one of which was in the area of education and career area. Based on the data from 342 Asian American college students, Chung found that Asian Americans who were more acculturated reported experiencing less conflict with their parents in the areas of education and career than both the low-acculturated and bicultural groups; with the SL-ASIA, individuals who scored neither high or low were classified as bicultural.

In a study that sampled participants beyond the college population, Leong (2001) examined the relations between acculturation and career adjustment among 56 Asian Americans working in several companies. The results showed that Asian Americans with high acculturation tended to be more satisfied and experience less stress and strain with their jobs than did their counterparts who were low acculturated. Also, the results showed that Asian Americans who were high acculturated tended to receive higher performance ratings from their supervisors than did their low acculturated counterparts.

The combined results of these studies provide support for the important role of acculturation in Asian Americans' career development. In particular, the studies highlighted some of the benefits in acculturating to the norms of mainstream U.S. culture, particularly in terms of career satisfaction. However, given that only one study (Leong, 2001) employed a non-college-based sample, more studies are needed that go beyond college students. Also, all of the studies used the unilinear SL-ASIA and hence it is not clear whether true biculturalism is associated with positive vocational outcomes.

Attitudes Toward Seeking Mental Health Services

Eight studies were found that examined the relations between acculturation and enculturation and help-seeking attitudes. These studies were conducted to try to explain the reasons why Asian Americans tended to underutilize psychological services (e.g., Leong, 1994; Snowden & Chueng, 1990). In a survey study of attitudes toward help-seeking among Asian Americans, Atkinson and Gim (1989) examined the relations between acculturation (assessed with the SL-ASIA) and attitudes toward seeking professional psychological services among 557 Chinese, Japanese, and Korean American college students. The results showed that respondents with high acculturation tended to be more likely to recognize personal need for professional psychological help, be tolerant of the stigma, and be open to discussing their problems with a service provider.

In a replication of Atkinson and Gim (1989), Tata and Leong (1994) examined the relations between acculturation (assessed with the SL-ASIA) and attitudes toward seeking professional psychology help. Based on a survey of 219 Chinese American college students, Tata and Leong found that, while controlling for gender, students who were more acculturated tended to have more positive attitudes toward seeking professional psychological help.

In a more recent replication of Atkinson and Gim (1989), Zhang and Dixon (2003) examined the relations between acculturation and attitudes toward seeking professional psychology help among 170 Asian international students. To assess acculturation, the authors used a modified version of the SL-ASIA in which eight items that were "irrelevant to the situation for the vast majority of Asian international students" (Zhang & Dixon, 2003, p. 211) were eliminated; a coefficient alpha of .74 was reported for the remaining 13 items. While controlling for the effects of several demographic variables (e.g., age, country of origin, gender, educational level, time since arrival, and previous therapy experience), the results indicated that more acculturated international students had more positive attitudes toward seeking help.

In a study of the relations between acculturation and willingness to see a counselor, a construct that may be more closely related to behavioral outcomes than attitudes toward help-seeking, Gim, Atkinson, and Whiteley (1990) examined Asian Americans' acculturation and its relations to willingness to see a counselor

and the level of reported severity of various types of psychological problems. Employing the SL-ASIA, the authors surveyed 816 Asian American college students and found that low-medium acculturated individuals were more willing to see a counselor than were high acculturated Asian Americans. Given the apparent contradiction with Atkinson and Gim's (1989) finding, the authors pointed out that because the respondents' ratings of the severity of problems were used as a covariate in the analysis, it is possible that when less acculturated students do acknowledge a concern, they are more willing to seek professional help. They speculated that this finding might reflect respect for authority on the part of less acculturated Asian Americans. Of course, the differences in the dependent variables also might account for this apparent contradiction.

In a similar study, Atkinson, Lowe, and Matthews (1995) investigated whether Asian Americans' level of acculturation is related to their willingness to see a counselor for personal and academic problems. The authors surveyed 187 Asian American college students and found no significant relation between acculturation and willingness to see a counselor.

In a study focusing on a specific type of mental health service, Leong, Wagner, and Kim (1995) examined the relations between acculturation and expectations for group counseling among 134 Asian American college students. To assess acculturation, the authors used a modified version of an acculturation scale that was developed as part of a doctoral dissertation for use with Koreans. This instrument yields a score for each of the four acculturation attitudes described earlier (assimilation, integration, separation, and marginalization). (Because of space limitation and the fact that it is not a published instrument, this scale is not reviewed in this chapter.) In addition to this instrument, this study employed the LOF to assess values enculturation. The results showed that, while controlling for gender and loss of face level, the integration attitude had a significantly positive relation to having positive attitudes toward group counseling. However, the results showed that the LOF score was not significantly related to positive group counseling attitudes.

In a study focusing on values enculturation, Kim and Omizo (2003) examined the relations among Asian American adherence to Asian cultural values, assessed by the AVS, attitudes toward seeking professional psychological help, and willingness to see a counselor. Based on the data from 242 Asian American college students, the results revealed that adherence to Asian cultural values was inversely related to both attitudes toward seeking professional psychological help and general willingness to see a counselor, above and beyond the effects of related demographic variables. The results also indicated that attitudes toward seeking professional psychological help was a perfect mediator on the relationship between adherence to Asian cultural values and willingness to see a counselor in general, and between adherence to Asian values and willingness to see a counselor for personal and health problems, in particular. This finding suggests that Asian American adherence to Asian cultural values influences one's willingness to see a counselor, a more behavior-oriented attitude, via its influence on attitudes toward professional psychological service.

In a partial replication of Kim and Omizo (2003), Gloria, Castellanos, Park, and Kim (in press) examined the relation between Korean American college students' adherence to Asian cultural values and attitudes toward seeking professional psychological help. Based on data from 228 Korean Americans, the results were consistent with Kim and Omizo's findings in that there was a significant inverse relationship between adherence to Asian values and positive help-seeking attitudes.

In summary, the results of these studies suggest that high acculturation is associated with increased positive help-seeking attitudes among Asian Americans. However, there is less clarity in terms of willingness to see a counselor, as one study found an inverse relation and another found a null relation. As for values enculturation, evidence suggests a negative relation between adherence to Asian cultural values and help-seeking attitudes and willingness to see a counselor. However, all of these findings are limited by their sole use of college-based samples. In addition, the measures of help-seeking used in these studies were attitudinal scales; hence, the results may not reflect actual service utilization rates.

Therapy Process

Although the research studies examining help-seeking attitudes and willingness to see a counselor are helpful in that they provide some explanations for Asian Americans' underutilization of services, they do not explain what occurs when Asian Americans do enter treatment. Scholars on Asian Americans and mental health services have observed that Asian Americans tend to prematurely terminate therapy if they are not provided with culturally credible treatment (e.g., Leong, Wagner, & Tata, 1995). In light of these observations, researchers have investigated ways in which the therapy process can be modified to become more culturally relevant, sensitive, and effective in meeting the psychological needs of Asian Americans. In many of these studies, acculturation and enculturation were examined to investigate whether people of different adaptation levels prefer different types of therapy intervention strategies. The summaries of findings from these studies are discussed next. The first study examined the role of acculturation within the therapy context, whereas the rest of the studies, except for Kim, Ng, and Ahn (2005), examined the role of enculturation. The Kim, Ng, et al. (2005) study examined the roles of both enculturation and acculturation.

Merta, Ponterotto, and Brown (1992) examined the relations between acculturation and ratings of effectiveness of two directive styles (authoritative or collaborative) of academic counseling with 50 Asian foreign students. Participants who have been in the United States longer than 2 months and who perceived their English proficiency as adequate were classified as being high acculturated. Participants who did not meet both conditions were classified as being low acculturated. The participants were assigned to a peer counselor who employed either authoritative style or collaborative style of counseling. Counterintuitively, the results showed that high acculturated students rated the authoritative peer counselors as more credible than the collaborative ones.

In an analogue study comparing cognitive therapy (CT) and time limited dynamic psychotherapy (TLDP), treatment rationales were examined for their perceived credibility among 136 Asian American college students and whether the credibility ratings related to participant enculturation level, as determined by the AVS and LOF (Wong, Kim, Zane, Kim, & Huang, 2003). Participants were randomly assigned to read a vignette describing the treatment rationale of either a CT or TLDP approach to treating persons with depression and then asked to rate the perceived credibility of the rationale. Contrary to what was hypothesized, the results revealed no relations with the two values enculturation variables.

In a study with Asian American college student clients, Kim and Atkinson (2002) investigated the effects of client adherence to Asian cultural values (values enculturation), counselor expression of cultural values, and counselor ethnicity on the counseling process. After completing the AVS, 112 Asian American clients engaged in a 30-minute career counseling session with either an Asian or European American counselor who expressed either Asian or U.S. cultural values. The results showed that, in general, clients with high adherence to Asian cultural values evaluated Asian American counselors as more empathic and credible than did clients with low adherence to Asian values. Clients who had low adherence to Asian values judged European American counselors to be more empathic than did clients with high adherence to Asian values.

In a similar study, 78 Asian American college students who were experiencing career uncertainty engaged in career counseling with a European American female counselor who focused on either immediate resolution of the problem or insight attainment through problem exploration and who emphasized client expression of either cognition or emotion (Kim, Li, & Liang, 2002). Across all conditions, clients with high adherence to Asian values (as determined by the AVS) perceived stronger counselor empathy and client-counselor working alliance than did clients with low adherence to Asian values, as expected. Among clients with high adherence to Asian values, those in the expression of emotion condition perceived greater counselor cross-cultural competence than did those in the cognition condition. This latter result was directly contradictory to what was hypothesized. Also interestingly, all clients who were

exposed to the immediate resolution condition perceived stronger working alliance than did the clients who were exposed to the insight attainment condition.

In a study on the effects of values enculturation and counselor self-disclosure, 62 East Asian American clients rated their counselor and session outcome after discussing personal issues with a European American counselor who either disclosed personal information or refrained from disclosing personal information (Kim et al., 2003). Before the session, all participants completed the AVS to indicate their enculturation level. Contrary to expectation, disclosure condition and client adherence to Asian values were not related to session outcome. However, in general, disclosures of strategies were perceived by the clients to be more helpful than disclosures of approval/reassurance, facts/credentials, and feelings, with disclosures of insight intermediate in helpfulness. Disclosures of strategies occurred more frequently in highly rated sessions than in sessions rated low. Client- and counselor-perceived intimacy of disclosures was related to client- and counselor-rated helpfulness of disclosures, respectively.

Li and Kim (2004) investigated the effects of counseling style and client adherence to Asian cultural values on the process of career-focused counseling with Asian American college students. Based on their scores on the AVS, 52 clients were classified as having either high or low adherence to Asian values and then randomly assigned to a European American female counselor who employed either a directive or a nondirective style. The results showed that clients exposed to the directive style, in comparison to those exposed to the nondirective style, rated the counselor as being more empathic and cross-culturally competent and reported stronger client-counselor working alliance and greater session depth, regardless of their level of adherence to Asian values. No relation was found between clients' AVS scores and session outcome.

In a study examining the effects of client expectation for counseling success, client-counselor worldview match, and clients' values acculturation and enculturation on counseling process, 88 Asian American volunteer clients with personal concerns engaged in single-session counseling with 1 of 11 female counselors who either matched or mismatched the client's worldview (Kim, Ng, et al., 2005). Client values enculturation was assessed using the AVS and values acculturation was assessed using the EAVS-AA-R. The results showed that adherence to Asian values was positively related to client-counselor working alliance, and adherence to U.S. values was positively associated with client-counselor working alliance and session depth. Also, an interaction effect was observed such that high expectation for counseling success and strong adherence to U.S. values were associated with increased perception of counselor empathy. Furthermore, clients in the worldview match condition perceived stronger client-counselor working alliance and counselor empathy than those in the mismatch condition.

In summary, the results of these studies show some support for the significant relations between Asian American acculturation and enculturation and therapy process. Four of the seven studies demonstrated significant relations between acculturation, enculturation, or both on client evaluation of session outcome. Among the five studies examining values enculturation, two of them yielded significant relations. In addition, the Kim, Ng, et al. (2005) study showed significant relations on both values acculturation and enculturation. However, it should be noted that all of the studies used college student samples and hence the results may not generalize to non-student populations. Also, all of the studies examined the outcome of the first session. Although the first session is critical in establishing therapeutic alliance, it would be valuable to examine the role of acculturation and enculturation on long-term therapy process and outcome.

SUMMARY, RECOMMENDATIONS, AND CONCLUSION

This chapter summarized the current literature on acculturation and enculturation. Based on this review, the following recommendations are offered.

1. There is a need to conduct more research on acculturation and enculturation as they relate to Asian Americans' experiences in the United States. This review found only 23 empirical studies across the four areas of focus, and some of these areas yielded inconsistent findings.

2. There is a need to improve the instrumentation in the assessment of acculturation and enculturation. The current measures assess mainly behaviors and values, and future psychometric research should focus on other dimensions of acculturation and enculturation such as knowledge and cultural identity. Also, the current and future instruments should be translated into various Asian languages and validated, so that they can be used to study individuals whose proficiency in English is limited (e.g., non–college student samples)

3. Given that almost all of the reviewed studies employed college student samples, particularly in the West Coast areas, future research should attempt to employ samples that represent community populations across a wider geographical area.

4. In terms of content areas, more theoretical and empirical work is needed to better understand the relations between acculturation and enculturation and psychological functioning. Specifically, the psychological outcomes of biculturalism need to be better understood. In addition, the process of biculturalism should be examined so that psychologists can help individuals to engage in this process while mitigating the effects of acculturative stress.

5. Research is needed to examine the relations between acculturation and enculturation and racial and ethnic identity and to identify the areas of overlap and distinctions.

6. For therapy research, studies are needed that examine the role of acculturation and enculturation on long-term process and outcome.

To conclude, the prediction from Heath et al.'s (1988) Delphi study that there would be more attention on acculturation (and enculturation) seems to be gradually materializing. However, more research is needed for this prediction to be fully realized. Therefore, it is hoped that this review and critique of the literature will foster more research in this important area of work within Asian American psychology.

REFERENCES

Abe-Kim, J., Okazaki, S., & Goto, S. G. (2001). Unidimensional versus multidimensional approaches to the assessment of acculturation for Asian American populations. *Cultural Diversity & Ethnic Minority Psychology, 7,* 232–246.

Atkinson, D. R. (2004). *Counseling American minorities* (6th ed.). Boston: McGraw-Hill.

Atkinson, D. R., & Gim, R. H. (1989). Asian-American cultural identity and attitudes toward mental health services. *Journal of Counseling Psychology, 36,* 209–212.

Atkinson, D. R., Lowe, S. M., & Matthews, L. (1995). Asian-American acculturation, gender, and willingness to seek counseling. *Journal of Multicultural Counseling and Development, 23,* 130–138.

Berry, J. W. (1980). Acculturation as varieties of adaptation. In A. M. Padilla (Ed.), *Acculturation: Theory, models, and some new findings* (pp. 9–25). Boulder, CO: Westview Press.

Berry, J. W., & Annis, R. C. (1974). Acculturative stress: The role of ecology, culture and differentiation. *Journal of Cross-Cultural Psychology, 5,* 382–406.

Chung, R. H. G. (2001). Gender, ethnicity, and acculturation in intergenerational conflict of Asian American college students. *Cultural Diversity & Ethnic Minority Psychology, 7,* 376–386.

Chung, R. H. G., Kim, B. S. K., & Abreu, J. M. (2004). Asian American Multidimensional Acculturation Scale: Development, factor analysis, reliability, and validity. *Cultural Diversity & Ethnic Minority Psychology, 10,* 66–80.

Cuellar, I., Arnold, B., & Maldonado, R. (1995). Acculturation rating scale for Mexican Americans–II: A revision of the original ARSMA scale. *Hispanic Journal of Behavioral Sciences, 17,* 275–304.

Cuellar, I., Harris, L. C., & Jasso, R. (1980). An acculturation scale for Mexican American normal and clinical populations. *Hispanic Journal of Behavioral Sciences, 2,* 199–217.

Gim, R. H., Atkinson, D. R., & Whiteley, S. (1990). Asian-American acculturation, severity of concerns, and willingness to see a counselor. *Journal of Counseling Psychology, 37,* 281–285.

Gloria, A. M., Castellanos, J., Park, Y. S., & Kim, D. (in press). The role of adherence to Asian cultural values and cultural fit in Korean American undergraduates' help-seeking attitudes. *Journal of Counseling & Development.*

Graves, T. D. (1967). Psychological acculturation in a tri-ethnic community. *Southwestern Journal of Anthropology, 23,* 337–350.

Hardin, E. E., Leong, F. T. L., & Osipow, S. H. (2002). Cultural relativity in the conceptualization of career maturity. *Journal of Vocational Behavior, 58,* 36–52.

Heath, A. E., Neimeyer, G. J., & Pedersen, P. B. (1988). The future of cross-cultural counseling: A Delphi poll. *Journal of Counseling & Development, 67,* 27–30.

Herskovits, M. J. (1948). *Man and his works: The science of cultural anthropology.* New York: Knopf.

Hofstede, G. (2001). *Culture's consequences: Comparing values, behaviors, institutions, and organizations across nations* (2nd ed.). Thousand Oaks, CA: Sage.

Hong, S., Kim, B. S. K., & Wolfe, M. M. (2005). A psychometric revision of the European American Values Scale for Asian Americans using the Rasch model. *Measurement and Evaluation in Counseling and Development, 37,* 194–207.

Kim, B. S. K., & Abreu, J. M. (2001). Acculturation measurement: Theory, current instruments, and future directions. In J. G. Ponterotto, J. M. Casas, L. A. Suzuki, & C. M. Alexander (Eds.), *Handbook of multicultural counseling* (2nd ed., pp. 394–424). Thousand Oaks, CA: Sage.

Kim, B. S. K., & Atkinson, D. R. (2002). Asian American client adherence to Asian cultural values, counselor expression of cultural values, counselor ethnicity, and career counseling process. *Journal of Counseling Psychology, 49,* 3–13.

Kim, B. S. K., Atkinson, D. R., & Umemoto, D. (2001) Asian cultural values and the counseling process: Current knowledge and directions for future research. *The Counseling Psychologist, 29,* 570–603.

Kim, B. S. K., Atkinson, D. R., & Yang, P. H. (1999). The Asian values scale: Development, factor analysis, validation, and reliability. *Journal of Counseling Psychology, 46,* 342–352.

Kim, B. S. K., Hill, C. E., Gelso, C. J., Goates, M. K., Asay, P. A., & Harbin, J. M. (2003). Counselor self-disclosure, East Asian American client adherence to Asian cultural values, and counseling process. *Journal of Counseling Psychology, 50,* 324–332.

Kim, B. S. K., & Hong, S. (2004). A psychometric revision of the Asian Values Scale using the Rasch model. *Measurement and Evaluation in Counseling and Development, 37,* 15–27.

Kim, B. S. K., Li, L. C., & Liang, C. T. H. (2002). Effects of Asian American client adherence to Asian cultural values, session goal, and counselor emphasis of client expression on career counseling process. *Journal of Counseling Psychology, 49,* 342–354

Kim, B. S. K., Li, L. C., & Ng, G. F. (2005). The Asian American Values Scale–Multidimensional: Development, reliability, and validity. *Cultural Diversity & Ethnic Minority Psychology, 11,* 187–201.

Kim, B. S. K., Ng, G. F., & Ahn, A. J. (2005). Effects of client expectation for counseling success, client-counselor worldview match, and client adherence to Asian and European American cultural values on counseling process with Asian Americans. *Journal of Counseling Psychology, 52,* 67–76.

Kim, B. S. K., & Omizo, M. M. (2003). Asian cultural values, attitudes toward seeking professional psychological help, and willingness to see a counselor. *The Counseling Psychologist, 31,* 343–361.

Kim, B. S. K., & Omizo, M. M. (2005). Asian and European American cultural values, collective self-esteem, acculturative stress, cognitive flexibility, and general self-efficacy among Asian American college students. *Journal of Counseling Psychology, 52,* 412–419.

Kim, B. S. K., & Omizo, M. M. (in press). Behavioral acculturation and enculturation and psychological functioning among Asian American college students. *Cultural Diversity & Ethnic Minority Psychology.*

Kim, B. S. K., Yang, P. H., Atkinson, D. R., Wolfe, M. M., & Hong, S. (2001). Cultural value similarities and differences among Asian American ethnic groups. *Cultural Diversity & Ethnic Minority Psychology, 7,* 343–361.

LaFromboise, T., Coleman, H. L K., & Gerton, J. (1993). Psychological impact of biculturalism: Evidence and theory. *Psychological Bulletin, 114,* 395–412.

Leong, F. T. L. (1994). Asian Americans' differential patterns of utilization of inpatient and outpatient public mental health services in Hawaii. *Journal of Community Psychology, 22,* 82–96.

Leong, F. T. L. (2001). The role of acculturation in the career adjustment of Asian American workers: A test of Leong and Chou's (1994) formulations. *Cultural Diversity & Ethnic Minority Psychology, 7,* 262–273.

Leong, F. T. L., & Tata, S. P. (1990). Sex and acculturation differences in occupational values among Chinese-American children. *Journal of Counseling Psychology, 37,* 208–212.

Leong, F. T. L., Wagner, N. S., & Kim, H. H. (1995). Group counseling expectations among Asian American students: The role of culture-specific factors. *Journal of Counseling Psychology, 42,* 217–222.

Leong, F. T. L., Wagner, N. S., & Tata, S. P. (1995). Racial and ethnic variations in help-seeking attitudes. In J. G. Ponterotto, J. M. Casas, L. A. Suzuki, & C. M. Alexander (Eds.), *Handbook of multicultural counseling* (pp. 415–438). Thousand Oaks, CA: Sage.

Li, L. C., & Kim, B. S. K. (2004). Effects of counseling style and client adherence to Asian cultural values on counseling process with Asian American college students. *Journal of Counseling Psychology, 51,* 158–167.

Mallinckrodt, B., Shigeoka, S., & Suzuki, L. A. (2005). Asian and Pacific Island American students' acculturation and etiology beliefs about typical counseling presenting problems. *Cultural Diversity & Ethnic Minority Psychology, 11,* 227–238.

Merta, R. J., Ponterotto, J. G., & Brown, R. D. (1992). Comparing the effectiveness of two directive styles in the academic counseling of foreign students. *Journal of Counseling Psychology, 39,* 214–218.

Moyerman, D. R., & Forman, B. D. (1992). Acculturation and adjustment: A meta-analytic study. *Hispanic Journal of Behavioral Sciences, 14,* 163–200.

Park, S. E., & Harrison, A. A. (1995). Career-related interests and values, perceived control, and acculturation of Asian-American and Caucasian-American college students. *Journal of Applied Social Psychology, 25,* 1184–1203.

Ponterotto, J. G., Baluch, S., & Carielli, D. (1998). The Suinn-Lew Asian self-identity acculturation scale (SL-ASIA): Critique and research recommendations. *Measurement and Evaluation in Counseling and Development, 31,* 109–124.

Ramirez, M., III (1984). Assessing and understanding biculturalism-multiculturalism in Mexican-American adults. In J. L. Martinez Jr. & R. H. Mendoza (Eds.), *Chicano psychology* (2nd ed., pp. 77–93). New York: Academic Press.

Rasch, G. (1960). *Probabilistic models for some intelligence and attainment tests.* Chicago: Mesa Press.

Redfield, R., Linton, R., & Herskovits, M. J. (1936). Memorandum on the study of acculturation. *American Anthropologist, 56,* 973–1002.

Ryder, A. G., Alden, L. E., & Paulhus, D. L. (2000). Is acculturation unidimensional or bidimensional? A head-to-head comparison in the prediction of personality, self-identity, and adjustment. *Journal of Personality and Social Psychology, 79,* 49–65.

Segall, M. H., Dasen, P. R., Berry, J. W., & Poortinga, Y. H. (1999). *Human behavior in global perspective: An introduction to cross-cultural psychology* (2nd ed.). Boston: Allyn & Bacon.

Smart, J. F., & Smart, D. W. (1995). Acculturative stress: The experience of the Hispanic immigrant. *The Counseling Psychologist, 23,* 25–42.

Snowden, L. R., & Cheung, F. H. (1990). Use of inpatient mental health services by members of ethnic minority groups. *American Psychologist, 45,* 347–355.

Sodowsky, G. R., & Maestas, M. V. (2000). Acculturation, ethnic identity, and acculturative stress: Evidence and measurement. In R. Dana (Ed.), *Handbook of cross-cultural and multicultural personality assessment* (pp. 131–172). Mahwah, NJ: Lawrence Erlbaum.

Suinn, R. M. (1998). Measurement of acculturation of Asian Americans. *Asian American and Pacific Islander Journal of Health, 6,* 7–12.

Suinn, R. M., Ahuna, C., & Khoo, G. (1992). The Suinn-Lew Asian self-identity acculturation scale: Concurrent and factorial validation. *Educational and Psychological Measurement, 52,* 1041–1046.

Suinn, R. M., Rickard-Figueroa, K., Lew, S., & Vigil, P. (1987). The Suinn-Lew Asian self-identity acculturation scale: An initial report. *Educational and Psychological Measurement, 47,* 401–407.

Szapocznik, J., Kurtines, W. M., & Fernandez, T. (1980). Bicultural involvement and adjustment in Hispanic-American youths. *International Journal of Intercultural Relations, 4,* 353–365.

Szapocznik, J., Scopetta, M. A., Kurtines, W., & Aranalde, M. A. (1978). Theory and measurement of acculturation. *Interamerican Journal of Psychology, 12,* 113–120.

Tang, M., Fouad, N. A., & Smith, P. L. (1999). Asian Americans' career choices: A path model to examine factors influencing their career choices. *Journal of Vocational Behavior, 54,* 142–157.

Tata, S. P., & Leong, F. T. L. (1994). Individualism-collectivism, social-network orientation, and acculturation as predictors of attitudes toward seeking professional psychological help among Chinese Americans. *Journal of Counseling Psychology, 41,* 280–287.

Triandis, H. C. (1994). *Culture and social behavior.* New York: McGraw-Hill.

Wolfe, M. M., Yang, P. H., Wong, E. C., & Atkinson, D. R. (2001). Design and development of the European American values scale for Asian Americans. *Cultural Diversity & Ethnic Minority Psychology, 7,* 274–283.

Wong, E., Kim, B. S. K., Zane, N. W. S., Kim, I. J., & Huang, J. S. (2003). Examining culturally-based variables associated with ethnicity: Influences on credibility perceptions of empirically supported interventions. *Cultural Diversity & Ethnic Minority Psychology, 9,* 88–96.

Yao, E. L. (1979). The assimilation of contemporary Chinese immigrants. *The Journal of Psychology, 101,* 107–113.

Zane, N. W. S., & Yeh, M. (2002). The use of culturally-based variables in assessment: Studies on loss of face. In K. S. Kurasaki & S. Okazaki (Eds.), *Asian American mental health: Assessment theories and methods* (pp. 123–138). New York: Kluwer Academic/Plenum.

Zhang, N., & Dixon, D. N. (2003). Acculturation and attitudes of Asian international students toward seeking psychological help. *Journal of Multicultural Counseling and Development, 31,* 205–222.

10

CAREER DEVELOPMENT AND VOCATIONAL BEHAVIORS OF ASIAN AMERICANS

FREDERICK T. L. LEONG

ARPANA GUPTA

As Leong (1985, 1991, 2004) has repeatedly observed, very little research has been done on Asian Americans' career choice and development. This deficit exists in spite of the high need for career counseling services expressed by Asian Americans. For example, 34% of the Asian American students taking the Scholastic Aptitude Test (SAT) in 1980 expressed an intention to seek vocational-career counseling when enrolled in college, compared to 27% of Whites, 24% of Blacks, and 30% of Mexican Americans (College Entrance Examination Board, 1980). In a more recent national survey conducted by the Gallup organization for the National Career Development Association (Brown, Minor, & Jepsen, 1991), it was found that large percentages of Asian-Pacific Islanders (71%) and Hispanics (75%) reported being interested in obtaining more information about careers if they could start over. Asian-Pacific Islanders (37%) were also significantly more likely to report using college career information centers than were Whites

(21%), African Americans (19%), or Hispanics (15%). Whites (71%) were significantly more likely than Asian-Pacific Islanders (61%) to report that the information they needed was available. When they found career information, 83% of Asian-Pacific Islanders found the information useful, compared to 88% of African Americans, 77% of Whites, and 83% of Hispanics.

In addition to their interest and need for career services, Asian Americans also constitute the fastest-growing minority groups in this country. The combination of these factors highlights the immense disparity between what is needed and what is available by way of career theory and research on Asian Americans. Career counselors need information on how Asian American clients may be different from European American students so that they can provide culturally relevant and effective services.

In a review of the career development of Asian Americans, we can focus on (a) an individual level of analysis, such as career interest and choice; and/or (b) a group and societal level of analysis, such as the role of macro-level processes including family influences, occupational stereotyping, occupational discrimination, occupational mobility, occupational segregation, and their potential impact on the career development of Asian Americans. Because of space limitations, for this chapter, we have limited our review to the former. This chapter on the career development of Asian Americans is divided into three sections. The first section consists of an in-depth individual level of analysis, in which we explore Asian Americans' career interests, career choices, occupational values, and vocational behaviors in professions and in organizations. This section also examines personality variables that impact Asian Americans' career development as well as work adjustment and vocational problems experienced by Asian Americans. In the second section, we briefly discuss group- and societal-level processes related to Asian Americans' career development. In the third section, we discuss the problems inherent in the current research, and we end the chapter with an outline of directions for future research.

INDIVIDUAL LEVEL OF ANALYSIS

Career Interests

Over the past 20 years, there have only been a handful of studies on the career interest patterns of Asian Americans. In a 1985 review of the literature, Leong (1985) was able to identify only three published empirical articles and one dissertation related to the career interests of Asian Americans. In a study of Chinese American students at the University of California, Berkeley, D. W. Sue and Kirk (1972) found that, based on the School and College Ability Test (SCAT), the Strong Vocational Interest Blank (SVIB), and the Omnibus Personality Inventory (OPI), Chinese American students had higher quantitative but lower verbal scores than the control group. Compared to the females, the males of both groups did better in quantitative scores. It is important to point out that, in general, students at Berkeley do better than the national norm.

Leong (1985), looking at the literature on career development of Asian Americans, found that Chinese American males showed more of an interest than all other males in areas of physical science, skilled technical trades, and business occupations. They tended to be less interested in social service and welfare, sales or business contact, and verbal-linguistic occupations (social). In comparison to all other males, the Chinese American males' vocational interests appeared more masculine and seemed to aspire to a lower level of occupational status and responsibility. On the other hand, the Chinese American females were more oriented toward the domestic occupations, such as housewifery, secretary, and elementary school teacher, than were White women. In addition, the Chinese American females exhibited more interest in technical-applied fields, biological and physical sciences, business and office type activities, and less interest in aesthetic-cultural fields, social sciences, and verbal-linguistic vocations.

In a more recent study, M. Tang, Fouad, and Smith (1999) discovered that Asian Americans display limited occupational choices, predominantly within the realistic and investigative arenas. Other factors contributing to occupational choice include level of acculturation, family background, and self-efficacy. This finding supports the theory proposed by Lent, Brown, and Hackett (1994) that self-efficacy dictates the ability to perform certain career tasks and that this, in turn, translates to career mobility and career options. In another study, by Leung, Ivey, and Suzuki (1994), Asian Americans displayed higher interests in the investigative versus the creative and enterprising arenas, and there were no differences found in the realistic and social fields.

D. W. Sue and Kirk (1973) found a similar pattern of vocational choices between Japanese American males and Chinese American males. The exception was that the Japanese American men did not express greater interest than did White men in physical sciences or lower interest in the social sciences. In addition, Japanese American women did not express greater interest than did White women in domestic fields. Sue and Kirk explained these differences between the Chinese and Japanese participants in terms of differential rates of acculturation and assimilation into American society between these two groups.

Using a typological analysis of the same Chinese American and Japanese American men who participated in the study discussed in the previous paragraph, D. W. Sue and Frank (1973) found that these students clustered into groups with characteristics quite different from those of Whites. They reconfirmed the findings of D. W. Sue and Kirk (1972) and M. Tang, Fouad, and Smith (1999) and concluded that those occupations that require "forceful self-expression, interaction with people, and communication in oral or written form" are the ones that Asian Americans feel most uncomfortable with and are most likely to avoid, given their preferences for "structured, logical, concrete and impersonal" work activities (D. W. Sue & Frank, 1973, p. 141).

In an unpublished dissertation on career development of Asian Americans, Kwak (1980) also examined the vocational interests of Asian American youths, using Holland's Self-Directed Search (Holland, 1971). He found that the Asian American students revealed vocational types predominantly in the Investigative (25.8%) and Social (25.0%) categories. Leong (1985) cautions the readers against the implications being highlighted in these studies, suggesting further empirical validation and cautious implementation. The bottom line is that more studies are needed in order to better serve the Asian American population.

Another study of interest along these lines is one conducted by Trusty, Ng, and Ray (2000), which looked at the choice of Holland's social careers within various ethnic/racial groups. This study had a sample size of 524 Asian-Pacific Islanders and showed that out of all the ethnic groups in this study, European Americans displayed career choices that were consistent with Holland's theoretical model. In other words, the structural validity of Holland's hexagonal structure was upheld within the European American group.

Another approach to understanding the career interests of Asian Americans would be to examine the courses they take and the academic majors they choose while in high school. Data from the 2004 National Science Foundation survey report indicated that Asian Americans were more likely to enroll in math, calculus, biology, chemistry or physics courses during their college time.

In terms of intended undergraduate major, Asian Americans were twice as likely to choose an engineering discipline. Within the sciences, Asians leaned more toward biology and computer science than did Whites. Asian Americans' greater interest in scientific majors was also paralleled by a high level of educational aspiration. More than two out of every five Asian American freshmen, compared to one of five European Americans, planned their highest degree to be either a doctorate or a medical degree (National Science Foundation [NSF], 2004, p. 43). According to the NSF (2004) report, more Asians aspired to become either engineers of physicians compared to Whites.

Occupational Values

On the whole, there is also a lack of empirical studies on the work values of Asian Americans. Leong and Tata (1990) examined the work values of Chinese American children, as well as the relation between the children's level of acculturation and work values. In this study, 177 Chinese American fifth and sixth graders in a Los Angeles inner-city elementary school were given the Ohio Work Values Inventory (OWVI) and the Suinn-Lew Asian Self-Identity Acculturation scale (SL-ASIA). The two most important values for Chinese American children were money and task satisfaction. Object orientation and solitude appeared to be considerably lower in importance. This emphasis on money is consistent with the finding of the importance of prestige in the career interests of Asian Americans (e.g., Leung, Ivey, & Suzuki, 1994). Boys valued object orientation, self-realization, and ideas-data more than did girls. Girls valued altruism more than did boys. These sex differences may represent non-culture-specific sex differences in work values.

Other studies that have directly compared the work values of Asian Americans and European Americans have yielded mixed results. For example, Park and Harrison (1995) used the Career Anchor Inventory (CAI) (Nordvik, 1991) to measure nine career-related values among Asian American (primarily East Asians, all U.S. citizens or permanent residents) and European American college students. These nine values were Autonomy/Freedom, Challenge, Creativity/ Entrepreneurship, Geographic Security, Organizational Security, Technical Competence, Managerial Competence, Lifestyle (e.g., balancing of work and family), and Service/Dedication to a Cause. Chi-square analyses revealed no differences in the proportions of Asian Americans and European Americans who endorsed each value as most or least important. For both groups, Service/Dedication to a Cause was selected most often as the most important value (28.1% of Asian Americans and 26.3% of European Americans). Other values chosen as most important by large numbers of participants included Managerial Competence (21.7% of Asian Americans and 16.9% of European Americans), Technical Competence (15.8% of Asian Americans and 11.3% of European Americans) and Lifestyle (14.9% of Asian Americans and 21.3% of European Americans). Asian Americans indicated Challenge most often as the least important value (21.1%, compared to 21.7% of European Americans), followed by Geographical Security (20.2%, compared to 22.3% of European Americans), and Creativity/Entrepreneurship (16.2%, compared to 23.5% of European Americans).

Another study, however, did find between-groups differences in work values. Leong (1991) used Rosenberg's (1957) Occupational Values Scale to compare the work values of 83 European American (46% male and 54% female) and 63 Asian American (38% male and 62% female) college students. Following the pattern used by Rosenberg (1957), Leong formed clusters of occupational values for analyses: Social, Extrinsic, Self-Expression, Power, and Security. Results revealed that Asian Americans placed greater emphasis on the Extrinsic and Security values than did the European Americans. Thus, although Park and Harrison (1995) found no differences in the proportions of Asian Americans and European Americans who endorse Security (Organizational or Geographical) as the *most important* work value, Asian Americans nonetheless do seem to value Security more than do their European American peers. Hence, Asian American college students, when compared to their European American peers, do show some significant differences on occupational values. Yet another

study (Weaver, 2000) that looked at attitudes toward managers, job unions, new occupations, and other related elements found that Asian Americans were, in general, less satisfied in their jobs than were European Americans. However, no differences were observed among Asian Americans, African Americans, and European Americans with regard to working hard in order to get ahead.

Taken together, these studies suggest that extrinsic factors, such as security, money, and service to others, are particularly important work values for many Asian Americans. This could be because of Asian American culture's emphasis on pragmatism, a collectivistic orientation in decision making, and a mindset influenced by the immigration experience. Career counselors therefore need to find ways of using a sufficiently structured approach that is mindful of the occupational values of Asian Americans. Asian American clients may not appreciate counselors who directly or indirectly promote the use of a more intrinsic set of work values with which to guide their career decision making.

Career Development

Research on career choice and development has been dominated by three major theoretical perspectives: (a) the person-environment interaction model, as exemplified by Holland's model; (b) the developmental approaches, as exemplified by Super's (1953) theory; and (c) social learning approaches, as delineated by Mitchell and Krumboltz (see Brown & Brooks, 1990). Within the developmental perspective, the level and correlates of career maturity have been the most researched construct. Crites (1978) defined career maturity as comprising five attitudinal components: "(a) decisiveness in career decision making, (b) involvement in career decision making, (c) independence in career decision making, (d) orientation to career decision making, and (e) compromise in career decision making" (p. 3). As is evident from these culture-bound components, there are likely to be cultural variations in the construct of career maturity among Asian Americans (Leong & Serafica, 2001).

In a study examining the differential career development attributes of Asian American (primarily of Chinese and Korean descent) and

European American college students, Leong (1991) used Crites's (1973) Career Maturity Inventory: Attitude Scale; Harren's (1978) Assessment of Career Decision-Making Style Subscale; and Holland, Daiger, and Power's My Vocational Situation (1980). The Asian Americans exhibited higher levels of dependent decision-making styles than did the European Americans. The Asian Americans also scored lower on career maturity. Despite this, however, there were no significant between-groups differences for vocational identity. Thus, Asian American college students, when compared to their European American peers, do show some significant differences on career development attributes and decision-making styles. These differences could be because of the Asian American's culture having a greater emphasis on a collectivistic orientation in decision making and could possibly be influenced by the acculturation process.

A later study (Hardin, Leong, & Osipow, 2001) examined this hypothesis by exploring the relation of acculturation, self-construal, and career maturity among Asian American and European American college students. Hardin et al. argued that Crites's Career Maturity Inventory (1973) may confuse interdependence and dependence and thus equate a lack of independence in career decision making with dependence. If so, Asian Americans who approach career decision making with culturally appropriate interdependence may be perceived instead as dependent and lacking in career maturity. Indeed, Hardin et al. found that interdependence, but not independence, was related to career maturity, with higher interdependence being associated with lower career maturity. Highly acculturated Asian Americans, who did not differ from the European Americans in terms of self-construal, also did not differ in terms of career maturity. Hardin et al. concluded that the Career Maturity Inventory is, in fact, unable to distinguish between dependence and interdependence and thus may be biased against more interdependent Asian Americans.

The major implication of these studies for counseling is that Asian Americans and European Americans seem to approach the career decision-making process differently but do not arrive at less crystallized vocational identities. Career counselors need to be mindful that Asian Americans may have preferences for different decision-making processes and may, on the surface, appear less "career mature" than Whites; however, it may be the case that these traditional definitions of career maturity are inappropriate for Asian Americans. Counselors must not assume that Asian American clients who consider the wishes of their family in making a career decision are exhibiting career immature "dependence." Rather, counselors must respect this culturally appropriate interdependence.

Career Choices

At first glance, it would seem that Asian Americans' career choices would be a direct reflection of their career interests. However, as Leong (1985, 1991) has pointed out, due to a host of factors, many of which have not yet been empirically investigated, Asian Americans' career choices may not be consistently related to their career interests. For example, many Asian American adolescents may be interested in artistic careers (reflected in measured interests) but may eventually choose a career in medicine or engineering (expressed interest or choice) because of parental guidance or pressure. This is consistent with the results of a recent study that applied Social Cognitive Career Theory (SCCT) (Lent et al., 1994) to explore the relative importance of interests and parental influence in the career choices of Asian American college students (M. Tang et al., 1999). The results showed that, contrary to the predictions of SCCT and most other theories of career choice, students' own interests were unrelated to their career choice. Parental involvement, however, was significantly related to career choice, with higher parental involvement predicting more traditional (i.e., science and technology related) career choice.

As noted by other authors (e.g., S. Sue & Okazaki, 1990), this is quite likely to occur, as many Asian American parents are aware that discrimination in the work world is quite common and that their children would have an easier time if they were in a respected and autonomous profession in which many Asian Americans have already succeeded. Hence, Asian American parents may be more likely than European

American parents to exert direct influence on the career aspirations and choices of their children. In addition, the Asian American youths would also be more likely than European American youths to defer to such parental guidance given the strong Asian value of respecting authority and submitting to the wisdom of the elderly. Therefore, in order to understand the career behavior of Asian Americans, it would be important to examine their career interests and career choices separately. It would also be important to examine when, why, and for whom the two processes do not often converge.

This parental influence seems to explain the overrepresentation of Asian Americans in math and science related fields. Data from the National Science Foundation (1996, cited in J. Tang, 1997) indicated that Asian Americans comprise nearly 9% of scientists and engineers in the United States, despite making up only 3.2% of the total population. Similarly, M. Tang et al. (1999) found that 75% of their Asian American participants chose occupations in which Asian Americans are proportionally represented or overrepresented. The three most popular choices—engineer, physician, and computer scientist—have an average of twice as many Asian Americans than in the general population. There is no doubt that Asian Americans are often viewed as a model minority. Wong, Lai, Nagasawa, and Lin (1998) looked at the self-perceptions and perceptions of other ethnic groups on Asian Americans. All the other racial/ethnic groups expected the Asian Americans to be more motivated to succeed, to have higher academic performances, and to be successful in their careers in comparison to other groups. Contrary to popular belief, grade point averages and SAT scores showed that compared to the other groups, Asian Americans were not more successful. Nor did the Asian Americans perceive themselves as more successful than the other ethnic students.

Based on data such as these, one can see why it is so common for the concept of the "model minority" to be applied to Asian Americans. Using the criterion of occupational attainment alone, Asian Americans as a group have fared quite well relative to other minority groups. However, such an observation overlooks important within-group differences. For example,

although Asian Americans as a group constitute 18.3% of professional occupations relative to the 12.3% for Whites, only 8.8% of Vietnamese Americans are in professional occupations. Furthermore, 29.3% of Vietnamese and 20.5% of Korean Americans are in operator/laborer occupations compared to 17.1% for European Americans and 14.2% for Asian Americans overall. The model minority concept also ignores the problem of discrimination against Asian Americans. Being successful is no guarantee against prejudice and discrimination. This problem of occupational discrimination is discussed later in the chapter.

Asian Americans in the Professions

In the book *Asian Americans in Higher Education and at Work,* Hsia (1988) discusses in detail the breakdown of Asian Americans in various professions. Some statistics are highlighted in order to bring attention to the profession choices of Asian Americans. Data collected since 1971 have shown that Asian Americans comprise less than 1% of the law student population. However, since 1973 a steady increase in these numbers has been observed. Recent immigrants were found to be at a certain disadvantage in terms of access to law school education because of their limited-English language ability. Asian Americans have been a very visible minority within the medical profession (Hsia, 1988). Census data show enrollments of 3% first-year students and 2.8% of the total medical student enrollment in the years 1979 to 1980. By 1984–1985, these numbers increased to 6.6% first-year students and 5.6% of the total medical student enrollment. These numbers suggest a high contrast to the 1.2% of the general U.S. population in the 1970s and the 3% representation for 1990s. The numbers clearly highlight the "overrepresentation" of Asian Americans in medical schools. However, Hsia (1988) also points out that, despite this overrepresentation, Asian Americans do experience a lower application-to-acceptance ratio in comparison to other racial/ethnic groups, which may suggest that some discriminatory admission policies are occurring. The bottom line is that Asian Americans seem to gravitate toward medicine as a career choice, but for some currently unknown and unexplained reasons, they are less likely to be accepted into medical schools despite meeting the necessary academic requirements. No information was examined or presented by Hsia (1988) on Asian American representation in business schools.

Personality Variables and Asian Americans' Career Development

There has been much debate in the literature about the extent to which the so-called personality structure hypothesis (Leung et al., 1994) accounts for the career behavior of Asian Americans. Although external factors such as discrimination must certainly be considered to fully understand Asian Americans' career development, numerous studies have identified internal factors related to Asian Americans' career behavior. In a review of the literature on the career development of Asian Americans, Leong (1985) noted that there were three personality variables that were repeatedly referred to in various studies concerning the vocational behavior of Asian Americans. These three personality variables were locus of control, social anxiety, and intolerance of ambiguity. With regard to locus of control, different studies have pointed out that Asian Americans tend to be less autonomous, more dependent, and more obedient to authority (D. W. Sue & Kirk, 1972, 1973). In line with this issue, D. W. Sue and Kirk (1972) administered the Omnibus Personality Inventory to 236 Chinese American students and found that they were significantly more conforming and socially introverted than the White students, which may be due to the traditional Chinese cultural values of respect for authority and submergence of individuality. These findings seem to suggest that Chinese Americans and Japanese Americans are more externally oriented in terms of how they view issues of control and reinforcement. Park and Harrison (1995) found that Asian Americans had lower personal and interpersonal control than did European Americans, as measured by Paulhus's (1983) Spheres of Control Scale. As suggested by Leong (1985), if indeed Asian Americans perceived the locus of control for reinforcement as external, it could certainly affect not only their career decision-making style but also the nature and scope of their career choices. Indeed, Park and Harrison found that higher perceived control in the personal and interpersonal domains was associated with greater Social and Enterprising career interests.

Social anxiety was the second personality characteristic that Leong (1985) had identified as a converging theme within the literature. Besides clinical impressions that Asian Americans are more emotionally withdrawn, socially isolated, and verbally inhibited (Sue, Sue & Sue, 1975), various empirical studies using objective and standardized personality instruments have found that Asian Americans do experience a greater degree of social anxiety (e.g., Hardin & Leong, 2005; Okazaki, 1997). Sue and Sue (1974), in an MMPI (Minnesota Multiphasic Personality Inventory) comparison of Asian American and European American students, found that the former exhibited greater social introversion. Using the Omnibus Personality Inventory, D. W. Sue and Kirk (1972) found that Chinese American students were significantly more inhibited, were more impersonal in their interpersonal relations, and appeared less socially concerned with other people. In a related study using the same database, D. W. Sue and Kirk (1973) found a similar pattern of social introversion and withdrawal among both Chinese American and Japanese American samples. They concluded that the social discomfort experienced by these Asian American students may be due to conflict between the informal nature of social relationships within American culture and their own, more formal and traditional cultural values and minority status.

D. W. Sue (1975), in his chapter in Picou and Campbell's book, *Career Behavior of Special Groups,* pointed out the relevance of Asian Americans' social anxiety to their career aspirations and plans. Sue (1975) observed that Asian Americans are often not discussed in the literature and the few times that they are, it is in an inferior manner. This thus leads to low self-esteem and ethnic pride, which, in turn, leads to withdrawal from social contacts and responsibility. Sue (1975) pointed out that the tendency of Asian Americans to choose occupations in the physical sciences and technical trades may be due to this social anxiety, discomfort, and inhibition. In any event, Sue noted that Asian

Americans are underrepresented in the social sciences and other vocations that require verbal/persuasive skills and high levels of social interactions, such as lawyers and psychologists. Park and Harrison (1995) similarly hypothesized that Asian Americans' underrepresentation in social occupations may be related to their lower levels of perceived control in the interpersonal sphere. Such hypotheses are consistent with the importance ascribed to self-efficacy in the Social Cognitive Career Theory (Lent et al., 1994) in predicting career interests and choices.

Besides the personality dimensions identified by Leong (1985), Hsia (1988) also discussed the role of a field-independent cognitive style among Asian Americans in the occupational segregation and limited occupational mobility. She noted that given their field-independent orientation, Asian Americans were much more likely to be limited to scientific and technical careers and were not likely to be successful in the people-oriented occupations such as managerial and administrative, those requiring more field-dependent cognitive styles. Her observation about cognitive style and career choices also points to the need to examine the role of cognitive styles in the career choices and behaviors of Asian Americans.

Some of the data from personality inventories already provide some support for Hsia's (1988) and Leong's (1985) hypotheses about personality variables' influence on the career behavior of Asian Americans. For example, the D. W. Sue and Frank study (1973) found that Asian males leaned toward occupations that had routine, business-detailed aspects to them. Thus, they were overrepresented in professions such as engineering and underrepresented in the social sciences. As the Asian men tended to score low in autonomy, they tended to be more conforming, more obedient to authority, and more connected to familial control and tended to dislike ambiguity. They also experienced strong feelings of isolation, loneliness, and rejection. Similarly, D. W. Sue and Kirk (1973) found that Japanese American students were less oriented to theoretical, abstract ideas and concepts than were European American students. Japanese American students also tended to dislike ambiguity in favor of structured situations. They tended to evaluate ideas based on immediate practical applications and were more socially conforming.

Leung et al. (1994) examined the sex stereotyping of the occupations in which Asian American and European American college students were interested. They found that Asian Americans aspired to careers that were significantly more masculine (in terms of percentage of men in the occupation, according to the 1985 statistics) than were European Americans. Further, despite the stronger emphasis of femininity in women that is placed by the Asian culture, Asian American women in this study, compared to the European American women, aspired to occupations that were significantly more masculine.

Work Adjustment and Vocational Problems

Asian Americans experience both a unique set of work adjustment problems as well as vocational problems common to many minority groups. One work adjustment problem that many Asian Americans have to deal with concerns their academic abilities. As measured by such tests as the SAT, Asian Americans tend to have lower levels of verbal skills in English than do European Americans. In 1988, Asian SAT verbal scores averaged 408, which is 37 points lower than the average for whites (445). On the other hand, the average math score for Asians (552) was 32 points higher than that for whites (490) (National Science Foundation, 1996, cited in J. Tang, 1997). Although never systematically investigated, it is easy to envision that many Asian Americans experience career-related problems due to their limited ability with the English language. For example, Asian Americans may be perceived as less intelligent or less competent than their White counterparts on the job because they are not able to articulate what they know fully. This, in turn, could lead to consequences such as being passed over for promotion to managerial or supervisory positions or receiving lower ratings in performance appraisal (see the next section for a discussion of occupational discrimination).

Asian Americans' higher ability with mathematics is also a double-edged sword. Whereas the higher math scores have helped balance out their lower verbal scores and have increased their chances of admission into colleges and graduate programs, the combination of the two also creates a certain image. The popular stereotypical version of this image is of Asian Americans being engineering or computer science "geeks": bespectacled, slide rule sticking out of their pockets, and spending all their time buried in books. However, if one chooses to characterize this image, the impression is that Asian Americans are best at being "technicians" and not managers and supervisors, as they lack the social skills due to their lower verbal skills. Indeed, Cheng (1996) found that in mini-assessment centers in organizational behavior classes, Asian American men were not selected by their peers to be team managers. Selectors explained that the Asian American men were "nerds" who, among other "deficits," were too soft-spoken and quiet.

There is some evidence that Asian Americans perceive themselves to be underemployed at work regardless of whether it is related to the previously mentioned stereotypes. In a national telephone survey, conducted by the Gallup organization, of 1,350 adults (African Americans, $n = 737$; Hispanics, $n = 310$; and Asian-Pacific Islanders, $n = 255$), Brown et al. (1991) reported that Asian-Pacific Islanders (47%) were less likely than Whites (54%), African Americans (60%), or Hispanics (63%) to report that their skills were being used very well. Other evidence supports this perception. Using data from the 1990 U.S. Census, Madamba and DeJong (1997) found that Asian American men were twice as likely as European American men, three times as likely as African American men, and four times as likely as Latino men to experience "job mismatch," or being overeducated for the requirements of one's job. Madamba and DeJong argue that higher levels of educational attainment among Asian Americans put them at greater risk for job mismatch, providing another example of the downside of the model minority model. Not surprisingly, given the objective and subjective underemployment experienced by Asian Americans, Brown et al. (1991) found that a large percentage of Asian-Pacific Islanders (71%) reported being interested in getting more information about careers if they could start over. Asian Americans also reported experiencing stress on the job more than did

other minority groups. These higher levels of job stress are reflected to some degree in the help-seeking behavior of Asian Americans. For example, Tracey, Leong, and Glidden (1986) found that Asian Americans were more likely to present vocational and career problems to a counselor than personal-emotional problems. They found that Asian American clients were more likely to endorse academic/vocational concerns as most important, but to a lesser degree if they had previous counseling.

Many Asian Americans face a unique work adjustment problem, namely, the stress from being unable to provide for extended family members. Traditional notions of filial piety dictate that it is the duty of children to honor and care for their parents (Ho, 1987), which often manifests in married couples providing financial support to their parents (particularly the husband's parents) and in elderly parents living with their married children (particularly the oldest son). However, some authors (e.g., Kim, Kim, & Hurh, 1991) have suggested that the economic realities of life in the United States for many immigrant Asians is such that this cultural ideal is unrealistic and places undue strain on families.

Yu and Wu (1985) investigated a unique work adjustment issue related to the stress experienced when caring for extended family. This study hypothesized that the ability to provide monetary support for the care of aged relatives was dependent on income and employment. The levels of stress experienced by American-born Chinese versus naturalized Chinese Americans were different. This study concluded that stress can be reduced when employment status is sufficient to meet the various family obligations. However, in these cases marital status also needs to be looked at and taken into consideration. Discomfort level and stress increases are more likely when parents-in-law are not supported. Finally, due to the reciprocal and relational effect of one spouse's feelings on the other spouse, both spouses' stress and discomfort levels need to be examined.

Redding and Ng (1982) investigated the role of "face" in the organizational perceptions of managers who were of Chinese nationality. According to these authors, face is particularly salient for the Chinese and is argued to be key in explaining much of their behavior. Face is the individual's assessments of how he or she is seen by close others. The salience of status and power becomes evident in this study, and the short-term reactions to losing face were as follows: shame (100%), worry (99%), feelings of uneasiness, anxiety, and tension (98%), difficulty in concentrating on work (72%), and symptoms such as blushing (64%). The long-term effects, such as loss of appetite or sleep, are rarely reported (33% and 21%, respectively). Having face and not having face are found to be strong influences in business (100% and 97% respectively). There is clear acknowledgment of the concept of face being present within the business world in the Chinese culture. Because the Western bureaucratic form of organization consists of the values of rationality and individualism, it is found to clash with the Chinese set of values. On these grounds, Redding and Ng (1982) argued that the introduction of Western managerial systems will either meet resistance or be subjected to extensive adaptation.

Demonstrating the relevance of these results for Asian Americans, Cheng (1996) found that Asian American men were, without exception, not selected as team managers in classroom mini-assessment centers. The Asian American men described their behavior during the assessment center interview as deferent, humble, polite, respectful, and "a team player," and indicated they thought these were characteristics of good managers. However, the students responsible for choosing the team managers described these same Asian American men as naïve, shy, soft-spoken, "too nice," passive, "too polite," "too respectful," and deferent. These qualities were seen as being in opposition to the qualities of an ideal manager, which included being "aggressive and assertive," competitive, "independent and self-reliant," individualistic, and having a strong personality.

In one of only a few studies that examined gender issues in the work adjustment of Asian Americans, Fujii, Fukushima, and Chang (1989) examined the experiences and thoughts of Asian women psychiatrists throughout the evolution of their careers within the context of such factors as gender, race, and culture. It was found that, as a general rule, the families of the women had disapproved of their career choice; they considered surgery more prestigious than psychiatry. In addition, racism and positive and negative stereotyping were issues experienced by these women, and, as a consequence, these women felt forced to address minority issues or to behave in culture-specific ways. All of the women reported satisfaction and a deep commitment to their professional lives. In most cases, these Asian women differed from Asian women both in the United States and in their native lands, as most had experienced unusual life circumstances, such as fleeing a native land, facing certain aspects of fatal illnesses, experiencing life-changing mentorships, or dealing with personal emotional stresses and mood disturbances.

Another common problem experienced by many Asian American groups concerns the impact of migration on their work adjustment in the host country. Kincaid and Yum (1987) examined some of the socioeconomic consequences of the migration of first-generation Samoans, Koreans, and Filipinos in Hawaii in contrast to local Japanese and Caucasian residents. These consequences were examined within the context of income level, occupational mobility, and difficulty of adjustment as indicated by stressful life events. It was observed that within each of these ethnic groups, the level of education corresponded to occupational status. According to Kincaid and Yum (1987), some of the main consequences of migration observed were a decline in the average occupational status/prestige, mobility issues within their occupations, differing degrees of stress, and differing degrees of personal achievement. In addition, the statistics suggests that the high numbers demonstrating an increased awareness of social agencies within this population did not correspond to equally high numbers in the use of these services. The bottom line is that migration led to a substantial lowering of occupational prestige for the immigrant groups and for the Caucasians. Kincaid and Yum (1987) also concluded that the needs of each immigrant group were different and that social policies needed to reflect these differences in their priorities.

There also are several studies that examined the work adjustment problems experienced by Southeast Asian immigrants and refugees. In the first of these studies, Nicassio and Pate (1984) examined the adjustment of Southeast Asian refugees in the United States. They sought to identify some major obstacles associated with the resettlement process, the interrelationships between adjustment issues, and the influence of certain sociodemographic factors on the various indices of adjustment. Problems of separation and immigration stress were highly emphasized. In addition, other serious issues included such things as learning to speak English, finances, job skills, and medical care, all of which were related in some way to the survival needs of the refugees. These problems were indicative and predictive of adjustment problems elsewhere. Some clear patterns of correlates emerged: Greater adjustment difficulties were reported in those refugees who were older, were less educated, had lower incomes, were unemployed, and had been in the United States for a short period of time. Socioeconomic level was also associated with social adjustment. The results also suggest that the socioeconomic, psychological, and cultural dimensions of adjustment among the refugees and immigrants are probably both interactive and mutually dependent. Nicassio and Pate (1984) concluded that particular attention needs to be given to the interventions that focus on consolidating and developing support systems and networks and to those practices that enhance the educational and job-related skills of refugees. This is because improvement in the socioeconomic area may, in turn, facilitate psychosocial adjustment. The results also indicated that work adjustment was a major problem.

In a similar study, Matsuoka and Ryujin (1989) found that, on one hand, some refugees were experiencing difficulties in adjustment issues associated with the acculturation process, and on the other hand, the younger refugees had fewer difficulties acculturating to the new lifestyle while leaving parts of their previous culture behind. There were differing expectations and hopes among the respondents, some believing that they would fare better in the new environment (40%), others believing otherwise (47%), most wanting more for their children (75%), and many wanting their children not to let go of their traditional culture (88%). In addition, many parents valued filial piety, expecting and hoping that their children would continue to value this aspect of the culture, yet also expecting that the opposite would happen. Many refugees have mixed feelings: Some enjoy the freedom, opportunities, and comforts provided by the United States, whereas others claim to like nothing about it and thus try to eliminate/minimize feelings of guilt by restricting material gratifications. Matsuoka and Ryujin advocate for the survival of these refugees by suggesting such things as language training, job training, access to employment, economic support, courses on U.S. culture, and counseling on how to obtain these things.

Haines (1987) found employment to be a major source of stress for Southeast Asian refugees. As a result of refugee exodus, refugees faced very severe employment problems on their arrival in the United States. These problems were then reflected in other forms such as in the decrease of public assistance, from initially high levels to that of approximately one-third in assistance over three years. The most crucial issue appeared to be the jobs that refugees obtained. There were three correlates related to occupational attainment: ability to understand and communicate in English, occupational background in place of origin, and education. All three categories can be used to indicate occupational status in the United States and they may have some overlap between them. To some extent, then, these correlations were not the separate effects of different variables but rather the effects of socioeconomic status (Haines, 1987).

In another study of Southeast Asians, J. Tang and O'Brien (1990) defined the vocational expectations of Indochinese refugees (529 subjects: 337 males and 192 females) by their readiness to remain in low-status jobs. Existing vocational data were provided by a social service organization (Center for Southeastern Asian Refugee Resettlement [CSEARR]) from the years 1981 to 1984. Status inconsistency was operationally defined as the difference between the previous position in the country of origin and the current position. Vocational success was defined as the time spent by the refugees on the current job. It was discovered that the subjects had a greater likelihood of vocational success dependent on length of time in the United States.

If the subjects had been in the United States for less than three years and if they previously held low-prestige positions in Asia, they worked longer than did their high-prestige counterparts. On the other hand, if they had been in the United States for more than three years, the situation was reversed, in that subjects who had previously held high-prestige positions worked much longer than did their previously low-prestige status counterparts. J. Tang and O'Brien's (1990) study provided evidence that status inconsistency affected the vocational success of these refugees. This is because the refugees who had been residing in the United States longer displayed fewer psychosocial problems than those who had been in the United States less than three years. The refugees would focus on attaining vocational goals that were in line with their self-concepts once they had acclimated to the present culture. For example, those who previously had high-prestige jobs would try to leave low-status jobs in the pursuit of a more congruent position to their self-image, so that ultimately the dissonance produced by status incongruence could be reduced. Inability to attain a high-prestige position could lead to high job turnover rates. This has important implications for those trying to intervene with this group in efforts to help enhance the self-esteem of this population. In addition, mental health workers can help enlighten refugees about the other important aspects of a job other than prestige, such as learning new skills, helping to fulfill the goals of the larger organization, and earning a wage or salary.

In the final study concerned with Southeast Asians, Anh and Healy (1985) examined the factors believed to affect the job satisfaction of 210 Vietnamese refugees. The authors used analysis of variance and chi-square to ascertain whether being employed and feeling satisfied with one's job related to length of time in the United States, estimated English proficiency, and views about job-seeking resources. On average, the immigrants were moderately satisfied with their jobs. Overall satisfaction related moderately and positively to wages and negatively to number of obstacles to having the desired job. The comparisons showed significant positive relationships between time in the United States and employment status and satisfaction. English

proficiency was not found to be related to employment or employment status, but it was significantly related to job satisfaction. Of the variables considered in Anh and Healy's (1985) study, time was the most consistent in its relation to the refugees' resettlement. Refugees who were in the United States longest were most likely to have jobs and to feel satisfied with their jobs. It is important, however, for future research to verify that increases in satisfaction over time do not indicate merely that refugees have settled for poor jobs.

In a more recent study that examined the job satisfaction of Asian Americans, Leong (2001) found that acculturation was related to job satisfaction. Asian Americans employed at two large companies (n = 24 and 15, respectively) and who were participating in a career development workshop completed measures of acculturation, job satisfaction, and job stress. In both groups, higher acculturation was associated with greater job satisfaction. Interestingly, higher acculturation was associated with less job strain for participants from one company but more job strain for participants at the other company, highlighting the important interaction of internal or individual-level factors with external or group-level factors in the career development of Asian Americans.

GROUP AND SOCIETAL LEVEL OF ANALYSIS

Psychology as a field of scientific inquiry has tended to employ an individual level of analysis. The few exceptions include social psychology, organizational psychology, and community psychology. This individual-level emphasis has also been true within the field of vocational psychology. However, as Leong and Brown (1995) have observed, the study of the experience of racial and ethnic minority members at the individual level of analysis misses many important factors (e.g., institutional racism, intergroup conflicts). Hence, although the analysis of the individual is the strength of psychology, a complete career psychology of the minority groups in general and Asian Americans in particular will only come about with an extension to higher levels of analyses such as group or societal phenomena.

Family Influences on the Career Development of Asian Americans

Psychologists and other social scientists have long indicated that the family plays a central role in the lives of Asian Americans (e.g., Chung, 2001). Yet, very little research has been conducted on the influence of the family on the career choices and behaviors of Asian Americans. There are, however, a few studies, all of which confirm the existence of significant family influence.

For example, M. Tang et al. (1999) found that higher levels of family influence predicted more traditional math- and science-related career choices for Asian American college students. Individual interests, however, were unrelated to career choice in this sample. It is often evident that family influence, particularly from parents, appears to be relevant across a range of Asian subgroups, although it is not without conflict. For example, Duong Tran, Lee, and Khoi (1996) found that high school students all indicated that high expectations from parents to do well in school were among their top five concerns. With regard to the medical profession, Asian Americans reported that they were more likely than any of the other underrepresented minorities to state that family influence was a significant factor in making the decision to go into medicine as a career (Bright, Duefield, & Stone, 1998). Consistent with these findings, Evanoski and Tse (1989) argued that education and career choices are of great importance to many Chinese and Korean families. The crucial role of Chinese and Korean parents in the career choice of their children makes it imperative that they not be omitted from the career counseling efforts of the educational institutions. M. Tang et al. (1999) describe a career awareness program for Chinese and Korean American parents. Another way in which parents influence the career choices of their children in Asian American families is by encouraging them to take over family-run businesses.

Occupational Stereotyping

Whereas it has been known for a long time that Asian Americans are often the victims of occupational stereotyping, no empirical study of this phenomenon had been undertaken until Leong and Hayes (1990). It is observable that occupational stereotyping by gender and race continues to exist despite the increasing sophistication among the public about the social undesirability of prejudicial attitudes. Leong and Hayes (1990) measured three aspects of stereotypes: (a) probability of success, (b) qualifications of training, and (c) acceptance by others. The study found both positive and negative stereotypes with regard to gender and race groupings. In fact, the study shows that Asian Americans were less likely to succeed as insurance sales persons. On the opposite end, Asians were more likely to succeed as engineers, computer scientists, and mathematicians. Further research is needed to determine how widespread these occupational stereotypes are before accepting the generalizability of the current findings. Future research is also needed to assess the psychological impact of these occupational stereotypes on Asian Americans and to study both internal and external barriers.

Occupational Discrimination

The myth that Asian Americans are a successful minority has been well documented and discussed within the social science literature (Leong, 1985). Many have questioned the myth, arguing that the stereotypes do not generalize to all Asian Americans and pointing out that labeling Asian Americans as a successful or model minority has resulted in their being neglected in terms of research or intervention programs (Chun, 1980; Hsia, 1988; Leong, 1985). The successful minority myth has arisen from the documentation of achievements Asian Americans have obtained in the United States. They have been portrayed as overcoming injustice and setbacks to become one of the most upwardly mobile minority groups in the country. These findings would lead one to believe that Asian Americans have successfully assimilated into American culture and, thus, do not experience discriminatory barriers to their success. Reference to their higher levels of educational attainment is often used as evidence of this successful assimilation. In addition, traditional Asian cultures often have emphasized the importance of educational performance in achieving success in society. As Chun (1980) has pointed out, the concept that Asian Americans are a successful or model minority has often covered up the occupational constraints and inequities experienced by Asian Americans.

Fernandez (1998) looked at Asian Indians in the San Francisco Bay Area from 1990 census data and found that, after controlling for variables such as human capital (e.g., education) and assimilation (e.g., fluency of the English language), males were less likely to be in management positions than were their White counterparts.

Evidence that Asian Americans may have higher academic competencies and yet be paid less than European Americans comes from another national data set. The National Science Foundation (2004) found that "Asian Americans reportedly earned more science and engineering bachelor degrees than the Whites in the 1990's" (p. 19). Furthermore, the same report revealed that there is also some evidence of occupational discrimination against Asian American scientists and engineers within U.S. universities. It is important to note that these disparities exist despite the fact that Asian Americans enter colleges and universities with much higher academic credentials (course grades and SAT/GRE scores) than European Americans.

In one study (Corbie Smith, Frank, Nickens, & Elon, 1999), out of 681 Asian Americans who responded to the U.S. Women Physicians' Health Study, 31% reported experiencing ethnic-based harassment, compared to 62% of African Americans, 20% Hispanic Americans, 36% other, and 6% European Americans. In addition, the Asian Americans claimed that the harassment led to work-related stress and less perceived control over their work environments. In contrast, in an earlier empirical study similar to Leong & Hayes's (1990) stereotyping study, Carroll, Feren, and Olian (1987) found no evidence of prejudice against Asian Americans as managers. In fact, it was found that non-Anglo-Saxon managers were preferred, mainly because of their interpersonal competence. In addition, women were found to be more sensitive to this kind of awareness than men were. However, the authors also highlighted the need for additional research in this area of study.

Occupational Segregation

As early as 1972, D. W. Sue and Kirk had observed that Asian Americans seem to be overrepresented in some occupations and underrepresented in others. Over the years, more and more data have been accumulated to demonstrate that occupational segregation is a major problem for Asian Americans as it has been for women. The notion that occupational segregation is a problem comes from the assumption that a skewed distribution of any group in the occupational structure may represent restricted access to certain occupations. At the very least, a pattern of occupational segregation among a racial/ethnic group calls for investigations to determine if there is differential access to various occupations.

In a review article, Chun (1980) noted occupational segregation was a prevalent problem among Asian Americans showing a pattern of occupational segregation and the tendency for Asian Americans to avoid the social sciences and humanities and gravitate toward the biological and physical sciences. Chun stated that this segregation is probably a result of the societal and cultural barriers to Asian Americans' occupational aspirations. In fact, in a national survey (U.S. Commission on Civil Rights, 1978), it was discovered that the Chinese, Filipino, and Japanese Americans exhibited the highest levels of occupational segregation among all minorities. In another article, Sue (1973) explains this occupational segregation in terms of Asian Americans' ethnic identity and cultural background, which emphasize reserve and formality in interpersonal relations, restraint and inhibition of strong feelings, and obedience to authority. A table in Hsia's 1988 book (p. 171, Table 7.4) concerning the representation of Asian Americans in selected occupations using the 1980 U.S. Census data provides a good illustration of the overall pattern of occupational segregation among Asian Americans. It is interesting to note that this pattern of occupational segregation among Asian Americans parallels the stereotyping literature, namely, that Asians are stereotyped as being more qualified to enter the physical, biological, and medical sciences and less qualified to enter or to be successful in the verbal, persuasive, social careers such as lawyer, judge, and teacher. Hence, there seems to be some numerical basis for the occupational stereotyping of Asian Americans. More recent data from the National Science Foundation (2004) document this problem of occupational segregation among Asian Americans. For example, the data show that in some cases, such as in the field of psychology, there were fewer than 50 weighted cases, so the results were suppressed and not calculated or recorded. One consequence of occupational segregation is that Asian Americans, like women, may be segregated into lower-paying occupations and denied access to higher-paying jobs.

Conclusions

Current Status of Career and Vocational Research on Asian Americans

As an update to the chapter by Leong (1998), this current review of the literature on the career development and vocational behavior of Asian Americans continues to find similar conceptual and methodological problems in the literature. First, there continues to be a relative dearth of empirical studies on the career choices of Asian Americans that provide useful information for career counselors and psychologists charged with helping Asian Americans with their career concerns. The dozen or so studies that have been published since the Leong (1998) review is a good start, but a great deal more research, and then implementation and evaluation of the research recommendations, is needed. Second, the uneven pattern of the studies of the career behavior of Asian Americans continues. There are many more studies on the work adjustment problems of Asian Americans than about the role of family influences on their career choices. Third, the limited research that does exist seems to be more problem-driven than theory-driven. For example, there are many more studies about the work adjustment problems of Asian Americans than about their career development processes and outcomes from a theoretical point of view. There is no question that problem-driven research is needed and has its value. Take the example of studies related to the work adjustment of Southeast Asian refugees; these studies were clearly in response to the large influx of this group of Asians into the United States. Yet, many of these studies were primarily descriptive in cataloging the problems experienced by this refugee group. What are also needed are studies that add to our theoretical knowledge base. For example, are there predictable cycles in the work adjustment of recent refugees? How do the various Southeast Asian groups fit this typical path? What cultural variables can account for deviations from the modal situations? There are many established career theories (see Brown & Brooks, 1990) that can be tested for their relevance to Asian Americans, and yet they are often ignored. One recent promising development in this arena is the attempt to test the relevance of social cognitive theory (Lent et al., 1994) for Asian Americans.

Finally, like much of the rest of the field of ethnic minority psychology, studies of the career development of Asian Americans continue to be stuck at the descriptive level. Most of the studies are based on the examination of ethnicity as a demographic and not a psychological variable. The former approach is characterized by studies that tend to examine a specific ethnic group's experience (e.g., the level of job-interviewing skills among Vietnamese refugees) or seeks to compare two groups based solely on ethnic designation (e.g., whether Chinese American engineers are more satisfied with their jobs than European American engineers). What are needed are studies that examine psychological variables that may be related to these ethnic groups' behaviors. For example, how does Berry's acculturation model relate to the type of work adjustment problems experienced by Vietnamese? Or does Rokeach's (1973) system of values moderate whether Japanese Americans are congruent in their measured and expressed career choices? Can Bogardus's (1925) social distance model account for a significant portion of the variance for the occupational discrimination of Asian Americans? Ethnicity per se is not a psychological variable and in the long run will yield very little information about the career behaviors of Asian Americans. What is needed are studies which identify, evaluate, and test the role and impact of various psychological variables which are believed to influence the work behavior and career development of Asian Americans. To be sure, there have been a handful of theoretical and empirical papers (Chung, 2001; Hardin et al., 2001; Leong, 1991, 2001; Leong & Tata, 1990; Park & Harrison, 1995) that have begun to examine the role of acculturation and its impact on the career choices and vocational behavior of Asian Americans

Directions for Future Research

Despite the fact that work constitutes a major portion of the activity of Asian Americans as with all other populations, surprisingly little empirical research has been conducted on this particular topic with Asian Americans. Hence, there continues to be a need for more systematic empirical studies of the career and vocational experience and problems encountered by Asian Americans.

In terms of the existing studies, there are several methodological issues that need to be attended to in order to improve our knowledge of the career behavior of Asian Americans. The first of them is to attempt wherever possible to collect data on the career behavior of Asian Americans such that data are available from subgroups so that we can examine if the same pattern of findings is true for Chinese Americans versus Korean Americans versus Filipino or Japanese Americans. In addition, limited research exists on the South Asian population. Further strides in research will need to be made in order to better understand these subgroups.

Currently most of the research is focused on Asian Americans as a global group with very little attention paid to intra- or subgroup differences. Worse still, much of the data collected from the federal statistical system uses the combined group of Asian and Pacific Islanders, which includes the Eastern Asian groups including Chinese, Japanese, Korean, and Filipino who are then combined with the Pacific Islanders, who are from a totally different culture including Samoans, Hawaiians, and so on. One possibility would be to mirror what has been done in the U.S. Census since 1980, which is to encourage the federal, state, and local statistical systems to collect data on not only the Asian subgroup but also the specific groups such that as in the 1980 census a person indicates whether he or she is Asian or Pacific Islander and then also designates his or her subgroup. This provides a more refined level of analysis and as we do particular levels of subgroup identification much more of our research and statistical data will be meaningful.

One recommendation for future research is to follow Leong and Brown's (1995) conceptual framework and conduct research on the career development of Asian Americans by examining BOTH cultural validity and cultural specificity. In terms of cultural validity, studies are needed that take the various existing models of career choice and adjustment to assess their validity for this population, namely how well or how poorly these models work when applied to Asian American populations. The integrative multidimensional model to cross-cultural counseling and psychotherapy introduced by Leong (1996) may be useful here as well. According to this model, the counselor or therapist needs to recognize that both the client and the therapist have a multidimensional identity that includes universal, group, and individual (unique) elements and that attention to only one dimension at the expense of the others would result in ineffective therapy. In applying this model to the existing career theories, it is highly unlikely that all aspects of these models which have been developed on European Americans will prove to be a good fit for Asian Americans. It would be a valuable contribution to identify which aspects are valid and which are not. In those areas of limited or poor validity, modifications to the model that are culturally relevant as well as culturally appropriate should then be identified and tested using the cultural accommodation approach suggested by Leong and his colleagues (Leong & Serafica, 2001; Leong & Tang, 2002).

The second part to Leong and Brown's (1995) conceptual framework is to examine culture-specific factors in the career development and vocational behavior of Asian Americans. These factors can come from the first set of studies where inadequacies in existing Western models need to accommodate for culture specific factors. Additionally, there are many studies that have sought to identify culture specific factors outside of career theories. Examples of these factors include individualism-collectivism, self-construal, loss of face, and so on.

Finally, cross-cultural and racial-ethnic minority research over the last couple of decades has also identified a couple of important moderator variables that should be integrated into future research on Asian American career behavior. The first of which is cultural identity or acculturation. There is now substantive research to show that Asian Americans either as an entire group or as subgroups experience this temporal variable which includes a process of acculturation that then differentiates these subgroups. Research is beginning to show that highly acculturated Asian Americans may not be the same as low level acculturated Asian Americans in terms of their occupational aspirations, interests, choices, and behavior. Hence, future research on the career behavior of Asian Americans will have to take into account this moderating effect of acculturation and cultural identity.

The second major moderator variable is that of socioeconomic status. We are in desperate need of research that separates out the effects of socioeconomic status from racial and ethnic minority group status. For Asian Americans as with many of the racial ethnic minority groups in this country, the two are often highly confounded. We do not know to what extent the career patterns are due to the fact that Asian Americans may be from lower working classes or to the fact of their being from a distinct cultural group, namely Asians in the United States. To achieve this purpose of identifying the effects of these two moderating variables we are in need of instruments that will also be able to accurately and reliably measure their effects. For acculturation there are already available instruments such as Suinn-Lew Asian Self-Identity Acculturation Scale (SL-ASIA; Suinn, Ahuna, & Khoo, 1992) or the more recent work of Phinney (2003) in terms of the multi group ethnic identity measure. Unfortunately we do not have a short, reliable, practical social class measure that we can use in our research, and that is certainly one area in need of further exploration. It would be very valuable if we could develop a short, highly reliable and useful social class measure for various racial/ethnic minority groups that will help us to provide comparable data on this very important moderated variable across various studies and different groups.

In conclusion, although slow and steady progress has been made in the research on the career development of Asian Americans, much remains to be done. The cultural validity of many existing career theories has not yet been tested with Asian Americans. Research on culture-specific variables that may increase our understanding of the vocational behavior of Asian Americans has only just begun. As progress is made on both fronts, the cultural accommodation approach (Leong & Serafica, 2001; Leong & Tang, 2002) can be used to build better theories and models of the career development of Asian Americans that would integrate the cultural validity and culture-specific strands of research.

References

Anh, N. T., & Healy, C. C. (1985). Factors affecting employment and job satisfaction of Vietnamese refugees. *Journal of Employment Counseling, 22,* 78–85.

Bogardus, E. S. (1925). Measuring social distance. *Journal of Applied Sociology, 9,* 299–308.

Bright, C. M., Duefield, C. A., & Stone, V. A. (1998). Perceived barriers and biases in the medical education experience by gender and race. *Journal of the National Medical Association, 90*(11): 681–688.

Brown, D., Minor, C. W., & Jepsen, D. A. (1991). The opinions of minorities about preparing for work: Report of the second NCDA National Survey. *Career Development Quarterly, 40,* 5–19.

Carroll, S. J., Feren, D. B., & Olian, J. D. (1987). Reactions to the new minorities by employees of the future: An experimental study. *Psychological Reports, 60*(3, Pt. 1), 911–920.

Cheng, C. (1996). We choose not to compete: The "merit" discourse in the selection process, and Asian and Asian American men and their masculinity. In C. Cheng (Ed.), *Masculinities in organizations* (pp. 177–200). Thousand Oaks, CA: Sage.

Chun, K. T. (1980, Winter-Spring). The myth of Asian American success and its educational ramifications. *IRCD Bulletin,* 2–13.

Chung, R. H. (2001). Gender, ethnicity, and acculturation in intergenerational conflict of Asian American college students. *Cultural Diversity & Ethnic Minority Psychology, 7,* 376–386.

College Entrance Examination Board. (1980). *National college-bound seniors, 1980.* Princeton, NJ: Author.

Corbie Smith, G., Frank, E., Nickens, H. W., & Elon, L. (1999). Prevalences and correlates of ethnic harassment in the U.S. Women Physicians' Health Study. *Academic Medicine, 74*(6), 695–701.

Crites, J. O. (1973). *Career maturity inventory.* Monterey, CA: McGraw-Hill.

Crites, J. O. (1978). *Career maturity inventory: Administration and use manual.* Monterey, CA: McGraw-Hill.

Duong Tran, Q., Lee, S., & Khoi, S. (1996). Ethnic and gender differences in parental expectations and life stress. *Child and Adolescent Social Work Journal, 13*(6), 515–526.

Evanoski, P. O., & Tse, F. W. (1989). Career awareness program for Chinese and Korean American parents. *Journal of Counseling and Development, 67,* 472–474.

Fernandez, M. (1998). Asian Indian Americans in the Bay area and the glass ceiling. *Sociological Perspectives, 41*(1), 119–149.

Fujii, J. S., Fukushima, S. N., & Chang, C. Y. (1989). Asian women psychiatrists. *Psychiatric Annals, 19,* 633–638.

Haines, D. W. (1987). Patterns in Southeast Asian refugee employment: A reappraisal of the existing research. *Ethnic Groups, 7,* 39–63.

Hardin, E. E., & Leong, F. T. L. (2005). Optimism and pessimism as mediators of the relations between self-discrepancies and distress among Asian and European Americans. *Journal of Counseling Psychology, 52,* 25–35.

Hardin, E. E., Leong, F. T. L., & Osipow, S. H. (2001). Cultural relativity in the conceptualization of career maturity. *Journal of Vocational Behavior, 58,* 36–52.

Harren, V. (1978). *Assessment of career decision making.* Unpublished manuscript, Southern Illinois University.

Ho, M. K. (1987). *Family therapy with ethnic minorities.* Newbury Park, CA: Sage.

Holland, J. L. (1971). A theory-ridden, computerless, impersonal vocational guidance system. *Journal of Vocational Behavior, 1*(2), 167–176.

Holland, J. L., Daiger, D. C., & Power, P. G. (1980). *My vocational situation.* Palo Alto, CA: Consulting Psychologist Press.

Hsia, J. (1988). *Asian Americans in higher education and at work.* Hillsdale, NJ: Lawrence Erlbaum.

Kim, K. C., Kim, S., & Hurh, W. M. (1991). Filial piety and intergenerational relationship in Korean immigrant families. *International Journal of Aging and Human Development, 33,* 233–245.

Kincaid, D. L., & Yum, J. O. (1987). A comparative study of Korean, Filipino and Samoan immigrants to Hawaii: Socioeconomic consequences. *Human Organization, 46,* 70–77.

Kwak, J. C. (1980). Vocational development of Asian American youth. *Dissertation Abstracts Online, 41*(05A), 00193.

Lent, R. W., Brown, S. D., & Hackett, G. (1994). Toward a unified social cognitive theory of career and academic interest, choice, and performance. *Journal of Vocational Behavior, 45,* 79–122.

Leong, F. T. (1985). Career development of Asian Americans. *Journal of College Student Personnel, 26,* 539–546.

Leong, F. T. L. (1991). Career development attributes and occupational values of Asian American and white American college students. *Career Development Quarterly, 39,* 221–230.

Leong, F. T. L. (1996). Towards an integrative model for cross-cultural counseling and psychotherapy. *Applied and Preventive Psychology, 5,* 189–209.

Leong, F. T. L. (1998). Career development and vocational behaviors. In L. C. Lee & N. W. S. Zane (Eds.), *Handbook of Asian American Psychology* (pp. 359–398). Thousand Oaks, CA: Sage.

Leong, F. T. L. (2001). The role of acculturation in the career adjustment of Asian American workers: A test of Leong and Chou's (1994) formulations. *Cultural Diversity & Ethnic Minority Psychology, 7,* 262–273.

Leong, F. T. L. (2004). Academic careers in Asia: A cross-cultural analysis. *Journal of Vocational Behavior, 64*(2), 346–357.

Leong, F. T. L., & Brown, M. T. (1995). Theoretical issues in cross-cultural career development: Cultural validity and cultural specificity. In W. B. Walsh & S. H. Osipow (Eds.), *Handbook of vocational psychology: Theory, research and practice* (2nd ed., pp. 143–180). Mahwah, NJ: Lawrence Erlbaum.

Leong, F. T. L., & Hayes, T. J. (1990). Occupational stereotyping of Asian Americans. *Career Development Quarterly, 39,* 143–154.

Leong, F. T. L., & Serafica, F. (2001). Cross-cultural perspectives on Super's career development theory: Career maturity and cultural accommodation. In F. T. L. Leong & A. Barak (Eds.), *Contemporary models in vocational psychology: A volume in honor of Samuel H. Osipow* (pp. 167–205). Mahwah, NJ: Lawrence Erlbaum.

Leong, F. T. L., & Tang, M. (2002). A cultural accommodation approach to career assessment with Asian Americans. In S. Okazaki, K. S. Kurasaki, & S. Sue (Eds.), *Asian American mental health: Assessment theories and methods* (pp. 77–94). New York: Kluwer Academic/Plenum.

Leong, F. T. L., & Tata, S. P. (1990). Sex and acculturation differences in occupational values among Chinese-American children. *Journal of Counseling Psychology, 37,* 208–212.

Leung, S., Ivey, D., & Suzuki, L. (1994). Factors affecting the career aspirations of Asian Americans. *Journal of Counseling and Development, 72*(4), 404–410.

Madamba, A. B., & De Jong, G. F. (1997). Job mismatch among Asians in the United States: Ethnic group comparisons. *Social Science Quarterly, 78,* 524–542.

Matsuoka, J. K., & Ryujin, D. H. (1989). Vietnamese refugees: An analysis of contemporary adjustment issues. *Journal of Applied Social Sciences, 14,* 23–45.

Mitchell, L. K., & Krumboltz, J. D. (1990). Social learning approach to career decision making: Krumboltz's theory. In D. Brown & L. Brooks (Eds.), *Career choice and development: Applying contemporary theories to practice* (2nd ed., pp. 145–196). San Francisco: Jossey-Bass.

National Science Foundation (NSF). (2004). *Women, minorities, and persons with disabilities in science and engineering* (Report No. NSF04–317). Washington, DC: Author.

Nicassio, P. M., & Pate, J. K. (1984). An analysis of problems of resettlement of the Indochinese refugees in the United States. *Social Psychiatry, 19,* 135–141.

Nordvik, H. (1991). Work activity and career goals in Holland's and Schein's theories of vocational personalities and career anchors. *Journal of Vocational Behavior, 38,* 165–178.

Okazaki, S. (1997). Sources of ethnic differences between Asian American and White American college students on measures of depression and social anxiety. *Journal of Abnormal Psychology, 106,* 52–60.

Park, S. E., & Harrison, A. A. (1995). Career-related interests and values, perceived control, and acculturation of Asian-American and Caucasian-American college students. *Journal of Applied Social Psychology, 25,* 1184–1203.

Paulhus, D. L. (1983). Sphere-specific measures of perceived control. *Journal of Personality and Social Psychology, 44,* 1253–1265.

Phinney, J. S. (2003). Ethnic identity and acculturation. In K. Chun, P. B. Organista, & G. Marin (Eds.), *Acculturation: Advances in theory, measurement, and applied research* (pp. 63–81). Washington, DC: American Psychological Association.

Redding, S. G., & Ng, M. (1982). The role of "face" in the organizational perceptions of Chinese managers. *Organization Studies, 3*(3), 201–219.

Rokeach, M. (1973). *The nature of human values.* New York: Free Press.

Rosenberg, M. (1957). *Occupations and values.* Glencoe, IL: Free Press.

Sue, D. W. (1973). Ethnic identity: The impact of two cultures on the psychological development of Asians in American. In S. Sue & N. Wagner (Eds.), *Asian Americans: Psychological perspectives* (pp. 14–149). Palo Alto, CA: Science & Behavior Books.

Sue, D. W. (1975). Asian Americans: Social-psychological factors affecting their lifestyles. In J. S. Picou & R. E. Campbell (Eds.), *Career behavior of special groups: Theory, research and practice* (pp. 97–121). Columbus, OH: Merrill.

Sue, S., Sue, D. W., & Sue, D. (1975). Asian Americans as a minority group. *American Psychologist, 30*(9), 906–910.

Sue, D. W., & Frank, A. C. (1973). A typological approach to the psychological study of Chinese and Japanese American college males. *Journal of Social Issues, 29,* 129–148.

Sue, D. W., & Kirk, B. A. (1972). Psychological characteristics of Chinese-American students. *Journal of Counseling Psychology, 19,* 471–478.

Sue, D. W., & Kirk, B. A. (1973). Differential characteristics of Japanese-American and Chinese-American college students. *Journal of Counseling Psychology, 20,* 142–148.

Sue, S., & Okazaki, S. (1990). Asian-American educational achievements: A phenomenon in search of an explanation. *American Psychologist, 45,* 913–920.

Suinn, R. M., Ahuna, C., & Khoo, G. (1992). The Suinn-Lew Asian Self-Identity Acculturation Scale: Concurrent and factorial validity.

Educational and Psychological Measurement, 52, 1041–1046.

Tang, J. (1997). The model minority thesis revisited: (Counter)evidence from the science and engineering fields. *Journal of Applied Behavioral Science, 33,* 291–315.

Super, D. E. (1953). A theory of vocational development. *American Psychologist, 8,* (185–190).

Tang, J., & O'Brien, T. P. (1990). Correlates of vocational success in refugee work adaptation. *Journal of Applied Social Psychology, 20*(17), 1444–1452.

Tang, M., Fouad, N. A., & Smith, P. L. (1999). Asian Americans' career choices: A path model to examine factors influencing their career choices. *Journal of Vocational Behavior 54*(1), 142–157.

Tracey, T. J., Leong, F. T. L., & Glidden, C. (1986). Help seeking and problem perception among Asian Americans. *Journal of Counseling Psychology, 33*(3), 331–336.

Trusty, J., Ng, K. M., & Ray, D. (2000). Choice of Holland's social type college majors for U.S. racial/ethnic groups. *Journal of Career Development, 27*(1), 49–64.

U.S. Commission on Civil Rights. (1978). *Social indicators of equality for minorities and women: A report of the United States Commission on Civil Rights.* Washington, DC: Author.

Weaver, C. N. (2000). Work attitudes of Asian Americans. *North American Journal of Psychology, 2*(2), 209–218.

Wong, P., Lai, C. F., Nagasawa, R., & Lin, T. (1998). Asian Americans as a model minority: Self-perceptions and perceptions by other racial groups. *Sociological Perspectives, 41*(1), 95–118.

Yu, L. C., & Wu, S. (1985). Unemployment and family dynamics in meeting the needs of Chinese elderly in the United States. *Gerontologist, 25,* 472–476.

PART III

SPECIFIC POPULATIONS

11

THE PSYCHOLOGY AND MENTAL HEALTH OF ASIAN AMERICAN WOMEN

DEBRA M. KAWAHARA

MICHI FU

According to the U.S. Census Bureau (2005), Asian or Asian in combination with one or more other races is one of the fastest-growing racial groups in the United States with an estimated 13.5 million U.S. residents. Women comprise 51% of this group (Nomura, 2003). The diversity among these women, however, is great. They differ in ethnicity, cultural values, language, generational level, residential status, education, and socioeconomic status (SES), as well as other demographic factors. In this chapter, we seek to illuminate these women's lives with the understanding that they are impacted by the overt and subtle historical, political, social, and economic realities in the United States that are imposed on all persons who are classified under this racial category. Furthermore, we address how these realities and the stereotypes projected onto Asian and Asian American (A/AA) women might impinge on the mental health of these women.

The use of the racial category of "Asian" or "Asian American" presents a dilemma for us as authors. Utilizing the category is, in some ways, buying into the Eurocentric hegemony that connotes an irrational and ignorant categorizing of persons that has no biological basis and is meaningless (Bradshaw, 1994). Yet, the racial category is the central focus of this book because A/AAs have been treated as one group politically, socially, and economically as seen in the U.S. Census. Given this reality, we chose to continue to use this grouping with the hope that the reader will be cognizant of the complexity among these vast ethnic groups and avoid overgeneralizing the similarities across ethnicities presented in this chapter.

HISTORICAL AND POLITICAL BACKGROUND OF ASIAN AMERICAN WOMEN

History plays an important role in the lives of A/AAs, particularly women. The historical and political barriers placed on A/AA women's immigration show the long-standing impact of preventing Asians from establishing themselves in the United States as well as embracing them into society at large (Root, 1995). Much of what revolves around the psychology of A/AA women deals with the construction of race, gender, and class within the social hierarchy. A/AA women must negotiate the tension between their culture and their gender role, contend with stereotypes and images, and integrate these multiple subjectivities into their whole being (Root, 1995). These historical and political realities, as well as the long-standing stereotypes situated in immigration patterns, still impact A/AA women today.

Immigration Patterns

As noted by Mazumdar (2003), immigration patterns of A/AA women are similar to those of immigrant women from Europe. Many of the women served domestic roles in the 1800s and early 1900s, while the men became sojourners to fill the labor needs of the global economy. However, unlike the European women, anti-miscegenation and exclusion laws prevented A/AA women from immigrating to the United States in larger numbers and even suppressed the number of Asian women immigrants, as compared to Asian men, as recently as the 1970 U.S. Census (Bradshaw, 1994).

The initial wave of immigration to the United States in the mid-1800s included Chinese women. Many were given false promises of the riches in the new land, sold by their family, or kidnapped to work as prostitutes. Because of the growing anti-Asian sentiment and the immorality of the Chinese "bachelor society," the larger U.S. society felt justified in passing laws that limited immigration. This atmosphere discouraged other Chinese women, such as wives, daughters, and mothers of the male sojourners, from making the move. The initial wave was followed by a wave of Japanese and Korean women before 1924. However, this second wave of immigration was curtailed by the Gentleman's Agreement in 1907 and the Emergency Quota Act of 1921 that set a quota system for immigrants per country. A larger flux of Korean women occurred after the Korean War (1950–1965). Another immigrant group consisted of women, primarily Japanese, who became wives of military personnel during the U.S. involvement in the Pacific from 1947 to 1977

(Bradshaw, 1994). The next wave of immigration came after the Immigration Act of 1965, which eased restrictions on Asian immigration. Women from China, Korea, the Philippines, South Asia, and Southeast Asia immigrated in large numbers; after 1965, these women were more educated than those in the earlier waves. For instance, Filipinas and South Asian women attained the highest educational levels statistically among all Asian immigrant groups (Bradshaw, 1994).

These waves of immigration seemed to have implications on A/AA women's ability to impact the larger societal structure. Legislation, as well as historical events, impacted immigration to the United States such that the growth or stagnation of specific ethnic communities in the United States was affected. Those women belonging to ethnic groups with longer histories in the United States were allowed more time and resources to establish themselves and make inroads into the larger U.S. society. In addition, these external circumstances created stereotypes about A/AAs, particularly women, which are still widely held.

Stereotypes of Asian American Women

One of the long-lasting effects of U.S. history and politics on minority groups is resultant stereotyping, both positive and negative, by the dominant group. These stereotypes emerge from the power inequities that are inherent in the hierarchical social, economic, and political structures in society. Regardless of the positive or negative nature, stereotypes are dangerous because they can promote certain characteristics that eventually lead to an internalization of them as reality (Chow, 1989). They also can be imposed on those who are seen to belong to the group, even if the person does not possess and/or adhere to the characteristic. This depersonalization consequently overrides the individual's unique personhood and rights (Root, 1995).

One such strongly held stereotype is the traditional gender role expectation of a "good" Asian female as being subservient, passive, and docile. Related to this is the stereotype of the childlike and innocent woman who needs to be dominated, taken care of, and guided by others.

Both of these stereotypes place the A/AA woman in an inferior or subservient position and unintentionally convey a lack of agency, action, or subjectivity. Another long-standing stereotype is the erotic or sensual A/AA woman. This perception was used as the reason for anti-immigration laws against Asian women in the 1800s (because of their assumed lack of morality), and it continues to objectify A/AA women as sex workers to be used and viewed as less than human. Countering that stereotype is that of the aggressive, mean, and manipulative A/AA woman. This stereotype is often perpetuated by media portrayals of the "Dragon Lady," sinister madam (Tajima, 1989), or more recently the "Ling" character on the television series *Ally McBeal*. This stereotype sends the message that one should not be intimately involved with, or trust, A/AA women because they are evil and bad. As Root (1995) noted, this stereotype can easily be relegated to those A/AA women who are assertive and independent and do not fit the first stereotype of being subservient and docile. This is similar to other women being called a "bitch" when they voice their opinions and advocate for their rights. The last prominent stereotype is the extremely conscientious, hardworking, sexless employee or "busy worker bee" (Root, 1995). This reflects the lack of employment opportunities for recent and older Asian women immigrants and refugees. These women are often invisible and dismissed by society-at-large and seldom heard.

Stereotypes of A/AA women have potentially detrimental effects on A/AA women, both individually and as a group. Root (1995) discussed the internalization of these stereotypes on A/AA women's self-esteem and self-determination. For example, because of the external expectations by both society and her family, an A/AA woman may be rewarded for being quiet and deferent to others and punished for being assertive and independent. Eventually, this shaping becomes part of her identity and primary way of interacting. Further, as A/AA women venture more into the mainstream, any one of these stereotypes or a combination of them can be projected onto her by others, especially when she finds herself to be the only Asian American woman in the environment (Kawahara & Van Kirk, 2004). The A/AA

women's movement has recognized the oppression and marginalization of A/AA women through stereotypes and other means and is working toward eradicating them within the A/AA community as well as within the society-at-large.

The Asian American Women's Movement

The feminist women's movement in the United States has focused primarily on the agenda of White middle-class women, and A/AA women—like other women of color—have not been as involved or as influential in it (Chow, 1989). Given the domination of White women in the feminist movement, many ignored or dismissed other oppressions such as race, class, and sexual orientation of other women's lived experiences and wanted these women to focus solely on the oppression of gender to the exclusion of the other factors impinging on their lives. As a result, many A/AA women felt that they had to align themselves with either the Asian or the feminist community to fight for social justice and equality (Fong, 1978); ultimately, many chose the Asian community (Root, 1995).

To further compound the A/AA women's movement, patriarchy in the A/AA community was an added barrier to A/AA women's visibility, empowerment, and activism. A/AA males tended to be the leaders and the prominent voice for the A/AA movement and its agenda, and A/AA women were relegated to a secondary role in terms of support (Root, 1995). Although many A/AA women may have desired a more activist role, much of their energy was spent in dealing with the contradictions between Asian cultural proscriptions of modesty, invisibility, passivity, and support of men (Root, 1995) and the Western values and behaviors in line with activism, such as independence, assertiveness, self-sufficiency, and identity separateness (Sue & Sue, 2003). Further, A/AA women participating in the women's movement were often seen as being disloyal to, and rejecting of, the A/AA community. Not adhering to the obligations and responsibilities of being a "good" A/AA woman (Root, 1995) was deemed as negatively reflecting on her parents and family. Additionally, for A/AA lesbians, the contradictions of being both a "good, dutiful" A/AA woman and an A/AA feminist activist may not have been as salient because of their triple oppressions of sexual orientation, race, and gender (Chan, 1987b). This may have permitted them to participate more openly in the White women's communities as well as in the A/AA community (Root, 1995).

Despite these barriers and obstacles, A/AA women organized and participated in grassroots efforts within various A/AA communities. By the mid-1970s, however, many of these activists were tired and pursuing other professional and personal interests; unfortunately, there were limited replacements for these activists, which led to the decline of the A/AA feminist movement (Root, 1995). The contribution of these women cannot be overlooked. They laid the important political groundwork for the present and future leaders by creating A/AA courses at several universities in California (Chu, 1986). Also, scholarship about A/AA women and their experiences were published in the 1970s, reflecting the noteworthy significance and contribution of these women (Fujitomi & Wong, 1973; Gee, 1976).

Currently, defining and refining the concepts of feminism within the context of one's ethnic community is a process that many A/AA feminists are engaged in. Dasgupta and Dasgupta (1993) clearly illustrate the complexities associated with incorporating the multiple marginalizations based in race, language, class, sexuality, and immigrant status and challenge the applicability of a "monolithic Women's Movement" (p. 130) to the A/AA community. Specifically, the historical and political experiences of A/AA women in the United States continue to impact these women's mental health by a continual subjugation to society's institutional actions and stereotypical attitudes. To understand A/AA women, these experiences must be considered when examining their position and experiences in society as well as their mental health.

CLINICAL ISSUES

Although the presenting issues for A/AA women, as a whole, are similar to those of all women (both ethnic and dominant), some are more specific to this broad cultural group, and still others are specific to subcultures within this group. For example, A/AA women, like other women, live in a society that presumes female inferiority (Westkott, 1998) and are more likely to exhibit and express depressive disorders than are men (Cook, 1990). Further, similar to other ethnic women, they are also affected by racism, sexism, social prejudice, acculturation, discrimination, stereotyping, and unequal access to education or employment (Lin-Fu, 1987). An example of such clinical issues may be a Cambodian refugee struggling with depression due to acculturative stress, underemployment, English language difficulties, and cultural conflicts with her second-generation children.

Whereas A/AA females are seeking mental health services in nearly equal proportion to A/AA men, their rates of mental health service utilization are still considerably lower than the rates of White women (True, 1991). It has been observed that gender research ignores racial/ethnic concerns while studies of racial/ethnic groups fail to address gender issues (Comas-Diaz & Greene, 1994; Robinson, 1993). Similarly, cross-cultural psychology, at times, fails to use rigorous scientific methods to develop theory while mainstream psychological theories often ignore culture and lack universality (Betancourt & Lopez, 1993). Therefore, it is necessary to glean information from a variety of sources, including studies that examine gender and ethnic minority issues separately. Because there is virtually no national data on A/AA females and mental health issues, it is often necessary to examine the data regarding Asian women internationally and regionally within the United States. The next section examines issues for A/AA women such as: multiple minority statuses, multiple roles, interracial issues, trauma, depression/anxiety, body image, sexuality, and domestic violence.

Multiple Minority Statuses

A/AA women face a double jeopardy of living within a racist and sexist society (Comas-Diaz & Greene, 1994; C. C. I. Hall, 1995). This double minority status affords them limited support among their A/AA peers and their female sisters from other cultures. At times, they may even suffer a "triple" stigma for being of a low

SES (Porter, 1995), sexual orientation, or another oppressed identity. Because the effects of race and social class are interactive (Kessler & Neighbors, 1986; Reid & Comas-Diaz, 1990), social and economic inequalities must not be overlooked when focusing on gender and ethnicity (Ryan 2002). For instance, despite the model minority myth, A/AA women tend to work out of necessity rather than choice and have significantly higher poverty rates than White women.

The double oppression experienced by A/AA women living in the United States may be further compounded by the conflicting gender stereotypes they face (Bradshaw, 1994). Although some may argue that it is adaptive to have different social contexts trigger different aspects of the self (Pittensky, Shih, & Ambady, 1999), this may not be true when the expectations of two cultures are vastly different. There also tend to be negative implications on women's mental health when they have internalized the expected standards and expectations set by their families, communities, and society, and they have failed in meeting them all.

For some A/AA women, negotiating between gender role expectations of the mainstream culture versus their culture of origin leads to conflicts (Inman, Constantine, & Ladany, 1999). Some believe they need to make personality accommodations based on their contexts and describe a pressure to conform to gender role expectations, which leads to a complaint that in ethnic settings, they cannot be who they truly are (Pyke & Johnson, 2003). This partial rejection of one's Asian culture may inadvertently reinforce White dominance and cause a feeling of tension between individualism of the dominant culture and the family obligations of the private sphere. At times, this conflict may lead to communication distortions between generations, for example, omitting information when communicating with one's parents to reduce potential parent-child conflicts (Kallivayalil, 2004).

Second-generation A/AA women face additional stressors in relation to their mothers (True, 1990). The cultural disparities often lead to intergenerational conflict of various issues, ranging from dating preferences to career aspirations (Fu, 2002; Inman, Howard, Beaumont, & Walker, 2005). While it has been noted that

A/AA women do not necessarily acculturate at the expense of their ethnic identification (Liu, Pope-Davis, Nevitt, & Toporek, 1999), Leong (1986) found that Asian women tend to acculturate at a faster rate than their male counterparts, sometimes leading to interpersonal and cultural conflicts within their family and community systems.

Balancing Multiple Roles

Even though the traditional Chinese saying "Men dominate the outside; women dominate the inside" is less apparent today than in the past, females are still responsible for the majority of traditionally female tasks in China and in the United States. Further, the less educated a woman is, the heavier the burden in the household is (Lu, Maume, & Bellas, 2000). Although the early Chinese women in the United States benefited from the new environment by being promoted from merely a breeder and caregiver to a joint family head and co-provider (Ling, 2000), there is still much discrepancy between homemaker and income-producing partner for the average A/AA female. Over a decade ago, Porter (1995) pointed out that "many Asian American women are beginning to reject the traditional role, but they are still struggling to achieve equal status and to overcome the inferiority complex, inculcated by traditional Asian thinking" (p. 186). We continue to see this struggle in many A/AA women today, especially in daughters of immigrant families. Additionally, A/AA women are often faced with conflicts regarding familial and gender roles when assimilating from native cultural patterns to the majority culture (Inman, Ladany, Constantine, & Morano, 2001). This is true, in part, because patriarchy had such an overwhelming influence on the inferior status of women throughout Asia. The culture conflict that ethnic minority women often face may lead to gender role conflict, identity crisis, feelings of isolation, alienation, or depression. Further, this culture clash may lead to problematic self-concept formation, which could contribute to depression (Shum, 1996).

The shift in lifestyle and changes in economic status when immigrating often forces women into the workforce. At times, highly trained individuals find themselves underemployed because of language barriers or difficulty transferring training from one country to another. Unlike White women who often work as an option, employment for many ethnic minority females has been more out of necessity to supplement the household income (Olmedo & Parron, 1981).

Ryan (2002) noted, however, that the most recent wave of Chinese female immigrants have quickly adapted to the workforce and have been able to take advantage of favorable economic opportunities in China prior to emigrating. Therefore, they tend to be less ambivalent about integrating their child-rearing responsibilities with their careers than are their Western counterparts. Ryan also found that women from Asia could flourish within self-employed or employer roles once removed from the constraints of Western employers.

Interracial Issues

Intermarriage is also increasing among A/AA females (True, 1997). Hirayama and Hirayama (1986) found that, although the outmarriage rate for first-generation Japanese Americans was less than 1%, the interracial marriage rate for third-generation Japanese Americans had increased to nearly 50%. Women who choose interracial partners may face greater stigma and loss of support from their own community, as engaging in an interracial marriage is seen as a sign of losing one's ethnic identity or "becoming Americanized" (Bradshaw, 1994; Root, 1990; Tewari, Inman, & Sandhu, 2003). This is especially so because women are usually considered the carriers of tradition; as a result, there is more pressure on them to uphold and transmit culture intergenerationally. This double standard for women may contribute to their sense of being ostracized by their Asian community. Additionally, they may even find themselves excluded from the majority culture, further contributing to their sense of isolation.

Trauma

Post-traumatic stress disorder (PTSD) has been highly prevalent among Southeast Asian refugees (True & Guillermo, 1996). It has been proposed that these refugees face the greatest levels of stress and difficulty adjusting to their postimmigration life in the United States (True, 1991), with women being more distressed than men (True, 1996). Many have suffered traumas in their countries of origin, during their involuntary escape out of their countries, and in refugee camps. The stress of migration and resettlement often manifests in physical and emotional symptoms (Tien, 1994). Traumas for females include, but are not limited to, being raped, witnessing family members being killed, separating from family and/or friends, and being physically and psychologically tortured.

Those who suffered multiple traumatic experiences before emigrating may experience severe PTSD (Pernice & Brook, 1996). For example, Rozée and Van Boemel (1989) examined the life experiences of a group of older Cambodian refugee women during and after the fall of Cambodia. They suspected the visual acuity loss might have been a reaction to the severe abuse they experienced. Also, years of servitude/internment were significantly related to the women's symptom severity. They further found a high incidence of depression and somatization among their Cambodian respondents.

Intergenerational transmission of trauma may also need to be considered for the children of those traumatized as well as the community. For example, Japanese Americans continue to be affected by being incarcerated during World War II as well as do subsequent generations who also may show symptoms of psychological trauma, humiliation, and fears about future persecution (Nagata, 1998). Nagata (2000) found that the camp effects influenced how Japanese American women raised their children by encouraging them to be "model Americans" and accelerated the rate of acculturation in third- and fourth-generation Japanese Americans.

Depression and Anxiety

Porter (1995) found that immigrant Asian women have higher rates of depression than immigrant Asian men. Shum (1996) believed that some of the traditional Asian cultural values for women might contribute to reinforcing dimensions of depression as defined by Western culture. It has been posited that postimmigration factors such as lack of social support and employability are associated with anxiety and depression scores more than are demographic characteristics (e.g., age, gender) for Southeast Asian refugees and Pacific Island immigrants moving to a Western country (Pernice & Brook, 1996).

Ethnic minority women have been found to experience high levels of depression, often associated with acculturation and immigration. Some stressors are specific to A/AA women (True & Guillermo, 1996; True, 1997). Additionally, feelings of helplessness and powerlessness stemming from being women and having minority status may lead to symptoms of depression (Baskin, Bluestone, & Nelson, 1981). Among these stressors are the intergenerational conflicts encountered during childrearing, for which women have the primary responsibility, and the lack of the traditional family networks that may have been available in the country of origin.

Although the suicide rates for A/AAs are relatively lower than those of the general U.S. population, there are certain ethnic/age specific groups that are at higher risk. For example, elderly A/AA women are at the highest risk for suicide among all A/AA women, especially after the death of their spouse; most likely this stems from low SES, social isolation, declining health, and the lack of supports/resources (True, 1996; True & Guillermo, 1996).

Body Image

Robinson et al. (1996) suggest that unhealthy eating attitudes are much more prevalent among A/AA females than previously recognized. Several factors have contributed to this prevalence. First, women in the United States are socialized to base their self-esteem on their physical appearance. The societal emphasis on a thinner ideal body shape for women exerts significant pressure on women to take extreme measures despite possible adverse effects (Garner, Garfinkel, Schwartz, & Thompson, 1980). This female standard of beauty that has often been based on the White female of European descent is not easily obtainable by A/AA females (C. C. I. Hall, 1995; Koff, Benavage, & Wong, 2001). Despite this, researchers have found that A/AA females reported significantly more body dissatisfaction and drive for thinness than A/AA males (Davis & Katzman, 1999). Except for the desire for thinness, A/AA females have expressed satisfaction with their body size in comparison with White females; however, they desired an increase of their breast size (Koff & Benavage, 1998; Lee, Leung, Lee, Yu, & Leung, 1996).

Second, factors associated with racism may increase vulnerability to eating disorders in order to be accepted by the dominant culture, even if messages from one's own culture are contradictory (Crago, Shisslak, & Estes, 1996; Root, 1990). A/AA women have been noted to be at higher risk for lower self-esteem and lower levels of satisfaction with racially defined features (e.g., eyes, face) (Mintz & Kashubeck, 1999). Inability to attain such racially specific standards may lead to stress, low self-esteem, and depression (Porter, 1995). Kaw (1993) found that, when seeking cosmetic surgery, A/AA women primarily sought to alter racial markers.

A third, related factor is acculturation. Although researchers have found more problematic eating among White women in comparison to A/AA women (Nevo, 1985), more acculturated A/AA women may begin to adopt more of the disordered eating behaviors of Westernized females (Furnham & Alibhai, 1983; Lee et al., 1996). This has been called the "culture change syndrome" due to the influence of acculturation and introduction of media across Asia (DiNicola, 1990).

The relatively low rate of eating disorders among A/AA women may actually be due to inaccurate data and misdiagnosis (C. C. I. Hall, 1995; Root, 1990). Researchers have suggested that ethnic or cultural background and SES may influence the prevalence and reporting of eating disorders symptoms (Lucero, Hicks, Bramlette, Brassington, & Welter, 1992; Osvold & Sodowsky, 1993). Likewise, Ritenbaugh (1982) argued that obesity may be a culture-bound syndrome and may increase with acculturation. Others have not confirmed that acculturation is associated with eating disturbance (Akan & Grilo, 1995; Dolan, 1991). Other factors that have been associated with disturbed eating among A/AA women include parental bonding (Haudek, Rorty, & Henker, 1999), hurtful racial teasing (Iyer & Haslam, 2003), and perceived level of maternal control (McCourt & Waller, 1995).

Sexuality

Traditional Asian values of sexuality have been shaped by Western culture. Although traditional Japanese society has been historically more sexually uninhibited than U.S. society, Japanese Americans began to acculturate to the host society, thereby accepting the moral positions toward sexual conduct advocated by the Catholic and Protestant churches (Hirayama & Hirayama, 1986). This translated into not only restricted physical demonstrations of affection and low tolerance for sexual education or conversation but also reinforcement of traditional sexual expectations for women. Therefore, while men were expected to assume more sexually aggressive roles, the women were expected to assume more submissive and passive roles.

More recently, studies of sexual practices of heterosexual A/AA young adults reflect sexual conservatism being limited to the initiation of sexual activity. However, once sexually active, A/AA young adult behaviors seem similar to those of their non-Asian peers. Thus, outreach should consider this subpopulation (Cochran, Mays, & Leung, 1991), especially considering the noncompliance rates among ethnic minorities in the treatment of sexually transmitted diseases (Oggins, 2003).

Cultural stereotypes have led to the sexual exploitation of A/AA women (Chan, 1987a). Historically, Asian women have been economic and sexual commodities, with war and media images and the Asian mail-order bride business contributing to the portrayal of A/AA women as exotic sexual objects. The initial psychological response of A/AA women being victimized by such stereotypes may result in feelings of helplessness, avoidance, self-blame, and guilt/ shame. The cultural norm that places a strong emphasis on silence or avoidance on topics of sexuality has severe health and social consequences for A/AA women. Not only have such views prohibited women from taking care of their bodies, but they also contribute to the perpetuation of domestic violence (Helstrom, Coffey, & Jorgannathon, 1998). The emphasis on group harmony and avoidance of shame may place A/AA females at particular risk of being sexually victimized. This may be further compounded by the patriarchal aspects of both Asian and U.S. cultures (G. C. N. Hall, Wondover, & Maramba, 1998). Out of fear or self-blame, A/AA females may be more likely to underreport and seek treatment for sexual assault; due to cultural influences, they may fail to recognize and label sexual victimization (Mori, Bernat, Glenn, Selle, & Zarate, 1995). Sexual victimization is but one of the ways in which A/AA women may be victimized. The next section examines certain aspects of domestic violence in this community.

Domestic Violence

There has been an increasing incidence of physical and sexual abuse among A/AA communities in the United States (True & Guillermo, 1996). Several risk factors have been identified in this regard: A/AA women's stereotypes as exotic, sexual creatures; changes in familial structures and roles as women enter the workforce and contribute to family finances; and stressors related to immigration, resulting from employment issues and social isolation (Yick, 2001). Despite these factors and increased risks, A/AAs have a reputation of having low incidence rates of domestic violence. This may be due to the denial of social problems within one's own community (Dasgupta, 2000), underutilization of mental health care services (Ho, 1990), underreporting (G. C. N. Hall, 2002), and culturally insensitive providers (Yeh, Inman, Kim, & Okubo, in press). Ayyub's 2000 survey showed that one in four South Asian women reported the occurrence of domestic violence in her home, an estimate that is most likely conservative. Literature suggests that the extent of domestic violence in the Asian community may actually be larger (Yick, 2001). Ho (1990) mentioned that cultural values of fatalism may also lead to silencing of this particular issue, and the acceptance of corporal punishment in the household may lead to the acceptance of violence as a means of negotiating power in the family. The stigma and shame attached to help-seeking and the need to save face within the community may result in a reluctance to seek help (Uba, 1994).

Various methods have been employed to enforce abuse patterns, including threatening to ruin a woman's reputation; using isolation;

refusing to grant women a religious divorce; and threatening to endanger immigration status (Abraham, 2000). The power imbalance inherent in traditional gender relations makes this particular group ripe for female abuse and leads to the subordination of women. Values that elevate group harmony above personal freedom also may serve to further isolate and oppress A/AA women (Preisser, 1999). Bradshaw (1994) noted that the emphasis on group harmony does not necessarily eradicate conflicts but merely prescribes how they are dealt with in the community. The protective factors of maintaining group harmony may be harnessed as a mechanism to both oppress and intervene on behalf of the domestic violence victim within the A/AA community. The clinical issues addressed in this section merely highlight the issues that plague A/AA women. The following section describes help-seeking patterns and behaviors of A/AA females who seek to improve their functioning.

HELP-SEEKING PATTERNS AND BEHAVIORS

A/AAs tend to underutilize mental health services; however, the mental health utilization pattern does not necessarily reflect a lack of need (Root, 1985). The therapist must understand that the values of counseling are antithetic to Asian philosophy of solving problems within the family/inner group (Toupin, 1980). Because of the contrasting value differences between their Asian heritage and U.S. culture, many A/AA women who want to seek help outside the family struggle with the dilemma of remaining loyal to their family and ethnic community while desiring validation and assistance with their own personal needs (True, 1997).

As a result, many Asian immigrant and refugee women often seek the help of extended family members, authority figures, indigenous healers, and medical professionals before they contact therapists, even if their issues are related to mental illness (Ying, 1990). Reasons for this vary from stigma to shame, loss of face, cultural mandates reinforcing personal suffering, lack of knowledge about services and resources, language mismatching (True & Guillermo, 1996), distrust, and unfamiliarity and/or unacceptability of psychotherapy (Chin, 1998). When

assistance is finally sought, presenting symptoms tend to be more severe than they would otherwise. As opposed to their male counterparts who tend to present with more serious psychotic illnesses, A/AA women's presenting issues tend to be related to depression and other affective disorders (True, 1997).

THE ASIAN AMERICAN WOMAN AND THERAPIST DYAD

Mental health providers' biases remain a major barrier to A/AA women seeking mental health services and remaining in treatment (Root, 1990). Mismatch of conceptualization of presenting issues may impede service delivery and compliance (Ying, 1990). For example, the Japanese concept of "amae" may be misinterpreted as dysfunctional dependence if the therapist is not able to understand the significance of interdependency in relationships (Mass, 2003). Furthermore, incompatible goals of the therapist and client also may serve as a barrier to treatment (Root, 1985). In the case of domestic violence, a more Western feminist intervention would be to encourage the woman to leave the perpetrator. This may be an incompatible option for an A/AA woman who sees her role as integral to her family. What has been found more effective with South A/AA women who sought help for domestic violence was providing interventions within the woman's community (Dasgupta, 2000; Dasgupta & Dasgupta, 1993).

The issue of ethnic (Atkinson, 1983) and gender matching has been examined with mixed results. Mintz and O'Neil (1990) found that females tend to prefer female therapists. While Brody (1987) argued that racial match is less important than gender match, so long as the therapist is mindful of culture and is able to create a trusting atmosphere, Fujino, Okazaki, and Young (1994) found that ethnic and/or gender match conditions were significantly associated with reduced premature termination and increased treatment duration when working with A/AA females. Moreover, they found that ethnic and gender match were more important for A/AA women than for A/AA men, White American women, and White American men.

THERAPEUTIC CONSIDERATIONS AND APPROACHES

To provide effective therapy, therapists need to understand how cultural conflict, SES, and stereotypical attitudes based on gender and race contribute to the psychological functioning of ethnic minority women (Porter, 1995). Initial phases of therapy should address cultural differences between client and therapist, which may include gender, race, ethnicity, language or dialect, immigration status, SES, and values (Fujino et al., 1994). For A/AA immigrant or refugee women, therapists can help them grieve the loss of their culture of origin. Often, loss of economic status, support networks, values, and other aspects of their lifestyle may be overlooked due to the need to acclimate to their host culture. Likewise, more culturally sensitive assessment measures need to be developed (Lee, 1995) to help alleviate the restrictions of using DSM (*Diagnostic and Statistical Manual of Mental Disorders*) criteria to diagnose clients outside of the Western culture.

Assertiveness training may be effective for those who need to negotiate with those outside the home, especially because less acculturated A/AA women are socialized to defer to others (Yanagida, 1979). Mastery experiences to increase self-efficacy, rather than anxiety management techniques, may be more effective when helping A/AA women develop assertive behaviors. Likewise, therapists can help clients understand that uncomfortable feelings are normative and need not inhibit assertiveness (Zane, Sue, Hu, & Kwon, 1991). Rather than denying the importance of the A/AA woman's community, therapists should consider self-care within the context of family care (Helstrom et al., 1998). This may be translated into convincing the A/AA woman of the benefits of routine gynecological/breast exams or other preventative health issues in relation to their ability to care for their families.

A more concrete, behavioral treatment approach may work better for A/AAs than examining the psychodynamics, which could enhance the individual's sense of shame (Tsui, 1985) by focusing on the deficiencies of one's parents (Bradshaw, 1994). It may be necessary to assess one's ethnic identity to determine appropriate treatment. For example, cognitive therapy was perceived as being more credible among A/AAs who indicated low levels of White identity (Wong, Kim, Zane, Kim, & Huang, 2003).

Less direct and nonthreatening therapeutic interventions, such as storytelling or narrative letters, also have been shown to be effective in modifying traditional therapy to work culturally sensitively (Bracero, 1996). Also, nonverbal therapy techniques (e.g., sand tray therapy, artwork) may be effective (Fu, in press). Relatedly, incorporating the family system may increase treatment outcomes (Rozeé & Van Boemel, 1989) by paying particular attention to the family structure (Kim, 1985; True, 1990). Incorporating the client's existing social/familial supports may be considered culturally appropriate, particularly when interventions involve a respected elder. This may be most helpful when the family system requires an intermediary to serve as a reconciler between two members, thus saving face (Kim, 1985).

To help combat domestic violence among A/AA families, Yick (2001) examined the merits and limitations of the feminist perspective and status inconsistency theory. Whereas feminist theory examines power structure imbalances, status inconsistency theory focuses on systems maintenance. Both have their merits, but status inconsistency theory has more immediate gains for family members by reducing stressors that lead to perceived imbalance of resources, whereas feminist theory addresses the macrosocietal level of oppression of women by men. Capitalizing on the cultural value of maintaining harmony within one's group also may help to counter domestic violence among A/AA communities.

Empowerment seems to be a repeated theme in the literature when examining effective ways of working with women, though this seems especially salient when discussing women of color. This perspective can help A/AA women understand and address how their position in society contributes to their problems. It is important for interventions that counteract the patriarchal aspects of Asian and U.S. cultures to be implemented (Hall et al., 1998). Feminist therapies can be applied, but the importance of sensitively integrating the values with the client's culture of origin cannot be overemphasized. Gender Aware Therapy is another option, which advocates that clients collaboratively choose their options in a nonsexist therapeutic environment (Good, Gilbert, & Scher, 1990). This orientation advocates that the therapist understands the contribution of worldviews and gender roles to counseling (Scher & Good, 1990). Both feminist therapy and Gender Aware Therapy are based on the premise that problems are considered within their societal context; therefore, the personal and political cannot be separated. However, some authors caution against the potential self-indulgent perspective of promoting the individual freedom of A/AA women (Bradshaw, 1994) in these approaches.

Although some women of color may benefit from self-help groups, due to the parallels of the group to the collective orientation among these women (Comas-Diaz & Greene, 1994), Leong (1986) and Toupin (1980) found negative outcomes for A/AAs who participated in group counseling. Groups may raise issues of trust and confidentiality; for example, the fear of gossip in the community can prevent these women from engaging in groups. Further, while certain treatment methods may be considered most effective when treating A/AA women, modifying traditional therapeutic approaches should be augmented to address the impact of the various factors affecting ethnic women (Olmedo & Parron, 1981). Likewise, True (1990) noted that various Asian therapists have advocated for a number of revised, eclectic therapeutic interventions rather than using a single method. This may be particularly helpful in order to tailor the modified approaches based on the client's particular needs and fit.

Conclusions and Recommendations

As the U.S. Surgeon General's (1999) report concluded, there are still great health disparities among ethnic minority groups in the United States, and A/AA women are no exception. Better and more accurate statistics about A/AA women and their specific ethnic groups are needed so that policymakers, researchers, and clinicians can address their particular issues and needs more effectively. Relatedly, research that integrates A/AA women's multiple subjectivities, such as gender, ethnicity, social class, and sexual orientation, is necessary. Both etic and emic research needs to be conducted to examine between- and within-group differences to assess the women's subjective interpretations of their lived experiences (Landrine, Klonoff, & Brown-Collins, 1992).

Considerable outreach is necessary to educate A/AA women about the benefits of self-care, importance of preventive health care, and ways to access the health care system (Lin-Fu, 1987; True & Guillermo, 1996). Bringing and expanding culturally competent services in A/AA communities will tremendously help those A/AA women who are less likely to seek out psychological help on their own (True, 1996). Likewise, coordinating with primary care physicians or other gateways for mental health referrals may help to facilitate services. In addition, formation of community multiservice centers targeted toward providing comprehensive services such as physical and mental health services, immigration assistance, child care activities, legal counsel, and vocational training would not only be convenient but may also minimize barriers, such as the sense of stigma and shame that potentially prevent A/AA women from seeking treatment (Ying, 1990). Once the A/AA woman seeks services, she needs to be assisted by culturally competent practitioners in a comfortable environment. Although multicultural training has increased across graduate psychology programs, there is still a huge demand for competent therapists to provide culturally appropriate services for A/AA women.

Advocacy and public policy remain the most crucial means by which to bring resources and services to A/AA women and their communities. It is the responsibility of those who are privileged to promote groups and issues to policymakers to advocate on behalf of A/AA women who are not given the opportunity to do so for themselves. For example, we cannot ignore the alarming numbers of women refugees, women sold as marriage partners, women kidnapped or indebted as sex slaves, and women exploited as factory workers or other deplorable employment conditions. The needs and issues affecting A/AA women are evident. These recommendations address the multiple levels of society that affect the lives of these women. Only a systemic approach to addressing these factors can result in reducing the barriers faced by A/AA women and allowing them to use their agency to live freely, optimally, and empowered in whatever manner they choose.

REFERENCES

Abraham, M. (2000). Isolation as a form of marital violence: The South Asian immigrant experience. *Journal of Social Distress and the Homeless, 9,* 221–236.

Akan, G. E., & Grilo, C. M. (1995). Sociocultural influences on eating attitudes and behaviors, body image, and psychological functioning: A comparison of African-American, Asian-American, and Caucasian college women. *International Journal of Eating Disorders, 18,* 181–187.

Atkinson, D. R. (1983). Ethnic similarity in counseling psychology: A review of research. *The Counseling Psychologist, 11,* 79–92.

Ayyub, R. (2000). Domestic violence in the South Asian Muslim immigrant population in the United States. *Journal of Social Distress and the Homeless, 9,* 237–248.

Baskin, D., Bluestone, H., & Nelson, M. (1981). Mental illness in minority women. *Journal of Clinical Psychology, 37,* 491–498.

Betancourt, H., & Lopez, S. R. (1993). The study of culture, ethnicity, and race in American psychology. *American Psychologist, 48,* 629–637.

Bracero, W. (1996). Ancestral voices: Narrative and multicultural perspectives with an Asian schizophrenic. *Psychotherapy, 33,* 93–103.

Bradshaw, C. K. (1994). Asian and Asian American women: Historical and political considerations in psychotherapy. In L. Comas-Diaz & B. Greene (Eds.), *Women of color: Integrating ethnic and gender identities in psychotherapy* (pp. 72–113). New York: Guilford Press.

Brody, C. M. (1987). White therapist and female minority clients: Gender and culture issues. *Psychotherapy, 24,* 108–113.

Chan, C. S. (1987a). Asian-American women: Psychological responses to sexual exploitation and cultural stereotypes. *Women & Therapy, 6,* 33–38.

Chan, C. S. (1987b). Asian lesbians: Psychological issues in the "coming out" process. *Asian American Psychological Association Journal,* 16–18.

Chin, J. L. (1998). Mental health services and treatment. In L. C. Lee & N. W. S. Zane (Eds.), *Handbook of Asian American psychology* (pp. 485–504). Thousand Oaks, CA: Sage.

Chow, E. N. (1989). The feminist movement: Where are all the Asian American women? In Asian Women United of California (Ed.), *Making waves: An anthology of writings by and about Asian American women* (pp. 362–377). Boston: Beacon Press.

Chu, J. (1986). Asian American women's studies course: A look back at our beginnings. *Frontiers, 8,* 96–101.

Cochran, S. D., Mays, V., M., & Leung, L. (1991). Sexual practices of heterosexual Asian-American young adults: Implications for risk of HIV infection. *Archives of Sexual Behavior, 20,* 381–391.

Comas-Diaz, L., & Greene, B. (1994). Overview: Gender and ethnicity in the healing process. In L. Comas-Diaz & B. Greene (Eds.), *Women of color: Integrating ethnic and gender identities in psychotherapy* (pp. 185–193). New York: Guilford Press.

Cook, E. P. (1990). Gender and psychological distress. *Journal of Counseling & Development, 68,* 371–375.

Crago, M., Shisslak, C. M., & Estes, L. S. (1996). Eating disturbances among American minority groups: A review. *International Journal of Eating Disorders, 19,* 239–248.

Dasgupta, S. D. (2000). Charting the course: An overview of domestic violence in the South Asian community in the United States. *Journal of Social Distress and the Homeless, 9,* 173–185.

Dasgupta, S., & Dasgupta, S. D. (1993). Journeys: Reclaiming South Asian feminism. In The Women of South Asian Descent Collective (Ed.), *Our feet walk the sky: Women of the South Asian diaspora* (pp. 123–130). San Francisco: Aunt Lute Books.

Davis, C., & Katzman, M. A. (1999). Perfection as acculturation: Psychological correlates of eating problems in Chinese male and female students living in the United States. *International Journal of Eating Disorders, 25,* 65–70.

DiNicola, V. (1990). Anorexia multiform: Self starvation in historical and cultural context. Part 2: Anorexia nervosa as a cultural reactive syndrome. *Transcultural Psychiatric Review, 27,* 254–286.

Dolan, B. (1991). Cross-cultural aspects of anorexic nervosa and bulimia: A review. *International Journal of Eating Disorders, 10,* 67–78.

Fong, K. M. (1978, Winter). Feminism is fine, but what's it done for Asia America? *Bridge: An Asian American Perspective,* pp. 21–22.

Fu, M. (2002). Acculturation, ethnic identity, and family conflict among first and second generation Chinese Americans. *Dissertation Abstracts International, 63*(2), 1024. (UMI No. AA13043465)

Fu, M. (in press). Expressive therapies for Asian-American clients: The value of nonverbal sand tray therapy. In E. Chen & G. Omatsu (Eds.), *Teaching about Asian Pacific Americans.* Lanham, MD: AltaMira Press.

Fujino, D. C., Okazaki, S., & Young, K. (1994). Asian-American women in the mental health system: An examination of ethnic and gender match between therapist and client. *Journal of Community Psychology, 22,* 164–176.

Fujitomi, I., & Wong, D. (1973). The new Asian-American woman. In S. Sue & N. N. Wagner (Eds.), *Asian Americans: Psychological perspectives* (pp. 252–263). Ben Lomond, CA: Science & Behavior Books.

Furnham, A., & Alibhai, N. (1983). Cross-cultural differences in the perception of female body shapes. *Psychological Medicine, 13,* 829–837.

Garner, D. M., Garfinkel, P. E., Schwartz, D., & Thompson, M. (1980). Cultural expectations of thinness in women. *Psychological Reports, 47,* 483–491.

Gee, E. (Ed.). (1976). *Counterpoint: Perspectives on Asian America.* Los Angeles: University of California, Asian American Studies Center.

Good, G. E., Gilbert, L. A., & Scher, M. (1990). Gender aware therapy: A synthesis of feminist therapy and knowledge about gender. *Journal of Counseling and Development, 68,* 376–380.

Hall, C. C. I. (1995). Asian eyes: Body image and eating disorders of Asian and Asian American women. *Eating Disorders: The Journal of Treatment and Prevention, 3,* 8–19.

Hall, G. C. N. (2002). Culture-specific ecological models of Asian American violence. In G. C. N. Hall & S. Okazaki (Eds.), *Asian American Psychology: The science of lives in context* (pp. 153–170). Washington, DC: American Psychological Association.

Hall, G. C. N., Wondover, A., K., & Maramba, G. G. (1998). Sexual aggression among Asian Americans: Risk and protective factors. *Cultural Diversity and Mental Health, 4,* 305–318.

Haudek, C., Rorty, M., & Henker, B. (1999). The role of ethnicity and parental bonding in the eating and weight concerns of Asian-American and Caucasian college women. *International Journal of Eating Disorders, 25,* 425–433.

Helstrom, A. W., Coffey, C., & Jorgannathon, P. (1998). Asian-American women's health. In E. A. Blechman & K. D. Brownell (Eds.), *Gender, culture, and health* (pp. 826–832). New York: Guilford Press.

Hirayama, H., & Hirayama, K. K. (1986). The sexuality of Japanese Americans. *Sexuality, Ethnoculture, and Social Work, 4,* 81–98.

Ho, C. K. (1990). An analysis of domestic violence in Asian American communities: A multicultural approach to counseling. In L. Brown & M. Root (Eds.), *Women and therapy: Diversity and complexity in feminist therapy* (pp. 129–150). New York: Haworth Press.

Inman, A. G., Constantine, M. G., & Ladany, N. (1999). Cultural value conflict: An examination of Asian Indian women's bicultural experience. In D. S. Sandhu (Eds.), *Asian and Pacific Islander Americans: Issues and concerns for counseling and psychotherapy* (pp. 31–41). Commack, NY: Nova Science.

Inman, A. G., Howard, E. E., Beaumont, R., & Walker, J. A. (2005). *Cultural transmission: Themes in Asian Indian parents' immigration experiences.* Poster presentation at the American Counseling Association convention in Atlanta, GA.

Inman A. G., Ladany, N., Constantine, M. G., & Morano, C. K. (2001). Development and preliminary validation of the cultural values conflict scale for South Asian women. *Journal of Counseling Psychology, 48,* 17–27.

Iyer, D. S., & Haslam, N. (2003). Body image and eating disturbance among South Asian-American women: The role of racial teasing. *International Journal of Eating Disorders, 34,* 142–147.

Kaw, E. (1993). Medicalization of racial features: Asian American women and cosmetic surgery. *Medical Anthropology Quarterly, 7,* 74–89.

Kawahara, D. M., & Van Kirk, J. J. (2004). Asian Americans in the workplace: Facing prejudice and discrimination in multiple contexts. In J. L. Chin

(Ed.), *The psychology of prejudice and discrimination* (pp. 37–63). Westport, CT: Praeger.

Kallivayalil, D. (2004). Gender and cultural socialization in Indian immigrant families in the United States. *Feminism and Psychology, 14,* 535–559.

Kessler, R. C., & Neighbors, H. W. (1986). A new perspective on the relationships among race, social class, and psychological distress. *Journal of Health and Social Behavior, 27*(2), 107–115.

Kim, S. C. (1985). Family therapy for Asian Americans: A strategic structural framework. *Psychotherapy: Theory, Research, and Practice, 22,* 342–348.

Koff, E., & Benavage, A. (1998). Breast size perception and satisfaction, body image, and psychological functioning in Caucasian and Asian American college women. *Sex Roles, 38,* 655–673.

Koff, E., Benavage, A., & Wong, B. (2001). Body-image attitudes and psychosocial functioning in Euro-American and Asian-American college women. *Psychological Reports, 88,* 917–928.

Landrine, H., Klonoff, E. A., & Brown-Collins, A. (1992). Cultural diversity and methodology in feminist psychology: Critique, proposal, empirical example. *Psychology of Women Quarterly, 16,* 145–163.

Lee, S. (1995). Self-starvation in context: Towards culturally sensitive understanding of anorexia nervosa. *Social Science Medicine, 41,* 25–36.

Lee, S., Leung, T., Lee, A. M., Yu, H., & Leung, C. M. (1996). Body dissatisfaction among Chinese undergraduates and its implications for eating disorders in Hong Kong. *International Journal of Eating Disorders, 20,* 77–84.

Leong, F. T. L. (1986). Counseling and psychotherapy with Asian-Americans: Review of the literature. *Journal of Counseling Psychology, 33,* 196–206.

Lin-Fu, J. S. (1987). Special health concerns of ethnic minority women. *Public Health Reports Supplement, 102,* 12–14.

Ling, H. (2000). Family and marriage of late-nineteenth and early-twentieth century Chinese immigrant women. *Journal of American Ethnic History, 19,* 43–63.

Liu, W. M., Pope-Davis, D. B., Nevitt, J., & Toporek, R. L. (1999). Understanding the function of acculturation and prejudicial attitudes among Asian Americans. *Cultural Diversity & Ethnic Minority Psychology, 5,* 317–328.

Lu, Z. Z., Maume, D. J., & Bellas, M. L. (2000). Chinese husband's participation in household labor. *Journal of Comparative Family Studies, 31,* 191–215.

Lucero, K., Hicks, R. A., Bramlette, J., Brassington, G. S., & Welter, M. G. (1992). Frequency of eating problems among Asian and Caucasian college women. *Psychological Reports, 71,* 255–258.

Mass, A. I. (2003). Asian-American women: Issues for clinical practice. In J. B. Sanville & E. B. Ruderman (Eds.), *Therapies with women in transition: Toward* relational perspectives with today's women (pp. 119–130). Madison, CT: International Universities Press.

Mazumdar, S. (2003). What happened to the women? Chinese and Indian male migration to the United States in global perspective. In S. Hune & G. M. Nomura (Eds.), *Asian/Pacific Islander American women: A historical anthology* (pp. 58–74). New York: New York University Press.

McCourt, J., & Waller, G. (1995). Developmental role of perceived parental control in the eating psychopathology of Asian and Caucasian schoolgirls. *International Journal of Eating Disorders, 17,* 277–282.

Mintz, L. B., & Kashubeck, S. (1999). Body image and disordered eating among Asian American and Caucasian college students. *Psychology of Women Quarterly, 23,* 781–796.

Mintz, L. B., & O'Neil, J. M. (1990). Gender roles, sex, and the process of psychotherapy: Many questions and few answers. *Journal of Counseling & Development, 68,* 381–387.

Mori, L., Bernat, J. A., Glenn, P. A., Selle, L. L., & Zarate, M. G. (1995). Attitudes toward rape: Gender and ethnic differences across Asian and Caucasian college students. *Sex Roles, 32,* 457–467.

Nagata, D. K. (1998). Internment and intergenerational relations. In L. C. Lee & N. W. S. Zane (Eds.), *Handbook of Asian American psychology* (pp. 433–456). Thousand Oaks, CA: Sage.

Nagata, D. K. (2000). World War II internment and the relationships of women. In J. L. Chin (Ed.), *Relationships among Asian American women* (pp. 49–70).

Nevo, S. (1985). Bulimic symptoms: Prevalence and ethnic differences among college women. *International Journal of Eating Disorders, 4,* 151–168.

Nomura, G. M. (2003). On our terms: Definitions and context. In S. Hune & G. M. Nomura (Eds.), *Asian/Pacific Islander American women: A historical anthology* (pp. 16–22). New York: New York University Press.

Oggins, J. (2003). Notions of HIV and medication among multiethnic people living with HIV. *Health and Social Work, 28,* 53–62.

Olmedo, E. L., & Parron, D. L. (1981). Mental health of minority women: Some special issues. *Professional Psychology, 12,* 103–111.

Osvold, L. L., & Sodowsky, G. R. (1993). Eating disorders of white American, racial and ethnic minority American, and international women. *Journal of Multicultural Counseling and Development, 21,* 132–142.

Pernice, R., & Brook, J. (1996). Refugees' and immigrants' mental health: Association of demographic and post-immigration factors. *The Journal of Social Psychology, 136,* 511–519.

Pittensky, T. L., Shih, M., & Ambady, N. (1999). Identity adaptiveness: Affect across multiple identities. *Journal of Social Issues, 55,* 503–518.

Porter, R. Y. (1995). Clinical issues and intervention with ethnic minority women. In J. Aponte, R. Y. Rivers, & J. Wohl (Eds.), *Psychological intervention and cultural diversity* (pp. 181–198). Needham Heights, MA: Allyn & Bacon.

Pressier, A. B. (1999). Domestic violence in South Asian communities in America. *Violence Against Women, 5,* 684–699.

Pyke, K. D., & Johnson, D. L. (2003). Asian American women and racialized femininities: "Doing" gender across cultural worlds. *Gender & Society, 17,* 33–53.

Ritenbaugh, C. (1982). Obesity as a culture-bound syndrome. *Culture, Medicine and Psychiatry, 6,* 347–361.

Reid, P. T., & Comas-Diaz, L. (1990). Gender and ethnicity: Perspectives on dual status. *Sex Roles, 22,* 397–408.

Robinson, T. (1993). The intersections of gender, class, race, and culture: On seeing clients whole. *Journal of Multicultural Counseling and Development, 21,* 50–58.

Robinson, T. N., Killen, J. D., Litt, I. F., Hammer, L. D., Wilson, D. M., Haydel, K. F., et al. (1996). Ethnicity and body dissatisfaction: Are Hispanic and Asian girls at increased risk for eating disorders? *Journal of Adolescent Health, 19,* 384–393.

Root, M. P. P. (1985). Guidelines for facilitating therapy with Asian American clients. *Psychotherapy, 22,* 349–356.

Root, M. P. P. (1990). Disordered eating in women of color. *Sex Roles, 22,* 525–536.

Root, M. P. P. (1995). The psychology of Asian American women. In H. Landrine (Ed.), *Bringing cultural diversity to feminist psychology: Theory, research, and practice* (pp. 265–301). Washington, DC: American Psychological Association.

Rozée, P. D., & Van Boemel, G. (1989). The psychological effects of war trauma and abuse on older Cambodian refugee women. *Women & Therapy, 8,* 23–50.

Ryan, J. (2002). Chinese women as transnational migrants: Gender and class in global immigration narratives. *International Migration, 40,* 93–114.

Scher, M., & Good, G. E. (1990). Gender and counseling in the twenty-first century: What does the future hold? *Journal of Counseling & Development, 68,* 388–391.

Shum, L. M. (1996). Asian-American women: Cultural and mental health issues. In J. Sechzer & S. Pfafflin (Eds.), *Women and Mental Health* (pp. 181–190). New York: Annals of the New York Academy of Sciences.

Sue, D. W., & Sue, D. (2003). *Counseling the culturally diverse: Theory and practice* (4th ed.). New York: Wiley.

Tajima, R. E. (1989). Lotus blossoms don't bleed: Images of Asian women. In Asian Women United of California (Ed.), *Making waves: An anthology of writings by and about Asian American women* (pp. 308–317). Boston: Beacon Press.

Tewari, N., Inman, A. G., & Sandhu, D. S., (2003). South Asian Americans: Culture, concerns and therapeutic strategies. In J. Mio & G. Iwamasa (Eds.), *Culturally diverse mental health: The challenges of research and resistance* (pp. 191–209). New York: Brunner-Routledge.

Tien, L. (1994). Southeast Asian American refugee women. In L. Comas-Diaz & B. Greene (Eds.), *Women of color: Integrating ethnic and gender identities in psychotherapy* (pp. 479–504). New York: Guilford Press.

Toupin, E. S. W. A. (1980). Counseling Asians: Psychotherapy in the context of racism and Asian-American history. *American Journal of Orthopsychiatry, 50,* 76–86.

True, R. H. (1990). Psychotherapeutic issues with Asian American women. *Sex Roles, 22,* 477–486.

True, R. H. (1991, August). *Psychosocial impact of immigration on Asian women.* Paper presented at the annual convention of American Psychological Association in San Francisco, CA.

True, R. H. (1996). Mental health issues of Asian/Pacific Island women. In D. Adams (Ed.), *Health issues for women of color* (pp. 89–111). Thousand Oaks, CA: Sage.

True, R. H. (1997). Asian American women. In E. Lee (Ed.), *Working with Asian Americans: A guide for clinicians* (pp. 420–427). New York: Guilford Press.

True, R. H., & Guillermo, T. (1996). Asian/Pacific Islander American women. In M. Bayne-Smoth (Ed.), *Race, gender, and health* (pp. 94–121). Thousand Oaks, CA: Sage.

Tsui, A. M. (1985). Psychotherapeutic considerations in sexual counseling for Asian immigrants. *Psychotherapy, 22,* 357–362.

Uba, L. (1994). *Asian Americans: Personality patterns, identity, and mental health.* New York: Guilford Press.

U.S. Census Bureau. (2005, April 29). *Facts for features: Asian/Pacific American Heritage month.* Retrieved June 5, 2005, from http://www.census.gov/Press-Release/www/releases/archives/facts_for_features_special_editions/004522.html

U.S. Surgeon General. (1999). *Mental health: Culture, race, ethnicity–supplemental.* Retrieved June 9, 2005, from http://www.mentalhealth.samhsa.org/cre/

Westkott, M. (1998). Culture and women's health. In E. A. Blechman & K. D. Brownell (Eds.), *Behavioral medicine and women: A comprehensive handbook* (pp. 816–820). New York: Guilford Press.

Wong, E. C., Kim, B. S., Zane, N. W. S., Kim, I. J., & Huang, J. S. (2003). Examining culturally based variables associated with ethnicity: Influences on credibility perceptions of empirically supported interventions. *Cultural Diversity & Ethnic Minority Psychology, 9,* 88–96.

Yanagida, E. H. (1979). Cross-cultural considerations in the application of assertive training. *Psychology of Women Quarterly, 3,* 400–402.

Yeh, C. J., Inman, A., Kim, A. B., & Okubo, Y. (in press). Asian American collectivistic coping in response to 9/11. *Cultural Diversity & Ethnic Minority Psychology.*

Yick, A. G. (2001). Feminist theory and status inconsistency theory: Application to domestic violence in Chinese immigrant families. *Violence Against Women, 7,* 545–562.

Ying, Y. W. (1990). Explanatory models of major depression and implications for help seeking among immigrant Chinese-American women. *Culture, Medicine and Psychiatry, 14,* 393–408.

Zane, N. W. S., Sue, S., Hu, L., & Kwon, J. (1991). Asian-American assertion: A social learning analysis of cultural differences. *Journal of Counseling Psychology, 38,* 63–70.

12

ASIAN AMERICAN MASCULINITIES

WILLIAM MING LIU

TAI CHANG

As counselors and psychologists explore the complexities surrounding Asian American masculinities, it is important to understand that psychology, in general, has not focused much attention on this topic. Of the research on Asian American men, most has focused on Chinese, Japanese, and Korean Americans, while little has addressed other Asian (e.g., South Asian, Filipino) or Pacific Islander communities. Additionally, the extant research on Asian American men has typically addressed differences between Asian American men and women (Fuertes, Sedlacek, & Liu, 1994; Liu, Pope-Davis, Nevitt, & Toporek, 1999; Liu & Sedlacek, 1999; Tsai, Ying, Lee, 2001). Some researchers have discussed issues among Asian American men (Chang & Yeh, 2003; Chang, Yeh, & Krumboltz, 2001; Chen, 1999; Chua & Fujino, 1999), others have developed theories on the construction of Asian American masculinity (C. S. Chan, 1989; D. B. Lee & Saul, 1987; Mok, 1998; D. Sue, 1996, 1999), and a few have examined Asian American masculinity specifically (E. J. Kim, O'Neil, & Owen, 1996; Levant, Wu, & Fischer, 1996; Liu, 2002).

This chapter provides an overview of some of the salient issues to be considered among Asian American men. First, the chapter addresses the historical construction of masculinity, especially

for men of color and, in particular, Asian American men. This context addresses the variables with which Asian American men contend. Second, the chapter addresses Asian American cultural notions of masculinity. This section focuses on how Asian American masculinity changes according to cultural contingencies. Third, the chapter provides an overview of current masculinity theories. Finally, we propose social identity theory as a consideration in our understanding of Asian American masculinity and suggest the multiple ways in which Asian American men negotiate and create positive masculine identities.

HISTORICAL CONSTRUCTIONS OF ASIAN AMERICAN MASCULINITIES

The term *Asian American* covers a broad range of peoples, ethnicities, and nationalities. The 2000 U.S. Census reports that the Asian American community comprises 10.9 million persons, representing approximately 4% of the entire U.S. population (Humes & McKinnon, 2000). The racial groups within the Asian American and Pacific Islander community have always been malleable to political forces and do not represent scientific notions of race, nationality, or ethnicity (Okihiro, 1994). For instance,

197

the aggregate racial group, Asian and Pacific Islander, was divided into two racial groups—Asian American and Native Hawaiian/Pacific Islander—due to political pressure by Pacific Islander communities (Humes & McKinnon, 2000). Although this development was to help ensure better representation for Pacific Islanders in various educational and economic settings, and to better quantify the diversity of the community, the division complicates the categories of race and ethnicity and further subdivides the Asian American community.

In this chapter, we use the term *Asian American* to reflect the "racialization" that occurs, regardless of ethnic identity. The process of racialization in the United States among people of color (i.e., African, Asian, Latino, Native Americans) creates "racial groups" regardless of ethnic or national origin. Consequently, all Asian Americans are treated as a unitary group. For Asian American men, this means that animosity toward one ethnic group (e.g., Vietnamese) is likely to be directed to anyone with Asian features. Furthermore, stereotypes of one Asian American ethnic group are likely to affect the image and perception of other Asian Americans.

Although Asian Americans have been a part of American history for hundreds of years, Asian Americans are still considered perpetual foreigners or aliens who cannot assimilate to U.S. culture, that is, not real Americans. Even though Asian Americans have been in the United States for many generations, they are still considered to be "not American" (Liang, Li, & Kim, 2004). To illustrate, in a series of six experimental studies investigating the connection between Whiteness and being American, Devos and Banaji (2005) found that Asian Americans, and to a lesser extent African Americans, were less associated with the notion of American than were Whites. The idea of Americanism is important, because being American is not only a national identity but also a raced and gendered cultural project. By "cultural project," we mean that there are societal actions and frameworks continually reinforcing the marginalization of Asian Americans. Perpetuating the image of Asian American men as asexual or overly feminine are examples of cultural projects. Television commercials that positively portray French, Australian, or British accents while denigrating Asian accents are another example of a cultural project. For Asian Americans, these cultural projects or socially marginalizing activities are multipronged attacks that target the gender, race, and social standing of these men. Hence, being marked as not-American has specific and different gendered consequences for Asian American men (Espiritu, 1997, 1998). For instance, the Asian American man is constructed as the asexual overachiever or the deviant sexual aggressor. By representing Asian American men, and other men of color (e.g, African Americans), as extreme and deviant forms of masculinity, White masculinity and White heterosexism remain normative.

Being marked as non-American is also related to how Asian American men identify and see themselves as men. The salience of knowing these contextual aspects of Asian American masculinity implies that contemporary masculinity theories (e.g., gender role strain or ideological subscription) need to incorporate specific cultural histories of men to capture, more fully, their specific struggles and negotiations.

Historically, masculinity, Whiteness, and citizenship have been confused and treated as one entity (Harris, 1995; Kimmel, 1996). This privilege conferred from White skin was codified in legislation and court decisions. Men of color were excluded from the benefits of citizenship and hence "manhood" because citizenship and manhood were historically one and the same. For example, men of color have been denied citizenship and thus access to historically masculine rights afforded to citizens, such as the ability to own property (S. Chan, 1991). The "bachelor societies" of Chinese American and Japanese American men during the late 19th and early 20th centuries were denied the right to have families because anti-miscegenation laws prevented men of color from marrying White women. This was true of Asian Indian men as well (Gupta, 1999). Exclusion from citizenship and property ownership meant that men of color could not participate in the economic and political growth of America. Because Whiteness and manhood represented the ideal citizen, men of color came to be enemies of the burgeoning nation state (Jacobson, 1998). Consequently, characteristics and stereotypes of men of color were used to buttress and reinforce dominant (i.e., normative) masculinity.

In contemporary society, Asian American men are often stereotyped as the "model minority," as effeminate, or "not quite men" (Liu, 1997). In one study, 178 college students were asked to list adjectives for Asian Americans. Participants described Asian Americans as "intelligent, industrious, gentle, selfish, nationalistic, and passive" (Stangor, Sullivan, & Ford, 1991, p. 364). The results supported particular stereotypes, such as the silent model minority or the perpetual foreigner. That is, the stereotypes reflected the image of Asian Americans as focused on academics and achievement, and un-American.

The model minority image of Asian Americans as being educationally and financially successful (S. Chan, 1991) also implies an "asexual" quality for Asian American men (J. W. Chan, 1998). That is, as a model minority man, the focus of time and energy is on career and work at the expense of one's personal relationships and sexuality. At one point, Asian American men were perceived to be "trophy boyfriends" (Nakamura, 2000) and portrayed as "sexy" and "cool" because they were not like traditional White men (Pan, 2000). This image was meant to disrupt the historical significance of Asian Americans as the newcomers, perpetual foreigners, and sexless (S. Chan, 1991) by relying on and emphasizing "exoticism" and "difference" from the norm (i.e., White masculinity) (Pan, 2000). But in this new construction, the Asian American men were relegated to the exoticized position that Asian American women have long endured, as the love interest for White consumption (S. Chan, 1991; Takaki, 1989). Thus, even in this reinterpretation of the Asian American man as a love interest and supposedly normal, the archetype of the feminized man lingers. Additionally, foreignness is not discarded because it is the outsider quality, the "not-like-other-White-men" quality that is the attraction.

For many Asian American men, negotiating masculinity is not a simple task. Asian American men are faced with a choice when confronted with the White masculine norm. For many Asian American men, the choice is either emulate and be like the dominant White male or "accept the fact we are not men" (J. W. Chan, 1998, p. 94). Within this context, negotiating a middle ground is difficult for Asian American men because they must simultaneously accept and repudiate the White masculine norm in search of alternative definitions of masculinity (J. W. Chan, 1998). This is a form of hegemonic negotiation or compromise (Chen, 1999) that Asian American men navigate—at times profiting from masculinity and at other times facing the prospect of marginalization because of their race and the historic "baggage" that comes from their racial history.

For example, in one attempt to reassert Asian American masculinity, the production of an Asian American men's calendar supposedly repudiates the "nerdy" and "geeky" stereotype by mirroring "beef-cake" poses (e.g., shirtless poses that accentuate pectoral and abdominal musculature) (Wong, 1993). This is a problem in that new masculinities are not formed; rather, old masculine ideals are rescued and recuperated for contemporary use (E. H. Kim, 1982, 1990). As one may infer, it is extremely difficult for Asian American men to define a sense of masculinity when faced with hurdles such as historical and contemporary negative images. Not being seen as a "total man" when compared to the White male norm, and being effeminized and emasculated, leaves Asian American men with few models of masculinity.

One important issue in the discourse over Asian American men is the problematic use of "feminization" as a negative characterization of Asian American men. Feminization is a pejorative description, used conventionally to describe the relative status and position of Asian American men as being beneath White men. Related to feminization is the notion that Asian American men have been emasculated; that is, the power to create their own images of and sense of masculinity has been taken away from Asian American men (Ling, 1997). Although feminization and emasculation typically connote low status and power when used in reference to Asian American men, femininity at the level of the individual has multiple meanings and need not have a negative connotation.

Thus far, the literature reviewed focuses on the historical critiques of masculinity. Although useful to initiate a discussion of Asian American men, to move the discourse further, we focus on the research on Asian Americans and masculinity. Specifically, we address how masculinity is conceptualized and how it evolves in different cultural contexts.

ASIAN AMERICAN CULTURAL NOTIONS OF MASCULINITY

Masculinity varies between and within cultures (Doss & Hopkins, 1998). However, there seem to be some common elements of masculinity for men of a particular racial and ethnic group (Doss & Hopkins, 1998). This is particularly true for Asian American men. Results from one study showed that, for Asian American men, masculinity was tied to being polite, obedient, and willing to do domestic tasks, whereas White men endorsed a more traditional notion of masculinity that avoided those attributes (Chua & Fujino, 1999). Asian American men, when compared to White American men, tended to see their masculinity differently in that they did not necessarily see their masculinity in opposition to femininity.

This notion that masculinity and femininity are complementary is consistent with traditional Confucian discourse, where men's gender roles are thought to be flexible and complex. Here, men are thought to be "yin" or submissive in the context of showing filial piety to their parents or deference to authority figures, but this is balanced by "yang" or masculine action when moral imperatives take precedence (Z. Zhou, 2004). Even though it appears that the Chua and Fujino (1999) study reveals a greater variability of masculinity among Asian American men than possessed by White men, the generalizability of the findings to all Asian American men is limited because the participants were all Chinese and Japanese. However, the Chua and Fujino (1999) study provides a springboard for thinking about how Asian American men cope with sometimes competing cultural notions of masculinity.

In contemporary society, Asian American men are brought up under stringent gender role expectations. Certain cultural values are imperative, such as a focus on group harmony and filial piety (Liu & Iwamoto, 2005), prominence in the family (Tang, 1997), risk taking, and courageous behavior (Nghe & Mahalik, 1998). For many Asian American men, keeping the adoration and admiration of the family entails fulfilling their filial duties, such as carrying on their family name, conforming to the expectations of their parents (S. J. Lee, 1996), and advancing the culture (Tang, 1997). Often, the need to please parents and the parental pressure on them to succeed lead to academic stress, poor self-image, poor performance, and interpersonal dysfunctions (Pang, 1991).

Among older men, especially Asian American fathers, threats to their patriarchal position (i.e., a loss of masculinity, stress and frustration, inability to be the "breadwinner") within the family may result in a reassertion of control over the family through physical abuse (Chow, 1998; Lum, 1998; Rimonte, 1991). For some men, domestic violence is justified or dismissed as a culturally congruent means to reinforce cultural and patriarchal structures (Rimonte, 1991).

Such threats to patriarchy have been noted among some Southeast Asian communities. Specifically, Southeast Asians (e.g., Vietnamese, Cambodians, and Laotians) fleeing political and economic turmoil in their homelands, who found themselves unprepared for a new culture and life as expatriates, were left with a distinct feeling of isolation from America as well as their homeland (Kibria, 1993). Many of these men lost their families, their jobs and earning ability, status and authority, community, and loved ones. Arrival in the United States typically meant the need for women to find work, which dissolved the patriarchal position of the male. A similar effect occurred among Japanese American men in the internment camps when they lost their ability to be providers and struggled with their sense of masculinity and loss of power (Nagata, 1998). For some Southeast Asian men, because a sense of powerlessness and depression often followed these changes, efforts to regain their masculinity sometimes entails brutal explosions of domestic violence or jealous outbursts that centered on the "American" man's (i.e., White) money (i.e., agency) as well as their sexual prowess (i.e., sexual potency) (Kibria, 1993). The end result tends to drive away loved ones and further magnify their marginal status as men in America.

Not all the conflicts over masculinity for Southeast Asians exist among adults. Masculinity also is an issue for boys and adolescents, particularly those who lost their parents and thus had to deal with acculturation, racism, and post-traumatic stress without much familial support or guidance (Long, 1996). But in discussing Asian American boys and adolescents, the problem with our current understanding is that the research, theory, and practice literature on this community, regardless of ethnic heritage, is quite sparse. Therefore, we are relying on ethnographic and sociological research to inform our understanding of one particular ethnic group. What we do know is that, for some Southeast Asian boys and adolescents, coping with acculturative stress can lead to dysfunction. This is the case among many Vietnamese boys who have lived their lives in America with no father and who may have a history of trauma. Typically, these young boys and adolescents turn to gangs because they long for paternal figures that mimic the "powerful, masculine allure" (Long, 1996, p. 70). Gangs represent quintessential male domains because women are usually excluded from these organizations but used as sexual objects (e.g., in gang rapes) to intensify the man's sense of masculinity (Chin, 1996). Without the father to offer discipline and guidance, and living within the context of poverty (Chin, 1996; Zhou & Bankston, 1998), gang life often offers the elements of stability: the promise of material benefits as well as a sense of family (Long, 1996; M. Zhou & Bankston, 1998). Consequently, many of these boys are socialized into a hypermasculine and violent environment that is difficult to leave (Long, 1996; M. Zhou & Bankston, 1998).

These cultural notions of masculinity point to some of the common links between "Asian" ideas of masculinity and those of the dominant group. Apparently, patriarchal privilege and power are artifacts within masculinity that many men struggle to retain or regain (Liu, 2005). Yet, even with knowledge that there are commonalties as well as differences in masculine ideologies, the understanding of how racism and class function in determining an Asian American man's sense of self is not well understood in psychology. Hence, even though there are different theories of masculinity, the lives of Asian American men may not be well understood through the experiences of dominant culture men.

THEORIES OF MASCULINITY

In general, masculinity theories examine the masculine standards in society and the belief, among many men, that living up to these expectations should be easy and without incongruencies or contradictions (Mosher & Tompkins, 1988). Some aspects of masculinity can be conceptualized as positive attributes, such as putting one's family first, protecting and taking care of others, and being loyal and dedicated (Levant, 1996). However, as men attempt to live up to all the masculine expectations, and as they are socialized into the dominant culture's definition of masculinity, psychological strain results. And because masculine expectations are many and varied, gender theorists speak of many masculinities rather than a singular masculinity. Finally, feminist discourse provides masculinity theorists with a tool to investigate the psychological strain and coping mechanisms of men within a society that demands compliance.

Pleck (1995) proposed three types of strain related to fulfilling masculine expectations: discrepancy, dysfunction, and trauma. In discrepancy strain, the person "fails to live up to one's internalized manhood ideal" (Levant, 1996, p. 261). Gender role conflict is an example of the discrepancy men may feel between real and ideal expectations of themselves as men. As Liu, Rochlen, and Mohr (2005) found, men who perceive a discrepancy between their real and ideal selves tend to report higher levels of psychological distress. Dysfunction strain occurs when men fulfill the expectations of contemporary masculinity but experience negative effects because the expectations for men are often psychologically toxic (Levant, 1996). Some of the toxic effects of fulfilling masculine expectations include (a) violence, especially spousal abuse, rape, and sexual assault; (b) promiscuity and "sexual excess" (Levant, 1996, p. 262); (c) irresponsible actions such as drug and alcohol abuse, and risk-taking behaviors; and (d) problematic relationships (Levant, 1996). Finally, trauma strain refers to the "male socialization process . . . which is recognized as inherently traumatic" (Levant, 1996, p. 261). The result of this traumatic socialization is estrangement from their affective life and development of sexual feelings and attitudes toward women to replace "caring emotions" (Levant, 1996, p. 263). Through these three types of strain, Pleck (1995) provided a developmental profile of masculine experiences men struggle through and the dysfunctional relational patterns resulting from adherence to society's masculine expectations.

The distinctions within the many masculinity theories are crucial in research and clinical practice. Eschewing the trait perspective, many current theorists investigate the kinds of expectations and standards dominant society holds for men. We present a brief overview of three such theories: Gender Role Conflict theory, Ideology theory, and Male Reference Group theory. Each theory takes a slightly different perspective on the normative approach to masculinity and offers unique insights into the issues facing men.

Gender Role Conflict Paradigm

Before the normative approach to investigating masculinity, much of the literature focused on masculine traits. In his book, *The Myth of Masculinity* (1981), Joseph Pleck suggested that the gender role identity (GRI) paradigm (i.e., trait) did not, and could not, explain the multitude of issues facing men. It was Pleck's (1981) opinion that the GRI paradigm reinforces, rather than critiques, gender roles.

The GRI paradigm proposes that people need to have a gender role identity and that this identity is related to the degree to which the individual subscribes to that gender role. Within this paradigm, gender roles are basically "behaviors, expectations, and values defined by society as masculine and feminine" (O'Neil, 1990, p. 24). The process of adopting a gender role is itself strenuous and conflicted, and it has negative effects on men (Pleck, 1995).

Pleck (1981) proposed an alternative theory of masculinity: gender role conflict. He theorized that gender roles are fluid, inconsistent, and often have contradictory expectations for men. O'Neil, Good, and Holmes (1995) further clarified gender role conflict as the "psychological state in which socialized gender roles have negative consequences on the person or others" (O'Neil et al., 1995, p. 166). Conflicts are

expected as a result of the gender role journey that brings a man from traditional masculinity through ambivalence, confusion, anger, and fear, to personal and professional advocacy (O'Neil et al., 1995). The conflicts affect the person's cognitions, emotional life, behaviors, and unconscious experiences and can be brought on by others, the self, or expressed toward others (O'Neil et al., 1995).

Gender role conflict is triggered when one (a) deviates from gender role norms; (b) tries, and meets or fails, gender role norms; (c) experiences a discrepancy between the real and ideal selves related to gender role norms; (d) personally devalues, restricts, or violates oneself; (e) experiences from others devaluation, restrictions, and violations; or (f) devalues, restricts, or violates others because of gender role stereotypes (O'Neil, Helms, Gable, David, & Wrightsman, 1986; O'Neil et al., 1995). The Gender Role Conflict measure focuses on four domains: (a) success, power, and competition; (b) restriction of emotions and a lack of emotional responsiveness; (c) homophobia; and (d) a restriction of affect toward other men (O'Neil et al., 1986).

Kim, O'Neil, and Owen (1996) found no other empirical study of Asian Americans and the Gender Role Conflict Scale (GRCS) (O'Neil, Egan, Owen, & Murry, 1993). Rather, many previous studies focused on gender roles, acculturation, or how Asian Americans differed from Caucasians. Kim and his colleagues administrated the GRCS and the Suinn-Lew Asian Self-Identity Acculturation Scale (SL-ASIA) (Suinn, Rickard-Figueroa, Lew, & Vigil, 1987) to 125 Asian American college students. Results generally showed no differences in acculturation scores along four patterns of gender role conflict. In a canonical correlation, the gender role conflict domains corresponding with higher acculturation scores were success, power, and competition. Acculturation was related to lower scores on restrictive emotionality. E. J. Kim et al. contend that restricting emotions is one of the costs that Asian American men experience as they assimilate.

Liu (2002) also explored the relationship between racial identity and gender role conflict among 323 Asian American college educated men. Using the People of Color Racial Identity Attitudes Scale (POCRIAS) (Helms, 1990, 1995), the GRCS, and the Male Role Norms Inventory (MRNI) (Levant & Fischer, 1998), Liu found that success, power, and competition attitudes were related to endorsement of traditional masculine role norms. This would suggest that success is related to being a traditional man. Additionally, moderate correlations were found between racial identity subscales, gender role conflict, and subscription to masculine role norms. Asian American men endorsing dissonance, immersion, and internalization attitudes tended to endorse traditional masculine role norms and gender role conflict. Similarly, dissonance, immersion, and internalization attitudes moderately positively predicted gender role conflict and masculine role norms. Thus, Asian American men's experience with racism and their view of themselves as racialized individuals were positively correlated with feelings of gender role conflict and higher endorsement of traditional male role norms. Another finding in the study was that the GRCS appeared to have better reliability than the MRNI among this sample of Asian American men and the POCRIAS may not have been sensitive enough to Asian American men's cultural attitudes.

Assessing for adherence to cultural values and its relationship to gender role conflict among 192 Asian American college-educated men, Liu and Iwamoto (2005) found that adherence to traditional Asian values, as measured by the Asian Values Scale (B. S. K. Kim, Atkinson, & Yang, 1999), was related to higher scores on gender role conflict; self-esteem was negatively related to psychological distress; and psychological distress was positively related to GRCS subscales. A simultaneous regression with GRCS subscales as the criterion suggests endorsing Asian cultural values was related most to gender role conflict scales. The relationship between gender role conflict and psychological distress supported previous research on this link (Liu, Iwamoto, & Hernandez, 2005).

Although the construct of gender role conflict and the measure developed for this construct are based primarily on White men, the theory and instrument may be applicable to Asian American men. For instance, some of the

research suggests that Asian American men do experience psychological distress related to gender role conflict, and so it may be inferred that Asian American men do negotiate dominant cultural expectations and Asian cultural values. But how do Asian American men construct a positive and healthy sense of self from these negotiations? Gender role conflict theory may be limited, as it addresses only the strain or sequelae associated with dominant masculine expectations. Additionally, gender role conflict does not specify the specific dimensions related to dominant masculinity; that is, gender role conflict does not delineate the ideology to which these men must subscribe.

Masculine Ideology

Masculine ideology is another theory that supports the belief that masculinity is socially constructed and that men endorse an ideology rather than possess traits (Thompson & Pleck, 1995). There are particular masculine standards (Pleck, 1995), including the ideas that men should (a) always succeed, (b) never show weakness, (c) be adventurous and risk takers, and (d) never be feminine (David & Brannon, 1976). Also, in enacting traditional masculinity, men are constantly negotiating the costs and benefits (Mahalik, Talmadge, Locke, & Scott, 2005). In one study, Levant et al. (1996) studied 232 mainland Chinese men and 135 White American men. The Male Role Norms Inventory (MRNI) (Levant et al., 1992) was used to assess endorsement of male role norms or traditional masculinity. The MRNI assessed traditional masculinity based on these subscales: Avoidance of Femininity, Rejection of Homosexuals, Self-Reliance, Aggression, Achievement/Status, Attitudes Toward Sex, Restrictive Emotionality, and Non-Traditional Attitudes Toward Masculinity. Although further research is required to examine whether these constructs and the scales that measure them are equivalent across cultures, the preliminary evidence suggests that Chinese men endorse traditional male role norms more than do White American men; that is, on the domains representing traditional masculinity, this research suggests that Chinese men are more traditional in their attitudes than are White men.

Addressing masculine ideology as well, Mahalik et al. (2003) developed the Conformity to Masculine Role Norms Inventory (CMNI), which measures the following masculine role norms: Winning, Emotional Control, Risk-Taking, Violence, Power Over Women, Dominance, Playboy, Self-Reliance, Primacy of Work, Disdain for Homosexuals, and the Pursuit of Status. In one study of 127 Asian American male college students and substance use, Liu et al. (2005) found that men who strongly endorse "Playboy" attitudes (e.g., anti-feminine, seeks sexual adventures, conceals emotions) are more likely to binge drink, use cocaine, and use marijuana in their lifetime. Interestingly, the strongest predictor of marijuana use in the past 30 days was the CNMI subscale, Disdain of Homosexuality.

Theories related to masculine role norms and ideology are necessary to explicate the dimensions and features of dominant masculinity. In these theories, we gain some understanding that there are many anti-feminine, homophobic, and power-related attitudes that constitute dominant masculinity. Although these ideology-based models are helpful, the expectations are focused on individual men subscribing to a dominant (i.e., White) cultural or social expectation. Particularly important to Asian American men, but left unanswered, is the role of peers and male relationships in the adoption of male role norms and ideology.

Male Reference Group Identity

To investigate the lives of men and understand why they adhere to some ideological elements of masculinity while neglecting others, Wade (1998) developed the theory of Male Reference Group Identity Dependence (MRGID). The impetus behind the MRGID was the speculation that demographic variables (e.g., race, class) are insufficient in providing a "causal explanation as to why a man socialized within a particular cultural context may or may not identify with the group of men to which he is demographically connected" (Wade, 1998, p. 351). The MRGID rests on the principle that a person, regardless of group membership (e.g., race), may find certain groups appealing and will psychologically orient himself or herself toward that group (Singer, 1992; Wade, 1998). As a result, the reference group helps establish an array of psychological and behavioral parameters to which the person aspires (Singer, 1992).

The MRGID model is predicated on the psychological (i.e., ego) readiness of the individual, the meaningfulness of the referent group, and the sense of being internally directed when participating in gender roles (Wade, 1998). The ego is important because its strength and resiliency help determine the man's flexibility toward gender roles and toward the group with whom he orients. Thus, the greater the ego maturity, the more likely the individual will resist conforming to conventional interpretations of gender roles and traditional groups (Wade, 1998).

To provide empirical evidence for this theory, the Reference Group Identity Dependency Scale (RGIDS) was developed (Wade & Gelso, 1998). A sample of 344 undergraduates were given the RGIDS, and results provided four general factors that accounted for 42.2% of the total variance:

1. No Reference Group—defined as feelings of disconnectedness from other males

2. Reference Group Nondependent Diversity—defined as appreciation of differences in males

3. Reference Group Nondependent Similarity—defined as feelings of connectedness

4. Reference Group Dependent—defined as feelings of connectedness with some males but not others. (Wade & Gelso, 1998, pp. 395, 397)

The final scale consists of 30 items in four subscales with internal reliabilities ranging from .70 to .78, but with low test-retest reliability (Wade & Gelso, 1998). What is not clear from the theory and scale are the effects of multiple referent groups; thus, it is difficult to ascertain which referent group research participants are using when responding to scale items (Eisler, 1998). While the psychometric properties of the RGIDS are moderate, further development will add promise to the scale and another dimension in the investigation of masculinities.

The MRGID theory is an important step in understanding the role that different groups have in mediating a man's sense of masculinity. The MRGID suggests that individuals may orient themselves toward a particular sense of masculinity depending on their cognitive resources and the salience of a certain group. Men are allowed, even within the same racial group, to subscribe to different notions of masculinity. So what does this mean for Asian American men? Some speculation or discussion of this issue would be helpful.

SOCIAL IDENTITY THEORY AND ASIAN AMERICAN MASCULINITIES

While many theories have been proposed that conceptualize masculinity as consisting of either gender roles (e.g., Eisler, 1995; Levant & Fischer, 1998; O'Neil et al., 1995; Pleck, 1981, 1995), ideology (e.g., Thompson & Pleck, 1995), or reference group identities (Wade, 1998), we believe these theories do not fully explain the identity development process for Asian American men. Gender role theories are based on the assumption that individuals have internalized schemas of societal notions of masculinity and femininity. Although gender roles are certainly a useful way to conceptualize an individual's cognitive representation of gender, they do not take into account the sociopolitical and hegemonic forces that influence identity. Wade's (1998) theory of male reference group identity dependence expanded on gender role theory in two main ways:

1. Gender role self-concept is associated with ego identity development and can take on many forms (i.e., no reference group, reference group dependent, reference group nondependent).

2. There exist many potential reference groups with which an individual can identify.

However, Wade's theory does not attempt to explain how power, status, and race influence the selection of groups (White men, Asian American men, etc.) that men use as their reference groups.

Dominant cultural ideals for men typically include White men and exclude Asian American men, and, as a result, race and gender are conflated (e.g., Chen, 1999). Chen used the term *hegemonic masculinities* to describe the dominant masculinities that are idealized in American society: White, middle class, heterosexual, young, educated, fully employed, handsome, and athletic. Thus, for Asian American men, aspects of masculine identities are inseparable from racial identities, and the motivational and developmental forces that influence Asian American masculine identities need to also capture the sociopolitical dynamics from which race and racial identity are formed. Although no single theory can fully capture the identity development of any group, including Asian American men, we believe Social Group Identity Theory (Tajfel & Turner, 1986) may help explain the esteem and status motives that drive identity development at the level of the individual as well as the dynamics of power and prejudice that determine the groups on whom prestige and status are conferred in the United States.

We propose that masculine identities are a form of social group identity. Our work draws on social identity theory (Tajfel & Turner, 1986), which posits that individuals derive a sense of social identity from membership in a social group. The main difference between social identity theory and other theories used to explain masculine identities and attitudes is that social groups are assumed to have status differences and their relative positions in the hierarchies of power and status have an impact on the identities of the individuals who belong to those groups. Evaluations of one's group, relative to other groups, influence the group's social prestige, which, in turn, influences the extent to which individuals identify with a group as well as the strategies they use to compare their social group to other outgroups. Ultimately, the goal for any individual is to enhance or preserve self-esteem and status; thus, status is a driving force behind individuals' decisions to identify with particular social groups.

Social Group Identity Theory also advances the discussion of Asian American masculinities beyond the deficit approach to understanding Asian American men and other men of color. The deficit approach essentially suggests Asian American men are constantly reacting to negative forces such as racism and stereotypes and, consequently, are limited in their ability to create a whole and healthy masculine self. The deficit approach assumes Asian American men are always conscious of a more positive identity and sense of self but cannot reveal or achieve this goal because of a hostile environment. As a counterpoint to the deficit approach, we believe that Asian American men are constantly shaping their masculinities and that the creation of their masculinities spans their lifetime. We also posit that Asian American men are in a state of praxis—constantly drawing from internal and external sources of information, reacting and being proactive in their environment, and shaping and being shaped by their situation and environment. While Social Group Identity Theory acknowledges that individuals respond to being delegated to low-status groups, it also theorizes that individuals play an active role in increasing their personal and group status.

According to Tajfel and Turner (1986), social status is based on the outcome of intergroup comparisons and is inherently subjective. Furthermore, the esteem individuals receive from their social group identities can be either global (e.g., Moyerman & Forman, 1992; Porter & Washington, 1993; Phinney, 1991, 1995; Phinney, Cantu, & Kurtz, 1997; Roberts et al., 1999) or specific to one's social group (e.g., Crocker and Luhtanen, 1990), and the esteem is directly related to the relative status of the group. Tajfel and Turner proposed three strategies group members use in response to negative or threatened social identity: individual mobility, social creativity, and social competition.

Individual Mobility

Individual mobility is an attempt to increase individual status and esteem by dissociating oneself from one's social group. Thus, personal status is enhanced while group status remains unchanged. The comparison to racial identity theory (Helms, 1990, 1995) is accurate insofar as this strategy seems similar to an individual in conformity status. But in conformity status, the individual is unaware of race, racism, and himself or herself as a racial being, while simultaneously rejecting affiliation with his or her racial group. In individual mobility, the individual may well be aware of himself or herself as a racial being and yet still reject affiliation. Specifically, the Asian American man recognizes the low status of his own racial group and seeks to move away or distance himself from other Asian Americans. Chen (1999) coined the term *hegemonic bargain* to describe how Chinese American men use their personal status–enhancing characteristics to distance themselves from their low-status groups (i.e., Chinese American men, Asian American men) to obtain status and esteem. In this sense, Asian American men make a bargain with hegemonic masculinity: They negotiate between positive aspects of masculinity as a dominant characteristic and the negative aspects of their racial group; that is, they buy into the idea that Asian American men or Chinese American men are inferior and then personally distance themselves from the group to achieve higher status.

Chen articulated three strategies Chinese American men use to increase their individual mobility: compensation, where individuals attempt to overcome negative stereotypes by trying to meet the ideals of hegemonic masculinity (e.g., trying to be a jock); deflection, where persons attempt to divert attention away from their perceived stereotypical behaviors by overcompensating in other areas (e.g., working harder to make up for perceived language deficits); and denial, where persons deny that racism or stereotypes exist or claim that they are the exception to those stereotypes (e.g., "I'm not one of those Chinese"). While Chen focused specifically on Chinese American men, the strategies he described are applicable to men from other Asian American ethnic groups (Chang & Yeh, 2003).

Using individual mobility strategies, the Asian American man may capitalize on his own interests, capabilities, and environment. He is not limited to a specific script of how to be an Asian American man, and he is able to find the environments and social groups that are most congruent with his interests and abilities. For instance, an Asian American man may be especially talented in athletics and may focus attention on developing his skills and abilities on a field or court. In this case, the Asian American man is "unlike" other Asian American men, is similar to other athletes he holds in high esteem, and is able to maintain a positive sense of self.

He may be unaware that his hegemonic bargain has led him into another script of being a male athlete, which could constrain other aspects of his sense of self (e.g., emotional expression, focus on aggression, homophobia).

Social Creativity

Tajfel and Turner's (1986) second class of strategies, social creativity, involves enhancing the status of one's group, by altering or redefining the basis of comparison to the dominant group without necessarily objectively changing the location of one's group in the status hierarchy. For example, to enhance group status, Asian American men might compare themselves to White men based on a characteristic on which Asian American men are superior. This strategy, however, also involves a hegemonic bargain because the de facto standard of comparison—White, middle class, heterosexual men—has not changed. Alternatively, Asian American men could reassign positive values to characteristics on which they have been perceived as negative. This strategy could include what Chen refers to as repudiation, where individuals reject the racial and gender premises of hegemonic masculinity by challenging the existing ideals of what it means to be a man. For example, Asian American men could reassign a positive value to the stereotype that they are "nerds" (Allis, 1991) or redefine masculinity to include nerdiness. Tajfel and Turner's strategy suggests group members can change the outgroup by which they are compared, so the comparisons result in favorable outcomes, thus enhancing esteem. This strategy also employs a hegemonic bargain because the increase in status for one group is gained at the expense of the lower-status group with which it is compared.

Social Competition

Tajfel and Turner's third class of strategies is based on social change and involves social competition between the nondominant group and the dominant group, with the purpose of changing the relative positions of the groups in the status hierarchy and achieving a positive distinctiveness. Unlike the second class of strategies, social competition involves a direct attempt to change the objective status location of the group in the hierarchy. These strategies may include social activism aimed at reducing oppression or redistributing resources.

Using social competition as a strategy to increase his status, the Asian American man may be involved in political and social action, campus activism, or a media-watch for negative stereotypes and images of Asian Americans. The Asian American man is activated to confront negative images and to seek redress from those perpetuating negative stereotypes. He may focus on demeaning dominant images and stereotypes of men as inferior and instead present Asian American men as a positive alternative. Moreover, the Asian American man may advocate for equality between Asian American, White, and other men of color.

Social identity theory is used here to add to the existing theoretical and empirical literature on men of color. Although extant theories on masculinity are premised on White, middle-class men's experiences, social identity theory injects into the discourse the importance of considering the environment and social groups. For many men of color, especially for Asian American men, social and peer groups are an important socializing force. Even though not all Asian American men affiliate with other Asian Americans as their reference group, they do need the affiliation of some particular group. Social identity theory allows psychologists to consider the important role these groups play in helping define and construct an Asian American man's identity and sense of masculinity.

CONCLUSION

This chapter presented literature to explore how Asian American men construct their sense of identity as a racialized and gendered group. Historically, racism and experiences of marginalization set the foundation for Asian American men. Yet, even though the historical and cultural contexts of Asian Americans have been negative (e.g., exclusion laws, anti-miscegenation laws, unfair taxation), Asian American communities have survived and thrived. The first immigrants were largely bachelor communities of male laborers (S. Chan, 1991; Takaki, 1990), and in the face of hostility, these men were able to thrive, albeit in limited ways. And just as they have done for generations, Asian American men have found ways to negotiate dominant and Asian cultural pressures and expectations.

For psychologists, our understanding of Asian American men is still limited, especially in the theoretical and empirical literature. Research is just beginning to explore the complexities and multiple masculinities within the Asian American community. Our effort in this chapter was to present possible theories to explain and explore Asian American masculinities. Although various other theories are certainly applicable, for our purpose, we focused on one specific theory: Social Identity Theory.

Our purpose in this chapter was to initiate a discussion of how Asian American men negotiate and construct their masculine and racialized selves. Keeping in mind the deficit model approach, we wanted to discuss possible ways Asian American men create positive masculine selves. Future research will need to examine more closely the process and outcome of Asian American men's endeavors to create a healthy sense of self. For clinicians, these issues will be important as more and more Asian American men find their way into therapy. It is not enough to focus on racial identity, acculturation, and traditional masculinity theories. Clinicians will need to understand how these variables intersect and how Asian American men contend with multiple expectations and pressures coming from masculine, racialized, and ethnic cultural groups. We hope to help Asian American men understand how they negotiate their identities, what sorts of compromises they make, and what the outcomes of their choices are.

REFERENCES

Allis, S. (1991, March 25). Kicking the nerd syndrome. *Time, 137*(12), 64–66.

Chan, C. S. (1989). Issues of identity development among Asian-American lesbians and gay men. *Journal of Counseling and Development, 68,* 6–20.

Chan, J. W. (1998). Contemporary Asian American men's issues. In L. R. Hirabayashi (Ed.), *Teaching Asian America: Diversity and the problem of community issues* (pp. 93–102). Lanham, MD: Rowman & Littlefield.

Chan, S. (1991). *Asian Americans: An interpretive history.* Boston: Twayne.

Chang, T., & Yeh, C. J. (2003). Using online groups to provide support to Asian American men: Racial, cultural, gender, and treatment issues. *Professional Psychology: Research and Practice, 34,* 634–643.

Chang, T., Yeh, C. J., & Krumboltz, J. D. (2001). Process and outcome evaluation of an online support group for Asian American male college students. *Journal of Counseling Psychology, 48,* 319–328.

Chen, A. S. (1999). Lives at the center of the periphery, lives at the periphery of the center: Chinese American masculinities and bargaining with hegemony. *Gender & Society, 13,* 584–607.

Chin, K. (1996). *Chinatown gangs: Extortion, enterprise, and ethnicity.* New York: Oxford University Press.

Chow, C. S. (1998). *Leaving deep water: The lives of Asian American women at the crossroads of two cultures.* New York: Dutton.

Chua, P., & Fujino, D. C. (1999). Negotiating new Asian American masculinities: Attitudes and gender expectations. *The Journal of Men's Studies, 7,* 391–413.

Crocker, J., & Luhtanen, R. (1990). Collective self-esteem and ingroup bias. *Journal of Personality and Social Psychology, 58,* 60–67.

David, D., & Brannon, R. (Eds.). (1976). *The forty-nine percent majority: The male sex role.* Reading, MA: Addison-Wesley.

Devos, T, & Banaji, M. R. (2005). American = White? *Journal of Personality and Social Psychology, 88,* 447–466.

Doss, B. D., & Hopkins, J. R. (1998). The multicultural masculine ideology scale: Validation from three cultural perspectives. *Sex Roles, 38,* 719–741.

Eisler, R. M. (1995). The relationship between masculine gender role stress and men's health risk: The validation of a construct. In R. F. Levant & W. S. Pollack (Eds.), *A new psychology of men* (pp. 207–228). New York: Basic Books.

Eisler, R. M. (1998). Male reference group identity dependence: Another concept of masculine identity to understand men? *The Counseling Psychologist, 26,* 422–426.

Espiritu, Y. L. (1997). *Asian American women and men.* Thousand Oaks, CA: Sage.

Espiritu, Y. L. (1998). All men are not created equal: Asian men in U.S. history. In M. S. Kimmel & M. A. Messner (Eds.), *Men's lives* (4th ed., pp. 35–44). Needham Heights, MA: Allyn & Bacon.

Fuertes, J., Sedlacek, W., & Liu, W. (1994). Using the SAT and non-cognitive variables to predict the grades and retention of Asian American university students. *Journal of Measurement and Evaluation in Counseling and Development, 27,* 74–84.

Gupta, S. (1999*). Emerging voices: South Asian American women redefine self, family and community.* New Delhi, India: Sage.

Harris, C. I. (1995). Whiteness as property. In K. Crenshaw, N. Gotanda, G. Pella, & K. Thomas (Eds.), *Critical race theory: The key writings that formed the movement* (pp. 276–291). New York: The New Press.

Helms, J. E. (1990). *Black and white racial identity: Theory, research, and practice.* Westport, CT: Greenwood Press.

Helms, J. E. (1995). An update of Helms' White and People of Color racial identity models. In J. G. Ponterotto, J. M. Casas, L. A. Suzuki, & C. M. Alexander (Eds.), *Handbook of multicultural counseling* (pp. 181–198). Thousand Oaks, CA: Sage.

Humes, K., & McKinnon, J. (2000). *The Asian and Pacific Islander population in the United States: Population characteristics* (U.S. Census Bureau Current Population Report No. P60–221). Washington, DC: U.S. Government Printing Office.

Jacobson, M. F. (1998). *Whiteness of a different color: European immigrants and the alchemy of race.* Cambridge, MA: Harvard University Press.

Kibria, N. (1993). *Family tightrope: The changing lives of Vietnamese Americans.* Princeton, NJ: Princeton University Press.

Kim, B. S. K., Atkinson, D. R., & Yang, P. H. (1999). The Asian Values Scale: Development, factor analysis, validation, and reliability. *Journal of Counseling Psychology, 46,* 342–352.

Kim, E. H. (1982). *Asian American literature: An introduction to the writings and their social context.* Philadelphia: Temple University Press.

Kim, E. H. (1990). "Such opposite creatures": Men and women in Asian American literature. *Michigan Quarterly Review, 29,* 68–93.

Kim, E. J., O'Neil, J. M., & Owen, S. V. (1996). Asian-American men's acculturation and gender-role conflict. *Psychological Reports, 79,* 95–104.

Kimmel, M. (1996). *Manhood in America: A cultural history.* New York: Free Press.

Lee, D. B., & Saul, T. T. (1987). Counseling Asian American men. In M. Scher, M. Stevens, G. Good, & G. A. Eichenfield (Eds.), *Handbook of counseling and psychotherapy with men* (pp. 180–191). Newbury Park, CA: Sage.

Lee, S. J. (1996). Perceptions of panethnicity among Asian American high school students. *Amerasia Journal, 22*(2), 109–125.

Levant, R. F. (1996). The new psychology of men. *Professional Psychology: Research and Practice, 27,* 259–265.

Levant, R. F., & Fischer, J. (1998). The Male Role Norms Inventory. In C. Davis, W. Yarber, R. Bauserman, G. Schreer, & S. Davis (Eds.), *Sexuality-related measures: A compendium* (2nd ed., pp. 469–472). Thousand Oaks, CA: Sage.

Levant, R. F., Hirsch, L., Celentano, E., Cozza, T., Hill, S., MacEachern, M., et al. (1992). The male role: an investigation of norms and stereotypes. *Journal of Mental Health Counseling, 14,* 325–337.

Levant, R. F., Wu, R., & Fischer, J. (1996). Masculinity ideology: A comparison between U.S. and Chinese young men and women. *Journal of Gender, Culture, and Health, 1,* 207–220.

Liang, C. T. H., Li, L. C., Kim, B. S. K. (2004). The Asian American Racism-Related Stress Inventory: Development, factor analysis, reliability, and validity. *Journal of Counseling Psychology, 51,* 103–114.

Ling, J. (1997). Identity crisis and gender politics: Reappropriating Asian American masculinity. In K. K. Chung (Ed.), *An interethnic companion to Asian American literature* (pp. 312–337). New York: Cambridge University Press.

Liu, W. M. (1997, Summer). Sex tour narratives: Narcissism and fantasy in determining Asian American sexuality. *Hitting Critical Mass: A Journal of Asian American Cultural Criticism, 4*(2), 87–110.

Liu, W. M. (2002). Exploring the lives of Asian American men: Racial identity, male role norms, gender role conflict, and prejudicial attitudes. *Psychology of Men and Masculinity, 3,* 107–118.

Liu, W. M. (2005). The study of men and masculinity as an important multicultural competency consideration. *Journal of Clinical Psychology, 61,* 685–697.

Liu, W. M., & Iwamoto, D. (2005). *Asian American men's gender role conflict: The role of acculturation, self-esteem, and psychological distress.* Unpublished manuscript.

Liu, W. M., Iwamoto, D. K., & Hernandez, J. (2005, August). *Acculturation, masculinity, distress, and substance abuse among Asian American men.* Poster presented at the 113th annual convention of the American Psychological Association, Washington, DC.

Liu, W. M., Pope-Davis, D. B., Nevitt, J., & Toporek, R. L. (1999). Asian American college students: Understanding the function of acculturation and prejudicial attitudes. *Cultural Diversity & Ethnic Minority Psychology, 5,* 317–328.

Liu, W. M., Rochlen, A., & Mohr, J. J. (2005). Real and ideal gender-role conflict: Exploring psychological distress among men. *Psychology of Men and Masculinity, 6,* 137–148.

Liu, W. M, & Sedlacek, W. E. (1999). Differences in leadership and co-curricular perception among male and female Asian Pacific American college students. *Journal of the Freshmen Year Experience, 11*(2), 93–114.

Long, P. D. P. (1996). *The dream shattered: Vietnamese gangs in America.* Boston: Northeastern University Press.

Lum, J. L. (1998). Family violence. In L. C. Lee & N. W. S. Zane (Eds.) *Handbook of Asian American psychology* (pp. 505–526). Thousand Oaks, CA: Sage.

Mahalik, J. R., Locke, B. D., Ludlow, L. H., Diemer, M. A., Scott, R. P. J., Gottfried, M., et al. (2003). Development of the Conformity to Masculine Norms Inventory. *Psychology of Men and Masculinity, 4,* 3–25.

Mahalik, J. R., Talmadge, W. T., Locke, B. D., & Scott, R. P. J. (2005). Using the Conformity to Masculine Norms Inventory to work with men in a clinical setting. *Journal of Clinical Psychology, 61,* 661–674.

Mok, T. A. (1998). Getting the message: Media images and stereotypes and their effect on Asian Americans. *Cultural Diversity and Mental Health, 4,* 185–202.

Mosher, D. L., & Tompkins, S. S. (1988). Scripting the macho man: Hypermasculine socialization and enculturation. *The Journal of Sex Research, 25,* 60–84.

Moyerman, D. R., & Foreman, B. D. (1992). Acculturation and adjustment: A meta-analytic study. *Hispanic Journal of Behavioral Sciences, 14,* 163–200.

Nagata, D. K. (1998). Internment and intergenerational relations. In L. C. Lee & N. W. S. Zane (Eds.), *Handbook of Asian American psychology* (pp. 433–456). Thousand Oaks, CA: Sage.

Nakamura, D. (2000). They're hot, they're sexy . . . they're Asian men. Retrieved February 15, 2006, from http://www.gapsn.org/project2/press/nakamura.asp

Nghe, L. T., & Mahalik, J. R. (1998, August). *Influences on Vietnamese men: Examining gender role socialization, acculturation, and racism.* Paper presented at the meeting of the American Psychological Association, San Francisco, CA.

Okihiro, G. (1994). *Margins and mainstreams: Asians in American history and culture.* Seattle: University of Washington Press.

O'Neil, J. M. (1990). Assessing men's gender role conflict. In D. Moore & F. Leafgren (Eds.), *Problem solving strategies and interventions for men in conflict* (pp. 23–38). Alexandria, VA: American Counseling Association.

O'Neil, J. M., Egan, J., Owen, S. V., & Murry, V. M. (1993). The gender role journey measure: Scale development and psychometric evaluation. *Sex Roles, 28,* 167–185.

O'Neil, J. M., Good, G. E., & Holmes, S. (1995). Fifteen years of theory and research on men's gender role conflict: New paradigms for empirical research. In R. F. Levant & W. S. Pollack (Eds.), *A new psychology of men* (pp. 164–206). New York: Basic Books.

O'Neil, J. M., Helms, B. J., Gable, R. K., David, L., & Wrightsman, L. S. (1986). Gender-role Conflict Scale: College men's fear of femininity. *Sex Roles, 14,* 335–350.

Pan, E. (2000, February 21). Asian-American men were told for many years by their own community to be dutiful sons. *Newsweek*, p. 50.

Pang, V. O. (1991). The relationship of test anxiety and math achievement to parental values in Asian-American and European-American middle school students. *Journal of Research and Development in Education, 24,* 1–10.

Phinney, J. S. (1991). Ethnic identity and self-esteem: A review and integration. *Hispanic Journal of Behavioral Sciences, 13,* 193–208.

Phinney, J. S. (1995). Ethnic identity and self-esteem. In A. M. Padilla (Ed.), *Hispanic psychology:*

Critical issues in theory and research (pp. 57–70). Thousand Oaks, CA: Sage.

Phinney, J. S., Cantu, C. L., & Kurtz, D. A. (1997). Ethnic and American identity as predictors of self-esteem among African American, Latino, and White adolescents. *Journal of Youth and Adolescence, 26,* 165–185.

Pleck, J. H. (1981). *The myth of masculinity.* Cambridge: MIT Press.

Pleck, J. H. (1995). The gender role strain paradigm: An update. In R. F. Levant & W. S. Pollack (Eds.), *A new psychology of men* (pp. 11–32). New York: Basic Books.

Porter, J. R., & Washington, R. E. (1993). Minority identity and self-esteem. *Annual Review of Sociology, 19,* 139–161.

Rimonte, N. (1991). A question of culture: Cultural approval of violence against women in the Pacific-Asian community. *Stanford Law Review, 43,* 1311–1362.

Roberts, R. E., Phinney, J. S., Masse, L. C., Chen, Y. R., Roberts, C. R., & Romero, A. (1999). The structure of ethnic identity of young adolescents from diverse ethnocultural groups. *Journal of Early Adolescence, 19,* 301–322.

Singer, E. (1992). Reference groups and social evaluations. In M. Rosenberg & R. H. Turner (Eds.), *Social psychology: Sociological perspectives* (pp. 66–93). New Brunswick, NJ: Transaction.

Stangor, C., Sullivan, L. A., & Ford, T. E. (1991). Affective and cognitive determinants of prejudice. *Social Cognition, 9,* 359–380.

Sue, D. (1996). Asian men in groups. In M. P. Andronico (Ed.), *Men in groups: Insights, interventions, psychoeducational work* (pp. 69–80). Washington, DC: American Psychological Association.

Sue, D. (1999). Counseling Asian American boys and adolescent males. In A. M. Horne & M. S. Kiselica (Eds.), *Handbook of counseling boys and adolescent males* (pp. 87–99). Thousand Oaks, CA: Sage.

Sue, D. W. (1990). Culture in transition: Counseling Asian-American men. In D. Moore & F. Leafgren (Eds.), *Problem solving strategies and interventions for men in conflict* (pp. 153–165). Alexandria, VA: American Counseling Association.

Suinn, R. M., Rickard-Figueroa, K., Lew, S., & Vigil, P. (1987). The Suinn-Lew Asian Self-identity Acculturation Scale: An initial report. *Educational and Psychological Measurement, 47,* 401–407.

Tajfel, H., & Turner, J. C. (1986). In S. Worchel & W. G. Austin (Eds.), *Psychology of intergroup relations.* Chicago: Nelson Hall.

Takaki, R. (1989). *Iron cages: Race and culture in 19th-century America.* New York: Oxford University Press.

Tang, N. M. (1997). Psychoanalytic psychotherapy with Chinese Americans. In E. Lee (Ed.), *Working with Asian Americans: A guide for clinicians* (pp. 323–341). New York: Guildford Press.

Thompson, E. H., Jr., & Pleck, J. H. (1995). *Masculinity ideologies: A review of research instrumentation on men and masculinities.* In R. F. Levant & W. S. Pollack (Eds.), *A new psychology of men* (pp. 129–163). New York: Basic Books.

Tsai, J. L., Ying, Y. W., & Lee, P. A. (2001). Cultural predictors of self-esteem: A study of Chinese female and male young adults. *Cultural Diversity & Ethnic Minority Psychology, 7,* 284–297.

Wade, J. C. (1998). Male reference group identity dependence: A theory of male identity. *The Counseling Psychologist, 26,* 349–383.

Wade, J. C., & Gelso, C. J. (1998). Reference Group Identity Dependence Scale: A measure of male identity. *The Counseling Psychologist, 26,* 384–412.

Wong, S. L. C. (1993). Subverting desire: Reading the body in the 1991 Asian Pacific Islander men's calendar. *Critical Mass, 1,* 63–74.

Zhou, M., & Bankston, C. L., III. (1998). *Growing up American: How Vietnamese children adapt to life in the United States.* New York: Russell Sage.

Zhou, Z. (2004). Aspiring to be *Da Zhangfu:* Masculinization in late Imperial Chinese literature. *Tamkang Review, 35,* 79–117.

13

The Psychology of Asian American Older Adults

Gayle Y. Iwamasa

Kristen H. Sorocco

In 2000, adults age 65 years and older comprised 7.8% of the Asian American population (U.S. Census Bureau, 2001). Given projected continuing increases in the population of Asian Americans, we may comfortably hypothesize that this percentage will increase over time (Fried & Mehrota, 1998). Who are Asian American older adults? The answer to this question is complex. Contrary to popular stereotypes, the group comprising Asian American older adults is vastly diverse. These older adults vary on a number of characteristics, including country of origin, generational status, use of language, acculturation level, religiosity/spirituality, education, socioeconomic status, and age. Consider the following two individuals:

Jessica Wong is a 67-year-old fourth-generation Chinese American attorney who celebrates both Chinese New Year and Christmas. She has been partner in her law firm for 31 years and is now semi-retired, only taking on cases that interest her—mainly those which involve copyright infringement. She is active in the California Bar Association, attends aerobics classes at the local Y three times a week, serves on the Board of Trustees for several prominent organizations and

one private university, speaks and writes fluently in Mandarin, and visits her two children and four grandchildren on a regular basis. Although agnostic most of her life, having attended a Unitarian Church for the past 10 years, Jessica is currently exploring Buddhism and Islam, for personal interest and also due to current global events. She and her Swedish American husband of 40 years, Stuart, a Los Angeles County circuit court judge, enjoy international travel. This includes yearly visits to the Shandong province of China, the area in which Jessica's family originated, skiing in Austria in the winter, spending time at their Lake Tahoe vacation home, and going on quarterly trips to Las Vegas with the Chinese American senior citizens group to which they belong. Jessica drives a 2006 Lexus; Stuart drives a 2005 Toyota Landcruiser. They live in a $1.2 million, 3,200 square foot home in Brentwood, a ritzy suburb of Los Angeles.

Nam Cher Pao is a 65-year-old immigrant from Xieng Khouang province in Laos. She and her husband, 69-year-old Cher Pao, lived in a relocation center, along with their now 30-year-old son and 33-year-old daughter, for two years before they relocated to Minneapolis in 1980. During the war in Laos, Cher Pao was able to avoid enlistment in the military due to the loss of his left arm, the result of a childhood farming accident. As far as they know, all of the rest of their family members were killed during the war, including their two oldest sons, who they last saw protecting their village from enemy soldiers as the rest of the family fled. On arrival in the United States, Nam Cher Pao and her family have lived in a close-knit, predominantly Hmong neighborhood. They have regularly attended the First Christian Church since 1984, when it began administering a refugee assistance program. Although her children speak English fluently, Nam Cher Pao speaks mainly Hmong and knows only a few words in English. She has been employed as a housekeeper for a local motel for the past 17 years, is paid hourly, and has no retirement benefits, thus has not considered retiring. Her employers value her because even though she does not speak English well, she is a reliable employee, arriving on time and doing her job without complaint. Nam Cher Pao cannot afford a car, lives in a one-bedroom apartment with Cher Pao, and takes public transportation to work each day.

Although both Jessica Wong and Nam Cher Pao are Asian American older adults, the life experiences of these two women are vastly different. Both Asian American psychology and geropsychology have increased in popularity over the past few decades, in large part due to the dramatic increases in these populations. However, Asian American elders who are members of both populations have unfortunately been largely ignored by researchers in these areas. For example, in Asian American psychology, ethnic identity, gender roles, and women's issues are currently popular research topics, yet there is no published research on these issues as they relate to Asian American older adults. Geropsychologists no longer focus solely on the cognitive impairment or bereavement that occurs during aging and have begun to focus on interpersonal issues such as caregiving, sexuality, and elder abuse. Furthermore, positive psychology has had its influence on geropsychology, so the field now attends to positive aspects of aging, such as models of successful aging, instead of focusing on declining physical and psychological attributes. Empirical research

on Asian American elders is nonexistent in these areas, an example of what Gutmann (1992) refers to as "a field without a literature."

Clearly, the lack of empirical research on Asian American older adults is problematic, given the continued growth of this group and that humans are living longer than ever. Stereotypes of Asian Americans are that they are fairly physically healthy and have greater longevity compared to other U.S. ethnic groups. Unfortunately, these assumptions typically ignore the vast differences in mortality among various Asian American older adults. For example, some researchers have lumped older adults from a large number of different ethnic groups into a monolithic "Asian/Pacific Islander" category (Takeuchi & Young, 1994), thus blurring distinctions between groups with lower rates of mortality (e.g., Chinese and Japanese Americans) with groups who have higher rates of mortality, such as Cambodians and the Hmong. The lack of research on Asian American older adults contributes to the stereotyping of this diverse and growing group.

The purpose of this chapter is to summarize the existing psychological research on Asian American older adults. In some areas, the differences are highlighted (e.g., acculturation level is a frequent influence on dependent measures and thus is not reviewed separately), whereas in others, commonalities are highlighted. However, we encourage researchers and practitioners to use the information presented here only as a guide and to attend to the individual cultural context and life experiences of those Asian American older adults they encounter. A comprehensive review of all of the aging issues of Asian American older adults is beyond the scope of this chapter. For more general reviews of life transitions and issues of Asian American older adults, please consult Yamamoto, Silva, and Chang (1998) and D. Yee (1997).

PSYCHOLOGICAL RESEARCH AND ASIAN AMERICAN OLDER ADULTS

In a review chapter such as this, it is important that research methodology issues are raised. An earlier work of ours (Iwamasa & Sorocco, 2002) provides an excellent summary of issues related to conducting research with Asian Americans. Given the heterogeneity of Asian American older adults, collapsing research participants into one monolithic group called Asian Americans is problematic. In addition to acknowledging ethnic group differences, psychologists also must be aware of differences such as age, educational level, socioeconomic status, work experience, language capability, and generational status among Asian American older adults. Gender differences also should be assessed, as the life experiences of men and women can be quite different, even among the same ethnic group and generation level.

We also suggest that when evaluating research on Asian American older adults, researchers and practitioners review the research design used to see if it is culturally appropriate. This involves understanding cultural beliefs, accessibility issues, and potential concerns that participants might have about the research. In our earlier work (Iwamasa & Sorocco, 2002), we reviewed a variety of methodologies, such as focus groups, interview studies, and survey studies and emphasized the need to use or develop culturally appropriate measures. Not only do measures often need to be revamped for older adults (e.g., increasing font size), but researchers also need to assess the appropriateness of measures developed on one ethnic group in assessing another ethnic group, especially when translating English language measures into Asian languages. Research that integrates the participants' perspective, from the design to the interpretation, is the ideal approach.

THE AGING PROCESS

Most models of the aging process include three components—physical, psychological/cognitive, and social, all of which interact dynamically with one another to influence the aging process (Fried & Mehrota, 1998). For example, Tran (1990) found that for Vietnamese immigrants, limited proficiency in English affected older adults' ability to engage in basic life skills such as grocery shopping and applying for aid. Tran further found that older Vietnamese

women had more difficulty learning English than did men, possibly the result of traditional patriarchal gender roles held by the women.

In terms of *physical aging,* little research exists on the physical health of Asian American older adults. As indicated previously, one stereotype of Asian American older adults is that they are physically healthier than other older adults. Studies that combine Asian ethnic groups into one Asian American/Pacific Islander category are not meaningful in terms of understanding the health status of Asian American older adults. Tanjasiri, Wallace, and Shibata's (1995) review of community-based research indicated that Korean American older adults believed their health to be poor, Vietnamese American older adults rated themselves as less healthy (compared to other ethnic groups' self-ratings), and many Chinese and Korean American older adults were without health insurance. Results of recent research also indicate that Asian American older adults' conceptualization of physical aging may depend on the type of physical problem. For example, in a qualitative study of Korean American women, Dickson and Kim (2003) found that participants perceived their arthritis-related pain to be a component of the aging process rather than disease-related. Additionally, Tang, Solomon, and McCracken (2000) found that insurance coverage and higher acculturation were significant predictors of mammograms among older Chinese American women.

Psychological aging among Asian American older adults has yet to be systematically studied. Although a number of models pertaining to the psychological functioning of older adults exist, such as Atchley's (1989) continuity theory, Erikson's (1982) life course theory, and George's (1990) model of life satisfaction, such theories are largely based on Eurocentric assumptions about aging; thus, it is not known how they may or may not be culturally relevant for ethnic minority elders. Park, Nisbett, and Hedden (1999) suggest that information processing differs cross-culturally; those of East Asian heritage process information in a holistic and contextual manner, while those from Western-based cultures process information in an analytical manner. They present a framework that incorporates the need to utilize culturally appropriate measures of information processing when examining older adults' cognition. Other psychological variables such as personality, identity issues (e.g., ethnic, gender, family, etc.) have yet to be examined among Asian American older adults.

B. W. K. Yee (1997) summarized the *social and cultural issues* related to aging Southeast Asian elders. Her review emphasizes a life-span developmental approach, in which the specific cultural group's age-related norms are used to examine adaptation to aging. Both personal characteristics and personal history are emphasized in interpreting how Southeast Asian elders experience life in the United States.

Given that many traditional Asian cultures view the mind-body as integrated, existing models that operationally define and examine various components of aging as distinct may not be as applicable to Asian American older adults. For example, well-being among many Asian ethnic groups is based on the interaction between the individual, nature, the universe, and other people (Matsumoto, 1996). Thus, in considering the aging process, separating such components may not be relevant. Instead, researchers may consider developing models based on such beliefs, rather than testing and revising models of aging based on predominantly European American older adults. An excellent example of such an approach is Kleinman, Eisenberg, and Good's (1978) explanatory model of illness, which suggests that a person's cultural framework influences one's beliefs and experiences of physical and psychological distress.

DISCRIMINATION ISSUES

In addition to the experience of racism, many Asian American older adults experience discrimination based on age. Ageism not only occurs across ethnic groups, but also from within one's own ethnic group. Crandall (1980) refers to this as double ethnic jeopardy. Additionally, some researchers have noted the deleterious effects of minority status, low socioeconomic status, and other ethnic and cultural factors on aging of Asian Americans and other ethnic minority elders (Jackson, Antonucci, & Gibson, 1995; Kiyak & Hooyman, 1994; Markides & Black,

1996). More research on the experience and impact of ageism and racism on the lives of Asian American older adults is needed.

MENTAL HEALTH ISSUES

Given the life changes associated with aging, it is no surprise that older age has been identified as a predictor of mental health problems among Asian Americans (Uba, 1994). In this section, we focus on the mental health issues of Asian American older adults that are either the most prevalent or that have received research attention: depression, anxiety, alcohol and tobacco use, and dementia.

Conceptualization of Mental Health Problems

There is a paucity of research on how Asian American older adults conceptualize mental health problems. Beliefs regarding mental health vary widely among Asian American communities and are dependent on subpopulation cultural beliefs as well as acculturation level. For example, some Asian Americans believe mental illness is due to loss of one's soul, demonic possession, or intervention of spirits (Kang & Kang, 1995). However, these supernatural views of mental illness are more often associated with less-acculturated Asian American immigrants and refugees (Cheung & Snowden, 1990). Asian Americans may also conceptualize mental health problems as an imbalance in bodily systems (Kang & Kang, 1995; Narikiyo & Kameoka, 1992; Ryan, 1985), which explains why many Asian Americans will often seek treatment for a mental health problem from their physician rather than from a mental health provider.

In fact, there is evidence to suggest that some Asian American older adults tend to express psychological distress by describing somatic symptoms more often than older adults from Western cultures do (Kleinman, 1977). More recent research has suggested that Asian American older adults do acknowledge symptoms of psychological distress, as well as somatic symptoms, when they are properly assessed. During an interview study designed to assess how Japanese American older adults conceptualize depression and anxiety, researchers found that Japanese American older adults in this sample defined anxiety and depression by describing primarily psychological symptoms, contradicting the popular belief that individuals from Asian cultures tend to express psychological complaints somatically (Iwamasa, Hilliard, & Osato, 1998). Additionally, Suen and Tusaie (2004) found, in a sample of 100 Taiwanese American older adults being assessed for depression with the Geriatric Depression Scale and individual interviews, that when given time to express themselves, the Taiwanese American older adults were able to report feelings of guilt, sadness, and anger, decreasing the symptoms of somatization.

Another common model used to explain Asian Americans' beliefs regarding mental health is a social model. The social model conceptualizes mental health problems as the result of interpersonal problems (Kuo, 1984; Marsella, Kinzie, & Gordon, 1973; Narikiyo & Kameoka, 1992). There is very little research examining how Asian Americans conceptualize specific types of mental health problems and whether their views of mental health diagnoses are consistent with Western diagnostic criteria. A few qualitative studies point to differences in how Asian American older adults conceptualize mental health problems compared to Western conceptualizations (Hilliard & Iwamasa, 2001; Iwamasa, Hilliard, & Osato, 1998).

Depression

Clinically significant depression is one of the more common mental health problems among older adults in general (Sorocco, Kinoshita, & Gallagher-Thompson, 2005). Depressive symptoms also appear to be a common mental health problem among Asian American older adults. Yamamoto et al. (1985) found that among community-dwelling Japanese American older adults, 27% had symptoms of dysthymia, and 3% had symptoms of major depression. Among Japanese American older adults living in an assisted-living facility, 39% had symptoms of dysthymia, and 16% had symptoms of major depression. Southeast Asian and Korean American older adults have also reported more

depressive symptomatology than younger adults, reporting higher levels of alienation (Nicassio & Pate, 1984) and unhappiness (Rumbaut, 1985) compared to younger Southeast Asian Americans. Korean American older adults report more feelings of alienation and powerlessness than their younger counterparts (Moon & Pearl, 1991).

Recent research suggests that assessment of depression within primary care settings serving Asian American older adults is vital. The prevalence of major depressive disorder among Chinese American older adults (mean age of 50 years) was 19.6% (Yeung et al., 2004). Although prior data have suggested that Chinese Americans have one of the lowest prevalence rates of depression compared to other ethnic groups, Yeung et al.'s (2004) study found that prevalence of major depressive disorders was equal to, and in some cases greater than, that in other ethnic groups.

Depressive symptoms alone also appear to have a significant influence on the health of Asian Americans. Depressive symptoms were found to be a risk factor for mortality among elderly Japanese American men participating in the Honolulu-Asia Aging Study (Takeshita et al., 2002). Of even more concern was that the risk was greatest for healthy Japanese American men. Furthermore, although not subgroup specific, Asian Americans were found to have the highest proportion of suicidal or death ideation within a primary care setting in comparison to other ethnic groups (Bartels et al., 2002). According to Bartels et al. (2002), among Asian Americans, those at the greatest risk were socially isolated geriatric outpatients with co-occurring depression and anxiety and of younger age (65–74 years).

Although more research is needed on culturally appropriate assessment of depression in Asian American older adults, the research that has been conducted suggests that some self-report measures have adequate psychometric properties among various Asian American subgroups. The Geriatric Depression Scale (GDS) (Yesavage et al., 1983) was found to have good internal consistency and reliability with coefficients similar to the original sample among healthy Japanese American older adults (Iwamasa, Hilliard, & Kost, 1998). The Diagnostic Interview

Schedule (Robins, Helzer, Croughan, & Ratcliff, 1981) also has been used successfully with Japanese American older adults. Many assessment measures have been translated into various Asian languages and maintain solid psychometric properties. For example, the Hopkins Symptom checklist-25 has been translated into the Hmong language and has demonstrated an internal consistency of .97, split-half coefficient of .92, and test-retest reliability of .90 among 159 Hmong adults with and without a mental health problem (Mouanoutoua & Brown, 1995). The Chinese version of the Beck Depression Inventory is a reliable and valid measure of depression among Asian Americans receiving services in a primary care setting (Yeung, et al., 2002). Yeung et al. (2002) also indicated that despite the literature on the somatization of mental health problems, Chinese Americans are able to self-report depressive symptoms in a questionnaire format.

Anxiety

The topic of anxiety among Asian American older adults has received very little research attention. One reason for the limited research attention is the possibility that anxiety symptoms do not appear to be a prevalent issue among Asian American older adults according to Western diagnostic criteria. However, Asian American older adults may conceptualize anxiety in a manner that is quite different from how traditional Western diagnostic criteria describe it. In an initial qualitative study to determine how Japanese American older adults define anxiety and depression, interview data suggested that there was no clear distinction between symptoms of anxiety and depression (Iwamasa, Hilliard, & Osato, 1998). In a follow-up study to examine whether anxiety was conceptualized by Japanese American older adults in a manner similar to Western diagnostic criteria, healthy participants were presented with a checklist composed of symptoms from Generalized Anxiety Disorder and Major Depressive Disorder in the *DSM-IV* (American Psychiatric Association, 1994) and from the earlier qualitative interview study (Hilliard & Iwamasa, 2001). Findings indicated that Japanese American older adults conceptualized anxiety by *describing* more depressive

symptoms than anxiety symptoms, and they described more cognitive symptoms of anxiety, as opposed to somatic symptoms, which is what past literature emphasized.

Despite the limited research on anxiety among Asian American older adults, at least some Asian American subgroups experience worry symptoms. Worry was examined in Japanese American older adults and European American older adults in community-based groups using the Penn State Worry Questionnaire (PSWQ) (Meyer et al., 1990), the Worry Scale-Revised (WSR) (Wisocki, 1995), and a self-report worry questionnaire adapted from Wisocki (Watari & Brodbeck, 1996). This cross-cultural study found that regardless of ethnicity, women scored higher on the PSWQ and WSR. This study highlights the need to examine gender differences among Asian American older adults—even when focusing on a single ethnic group of the same generation level.

Alcohol and Tobacco Use

There is very little research available on the prevalence of alcohol use and related problems among Asian American elders. What little research that exists is consistent with studies on European Americans—gender and age differences are apparent in drinking and smoking patterns among Asian Americans. Among Japanese Americans, men drink more alcohol than women, and heavier and problem drinkers are more prevalent among young adults (Higuchi et al., 1994). However, middle-aged men consumed more alcohol and had a higher proportion of heavier drinkers than other age groups.

A few studies have suggested the benefits of moderate alcohol use on cognitive performance. A positive relationship was found between light to moderate drinking and cognitive performance among Japanese American men and women aged 65 and older (Bond, Burr, McCurry, Graves, & Larson, 2001; Galanis et al., 2000). A follow-up study found that current drinkers scored significantly higher on the Cognitive Abilities Screening Instrument over time than past drinkers or abstainers (Bond et al., 2004). However, Galanis et al. (2000) also emphasized that the health risks associated with drinking may outweigh any potential cognitive benefits of moderate alcohol consumption.

Although Asian Americans in general tend to have the lowest prevalence rates of smoking compared to other ethnic groups, there are significant subgroup differences (Hee-Soon et al., 2003). The prevalence of tobacco use among Chinese Americans aged 18–74 years was found to be 29% of men and 4% of women (Shelley et al., 2004). Interestingly, level of acculturation, being older than age 35, and high levels of tobacco-related knowledge were all found to be positively associated with history of never smoking (Shelley et al., 2004). Among Korean American men, the prevalence of smoking was found to be 26.1% current smokers and 42.3% former smokers (Hee-Soon et al., 2003). Men older than age 40 were more likely to have quit smoking than younger Korean Americans. Similarly, acculturation was found to have a positive association with smoking status. Those with higher levels of acculturation were less likely to be current smokers.

Dementia

Of mental health issues among Asian American elders, the topic of dementia has received the most research attention. Basic information is available on the conceptualization of dementia among Asian American older adults and their families, as well as assessment and treatment recommendations (Yeo & Gallagher-Thompson, 1996). Western-trained health care providers define dementia differently than Asian American older adults and their families do. Chinese American older adults and their families view dementia as a mental illness rather than a biological disease (Elliott, DiMinno, Lam, & Tu, 1996). In fact, the Chinese characters used to represent dementia mean "crazy" and "catatonic" (Elliott et al., 1996). Thus, it is no surprise that Chinese American dementia caregivers have identified stigmatization of a diagnosis of Alzheimer's disease to be a barrier in seeking treatment (Zhan, 2004). Perhaps as a result of the stigma, dementia-related symptoms also have been defined as part of the normal aging process among Chinese American family caregivers (Hinton, Guo, Hillygus, & Levkoff, 2000). Among Japanese Americans, particularly the Issei and Nisei generations, the diagnosis of dementia also carries a stigma and is defined as a mental illness (Tempo & Saito, 1996).

The Honolulu-Asia Aging Study provides some data on the prevalence of dementia among Asian American older adults. The prevalence of dementia was assessed in older Japanese American men (N = 3,734) aged 71 to 93 years and living within the community or institutions (Lon et al., 1996). The inclusion criteria for dementia were based on *DSM-III-R* diagnostic criteria. In men aged 71 to 74 years, the prevalence of dementia was 2.1%, but the prevalence increased with age to 33.4% in men aged 85 to 93 years (Lon et al., 1996). Overall, the prevalence for Alzheimer's disease in older Japanese Americans men in Hawai'i was found to be similar to European American populations and higher than for men in Japan (Lon et al., 1996). However, the prevalence of vascular dementia was found to be higher than in European American populations (Lon et al., 1996). In general, the prevalence of dementia among older Japanese American men appears to be comparable to other populations, but there appear to be differences in the prevalence of the type of dementia.

Mild cases of dementia among Japanese American elders and their families tend to go unrecognized (Ross et al., 1997). Additionally, Korean Americans have been found to wait three to four years before seeking help (Watari & Gatz, 2004). This is of concern given that individuals with a potentially treatable dementia will not receive the early interventions necessary to alleviate symptoms and slow the progression of the disease. Proper diagnosis of dementia must include going into the Asian American community in order to conduct cognitive screening programs for the elderly and public education programs on the early signs and symptoms of dementia (Ross et al., 1997). Such community programs appear to be successful, as Korean Americans who have more knowledge about dementia have been found to be more willing to seek help and to benefit from public education (Watari & Gatz, 2004).

Overall Risk Factors for Mental Health Problems Among Asian American Older Adults

As is evident from the previous sections, a paucity of research has been conducted on

Asian American older adults with regard to mental health issues. However, several risk factors are apparent from the existing research. Loneliness and the experience of loss among Asian American older adults might place them at a greater risk for mental health disorders, in particular depression (Uba, 1994). Asian American older adults who were refugees also might be at a greater risk for mental health problems. Older Indo-Chinese refugees (including ethnic Vietnamese, Chinese Vietnamese, and Lowland Laotians) were found to have lower social adjustment scores than younger cohorts (Tran, 1991). Additionally, recent immigration status was also found to be associated with higher depression scores among older Chinese Americans (Ying, 1988). Despite limited research on examining the comorbidity of mental health problems with physical health problems among Asian American older adults, mental health problems should also be assessed when certain physical health conditions, such as cardiovascular disease, are present. Mental health assessment within primary care settings is also warranted, given that many Asian American elders likely feel more comfortable seeking help from their primary care physician.

CAREGIVING ISSUES

Caregiving among elders has received increased attention in the past few years (Coon, Ory, & Schulz, 2003). Among many traditional Asian cultures, filial piety (respect, responsibility, and personal sacrifice for one's family) influences caregiving of elders (Sung, 1990). This often results in multigenerational families in one household. However, there is some evidence that such influences are declining both in the United States and in Asia (Fried & Mehrota, 1998).

Some evidence suggests that for some Asian American elders, higher levels of acculturation, medical benefits such as Medicaid, and independent thinking are related to more acceptance of formal long-term care outside the family home (Min, 2005) and that, among Chinese American elders, within-group differences exist in the use of aging-related services (Liu, 2003). However, statistics do indicate

that Asian American elders underutilize adult day care centers and assisted living facilities (Aroian, Wu, & Tran, 2005; Yu, Kim, Liu, & Wong, 1993), which also suggests that many Asian American families are informally caregiving for their elders. Barriers to the use of more formal caregiving resources include cultural values, lack of knowledge about available resources, language differences, availability of culturally sensitive services, staff, facilities, and finances.

Research has demonstrated that when caregiving is designed to be culturally sensitive, Asian American elders are able to receive good care (Van Steenberg, Ansak, & Chin-Hansen, 1993). Further, culture-specific caregiving programs that incorporate the cultural values and activities of the cultural group result in the increased trust and comfort of those Asian American elders who utilize the services (Edgerly et al., 2003).

Treatment Implications

General barriers to treatment. There are a number of barriers to service utilization facing Asian American older adults in need of mental health services (AARP Minority Affairs, 1995). First, research suggests that Asian American older adults have limited knowledge about mental health services (Kang & Kang, 1995; Salcido, Nakano, & Jue, 1980; Yeatts, Crow, & Folts, 1992), and even when they are aware of mental health services, knowledge about how to gain access to services is limited (Cunningham, 1991). Second, as with the older adult population in general, limited financial resources (Cheung & Snowden, 1990; Kang & Kang, 1995; Padgett, 1988; Yeatts et al., 1992), including the lack of access to medical insurance, also serves as a significant barrier to treatment. Third, the Western model of therapy is not consistent with Asian cultural norms (Kang & Kang, 1995). Traditional Western counseling practices that conflict with Asian cultural norms include the typically unstructured nature of the therapy and the expectations that clients exhibit openness and psychological mindedness; share intimate personal details; focus on insight rather than problem solving (Sue & Sue, 2003). Lastly, the lack of bilingual mental health professionals and service providers trained in culturally appropriate treatment strategies are profession-generated barriers to treatment (Kang & Kang, 1995).

Culturally appropriate treatment interventions. Many Asian American elders and their families perceive mental health problems as conditions that bring shame on the family (Kleinman, 1986). As a result of the stigma associated with mental health problems, it is no surprise that research on service utilization indicates that Asian Americans in general have lower rates of utilization of mental health services than other ethnic groups (Tsai, Teng, & Sue, 1981). Yamamoto et al. (1996) found that Asian Americans who were seen at psychiatry clinics were very rarely self-referred or referred by their families. This suggests that it is important for mental health practitioners to bring mental health services to the Asian American community in order to prevent and treat common mental health problems, as well as reduce the stigma associated with mental health problems.

Providing psychoeducational material to Asian American communities has been shown to be an effective, culturally appropriate strategy to educate Asian American older adults and their families about mental health issues. Language-specific educational material has been shown to reduce the stigma of mental illness (Watari & Gatz, 2004), improve knowledge of warning signs of mental health problems (Shelley et al., 2004), and increase the use of mental health services (Watari & Gatz, 2004) among Asian American elders.

Cognitive behavioral therapy (CBT) has been found to be effective with Chinese American older adults. The effectiveness of a CBT package developed by Ricardo Muñoz was examined with non-patient, community-dwelling Chinese Americans older than age 40 (Dai et al., 1999). A Chinese language manual reviewing the content of eight "classes" was provided to the participants. The experimental group, who received CBT, showed significant improvement as indicated by their pre-post Hamilton Depression Scale scores and scores on the Somatic subscale in the Hamilton Anxiety Scale; such improvement was not seen in the control group. Thus, CBT may be an effective treatment approach for treating depression among Chinese American elders when presented in a psychoeducational class format.

Culture-specific treatment interventions also should be considered when working with Asian American older adults. Itai and McRae (1994) discuss the possible benefits of using therapy techniques developed in Japan when working with Japanese American older adults. For example, Morita therapy was developed to treat anxiety-related disorders, and Naikan therapy emphasizes introspection. Other nontraditional forms of therapy that might be culturally appropriate when working with Japanese American elders include dance movement therapy, horticultural therapy, and food therapy (Itai & McRae, 1994).

Guidelines for working with Asian American elders. To determine the most effective treatment approach to working with Asian American elders, it is important to be knowledgeable about how to work with older adults, in general, as well as have a solid understanding of the impact of Asian American culture on the therapeutic process (Iwamasa, 2003). The American Psychological Association (1998) published general principles for conducting psychological interventions with older adult clients:

1. Older adults tend to be referred by a third party, so it is important to assess their understanding and expectations of treatment.

2. Embarrassment, shame, and stigma concerning mental health treatment need to be addressed more often with older adults.

3. Older adults may need more education regarding the process of mental health treatment.

4. Psychologists need to be aware of possible sensory deficits that might interfere with communication.

5. Psychologists should work with the client's other service providers, whenever possible, to coordinate care.

6. Psychologists themselves need to be aware of their own negative biases or stereotypes about older adults.

The next step is to examine the effectiveness of these principles with Asian American elders.

Itai and McRae (1994) wrote one of the few overview articles on counseling older Asian American clients. They discussed basic counseling strategies for working with Japanese American older adults in terms of preparation for counseling, early stages of counseling, access to services, ethical issues, diagnostic concerns, and culture-specific interventions. When preparing a client for counseling, it is important to understand significant aspects of culture, specifically the role of respect, because demonstrating knowledge of the culture will determine the credibility of the counselor and outcome of treatment. Additionally, in the preparation phase, it is important to educate the client about the therapy process and expectations for therapy.

According to Itai and McRae (1994), during the early stages of counseling, the counselor should discuss the rationale for therapy and cost of counseling. It is imperative to create a safe environment to foster self-disclosure and to be flexible when helping the client establish therapeutic goals. Therapy goals may not adhere to the Western values of individualism but instead may be family-oriented. In order to facilitate access to services, counseling services should be offered within the Asian American community, or transportation to services should be available. Another aspect of therapy that should be discussed early on is the structure and length of therapy. Most Asian American elders would probably not be interested in an unstructured and long-term treatment approach. Clarifying the role of silence during therapy also should be done prior to using it as a treatment technique. Silence can be interpreted as a sign of respect, identify confusion or boredom, or signify resistance to counseling.

Two primary ethical issues that might arise during therapy with Japanese American older adults include confidentiality and gift giving. Such issues should be addressed when the occasion arises in treatment. Counselors working with Japanese American elders also need to be cautious when making a clinical diagnosis: Depending on the client's situation, Western diagnostic criteria may not be culturally appropriate. Lastly, it is important to learn about culture-specific treatment interventions that might be appropriate to use with Japanese American clients based on their conceptualization of mental illness, such as those techniques derived from Morita and Naikan therapy.

CONCLUSION

In this chapter, we provided a summary of existing psychological research on Asian American older adults. We reviewed issues related to research methodology and several topics on which research exists. Clearly, more research on Asian Americans is needed, as both Asian American psychology and geropsychology have largely ignored this increasing group. Qualls and Abeles (2000) discuss the importance of understanding the aging process given the "aging revolution" occurring in the United States. We agree and hope this chapter will inspire others to conduct further research on Asian American elders, so that we can better understand their life experiences. That understanding will influence our research and the services we provide to them.

REFERENCES

American Association of Retired Persons (AARP) Minority Affairs. (1995). *A portrait of older minorities*. Retrieved September 26, 2005, from http://www.aarp.org/research/reference/minorities/aresearch-import-509.html#

American Psychiatric Association. (1994). *Diagnostic and statistical manual of mental disorders* (4th ed.). Washington, DC: Author.

American Psychological Association. (1998). *What practitioners should know about working with older adults*. Washington, DC: Author.

Aroian, K. J., Wu, B., & Tran, T. V. (2005). Health care and social service use among Chinese immigrant elders. *Research in Nursing and Health, 28,* 95–105.

Atchley, R. C. (1989). A continuity theory of normal aging. *The Gerontologist, 29,* 183–190.

Bartels, S. J., Coakley, E., Oxman, T. E., Constantino, G., Oslin, D., Chen, H., et al. (2002). Suicidal and death ideation in older primary care patients with depression, anxiety, and at-risk alcohol use. *American Journal of Geriatric Psychiatry, 10*(4), 417–427.

Bond, G. E., Burr, R., McCurry, S. M., Graves, A. B., & Larson, E. B. (2001). Alcohol, aging, and cognitive performance in a cohort of Japanese Americans aged 65 and older: The Kame project. *International Psychogeriatrics, 13*(2), 207–223.

Bond, G. E., Burr, R., McCurry, S. M., Rice, M. M., Borenstein, A. R., Kukull, W. A., et al. (2004). Alcohol, gender, and cognitive performance: A longitudinal study comparing older Japanese and non-Hispanic white Americans. *Journal of Aging and Health, 16*(5), 615–640.

Cheung, F. K., & Snowden, L. R. (1990). Community mental health and ethnic minority populations. *Community Mental Health Journal, 20,* 277–291.

Coon, D. W., Ory, M. G., & Schulz, R. (2003). Family caregivers: Enduring and emergent themes. In D. W. Coon, D. Gallagher-Thompson, & L. W. Thompson (Eds.), *Innovative interventions to reduce dementia caregiver distress: A clinical guide* (pp. 3–27). New York: Springer.

Crandall, R. C. (1980). *Gerontology: A behavioral science approach.* Reading, MA: Addison-Wesley.

Cunningham, C. V. (1991). Reaching minority communities: Factors impacting on success. *Journal of Gerontological Social Work, 17,* 125–135.

Dai, Y., Zhang, S., Yamamoto, J., Ao, M., Belin, T. R., Cheung, F., et al. (1999). Cognitive behavioral therapy of minor depressive symptoms in elderly Chinese Americans: A pilot study. *Community Mental Health Journal, 35*(6), 537–542.

Dickson, G. L., & Kim, J. I. (2003). Reconstructing a meaning of pain: Older Korean American women's experiences with the pain of osteoarthritis. *Qualitative Health Research, 13,* 675–688.

Edgerly, E., Montes, L., Yau, E., Stokes, S. C., & Redd, D. (2003). Ethnic minority caregivers. In D. W. Coon, D. Gallagher-Thompson, & L. W. Thompson (Eds.), *Innovative interventions to reduce dementia caregiver distress: A clinical guide* (pp. 223–242). New York: Springer.

Elliott, K. S., Di Minno, M., Lam, D., & Tu, A. M. (1996). Working with Chinese families in the context of dementia. In G. Yeo & D. Gallagher-Thompson (Eds.), *Ethnicity and the dementias* (pp. 89–108). Washington, DC: Taylor & Francis.

Erikson, E. (1982). *The lifecycle completed: A review.* New York: Norton.

Fried, S. B., & Mehrota, C. M. (1998). *Aging and diversity: An active learning experience.* Washington, DC: Taylor & Francis.

Galanis, D. J., Joseph, C., Masaki, K. H., Petrovitch, H., Ross, G., & White, L. (2000). A longitudinal study of drinking and cognitive performance in elderly Japanese American men: The Honolulu-Asia aging study. *American Journal of Public Health, 90*(8), 1254–1259.

George, L. K. (1990). Social structure, social processes, and social-psychological states. In R. H. Binstock & L. K. George (Eds.), *Handbook of aging and the social sciences* (3rd ed., pp. 186–204). San Diego, CA: Academic Press.

Gutmann, D. (1992). Culture and mental health in later life revisited. In J. E. Birren, R. B. Sloane, & G. D. Cohen (Eds.), *Handbook of mental health and aging* (2nd ed., pp. 75–98). San Diego, CA: Academic Press.

Hee-Soon, J., Miyong, K., Haera, H., Jai, P. R., & Wolmi, H. (2003). Acculturation and cigarette smoking among Korean American men. *Yonsei Medical Journal, 44*(5), 875–882.

Higuchi, S., Parrish, K. M., DuFour, M. C., Towle, L. H., & Harford, T. C. (1994). Relationship between age and drinking patterns and drinking problems among Japanese, Japanese-Americans, and Caucasians. *Alcohol Clinical and Experimental Research, 18*(2), 305–310.

Hilliard, K. M., & Iwamasa, G. Y. (2001). The conceptualization of anxiety: An exploratory study of Japanese American older adults. *Journal of Clinical Geropsychology, 7,* 53–65.

Hinton, L., Guo, Z., Hillygus, J., & Levkoff, S. (2000). Working with culture: A qualitative analysis of barriers to the recruitment of Chinese-American family caregivers for dementia research. *Journal of Cross-Cultural Gerontology, 15,* 119–137.

Itai, G., & McRae, C. (1994). Counseling older Japanese American clients: An overview and observations. *Journal of Counseling and Development, 72,* 373–377.

Iwamasa, G. Y. (2003). Recommendations for the treatment of Asian American/Pacific Islanders. In Council of National Psychological Associations for the Advancement of Ethnic Minority Issues (Eds.), *Psychological treatment of ethnic minority populations.* Washington, DC: Association of Black Psychologists.

Iwamasa, G. Y., & Sorocco, K. H. (2002). Aging and Asian Americans: Developing culturally appropriate research methodology. In G. N. Hall & S. Okazaki (Eds.), *Asian American psychology:*

The science of lives in context (pp. 105–130). Washington, DC: American Psychological Association.

Iwamasa, G. Y., Hilliard, K., & Kost, C. (1998). The Geriatric Depression Scale and Japanese American older adults. *Clinical Gerontologist, 19*(3), 13–24.

Iwamasa, G. Y., Hilliard, K. M., & Osato, S. S. (1998). Conceptualizing anxiety and depression: The Japanese American older adult perspective. *Clinical Gerontologist, 19,* 77–93.

Jackson, J. S., Antonucci, T. C., & Gibson, R. C. (1995). Ethnic and cultural factors in research on aging and mental health: A life-course perspective. In D. K. Padgett (Ed.), *Handbook on ethnicity, aging, and mental health* (pp. 22–46). Westport, CT: Greenwood Press.

Kang, T. S., & Kang, G. E. (1995). Mental health status and needs of the Asian American elderly. In D. K. Padget (Ed.), *Handbook on ethnicity, aging, and mental health* (pp. 113–131). Westport, CT: Greenwood Press.

Kiyak, H., & Hooyman, N. R. (1994). Minority and socioeconomic status: Impact on quality of life in aging. In R. P. Abeles, H. C. Gift, & M. G. Ory (Eds.), *Aging and quality of life* (pp. 295–315). New York: Springer.

Kleinman, A. (1977). Depression, somatization, and the "new cross-cultural psychiatry." *Social Science and Medicine, 11,* 3–10.

Kleinman, A. (1986). *Social origins of distress and disease: Depression, neurasthenia and pain in modern China.* New Haven, CT: Yale University Press.

Kleinman, A., Eisenberg, L., & Good, B. (1978). Culture, illness, and care: Clinical lessons from anthropologic and cross-cultural research. *Annals of Internal Medicine, 88,* 251–258.

Kuo, W. H. (1984). Prevalence of depression among Asian Americans. *Journal of Nervous and Mental Disease, 172,* 449–457.

Liu, Y. (2003). Aging service need and use among Chinese American seniors: Intragroup variations. *Journal of Cross-Cultural Gerontology, 18,* 273–301.

Lon, W., Petrovitch, H., Ross, G., Webster, M. D., Masaki, K. H., Abbott, R. D., et al. (1996). Prevalence of dementia in older-Japanese American men in Hawaii: The Honolulu-Asia aging study. *Journal of the American Medical Association, 276*(12), 955–960.

Markides, K. S., & Black, S. A. (1996). Race, ethnicity, and aging: The impact of inequality. In R. H. Binstock & L. K. George (Eds.), *Handbook of aging and the social sciences,* (4th ed., pp. 153–170). San Diego, CA: Academic Press.

Marsella, A. J., Kinzie, J., & Gordon, P. (1973). Ethnocultural variations in the expression of depression. *Journal of Cross-Cultural Psychology, 4,* 453–458.

Matsumoto, D. (1996). *Culture and psychology.* Pacific Grove, CA: Brooks/Cole.

Meyer, T., Miller, M., Metzger, R., & Borkovec, T. (1990). Development and validation of the Penn State Worry Questionnaire. *Behaviour Research and Therapy, 28,* 487–495.

Min, J. W. (2005). Preference for long-term care arrangement and its correlates for older Korean Americans. *Journal of Aging and Health, 17,* 363–395.

Moon, J. H., & Pearl, J. H. (1991). Alienation of elderly Korean American immigrants as related to place of residence, gender, age, years of education, time in the U.S., living with or without children, and living with or without a spouse. *International Journal of Aging and Human Development, 32*(2), 115–124.

Mouanoutoua, V. L., & Brown, L. G. (1995). Hopkins symptom checklist-25, Hmong version: A screening instrument for psychological distress. *Journal of Personality Assessment, 64*(2), 376–383.

Nicassio, P. M., & Pate, J. K. (1984). An analysis of problems of resettlement of the Indochinese refugees in the United States. *Social Psychiatry, 19*(3), 135–141.

Narikiyo, T. A., & Kameoka, V. A. (1992). Attributions of mental illness and judgments about help seeking among Japanese-American and white American students. *Journal of Counseling Psychology, 39,* 363–368.

Padgett, D. (1988). Aging minority women: Issues in research and health policy. *Women and Health, 14,* 213–225.

Park, D. C., Nisbett, R., & Hedden, T. (1999). Aging, culture, and cognition. *Journals of Gerontology: Series B: Psychological Sciences & Social Sciences, 54B,* 75–84.

Qualls, S. H., & Abeles, N. (2000). *Psychology and the aging revolution: How we adapt to longer life.* Washington, DC: American Psychological Association.

Robins, L. N., Helzer, J. E., Croughan, J., & Ratcliff, K. (1981). National Institute of Mental Health diagnostic interview schedule: Its history, characteristics, and validity. *Archives of General Psychiatry, 38,* 381–389.

Ross, G., Webster, M. D., Abbott, R. D., Petrovitch, H., Masaki, K. H., Murdaugh, C., et al. (1997). Frequency and characteristics of silent dementia among elderly Japanese-American men: the Honolulu-Asia aging study. *Journal of the American Medical Association, 277*(10), 800–805.

Rumbaut, R. (1985). Mental health and the refugee experience: A comparative study of Southeast Asian refugees. In Tom Owan (Ed.), *Southeast Asian mental health: Treatment prevention, services, training, and research* (pp. 433–456). Washington, DC: U.S. Department of Health and Human Services.

Ryan, A. S. (1985). Cultural factors in casework with Chinese-Americans. *Social Casework, 66,* 333–340.

Salcido, R. M., Nakano, C., & Jue, S. (1980). The use of formal and informal health and welfare services of the Asian-American elderly: An exploratory study. *California Sociologist, 3,* 213–229.

Shelley, D., Fahs, M., Scheinmann, R., Swain, S., Qu, J., & Burton, D. (2004). Acculturation and tobacco use among Chinese Americans. *American Journal of Public Health, 94*(2), 300–307.

Sorocco, K. H., Kinoshita, L., & Gallagher-Thompson, D. (2005). Mental health and aging: Current trends and future directions. In J. Maddux & B. Winstead (Eds.), *Psychopathology: Contemporary issues, theory, and research.* Mahwah, NJ: Lawrence Erlbaum.

Sue, D. W., & Sue, D. (2003). *Counseling the culturally diverse: Theory and practice* (4th ed.). New York: Wiley.

Suen, L. J., & Tusaie, K. (2004). Is somatization a significant depressive symptom in older Taiwanese Americans? *Geriatric Nursing, 25*(3), 157–163.

Sung, K. (1990). A new look at filial piety. *The Gerontologist, 30,* 610–617.

Takeshita, J., Masaki, K., Ahmed, I., Foley, D. J., Qing Li, Y., Chen, R., et al. (2002). Are depressive symptoms a risk factor for mortality in elderly Japanese American men? The Honolulu-Asia aging study. *American Journal of Psychiatry, 159*(7), 1127–1132.

Takeuchi, D. T., & Young, K. N. J. (1994). Overview of Asian and Pacific Islander Americans. In N. W. S. Zane, D. T. Takeuchi, & K. N. Y. Young (Eds.), *Confronting critical issues of Asian and Pacific Islander Americans* (pp. 3–21). Thousand Oaks, CA: Sage.

Tang, T. S., Solomon, L. J., & McCracken, L. M. (2000). Cultural barriers to mammography, clinical breast exam and breast self-exam among Chinese-American women 60 and older. *Preventive Medicine: An International Journal Devoted to Practice and Theory, 31,* 575–583.

Tanjasiri, S. P., Wallace, S. P., & Shibata, K. (1995). Picture imperfect: Hidden problems among Asian Pacific Islander elderly. *The Gerontologist, 35,* 753–760.

Tempo, P. M., & Saito, A. (1996). Techniques for working with Japanese American families. In G. Yeo & D. Gallagher-Thompson (Eds.), *Ethnicity and the dementias* (pp. 109–122). Washington, DC: Taylor & Francis.

Tran, T. V. (1991). Family living arrangement and social adjustment among three ethnic groups of elderly Indochinese refugees. *International Journal of Aging and Human Development, 32,* 91–102.

Tran, T. V. (1990). Language acculturation among older Vietnamese refugee adults. *The Gerontologist, 30,* 94–99.

Tsai, M., Teng, N. L., & Sue, S. (1981). Mental health status of Chinese in the U.S. In L. Maldonado & J. Moore (Eds.), *Urban ethnicity in the U.S.* (pp. 211–247). Beverly Hills, CA: Sage.

Uba, L. (1994). *Asian Americans: Personality patterns, identity, and mental health.* New York: Guilford Press.

U.S. Census Bureau. (2001). *Total population by age, race, and Hispanic or Latino origin for the United States: 2000.* Retrieved July 12, 2005, from http://www.census.gov/population/cen2000/phc-t9/tab01.pdf

Van Steenberg, C., Ansak, M. L., & Chin-Hansen, J. (1993). On Lok's model: Managed long-term care. In C. M. Barresi & D. E. Stull (Eds.), *Ethnic elderly and long-term care* (pp. 178–190). New York: Springer.

Watari, K., & Brodbeck, C. (1996). *A comparison of worry in older Japanese Americans and older European Americans.* Poster presented at the 30th Annual Meeting of the Association for the Advancement of Behavior Therapy, New York.

Watari, K., & Gatz, M. (2004). Pathways to care for Alzheimer's disease among Korean Americans. *Cultural Diversity & Ethnic Minority Psychology, 10,* 23–38.

Wisocki, P. (1995). The Worry Scale-Revised. Unpublished manuscript.

Yamamoto, J., Chung, C., Nukariya, K., Ushijima, S., Kim, J. H., Dai, Y., et al. (1996). *Depression, prevention, suicide prevention.* Paper presented at the 149th Annual Meeting of the American Psychiatric Association, New York.

Yamamoto, J., Machizawa, S., Araki, F., Recce, S., Steinberg, A., Leung, J., et al. (1985). Mental health of elderly Asian Americans in Los Angeles. *American Journal of Social Psychiatry, 1,* 37–46.

Yamamoto, J., Silva, J., & Chang, C. Y. (1998). Transitions in Asian-American elderly. In G. H. Pollock & S. I. Greenspan (Eds.), *The course of life: Vol. 7. Completing the journey* (pp. 135–159). Madison, CT: International Universities Press.

Yeatts, D. E., Crow, T., & Folts, E. (1992). Service use among low-income minority elderly: Strategies for overcoming barriers. *The Gerontologist, 32,* 24–32.

Yee, B. W. K. (1997). The social and cultural context of adaptive aging by Southeast Asian elders. In J. Sokolovsky (Ed.), *The cultural context of aging: Worldwide perspectives* (pp. 293–303). Westport, CT: Bergin & Garvey.

Yee, D. (1997). Issues and trends affecting Asian Americans, women, and aging. In J. M. Coyle (Ed.), *Handbook on women and aging* (pp. 316–334). Westport, CT: Greenwood Press.

Yeo, G., & Gallagher-Thompson, D. (Eds.). (1996). *Ethnicity and the dementias.* Washington, DC: Taylor & Francis.

Yesavage, J. A., Brink T. L., Rose, T. L., Lum, O., Huang, V., Adey, M., et al. (1983). Development and validation of a geriatric depression screening scale: A preliminary report. *Journal of Psychiatric Research, 17,* 37–49.

Yeung, A., Chan, R., Mischoulon, D., Sonawalla, S., Wong, E., Nierenberg, A. A., et al. (2004). Prevalence of major depressive disorder among Chinese Americans in primary care. *General Hospital Psychiatry, 26,* 24–30.

Yeung, A., Howarth, S., Chan, R., Sonawalla, S., Nierenberg, A. A., & Fava, M. (2002). Use of the Chinese version of the Beck Depression Inventory for screening depression in primary care. *Journal of Nervous and Mental Disease, 190*(2), 94–99.

Ying, Y. W. (1988). Depressive symptomatology among Chinese-Americans as measured by the CES-D. *Journal of Clinical Psychology, 44,* 739–746.

Yu, E. S. H., Kim, K., Liu, W. T., & Wong, S. C. (1993). Functional abilities of Chinese and Korean elders in congregate housing. In C. M. Barresi & D. E. Stull (Eds.), *Ethnic elderly and long-term care* (pp. 87–100). New York: Springer.

Zhan, L. (2004). Caring for family members with Alzheimer's disease: Perspectives from Chinese American caregivers. *Journal of Gerontological Nursing, 30*(8), 19–29.

14

ASIAN IMMIGRANTS AND REFUGEES

RITA CHI-YING CHUNG

FRED BEMAK

The U.S. Census 2000 showed that one in ten people in the United States come from an immigrant/refugee background and that one in five people was either born in another country or has at least one parent who was born outside the United States. The Asian American population is one of the fastest-growing ethnic groups in the United States, in part due to the Asian immigrant and refugee population (Reeves & Bennett, 2004). Asian immigrants account for 8.9 million, or 26%, of the foreign-born population in the United States (Capps & Passel, 2004). Given these statistics, it is vital that mental health professionals understand the challenges encountered by this group in order to work effectively with this population. Although immigrants and refugees encounter similar experiences in adjustment and adaptation, refugees have unique experiences that define them as refugees. Therefore, to clearly understand this population, it is important to first distinguish between immigrant and refugee status.

Hence, we begin the chapter with a brief discussion on the differences between immigrants and refugees and follow it with a brief overview of the unique challenges encountered by refugees. Given that there are similarities in the postmigration psychosocial adjustment and adaptation process for both groups, in the next section we discuss the commonalities in the adjustment process as they relate to both Asian immigrants and refugees and explore psychosocial adjustment and adaptation challenges. Whereas other chapters in the handbook review barriers to mental health services, differing cultural beliefs, and cultural responsive techniques for helping Asian Americans who seek mental health services, this chapter addresses the unique experiences of refugees and immigrants as they relate to mental health and help-seeking behavior. We end the chapter with a brief overview of the current issues encountered by this population, such as Asian gangs and intergenerational conflict.

IMMIGRANTS VERSUS REFUGEES

As stated in the introduction, it is critical to make a clear distinction between immigrant and refugee status. Immigrants voluntarily migrate to other countries seeking better economic, political, social, cultural, educational conditions, and religious freedom. In contrast, refugees involuntarily migrate to another country, usually as a result of war, persecution, or disaster. To distinguish between the two groups, Murphy (1977) used the phrase "forced versus free" migration. Within the Asian American population, Southeast Asian refugees were forced to leave their country due to the Vietnam War and associated fighting in Cambodia and Laos. Subsequently, the Southeast Asian refugees consist mainly of Cambodians, Vietnamese, Hmong, and Laotians. Their departure from their home countries was due to events outside of their own control and was sudden, involuntary, and forced. This group differs from other Asian immigrants or sojourners in the involuntary nature of their departure from their home country (Chung & Bemak, 2006). To fully understand the challenges encountered by Southeast Asian refugees and how the refugee experience differs from that of immigrants who voluntarily migrate to another country, it is important to understand the historical and sociopolitical context surrounding this population. In the next section, therefore, we provide a brief overview of the Southeast Asian refugee experience.

SOUTHEAST ASIAN REFUGEES: HISTORICAL PERSPECTIVE

Even though the Vietnam War ended approximately 30 years ago, the challenges of Southeast Asian refugees in the United States are still prominent issues. After the end of the war in 1975, due to political turmoil and genocide, there was a mass exodus of Southeast Asian refugees. Over 1.5 million fled their homes and sought refuge in the United States. This resulted in the Southeast Asian refugee population becoming one of the fastest-growing ethnic groups in the United States (Chung & Bemak, 2006). The Southeast Asians entered the United States in two main time periods. Each group had different demographic characteristics and premigration experiences, which had a bearing on their postmigration adjustment to the United States. The first wave of Southeast Asian Americans was mainly Vietnamese and tended to be relatively well educated, was generally affiliated with the U.S. government and military in Vietnam, and consequently had a degree of English proficiency (Chung & Bemak, 2006). During the fall of Saigon, due to their close association with the U.S. forces, South Vietnamese forces, or both, this group was assisted by the American government and hastily evacuated by helicopters or sea-lifts (Chung & Okazaki, 1991). The first wave left Vietnam prior to the fall of Saigon in 1975 and entered the United States directly from Vietnam or from refugee camps.

Similar to other Western resettlement countries after the Vietnam War, the United States felt a responsibility and obligation to resettle this population. Between 1978 and 1980, the second main wave of Southeast Asian refugees entered the United States. This wave consisted of mainly Vietnamese, Laotians, Hmong, and Cambodians. Unlike their first wave counterparts, these refugees made hazardous escapes by sea or through the jungle in life-threatening circumstances. The Vietnamese left their country in small, overcrowded, and poorly constructed boats, and were known as the "boat people." This group was subjected to brutal attacks by sea pirates; many were raped and killed or otherwise victims of severe violence (Chung & Okazaki, 1991). The Cambodians, Hmong, and Laotians escaped by land through jungles, crossing mine fields and avoiding ambushes and hence death by military soldiers. During their flight, they experienced tropical diseases, death, hunger, starvation, and exhaustion. Their escape to refugee camps in nearby countries, such as Thailand, the Philippines, or Hong Kong, compounded their traumatic war and escape experiences, as they were forced to wait in overcrowded and unsanitary refugee camps for periods of time ranging from months to years before they were permanently resettled in the United States or other resettlement countries (Chung & Bemak, 2006).

After the fall of Saigon in 1975, the political repression intensified in Cambodia, Vietnam, and Laos. Many in the second wave experienced or witnessed atrocities, genocide, brutal beatings, violence, sexual abuse, rape, and starvation. They were victims of incarceration and torture and were forced to commit human atrocities themselves (Mollica, Wyshak, & Lavelle, 1987). Unfortunately, the violence, sexual abuse, and rape continued in the refugee camps (Mollica & Jalbert, 1989), with frequent incidents of domestic violence, beatings, rapes, knifings and axings, and suicide. A well-known example of the degree of atrocities and genocide experienced by the second wave is the Cambodian "killing fields." The Pol Pot Khmer Rouge government orchestrated mass genocide, violence, and atrocities on the Cambodian people from 1975 to 1979 (Chung, 2001). An estimated one to three million of Cambodia's seven million people died from execution, starvation, or illness, resulting in the virtual extermination of Cambodian people and culture (Kinzie & Leung, 1989; White, 1982). Hence, the second wave experienced multiple traumatic events before migrating to the United States.

Due to the influx of the second, and subsequent, waves of Southeast Asian refugees, the U.S. government initially made an effort to cluster the refugees throughout the country so as not to overburden any particular community (Chung & Okazaki, 1991). However, this population undertook a secondary migration and moved from their original resettlement areas in search of warmer weather, better opportunities, closer family ties, and larger refugee communities (S. Nguyen, 1982). Although this population settled in every state in the United States, they are especially concentrated in 14 states, including California, Texas, and Washington (Chung & Okazaki, 1991). To date, Southeast Asians are the largest refugee group (36% of all refugees who arrived since 1983) among recent arrivals (ORR, 2001).

The second wave tended to be less educated than the first wave and came with minimal or no English language skills. Many, especially those from the rural areas, had little or no exposure to Western culture prior to arriving in the United States (Chung & Okazaki, 1991). The first wave of Southeast Asian refugees came with less premigration trauma, more education, and more wealth and resources than the second wave, which had fewer professional skills, minimal or no language skills, and no financial safety net or savings (S. Nguyen, 1982). Given the differences between the first and second waves during their escape and premigration experiences, the first wave of Southeast Asian Americans adjusted more successfully than the second wave (Chung & Bemak, 2006). According to the Office of Refugee Resettlement Annual Report to Congress (2001), only 33% of the refugees who entered the United States in the late 1980s and early 1990s were employed.

IMPACT OF PREMIGRATION TRAUMA ON PSYCHOSOCIAL ADJUSTMENT

Studies show a relationship between the premigration trauma experiences and the level of adjustment and adaptation to the United States, a country that is significantly different from Southeast Asia (Bemak, 1989; Chung & Bemak, 2006; Chung & Kagawa-Singer, 1993; K. M. Lin, Masuda, & Tazuma, 1982; Nicholson, 1997). The challenge this population encountered can be measured by the frequency and severity of premigration traumatic experiences and the level of difficulty in adjusting to the United States. Consequently, it is critical to be aware of, acknowledge, and understand the actual premigration traumatic experiences of Southeast Asians and their linkage with psychosocial adjustment and adaptation during postmigration. A good illustration of the interaction between premigration trauma and postmigration adjustment is that of some older Cambodian women, who displayed nonorganic or psychosomatic blindness in the United States (Van Boemel & Rozee, 1992). The number of years the women were interned in the refugee camps and the degree and level of traumatic events they experienced resulted in subjective visual impairment.

Many refugees experienced multiple traumatic events. These situations were not single isolated incidents but rather multiple events experienced during the war, the escape process, and in refugee camps (Mollica & Jalbert, 1989). This population's premigration traumatic events were classified into four categories: (a) deprivation (e.g., food and shelter), (b) physical injury and torture, (c) incarceration and reeducation camps, and (d) witnessing killing, experiencing torture, or both (Mollica, Lavelle, & Khoun, 1985). Understanding the relationship between premigration traumatic experiences and postmigration adjustment is critical, in that it not only affects the individual and his or her family but also may have a long-term impact. That is, the premigration experiences of Southeast Asian Americans may affect future generations through the effects of intergenerational trauma (Apprey, 1998; Nagata, 1998).

Once they migrated to the United States, Southeast Asian refugees, like other refugees, employed familiar coping strategies based on skills that they had mastered in their home countries (Bemak, 1989). Trying to transpose these skills to a very new and different country oftentimes presented problems and resulted in behaviors that could be viewed as inappropriate and peculiar (Chung & Bemak, 2006). For example, Cambodians learned to survive the oppressive conditions of the Pol Pot regime by complying with sometimes brutal orders without showing any signs of reaction, asking questions, or complaining. Speaking up or showing any signs of intelligence or feeling resulted in instantaneous torture or death. Therefore, learning to "act dumb," that is, appearing to be deaf, foolish, stupid, confused, or dumb, was a means of survival (Mollica & Jalbert, 1989). To duplicate these coping skills by "acting dumb" or unresponsive in the United States would be inappropriate and may even be viewed as antisocial and pathological (Stein, 1986). Postmigration allowed refugees to feel safe enough psychologically to subsequently change their former coping strategies. Thus, the Cambodians relearned how to express feelings and express personal reactions. Similar to Cambodian refugees, Vietnamese Amerasians (children with American fathers and Vietnamese mothers) survived harsh conditions by developing strong defenses and by showing no physical or psychological reactions while in Vietnam. However, once they were in the United States and began to experience personal, familial, and psychological safety, they began to display more openness and to develop new coping strategies that were antithetical to their past ways of behaving. This has been termed the *psychological recoil effect* (Bemak & Chung, 1998).

At-Risk Groups

Specific subgroups within this population have been identified as being at high risk for developing serious mental health problems due to their unique premigration experiences and/or postmigration challenges. One group is the elderly, who, in general, have a more difficult time during postmigration adjustment. This group was accustomed to their daily routines and lives in their home countries. The change of well-established routines and patterns, the demands of learning a new language and new customs, and the change of the very foundation for daily survival is an enormous challenge for the elderly. Coming to terms with changes in socioeconomic status at a later stage in life—which frequently results in not being able to maintain the same lifestyle, financial stature, and subsequent position as a family and community elder that they may have held in their home country—compounds the situation. Studies have found a correlation between limited English proficiency, employment status, and depression (Chung & Kagawa-Singer, 1993; Hinton, Tiet, Tran, & Chesney, 1997). The inability to speak English in the United States frequently presented unique problems for the elderly, who were already limited in finding adequate employment. Simultaneously, the elderly are faced with changing family dynamics (Buchwald et al., 1993; Chung & Bemak, 2006; Chung & Kawaga-Singer, 1993; Yee, 1992). As the younger generations acculturate more quickly and become "cultural brokers" for the family, the elderly lose stature and credibility within the family and community and can no longer offer guidance or wisdom in the new environment.

A second group identified as being at high risk is women, in large part due to their premigration war experiences of rape, sexual abuse, and other violence (Refugee Women in Development, 1990). Their premigration experiences created significant challenges in successful postmigration adjustment. Within this group, Cambodian women were found to be at greater risk for developing serious mental health problems (Chung, 2001), experiencing nearly nine times more trauma than other Southeast Asian American groups (Mollica et al., 1985). In a community sample of 300 Cambodian women (mean age 38 years) who have lived in the United States for an average of 3.68 years, 22% reported death of a spouse and 53% reported loss or death of other family members (Chung, 2001). In another study using a clinical population, 95% of the Cambodian women reported that they had been sexually abused or raped (Caspi, Pool, Mollica, & Frankel, 1998). Furthermore, three subgroups were identified as being at extreme risk for developing serious psychological problems: (a) those who were raped or victims of sexual abuse, (b) those who were widowed, and (c) those who lost their children.

A third at-risk group within this population is children and adolescents. Those adolescents who arrived in the United States in the second wave were found to have more difficulties with adjustment compared to those who arrived in the first wave (Chung, Bemak, & Wong, 2000). This was, in large part, due to their age at arrival. The average age of the first wave was 3 years, compared to an average age of 11 for the second wave. The results also found that the first wave was more acculturated and reported better quality of social support. Because research has found a correlation between parents' and children's psychological well-being, the greater degree of premigration trauma experienced by the second wave parents may contribute also to higher degrees of at-risk behavior for second wave youth. Two other groups of children were identified as at risk for developing serious psychological problems: (a) unaccompanied minors (those who migrated alone because of loss or separation of family members) and (b) Vietnamese Amerasians (who experienced significant discrimination in Vietnam because of their American fathers) (Chung & Bemak, 2006; Bemak & Chung, 1998, 1999).

Psychological Distress

It is not surprising to find that premigration trauma is a major predictor of psychological distress for Southeast Asian refugees (Chung & Kagawa-Singer, 1993; Hinton et al., 1997; Mollica et al., 1987). The major psychological problems exhibited by this group are post-traumatic stress disorder (PTSD), depression, somatization, and suicide (Chung & Kagawa-Singer, 1995; Fawzi et al., 1997; Nicholson, 1997). Studies have found that there may be a delay in the onset of PTSD and other manifestations of premigration trauma, as this group initially coped with postmigration tasks of finding employment and housing (Sack, Him, & Dickason, 1999). Nevertheless, it was clearly established that premigration trauma has a long-standing, negative impact on mental health after resettlement (Chung & Kagawa-Singer, 1993; Hauff & Valgum, 1995; Hinton et al., 1997).

Associated with resettlement and premigration trauma is the issue of loss and grief. Loss of family ties and family support has been correlated with psychological distress (Barudy, 1989; Bemak & Chung, 1998) and demonstrated in studies, such as the study of children in Bosnia-Herzegovina that found a relationship between the loss of a loved one and self-reported grief (Dyregov & Yule, 1995). The literature on refugee mental health has clearly identified the effect of losing one's family, friends, community, livelihood, culture, and language on psychological well-being (Bemak, 1989; Bemak & Chung, 2000; Chung, 2001; Chung & Bemak, 2006).

There are also intergroup differences in the level of distress experienced by this population. Cambodians were found to experience greater psychological distress compared to other Southeast Asian groups (Chung, 2001; Chung & Bemak, 2002b; Chung & Kagawa-Singer, 1993; Mollica et al., 1987), which has been attributed to their experiences during the Pol Pot regime. In comparison, the Vietnamese and Chinese-Vietnamese have been found to be the least distressed, which was associated with higher levels of education, better English language skills, the fact that some had managed to arrive with financial assets, and access into the already established Chinatown communities in the United States (Chung & Kagawa-Singer, 1993). It was suggested that there is a correlation between size of ethnic communities and the degree of depression. A larger ethnic community provides more social support, thus buffers stress and reduces depression (Bieser, 1988). There are also gender differences in psychological distress, with women reporting a significantly higher level of psychological distress than their male counterparts (Chung et al., 1998; Chung & Bemak, 2002b).

AN OVERVIEW OF ASIAN AMERICAN IMMIGRANTS

The 2000 census showed that the U.S. population was 281.4 million. One of the fastest-growing ethnic groups is Asian, comprising 4.2% of the total population or 11.9 million people (Reeves & Bennett, 2004). We begin this section with a review of the history of Asian American immigrants, and we follow it with a brief summary of the migration process and, finally, an overview focusing on current demographics and the characteristics of this population.

Historical Perspective of Asian American Immigrants

This section provides only a brief overview of the history of Asian Americans in the United States; more detailed information can be found elsewhere (Takaki, 1998). The first Asians who came to the United States were approximately 100,000 Chinese who immigrated during the California gold rush (Chang, 2003). Between 1848 and 1882, more than 300,000 Chinese arrived in the United States to work in mines and on the railroads (K. Huang, 1991). In the later 1800s, Japanese immigrants came to Hawai'i and worked as cheap laborers on sugar plantations. Asian immigrants encountered discrimination and racism early on in their arrival in the United States. During the economic depression in the 19th century, White laborers killed Chinese competitors and lobbied politicians to pass the Chinese Exclusion Act of 1882. This act had a major effect on the Chinese population, since it stopped Chinese immigration for 80 years, until new legislation was passed in the middle of the 20th century that permitted second and third waves of Chinese immigrants (Chang, 2003). Similarly, in 1907 and 1908, a Gentleman's Agreement placed parallel limits on Japanese and Korean immigration, and in 1917, an immigrant act restricted entry of Asian Indians. Asian immigration restrictions continued with the Tydings-McDuffie Act of 1934, which denied entry to Filipinos in response to concerns by White Americans about growing numbers of Filipino immigrants working as day agricultural laborers in California. During World War II, as anti-Japanese sentiments and fears for national security grew, President Franklin Roosevelt signed Executive Order 9066, which incarcerated over 120,000 people of Japanese heritage, including more than 70,000 U.S.-born citizens (Takaki, 1998).

It was not until the 1965 Immigrant Act, which focused on family reunification, that the second wave of Asian immigrants came to the United States. In 1971, new legislation eliminated all quotas on countries of origin and replaced them with a general limit of 290,000 immigrants a year, opening doors for Asians and changing the ethnic configuration of Asian immigrants. As a result, the Asian American population soared from less than 1% (one million) in 1965 to 2% in 1985. In 1960, there were 52% Japanese, 27% Chinese, 20% Filipino, 1% Korean, and 1% Asian Indian immigrants. In 1985, 21% of Asian Americans were Chinese, 21% Filipino, 15% Japanese, 12% Vietnamese, 11% Korean, 10% Asian Indians, 4% Laotian, 3% Cambodian, and 3% "other" (Takaki, 1998). The second wave was very different from the earlier immigrants in that it included many professionals and people from cities while the first wave was composed of farmers and people from rural areas.

Migration Process

Five stages of the migration process have been identified (Sluzki, 1979). They include (a) preparation; (b) the actual act of migration; (c) the focus is on tasks related to survival and meeting primary needs; (d) the crisis period, when one is confronted with the reality of migrating to a new, foreign culture while trying to integrate the old and new cultures, bringing doubts and disappointment and a sense of loss; and (e) the period of intercultural and intergenerational clashes, characterized by attempts to adjust to a new culture while maintaining traditional cultural values. Children are in a unique position, as exposure and acculturation to differences of the new culture foster questions about their traditional culture and its values. During this final period, Asian families are likely to contact mental health services (L. N. Huang, Ying, & Arganza, 2003).

Current Demographics of Asian Americans

In this section, we discuss the characteristics of Asian Americans based on the U.S. Census 2000 (Reeves & Bennett, 2004). The Census 2000 differs from Census 1990 in that the 1990 category "Asian or Pacific Islanders" were separated into two categories: "Asian" and "Native Hawaiian or other Pacific Islanders." The term *Asian,* according to Census 2000, refers to people having origins in the Far East, Southeast Asia, or the Indian subcontinent, for example,

Cambodia, China, India, Japan, Korea, Malaysia, Pakistan, Philippines, Thailand, and Vietnam. The category is not limited to nationalities but includes ethnic categories as well, such as Hmong. Therefore, this category accounts for as many as 43 different ethnic groups (S. M. Lee, 1998). According to Census 2000, a majority of the Asian American population (49%) lived in the West, with 20% residing in the Northeast, 19% in the South, and 12% in the Midwest. Over half (51%) of this population lived in just three states: California, New York, and Hawaii. The seven states with the next largest Asian population in 2000 were Texas, New Jersey, Illinois, Washington, Florida, Virginia, and Massachusetts. Chinese (2.7 million, or 23.8%) is the largest Asian American group, followed by Filipino Americans (2.4 million, or 18.3%) and Asian Indians (1.9 million or 16.2). Each of the Vietnamese American and Korean American groups accounted for approximately 10% (1.2 million) of the Asian population. Japanese Americans, Cambodians, Hmong, Laotian, Pakistani, and Thai collectively accounted for 15% of the Asian population.

The mean age of the U.S. population is 35.3 years; for Asian Americans the mean age is 32.7. Sixty-nine percent of all Asian Americans were foreign-born, while approximately 40% of Japanese Americans were foreign-born, compared to approximately 75% of Vietnamese, Koreans, Asian Indians, Pakistanis, and Thai. Compared with the total U.S. population (54%), 60% of Asian Americans were married. Over 60% of Asian American households were maintained by married couples, compared with 53% of the U.S. population. However, Cambodians had the highest (21%) proportion of female-headed households with no husband present. The average U.S. household size was 3.2. For Asian Americans the household size ranged from 2.25 for Japanese to 4.41 for Cambodians, 4.23 for Laotian and 6.14 for Hmong. The proportion of Asians who spoke another language other than English at home ranged from 47% for Japanese to 90%–96% for Cambodians, Hmong, Laotians, Pakistanis, and Vietnamese.

Over 80% of Asians had a high school diploma, a percentage similar to that of the general U.S. population. A higher proportion of Asians (44%), compared with the total U.S. population (24%), had earned at least a bachelor's degree. These statistics can be misleading and provide inaccurate support for the model minority myth, since an examination of the intergroup differences showed that there is great heterogeneity within the Asian population. For example, Asian Indians had the highest percentage (64%) with a bachelor's degree and the Japanese had the highest (91%) with at least a high school education. In contrast, approximately 60% of the Hmong, 50% of the Cambodians and Laotians, and 38% of Vietnamese had less than a high school education.

Although 45% of Asians were employed in management, professional, and related occupations (compared with 34% of the U.S. population), the percentage varied among subgroups. For example, the range was from 60% for Asian Indians to less than 20% for Cambodians and Hmong and only 13% of Laotians holding such positions. Similarly, the median Asian family income is higher ($59,300) than that of the total U.S. population ($50,000); however, Asian families have a greater number of people working in their households. Furthermore, Cambodians, Hmong, Vietnamese, Laotians, Koreans, and Thai median family incomes were substantially lower, ranging from $32,400 to $47,624. The poverty rate for Asians and the total U.S. population were similar (12%), even though median earning for Asians was higher. Intergroup differences were such that Hmong (37.8%) had the highest poverty rates, followed by Cambodians (29.3%), Laotians (18.5%), Pakistani (16.5%), and Vietnamese (16%). Filipinos (6.3%), Japanese (9.7%), and Asian Indians (9.8%) had the lowest poverty rates within this population.

Intergroup and Intragroup Differences

Because Asian Americans comprise so many different groups, examining overall statistics for the total Asian American population provides inaccurate and misleading information that does not reflect differences among the subgroups. Although there are similarities among different Asian cultures, there are also differences in the unique challenges encountered by these groups. It is critical to acknowledge, understand, and be aware of the inter- and intragroup differences

234 • SPECIFIC POPULATIONS

within this population (Chung & Bemak, 2002b; Root, 1998). For example, the refugee experience has impacted the Southeast Asian refugees' mental health and psychosocial adjustment (U.S. Department of Health & Human Services, 2001). It is also important to recognize that there are gender differences within and between Asian groups, as well as different experiences between those who are foreign-born versus U.S.-born. Thus, it is important to understand historical, sociopolitical, psychosocial, cultural, and socioeconomic factors that influence immigrant and refugee life experiences. In the next section, we discuss the similarities between immigrants and refugees in their psychosocial adjustment adaptation to the United States.

PSYCHOSOCIAL
ADJUSTMENT CHALLENGES

Any group that migrates to a foreign country will face issues of adjustment and adaptation. Successful adjustment is dependent on how migrants cope with the phases of resettlement (Beiser & Hou, 2001). The general pattern of resettlement typically begins within the first two years, when the focus is on meeting basic needs such as housing and employment. During this period, immigrants may experience a loss of control over decision-making about basic life issues, such as choices about work. Everyday tasks become a challenge: navigating local transportation, handling money, or going shopping have the potential to become major ordeals (Chung & Okazaki, 1991). These difficulties accentuate adaptation difficulties and regrets about leaving one's home country, friends, and family, thus hindering the enthusiasm and optimism that is helpful in acculturation. This in turn may create emotional and psychological problems associated with the loss of one's culture and former identity (Bemak & Chung, 2000). Subsequently, immigrants may undergo acculturative stress (Miranda & Matheny, 2000), a unique type of distress that involves multiple factors in adjusting to a foreign culture and the transformation of one's identity, values, behaviors, cognitions, attitudes, and affect (Berry, 1990; Berry & Anis, 1974; Liebkind, 1996; Miranda & Matheny, 2000).

English Language
Proficiency and Employment

To successfully adapt and adjust in the United States, immigrants must acquire proficiency in English, especially given that education level and English language proficiency correlates with accessing mainstream mental health services (Chung & Lin, 1994). The ability to communicate in English plays a vital role in obtaining gainful employment and influences one's ability to successfully access available resources and opportunities. Thus, Asian immigrants may find themselves in a "catch-22" situation; to find gainful employment, they must have some aptitude in English, yet to become competent in English requires English language classes, which detract from time spent earning money. This is particularly difficult when the immigrant is the sole breadwinner, and family members are dependent on his or her earnings. The problem of language affects 39.5% of the Asian American population, who reported in the 2000 Census that they spoke English "less than very well." Within this population, 62.4% Vietnamese, 58.6% Hmong, 53.5% Cambodian, 52.8% Laotian, 50.5% Korean, and 49.6% Chinese reported that they spoke limited English. Chung and Kagawa-Singer (1993) found that for Southeast Asian refugees, attendance in English language classes was a significant predictor of psychological distress and hypothesized that not only was there a need in many instances to forfeit income to learn English, but that learning English may prove to be a significant challenge for those who were illiterate in their own language. Furthermore, for the refugee population, learning English may be hindered by emotional and mental fatigue and memory and concentration difficulties associated with premigration trauma (Mollica & Jalbert, 1989). Hence, a large percentage of Southeast Asian refugees were dependent on welfare for a long period of time (Chung & Bemak, 1995, 2006).

Even those who are proficient in English may encounter difficulties in obtaining a position reflective of their educational qualifications. Education, training, and skills obtained in one's home country are not necessarily transferable to the United States (even if the immigrant possesses adequate command of English), causing a dramatic change in socioeconomic status (Bemak, Chung, & Pedersen, 2003). This results in immigrants taking jobs for which they are overqualified, causing them to be underemployed and thus experience a relative decrease in social standing. The relative downward economic status, coupled with the Asian cultural value of losing face, causes some Asian immigrants to remain unemployed while waiting for a suitable position that will match their skills (Chung & Bemak, 2006). Although some Asian immigrants do remarkably well, Lin and his colleagues found that only a small percentage of Southeast Asian refugees regained their former socioeconomic status (K. M. Lin, Tazuma, & Masuda, 1979; K. M. Lin, Inui, Kleinman, & Womack, 1982; K. M. Lin, Masuda, et al., 1982).

Changing Family Dynamics

Migration to a foreign country frequently brings about changes in family structure and family dynamics. These changes occur for a number of reasons. If men cannot find employment, or are underemployed, women are forced to seek employment to help meet expenses. Paradoxically, while the men may experience a downward turn in their socioeconomic status, women may experience upward mobility in theirs (Chung & Bemak, 2006). As a result of working outside the home and community, Asian refugee and immigrant women are simultaneously exposed to the American culture and different perspectives regarding gender roles. These new ideas may generate questions about traditionally defined gender roles, and as some women seek greater independence, this may lead to changes in family roles and relationships (Chung & Bemak, 2006). In turn, the changes in gender roles and attitudes may lead to marital conflict as the women assert their authority and control and contribute to the family's financial well-being. This sometimes results in spousal abuse and domestic violence (Luu, 1989). Thus it is no surprise that research shows women acculturating faster than men (Chung et al., 2000).

In some cases, Asian families may not come to the United States as intact family units. One or both parents may come to get established and then bring their spouses, extended family members, and/or children at a later date. In turn,

children may be sent to the United States to live with relatives and be joined by parents and other family members later. The age of the children's migration and the years of separation from their parents may influence their acculturation, psychosocial adjustment, and adaptation (L. N. Huang et al., 2003), causing tension, isolation, loss of traditional family roles and structure, and vulnerability. The fragmentation of Asian families through separation may be particularly challenging given the collectivistic basis of Asian cultures and the emphasis on filial piety and interdependence. This situation may confound the migration process and contribute to potential mental health issues.

Compounding the changing family structure and dynamics is the faster pace of acculturation experienced by children and adolescents (L. N. Huang et al., 2003), who are exposed to immersion in English language training and American customs in school. The more rapid adaptation by youth may reverse traditional family roles so that adults are guided and taught by children how to manage and cope in the new country. As the children support and guide their parents and elders, they assume the role of language and *cultural translators* (Bemak et al., 2003). Children may at times feel ashamed and embarrassed by their parents because they lack English language skills and dress and exhibit "funny" or different behaviors from mainstream culture. Furthermore, children may also be embarrassed to publicly speak in their mother tongue with parents or family members because of the fear of being ridiculed by their American peers (Chung & Bemak, 2006). Thus, the family dynamics may change as children witness a transformation of their parents and other adults from previously competent and autonomous caretakers to potentially overwhelmed and dependent individuals. Of equal importance is the fact that many immigrant and refugee families provide social support that is essential in successful adjustment and acculturation and play a vital role in transmitting culture to younger family members.

Child-Rearing Practices

Adding to family stress are traditional child-rearing practices that are sometimes misunderstood in the United States. Barriers against raising children in ways that have been culturally acceptable for generations may add to Asian immigrants' feelings of being diminished as parents and community members. Traditional disciplinary practices that use corporal punishment and healing methods may be prohibited by U.S. laws and viewed as forms of abuse. For example, coining is a traditional healing method that leaves temporary bruises on the body. Due to the lack of knowledge of this Asian traditional form of healing, there have been reports of child and elderly abuse by teachers and health and social service workers (Chung & Bemak, 2006). Cultural practices such as coining may hinder successful adjustment and adaptation. This may be further compounded by intergenerational conflict between parents and children, as the youth acculturate more rapidly and attempt to balance new values and peer norms with parental and community traditional values and practices that are rooted in long standing cultural traditions (Ying, 1999; Ying & Chao, 1996). Parents who believe in obedience and respect for elders, based on Confucianism, where a strong emphasis is placed on family roles, proper behavior, clear expectations, and harmony, may find their world shaken by children who openly question their authority, rules, and values. In an attempt to maintain traditional values, parents may revert to stricter practices, sometimes causing more tension and problems within the family. Regardless, many Asian immigrant parents experience the loss of traditional authority and control as their children become more outspoken and challenge their authority and the "old culture" (Chung & Bemak, 2006).

School

Educational data presented previously clearly shows a disparity within the Asian population with regard to educational attainment. Regardless of the level of educational attainment, Asian students encounter similar problems in schools. Although Asian immigrant and refugee children may want to acculturate and to adopt U.S. customs and values, this may prove to be very challenging. Not only might there be a lack of acceptance by American peers, but racial prejudice, discrimination, and harassment that includes fights, being punched, mimicked, or even robbed by non-Asian students may also occur in schools (L. N. Huang, 1989). In addition, the norms regulating classroom and school behavior are typically different from those in their home countries. Although the acquisition of a new language is one of the most important variables in acculturation, it is also closely related to other issues associated with adjustment. Learning English may symbolize rejection of their native language and hence their traditional culture (Bemak & Chung, 2003), and older children who immigrate to the United States may find learning English as a second language stressful.

Some parents see education as a tool for upward mobility, hence their decision to immigrate to the United States. They push children to achieve academically at the expense of other extracurricular activities. Not being permitted to participate in school activities outside of the classroom combined with the desire to belong and adjust may generate internalized and externalized tensions and conflicts for Asian children and adolescents that result in psychological problems (Chung & Bemak, 2006). Furthermore, it has been found that poor psychological health of parents has a negative impact on children's psychosocial adjustment and academic achievement, resulting in increased high school dropout rates and low grade point averages (Ima & Rumbaut, 1989; Rumbaut, 1989).

Racism

Not only did Asians encounter racism over 150 years ago during migration, but also they continue to encounter discrimination and racism today. The pain of the Vietnam War is still strong within the American psyche, as are the fears of Communism and espionage, evident in the recent Wen Ho Lee alleged spy incident. Subsequently, Asian migrants may encounter hostility and racism in the United States (U.S. Commission on Civil Rights, 1992), which may manifest as resentment towards Asian immigrants based on the perception that services, resources, and jobs are being taken away from American citizens (Young & Takeuchi, 1998).

In addition, there may be resentment because of government support and assistance to immigrant groups as they make the transition to self-sufficiency and economic independence.

Because Asian immigrants and refugees are one of the principal groups migrating to the United States, they may experience racism and discrimination, which are exacerbated during economic difficulties or national crises. For example, in 2001, there was a 23% increase in reported hate crimes against Asian Pacific Americans (National Asian Pacific American Legal Consortium, 2001). The increase was primarily a backlash after September 11, 2001. Another form of discrimination is evident in the "bamboo ceiling" (similar to the "glass ceiling"), where Asians who attain professional positions are prevented from advancing to top managerial positions due to the stereotype that links Asians with poor communication and leadership skills. More insidious is that Asian Americans may internalize this type of racism (Steele & Aronson, 1995). Frank Wu (2002), a prominent lawyer and author, stated that Asians, including those who have been in the U.S. for multiple generations, are seen as the perpetual foreigner. This is based on the ongoing overt and covert racism and discrimination that are regularly encountered by Asian Americans.

Gangs

One of the growing concerns in the Asian immigrant and refugee population is youth gang activity. There are approximately 25,000 Asian gang members in the United States (California Department of Justice, 1998). The gangs are reported to be more dangerous because the members grew up in the war-torn countries and were victims of, witnessed, or were forced to commit atrocities (L. C. Lee & Zhan, 1998). Some of the reasons why Asian refugees and immigrants join gangs include being disappointed with life in the U.S., experiencing difficulties academically and socially, experiencing conflicts at home (Furuto & Murase, 1992), believing that gangs will offer protection (Hays, 1990), and being impoverished while having a strong desire to acquire money and material goods (Vigil, Yun, & Long, 1992).

CULTURAL BELIEF SYSTEMS

There is a significant stigma attached to mental illness in Asian cultures because it is viewed as a genetic defect that affects past and future generations of families (Cheung, 1989). This may account for Asian immigrants and refugees exhibiting mental illness in a culturally sanctioned manner through idioms of bodily complaints (Kleinman & Kleinman, 1985), such as headaches, weakness, dizziness, pressure on the chest or head, abdominal pain, and fatigue, that have no apparent organic pathology (Caspi et al., 1998; E. H. Lin, Carter, & Kleinman, 1985). These symptoms, combined with depression, anxiety, and psychosocial dysfunctions, have been labeled *neurasthenia* (Chung & Kagawa-Singer, 1995). Hence, neurasthenia allows for the combination of somatic and psychological manifestations of distress that are compatible with the holistic mind/body complementarity concept of health and illness found in traditional Asian medical paradigms (Cheung, 1989). Neurasthenia therefore presents ambiguity, allowing for the implicit and discreet admission of a variety of less socially acceptable symptoms while still leaving room for saving face; thus, it is considered a culturally sanctioned idiom of distress used by Asians (Chung & Kagawa-Singer, 1993; Kleinman, 1982).

Neurasthenia is a good illustration of how the cultural conceptualization of mental health influences help-seeking behavior and, hence, treatment expectations and outcome. Asian migrants may be unfamiliar with Western mental health concepts due to little or no exposure to Western mental health treatment in their home countries (Bemak et al., 2003; Chung & Kagawa-Singer, 1995; Chung & Lin, 1994). To be effective, the psychotherapist must be aware of, acknowledge, and understand the client's cultural conceptualization of problems and employ culturally sensitive therapeutic interventions and skills (Chung & Bemak, 2006; Kleinman & Good, 1985; Pedersen, 2000).

Preference in Treatment Modalities

Asian immigrants and refugees may not understand nor believe in Western psychotherapy as a means of healing and support, leading to the rejection of Western mental health practices. Consequently, a number of Asian immigrants prefer traditional healing that is influenced by religious (e.g., Buddhism, Taoism, and Confucianism) and cultural beliefs involving possession, soul loss, and witchcraft (Chung & Lin, 1994). Rituals for exorcism are performed by shamans and Taoist priests in Vietnam (Hickey, 1964) and by Buddhist monks in Laos and Cambodia (Westermeyer, 1973). These rituals, which are common practice in Vietnam, consist of calling back the soul of individuals believed to be suffering from soul loss and asking local guardian gods for protection. Laotians strongly subscribe to animism (belief in the supernatural, gods, demons, and evil spirits) as an essential part of everyday life (Muecke, 1983).

Fortune-telling with cards and coins, the Chinese horoscope, and physiognomy (palm reading and reading of facial features) are also popular methods of treatment (Chung & Bemak, 2006). Chinese medical practices, such as the use of folk remedies including herbal concoctions and poultices, forms of acupuncture, acupressure and massage, and the dermabrasive practices of cupping, pinching, rubbing, and burning, are also popular (D. L. Nguyen, Nguyen, & Nguyen, 1987). Because mental illness is perceived as a disturbance of the internal vital energy, acupuncture is often used as a remedy for depression and psychosis. In seeking help from Western psychotherapists, Asians expect a medical approach and quick symptom relief (Bemak et al., 2003). Often, mental health problems are viewed as being physical disorders, so Asians request injections, medication, or both (Chung & Okazaki, 1991).

Barriers to Mainstream Mental Health Services

Only a small percentage of Asian immigrants utilize mainstream mental health services (Sue, Fujino, Hu, Takeuchi, & Zane, 1991). Some authors assert that lack of cultural responsiveness is the reason for the low utilization of mainstream mental health services (Kagawa-Singer & Chung, 1994; Sue et al., 1991). Other cultural barriers also exist: language barriers between the client and psychotherapist, verbal differences (e.g., tone and volume when speaking), and nonverbal disparities (e.g., eye contact

and culturally sanctioned personal space). For example, Buddhist Asians would consider it extremely offensive if the therapist's sole faced the Asian client or if the therapist pats a child's head. Poor accessibility may also hinder the utilization of mainstream mental health services. Interestingly, when Asian immigrants do use mainstream services, they frequently utilize traditional and Western mainstream health care methods concurrently (Chung & Lin, 1994). Given this population's cultural beliefs and preference for traditional health care, it is essential that psychotherapists work cooperatively with bilingual/bicultural mental health professionals, community leaders, elders, and traditional healers (e.g., spiritual leaders, monks, priests, herbalists, and shamans) (Chung & Bemak, 2006).

CULTURALLY RESPONSIVE TECHNIQUES

To be effective with this population and avoid premature termination, the psychotherapist must gain both ascribed and achieved credibility from their Asian immigrant and refugee clients (Sue & Zane, 1987). To gain both types of credibility, psychotherapists must be culturally sensitive (Chung & Bemak, 2002a) and aware of the Asian immigrant's cultural beliefs about health and mental health, premigration history, and postmigration challenges as they implement traditional Western methods of health care. It is also important for mental health professionals to take into account cultural styles of grief and bereavement since culture influences their expression, and loss is a major aspect of an Asian immigrant's life. Thus, paying respect to deceased ancestors may be an important aspect of healing.

Various treatment strategies and interventions have been found to be effective when working with this population. For example, cognitive-behavioral interventions (Beiser, 1988; Bemak & Greenberg, 1994), as well as other therapeutic techniques such as storytelling and projective drawing (Pynoos & Eth, 1984), dream work (Bemak & Timm, 1994), gestalt, relaxation, role playing, psychodrama, and group and family therapy (Bemak, 1989; Friedman & Jaranson, 1994; Kinzie et al., 1988) have all been recognized for their effectiveness. The use of these strategies has been related to culturally sensitive modifications and applications such as Kinzie's (1985) work with PTSD.

Bemak and Chung developed the Multi-Level Model (MLM) of social justice, human rights, and psychotherapy to work with immigrant and refugee populations. The MLM not only involves utilizing culturally responsive techniques, but also forming partnerships with indigenous healers, the cultural empowerment of clients, advocacy and assuming an added role of being a change agent (Bemak et al., 2003). Thus, an Asian immigrant who seeks counseling but does not know how to access support to find adequate housing would be assisted by the psychotherapist to better understand where or whom to call (*cultural empowerment*), or there may be a coordinated effort between the psychotherapist and a Buddhist monk to assist the Asian refugee who is grieving for family members who were killed in a conflict at home and who believes in healing rituals rooted in Buddhist practices (*partnership with an indigenous healer*).

CONCLUSION

In summary, the Asian immigrant and refugee population is a diverse group requiring that psychotherapists thoroughly examine the inter- and intragroup differences, as well as gender differences, with regard to their premigration experiences, postmigration challenges, the type of distress predictors, and the level and degree of psychological distress (Chung & Bemak, 2006; Hsu, Davies, & Hansen, 2004). It is critical that there is awareness, understanding, acceptance, and acknowledgment of cultural differences in the conceptualization of mental illness, the expression of distress, help-seeking behavior, coping, grieving, and bereavement. Furthermore, it is also necessary to understand and appreciate the strength and resiliency of this population and incorporate these interpersonal resources into mental health interventions.

REFERENCES

Apprey, M. (1998). Reinventing the self in the face of received transgenerational hatred in African American community. *Mind and Human Interaction, 9,* 30–37.

Barudy, J. A. (1989). A programme of mental health for political refugees: Dealing with the invisible pain of political exile. *Social Science & Medicine, 28,* 715–727.

Beiser, M. (1988). Influences of time, ethnicity, and attachment on depression in Southeast Asian refugees. *American Journal of Psychiatry, 145*(1), 46–51.

Beiser, M., & Hou, F. (2001). Language acquisition, unemployment, and depressive disorder among Southeast Asian refugees: A 10-year study. *Social Science & Medicine, 53,* 1321–1334.

Bemak, F. (1989). Cross-cultural family therapy with Southeast Asian refugees. *Journal of Strategic and Systemic Therapies, 8,* 22–27.

Bemak, F., & Chung, R. C.-Y. (1998). Vietnamese Amerasians: Predictors of distress and self-destructive behavior. *Journal of Counseling & Development, 76,* 452–458.

Bemak, F., & Chung, R. C.-Y. (1999). Vietnamese Amerasians: The relationship between biological father, psychological distress, and self-destructive behavior. *Journal of Community Psychology, 27,* 443–456.

Bemak, F., & Chung, R. C.-Y. (2000). Psychological interventions with immigrants and refugees. In J. F. Aponte & J. Wohl (Eds.), *Psychological interventions and cultural diversity* (pp. 200–213). Boston: Allyn & Bacon.

Bemak, F., & Chung, R. C.-Y. (2003). Multicultural counseling with immigrant students in schools. In P. B. Pedersen & J. C. Carey (Eds.), *Multicultural counseling in schools: A practical handbook* (pp. 84–104). Boston: Allyn & Bacon.

Bemak, F., Chung, R. C.-Y., & Pedersen, P. B. (2003). *Counseling refugees: A psychosocial approach to innovative multicultural interventions.* Westport, CT: Greenwood Press.

Bemak, F., & Greenberg, B. (1994). Southeast Asian refugee adolescents: Implications for counseling. *Journal of Multicultural Counseling and Development, 22,* 115–124.

Bemak, F., & Timm, J. (1994). Case study of an adolescent Cambodian refugee: A clinical, developmental and cultural perspective. *International Journal of the Advancement of Counseling, 17,* 47–58.

Berry, J. W. (1990). Psychology of acculturation. In R.W. Brislin (Ed.), *Applied cross-cultural psychology* (pp. 232–253). Newbury Park, CA: Sage.

Berry, J. W., & Anis, R. C. (1974). Acculturative stress: The role of ecology, culture, and differentiation.

Journal of Cross-Cultural Psychology, 5, 382–406.

Buchwald, D., Manson, S. M., Ginges, N. G., Keane, E. M., & Kinzie, D. (1993). Prevalence of depressive symptoms among established Vietnamese refugees in the United States. *Journal of General Internal Medicine, 8,* 76–81.

California Department of Justice. (1998). *Bureau of Investigations 1998 report on gang activity.* Los Angeles, CA: California Department of Justice.

Caspi, Y., Poole, C., Mollica, R. F., & Frankel, M. (1998). Relationship of child loss to psychiatric and functional impairment in resettled Cambodian refugees. *Journal of Nervous and Mental Disease, 186*(8), 484–491.

Capps, R., & Passel, J. S. (2004). *Describing immigrant communities.* Washington, DC: Urban Institute, Immigration Studies Program.

Chang, I. (2003). *The Chinese in America.* New York: Penguin Books.

Cheung F. H. (1982). Psychological symptoms among Chinese in urban Hong Kong. *Social Science & Medicine, 16,* 1339–1344.

Cheung, F. H. (1989). The indigenization of neurasthenia in Hong Kong. *Culture, Medicine & Psychiatry, 13,* 227–241.

Chung, R. C.-Y. (2001). Psychosocial adjustment of Cambodian refugee women: Implications for mental health counseling. *Journal of Mental Health Counseling, 23,* 115–126.

Chung, R. C.-Y., & Bemak, F. (1995). The effects of welfare status on psychological distress among Southeast Asian refugees. *Journal of Nervous and Mental Disease, 184,* 346–353.

Chung, R. C.-Y., & Bemak, F. (2002a). The relationship between culture and empathy. *Journal of Counseling & Development, 80,* 154–159.

Chung, R. C.-Y., & Bemak, F. (2002b). Revisiting the California Southeast Asian mental health needs assessment data: An examination of refugee ethnic and gender differences. *Journal of Counseling & Development, 80,* 111–119.

Chung, R. C.-Y., & Bemak, F. (2006). Counseling Americans of Southeast Asian descent: The impact of the refugee experience. In C. C. Lee (Ed.), *Multicultural issues in counseling: New approaches to diversity* (3rd ed., pp. 151–170). Alexandria, VA: American Association for Counseling and Development.

Chung, R. C.-Y., Bemak, F., & Kagawa-Singer, M. (1998). Gender differences in psychological distress among Southeast Asian refugees. *Journal of Nervous and Mental Disease, 186,* 112–119.

Chung, R. C.-Y., Bemak, F., & Wong, S. (2000). Vietnamese refugees' level of distress, social support and acculturation: Implications for mental health counseling. *Journal of Mental Health Counseling, 22,* 150–161.

Chung, R. C.-Y., & Kagawa-Singer, M. (1993). Predictors of psychological distress among Southeast Asian refugees. *Social Science & Medicine, 36*(5), 631–639.

Chung, R. C.-Y., & Kagawa-Singer, M. (1995). Interpretation of symptom presentation and distress: A Southeast Asian refugee example. *Journal of Nervous and Mental Disease, 183,* 639–648.

Chung, R. C.-Y., & Lin, K. M. (1994). Help-seeking behavior among Southeast Asian refugees. *Journal of Community Psychology, 22,* 109–120.

Chung, R. C.-Y., & Okazaki, S. (1991). Counseling Americans of Southeast Asian descent: The impact of the refugee experience. In C. C. Lee (Ed.), *Multicultural issues in counseling: New approaches to diversity* (pp. 107–126). Alexandria, VA: American Association for Counseling and Development.

Dyregov, A., & Yule, W. (1995, November). *Screening measures—The development of the UNICEF screening battery.* Paper presented at the Symposium on War-Affected Children in Former Yugoslavia at the Eleventh Annual Meeting of the International Society for Traumatic Stress Studies, Boston.

Fawzi, M. C. S., Pham, T., Lin, L., Nguyen, T. V., Ngo, D., Murphy, E., et al. (1997). The validity of posttraumatic stress disorder among Vietnamese refugees. *International society for traumatic stress studies, 10*(1), 101–108.

Furuto, S. M., & Murase, K. (1992). *Asian Americans in the future.* In S. M. Furuto, R. Biswas, D. K. Chung, K. Murase, & F. Ross-Sheriff (Eds.), *Social work practice with Asian Americans* (pp. 240–253). Thousand Oaks, CA: Sage.

Hauff, E., & Vaglum, P. (1995). Organized violence and the stress of exile. *British Journal of Psychiatry, 166,* 360–367.

Hays, C. L. (1990, July 31). Amid gang violence, Chinatown casts off quiet image. *The New York Times,* p. B1.

Hickey, G. G. (1964). *Village in Vietnam.* New Haven, CT: Yale University Press.

Hinton, W. L., Tiet, Q., Tran, C. G., & Chesney, M. (1997). Predictors of depression among refugees from Vietnam: A longitudinal study of new arrivals. *Journal of Nervous and Mental Disease, 185(1),* 39–45.

Hsu, E., Davies, C. A., & Hansen, D. (2004). Understanding mental health needs of Southeast Asian refugees: Historical, cultural, and contextual challenges. *Clinical Psychology Review, 24*(2), 193–213.

Huang, K. (1991). Chinese Americans. In N. Mokuau (Ed.), *Handbook of social service for Asian and Pacific Islanders* (pp. 79–96). Westport, CT: Greenwood Press.

Huang, L. N. (1989). Southeast Asian refugee children and adolescents. In J. T. Gibbs & L. N. Huang (Eds.), *Children of color: Psychological interventions with minority children* (pp. 250–260). San Francisco: Jossey-Bass.

Huang, L. N., Ying, Y.-W., & Arganza, G. (2003). Chinese American children and adolescents. In. J. T. Gibbs & L. N. Huang (Eds.), *Children of color: Psychological interventions with minority children* (2nd ed., pp. 187–228). San Francisco: Jossey-Bass.

Ima, K., & Rumbaut, R. (1989). Southeast Asian refugees in American schools: A comparison of fluent English-proficient and limited-English proficient students. *Topics in Language Disorders, 9*(3), 54–75.

Kagawa-Singer, M., & Chung, R. C.-Y. (1994). A paradigm for culturally based care in ethnic minority populations. *Journal of Community Psychology, 22,* 192–208.

Kinzie, J. D. (1985). Overview of clinical issues in the treatment of Southeast Asian refugees. In T. C. Owan (Ed.), *Southeast Asian mental health: Treatment, prevention, services, training and research* (pp. 113–135). Washington, DC: U.S. Department of Health and Human Resources.

Kinzie, J. D., Leung, P., Bui, A., Ben, R., Keopraseuth, K. O., Riley, C., et al., (1988). Group therapy with Southeast Asian refugees. *Community Mental Health Journal, 23,* 157–166.

Kinzie, J. D., & Leung, P. (1989). Cloindine in Cambodian patients with post-traumatic stress disorder. *Journal of Nervous and Mental Disease, 175,* 546–550.

Kleinman, A. (1982). Neurasthenia and depression: A study of somatization and culture in China. *Culture, Medicine and Psychiatry, 6,* 117–190.

Kleinman, A., Eisenberg, L., & Good, B. (1978). Culture, illness and care. *Annals of Internal Medicine, 88,* 251–258.

Kleinman, A., & Good, B. (1985). *Culture and depression: Studies in the anthropology and cross-cultural psychiatry of affect and disorder.* Berkeley: University of California Press.

Kleinman, A., & Kleinman, J. (1985). Somatization: The interconnections in Chinese society among culture, depressive experiences, and the meaning of pain. In A. Kleinman & B. Good (Eds.), *Culture and depression.* Berkeley: University of California Press.

Lee, L. C., & Zhan, G. (1998). Psychosocial status of children and youths. In L. C. Lee & N. W. S. Zane (Eds.), *Handbook of Asian American psychology* (pp. 137–163). Thousand Oaks, CA: Sage.

Lee, S. M. (1998). Asian Americans: Diverse and growing. *Population Bulletin, 53*(2), 1–40. Washington, DC: Population Reference Bureau.

Liebkind, K. (1996). Acculturation and stress: Vietnamese refugees in Finland. *Journal of Cross-Cultural Psychology, 27,* 161–180.

Lin, E. H., Carter, W. B., & Kleinman, A. M. (1985). An exploration of somatization among Asian refugees and immigrants in primary care. *American Journal of Public Health, 75,* 1080–1084.

Lin, K. M., Inui, T. S., Kleinman, A. M., & Womack, W. (1982). Sociocultural determinants of the help-seeking behavior of patients with mental illness. *Journal of Nervous and Mental Disease, 170*(2), 78–85.

Lin, K. M., Masuda, M., & Tazuma, L. (1982). Adaptational problems of Vietnamese refugees, III: Case studies in clinic and field: Adaptive and maladaptive. *Psychiatric Journal of University of Ottawa, 7*(3), 173–183.

Lin, K. M., Tazuma, L., & Masuda, M. (1979). Adaptation problems of Vietnamese refugees, II: Life changes and perception of life events. *Archives of General Psychiatry, 37,* 447–450.

Luu, V. (1989). The hardships of escape for Vietnamese women. In Asian Women United of California (Ed.), *Making waves: An anthology of writings by and about Asian American women* (pp. 60–72). Boston: Beacon Press.

Miranda, A. O., & Matheny, K. B. (2000). Sociopsychological predictors of acculturative stress among Latino adults. *Journal of Mental Health Counseling, 22,* 306–317.

Mollica, R. F., & Jalbert, R. R. (1989). *Community of confinement: The mental health crisis in Site Two: Displaced persons' camps on the Thai-Kampuchean border.* Boston: Committee on World Federation for Mental Health.

Mollica, R. F., Lavelle, J., & Khoun, F. (1985, May). *Khmer widows at highest risk.* Paper presented at the Cambodian Mental Health Conference, New York.

Mollica, R. F., Wyshak, G., & Lavelle, J. (1987). The psychosocial impact of war trauma and torture on Southeast Asian refugees. *American Journal of Psychiatry, 144*(12), 1567–1572.

Muecke, M. A. (1983). Caring for Southeast Asian refugees in the U.S.A. *American Journal of Public Health, 73*(4), 431–438.

Murphy, H. B. (1977). Migration, culture and mental health. *Psychological Medicine, 7,* 677–681.

National Asian Pacific American Legal Consortium. (2001). *2001 Audit of violence against Asian Pacific Americans: Ninth Annual Report.* Washington, DC: National Asian Pacific American Legal Consortium.

Nagata, D. K. (1998). Internment and intergenerational relations. In L. C. Lee & N. W. S. Zane (Eds.), *Handbook of Asian American psychology* (pp. 433–456). Thousand Oaks, CA: Sage.

Nguyen, D. L., Nguyen, P. H., & Nguyen, L. H. (1987). *Coin treatment in Vietnamese families: Traditional medical practice vs. child abuse.* Unpublished manuscript.

Nguyen, S. (1982). Psychiatric and psychosomatic problems among Southeast Asian refugees. *Psychiatric Journal of the University of Ottawa, 7*(3), 163–172.

Nicholson, B. F. (1997). The influence of premigration and postmigration stressors on mental health: A study of Southeast Asian refugees. *Social Work Research, 21,* 19–31.

Office of Refugee Resettlement (ORR). (2001). *Office of Refugee Resettlement (ORR) annual report to Congress 2001.* Washington, DC: U.S. Department of Health and Human Services.

Pedersen, P. (2000). *A handbook for developing multicultural awareness.* Alexandria, VA: American Association for Counseling and Development.

Pynoos, R., & Eth, S. (1984). Children traumatized by witnessing acts of personal violence: Homicide, rape or suicide behavior. In S. Eth & R. Pynoos (Eds.), *Post-traumatic stress disorder in children* (pp.17–44). Washington DC: American Psychiatric Press.

Reeves, T. J., & Bennett, C. E. (2004). *We the People: Asians in the United States* (Census 2000 Special Report No. CENSR–17). Washington, DC: U.S. Census Bureau.

Refugee Women in Development. (1990). *What is a refugee?* Available at www.refwid.org

Root, M. P. P. (1998). Women. In L. C. Lee & N. W. S. Zane (Eds.), *Handbook of Asian American psychology* (pp. 211–232). Thousand Oaks, CA: Sage.

Rumbaut, R. G. (1989). Portraits, patterns and predictors of the refugee adaptation process: A comparative study of Southeast Asian refugees. In D. W. Haines (Ed.), *Refugees and immigrants: Cambodians, Laotians, and Vietnamese in America* (pp. 138–190). Totwa, NJ: Rowman & Littlefield.

Sack, W. H., Him, C., & Dickason, D. (1999). Twelve-years follow-up study of Khmer youths who suffered massive war trauma as children. *Journal of American Academic Child Adolescent Psychiatry, 38*(9), 1173–1179.

Sluzki, C. (1979). Migration and family conflict. *Family Process, 18*(4), 379–390.

Steele, C. M., & Aronson, J. (1995). Stereotype threat and the intellectual test performance of African Americans. *Journal of Personality & Social Psychology, 69*(5), 797–811.

Stein, B. N. (1986). The experience of being a refugee: Insights from the research literature. In C. L. Williams & J. Westermeyer (Eds.), *Refugee mental health in resettlement countries* (pp. 5–23). Washington, DC: Hemisphere.

Sue, S., Fujino, D., Hu, L., Takeuchi, D., & Zane, N. (1991). Community mental health services for ethnic minority groups: A test of cultural responsive hypothesis. *Journal of Consulting and Clinical Psychology, 59*(4), 533–540.

Sue, S., & Zane, N. (1987). The role of culture and cultural techniques in psychotherapy: A critique and reformulation. *American Psychologist, 42*(1), 37–45.

Takaki, R. (1998). *Strangers from a different shore: A History of Asian Americans.* New York: Penguin Books.

U.S. Commission on Civil Rights. (1992). *Civil rights issues facing Asian Americans in the 1990s.* Washington, DC: Government Printing Office.

U.S. Department of Health and Human Services. (2001). *Mental health: Culture, race, and ethnicity.* A supplement to *Mental health: A report of the Surgeon General.* Rockville, MD: U.S. Department of Health and Human Services.

Van Boemel, G., & Rozee, P. D. (1992). Treatment for psychosomatic blindness among Cambodian refugee women. In E. Cole, O. M. Espin, & E. D. Rothblum (Eds.), *Refugee women and their mental health: Shattered societies, shattered lives* (pp. 239–266). New York: Haworth Press.

Vigil, J. D., Yun, S., & Long, J. M. (1992, June). *Youth gangs, crime, and the Vietnamese in Orange County.* Paper presented at the convention of the Association of Asian American Studies, San Jose, CA.

Westermeyer, J. (1973). Lao Buddhism, mental health, and contemporary implications. *Journal of Religion and Health, 12,* 181–187.

White, P. T. (1982). Kampuchea wakes from a nightmare, *National Geographic, 161,* 590–623.

Wu, F. H. (2002). *Yellow: Race in America beyond black and white.* New York: Basic Books.

Yee, B. W. (1992). Elders in Southeast Asian refugee families. *Generations: Journal of the American Society on Aging, 16*(3), 24–27.

Ying, Y. (1999). Strengthening intergenerational/intercultural ties in migrant families: A new intervention for parents. *Journal of Community Psychology, 27*(1), 89–96.

Ying, Y., & Chao, C. (1996). Intergenerational relationships in Iu Mien American families. *Amerasia Journal, 22*(3), 47–64.

Young, K., & Takeuchi, D. T. (1998). Racism. In L. C. Lee & N. W. S. Zane (Eds.), *Handbook of Asian American psychology* (pp. 401–432). Thousand Oaks, CA: Sage.

15

INTERNATIONAL STUDENTS FROM ASIA

YU-WEI WANG

JUN-CHIH GISELA LIN

LAN-SZE PANG

FRANCES C. SHEN

Mei's home in rural China had no electricity and no roads. When she walked over the mountains to school at the beginning of every semester, her older sister escorted her before dawn with a torch. From this remote beginning, Mei has made it to a university in upstate New York. . . . "I encounter so many difficulties. . . . Sometimes I even do not understand what is the teacher's assignment. But I am a little Chinese bamboo, and here, there are a lot of sunlight, rain, breeze, and so on. . . . I will grow up quickly."

Anna (2005, p. 3E)

This is a real-life story about an international student from Asia who is pursuing a master's degree in educational leadership in the United States. She is determined to go back home, to the remote village in the mountains where her life started, equipped with her new degree and an inexorable passion for serving her people and community as an educator. During the past two years, other than being separated from her family (including her 3-month-old daughter), Mei has overcome many barriers while living and learning in a

foreign country with a very different culture from her own. Although each student has a different story of studying abroad, the many difficulties that Mei has encountered are very familiar to other international students from Asia.

In this chapter, we review the literature on the adaptation experiences of international students from Asia and outline recommendations for mental health professionals who work and conduct research with this population. First, we briefly define this population and present a profile of international students from Asia.

Next, we summarize the common problems and difficulties encountered by international students during the cultural adaptation process and discuss relevant theoretical models and empirical research. Subsequently, we outline implications for counseling with this population. We conclude with directions for future research.

DEFINING THE POPULATION

It is first and foremost important to define the population—international students from Asia—because vague or inconsistent definitions in the extant literature have made it extremely challenging to interpret and generalize previous research findings. *International students* (also previously termed *foreign students*) are students who study abroad for sojourns in a host country. It is important to note that *the* international student simply does not exist, because this population represents a very diverse group of students who study abroad with different motives and goals (Klineberg & Hull, 1979). International students hold a temporary visa (e.g., F-1, J-1) while studying in the United States for a variety of reasons (e.g., pursuing an academic degree, participating in an exchange program, seeking political refuge, being pressured by parents). They are confronted with varying degrees of academic, economic, and political pressure during their sojourns. Even when we only focus on the international students from Asia, this group of students still represents a diverse population from various ethnic and cultural backgrounds. About 50 different countries are located in Asia; each has its own rich religious and spiritual traditions (e.g., Christianity, Islam, Hinduism, Buddhism, Sikhism, and Judaism). Therefore, defining international students by their visa status (as is done in most studies) or the geographical location of their home countries, without acknowledging the heterogeneous nature of this population, introduces much ambiguity in the validity of research findings.

In this chapter, we adopt the broad definition of *international students* commonly utilized in the extant literature, that is, students who come from abroad and study in the United States with temporary visa status. Due to space limitations and availability of research on students from certain ethnic backgrounds, most of the literature discussed in this chapter focuses on students from East, Southeast, and South Asia (i.e., the countries that have sent the largest number of international students to the United States). Yet, it should be noted that some studies did not specify the students' countries of origin, and some included students from various countries without exploring ethnic differences. In sum, we discuss international students from Asia in general but would like to acknowledge the inherent heterogeneity of this population, as well as the overinclusiveness of categorizing these students by using the geographical region of their home countries.

PROFILE OF INTERNATIONAL STUDENTS FROM ASIA

For decades, international students from Asia have constituted the largest segment of international students in the United States, making strong contributions to the U.S. economy. According to *Open Doors 2004* (Gardner & Witherell, 2004), the most recent annual report by the Institute of International Education, there were over 570,000 international students studying in the United States from 2003 to 2004, and approximately 57% of them came from Asia. Even though the United States still remains the largest hosting country for international students, there has been a decline in the international student enrollment for the first time in decades (Gardner & Witherell, 2004). During the 2003–2004 academic year, Asian student enrollments fell by 3% from the previous year, and there has been a sharp decrease (5–15%) in the number of new students from the top ten sending countries. The sudden decrease in international student enrollment has been linked to a variety of factors: increasing costs of U.S. tuition and fees, weak economic growth in certain Asian nations, aggressive recruitment efforts by other English-speaking countries (e.g., Britain, Canada), actual and perceived difficulties in obtaining student visas, and suspicion that the United States may no longer welcome international students after the September 11 terrorist attacks, 2001, (Arnone, 2004; Gardner & Witherell, 2004; Zakaria, 2004).

These alarming statistics and anecdotal accounts about the drastic decline of new international students from Asia suggest that a closer look at the services and training experiences provided to international students is warranted. It is important to ask: Has the United States been a warm and welcoming place for international students? What and how much do we actually know about the adaptation processes and outcomes of international students from Asia? Do we have adequately trained mental health professionals, educators, and student support personnel to work with international students? These professionals and educators play a major role in responding to the needs of international students, and thus they are invited to examine their own competencies of working with this diverse student body (Arthur, 2004). The following theories and empirical studies are presented to facilitate the understanding of and work with international students who cope with the daily challenges associated with living and learning in a different culture.

COMMON PROBLEMS AND DIFFICULTIES

Following the waves of international students studying abroad after World War II, earlier researchers and practitioners documented the observed maladjustment outcomes of this population (Leong & Chou, 2002). Based on the medical model, several terminologies have been coined to describe the psychological and physical symptoms reported by international sojourners. These early conceptualizations will be introduced first, followed by a discussion of the common stressors facing international students.

Early Conceptualizations: Culture Shock and Foreign Student Syndrome

The term *culture shock* has been used extensively to describe the cross-cultural adjustment

stressors confronting international students. It was originally defined by two anthropologists, Kalervo Oberg and George Foster, in the late 1950s as "a medical condition describing feelings of disorientation following entry into a new culture, feelings often so strong as to degenerate into physical symptoms" (Anderson, 1994, p. 294). As a result of losing familiar cultural cues during social interactions (e.g., customs, facial or verbal expressions) and lacking social support in the host culture, international sojourners may develop an array of symptoms (e.g., anxiety, depression, *cultural fatigue* associated with being overloaded with new information) and yearn for a more familiar and predictable environment (Church, 1982).

Related to the concept of culture shock, *foreign student syndrome* refers to the tendency for international students to report "vague physical complaints" with a "regression to oral aggressive dependence, a passive withdrawn attitude," "a marked reluctance to converse," a "general disheveled appearance and a restriction of body movements" (Ward, 1967, p. 362, as cited in Allen & Cole, 1987). Medical professionals observed international students' tendency to somatize their problems with anxiety, loneliness, or distress; it appeared that, for these students, seeking medical care vis-à-vis seeking psychotherapy was more culturally acceptable (Allen & Cole, 1987). Consistent with this contention is the documented international students' overutilization of university health services (Ebbin & Blankenship, 1986) and underutilization of mental health services in the United States (Bradley, Parr, Lan, Bingi, & Gould, 1995; Nilsson, Berkel, Flores, & Lucas, 2004). The tendency for Asians to report somatic complaints about their psychological distress also has been discussed extensively in the counseling literature (Mori, 2000; Sue & Sue, 2003).

These early conceptualizations, however, have been questioned for their misrepresentation or oversimplicity. In the extant literature, the term *culture shock* has been redefined and broadened to include the psychological and physiological reactions to "the multiple demands for adjustment that individuals experience at the cognitive, behavioral, emotional, social, and psychological levels when they relocate to another culture" (Chapdelaine & Alexitch, 2004, p. 168). It has become a common awareness that international students experience culture shock as they face adjustment to different food, climate, dress codes, values, beliefs, language, and social norms upon arriving in the United States (Arthur, 2004). Yet, Anderson (1994) argued that the term *culture shock* has been overgeneralized to "become more than a catch-all phrase encompassing a host of different reactions to a host of different problems" (p. 297). *Culture shock* should be rephrased as *change shock*, because people who go through major transitions in their lives report similar psychological and physical symptoms. Anderson (1994) also indicated that the concept of culture shock does not explain why certain international students experience maladjustment difficulties, but others do not.

In addition, Allen and Cole (1987) contended that *foreign student syndrome* is a fable rather than fact. In their study, which was conducted in Australia, they found that after controlling for the students' age, sex, and proximity to the health center, Asian international students, compared with their Australian peers and Asian counterparts in Asia, did not seek more medical consultations. Leong and Chou (2002) concluded that "the nature and the degree of somatization among international students remain controversial" (p. 188) due to the methodological issues in assessing actual utilization rates of medical services (e.g., failure to take into account the issue of repeat users) (Furnham & Bochner, 1986) and the fact that international students may tend to get "ill" due to the climate differences between Asia and the host country (Allen & Cole, 1987).

Finally, the use of the term *foreign student syndrome* may divert attention away from the other important factors that influence Asian international students' help-seeking behaviors: (a) the Eurocentric notion of appropriate help-seeking behaviors (e.g., psychotherapy may not be a familiar or culturally appropriate help-seeking venue for international students from certain Asian countries) (Furnham & Bochner, 1986); (b) the holistic view of mind-body connection in Asian culture (Sue & Sue, 2003); (c) the lack of culturally sensitive physical and mental health services in the United States (Oropeza, Fitzgibbon, & Barón, 1991); (d) different health care systems and indigenous healing traditions in Asia (Ebbin & Blankenship, 1986); and (e) the common barriers for international students to seek any type of services in the host countries (e.g., unfamiliarity with the resources available, limited vocabulary in explaining one's needs and medical conditions, and lack of transportation) (Allen & Cole, 1987).

To sum up, it seems questionable to attribute the maladjustment outcomes of Asian international students simply to *culture shock*. It is also problematic to conclude that Asian international students *over-/under*-utilize health services because the comparisons may not be meaningful (e.g., Who should serve as the baseline, U.S. nationals or Asian students in Asia? Is it natural that they would experience more health problems due to the change of their living environment?). The more meaningful questions may be: what are the common stressors facing international students and the factors that influence their help-seeking process and outcome?

Common Stressors

Despite the problematic nature of these early theorizations derived from the medical model, they have called attention to the challenges facing international students during the cultural transition process. In addition to the normal developmental issues facing every college student, international students are confronted with additional stressors due to their sojourn status (Mori, 2000). The extensive reports of these common stressors have remained consistent during the last half of the 20th century (for reviews, see Alexander, Klein, Workneh, & Miller, 1981; Arthur, 2004; Church, 1982; Klineberg & Hull, 1979; Leong & Chou, 2002; Pedersen, 1991; Thomas & Althen, 1989). This wide range of stressors can be roughly divided into the following areas: (a) academic difficulties, (b) personal and vocational issues, and (c) sociocultural barriers.

Academic difficulties. Academic difficulties are considered one of the major barriers confronting international students (Chen, 1999;

Thorstensson, 2001). International students from Asia reported a myriad of stressors in U.S. higher education institutions: second language anxiety, culture-specific demands in educational system and learning styles, the constraints unique to their sojourn status, and the pressure to excel academically.

International students' self-perceived English proficiency is related to their appraisal of the cross-cultural adjustment stress (Swagler & Ellis, 2003; Wan, Chapman, & Biggs, 1992). Compared to international students who are more confident in their English proficiency, those who report weak English skills are more likely to perceive their academic experience as stressful or feel that they lack the ability to cope with stress. Also, international students have to adjust to the novelty of the U.S. educational system and learning styles (Wong, 2004). Yet, their length of stay is limited by the visa regulations imposed by the U.S. Immigration and Naturalization Services (INS). In addition, international students are not qualified for financial aid or allowed to work off-campus due to their visa status. Therefore, these students generally face huge financial commitments and restraints (Arthur, 2004); academic restrictions are often identified as the main concern among international students (Charles & Stewart, 1991). Finally, Asian international students, in particular, may face familial pressure to succeed academically due to the traditional cultural values of educational achievement, filial piety, and conformity to family and social expectations (Hanassab & Tidwell, 2002; Kim, Atkinson, & Umemoto, 2001).

With the language challenges, differences in learning styles and the educational system, unique academic and financial constraints, and the fear of disappointing others, many Asian international students develop performance anxiety (Chen, 1999; Thomas & Althen, 1989). These additional stressors interfere with the achievement of their academic goals (Hanassab & Tidwell, 2002) and may lead to psychological maladjustment (e.g., depression) during their stay in the United States (Nilsson et al., 2004; Yang & Clum, 1995).

Personal and vocational concerns. Beside academic stressors, international students are confronted with a wide range of personal and vocational issues: arrival confusion, adjustment to food and climate, housing issues during sojourns, somatic complaints, family problems, the development of their home countries, homesickness, loneliness, struggle to maintain one's self-esteem, and career decision regarding whether to stay in the United State or return to home countries (Arthur, 2004; Church, 1982; Pedersen, 1991; Thomas & Althen, 1989).

In particular, international students face several unique challenges in the area of career development (Hanassab & Tidwell, 2002; Thomas & Althen, 1989). Upon graduation, they have a number of options, such as staying permanently in the United States, returning to their home countries, staying temporarily in the United States and then moving back to their home countries, or moving to a third country after completing their studies in the United States. This decision-making process may be further complicated by numerous factors: personal or family backgrounds (e.g., whether or not they have children with them, marketability of their degrees in the home or host countries), their previous training and work experiences, resources available for the job search, immigration regulations on employment, and re-entry preparation (Mori, 2000; Shen & Herr, 2004). All of these unique career development issues suggest that Asian international students, compared to domestic students, may have greater need for career services, as demonstrated in an earlier study (Leong & Sedlacek, 1989).

Sociocultural issues. The final type of stressors pertain to sociocultural issues: accommodating to the social norms in the host country, political/religious/cultural value clashes, struggle with one's ethnic identity and role as an international student, lack of social support and personal guidance, cross-cultural friendship and romantic relationships, loss or change of social status, and stereotypes and discrimination against international students or students from certain ethnic backgrounds (Al-Sharideh & Goe, 1998; Brinson & Kottler, 1995; Church, 1982; Pedersen, 1991; Spencer-Rodgers, 2001; Thomas & Althen, 1989). The September 11 terrorist attacks also have exacerbated discrimination against international students from

Asia. Because some of the hijackers were identified as Muslims with student visas, negative stereotypes toward individuals from particular ethnic backgrounds apparently have been transferred to international students through subtle and overt hostility (Arthur, 2004; Chepesiuk, 2002; Hartle, 2004; Kong, 2001). Perceived and actual discrimination may have serious implications for these students' adjustment outcomes (Schmitt, Spears, & Branscombe, 2003).

Summary of common stressors. The common stressors facing international students during their cross-cultural transition are interrelated, which means a single concern cannot be completely separated from other adjustment concerns. It is also important to acknowledge that the impact of psychological stressors may not only be additive, but these stressors interact synergistically to affect the adjustment outcomes. In other words, common developmental issues experienced by college students (e.g., homesickness) may be exacerbated due to the unfamiliarity with the host culture and the lack of problem-solving resources available; common issues that most sojourners have to deal with (e.g., communication barriers) may limit the emotional resources available to international students for coping with academic difficulties. These various cross-cultural challenges create substantial barriers for international students in the pursuit of their educational and career goals. Finally, it is important to note that previous studies often did not differentiate between stressors and maladjustment outcomes. Yet, in dealing with these common stressors, some students were able to overcome the myriad barriers, whereas others developed serious maladaptive behaviors. The following models have been developed to explain the variations in international students' adjustment processes and outcomes.

THEORIES AND RESEARCH ABOUT ADJUSTMENT PROCESSES AND OUTCOMES

Numerous theories have been developed to explain the adjustment processes and outcomes for international students: (a) recuperation models, (b) cultural learning and social support models, (c) identity development and acculturation models, and (d) sociopsychological adjustment and coping models (Anderson, 1994; Berry, 1997; Furnham & Bochner, 1986). All of these models describe a common process of adapting to or recovering from the stress related to cultural adjustment with emphases on different aspects (or mechanisms) of this adaptation process. A discussion of these models and relevant research is presented below.

Recuperation Models

The recuperation models emphasize "recovery from the shock to be the mechanism for accommodation to life in strange new lands" (Anderson, 1994, p. 293). During this recuperation process, sojourners go through different phases characterized with various adjustment outcomes. Also, international students relocating to a host culture that is significantly different from their home cultures (i.e., greater *culture distance*) are hypothesized to experience more difficulties than their counterparts (Furnham & Bochner, 1986). Remedial approaches were recommended for international sojourners in order to help them recuperate and recover from culture shock.

Two earlier models proposed by Oberg (1960) and Lysgaard (1955) indicate that international students may experience initial excitement at cultural entry. Subsequently, having to deal with major life changes without adequate social support leads to feelings of confusion, isolation, and distress; culture shock as manifested in role ambiguity and strain, culture fatigue, and depression is at its peak during this crisis stage. As individuals spend more time in the host country, they may start to appreciate and accept the new culture, which results in a recuperation or recovery from culture shock. These stages are considered "both sequential and cyclical" depending on whether new crises emerge, but sojourners eventually enter the permanent adjustment stage once they "become effectively bicultural" (Winkelman, 1994, p. 122). Gullahorn and Gullahorn (1963) later extended the U-curve theory to the W-curve theory by adding a re-entry adjustment phase;

they suggested that a similar readjustment process (a second U-curve) would occur when international students return to their home country.

However, the recuperation models have been criticized for several reasons. First, these models lack explanatory power for individual differences in adjustment outcomes as well as differences in the causes and levels of culture shock (Anderson, 1994; Furham & Bochner, 1986). Next, previous studies on the stages of the recuperation process are mostly cross-sectional in nature; several longitudinal studies did not find support for the progressive stages of the cultural adjustment process (Klineberg & Hull, 1979; Nash, 1991). The concept of culture distance also received mixed empirical support. Some studies found that culture distance is related to psychological or sociocultural adjustment outcomes (Hanassab & Tidwell, 2002; Seale & Ward, 1990), whereas others did not support this hypothesis (Wan et al., 1992). The mixed findings may be associated with how culture distance is defined (e.g., language, religion, social class, technological development) (Furnham & Bochner, 1986).

In sum, the recuperation models seem to be overly simplistic and predominately focused on the "noxious aspects of cross-cultural contact" (Furnham & Bochner, 1986, p. 12). The varying innate abilities for international students to cope with the external culture and environment change are also overlooked. The culture-learning and social support models were subsequently developed to address these limitations.

Culture-Learning and Social Support Models

The next generation of researchers developed the culture-learning/social support models to explain the variability in the adjustment outcomes of international students. These models emphasize that international students have the capacity to learn new cultural skills and that general social support can buffer or offset the stress experienced by international students during the cultural transition process.

The culture-learning model stresses that "cross-cultural problems arise because sojourners have trouble negotiating certain social situations" (Furnham & Bochner, 1986, p. 15). It de-emphasizes the difficulties experienced by international sojourners as symptoms that require treatment (e.g., psychotherapy) and challenges the notion that newcomers need to adjust to and embrace the cultural values and norms of the host countries in order to function well. Therefore, scholars adhering to this model focus on ways to help sojourners develop appropriate skills in dealing with certain social situations effectively. Newcomers either could receive formal social-skills training or they would need to have connections with supportive host nationals who could serve as culture informants or mediators. The culture-learning model is associated with the subsequent work on friendship network of international sojourners, outreach programming, cultural sensitivity training, and cross-cultural communications (Chapdelaine & Alexitch, 2004; Furnham & Alibhai, 1985; Jacob, 2001; Triandis, Brislin, & Hui, 1988).

The social support model addresses "the supportive functions of interpersonal relationships" in psychological and physical well-being and is largely based on attachment theory, social-network theory, and psychotherapy literature (Furnham & Bochner, 1986, p. 185). According to this model, being deprived of the established social support in the home country may lead to psychological and physical maladjustment outcomes. Pedersen (1991) argued that the loss of social support significantly impacts the psychological well-being of international students, and commonly results in feelings of anxiety, disorientation, loss, and pain. Social alienation may be a particular concern for Asian international students who are thousands of miles away from home (Yang, Teraoka, Eichenfield, & Audas, 1994).

One major area of research on social support emphasizes the sources of support. Many international students from Asia naturally tend to identify and socialize with co-nationals who share similar cultural values (Klineberg & Hull, 1979). Interactions with such a group may provide international students a venue to establish their social support in the host country, to find a sense of belonging, and to share familiar cultural practices (Mori, 2000). Additionally, levels of interactions with U.S. nationals reported by international students are positively related to their levels of adjustment and negatively associated with feelings of alienation and levels of strain (Hechanova-Alampay, Beehr, Christiansen, & van Horn, 2002; Schram & Lauver, 1988).

Yet, the formation of cultural subgroups may isolate international students from American students (Hayes & Lin, 1994); it also appears extremely challenging for international sojourners to establish meaningful relationships with host nationals. For example, based on the findings of a longitudinal study with 2,536 international students who studied abroad in 11 countries, Klineberg and Hull (1979) concluded that "those foreign students satisfied and comfortable with their interactions with local people and the local culture during their sojourn will report broader and more general satisfaction with their total sojourn experience, both academically and nonacademically" (p. 178). However, their respondents reported a remarkable amount of disappointment and discouragement while seeking social interactions with host nationals. This earlier finding was replicated in a later study by Yang and colleagues (1994). When asked to identify barriers to developing more meaningful relationships with Americans, participants who reported having only superficial relationships with Americans ranked "lack of opportunities to interact with U.S. students" as the greatest barrier, followed by "differences in ways of living" (Yang et al., 1994, p. 110). In a word, the existing literature suggests that many Asian international students struggle with the development of meaningful relationships with Americans and may perceive a lack of opportunities and cultural differences as potential barriers.

Moreover, findings from empirical studies that examined the impact of social support have been mixed. On the one hand, research has found that lower levels of perceived social support are associated with higher levels of acculturative stress, depression, hopelessness, and suicidal ideation (Choi, 1997; Yang & Clum, 1995; Yeh & Inose, 2003). Perceived support from graduate programs (e.g., relationship with faculty members) was a strong buffer against the development of stress symptoms among international graduate students (Mallinckrodt & Leong, 1992). In addition,

international students who reported more social support, compared to their counterparts, expressed more confidence in their ability to cope with stressful academic situations (Wan et al., 1992). Yet, on the other hand, several studies found that the relationship between perceived social support and symptoms of psychological distress is rather complex. For example, one longitudinal research with 106 international students from 37 countries found no direct relationship between the level of social support and psychological adjustment or distress (Hechanova-Alampay et al., 2002). In a study with 74 Korean international students, social support served as a buffer against the development of mental health symptoms only for students who experience high levels of acculturative stress (Lee, Koeske, & Sales, 2004). Findings from another longitudinal study with 199 Japanese exchange students revealed that the likelihood of developing psychiatric morbidity during sojourns is positively correlated with perceived social support measured before departure and yet negatively correlated with the social support assessed during sojourns; neither of the levels of social support measured before departure and during sojourns is correlated with distress level after the students returned to the home country (Furukawa, 1997). One study with 52 East Asian international students reported that the perceived support from their International Student Office helped to decrease the negative impact of racism on those students who experienced racist events, and yet no buffering effects were found for other sources of social support or stressors (Chen, Mallinckrodt, & Mobley, 2002).

Overall, the models of culture learning and social support have their limitations and contributions. For example, the culture-learning model addresses only part of the cultural adaptation process because successful cultural adaptation requires much greater efforts than learning to function well in a new culture (Anderson, 1994); culture learning does not take away the homesickness, the need for having loved ones around, or the challenge to resolve value clashes and to develop friendship with host-nationals. Also, the relationship between social support and international students' well-being is complicated by a number of factors (e.g., students' personalities and interpersonal styles, needs for social support, situational factors). Nonetheless, the culture-learning and social support models explain, in part, the variations in the adjustment outcomes of international sojourners and underscore the potential for international students to actively adapt to the transitional process (instead of passively reacting to culture shock) with the resources available to them.

Identity Development and Acculturation Models

Other types of models that may explain the varying sojourner adaptation outcomes are the identity development and acculturation models. These models emphasize the mechanisms of identity shifting and cultural adaptation during the transitional process.

Adler (1975) described the progressive change in the level of cultural awareness among sojourners with five phases: contact, disintegration, reintegration, autonomy, and independence. The loss of familiar behavioral cues and the underpinning of one's sense of self in a new culture may lead to "disintegration" of one's personality and push individuals toward forming a more integrated and "multicultural" self. The cultural concept of the "self" may play a significant role in the adjustment process of international students (Cross, 1995). A multicultural person is capable of constantly adapting to new roles and values while developing an integrated cultural identity (Adler, 1985, as cited in Pedersen, 1991).

Similarly, scholars in cross-cultural psychology have also attempted to examine this cultural adaptation or acculturation process (Berry, 1997). Based on the early conceptualization of acculturation (Redfield, Linton, & Herskovits, 1936, as cited in Berry, 1985), acculturation was defined as "those modifications which occur due to continuous first-hand contact with another culture, resulting in both sociocultural (group-level) and behavioral (individual-level) changes" (Berry, 1985, p. 236). Berry (1997) maintained that four acculturation strategies (i.e., assimilation, separation, integration, and marginalization) are formed depending on two

issues: "*cultural maintenance* (to what extent are cultural identity and characteristics considered to be important, and their maintenance strived for); and *contact and participation* (to what extent should they become involved in other cultural groups, or remain primarily among themselves)" (p. 9). According to Berry (1997), one may explore different strategies and develop an overall preference for one particular strategy. Individuals may use different strategies according to the situations (e.g., family issues), and the four strategies do not represent a progressive sequence that sojourners would go through. The large sociocultural context (e.g., national policy) may also affect the acculturation options available to individuals. Sojourners may experience acculturative stress when serious conflicts arise in the acculturation process and may develop psychological maladjustment outcomes (e.g., depression and anxiety) if the acculturative stress exceeds their coping capacity and resources (William & Berry, 1991).

The identity development and acculturation models have inspired subsequent scholarly endeavors in assessing international students' adaptation processes and outcomes. It should be noted that most of the studies used unidimensional assessments that focus on acculturative stress (Sandhu & Asrabadi, 1994) or the level of assimilation in one or multiple domains (Suinn, Ahuna, & Khoo, 1992). Bicultural identity is represented as the mid-point score in the acculturation continuum with highly traditional at one end and highly assimilated at the other end (Ryder, Alden, & Paulhus, 2000). Previous studies have demonstrated that a higher assimilation level among international students is associated with a greater length of residency in the United States (Shih & Brown, 2000; Sodowsky & Plake, 1992; Yasuda & Duan, 2002). Yeh and Inose (2003) found that international students with higher levels of self-evaluated English proficiency, social connection, and satisfaction with their social networks reported less acculturative stress. Also, among a group of international students from South Asia, higher levels of acculturative stress (i.e., perceived prejudice) are related to higher levels of self-reported depressive symptoms (Rahman & Rollock, 2004).

Although the aforementioned studies suggest that high levels of assimilation and low levels of acculturative stress are associated with positive psychological well-being of international students, some researchers have called attention to other aspects of acculturation and its complex relationship with psychosocial adjustment outcomes. First, the *process* of assimilating to a new culture can be an extremely stressful experience for international students (Oh, Koeske, & Sales, 2002), which cannot be assessed using one-shot, cross-sectional research. Also, a lower level of assimilation was associated with clearer vocational identity among 112 graduate and undergraduate international students from Taiwan (Shih & Brown, 2000). Additionally, using a bidimensional assessment of acculturation measure, Ryder and colleagues (2000) demonstrated that higher adherence to mainstream value is related to greater adjustment, whereas stronger adherence to one's own Asian heritage is related to family life satisfaction for a group of Asian students.

To sum up, although much research has been conducted to examine the relationship between acculturation and the psychosocial well-being of Asian international students, the use of unidirectional conceptualization and different operational definitions of acculturation may have contributed to the inconsistent research findings. Most of the studies are cross-sectional in nature, which makes it difficult to infer causality or understand the acculturation dynamics. Other situational variables were often not considered (e.g., the impact of international students' partners or children on their acculturation process). Therefore, there is a dire need for more in-depth process and outcome research on sojourners' acculturation processes and outcomes.

Sociopsychological Adjustment and Coping Model

The sociopsychological adjustment model maintains that "all adjustment is a cyclical and recursive process of overcoming obstacles and solving problems in person-environment transactions" (Anderson, 1994, p. 293). Anderson (1994) asserts that "it is the individual who

chooses how to respond, and in so doing creates his or her own adjustment" (p. 293). Based on the sociopsychological adjustment model, six principles are applicable to the cross-cultural adaptation processes and outcomes: (a) involves adjustments; (b) implies learning; (c) implies a stranger-host relationship; (d) is cyclical, continuous, and interactive; (e) is relative; and (f) implies personal development (Anderson, 1994). This model brought additional insights into the individual sojourner adjustment process and emphasizes the role of individual will in choosing the coping responses to cultural adjustment stress.

Two recent studies identified several coping mechanisms that international students use to cope with their educational and cultural struggles. Specifically, international students reported coping with their adjustment problems by seeking advice and support from family and friends from their home country as well as from local U.S. nationals (Constantine, Kindaichi, Okazaki, Gainor, & Baden, 2005; Myburgh, Nihaus, & Poggenpoel, 2002). In a qualitative study conducted with 15 Asian female international students (Constantine et al., 2005), participants typically reported learning to be more independent and self-sufficient as well as minimizing or denying their adjustment difficulties in order not to burden others with their problems. A few participants reported seeking counseling to address adjustment concerns only as a last resort. Another study using a focus group with 18 international students from 10 different countries found that international students use a variety of strategies to cope with feelings of isolation, loneliness, and insecurity: (a) believing in their social competence and interpersonal skills to join social circles and develop new friendships, (b) perceiving obstacles as challenges, (c) coping with challenges "by acknowledging personal worth" and taking good care of themselves, (d) focusing on the actualization of their personal goals and expectations, and (e) enjoying local food and culture (Myburgh et al., 2002, p. 125).

In summary, present research primarily focuses on the identification of the coping strategies used by international students in adjusting to a new culture. However, more research is needed to better understand the coping strategies and mechanisms used by Asian international students from different Asian cultures, as well as the impact of these coping processes on their cultural adjustment outcomes during their sojourns.

Conclusion of Theoretical Models and Empirical Research

The aforementioned theoretical frameworks have contributed to our knowledge about the adjustment and adaptation processes and outcomes for international students. These models and empirical studies have helped us understand different aspects (or mechanisms) of the cross-cultural transition process for international sojourners. Unfortunately, often "isolated, uncoordinated, and fragmentary studies" with contradictory findings were produced due to the lack of an integrated theory, incongruent definitions of fundamental concepts, diverse backgrounds of international students, and methodological issues (Pedersen, 1991, p. 50).

This is also reflected in the mixed findings from research on counseling international students (Leong & Chou, 2002). For example, results from studies that examine international students' preferences for help sources and helping styles have been equivocal. Some researchers have suggested that international students prefer to seek help from co-nationals and typically seek counseling only after they have exhausted other personal resources (Mau & Jepsen, 1990), whereas others have found that preferred help sources for international students are faculty members and counselors for both educational-vocational and emotional-social issues (Leong & Sedlacek, 1986). Studies on international students from Hong Kong and Taiwan reported that sojourners expressed strong preference for a directive rather than non-directive counseling approach (Exum & Lau, 1988; Mau & Jepsen, 1988). Yet, another study found that Asian international students who have stayed in the United States for more than two months and perceived their English proficiency to be adequate rated authoritative peer counselors as more effective, whereas their counterparts rated collaborative peers as more effective (Merta, Ponterotto, & Brown, 1992). In another study using a single-subject design, six international students reported no preference for either a problem-solving approach or a client-centered approach (Yau, Sue,

& Hayden, 1992). These seemingly contradictory findings suggest that there are multiple factors that interact with each other in affecting international students' preferences for help sources and counseling styles and that there is a dearth of in-depth research on international students' help-seeking processes and outcomes.

With the complexity of conducting research with Asian international students from extremely diverse backgrounds, "counselors who work with international students cannot wait for the fruits of scientific research but instead must 'muddle through' with the existing knowledge base and a great deal of improvisation" (Leong & Chou, 2002, p. 203).

COUNSELING INTERNATIONAL STUDENTS FROM ASIA

Presenting concerns of international students include but are not limited to: depression, anxiety, academic concerns, relationship problems, vocational issues, and personality pathology (Oropeza et al., 1991; Nilsson et al., 2004). Because a large percentage of international students tend to prematurely terminate counseling and choose not to return after the first session (Nilsson et al., 2004; Pedersen, 1991), it is crucial for mental health professionals to prepare themselves for the next international student who knocks on their doors.

Numerous recommendations have been made about counseling international students (Alexander et al., 1981; Church, 1982; Lin, 2000; Leong & Chou, 2002; Pedersen, 1991; Thomas & Althen, 1989; Wehrly, 1986). Recently, Arthur (2004) presented counseling applications for international students based on the multicultural counseling competencies (MCC) model (Sue, Arredondo, & McDavis, 1992; Sue et al., 1998) and her years of experience working with international students. Next, we will present our and other scholars' suggestions about counseling international students along various dimensions of the MCC model (i.e., counselors' self-awareness, knowledge, and skills, as well as systemic interventions).

First, in terms of counselors' self-awareness, counselors should be aware of their cultural encapsulation and unintentional stereotypes against international students as well as the existence of racism and discrimination against this population (Arthur, 2004; Church, 1982). An attempt should be made to minimize culture shock in counseling, particularly when there is large culture-distance between counselors and clients. Counselors are, however, cautioned against overemphasizing cultural dimensions of the clients' presenting concerns. Aside from the unique issues confronting international sojourners and general sojourners, international students also deal with the typical developmental issues facing all college students and early adults (Leong & Chou, 2002).

Second, in the area of knowledge, Arthur (2004) advocated that counselors should acquire culture-specific knowledge about international students by utilizing community resources and learning directly from international students without "exploiting international students as cultural teachers" (p. 76). Awareness of Asian cultural values (Kim et al., 2001) and the stigma attached to seeking mental health services for Asian international students (Church, 1982; Wehrly, 1986) may facilitate the development of a working alliance and decrease the likelihood of misinterpreting international students' expressions and behaviors. Knowledge about the theoretical frameworks and relevant research would help counselors to address the common stressors (e.g., academic difficulties, personal and vocational issues, and sociocultural barriers) encountered by international students. Understanding the identity development and acculturation models sensitizes counselors so that they can better help international students deal with acculturative stress and value clashes with their family, significant others, or friends. In addition, counselors should recognize the impact that heterogeneous backgrounds and large individual differences (e.g., religious affiliation, political beliefs, socioeconomic status, sex-role socializations) have on international students. These factors affect their presenting concerns, as well as their help-seeking behaviors and expectations.

Third, in order to enhance one's multicultural counseling skills, counselors should develop culturally responsive communication skills (e.g., culturally appropriate ways of verbal and non-verbal communication with international students from different cultures) (Arthur, 2004).

Counselors need to be adept at changing between multiple roles (e.g., teacher, consultant, advocate, mentor, mediator) while working with international students (Lin, 2000) and adapt their counseling interventions (e.g., incorporating cultural views in interpreting assessment results) to fit the needs of international clients. Consistent with the theorization of the culture-learning/social support models, Pedersen (1991) suggested that counselors help international students to identify specific skills required for specific cross-cultural situations and encourage international students to establish supportive relationships in the hosting country. Teaching international students about the sociopsychological adjustment processes will also help them understand the transition process, broaden their repertoire of coping strategies, and empower them to deal with multiple demands by utilizing their own strengths (Lin & Yi, 1997).

Finally, in terms of systemic interventions, counselors should help to internationalize counseling services and contribute to campus internationalization in order to improve the overall campus climate for international students (Arthur, 2004). Bilingual services and outreach programming for international students are examples of culturally sensitive, systemic interventions. In addition, counselors should be familiar with the visa regulations for international students and establish collaborative relationships with other relevant student services on campus (e.g., International Student Office, Learning Center) in order to effectively work with international students whose adjustment difficulties are often intertwined with academic concerns and restraints due to their sojourner status. An extensive network with various constituencies that provide services for international students (e.g., international student organizations, churches well-attended by international students) may also help to familiarize students with the counseling services and decrease the stigma attached to seeking mental health services. Finally, counseling services should be marketed to international students in creative ways (e.g., providing outreach programs during international student orientation sessions, co-sponsoring international festivals with other international student organizations, translating the self-help materials into different languages).

In addition to the aforementioned recommendations, experts have advocated the use of critical incident methodology as a tool to learn about the unique issues facing international students and possible culturally-sensitive interventions (Leong & Chou, 2002). Excellent case discussions may be found in Arthur (2004), Cushner and Brislin (1996), and Pedersen (1991). We suggest that counselors familiarize themselves with these case studies, because they may facilitate the decision-making process in counseling and aid understanding of the dynamics in intercultural interactions. Various culture-specific counseling services and outreach programs also have been published. For example, Yang, Wong, Hwang, and Heppner (2002) presented a creative career counseling service for international students. Lin (2000) also introduced a culturally sensitive support group for international students. These culture-specific interventions use proactive methods to market and provide counseling services to Asian international students (e.g., conducting focus group interviews and surveys about international students' needs, translating career service brochures into different languages, having counselors who are international graduate students from Asia available, using culturally sensitive assessments, networking with Asian international student organizations, and collaborating with language partner programs). In the surveys and focus group interviews with international students, the participants reported that the support group experiences helped them improve their academic and social life (Lin, Orozco, Quick, Roberts, & Helms, 1999). This type of intervention also has been shown to increase the utilization of counseling services by international students (Yi, Lin, & Kishimoto, 2003).

CONCLUSION AND IMPLICATIONS FOR FUTURE RESEARCH

In his major contribution on counseling international students, Pedersen (1991) concluded that "there is no Grand Theory, in the mode of natural sciences, to direct research on multicultural interactions, such as those between international students and their host environment" (p. 27). Review of the literature 15 years later still confirmed that there is the lack of an integrative theory accompanied with methodological issues (Church, 1982; Yoon & Portman, 2004), which have led to fragmented and inconsistent research findings.

The research findings accumulated during the past five decades, albeit remaining inconclusive, have provided evidence for the impact of the complex interactions among social, psychological, and interpersonal influences on an individual student's adjustment outcomes. Despite historically being grouped together by their visa status as international students, this population represents an extremely heterogeneous group of sojourners with various ethnic, cultural, religious, and socioeconomic backgrounds. Each individual student also has her/his own personal histories, cultural values, and personalities, and is at varying developmental stages on arriving in the United States. The people who they meet during their sojourns and the academic institutions where they study all have potentially significant impacts on the international students' experiences during academic sojourns.

These differences in demographic backgrounds, personal characteristics, and situational contexts are important factors to consider in theorizing the development processes and adjustment outcomes of Asian international students (Yoon & Portman, 2004). Within-group differences (e.g., pre-arrival preparation and psychosocial adjustments, academic goals, countries of origin, age, gender, marital status, religious/spiritual affiliations, socioeconomic backgrounds, identity development) and environmental factors (e.g., cultural sensitivity of the training programs and campus climate) should be attended to. Also, there is a dearth of research on issues related to international students' significant others and families and how they affect sojourners' adjustment processes. In addition, clinical and research instruments should be validated among various international student subgroups. It should not be assumed that assessments developed for and based on the U.S. population and culture will be valid for international students from different Asian countries just because most international students have the basic level of English fluency to respond to items written in English.

Furthermore, the extant literature tends to focus on the pathology, rather than the strengths, of international students (Pedersen, 1991); more research is needed to examine international students' successful experiences and other life roles (e.g., helpers). Finally, there is a dire need for more in-depth process and outcome research on the coping and counseling issues of international students (Leong & Chou, 2002). More sophisticated research methodology (e.g., longitudinal design) (Ying, & Liese, 1991), statistical analysis methods (e.g., structural equation modeling), and qualitative research methods show great promise in advancing our knowledge about the impact of these complex factors on international student development.

With our continuous efforts to understand cultural transition processes and outcomes, we hope every international student will thrive like "a little Chinese bamboo," enjoy a meaningful journey in quest of knowledge, and eventually contribute to the collective well-being and closer cross-cultural relationships across the globe.

REFERENCES

Adler, P. S. (1975). The transitional experience: An alternative view of culture shock. *Journal of Humanistic Psychology, 15*(4), 13–23.

Alexander, A. A., Klein, M. H., Workneh, F., & Miller, M. H. (1981). Psychotherapy and foreign students. In P. B. Pedersen, J. G. Draguns, W. H. Lonner, & J. E. Trimble (Eds.), *Counseling across cultures* (Rev. ed., pp. 227–243). Honolulu: University Press of Hawaii.

Allen, F. C. L., & Cole, J. B. (1987). Foreign student syndrome: Fact or fable? *Journal of American College Health, 35,* 182–186.

Al-Sharideh, K. A., & Goe, W. R. (1998). Ethnic communities within the university: An examination of factors influencing the personal adjustment of international students. *Research in Higher Education, 39*(6), 699–723.

Anderson, L. E. (1994). A new look at an old construct: Cross-cultural adaptation. *International Journal of Intercultural Relations, 18*(3), 293–328.

Anna, C. (2005, September 11). Long road: From a remote Chinese village to laptops and launderettes, one student eager to go back home. *The Southern Illinoisan,* p. 3E.

Arnone, M. (2004). Security at home creates insecurity abroad: With fewer foreign students applying to U.S. colleges, federal visa rules get the blame. *The Chronicle of Higher Education, 50*(27), pp. A21–A22.

Arthur, N. (2004). *Counseling international students: Clients from around the world.* New York: Kluwer Academic/Plenum.

Berry, J. W. (1985). Psychological adaptations of foreign students. In R. J. Samuda & A. Wolfgang (Eds.), *Intercultural counselling and assessment: Global perspectives.* Lewiston, NY: C. J. Hogrefe.

Berry, J. W. (1997). Immigration, acculturation, and adaptation. *Applied Psychology: An International Review, 46*(1), 5–68.

Bradley, L., Parr, G., Lan, W. Y., Bingi, R., & Gould, L. J. (1995). Counseling expectations of international students. *International Journal for the Advancement of Counseling, 18,* 21–31.

Brinson, J. A., & Kottler, J. (1995). International students in counseling: Some alternative models. *Journal of College Student Psychotherapy, 9*(3), 57–70.

Chapdelaine, R. F., & Alexitch, L. R. (2004). Social skills difficulty: Model of culture shock for international graduate students. *Journal of College Student Development, 45*(2), 167–184.

Charles, H., & Stewart, M. A. (1991). Academic advising of international students. *Journal of Multicultural Counseling and Development, 19*(4), 173–181.

Chen, C. P. (1999). Common stressors among international college students: Research and counseling implications. *Journal of College Counseling, 2,* 49–65.

Chen, H.-J., Mallinckrodt, B., & Mobley, M. (2002). Attachment patterns of East Asian international students and sources of perceived social support as moderators of the impact of U.S. racism and cultural distress. *Asian Journal of Counselling, 9*(1–2), 27–48.

Chepesiuk, R. (2002, November). Dealing with discrimination. *Graduating Engineer and Computer Careers Online: International Insights.* Retrieved November 8, 2004, from http://graduatingengineer.com/ intl_insights/ nov2002.html

Choi, G. (1997). Acculturative stress, social support, and depression in Korean-American families. *Journal of Family Social Work, 2*(1), 81–97.

Church, A. T. (1982). Sojourner adjustment. *Psychological Bulletin, 91*(3), 540–572.

Constantine, M. G., Kindaichi, M., Okazaki, S., Gainor, K. A., & Baden, A. L. (2005). A qualitative investigation of the cultural adjustment experiences of Asian international college women. *Cultural Diversity & Ethnic Minority Psychology, 11*(2), 162–175.

Cross, S. E. (1995). Self-construals, coping, and stress in cross-cultural adaptation. *Journal of Cross-Cultural Psychology, 26*(6), 673–697.

Cushner, K., & Brislin, R. W. (1996). *Intercultural interactions: A practical guide* (2nd ed.). Thousand Oaks, CA: Sage.

Ebbin, A. J., & Blankenship, E. S. (1986). A longitudinal health care study: International versus domestic students. *Journal of American College Health, 34,* 177–182.

Exum, H. A., & Lau, E. Y. (1988). Counseling style preference of Chinese college students. *Journal of Multicultural Counseling and Development, 16,* 84–92.

Furnham, A., & Alibhai, N. (1985). The friendship networks of foreign students: A replication and extension of the functional model. *International Journal of Psychology, 20,* 709–722.

Furnham, A., & Bochner, S. (1986). *Culture shock: Psychological reactions to unfamiliar environment.* New York: Methuen.

Furukawa, T. (1997). Sojourner readjustment: Mental health of international students after one year's foreign sojourn and its psychosocial correlates. *Journal of Nervous and Mental Disease, 185*(4), 263–268.

Gardner, D., & Witherell, S. (2004). Open door 2004: International students in the U.S. *Institute of International Education Network.* Retrieved April 22, 2005, from http://opendoors.iienetwork.org/?p=49929

Gullahorn, J. T., & Gullahorn, J. E. (1963). An extension of the U-curve hypothesis. *Social Issues, 19,* 33–47.

Hanassab, S., & Tidwell, R. (2002). International students in higher education: Identification of needs and implications for policy and practice. *Journal of Studies in International Education, 6*(4), 305–322.

Hartle, T. (2004, Spring). Foreign students and scholars: Do not pass go. *The Presidency,* pp. 14–16.

Hayes, R. L., & Lin, H. (1994). Coming to America: Developing social support systems for international students. *Journal of Multicultural Counseling and Development, 22*(1), 7–16.

Hechanova-Alampay, R., Beehr, T. A., Christiansen, N. D., & van Horn, R. K. (2002). Adjustment and strain among domestic and international student sojourners. *School Psychology International, 23*(4), 458–474.

Jacob, E. J. (2001). Using counselor training and collaborative programming strategies in working with international students. *Journal of Multicultural Counseling and Development, 29*(1), 73–88.

Kim, B. S. K., Atkinson, D. R., & Umemoto, D. (2001). Asian cultural values and the counseling process: Current knowledge and directions for future research. *The Counseling Psychologist, 29*(4), 570–603.

Klineberg, O., & Hull, W. F. (1979). *At a foreign university.* New York: Praeger.

Kong, D. (2001, November 1). Post-Sept. 11 harassment: Civil rights complaints up. *The Associated Press.* Retrieved November 8, 2004, from http://www.asianweek.com/2001_11_1/news_harassment.html

Lee, J., Koeske, G. F., & Sales, E. (2004). Social support buffering of acculturative stress: A study of mental health symptoms among Korean international students. *International Journal of Intercultural Relations, 28,* 399–414.

Leong, F. T. L., & Chou, E. L. (2002). Counseling international students and sojourners. In P. B. Pedersen, W. J. Lonner, J. E. Trimble, & J. Draguns (Eds.), *Counseling across cultures* (5th ed., pp. 185–207). Alexandria, VA: American Counseling Association.

Leong, F. T. L., & Sedlacek, W. (1986). A comparison of international and U.S. students' preferences for help sources. *Journal of College Student Personnel, 27,* 426–430.

Leong, F. T. L., & Sedlacek, W. (1989). Academic and career needs of international and United States college students. *Journal of College Student Development, 30,* 106–111.

Lin, J. C. G. (2000). College counseling and international students. In K. Humphrey & D. Davis (Eds.), *College counseling: Issues and strategies for a new millennium* (pp. 169–183). Alexandria, VA: American Counseling Association.

Lin, J. C. G., Orozco, C., Quick, C., Roberts, K., & Helms, L. (1999, April). *Modifying Traditional Counseling Groups for International Students.* Workshop presented at the annual convention of the American Counseling Association, San Diego, CA.

Lin, J. C. G., & Yi, J. (1997). Asian international students' adjustment: Issues and programs suggestions. *College Student Journal, 31,* 473–479.

Lysgaard, S. (1955). Adjustment in a foreign society: Norwegian Fulbright grantees visiting the United States. *International Social Science Bulletin, 10,* 45–51.

Mallinckrodt, B., & Leong, F. T. L. (1992). International graduate students, stress, and social support. *Journal of College Student Development, 33,* 71–78.

Mau, W., & Jepsen, D. A. (1988). Attitudes toward counselors and counseling processes: A comparison of Chinese and American graduate students. *Journal of Counseling & Development, 67,* 189–192.

Mau, W., & Jepsen, D. A. (1990). Help-seeking perceptions and behaviors: A comparison of Chinese and American graduate students. *Journal of Multicultural Counseling and Development, 18,* 94–104.

Merta, R. J., Ponterotto, J. G., & Brown, R. D. (1992). Comparing the effectiveness of two directive styles in the academic counseling of foreign students. *Journal of Counseling Psychology, 39,* 214–218.

Mori, S. (2000). Addressing the mental health concerns of international students. *Journal of Counseling & Development, 78,* 137–144.

Myburgh, C. P. H., Nihaus, L., & Poggenpoel, M. (2002). International learners' experiences and coping mechanisms within a culturally diverse context. *Education, 123,* 107–129.

Nash, D. (1991). The course of sojourner adaptation: A new test of the U-curve hypothesis. *Human Organization, 50*(3), 283–286.

Nilsson, J. E., Berkel, L. A., Flores, L. Y., & Lucas, M. S. (2004). Utilization rate and presenting concerns of international students at a university counseling center: Implications for outreach programming. *Journal of College Student Psychotherapy, 19*(2), 49–59.

Oberg, K. (1960). Culture shock: Adjustment to new cultural environments. *Practical Anthropology, 4,* 177–182.

Oh, Y., Koeske, G. F., & Sales, E. (2002). Acculturation, stress, and depressive symptoms among Korean immigrants in the United States. *Journal of Social Psychology, 142*(4), 511–526.

Oropeza, B. A. C., Fitzgibbon, M., & Barón, A. (1991). Managing mental health crises of foreign college students. *Journal of Counseling & Development, 69,* 280–284.

Pederson, P. B. (1991). Counseling international students. *The Counseling Psychologist, 19*(1), 10–58.

Rahman, O., & Rollock, D. (2004). Acculturation, competence, and mental health among South Asian students in the United States. *Journal of Multicultural Counseling and Development, 32,* 130–142.

Ryder, A. G., Alden, L. E., & Paulhus, D. L. (2000). Is acculturation unidimensional or bidimensional? A head-to-head comparison in the prediction of personality, self-identity, and adjustment. *Journal of Personality and Social Psychology, 79*(1), 49–65.

Sandhu, D., & Asrabadi, B. (1994). Development of an acculturative stress scale for international students: Preliminary findings. *Psychological Reports, 75,* 435–448.

Schmitt, M. T., Spears, R., & Branscombe, N. R. (2003). Constructing a minority group identity out of shared rejection: The case of international students. *European Journal of Social Psychology, 33,* 1–12.

Schram, J. L., & Lauver, P. J. (1988). Alienation in international students. *Journal of College Student Development, 29,* 146–150.

Seale, W., & Ward, C. (1990). The prediction of psychological and sociocultural adjustment during cross-cultural transitions. *International Journal of Intercultural Relations, 14,* 449–463.

Shen, Y.-J., & Herr, E. L. (2004). Career placement concerns of international graduate students: A qualitative study. *Journal of Career Development, 31*(1), 15–29.

Shih, S. F., & Brown, C. (2000). Taiwanese international students: Acculturation level and vocational identity. *Journal of Career Development, 27*(1), 35–47.

Sodowsky, G. R., & Plake, B. S. (1992). A study of acculturation differences among international people and suggestions for sensitivity to within-group differences. *Journal of Counseling & Development, 71*(1), 53–59.

Spencer-Rodgers, J. (2001). Consensual and individual stereotypic beliefs about international students among American host nations. *International Journal of Intercultural Relations, 25,* 639–657.

Sue, D. W., Arredondo, P., & McDavis, R. J. (1992). Multicultural competencies/standards: A call to the profession. *Journal of Counseling & Development, 70*(4), 477–486.

Sue, D. W., Carter, R. T., Casa, J. M., Fouad, N. A., Ivey, A. E., Jensen, M., et al. (1998). *Multicultural counseling competencies: Individual and organizational development.* Thousand Oaks, CA: Sage.

Sue, D. W., & Sue, D. (2003). *Counseling the culturally diverse: Theory and practice* (4th ed.). New York: Wiley.

Suinn, R. M., Ahuna, C., & Khoo, G. (1992). The Suinn-Lew Self-Identity Acculturation Scale: Concurrent and factorial validation. *Educational and Psychological Measurement, 52,* 1041–1046.

Swagler, M. A., & Ellis, M. V. (2003). Crossing the distance: Adjustment of Taiwanese graduate students in the United States. *Journal of Counseling Psychology, 50,* 420–437.

Thomas, K., & Althen, G. (1989). Counseling foreign students. In P. B. Pedersen, J. G. Draguns, W. J. Lonner, & J. E. Trimble (Eds.), *Counseling across cultures* (3rd ed., pp. 205–241). Honolulu: University of Hawaii Press.

Thorstensson, L. (2001). This business of internationalization: The academic experiences of 6 Asian MBA international students at the University of Minnesota's Carlson School of Management. *Journal of Studies in International Education, 5*(4), 317–340.

Triandis, H. C., Brislin, R., & Hui, C. H. (1988). Cross-cultural training across the individualism-collectivism divide. *International Journal of Intercultural Relations, 12,* 269–289.

Wan, T., Chapman, D. W., & Biggs, D. A. (1992). Academic stress of international students attending U.S. universities. *Research in Higher Education, 33*(5), 607–623.

Wehrly, B. (1986). Counseling international students: Issues, concerns, and programs. *International Journal for the Advancement of Counselling, 9,* 11–22.

William, C. L., & Berry, J. W. (1991). Primary prevention of acculturative stress among refugees: Application of psychological theory and practice. *American Psychologist, 46*(6), 632–641.

Winkelman, M. (1994). Cultural shock and adaptation. *Journal of Counseling & Development, 73,* 121–126.

Wong, J. K. (2004). Are the learning styles of Asian international students culturally or contextually based? *International Education Journal, 4*(4), 154–166.

Yang, B., & Clum, G. A. (1995). Measures of life stress and social support specific to an Asian student population. *Journal of Psychopathology and Behavioral Assessment, 17*(1), 51–67.

Yang, B., Teraoka, M., Eichenfield, G. A., & Audas, M. C. (1994). Meaningful relationships between Asian international and U.S. college students: A descriptive study. *College Student Journal, 28*(1), 108–115.

Yang, E., Wong, S. C., Hwang, M., & Heppner, M. J. (2002). Widening our global view: The development of career counseling services for international students. *Journal of Career Development, 28,* 203–213.

Yasuda, T., & Duan, C. (2002). Ethnic identity, acculturation, and emotional well-being among Asian American and Asian international students. *Asian Journal of Counselling, 9*(1–2), 1–26.

Yau, T. Y., Sue, D., & Hayden, D. (1992). Counseling style preference of international students. *Journal of Counseling Psychology, 39*(1), 100–104.

Yeh, C. J., & Inose, M. (2003). International students' reported English fluency, social support satisfaction, and social connectedness as predictors of acculturative stress. *Counselling Psychology Quarterly, 16,* 15–28.

Yi, J., Lin, J. C. G., & Kishimoto, Y. (2003). Utilization of counseling services by international students. *Journal of Instructional Psychology, 30*(4), 333–342.

Ying, Y.-W., & Liese, L. H. (1991). Emotional well-being of Taiwan students in the U.S.: An examination of pre- to post-arrival differential. *International Journal of Intercultural Relations, 15,* 345–366.

Yoon, E., & Portman, T. A. A. (2004). Critical issues of literature on counseling international students. *Journal of Multicultural Counseling and Development, 32,* 33–43.

Zakaria, F. (2004, November 29). Rejecting the next Bill Gates. *Newsweek,* p. 33.

PART IV

SOCIAL AND PERSONAL ADJUSTMENT

16

In Search of Personality in Asian Americans: What We Know and What We Don't Know

Edward C. Chang

Rita Chang

Joyce P. Chu

In this chapter, we look at studies of personality in Asian Americans. We begin with a brief introduction to the study of personality and then critically appraise the extant empirical literature on personality to determine what we do and don't know about the form and function of some popular personality constructs within Asian Americans. Following this, we turn to a discussion regarding the limits of research on personality in Asian Americans and what factors need to be considered in future efforts to develop an understanding of Asian American personality.

What Is Personality and Who Is Asking the Question?

What is personality? Although there are a number of different definitions of personality, most would agree that personality refers to a set of important and relatively stable attributes that distinguish one individual from another (Ewen, 2003). However, what individual difference attributes are deemed important depends on the specific theoretical framework applied. For example, the psychodynamic framework focuses on a notion of personality that is

Authors' Note: The first author would like to acknowledge Chang Suk-Choon and Tae Myung-Sook for their encouragement and support throughout this project.

believed to result from a host of early childhood experiences and intrapsychic forces (Freud, 1933/1965). Accordingly, attributes associated with unique challenges faced by the child as she or he maneuvers through different psychosexual stages are believed to result in the establishment of distinct personality types (e.g., anal-retentive vs. anal-expulsive). In contrast, the dispositional framework focuses on a notion of personality as enduring. Thus, dispositionists tend to believe that individuals possess distinct traits (e.g., extroversion, neuroticism) that remain largely robust despite an individual's movement across time and space (McCrae et al., 1999). Any meaningful understanding of personality must always get back to addressing this question: What is the theoretical framework from which one is to identify and study personality?

LOCATING PERSONALITY (STUDIES) OF ASIAN AMERICANS OVER THE PAST FORTY YEARS

To get an impression of what we do and do not know about the study of personality in Asian Americans, we began with a broad snapshot look at the empirical literature. Using the PsycINFO database limited to peer-reviewed journals published between 1960 and 2004, we entered for our subject search "Personality Traits" and looked for the words "Asian" or "Asian American" anywhere in the text. The results were surprising (see Figure 16.1). Although we did not expect to find hundreds of empirical studies on Asian American personality, we were nevertheless alarmed by the paucity of research focusing on Asian Americans and Asians. For example, out of the 373 studies published between 1960 and 1969, there were no studies focusing on either Asian Americans (0%) or Asians (0%). More than three decades later, and despite the 15-fold increase in publications involving the study of personality between 1990 and 1999, the pattern had not changed much. Out of the 5,698 studies published in those 10 years, only 6 studies involved Asian Americans (.1%), and only 26 studies involved Asians (.4%). It seems apparent that researchers have done little to expand their empirical studies of personality to more diverse ethnic groups over the past 40 years, as indicated in Figure 16.1.

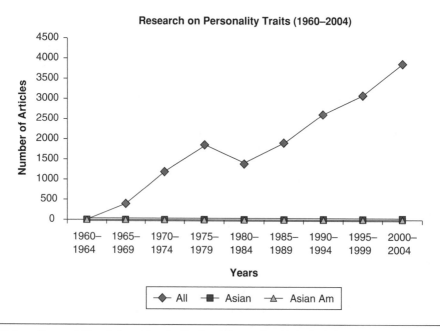

Research on Personality Traits (1960–2004)

Figure 16.1 Research Trends Involving the Study of Personality Traits in Asians and Asian Americans, Compared With Total Number of Published Articles

The Little That We Know: Locating Key Personalities in Asian Americans

Given the little that we know about studies of personality in Asian Americans, we decided to focus on identifying relevant personality studies looking at research published from 1990 to the present. First, after identifying the 90 distinct constructs classified by the PsycINFO database as "Personality Traits," we applied two criteria to identify which of these personality traits were relevant for our comprehensive review of individual differences in Asian Americans: (a) importance in the field as defined by abundance of empirical research produced, and (b) generation of research interest for Asian American communities in particular. We then executed a PsycINFO search to determine how many peer-reviewed research works were published from the year 1990 to present that included the trait as a key concept. We also recorded the number of empirical articles in the PsycINFO database that examined each personality trait with Asian American groups. That number was obtained by performing a keyword search using both the trait name and "Asian American" as keywords. Many articles regarding Asian Americans, though, were classified as "Asian." To ensure that all Asian American articles were surveyed, we perused each Asian article to reclassify those works that actually examined an Asian American sample. The "Asian American" article counts reflected those changes. For this study, inclusion criteria for "Asian American" included birth in, or immigration to, the North American continent.

Six of the ninety personality traits were selected for the present review by choosing traits that both generated the greatest number of empirical articles since 1990 and showed the presence of any number of articles concerning Asian Americans and the relevant personality trait. This selection procedure yielded the following six traits (listed from most to least number of publications generated): risk taking, cognitive style, sexuality, locus of control, empathy, and self-control. What follows next are summaries based on our review of the general and Asian American–specific literature for each of these six traits. These summaries are provided in Table 16.1.

Risk Taking

Risk taking involves taking a chance on a game, an event, a happening, or a venture that lacks certainty (Peck, 1986). In research, risk taking often includes behaviors like engaging in acts involving unhealthy weight loss, substance abuse, delinquency, and early/unsafe sexual activity (Neumark-Sztainer, Story, French, & Cassuto, 1996). A meta-analysis of gender differences in risk taking showed that for 14 out of 16 types of risk taking, there was greater risk taking among male participants, but certain types (e.g., intellectual risk taking and physical skills) produced larger gender differences than others (e.g., smoking). There were also significant shifts in the size of the gender gap between successive age levels, with the gap becoming smaller over time (Byrnes, Miller, & Schafer, 1999). Overall, it seems that risk taking in excess is maladaptive. In HIV/AIDS prevention research, individuals who use drugs and do not use condoms score significantly higher on a scale assessing characteristic impulsivity, risk taking, and sensation seeking than other individuals (Schafer, Blanchard, & Fals-Stewart, 1994). Middle adolescent risk-taking behavior also mediated the influence of early adolescent parental warmth-involvement and deviant-peer affiliations on involvement in a pregnancy by 12th grade (Scaramella, Conger, Simons, & Whitbeck, 1998).

Several large-scale survey studies have compared risk taking in adolescents of different ethnic groups, and Asian Americans usually report less risky behaviors (e.g., unsafe/early sex, gambling, alcohol/drug abuse) than African, Latino, European, and Native Americans (e.g., Neumark-Sztainer et al., 1996; Stinchfield, 2000). Similar results have emerged for the college population (e.g., McLaughlin, Chen, Greenberger, & Biermeier, 1997). Although Asian Americans appear less likely to contract HIV as a result of their sexual behavior, Strunin (1991) found that the Asian American adolescents in his sample were also much less knowledgeable about HIV transmission methods than were European American and African American students.

The lower rates of risk taking among Asian Americans may reflect a cultural tendency, stricter parenting styles, or more realistic/

Table 16.1 Summary Table of Personality Traits and Patterns Identified in the Empirical Literature From 1990 to 2005

Trait/Related Terms	Total N	European American (EA) Findings	AA N	Asian American (AA) Findings
Risk taking: Taking a chance on an uncertain event or venture. **Related terms**: gambling, sexual risk taking, risk perception.	2728	Males > females in risk taking (Byrnes, Miller, & Schafer, 1999). High risk takers more likely to use drugs and have unprotected sex. Higher risk for HIV infection and early pregnancy (Scaramella, Conger, Simons, & Whitbeck, 1998; Schafer, Blanchard, & Fals-Stewart, 1994).	10	AAs < EAs in risky behaviors like substance abuse and early sexual activity (e.g., Neumark-Sztainer, Story, French, & Cassuto, 1996). **Further Questions:** Stricter parenting styles of AA parents? General cultural tendency? More realistic/pessimistic expectations of the outcomes of risks?
Cognitive style: A preferred or habitual style of learning or thinking. **Related terms:** learning style, cognitive complexity, field dependence, impulsiveness, reflectiveness.	1977	Depressed individuals > nondepressed individuals in external locus of control (LOC) and depressive attributional styles (e.g., McCauley, Mitchell, Burke, & Moss, 1988). "Looming maladaptive style" as a danger schema to produce specific vulnerability to anxiety (Riskind, Williams, Gessner, Chrosniak, & Cortina, 2000).	7	AAs ≠ other ethnic groups and AAs ≠ Asians in preferred learning modalities (Dunn et al., 1990; Ewing & Yong, 1992; Hong & Suh, 1995). **Further Questions:** How does the setup of the American school system facilitate or impair academic success of Asian American children?
Sexuality: Includes components like sexual behavior, sexual attitudes, affects, cognitions, or sexual responses (Andersen & Cyranowski, 1995). **Related terms**: sex, sexual fantasy, sexual satisfaction.	1951	Males ≠ females in arousal process; for women, feelings more closely tied to sexual affects (e.g., Joseph, Markus, & Tafarodi, 1992). Physical factors predominant in men's sexuality; sociocultural factors predominant in women's (Baumeister, 2000).	5	AAs > EAs in sexual conservativeness (e.g., Cochran, Mays, & Leung, 1991; Kennedy & Gorzalka, 2002), though conservativeness decreases with acculturation (Meston, Trapnell, & Gorzalka, 1998). **Further Questions:** Impact of minority status on sexuality for AAs?

Construct	Articles	Findings	Rank	Cultural findings / Further Questions
Locus of control: An overall sense of control over one's environment (Bandura, 1977). **Related terms:** attribution, helplessness, self-determination.	1659	People with internal LOC > people with external LOC in academic success (e.g., Rotter, 1966). Internal LOC → well-being (e.g., Fisher, 1984); external LOC → negative health and depression (e.g., Seligman, 1975).	3	AAs = EAs (Moneta, Schneider, & Csikszentmihalyi, 2001). AAs > EAs in external LOC (Meredith, 1966). **Further Questions:** AAs more community focused and emphasize conformity—different meaning of "external control"? External LOC may be more realistic/adaptive for AAs.
Empathy: Ability to take another's viewpoint, ability to vicariously experience the feelings of another, or both (Davis, 1983; Mehrabian & Epstein, 1972). **Related terms:** sympathy, agreeableness.	1415	Empathic responding negatively related to aggression (Miller & Eisenberg, 1988). Empathy positively related to prosocial/helping behaviors. Altruistic or self-serving (e.g., Batson et al., 1988; Cialdini et al., 1987)? Empathy is stronger predictor of helping when recipient is ingroup (Stürmer, Snyder, & Omoto, 2005).	1	One study on empathy with AAs. No ethnic differences reported (Schewe & O'Donohue, 1996). **Further Questions:** Predictors of empathy's relationship with helping may be differ for AAs. Asian cultures emphasize ingroup and greater good—greater tendency to empathize with and help certain people?
Self-control: Ability to regulate one's own impulses, affect, and behavior, perhaps to obtain some future reward (Metcalfe & Mischel, 1999). **Related terms:** anger control, emotional control, self-regulation.	1283	Low self-control positively related to criminal behavior (DeLisi, 2001). Self-control in childhood → later academic/social competence (e.g., Laursen, Pulkkinen, & Adams, 2002). Deficits in self-control → depression? Depressed individuals don't maintain desired behavior in the absence of external reinforcement (Rehm, 1977).	2	Ethnic minority families > EA families in emphasizing self-control in children (Julian, McKenry, & McKelvey, 1994). EAs > AAs in self-reinforcing to regulate affect when external reinforcements delayed (Wong, Heiby, Kameoka, & Dubanoski, 1999). **Further Questions:** Self-control—more social function in AAs because of importance of harmonious social relationships?

pessimistic expectations on the outcomes of risks. Chang and Asakawa (2003), for example, have shown that Japanese have a pessimistic bias for negative outcomes. Pessimistic expectations for consequences of risk taking may thus have a positive effect on Asian Americans, deterring them from potentially self-destructive behaviors.

Cognitive Style

Cognitive style is a broad term that refers to an individual's preferred or habitual way of thinking/learning and includes constructs like reflective versus impulsive thinking styles, field dependence versus independence, and uncertainty versus certainty orientations (Sternberg & Grigorenko, 1997). Cognitive style also can influence the emotional or interpersonal aspects of one's life. For example, Sorrentino, Holmes, Hanna, and Sharp (1995) found that certainty-oriented individuals tend to have either a high or low level of trust for their significant others because of their need for cognitive closure, whereas uncertainty-oriented individuals typically have a moderate level of trust. In psychopathology research, cognitive style specifically refers to ways of thinking that promote or maintain certain disorders (e.g., Carver, Ganellen, & Behar-Mitrani, 1985). Cognitive styles frequently implicated in depression research are an external locus of control and depressive attibutional styles (e.g., Rotheram-Borus, Trautman, Dopkins, & Shrout, 1990), and in studies of anxiety, researchers have proposed a "looming maladaptive style" that functions as a danger schema to produce specific vulnerability to anxiety (Riskind, Williams, Gessner, Chrosniak, & Cortina, 2000).

Much of the research on the cognitive styles of Asian Americans has focused on learning orientations. It appears that Asian Americans' learning style differs most from that of African Americans, followed by those of Greek Americans and Mexican Americans (Dunn, Gemake, Jelali, & Zenhausern, 1990). Comparing Korean with Korean American students, Hong and Suh (1995) found that the preferred styles of Korean Americans tended to be more similar to those of European American students than to those of Korean students. Korean American students preferred warmer temperatures while studying, less formal class designs, less auditory learning, working in the evenings, and more classroom mobility. Ewing and Yong (1992) examined learning styles in gifted minority students and found that persistence, responsibility, and preferences for studying in the afternoon and bright lighting most characterized the styles of Chinese American children. Similar results emerged in a study by Hickson, Land, and Aikman (1994), where Asian Americans also preferred less intake (eating/drinking), less noise and auditory learning, and more parental motivation, direction from authorities, and visual learning than other groups.

Non-learning research has shown that Japanese are more likely to give "intermediate answers" (unclear answers that do not take any one side) than Japanese Americans, followed by European Americans; this tendency may reflect a higher tolerance for ambiguity. But Yamaoka (2000) also observed that third-generation Japanese Americans gave more intermediate answers than the second-generation group, even though the former is presumably more acculturated than the latter. Yamaoka suggested there may be a tendency to return to a Japanese way of thinking for that cognitive style.

In a study on self- and group-enhancing cognitive styles, Heine and Lehman (1997) compared Japanese, Asian Canadian, and European Canadian college students and showed that Japanese participants did not exhibit a group-serving bias when evaluating a close family member or the university they were attending, countering the idea that Japanese make up for their lack of self-enhancement through group enhancement.

Because cognitive style is a broad term that refers to many constructs, it is hard to speculate how the cognitive styles of Asian Americans and European Americans differ. Still, dissimilarities do exist, and it will be helpful to clarify the functions of certain ways of thinking for the two groups to facilitate drawing conclusions about the adaptive/maladaptive value of any cognitive style.

Sexuality

The study of human sexuality has lacked a consistent theoretical or conceptual framework (Abramson, 1990; Andersen & Cyranowski, 1995). In our examination of the literature, although we found an absence of one cohesive sexuality definition used consistently across studies, we found that most researchers assess sexuality using different combinations of the following components: sexual behavior, attitudes, affects, cognitions, and responses (Andersen & Cyranowski, 1995). For example, sexual behaviors may chronicle the range of sexual activities one has engaged in, such as incidence of heterosexual intercourse, homosexual behavior, oral-genital behavior, and so on, as well as other factors, such as age of first intercourse, number of sexual partners, or frequency of intercourse (e.g., Andersen & Cyranowski, 1995; Oliver & Hyde, 1993). Sexual attitudes characterize one's attitudes and affective responses toward sex, such as sexual permissiveness, attitudes about homosexuality, attitudes about extramarital sex, anxiety about sex, sexual satisfaction, double-standard attitudes, and attitudes about masturbation (e.g., Oliver & Hyde, 1993; Simpson & Gangestad, 1991). Sexuality, as defined in cognitive terms, may encompass one's self-views on sexuality, or sexual self-schemas (Andersen & Cyranowski, 1995). Sexuality also may be defined by how the sexual response cycle relates to stages of sexual engagement such as desire, excitement, orgasm, and resolution (e.g., Kaplan, 1979; Masters & Johnson, 1966). A developmental course of sexuality that results in healthy sexual adjustment may include confidence, competence and responsibility regarding sexuality (Maddock, 1983; Mrazek & Mrazek, 1981).

Many studies have documented clear differences between Asian Americans and other diverse ethnic groups in sexuality attitudes and behaviors. For example, sexuality is connected to procreation within the context of marriage in most Asian cultures, with limited discussions and education about premarital sexual activity (e.g., Chan, 1986; Kulig, 1994). Additionally, several studies have found that Asian Americans report more conservative attitudes about sexuality and

have later timetables for initiation of sexual activity and later acquisition of knowledge about sex (e.g., Kennedy & Gorzalka, 2002; Meston, Trapnell, & Gorzalka, 1998). These more conservative sexual attitudes affect behavior, with Asian Americans reporting more conservative sexual behaviors, such as less likelihood to initiate sex at an early age, higher percentage of people reporting to be virgins, lower percentage of people being sexually active, and lower number of reported lifetime sexual partners (e.g., Cochran, Mays, & Leung, 1991; McLaughlin et al., 1997; Schuster, Bell, Nakajima, & Kanouse, 1998). With the documentation of these basic differences in sexual behaviors and attitudes, further research is needed to better understand their implications of these sexuality differences for mental health treatment and the meaning of healthy sexual development in Asian Americans. Additionally, more research is needed to study the impact of minority status on sexuality for this ethnic group (Okazaki, 2002).

Locus of Control

The term *locus of control* was originally defined by Rotter (1966) as a cognitive construct, as one's overall sense of control over one's environment. External control is the view that control lies in forces external to the self, such as fate, luck, or other, whereas internal control is the view that action consequences are a function of one's own behavior. Rotter's (1966) Internal/External scale measures locus of control along one dimension, classifying someone as either internal or external. Levenson (1974) later broadened Rotter's measure of locus of control to a three-dimensional scale that not only measures the dimension of internal locus of control but also expands assessment of external control into the two dimensions of Powerful Others and Chance. Since the original conception of the locus of control construct, additional research has suggested that measures of locus of control may actually be a marker of a higher-order concept such as the broad dispositional trait of "positive self-concept" (Judge, Erez, Bono, & Thoresen, 2002). Taken together, locus of control, self-esteem, generalized self-efficacy, and emotional stability may be components of an overall positive self-concept (Judge et al., 2002).

Specifically, internal locus of control has been found to have positive associations with well-being (e.g., Fisher, 1984). External locus of control, with its perceptions of uncontrollability, has been linked with negative health, such as anxiety, stress, perceived illness, and especially depression (e.g., Seligman, 1975).

Ethnicity has been shown to have clear effects on locus of control. For example, African Americans have been consistently shown to have lower internal control than European Americans (e.g., Garcia & Levenson, 1975; Shaw & Uhl, 1971). Findings for Asian Americans, on the other hand, have been limited and inconsistent. For example, though some studies found greater external locus of control in Asian Americans compared to European Americans (e.g., Meredith, 1966; Padilla, Wagatsuma, & Lindholm, 1985), others found no differences between the two groups (e.g., Moneta, Schneider, & Csikszentmihalyi, 2001; Yong, 1994). Another study found that Asian Americans expressed less internal control than European Americans but more internal control than other minority groups (Coleman, 1966).

These inconsistencies in findings on locus of control for Asian Americans make it difficult to draw any conclusions, and further research (e.g., a meta-analysis) is needed to determine whether Asian Americans do tend to be more externally oriented. Research also should explore the source of these inconsistencies, such as the possibility that Asian Americans may exercise more variability in internal versus external control, depending on the context and situation. Finally, more research is needed to understand differing meanings of, and the adaptive versus maladaptive nature of, locus of control for Asian Americans.

Empathy

Researchers have approached the study of empathy from many different directions, and, as a result, no consensus exists on the definition of the construct. Some view empathy as a trait that certain individuals have more of than others, and others view empathy as a situation-specific, cognitive-affective state that one can manipulate in experiments. Empathy in the clinical context has also been the focus of a few studies, but therapeutic empathy is not so much an individual difference but a "multistage interpersonal process" (Duan & Hill, 1996). There has also been disagreement over whether empathy is the ability to take another's viewpoint or the ability to vicariously experience the feelings of another (Mehrabian & Epstein, 1972), though some studies have pushed for a multidimensional conceptualization of empathy (e.g., Davis, 1983).

Empathy has long been positively associated with prosocial helping behavior (e.g., Batson et al., 1988) and negatively associated with aggression (e.g., Miller & Eisenberg, 1988), but it is unclear whether the relation between empathy and helping behavior is the result of altruism (e.g., Fultz, Batson, Fortenbach, McCarthy, & Varney, 1986) or egoistic motives like relief of feelings of sadness or guilt (Cialdini et al., 1987). Empathy also appears to be a stronger predictor of helping when the recipient of assistance is an ingroup member than when that person is an outgroup member (Stürmer, Snyder, & Omoto, 2005). But helping behavior may have a downside, as people who experience high empathy may allocate more resources to the target of empathy even though it reduces resources for the collective good (Batson et al., 1995).

Virtually no research is available on empathy in Asian Americans. Schewe and O'Donohue (1996) examined the effects of a rape prevention program on a group of college males that included Asian Americans, but they did not report any ethnic differences in levels of empathy or program effectiveness. In the future, researchers may want to see if empathy and its correlates (e.g., helping behavior) are the same in Asian Americans. For example, given the emphasis Asian cultures traditionally place on the ingroup (Markus & Kitayama, 1991), perhaps the effect found by Stürmer et al. (2005) would be greater for Asian Americans. And given the importance of the collective good in certain Asian cultures, perhaps Asian Americans high in empathy would be less likely to devote resources to a target of empathy if they knew the action would detract from the group's well-being.

Self-Control

Self-control refers to an individual's ability to regulate his or her own impulses, affect, and behavior in the present to obtain some future reward—for example, through delay of gratification. Metcalfe and Mischel (1999) have suggested that one's level of self-control arises from the balance between the emotional "go" system and the cognitive "know" system. Researchers have mostly examined self-control from a childhood and developmental perspective (Mischel & Mischel, 1983), but studies also show a relationship between the ability to exercise self-control in childhood and academic/social competence and coping ability in adolescence (Shoda, Mischel, & Peake, 1990). Additionally, studies with European American adults find a relationship between low self-control and criminal behavior (DeLisi, 2001).

Julian, McKenry, and McKelvey (1994) looked at parenting styles among Asian, African, European, and Latino American families and found that the ethnic minority families were more likely than the European American families to emphasize self-control in their children. The emphasis may be an adaptive response to societal racism. Wong, Heiby, Kameoka, and Dubanoski (1999) examined the relationship of self-control to depressive symptoms in a geriatric population and found that for both Asian Americans and European Americans, the ability to regulate affect through self-reinforcement when environmental reinforcements were delayed negatively predicted depression five months later. The European Americans had higher levels of self-reinforcement than the Asian Americans, though the two groups did not differ in degree of depression. Results suggest that there may be cultural norms for engaging in self-reinforcing behavior, and the relation between self-reinforcement and depression may not be the same across cultures.

From "What Has Been Missed" to "What Needs to Be Done"

In our brief but critical look at some of the personality variables that have been of popular interest to researchers over the past four decades, at least two clear patterns seem apparent to us with regard to the study of Asian Americans. First, personality psychologists

have understudied Asian Americans. In the present review of the top six personality variables that have been studied over the past four decades, only 28 out of 11,041 studies ($< .25\%$) specifically involved the study of Asian Americans. Indeed, despite the growing public appreciation that Asian Americans represent a distinct and important ethnic group living within the United States (Uba, 1994; Zhang, 2003; Zia, 2000), it appears that most researchers, including personality researchers, have failed to spend much time and effort in studying this unique and complex population. Accordingly, even when findings for a given personality variable (e.g., risk taking) appear consistent across the less than a dozen studies conducted on Asian Americans, it is difficult to have great confidence in the reliability of such findings in the absence of many more studies that use multiple measures and methods of personality assessment (Okazaki & Sue, 1995). Of course, we realize that in some cases, it is difficult for researchers to conduct comprehensive large-scale studies of Asian Americans. Yet, Asian Americans represent an increasingly accessible population of study. So, why have efforts by mainstream researchers to study Asian American personality been so limited or unsuccessful despite the ever-growing presence of Asian Americans in the United States? Clearly, if researchers are interested in developing a complete understanding of personality within Asian Americans, then researchers must work on finding effective ways to assess this rich and ethnically diverse group. Such efforts may include collaborating with other researchers who have greater access to Asian American populations, working with various Asian American organizations and communities to solicit research participation, and seeking grants that provide funding to survey large representative samples of Asian Americans throughout the country.

Second, of the limited number of personality studies we have identified involving Asian Americans, most have been based on extending dominant (i.e., Eurocentric) models and measures of personality onto the study of Asians and Asian Americans (Cheung, Cheung, Wada, & Zhang, 2003). Put another way, although most personality researchers do appreciate that some important group differences may be present (e.g., McCrae, Terracciano, & 79 Members of the Personality Profiles of Cultures Project, 2005), they often do not question the general usefulness of applying their model or measure of personality to different groups (Allik, 2005). Thus, most personality researchers appear to be interested in asking questions that focus more on finding out what is most common across different groups (e.g., can the structure of a given personality variable be replicated in different ethnic groups?), rather than in asking questions that focus more on finding out what is most different across them (e.g., are there different antecedents, consequences, or functions of a given personality variable across different ethnic groups?). This is because most (Western) personality researchers, despite their use of different theoretical frameworks, tend to implicitly endorse a universalistic view of personality (Quinones-Vidal, Lopez-Garcia, Penaranda-Ortega, & Tortosa-Gil, 2004). Indeed, even within the bold and emerging framework of positive psychology (e.g., Seligman & Csikszentmihalyi, 2000; Sheldon & King, 2001), there appears to be greater emphasis on identifying important character strengths believed to be present across all groups (Peterson & Seligman, 2004; cf. Bacon, 2005) and less emphasis on identifying virtues that are believed to be specific to certain groups. Consequently, adding to earlier concerns about the need for a multicultural framework in studying Asian Americans (Leong, 1996), some researchers have begun to raise questions about the apparent lack of a multicultural framework within positive psychology (Sandage, Hill, & Vang, 2003). Given that conventional top-down approaches may not shed sufficient light on what is relevant to the study of Asian American personality, it may be useful for researchers to consider bottom-up approaches that include, among other things, an appreciation for how Eastern cultures may impact our understanding and study of personality in Asian Americans.

FROM EASTERN CULTURES TO A PSYCHOLOGY OF ASIAN PERSONALITY

Typically, Western cultures, or the cultures of Europe and North America (the United States and Canada), are considered to be individualistic, given their emphasis on attending to the needs of the self over others (Greenwald, 1980; Weisz, Rothbaum, & Blackburn, 1984). Thus, for most Westerners, it is the attainment of personal happiness, rather than group happiness, that is highly regarded and sought after, as codified and expressed in historical works ranging from Aristotle's *Nicomachean Ethics* to the United States' *Declaration of Independence.* As noted by Markus and Kitayama (1991), the self that emerges from Western cultures is one that perceives itself as independent of others, including of family members (e.g., parents, siblings), friends, and of coworkers. In contrast, Eastern cultures or cultures found in many Asian countries, have been considered collectivist with a focus on fostering a view of the self as fundamentally interrelated with significant others (Doi, 1971/1973; Markus & Kitayama, 1991). Hence, attending to significant others, harmonious interdependence with them, and fitting in are not only valued but also often strongly expected among members living within these cultures. In turn, one finds that the self fostered in Eastern cultures, as in Japan, is interdependent with significant others, such that important others "participate actively and continuously in the definition of the interdependent self" (Markus & Kitayama, 1991, p. 227).

Given such apparent differences between Easterners and Westerners, it is not surprising that efforts to develop emic conceptualizations of Asian personality using bottom-up approaches have pointed to important group differences. For example, Yang and Bond (1990) selected 150 trait adjectives from the Chinese language and 20 sets of bipolar Big Five adjectives for factor analysis, and five factors emerged: social orientation versus self-centeredness, competence versus incompetence, expressiveness versus conservatism, self-control versus impulsiveness, and optimism versus neuroticism. Comparing the Chinese Big Five to the American Big Five, Yang and Bond found that combinations of the American factors could adequately explain four of the Chinese factors (all except optimism). Additionally, there was a one-to-one correspondence for only one of those four factors (social orientation with agreeableness), suggesting that the American Big Five slices the Asian personality into different segments than the Chinese Big Five does. Similarly,

Cheung et al. (1996) also identified some important differences in developing the Chinese Personality Assessment Inventory (CPAI) from indigenous Chinese material. Factor analysis revealed four factors, three of which roughly mapped onto the American factors of extraversion, neuroticism, and conscientiousness. These researchers titled the remaining factor "Chinese tradition," which describes personality styles related to the maintenance of interpersonal harmony and *Ren Qin* (literally, "interpersonal affection"). Cheung et al. (1996) then combined the Chinese translation of the NEO-PI-R and the CPAI for a factor analysis and found six factors, the American factors plus the Chinese tradition factor. None of the NEO-PI-R scales loaded on the Chinese tradition factor, and none of the CPAI scales loaded on the openness factor. These findings point to the possibility that researchers using Western instruments may have overlooked one important aspect of personality in Chinese and that openness may not be a relevant personality dimension for Chinese individuals. Accordingly, one might expect most Asian Americans who maintain some aspect of Eastern cultures and traditions to display personality attributes that are reflective of their distinct heritage.

Some Promising Signs of a Psychology of Asian American Personality

Notions about personality variables that may be specific to Asian Americans can be culled from at least three different sources:

1. Literature about Asian American cultural values and practices

2. Studies of general personality assessment instruments with Asian American samples

3. Studies of personality assessment instruments that were developed specifically with Asian Americans.

Each of these literatures is described briefly here.

First, several consistent themes exist in the psychological literature about Asian American culture. Because these Asian American–specific cultural values and practices may influence the development of personality traits, an examination of these cultural constructs yields valuable information about the Asian American personality. For example, family structure in Asian American cultures often revolves around respect, order, hierarchical authority, and duty (Uba, 1994). Communication may be indirect or inferred through behavior, with little open affection in the family. Gender roles may be scripted, with women playing the nurturing role and men playing the strong stoic role. This culture of the family, with its concomitant gender roles or expectations, may shape personality traits such as masculinity, femininity, emotionality, or obedience. As noted earlier, Eastern cultural emphasis on the precedence of the group over the individual, with emphasis on interpersonal harmony, also bears great importance on Asian American personalities. Asian Americans' perceptions and behaviors in social situations may revolve around the group or others' needs. They may appear accommodating and conforming, which is often mistaken for lack of assertiveness or submissiveness. Importantly, Kim, Li, and Ng (2005) developed an assessment tool of Asian American cultural values that exemplifies many of these personality influences. The 42-item Asian American Values Scale–Multidimensional (AAVS-M) measures Asian American–specific cultural values that are commonly observed among Asian Americans. Specifically, the AAVS-M comprises five main categories of cultural values that are most often endorsed by highly enculturated Asian Americans (i.e., first-generation Asian Americans): collectivism, conformity to norms, emotional self-control, family recognition through achievement, and humility. An additional dimension, filial piety, was included in the original Asian Values Scale (Kim, Atkinson, & Yang, 1999).

Second, several studies have explored how Asian Americans score on Western-based personality assessment instruments, comparing their responses to those of a European American comparison group. Many of these studies found significant differences in rates of endorsement. For example, studies looking at the Minnesota Multiphasic Personality Inventory (MMPI), one of the best known and widely used personality instruments, have found elevated reports on scale 2, depression, in normal Chinese American and

Japanese American males compared to European American males (Marsella, Sanborn, Kameoka, Shizuru, & Brennan, 1975), and more somatic complaints, depression, isolation, and anxiety in Asian American students compared to European American students (Chun, Enomoto, & Sue, 1996). Using Cattell's 16 Personality Factor questionnaire, Meredith (1966) found that Japanese American male students were more submissive, different, reserved, serious, regulated, tense, and affected by feelings and social pressures, and Japanese American females were more suspicious, group-dependent, submissive, different, reserved, and apprehensive, than their European American counterparts. Finally, in their study using the Omnibus Personality Inventory, Sue and colleagues (Sue & Frank, 1973; Sue & Kirk, 1973) found that compared to European Americans, Asian Americans scored higher on isolation, loneliness, anxiety, uncomfortableness, dislike for uncertainty and ambiguity, conformity, and obedience to authority, and lower on orientation to abstract concepts, independence, and social extraversion. Together, these results concerning differential scores on general personality assessment measures portray Asian American personalities in a negative light. In particular, researchers interpreted Asian Americans to be either maladjusted (e.g., reserved, submissive, serious) or elevated in distress and psychological symptomatology (e.g., anxious, depressed, lonely). Little research has attempted to examine and interpret these differences in terms of Asian American–specific personalities, understanding them instead in a culturally specific and possibly positive light. Additionally, few studies have integrated these general personality assessment studies to make overall conclusions about the basic personality structure for Asian Americans. As noted earlier, studies with the Chinese found a sixth personality factor in addition to the Big Five (Cheung, 2002). Similar research should be conducted to develop a better understanding of the structure and function of personality in Asian Americans.

Lastly, besides studies with general Western-based personality measures, research with new assessment tools developed specifically for Asian Americans can and should also inform ideas about Asian American personalities.

For example, the Loss of Face Scale (Zane & Yeh, 2002) points to the importance of considering shame or threat to one's social integrity in interpersonal dynamics as an important personality construct. Additionally, one of the most common concepts discussed in the psychological literature with regard to Asian Americans is enculturation and acculturation. The presumption is that those less acculturated to the mainstream culture, such as more recent immigrants, may be more likely to possess traits consistent with traditionally Asian values. Acculturation has an important influence on Asian American personalities, and acculturation scales such as the Suinn-Lew Asian Self-Identity Acculturation Scale (Suinn, Rickard-Figueroa, Lew, & Vigil, 1987) have been developed for Asian Americans specifically.

Taken together, these sources indicate that any meaningful study of Asian American personality must include (a) a clear understanding of how Eastern culture influences the form and function of personality in Asian Americans, (b) an appreciation that measures developed and normed from European American or non–Asian American samples may not represent valid or useful measures when used with Asian Americans, and (c) an understanding that we need more culture-specific models and measures of Asian Americans.

CONCLUDING COMMENT

In recent years, we have seen a growing appreciation for the study of personality and individual differences. Yet, such efforts appear to continue a popular strategy used by many personality researchers, namely, of focusing on what is most common rather than what is most specific across and within individuals from different groups. Perhaps as a consequence, most mainstream researchers have neglected to consider models and measures of personality that may be specific to particular ethnic groups. If this is the case, then it appears that one important way in which we will see greater progress toward the development of more thoughtful and comprehensive models and measures of Asian American personalities will be when researchers appreciate that even a universalistic framework for understanding

personality is only one of many conceptual frameworks available to them.

REFERENCES

Abramson, P. R. (1990). Sexual science: Emerging discipline or oxymoron? *The Journal of Sex Research, 27,* 147–165.

Allik, J. (2005). Personality dimensions across cultures. *Journal of Personality Disorders, 19,* 212–232.

Andersen, B. L., & Cyranowski, J. C. (1995). Women's sexuality: Behaviors, responses, and individual differences. *Journal of Consulting and Clinical Psychology, 63,* 891–906.

Bacon, S. F. (2005). Positive psychology's two cultures. *Review of General Psychology, 9,* 181–192.

Bandura, A. (1977). Self-efficacy: Toward a unifying theory of behavior change. *Psychological Review, 84,* 191–215.

Batson, C. D., Batson, J. G., Todd, R. M., Brummett, B. H., Shaw, L. L., & Aldeguer, C. M. R. (1995). Empathy and the collective good: Caring for one of the others in a social dilemma. *Journal of Personality and Social Psychology, 68,* 619–631.

Batson, C. D., Dyck, J. L., Brandt, J. R., Batson, J. G., Powell, A. L., McMaster, M. R., et al. (1988). Five studies testing two new egoistic alternatives to the empathy-altruism hypothesis. *Journal of Personality and Social Psychology, 55,* 52–77.

Baumeister, R. F. (2000). Gender differences in erotic plasticity: The female sex drive as socially flexible and responsive. *Psychological Bulletin, 126,* 347–374.

Byrnes, J. P., Miller, D. C., & Schafer, W. D. (1999). Gender differences in risk taking: A meta-analysis. *Psychological Bulletin, 125,* 367–383.

Carver, C. S., Ganellen, R. J., & Behar-Mitrani, V. (1985). Depression and cognitive style: Comparisons between measures. *Journal of Personality and Social Psychology, 49,* 722–728.

Chan, D. W. (1986). Sex misinformation and misconceptions among Chinese medical students in Hong Kong. *Medical Education, 20,* 390–398.

Chan, C. S. (1989). Issues of identity development among Asian-American lesbians and gay men. *Journal of Counseling & Development, 68,* 16–20.

Chang, E. C., & Asakawa, K. (2003). Cultural variations on optimistic and pessimistic bias for self versus a sibling: Is there evidence for self-enhancement in the West and for self-criticism in the East when the referent group is specified? *Journal of Personality and Social Psychology, 84,* 569–581.

Cheung, F. M. (2002). Universal and indigenous dimensions of Chinese personality. In K. S. Kurasaki & S. Okazaki (Eds.), *Asian American mental health: Assessment theories and methods* (pp. 123–138). New York: Kluwer Academic/ Plenum.

Cheung, F. M., Cheung, S. F., Wada, S., & Zhang, J. (2003). Indigenous measures of personality assessment in Asian countries: A review. *Psychological Assessment, 15,* 280–289.

Cheung, F. M., Leung, K., Fan, R. M., Song, W., Zhang, J. X., & Zhang, J. P. (1996). Development of the Chinese Personality Assessment Inventory. *Journal of Cross-Cultural Psychology, 27,* 181–199.

Chun, C.-A., Enomoto, K., & Sue, S. (1996). Health care issues among Asian Americans: Implications of somatization. In P. M. Kato & T. Mann (Eds.), *Handbook of diversity issues in health psychology* (pp. 347–365). New York: Plenum Press.

Cialdini, R. B., Schaller, M., Houlihan, D., Arps, K., Fultz, J., & Beaman, A. L. (1987). Empathy-based helping: Is it selflessly or selfishly motivated? *Journal of Personality and Social Psychology, 52,* 749–758.

Cochran, S. D., Mays, V. M., & Leung, L. (1991). Sexual practices of heterosexual Asian-American young adults: Implications for risk of HIV infection. *Archives of Sexual Behavior, 20,* 381–391.

Coleman, J. S. (1966). *Equality of educational opportunity.* Washington, DC: U.S. Department of Health, Education, and Welfare, Office of Education, Government Printing Office.

Davis, M. H. (1983). Measuring individual differences in empathy: Evidence for a multidimensional approach. *Journal of Personality and Social Psychology, 44,* 113–126.

DeLisi, M. (2001). Designed to fail: Self-control and involvement in the criminal justice system. *American Journal of Criminal Justice, 26,* 131–148.

Doi, T. (1973). *The anatomy of dependence* (J. Bester, Trans.). Tokyo: Kodansha. (Original work published 1971)

Duan, C., & Hill, C. E. (1996). The current state of empathy research. *Journal of Counseling Psychology, 43,* 261–274.

Dunn, R., Gemake, J., Jalali, F., Zenhausern, R., Quinn, P., & Spiridakis, J. (1990). Cross-cultural differences in learning styles of elementary-age students from four ethnic backgrounds. *Journal of Multicultural Counseling and Development, 18*, 68–93.

Ewen, R. B. (2003). *An introduction to theories of personality* (6th ed.). Mahwah, NJ: Lawrence Erlbaum.

Ewing, N. J., & Yong, F. L. (1992). A comparative study of the learning style preferences among gifted African-American, Mexican-American, and American-born Chinese middle grade students. *Roeper Review, 14*, 120–123.

Fisher, S. (1984). *Stress and the perception of control.* London: Lawrence Erlbaum.

Freud, S. (1965). *New introductory lectures on psychoanalysis* (J. Strachey, Trans.). New York: Norton. (Original work published 1933)

Fultz, J., Batson, C. D., Fortenbach, V. A., McCarthy, P. M., & Varney, L. L. (1986). Social evaluation and the empathy-altruism hypothesis. *Journal of Personality and Social Psychology, 50*, 761–769.

Garcia, C., & Levenson, H. (1975). Differences between blacks' and whites' expectation of control by chance and powerful others. *Psychological Reports, 37*, 563–566.

Greenwald, A. G. (1980). The totalitarian ego: Fabrication and revision of personal history. *American Psychologist, 35*, 603–618.

Heine, S. J., & Lehman, D. R. (1997). The cultural construction of self-enhancement: An examination of group-serving biases. *Journal of Personality and Social Psychology, 72*, 1268–1283.

Hickson, J., Land, A. J., & Aikman, G. (1994). Learning style differences in middle school pupils from four ethnic backgrounds. *School Psychology International, 15*, 349–359.

Hong, E., & Suh, B. K. (1995). An analysis of change in Korean-American and Korean students' learning styles. *Psychological Reports, 76*, 691–699.

Josephs, R. A., Markus, H. R., & Tafarodi, R. W. (1992). Gender and self-esteem. *Journal of Personality and Social Psychology, 63*, 391–402.

Judge, T. A., Erez, A., Bono, J. E., & Thoresen, C. J. (2002). Are measures of self-esteem, neuroticism, locus of control, and generalized self-efficacy indicators of a common core construct? *Journal of Personality and Social Psychology, 83*, 693–710.

Julian, T. W., McKenry, P. C., & McKelvey, M. W. (1994). Cultural variations in parenting: Perceptions of Caucasian, African-American, Hispanic, and Asian-American parents. *Family Relations: Interdisciplinary Journal of Applied Family Studies, 43*, 30–37.

Kaplan, H. S. (1979). *Disorders of sexual desire.* New York: Brunner/Mazel.

Kennedy, M. A., & Gorzalka, B. B. (2002). Asian and non-Asian attitudes toward rape, sexual harassment, and sexuality. *Sex Roles, 46*, 227–237.

Kim, B. S., Atkinson, D. R., & Yang, P. H. (1999). The Asian Values Scale: Development, factor analysis, validation, and reliabiliy. *Journal of Counseling Psychology, 46*, 342–352.

Kim, B. S. K., Li, L. C., & Ng, G. F. (2005). The Asian American Values Scale–Multidimensional: Development, reliability, and validity. *Cultural Diversity & Ethnic Minority Psychology, 11*, 187–201.

Kulig, J. C. (1994). Sexuality beliefs among Cambodians: Implications for health care professionals. *Health Care for Women International, 15*, 69–76.

Laursen, B., Pulkkinen, L., & Adams, R. (2002). The antecedents and correlates of agreeableness in adulthood. *Developmental Psychology, 38*, 591–603.

Leong, F. T. L. (1996). MCT theory and Asian-American populations. In D. W. Sue, A. E. Ivey, & P. B. Pedersen (Eds.), *A theory of multicultural counseling and therapy* (pp. 204–216). Pacific Grove, CA: Brooks/Cole.

Levenson, H. M. (1974). Activism and powerful others: Distinctions within the concept of internal-external control. *Journal of Personality Assessment, 38*, 377–383.

Maddock, J. W. (1983). Human sexuality in the life cycle of the family system. *Family Therapy Collections, 5*, 1–31.

Markus, H. R., & Kitayama, S. (1991). Culture and the self: Implications for cognition, emotion, and motivation. *Psychological Review, 20*, 568–579.

Marsella, A. J., Sanborn, K. O., Kameoka, V. A., Shizuru, L. S., & Brennan, J. M. (1975). Cross-validation of self-report measures of depression among normal populations of Japanese, Chinese, and Caucasian ancestry. *Journal of Clinical Psychology, 31*, 281–287.

Masters, W. H., & Johnson, V. E. (1966). *Human sexual response.* Boston: Little, Brown.

McCauley, E., Mitchell, J. R., Burke, P. M., & Moss, S. J. (1988). Cognitive attributes of depression in children and adolescents. *Journal of Consulting and Clinical Psychology, 56,* 903–908.

McCrae, R. R., Costa, P. T., Jr., de Lima, M. P., Simões, A., Ostendorf, F., Angleitner, A., et al. (1999). Age differences in personality across the adult life span: Parallels in five cultures. *Developmental Psychology, 35,* 466–477.

McCrae, R. R., Terracciano, A., & 79 Members of the Personality Profiles of Cultures Project. (2005). Personality profiles of cultures: Aggregate personality traits. *Journal of Personality and Social Psychology, 89,* 407–425.

McLaughlin, C. S., Chen, C., Greenberger, E., & Biermeier, C. (1997). Family, peer, and individual correlates of sexual experience among Caucasian and Asian American late adolescents. *Journal of Research on Adolescence, 7,* 33–53.

Mehrabian, A., & Epstein, N. (1972). A measure of emotional empathy. *Journal of Personality, 40,* 525–543.

Meredith, G. M. (1966). Amae and acculturation among Japanese American college students in Hawaii. *Journal of Social Psychology, 70,* 171–180.

Meston, C. M., Trapnell, P. D., & Gorzalka, B. B. (1998). Ethnic, gender, and length-of-residency influences on sexual knowledge and attitudes. *The Journal of Sex Research, 35,* 176–188.

Metcalfe, J., & Mischel, W. (1999). A hot/cool-system analysis of delay of gratification: Dynamics of willpower. *Psychological Review, 106,* 3–19.

Miller, P. A., & Eisenberg, N. (1988). The relation of empathy to aggressive and externalizing/antisocial behavior. *Psychological Bulletin, 103,* 324–344.

Mischel, H. N., & Mischel, W. (1983). The development of children's knowledge of self-control strategies. *Child Development, 54,* 603–619.

Moneta, G. B., Schneider, B., & Csikszentmihalyi, M. (2001). A longitudinal study of the self-concept and experiential components of self-worth and affect across adolescence. *Applied Developmental Science, 5,* 125–142.

Mrazek, D. A., & Mrazek, P. B. (1981). Psychosexual development within the family. In P. B. Mrazek & C. H. Kempe (Eds.), *Sexually abused children and their families* (pp. 17–32). Oxford, UK: Pergamon.

Neumark-Sztainer, D., Story, M., French, S., & Cassuto, N. (1996). Patterns of health-compromising behaviors among Minnesota adolescents: Sociodemographic variations. *American Journal of Public Health, 86,* 1599–1606.

Okazaki, S. (2002). Influences of culture on Asian Americans' sexuality. *The Journal of Sex Research, 39,* 34–41.

Okazaki, S., & Sue, S. (1995). Methodological issues in assessment research with ethnic minorities. *Psychological Assessment, 7,* 367–375.

Okazaki, S., & Sue, S. (2000). Implications of test revisions for assessment with Asian Americans. *Psychological Assessment, 12,* 272–280.

Oliver, M. B., & Hyde, J. S. (1993). Gender differences in sexuality: A meta-analysis. *Psychological Bulletin, 114,* 29–51.

Padilla, A. M., Wagatsuma, Y., & Lindholm, K. J. (1985). Acculturation and personality as predictors of stress in Japanese and Japanese-Americans. *Journal of Social Psychology, 125,* 295–305.

Peck, C. P. (1986). A public mental health issue: Risk-taking behavior and compulsive gambling. *American Psychologist, 41,* 461–465.

Peterson, C., & Seligman, M. E. P. (2004). *Character strengths and virtues: A handbook and classification.* New York: Oxford University Press.

Quinones-Vidal, E., Lopez-Garcia, J. J., Penaranda-Ortega, M., & Tortosa-Gil, G. (2004). The nature of social and personality psychology as reflected in *JPSP,* 1965–2000. *Journal of Personality and Social Psychology, 86,* 435–452.

Rehm, L. P. (1977). A self-control model of depression. *Behavior Therapy, 8,* 787–804.

Riskind, J. H., Williams, N. L., Gessner, T. L., Chrosniak, L. D., & Cortina, J. M. (2000). The looming maladaptive style: Anxiety, danger, and schematic processing. *Journal of Personality and Social Psychology, 79,* 837–852.

Rotheram-Borus, M. J., Trautman, P. D., Dopkins, S. C., & Shrout, P. E. (1990). Cognitive style and pleasant activities among female adolescent suicide attempters. *Journal of Consulting and Clinical Psychology, 58,* 554–561.

Rotter, J. B. (1966). Generalized expectancies for internal versus external control of reinforcement. *Psychological Monographs, 80* (1, Whole No. 609).

Sandage, S. J., Hill, P. C., & Vang, H. C. (2003). Toward a multicultural positive psychology:

Indigenous forgiveness and Hmong culture. *The Counseling Psychologist, 31,* 564–592.

Scaramella, L. V., Conger, R. D., Simons, R. L., & Whitbeck, L. B. (1998). Predicting risk for pregnancy by late adolescence: A social contextual perspective. *Developmental Psychology, 34,* 1233–1245.

Schafer, J., Blanchard, L., & Fals-Stewart, W. (1994). Drug use and risky sexual behavior. *Psychology of Addictive Behaviors, 8,* 3–7.

Schewe, P. A., & O'Donohue, W. (1996). Rape prevention with high-risk males: Short-term outcome of two interventions. *Archives of Sexual Behavior, 25,* 455–471.

Schuster, M. A., Bell, R. M., Nakajima, G. A., & Kanouse, D. E. (1998). The sexual practices of Asian and Pacific Islander high school students. *Journal of Adolescent Health, 23,* 221–231.

Seligman, M. E. P. (1975). *Helplessness.* San Francisco: Freeman.

Seligman, M. E. P., & Csikszentmihalyi, M. (2000). Positive psychology: An introduction. *American Psychologist, 55,* 5–14.

Shaw, R. L., & Uhl, N. P. (1971). Control of reinforcement and academic achievement. *Journal of Educational Research, 64,* 226–228.

Sheldon, K. M., & King, L. A. (2001). Why positive psychology is necessary. *American Psychologist, 56,* 216–217.

Shoda, Y., Mischel, W., & Peake, P. K. (1990). Predicting adolescent cognitive and self-regulatory competencies from preschool delay of gratification: Identifying diagnostic conditions. *Developmental Psychology, 26,* 978–986.

Simpson, J. A., & Gangestad, S. W. (1991). Individual differences in sociosexuality: Evidence for convergent and discriminant validity. *Journal of Personality and Social Psychology, 60,* 870–833.

Singh, G. K., & Kochanek, K. D., & MacDorman, M. F. (1996). Advance report of final mortality, 1994. *Monthly Vital Statistics Reports, 45*(3, Suppl.). Hyattsville, MD: National Center for Health Statistics.

Sorrentino, R. M., Holmes, J. G., Hanna, S. E., & Sharp, A. (1995). Uncertainty orientation and trust in close relationships: Individual differences in cognitive styles. *Journal of Personality and Social Psychology, 68,* 314–327.

Sternberg, R. J., & Grigorenko, E. L. (1997). Are cognitive styles still in style? *American Psychologist, 52,* 700–712.

Stinchfield, R. (2000). Gambling and correlates of gambling among Minnesota public school students. *Journal of Gambling Studies, 16,* 153–173.

Stürmer, S., Snyder, M., & Omoto, A. M. (2005). Prosocial emotions and helping: The moderating role of group membership. *Journal of Personality and Social Psychology, 88,* 532–546.

Strunin, L. (1991). Adolescents' perceptions of risk for HIV infection: Implications for future research. *Social Science & Medicine, 32,* 221–228.

Sue, D. W., & Frank, A. C. (1973). A typological approach to the psychological study of Chinese and Japanese American college males. *Journal of Social Issues, 29,* 129–148.

Sue, D. W., & Kirk, B. A. (1973). Differential characteristics of Japanese-American and Chinese-American college students. *Journal of Counseling Psychology, 20,* 142–148.

Suinn, R. M., Rickard-Figueroa, K., Lew, S., & Vigil, P. (1987). The Suinn-Lew Self-Identity Acculturation Scale: An initial report. *Education and Psychological Measurement, 47,* 401–407.

Uba, L. (1994). *Asian Americans: Personality patterns, identity, and mental health.* New York: Guilford Press.

Weisz, J. R., Rothbaum, F. M., & Blackburn, T. C. (1984). Standing out and standing in: The psychology of control in America and Japan. *American Psychologist, 39,* 955–969.

Wong, S. S., Heiby, E. M., Kameoka, V. A., & Dubanoski, J. P. (1999). Perceived control, self-reinforcement, and depression among Asian American and Caucasian American elders. *Journal of Applied Gerontology, 18,* 46–62.

Yamaoka, K. (2000). Variation in attitudes and values among Japanese Americans and Japanese Brazilians across generations. *Behaviormetrika, 27,* 125–151.

Yang, K., & Bond, M. H. (1990). Exploring implicit personality theories with indigenous or imported constructs: The Chinese case. *Journal of Personality and Social Psychology, 58,* 1087–1095.

Yong, F. L. (1994). Self-concepts, locus of control, and Machiavellianism of ethnically diverse middle school students who are gifted. *Roeper Review, 16,* 192–194.

Zane, N. W. S., & Yeh, M. (2002). The use of culturally-based variables in assessment: Studies on loss of face. In K. S. Kurasaki & S. Okazaki (Eds.), *Asian American mental health: Assessment theories and methods* (pp. 123–138). New York: Kluwer Academic/Plenum.

Zhang, L. (2003). *Asian Americans: Vulnerable populations, model interventions, and clarifying agendas.* Boston: Jones & Bartlett.

Zia, H. (2000). *Asian American dreams: The emergence of an American people.* New York: Farrar, Straus & Giroux.

17

Interpersonal Effectiveness Among Asian Americans: Issues of Leadership, Career Advancement, and Social Competence

Nolan Zane

Anna Song

As more Asian Americans become upwardly mobile in terms of jobs and careers, and as they expand on their social options in terms of interracial marriage and other social relationships, they have become increasingly concerned about efficacy in interpersonal situations (Guimares, 1980; Sue, 1977). Bakan (1966) has noted that life experiences, especially with respect to social relations, can be characterized in terms of agency or communion. Agency "manifests itself in self-protection, self-assertion, and self-expansion; communion manifests itself in the sense of being at one with other organisms. . . . Agency manifests itself in the urge to master; communion in noncontractual cooperation" (pp. 14–15). This distinction can be helpful in examining issues about interpersonal or social effectiveness. On the one hand, to be interpersonally effective, people often have to assert themselves and exert influence on others' behaviors, attitudes, or both. On the other hand, social effectiveness can involve developing and maintaining meaningful and high-quality social bonds and attachments. Thus, interpersonal effectiveness refers to the person's capacity to initiate, maintain, and enhance social relationships (communion) as well as the ability to influence others (agency). Although Asian Americans come from cultures that reputedly emphasize communion in terms of collectivism and sense of belongingness (Triandis, Bontempo, & Villareal, 1988), social connectiveness and harmonious interdependence (Markus & Kitayama, 1991), and maintaining face or social integrity among others (Heine, Lehman, Markus, & Kitayama, 1999), Asian Americans often experience difficulties and challenges in agency, at least within the context of American society.

DIFFICULTIES IN CAREER ADVANCEMENT AND IN ATTAINING LEADERSHIP/MANAGERIAL POSITIONS

Over the years, a consistent pattern has been documented with respect to Asian Americans in the workplace: Despite their high levels of education and technical training (relative to other ethnic groups and, at times, Whites), Asian Americans are not represented in high-level administrative or managerial positions in proportion to their numbers in a particular work-force. Referred to as the "glass ceiling" effect, this pattern of underrepresentation in esteemed positions, management, and administration has been found in professions and organizations in both the private and public sectors. In 1980, the U.S. Commission on Civil Rights reported on a number of analyses and studies that addressed Asian American career advancement. Using data from the U.S. Department of Labor, Cabezas (1980, cited in Bass, 1990) found that Asian Americans were seriously underrepresented as top administrators and decision makers. Even when Asian Americans were well represented in professional corporate jobs, few were promoted to top executive positions compared to White Americans (Minami, 1980).

This trend has continued into the 1990s and through the turn of the century. For example, a study of high-level executives in Fortune 500 companies found that 0.3% of these corporate officers were Asian American (Korn/Ferry International, 1990, Table 61, p. 23). The representation of Asian Americans in executive corporate positions was one-tenth of what would be expected given their population, since Asians constituted 2.9% of the general population in the 1990 Census. A study of engineers showed that Asian American engineers had job qualifications (i.e., educational level, years of experience, field of engineering) similar to those of their White American counterparts but were less likely to be in management or to be promoted to management positions (Tang, 1991). A study of the aerospace industry by the U.S. General Accounting Office (U.S. GAO) found that Asian Americans had a higher percentage of aerospace professionals than either African Americans or Hispanics. However, both of these ethnic minority groups had a higher percentage of managers than aerospace professionals (U.S. GAO, 1989). The findings suggest that Asian Americans may experience difficulties in advancing from professional to managerial positions in this industry, although it is also possible that nonprofessional African American and Hispanic workers were taking low-level managerial positions. Similar patterns of underrepresentation in managerial and administrative positions have been found in the legal profession (Jensen, 1990; Glater, 2001) and in the television media (U.S. Commission on Civil Rights, 1992).

With respect to the public sector, one study examined the city of San Francisco's civil service (Der & Lye, 1989). The investigators found that the ratio of administrators to professionals was lower for Asian Americans than for any other ethnic minority group, whereas Whites had the highest ratio. Not surprisingly, Asian Americans were underrepresented among local political leaders. In 1989, 35% of San Francisco's general population was Asian American, but only 1 member of the 11 elected to the city council was Asian American (U.S. Commission on Civil Rights, 1992).

Contrary to what many believe, this pattern of underrepresentation in leadership, managerial, and administrative positions does not appear to be a phenomenon solely associated with the problems concomitant with being an immigrant—learning a new lifestyle, communicating in English, and accessing useful social networks. In the study of engineers, the pattern of underrepresentation in managerial positions was found for both immigrants and U.S.-born Asians (Tang, 1991). A study of only U.S.-born Asian American men in various occupations revealed that Asian American men were 7% to 11% less likely to be in managerial occupations, even after accounting for ethnic variations in factors such as education level, English ability, work experience, region, marital status, disability, and type of industry. Thus, there appears to be compelling and convergent evidence that for many Asian Americans, both immigrants and U.S.-born individuals are experiencing significant career advancement difficulties in many professions and in work organizations within both the private and public sector.

It also appears that Asian Americans themselves perceive racial, ethnic, and/or cultural issues as major factors that contribute to their difficulties in career advancement. One study surveyed Asian Americans working in computer industries in Santa Clara County (Asian Americans for Community Involvement, 1993). Half of those sampled believed that their promotion to managerial positions was limited by their ethnicity or race, and 17% thought perceptions of their interactional styles adversely affected their career advancement. Cabezas, Tam, Lowe, Wong, and Turner (1989) surveyed over 300 Asian American professionals and managers in the San Francisco Bay Area and found that a majority of the Japanese Americans and a large majority (over 67%) of the Chinese and Filipino Americans considered racism a major factor limiting their career advancement. In New York, the majority of Asian American attorneys maintained that minority lawyers have fewer opportunities for promotion or choice cases and are less likely to attain partnership (New York Judicial Commission on Minorities, 1991).

DIFFICULTIES IN SOCIAL SKILLS AND IN BEHAVIORS RELATED TO AGENCY

A number of investigators have noted that Asian Americans tend to be quiet, verbally inhibited, nonassertive, and compliant. They also have a wide range of apparent social deficits and problems: Greater social anxiety and more apprehension over social encounters (Sue, Ino, & Sue, 1983), more social anxiety in situations requiring assertiveness (Zane, Sue, Hu, & Kwon, 1991), lack of adequate public speaking skills (Klopf & Cambra, 1979b), discomfort in situations demanding interpersonal fluency (Callao, 1973), lowered mental health, overconformity, feelings of inadequacy (Sue, Zane, & Sue, 1985), and a lower preference for Asian males as dating partners by Asian females (Weiss, 1970). Reviews of research on psychological distress also have found that Asian Americans experience higher levels of social anxiety and report more interpersonal difficulties. For example, Leong (1985) reviewed the career development research and concluded that Asian Americans tended to differ from White Americans on three personality characteristics: social anxiety, locus of control, and tolerance of ambiguity. Abe and Zane (1990) specifically tested for ethnic differences on psychological distress while controlling for other possible ethnic differences in demographics (e.g., age, sex, socioeconomic status), response style (e.g., social desirability), and personality style (e.g., self-consciousness, extraversion, and other-directedness). The investigators still found more interpersonal or social, as well as intrapersonal (e.g., peculiar thoughts, depression), distress among foreign-born Asian Americans compared to White Americans, even after accounting for ethnic differences on the other psychological factors.

The Abe-Zane finding of ethnic differences on both social distress and depression raises the question of whether one distress pattern is more primary than the other. Other studies have indicated that Asian Americans also report more depression than Whites (Aldwin & Greenberger, 1987; Kinzie, Ryals, Cottington, & McDermott, 1973; Kuo, 1984). Because social anxiety and depression are both negative affects, and they are often correlated or comorbid conditions, it is unclear if the distress differential among Asians and Whites primarily involves depression or social anxiety or both. Okazaki (1997) tested if the Asian-White difference was due more to social anxiety or depression variations. She found that Asian Americans reported more social anxiety and depression than Whites. However, once the association between these two types of distress was accounted for, ethnic differences were found for social anxiety but not for depression. Evidence also suggests that work-related adjustment is a major factor in the mental health of Asian Americans. For example, Hurh and Kim (1990) surveyed Korean male immigrants and found that job satisfaction was the major correlate of mental health adjustment.

In sum, issues about interpersonal effectiveness involving career advancement and social relations have become major concerns for Asian Americans. With respect to the former, compelling evidence exists that Asian Americans are not being hired and promoted at rates commensurate with their proportion in the workforce. As for the latter, numerous studies have documented that Asian Americans have higher levels of social distress and interpersonal adjustment problems relative to other ethnic groups, especially Whites. Despite this evidence, considerable debate exists over why Asian Americans are experiencing difficulties and challenges in interpersonal effectiveness and agency.

There are at least three possible explanations for these problems in career advancement and interpersonal relations. First, as members of an ethnic minority group and of a predominantly immigrant group, such problems may occur for Asian Americans as a consequence of negative ethnic stereotyping, prejudice, discrimination, marginalization, and tokenism. This explanatory framework, which we will refer to as the marginalization hypothesis, posits that problems of interpersonal effectiveness for Asian Americans primarily result from individual and institutional racism designed to preserve racial and cultural hegemony by keeping Asians on the social margins of society. Some have argued, though, that Asian Americans often lack certain social and interpersonal skills considered instrumental for leadership positions and for establishing and maintaining good social relations. The second factor, which we will refer to as the skills deficit hypothesis, may better explain these problems in interpersonal effectiveness. It should be noted that the first two factors may be related in that marginalization experiences may prevent Asian Americans from developing the requisite skills for interpersonal effectiveness.

Finally, a third explanation centers on how behavioral performances can be adversely affected. It is a well-known fact that one of the most effective ways of inhibiting a behavior is to have the person perform a behavior incompatible with the targeted behavior so that the performance of the former prevents the occurrence of the latter. For example, reasoning that relaxation responses were incompatible with anxiety reactions, Wolpe (1958) developed a therapy for phobic anxiety disorders, systematic desensitization, which applied the anxiety-inhibiting effects of deep muscle relaxation to allow clients to tolerate greater levels of anxiety-eliciting stimuli. In a similar fashion, for Asian American individuals, culturally reinforced and socialized behavioral tendencies may

be incompatible or inhibit the learning or use of certain skills and behaviors needed for greater interpersonal effectiveness in Western cultural contexts. If, in certain Asian cultures, a person is taught and socialized to be modest, self-effacing, respectful to authority figures, and mindful of preserving interpersonal harmony, these tendencies may inhibit or prevent the performance of the behaviors and skills considered essential for career advancement and effective social relations in Western societies and cultures. Essentially, this may be the behavioral outcome or end product of the effects of cultural conflicts in values and worldviews for bicultural individuals such as Asian Americans. This third factor, which we refer to as the incompatible behavior hypothesis, may also be a compelling explanation for the interpersonal issues concerning Asian Americans. In this chapter, we address the challenges and difficulties faced by Asian Americans in interpersonal issues of agency (leadership and career advancement) and critically review the research using the three hypotheses as possible explanatory frameworks for understanding the ethnocultural issues in this area of interpersonal effectiveness.

THE PARADOX OF ASIAN AMERICAN LEADERSHIP

The case of Asian Americans in leadership presents an interesting paradox. As a group, they are the most educated in the United States: According to the U.S. Census Bureau (2004), 50% of Asian adults have college degrees (national average, 27%), and 19% have advanced degrees (national average 9%). Adolescents score higher on standardized tests, such as the SATs, than other ethnic groups (College Board National Report, 2002). In addition, portrayals of Asians in mass media since the 60s have been of a group exhibiting strong family values, determination, industriousness, high socialization, and conciliatory behavior (Mok, 1998). By all accounts, it seems that Asian Americans are enormously successful in American society. Herein lies the paradox: Although the Asian American stereotype is that of a successful, industrious ethnic group, they are rarely seen in positions of leadership. Indeed, leadership researchers, including Bass (1990), have argued that even though Asian Americans, as a group, possess the traits and management decision-making skills necessary for leadership positions, they are very much underrepresented in corporate management, as they represent 6% of all college graduates (National Center for Education, 2000) but only 0.3% of American corporate executives (Xin, 2004).

The paradoxical lack of Asian American leaders becomes more comprehensible when the role of culture is considered. Most theoretical models are based on Western conceptions of leadership and therefore are more likely to incorporate traits and behaviors that are socially valued in European American societies. Many of these traits may not be valued by Asian cultures, and in some cases, may conflict with Asian values. Subsequently, these potential conflicts may obstruct Asian Americans' ability to be recognized as leaders, and perform in leadership roles. Moreover, these incongruities may also increase negative stereotyping against Asians, which, in turn, increases the likelihood of discrimination.

The following sections explore different explanations for the glass ceiling that Asians can't seem to penetrate. First, general theories on leadership and empirical studies that isolate traits and behaviors conducive to advancement in organizations are described. Second, the possibility that prejudice, discrimination, and racism form a plausible basis for the lack of Asian leaders and managers is considered. Third, relevant research is reviewed to determine if skill deficits in interpersonal qualities can account for these challenges in interpersonal effectiveness among Asian Americans. Lastly, the discussion turns to how several cultural factors may be incompatible with Western conceptions of leadership. In this regard, several hypotheses are presented on how culture-specific factors, such as face-saving orientation and dialectical thinking, might occlude organizational advancement.

What Is a Leader?

Even though there are several theories of leadership development, several common threads regarding the nature of leadership unite most perspectives. Most apparent is the influence of economist-sociologist Max Weber's (1918) description of charismatic leadership: "Devotion to the charisma of the prophet . . . means that the leader is personally recognized as the innerly 'called' leader of men. Men do not obey him by virtue of tradition or statute, but because they believe in him" (p. 17). Furthermore, Weber expanded his conception of charismatic leadership as a relationship where one person (leader) influences another or others (followers). Charismatic leaders emerge when there is a crisis or special problem. During this time of need, leaders are the individuals who provide clear solutions to problems and effectively relay these ideas to followers.

Current leadership researchers have expounded on Weber's theory of charismatic leadership to apply it to modern-day, leader-follower environments. Bass's (1990, 1997) theory of transformational leadership is one of the most widely cited frameworks for charismatic leadership in organizational systems. According to Bass, two leadership styles emerge in hierarchical organizations: transactional and transformational. Transactional leadership is based on reward contingencies, and acts are rewarded on fixed, one-to-one schedules. Transformational leadership is based on persuading and motivating individuals to change their personal goals and accept collective goals. "People jockey for positions in a transactional group, whereas they share common goals in a transformational group. Rules and regulations dominate the transactional organization; adaptability is a characteristic of the transformational organization" (p.131). Although transactional leadership is common within hierarchical organizations, transformational leadership is the ideal form of leadership and can turn an ordinary leader into an icon.

Several empirical works have elucidated the nature of transformational leadership. Conger and Kanungo (1994) define leadership as a transformation of followers from one position to an improved position. A leader accomplishes this by clearly articulating a clear vision, showing sensitivity to others' needs, and demonstrating creativity and vision. Riggio (1986) and Groves (2005) argue that charismatic leaders' influence over followers lies in their social and emotional skills. Social control, as conceptualized by Riggio (1986) is a social self-presentation skill that involves self-monitoring and social adaptability. People who have high social control adjust their behavior to fit varying social settings and situations. Grace, tactfulness, confidence, and acting abilities are all within a charismatic leader's repertoire of traits. In addition, validation studies conducted by Riggio (1986) have demonstrated convergent validity: Self-control is positively correlated with extraversion and negatively correlated with other-directedness, two dimensions that should contrast with one another.

Effective leaders also seem to be skilled in emotional expressivity, which is the ability to communicate emotional states using nonverbal gestures and expressions. According to several investigators, charismatic delivery style is characterized by appropriate eye contact, animated facial expressions, body gestures, and posture. Using these skills, leaders establish connections with followers and communicate their plans and influence. This argument has been supported by other empirical studies demonstrating the importance of body posture and gestures, speaking rate, smiles, eye contact, facial expressions, verbal tone, and touch to charismatic leadership (Gardner & Avolio, 1998; Riggio, 1992). These aspects of nonverbal communication are so important that without them, visionary speeches are rated uncharismatic and with them, nonvisionary speeches charismatic (Holladay & Coombs, 1994).

To summarize the empirical findings discussed in this section, charismatic leadership is characterized by extraversion, high social control, high emotional expressivity, and the ability to create group cohesion. Returning to our original line of inquiry, if we know what it takes to be a leader, why are there so few Asian American leaders? And why do Asian Americans seem to experience relatively more problems in advancing their careers than Whites do? As indicated earlier, several hypotheses may explain this differential pattern in interpersonal effectiveness. First, it is possible that Asians Americans face social marginalization through direct and indirect discrimination, thereby preventing mobility to upper-level management occupations. Second, contrary to Bass's (1990) assertion, Asians

may lack the general traits and skills necessary for leadership or consideration for leadership positions. To be more specific, although Asians are highly educated and motivated as a group, they may not have the "soft skills" necessary to be noticed and promoted to upper management levels. Lastly, Asians may have certain culturally socialized characteristics, attitudes, or values that conflict with or are incompatible with routes to leadership positions. Particularly pertinent would be characteristics or orientations such as face-saving concerns (Liem, 1997; Lutwak, Razzino, & Ferrari, 1998; Zane, Sue, Hu, & Kwon, 1991) that would conflict with essential leadership characteristics such as assertiveness and charisma. In the following discussion, all three hypotheses are examined as separate explanations for Asian American underrepresentation in leadership roles and problems in career advancement. It is highly likely that the three hypotheses are not mutually exclusive, so the interdependence among these processes is also considered.

SOCIAL MARGINALIZATION: EFFECTS OF RACISM AND DISCRIMINATION

With regard to racism and discrimination, times have both dramatically changed and stayed the same. On the one hand, blatant discrimination, overt prejudice, and explicit racial hostility are no longer acceptable in American culture. Federal laws prohibiting discrimination based on race, including The Civil Rights Act of 1964 that established Equal Employment Opportunities and the Civil Rights Acts of 1991 that paved way for monetary damages in cases of employment discrimination, have served as deterrents to obvious prejudiced behaviors. A cursory inspection of Whites' attitudes toward minority groups, particularly toward Black Americans, suggests that "old fashioned" overt racism is gone (Kinder & Sanders, 1996; Schuman, Steeh, Bobo, & Krysan, 1997). On the other hand, experts have theorized that prejudice is not dead. Instead, its manifestation has changed. In this case, explicit prejudice has turned into *symbolic racism,* a cluster of beliefs and attitudes based on the denial that racism exists (Kinder & Sears, 1985; Sears & Kinder, 1985). The line of reasoning behind symbolic racism is as follows: if one believes that racism has been eliminated in society, a minority individual's failure to succeed cannot be due to systemic obstacles, but instead is due to laziness and personality flaws. This kind of reasoning can lead to other attitudes, such as thinking that minorities' expectations are unrealistic and that social programs, such as affirmative action, provide more advantages to minorities than they deserve (Henry & Sears, 2002). Outcomes of such belief structures reflect subtle acts of discrimination, such as support for conservative candidates and opposition to race-related policies (Bobo, 1998; Sidanius, Devereux, & Pratto, 1992).

Although most of the studies on symbolic racism used White and Black American relations as its focus, symbolic racism may nevertheless affect Asian Americans. Just as overt racist behavior has transformed into covert racism toward Black Americans, racial discrimination has taken a subtle form toward Asian Americans as well. Researchers have documented increases in anti-Asian sentiment in the auto industry's "buy American" campaigns, which were directed specifically against Japanese car companies—despite the fact that foreign car companies are multinational conglomerates that employ American assembly workers (Omi, 1993). In addition, the Western half of the United States closed out the 21st century embroiled in controversial debates on English Only initiatives. Since the 1960s, Western states accommodated bilingual citizens by making information available in various languages, such as Spanish or Japanese. For example, as the governor of California, Ronald Reagan authorized bilingual education in 1967, allowing children to be taught in both English and their native language. The English Only movement sought to abolish government-supported bilingualism and make English the sole means of communication between governmental agencies and its citizens. Numerous groups, including the American Civil Liberties Union and cultural advocacy groups, opposed the movement, suggesting that the English Only movement was racism cloaked in progressivism (Johnson & Martinez, 2000).

In addition to symbolic racism, several stereotypes about Asian Americans may contribute to discrimination. Asian Americans are frequently stereotyped as the model minority. This image is of educationally successful, achievement-oriented Asians who excel in mathematics and science (Kao, 2000). But other, negative stereotypes also accompany attitudes toward Asians. For example, Fujino (1993) found that Asian men are frequently described as less attractive, sexless, and lacking in social skills. White and Chan (1983) conducted one study in which Asian American men reported feeling less attractive than White Americans feel. In addition, Sue and Sue (1971) describe several incidents where Chinese American men develop "racial self hatred" and begin to despise their own racially related physical characteristics. In contrast to the sexless image of the Asian male discussed by Fujino (1993), White and Chan (1983), and Sue and Sue (1971), Shah (2003) argues that Asian women often must contend with a dualistic stereotype, both sides laden with sexuality. The "dragon lady" image is that of an Asian woman who wields sexual powers to diabolically manipulate and ruin White men. As Shah contends, this image appears in popular media in the form of sexually aggressive Asian women who scheme and connive against the protagonist. The other image is the "lotus blossom," a meek, submissive Asian woman who dutifully experiences great emotional suffering without any complaints.

Although these stereotypes do not seem overtly negative or detrimental, they do have the potential to have adverse consequences on Asian American performance in the workforce, as shown by Steele (1998) and his work on stereotype threat. According to Steele, success in any domain requires a psychological investment in that people normally incorporate achievements within a domain as a part of their self-identity. Many members of various ethnic groups have stereotypic expectations about success or failure based on ethnicity. A common expectation based on stereotypes would be that Asians will perform well on math tests and African Americans will not. For the African American student, the mere existence of this expectation leads to impediments in math performance. According to Steele, just being cognizant of one's ethnic affiliation is enough to prime these negative stereotypes. In turn, the activation of a stereotype, or stereotype threat, will increase anxiety and fear, particularly because the individual fears he or she will prove the stereotype true. The result of such high anxiety is underperformance on the identified task.

For Asians, stereotype threat could possibly cause underperformance in leadership-related behaviors. It can be assumed that Asians in business organizations are invested in their performance and want to advance in their work environment. Indeed, empirical evidence supports the idea that Asian self-identity and esteem tend to be rooted in achievement and accomplishments (Oyserman & Sakamoto, 1997). Given this investment in work and performance, Steele's (1998) model of stereotype threat would predict that Asian ethnicity, even implicit attention to Asian identity, might be associated with negative character associations, such as submissiveness, social awkwardness, and unattractiveness. In this case, Asians would underperform on behaviors such as appearing assertive or social networking, thus making them seem less capable of leading their colleagues. It is possible that these achievements or performances may be influenced by identity and acculturation processes.

Shih, Pittinsky, and Ambady (1999) presented evidence that negative stereotyping can impede performances among Asian Americans. They examined the influence of identity salience on one type of academic achievement, quantitative achievement. They reasoned that if a certain type of identity were implicitly activated, this identity would either facilitate or impede quantitative performance. Moreover, the specific effect of the activated identity on performance would depend on the stereotypes associated with that identity. In the case of Asian American women, the salience of ethnic identity would facilitate performance, due to the stereotype of Asian Americans as being adept in quantitative skills, whereas the salience of gender identity would impede performance based on the stereotype of women as being less quantitatively skilled than men. It was assumed that the identity effects were due to stereotypes related to one's particular identity. The investigators invoked or activated a particular identity by having Asian American women participants complete questionnaires that made one's female

gender or Asian ethnicity salient. As hypothesized, Asian females with activated gender identity performed worse than the controls, whereas Asian females with the activated ethnic identity performed better than the controls. These differences could not be attributed to differences in effort or ability. These findings strongly suggest that the negative social stereotypes of Asian Americans can serve as stereotype threats that can adversely affect performance in situations requiring them to exert leadership and management qualities. The findings also suggest that these stereotype effects have the most impact in work conditions that make the ethnic status or ethnic identity of an Asian American individual salient.

Lin, Kwan, Cheung, and Fiske (2005) have further examined how stereotypes might contribute to prejudice and discrimination. If Asians are perceived as highly competent yet socially awkward, it is possible that a corporate system can reward Asian Americans for work-related competence, but simultaneously exclude them from the important social networking necessary for upward mobility (Glick & Fiske, 2001; Jost, Burgess, & Mosso, 2001). More specifically, Lin et al. identified anti-Asian prejudice as envious discrimination most commonly used against out-groups categorized as competent but emotionally cold. Moreover, they theorized that discrimination against Asian Americans is a culmination of two basic attitudes: Asian Americans are competent and socially awkward or emotionally constrained. The researchers found that competence was related to out-group envy, but did not manifest itself as discrimination or rejection of Asian Americans. Instead, rejection of Asian Americans as members of an out-group may be due to the perception that Asians are *not sociable*.

If Asian Americans, as a group, tend to be socially marginalized, it would be expected that the individuals of that group who have characteristics and behavioral tendencies least like normative behaviors in White American culture would be the most affected. Leong (2001) used similar reasoning and tested the relationship between acculturation and career adjustment among Asian American workers in two studies. As predicted, he found that acculturation was negatively associated with job stress and strain, whereas acculturation was positively associated with job satisfaction among Asian American workers. In other words, the least Westernized workers reported more occupational stress and less job satisfaction than their more Westernized counterparts. In the second study, he found compelling evidence for the effect of acculturation. The study examined the actual supervisor ratings of both Asian American and Hispanic workers. Leong found that acculturation was positively related to job evaluations in that the least-Westernized Asian and Hispanic workers tended to receive lower job performance ratings from their predominantly White supervisors (94%) than did the more Westernized minority workers. Consistent with the social marginalization hypothesis, Leong asserted that the lower-career adjustment and poorer job performance ratings of less-acculturated Asian workers could be attributed to in-group bias on the part of the predominantly White American management. However, as indicated later in this chapter, these acculturation effects also could be due to Asian Americans having certain cultural tendencies that were incompatible with the manifestation of Westernized leadership behaviors and skills.

The previous discussion of leadership skills and traits noted that leaders are individuals who identify conflict, effectively communicate a solution to others, and motivate others to work for the common good. Individuals who are able to accomplish these tasks also need to be extraverted in order to be noticed, socially malleable to adjust to volatile political climates, masters of nonverbal emotional cues, and Machiavellian enough to accomplish tasks for individual advancement. However, Asian Americans, like most other ethnic minority groups, are frequently associated with negative stereotypes. Particularly, Asians are often thought of as socially awkward, unattractive, submissive, docile, and emotionally constrained.

Given the negative attributes associated with Asian stereotypes, it becomes clearer why Asians are passed over for leadership positions. This line of research suggests that Asian Americans may not reach upper levels of management or other leadership positions because they may be perceived as unsocial and possibly are precluded from important network functions or overlooked as potential leaders. But these findings also lead to another line of important questioning. What is fueling these negative attitudes and the perception that Asians lack leadership qualities? Do Asians really lack charismatic attributes or are there culturally related obstacles that impede expression of leadership traits?

SKILL DEFICITS IN INTERPERSONAL QUALITIES

A cursory investigation of the skills deficits hypothesis does garner some empirical support. There is gathering evidence that Asians tend to be emotionally constrained (Tsai et al. 2002), introverted, traditional, and compliant (McCrae, 2002), less assertive (Fukuyama & Greenfield, 1983; Johnson & Marsella, 1978), more accepting of hierarchies (Shon & Ja, 1982), and place group interests before self-interests (Allik & McCrae, 2004). Indeed, several investigators concluded that behavioral deficits may lead to other deficits in leadership-related skills such as public speaking abilities (Klopf & Cambra, 1979a) or interpersonal fluency (Callao, 1973). If Asians do lack these important leadership traits, then trait deficits could be blamed for the underrepresentation of Asians in leadership roles.

However, a number of studies indicate that Asian Americans may have the skills necessary to be interpersonally effective. For example, Sue, Ino, and Sue (1983) found that when Asian students were asked to role-play assertive responses, they were behaviorally as assertive as their Caucasian counterparts. Brief role-plays usually reflect the person's assertion capability and not the individual's actual tendency to respond assertively in the natural environment (Higgins, Frisch, & Smith, 1983; Linehan, Goldfried, & Goldfried, 1979). The conditions in the Sue et al. (1983) study would tend to be optimal for assessing skill ability for assertive behavior on the part of Asian Americans, but this capability may not correspond to actual tendencies outside the laboratory. In other words, although Asian Americans have the *capacity and requisite skills* to be assertive, they may not perform or behave assertively. The distinction between skill capacity and actual skill performance is a helpful one to make because other research shows that Asian Americans may have the abilities to take on leadership positions and to manage other interpersonal situations, even if they are under-represented. Zane, Sue, Hu, and Kwon (1991) found that Asian Americans were as assertive as Whites with acquaintances (e.g., coworker, friend) and close relations (e.g., boyfriend/girlfriend, spouse, family member), and assertion differences occurred only when interacting with total strangers (e.g., salesperson, fellow customer). Similarly, Zea, Jarama, and Bianchi (1995) found no differences between Asian American, African American, Latino, and White college students on psychosocial competence or in adaptation to college demands. As these cases show, there is growing evidence against the deficit hypothesis since Asians may possess the requisite skills to behave as assertively as Whites. Instead, it may be that culture-related factors may prohibit the expression of these behaviors and traits.

CULTURAL TENDENCIES INCOMPATIBLE WITH WESTERN-BASED SOCIAL COMPETENCE

In view of the research strongly suggesting that Asians actually may possess the necessary characteristics to be noticed and promoted, it is more likely that cultural factors can suppress or inhibit the expression of leadership traits and skills (Triandis & Suh, 2002; Zane, Sue, Hu, & Kwon, 1991). We outline several studies that provide evidence for ethnic differences in key leadership traits: Emotional expressivity, extra-version, and conflict negotiation. In addition, we provide several possible ways cultural variables might impact the expression of these traits in potential leadership situations.

Emotional Expressivity and Emotional Moderation/Constraint

Even though emotions are thought to be universal and biologically based (Ekman, 1999), several investigators have recently discovered ethnic differences in emotional experience. Specifically, Mesquita (2001) has demonstrated group differences in emotional appraisal,

recognition of emotional expressions (Matsumoto, 1993), and expression of self-conscious emotions (Tracy & Robins, 2004). One of the most enduring findings in the emotions-culture literature is that Asian cultures have different behavioral scripts for expressing emotions than American, or Western, culture. In particular, Asian emotional expression tends to center on balance, moderation, and self-constraint. Although inner states may differ, emphasis is placed on controlling behavior, rather than releasing it. Conversely, Western cultures more often value emotional expressivity and release, even if it means confrontation (Lutz, 1989).

According to Markus & Kitayama (1991), the difference in emotional expression lies in how a culture values groups. Asian cultures are described as collectivistic, meaning that individuals' orientation is toward the group, and so they adjust personal needs to fit members' considerations. In this case, the concern surrounding emotional expression is not whether the individual feels better or accomplishes some goal, but rather on how behaviors might affect the group or members within the group. Therefore, to reduce the risk of offending the group or throwing off its balance, members within the collective rein in emotional expressions. In stark contrast to the Asian model, Western culture is described as individualistic. The goal is not necessarily to fit in, but to stand out and be recognized for uniqueness. Therefore, the concern is not on impact on others, but on how expressions might differentiate the individual from the group. In a way, emotion-based behaviors are an assertion of the individual (Tsai et al., 2002).

Extraversion/Assertiveness and Face Concerns

As suggested by Markus and Kitayama (1991), assertion of individuality is a Western ideal and not necessarily accepted in Eastern cultures. This cultural difference speaks to possible cultural differences in personality, such as extraversion and assertiveness. The topic of personality differences across cultures seems to be a divisive issue in personality psychology. On one side, researchers argue that personality cannot be generalized across cultures. Instead, behavioral patterns are context specific, as evidenced by low correlations on characteristics across situations (Mischel, 1969; Shweder, 1991). On the other side, McCrae et al. (2000) contend that the Five Factor personality traits—extraversion, agreeableness, conscientiousness, neuroticism, and openness to experience—are universal and are traceable to biological temperament. These two lines have been merged to form a cross-cultural perspective of personality. Triandis and Suh (2002) explain that this perspective accepts the universality of personality traits but also argue that culture influences patterns of behavior.

McCrae, Costa, Del Pilar, Rolland, and Parker (1998) provide evidence for both universality and cultural differences. In their study, European American participants scored higher on extraversion and openness to new experience than Asians. Moreover, Americans were also characterized as antagonistic, individualistic, and more likely to reject social hierarchies. In contrast, Asians tended to be more introverted, traditional, and compliant. Asians also tended to put group-interest before self-interest demonstrating high collectivism. These findings have been corroborated by several other studies, including Okazaki, Liu, Longworth, and Min's (2002) study on social anxiety and Fukuyama and Greenfield's (1983) work on assertiveness. Both studies reported that Asians demonstrated more muted behaviors than their White counterparts.

Even though some researchers suggest that Asians lack the ability to be demonstrative or assertive, other findings, such as Sue et al.'s (1983) study, suggest Asians do possess the ability to act forcefully. Because role-play situations, like the ones used by Sue et al., are more likely to prompt assertiveness at levels not seen in naturalistic settings, Zane et al. (1991) tested whether nonassertiveness transcended situational contexts. Specifically, since Asians demonstrate the ability to act assertively, they tested whether situational variables, such as self-efficacy or outcome expectancies, could influence assertion. Across 9 situations, Zane and colleagues found that self-efficacy and expectancies were strong predictors of assertion. In particular, Asians were less likely to be assertive in situations involving interactions with strangers or unknown persons, especially if they felt less efficacious. Moreover, the

investigators argue that the results dispute previous notions of Asian's abilities to act assertively. Specifically, although Asians may feel more anxious and guilty when asserting themselves, they will act forcefully—but mostly with intimates or acquaintances. This suggests that it is not the case that Asians lack the capacity for assertion, but they may avoid asserting themselves if they feel that they have little control over the situation.

In the context of leadership, Zane et al.'s (1991) findings are particularly useful in understanding why Asians are frequently overlooked as leaders. As Bass (1990) and others have theorized, a large component of leadership is the ability to distinguish oneself from the masses. Also, leaders are the individuals who convince others to follow their plans or, at a basic level, impose their will on others. It is possible, as in the previous discussion on discrimination demonstrates, Asians may not feel efficacious in the work environment. More specifically, the workplace is frequently comprised of strangers or nonintimates. Also, as Steele's (1998) work showed, stereotypes increased anxiety related to outcome expectancies. All of these factors may work to prevent Asians from asserting themselves, which then makes them unlikely candidates for leadership positions.

It is also possible that other culturally sanctioned tendencies can inhibit efforts to be assertive and to control others. Specifically, the tendency to self-efface and be modest may compete with and suppress assertiveness. Akimoto and Sanbonmatsu (1999) examined very acculturated Asian Americans (third- and later-generation Japanese Americans) to see if they still self-effaced more than White American college students. All participants took a set of cognitive problem solving tasks (e.g., anagrams, cryptograms, perceptual reasoning problems) that were presented as new psychological measures of future job success. Regardless of their actual performance, all participants were told that they scored in the 89th percentile relative to college students from their region, and this feedback was found to be credible. Asian and White American participants then were randomly assigned to either a private or public condition in which they completed a questionnaire rating their performance on that creativity task. The investigators hypothesized that if Japanese Americans were simply more self-critical than White Americans, they would rate themselves as lower in performance in both the public and private conditions. However, if Japanese Americans were more self-effacing, they would only rate themselves lower in the public condition. Support for ethnic differences in self-effacing tendencies was found as Japanese Americans rated themselves similar in performance to Whites in the private condition but lower in performance when asked to do so publicly. A follow-up study determined that self-effacing behaviors actually affected evaluations of competence. White American judges who had not participated in the previous study rated the audiotaped responses of the Japanese and White participants self-evaluating their performances from the first study. The judges rated the Japanese Americans (who had been shown to be more self-effacing as a group in the first study) as less competent, having performed less well, less likely to be hired, and less likeable than the White American participants. These findings suggest that the culturally based tendency to self-efface and be modest may mitigate the tendency to be assertive among Asian Americans. What is especially important to note is that the tendency among Asian Americans to self-efface about one's achievements and performance may be interpreted as signs of lower competence, poorer performance, less suitability for a job, and less likability in work situations. In this case, this cultural tendency may directly affect job evaluations of Asian Americans.

Conflict Negotiation and Loss of Face

In addition to Asians not displaying traits commonly associated with Western ideals of leadership, another reason that Asians are not perceived as leaders may be the strategies they use in dealing with conflicts. As several theorists have argued, the process of conflict resolution is dualistic. On the one hand, an individual can dangle threats of imposing costs in order to coerce other parties. As Schelling (1960) points out, coercion may be useful in accomplishing shortsighted goals, but it also poses high risks in the long term. It is possible that coercion will produce resentment, which will produce

retaliation or noncooperation in the future. Also, coercion commonly induces shame and loss of face on the part of the losing party. On the other hand, an individual can use bargaining techniques to show cooperative solutions that allow opposing parties to maintain their sense of respect. Tanter (1999) describes this type of conciliatory bargaining as appeasement, a tactic that requires negotiators to demonstrate a willingness to give up possible benefits and trust that their appeasement will not be taken advantage of in the future.

According to Western models of leadership, coercion is perceived as an indication of resolve, assertiveness, and strength. People who are willing to coerce are perceived as competent leaders, because they are willing to make their opposition lose face in order to fulfill their individual goals (Tanter, 1999). As Triandis and Suh (2002) argue, coercive tactics are not characteristic of Eastern styles of communication. Indeed, since Eastern cultures are collectivistic and emphasize respect, negotiators often engage in communication strategies that allow opposing parties to save face, but at the cost of clarity and the possible sacrifice of their own goals.

The difference in conflict negotiation tactics can be better understood when we consider how Western and Eastern cultures differ in self-identity reference points and the concept of face. Westerners frequently use the individual as an identity reference point. For example, according to Ting-Toomey (2004), Americans associated respect, reputation, and credibility to the individual, most commonly to themselves. Respect, in this context, is related to the ego of the individual. In contrast, Asians tended to use group affiliation as the identity reference point. For members of Eastern cultures, respect and reputation was associated with family or social group, not necessarily with the individual.

The contrast between Western and Eastern concepts of face is particularly poignant when considering the act of face-giving. According to Ting-Toomey, when Asians engaged in negotiations, they frequently offered opposing parties an option to maintain their respect or dignity. In this regard, Asians saw face as a relational concept that included their opponent's respect, as well as their own. Alternatively, Americans could not offer a definition for "face giving." In her sample, American students were not able to discuss the terms of giving face to opponents in negotiations. During the conflict-resolution process, maintaining self-pride and esteem seemed to be the goal for American students. In this regard, American students focused on win-lose strategies that allowed them to maintain their own esteem, but at the cost of their opponent's respect. For Asian students, loss of face was less attached to the self, instead it was attached to family, groups, or a company. Instead of engaging in win-lose strategies, Asian students focused on win-win strategies and preferred tactics that allowed their opponents to maintain their respect and esteem.

Face-giving strategies frequently employed by Asians may be problematic in the context of Western leadership. Consider the fact that these models of leadership hold that individuals rise from conflict by emphasizing their individuality and demonstrating to peers that they hold the solution to the problem. To promote their solutions or plans, individuals usually compete against others who offer solutions and engage in win-lose tactics. The individual who gains the most respect, even if it is at the cost of the opponent losing respect, becomes the leader. This strategy may be incompatible with Asian styles of negotiation. Instead of engaging in tactics that will bring attention to their individuality, Asians may seek alternatives that are acceptable to all parties and allow people to save face. If they are working in a Western context, Asians using win-win strategies will not be able to garner the attention needed to stand out. In addition, since the Western perception of winning is that the opponent loses, the tactics employed by Asians may yield ambiguous results. In other words, even when Asians succeed in conflict negotiations, because there are no clear losers, Asians may not be seen as winners.

Self-Enhancement and Self-Criticism

Underlying these tendencies to express oneself, assert oneself, and exert control over others is what is seen as the basic, general need for positive self-regard—essentially the motivation to "possess, enhance, and maintain positive self-views" (Heine, Lehman, Markus, & Kitayama,

1999). Psychological research indicates that this is a core, normative need in Western societies (Diener & Diener, 1996; Steele, 1988; Taylor & Brown, 1988; Tesser, 1988). Accordingly, it is not surprising that Western notions of leadership involve enhancing, promoting, and extending one's self interests over others. However, some cross-cultural research has called into question whether or not this motivation for positive self-regard is truly universal in nature. Research in Japan and other East Asian societies indicates that rather than positive self-regard, the basic underlying motivation is to be self-critical and to make continual efforts to improve oneself and to reduce one's shortcomings (e.g., DeVos, 1985; Kashiwagi, 1986). There is an emphasis on performing up to and meeting certain socially shared standards or role expectations. In this way, the self-critical orientation reinforces and affirms the sense of belongingness, inter-group harmony, and interdependent relations so valued in these collectivistic societies. Similar to how positive self-regard has been linked to mental health in Western cultures (e.g., Baumeister, 1993; Taylor & Brown, 1988), self-criticism has been linked to adaptive coping among Asian Americans (Chang, 1996).

This interesting cultural difference in basic motives and needs points to another reason why Asian Americans may not perform well or excel in Western leadership and management roles. The behaviors and skills required of leaders and managers are essentially self-enhancement strategies designed to increase or maintain positive self-regard. As a consequence, Asian Americans, who are more likely to be oriented to self-critical and self-improvement concerns, may not be as motivated to excel in these situations. Needless to say, this explanation remains speculative, as there has been no research to test this possibility.

CONCLUSION

There is compelling evidence that many Asian Americans are experiencing difficulties in interpersonal effectiveness, especially as these issues affect their career advancement and opportunities for attaining leadership positions. Moreover, Asian Americans themselves perceive problems in career advancement and often believe they are less effective in influencing people and having an impact on others. Three hypotheses were considered as possible explanations for why many Asian Americans experience challenges in interpersonal effectiveness. There appears to be little evidence that these interpersonal difficulties result from deficits in the skills needed to be interpersonally effective. In fact, there is evidence to the contrary showing that Asian Americans have the capacity to be assertive and to influence others in work situations.

More evidence exists for the other two hypotheses, social marginalization, and culturally reinforced incompatible behaviors. First, it is highly likely that Asian Americans, like other ethnic minorities, are adversely affected by racist attitudes, beliefs, and practices that keep them on the social margins and prevent them from fully participating in managerial and leadership opportunities. Second, certain cultural tendencies on the part of Asian Americans, such as modesty, self-effacing behaviors, and face giving/saving, may be incompatible with and inhibit behaviors considered instrumental for effective leadership and management. There is even some evidence that certain tendencies such as self-effacing behavior may be interpreted in a way that results in negative job-related evaluations concerning competence, performance, likelihood of being hired, and likability. Moreover, the basic motivation that drives Western leadership behaviors, the need for positive self-regard, may not hold as much valence for Asian Americans, who tend to be grounded and socialized in cultures that emphasize a more self-critical orientation. Lastly, it is highly possible that social marginalization and cultural incompatibilities can interact and build on one another to create major interpersonal challenges for Asian Americans. Specifically, due to cultural incompatibilities, Asians may not manifest behaviors and performances associated with leaders and influential people, and these perceived deficits, in turn, reinforce the already negative social stereotypes of Asians. Moreover, negative stereotyping and other racist practices may differentially reinforce and strengthen those Asian cultural tendencies that are incompatible with, or inhibit behavior considered interpersonally effective in, Western cultural contexts.

One fact to keep in mind with respect to these issues of interpersonal effectiveness is the possibility that many Asian Americans are or can become bicultural in their adaptation. As bicultural individuals, they have opportunities to develop competencies and skills to function and perform well in two or more different cultures. However, this review suggests that at least in the area of interpersonal effectiveness in job and career situations, many Asian Americans continue to be challenged and, at times, frustrated in negotiating the American work culture. The normative tendency is for people to become bicultural (Hurh & Kim, 1984; Hurh & Kim, 1990). Then why do many bicultural Asian Americans continue to experience challenges in the workplace, even though they supposedly have access to behavioral competencies from both Asian and Western cultures?

A number of factors may be operating to limit bicultural individuals' access to the Western-based competencies that they may possess. First, even bicultural individuals are not immune to the effects of ethnic stereotyping and in-group bias, in that these effects are predicated on minority group membership. Moreover, group stereotyping and bias may differentially reinforce Asians to behave in an "Asian" or "non-Western" manner, since that is what is expected of them. Behaviors not consistent with these expectations are not reinforced or punished. Second, most performances related to leadership and management usually take place in a public context and involve complex behaviors that usually elicit high social anxiety. Under these conditions (i.e., presence of others, performance of complex behaviors, and high anxiety level), social facilitation effects are likely to occur (Zajonc, 1965). Social facilitation is a well-established psychological principle that may have universal applicability across cultures (Norenzayan & Heine, 2005). In social facilitation, the presence of others induces arousal (Martens, 1969). This heightened arousal facilitates the performance of the dominant response in one's behavioral repertoire and inhibits the non-dominant responses (Zajonc & Sales, 1966). Given that the large majority of Asian Americans are immigrants or are children of immigrant parents, it would be safe to assume that the behaviors learned and reinforced in East

Asian cultures would be the most well-learned behaviors, whereas the more recently learned behaviors tied to Western culture would be non-dominant. Consequently, in the context of career and work situations in American society, social facilitation may affect bicultural Asian individuals by enhancing their dominant East Asian tendencies over their subordinate Western-based competencies. This analysis raises a number of interesting hypotheses that remain to be tested in future research.

In their review of the research on biculturalism, LaFromboise, Coleman, and Gerton (1993) note that the alternation model of biculturalism seems to be the most adaptive. In alternation functioning, the individual knows and develops proficiency in both cultures without losing functional connections or identification with either culture. Alternation also involves the ability to alter one's behavior to fit a particular sociocultural context. Indeed, it seems that a major psychosocial challenge for bicultural individuals involves breaking out of the negative cycle of stereotyping/in-group bias and selectively alternating between Eastern and Western behavioral tendencies so that they can function more effectively in the workplace.

REFERENCES

Abe, J. S., & Zane, N. W. S. (1990). Psychological maladjustment among Asian and white American college students: Controlling for confounds. *Journal of Counseling Psychology, 37,* 437–444.

Akimoto, S. A., & Sanbonmatsu, D. M. (1999). Differences in self-effacing behavior between European and Japanese Americans. *Journal of Cross-Cultural Psychology, 30,* 159–177.

Aldwin, C., & Greenberger, E. (1987). Cultural differences in the predictors of depression. *American Journal of Community Psychology, 15,* 789–813.

Allik, J., & McCrae, R. R. (2004). Toward a geography of personality traits: Patterns of profiles across 36 cultures. *Journal of Cross-Cultural Psychology, 35*(1), 13–28.

Asian Americans for Community Involvement (1991). *Qualified, but: A report on glass ceiling issues facing Asian Americans in Silicon Valley.* San Jose: Author.

Bakan, D. (1966). *The duality of human existence: Isolation and communion in Western man.* Boston: Beacon Press.

Bass, B. M. (1990). From transactional to transformational leadership: Learning to share the vision. *Organizational Dynamics, 18*(3), 19–31.

Bass, B. M. (1997). Does the transactional-transformational leadership paradigm transcend organizational and national boundaries? *American Psychologist, 52*(2), 130–139.

Baumeister, R. F. (1993). Understanding the inner nature of low self-esteem: Uncertain, fragile, protective, and conflicted. In R. F. Baumeister (Ed.), *Self-esteem: The puzzle of low self-regard* (pp. 201–218). New York: Plenum.

Bobo, L. (1998). Race, interests, and beliefs about affirmative action: Unanswered questions and new directions. *American Behavioral Scientist, 41*(7), 985–1003.

Cabezas, A. (1980). Disadvantaged employment status of Asian and Pacific Americans. In U.S. Commission on Civil Rights (Ed.), *Civil rights issues of Asian and Pacific-Americans: Myths and realities* (pp. 434–444). Washington, DC: U.S. Government Printing Office.

Cabezas, A., Tam, T. M., Lowe, B. M., Wong, A., & Turner, K. O. (1989). Empirical study of barriers to upward mobility of Asian Americans in the San Francisco Bay Area. In G. M. Nomura, R. Endo, S. H. Sumida, & R. C. Leong (Eds.), *Frontiers of Asian American Studies: Writing research and commentary* (pp. 85–97). Pullman: Washington State University Press.

Callao, M. J. (1973). Culture shock; West, East, and West again. *Personnel and Guidance Journal, 51,* 413–416.

Chang, E. C. (1996). Cultural differences in optimism, pessimism, and coping: Predictors of subsequent adjustment in Asian American and Caucasian American college students. *Journal of Counseling Psychology, 43,* 113–123.

College Board National Report. (2002). *College-bound seniors: A profile of SAT program test takers.* New York: College Entrance Examination Board.

Conger, J. A., & Kanungo, R. N. (1994). Charismatic leadership in organizations: Perceived behavioral attributes and their measurement. *Journal of Organizational Behavior, 15*(5), 439–452.

Der, H., & Lye, C. (1989). The broken ladder '89: Asian Americans in city government. *San Francisco: Chinese for Affirmative Action.*

De Vos, G. A. (1985). Dimensions of the self in Japanese culture. In A. J. Marsella, G. A. De Vos, & F. L. K. Hsu (Eds.), *Culture and self: Asian and Western perspectives* (pp. 141–182). New York: Tavistock.

Diener, E., & Diener, C. (1996). Most people are happy. *Psychological Science, 7,* 181–185.

Ekman, P. (1999). *Basic emotions.* New York: Wiley.

Fujino, D. C. (1993). Extending exchange theory: Effects of ethnicity and gender on Asian American heterosexual relationships. *Dissertation Abstracts International, 53,* 4932B.

Fukuyama, M. A., & Greenfield, T. K. (1983). Dimensions of assertiveness in an Asian-American student population. *Journal of Counseling Psychology, 30,* 429–432.

Gardner, W. L., & Avolio, B. J. (1998). The charismatic relationship: A dramaturgical perspective. *Academy of Management Review, 23*(1), 32–58.

Glater, J. D. (2001, August 7). Law firms are slow in promoting minority lawyers to partnerships. *The New York Times,* p. A1.

Glick, P., & Fiske, S. T. (2001). *Ambivalent stereotypes as legitimizing ideologies: Differentiating paternalistic and envious prejudice.* New York: Cambridge University Press.

Groves, K. S. (2005). Linking leader skills, follower attitudes, and contextual variables via an integrated model of charismatic leadership. *Journal of Management, 31*(2), 255–277.

Guimares, B. L. (1980). Employment issues—Federal and state policy. In U.S. Commission on Civil Rights (Ed.), *Civil rights issues of Asian and Pacific-Americans: Myths and realities* (pp. 560–566). Washington, DC: U.S. Government Printing Office.

Heine, S. J., Lehman, D. R., Markus, H. R., & Kitayama, S. (1999). Is there a universal need for positive self-regard? *Psychological Review, 106,* 766–794.

Henry, P. J., & Sears, D. O. (2002). The symbolic racism 2000 scale. *Political Psychology, 23*(2), 253–283.

Higgins, R. L., Frisch, M. B., & Smith, D. (1983). A comparison of role-played and natural responses to identical circumstances. *Behavior Therapy, 14,* 158–169.

Holladay, S. J., & Coombs, W. T. (1994). Speaking of visions and visions being broken: An exploration of the effects of content and delivery on perceptions of leader charisma. *Management Communication Quarterly, 8,* 165–189.

Hurh, W. M., & Kim, K. C. (1984). *Korean immigrants in America.* Cranbury, NJ: Associated University Press.

Hurh, W. M., & Kim, K. C. (1990). Correlates of Korean immigrants' mental health. *Journal of Nervous and Mental Disease, 178,* 703–711.

Jensen, R. H. (1990, February 19). Minorities didn't share in firm growth. *National Law Journal,* pp. 1, 28–31, 35.

Johnson, F. A., & Marsella, A. J. (1978). Differential attitudes toward verbal behavior in students of Japanese and European ancestry. *Genetic Psychology Monographs, 97,* 43–76.

Johnson, K. R., & Martinez, G. A. (2000). Discrimination by proxy: The case of Proposition 227 and the ban on bilingual education. *The University of California, Davis Law Review, 33,* 1227–1276.

Jost, J. T., Burgess, D., & Mosso, C. O. (2001). *Conflicts of legitimation among self, group, and system: The integrative potential of system justification theory.* New York: Cambridge University Press.

Kao, G. (2000). Group images and possible selves among adolescents: Linking stereotypes to expectations by race and ethnicity. *Sociological Forum, 15*(3), 407–430.

Kashiwagi, K. (1986). Personality development of adolescents. In H. Stevenson, H. Azuma, & K. Hakuta (Eds.), *Child development and education in Japan* (pp. 167–185). New York: Freeman.

Kinder, D. R., & Sanders, L. M. (1996). *Divided by color: Racial politics and democratic ideals.* Chicago: University of Chicago Press.

Kinder, D. R., & Sears, D. O. (1981). Prejudice and politics: Symbolic racism versus racial threats to the good life. *Journal of Personality and Social Psychology, 40*(3), 414–431.

Kinzie, J. D., Ryals, J., Cottington, F., & McDermott, J. F. (1973). Cross-cultural study of depressive symptoms in Hawaii. *International Journal of Social Psychiatry, 19,* 19–24.

Klopf, D., & Cambra, R. (1979a). Apprehension about speaking in the organizational setting. *Psychological Reports, 45*(1), 58.

Klopf, D. W., & Cambra, R. E. (1979b). Communication apprehension among college students in America, Australia, Japan, and Korea. *Journal of Psychology, 102,* 27–31.

Korn/Ferry International. (1990). *Korn/Ferry's international executive profile: A decade of change in corporate leadership.* New York: Author.

Kuo, W. H. (1984). Prevalence of depression among Asian-Americans. *Journal of Nervous and Mental Disease, 172,* 449–457.

LaFromboise, L., Coleman, H. L. K., and Gerton, J. (1993). Psychological impact of biculturalism: Evidence and theory. *Psychological Bulletin, 114,* 395–412.

Leong, F. T. L. (1985). Career development of Asian Americans. *Journal of College Student Personnel, 26,* 539–546.

Leong, F. T. L. (2001). The role of acculturation in the career adjustment of Asian American workers: A test of Leong and Chou's (1994) formulations. *Cultural Diversity & Ethnic Minority Psychology, 7,* 262–273.

Liem, R. (1997). Shame and guilt among first- and second-generation Asian Americans and European Americans. *Journal of Cross-Cultural Psychology, 28*(4), 365–392.

Lin, M. H., Kwan, V. S. Y., Cheung, A., & Fiske, S. T. (2005). Stereotype content model explains prejudice for an envied outgroup: Scale of anti-Asian American stereotypes. *Personality and Social Psychology Bulletin, 31*(1), 34–47.

Linehan, M. M., Goldfried, M. R., & Goldfried, A. P. (1979). Assertion therapy: Skill training or cognitive restructuring. *Behavior Therapy, 10,* 372–388.

Lutwak, N., Razzino, B. E., & Ferrari, J. R. (1998). Self-perceptions and moral affect: An exploratory analysis of subcultural diversity in guilt and shame emotions. *Journal of Social Behavior and Personality, 13*(2), 333–348.

Lutz, C. (1989). *Unnatural emotions: Everyday sentiments on a Micronesian atoll and their challenge to Western theory.* Chicago: University of Chicago Press.

Markus, H. R., & Kitayama, S. (1991). Culture and the self: Implications for cognition, emotion, and motivation. *Psychological Review, 98*(2), 224–253.

Martens, R. (1969). Palmar sweating and the presence of an audience. *Journal of Experimental Social Psychology, 5,* 371–374.

Matsumoto, D. (1993). Ethnic differences in affect intensity, emotion judgments, display rule attitudes, and self-reported emotional expression in an American sample. *Motivation and Emotion, 17*(2), 107–123.

McCrae, R. R. (2002). *NEO-PI-R data from 36 cultures: Further intercultural comparisons.* New York: Kluwer Academic/Plenum.

McCrae, R. R., Costa, P. T. J., Del Pilar, G. H., Rolland, J., & Parker, W. D. (1998). Cross-cultural assessment of the five-factor model: The revised NEO personality inventory. *Journal of Cross-Cultural Psychology, 29*(1), 171–188.

McCrae, R. R., Costa, P. T. J., Ostendorf, F., Angleitner, A., Hrebíčková, M., & Avia, M. D., et al. (2000). Nature over nurture: Temperament, personality, and life-span development. *Journal of Personality and Social Psychology, 78*(1), 173–186.

Mesquita, B. (2001). Emotions in collectivist and individualist contexts. *Journal of Personality and Social psychology, 80*(1), 68–74.

Minami, D. (1980). Discrimination against Asian and Pacific Americans in federal and civil rights enforcement. In U.S. Commission on Civil Rights (Ed.), *Civil rights issues of Asian and Pacific-Americans: Myths and realities* (pp. 555–559). Washington, DC: U.S. Government Printing Office.

Mischel, W. (1969). Continuity and change in personality. *American Psychologist, 24*(11), 1012–1018.

Mok, T. A. (1998). Getting the message: Media images and stereotypes and their effect on Asian Americans. *Cultural Diversity & Mental Health, 4*(3), 185–202.

New York Judicial Commission on Minorities. (1991). *Report of the New York Judicial Commission on Minorities* (Vol. 4). New York: Author.

Norenzayan, A., & Heine, S. J. (2005). Psychological universals: What are they and how can we know? *Psychological Bulletin, 131,* 763–784.

Okazaki, S. (1997). Sources of ethnic differences between Asian American and white American college students on measures of depression and social anxiety. *Journal of Abnormal Psychology, 106,* 52–60.

Okazaki, S., Liu, J. F., Longworth, S. L., & Minn, J. Y. (2002). Asian American-White American differences in expressions of social anxiety: A replication and extension. *Cultural Diversity & Ethnic Minority Psychology, 8*(3), 234–247.

Omi, M. (1993). Out of the melting pot and into the fire: Race relations policy. In Leadership Education for Asian Pacifics (LEAP) (Eds.), *The state of Asian Pacific America* (pp. 199–214). Los Angeles: LEAP and UCLA Asian American Studies Center.

Oyserman, D. & Sakamoto, I. (1997). Being Asian American: Identity, cultural constructs, and stereotype perceptions. *Journal of Applied Behavioral Science, 33,* 435–453.

Riggio, R. E. (1986). Assessment of basic social skills. *Journal of Personality and Social Psychology, 51*(3), 649–660.

Riggio, R. E. (1992). Social interaction skills and nonverbal behaviors. In R. S. Feldman (Ed.), *Applications of nonverbal behavioral theories and research* (pp. 3–30). Hillsdale, NJ: Lawrence Erlbaum.

Schelling, T. C. (1960). *The strategy of conflict.* Cambridge, MA: Harvard University Press.

Schuman, H., Steeh, C., Bobo, L., & Krysan, M. (1997). *Racial attitudes in America: Trends and interpretations* (Rev. ed.). Cambridge, MA: Harvard University Press.

Sears, D. O., & Kinder, D. R. (1985). Whites' opposition to busing: On conceptualizing and operationalizing group conflict. *Journal of Personality and Social Psychology, 48*(5), 1148–1161.

Shah, H. (2003). "Asian culture" and Asian American identities in the television and film industries of the United States. *Studies in Media and Information Literacy Education, 3,* 3.

Shon, S. P., & Ja, D. Y. (1982). Asian families. In M. McGoldrick, J. K. Pearce, & J. Giordano (Eds.), *Ethnicity and family therapy* (pp. 208–228). New York: Guilford Press.

Shweder, R. A. (1991). *Thinking through cultures: Expeditions in cultural psychology.* Cambridge, MA: Harvard University Press.

Shih, M., Pittinsky, T. L., & Ambady, N. (1999). Stereotype susceptibility: Identity salience and shifts in quantitative performance. *Psychological Science, 10*(1), 80–83.

Sidanius, J., Devereux, E., & Pratto, F. (1992). A comparison of symbolic racism theory and social dominance theory as explanations for racial policy attitudes. *Journal of Social Psychology, 132*(3), 377–395.

Steele, C. M. (1988). The psychology of self-affirmation: Sustaining the integrity of the self. In L. Berkowitz (Ed.), *Advances in experimental social psychology* (Vol. 21, pp. 261–302). San Diego, CA: Academic Press.

Steele, C. M. (1998). Stereotyping and its threat are real. *American Psychologist, 53*(6), 680–681.

Sue, D., Ino, S., & Sue, D. M. (1983). Nonassertiveness of Asian Americans: An inaccurate assumption? *Journal of Counseling Psychology, 30,* 581–588.

Sue, S. (1977). Psychological theory and implications for Asian-Americans. *Personnel and Guidance Journal, 55,* 381–389.

Sue, S., & Sue, D. (1971). Chinese-American personality and mental health. *Amerasia Journal, 1,* 36–49.

Sue, S., Zane, N., & Sue, D. (1985). Where are the Asian American leaders and top executives? *Pacific/Asian Mental Health Research Center Review, 4,* 12–14.

Tang, J. (1991, August). *Asian American Engineers: Earnings, Occupational Status, and Promotions.* Paper presented at the 86th annual meeting of the American Sociological Association, Cincinnati, OH.

Tanter, R. (1999). *Rogue regimes: Terrorism and proliferation.* New York: St. Martin's Press.

Taylor, S. E., & Brown, J. D. (1988). Illusion and well-being: A social psychological perspective on mental health. *Psychological Bulletin, 103,* 193–210.

Tesser, A. (1988). Toward a self-evaluation maintenance model of social behavior. In L. Berkowitz (Ed.), *Advances in experimental social psychology* (Vol. 21, pp. 181–227). San Diego, CA: Academic Press.

Ting-Toomey, S. (2004). The matrix of face: An updated face-negotiation theory. In W. B. Gudykunst (Ed.), *Theorizing about intercultural communication* (pp. 71–92). Thousand Oaks, CA: Sage.

Tracy, J. L., & Robins, R. W. (2004). Putting the self into self-conscious emotions: A theoretical model. *Psychological Inquiry, 15*(2), 103–125.

Triandis, H. C., Bontempo, R., & Villareal, M. J. (1988). Individualism and collectivism: Cross-cultural perspectives on self-ingroup relationships. *Journal of Personality and Social Psychology, 54,* 323–338.

Triandis, H. C., & Suh, E. M. (2002). Cultural influences on personality. *Annual Review of Psychology, 53*(1), 133–160.

Tsai, J. L., Chentsova-Dutton, Y., Freire-Bebeau, L., & Przymus, D. E. (2002). Emotional expression and physiology in European Americans and Hmong Americans. *Emotion, 2*(4), 380–397.

U.S. Census Bureau. (2004). Current population survey: Educational attainment. Washington, DC: U.S. Government Printing Office.

U.S. Commission on Civil Rights. (1992). *Civil rights issues facing Asian Americans in the 1990s.* Washington, DC: U.S. Government Printing Office.

U.S. Department of Education. (2000). *Bachelor's degrees conferred by Title IV degree-granting postsecondary institution by race/ethnicity, field, and gender: 50 states and District of Columbia, academic year 1999–2000*. Washington, DC: National Center for Education Statistics.

U.S. General Accounting Office. (1989). *Equal employment opportunity: Women and minority aerospace managers and professionals, 1979–86*.

Weber, M. (1965). *Politics as a vocation*. Philadelphia: Fortress Press. (Original work published 1918)

Weiss, M. S. (1970). Selective acculturation and the dating process: The pattern of Chinese-Caucasian interracial dating. *Journal of Marriage and the Family, 32*, 273–278.

White, W. G., & Chan, E. (1983). A comparison of self-concept scores of Chinese and white graduate students and professionals. *Journal of Non-White Concerns in Personnel and Guidance, 11*(4), 138–141.

Wolpe, J. (1958). *Psychotherapy by reciprocal inhibition*. Stanford, CA: Stanford University Press.

Xin, K. R. (2004). Asian American managers: An impression gap? An investigation of impression management and supervisor-subordinate relationships. *Journal of Applied Behavioral Science, 40*(2), 160–181.

Zajonc, R. B. (1965). Social facilitation. *Science, 149*, 269–274.

Zajonc, R. B., & Sales, S. M. (1966). Social facilitation of dominant and subordinate responses. *Journal of Experimental and Social Psychology, 2*, 160–168.

Zane, N. W., Sue, S., Hu, L., & Kwon, J. (1991). Asian-American assertion: A social learning analysis of cultural differences. *Journal of Counseling Psychology, 38*(1), 63–70.

Zea, M. C., Jarama, S. L., and Bianchi, F. T. (1995). Social support and psychosocial competence: Explaining the adaptation to college of ethnically diverse students. *American Journal of Community Psychology, 23*, 509–531.

18

HEALTH PSYCHOLOGY AND ASIAN PACIFIC ISLANDERS: LEARNING FROM CARDIOVASCULAR DISEASE

ANGELA EBREO

YUKIKO SHIRAISHI

PAUL LEUNG

JENNY KISUK YI

Health psychology has contributed to the biomedical sciences by inclusion of behavioral and psychological factors in the understanding of disease processes, disease prevention, and disease management. Physicians and biomedical researchers now recognize the significance of psychosocial factors in "the natural history of disease, prevention of disability and illness, and promotion of recovery" (Adler & Matthews, 1994, p. 230). In addition to their interest in individual-level variables, health psychologists also have shown an increasing interest in the role of contextual factors (Adler &

Matthews, 1994; Krantz & McCeney, 2002; Taylor, Repetti, & Seeman, 1997). A growing number of researchers hypothesize that contextual factors are important variables in understanding the health of ethnic minority populations.

Studies of chronic conditions and illnesses provide health psychologists an opportunity to study the interplay of psychosocial variables and contextual factors. Chronic conditions range from relatively mild ones, such as partial hearing losses, to severe and life-threatening disorders, such as cancer. Chronic illnesses, such as cardiovascular diseases (CVDs), that result in full or

Authors' note: This chapter is respectfully dedicated in memory of Patrick Okura, Japanese American psychologist and activist, and his wife Lily Okura. The authors acknowledge the staff of the Institute for Research on Race and Public Policy for clerical support. The authors also express their appreciation to Carrol Smith and Sharon Telleen who provided useful comments on earlier drafts of this manuscript.

partial disability also have far-ranging consequences in terms of the patient's employment and financial circumstances.

This chapter provides examples of issues of relevance to health psychologists. We examined current etic explanations of the relationship between psychological factors and biological pathways leading to illness, including chronic diseases such as cancer and cardiovascular disease. These etic explanations neglect to consider social factors such as culture and socioeconomic status and contextual factors such as linguistic isolation and residential segregation, all of which are of particular importance to ethnic minority populations. We have chosen to focus our discussion on CVDs, which are among the leading largely preventable causes of death globally. There are several different types of CVD: atherosclerosis (fatty plaque buildup in the arteries), coronary heart disease, chest pain (angina pectoris), irregular heartbeat (arrhythmia), congestive heart failure, congenital and rheumatic heart disease, and stroke. We limit our presentation to cardiovascular conditions that are amenable to psychosocial or behavioral interventions. We do not provide a comprehensive overview of the pathophysiology of individual cardiovascular conditions; interested readers are thus referred to other sources (e.g., Allan & Scheidt, 1996; Suchday, Tucker, & Krantz, 2002).

EPIDEMIOLOGY OF CARDIOVASCULAR DISEASES: MORTALITY RATE AND PREVALENCE IN ASIAN PACIFIC ISLANDERS

Cardiovascular disease is a global problem in both developed and developing nations. Heart disease and stroke kill some 17 million people a year, which is almost one-third of all deaths globally. By 2020, heart disease and stroke will become the leading cause of both death and disability worldwide, with the number of fatalities projected to increase to more than 20 million a year and, by 2030, to more than 24 million a year (Mackay & Mendis, 2004). One-half of all deaths in developed nations are from heart disease. In India and China, which together account for more than 50% of the world's population, more deaths are attributed to CVD than in all other industrialized nations combined. Coronary heart disease, hypertension, and stroke account for approximately 70% of the deaths caused by CVD.

Despite the fact that CVD is the leading cause of death for APIs in the United States (American Heart Association [AHA], 2005; National Heart, Lung, and Blood Institute, 2000), the profile on the cardiovascular health status of APIs is not clear. National data on CVD among Asian ethnic subgroups are very limited, posing a problem in assessing the needs of the population. The principal sources of ethnically specific epidemiological data will most likely be limited to California and Hawaii. In addition, the true death rates among APIs (especially subgroups) with CVD are not clear due to inaccurate reporting of the race and ethnicity of decedents on death certificates. Prevalence data for CVD among Asian immigrants and U.S.-born APIs are also limited, but studies have shown that the risk for developing CVD increases with the length of residency in the United States.

In 2000, CVD accounted for 36.2% of deaths among API males and 36.3% among API females (AHA, 2005). Among APIs ages 18 and older, 5.4% have heart disease and 2.2% have had a stroke (National Center for Health Statistics [NCHS], 2004). The 2000 overall death rate for stroke for APIs was 52.4 per 100,000, compared to 56.2 per 100,000 for the general population (AHA, 2005).

PATHOGENESIS OF CARDIOVASCULAR DISEASE: LINKING STRESS TO BIOLOGICAL PATHWAYS

Stress, negative emotions, dispositional factors, and social factors such as social support are thought to be interconnected in the etiology and progression of various illnesses, including CVD, cancer, and infectious diseases (Suchday et al. 2002). The role of stress in the etiology of CVD has been well documented (for reviews, see Adler & Matthews, 1994; Everson-Rose & Lewis, 2005). Types of stress that have been studied in relation to CVD include extreme acute stress, chronic stress, work-related stress, and stressful life events. Stress may exert its deleterious effects on cardiovascular health by affecting behavioral pathways, that is, health-related behavior such as smoking, which increases the risk of disease. Yet in general, controlling for behavioral risk factors does not sufficiently explain the effects of stress on CVD. Thus, researchers hold the view that psychosocial factors such as stress may contribute to the etiology of CVD through a biological pathway linking psychosocial factors to the biological pathogenesis of CVD. In recent years, a growing body of research has explored biological pathways through which psychosocial stress may contribute to the development of CVD. Similar mechanisms have been proposed for other conditions such as cancer and infectious diseases, and these mechanisms are viewed as being etic in nature.

Everson-Rose and Lewis (2004) describe the mechanisms wherein activation of the HPA (hypothalamic-pituitary-adrenal) axis and the autonomic nervous system (ANS), serotonergic dysfunction, proinflammatory cytokines (e.g., IL-1, IL-6), and platelet activation play key roles in the pathophysiology of CVD. Studies have long linked the activation of the HPA-axis and the ANS as a central biological response to stressors. Serotonin is a neurotransmitter that has a major role in mood regulation. Chronic stress can result in serotonergic dysfunction, which can have vascular implications. Inflammation has been known to play a critical role in the development of atherosclerosis. Proinflammatory cytokines can result in vascular damage both directly and indirectly through their influence on the HPA axis. Together, HPA-axis activation, ANS activation, and an increased production of proinflammatory cytokines contribute to platelet activation, which leads to atherogenesis and formation of plaque.

Psychological factors other than stress such as negative emotions (e.g., depression, hopelessness, anger, hostility, anxiety) and social factors (e.g., a lack of social ties or social support), can activate the HPA-axis, the ANS, and stimulate the production of proinflammatory cytokines. Activation of the HPA-axis results in increased levels of ACTH (adrenocorticotropin hormone) and elevated cortisol levels. HPA-axis activation and dysregulation and increased proinflammatory cytokines appear to play key roles in linking psychosocial factors to vascular damage, platelet activation, and the resultant increase in atherogenesis and plaque formation. Psychosocial factors, such as stress, can lead to ANS activation, increased blood pressure, and elevated heart rate, which indirectly contribute to platelet activation. Depression has been found to be associated with serotonergic dysfunction, which is related to atherogenesis as well. Psychosocial factors, such as stress and negative emotions, are related to increased inflammation and increased production of proinflammatory cytokines, which, **in turn**, can activate the HPA-axis.

Researchers have begun to see beyond the traditional psychosocial factors to see how larger social and environmental contexts may be related to the pathogenesis of CVD. In studying Asian Pacific Islanders and CVD, understanding how these contextual factors are interrelated with psychosocial factors, behavioral pathways and risk factors, and biologic pathways is key to understanding the etiology and progression of CVD in this population. Next, we present a conceptual model proposed by Myers, Lewis, and Parker-Rodriguez (2003) so that we can critically examine the status of current research on CVD and Asian Pacific Islanders in the remainder of this chapter.

Contextualizing Biopsychosocial Models of Stress and Disease: Explicit Inclusion of Emic Factors Influencing Health

Racial and Ethnic Disparities in Health

Subgroup differences in the incidence, prevalence, treatment responses, and health status outcomes of CVD were at one time attributed primarily to biological factors, such as physiological processes. More recently, health psychologists and other behavioral scientists have added contextual factors to models that link these biological mechanisms to psychological factors that can be assessed at the level of individuals (e.g., Adler & Ostrove, 1999; Anderson

& Armstead, 1995; Goodman, McEwen, Huang, Dolan, & Adler, 2005; Kawachi, Kennedy, & Glass, 1999; Schnittker & McLeod, 2005; Williams, 1999; Williams & Rucker, 1996). Including contextual factors in biopsychosocial models enables researchers to consider social, economic, and political forces that systematically exert negative influences on the health of ethnic and racial minority individuals.

Contextual factors are important to understanding the health of ethnic minority groups, persons living in poverty, and other low-status social groups. Members of low-status groups, including ethnic minorities, often are restricted in where they can reside. They live in different locations and thus experience different social environments than members of higher-status groups. For instance, economically challenged persons live in poorer communities, which are likely to lack health system infrastructures, leading to poorer health outcomes for the residents of those communities. Contextual factors, such as neighborhood context and social status, are commonly found in theories and models focusing on the elimination of health disparities across social groups. Health disparity models can serve as useful heuristic devices, providing some insight into possible mechanisms through which social ecologies affect health. For APIs, models of racial and ethnic disparities in health might examine ecological factors such as language and linguistic isolation and residential segregation. Health disparities models might also include cultural factors, such as level of acculturation, and other variables that are related to health access, such as immigration status. From among the several extant health disparity models, we selected a conceptual model by Myers et al. (2003) to guide our discussion, as this model includes variables that are important in understanding the health of API populations. This model, adapted to the study of CVD, is depicted in Figure 18.1.

The Myers, Lewis, and Parker-Dominguez Model of Health Disparities

Current psychological and behavioral science literature supports the notion that individual health behaviors and psychological characteristics are major contributors to health status, regardless of one's racial or ethnic background. There is some evidence to suggest that these factors might vary across racial and ethnic groups as well as across subethnic groups. Regardless of racial or ethnic group, stress contributes to individual health status. However, sources of chronic and acute stress and the strategies used to cope with stress are mediated by the cultural and/or racial and ethnic group to which one belongs (e.g., Inman & Yeh, Chapter 19, this volume). Thus, existing etic models of the relationship between stress and biological pathways leading to disease can be augmented by including emic psychological, social, and lifestyle factors.

Myers, Lewis and Parker-Rodriguez's (2003) integrative biopsychosocial model explicitly incorporates the influence of macrosocial factors and social environments on stress experienced by ethnic minorities. Social status factors (i.e., macrosocial factors), such as social class, race, ethnicity, and environmental sources of stress (e.g., neighborhood disorganization, family contexts, and work environments), independently contribute to the chronic stress experienced by members of ethnic minority groups. Chronic stressors can be categorized as etic (i.e., general life stresses) or emic (i.e., stresses, such as racism and discrimination, that are linked to one's race or ethnicity). Chronic stress is viewed as affecting physiological and psychological responses that, in turn, may interact with individual genetic factors, leading to an increase in the load on various physiological systems (e.g., the HPA-axis, the immune system, the cardiovascular system). The overstimulation of these physiological systems leads to cumulative vulnerability, which, over time, results in disease. The Myers et al. model also acknowledges the role of psychosocial and lifestyle factors.

To illustrate the concepts in the Myers et al. (2003) model as they might apply to APIs, we examined the psychological and health sciences literatures. Our goal was not to conduct a comprehensive review but to look for examples of studies on CVD conducted in API populations. Most frequently, we located, and share findings from, studies that have been conducted on members of one or, at most, a few Asian subethnic group(s) who reside in a particular geographic location. Note that data on API

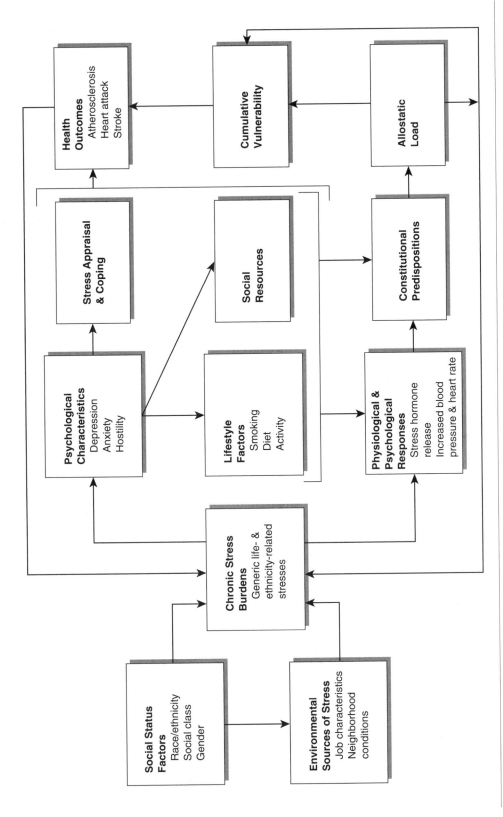

Figure 18.1 Conceptual Model of Social Status Factors, Etic and Emic Sources of Stress, and Ethnic Minority Health

Source: Adapted from Myers, Lewis, and Parker-Dominguez (2003).

subgroups are extremely limited, especially with respect to population-based studies such as those represented by national databases. It should be noted that most data on API ethnic subgroups are based on community and local surveys. Because these surveys are geographically and perhaps cohort-limited, the information provided by them should be viewed with caution in terms of their generalizability and application to other subgroups. The relatively small proportion of APIs in the general population, compounded by the heterogeneity within API populations, has contributed to the current paucity of empirical research.

When necessary, we illustrate a topic area by including findings from studies conducted outside of the United States, particularly when the findings are consistent with other research. We acknowledge the differences between the United States and other countries in terms of social and contextual factors, but we feel that when few or no U.S. studies are available, non-U.S. studies might still provide useful information at the population level. Nonetheless, readers are cautioned to consider the unique circumstances of API populations in the United States when interpreting findings from non-U.S. studies.

We focus our presentation on four areas pertinent to CVD that are amenable to psychological or behavioral intervention: psychosocial factors, behavioral (i.e., lifestyle) risk factors, social-environmental factors, and patient quality of life. Before we share these research examples, it is important to consider evidence (or the lack thereof) for the existence of health disparities related to API populations. The inadequacy and inaccuracy of existing health data for API subgroups, and for APIs as a whole, make it difficult to assess the full extent of health disparities for various conditions, including CVD. Overall, APIs appear to be healthier than members of other racial and ethnic minority groups. For instance, API females have the lowest overall rates of coronary heart disease, followed by Latinos and Native Americans, African Americans, and European Americans (Casper et al., 2000). However, misreporting of race and ethnicity on death certificates may have led to spuriously lower heart disease death rates for APIs, compared with African Americans and European Americans.

A more complex picture of the health of APIs appears when data are disaggregated, with some API subgroups faring less well than others. For example, South Asians appear to have higher rates of CVD than members of other API subethnic groups. In addition, the rate of coronary artery disease among Native Hawaiians is double that of European Americans. Researchers have also found that more Filipino Americans than members of other API groups are hypertensive (Esperat, Inouye, Gonzales, Owen, & Feng, 2004). Despite the diversity within API communities, there are few published research studies (Institute of Medicine, 2002) and more research needs to be conducted to describe the similarities and differences between Asian subethnic groups. In the next section, we present examples of the issues that frequently appear in the literature.

PSYCHOSOCIAL, BEHAVIORAL, AND SOCIAL-ENVIRONMENTAL RISK FACTORS FOR CARDIOVASCULAR DISEASES

Our examination of the literature on APIs and CVD indicates that the majority of research of interest to psychologists has been conducted on modifiable factors, that is, on patient behaviors and on psychosocial variables affecting patients. The major psychosocial risk factors associated with CVD include negative emotions and emotional states (e.g., depression, anxiety, anger), chronic and acute stress, and low levels of social support. The major risk factors associated with CVD that are amenable to behavioral intervention are tobacco use, dietary factors, inadequate physical activity and the prevention and management of conditions related to CVD such as diabetes, obesity, and hypertension.

Psychosocial Factors

Negative emotions and emotional states. Depression has been shown to be a risk factor for developing a future heart attack (Pratt et al., 1996) and to be a predictor of poorer health outcomes among current heart disease patients (e.g., Frasure-Smith, Lesperance, & Talajic, 1993; Glassman & Shapiro, 1998). Subclinical

cholesterol levels were lowest in "other Asian" and highest in Japanese, compared with other API ethnic groups. Whereas Klatsky and Armstrong found no significant differences between the cholesterol levels of U.S.-born Asians and foreign-born Asians, other researchers (e.g., Bates, Hill, & Barrett-Connor, 1989; Yao et al., 1988) have found such differences. The limited number of APIs who have their blood cholesterol checked indicates a gap in knowledge and access to information. More importantly, it indicates a significant number of APIs who are unaware of their risk for heart disease.

Diabetes management and prevention. Diabetes is another major risk factor for CVD (Carter, Pugh, & Monterrosa, 1996; Klastsky et al., 1996; Kumantika, 1990). Because diabetic patients without existing heart disease are just as likely as cardiac patients to suffer a heart attack, the detection and management of diabetes is important. In addition, diabetics are strongly encouraged to lower their LDL cholesterol and triglyceride levels and to raise their HDL cholesterol levels. For APIs as a whole, diabetes is ranked as the fifth-highest cause of death for people between the ages of 45 and 54 (fourth for ages 55–65) (National Center for Health Statistics, 2003). Prevalence data are limited, but diabetes prevalence may be higher than currently reported due to a low level of awareness of symptoms and risk factors for diabetes among APIs (Fujimoto, 1995; Kumantika, 1990; UCLA Center for Health Policy Research, 2001). Researchers attribute the increase in the incidence of diabetes among APIs to changes in food habits and rising rates of obesity (UCLA Center for Health Policy Research, 2001). Physical activity levels were positively associated with lower levels of diabetes prevalence among Japanese American men enrolled in the Honolulu Heart Study (Burchfiel et al., 1995). In postmenopausal API women, however, physical activity was not associated with decreased incidence of type 2 diabetes as was observed in White postmenopausal women (Hsia et al., 2005).

Inadequate physical activity. Numerous studies have demonstrated that an increased level of physical activity lowers blood levels of LDL cholesterol, raises levels of HDL cholesterol,

and regulates blood glucose levels. Data on physical activity in APIs, however, are lacking. Increased Westernization and urbanization has greatly reduced physical activity in the API population, along with changes from a lifestyle characterized by hard labor to a more sedentary one (Klatsky & Armstrong, 1991; Klatsky et al., 1996; UCLA Center for Health Policy Research, 2001). Other researchers (e.g., Hall, Kuga, & Jones, 2002; Wolf et al., 1993) have found that API school-aged and college-aged females engage in lower levels of physical activity, compared to females of other ethnic groups, and that low levels of physical activity may be related to cultural beliefs and acculturation. Recent Asian immigrants are much less likely to meet national recommendations for regular leisure time physical activity than U.S.-born APIs (UCLA Center for Health Policy Research, 2001). Low levels of exercise among older API women may be due to cultural beliefs about exercise and physical activities (Eyler et al., 1998; Wilcox, 2002). Poor diet and a sedentary lifestyle contribute to chronic illnesses such as diabetes and heart disease. However, this relationship may not be as clear cut for API women, compared to White postmenopausal women in relationship to diabetes incidence (Hsia et al., 2005). Though the incidence of CHD and type 2 diabetes among South Asians are high in the United Kingdom, the clear relationship between physical activity and reduced risk of CHD and type 2 diabetes were reported to be stronger in Europeans (Hayes et al., 2002).

Prevention and management of hypertension. Hypertension, or high blood pressure, is strongly related to the risk of having a heart attack or stroke and developing congestive heart failure and atherosclerosis. Untreated hypertension can adversely affect cognitive functioning, producing problems in learning, attention, and other cognitive skills. It is particularly insidious because many persons are asymptomatic and unaware that they are hypertensive until diagnosed by a health professional.

Within-group variation in hypertension in API populations is summarized in Havas et al. (1996). Filipinos have systematically higher mean systolic and diastolic blood pressures than Japanese, Chinese, and "other Asians." Filipino men's systolic and diastolic blood pressures were comparable to those of African Americans. The lack of knowledge about the causes of hypertension among Vietnamese Americans with high prevalence of hypertension (43.78% of the respondents) indicates a need for education as an important part of prevention and management of hypertension (Duong, Bohannon, & Ross, 2001). In a study of managing hypertension through medications, Hui and Pasic (1997) found that API patients, in comparison to Whites, more frequently reported side effects attributed to their antihypertensive medication.

Acculturation may play a role in the development of hypertension. Previous studies have suggested that cultural stress and recent immigration were among the possible reasons for high blood pressure levels (Klatsky & Armstrong, 1991; Stavig et al., 1984, 1988). Acculturation in terms of duration of residence in Canada was also found to be a significant predictor of hypertension among Asian immigrants in Canada, controlling for factors such as smoking, alcohol use, physical activity, psychological distress, access to health services, and sociodemographic characteristics such as gender and education level (Kaplan, Chang, Newsom, & McFarland, 2002).

In comparison to most Americans, APIs are less likely to be aware of hypertension or to be undergoing treatment. Lack of culturally appropriate health education materials and programs adversely impacts this community's ability to increase understanding of CVD risks and the management of CVD.

Social-Environmental Risk Factors

As mentioned earlier, Myers et al. and other researchers propose that individual difference predictors of chronic disease (e.g., health behaviors) or individual psychological propensities (e.g., depression) "are nested within geographic, developmental, occupational, and social environments" (Taylor et al., 1997, p. 413). Several contextual variables are contributors to health disparities in general, and it is probable that these same factors play a role in more specific diseases such as CVD. Due to the lack of studies in the existing literature that directly address the links between social-environmental risk factors and the health status of APIs, we present a more general, brief overview of the influence of social-environmental factors on health.

Socioeconomic status. Socioeconomic status has already been documented as one of the most powerful predictors of health status, with economically disadvantaged persons experiencing the worst health (e.g., Adler, Boyce, Chesney, Cohen, & Folkman, 1994; Williams & Collins, 1995). Whether measured at the level of individuals or at the level of neighborhoods, economic deprivation has consistently been found to be negatively related to measures of health such as mortality, morbidity, and disability. It also appears that even when a particular condition is initially more prevalent in groups of higher socioeconomic status, over time the condition becomes prevalent among lower-status groups, as is the case with heart disease (Williams & Rucker, 1996). Socioeconomic status most probably contributes to health disparities across API subethnic groups, which vary substantially on indicators such as poverty level, employment status, and occupation.

Race-related factors. Various researchers (e.g., Jackson & Sellers, 1996; Kreiger, 2003; Williams, 1999; Williams, Neighbors, & Jackson, 2003) have advanced the notion that societal processes related to "race" contribute to health disparities. For instance, Jackson and Sellers (1996) discuss how racialization, the process of defining a group of people as a race, results in racism, which, in turn, leads to discrimination toward the group(s) that is considered to be inferior. Central to their thesis is the idea that race is a social construct. Given that racialization is a societal process that most probably varies across different racial and ethnic groups, it is important to consider the effects of these differences in social status. For example, perceptions and experiences of racism have been found to have initially adverse effects on the physical health of African Americans, who, as a group, have low status compared to other groups. Over time, acquiring a sense of "system or societal" blame for discriminatory treatment acts as a protective factor; in other words, this orientation may lead to health-protective behaviors but not without some psychological costs (Jackson et al., 1996). At present, it is not clear whether a similar process may be at work that might explain some of the health disparities that affect API ethnic groups.

Interaction of socioeconomic and race-related factors. Differences in socioeconomic status by themselves do not account for all of the variance in health inequalities. When socioeconomic status is controlled, racial disparities in health persist. In fact, an increasing number of researchers have argued that socioeconomic measures are indicators of social status (i.e., the location of one's position in the prevailing social hierarchy), and it is one's social status that determines access to resources that promote health (e.g., Williams & Rucker, 1996). Carter-Pokras and Woo (1999) offer three reasons why racial and ethnic disparities in health persist after adjusting for socioeconomic indicators. First, commonly used indicators of socioeconomic status focus on income rather than on assets. Second, racism and discrimination can operate differently across racial and ethnic groups such that socioeconomic status may have less of an effect in some groups than in others. Finally, some racial and ethnic groups may experience greater degrees of psychological stress as a result of racism and discrimination. For APIs, racism and discrimination may be more or less salient in some groups than in others (e.g., recent immigrants, persons with limited English proficiency).

Aggregation of health data across API subethnic groups can disguise disparities within the overall API population, by the masking of socioeconomic differences across groups. For instance, APIs overall have high levels of educational attainment and income compared to the general U.S. population and other racial and ethnic minorities. However, disaggregated data also indicate that socioeconomic indicators vary widely among subethnic groups. As Carter-Pokras and Woo (1999) suggest, more research needs to be conducted to understand factors that affect the health status of the less affluent and less educated API groups. In addition, it is unclear how exposure to racism and discrimination, in the forms of phenomena such as "underemployment," "the glass ceiling," the "model minority stereotype" and "stereotype threat," might have on the health of more affluent and more highly educated API groups.

CARDIOVASCULAR DISEASES AND PATIENT QUALITY OF LIFE

In this last section, we address some issues related to the quality of life of patients diagnosed with, and undergoing treatment for, cardiovascular disease. Assessment of patients' quality of life can assist psychologists in designing and implementing appropriate interventions for enhancing their patients' well-being.

Conceptualizing "quality of life" is not as simple as it may seem, particularly when patients' experiences are influenced by race, ethnicity, culture, social status, and lack of access to health care (Lau & McKenna, 2001). First, quality of life has both objective and subjective aspects. Objective aspects of quality of life include elements such as the patient's functional status and socioeconomic status, and subjective aspects include the patient's appraisal of his or her situation (e.g., self-esteem, sense of control) and emotional well-being. Quality of life is also multidimensional, encompassing a range of domains such as physical well-being, functional well-being, psychological well-being, social well-being, economic well-being, and spiritual well-being.

Because of their chronic nature and likelihood of causing disability in diagnosed patients, cardiovascular diseases provide ample opportunities for examining quality of life as it relates to the long-term progression of chronic illness and the treatments offered to patients. Thus, we examine the extant literature on CVD-related disabilities as they affect API populations.

Disability and Cardiovascular Disease

Definition of disability. As defined in the Americans With Disabilities Act (ADA), the term *disability,* as applied to an individual, means (a) a physical or mental impairment that substantially limits one or more of the major life activities of such individual, (b) a record of such an impairment, or (c) being regarded as having such an impairment. The ADA definition or description of disability has little meaning to most Americans of Asian or Pacific Islander descent. Anecdotal evidence suggests that many APIs acquiring disability from cardiovascular and related diseases will attempt to go on and do what they have been doing as long as possible and will deny the existence of disability as long as possible.

The etiology of disability from CVD among APIs varies greatly across individuals and is often dependent on factors such as age, severity of disease involvement, premorbid physical conditioning, and the presence of other medical conditions. Disability as a result of CVD is more generalized and diffuse (e.g., an individual feels fatigued and has less strength/tolerance) than is disability caused by cerebrovascular disease or stroke, which may be quite specific (paralysis or weakness of arms and legs, aphasia). Patients and their significant others sometimes find the generalized forms of disability difficult to understand, as there may be no visible reason for the patients' limitations.

The literature on APIs and disability related to CVD is essentially nonexistent. Research on the quality of life of stroke patients has been conducted in Asian countries such as China (e.g., Chow, 1997; Cheung, 2002; Lau, McKenna, Chan, & Cummins, 2003), Japan (e.g., Kobayashi et al., 2000), and Taiwan (e.g., Chien et al., 2002; Shih & Shih, 1999) and in the United Kingdom (e.g., Perry, Hsu, Brooks, & Cherry, 1999).

Consequences of a stroke may involve the entire body and the ability to ambulate. The resulting disabilities include paralysis, cognitive difficulties, speech problems, emotional behaviors, daily living problems, and sometimes pain. Individuals may have problems with the simplest daily activities (e.g., walking, eating, using the bathroom). Problems with thinking, awareness, attention, learning, judgment, and memory can occur following a stroke and, to a lesser extent, following heart disease. Stroke patients may be unaware of their surroundings or the cognitive sequela resulting from the stroke. They may have difficulty controlling emotions or may express inappropriate emotions in certain contexts. Depression, which commonly occurs after a stroke or heart attack, can be a clinical behavioral problem interfering with recovery and rehabilitation. Treatment for post-stroke depression is similar to treatment for any depression; likely interventions are antidepressant medications and psychological therapy.

Psychosocial Aspects of Cardiovascular-Related Disabilities

Some anecdotal evidence suggests that APIs may engage in denial of the existence of their disability and may continue to work because of economic necessity. Individuals might also believe that as long as they can perform job tasks, they should continue as long as they can. There is little in the literature specific to APIs that would serve as a resource or guide for supporting and assisting the individual and family in these situations.

APIs may believe disability to be a function of fate. This is an Asian philosophical perspective that provides a way to cope with the vagaries of life and living and not to let possibly negative after-effects of an event deter one from acting virtuously. The belief that disability is inevitable also suggests that little can be done to either prevent or ameliorate the disabling condition.

Other beliefs that impact on how disability is perceived include the notion that disability is the result of behaviors (sins) by parents or ancestors. This belief is almost universal in scope; it is the same sentiment expressed in Western society in answer to the "why me" question that is often asked following a traumatic event. A penchant for keeping things within the family—the primary hallmark of many Asian societies—and a desire to avoid a loss of face lead to keeping disability under wraps and a private matter. Although many APIs no longer believe in these notions, their behavior continues to be influenced by them, sometimes in subtle ways.

The consequences of these beliefs may determine the course of action of the individual with the disability and his or her family following the acquisition of a disability. For example, adults may not see themselves as "worthy," because the disability was the result of their own actions. APIs of Chinese descent may use a term that translates as "useless" to describe themselves if there is loss of function. An individual views self in terms of what one can do and what one can contribute to the family. Loss of function suggests an inability to contribute to the needs of the family unit, and the individual may be considered a burden. Only children with physical disabilities are worthy of receiving services, as children are not seen as being responsible for what has happened to them.

Because of the belief in the significance of the family within most Asian cultures and the collective belief that disability reflects on family, considerable pressure is placed on not calling attention to disability and even to keeping it as low key as possible. There is the feeling that disability is a private matter to be dealt with within the family if at all possible. For example, a Korean American mother with a child who has a disability was quoted in one study (Cho, Singer, & Brenner, 2000) as saying, "I was furious and ashamed to have an autistic child. . . . I was hopeless and lost the meaning of my life when I learned that my daughter has autism." Nearly one-third of the participants in Cho et al.'s study attributed disability to their own behavior. It may be significant that a large percentage of the Korean American parents in Cho et al.'s study (63%) were Christians and viewed disability as part of a divine plan that would ultimately benefit the child and family. Although Westernized, in part, by their religious beliefs, these parents nevertheless also retained some of their traditional Asian perspectives. This perspective is not limited to Koreans. Filipinos traditionally view severe disabilities with considerable stigma as well. Such stigma derives, in part, from traditional attributions linking specific disabilities to different strategies, including past sins and behaviors.

Centuries of tradition can be passed on and continue to affect attitudes. For example, Paris (1993), studying professional health care providers, found that "Asians generally had the least positive attitudes [toward people with disabilities], even when healthcare professionals are the subjects of research" (p. 823).

As Hong (1995) explained,

Many [Asian Pacific Islanders] believe in supernatural or metaphysical forces which could play a role in health and disease, and in fortune and misfortune. Such beliefs have strong implications in the perception of the causes of disability, in the treatment of disability, and in the feelings of guilt, responsibility or shame associated with having a person with a disability in the family. (p. 61)

In discussing Americans of Chinese descent, Chan, Lam, Wong, Leung, and Fung (1988) contrasted the individualistic orientation of U.S. mainstream culture with "the Chinese preoccupation with social order (collectivist orientation). The concern of Chinese people for harmony-within-hierarchy is strongly influenced by Confucian philosophy and often continues to be an influence on Americans of Chinese descent" (p. 21). The emphasis in traditional Chinese society on "functioning within well-defined and structured social relationships" may lead some Chinese Americans to "expect the same well-defined structure and role in a [rehabilitation] counseling relationship." Similarly, McFarlane, Farley, Guerrero, and Galea'i (1996), describing Pacific cultures in areas served by the Rehabilitation Research and Training Center of the Pacific, portray how a collectivistic orientation may influence concepts such as independent living. "The concept of independent living when described by such terms as empowerment, advocacy, personal choice, and living independently, goes against Pacific Island cultural practices of respect, being humble . . . , family choice and involvement, and living and being with the family" (p. 24).

Traditional APIs often seek help through sources other than, or in addition to, the Western medical or rehabilitation system. Hong observes that "a family will often want to pursue traditional Asian cures, such as herbal medicine, or take certain actions to restore the balance of nature" (p. 61). Liu (1995) notes that "Asian Pacific Islanders rely more heavily on informal social networks" than do most other minority groups (p. 125).

To serve as a resource to the individual involved in the rehabilitation process, as well as to his or her family and other professional team members, psychologists need to understand the unique interface—that is, the various factors that join together or become interconnected—that may occur when working with persons of API background. Family involvement is necessary, including discussion of their perspective of the disability and expectations of both the individual with the disability and family members. Individuals and families whose primary language is not English may need not only a translator but also additional time to explore the rehabilitation process and all that it entails.

SUMMARY AND CONCLUSION

One goal in writing this chapter was to introduce readers to some of the issues that health psychologists must consider in understanding the health of API populations. We attempted this by focusing our discussion on CVD, given its personal, economic, and societal impact. We presented an etic biopsychological model of the relationship between health status and psychological factors along with a more emic model, which includes social-environmental (i.e., contextual) factors that can be used to explain differences across racial and ethnic minority populations.

Health disparity models (e.g., Myers et al., 2003) indicate how the health of ethnic minority populations is influenced by societal forces, such as racism, discrimination, and barriers to health care access; individual characteristics, such as personality or perceived social support; individual behaviors, such as smoking and dietary habits; and biological factors, such as genetic predispositions toward a given disease. In addition, these models encourage researchers to consider cultural influences in the promotion of healthy behaviors. The inclusion of societal and other contextual factors within health disparity models results in a more inclusive framework for understanding the health of ethnic minority groups, including APIs. Our application of the Myers et al. model to the investigation of CVD in APIs shows that there are many areas amenable to further research and theoretical developments beyond CVD.

Existing data sets have their limitations especially for APIs. Comprehensive health data for APIs are limited in most cases. Historically, researchers have treated APIs as one homogenous group, ignoring the disparities and differences that exist within the population. The heterogeneity of APIs, with respect to distribution of cardiovascular risk factors and mortality, cannot be neglected, and future studies should take this into account. Because of small samples of APIs in national surveys, researchers and practitioners are often unable to formulate comprehensive analyses of API health profiles. In addition to insufficient data, inconsistencies in coding for race and ethnicity within existing data have been noted by researchers and clinicians.

The lack of reliable, ethnic-specific data on API cardiovascular health status impedes the ability of researchers and clinicians to assess the varying cardiovascular health needs of individuals within each ethnic group.

We utilized CVD as one example of health-related conditions among API populations needing attention from health psychology. Studying API groups within the United States and Canada, along with worldwide ethnic differences in the incidence and prevalence of CVD and other chronic health conditions including mortality rates, and migration patterns, may provide us with a clearer picture of the factors related to the etiology of these conditions. Future studies focusing on understanding the interactions between social-environmental, group-level, and individual risk factors cannot only contribute to theory but may also suggest the appropriate levels for different intervention strategies and approaches.

In addition to incorporating multilevel, longitudinal, prospective designs, future research will need to address issues at a population level. Clearly, larger, more comprehensive epidemiological studies are needed to understand factors related to the disease process, particularly if comparisons across API subgroups are to be made. Ideally, such studies will involve collaborations among teams of researchers located in various geographical regions of the United States. This is not to say that smaller and more qualitative studies are not useful. On the contrary, smaller studies of single subethnic groups can provide a level of detail that cannot be obtained in nationwide or regional studies.

Our review revealed that research on psychosocial issues as they relate to CVD and other health conditions in API populations to be quite limited. Our major impression is that there is significant need to test health psychology models that incorporate physiological, psychological, cultural, and social factors for API populations. Further, studies typically do not present a conceptual framework that can be used to test hypotheses about how these factors are interrelated. Biopsychosocial models that include emic factors are sorely needed in order to uniquely address API health concerns.

REFERENCES

Adler, N. E., Boyce, T., Chesney, M. A., Cohen, S., & Folkman, S. (1994). Socioeconomic status and health: The challenge of the gradient. *American Psychologist, 49,* 15–24.

Adler, N. E., & Mathews, K. (1994). Health psychology: Why do some people get sick and some stay well? *Annual Review of Psychology, 45,* 229–259.

Adler, N. E., & Ostrove, J. M. (1999). Socioeconomic status and health: What we know and what we don't. *Annals of the New York Academy of Sciences, 896,* 3–15.

Allan, R., & Scheidt, S. (1996). *Heart and mind: The practice of cardiac psychology.* Washington, DC: American Psychological Association.

American Heart Association. (2005). *Heart disease and stroke statistics—2005 update.* Dallas, TX: Author.

Anderson, N. B., & Armstead, C. A. (1995). Toward understanding the association of socioeconomic status and health: New challenges for the biopsychosocial approach. *Psychosomatic Medicine, 57,* 213–225.

Baluja, K. F., Park, J., & Myers, D. (2003). Inclusion of immigrant status in smoking prevalence statistics. *American Journal of Public Health, 93,* 642–646.

Bates, S. R., Hill, L., & Barrett-Connor, E. (1989). Cardiovascular disease risk factors in an Indochinese population. *American Journal of Preventive Medicine, 5,* 15–20.

Berkman, L. F., Leo-Summers, L., & Horwitz, R. I. (1992). Emotional support and survival after myocardial infarction: A prospective, population-based study of the elderly. *Annals of Internal Medicine, 117,* 1003–1009.

Bishop, G., D., & Robinson, G. (2000). Anger, harassment, and cardiovascular reactivity among Chinese and Indian Men in Singapore. *Psychosomatic Medicine, 62,* 684–692.

Bland, S. H., Krogh, V., Winkelstein, W., & Trevisan, M. (1991). Social network and blood pressure: A population study. *Psychosomatic Medicine, 53,* 598–607.

Burchfiel, C. M., Sharp D. S., Curb J. D., Rodriguez B. L., Hwang L. J., Marcus E. B., et al. (1995). Physical activity and incidence of diabetes: the Honolulu Heart Program. *American Journal of Epidemiology, 141,* 360–368.

Carter J. S., Pugh J. A., & Monterrosa A. (1996) Non-insulin dependent diabetes mellitus in minorities in the United States. *Annals of Internal Medicine, 16,* 157–177.

Carter-Pokras, O., & Woo, V. (1999). Health profile of racial and ethnic minorities in the United States. *Ethnicity & Health, 4,* 117–120.

Casper, M. L., Barnett, E., Halverson, J. A., Elmes, G. A., Braham, V. E., Majeed, Z. A., et al. (2000). *Women and heart disease: An atlas of racial and ethnic disparities in mortality* (2nd ed.) Morgantown, WV: Office for Social Environment and Health Research, West Virginia University.

Centers for Disease Control and Prevention. (2003). Tobacco use among middle and high school students—United States, 2002. *Morbidity and Mortality Weekly Reports, 52.*

Centers for Disease Control and Prevention. (2004). Cigarette smoking among adults—United States, 2002. *Morbidity and Mortality Weekly Reports, 53.*

Chan, F., Lam, C. S., Wong, D., Leung, P., & Fung, X.-S. (1988). Counseling Chinese Americans with disabilities. *Journal of Applied Rehabilitation Counseling, 19,* 21–25.

Chen, X., Unger, J. B., Cruz, T. B., & Johnson, C. A. (1999). Smoking patterns of Asian-American youth in California and their relationship with acculturation. *Journal of Adolescent Health,* 321–328.

Cheung, R. T. F. (2002). Sexual functioning in Chinese stroke patients with mild or no disability. *Cerebrovascular Diseases, 14,* 122–128.

Chew, T. (1983). Sodium values of Chinese condiments and their use in sodium restricted diets. *Journal of the American Dietetic Association, 82,* 397–401.

Chien, K., Huang, P. Chen, M., Chiang, F., Lai, L., & Lee, Y. (2002). Assessment of quality of life in a double-blind, randomized clinical trial of imidapril and captopril for hypertensive Chinese in Taiwan. *Cardiovascular Drugs and Therapy, 16,* 221–226.

Cho, S., Singer, G. H. S., & Brenner, M. (2000). Adaptation and accommodation to young children with disabilities: A comparison of Korean and Korean American parents. *Topics in Early Childhood Special Education, 20,* 236–249.

Chow, E. O. W. (1997). Quality of life and associated factors in Chinese stroke survivors in Hong Kong. *Health Care in Later Life, 2,* 227–238.

Cohen, J. B., & Reed, D. (1985). The type A behavior pattern and coronary heart disease among Japanese men in Hawaii. *Journal of Behavioral Medicine, 8,* 343–852.

Cottington, E. M., Matthews, K. A., Talbott, E., & Kuller, L. H. (1980). Environmental agents preceding sudden death in women. *Psychosomatic Medicine. 42,* 567–574.

Duong, D. A., Bohannon, A. S., & Ross, M. C. (2001). A descriptive study of hypertension in Vietnamese Americans. *Journal of Community Health Nursing, 18,* 1–11.

Eaker, E. D., Pinsky, J., & Castelli, W. P. (1992). Myocardial infarction and coronary death among women: psychosocial predictors from a 20-year follow-up of women in the Framingham Study. *American Journal of Epidemiology, 135,* 854–64.

Egusa, G., Murakami, F., Ito, C., Matsumoto, Y., Kado, S., Okamura, M., et al. (1993). Westernized food habits and concentrations of serum lipids in the Japanese. *Atherosclerosis, 100,* 249–255.

Esperat, M. C., Inouye, J., Gonzales, E. W., Owen, D. C., & Feng, D. (2004). Health disparities among Asian Pacific Islanders and Pacific Islanders. *Annual Review of Nursing Research,* 135–159.

Everson-Rose, S. A., & Lewis, T. T. (2005). Psychosocial factors and cardiovascular diseases. *Annual Review of Public Health, 26,* 445–467.

Eyler, A. A., Baker, E., Cromer, L., King, A. C., Brownson, R. C., & Donatelle, R. J. (1998). Physical activity and minority women: a qualitative study. *Health Education Behavior, 25,* 640–652.

Frasure-Smith, N., Lesperance, F., & Talajic, M. (1993). Depression, following myocardial infarction: Impact on 6-month survival. *Journal of the American Medical Association, 270,* 1819–1825.

Fuh, J. L., Liu, H. C., Wang, S. J., Liu, C. Y., & Wang, P. N. (1997). Poststroke depression among the Chinese elderly in a rural community. *Stroke, 28,* 1126–1129.

Fujimoto, W. Y. (1995). Diabetes in Asian and Pacific Islander Americans. In *National Diabetes Data Group. Diabetes in America.* (NIH Publication No. 95–1468, 2nd ed., pp. 661–681). Bethesda, MD: National Institute of Diabetes and Digestive and Kidney Diseases, National Institutes of Health.

Glassman, A. H., & Shapiro, P. A. (1998). Depression and the course of coronary artery disease. *American Journal of Psychiatry, 155,* 4–11.

Goodman, E., McEwen, B. S., Huang, B., Dolan, L. M., & Adler, N. E. (2005). Social inequalities in biomarkers of cardiovascular risk in adolescence. *Psychosomatic Medicine, 67,* 9–15.

Hall, A. E., Kuga, D., & Jones, D. F. (2002). A multivariate study of determinants of vigorous physical activity in a multicultural sample of college students. *Journal of Sport & Social Issues, 26,* 66–84.

Hance, M., Carney, R. M., Freedland, K. E., & Skala, J. (1996). Depression in patients with coronary heart disease. A 12-month follow-up. *General Hospital Psychiatry, 18,* 61–65.

Havas, S., Fujimoto, W., Close, N., McCarter, R., Keller, J., & Sherwin, R. (1996). The NHLBI workshop on hypertension in Hispanic Americans, Native Americans, and Asian/Pacific Islander Americans, *Public Health Reports, 111,* 451–458.

Hayes, L., White, M., Unwin, N., Bhopal, R., Fischbacher, C., Harland, J., et al. (2002). Patterns of physical activity and relationship with risk markers for cardiovascular disease and diabetes in Indian, Pakistani, Bangladeshi and European adults in a UK population. *Journal of Public Health Medicine, 24,* 170–178.

Haynes, S. B., Feinlieb, M. (1980). Women, work, and coronary disease: Prospective findings from the Framingham Heart Study. *American Journal of Public Health, 700,* 133–141.

Hong, G. K. (1995). Cultural considerations in rehabilitation counseling for Asian Pacific Islanders. *NARPPS Journal, 19,* 59–64.

Hsia, J., Wu, L., Allen, C., Oberman, A., Lawson, W. E., Torrens, J., et al. (2005). Physical activity and diabetes risk in postmenopausal woman. *American Journal of Preventive Medicine, 28,* 19–25.

Huang, B., Rodriguez, B., Burchfiel, C., Chyou, P., Curb, J. D., & Yano, K. (1996). Acculturation and prevalence of diabetes among Japanese-American men in Hawaii. *American Journal of Epidemiology, 144,* 674–681.

Hui, K. K., & Pasic, J. (1997). Outocome of hypertension management in Asian Americans. *Archives of Internal Medicine, 23,* 1345–1348.

Institute of Medicine. (2002). *Unequal treatment: Confronting racial and ethnic disparities in health care.* Washington, DC: National Academy Press.

Iwasaki, M., Otani, T., Sunaga, R., Miyazaki, H., Xiao, L., & Wang, N., et al. (2002). Social networks and mortality based on the komo-ise cohort study in Japan. *International Journal of Epidemiology, 31,* 1208–1218.

Jackson, J. S., Brown, T., Williams, D., Torres, M., Sellers, S., & Brown, K. (1996). Perceptions and experiences of racism and the physical and mental health status of African Americans: A thirteen-year national panel study. *Ethnicity & Disease, 6*, 132–147.

Jackson, J. S., & Sellers, S. L. (1996). African American health over the life course: A multidimensional framework. In. P. M. Kato & T. Mann (Eds.), *Handbook of diversity issues in health psychology* (pp. 301-317). New York: Plenum Press.

Kaplan, M. S., Chang, C., Newsom, J. T., & McFarland, B. H. (2002). Acculturation status and hypertension among Asian immigrants in Canada. *Journal of Epidemiology and Community Health, 56*, 455–456.

Kaprio, J., Koskenvuo, M., & Rita, H. (1987). Mortality after bereaved: A prospective study of 5,647 widowed persons. *American Journal of Public Health, 77*, 283–287.

Karasek, R. A., & Theorell, T. G. (1990). *Health, work, stress, productivity, and the reconstruction of working life*. New York: Basic Books.

Kawachi, I., Colditz, G. A., Ascherio A., Rimm, E. B., Giovannucci E., Stamfer, J. J., et al. (1996). A prospective study of social networks in relation to total mortality and cardiovascular disease in men in the USA. *Journal of Epidemiology and Community Health, 50*, 245–51.

Kawachi, I., Kennedy, B. P., & Glass, R. (1999). Social capital and self-rated health: A contextual analysis. *American Journal of Public Health, 89*, 1187–1193.

Kim, K. K., Yu, E., Chen, E. H., Kim, J., Brintnall, R., & Vance, S. (2000). Smoking behavior, knowledge and beliefs among Korean Americans. *Cancer Practice, 8*, 223–230.

Klatsky, A. L., & Armstrong, M. A. (1991). Cardiovascular risk factors among Asian Americans living in Northern California. *American Journal of Public Health, 81*, 1423–1428.

Klatsky A. L., Tekawa I. S., & Armstrong M. A. (1996) Cardiovascular risk factors among Asian Pacific Islanders. *Public Health Reports, 111*, 62–64.

Kobayashi, R., Kai, N., Hosoda, M., Minematsu, A., Sasaki, H., Maejima, H., et al. (2000). *Journal of Physical Therapy Science, 12*, 13–17.

Kolonel, L. N., Henderson, B. E., Hankin, J. H., Nomura, A. M. Y., Wilkens, L. R., Pike, M. C., et al. (2000). A multiethnic cohort in Hawaii and Los Angeles: Baseline characteristics. *American Journal of Epidemiology, 151*, 346–357.

Krantz, D. S., & McCeney, M. K. (2002). Effects of psychological and social factors on organic disease: A critical assessment of research on coronary heart disease. *Annual Review of Psychology, 53*, 341–369.

Kreiger, N. (2003). Does racism harm health? Did child abuse exist before 1962? On explicit questions, critical science, and current controversies: An ecosocial perspective. *American Journal of Public Health, 93*, 194–199.

Kumantika S. (1990). Diet and chronic disease issues for minority populations. *Journal of Nutrition Education, 22*, 89–96.

LaCroix, A. Z., & Haynes, S. G. (1987). Gender differences in the health effect of workplace roles. In R. C. Barnett, L. Biener, & G. K. Baruch (Eds.), *Gender and stress* (pp. 96–121). New York: Free Press.

Lau, A., & McKenna, K. (2001). Conceptualizing quality of life for elderly people with stroke. *Disability and Rehabilitation, 23*, 227–238.

Lau, A. L. D., McKenna, K., Chan, C. C. H., & Cummins, R. A. (2003). Defining quality of life for Chinese elderly stroke survivors. *Disability and Rehabilitation, 25*, 699–711.

Leor, J., & Kloner, R. A. (1996). The Northridge earthquake as a trigger for acute myocardial infarction. *American Journal of Cardiology, 77*, 1230–1232.

Liu, M. (1995). Ethnicity and information seeking. *The Reference Librarian, 49–50*, 123–134.

Ma, G., Tan, Y. Freeley, R., & Thomas, P. (2002). Perceived risks of certain types of cancer and heart disease among Asian American smokers and non-smokers. *Journal of Community Health, 27*, 233–246.

Mackay, J., & Mendis, G. (2004). *Atlas of heart disease and stroke*. Geneva, Switzerland: World Health Organization Press.

Markovitz, J. H., Matthews, K. A., Kannel, W. B., Cobb, J. L., & D'Agostino, R. B. (1993). Psychological predictors of hypertension in the Framingham Study: Is there tension in hypertension? *Journal of the American Medical Association, 270*, 2439–2443.

Marmot, M. G. (1983). Stress, social and cultural variations in heart disease. *Journal of Psychosomatic Research, 27*, 377–384.

Maxwell, A., Bastani, R., Vida, P., & Warda, U. (2002). Physical activity among older Filipino-American women. *Women & Health, 36*, 67–79.

McFarlane, F.R., Farley, T. H., Guerrero, J. L., & Galea'i, K. E. (1996). Embracing diversity in rehabilitation in Pacific cultures. *American Rehabilitation, 22,* 20–28.

Miller, T. Q., Smith, T. W., Turner, C. W., Guijarro, M. L., & Hallet, A. J. (1996). A meta-analytic review of research on hostility and physical health. *Psychological Bulletin, 119,* 168–174.

Myers, H. F., Lewis, T. T., & Parker-Dominguez, T. (2003). Stress, coping and minority health: Biopsychosocial perspective on ethnic health disparities. In G. Bernal, J. E. Trimble, A. K. Burlew, & F. T. L. Leong (Eds.), *Handbook of racial and ethnic minority psychology* (pp. 377–400). Thousand Oaks, CA: Sage.

National Center for Health Statistics. (2003). Health, United States, 2003. Hyattsville, MD: Author, Centers for Disease Control and Prevention, U.S. Department of Health and Human Services.

National Center for Health Statistics. (2004). National Health Interview Survey (NHIS) Series 10, No. 219. Hyattsville, MD: Centers for Disease Control and Prevention, National Center for Health Statistics.

National Heart, Lung, and Blood Institute. (2000). *Addressing cardiovascular health in Asian Pacific Islanders and Pacific Islanders: A background report.* (NIH Publication No. 00–3647). Washington, DC: U.S. Government Printing Office.

Ohira, T., Iso, H., Satoh, S., Sankai, T., Tanigawa, T., Ogawa, Y., et al. (2001). Prospective study of depressive symptoms and risk of stroke among Japanese. *Stroke, 32,* 903–908.

Paris, M. J. (1993). Attitudes of medical students and healthcare professionals towards people with disabilities. *Archives of Physical Medicine and Rehabilitation, 74,* 818–825.

Perry, S. I., Hsu, R. T., Brooks, W., & Cherry, D. (1999). Perceptions of community services among Asian and white survivors and their carers: An exploratory study. *Ethnicity & Health, 4,* 101–105.

Petticrew, M., Gilbody, S., & Sheldon, T. A. (1999). Relation between hostility and coronary heart disease. Evidence does not support link [Comment]. *British Medical Journal, 319,* 917–918.

Pratt, L. A., Ford, D. E., Crum, R. M., Armenian, H. K., Gallo, J. J., & Eaton, W. W. (1996). Depression, psychotropic medication, and risk of myocardial infarction: Prospective data from Baltimore ECA follow-up. *Circulation, 94,* 3123–3129.

Rozanski, A., Blumenthal, J. A., & Kaplan, J. (1999). Impact of psychological factors on the pathogenesis of cardiovascular disease and implications for therapy. *Circulation, 99,* 2192–2197.

Satia-Abouta, J., Patterson, R. E., Kristal, A. R., Teh, C., & Tu, S. P. (2002). Psychosocial predictors of diet and acculturation in Chinese American and Chinese Canadian woman. *Ethnicity & Health, 7,* 21–39.

Schnittker, J., & McLeod, J.D. (2005). The social psychology of health disparities. *Annual Review of Sociology, 31,* 75–103.

Schoenborn, C.A. (2004). Health behaviors of adults: United States, 1999-2001. Hyattsville, MD: Centers for Disease Control and Prevention, U.S. Department of Health and Human Services, National Center for Health Statistics.

Seeman, T. E., & McEwen, B. S. (1996). Impact of social environment characteristics on neuroendocrine function. *Psychosomatic Medicine, 58,* 459–471.

Shih, S., & Shih, F. (1999). Health needs of lone elderly Chinese men with heart disease during their hospitalization. *Nursing Ethics, 6,* 58–72.

Shumaker, S. A., & Czajkowski, S. M. (1994). *Social support and cardiovascular disease.* New York: Plenum Press.

Stavig, G., Igra, I., & Leonard, A. (1984). Hypertension among Asians and Pacific Islanders in California. *American Journal of Epidemiology, 119,* 677–691.

Stavig, G., Igra, I., & Leonard, A. (1988). Hypertension and related health issues among Asians and Pacific Islanders in California. *Public Health Reports, 103,* 23–37.

Suchday, S., Tucker, D. L., & Drantz, D. S. (2002). Diseases of the circulatory system. In T. J. Boll, S. B. Johnson, N. W. Perry, & R. H. Rozensky (Eds.), *Handbook of clinical health psychology:. Vol. 1. Medical disorders and behavioral applications* (pp. 203–238). Washington, DC: American Psychological Association.

Takeshita, J., Masaki, K., Ahmed, I., Foley, D. J., Li, Y. Q., Chen, R., et al. (2002). Are depressive symptoms a risk factor for mortality in elderly Japanese American men? The Honolulu-Asia aging study. *American Journal of Psychiatry, 159,* 1127–1132.

Tang, W. K., Ungvari, G. S., Chiu, H. F., Sze, K. H., Woo, J., & Kay, R. (2002). Psychiatric morbidity in first time stroke patients in Hong Kong: A pilot study in a rehabilitation unit. *Australian and New Zealand Journal of Psychiatry, 36,* 544–549.

Taylor, S. E., Repetti, R. L., & Seeman, T. (1997). Health psychology: What is an unhealthy environment and how does it get under the skin? *Annual Review of Psychology, 48,* 411–447.

Torres-Schow, R. M., Suen, S., Yeh, I., & Tam, C. F. (1999). A comparison of atherogenic potential of diets between Asian and Hispanic college students and their parents. *Nutrition Research, 19,* 555–568.

UCLA Center for Health Policy Research. (2001). *California Health Interview Survey (CHIS).* Los Angeles: Author.

Unger, J. B., Reynolds, K., Shakib, S., Spruiji-Metz, D., Sun, P., & Johnson, C. A. (2004). Acculturation, physical activity, and fast-food consumption among Asian-American and Hispanic adolescents. *Journal of Community Health, 29,* 467–481.

U.S. Department of Health and Human Services. (1998). *Tobacco use among U.S. racial/ethnic minority groups–African Americans, American Indians and Alaska natives, Asian Americans and Pacific Islanders, and Hispanics: A report of the Surgeon General.* Atlanta: U.S. Department of Health and Human Services, Centers for Disease Control and Prevention.

WHO Expert Consultation. (2004). Appropriate body-mass index for Asian populations and its implications for policy and intervention strategies. *Lancet, 363,* 157–163.

Wilcox, S. (2002). Physical activity in older women of color. *Topics in Geriatric Rehabilitaion, 18,* 21–33.

Williams, D. R. (1999). Race, socioeconomic status, and health: The added effects of racism and discrimination. In N. E. Adler & M. Marmot (Eds.), *Socioeconomic status and health in industrial nations: Social, psychological and biological pathways* (pp. 173–188). New York: New York Academy of Sciences.

Williams, D. R., & Collins, C. (1995). U.S. socioeconomic and racial differences in health: Patterns and explanations. *Annual Review of Sociology, 21,* 349–386.

Williams, D. R., Neighbors, H. W., & Jackson, J. S. (2003). Racial/ethnic discrimination and health: Findings from community studies. *American Journal of Public Health, 93,* 200–208.

Williams, D. R., & Rucker, T. (1996). Socioeconomic status and the health of racial minority populations. In P. M. Kato & T. Mann (Eds.), *Handbook of diversity issues in health psychology* (pp. 407–423). New York: Plenum Press.

Wolf, A. M., Gortmaker, S. L., Cheung, L., Gray, H., Herzog, D. B., & Coldits, G. A. (1993). Activity, inactivity, and obesity: Racial, ethnic, and age differences among schoolgirls. *American Journal of Public Health, 83,* 1625–1627.

Yao, C. H., Wu, Z. S., Hong, Z. G., Xu, X. M., Zhang, M., Wu, Y. Y., et al. (1988). Risk factors of cardiovascular diseases in Beijing. *Chinese Medical Journal, 101,* 901–905.

Yu, E. S. H., Chang, C. F., Liu, W. T., & Kan, S. H. (1985). Asian-white mortality differences: Are there excess deaths? In M. Heckler (Ed.), *Report of the Secretary's Task Force on Black and Minority Health* (Vol. 2, pp. 209–281). Rockville, MD: U.S. Department of Health and Human Services.

19

ASIAN AMERICAN STRESS AND COPING

ARPANA G. INMAN

CHRISTINE J. YEH

The changing demographics of the United States and the focus on multicultural competencies in the counseling literature have provided a strong impetus for challenging European American theoretical and empirical perspectives and examining how perceptions and approaches to life's issues may be imbedded in cultural and symbolic structures of specific ethnic groups (Kakar, 1982; D. W. Sue & Sue, 2003). In this chapter, we explore concepts of stress and coping among Asians/Asian Americans. Several major assumptions guide this chapter.

First, stress and coping cannot be separated from the cultural context in which they arise (Lazarus & Folkman, 1984). Asian Americans are an ethnically diverse group with specific cultural values and beliefs that influence their worldviews and ways of living. As a result, understanding how stress and coping may be defined from an Asian/Asian American cultural perspective becomes relevant. Second, because culture is central to the experience of stress and coping, understanding the cultural values and beliefs that influence the types of stressors that Asian Americans face and the coping strategies that they employ to deal with the changing demands of life (e.g., immigration, discrimination) become important. Third, because of the collective nature of Asian communities (Markus & Kitayama, 1991; Yeh, Inman, Kim, & Okubo, 2006), stress and coping need to be understood not only from an individual perspective but also from a systemic and sociocultural context. Intrinsic to this context is the experience of immigration. The literature suggests that immigration poses significant pressures on first and subsequent generations (Berry, 1993; Inman, Howard, Beaumont, & Walker, 2005). Thus, we examine, in this chapter, the stressors and coping styles inherent in these generational differences. Furthermore, although there is much diversity within and between Asian ethnic groups with regard to cultural practices, language, and histories of immigration to the United States, these groups are similar in terms of their collectivistic ideologies, family values, and the religious philosophies that guide their perspectives on life's experiences and challenges. This chapter focuses on these similarities in relation to stress and coping among Asian/Asian American ethnic groups.

CULTURE AND STRESS

Stress is an inevitable aspect of everyday life. Stress has been conceptualized as an interaction between the demands of the environment and the resources within an individual (Tweed, White, & Lehman, 2004). An individual's response to stressful situations may be positive or negative, depending on the meaning, intrinsic value, and appraisal of the events (Coll & Magnuson, 1997); these aspects are largely affected by one's cultural values and beliefs. Furthermore, whether stress has repercussions beyond the immediate context can depend on a number of factors, such as personal characteristics, immigrant group characteristics, environmental factors, and the interaction between these factors (Coll & Magnuson, 1997; Sodowsky & Lai, 1997). Thus, in order to better understand the different stressors, it is important to first understand the cultural values that may influence Asian/Asian American lives and how stress may be conceptualized within these communities.

ASIAN AMERICAN CULTURAL VALUES AND STRESS

While the Western American culture has been predominantly described as individualistic, with individuals seeking independence from each other, the Asian culture has historically been known to foster a collectivistic perspective, wherein individuals are seen as maintaining a fundamental relatedness to each other (Markus & Kitayama, 1991). Within this context, attending to others, maintaining interdependence and harmony in relations, and fitting in are not only valued but also expected (Chang, 2001; Cheng 1990; Yee, 1992). Thus, the belief in privacy, personal space, and individualism are antithetical to this collective value orientation (Hines, Gracie-Preto, McGoldrick, Almeida, & Weltman, 1992; Prathikanti, 1997). Additionally, the notion of filial piety based in clear hierarchies, roles, duties, and moral obligations is considered important in Asian families. Individuals are raised to have unconditional respect and loyalty toward their parents and elders (Buriel & De Ment, 1997; Chang, 2001). Intrinsic to these values is the belief that individuals' actions and behaviors

reflect the welfare and integrity of the family. Family needs supersede individual needs, and having an identity separate from the family is discouraged (Inman & Tewari, 2003). Thus, when stressors evolve from life issues, they are primarily discussed within a familial context (Froggett, 2001). Additionally, maintaining social and emotional restraint is considered important when dealing with life's difficulties (Hastings, 2000).

This philosophy of self and relationships is further influenced by different religions and spiritual perspectives on life, health, and illness. Commensurate with this is the belief that pain (or stress) and pleasure are part of suffering, with suffering being a lifelong process. Within this context, suffering is to be accepted and tolerated and is even seen as necessary for salvation (Palsane & Lam, 1996). Asians/Asian Americans perceive health and well-being holistically, with mental, physical, and spiritual components included in this conceptualization (Hilton et al., 2001; Mullatti, 1995). Thus, not only are symptoms presented somatically, but they may also be embedded within a religious context (Inman, Yeh, Madan-Bahel, & Nath, 2006). For example, according to Hinduism, the "cosmic process is one of universal and unceasing change and is patterned on the duality which is perpetually in conflict" (Rhys Davids, 1972, p. 148). According to Buddhism, suffering is inevitable in the physical world. The path to happiness (freedom from suffering) is seen as an absence of desire rather than a result of symptom reduction in the physical world. Like Hinduism, Taoism teaches one to adapt to the ever-changing environment (Tweed et al., 2004). In the Islamic tradition, suffering is an inherent part of one's life, and God is conceived as someone who inflicts suffering to punish individuals for their sins or to test their faith. The sufferer is expected to be patient, maintain faith, and endure the suffering (Bowker, 1970). The Japanese who follow Zen Buddhism believe that suffering is an essential part of existence and stems from desires and individual self-centeredness that need to be controlled through discipline. Similarly, the Chinese philosopher Mencius suggests that life without stress is no life at all. In fact stress and its byproducts are seen to strengthen a person's psychological makeup (Palsane & Lam, 1996).

Suffering is also linked to rebirth within the Hindu and Chinese philosophies. For all actions that individuals engage in, there is positive or negative credit, and the accumulation of these credits is considered part of one's Karma. Within the Chinese philosophy, these credits are sometimes called "accumulated blessings" that are carried forward from life to life (Palsane & Lam, 1996). Thus, faith in God, fate, rebirth, and suffering as preordained from a previous life are some of the factors that affect the conceptualization of pain, suffering, and stress.

Types of Stressors

In considering Asian/Asian American stress and coping, one needs to examine these constructs within a sociocultural context. Specifically, immigration has been identified as having a significant impact on immigrant family processes and their experiences. The immigration process and the resultant acculturative experience have their own unique challenges and stressors. Berry (1990) termed this *acculturative stress*. Acculturative stress is impacted by factors such as length of stay in the United States, the extent and quality of interaction between the members of the culture of origin and the host culture, societal discrimination, educational and employment opportunities, opportunities to participate in one's own cultural activities and traditions, as well as the historical relationships between the original culture and the host culture. Furthermore, the literature suggests that there is much diversity in the extent to which Asian/Asian Americans might be involved with their own culture and the American culture (Buriel & De Ment, 1997; Ramisetty-Mikler, 1993; Uba, 1994). This variation in cultural involvement has been noted to result in several context-specific forms of acculturative stress (e.g., family, personal identity, minority status as it pertains to social/educational contexts, and discrimination within an environmental context) (Sluzki, 1979). This section addresses the different context-specific stressors experienced by the Asian American community and highlight particular generational issues that may evolve. In addressing generational differences, we use the term *Asian* for first generation and the term *Asian American* will be used for second and subsequent generations.

Familial and intergenerational stress. The literature suggests that immigration poses significant challenges to the Asian family. Specifically, Asian immigrants experience numerous shifts as a function of the new social norms that they encounter. Within this context, difficulties encountered in transitioning from one culture to another can result in significant familial acculturative conflicts (Lee, Choe, Kim, & Ngo, 2000).

One area that has created stressors is the change in family roles (Uba, 1994). Traditionally, Asian families have clear gender roles, with men working outside the family and women working within the household. However, immigration may result in both partners needing to work outside the household. Given that employment opportunities for foreign-born Asians may be limited due to language barriers or institutional racism, Asian men may find themselves experiencing downward occupational mobility (Uba, 1994). For example, Kibria (1993) noted a shift in household roles for Vietnamese refugee men and women. Many of the men who had middle-class careers in Vietnam have been forced to take on lower-level service jobs in the United States, resulting in less access to economic power. Conversely, Vietnamese women in the United States have had to increase their contact with the outside world, resulting in greater control over social and economic resources. Although these changes did not result in the restructuring of gender roles within the family, the shift in power was seen as likely to create marital tension in the family.

A second and related area that has been a source of stress is related to family expectations of parenting and its resulting influence on the family structure/hierarchy. Kibria's (1993) study on Vietnamese refugee families revealed that participants perceived immigration as having eroded parental authority over children. Parents attributed this to socializing agents such as the school, peers, and the media. Similarly, Inman et al. (2005) found that many Asian Indian parents felt that the U.S. cultural environment undermined their efforts to socialize their children with the appropriate values and norms of their ethnic culture. An intrinsic fear here was that their children will lose their ethnic roots and become Americanized (Dasgupta & Dasgupta, 1996; Sodowsky & Carey, 1988; Uba, 1994). Experiencing the loss of their extended familial as well as societal support systems, these parents perceive themselves as having the sole responsibility in parenting and imparting their cultural values/beliefs (Sodowsky & Carey, 1988). The fear of cultural dilution results in parents placing a great emphasis on cultural transmission (Inman et al., 2005; Uba, 1994) leading to greater intergenerational stress (Inman, Constantine, & Ladany, 1999).

One aspect that has been identified as contributing to these challenges is the different rates at which family members tend to acculturate. The literature suggests that children seem to adopt Western cultural values at a more rapid pace than their immigrant parents (Uba, 1994). According to Lee et al. (2000), acculturative conflicts in families are more likely to occur in immigrant families when the gap between parents and children is the greatest and among older immigrant and later generation families where parents have maintained traditional cultural values. These different patterns of acculturation tend to be more evident in parenting beliefs and practices (Lin & Fu, 1990; Phinney, Ong, & Madden, 2000).

Specifically, traditional values influence parenting practices for immigrant parents. Parents tend to selectively acculturate by holding onto core cultural values (e.g., gender roles, marriage, interdependence, family relations) while acculturating to the more practical values such as dress, language, home décor, independence in career achievement (Buriel & De Ment, 1997; Lin & Fu, 1990). These generational differences in acculturation result in different choices and options for parents and their children, producing significant intergenerational conflicts (Inman et al., 2005; Sodowsky & Lai, 1997; Uba, 1994). Immigrant parents expect their children to be dutiful and adhere to the traditional lifestyles and cultural values, whereas their children may feel more inclined toward the Western-oriented, individualistic values that they adopt while growing up in the United States. Thus, the generational gap that typically exists in the

parent-child relationship is further exacerbated by these acculturative differences (Nguyen & Williams, 1989).

Lee et al. (2000) developed the Family Conflict Scale (FSC) to assess the likelihood of intergenerational family conflict and the seriousness of problems between Asian American children and their parents. They found that highly acculturated Asian American children who perceived their parents to be less acculturated reported more frequent conflict than highly acculturated children who perceived their parents to also be highly acculturated. In keeping with this, their study revealed that more recent Asian immigrants (e.g., Southeast Asians) tended to experience more acculturative stress than U.S.-born families or families that had lived in the United States for multiple generations (e.g., Japanese Americans) (Rumbaut, 1994). In particular, children's inability to communicate their needs and expectations within the context of a rigid family structure seemed to compound the changing family dynamics, resulting in more familial conflicts (Lee et al., 2000).

These acculturative differences become even more difficult when children serve as linguistic and cultural interpreters for their immigrant parents, shifting the family hierarchy and structure within the Asian family (Coll & Magnuson, 1997; Tran, 1988). Such intergenerational conflict can have a detrimental psychological effect not only on the family as a whole; it also can create significant cultural conflicts for Asian American children growing up in a bicultural society (Lee, & Liu, 2001) and has been noted to contribute to mental health concerns such as depression and anxiety among Chinese immigrant youth (Yeh, Ma, et al., 2004).

Cultural conflicts and bicultural identities. An integral part of any culture is its values and philosophy of life. Cultural values affect individuals' socialization by influencing their psychological and social identities (Tewari, Inman, & Sandhu, 2003). Whether born in Asia or in the United States, Asian/Asian Americans living in the United States are socialized within their own ethnic culture (i.e., enculturation) as well as the American culture (i.e., acculturation) (Inman, Ladany, Constantine, Morano, 2001). An added element that affects Asians/Asian Americans in the United States is the sociopolitical role of race and race relations (Alvarez & Helms, 2001; Inman, in press). Forging an identity within the context of cultural/ethnic and racial socializations can create unique choices and opportunities. Authors have suggested that the inconsistencies that arise from the negotiation of these different cultural expectations are likely to result in cultural conflicts (Berry, 1993; Inman et al., 1999, 2001). Asians and Asian Americans may struggle to balance these competing cultural identities and values (Yeh, Arora, et al., 2004; Yeh, Ma, et al. 2005). Researchers have discussed the stress of negotiating two cultural contexts, in terms of acculturative stress (Berry & Annis, 1974; Smart & Smart, 1995).

According to S. Sue and Chin (1983), acculturative stress can result when members of distinct cultures come in contact with each other's cultural values, norms, and behavioral patterns. Specifically, Berry (1993) suggested that acculturative changes involving inconsistencies and conflicts may be a source of distress for individuals acculturating within two distinct cultures. Such stress is exacerbated by the fact that conformance to the specific cultural values is rewarded and socialized by each culture. Stress resulting from this acculturative process can infiltrate different aspects of one's life, creating significant adjustment difficulties (Sodowsky & Lai, 1997). A meta-analytic study involving 49 studies of acculturation and adjustment revealed acculturative stress to be positively correlated with psychosocial and health problems (Moyerman & Forman, 1992). Specifically, acculturative stress has been noted to result in feelings of marginality and alienation, identity confusion, increased anxiety and depression, and heightened levels of psychosomatic symptoms (Berry & Annis, 1974; Berry, Kim, Minde, & Mok, 1987; Smart & Smart, 1995).

Furthermore, research in the area of cultural conflicts arising from acculturative stress suggests that such conflicts can be a significant source of psychological stress. For example, several authors (Inman et al., 1999, 2001; Sung, 1985; Tewari, 2000; Uba, 1994) have noted that Asian American (e.g., Chinese, South Asian, Thai) men and women experienced bicultural conflicts in several areas, including assertion of independence and individualism, involvement in academics and sports, expression of sexuality and involvement in dating, and expression of ethnic identity, physical difference, and sex role expectations.

In her interviews with Asian American college students, Uba (1994) noted that students struggled to express their thoughts and feelings for fear of appearing disrespectful and going against their familial cultural values. Given the conflicting emphasis on modesty and social restraint within Asian cultures and assertiveness and outspokenness within the dominant culture, a substantial conflict was identified among these students. Their struggles were noted in their compartmentalization of behaviors outside their homes and behaviors inside their homes and the increased tension between these students and their families.

Academically, Asian American students reported that they felt torn when selecting a career based on personal choice rather than on their parent's academic expectation (Ma & Yeh, 2005; Okubo, Yeh, Lin, Fujita, & Shea, in press; Sung, 1985; Tewari, 2000; Uba, 1994). This seemed consistent with Asian parents' own bicultural struggles to provide a secure financial future for their children (Inman et al., 2005). Specifically, Asian Indian parents discussed the sacrifices made in coming to the United States in order to provide a better life for their children. In addition to Asian traditional values of respect for authority, filial piety, and suppression of individual desires, these parents recognized that, as a minority, their children might have more stable futures if they got the right education, and hence they encouraged certain careers over others (Inman et al. 2005; Uba, 1994).

Cultural conflicts have also been noted with regard to expression of sexuality and other related behaviors (e.g., dating, premarital sex, marriage, sexual orientation). Tewari's (2000) review of mental health concerns presented by Asian American students revealed that they experienced significant stress when dating. Uba (1994) found similar stressors in her interviews with Asian American students, who felt compelled to hide their dating from their parents. Having frequently heard messages that dating would interfere with education and a successful career, Asian Americans reported experiencing significant internal conflict when going against their parents' wishes. Similarly, Inman et al. (1999, 2001) found that the struggle for many South Asian Americans to understand and "fit" into the American culture, while still maintaining their South Asian traditions and beliefs, resulted in significant conflicts when they associated with members of the opposite sex, engaged in premarital relations, and made choices related to marriage. Specifically, Inman (in press) found that the more strongly ethnically identified South Asian women were, the greater the conflict they experienced in the expression of intimate relations. Thus, another area of conflict for Asian Americans is the impact of a minority status on identity development (Coll & Magnuson, 1997).

Being raised within multiple social systems, Asian Americans have the developmental task of constructing ethnic and racial identities in addition to personal identities. The development of an ethnic and racial identity then becomes part of forging an adequate personal identity. Several factors have been deemed to influence the development of these identities. In particular, prejudicial or discriminatory experiences, and experiences of rejection and exclusion based in the relationship between the immigrant community and the larger dominant community have been reported to significantly influence the struggles inherent in Asian/Asian American ethnic and racial identity development (Rumbaut, 1994; D. W. Sue & Sue, 2003). For example, Tewari (2000) found that the Asian Americans in her study expressed significant stressors when their physical image was considerably different from mainstream America. Being seen as "outsiders" due to their physical appearances resulted in experiences of isolation and depression among these students. Furthermore, Inman (in press) found that prejudicial encounters based on external appearances resulted in greater dissonance when engaging in traditional sex-role behaviors for second-generation South Asian women. Thus, developing a minority identity based in ethnic and racial socialization has significant implications for Asian Americans in the United States.

Model minority stress. The seemingly positive stereotype of "model minority," a phrase first coined by William Peterson (1966), ascribed to Asian Americans has not been devoid of negative influence on this community. The term *model minority* suggests that Asian Americans have embodied the "American dream." They are seen as hard-working, high-achieving individuals with few psychological difficulties. This is further substantiated by statistics that show an underutilization of mental health services by Asian Americans when compared to other Americans (Atkinson, Lowe, & Matthews, 1995; Durvalsula & Mylvaganam, 1994; Matsuoka, Breaux, & Ryujin, 1997). Furthermore, according to Hune and Chan (1997), the image portrays Asian Americans as "educationally successful despite socioeconomic and linguistic barriers" (p. 44).

However, within the confines of the myth of the model minority, there is a failure to recognize the cultural and racial realities for this group (Kim & Yeh, 2002). Specifically, with regard to mental health use, several authors have identified cultural factors that may influence Asian American underutilization of services: shame and stigma associated with personal problems, the mind-body duality espoused in the Western cultural perspective, reliance on family/community, availability and preference for alternative indigenous resources to traditional counseling, linguistic barriers, and a shortage of culturally sensitive personnel (Froggett, 2001; Inman et al., 2006; Morrissey, 1997; D. W. Sue & Sue, 2003; Yeh et al., 2006).

In terms of educational and employment success, there is a failure to perceive the gap between striving and achieving. Often, Asian Americans are compared to other minorities and perceived as being successful and not needing assistance. Due to being geographically concentrated in areas where both income and cost of living are high (e.g., California), they are perceived as financially well off despite disparities in SES levels among different Asian groups (e.g. Vietnamese, Hmong). Success perceived within the context of a cultural emphasis on education and hard work masks the real social, economic, and psychological problems encountered by the various members of this community (D. W. Sue, 1994).

The literature suggests that Asians are more educated than Whites, yet Whites earn considerably more than native-born Asian Americans as well as immigrant Asians, undermining the model minority myth (Barringer, Takeuchi, &

Xenos, 1990). Furthermore, Asian Americans are known to encounter a glass ceiling at work (Morrison & von Glinow, 1990). The perception that mere high-labor force participation is a sign of successful employment results in a lack of connection between return on educational investment and income. Education may improve chances for success, but it does not promise the American Dream. Asian Americans continue to be seen as foreigners in their own land. According to authors (D. W. Sue, 1994; Wu, 2002), the model minority myth is an oversimplification, because it (a) does not represent the millions of Asian/Asian Americans in the United States, (b) marginalizes the cultural context of coping, and (c) denies the experience of racial discrimination that Asian Americans face. Thus the positive façade associated with the model minority myth can have significant negative implications for Asian/Asian American communities.

Stress related to racism and discrimination. Despite having been in the United States for over 150 years and being perceived as the model minority, Asian/Asian Americans are not immune from experiences of racism, discrimination, and prejudice. Throughout their history in the United States, Asian/Asian Americans have confronted a long legacy of exclusion and inequity in relation to school policies and practices, work, intergroup relations, acquisition of land, occupations, immigration policies, and racism—particularly during periods of changing demographics, economic recession, or war. Experiences ranging from the anti-Chinese sentiments in the 1800s, Japanese internment camps during World War II, to the more recent post-9/11 anti-South Asian sentiment suggest that discrimination and prejudice continue to be a significant source of stressors among these groups (Chan, 1991; Gupta, 1999; Inman et al., 2006; National Asian Pacific American Legal Consortium, 2002; Takaki, 1994). Anti-Asian incidents continue to occur in the form of vandalism, intimidation and threats, aggravated assaults and incidents involving bodily harm, harassment, racial slurs, and religious prejudices with bias-motivated crimes increasing in brutality in recent years (National Asian Pacific American Legal Consortium, 2002).

Furthermore, the non-European phenotype of Asian/Asian Americans has triggered significant stereotypes and prejudice of "the perpetual foreigner," creating social barriers to full integration into the American society (Buriel & Ment, 1997; Takaki, 1994). Gender stereotypes of women as exotic dragon ladies, while at the same time unassertive and compliant, and men as hard-working and asexual have had further repercussions in terms of opportunities for exploitation and oppression (Uba, 1994). The "tendency to see racist acts as isolated incidents rather than as systematic attempts" (Young & Takeuchi, 1998, p. 403) against Asian/Asian Americans results in a minimization of discriminatory experiences. Furthermore, in understanding the impact of these experiences, one needs to keep in mind generational differences. As native-born minorities, Asian Americans develop a minority identity through varying socialization agents (parents, peers, media) and thus grow up with a vocabulary for describing discrimination (Demo & Hughes, 1990). On the other hand, Asian immigrants and refugees develop a minority identity with little or no anticipatory socialization about prejudice and discrimination. The process of developing an ethnic and racial identity thus occurs through a resocialization of social identities (Hein, 2000).

Although scarce, a growing number of empirical studies have started to examine the role of racism and discrimination on Asian/Asian American lives. In particular, authors (Ramisetty-Mikler, 1993; Sodowsky & Carey, 1987) have identified perceived prejudice in social/professional settings (being of a minority status), negative stereotyping (math geniuses, snake worshippers, bride burners, etc.) and physical differences (ethnicity, clothing style, accents) as factors negatively affecting Asian Americans. Specifically, Asian Indians, Chinese Americans, and Hmong immigrants perceiving prejudice in U.S. society attributed it to their physically different appearance, ethnicity, race, and nonfluent English (Goto, Gee, & Takeuchi, 2002; Hein, 2000; Sodowsky & Carey, 1988). These experiences have been noted to result in feelings of isolation, defensiveness, and inferiority within a majority-minority context (Inman, in press; Ramisetty-Mikler, 1993).

Owyoung (1999) interviewed Chinese and Japanese Americans and noted that both direct and indirect hate crime victims reported having emotional difficulties long after their experience. Other research suggests discrimination and perceived prejudice as significantly affecting self-esteem (Asamen & Berry, 1987; Uba, 1994). For example, Asamen and Berry (1987) reported a significant negative relationship between perceived prejudice and self-concept among Japanese Americans. Perceived prejudice was also found to be significantly related to depression and stress among Asian Americans (Kim, 2002) and South Asian International students (Rahman & Rollock, 2004). Lee (2003) found that discrimination, particularly when directed personally at an individual, correlated negatively with psychological well-being and correlated positively with distress. In a study examining the role of racial and gender discrimination experiences in the psychological well-being of Asian American female college students, Patel (1999) found that lifetime experiences of racial and gender discrimination were positively related to psychological symptoms and negatively related to self-esteem, with racial discrimination being more predictive of psychological outcomes than gender discrimination. Finally, other research has found a link between perceived discrimination and negative mental health outcomes for Southeast Asian refugee populations in Canada (Noh, Beiser, Kaspar, Hou, & Rummens, 1999) and a Chinese Canadian student sample (Dion, Dion, & Pak, 1992). Thus, research clearly reveals the impact that discrimination and racism can have on the daily function and overall well-being of Asian Americans (Ying, Lee, & Tsai, 2000).

Coping From an Asian American Perspective

The vast literature and research on Asian American coping has been conceptualized primarily around seeking professional psychological help and the underuse of mental health services (Chun, Enomoto, & Sue, 1996; Gallo, Marino, Ford, & Anthony, 1995; Kessler, Mikelson, & William, 1996). Due to this strong focus in Asian American psychology, researchers have only recently begun to explore the Asian cultural underpinnings associated with coping processes and naturalistic and indigenous forms of managing stress (Inman, et al. 2006; Lee & Liu, 2001; Yeh, Hunter, Madan-Bahel, Chiang, & Kwong, 2004; Yeh et al., 2006; Yeh & Inose, 2002; Yeh & Wang, 2000). Much of this work has highlighted the Asian American tendency to cope using social support networks, familial ties, indigenous healers, religious and spiritual outlets. Moreover, the coping literature has underscored the need to consider cultural norms and patterns in coping (Lam & Zane, 2004; Marsella & Dash-Scheuer, 1988).

For example, in individualistic cultures (such as the United States) there is a strong emphasis on personal autonomy and control (Markus & Kitayama, 1991) whereas, in collectivistic cultures (such as China, Japan, Thailand, etc.), there is a focus on interpersonal harmony and connectedness (Chang, Chua, & Toh, 1997; Lam & Zane, 2004; Morling & Fiske, 1999; Weisz, Rothbaum, & Blackburn, 1984). Hence, in individualistic cultures, coping strategies may correspond with cultural priorities such as confrontation, problem solving, and taking direct action. Conversely, in collectivistic cultures, a cultural mandate is to achieve group harmony with others so attendant coping methods may highlight adjusting ones own behavior, rather than trying to control the situation (Weisz et al., 1984; Yang, 1986).

Previous coping research has been criticized for incorporating an individualistic perspective and using primarily White American participants as a normative sample (Bjorck, Cuthbertson, Thurman, & Lee, 2001; Dunahoo, Hobfoll, Moniier, Hulsizer, & Johnson, 1998). A dominant finding in coping research is that of the relationship between action-oriented coping and positive psychological outcomes, whereas avoidance and emotion-focused strategies are tied to mental health symptoms (Endler & Parker, 1990; Seiffge-Krenke, 1993; Stern & Zavon, 1990). Due to strong differences in cultural orientation, Asian Americans have been characterized in the coping literature as avoidant and indirect in their coping methods (Chang, 1996). Another possible interpretation of this finding is that Asian Americans may employ culturally valid forms of coping that are grounded in collectivistic intentions (Yeh, Arora, & Wu, 2005).

Individuals from collectivistic cultures are socialized to cope in ways that emphasize group cohesion, family privacy, and social harmony. This chapter will focus primarily on Asian American coping in terms of indigenous help-seeking, familial support, religious and spiritual coping, and use of social support networks. Asian cultural values as they pertain to coping strategies will be illuminated.

Indigenous Healers

Recent research on Asian and Asian American patterns of coping has revealed their strong cultural preference for using indigenous healers. For example, in a study on how South Asian families (Inman et al., 2006) have coped with the loss of family members in the World Trade Center attacks, the authors found that almost all Hindu participants sought consultation from healers such as astrologers, religious leaders, face readers, and palmists. In a similar study of Asian American family members of the victims of the 9/11 attacks, Yeh et al. (2006) found that many Asian immigrants sought help from traditional Chinese medicine doctors and chi-gong healers.

The consistent findings on mental health underutilization among Asian Americans suggests that current mental health practices, such as talking to a counselor, psychologist, or psychiatrist, may be inadequate in meeting the needs of these groups. One possible explanation is that these groups may feel more comfortable using indigenous and interdependent forms of healing than Western psychological services. In fact, studies have found that many Asian American ethnic groups turn more often to informal sources of care such as clergy, traditional healers, family, and friends (Yeh & Wang, 2000).

An interdependent perspective is essential for understanding why Asian Americans may prefer using indigenous healing approaches. Asian cultures differ from Western European cultures in that they emphasize the self in relation to, rather than as separate from, others (Markus & Kitayama, 1991; Yeh & Hwang, 2000). This view of self and the relationship between the individual and others highlights self not as separate from the social context but as more connected to and less differentiated from others (Markus & Kitayama, 1991).

Research on the use of traditional or indigenous healers in 16 non-Western countries (Lee, Oh, & Mountcastle, 1992) reveal three approaches underscoring the cultural relevance of an interdependent perspective. First, there is strong preference for community, group, and family networks to support the individual in need, and to address concerns as a group. Second, spiritual and religious beliefs and traditions of the community are used as part of the healing process. Third, the use of shamans, who are known as holding timeless wisdom, is the norm. In fact, in many cases, the person conducting a healing ceremony may be someone already related to the person, such as a family member or a respected elder in the community (D. W. Sue & Sue, 2003). Many Asian cultures do not separate the observer from the observed and believe that all life forms are interrelated with one another (Yeh, Hunter, et al., 2004).

The Asian cultural emphasis on interrelatedness may also be used to explain illness, including mental illness (Lee et al., 1992). For example, illness may be a result of family dynamics, fate, or possession by malevolent spirits. The strong belief in the unity of spirit, mind, and body does not differentiate between physical and mental functioning. In addition, it is believed that life forms are interrelated with one another, the environment, and the cosmos (Lee & Armstrong, 1995; D. W. Sue & Sue, 2003). Based on these assumptions of interdependence, it follows that illnesses, distress, or problematic behaviors are seen as an imbalance in human relationships, a disharmony between the individual and his/her group, or of being out of synchrony with internal or external forces. The pursuit of group harmony or balance is often the healer's goal (D. W. Sue & Sue, 2003).

Familial Support

Traditional Asian cultural values also highlight the strong preference for keeping family matters private (Uba, 1994). Family relationships, roles, and positions are essential in informing Asian American identities and obligations. How an individual copes, then, reflects on the family as a whole. Since many Asian Americans have strong familial ties, coping strategies reflect cultural stigmas and shame concerning the use of professional services and underscore the need to deal with matters as a family (D. W. Sue, 1994). Families then serve a vital supportive and caring function for the members within (Yeh & Wang, 2000).

Specifically, in collectivistic cultures, the family serves as a social support system to buffer individuals against stressful events (Pierce, Sarason, & Sarason, 1992; Treharne, Lyons, & Tupling, 2001). The central role of the family to support and care for family members has been noted across numerous Asian ethnic groups and cultures, including South Asian, Chinese, Korean, Japanese, Taiwanese, and Thai (Ben-Ari & Lavee, 2004; Erickson & Al-Timimi, 2001; Inman et al., 2006; McCarty et al., 1999; Yeh & Wang, 2000). For example, in the highly interdependent Japanese culture, involvement in family activities aids in coping with stress (Homma-True, 1997). Yeh and Wang (2000) found that Asian Americans tended to use coping sources and practices that emphasized talking with familial and social relations rather than professionals such as counselors.

Using family support to cope with stress is culturally reinforced among Asian Americans who are strongly connected with family members; however, when there are intergenerational differences, conflicts in values and norms arise. Asian Americans have been reported to have higher levels of family conflict in comparison to Hispanic and European American college students (Lee & Liu, 2001) and adolescents (Greenberger & Chen, 1996). Due to tensions across generations, Asian Americans must find coping methods that extend beyond the family.

Social Support and Coping

The strong emphasis on interdependence in Asian cultures helps to inform coping styles that involve using social support as a critical means of managing stressors (Liu, 1986; Mau & Jepsen, 1988; Solberg, Choi, Ritsma, & Jolly, 1994; Yeh & Inose, 2002; Yeh & Wang, 2000). Specifically, Yeh and Wang (2000) found that Asian American college students tended to endorse coping sources and practices that emphasized talking and connecting with social relations rather than mental health professionals such as psychologists. This tendency to spend time with friends and social networks when coping with mental health problems was also found among Japanese college students (Yeh, Inose, Kobori, & Chang, 2001), Chinese, Japanese, and Korean immigrant adolescents (Yeh & Inose, 2002), Filipino Americans (Edman & Johnson, 1999), and South/Asian Americans who lost a family member in the World Trade Center attacks (Inman et al., 2006; Yeh et al., 2006). However, research comparing Asians and Asian Americans versus European Americans has found that Asian and Asian Americans tend to use social support less than European Americans (Taylor et al., 2004). Although, conceptually, it seems that collectivistic, versus individualistic cultures, may utilize interpersonal supports more frequently in times of stress, the authors suggest that fear of shame and the strong cultural emphasis on group harmony may also serve to impede Asian American social support seeking.

Culturally similar peers and support networks, which extend beyond the family, have also been found to comfort immigrants who have largely come from Asian cultures (Roysircar-Sodowsky, & Frey, 2003). Intracultural coping refers to the use of supportive networks comprised of racially similar individuals, such as one's family network or community-based social groups (Yeh, Arora, et al., 2005). Wong (1993) also referred to an aspect of intracultural coping in his resource-congruence coping model with the idea of collective coping, a form of coping extending beyond social support that encompasses the action of multiple group members to resolve a single problem. Since Asian Americans tend to define in-group members more narrowly and with more overt impermeability than other racial groups (Hall, 2003; Triandis, 1989), they may maintain more cohesive bonds with in-group members that are then utilized when stressors are present. Hence, Asian Americans may not only seek social support when dealing with stress, but they may specifically try to find comfort and support through racially and ethnically similar individuals.

Religious and Spiritual Support

Asian Americans not only cope by using supportive cultural networks, but also through religious and spiritual connections. Belonging to a religious organization, group, or institution is consistent with Asian cultural values, which emphasize respect for authority, fatalism, and intergroup harmony. Specifically, a collectivistic cultural orientation may shape a holistic worldview and a belief that control may lie in contextual or external forces (Morling & Fiske, 1999). Relatedly, there is a cultural appreciation for luck, fate, and a higher being (such as God or Buddha) (Morling & Fiske, 1999).

Asian Americans have been found to use spirituality and religion as an important means of coping with daily stressors and problems, such as concerns related to adjustment, immigration, and adaptation (Kim, Brenner, Liang, & Asay, 2003). In a study of Asian Americans coping with the loss of a family member, Inman et al. (2006) found that participants coped with their loss through the use of prayer, spiritualistic behaviors (e.g., praying, lighting lamps, reading prayer books), and belief in a higher power such as God, Lord Krishna, and Bhagwat Geeta. Similarly, Yeh and colleagues (2006) found that Asian American family members of victims of the World Trade Center attacks used fatalistic beliefs as a way of understanding their significant losses. For example, all of the Korean and Filipino participants and two of the Chinese participants in their study reported an increase in religious or spiritual activity, such as prayer, going to church, speaking with a pastor, and/or attending religious functions. Moreover, when asked how the participants made sense of their tragic losses, many of them described the events in fatalistic terms ("happened for a reason," "was out of their hands/control," "was in God's hands," "was part of a natural order," "was part of a larger will").

The use of religion and spirituality as a means for coping among Asian Americans may not only reflect strong personal ties to religious and spiritual beliefs. Asian American involvement in churches and other religious organizations may also reflect a cultural need for community, unity, and interrelatedness with others. Religious engagement represents spiritual connection as well as relationship activities and duties, which may appeal to Asian Americans. Hence, when dealing with stress, seeking support from a religious or spiritual community may come naturally for Asian Americans.

Conclusion

The heterogeneity of the Asian American population underscores the need for complex models of coping that incorporate the various stressors faced by this unique racial group. Specifically, Asian Americans face numerous challenges and difficulties as related to immigration, adaptation, adjustment, racism, discrimination, and intergenerational differences. These challenges often inform multiple approaches to coping that may involve the use of social support networks, family systems, religious institutions, or indigenous healers. A common thread, linking these coping methods, is the Asian priority on interconnectedness with others. Hence, Asian American coping must be conceptualized interdependently rather than as an agentic, directive act of problem solving. Moreover, since Asian American selves are contextually embedded (Yeh & Hwang, 2000), it follows that cultural strategies for coping may also be situationally driven.

References

Alvarez, A. N., & Helms, J. E. (2001). Racial identity and reflected appraisals as influences on Asian Americans' racial adjustment. *Cultural Diversity & Ethnic Minority Psychology, 7,* 217–231.

Asamen, J. K., & Berry, G. L. (1987). Self-concept, alienation, and perceived prejudice: Implications for counseling with Asian Americans. *Journal of Multicultural Counseling and Development, 15,* 140–160.

Atkinson, D. R., Lowe, S., & Matthews, L. (1995). Asian-American acculturation, gender, and willingness to seek counseling. *Journal of Multicultural Counseling and Development, 23,* 130–138.

Barringer, H. R., Takeuchi, D. T., & Xenos, P. (1990). Educational, occupational prestige, and income of Asian Americans. *Sociology of Education, 63,* 27–43.

Ben-Ari, A., & Lavee, Y. (2004). Cultural orientation, ethnic affiliation, and negative daily occurrences: A multidimensional cross-cultural analysis. *American Journal of Orthopsychiatry, 74,* 102–111.

Berry J. W. (1990). Acculturation and adaptation: A general framework. In W. H. Holtzman & T. H. Bornemann (Eds.), *Mental health of immigrants and refugees* (pp. 90–102). Austin, TX: Hogg Foundation for Mental Health.

Berry, J. W. (1993). Ethnic identity in plural societies. In M. E. Bernal & G. P. Knight (Eds.), *Ethnic identity: Formation and transmission among Hispanics and other minorities* (pp. 271–296). Albany: State University of New York Press.

Berry, J. W., & Annis, R. C. (1974). Acculturative stress: The role of ecology, culture and differentiation. *Journal of Cross-Cultural Psychology, 5,* 382–406.

Berry, J. W., Kim, U., Minde, T., & Mok, D. (1987). Comparative studies of acculturative stress. *International Migration Review, 21,* 491–511.

Bjorck, J. P., Cuthbertson, W., Thurman, J. W., & Lee, Y. S. (2001). Ethnicity, coping, and distress among Korean Americans, Filipino Americans, Caucasian Americans. *The Journal of Social Psychology, 141,* 421–442.

Bowker, J. (1970). *Problems of suffering in religions of the world.* Cambridge, UK: Cambridge University Press.

Buriel, R., & De Ment, T. (1997). Immigration and sociocultural change in Mexicans, Chinese, and Vietnamese American families. In A. Booth, A. C. Crouter, & N. Landale (Eds.), *Immigration and the family: Research and policy on U.S. immigrants* (pp. 165–200). Mahwah, NJ: Lawrence Erlbaum.

Chan, S. (1991). *Asian Americans: An interpretive history.* Boston: Twayne.

Chang, E. C. (1996). Cultural differences in optimism, pessimism, and coping: Predictors of subsequent adjustment in Asian American and Caucasian American college students. *Journal of Counseling Psychology, 43,* 113–123

Chang, E. C. (2001). A look at the coping strategies and styles of Asian Americans: Similar and different? In C. R. Snyder (Ed.), *Coping with stress: Effective people and processes.* New York: Oxford University Press.

Chang, W. C., Chua, W. L., & Toh, Y. (1997). The concept of psychological control in the Asian context. In K. Leung, U. Kim, S. Yamaguschi, & Y. Kashima (Eds.), *Progress in Asian social psychology* (pp. 95–118). New York: Wiley.

Cheng, S. K. (1990). Understanding the culture and behavior of East Asians: A Confucian perspective. *Australian and New Zealand Journal of Psychiatry, 24,* 510–515.

Chun, C., Enomoto, K., & Sue, S. (1996). Healthcare issues among Asian Americans: Implications of somatization. In P. M. Kata & T. Mann (Eds.), *Handbook of diversity issues in health psychology* (pp. 347–366). New York: Plenum.

Coll, C. G., & Magnuson, K. (1997). The psychological experience of immigration: A developmental perspective. In A. Booth, A. C. Crouter, & N. Landale (Eds.), *Immigration and the family: Research and policy on U.S. immigrants* (pp. 91–132). Mahwah, NJ: Lawrence Erlbaum.

Dasgupta, S. D., & Dasgupta, S. (1996). Public face, private space: Asian Indian women and sexuality. In N. B. Maglin & D. Perry (Eds.), *Bad girls, good girls: Women, sex, and power in the nineties* (pp. 226–243). New Brunswick, NJ: Rutgers University Press.

Demo, D. H., & Hughes, M. (1990). Socialization and racial identity among Black Americans. *Social Psychological Quarterly, 53,* 364–374.

Dion, K. L., Dion, K. K., & Pak, A. (1992). Personality-based hardiness as a buffer for discrimination related stress in members of Toronto's Chinese community. *Canadian Journal of Behavioral Science, 24*(4), 517–536.

Dunahoo, C. L., Hobfoll, S. E., Moniier, J., Hulsizer, M. R., & Johnson, R. (1998). There's more than rugged individualism in coping: Part 1. Even the Lone Ranger had Tonto. *Anxiety, Stress, and Coping, 11,* 137–165.

Durvasula, R. S., & Mylvaganam, G. A. (1994). Mental health issues of Asian Indians: Relevant issues and community implications. *Journal of Comparative Psychology, 22,* 97–108.

Edman, J. L., & Johnson, R. C. (1999). Filipino American and Caucasian American beliefs about the causes and treatment of mental problems. *Cultural Diversity & Ethnic Minority Psychology, 5,* 380–386.

Endler, N. S., & Parker, J. D. A. (1990). Multidimensional assessment of coping: A critical evaluation. *Journal of Personality and Social Psychology, 58,* 844–854.

Erickson, C. D., & Al-Timimi, N. R. (2001). Providing mental health services to Arab Americans: Recommendations and considerations. *Cultural Diversity & Ethnic Minority Psychology, 7,* 308–327

Froggett, L. (2001). From rights to recognition: Mental health and spiritual healing among older Pakistanis. *Psychoanalytic Studies, 3,* 177–186.

Gallo, J. J., Marino, S., Ford, D., & Anthony, J. C. (1995). Filters on the pathway to mental health care: II. Sociodemographic factors. *Psychological Medicine, 25,* 1149–1160.

Goto, S. G., Gee, G. C., & Takeuchi, D. T. (2002). Strangers still? The experience of discrimination among Chinese Americans. *Journal of Community Psychology, 30,* 211–224

Greenberger, E., & Chen, C. (1996). Perceived family relationships and depressed mood in early and late adolescence: A comparison of European and Asian Americans. *Developmental Psychology, 32,* 707–716.

Gupta, S. (1999). *Emerging voices: South Asian American women redefine self, family, and community.* New Delhi, India: Sage.

Hall, G. C. N. (2003). The self in context: Implications for psychopathology and psychotherapy. *Journal of Psychotherapy Integration, 13,* 66–82.

Hastings, S. O. (2000). Asian Indian "self-suppression" and self-disclosure: Enactment and adaptation of cultural identity. *Journal of Language and Social Psychology, 19,* 85–109.

Hein, J. (2000). Interpersonal discrimination among Hmong Americans: Parallels and variations in microlevel racial inequality. *The Sociological Quarterly, 41,* 413–429.

Hilton, B. A., Grewal, S., Popatia, N., Bottorff, J. L., Johnson, J. L., Clarke, H., et al., (2001). The desi way: Traditional health practices of South Asian women in Canada. *Health Care for Women International, 22,* 553–567.

Hines, P. M., Garcia-Preto, N., McGoldrick, M., Almeida, R., & Weltman, S. (1992). Intergenerational relationships across cultures. *Families in Society, 73,* 323–338.

Homma-True, R. (1997). Japanese American families. In E. Lee (Ed.), *Working with Asian Americans: A guide for clinicians* (pp. 114–124). New York: Guilford Press.

Hune, S., & Chan, K. S. (1997). Special focus: Asian Pacific American demographic and educational trends. In D. J. Carter & R. Wilson (Eds.), *Minorities in higher education: Fifteenth annual status report* (pp. 39–67). Washington, DC: American Council on Education.

Inman, A. G. (in press). South Asian Women: Identities and conflicts. *Cultural Diversity & Ethnic Minority Psychology.*

Inman, A. G., Constantine, M. G., & Ladany, N. (1999). Cultural value conflict: An examination of Asian Indian women's bicultural experience. In D. S. Sandhu (Ed.), *Asian and Pacific Islander Americans: Issues and concerns for counseling and psychotherapy* (pp. 31–41). Commack, NY: Nova Science.

Inman, A. G., Howard, E. E., Beaumont, R., & Walker, J. A. (2005). *Cultural transmission: Themes in Asian Indian parents' immigration experiences.* Poster presented at the annual convention of the American Counseling Association, Atlanta, GA.

Inman, A. G., Ladany, N., Constantine, M. G., & Morano, C. K. (2001). Development and preliminary validation of the cultural values conflict scale for South Asian women. *Journal of Counseling Psychology, 48,* 17–27.

Inman, A. G., & Tewari, N. (2003). The power of context: Counseling South Asians within a family context. In G. Roysircar, D. S. Sandhu, & V. B. Bibbins (Eds.), *A guidebook: Practices of multicultural competencies* (pp. 97–107). Alexandria, VA: American Counseling Association.

Inman, A. G., Yeh, C. J, Madan-Bahel A., & Nath, S. (2006). *Bereavement and coping practices of South Asian families post-9/11.* Manuscript submitted for publication.

Kakar, S. (1982). *Shamans, mystics, and doctors: A psychological inquiry into India and its healing traditions.* New Delhi, India: Oxford University Press.

Kessler, R. C., Mikelson, K. D., & William, D. R. (1996). The prevalence, distribution, and mental health correlates of perceived discrimination in the United States. *Journal of Health and Social Behavior, 40,* 208–230.

Kibria, N. (1993). *Family tightrope: The changing lives of Vietnamese Americans.* Princeton, NJ: Princeton University Press.

Kim, J. G. S. (2002). Racial perceptions and psychological well-being in Asian and Hispanic Americans. *Dissertation Abstracts International: Section B: The Sciences & Engineering, 63*(2-B), 1033.

Kim, A., & Yeh, C. J. (2002). *Stereotypes of Asian American children and youth in schools.* New York: Teachers College, Columbia University. (ERIC Document Reproduction Services No. ED462510)

Kim, B. S. K., Brenner, B. R., Liang, C. T., & Asay, P. A. (2003). A qualitative study of adaptation experiences of 1.5-generation Asian Americans, *Cultural Diversity & Ethnic Minority Psychology, 9,* 156–170.

Lam, A. G., & Zane, N. W. S. (2004). Ethnic differences in coping with interpersonal stressors. *Journal of Cross-Cultural Psychology, 35,* 446–459.

Lazarus, R. S., & Folkman, S. (1984). *Stress, appraisal, and coping.* New York: Springer.

Lee, C. C., & Armstrong, K. L. (1995). Indigenous models of mental health interventions: Lessons from traditional healers. In J. G. Ponterotto, J. M. Casas, L. A. Suzuki, & C. M. Alexander (Eds.), *Handbook of multicultural counseling* (pp. 441–456). Thousand Oaks, CA: Sage.

Lee, R. M., Choe, J., Kim, G., & Ngo, V. (2000). Construction of the Asian American family conflict scale. *Journal of Counseling Psychology, 47,* 211–222.

Lee, C. C., Oh, M. Y., & Mountcastle, A. R. (1992). Indigenous models of helping in nonwestern countries: Implications for multicultural counseling. *Journal of Multicultural Counseling and Development, 20,* 1–10.

Lee, R. M. (2003). Do ethnic identity and other-group orientation protect against discrimination for Asian Americans? *Journal of Counseling Psychology, 50,* 133–141.

Lee, R., & Lui, H. T. (2001). Coping with intergenerational family conflict: Comparison of Asian American, Hispanic, and European American college students. *Journal of Counseling Psychology, 48*(4), 410–419.

Lin, C. Y., & Fu, V. (1990). A comparison of child-rearing practices among Chinese, immigrant Chinese, and Caucasian-American parents. *Child Development, 61,* 429–433.

Liu, W. T. (1986). Culture and social support. *Research on Aging, 8,* 57–83.

Ma, P.-W., & Yeh, C. J. (2005). Factors influencing the career decision status of Chinese American youth. *Career Development Quarterly, 53,* 337–347.

Markus, H. R., & Kitayama, S. (1991). Culture and the self: Implications for cognition, emotion, and motivation. *Psychological Review, 98,* 224–253.

Marsella, A. J., & Dash-Scheuer.A (1988). Coping, culture, and healthy human development: A research and conceptual overview. In P. R. Dasen, J. W. Berry, & N. Sartorius (Eds.), *Health and cross-cultural psychology: Toward applications* (pp. 162–178). Thousand Oaks, CA: Sage.

Matsuoka, J. K., Breaux, C., & Ryujin, D. H. (1997). National utilization of mental health services by Asian Americans/Pacific Islanders. *Journal of Community Psychology, 25,* 141–145.

Mau, W.-C., & Jepsen, D. A. (1988). Attitudes toward counselors and counseling processes: A comparison of Chinese and American graduate students. *Journal of Counseling and Development, 67,* 189–192.

McCarty, C. A., Weisz, J. R., Wanitromanee, K., Eastman, K., Suwanlert, S., Chaiyasit, W., et al. (1999). Culture, coping, and context: Primary and secondary control among Thai and American youth. *Journal of Child Psychology and Psychiatry, 40,* 809–818.

Morling, B., & Fiske, S. T. (1999). Defining and measuring harmony control. *Journal of Research in Personality, 33,* 379–414.

Morrison, A. M., & von Glinow, M. A. (1990). Women and minorities in management. *The American Psychologist, 45,* 200–208.

Morrissey, M. (1997). The invisible minority: Counseling Asian Americans. *Counseling Today, 40,* 21–22.

Moyerman, D. R., & Forman, B. D. (1992). Acculturation and adjustment: A meta-analytic study. *Hispanic Journal of Behavioral Sciences, 14,* 163–200.

Mullatti, L. (1995). Families in India: Beliefs and realities. *Journal of Comparative Family Studies, 26,* 11–25.

National Asian Pacific American Legal Consortium. (2002). *Backlash: When America turned on its own.* Washington, DC: Author.

Nguyen, N. A., & Williams, H. L. (1989). Transition from east to west: Vietnamese adolescents and their parents. *Journal of American Academy of Child and Adolescent Psychiatry, 28,* 505–515.

Noh, S., Beiser, M., Kasper, V., Hou, F., & Rummens, J. (1999) Perceived racial discrimination, depression, and coping: A study of Southeast Asian refugees in Canada. *Journal of Health & Social Behavior, 40,* 193–207.

Okubo, Y., Yeh, C. J., Lin, P.-Y., Fujita, K., & Shea, J. M.-Y. (in press). The career decision-making process of Chinese American youth. *Journal of Counseling & Development.*

Owyoung, B. H. (1999). The psychological effects and treatment of hate crime victimization on Chinese-Americans and Asian-Americans residing in Castro Valley, California. *Dissertation Abstracts International: Section B: The Sciences & Engineering, 59* (9-B), 5103.

Palsane, M. N., & Lam, D. J. (1996). Stress and coping from traditional Indian and Chinese perspectives. *Psychology and Developing Societies, 8,* 29–53.

Patel, N. R. (1999). The role of racial and gender discrimination in the psychological well-being of Asian-American female college students. *Dissertation Abstracts International: Section B: The Sciences & Engineering, 59* (8-B), 4479.

Peterson, W. (1966, January 9). Success story: Japanese American style. *The New York Times,* vi–20.

Phinney, J. S., Ong, A., & Madden, T. (2000). Cultural values and intergenerational value discrepancies in immigrant and non-immigrant families. *Child Development, 71,* 528–539.

Pierce, G. R., Sarason, B. R., & Sarason, I. G. (1992). General and specific support expectations and stress as predictors of perceived supportiveness: An experimental study. *Journal of Personality and Social Psychology, 63,* 297–307.

Prathikanti, S. (1997). East Indian American families. In E. Lee (Ed.), *Working with Asian Americans: A guide for clinicians* (pp. 79–100). New York: Guilford Press.

Rahman, O., & Rollock, D. (2004). Acculturation, competence, and mental health among South Asian students in the United States. *Journal of Multicultural Counseling & Development, 32,* 130–142.

Ramisetty-Mikler, S. (1993). Asian Indian immigrants in America and sociocultural issues in counseling. *Journal of Multicultural Counseling and Development, 21,* 36–49.

Rhys Davids, T. W. (1972). *Buddhist Sutras* (English translation of *Dhamma-Chakkappavattana-sutta*). Delhi: Motilal Banarsidass.

Roysircar-Sodowsky, G. & Frey, L. L. (2003). Children of immigrants: Their worldviews value conflicts. In P. B. Pedersen & J. C. Corey (Eds.), *Multicultural counseling in schools: A practical handbook* (2nd ed., pp. 61–83). Boston: Pearson Education.

Rumbaut, R. (1994). The crucible within: Ethnic identity, self-esteem, and segmented assimilation among children of immigrants. *International Migration Review, 28,* 748–794.

Seiffge-Krenke, I. (1993). Coping in normal and clinical samples: More similarities than differences? *Journal of Adolescence, 16,* 285–305.

Sluzki, C. (1979). Migration and family conflict. *Family Process, 18,* 379–390.

Smart, J. F., & Smart, D. W. (1995). Acculturative stress: The experience of the Hispanic immigrant. *The Counseling Psychologist, 23,* 25–42.

Sodowsky, G. R., & Carey, J. C. (1987). Asian Indian immigrants in America: Factors related to adjustment. *Journal of Multicultural Counseling and Development, 15,* 129–141.

Sodowsky, G. R., & Carey, J. C. (1988). Relationship between acculturation-related demographics and cultural attitudes of an Asian Indian immigrant group. *Journal of Multicultural Counseling and Development, 16,* 117–136.

Sodowsky, G. R., & Lai, E. W. M. (1997). Asian immigrant variables and structural models of cross-cultural distress. In A. Booth, A. C. Crouter, & N. Landale (Eds.), *Immigration and the family: Research and policy on U.S. immigrants* (pp. 211–234). Mahwah, NJ: Lawrence Erlbaum.

Solberg, V. S., Choi, K.-H., Ritsma, S., & Jolly, A. (1994). Asian-American college students: It is time to reach out. *Journal of College Student Development, 35,* 296–301.

Stern, M., & Zavon, M. (1990). Stress, coping, and family environment: The adolescent's response to naturally occurring stressors. *Journal of Adolescent Research, 5,* 290–305.

Sue, D. W. (1994). Asian-American mental health and help-seeking behavior: Comment on Solberg et al. (1994), Tata and Leong (1994), and Lin (1994). *Journal of Counseling Psychology, 41,* 292–295.

Sue, D. W., & Sue, D. (2003). *Counseling the culturally diverse: Theory and practice.* (4th ed.). New York: Wiley.

Sue, S., & Chin, R. (1983). The mental health of Chinese American children: Stressors and resources. In G. J. Powell (Ed.), *The psychosocial development of minority group children.* (pp. 385–397). New York: Brunner/Mazel.

Sung, B. L. (1985). Bicultural conflicts in Chinese immigrant children. *Journal of Comparative Family Studies Special Issue: Family, Kinship and Ethnic Identity Among the Overseas Chinese, 16,* 255–269.

Takaki, R. (1994). *A different mirror: A history of multicultural America.* New York: Little, Brown.

Taylor, S. E., Sherman, D. K., Heejung, S., Jarcho, J. Takagi, K., & Dunagan, M. S. (2004, September). Culture and social support: Who seeks it and why? *Journal of Personality and Social Psychology, 87,* 354–362.

Tewari, N. (2000). *Asian Indian American clients presenting at a university counseling center: An exploration of their concerns and a comparison to other groups.* Unpublished doctoral dissertation, Southern Illinois University, Carbondale.

Tewari, N., Inman, A. G., & Sandhu, D. S. (2003). South Asian Americans: Culture, concerns and therapeutic strategies. In J. Mio & G. Iwamasa (Eds.), *Culturally diverse mental health: The challenges of research and resistance* (pp. 191–209). New York: Brunner/Routledge.

Tran, T. V. (1988). Sex differences in English language acculturation and learning strategies among Vietnamese adults aged 40 and over in the United States. *Sex Roles, 19,* 747–758.

Treharne, G. J., Lyons, A. C., & Tupling, R. E. (2001). The effects of optimism, pessimism, social support, and mood on the lagged relationship between daily stress and symptoms. *Current Research in Social Psychology, 7,* 60–81.

Triandis, H. C. (1989). The self and social behavior in differing cultural contexts. *Psychological Review, 96,* 506–520.

Tweed, R. G., White, K., & Lehman, D. R. (2004). Culture, stress, and coping: Internally- and externally-targeted control strategies of European Canadians, East Asian Canadians, and Japanese. *Journal of Cross-Cultural Psychology, 35,* 652–668.

Uba, L. (1994). *Asian Americans: Personality patterns, identity, and mental health.* New York: Guilford Press.

Weisz, J. R., Rothbaum, F. M., & Blackburn, T. C. (1984). Standing out and standing in: The psychology of control in America and Japan. *The American Psychologist, 39,* 955–969.

Wong, P. T. P. (1993). Effective management of life stress: The resource-congruence model. *Stress Medicine, 9,* 51–60.

Wu, F. H. (2002). The model minority: Asian American "success" as a race relations failure. In F. H. Wu (Ed.), *Yellow: Race in America beyond black and white* (pp. 39–77). New York: Basic Books.

Yang, K. S. (1986). Chinese personality and its change. In M. H. Bond (Ed.), *Psychology of the Chinese people* (pp. 107–170). Hong Kong: Oxford University Press.

Yee, A. H. (1992). Asians as stereotypes and students: Misperceptions that persist. *Educational Psychology Review, 4,* 95–132.

Yeh, C. J., Arora, A., Inose, M., Okubo, Y., Li, R., & Greene, P. (2004). The cultural adjustment and mental health of Japanese immigrant youth. *Adolescence, 38,* 481–500.

Yeh, C. J., Arora, A. K., & Wu, K. A. (2005). A new theoretical model of collectivistic coping. In P. T. P. Wong & L. C. J. Wong (Eds.), *Handbook of multicultural perspectives on stress and coping* (pp. 53–70). New York: Springer.

Yeh, C. J., Hunter, C. D., Madan-Bahel, A., Chiang, L., & Kwong, A. (2004). Indigenous and interdependent perspectives of healing: Implications for counseling and research. *Journal of Counseling and Development, 82,* 410–419.

Yeh, C. J., & Hwang, M. (2000). Interdependence in ethnic identity and self: Implications for theory and practice. *Journal of Counseling and Development, 78,* 420–429.

Yeh, C. J., Inman, A., Kim, A. B., & Okubo, Y. (2006). Asian American collectivistic coping in response to 9/11. *Cultural Diversity & Ethnic Minority Psychology, 12,* 134–148.

Yeh, C. J., & Inose, M. (2002). Difficulties and coping strategies of Chinese, Japanese, and Korean immigrant students. *Adolescence, 37*(145), 69–82.

Yeh, C. J., & Inose, M. (2003). International students' reported English fluency, social support satisfaction, and social connectedness as predictors of acculturative stress. *Counselling Psychology Quarterly, 16*(1), 15–28.

Yeh, C. J., Inose, M., & Kobori, A., & Chang, T. (2001). Self and coping among college students in Japan. *Journal of College Student Development, 42,* 242–256.

Yeh, C. J., Ma, P.-W., Madan, A., Hunter, C. D., Jung, S., Kim, A., et al. (2005). The cultural negotiations of Korean immigrant youth. *Journal of Counseling and Development, 83,* 172–181.

Yeh, C. J., Ma, P-W., Okubo, Y., Maden-Bahel, A., Cort, K. A., Shea, M., et al. (2004). *The cultural adjustment of low-income, urban, Asian immigrant high school students.* Poster presented at the annual convention of the American Psychological Association, Honolulu, Hawaii.

Yeh, C. J., & Wang, Y. W. (2000). Asian American coping attitudes, sources, and practices: Implications for indigenous counseling strategies. *Journal of College Student Development, 41,* 94–103.

Ying, Y. W., Lee, P. A., & Tsai, J. L. (2000). Cultural orientation and racial discrimination: Predictors of coherence in Chinese American young adults. *Journal of Community Psychology, 28,* 427–442.

Young, K., & Takeuchi, D. T. (1998). Racism. In L. C. Lee & N. W. S. Zane (Eds.), *Handbook of Asian American psychology* (pp. 401–432). Thousand Oaks, CA: Sage.

20

Racism Against Asian/Pacific Island Americans

Jeffery Scott Mio

Donna K. Nagata

Amy H. Tsai

Nita Tewari

A Filipina friend of mine said she was talking with another friend on a bench outside of a large department store. All of a sudden, a White woman sitting on a bench a few feet from her got up and said, "I hate Japs!" and walked away.

JSM

In recent years, Asian/Pacifics and Asian/Pacific Island Americans[1] have not been targets of racism as much as they had been decades ago nor as much as some other ethnic minority groups (Mio & Awakuni, 2000). Still, such targeting does exist, and the chapter-opening example characterizes at least three different ways in which APIAs are targeted:

1. Some individuals still do not accept non-White people in America.

2. APIAs tend to be grouped into a single group with little understanding of the heterogeneity of ancestral national origin.

3. Some people fail to distinguish between APIAs and Asians living overseas.

In this chapter, we discuss these three attitudes, the "model minority" stereotype, the history of racism against APIAs in the United States (which had been primarily expressed around immigration issues), the special case of Hawaii, the injustice of the internment of Japanese Americans during World War II, and the emerging issue of racism against South Asians.

APIAs represent the largest diversity of nations within one of the traditional "racial/ethnic" groups. Within the APIA categorization are four major groups: East Asians, Southeast

Asians, South Asians, and Pacific Islanders. Traditionally, people thought of the general category of Asians as being people of East Asian descent. The earliest major groups of Asian immigrants were from China, then Japan. During the Korean War, large groups of Koreans began immigrating to the United States. These three countries represent the East Asian group within the general APIA categorization (Chin, Mio, & Iwamasa, in press). There is considerable diversity even within this group, particularly those from China. Besides having a large population of U.S.-born people of Chinese descent, Chinese immigrants have come from Hong Kong, Taiwan, East Mainland China, and Vietnam. Chinese from the Western regions of China typically have not immigrated to the United States. These individuals are more related to South Asians and Middle Easterners than they are to East Mainland Chinese. Individuals of Japanese descent have the largest percentage born in the United States of any APIA group. In fact, those of Japanese descent are the only APIA group in which more than 50% were born in the United States. Thus, issues of immigration are not as relevant to this group of people as they are to other APIA groups. Immigrants from Korea are primarily from South Korea. Whereas those from other East Asian countries have generally maintained religious beliefs from traditionally Asian religions (e.g., Taoism, Confucianism, and Buddhism), most of the Korean immigrants were sponsored by Christian churches, so these immigrants primarily follow Christian beliefs. It is important for people to know that because of Japanese military aggression between the periods of the Sino–Japanese War through World War II, there had been traditional animosity from those of Chinese and Korean descent toward those of Japanese descent. Although these antipathies have less relevance in the United States—particularly among those of Chinese, Korean, and Japanese descent who were born in the United States—many older Chinese and Koreans still harbor these negative feelings.

The second subset of those categorized as APIAs are from the Southeast Asian countries of Vietnam, Cambodia, Laos, Thailand, and Myanmar (formerly Burma) (Chin et al., in press; Hong & Ham, 2001). Large numbers of immigrants from these countries came during and after the war in Vietnam. Because of the historical influence of French colonization, many immigrants from these Southeast Asian countries follow the Catholic religion. However, Buddhism is a major cultural influence in these countries, so even though many immigrants may be members of Catholic churches at a formal level, they may also follow cultural beliefs heavily influenced by Buddhism.

The third subset of those categorized as APIAs are from South Asia (Chin et al., in press; Tewari, Inman, & Sandhu, 2003). This area includes India, Pakistan, Bangladesh, Sri Lanka, Nepal, Bhutan, and the Maldives. The two dominant religions influencing people from these countries are Hinduism and Islam, although Christianity, Sikhism, and Buddhism are also major influences in this region of the world. Just as there had been historical animosities between Koreans and Japanese, there had been, and still are, animosities between Indians and Pakistanis. Again, although these antipathies are less relevant to those born in the United States, negative feelings still exist among older immigrants.

By far, the most diverse subset included in the APIA category is the Pacific Islander population (Chin et al., in press; Espiritu & Omi, 2000). This subset includes descendents from the Philippines, Malaysia, Indonesia, Samoa, Fiji, Hawaii, Tahiti, Guam, and numerous other island nations. According to the U.S. Census Bureau (Barnes & Bennett, 2002), individuals of Filipino descent constitute the second largest number of APIAs in the United States. However, besides Filipinos, other Pacific Islanders constitute a very small portion of the overall APIA population. For example, whereas 1,850,314 individuals claimed Filipino descent, the next highest Pacific Island group was from Indonesia; only 39,757 individuals claimed Indonesian descent.[2] Dominant religions influencing these island nations are Catholicism, Islam, Christianity, and indigenous religions.

Forms of Categorization

Before delving much more into issues of racism, we would like to go over some terms of categorization that are sometimes confused: stereotypes, prejudice, discrimination, and racism. Our definitions conform to social psychological distinctions (Mio, 2003; Mio & Awakuni, 2000; Myers, 2005). *Stereotypes* are generalizations about people in an identifiable group. These generalizations are often inaccurate and resistant to change when new information is experienced. For example, if one has a view that a particular group of people are lazy and then one is exposed to many hard-working people from that group, the "lazy" stereotype is not changed. Stereotypes can also be positive and resistant to change. For example, if one has a view that a particular group of people are smart and then one is exposed to many not-so-smart people from that group, the "smart" stereotype can still remain. A corollary to stereotypes is that the one who stereotypes another group does not allow for variation in that group. In other words, a particular norm may apply to one group and actually be measurable. For example, APIAs may be less talkative than their White[3] counterparts. However, someone who might stereotype APIAs as being quiet may believe that *all* APIAs are quiet or that the difference in talkativeness between APIAs and Whites is exaggerated. Stereotypes are therefore the cognitive component of group categorization.

Prejudice refers to an evaluation of someone or some people on the basis of their categorization. It is a negative or positive feeling about the person or group merely because of their category membership. For example, if it is the case that APIAs tend to talk less than their White counterparts, a teacher may like APIAs because of this because they tend to be less disruptive in the class. On the other hand, a teacher may dislike APIAs because of this because they will not contribute as much to the class discussion. This liking or disliking merely because of category membership is what we mean by "prejudice." Of course, when this term is typically used, it is meant to refer to the negative evaluation on the basis of category membership. Prejudice is therefore the evaluative component of group categorization.

Discrimination refers to behavior based on prejudice. Thus, if one feels negatively toward someone on the basis of that person's group membership, one will act negatively toward that person, whereas positive feelings will lead to positive behaviors. Again, this term is typically used negatively. To use our preceding example, if a teacher does not like APIAs because the teacher feels that APIAs, in general, do not contribute very much to class discussion, and if this teacher therefore gives APIA students poor class participation grades regardless of their contribution to the class, this teacher is acting in a discriminatory manner. Discrimination is therefore the behavioral component of group categorization. Notice that if stereotypes and prejudice are not acted on, they do not hurt the target of the stereotype or produce prejudicial feelings. Therefore, people are not hurt by stereotypes or prejudice alone; they are only hurt if the stereotype or prejudice is acted on through discriminatory practices. Of course, if one feels negatively toward another person on the basis of that person's category membership, it is likely that discrimination will follow.

Finally, *racism* is a routine mistreatment of a person or a group of people on the basis of his/her/their racial/ethnic category membership. Many people see this as discrimination plus the power to discriminate. In our previous example of discrimination, the teacher may act in a discriminatory manner, but if this teacher does not have institutional support, he or she can get into trouble. However, if the institution supports this teacher's discriminatory practices, this situation will be an example of racism. Some people distinguish individual racism versus institutional racism, contending that the teacher in our example is acting in a racist manner, even though the institution does not support his or her racism. However, other people contend that racism *only* involves institutional support. Therefore, racism can only be applied when someone from a group on the upside of power has institutional support to discriminate against people on the downside of power. According to Jones (1997), this latter conception of racism was coined by Carmichael and Hamilton (1967) when they introduced the term *institutional racism*. From this conception, racism is the institutional component of group categorization.

Jones (1997) allows for both definitions of racism. He contends that racism is a complex term that has multiple layers:

> Racism is organized and occurs at a societal level. That it is exemplified by segregation, persecution, and domination is stated explicitly. Because "racism" is also a *doctrine,* it occurs at the cultural level. And because racism also involves a "feeling of superiority" and "antagonisms," it occurs at an individual level. (p. 367)

THE "MODEL MINORITY" STEREOTYPE

In the 1960s, the popular media began to take notice that many high school valedictorians were of Asian/Pacific descent. They began to label APIAs as the "model minority" (Kasindorf et al., 1982; Petersen, 1966; "Success Story," 1966). However, many in the APIA community began seeing this popular label as a straitjacket as opposed to a tailored suit (Danico & Ng, 2004; Suzuki, 1977, 1989, 2002). For example, Danico and Ng indicated that this stereotype was designed to counteract arguments about institutional racism. How could the United States be racist if some of its ethnic minorities are successful? Moreover, this implicit comparison between APIAs and other ethnic minority populations had the effect of causing resentment among the other groups. The broader community was essentially saying: If APIAs can be successful, why can't you?

One of the leading voices in the examination of the model minority stereotype has been Suzuki (1977, 1989, 2002). Suzuki (1989) indicated that this label was a direct response to the civil unrest in the mid-1960s. Up until that point, the influx of APIAs was seen as a "yellow peril" that threatened to overtake the country. However, when major cities in the United States experienced riots and other forms of civil unrest, at least two popular articles (Petersen, 1966; Success Story, 1966) immediately labeled Asians as the model minority. This label ignored the fact that, whereas many APIAs experienced some degree of success, a higher percentage of APIAs than Whites lived below the poverty level. Also, while APIAs tended to achieve a great deal of success academically, this did not translate into job opportunities, as APIAs tended to be underemployed given their level of education. They tended to take jobs below their education level and to advance more slowly or hit a glass ceiling sooner than workers of other ethnicities. Fong (2002) stated, "The images of Asian Americans in school are that they are hard working, eager to learn, and achievement oriented. But the educational stereotypes of Asian Americans seem to disappear when they enter the workplace" (p. 118).

Suzuki (2002) also noted that the image of APIAs as the model minority tended to mask the needs of the community. For example, when he was an administrator at one university, despite the fact that APIAs comprised more than 15% of the student body, there were no APIA therapists in the student counseling center. When he inquired about this, the director of the center said that APIAs did not need therapy, as indicated by the fact that almost no such students sought therapy. However, when he persisted that there should be at least one APIA therapist on staff, the center finally hired such a therapist. Soon, this therapist became inundated with APIA students exhibiting a wide range of mental health issues. On investigation, it seemed that the existing therapists were not sensitive to APIA needs, and word got out that the center was not responsive to APIAs. When the new therapist arrived, she displayed the needed sensitivity, and APIA students began to realize that the center was now responsive. When she became so overloaded that she stayed long hours past the normal center's hours, the therapist requested that the center either hire another APIA therapist or that she be allowed to train her colleagues to be more sensitive to APIA needs and issues. The director of the center opted for this second option, and soon the other therapists became skilled in treating APIA students. Thus, the clinical staff became more diversified and more skilled in dealing with APIA clients. Moreover, they saw how their perception of APIA students being a model minority masked the needs of such students. More broadly, when society views APIAs as being a model minority and a success story in America, such views can overlook the real needs of some members of the community.

RACISM AGAINST ASIAN/PACIFIC ISLAND AMERICANS: PAST AND PRESENT

In the first edition of the *Handbook of Asian American Psychology,* Young and Takeuchi (1998) discussed racism against specific APIA groups. It is not our objective to reiterate these forms of racism. However, we would like to discuss a few overarching issues and also provide some specific examples of racism directed against APIA populations. We might point out that racism against APIA groups seems to wax and wane according to the political winds. For example, racism against APIA groups increased during the Korean War, the Vietnam War, the

Japanese economic upturn (and concomitant American economic downturn) in the 1970s and 1980s, fear of Chinese communism which supplanted Russian communism in the 1990s (cf., the Wen Ho Lee case; W. H. Lee, 2001), the aftermath of the terrorism experienced on September 11, 2001, and the scapegoating of South Asians for American companies' decisions to outsource work abroad. Because the general population tends not to make distinctions among different Asian groups, racism against one group reverberates among all APIA groups.

Anti-Asian Laws

Throughout most of the history of Asian immigration to the United States, there have been anti-Asian restrictions to this immigration. When it was convenient or desirable for Asians to enter the United States, they were allowed to immigrate to this country. However, once their utility was over, laws were passed to prevent them from immigrating to, or staying in, the United States. Kitano and Daniels (1995) and Young and Takeuchi (1998) discussed many such relevant laws restricting Asian immigration.

The early years. As most people know, the initial Chinese immigrants came to the United States as a result of the gold rush in California beginning in 1848 and the need for Chinese laborers to help build the coast-to-coast railroad, completed at Promontory Summit, Utah, in 1869 (E. Lee, 1996). The Chinese immigrants who initially came to the United States because of the gold rush were in search of *Gam Saan* or the "Gold Mountain," where their hopes were to become rich with gold and return to China. The laborers who came to build the railroads primarily were recruited from two very poor regions in China. Building the railroad in the Western region of the United States was very dangerous work because it involved having to build the railroad tracks over and through the Rocky Mountains. Because of this danger and the relatively scarce number of American citizens in the Western region, Chinese laborers were drawn to the United States in hopes of making a better living than they were making in China. Because of the need for hard labor both in the mines and the railroads, almost all of the Chinese immigrants were men. Moreover, because the United

States did not want these immigrants to settle permanently, women were initially not allowed to immigrate; this was so that the men would be encouraged to leave when their work was done or so that they would not start families in the United States. Because Chinese men were not allowed to marry White women nor even have sexual relations with them, a few Chinese women were allowed to immigrate to the United States to serve as prostitutes. In 1900, nearly 90,000 Chinese were in the United States, but only 5% were women (E. Lee, 1996).

In 1870, Congress "made 'white persons and persons of African descent' eligible for citizenship" through naturalization (Kitano & Daniels, 1995, p. 13). This effectively prevented only Asians from becoming naturalized American citizens. "Attempts by Charles Sumner, the radical Republican senator from Massachusetts, and a few others to make naturalization color-blind were overwhelmingly voted down by Congress" (Kitano & Daniels, 1995, p. 13). Although some judges allowed citizenship to some specific Asians, two Supreme Court decisions in 1922 and 1923 prevented *any* Asians from becoming naturalized citizens.

The Chinese Exclusion Act of 1882. The Chinese Exclusion Act of 1882 only excluded immigrants from China from entering the U.S. for 10 years (Kitano & Daniels, 1995). This exclusion was extended in 1892 by the Geary Act for another 19 years, and then finally extended indefinitely in 1902. When attempts were made in the mid-1800s to block immigration from Ireland and Germany, the U.S. Supreme Court ruled in 1849 that these laws were unconstitutional. However, the Chinese Exclusion Act of 1882 was not challenged.

The "Gentleman's Agreement." Although Japanese were not formally barred from immigrating to the United States, around 1907–1908 there was a "Gentleman's Agreement" between the United States and Japan (Kitano & Daniels, 1995). This agreement was one-sided where Japan agreed to limit the number of immigrants to the United States to a trickle.

The Immigration Act of 1924. The Immigration Act of 1924 codified immigration restrictions, allowing thousands of immigrants from

Northern and Western Europe (between 18,000 and 65,000 depending on the specific country) and restricting immigrants from Southern and Eastern Europe (approximately 6,000 per country). Asian countries were allowed 100 immigrants per country. However, no one of discernible Asian ancestry was allowed to immigrate to the United States, despite the nominal number of 100 "allowed" per country. An Asian born in England could not be considered as an English immigrant, and the only ones who could emigrate from Asian countries were White individuals who were born in Asian countries (Higham, 1955; Kitano & Daniels, 1995).

Filipino independence. When the United States won the Spanish-American War of 1898, the Philippine Islands became a territory of the United States (Kitano & Daniels, 1995). Thus, Filipinos were American nationals and were allowed to enter the United States without restrictions. However, in 1934, a law was passed that promised Filipino independence by 1945. This law also limited Filipino immigration to 50 per year. However, Filipinos living in the United States could repatriate to the Philippines at public expense. Thus, while Filipino immigration to the United States was severely restricted, Filipinos were almost encouraged to emigrate from the United States back to the Philippines.

Executive Order 9066. In 1942, after the Japanese attack on Pearl Harbor in December 1941, President Franklin Delano Roosevelt signed Executive Order 9066. This order allowed the incarceration of 120,000 individuals of Japanese descent in the name of national security (Nagata, 1998). Because this episode is so unique and important, we dedicate an entire section to this topic later in the chapter.

The Magnuson Act. In 1943, the Magnuson Act repealed limitations on Chinese immigration, mainly to allow family reunification. Chinese men living in the United States were allowed to return to Hong Kong in order to find wives and return to this country. In reality, these women were mostly arranged by matchmakers or were relatives of the men (Kitano & Daniels, 1995; Riggs, 1950).

President Truman's proclamation. In 1946, President Truman raised the Filipino quota from 50 to 100 per year. Congress also passed a law allowing Filipinos to become naturalized citizens (Kitano & Daniels, 1995).

The McCarran-Walter Act. In 1952, the McCarran-Walter Act was passed. This law allowed Asians to become naturalized citizens, as it removed all racial and ethnic barriers to naturalized citizenship. It also allowed for family reunification, so while all Asian countries had severe immigration quotas (100–185 immigrants per country per year), many more immigrants entered the United States as non-quota immigrants for reunification purposes (Bruce, 1954; Kitano & Daniels, 1995).

The Refugee Act of 1953. The Refugee Act of 1953 allowed refugees to enter the United States as non-quota immigrants if they were fleeing from Communist countries. This, in effect, opened up immigration from China for those opposed to the Communist government, as certified by the nationalist Chinese government in Taiwan (Kitano & Daniels, 1995).

The 1965 Immigration Act. In 1965, Congress opted to substitute regions of the world for specific countries. Immigration from countries in the Western hemisphere was limited to 120,000 per year with no limitations from any one country. Immigration from countries in the Eastern hemisphere was limited to 170,000 per year, although there was a limitation of 20,000 from any one country (Kitano & Daniels, 1995). Figure 20.1 displays a timeline of important immigration dates, including those relevant to South Asians.

Hawaii Under U.S. Control

Fuchs (1961) discussed the history of Hawaii shortly after it became the 50th state of the United States in 1959. Hawaii was thought to be settled by Polynesians in about A.D. 750. It experienced relative stability for over 1,000 years. Its first contact with Western cultures came when Captain James Cook of England came on the islands in 1778 on his search for a short passage to Alaska. After this contact, radical change soon ensued. Moreover, the native population dropped from about 300,000 to about 57,000 in 1889 due to disease and social problems introduced by Western ways of conduct.

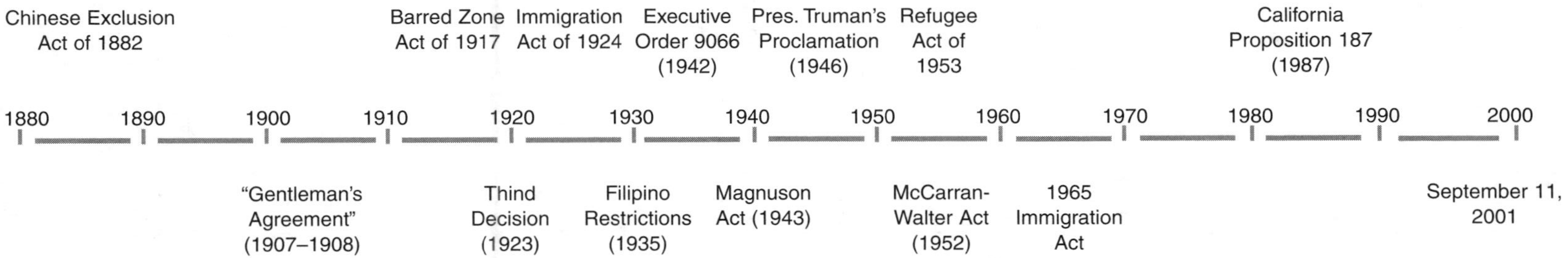

Figure 20.1 Timeline of Immigrant-Relevant Dates.

The United States first made contact with Hawaii in 1887 through a series of commercial treaties. However, the United States helped to overthrow the ruling Queen Liliuokalani in 1893. Sanford B. Dole, who controlled pineapple interests in Hawaii, led a provisional government and worked to have Hawaii annexed by the United States. However, then-President Grover Cleveland was against imperialism and denied annexation. After Cleveland left office in 1897 and after the Spanish-American War in 1898, Dole was successful in getting Hawaii annexed; it was a territory of the United States from 1898 until it gained statehood in 1959. The drive to statehood began in 1935. Congress held 20 hearings about Hawaiian statehood between 1935 and 1958.

Some opposition to Hawaii statehood came from residents of the islands, but most of the opposition came from the mainland and seemed rooted in racism. "American politicians rightly assumed that polyethnic Hawaii would send non-white representatives to Congress" (Kitano & Daniels, 1995, p. 139). One of the latter main opponents, Republican Representative John Pillion of New York, was against statehood, ostensibly because he contended that Hawaii was run by Communists through the strong union movement. He also suggested that "Hawaii's Oriental population would never be fully assimilated into American life" (Fuchs, 1961, p. 411).

Since statehood, one important issue has been the degree to which Hawaiian lands were taken from their original inhabitants. In the 1970s, "ceded lands" from Hawaii were seen as stolen property. Hence, Hawaiians sought an apology and reparations from the U.S. government. The U.S. Congress set up the Native Hawaiians Study Commission to make recommendations on this matter. The Carter administration appointed six individuals from Hawaii and three from the mainland to this commission. However, before this commission could complete its task, President Carter was swept out of office. The Reagan administration dismissed the Carter appointees and replaced them with six individuals from the mainland and three from Hawaii. Not surprisingly, the commission found in favor of the U.S. government. "Their draft report of 1982 outraged native Hawaiians, because it absolved the USA of any guilt or responsibility for the overthrow of the monarchy and essentially concluded that the USA owed the Hawaiians nothing" (Fischer, 2002, p. 254). The final report in 1983 offered a two-volume conclusion, with the six members from the mainland affirming the draft report and the three members from Hawaii offering a rebuttal.

The issue of ceded lands and self-determination continues to be an issue. Senator Akaka from Hawaii introduced a bill to give Native Hawaiians the same rights as Native Americans, but the vote was never taken. A vote on this bill was supposed to have taken place in July 2005, but "a small group of Republican senators who opposed the bill placed holds on it, keeping it from going to the Senate floor for a full debate" ("Senate to Consider Akaka Bill Vote," 2005; see also Kaste, 2005). This underscores the continued tension between Native Hawaiians and White majority political dominance.

World War II and Japanese American Internment

The definitions of racism presented earlier in this chapter indicate that racism can be directed toward an individual or to a group of people. The "group" can range from including as few as two people to an entire ethnic or racial group. One of the most dramatic examples of racism directed toward an entire Asian ethnic group in the United States was the internment of Japanese Americans during World War II. Ten weeks after Japan's military attacked Pearl Harbor, President Franklin Roosevelt signed Executive Order 9066, which authorized the removal of all persons of Japanese ancestry from the entire West Coast of the United States (see Appendix A). As a result, over 90% of mainland Japanese Americans were ordered to leave their homes and were placed in incarceration camps located in remote desert and swamp areas of the country's interior. "Evacuees" (as the government euphemistically referred to the affected Japanese Americans) were allowed to take only what they could carry and often had little more than a week's notice to dispose of their life possessions, homes, businesses, and farmlands. Most suffered two uprootings, being sent first to temporary assembly centers within racetracks and fairgrounds where they were kept for several months and later to the more permanent camps. Labeled as potentially disloyal based only on their Japanese heritage, 120,000 Japanese Americans endured the isolated camps for an average of two to three years surrounded by barbed wire and armed guards. An average-sized camp held 10,000 internees within a single square mile of space, with each family assigned to a single barrack room that ranged from 20 by 8 feet for the smallest to 20 by 24 feet for the largest. Eating, bathing, and laundering took place in communal facilities (CWRIC, 1997; Daniels, 1988).

Two-thirds of the imprisoned were U.S. citizens by birth. Many were young children and teenagers. Yet, neither citizenship nor age mattered, and Japanese Americans had no opportunity for an individual review of their loyalty. The government portrayed the mass incarceration as a military necessity to protect the country from any acts of sabotage or espionage that might be committed by Japanese Americans living along the Pacific Ocean and close to Japan. However, more than 40 years later, the Commission on Wartime Relocation and Internment of Civilians (CWRIC) thoroughly investigated the circumstances surrounding Roosevelt's executive order decision and found no evidence to support the claim of military necessity. Instead, the commission cited "race prejudice, war hysteria, and a failure of political leadership" as the primary forces behind the move to imprison Japanese Americans (CWRIC, 1997, p. 18).

The mass incarceration of Japanese Americans stands as one of the most compelling examples of injustice in U.S. history. It also represents a significant episode in Asian American history and provides a dramatic example of prejudice and discrimination directed against a specific Asian ethnic group. As such, it is useful to examine how the internment reflected racism toward Japanese Americans, the psychological consequences that emerged in its wake, and its broader implications for Asian Americans.

The CWRIC conclusions emphasize that racism played a central role in the internment. Although Italy and Germany were also enemies of the United States during World War II, neither German Americans nor Italian Americans were subjected to mass internment. Japanese

Americans had been the targets of racism and discrimination well before the attack on Pearl Harbor, and previous decades of anti-Asian sentiment and policies provided fertile ground for implementation of the internment. As scholar Roger Daniels noted, "The wartime abuse of Japanese Americans . . . was merely a link in a chain of racism that stretched back to the earliest contacts between Asians and Whites on American soil" (Daniels, 1993, p. 3). Stereotypes of Asians as inferior, foreign, and inassimilable were ongoing, and segregation and systematic discrimination (as reflected in the forms of anti-Asian legislation described earlier) characterized the experiences of many Asians in the United States before the war. Following Pearl Harbor, however, specific antagonisms toward Japanese Americans quickly escalated. The Japanese were perceived to be sneaky, untrustworthy, and treacherous.

Many Americans, including those in key positions of the military, failed to make distinctions between the Japanese abroad and Japanese Americans living in the United States. The following quote from the commanding general in charge of West Coast security, Lieutenant General John L. DeWitt, illustrates the extremity of this thinking:

> In the war in which we are now engaged racial affinities are not severed by migration. The Japanese race is an enemy race, and while many second and third generation Japanese born on United States soil, possessed of United States citizenship, have become "Americanized," the racial strains are undiluted. (quoted in CWRIC, 1997, p. 82)

General DeWitt goes on to state that "the very fact that no sabotage has taken place to date is a disturbing and confirming indication that such action will be taken" (quoted in CWRIC, 1997, p. 82).

Internees experienced a wide range of consequences stemming from their incarceration. Inside the camps, Japanese Americans dealt with severe weather conditions, boredom, and the uncertainty of their future. The cramped conditions and communal lifestyle severely limited privacy and contributed to a breakdown of the nuclear family role structures that had been central to their culture prior to incarceration

(Morishima, 1973). Because everyone ate in the mess halls, children tended to eat with friends and moved from mess hall to mess hall. The dislocation of the typical family meal eroded the dignity and authority of parents. In addition, the Nisei's (second-generation Japanese Americans) higher English proficiency placed them in a position of power over their Issei (first-generation) parents because business within the camp bureaucracy was conducted in English (CWRIC, 1997) and gender roles shifted as Issei men were no longer family breadwinners (Matsumoto, 1984).

Psychological impacts continued well beyond the closing of the camps after the war. Although the internment is seen as the most critical historical event that has shaped the Japanese Americans and their identity in this country, silence shrouded the topic of "the camps" for decades within their families and communities. Most who had been interned went on to lead successful lives that revealed little indication of postinternment effects. It was not until the testimonies of the 1980 Commission on Wartime Relocation and Internment of Civilians hearings that Japanese Americans began to speak publicly about their past pain and trauma (CWRIC, 1997; Furutani, 1981). Former internees revealed a wide range of psychological effects stemming from their unjust imprisonment. Some reported undeserved feelings of shame and humiliation, similar to those reported by rape victims, and that they were somehow to blame for their treatment (Hansen & Mitson, 1974). Others shared painful experiences of having lost loved ones from inadequate health care and harsh living conditions. Still others described the anxiety of being away from family members sent to separate camps. Many felt a pressure to become "super Americans" after the war and to minimize their Japanese culture. The government's actions left them self-conscious about their heritage and uncertain about their place in postwar American society. Related to such impacts on their identities, others reported a lowered sense of self-esteem (CWRIC, 1997; Mass, 1991; Maykovitch, 1972).

Additional testimonies from the CWRIC hearings and subsequent writings suggested that the impacts on identity and family were extensive enough to have long-term effects on subsequent generations, including those third-generation Japanese Americans (Sansei) born after the war (CWRIC, 1997; Furutani, 1981). Sansei writer David Mura (1991) stated that, instead of inheriting a sense of "Japaneseness," his generation had inherited a sense of shame about their ethnic identity. Similarly, family therapist Nobu Miyoshi (1980) described the Sansei as "heirs" to their internment camp legacy. Nagata's (1990, 1993) survey and interview data support the existence of these cross-generational effects. Her research found that the adult Sansei children of former internees felt a gap in their own personal history because their parents rarely discussed their internment. These Sansei attributed the loss of the Japanese language and culture that typifies most of their generation to the fact that, after the war, Nisei parents tried to minimize anything related to Japan. Many felt their parents' need to demonstrate the "worth" of Japanese Americans transferred into parenting pressures that urged the Sansei to excel in school and careers. Virtually all Sansei carried an internal sense of sadness and anger about what their parents had experienced, and those who had a parent interned were significantly less confident about their rights in this country than Sansei who did not have a parent interned (Nagata, 1993). This last finding challenges any assumption that all third-generation Japanese Americans feel fully comfortable in mainstream U.S. society.

Even though the Civil Liberties Act of 1988 eventually provided for $20,000 redress and an official apology for each of the 60,000 surviving internees following the 1980 CWRIC review, anti-Japanese sentiment continued to have broader implications in the postwar United States whenever Japan was viewed as an economic enemy. It is particularly at these times that Japanese Americans and other Asian Americans are targets for "Japan bashing" and anti-Asian violence. For example, in 1982, a time when tensions between U.S. and Japanese automakers were high, two White factory workers severely beat Vincent Chin, a Chinese American, with a baseball bat because they apparently mistook him for a "Jap." Chin died four days later, but neither of his assailants went to prison for his killing (AALDEF, 2005). The tragedy served as a grim reminder to all generations of Japanese Americans and other Asian Americans that the forces of racism and anger underlying the internment could resurface in postwar America.

More recently, the tragedies of September 11, 2001, have raised issues associated with the internment once again. News reports compared the terrorist attacks to the Japanese attack on Pearl Harbor. These comparisons are addressed in Leong and Nakanishi's (2002) edited volume *Asian Americans on War and Peace.* In an atmosphere of contemporary panic and fear following the terrorist attacks of 2001, the calls to round up "suspect" Arab Americans and Muslims to ensure national security paralleled the calls to round up Japanese Americans in 1941. Innocent individuals, including South Asians, mistakenly viewed as potential terrorists have been targets of violence and anger. These developments are reminders that the Japanese American internment remains relevant to Asian Americans. However, racism against South Asians did not begin with 9/11; racism against this population has had a long history.

RACISM AGAINST SOUTH ASIANS AND SOUTH ASIAN AMERICANS

Early Racism

Migration of South Asians, like migration of other Asians, began as early as the 1700s and 1800s, although the number of immigrants was small (Sheth, 1995). About 7,000 to 10,000 came to the United States from India at the end of the 19th century and beginning of the 20th century (1890s and 1900s). In early history, South Asians arrived to the West Coast where they served as indentured servants, were sold as slaves, and worked on the California railroad and farms (Leonard, 1997; Sheth, 1995; Takaki, 1998). About 200 Indian laborers (primarily from the Punjab region of India due to military affiliations) arrived between 1820 and 1870. Some Indians arriving in the West migrated to Canada, until Canada prevented Indians from landing on Canadian shores (Sheth, 1995). Such racism in the 1900s led many Indians to migrate to the United States from 1907 to 1910 for labor opportunities (Rao, 1999).

Although there was a small window of opportunity for Indians to serve as migrant workers and laborers, anti-miscegenation laws prevented interracial unions. The 1661 anti-miscegenation laws that prohibited marriage between Caucasian women and African American slaves were extended, in the 1900s, to Asians (Takaki, 1998). Similarly, with other Asians in the 1900s, there was a movement toward formalized exclusion of Asians from immigrating and gaining U.S. citizenship (Lal, 1999; Uba, 1994). This time period was also characterized by discriminatory laws and regulations barring Indians from entering the United States. The media, trade unions, politicians, and White workers pressured the government to pass exclusionary laws against Indians as well. Two laws, the Barred Zone Act of 1917 and the Asian Exclusion Act of 1924, were mainly responsible for restricting migration from India (Ibrahim, Ohnishi, & Sandhu, 1997; Lal, 1999). In the 1800s, a California senator campaigned to have the Chinese Exclusion Act apply to Indians as well as Chinese. Later, Congress passed the Immigration Regional Restriction Act in 1917, and attempts were made to deport all Indians. Then in the 1923 Thind Decision, the Supreme Court ruled that Indians, although Caucasian, were not White and not entitled to citizenship, revoking all prior Indian citizenships. White individuals also ruled that Indians could not own or lease land (Lal, 1999). With the enforcement of the Asian Exclusion Act, only about 100 Indians arrived on the shores of the United States in the 1930s. Whereas the Chinese Exclusion Act was repealed toward the end of World War II under Roosevelt, the Indian Regional Exclusion Act was overlooked by the congressional committee, and requests were made to lift the ban on Indians (Rao, 1999).

Because of an increased number of Asian laborers, railroad laborer disputes, and economic depression, Asians and Indians became scapegoats during the California gold rush period and were blamed for taking away local jobs. In 1907 and 1908, mobs of Whites drove hundreds of Indian farm workers from their communities on the West Coast regions of Bellingham, Washington, and Live Oak, California (L. C. Lee,

1998; Takaki, 1998). Racist sentiments and the slow overturning of institutional laws against Asians continued into later decades. In July of 1946, Congress passed an act allowing persons of races indigenous to India to immigrate in the United States with the right of naturalization (Young & Takeuchi, 1998).

Racism in the 1980s

Immigration of Indians and other South Asians to the United States in larger waves began with the 1965 Immigration Act (Inman & Tewari, 2003; Takaki, 1998; Tewari et al., 2003). South Asians arriving in the United States post 1965 were believed to be the "cream of the crop" from their respective countries, and jealousies, resentment, and competitiveness were on the rise in the 1980s, with South Asians being targeted once again (Tewari et al., 2003). The 1980s represent a time with much anti-Asian sentiment that was related to the large car import business with Asia, especially Japan (cf. Vincent Chin discussion, earlier in this section). American companies and the media quickly jumped onto the phrase "Made in America" as a way to support U.S. locals rather than the labor and products of Asian companies (AALDEF, 2005).

Indians and South Asians were blamed for taking away jobs from locals, and racism was at its height in cities largely populated by Indians. Jersey City, New Jersey, was one such city, where approximately 15,000 Indians resided during the 1980s. Numerous racist incidents occurred among the Indian community despite their educational and occupational status (Das & Kemp, 1997). During this time, a gang, the "Jersey City Dot Busters" formed to target Indian immigrants with harassment and violent intimidation (Sheth, 1995; Tewari et al., 2003). ("Dot" refers to the bindi Indian Hindu women wear on their foreheads as part of their ethnic cultural dress and identity.) In July 1987, a local New Jersey newspaper reported the rising number of harassment incidents in the Indian community of Jersey City (Pluralism Project, 2005). One month later, racism against Indians led to two deaths; first, a 30-year-old Indian immigrant bank manager, Navroze Mody, was beaten to death by a gang chanting "Hindu, Hindu!" Second, a few weeks after Mody's death,

a young medical resident, Dr. Sharan, was assaulted by three young men with baseball bats when walking home late one night yelling, "There's a dothead! Let's get him!" Sharan was beaten severely and left unconscious with a fractured skull and permanent neurological damage (Pluralism Project, 2005).

Such incidents shocked the South Asian community, as discrimination was aimed at Indian professionals, taxi drivers, grocery store owners, and the like. Business and hotel owners were also targeted, and hotels/motels were often stereotyped as being "Potels, hotels, and motels" where Gujarati Indians owned several real estate properties (Sheth, 1995). As the population of all Asians began to increase, so did the number of violations against Asians. In the 1980s, the Asian American Legal Defense and Education Fund (AALDEF) was formed to provide support for individuals of Asian descent who were victims of hate crimes and racist incidents.

Racism in the 1990s

Anti-Indian attitudes surfaced in the 1990s with the technology boom, especially in Silicon Valley (including and surrounding San Jose, California) and other IT (information technology) cities. IT companies and industries in the area were targeted for favoring Indians and discriminating against those who were not South Asian (Brown, 2001; Jayadev, 2001). Presidents and chief executive officers of IT companies were asked to comment on their hiring practices, policies, and procedures in explaining and justifying the large numbers of Indians employed in such organizations. Not only were Indians perceived as discriminating against others but also, ironically, Indians themselves believed they were discriminated against within such companies; several Indians and Asian workers in the IT industry believed in the "glass ceiling" as inhibiting their professional advancement in their workplaces (Rivlin, 2000; Sandhu, Kaur, & Tewari, 1999). Although West Coast areas like Silicon Valley in California recruited Indians and other Asian immigrants because of their abilities in technology, the model minority stereotype undoubtedly had an influence in this recruitment in that these workers would produce well for the corporations while not causing problems socially. However, the anti-immigrant mood in California in the 1990s resulted in the passing of Proposition 187, a proposition aimed at the illegal immigration of Mexican migrant workers that denied public services (e.g., schooling, emergency room services) to these immigrants. Several Indians feared negative reactions toward them as immigrants and part of the scapegoating mood of the country toward people of color.

The East Coast also continued to struggle with discrimination. In New Jersey in 1991, there were 58 cases of hate crimes against Indians who were physicians, businessmen, and other professionals (Pluralism Project, 2005). This time, a group called Indian Youth Against Racism (IYAR), based at Columbia University, documented instances of violence against Indians in New Jersey and helped implement a series of educational programs on South Asian cultures for students and faculty at a Jersey City high school. The group also helped get a bill passed in the New Jersey legislature that raised the mandatory penalties for "bias crimes." In the 1990s, anti-Asian sentiments were not condoned in the United States, but certainly discrimination and racism continued to affect the lives of South Asian individuals and other Asian American communities (Alvarez, 1998).

Racism Now

9/11. Political strife and terrorism—whether domestic or abroad—have the tendency to contribute to subtle, overt or covert prejudice, racism, and discrimination. Racial prejudice, war, economic competition, and media stereotypes have been known to trigger acts of hate in society. As mentioned previously, the aftermath of the terrorist events of September 11, 2001, in New York City not only had a tremendous impact on the American community, but it also resulted in a backlash toward the South Asian community. Not only have there been direct acts of racism against South Asians as part of the aftermath, but there also continue to be ongoing fears among those who are South Asian (Inman, Yeh, Madan-Bahel, & Nath, 2005; National Asian Pacific American Legal Consortium, 2002).

One of the many consequences of 9/11 has been with immigration. Immigration to the United States and U. S. citizenship have been under great scrutiny, affecting individuals in South Asian communities and abroad (Inman et al., 2005). In December 2002, a notice of "Special Registration" was placed by the U.S. Department of Justice requesting that individuals appear at the Immigration and Naturalization Service with the risk of being detained or deported based on their ethnicities—some South Asian subgroups were included in this notice (see Appendix B).

In times of fear and hatred, such as post-9/11, innocent individuals who resemble the "enemy" are targeted (Inman et al., 2005; Jayadev, 2001). One such group among many who have been victimized is the Sikh community. In a qualitative analysis of the concerns and issues facing South Asian Americans seeking psychological services at a university counseling center, Tewari (2000) found that racism was a salient issue for several Sikh students attempting to manage life in America while maintaining their cultural and religious identity, even before 9/11. The turbans have traditionally distinguished Sikh individuals from other ethnic minority groups, thus subjecting them to increased prejudice and ridicule. Such targeting has contributed to the psychological distress of Sikh Indians living in the United States (Tewari, 2000). After 9/11, because Sikhs wear turbans like some male Muslims, they have been subject to greater attack. Male Sikhs have not been the only victims of racism due to their cultural dress; South Asian women have also feared wearing their traditional *salvar kameez* (long shirt and pants) due to being perceived as terrorists or being identified as Muslim. In fact, immediately following 9/11, the New York–based AALDEF documented over 100 bias-related incidents toward South Asian individuals, half of which were of a violent nature (AALDEF, 2005; AsianWeek, 2001).

Over the decades, there has been a loss of ethnic/cultural identity among South Asians; many do not feel safe enough to express themselves in dress, religion, and culture—previously with the dot, and now with turbans or traditional loose clothing such as salvar kameezs and kurtas. Since 9/11, South Asians have worried about their safety, both in their visibility in the media and suspicion by the government (Inman et al., 2005). Clearly, incidents of hate crimes toward South Asians have been documented, and several South Asians feel victimized by racial profiling and also feel the need to justify their nonterrorist stance years later. The terrorist events of 9/11 have impacted the South Asian subgroup, both psychologically and physically. According to the AALDEF, racial profiling and violence against South Asians continue to be reported and discussed.

Outsourcing

Most recently, due to the U.S. elections in 2004 and the changing economy, attention has been directed toward globalization and outsourcing to foreign countries. Outsourcing has been a controversial topic of discussion among politicians, business owners, U.S. citizens, and people around the world. Call centers and new companies have been expanding in India, Mexico, and other foreign countries. Such growth has propelled many Americans to once again blame foreigners for taking jobs away from the American people. There is increasing prejudice among Americans toward companies moving globally and taking businesses across the world to places such as India and other foreign labor markets. Lou Dobbs, Ralph Nader, John Kerry, and other notable figures have commented on the pros and cons of outsourcing and have mentioned India as a booming economy due to the globalization. Several articles, news shows, and Web sites have referenced outsourcing and its impact on American workers.

On February 9, 2004, *The New York Times* featured an article, "Indians Fearing Repercussions of U.S. Technology Outsourcing" (Rai, 2004), and pictured an Indian call center where Indians were answering phone calls, with the following description underneath the photograph: "At Spectramind, a call center in Powai, outside Bombay, employees assist American customers. Such outsourcing of white-collar work is under fire in United States." The article went on to discuss how the U.S. political reaction has been building up against such outsourcing in recent years and nearly two dozen states have voted on legislation to ban government work from being contracted to non-Americans. Not only have legislative attempts been made, but the article also

noted that the U.S. Senate approved a bill aimed at restricting outsourcing of contracts from two federal departments. Although the House has not acted on similar legislation, there has been a campaign against moving work to low-cost destinations. As of March 2004, 170,000 American jobs had moved to India and researchers are predicting that by 2015, more than 3 million jobs will move out of the United States (Haidar, 2004). Such domestic and global changes will result in differential attitudes toward foreigners—as has been recently noted, some Americans view outsourcing as "job-snatching." Colin Powell commented on outsourcing while in India in March 2004, stating "Outsourcing is a reality in the 21st century global environment," and that "outsourcing invariably does result in the loss of jobs and we have to do a better job in the United States of creating opportunity in the United States to provide more jobs so that those who have lost jobs will have opportunities in the future" (Haidar, 2004, p. 1). It is precisely the job losses that have contributed to the fear, animosity, and negative feelings toward Indians and other foreigners.

These fears have contributed to the material placed on Web sites, in the media, and in newspapers. One such Web site article mentions outsourcing in the following context of an advice column focused on helping employees improve their marketability through networking. In an opening description of NetWorking with Jane Lommel (April, 2004) was the following:

> For years, you have heard me harp on the need to upgrade your skills. Nothing like having several hundred million Indian Brahmins who value education as a ticket to a better life to prompt Americans who have become sloppy and complacent to open a book and master the computer. Coming alive, however, should not mean crying for protectionism and unions to keep them from upgrading their skills. No, Americans are too creative and full of entrepreneurial spirit and dynamism to capitulate to the competition from high-quality Indian scientists and engineers. So, don't complain about Indians taking away jobs. Be glad that someone is willing to do the lower end manufacturing, call center, and even programming jobs. This saves our fine brains for even more creative endeavors! (p. 1)

In the same month, *The Washington Times* published an article titled "Fear and Outsourcing" (Richman, 2004), attempting to dispel some of the fears of outsourcing and giving jobs to Indians abroad. Outsourcing and globalization will continue; with such movement, there is a great likelihood of increased prejudice, discrimination, and racism toward Indians and other South Asians taking away American jobs. Currently, South Asians are not only experiencing the backlash of 9/11, but they are also facing the impact of U.S. attitudes toward foreigners. Concern occurs when fears turn into acts of racism and violence as a direct result of what has been happening around the world and with the U.S. economy. Psychologically, the impact of others' misperceptions and actions toward any ethnic or cultural group is likely to cause emotional distress. Historically, South Asians have been targets of prejudice and discrimination, and it is clear that this group has not been spared, as evidenced by the incidents occurring in the 1980s, the 1990s, in the post-9/11 years, and now with outsourcing. Such domestic and world events have increased the heightened fear, sensitivity, and cautions within the South Asian American community.

Summary and Future Directions

The history of the United States reflects multiple periods of high anti-Asian sentiment over time. This sentiment emerged interpersonally and legislatively. Since the inception of contact with Asians in the 1800s, White Americans have sought to limit the rights of Asians and Asian Americans. This situation is historically ironic, given that the Americas were "discovered" as a result of European desire to find a shortcut to Asian countries. Of greatest concern is the fact that racism and stereotyped attitudes toward APIA groups have continued to exist in more recent history as well. This chapter highlighted two examples that reflect more contemporary racism toward APIAs—the World War II internment of Japanese Americans and the ongoing suspicions, prejudices, and violence toward South Asians. Both cases illustrate how racism can spring to the surface under conditions of perceived economic and security threats.

Individuals of Japanese descent, regardless of U.S. citizenship, were labeled potentially disloyal and targeted for mass incarceration soon after Japan attacked Pearl Harbor. Those who directly experienced the unjust internment live with the memory of having been imprisoned by their own country because of their ethnic heritage, and the psychological impacts of this injustice continue to be felt generations later.

We also noted how the more recent terrorist events of September 11, 2001, have renewed suspicion of APIAs, particularly South Asians. Many South Asians were mistaken for being Arab; moreover, Islam is the second largest religion among South Asians. Therefore, Muslim individuals became the targets of anti-Arab feelings in the country as well. Such suspicions and fears in the post-9/11 atmosphere have continued and have taken a psychological toll among South Asians. These feelings may also be merged with feelings of resentment toward South Asians for the outsourcing of jobs due to economic globalization.

Part of the history of APIAs in the United States has included a period of time when a seemingly positive portrayal of APIAs—that of the model minority—dominated. However, this depiction was both a myth and a straitjacket. It was a myth because there was a higher percentage of APIAs living below the poverty level than their White counterparts. This myth also served to lead those in power to ignore some of the very real needs of the various APIA communities. Additionally, it was seen as a straitjacket because implicit in this label was a comparison between APIAs and other ethnic minority groups, thus engendering resentment and hostility from these comparison groups.

As APIAs become interwoven into the fabric of American society, there is hope that they can be perceived as part of the society and not distinct from it. There is optimism and pessimism for this sentiment. There is optimism for it because there has been progress in accepting APIAs over the course of the past several decades, particularly since the end of World War II. However, there is pessimism for this sentiment because such acceptance seems to wax and wane with the political climate. Periods of fear and suspicion of the

APIA communities have been related to the Korean War, the Vietnam War, the Japanese economic threat of the 1970s and 1980s, fear of Chinese communism supplanting fear of Soviet communism in the 1990s, the events of 9/11 in the early 2000s, and the very recent economic fear of outsourcing to foreign countries, including India. Historically and currently, prejudice, discrimination, and racism have had and continue to have a place in U.S. society. Additionally, APIAs have been perceived as foreigners because they look phenotypically different from other Americans; APIAs continue to be perceived as different from White and other Americans. Future social, political, and economic events will influence the degree to which APIA communities are accepted into American society—perhaps in 2050, with the browning of America and the increase in the number of multiracial individuals in the United States, there will be a movement toward accepting different races and multiple ethnicities of Asian ancestry.

NOTES

1. Henceforth we will be referring to Asians, Asian/Pacific Islanders, and Asian/Pacific Island Americans as "APIAs."

2. These numbers reflect those claiming only Filipino or Indonesian backgrounds. Those who claimed Filipino ancestry in combination with any other race or ethnicity bring the Filipino total in the United States to 2,364,815, and those who claimed Indonesian ancestry in combination with any other race or ethnicity bring the Indonesian total to 63,073.

3. We use the terms *Whites, White Americans,* and *Caucasians* interchangeably.

REFERENCES

Alvarez, A. (1998). *Asian American racial identity and racial adjustment.* Poster presentation at the 106th annual convention of the American Psychological Association, San Francisco, CA.

Asian American Legal Defense and Education Fund (AALDEF). (2005). *Anti-Asian violence.* Retrieved May 14, 2005, from http://www.aaldef.org/violence.html

AsianWeek.com. (2001, September 21–27). *South Asians face violent backlash after WTC attacks.* Retrieved May 14, 2005, from http://www.asianweek.com/2001_09_21/news_backlash.html

Barnes, J. S., & Bennett, C. E. (2002). *The Asian population: 2000.* (Census 2000 Brief No. C2KBR-01-16). Retrieved January 17, 2005, from www.census.gov/prod/2002pubs/c2kbr01-16.pdf

Brown, T. (2001). *Why Indian H-1B's are not superior and Aframericans are not cry babies.* Retrieved May 15, 2005, from http://www.zazona.com/shameH1B/Library/Archives/Tony Brown.htm

Bruce, J. C. (1954). *The golden door: The irony of our immigration policy.* New York: Random House.

Carmichael, S., & Hamilton, C. V. (1967). *Black power: The politics of liberation in America.* New York: Vintage Books.

Chin, J. L., Mio, J. S., & Iwamasa, G. Y. (in press). Ethical conduct of research with Asian and Pacific Island American populations. In C. B. Fisher & J. E. Trimble (Eds.), *Ethical conduct of research with ethnic minority populations.* Thousand Oaks, CA: Sage.

Commission on Wartime Relocation and Internment of Civilians (CWRIC). (1997). *Personal justice denied: Report of the Commission on Wartime Relocation and Internment of Civilians.* Washington, DC: The Civil Liberties Public Education Fund, and Seattle: University of Washington Press.

Danico, M. Y., & Ng, F. (2004). *Asian American issues.* Westport, CT: Greenwood Press.

Daniels, R. (1988). *Asian America: Chinese and Japanese in the United States since 1850.* Seattle: University of Washington Press.

Daniels, R. (1993). *Prisoners without trial—Japanese Americans in World War II.* New York: Hill and Wang.

Das, A. K., & Kemp, S. F., (1997). Between two worlds: Counseling South Asian Americans. *Journal of Multicultural Counseling and Development, 25,* 23–33.

Espiritu, Y. L., & Omi, M. (2000). "Who are you calling Asian?" Shifting identity claims, racial classifications, and the census. In P. M. Ong (Ed.), *The state of Asian Pacific America: Transforming race relations: A public policy report.* Los Angeles: LEAP Asian Pacific American Public Policy Institute and the UCLA Asian American Studies Center.

Fischer, S. R. (2002). *A history of the Pacific Islands.* New York: Palgrave.

Fong, T. P. (2002). *The contemporary Asian American experience* (2nd ed.). Upper Saddle River, NJ: Prentice Hall.

Fuchs, L. (1961). *Hawaiian pono: A social history of Hawaii.* New York: Harcourt, Brace and World.

Furutani, W. (1981). The Commission on Wartime Relocation and Internment of Civilians: Selected testimonies from Los Angeles and San Francisco hearings. *Amerasia, 8,* 101–105.

Haidar, S. (2004, March 14). *Powell tackles hot topic in India.* CNN.com, World Business. Retrieved February 16, 2006, from http://www.cnn.com/2004/BUSINESS/03/16/india.outsourcing/index.html

Hansen, A. A., & Mitson, B. E. (1974). *Voices long silent: An oral inquiry into the Japanese American evacuation.* Fullerton: California State University Oral History Program.

Higham, J. (1955). *Strangers in the land.* New Brunswick, NJ: Rutgers University Press.

Hong, G. K., & Ham, M. D. C. (2001). *Psychotherapy with Asian American clients: A practical guide.* Thousand Oaks, CA: Sage.

Ibrahim, F., Ohnishi, H., & Sandhu, D. (1997). Asian American identity development: A culture specific model for South Asian Americans. *Journal of Multicultural Counseling and Development, 25,* 34–50.

Inman, A. G., & Tewari. N. (2003). The power of context: Counseling South Asians within a family context. In G. Roysircar, D. S. Sandhu, & V. B. Bibbins (Eds*.),* *A guidebook: Practices of multicultural competencies* (pp. 97–107). Alexandria, VA: American Counseling Association.

Inman, A. G., Yeh, C. J, Madan-Bahel A., & Nath, S. (2005). *A qualitative exploration of the post 9/11 bereavement and coping of South Asian families.* Unpublished manuscript, Lehigh University, Bethlehem, PA.

Jayadev, R. (2001, November 23). Leadership vacuum in Silicon Valley. Pacific News Service. Retrieved May 4, 2005, from http://model minorty.com/modules.php?name=News&file=article&sid=52

Jones, J. M. (1997). *Prejudice and racism* (2nd ed.). New York: McGraw-Hill.

Kasindorf, M., Chin, P., Weathers, D., Foltz, K., Shapiro, D., & Junkin, D. (1982, December 6). Asian Americans: A "model minority." *Newsweek,* 39ff.

Kaste, M. (2005, August 16). Native Hawaiians seek self-rule. On National Public Radio's *Morning Edition.* Retrieved September 5, 2005, from http://www.npr.org/templates/story/story.php?storyId=4801431

Kitano, H. H. L., & Daniels, R. (1995). *Asian Americans: Emerging minorities* (2nd ed.). Englewood Cliffs, NJ: Prentice Hall.

Lal, V. (1999). *A political history of Asian Indians in the United States.* Retrieved May 6, 2005, from http://www.punjabilok.com/heritage/political_history_asian_indians_united_states.htm.

Lee, E. (1996). Chinese families. In M. McGoldrick, J. Giordano, & J. K. Pearce (Eds.), *Ethnicity and family therapy* (2nd ed., pp. 249–267). Thousand Oaks, CA: Sage.

Lee, L. C. (1998). Overview. In L. C. Lee & N. W. S. Zane (Eds.), *Handbook of Asian American psychology* (pp. 1–20). Thousand Oaks, CA: Sage.

Lee, W. H. (2001). *My country versus me.* New York: Hyperion.

Leonard, K. I. (1997). *The South Asian Americans.* Westport, CT: Greenwood Press.

Leong, R.C., & Nakanishi, D.T. (Eds.). (2002). *Asian Americans on war and peace.* Los Angeles: UCLA Asian American Studies Center Press.

Lommel, J. (April, 2004). *Feeling outsourced and outsmarted in your job search? Here are 6 trends to help you succeed.* In NetWorking with Jane Lommel. Retrieved May 12, 2005, from http://www.newwork.com/Pages/Networking/2004/Fear%20of%20outsourcing.html

Mass, A. I. (1991). Psychological effects of the camps on the Japanese Americans. In R. Daniels, S. C. Taylor, & H. H. L. Kitano (Eds.), *Japanese Americans: From relocation to redress* (Rev. ed., pp. 159–162). Seattle: University of Washington Press.

Matsumoto, V. (1984). Japanese American women during World War II. *Frontiers, 8,* 6–14.

Maykovitch, M. K. (1972). *Japanese American identity dilemma.* Tokyo: Waseda University Press.

Mio, J. S. (2003). Modern forms of resistance to multiculturalism: Keeping our eyes on the prize. In J. S. Mio & G. Y. Iwamasa (Eds.), *Culturally diverse mental health: The challenges of research and resistance* (pp. 3–16). New York: Brunner/Routledge.

Mio, J. S., & Awakuni, G. I. (2000). *Resistance to multiculturalism: Issues and interventions.* Philadelphia: Brunner/Mazel.

Miyoshi, N. (1980, December 19–26). Identity crisis of the Sansei and the American concentration camp. *Pacific Citizen,* pp. 41–41, 50, 55.

Morishima, J. (1973). The evacuation: Impact on the family. In S. Sue & N. N. Wagner (Eds.), *Asian Americans: Psychological perspectives* (pp. 13–19). Palo Alto, CA: Science & Behavior Books.

Mura, D. (1991). *Turning Japanese: Memoirs of a Sansei.* New York: Atlantic Monthly.

Myers, D. G. (2005). *Social psychology* (8th ed.). Boston: McGraw-Hill.

Nagata, D. K. (1990). The Japanese American internment: Exploring the transgenerational consequences of traumatic stress. *Journal of Traumatic Stress, 3,* 47–69.

Nagata, D. K. (1993). *Legacy of silence: Exploring the cross-generational impact of the Japanese American internment.* New York: Plenum.

Nagata, D. K. (1998). Internment and intergenerational relations. In L. C. Lee & N. W. S. Zane (Eds.), *Handbook of Asian American psychology* (pp. 433–456). Thousand Oaks, CA: Sage.

Petersen, W. (1966, January 9). Success story: Japanese-American style. *New York Times Magazine,* p. 21.

Pluralism Project. (2005). *Dot busters in New Jersey.* Retrieved May 17, 2005, from http://www.pluralism.org/ocg/CDROM_files/hinduism/dot_busters.php

Rai, S. (2004, February 9). Indians fearing repercussions of U.S. technology outsourcing. *The New York Times,* p. C4.

Rao, R. N. (1999). *Disjunctured identity of Indian Americans: Part I.* Retrieved April 29, 2005, from http://rameshnrao.com/culture-disjunctured-1.html

Richman, S. (2004, April). Outside view: Fear and outsourcing. *The Washington Times.* Retrieved May 2, 2005, from http://washingtontimes.com/upi breaking/20040415–125514–8237r.htm

Riggs, F. W. (1950). *Pressures on Congress: A study of the repeal of Chinese exclusion.* New York: King's Crown.

Rivlin, G. (2000). Busting the myth of meritocracy. *In model minority: A guide to empowerment.* Industry News. Retrieved April 14, 2005, from http://modelminority.com/modules.php?name=News&file=article&sid=101

Sandhu, D. S., Kaur, K. P, & Tewari, N. (1999). Acculturative experiences of Asian and Pacific Islander Americans: Considerations for counseling and psychotherapy. In D. S. Sandhu (Ed.), *Asian and Pacific Islander Americans: Issues and concerns for counseling and psychotherapy,* (pp. 3–20). New York: Nova Science.

Senate to consider Akaka bill vote in September. (2005). Retrieved September 5, 2005, from http://www.nativehawaiians.com

Sheth, M. (1995). Asian Indian Americans. In P. G. Min (Ed.), *Asian Americans: Contemporary trends and issues* (pp. 169–198). Thousand Oaks, CA: Sage.

Success story of one minority group in the United States. (1966, December 26). *U.S. News and World Report,* 73–76.

Suzuki, B. H. (1977). Education and the socialization of Asian Americans: A revisionist analysis of the "model minority" thesis. *Amerasia Journal, 4,* 23–51.

Suzuki, B. H. (1989, November/December). Asian Americans as the "model minority": Outdoing Whites? Or media hype? *Change,* 12–19.

Suzuki, B. H. (2002). Revisiting the model minority stereotypes: Implications for student affairs practice and higher education. In M. K. McEwen, C. M. Kodama, A. N. Alvarez, S. Lee, & C. T. H. Liang (Eds.), *Working with Asian American college students* (pp. 21–32). San Francisco: Jossey-Bass.

Takaki, R. T. (1998). *A larger memory: A history of our diversity, with voices.* Boston: Little, Brown.

Tewari, N. (2000). *Asian Indian Americans clients presenting at a university counseling center: An exploration of their concerns and a comparison to other groups.* Unpublished doctoral dissertation, Southern Illinois University, Carbondale.

Tewari, N., Inman, A. G., & Sandhu, D. S. (2003). South Asian Americans: Culture, concerns and therapeutic strategies. In J. Mio & G. Iwamasa (Eds.), *Culturally diverse mental health: The challenges of research and resistance* (pp. 191–209). New York: Brunner/Routledge.

Uba, L. (1994). *Asian Americans: Personality patterns, identity and mental health.* New York: Guilford Press.

Yamamoto, M. (2001, August 14). *So much for a colorblind meritocracy.* CNET News.Com. Retrieved February 16, 2006, from http://news.com.com/So+much+for+a+colorblind+meritocracy/2010-1071_3-281531.html

Young, K., & Takeuchi, D. T. (1998). Racism. In L. C. Lee & N. W. S. Zane (Eds.), *Handbook of Asian American psychology* (pp. 401–432). Thousand Oaks, CA: Sage.

Appendix A

WESTERN DEFENSE COMMAND AND FOURTH ARMY
WARTIME CIVIL CONTROL ADMINISTRATION

Presidio of San Francisco, California
May 3, 1942

INSTRUCTIONS
TO ALL PERSONS OF
JAPANESE
ANCESTRY

Living in the Following Area:

All of that portion of the City of Los Angeles, State of California, within that boundary beginning at the point at which North Figueroa Street meets a line following the middle of the Los Angeles River; thence southerly and following the said line to East First Street; thence westerly on East First Street to Alameda Street; thence southerly on Alameda Street to East Third Street; thence northwesterly on East Third Street to Main Street; thence northerly on Main Street to First Street; thence northwesterly on First Street to Figueroa Street; thence northeasterly on Figueroa Street to the point of beginning.

Pursuant to the provisions of Civilian Exclusion Order No. 33, this Headquarters, dated May 3, 1942, all persons of Japanese ancestry, both alien and non-alien, will be evacuated from the above area by 12 o'clock noon, P. W. T., Saturday, May 9, 1942.

No Japanese person living in the above area will be permitted to change residence after 12 o'clock noon, P. W. T., Sunday, May 3, 1942, without obtaining special permission from the representative of the Commanding General, Southern California Sector, at the Civil Control Station located at:

> Japanese Union Church,
> 120 North San Pedro Street,
> Los Angeles, California.

Such permits will only be granted for the purpose of uniting members of a family, or in cases of grave emergency.

The Civil Control Station is equipped to assist the Japanese population affected by this evacuation in the following ways:

1. Give advice and instructions on the evacuation.
2. Provide services with respect to the management, leasing, sale, storage or other disposition of most kinds of property, such as real estate, business and professional equipment, household goods, boats, automobiles and livestock.
3. Provide temporary residence elsewhere for all Japanese in family groups.
4. Transport persons and a limited amount of clothing and equipment to their new residence.

The Following Instructions Must Be Observed:

1. A responsible member of each family, preferably the head of the family, or the person in whose name most of the property is held, and each individual living alone, will report to the Civil Control Station to receive further instructions. This must be done between 8:00 A. M. and 5:00 P. M. on Monday, May 4, 1942, or between 8:00 A. M. and 5:00 P. M. on Tuesday, May 5, 1942.
2. Evacuees must carry with them on departure for the Assembly Center, the following property:
    (a) Bedding and linens (no mattress) for each member of the family;
    (b) Toilet articles for each member of the family;
    (c) Extra clothing for each member of the family;
    (d) Sufficient knives, forks, spoons, plates, bowls and cups for each member of the family;
    (e) Essential personal effects for each member of the family.

All items carried will be securely packaged, tied and plainly marked with the name of the owner and numbered in accordance with instructions obtained at the Civil Control Station. The size and number of packages is limited to that which can be carried by the individual or family group.

3. No pets of any kind will be permitted.
4. No personal items and no household goods will be shipped to the Assembly Center.
5. The United States Government through its agencies will provide for the storage, at the sole risk of the owner, of the more substantial household items, such as iceboxes, washing machines, pianos and other heavy furniture. Cooking utensils and other small items will be accepted for storage if crated, packed and plainly marked with the name and address of the owner. Only one name and address will be used by a given family.
6. Each family, and individual living alone, will be furnished transportation to the Assembly Center or will be authorized to travel by private automobile in a supervised group. All instructions pertaining to the movement will be obtained at the Civil Control Station.

Go to the Civil Control Station between the hours of 8:00 A. M. and 5:00 P. M., Monday, May 4, 1942, or between the hours of 8:00 A. M. and 5:00 P. M., Tuesday, May 5, 1942, to receive further instructions.

> J. L. DeWITT
> Lieutenant General, U. S. Army
> Commanding

SEE CIVILIAN EXCLUSION ORDER NO. 33

Appendix B

[December, 2002]

IMPORTANT NOTICE
'SPECIAL REGISTRATION'

The **Department of Justice** now requires certain people to **appear at an INS office** for 'Special Registration.' Those who miss the deadline face a **serious risk of being detained and/or made deportable and inadmissible**. Please examine the requirements below carefully. If you are **clearly not** among the groups required to appear, it is not advisable to appear. If you think that you have violated your current status or have any uncertainty, consult with an immigration attorney prior to registering. You are entitled to bring a lawyer to your interview.

WHO IS REQUIRED TO APPEAR?

GROUP 1:   Male nationals or citizens of:

IRAN   IRAQ   LIBYA   SUDAN   SYRIA

Born on or before Nov 15, 1986 and
arrived in the US on or before Sep 10, 2002 and
staying in the US at least until Dec 16, 2002

REGISTRATION DEADLINE: DECEMBER 16, 2002

GROUP 2: Male nationals or citizens of:

SOMALIA, AFGHANISTAN, ALGERIA, BAHRAIN, ERITREA, LEBANON, MOROCCO, NORTH KOREA, OMAN, QATAR, TUNISIA, UNITED ARAB EMIRATES, YEMEN

Born on or before Dec 2, 1986 and
arrived in the US on or before Sep 30, 2002 and
staying in the US at least until Jan 10, 2003

****REGISTRATION DEADLINE: JANUARY 10, 2003****

GROUP 3: Male nationals or citizens of:

PAKISTAN, SAUDI ARABIA

Born on or before Jan 13, 1987 and
arrived in the US on or before Sep 30, 2002 and
staying in the US at least until Feb 21, 2003.

****REGISTRATION BETWEEN JANUARY 13 AND FEBRUARY 21, 2003****

THE FOLLOWING APPLIES TO ALL GROUPS:

EXCEPTIONS: (Those who do NOT have to register)
- US citizens
- Lawful Permanent Residents
- Refugees and Asylees
- Asylum seekers who applied for asylum on or before Nov 6, 2002 (Group 1)
                                        on or before Nov 22, 2002 (Groups 2 & 3)
- Diplomats and their dependents / Those admitted under A or G visa

THE REQUIREMENTS ARE:
Appear at an INS office Monday through Friday. The Seattle facility, 815 Airport Way South, is open Wed 10:30 to 2:30; Mon, Tue, Thu, and Fri from 7:30 to 2:30. You will have to wait in line, but tell the guard you are there for special registration. At the interview, you will be photographed and fingerprinted. The INS may ask you questions about your status as well as personal information such as your name, address, etc.

BRING WITH YOU:
- Travel Documents, including your passport, I-94, and any other form of government-issued ID
- Proof of residence in the US: printed mail with your address or your host's address, lease agreement, etc.
- If you are on a student visa, proof you are attending school
- If you are on a work visa, proof you are working
- An interpreter if you need one – interpretation is not provided

DO NOT bring extra materials. The INS may inspect any of your belongings.

NEXT YEAR: If you are still in the US, you will be required to appear again each year between 10 days before and after the one year anniversary of your initial registration.
  Example: If you registered Dec 10, 2002, you need to appear every year between Nov 30 and Dec 20.

IF YOU MOVE, CHANGE JOBS OR SCHOOLS: You have only 10 days to notify the INS by certified mail with form AR-11 SR. (www.ins.usdoj.gov)
  ALWAYS KEEP A COPY FOR YOUR RECORDS!

TRAVELING
These regulations affect your travel plans to other nations. There are only 18 ports you may leave the US through. At these ports, you must notify the INS in person of your departure. You will be interviewed, photographed and fingerprinted each time you return to the US. Please consult www.ins.usdoj.gov or call 1-800-375-5283 for a list of designated ports or for more information.

21

FAMILY VIOLENCE AMONG ASIAN AMERICANS

IRENE J. KIM

ANNA S. LAU

DORIS F. CHANG

The right to be free from domestic violence or threat of domestic violence is a fundamental and universal human right.

United Nations Office
at Vienna (1993, p. 11)

The power of naming is at least twofold: naming defines the quality and value of that which is named. . . . That which has no name, that for which we have no words or concepts, is rendered mute and invisible: powerless to inform or transform our consciousness or our experience, our understanding, our vision; powerless to claim its own existence. . . . This has been the situation of women [and children] in our world.

Du Bois (1983, p. 106)

Although Asian American families have shown considerable strength and resilience through their varied experiences in adapting to different cultural and environmental contexts in the United States, they have also encountered problems that are often left un-named. One such problem is that of family violence. Through mounting advocacy and intervention efforts, the women's movement, media attention, and research efforts, the problem of family violence has gained national and international attention over the past three decades. Our general aim in this chapter is to specifically name many of the challenging issues involved in family violence among Asian Americans. Although family violence covers many types of physical, sexual, emotional, financial, and psychological abuse among various members of the kinship system, we focus primarily on intimate partner violence and child abuse in Asian American communities. Specifically, we examine the following issues with regard to intimate partner violence and child abuse: (a) the scope and significance of these problems, (b) factors that may be especially salient for Asian Americans, and (c) empirical research on variables that increase risk for these two types of family violence. By naming these problems, we hope to contribute to the growing literature on intimate partner violence and child abuse among Asian Americans and to break the silence that often shrouds Asian American communities around issues of family violence.

Intimate Partner Violence[1]

Scope and Significance of the Problem in the General Population

Intimate partner violence is a serious problem in the United States. Approximately 1.8 million women are physically beaten by an intimate partner each year (Straus & Gelles, 1990). Lifetime prevalence rates of intimate partner violence for women range from 9% to 34% (Browne, 1993; Tjaden & Thoennes, 2000). According to the National Crime Victimization Survey, women, compared to men, are six times more likely to be victimized by an intimate partner (Bachman & Saltzman, 1995).

These statistics are corroborated by findings from the National Violence Against Women Survey, the largest national probability sample study to date with 8,000 men and 8,000 women (Tjaden & Thoennes, 2000). Lifetime prevalence rates of physical violence for women were 20.4%, and for men 7.0%; that is, women were significantly (2.9 times) more likely than men to report being victimized by a current or former spouse or by an opposite-sex cohabitating partner. Annual prevalence rates of physical assault for women have ranged from 1.4% to 12% (Tjaden & Thoennes, 2000; Straus, 1977–1978; Straus & Gelles, 1986). Some of the variance in annual prevalence rates may be due to the framing of questions in these surveys.[2] These alarming statistics reveal only the tip of the iceberg, however, due to both underreporting of intimate partner violence and limitations inherent in different sampling methods. Individuals (e.g., both the batterers and the victims) typically avoid reporting occurrences of abuse because it is socially undesirable or stigmatized. Such social desirability factors often lead to underreporting, such that estimates of intimate partner violence are often lower than they are in reality.

When women are assaulted by their intimate partners, consequences are severe and encompass psychological and physical sequelae, including death (Bachman & Saltzman, 1995). Psychological effects of wife battering in women include lowered self-esteem, depression, suicidal ideation and attempts, alcohol and other substance abuse, and post-traumatic stress disorder (Holtzworth-Munroe, Smutzler, & Sandin, 1997; National Research Council, 1996). Tjaden and Thoennes (2000) also found that women who are physically assaulted are significantly more likely than their male counterparts to incur injuries, require medical treatment and mental health services, experience loss of time from work, place a restraining order, and report that the perpetrator was prosecuted.

Not only are women affected, but children who witness parental violence also suffer psychological and behavioral consequences (Rosenberg & Rossman, 1990), as manifested by the pattern of intergenerational transmission of violence (e.g., Kaufman Kantor & Jasinski, 1998). Witnessing parental aggression or experiencing abuse as a teenager in the family-of-origin has been significantly related to marital aggression in the next generation (Kalmuss, 1984). Children who are exposed to domestic violence are also at significantly higher risk for developing comorbid (both externalizing and internalizing) psychological disorders (Jaffee, Moffitt, Caspi, Taylor, & Arseneault, 2002).

Intimate Partner Violence Among Asian Americans

Although the problem of domestic violence has begun to garner the attention it deserves, some groups have remained "hidden" to both researchers and care providers. Asian Americans are one such population, particularly in the area of wife battering. This is apparent in the paucity of empirical research conducted on intimate partner violence among Asian Americans. At the community level, silence perpetuates a similar perception that wife battering is not a major concern. For example, Dasgupta and Warrier (1996) reported that the South Asian community "turns a blind eye to many troublesome issues . . . [and] has denied abuse of women in particular" (p. 240). However, there is mounting evidence that wife battering is a significant concern in Asian American communities (e.g., Dasgupta, 2000; J. Y. Kim & Sung, 2000; Lum, 1998; Tran & DesJardins, 2000; Yoshihama, 1999), demanding immediate attention.

Currently, no nationally representative studies have yet examined prevalence rates for domestic violence among Asian Americans. However, several smaller-scale studies have estimated the prevalence of wife abuse in various Asian ethnic groups. For example, Yoshihama (1999) found a lifetime prevalence rate of 33.6% among women of Japanese descent in Los Angeles using standardized measures (i.e., the Conflict Tactics Scale developed by Straus and Gelles). However, using a new contextualized method for assessing physical violence, Yoshihama found a lower prevalence rate of 26.5% for Japanese women in the United States. One critical lesson from this study is that current measures of physical violence may not capture culturally rooted forms of intimate partner violence. Yoshihama stressed the importance of considering the participants' perceptions of abuse and their own meaning systems because there are sociocultural variations in how intimate partner violence is perceived and manifested. For example, in Yoshihama's (1999) study, she included items from a previous study in Japan that inquired about throwing water on the woman or overturning the dining table, because these acts are perceived to be abusive in the Japanese cultural context.

Song (1996) found that 60% of the Korean immigrant women ($N = 150$) sampled in her survey reported being abused by her partner in the past year. Song used a snowball sampling method, as well as local directories in the Chicago area, to obtain these participants. Given the biased sampling method, definitive conclusions cannot be reached about whether or not prevalence rates in Chicago are higher than those of nationally representative samples; however, Song's study demonstrates that wife battering does indeed exist within the Korean immigrant community. In a more recent study, J. Y. Kim and Sung (2000) found high rates of severe marital violence between Korean American husbands and wives, with 6.3% of husbands (compared to 1.5% of husbands in a nationally representative sample) committing severe[3] acts of violence against their wives (Straus & Gelles, 1986).

One of the fastest-growing areas of research in intimate partner violence is research on the South Asian community. For example, Ahmad, Riaz, Barata, and Stewart (2004) found that 24.1% of women in their sample ($N = 47$ South Asian women) reported physical abuse in the past five years. Dasgupta's (2000) historical overview of the domestic violence movement in the South Asian American community helps shed light on the progress made, as well as the unresolved issues and unmet needs that this community continues to face.

Another study (Tran, 1997) estimated a lifetime prevalence rate of 53% for domestic violence among Vietnamese female refugees and immigrants ($N = 30$) in Boston, as well as a current prevalence rate of 37%. These participants were recruited consecutively through a local civic association based on the following criteria: (a) currently living with a partner (or had lived with a partner during the past year) and (b) speaks Vietnamese fluently. Thus, domestic violence prevalence rates may be higher than (even twice as high as) the rate cited for the general U. S. population; yet, without comparable sampling strategies, valid conclusions are difficult to draw. Nevertheless, these studies at least reveal the existence, if not urgency, of the problem of domestic violence in Asian American families.

Given the international and national scope of the problem of violence against women, and more specifically, the issue of wife battering, identification of the causes of the problem is an important issue for researchers. Identification of correlates and predictors of intimate partner violence for specific populations allows for the design of empirically based prevention and intervention programs that are more culturally sensitive. Although past theories of intimate partner violence have tended to focus on single causes, more current models, based on ecological and systemic paradigms, are more integrative and account for multiple factors in the risk context. These integrative models often incorporate psychological, family, and macrosocial variables that are especially useful in studying ethnic minority populations such as Asian Americans and can help elucidate some of the factors that may increase risk for intimate partner violence.

The Context of Risk for Intimate Partner Violence in Asian American Communities

Although researchers have identified risk factors for family violence in the general population, less empirical research has been conducted on sources of vulnerability for Asian Americans. In this section, we examine the unique ecology of intimate partner violence among Asian Americans by considering two themes in the literature. First, the stressors involved in immigration and acculturation may increase vulnerability to intimate partner violence.[4] Second, traditional attitudes toward marriage and gender roles may perpetuate patriarchal norms related to risk.

The context of immigration and acculturative stress. Acculturation has been broadly defined as "the changes in cultural attitudes, values, and behaviors due to contact between two cultures" (Berry, Trimble, & Olemedo, 1986). Song (1996) found that acculturation level is related to domestic violence among Asian Americans, with more recent immigrant women experiencing higher levels of intimate partner violence three to five years after their arrival in the United States. *Acculturative stress* results when the process of acculturation, often fraught with multiple stressors, causes problems for individuals or groups (Berry, 1998). For instance, as Asian families immigrate and adjust to a new country, they may encounter physical, material, cognitive, and affective stressors (Shon & Ja, 1992). Recent immigrants are faced with language barriers, limited economic resources, lack of familiarity with service systems, minority status and related prejudice/discrimination/racism, changes in gender roles, clashing cultural values, and social isolation. As found in earlier studies (see review by Tolman & Bennett, 1990), higher stress levels are indirectly related to higher levels of intimate partner violence.

Some salient immigration-related stressors in Asian American communities dealing with intimate partner violence include premigration and migration trauma, status inconsistency, traditional gender role expectations, social isolation, and alcohol abuse. Premigration and migration trauma are highlighted in the domestic violence literature, especially for Vietnamese refugee women. The importance of assessing their preimmigration experiences, particularly given the traumas of fleeing a war-torn country and witnessing the atrocities of war, has been raised in some reports (Norton & Manson, 1992; Tran, 1997). Other studies have noted the possible connection between the occurrence of a recent war and higher levels of family violence (Archer & Gartner, 1976).

Status inconsistency occurs when an individual's preimmigration level of education or occupation is inconsistent with his or her current occupation. Increased tensions between partners, resulting from one partner's status inconsistency, may contribute to intimate partner violence (e.g., Hornung, McCullough, & Sugimoto, 1981). Yick (2001) argues for the applicability of status inconsistency theory to Asian immigrant families in the context of immigration and the accompanying stresses of downward mobility, especially for husbands. For example, Song (1996) found that status inconsistency in male batterers, compared to nonbattering men, is associated with wife abuse in Korean immigrant families. That is, significantly more battering men in Song's study had lower employment levels after immigration as compared to nonabusive men.

Traditional gender role expectations may also cause stress within the marital subsystem, especially when these gender roles no longer fit the immigrant family's circumstances once they are in the United States. Moreover, husbands and wives may experience differential acculturation rates, producing discrepancies in their gender role beliefs. For example, in a study by Bui and Morash (1999), Vietnamese women reported that their husbands tended to adhere strongly to traditional Vietnamese gender roles, whereas the majority of women themselves indicated that they did not. As clashing gender role expectations increase marital stress, the risk for marital violence may also increase.

Another immigration-related stressor is social isolation. There are some data to suggest that isolation in and of itself can be a form of marital violence (Abraham, 2000). Some quantitative data reveal that an abused woman's lack of social contact is related to her inability to leave the abusive situation. Song's (1996) results reveal a significant difference between battered versus nonbattered women in their frequency of going out, participation in clubs/organizations, and frequency of talking to friends/relatives, with battered women being more socially isolated than nonbattered women. This result has been seen in the general literature as well (cf. Walker, 1979).

Alcohol use and abuse, which may be one way of coping with the stress of immigration and adaptation, have been linked to the physical abuse of wives in the general domestic violence literature (e.g., Hotaling & Sugarman, 1990). In the Asian American community, this association has been observed in Vietnamese (Tran, 1997) and Korean immigrant samples (Rhee, 1997). Abused women reported a higher frequency of partner drinking behavior, when compared to nonabused women, and a significant positive relationship was found between severity of verbal abuse and frequency of partner drinking (Tran, 1997). Rhee (1997) noted "a strong relationship between drinking and wife battering in Korean immigrant families" (p. 72). She made a cultural argument by citing high tolerance and permissiveness toward male drinking in Korean culture (Chi, Lubben, & Kitano, 1989).

Whereas the bulk of the research reviewed thus far involves victims of domestic violence, alcohol use represents a perpetrator-linked characteristic. Almost no published studies are available that focus on Asian American male batterers, and more research is certainly needed. One exception is a study by I. J. Kim and Zane (2004), which examined risk factors for intimate partner violence among Korean American and European American male batterers. One of their key findings is that the effect of ethnicity on anger regulation (a risk factor for battering) is mediated by culturally based self-construal (i.e., independent self-construal). This study underscores the importance of examining culturally based variables when examining vulnerability for intimate partner violence among Asian Americans.

The context of patriarchal ideology. Some Confucian-based teachings about marriage and traditional gender roles may be conducive to perpetuating patriarchal norms, which, in turn, are associated with greater tolerance of intimate partner violence (Ahmad et al., 2004; Yoshioka, DiNoia, & Ullah, 2001). Within the Asian family structure, specific roles and obligations are prescribed for different family members according to cultural values rooted in Confucianism (Uba, 1994). For example, Confucian teachings exhort a woman to follow a doctrine of "three obediences" during her lifetime: to obey her father before marriage, her husband after marriage, and her son after her husband's death (Chan & Leong, 1994). Self-sacrifice, silent suffering, and perseverance are held up as valued virtues for women (C. K. Ho, 1990), especially in marriage because "divorce is rare and brings family shame" (E. Lee, 1989, p. 105). Gender role expectations are equally strong for men. In Asian families, the father is expected to be the family's provider and tends to be the dominant authority figure (Uba, 1994).

In a review of the general literature on domestic violence, Feldman and Ridley (1995) noted mixed findings on the associations between sex-role expectations and wife battering. For example, some research (Hotaling & Sugarman, 1986) has found that men's traditional sex-role expectations and male-dominated decision making are "consistently unrelated" to wife assault. However, other investigators have found positive associations (Finn, 1986) between traditional sex role preferences and attitudes supporting domestic violence. Thus, the consistent findings of associations between domestic violence and rigid sex-role adherence among Asian Americans appear to be somewhat unique, in that the general domestic violence literature findings are more ambiguous. This discrepancy between findings among Asian Americans and White Americans highlights the importance of considering the effects of immigration and acculturation, especially with regard to gender role expectations.

Traditional attitudes toward marriage also may perpetuate patriarchal norms (C. K. Ho, 1990). Within patriarchal societies, marriage is male dominated, and the female is looked on as the husband's property or possession (Almirol, 1982; Cimmarusti, 1996; Dasgupta & Warrier, 1996). Wives tend to believe that they have no rights to property, wealth, or their own children

(Ayyub, 2000; Dasgupta & Warrier, 1996; C. K. Ho, 1990). Additionally, traditional marriages are often prearranged to safeguard family prosperity and to extend the male's patrilineage rather than to vouchsafe romantic love (E. Lee, 1989). When a woman marries, she is to leave her family-of-origin to join her husband and her in-laws. Overall, these traditional attitudes toward marriage reinforce the notion of lack of control or power.

Patriarchal beliefs can also shape whether or not an Asian American woman perceives an act to be abusive (e.g., Ahmad et al., 2004). For instance, given a story to read about a South Asian immigrant woman who sustained an injury during an argument with her husband, women who agreed with patriarchal norms (e.g., a man should decide whether or not his wife should work outside the home) were less likely to label this scenario as spousal abuse (Ahmad et al., 2004). As Huisman (1996) noted, the patriarchal ideology embedded in cultural norms has sanctioned or minimized the problem of domestic violence in the Asian American community.

Power differentials between the sexes may also result from, and perpetuate, patriarchal norms (Abraham, 1995; Bui & Morash, 1999; Campbell, 1992; Dasgupta & Warrier, 1996; C. K. Ho, 1990; Huisman, 1996; J. Y. Kim & Sung, 2000; Song, 1996; Tran, 1997; Yim, 1978). J. Y. Kim and Sung (2000) examined the marital power differentials in Korean American couples and found that male-dominant marriages incurred the highest rates of violence, with 33% of these couples experiencing at least one physical assault within the past year.

In sum, the contexts of immigration and patriarchal ideology are important variables to consider in the examination of intimate partner violence among Asian Americans. However, most of the studies reviewed tend to be more descriptive than explanatory and, thus, are limited in their ability to shed light on *why* intimate partner violence occurs among Asian Americans. Although useful, the concept of acculturative stress has not been explicitly linked to any underlying models of intimate partner violence. Nevertheless, these studies point to the need to carefully account for cultural orientations and varying levels of acculturation in future research on risk factors for intimate partner violence among Asian Americans.

Emerging Research on Intimate Partner Violence Among Asian Americans

In a recent investigation (Chang, Shen, & Takeuchi, 2005), associations between immigration-related stressors and risk for domestic violence were examined in 1,470 married or cohabitating Asian Americans using a sample from the larger National Latino and Asian American Study (NLAAS). The NLAAS is the first nationally representative community epidemiological household survey that estimates the prevalence of mental disorders, social problems, and rates of service utilization by Latinos and Asian Americans in the United States (Alegria et al., 2004). Participants were predominantly immigrants (84.2%), married (93.6%), and approximately 44% had a high school level of education or higher. The diverse sample included Asian Americans of Vietnamese (24.4%), Filipino (22.0%), Chinese (25.9%), and other Asian ancestry (21.0%).

One surprising finding is that, in general, both male and female respondents were more likely to admit being a perpetrator rather than a victim of violence, contradicting previous research on the general population (e.g., Kessler, Molnar, Feuer, Appelbaum, 2001). This finding lends some support to the notion that domestic violence may be more normalized in Asian American communities due to cultural traditions that view it as an acceptable response to norm violations within the marital relationship. Additional analyses provide empirical support for the role that family-level acculturation processes play in risk for intimate partner violence among Asian Americans, in general, and Asian American women, in particular.

Specifically, two aspects of the family cultural climate were found to be positively related to risk for minor violence: household gender role division and family conflict. First, a more traditional division of decision-making power (with women having less power) was associated with women's decreased risk for *perpetrating* intimate partner violence, as expected. However, a more traditional division of household chores (with women bearing greater responsibility) was associated with women's increased risk for being both a perpetrator and victim of violence. In contrast, there was no relationship between household gender role division and minor violence for men. Second, as acculturation-related family conflict increased, the risk for committing and being a victim of minor violence increased for both men and women.

CHILD PHYSICAL ABUSE

Scope and Significance of the Problem in the General Population

It is widely accepted that child physical abuse poses a major threat to public health. The psychological sequelae of physical abuse are widely recognized, with elevated risk for psychiatric diagnoses among victims across the life span (Cohen, Brown, & Smailes, 2001). For example, physically abused children and adult victims of childhood abuse have increased rates of depression (e.g., Bemporad & Romano, 1992; Brown, Cohen, Johnson, & Smailes, 1999) and anxiety disorders (e.g., Flisher, Kramer, Hoven, & Greenwald, 1997). Perhaps the most compelling longitudinal evidence is the link between childhood physical abuse and aggression and conduct problems (e.g., Dodge, Pettit, & Bates, 1997). Indeed, abuse broadly compromises public safety through increased antisocial behavior, violence, delinquency, and adult criminality among victims (e.g., Jaffee, Caspi, Moffitt, & Taylor, 2004; Widom, 1989).

Furthermore, the impact of child physical abuse on physical health is only recently beginning to be understood. Beyond immediate physical injuries, child physical abuse victimization is associated also with numerous chronic illnesses and health impairments throughout the life span (Goodwin & Stein, 2004; Sachs-Ericsson, Blazer, Plant, & Arnow, 2005); it also is a leading cause of mortality (Felitti et al., 1998). Given these far-reaching consequences of child physical abuse, it is perhaps not surprising that the annual societal cost of child abuse is estimated to exceed $72 billion, incurred by health care, judicial, and correctional systems alone (Fromm, 2001).

The scope of this public health problem can be described as epidemic. In 2003, nearly 149,000 children were identified as victims of physical abuse by child protective services (CPS), and an estimated 1,500 child fatalities were attributable to child maltreatment (U.S. Department of Health and Human Services, 2005). It is, of course, extremely difficult to estimate the extent of victimization that goes undetected by authorities. The epidemiology of child maltreatment is complex, and estimates of the prevalence of abuse vary widely by data source, which include officially reported and substantiated abuse in child protective services, parent reports of perpetration, and child self-reports of victimization. Thus, there are, as yet, no reliable estimates of the prevalence of the problem among Asian Americans or other racial ethnic groups in the United States. Conclusions about differences in rates of victimization among the major racial ethnic groups are also highly dependent on the data source examined.

Child Physical Abuse Among Asian Americans: Rates of Victimization

Analyses of official reports of maltreatment filed with CPS agencies in the United States yield large and robust racial differences in rates of abuse. The most recent national data, based on counts of substantiated maltreatment reports compared to race-specific child population estimates, indicate that victimization rates are highest for Pacific Islander, American Indian, and African American children (21.4, 21.3, and 20.4 per 1,000 children, respectively). Rates are lower among White and Hispanic children (11.0 and 9.9 per 1,000). Finally, Asian American children had the lowest rate of 2.7 per 1,000 children (U.S. Department of Health and Human Services, 2005). From these data, one might conclude that Asian Americans represent the group at the lowest risk of child abuse. However, these statistics on officially reported abuse may not reflect actual rates of victimization but institutional or community factors that funnel certain minority groups into CPS while others are kept out of the system (Chand, 2000; A. S. Lau et al., 2003). There is compelling evidence that race influences the likelihood of maltreatment reporting (Chasnoff, Landress, &

Barrett, 1990). There has been some speculation that Asian American families may be less likely to make contact with CPS, as community norms regarding reporting may differ. For example, Chinese Americans have been found to be more tolerant of vignettes depicting physical beating as a disciplinary strategy for child misbehavior compared to Whites and Hispanics and report lower willingness to report offending parents to authorities (Hong & Hong, 1991). This conservative classification of physical abuse and reluctance to report abuse has also been noted among Hong Kong Chinese (J. T. F. Lau, Liu, Yu, & Wong, 1999).

Clearly then, it is problematic to draw conclusions about rates of abuse across racial groups by relying exclusively on official reports of abuse. However, there are few population-based surveys of abuse victimization in the general community, and none has ascertained prevalence or incidence estimates separately for Asian Americans. There have been nonrepresentative surveys of parents focusing on racial ethnic differences in rates of self-reported use of physical punishment. Often, ethnic minority parents, including Asian Americans, acknowledge, more than do White parents, physically aggressive acts toward their children (Straus & Gelles, 1990) and endorse greater acceptance and use of corporal punishment in their child-rearing practices (e.g., Hong & Hong, 1991; Jambunathan, Burts, & Pierce, 2000; Kelley & Tseng, 1992). While Asian Americans report more reliance on physical control, it is difficult to conclude whether these differences constitute higher rates of abuse, per se.

Studies that survey children regarding abuse victimization are less frequent and have often omitted racial/ethnic comparisons (e.g., Brown et al., 1999; MacMillan et al., 1997). One recent exception is the Developmental Victimization Survey, a national telephone survey which found significant racial differences in physical abuse, with victimization rates highest among Hispanic youth and lowest among African American youth (Finkelhor, Ormrod, Turner, & Hamby, 2005). Unfortunately, there was not sufficient representation of Asian American families in the sample to disaggregate them from the "Other" category. The only published study to include separate rates of abuse victimization among Asian Americans

focused on a sample of high-risk youth involved in public health and social services (A. S. Lau et al., 2003). In this survey, no significant racial differences were found in rates of physical abuse. A lifetime history of moderate physical abuse was reported by 23.7% of Whites, 28.3% of African Americans, 21.6% of Hispanics, and 22.0% of Asian Americans. However, these results may only be representative of high-risk groups and not the general community.

Culling these limited sources of data together, there is little convergence on which to draw conclusions regarding the relative risk of child physical abuse among Asian American children and families. This uncertainty stems both from a lack of inclusion of Asian Americans in most epidemiologic surveys of abuse victimization and from the marked variability in findings owing to reliance on different data sources. In comparative studies on parenting Asian American adults report greater frequency and acceptance of physical discipline, indicating the potential for elevated risk of abuse. In contrast, examination of officially reported physical abuse suggests very low rates of victimization among Asian Americans. Finally, the meager data on youth self-reported victimization may suggest levels of abuse comparable to youth from other racial groups.

The Context of Risk for Child Physical Abuse in Asian American Communities

Consistent with the paucity of knowledge about the prevalence of child physical abuse in Asian American communities, there is, likewise, very little known about what might predispose these families to risk. The study of factors that heighten vulnerability in our growing Asian American communities is important for at least two reasons. First, families of Asian descent may bring a diverse range of cultural traditions in child rearing that are related to risk. Second, these families are subject to a variety of stressors in adjusting to the environmental demands of immigration and adaptation.

Cultural orientations regarding child rearing. Some observers have speculated that certain traditions, values, and expectations associated with Asian cultures may exacerbate risk of parental aggression, even physical abuse (Tang, 1998). For example, the traditional Confucian ethic of filial piety (*xiào shùn*)[5] is sometimes interpreted as a dictate that children must be unquestioningly loyal and obedient to their parents and look after their parents' needs (Chan, 1992; Yeh & Bedford, 2004). Socialization in Chinese families may thus focus on training children in proper conduct, impulse control, respect for elders (*jìng lao*), and fulfillment of obligations (*fù zhe rèn*), with less emphasis on children's autonomy and expressiveness (Gorman, 1998; D. Y. F. Ho, 1986). Some observers describe this cultural orientation as parent focused, restrictive, and authoritarian, marked by firm control of the parent over the child (Jose, Huntsinger, Huntsinger, & Liaw, 2000). Tang (1998) suggests that a rigid emphasis on filial piety may be conducive to child abuse by promoting absolute control of the parent over the child.

Asian American parents may share cultural values with parents in Asian nations that may contextualize the use of physical control in discipline. For example, in comparison to White parents, Chinese American parents appear more "authoritarian" (Wang & Phinney, 1998), emphasize achievement expectations (Lin & Fu, 1990), and endorse greater use of restrictive and physical control (Kelley & Tseng, 1992). Therefore, collectivistic values, including an emphasis on shame, filial piety, and use of physical control, are salient for Asian American parents. Surveys of parental attitudes indicate that Asian American parents hold more favorable attitudes toward corporal punishment (Hong & Hong, 1991; Jambunathan et al., 2000) compared to Whites and Hispanics. Given these child-rearing values, there is some concern that Asian American parents may be intolerant of misbehavior and may feel entitled to use harsh physical discipline, without interference from outsiders, to fulfill the parental duty to inculcate morality (Ima & Hohm, 1991).

However, others object to deficit characterizations of Asian parenting and have described traditions that emphasize parental sacrifice, support, and close involvement (Chao, 1994). Indeed, D. Y. F. Ho (1986) observed that Chinese parents promote filial piety in two ways: through the inducement of physical and emotional closeness, ensuring a lifelong bond, and by establishing parental authority and child obedience through strict discipline. Themes of balancing disciplinary responsibilities with parental affection are common across Asian cultures influenced by Confucian tradition (Chan, 1992). Indeed, parental use of force may be seen as reflecting parental devotion (Ima & Hohm, 1991). For example, Park (2001) found that Korean immigrant mothers who reported that children are highly valued in Korean culture also reported more favorable attitudes about physical control of children. Among Korean Americans, child-focused parents place great value in physical punishment for the desirable growth of children (Park, 2001). Given these descriptions, it is possible that the family climate and set of parental motivations in which the use of physical force occurs may be qualitatively different in families of Asian descent.

The immigrant family context. Ecological models of risk for child maltreatment have been widely accepted as holding greater potential to explain and predict the occurrence of child abuse and neglect (National Research Council, 1993). These models represent a move away from the conceptualization of abuse as a function of isolated sets of personal characteristics among offending parents. Ecological models view child abuse within a system of vulnerability and resilience processes interacting across ecological levels, including the parent, the child, the immediate context of parent-child interactions, the community, and the broader society and culture (Belsky, 1993). Therefore, child abuse in Asian American communities may not be well understood by considering only the factors associated with cultural values, beliefs, and preferences. We must look beyond intra-individual cognitions and attitudes at the broader contexts in which families reside.

An important potential source of risk for immigrant families involves the stress inherent in migration, acculturation, and minority status. As discussed previously in the review of intimate partner violence research, distress can stem from a wide range of problems in acculturation, such as communication barriers, lack of understanding of cultural norms, discomfort with individualistic values, lack of social support network, or downward social mobility stemming from loss of status when previous foreign occupational experience and education are unrecognized. High levels of acculturative stress among Asian American families may elevate risk of a variety of adjustment problems including family violence. Acculturative stress among immigrant parents may be associated with a variety of reductions in health status, including anxiety, depression, feelings of marginality, and alienation (C. L. Williams & Berry, 1991).

Furthermore, for many immigrant Asian American families, arrival as newcomers to the United States means that they are socially positioned as members of an ethnic, racial, or linguistic minority group for the first time. Minority status, in turn, is accompanied by new or expanded opportunities for real and perceived discrimination, prejudice, and intergroup tension. There is a large body of literature linking discrimination with mental health problems (Adler, Epel, Castellazzo, & Ickovics, 2000; D. R. Williams, Neighbors, & Jackson, 2003). Because stress and distress generally compromise the quality of parenting behavior, these strains of acculturative stress, minority status, and limited social mobility may contribute to the risk of abuse among immigrant Asian American parents when their coping resources are overwhelmed.

At the level of parent-child interactions, acculturative stress may be experienced as a dyadic or family-wide process. In immigrant families, stress and conflict can arise when parents and children become acculturated at different rates (Farver, Narang, & Bhadha, 2002). Children adapt to host culture language, values, and norms more quickly than do their parents (Szapocznik & Truss, 1978). Immigrant parents may disapprove of their children's adaptation, and conflict may arise between less acculturated parents and their more acculturated children (Szapocznik & Kurtines, 1993). This gulf can widen as parents attempt to restrict the child's acculturation, further alienating the child and precipitating an untimely rejection of the parental culture and fuller adherence to the host culture. The development of these intergenerational acculturation conflicts may be normative in immigrant families; however, the failure to resolve these differences may result in disrupted family relations (R. M. Lee, Choe, Kim, & Ngo,

2000). Furthermore, the risk of physical abuse by parents may be heightened, directly due to a breakdown of effective parenting in the face of this conflict. Indeed, Park (2001) reported that family acculturation conflict was related to the occurrence of physical aggression during mother-child disputes in Korean immigrant families.

Emerging Research on Child Physical Abuse Among Asian Americans

Consistent with a broader ecological model, recent analyses of data emerging from the NLAAS suggest that child physical abuse may not be largely a product of heritage cultural patterns but may emerge amid contextual stressors in Asian American families. Recent analyses provided a preliminary examination of the context of risk of child physical abuse as reported by 1,292 Asian American parents in the NLAAS sample (A. S. Lau, Takeuchi, & Alegria, 2005). This sample included Vietnamese, Filipino, Chinese, and Other Asian parents. The Other Asian group included Korean, Japanese, Asian Indian, and individuals of other Asian ancestry.

Somewhat contrary to the notion that adherence to traditional cultural values and child-rearing norms promote child abuse among Asian Americans, sociodemographic correlates of parent-reported lifetime history of parent-to-child aggression suggest that risk may be greater among more highly acculturated parents. Asian American parents who were born in the United States or who immigrated in their youth were more likely to report aggression than those who immigrated as adults and older adults. Further, parents with greater English use and proficiency were more likely to report minor parental aggression. This may suggest that physical abuse by Asian American parents is likely multiply determined and may not be driven primarily by heritage cultural patterns. Risk increased rather than decreased with increasing exposure to U.S. culture.

Risk of child physical abuse appeared related to two aspects of contextual stress. First, although family income and parental education were unrelated to abuse, parents' subjective appraisal of low social standing in the United States increased risk of parent-reported child abuse. Among Asian American families, frustration over limited social mobility in the United States may convey more risk than one's actual financial situation. Second, cultural family conflicts in negotiating personal goals and family priorities and the erosion of family unity were associated with parent-reported child physical abuse. Severe parent-child physical encounters may indeed occur in the context of distress marked by disputed priorities in matters of family and culture.

This initial examination of risk for child abuse among Asian Americans yielded some preliminary impressions requiring further inquiry. The data do not provide strong support for a "cultural explanation" for child abuse whereby traditional Asian cultural orientations promote parental aggression. Instead, salient aspects of the immigrant family context, including limited social mobility, and cultural family conflicts in navigating a new sociocultural landscape were associated with risk.

Implications for Practice

In terms of clinical practice, the United Nations (1993) has issued a call for more treatment outcome, efficacy, and effectiveness studies that can examine current strategies for treating family violence and respond to questions of how we can improve services. For instance, there is currently a lack of research on treatment efficacy of culturally responsive interventions for Asian American batterers, and this gap should be examined. However, there is emerging work addressing culture in batterers' intervention programs; for example, the Cultural Context Model (Almeida & Dolan-Delvecchio, 1999) incorporates social justice concerns related to race, gender, class, ethnicity, and sexual orientation into family therapy practice.

There is also a growing literature on interventions and services for Asian American survivors of domestic violence. One example of this emerging work comes out of the advocacy and organizing efforts of the South Asian community (Dasgupta, 2000). Although there are myriad factors to consider in the culturally competent delivery of services and outreach to Asian American victims of intimate partner violence, some fundamental issues for service providers

include (a) the recognition of various types of abuse, (b) potential barriers to help-seeking among Asian immigrant women, and (c) critical ingredients of effective interventions. Dasgupta (2000) identifies not only physical abuse, but also emotional, sexual, financial, "mother-in-law" (i.e., a woman's mother-in-law also inflicts abuse), and "immigration" abuse (i.e., using a woman's illegal or undocumented status in the United States as leverage to maintain control over her). Three types of barriers to services for South Asian women have been described by Dasgupta (2000), including (a) personal barriers (e.g., fear of losing face, financial insecurity, lack of social support), (b) institutional barriers (e.g., immigration policies, language barriers, racism, cultural insensitivity, cost of legal services), and c) cultural barriers (e.g., views of family, marriage/divorce, motherhood; belief in keeping one's family intact; glorification of women's suffering for the sake of family; the idea of "fate" or "karma" in tolerating abuse). The literature also suggests some specific ways in which outreach and delivery of services to Asian immigrant survivors of domestic violence can become more culturally competent. For instance, employing bilingual staff, offering Asian food, and providing detailed explanations of the unfamiliar service system at women's shelters (C. K. Ho, 1990; Huisman, 1996) have been suggested. C. K. Ho (1990) has recommended the use of cultural resources, such as elders in the community who can intervene or offer support, as well as cultural mechanisms of social control such as guilt/shame to inhibit future abuse. At the same time, service providers are cautioned against the use of culture as an excuse or pretext for abuse (Dasgupta, 2000; C. K. Ho, 1990). Finally, service providers are urged to tailor traditional Western methods of empowerment or therapeutic approaches to the cultural contexts of Asian immigrant women (Tran & DesJardins, 2000).

DIRECTIONS FOR FUTURE RESEARCH

In conclusion, this review of the literature on intimate partner violence and child physical abuse in Asian American communities points to some directions for future research as well as implications for practice. First, there is an urgent need for more empirical research on family violence among Asian American families. More nationally representative information is needed on the epidemiology of intimate partner violence and child physical abuse among Asian Americans as a whole, as well as baseline prevalence rates among specific Asian ethnic groups (particularly in light of differing cultural norms). From our review of the research literature, it appears that one consistent theme in both intimate partner violence and child physical abuse is that acculturation and acculturative stress may play pivotal roles. However, it is still unclear as to whether or not acculturation acts as a risk factor or as a protective factor. As emerging research has revealed somewhat contradictory findings (compared to previous studies, which show higher acculturation levels may be associated with higher levels of violence), this represents an area where further empirical investigation is required. There is also a paucity of research addressing the complexities involved in elder abuse among Asian Americans—a topic beyond the scope of this chapter. Furthermore, the theoretical basis of the family violence literature requires strengthening (e.g., the mere definitions of abuse and violence require clarification), and more specific explanatory models of family violence with Asian Americans should be empirically tested, especially with regard to identification of causal mechanisms and related risk contexts. Prospective studies would aid in this effort.

The United Nations (1993) has also outlined research priorities for the study of domestic violence worldwide. For example, cross-cultural research is strongly encouraged. Specifically, the United Nations calls for more comparative studies of different ethnic groups within the same society; studies that assess the relationship between family violence and specific social, economic, and cultural contexts; culture-specific case studies; longitudinal studies of families in specific cultural contexts; and worldwide comparisons of family violence in various societies. Hopefully, with this increased attention to family violence at both global and local levels, we can begin to break the silence, name that which was previously un-named, and make progress toward a society where all individuals can be free from domestic violence.

NOTES

1. Various terms have been used to describe violence between intimates. We will use the term *intimate partner violence* as it is an inclusive term, encompassing husband-to-wife violence as well as boyfriend-girlfriend and ex-partner violence. As is usually done in the literature, we are referring to violence in heterosexual relationships, although there is emerging literature on violence in same-gender relationships.

2. For example, in the National Family Violence Survey by Straus and Gelles (1990), participants initially heard an introductory statement about the pervasiveness of conflict in couples before they answered questions about violent acts, whereas in the National Violence Against Women Survey (Tjaden & Thoennes, 2000), no such statement was read.

3. In this study, "severe" violence was operationalized through the following subset of items from the Conflict Tactics Scale (Straus, 1979): "kicked, bit or hit with a fist; hit or tried to hit with something; beat up the other one; threatened with a knife or gun; used a knife or gun" (J. Y. Kim & Sung, 2000, p. 336).

4. Similar contexts for risk can also be observed in the literature on child physical abuse, as seen later in this chapter.

5. Italicized terms reference standard Chinese referents for the Confucian-based values. However, these values are common across many Confucian-based East Asian cultures, including those of Korea, Japan, and Vietnam.

REFERENCES

Abraham, M. (1995). Ethnicity, gender, and marital violence: South Asian women's organizations in the United States. *Gender & Society, 9,* 450–468.

Abraham, M. (2000). Isolation as a form of marital violence: The South Asian immigrant experience. *Journal of Social Distress and the Homeless, 9,* 221–236.

Adler, N., Epel, E., Castellazzo, G., & Ickovics, J. (2000). Relationship of subjective and objective social status with psychological and physiological functioning: Preliminary data in healthy white women. *Health Psychology, 19,* 586–592.

Ahmad, F., Riaz, S., Barata, P., & Stewart, D. (2004). Patriarchal beliefs and perceptions of abuse among South Asian immigrant women. *Violence Against Women, 10,* 262–282.

Alegria, M., Takeuchi, D., Canino, G., Duan, N., Shrout, P., Meng, X.-L., et al. (2004). Considering context, place and culture: The National Latino and Asian American Study. *International Journal of Methods in Psychiatric Research, 13,* 208–220.

Almeida, R. V., & Dolan-Delvecchio, K. (1999). Addressing culture in batterers intervention: The Asian Indian community as an illustrative example. *Violence Against Women, 5,* 654–683.

Almirol, E. B. (1982). Rights and obligations in Filipino American families. *Journal of Comparative Family Studies, 13,* 291–306.

Archer, D., & Gartner, R. (1976). Violent acts and violent times: A comparative approach to postwar homicide rates. *American Sociological Review, 41,* 937–963.

Ayyub, R. (2000). Domestic violence in the South Asian Muslim immigrant population in the United States. *Journal of Social Distress and the Homeless, 9,* 237–248.

Bachman, R., & Saltzman, L. E. (1995). *Violence against women: Estimates from the redesigned survey* (Special Report No. NCJ-154348). Washington, DC: Bureau of Justice Statistics.

Belsky, J. (1993). Etiology of child maltreatment: A developmental-ecological analysis. *Psychological Bulletin, 114,* 413–434.

Bemporad, J. R., & Romano, S. J. (1992). Childhood maltreatment and adult depression: A review of research. In D. Cicchetti & S. L. Toth (Eds.), *Developmental perspectives on depression. Rochester symposium on developmental psychopathology* (Vol. 4, pp. 351–375). Rochester, NY: University of Rochester Press.

Berry, J. W. (1998). Acculturative stress. In P. B. Organista, K. M. Chun, & G. Marin (Eds.), *Readings in ethnic psychology* (pp. 117–122). New York: Routledge.

Berry, J. W., Trimble, J. E., & Olemedo, E. L. (1986). Assessment of acculturation. In W. J. Lonner & J. W. Berry (Eds.), *Field methods in cross-cultural research* (pp. 291–324). Beverly Hills, CA: Sage.

Brown, J., Cohen, P., Johnson, J. G., & Smailes, E. M. (1999). Childhood abuse and neglect: Specificity and effects on adolescent and young adult depression and suicidality. *Journal of the American Academy of Child & Adolescent Psychiatry, 38*(12), 1490–1496.

Browne, A. (1993). Violence against women by male partners: Prevalence, outcomes, and policy implications. *American Psychologist, 48,* 1077–1087.

Bui, H. N., & Morash, M. (1999). Domestic violence in the Vietnamese immigrant community. *Violence Against Women, 5,* 769–795.

Campbell, J. C. (1992). Prevention of wife battering: Insights from cultural analysis. *Response to Victimization in Women and Children, 14,* 18–24.

Chan, S. (1992). Families with Asian roots. In E. W. Lynch & M. J. Hanson (Eds.), *Developing cross-cultural competence: A guide for working with children and their families* (pp. 181–257). Baltimore: Brookes.

Chan, S., & Leong, C. W. (1994). Chinese families in transition: Cultural conflicts and adjustment problems. *Journal of Social Distress & the Homeless, 3,* 263–281.

Chand, A. (2000). The over-representation of black children in the child protection system: Possible causes, consequences and solutions. *Child & Family Social Work, 5,* 67–77.

Chang, D. F., Shen, B. J., & Takeuchi, D. T. (2005, August). Prevalence and predictors of domestic violence in Asian Americans. In A. S. Lau (Chair), *Vulnerability to public health problems among Asian Americans: Findings from the National Latino and Asian American Study.* Symposium conducted at the annual meeting of the American Psychological Association, Washington, DC.

Chao, R. K. (1994). Beyond parental control and authoritarian parenting style: Understanding Chinese parenting through the cultural notion of training. *Child Development, 65,* 1111–1119.

Chasnoff, I. J., Landress, H. J., & Barrett, M. E. (1990). The prevalence of illicit-drug or alcohol use during pregnancy and discrepancies in mandatory reporting in Pinellas County, Florida. *New England Journal of Medicine, 322,* 1202–1206.

Chi, I., Lubben, J. E., & Kitano, H. H. L. (1989). Differences in drinking behavior among three Asian-American groups. *Journal of Studies on Alcohol, 50,* 15–23.

Cimmarusti, R. A. (1996). Exploring aspects of Filipino-American families. *Journal of Marital & Family Therapy, 22,* 205–217.

Cohen, P., Brown, J., & Smailes, E. (2001). Child abuse and neglect and the development of general disorders in the general population. *Development and Psychopathology, 13,* 981–999.

Dasgupta, S. D. (2000). Charting the course: An overview of domestic violence in the South Asian community in the United States. *Journal of Social Distress and the Homeless, 9,* 173–185.

Dasgupta, S. D., & Warrier, S. (1996). In the footsteps of "Arundhati": Asian Indian women's experience of domestic violence in the United States. *Violence Against Women, 2,* 238–259.

Dodge, K. A., Pettit, G. S., & Bates, J. E. (1997). How the experience of early physical abuse leads children to become chronically aggressive. In D. Cicchetti & S. L. Toth (Eds.), *Developmental perspectives on trauma: Theory, research, and intervention. Rochester symposium on developmental psychology* (Vol. 8, pp. 263–288). Rochester, NY: University of Rochester Press.

Du Bois, B. (1983). Passionate scholarship: Notes on values, knowing and method in terminal-social science. In G. Baules & R. D. Klein (Eds.), *Theories of Women's Studies,* London: Routledge.

Farver, J. A. M., Narang, S. K., & Bhadha, B. R. (2002). East meets West: Ethnic identity, acculturation, and conflict in Asian Indian families. *Journal of Family Psychology, 16*(3), 338–350.

Feldman, C. M., & Ridley, C. A. (1995). The etiology and treatment of domestic violence between adult partners. *Clinical Psychology: Science and Practice, 2,* 317–348.

Felitti, V. J., Anda, R. F., Nordenberg, D., Williamson, D. F., Spitz, A. M., Edwards, V., et al. (1998). Relationship of childhood abuse and household dysfunction to many of the leading causes of death in adults: The adverse childhood experiences (ACE) study. *American Journal of Preventive Medicine, 14,* 245–258.

Finkelhor, D., Ormrod, R., Turner, H., & Hamby, S. L. (2005). The Victimization of Children and Youth: A Comprehensive, National Survey. *Child Maltreatment, 10*(1), 5–25.

Finn, J. (1986). The relationship between sex role attitudes and attitudes supporting marital violence. *Sex Roles, 14,* 235–244.

Flisher, A. J., Kramer, R. A., Hoven, C. W., & Greenwald, S. (1997). Psychosocial characteristics of physically abused children and adolescents. *Journal of the American Academy of Child & Adolescent Psychiatry, 36*(1), 123–131.

Fromm, S. (2001). *Total estimated cost of child abuse and neglect in the United States: Statistical evidence.* Retrieved February 28, 2005, from www.preventchildabuse.org/learn_more/research_docs/cost_analysis.pdf.

Goodwin, R. D., & Stein, M.B. (2004). Association between childhood trauma and physical disorders among adults in the United States. *Psychological Medicine, 34,* 509–520.

Gorman, J. C. (1998). Parenting attitudes and practices of immigrant Chinese mothers of adolescents. *Family Relations, 47,* 73–80.

Ho, C. K. (1990). An analysis of domestic violence in Asian American communities: A multicultural approach to counseling. *Women & Therapy, 9,* 129–150.

Ho, D. Y. F. (1986). Chinese patterns of socialization: A critical review. In M. H. Bond (Ed.), *The psychology of the Chinese people* (pp. 1–37). Hong Kong: Oxford University Press.

Holtzworth-Munroe, A., Smutzler, N., & Sandin, E. (1997). A brief review of the research on husband violence. Part II: The psychological effects of husband violence on battered women and their children. *Aggression and Violent Behavior, 2,* 179–213.

Hong, G. K., & Hong, L. K. (1991). Comparative perspectives on child abuse and neglect: Chinese versus Hispanics and Whites. *Child Welfare, 70,* 463–475.

Hornung, C. A., McCullough, B. C., & Sugimoto, T. (1981). Status relationships in marriage: Risk factors in spouse abuse. *Journal of Marriage and the Family, 43,* 675–692.

Hotaling, G. T., & Sugarman, D. B. (1986). An analysis of risk markers in husband to wife violence: The current state of knowledge. *Violence and Victims, 1,* 101–124.

Hotaling, G. T., & Sugarman, D. B. (1990). A risk marker analysis of assaulted wives. *Journal of Family Violence, 5,* 1–13.

Huisman, K. A. (1996). Wife battering in Asian American communities. *Violence Against Women, 2,* 260–283.

Ima, K., & Hohm, C. F. (1991). Child maltreatment among Asian and Pacific Islander refugees and immigrants: The San Diego case. *Journal of Interpersonal Violence, 6*(3), 267–285.

Jaffee, S. R., Caspi, A., Moffitt, T. E., & Taylor, A. (2004). Physical maltreatment victim to antisocial child: Evidence of an environmentally mediated process. *Journal of Abnormal Psychology, 113*(1), 44–55.

Jaffee, S. R., Moffitt, T. E., Caspi, A., Taylor, A., & Arseneault, L. (2002). The influence of adult domestic violence on children's internalizing and externalizing problems: An environmentally informative twin study. *Journal of the American*

Academy of Child & Adolescent Psychiatry, 41, 1095–1103.

Jambunathan, S., Burts, D. C., & Pierce, S. (2000). Comparisons of parenting attitudes among five ethnic groups in the United States. *Journal of Comparative Family Studies, 31*(4), 395–406.

Jose, P. E., Huntsinger, C. S., Huntsinger, P. R., & Liaw, F.-R. (2000). Parental values and practices relevant to young children's social development in Taiwan and the United States. *Journal of Cross-Cultural Psychology, 31*(6), 677–702.

Kalmuss, D. S. (1984). The intergenerational transmission of marital aggression. *Journal of Marriage and the Family, 46,* 11–19.

Kaufman Kantor, G. F., & Jasinski, J. L. (1998). Dynamics and risk factors in partner violence. In J. L. Jasinski & L. M. Williams (Eds.), *Partner violence: A comprehensive review of 20 years of research* (pp. 184–209). Thousand Oaks, CA: Sage.

Kelley, M. L., & Tseng, H.-M. (1992). Cultural differences in child rearing: A comparison of immigrant Chinese and Caucasian American mothers. *Journal of Cross-Cultural Psychology, 23*(4), 444–455.

Kessler, R. C., Molnar, B. E., Feurer, I. D., & Appelbaum, M. (2001). Patterns and mental health predictors of domestic violence in the United States: Results from the National Comorbidity Survey. *International Journal of Law & Psychiatry, 24*(4–5), 487–508.

Kim, I. J., & Zane, N. W. S. (2004). Ethnic and cultural variations in anger regulation and attachment patterns among Korean American and European American male batterers. *Cultural Diversity & Ethnic Minority Psychology, 10,* 151–168.

Kim, J. Y., & Sung, K. (2000). Conjugal violence in Korean American families: A residue of the cultural tradition. *Journal of Family Violence, 15,* 331–345.

Lau, A. S., McCabe, K., Yeh, M., Garland, A. F., Hough, R. L., & Landsverk, J. (2003). Race/ethnicity and rates of self-reported maltreatment among high-risk youth in public sectors of care. *Child Maltreatment, 8*(10), 1–9.

Lau, A. S., Takeuchi, D. T., & Alegria, M. (2005, August). *Parent-to-child aggression in Asian American families: Culture, context, and vulnerability.* Paper presented at the 113th Annual Convention of the American Psychological Association. Washington, DC.

Lau, J. T. F., Liu, J. L. Y., Yu, A., & Wong, C. K. (1999). Conceptualization, reporting and underreporting of child abuse in Hong Kong. *Child Abuse & Neglect, 23*(11), 1159–1174.

Lee, E. (1989). Assessment and treatment of Chinese-American immigrant families. *Journal of Psychotherapy & the Family, 6 ,* 99–122.

Lee, R. M., Choe, J., Kim, G., & Ngo, V. (2000). Construction of the Asian American Family Conflicts Scale. *Journal of Counseling Psychology, 47*(2), 211–222.

Lin, C.-Y. C., & Fu, V. R. (1990). A comparison of child-rearing practices among Chinese, immigrant Chinese, and Caucasian-American parents. *Child Development, 61*(2), 429–433.

Lum, J. L. (1998). Family violence. In L. Lee & N. W. S. Zane (Eds.), *Handbook of Asian American psychology* (pp. 505–525). Thousand Oaks, CA: Sage.

MacMillan, H. L., Fleming, J. E., Trocme, N., Boyle, M. H., Wong, M., Racine, Y., et al. (1997). Prevalence of child physical and sexual abuse in the community. *Journal of the American Medical Association, 278,* 131–135.

National Research Council. (1993). *Understanding child abuse and neglect.* Washington, DC: National Academy Press.

National Research Council. (1996). *Understanding violence against women.* Washington, DC: National Academy Press.

Norton, I. M., & Manson, S. M. (1992). An association between domestic violence and depression among Southeast Asian refugee women. *Journal of Nervous and Mental Disease, 180,* 729–730.

Park, M. S. (2001). The factors of child physical abuse in Korean immigrant families. *Child Abuse & Neglect, 25,* 945–958.

Rhee, S. (1997). Domestic violence in the Korean immigrant family. *Journal of Sociology & Social Welfare, 24,* 63–77.

Rosenberg, M. S., & Rossman, B. B. R. (1990). The child witness to marital violence. In R. T. Ammersman & M. Herson (Eds.), *Treatment of family violence* (pp. 183–210). New York: Wiley.

Sachs-Ericsson, N., Blazer, D., Plant, E.A., & Arnow, B. (2005). Childhood sexual and physical abuse and the 1-year prevalence of medical problems in the National Comorbidity Survey. *Health Psychology, 24,* 32–40.

Shon, S. P., & Ja, D. Y. (1992). Asian families. In A. S. Skolnick & J. H. Skolnick (Eds.), *Family in transition: Rethinking marriage, sexuality, child rearing, and family organization* (7th ed., pp. 439–535). New York: HarperCollins.

Song, Y. I. (1996). *Battered women in Korean immigrant families: The silent scream.* New York: Garland.

Straus, M. A. (1977–1978). Wife beating: How common and why? *Victimology, 2,* 443–458.

Straus, M. A. (1979). Measuring intrafamily conflict and violence: The Conflict Tactics (CT) Scales. *Journal of Marriage and the Family, 41,* 75–88.

Straus, M. A., & Gelles, R. J. (1986). Societal change and change in family violence from 1975 to 1985 as revealed by two national surveys. *Journal of Marriage and the Family, 48,* 465–479.

Straus, M. A., & Gelles, R. J. (1990). How violent are American families? Estimates from the National Family Violence Resurvey and other studies. In M. A. Straus & R. J. Gelles (Eds.), *Physical violence in American families: Risk factors and adaptations to violence in 8,145 families.* New Brunswick, NJ: Transaction.

Szapocznik, J., & Kurtines, W. M. (1993). Family psychology and cultural diversity: Opportunities for theory, research, and application. *American Psychologist, 48*(4), 400–407.

Szapocznik, J., & Truss, C. (1978). Intergenerational sources of conflict in Cuban mothers. In M. Montiel (Ed.), *Hispanic families: Critical issues for policy and programs in human services* (pp. 41–65). Washington, DC: National Coalition of Hispanic Mental Health and Human Services Organizations.

Tang, C. S.-K. (1998). The rate of physical child abuse in Chinese families: A community survey in Hong Kong. *Child Abuse & Neglect, 22*(5), 381–391.

Tjaden, P., & Thoennes, N. (2000). Prevalence and consequences of male-to-female and female-to-male intimate partner violence as measured by the National Violence Against Women Survey. *Violence Against Women, 6,* 142–161.

Tolman, R. M., & Bennett, L. W. (1990). A review of quantitative research on men who batter. *Journal of Interpersonal Violence, 5,* 87–118.

Tran, C. G. (1997). Domestic violence among Vietnamese refugee women: Prevalence, abuse characteristics, psychiatric symptoms, and psychosocial factors. (Doctoral dissertation, Boston University, 1997). *Dissertation Abstracts International, 57,* 7239.

Tran, C. G., & DesJardins, K. (2000). Domestic violence in Vietnamese refugee and Korean immigrant communities. In J. L. Chin (Ed.), *Relationships among Asian American women* (pp. 71–96). Washington, DC: American Psychological Association.

Uba, L. (1994). Families. In L. Uba (Ed.), *Asian Americans: Personality patterns, identity, and mental health* (pp. 26–55). New York: Guilford Press.

United Nations Office at Vienna, Centre for Social Development and Humanitarian Affairs. (1993). *Strategies for confronting domestic violence: A resource manual* (ST/CSDHA/20). New York: United Nations.

U.S. Department of Health and Human Services, Administration on Children, Youth, and Families. (2005). *Child maltreatment 2003.* Washington, DC: U.S. Government Printing Office.

Walker, L. E. (1979). *The battered woman.* New York: Harper & Row.

Wang, C.-H. C., & Phinney, J. S. (1998). Differences in child rearing attitudes between immigrant Chinese mothers and Anglo-American mothers. *Early Development & Parenting, 7*(4), 181–189.

Widom, C. S. (1989). Does violence beget violence? A critical examination of the literature. *Psychological Bulletin, 106*(1), 3–28.

Williams, C. L., & Berry, J. W. (1991). Primary prevention of acculturative stress among refugees: Application of psychological theory and practice. *American Psychologist, 46,* 632–641.

Williams, D. R., Neighbors, H. & Jackson, J. S. (2003). Racial/ethnic discrimination and health: Findings from community studies. *American Journal of Public Health, 93,* 200–208.

Yeh, K. H., & Bedford, O. (2004). Filial belief and parent-child conflict. *International Journal of Psychology, 39,* 132–144.

Yick, A. G. (2001). Feminist theory and status inconsistency theory: Application to domestic violence in Chinese immigrant families. *Violence Against Women, 7,* 545–562.

Yim, S. B. (1978). Korean battered wives: A sociological and psychological analysis of conjugal violence in Korean immigrant families. In H. H. Sunoo & D. S. Sunoo (Eds.), *Korean women: In a struggle for humanization* (pp. 171–189). Memphis, TN: Association of Korean Christian Scholars.

Yoshihama, M. (1999). Domestic violence against women of Japanese descent in Los Angeles. *Violence Against Women, 5,* 869–897.

Yoshioka, M. R., DiNoia, J., & Ullah, K. (2001). Attitudes towards marital violence: An examination of four Asian communities. *Violence Against Women, 7,* 900–926.

22

PSYCHOPATHOLOGY AMONG ASIAN AMERICANS

LAWRENCE HSIN YANG

AHTOY J. WONPAT-BORJA

Research on Asian American mental health has proliferated within recent years, culminating with the surgeon general's *Supplement to Mental Health: Culture, Race, and Ethnicity* (U.S. Department of Health and Human Services, 2001), which provided a much-needed review of research and set of policy recommendations concerning mental health care for Asian Americans. Studies of psychopathology within Asian American groups, such as those reviewed by the surgeon general's supplement, serve two critical purposes. First, these investigations have vital implications for establishing mental health care policy for this population. Second, such studies can take up central questions concerning the nature, manifestation, and prevalence of psychopathology among Asian Americans, along with addressing how key factors—such as ethnicity, race, acculturation, and social stresses related to immigration—impact these variables.

In this chapter, we seek to address these critical questions by first describing how cultural processes shape psychopathology by infusing experiences of distress with meaning and organizing distress in ways coherent with the social context. We examine how Asians, in particular, may employ somatic metaphors as a culturally mediated form of distress that conveys communal bodily, emotional, and social meanings, and we evaluate to what extent Asian Americans consequently somatize mental illness symptoms. In the next major section, we evaluate evidence relevant to the prevalence and manifestation of psychopathology among Asian Americans. We begin by reviewing how prevalent mental disorders are within Asian countries and how the experience of psychopathology may change among Asian Americans due to processes linked with immigration to the United States. We then briefly review the major principles of constructing cross-cultural assessments of psychiatric disorders before evaluating psychopathology research on Asian Americans, specifically focusing on mental health utilization studies and research on neurasthenia, anxiety, schizophrenia-spectrum,

Authors' Note: We would like to thank Dr. David Takeuchi for his helpful advice in the preparation and editing of this manuscript. The preparation of this manuscript was also supported, in part, by National Institute of Mental Health grant K01 MH73034–01, which has been awarded to the first author.

and major depressive disorders. We conclude by returning to our original questions regarding prevalence and manifestation of psychopathology among Asian Americans and identifying areas that need further study.

CULTURE AND PSYCHOPATHOLOGY

How Culture Affects Psychopathology

Early uses of the concept of culture referred to shared patterns of life that characterized social groups. However, rather than consisting of an unchanging variable as these earlier definitions implied, culture can better be understood as a dynamic process that manifests itself through, and becomes critically intertwined with, larger-scale (economic, political) and smaller-scale (psychological, biological) social forces. Culture can be viewed as a process by which everyday activities become embedded with emotional meanings for actors in local worlds (A. Kleinman, 2004). Central to this process is the concept of moral experience, where meanings of events such as illness become interpretable by understanding what is most at stake for participants in their social contexts.

Because cultural processes imbue subjective experiences of physiology and distress with meaning, culture accordingly influences how psychopathology is experienced and expressed. First, culture shapes the manifestation and experience of symptoms, which, in turn, may influence the course of illness. Second, whereas certain symptoms may appear to be similar across cultures, the interpretation of these symptoms is determined by cultural values and meanings. Third, identical constellations of symptoms may be organized into differing syndromes according to historical and sociopolitical influences (Lee, 2002). In sum, cultural meanings and practices shape how discomfort associated with mental illness is expressed, interpreted, and organized within a particular social context.

Culture and Somatization

Somatization, in addition to its use as a family of psychiatric disorders within the *Diagnostic and Statistical Manual of Mental Disorders* (DSM-IV), has held several meanings within psychological discourse (Kirmayer & Young, 1998). In one common definition, unacknowledged psychological conflict is transformed by the sufferer into physical symptoms. Thus, what might be interpreted as an underlying affective or anxiety disorder instead is expressed as bodily discomfort. In another usage, somatization is used to describe a particular clinical presentation in which somatic symptoms are focused on to the exclusion of psychological, emotional, or social difficulties. This definition does not presume an active denial of psychosocial distress or an inability to express emotional conflict by the patient, and it acknowledges that affective and somatic symptoms can co-occur (even if one is presently emphasized over the other).

By this last definition, somatization is prevalent in all cultural groups; indeed, Kirmayer and Young (1998) assert that " somatic symptoms are the most common clinical expression of emotional distress worldwide" (p. 421). From their perspective, somatization reflects a culturally mediated way of expressing distress that is embedded in interpersonal and wider social processes and thus comprises somatic, emotional, and social meanings. Local ideas about how the body and physiology communicate suffering result in culture-specific syndromes of somatic complaints; hence, medical complaints about the body tap into larger cultural models of sickness and are accorded shared affective meaning and significance. These cultural models, in turn, provide explanations for symptoms that can be understood by those within a social context but may be interpreted differently by outsiders.

Although somatization is common across all cultures, significant cultural variations in prevalence and form also exist. Cultural preferences in how emotions are experienced and expressed occur within Asian societies. In Chinese cultures, for example, emotional communication takes place not in words that symbolize emotion but instead through metaphors that are often associated with the body (Cheung, 1995). This integration of affect expressed through the body is shown in factor analyses of the Center for Epidemiologic Studies–Depression (CES-D) Scale among immigrant Asian American groups.

Whereas the Somatic and Depressed Affect factors appeared as two independent factors when the CES-D was administered to Anglo populations in the United States (Radloff, 1977), these factors clustered into one combined factor when administered to less acculturated Asian American groups (Kuo, 1984; Ying, 1988). This association seems to vary with exposure to Western norms; when the CES-D was given to more Western-acculturated Chinese American college students, Depressed Affect and Somatic factors loaded as separate factors (Kuo, 1984; Ying, Lee, Tsai, Yeh, & Huang, 2000).

Despite this tendency to utilize bodily metaphors to express emotional distress, it remains unresolved whether Asians and Asian Americans report more somatic symptoms when presenting symptoms of mental illness than do Western groups (Yen, Robins, & Lin, 2000). Several studies have reported higher rates of somatization among Chinese samples, but these used either open-ended questioning of patient populations without a comparison group (A. M. Kleinman, 1977) or unstandardized interviews on clinically unmatched Chinese American and comparison samples (Hsu & Folstein, 1997). Results utilizing outpatients may be affected by help-seeking patterns because when patients in a certain society lack easy access to psychiatric services, they may highlight somatic distress in medical encounters in order to make certain they receive appropriate attention. Somatization may also be seen as a construction of illness meaning by the patient to avoid the severe stigma attached to psychiatric treatment and to obtain aid that is judged as acceptable. For example, Chinese Americans have been found to attribute more shame to using Western psychiatric services for mental illness as compared to using traditional Chinese medicine (Yang, 2003b).

Although Chinese patient groups may present greater somatic symptoms in lieu of emotional distress, this pattern does not appear to extend to the Chinese general community. In a study by Yen et al. (2000) in China, mental health outpatients emphasized somatic symptoms on the CES-D to a greater degree than did a sample of nonpatient college students. Further, Chinese ethnic community groups do not appear to endorse a greater amount of somatic symptoms than do Western community groups. In fact, Zhang, Snowden, and Sue (1998) found in a community sample of the Los Angeles site of the Epidemiological Catchment Area (ECA) study that the Asian American group ($n = 161$) reported fewer average somatic symptoms than did the Anglo group ($n = 1332$) (.8 vs. 1.2 symptoms). Also, Yen et al. (2000) found that their sample of Chinese students actually endorsed significantly fewer somatic symptoms than a matched set of non-Chinese U.S. students.[1]

The manner used in interviewing respondents about symptoms is also critical to apparent clinical presentations of somatization. Whereas open-ended questions may result in elevated report of somatic symptoms among Asians and Asian Americans, structured questioning may elicit responses about psychological distress either as symptom or possible cause. Yeung, Chang, Gresham, Nierenberg, and Fava (2004) found, among their sample of depressed Chinese Americans in primary care, that although 76% (22 out of 29 study participants) complained chiefly of somatic complaints, none complained spontaneously about depressed mood. However, 93% (27 out of 29) of this sample subsequently endorsed depressed mood in response to a structured screening tool. Similarly, Yen et al. (2000) found that when responding to a structured interview, three ethnic Chinese groups (Chinese patients, Chinese college students, and Chinese American college students) endorsed the same level of affective symptoms when compared with a group of European American college students. Data from Zhang et al. (1998) further illustrate how somatic distress co-signals emotional distress as the number of somatic symptoms endorsed positively predicted disclosure of mental health problems among the Asian American group. Thus, for Asian Americans, it appears that somatic complaints parallel affective complaints as a form of expression rather than acting against emotional expression. In sum, somatization does not seem to be a conscious denial of affective distress among Asians and Asian Americans but instead an initial culturally accepted "negotiating tactic" (Parker, Gladstone, & Chee, 2001) that is not necessarily sustained on continued questioning.

PREVALENCE AND MANIFESTATION OF PSYCHOPATHOLOGY AMONG ASIAN AMERICANS

Prevalence of Psychopathology in Asian Countries

To frame a discussion on psychopathology within Asian American groups, it is essential to review how prevalent mental disorders are within Asian countries and to examine how these rates compare with those within the United States. By establishing baseline prevalence of psychiatric disorders in these two contexts, we can examine the potential influence of immigration and acculturation on the prevalence of psychopathology among Asian Americans. Assuming that prevalence differs between these two contexts, does risk of developing a mental disorder start low in Asian countries and then increase when Asians immigrate to the United States? Or is the reverse true—that migration and acculturation to U.S. society are associated with a lower risk of developing psychiatric disorders?

One critical recent study that examined prevalence of psychiatric disorders cross-nationally was conducted by the World Health Organization (World Mental Health Survey Consortium, 2004). This international study conducted face-to-face household surveys among 60,463 community adults in 14 countries from 2001 to 2003 using the World Mental Health–Composite International Diagnostic Interview (WMH-CIDI), a fully structured diagnostic interview that has demonstrated good reliability and validity in Western settings. Using DSM-IV criteria, various disorders were assessed, including anxiety, mood, "impulse–control" (e.g., bulimia, adult-persistent attention deficit and hyperactivity disorder [ADHD]), and substance abuse disorders. All surveys were conducted using a multistage household probability sample design. Countries participating from Asia included Japan ($n = 1,663$) and China (Beijing and Shanghai, $n = 2,633$ and $2,568$, respectively); the U.S. sample was nationally representative ($n = 9,282$).

The study's results indicate that prevalence of mental disorders within Japan and China is far

less than that in the United States. The 12-month point prevalence and 95% confidence intervals (CIs) of all mental disorders included in the study in Japan (8.8%) (95% CI = 6.4–11.2%), Beijing (9.1%) (95% CI = 6.0–12.1%), and Shanghai (4.3%) (95% CI = 2.7–5.9%) were far less than the proportion of people in the United States who were diagnosed in the past year at time of interview with having a mental disorder (26.4%) (95% CI = 24.7–28.0%). Similarly, the proportion of cases who were classified as being either moderate or serious in nature was far lower in Japan and China when compared with the United States. Potential methodological issues that may account for these findings include instrumentation differences, as the concepts and wording used to describe psychiatric symptoms by the WMH-CIDI may not have matched indigenous cultural notions of illness. Further, the lower response rate obtained in the Japanese sample may have contributed to findings of decreased prevalence, as survey nonrespondents, in general, have been found to demonstrate higher rates of mental illness than respondents (Kessler et al., 1994). Even after considering these methodological concerns, however, the results remain strongly suggestive that prevalence of mental disorders (as defined by DSM- IV) is lower in Asian countries than in the United States. These results are consistent with an earlier group of studies that reported a low prevalence of psychiatric disorders in Asian countries (Parker et al., 2001; Simon, Goldberg, Von Korff, & Ustun, 2002; Weissman et al., 1996, 1997).

Immigration and Psychopathology

There are currently two alternative theories for how immigration to the United States might affect psychopathology among Asian Americans (Hwang, Chun, Takeuchi, Myers, & Siddarth, 2005). New immigrants typically face multiple adverse conditions, such as language barriers, low-paying jobs with long working hours, and loss of social support networks. These and other stressors linked with transitioning and adapting to a new setting, termed *acculturative stress,* might directly increase risk of psychopathology among new immigrants. On the other hand, as immigrants are exposed to U.S. norms, they may gradually absorb characteristics of psycho-pathology found in the general U.S. population (i.e., having a higher prevalence of disorders). This process of *cultural assimilation* implies that risk of psychopathology gradually increases as culturally protective factors slowly erode with greater acculturation.

Consistent with the cultural assimilation hypothesis is the notion termed *the immigrant paradox*—the finding that among certain ethnic groups, being foreign-born and having lower levels of acculturation to U.S. culture appear to decrease risk of developing mental disorders. The paradox is that as access to socioeconomic opportunities and health care services typically increase with acculturation, mental health should also improve (Ying & Hu, 1994). Contrary to this view, Latino (and in particular, Mexican) immigrants have shown a lower prevalence of various psychiatric disorders when compared with both U.S.-born Latinos and the U.S. general population (Escobar et al., 2000). However, such an association has not yet been tested among Asian Americans.

"Asian Americans" as Classification

For demographic purposes, the U.S. government has classified persons of Asian descent and those from the Pacific islands as "Asian American." However, this created category has grouped together more than 50 different ethnic groups who speak more than 30 different languages, and it has obscured differences in national ethnic backgrounds, socioeconomic status (SES), race, and history of migration (S. Sue, 2002). This practice has persisted in most psychiatric epidemiology studies to date. For example, two studies, the ECA study (Robins & Regier, 1991) and the National Comorbidity Study (Kessler et al., 1994), which examined prevalence of mental disorders at the regional and national levels, did not report results for specific Asian American ethnicities, instead collapsing Asian Americans into one homogenous group. This, in turn, has made it particularly difficult to draw any conclusions about how rates of psychopathology and need for mental health services may differ among Asian American subgroups.

Diagnostic Measures

Central to the question of prevalence of psychiatric disorders among Asian Americans is a consideration of the measures used to assess psychopathology in this group. Neglecting to modify assessment tools to consider the cultural background of individuals can lead to either an inaccurate diagnosis of pathology or failure to detect a present disorder. Ensuring language equivalence of measures is not sufficient, as the translated measure must still be evaluated as to whether it taps the same underlying theoretical construct. To address this, most researchers have attempted to establish *construct validity* for measures adapted to Asian American groups, that is, to examine whether the adapted measure is associated with, or predicts, other related constructs in a manner consistent with the original measure. Recent examples of adaptation of symptom scales for use with Asian American youth and adults that demonstrate at least some evidence for construct validity include Choi, Stafford, Meininger, Roberts, and Smith (2002) and Yeung, Howarth, et al. (2002), respectively.

D. Sue and Sue (1987), in their classification of cross-cultural measurement, distinguished between measurement strategies developed in one culture and then applied to another as opposed to when a measure has been developed emically. An advantage of adapting instruments developed in Western cultures is the possibility of accessing accumulated evidence of psychometric and construct validity of the instrument. Yet, one critical shortcoming of translated measures is the potential failure to incorporate culturally relevant emic constructs that are meaningful to the local culture (Cheung, Cheung, & Zhang, 2004). An example of a psychopathology assessment designed by a combined etic-emic approach is the Chinese Personality Assessment Inventory, an instrument that mirrors the Minnesota Multiphasic Personality Inventory–2 in structure but has been developed using a representative sample from China and Hong Kong (Cheung et al., 1996). This measure includes several personality scales indigenous to China, such as Harmony, Face, and Relationship Orientation.

Including such emic constructs with diagnostic interviews is vital to accurately identifying prevalence of mental disorders among Asian Americans. Deep cultural knowledge of a group can enable more culturally sensitive stem questions of interview modules that may significantly impact the rate of identified psychiatric disorders (Lee, 2002). For example, Koreans use "black" as a metaphor for depressed feelings rather than "feeling blue" (M. T. Kim, 1995); hence, ignorance of such unique idioms may lead to underdiagnosis of depression among Korean Americans. Care in ensuring cultural equivalence in symptom probes is critical to accurate cross-cultural comparison.

Several investigators using diagnostic interviews with Asian Americans have taken steps to make their probes culturally appropriate. Takeuchi et al. (1998), in the Chinese American Psychiatric Epidemiology Study (CAPES), adapted the University of Michigan's version of the Composite International Diagnostic Interview (UM-CIDI) (Kessler et al., 1994) to measure rates of depressive disorders among Chinese Americans. The UM-CIDI is a structured interview schedule that begins with a series of screening questions that lead to more detailed probes if responded to affirmatively. In addition to rigorous translation and back-translation, Takeuchi et al. undertook a set of focus groups to examine whether the phrases used to describe depressive symptoms made sense to Chinese American subjects. Resulting from these focus groups, additional probes were developed to aid respondents in comprehending key words or idioms.

Building on this work, Alegria et al. (2004), in the National Latino and Asian American Study (NLAAS), incorporated emic expressions of disorders into the translated UM-CIDI by engaging in extensive qualitative research to generate one additional screening question for each of four disorders that entered respondents into specific diagnostic sections. These additional probes were created by asking respondents to offer probes that indicated similar symptoms and by examining how the subjects interpreted the original screener probes. By locating emic concepts within each ethnic group, these investigators included culture-specific symptom expression not covered by DSM-IV criteria in the potential identification of a disorder.

Mental Health Service Utilization Studies

We first review a set of mental health service utilization studies that suggest some directions regarding the nature and prevalence of psychiatric disorders among Asian Americans. Table 22.1 lists studies of large mental health systems that detail rates of mental health service use in this group. The first seven studies (listed from the top) compared mental health service use among Asian Americans with rates of use among Anglos. These seven studies consistently show, with only one incongruent finding, that Asian Americans use almost all types of mental health services to a significantly lesser degree when compared with Anglos. This finding applies to Asian American youth, adults, and elders, and holds true when examining both regional- and national-level data.

More informative data arise from studies that compare the proportion of Asian Americans who enter a mental health service system with the proportion of Asian Americans who comprise that system's catchment area (summarized by the last six studies in Table 22.1). Because Anglos' mental health utilization rates appear to equal their respective population rates for both adults (S. Sue, Fujino, Hu, Takeuchi, & Zane, 1991) and adolescents (Bui & Takeuchi, 1992), Asian Americans are seen to underutilize mental health services if their rates of service use are greatly lower than their population proportion. These six studies consistently demonstrate that the proportion of Asian Americans who use inpatient and outpatient mental health services are approximately one-third of what might be expected given their population proportion. The sole exception is a study by O'Sullivan, Peterson, Cox, and Kirkeby (1989), who showed in a 10-year follow-up to S. Sue's (1977) study that mental health service use by Asian Americans had increased to their population proportion in the Seattle area, presumably due to the development of culture-specific outreach programs to ethnic minority groups. Aside from this finding however, these studies

Table 22.1   Services Utilization Studies

Study	Ethnicity	Sample & Time Frame	Utilization Rates/Main Findings
Snowden & Cheung, 1990	Asian-Am	National-level survey data for inpatient mental health service use; 1980	Asian-Am use inpatient mental health services at 1/2 rate nationally vs. Anglos
Hu et al., 1991	Asian-Am	3,825 adult inpatients and outpatients from San Francisco & Santa Clara Counties' Public Mental Health Systems; 1987–1988	Asian-Am utilization < Anglos for emergency room, inpatient, and case management; Asian-Am utilization > Anglos for outpatient services
Matsuoka et al., 1997	Asian-Am	National Institute of Mental Health survey data for overall mental health services use (5,852,098 Asian-Am); 1986	Asian-Am use overall mental health services at 1/3 rate nationally vs. Anglos
Zhang et al., 1998	Asian-Am	161 community respondents randomly selected from the Los Angeles area; Epidemiological Catchment Area; early 1980s	Asian-Am use almost all outpatient mental health services significantly < Anglos
Virnig et al., 2004	Asian-Am	68,865 elders enrolled in U.S. Medicare managed care plans; 1999	Overall rates of mental health services use (inpatient & outpatient) significantly lower among Asian-Am vs. Anglos
McCabe et al., 1999	Asian-, Pacific Islander-Am	546 youth from San Diego Youth Mental Health Care in Public Services Systems Project; 1996–1997	Asian-, Pacific Islander-Am use < Anglos in child welfare, mental health, and juvenile justice services; equal rate for alcohol & drug services
Leong, 1994	Asian-Am (Chinese-, Japanese-, Filipino-Am)	Archival data from 7,577 adult inpatients & outpatients from Hawaii Mental Health Division; 1972–1981	All groups of Asian-Am use < Anglos in inpatient & outpatient services
S. Sue, 1977	Asian-Am	100 adult inpatients and outpatients from community mental health centers in the greater Seattle Area; 3-year period early 1970s	0.7% use vs. 2.4% population rate
O'Sullivan et al., 1989	Asian-Am	742 adult outpatients from Washington State Mental Health Management Information System; 1983	5.4% use vs. 4.6 % population rate
Loo et al., 1989	Chinese-Am	108 community respondents from San Francisco's Chinatown; area sample	5% use vs. 12% general population rate
S. Sue et al., 1991	Asian-Am (Chinese-, Japanese-, Filipino-, Korean-, SE Asian-Am)	3,344 adult outpatients from the Los Angeles County Public Mental Health System; 1983–1988	3.1% use vs. 8.7% population rate
Bui & Takeuchi, 1992	Asian-Am	704 adolescent outpatients from the Los Angeles County Public Mental Health System; 1983–1988	2.7% use vs. 10.2% population rate
Yeh et al., 2002	Asian-Am	122 youth from the San Diego County Mental Health Services public outpatient department; 1996–1997	3.1% use vs. 9.0% population rate

strongly indicate that Asian American youth and adults demonstrate a striking pattern of mental health underutilization that has persisted through several decades.[2]

This underutilization phenomenon has been accompanied by the finding that Asian American youth and adults who enter treatment systems have scored lower on global functioning measures and received a significantly greater proportion of severe psychiatric diagnoses (e.g., psychotic features) than Anglos, even after controlling for the effects of other SES variables (Durvasula & Sue, 1996; Yeh et al., 2002). One explanation proposed for this greater severity of disorders is that delayed help-seeking among Asian Americans may lead to increased severity of symptoms (Lin, Inui, Kleinman, & Womack, 1982). Due to these findings, it has been thought that underutilization does not indicate a paucity of need but instead reflects a reluctance to use mental health services.

These findings suggest the following: (a) Asian American groups may have lower rates of psychopathology than Anglos, or (b) the same (or higher) rate of psychiatric problems exists among Asian American groups, but culture-specific help-seeking patterns reduce mental health service use (Bui & Takeuchi, 1992). In considering usage pattern data alone, both explanations are plausible; yet, the higher proportion of severe disorders among Asian Americans who do enter treatment suggests an unmet need in the community. To further investigate this issue, we next examine data establishing the need and demand for psychiatric services in the Asian American community.

Prevalence and Correlates of Psychopathology Within Asian American Groups

We begin this section by reviewing the literature on neurasthenia among Asian American groups, followed by anxiety disorders and then schizophrenia-spectrum disorders. Due to the relatively large literature on major depression among Asian Americans, we review this disorder last, concluding with suicide. Within each class of disorders, we note evidence regarding prevalence among Asian American groups compared with European American norms. We next describe cultural differences in manifestation of the disorder among Asian Americans. This selective review excludes disorders such as eating disorders and personality disorders due to the paucity of research on Asian Americans, and topics such as mental disorders among high-risk groups (i.e., Southeast Asian refugees) because other chapters in this handbook address such topics.

Neurasthenia

Although no longer an official DSM classification, neurasthenia remains a particularly relevant diagnosis among Asian and Asian American groups. Neurasthenia is characterized in the International Classification of Disease, 10th Edition (ICD-10) by weakness symptoms, including physical fatigue, memory loss, and concentration problems; emotional symptoms, including dysphoria, worry, and irritability; excitability; nervous pain; and sleep disturbances (ICD-10). In Asia, neurasthenia was introduced as a diagnosis in mainland China in the early 1900s and has been used more as a generic label to describe a cluster of somatic, cognitive, emotional, and depressive symptoms rather than as a somatization disorder per se (Parker et al., 2001). Because neurasthenia is conceptually distant from psychiatric disorders and their accompanying stigma, it has gained popular use as a nonstigmatizing diagnosis. The use of neurasthenia as a diagnosis since the mid-1980s has decreased in China, whereas use of depression has increased. Despite this trend, neurasthenia is still used widely in Asian countries and remains prevalent in Chinese societies, with a rate of 10% in the general population (Young, 1989). In the Chinese-American Psychiatric Epidemiology Study (CAPES), a community epidemiology study of 1,747 Chinese Americans in the Los Angeles area, 6.4% of this sample reported a 12-month prevalence rate for neurasthenia when assessed by ICD-10 criteria (Zheng et al., 1997). Despite its applicability to Asian and Asian American groups, neurasthenia as a diagnosis has gradually fallen into disuse in the West and was omitted from both DSM-III and DSM-IV (Zheng et al., 1997).

Although neurasthenia is conceptually heterogenous, it appears to be distinguishable from depressive, anxiety, and somatoform disorders (Young, Zhang, Li, Lin, & Zheng, 1997). In Zheng et al.'s (1997) study, 3.6% of the Chinese Americans sampled met 12-month prevalence for neurasthenia when all other current and lifetime DSM-III-R diagnoses were excluded. The fact that more than 56% of overall neurasthenia diagnoses met such criteria for "pure" neurasthenia, and that the 3.6% 12-month prevalence was higher than any other DSM-III-R defined mental disorder in this group, suggests that neurasthenia constitutes a relatively prevalent disorder among Chinese Americans that is distinct from diagnoses such as depression and anxiety.

Anxiety Disorders

Few studies are available that address prevalence of anxiety disorders among Asian Americans. Zhang and Snowden (1999) utilized data from the ECA, which sampled five urban sites in the United States, and found a lifetime prevalence of 1.0% for obsessive-compulsive disorder and 6.6% for phobia among Asian Americans. Although these rates did not differ significantly when compared with an Anglo reference group, Asian Americans did exhibit lower rates of panic disorder than the European American group. The CAPES study also found quite low prevalence of anxiety disorders among their sample of Chinese Americans when compared with the U.S. general population (Kessler et al., 1994). S. Sue, Sue, Sue, and Takeuchi (1995) reported that Chinese Americans showed lower lifetime prevalence of generalized anxiety disorder (1.7% vs. 5.1% for Anglos), agoraphobia (1.6% vs. 5.3%), simple phobia (1.1% vs. 11.3%), social phobia (1.2% vs. 13.3%) and panic disorder (.4% vs. 3.5%).

The majority of studies on anxiety in Asian American groups have focused on social anxiety among college students. D. Sue, Ino, and Sue (1983) found that, compared with Anglo college students, male Chinese American college students endorsed a significantly greater tendency to avoid and to feel anxious in social situations and to worry about how others would evaluate them interpersonally. Okazaki (1997) replicated these results in another college sample and also found that differences among Asian Americans and Anglos on depressive symptom

measures were no longer significant after controlling for levels of social anxiety. However, symptoms of social avoidance and distress were still higher among Asian Americans even after depressive symptoms were controlled for. Because ethnic differences persist in social anxiety, these symptoms may constitute a way of expressing distress that is especially sensitive to cultural variation among Asian Americans. Although Okazaki, Lui, Longworth, and Minn (2002) found greater reporting on trait and state self-report measures of social anxiety among a sample of Asian American college students when compared with their Anglo counterparts, Okazaki et al. also found no significant ethnic differences in behavioral cues of social anxiety as measured by ratings of a social performance task. The authors thus suggest that elevated subjective report of social anxiety may not translate into observable impairment among Asian Americans.

The two studies we located on anxiety among the elderly sampled Japanese American groups specifically. Yamamoto et al. (1985) utilized a structured clinical interview with a sample obtained from a retirement home and the broader community and found that 9% of respondents were diagnosed with panic disorder. Iwamasa, Hilliard, and Kost (1998) interviewed a sample of elderly English-speaking Japanese Americans from a senior center and found that their conceptualizations of anxiety overlapped somewhat with that of depression; elders described anxiety with terms such as irritability, difficulties in sleeping, and low mood. These two studies suggest that prevalence of anxiety disorders and cultural differences in perceptions of anxiety among older adults warrant further examination.

Schizophrenia-Spectrum Disorders

We found only one study that addressed prevalence of schizophrenia-spectrum disorders (i.e., schizophrenia, schizoaffective, and schizophreniform disorders) among Asian Americans. Zhang and Snowden's (1999) reanalysis of the ECA study data found that Asian Americans demonstrated a lifetime prevalence of .2% for schizophrenia, which did not significantly differ from the rates found in an Anglo comparison group after controlling for sociodemographic variables. However, Asian Americans did demonstrate a significantly lower prevalence of schizophreniform than did the Anglo reference group.

Other than clinical case studies of Asians and Asian immigrants with schizophrenia (D. H. Lam, Chan, & Leff, 1995; Yang & Pearson, 2002), the scant literature on schizophrenia-type disorders among Asian Americans has focused on treatment delay due to stigma among patients and family members (Yang, in review). Lin and Lin (1980) identified five phases of help-seeking among families of Chinese Canadian patients diagnosed with psychotic disorders which result from the intense stigma attached to mental illness: (1) exclusive intrafamilial coping; (2) inclusion of trusted outsiders; (3) use of outside agencies, physicians and finally psychiatrists; (4) labeling of mental illness and hospitalization; and (5) scapegoating and rejection of the patient. In a study of how stigma contributes to help-seeking delay among psychotic patients, Okazaki (2000) found that a sample of Asian American patients diagnosed with psychotic-spectrum disorders and treated in community mental health centers had an average treatment delay of 17.3 months. Further, although patients' and family members' perceptions of stigma were lower than expected, an increase in relatives' reported level of stigma was significantly related to greater treatment delay for patients. In the sole treatment study, psychoeducational group sessions were provided to a group of Korean American patients diagnosed with a schizophrenia-spectrum disorder in addition to weekly individual supportive sessions (Shin & Lukens, 2002). The treatment group showed a greater reduction in psychotic symptoms, expressed less perceived stigma, and perceived more improvements in specific coping skills when compared with a control group, suggesting that psychoeducation is effective in facilitating use of mental health services among Asian Americans who suffer from schizophrenia-spectrum disorders.

Major Depressive Disorders

By far, the most extensive psychopathology research among Asian American groups has occurred with depressive disorders. This section is organized broadly, according to three age groups: youth, adult, and elderly. Within each age group, we first review studies that examine depressive symptoms. We then review studies that utilize DSM criteria to identify prevalence of major depressive disorder (MDD) found in Asian Americans. Although assessing prevalence of depressive symptoms is useful, use of diagnostic interviews to assess psychiatric disorders is more commonly used as the standard by which to detect psychopathology. The advantages to diagnostic interviewing include minimizing criterion variance, assessing a range of symptoms typically not examined by self-report measures alone, and allowing raters to judge whether reported symptoms meet diagnostic criteria (C. Y. Lam, Pepper, & Ryabchenko, 2004). After reviewing research on depressive symptoms and MDD diagnoses, we conclude this section by presenting research on suicide among Asian American groups.

In each section, we review evidence to address key questions:

1. Is the prevalence of depressive disorders higher, lower, or the same among Asian Americans when compared with rates found in the United States and in Asia? Is there any evidence for interethnic differences among Asian Americans?

2. Do correlates of major depressive disorders among Asian Americans follow gender patterns evidenced in most other contexts (i.e., being strongly associated with female gender)?

3. Does prevalence of major depressive disorders vary by immigration status; that is, do the findings inform us of how processes related to ethnicity and immigration may protect against or predispose Asian Americans to developing depression?

Youth (symptoms). The top section of Table 22.2 summarizes studies of depressive symptoms among Asian American youth identified by our literature review. Table 22.2 assesses key aspects of each study, including sample characteristics (ethnic composition, number of respondents, and sampling strategy), assessment measure, and main finding (prevalence of depressive symptoms and whether an Anglo reference group was provided). In comparing prevalence among Asian Americans versus Anglos, whenever possible we utilize scores obtained from Anglo comparison groups within the study itself to minimize sampling and measurement differences. Because the generalizability of studies relies on their sampling strategy and frame, we group studies based on representativeness of the national Asian American community (top of chart, probability sampling,[3] such as an area probability sample to bottom of chart, nonrandom or convenience sampling such as snowball technique). Further, given that estimates of prevalence depend on the validity of assessment measures, we evaluate the reliability and validity of each measure in its use with the specific Asian American sample. Because of the potential importance of incorporating culture-specific idioms of distress when assessing for depression, we also noted whether emic items were developed and if reliability and validity for the adapted measure were assessed.

When examining the seven studies under "Youth Symptoms Scale Studies" (Table 22.2), four studies can be considered representative of a school or area (i.e., are probability samples), whereas the other three studies selected subjects nonrandomly. Each study used an established Western depression symptom scale (although none developed emic items) to measure depressive symptoms. All studies sampled community (or nonmedical-setting) respondents and provided an Anglo comparison group (or referenced an Anglo normative sample for the measure). Six of the seven studies detected no significant differences in depressive symptoms when comparing Asian American youth with an Anglo reference group. The one study that did report more depressive symptoms among Korean youth when compared with Anglos must be viewed with caution due to its use of a convenience sample (Choi et al., 2002). When examining interethnic differences among Asian Americans, Chinese American adolescents appeared to report fewer depressive symptoms when compared with Indian American, Pakistani American, and Vietnamese American adolescents (Roberts, Roberts, & Chen, 1997), although whether this difference reached statistical significance was not reported.

In terms of gender, three studies (one not listed) report a significant association between depressive symptoms and female gender among Hawaiian (Makini et al., 1996), Chinese American (Greenberger & Chen, 1996), and Filipina American youth (Edman et al., 1998), although two studies report no gender differences (Chang, Morrissey, & Koplewicz, 1995; Siegel, Aneshensel, Taub, Cantwell, & Driscoll, 1998). The limited evidence that examines the effect of immigration on depressive symptoms among youth is divided. One study reports higher levels of depressive symptoms among less acculturated Chinese American and Korean American youth (Greenberger & Chen, 1996), whereas another study reports higher levels of anxious/depressed symptoms among a more acculturated sample of Chinese American boys (Chang et al., 1995). One last study found no differences by immigration status (Choi et al., 2002).

Youth (MDD diagnosis). Only two studies (Table 22.2, "Youth Diagnostic Interview Studies") were identified that used DSM criteria to diagnose MDD among Asian American youth. One study found that six-month prevalence of MDD based on records of 954 Asian American mental health outpatients was greater among Asian than Caucasian female adolescents (9.7% vs. 5.7%) but that no significant ethnic differences existed among the male adolescents (L. S. Kim & Chun, 1993). Of note is that this finding among Asian female adolescents took place in a treatment setting and thus may not reflect community patterns of depression. The second study administered the Diagnostic Interview Schedule for Children (DISC) to a sample of high school students and found no differences between Hawaiian and non-Hawaiian adolescents in their rates of current MDD (8.4% vs. 8.5%). However, a direct ethnic comparison is made complicated in that the non-Hawaiian group largely was of mixed or full Asian ethnicity. In terms of interethnic differences, L. S. Kim and Chun (1993) report that Korean Americans had significantly higher rates of MDD whereas Filipino American, Vietnamese American, and "Other" Asian American male adolescents reported lower rates of MDD relative to the larger Asian American group. When comparing prevalence of MDD

Table 22.2 Youth Depression Studies

Study	Ethnicity	Sample & Source	Measure	Main Finding/Prevalence
Symptom Scale Studies				
Gore & Aseltine, 2003	Asian-Am	93 high school respondents; probability sample of nine public schools	Shortened 12-item Center for Epidemiologic Studies–Depression Scale (CES-D)[2]	Asian-Am = Anglos in depressive symptoms at 2-yr follow-up*
Siegel et al., 1998	Asian-Am	93 adolescents (ages 12–17); stratified area probability sample	Children's Depression Inventory (CDI)[1]	No significant differences in depressive symptoms between Asian-Am and Anglos*
Edman et al., 1998	Filipino-Am	285 high school respondents; probability sample	CES-D[1]	No significant differences in depressive symptoms between Filipino-Am and Anglos*
Roberts et al., 1997	Indian-Am	184 school respondents; probability sample of five schools in one district	DSM Scale for Depression[3]	7.6% screened positive for depression; Anglo prevalence = 6.3%*
	Pakistani-Am	146 school respondents	DSM Scale for Depression[3]	6.9% screened positive for depression*
	Vietnamese-Am	288 school respondents	DSM Scale for Depression[3]	6.3% screened positive for depression*
	Chinese-Am	174 school respondents	DSM Scale for Depression[3]	2.9% screened positive for depression*
Choi et al., 2002	Korean-Am	104 community respondents; convenience sample	Adapted DSM Scale for Depression[3]	Korean-Am > Anglos in depressive symptoms
Greenberger & Chen, 1996	Asian-Am (Chinese-, Korean-Am)	89 school respondents (Grades 7 & 8); convenience sample	Shortened 16-item CES-D[1]	No significant differences in depressive symptoms between Asian-Am and Anglos*
L. Chang et al., 1995	Chinese-Am	181 school respondents (ages 5–17); convenience sample	Child Behavior Checklist (CBCL)[3]	No significant differences in depressive symptoms between Asian-Am and those reported for U.S. community

Diagnostic Interview Studies

Study	Group	Sample	Instrument	Findings
Prescott et al., 1998	Hawaiian	321 high school respondents, probability sample	Diagnostic Interview Schedule for Children (DISC)[1]	6-month major depressive disorder (MDD): Hawaiian 8.4%, non-Hawaiian 8.5%
L. S. Kim & Chun, 1993	Asian-Am total	954 mental health outpatients; convenience sample	Clinician-rated (DSM-III)	Current MDD: Asian-Am females 9.7% > Anglo females 5.7%; Asian-Am males 5.3% = Anglo males 3.8%
	Chinese-Am	146 mental health outpatients	Clinician-rated (DSM-III)	Current MDD: females 12.5%, males 4.4%
	Japanese-Am	110 mental health outpatients	Clinician-rated (DSM-III)	Current MDD: females 12.8%, males 6.4%
	Korean-Am	76 mental health outpatients	Clinician-rated (DSM-III)	Current MDD: females 9.1%, males 20.9%
	Filipino-Am	180 mental health outpatients	Clinician-rated (DSM-III)	Current MDD: females 13.6%, males 2.6%
	Vietnamese-Am	106 mental health outpatients	Clinician-rated (DSM-III)	Current MDD: females 7.9%, males 2.7%
	Other Asian-Am (Southeast Asians & Pacific Islanders)	305 mental health outpatients	Clinician-rated (DSM-III)	Current MDD: females 4.9%, males 3.9%

[1] Instrument directly translated, no reliability or validity data for translated instrument; or original version of instrument used with no reliability or validity data for use with new group

[2] Instrument directly translated, reliability of translated instrument assessed with new group but no validity data

[3] Instrument directly translated, reliability and validity of translated instrument assessed with new group

[4] Emic items added to instrument, no reliability or validity data for adapted instrument

[5] Emic items added to instrument, reliability of adapted instrument assessed but no validity data

[6] Emic items added to instrument, reliability and validity assessed for adapted instrument

*Study provides Anglo comparison group

among genders, both studies report that MDD is more likely to be diagnosed among females than males. Neither study examines the effect of immigration on MDD diagnoses.

Adults (symptoms). Table 22.3 summarizes the key features of studies among Asian American adults in an identical fashion to Table 22.2. Among the 15 studies under "Adult Symptom Scale Studies" (Table 22.3), the 5 studies at the top of the chart solely utilized probability sampling, whereas the other 10 studies chiefly used convenience sampling. Thirteen studies utilized Western-validated measures of depressive symptoms, whereas two studies combined portions of such assessments to form their measures. One study added emic items to detect depressive symptoms among Chinese American respondents (Loo, Tong, & True, 1989).

To address issues of depressive symptom prevalence, the 15 studies used three different types of samples: primary care patients ($n = 3$), community samples with both genders ($n = 10$), and female-only community respondents ($n = 2$). Among the primary care studies, one study showed greatly elevated rates of Chinese immigrants screening positive for depressive symptoms (41.6%), whereas the two other studies found more moderate rates among Chinese immigrants (15%) (Yeung, Chan, et al., 2002) and an Asian American group (12.9%), which did not differ significantly from an Anglo comparison rate of 14.5% (Jackson-Triche et al., 2000). The use of convenience sampling in two of the three studies and the use of different measures make drawing definitive conclusions difficult. Among the 10 studies based on community samples of both genders, 5 directly compare depressive symptoms among Asian American and Anglo groups. Four of these studies indicated greater levels of depressive symptoms among Asian American adults, whereas one study reported no differences. However, all five of these studies utilized convenience sampling with college student samples; thus, these findings may not generalize to the larger community. Of the remaining five community studies (none of which sampled an Anglo reference group), four studies reported higher levels of depressive symptoms among Asian American adults (Chinese and Korean Americans specifically)

when compared with U.S. community norms, whereas one study showed no differences. Three of the four studies with positive findings were area probability samples and thus increase our confidence in these results. In the two studies that sampled Asian American women only, results varied by specific ethnicity. Bromberger, Harlow, Avis, Kravitz, and Cordal (2004) found that after controlling for SES, Chinese American women screened at lower levels, but Japanese American women reported similar levels of depressive symptoms as an Anglo reference group. In the second study, S. Kim and Rew (1994) found that a greater proportion of Korean women screened positive for depressive symptoms when compared with U.S. community norms.

The one study that examined group differences among Asian Americans found that Korean Americans scored highest in depressive symptoms among four Asian American groups (Kuo, 1984). In examining gender differences, one study reported female gender being significantly related with higher levels of depressive symptoms among Chinese Americans (Ying, 1988). On the other hand, two studies did not find any gender differences (Hurh & Kim, 1990; Loo et al., 1989). In examining how immigration relates to depressive symptoms, two studies showed that less acculturation to U.S. society is associated with higher levels of depressive symptoms among Korean (Oh, Koeske, & Sales, 2002) and Japanese Americans (Kuo, 1984). However, Kuo et al. also found that lower levels of acculturation were linked with fewer depressive symptoms among Chinese Americans. Lastly, after controlling for SES variables, three studies found no effect of immigration on depressive symptoms (S. Kim & Rew, 1994; Loo et al., 1989; Ying, 1988).

Adult (MDD diagnosis). Six studies (Table 22.3, "Adult Diagnostic Interview Studies") used DSM criteria to identify MDD among Asian American adults. Four of the six utilized probability sampling, and the two others used convenience sampling. All but one study employed Western-developed structured interviews to establish diagnoses, and one study also included emic symptom probes in the diagnostic measure (Takeuchi et al., 1998). Three of the six studies sampled primary care patients. Two of these

Table 22.3   Adult Depression Studies

Ethnicity	Sample & Source	Measure	Prevalence	Main Finding/Study
Symptom Scale Studies				
Jackson-Triche et al., 2000	Asian-Am	527 insured general medical population; probability sample of three health systems	Combined Diagnostic Interview Schedule (DIS) and CES-D[1]	12.9% screened positive for depression (Anglo sample = 14.5%; not significant)*
Hurh & Kim, 1990	Korean-Am	622 community respondents; probability sample of phone and household directories	Adapted CES-D[2]	Average Korean-Am scores (12.3%, male; 12.9%, female) > those reported for U.S. community (7.9%–9.2%) (Radloff, 1977)
Loo et al., 1989	Chinese-Am	108 community respondents; area probability sample	Langer Scale[4]	20% reported > six symptoms vs. 11% Manhattan study
Ying, 1988	Chinese-Am	360 community respondents; probability sample for telephone directory	Adapted CES-D[2]	24.2% screened positive for depression; Radloff (1977) = 19%
Bromberger et al. 2004	Japanese-Am	262 female community respondents; probability sample	Adapted CES-D[2]	14% screened positive for depression (= rate in Anglo sample)*
	Chinese-Am	224 female community respondents	Adapted CES-D[2]	14% screened positive for depression (< rate in Anglo sample)*
Kuo, 1984	Asian-Am (Chinese-, Filipino-, Japanese-, Korean-Am)	484; probability, convenience, and snowball samples combined	CES-D[1]	19.1% screened positive for depression; Radloff (1977) = 19%
Lam et al., 2004	Asian-Am	238 college students; convenience sample	Beck Depression Inventory (BDI)[1]	20.6% screened positive for depression (> Anglo sample)*
			Mood Behavior Questionnaire (MBQ)[1]	21.8% screened positive for depression (= Anglo sample)*

(Continued)

393

Table 22.3 (Continued)

Study	Ethnicity	Sample & Source	Measure	Main Finding/Prevalence
Chung et al., 2003	Chinese-Am	91 primary care patients of participating physicians; convenience sample	CES-D[3]	41.6% screened positive for depression
Oh et al., 2002	Korean-Am	157 community respondents; convenience sample	Adapted CES-D[2]	40% screened positive for depression; Radloff (1977) = 19%
Yeung, Chan, et al., 2002	Chinese-Am	503 primary care clinic patients; convenience sample	Adapted BDI[3]	15% screened positive for depression
Greenberg & Chen, 1996	Asian-Am (Chinese-, Korean-Am)	129 college respondents; convenience sample	Shortened 16-item CES-D[1]	Asian-Am scores > Anglos*
Gratch et al., 1995	Asian-Am	127 college respondents; convenience sample	BDI[1]	Asian-Am scores > Anglos*
E. Chang, 1996	Asian-Am	111 college respondents; convenience sample	BDI[1]	No significant differences in depressive symptoms between Asian-Am and Anglos*
S. Kim & Rew, 1994	Korean-Am	76 females; convenience sample	CES-D[1]	48% screened positive for depression
Aldwin & Greenberger, 1987	Korean-Am	61 college respondents; convenience sample	Scale derived from Langer-22 & Psychiatric Epidemiology Research Interview (PERI)[1]	Korean-Am scores > Anglos*

Diagnostic Interview Studies

Study	Ethnicity	Sample & Source	Measure	Main Finding/Prevalence
Takeuchi et al., 1998	Chinese-Am	1,747 community respondents; probability sample of greater L.A. area	Composite International Diagnostic Interview (CIDI)[4]	12-month major depressive disorder (MDD): 3.4%; U.S. 12-month MDD: 6.6% (Kessler et al., 2003)

Study	Group	Sample	Instrument	Findings
Zhang & Snowden, 1999	Asian-Am	242 community respondents; probability sample of 5 urban communities	Diagnostic Interview Schedule–3rd Edition (DIS-III)[3]	Lifetime MDD: 3.4%; Anglos 4.8% (not significant)*
Hicks & Li, 2003	Chinese-Am	178 female community respondents; probability sample	CIDI[3]	12-month MDD: 7%
Jackson-Triche et al., 2000	Asian-Am	527 insured general medical population; probability sample of 3 healthcare systems	DIS-III[1]	Current MDD: 0.9% < 3.4% Anglo sample*
Chung et al., 2003	Chinese-Am	91 primary care patients of participating physicians; convenience sample	CES-D[3]	17.2% screened positive on the CES-D and were identified by physicians as having an emotional/psychiatric problem
Yeung, Chan, et al., 2002	Chinese-Am	180 primary care patients; convenience sample	Structured Clinical Interview for DSM-III-R Diagnoses (SCID- for DSM-III-R)[2]	Current MDD: 19.6%

[1] Instrument directly translated, no reliability or validity data for translated instrument; or original version of instrument used with new group with no reliability or validity data for use with new group

[2] Instrument directly translated, reliability of translated instrument assessed with new group but no validity data

[3] Instrument directly translated, reliability and validity of translated instrument assessed with new group

[4] Emic items added to instrument, no reliability or validity data for adapted instrument

[5] Emic items added to instrument, reliability of adapted instrument assessed but no validity data

[6] Emic items added to instrument, reliability and validity assessed for adapted instrument

* Study provides Anglo comparison group

studies found that prevalence of current MDD was higher among immigrant Chinese medical patients (17.2%–19.6%) (Chung et al., 2003; Yeung, Howarth, et al., 2002) when compared with estimates of MDD among primary care patients in general (5%–10%) (Katon & Schulberg, 1992). The third study, however, found a significantly lower prevalence of current MDD among Asian Americans (.9%) when compared with an Anglo reference group (3.4%) (Jackson-Triche et al., 2000). The contrary findings in this last study may be attributable to sample differences, as the subjects were selected from fee-for-service and managed care insurance systems and thus came from more advantaged SES conditions than the recent immigrants surveyed in the studies by Chung et al. and Yeung et al. Among the three studies utilizing community samples, one found a 12-month MDD prevalence of 7% among a probability sample of Chinese American women in the greater Boston area (Hicks & Li, 2003). In the second study, Zhang and Snowden (1999) reanalyzed the ECA data and found that Asian Americans did not differ significantly in lifetime prevalence of MDD (3.4%) when compared with an Anglo reference group (4.8%). In the third study (CAPES), Takeuchi et al. (1998) found a 3.4% 12-month prevalence of MDD in a three-stage probability sample of 1,747 Chinese Americans in the greater Los Angeles area. The rate found in CAPES is lower than the 6.6% 12-month prevalence of MDD reported in the U.S. community by the NCS-Replication (Kessler et al., 2003).

None of these six studies examined group differences among Asian Americans. In terms of gender, somewhat surprisingly, Takeuchi et al. (1998) reported that female gender among their representative sample of Chinese Americans was not related to either 12-month or lifetime prevalence of MDD. However, when examining gender and immigration effects together, women were more likely than men to suffer lifetime MDD in the high-acculturation but not in the low-acculturation group. One other study (Hicks & Li, 2003), after controlling for SES variables, found no effect of acculturation on prevalence of MDD.

Elderly (depressive symptoms). Of the seven studies included under "Elderly Symptom Scale Studies" (Table 22.4), one is a regional probability sample whereas the other six used convenience sampling. Each study used a Western-developed depression scale, although none included emic items. All seven studies utilized community respondents; only one sampled an Anglo comparison group. Regarding prevalence, results varied a great deal among the six studies that used convenience samples. In comparison with the reported 15%–20% rate of the general elder population who suffer significant depressive symptoms (Gallo & Lebowitz, 1999), three of the six studies reported lower rates among Asian American elders, and two found similar rates of depressive symptoms. The last study found elevated levels of depressive symptoms among a sample of Korean American elders (Mui, 2001). The single regional probability sample found greatly increased rates of positive screens for depression among six elder Asian American groups (average = 40.5%; range = 15%–76%), suggesting that Asian American elders are at strong risk for depression (Mui, Kang, Chen, & Domanski, 2003). Heterogeneity of depression scores among this sample existed, as Japanese American elders reported significantly higher scores and Korean American and Filipino American elders reported the least.

When examining the effect of gender, Mui (2001) found that females tended to score higher on depressive symptoms in a sample of Korean American elders, although Raskin, Chien, and Lin (1992) and Iwamasa et al. (1998) did not find significant gender differences among Chinese American and Japanese American elders, respectively. The lone study that examined the effect of immigration reported that acculturation was not related with depression scores among Japanese American elders (Shibusawa & Mui, 2001).

Elderly (MDD diagnosis). We found only one study (Table 22.4, "Elderly Diagnostic Interview Studies") that used DSM criteria to diagnose MDD among Asian American elders. Yamamoto, Rhee, and Chang (1994) used a structured clinical interview to assess current MDD in a convenience sample of 100 Korean American community elders and found a prevalence of 2.1% among females and 0% among males. These findings are roughly comparable to a stratified random sample of Anglo elderly in

Table 22.4 Elderly Depression Studies

Study	Ethnicity	Sample & Source	Measure	Main Finding/Prevalence
Symptom Scale Studies				
Mui et al., 2003	Asian-Am (Chinese-, Korean-, Filipino-, Vietnamese-, Japanese-Am)	407 community respondents; regional probability sample	Adapted Geriatric Depression Scale (GDS)[2]	40.5% screened positive for depressive symptoms
Mui, 2001	Korean-Am	67; convenience sample	GDS[2]	44.8% screened positive for depressive symptoms
Shibusawa & Mui, 2001	Japanese-Am	131; convenience sample	GDS[2]	19.8% screened positive for depressive symptoms
Iwamasa et al., 1998	Japanese-Am	120; convenience sample from one community center	GDS[1]	No depressed subjects
Mui, 1996	Chinese-Am	50 community respondents; convenience sample	Adapted GDS[2]	18% screened positive for depressive symptoms
Raskin et al., 1992	Chinese-Am	113 community respondents; convenience sample	Inventory of Psychic and Somatic Complaints–Elderly, Global Assessment of Psychopathology Scales–Elderly, Mood States–Elderly[1]	Chinese-Am < Anglos on depressive symptoms*
Suen & Tusaie, 2004	Taiwanese-Am	100 community respondents; convenience sample	GDS[2]	9% screened positive for depressive symptoms
Diagnostic Interview Study				
Yamamoto et al., 1994	Korean-Am	100; convenience sample from one organization	Diagnostic Interview Schedule– 3rd Edition (DIS-III)	Current major depressive disorder (MDD): females 2.1%, males 0%

[1] Instrument directly translated, no reliability or validity data for translated instrument; or original version of instrument used with no reliability or validity data for use with new group

[2] Instrument directly translated, reliability of translated instrument assessed with new group but no validity data

* Study provides Anglo comparison group

397

St. Louis, Missouri, whose prevalence of MDD was .8% (sexes combined) (Robins et al., 1984). Yamamoto et al. (1994) did not report whether the differences among genders are statistically significant; nor did they examine effects of immigration on prevalence of MDD.

Suicide

Overall, the national suicide rates (per 100,000) for Asian Americans have been slowly decreasing from 1980 to 2002 from 10.7 to 8.0 among males and 5.5 to 3.0 among females (National Center for Health Statistics, 2004). These rates have remained at or below the rates for Anglos except for elevated rates among elderly Asian Americans. Earlier studies have reported similar findings among specific Asian American ethnicities, as Bourne (1973) found that the completed suicide rates for Chinese Americans were similar to the rates for Anglos except for higher rates of suicide in Chinese Americans over 50 years old. Further, whereas non-elder Japanese Americans in Hawai'i and Los Angeles have not shown more frequent suicide attempts than other ethnic groups (Rogers & Izutsu, 1980), the suicide rates for Japanese American elders is 2.5 times higher than that of their White counterparts (Baker, 1994).

In examining how gender relates with suicide, the female-to-male ratio for the national suicide rate for Asian Americans has slightly increased from 1980 to 2002 (National Center for Health Statistics, 2004). The gender balance of suicide among elderly Asian Americans has also shifted over time. At first, Bourne (1973) found in the completed suicide rates for Chinese Americans over 50 years old, females had increasing rates of 35.1 (65–74 yrs.) to 43.3 (> 75 yrs.) while males had the highest rate at 63 (> 75 yrs.). Over 20 years later, Shiang et al. (1997) found that Asian American males showed much lower rates overall than Anglo males (18.45 vs. 68.25). Although the rate peaks at 50 per 100,000 for Asian American males at age 75–84, that rate was still lower than their Anglo counterparts (83 per 100,000). While Asian American females had lower rates overall than Anglo females, differences emerged in females older than 85 years, where the rate for Asian Americans rose to 67 compared to 27 for Anglos. Currently, it is thus the female elderly Asian American group who faces a particularly elevated risk of suicide.

Despite findings that non-elder Asian Americans as a group do not evidence a higher risk of suicide than other ethnic groups, Asian American adolescents and young adults may face culture-specific risk factors for suicide. First of all, there is initial evidence that suicidal ideation, an often-understudied cognition that predisposes suicidal behavior, is higher among Asian American adults. One study found that Asian American college students reported more suicidal ideation than Anglo students (Muehlenkamp, Gutierrez, Osman, & Barrios, 2005); this finding was attributed to the way Asian Americans responded to items relating disparity in achievement standards. Second, certain Pacific Islander adolescent groups are at greater risk of suicide. Micronesian youth have experienced a suicide epidemic for the past 30 years with rates from 10 to 13 times the rate for U.S. youth (Hezel, 1987; Rubinstein, 1995). Lowe (2003) attributes this epidemic to compromised social functioning due to rapid socioeconomic changes in these communities after World War II, which has also manifested in increased substance abuse, peer violence, and social delinquency (Hezel, 1987; Marshall, 1979; Rubinstein, 1995). Native Hawaiian adolescents are also at greater risk of attempting suicide than their peers in Hawaii (Yuen, Nahulu, Hishinuma, & Miyamoto, 2000). Further, Hawaiian cultural affiliation was a more accurate predictor of suicide attempts than ethnicity per se, which may speak to the effects of acculturative stress on mental health for those who are culturally Hawaiian. Other subgroups of Asian American adolescents have not been well studied, although Roberts et al. (1997) reported that Pakistani American and Vietnamese American adolescents were found to have elevated levels of suicidal ideation, plans, and attempts.

Conclusions: Depressive Disorders Among Asian Americans

In considering the evidence presented, in conjunction with findings from the CAPES study (Hwang et al., 2005; Takeuchi et al., 1998), several initial conclusions can be drawn:

1. Elevated depression scale scores do not necessarily signal greater prevalence of MDD among Asian Americans, as the adult studies indicate elevated rates of depressive symptoms but moderate or low prevalence of MDD in this group. Scores over "case" thresholds on depression scales may instead detect distress or demoralization (Coyne, 1994).

2. When considering prevalence of MDD, there is evidence that recent immigrant Chinese American adults within primary care and Asian American girls in mental health treatment samples are at higher risk of developing MDD. However, evidence from community samples suggests that prevalence of MDD among Asian Americans is equal to or less than general U.S. population rates, but still higher than rates found in Asia. One notable finding is that almost all the community studies with Asian American youth find no differences in depressive disorders between this group and Anglo comparison groups.

3. The greater risk of suicide among the Asian American elderly, particular elderly females, highlights a need to conduct more research in this group using DSM criteria for MDD.

4. Except for one study with elders, Korean Americans in particular showed higher levels of depressive symptoms relative to Anglo and other Asian American groups.

5. The data are divided when considering an association between female gender and depressive disorders among Asian Americans. Takeuchi et al.'s (1998) findings that gender differences only occurred in the high-acculturation group may explain why this association is detected in some studies (which may vary by acculturation status) but not in others.

6. The data on the effect of immigration on depressive disorders is also mixed, and mainly finds no association after accounting for other SES variables. Hwang et al. (2005) was able to test effects of acculturation more powerfully than most other studies via the large CAPES sample size; they found that as length of time in the United States increased, risk of developing depression decreased. They also found that Chinese immigrants faced their greatest risk of developing depression at, or soon after, migration. Thus, Chinese immigrants initially face a greater risk for depression as they confront migration stresses, but gradually they are at less risk for developing depression as they acclimate to life in the United States.

SUMMARY AND FUTURE DIRECTIONS

Having reviewed how cultural processes shape psychopathology and the literature on prevalence and manifestation of several major mental disorders among Asian Americans, we return to our original questions regarding how psychopathology may change in form as Asian Americans arrive and settle in the United States. We also suggest areas of future investigation.

1. Although people from Asian groups tend to use bodily metaphors to convey emotional distress, it remains unresolved whether Asian American community members report more somatic symptoms than Anglo community members. Among Asian Americans, continued structured questioning appears to elicit endorsement of affective as well as physical types of distress.

2. The relatively small size, heterogeneity, and changing demographic composition of the Asian American population pose particular challenges to our ability to accurately categorize the experiences of this group (S. Sue, 2002). Because studies of Asian Americans often are based on different types of samples, estimates of psychopathology in specific subgroups may vary widely and may sometimes even conflict.

3. With this limitation in mind, in studies that utilize probability sampling techniques and DSM criteria for diagnosis, Asian Americans generally appear to show rates of psychopathology that are similar to, or lower than, the larger U.S. population. However, these estimates do not include occurrence of culture-specific syndromes (such as neurasthenia) or diagnoses that incorporate emic symptom expression.

4. Estimates of psychopathology among Asian Americans appear higher than rates found in Asia, which suggest that acculturative stress

during the immigration process may contribute to higher prevalence of mental disorders. Initial evidence from the CAPES study suggests that when Chinese Americans immigrate to the United States, they may face a higher risk of developing mental disorders (Hwang et al., 2005). However, this study also suggests that subsequent acculturation to U.S. society provides an overall protective effect against developing a psychiatric disorder.

5. Although a great deal of research has been conducted on depressive disorders, research on other diagnoses such as anxiety and schizophrenia-type disorders has been neglected. Examination of factors particular to Asian American culture that may directly affect manifestation and course of illness deserve special attention. For example, how patient-family interactions influence the course of schizophrenia has been widely established but has yet to be examined among Asian Americans (Yang, Phillips, Licht, & Hooley, 2004; Yang, 2003a). Further research should also address the measurement of emic expressions of mental health symptoms and diagnoses among Asian Americans.

This chapter has attempted to summarize the current state of psychopathology research among Asian Americans. Many unresolved empirical issues will soon be addressed more adequately by the NLAAS study, which estimates the prevalence of mental disorders among Asian American groups using a nationally representative household sample and directly examines the mechanisms by which acculturation may be linked to psychiatric disorders among this group. It is our hope that this review and studies such as NLAAS will spur further innovation in psychopathology research among Asian Americans in future studies to come.

Notes

1. However, there is one finding counter to the previously mentioned findings. In a study of a multiethnic community sample of 2,246 residents of Montreal, Canada, the Vietnamese and Filipino groups endorsed higher levels of somatic symptoms than did the other ethnic groups studied when level of emotional distress was controlled for (Kirmayer & Young, 1998).

2. One study not listed in Table 22.1 compared utilization rates among Asian American subgroups (Ying & Hu, 1994). Filipinos were reported to be underrepresented relative to other Asian American groups in one public mental health care system, which is attributable to their increased access to private health insurance due to their greater likelihood of employment and English proficiency. On the other hand, Southeast Asians were overrepresented relative to other Asian American groups, which likely reflects their history of premigration trauma and correspondingly higher proportion of anxiety disorders (e.g., post-traumatic stress disorder).

3. In our definition of probability sampling, we include random selection of respondents from nonrandom sampling frames such as telephone directories and health insurance plans due to the paucity of studies among Asian American groups that attempt to minimize selection bias by the respondents into the sample.

References

Aldwin, C., & Greenberger, E. (1987). Cultural differences in the predictors of depression. *American Journal of Community Psychology, 15,* 789–813.

Alegria, M., Takeuchi, D., Canino, G., Duan, N., Shrout, P., Meng, X., et al. (2004). Considering context, place and culture: The National Latino and Asian American Study. *International Journal of Methods in Psychiatric Research, 13*(4), 208–220.

Baker, F. M. (1994). Suicide among ethnic minority elderly: A statistical and psychosocial perspective. *Journal of Geriatric Psychiatry, 27,* 241–264.

Bourne, P.G. (1973). Suicide among Chinese in San Francisco. *American Journal of Public Health, 8,* 744–750.

Bromberger, J. T., Harlow, S., Avis, N., Kravitz, H. M., & Cordal, A. (2004). Racial/ethnic differences in the prevalence of depressive symptoms among middle-aged women: Study of Women's Health Across the Nation (SWAN). *American Journal of Public Health, 94*(8), 1378–1385.

Bui, K. V., & Takeuchi, D. T. (1992). Ethnic minority adolescents and the use of community mental health care services. *American Journal of Community Psychology, 20*(4), 403–417.

Chang, E. (1996). Cultural differences in optimism, pessimism, and coping: Predictors of subsequent adjustment in Asian-American and Caucasian-American students. *Journal of Counseling Psychology, 43,* 113–123.

Chang, L., Morrissey, R. F., & Koplewicz, H. S. (1995). Prevalence of psychiatric symptoms and their relation to adjustment among Chinese-American youth. *Journal of the American Academy of Child & Adolescent Psychiatry, 34,* 91–99.

Cheung, F. (1995). Facts and myths about somatization among the Chinese. In T. Y. Lin, W. S. Tseng, & E. K. Yeh (Eds.), *Chinese societies and mental health* (pp. 141–180). Hong Kong: Oxford University Press.

Cheung, F. M., Cheung, S. F., & Zhang, J. (2004). Convergent validity of the Chinese Personality Assessment Inventory and the Minnesota Multiphasic Personality Inventory–2: Preliminary findings with a normative sample. *Journal of Personality Assessment, 82*(1), 92–103.

Cheung, F. M., Leung, K., Fan, R. M., Song, W. Z., Zhang, J. X., & Zhang, J. P. (1996). Development of the Chinese Personality Assessment Inventory. *Journal of Cross-Cultural Psychology, 27,* 143–164.

Choi, H., Stafford, L., Meininger, J. C., Roberts, R. E., & Smith, D. P. (2002). Psychometric properties of the DSM scale for depression (DSD) with Korean-American youths. *Issues in Mental Health Nursing, 23*(8), 735–756.

Chung, H., Teresi, J., & Guarnaccia, P., Meyers, B., Holmes, D., Bobrowitz, T., et al. (2003). Depression symptoms and psychiatric distress in low-income Asian and Latino primary care patients: Prevalence and recognition. *Community Mental Health Journal, 39,* 33–46.

Coyne, J. C. (1994). Self-reported distress: Analog or ersatz depression? *Psychological Bulletin, 116,* 29–45.

Durvasula, R., & Sue, S. (1996). Severity of disturbance among Asian American outpatients. *Cultural Diversity and Mental Health, 2*(1), 43–51.

Edman, J. L., Andrade, N. N., Glipa, J., Foster, J., Danko, G. P., Yates, A., et al. (1998). Depressive symptoms among Filipino American adolescents. *Cultural Diversity and Mental Health, 4*(1), 45–54.

Escobar, J. I., Hoyos Nervi, C., & Gara, M. A. (2000). Immigration and mental health: Mexican Americans in the United States. *Harvard Review of Psychiatry, 8,* 64–72.

Gallo, J. J., & Lebowitz, B. D. (1999). The epidemiology of common late-life mental disorders in the community: Themes for the new century. *Psychiatric Services, 50,* 1158–1166.

Gore, S., & Aseltine, R. H., Jr. (2003). Race and ethnic differences in depressed mood following the transition from high school. *Journal of Health and Social Behavior, 44*(3), 370–389.

Gratch, L. V., Bassett, M. E., & Attra, S. L. (1995). The relationship of gender and ethnicity to self-silencing and depression among college students. *Psychology of Women Quarterly, 19,* 509–515.

Greenberger, A., & Chen, C. (1996). Perceived family relationships and depressed mood in early and late adolescence: A comparison of European and Asian-Americans. *Developmental Psychology, 32,* 707–716.

Hezel, F. X. (1987). Truk suicide epidemic and social change. *Human Organization, 46,* 283–291.

Hicks, M. H., & Li, Z. (2003). Partner violence and major depression in women: A community study of Chinese Americans. *Journal of Nervous and Mental Disease, 191*(11), 722–729.

Hsu, L. K., & Folstein, M. F. (1997). Somatoform disorders in Caucasian and Chinese Americans. *Journal of Nervous and Mental Disease, 185*(6), 382–387.

Hu, T. W., Snowden, L. R., Jerrell, J. M., & Nguyen, T. D. (1991). Ethnic populations in public mental health: Services choice and level of use. *American Journal of Public Health, 81*(11), 1429–1434.

Hurh, W. M., & Kim, K. C. (1990). Correlates of Korean immigrants' mental health. *Journal of Nervous and Mental Disease, 178*(11), 703–711.

Hwang, W. C., Chun, C. A., Takeuchi, D. T., Myers, H. F., & Siddarth, P. (2005). Age of first onset major depression in Chinese Americans. *Cultural Diversity & Ethnic Minority Psychology, 11*(1), 16–27.

Iwamasa, G. Y., Hilliard, K. M., & Kost, C. (1998). The Geriatric Depression Scale and older Japanese American adults. *Clinical Gerontologist, 19,* 13–26.

Jackson-Triche, M. E., Greer Sullivan, J., Wells, K. B., Rogers, W., Camp, P., & Mazel, R. (2000). Depression and health-related quality of life in ethnic minorities seeking care in general medical settings. *Journal of Affective Disorders, 58*(2), 89–97.

Katon, W., & Schulberg, H. (1992). Epidemiology of depression in primary care. *General Hospital Psychiatry, 14,* 237–247.

Kessler, R. C., Berglund, P., Demler, O., Jin, R., Koretz, D., Merikangas, K. R., et al. (2003). The epidemiology of major depressive disorder: Results from the National Comorbidity Survey Replication (NCS-R). *Journal of the American Medical Association, 289*(23), 3095–3105.

Kessler, R. C., McGonagle, K. A., Zhao, S., Nelson, C. B., Hughes, M., Eshleman, S., et al. (1994). Lifetime and 12-month prevalence of DSM-III-R psychiatric disorders in the United States. Results from the National Comorbidity Survey. *Archives of General Psychiatry, 51*(1), 8–19.

Kim, L. S., & Chun, C. A. (1993). Ethnic differences in psychiatric diagnosis among Asian American adolescents. *Journal of Nervous and Mental Disease, 181*(10), 612–617.

Kim, M. T. (1995). Cultural influences on depression in Korean-Americans. *Journal of Psychosocial Nursing and Mental Health Services, 33*(2), 13–18.

Kim, S., & Rew, L. (1994). Ethnic identity, role integration, quality of life, and depression in Korean-American women. *Archives of Psychiatric Nursing, 8,* 348–356.

Kirmayer, L. J., & Young, A. (1998). Culture and somatization: Clinical, epidemiological, and ethnographic perspectives. *Psychosomatic Medicine, 60,* 420–430.

Kleinman, A. (2004). Culture and depression. *New England Journal of Medicine, 351*(10), 951–953.

Kleinman, A. M. (1977). Depression, somatization and the "new cross-cultural psychiatry." *Social Science & Medicine, 11*(1), 3–10.

Kuo, W. H. (1984). Prevalence of depression among Asian-Americans. *Journal of Nervous and Mental Disease, 172,* 449–457.

Lam, C. Y., Pepper, C. M., & Ryabchenko, K. A. (2004). Case identification of mood disorders in Asian American and Caucasian American college students. *Psychiatric Quarterly, 75*(4), 361–373.

Lam, D. H., Chan, N., & Leff, J. (1995). Family work for schizophrenia: Some issues for Chinese immigrant families. *Journal of Family Therapy, 17,* 281–297.

Lee, S. (2002). Socio-cultural and global health perspectives for the development of future psychiatric diagnostic systems. *Psychopathology, 35,* 152–157.

Leong, F. T. L. (1994). Asian-Americans' differential patterns of utilization of inpatient and outpatient public mental health services in Hawaii. *Journal of Community Psychology, 22,* 82–89.

Lin, K. M., Inui, T. S., Kleinman, A. M., & Womack, W. M. (1982). Sociocultural determinants of the help-seeking behavior of patients with mental illness. *Journal of Nervous and Mental Disease, 170,* 78–85.

Lin, K. M., & Lin, M.C. (1980). Love, denial, and rejection: Responses of Chinese families to mental illness. In A. M. Kleinman & T. Y. Lin (Eds.), *Normal and deviant behavior in Chinese culture* (pp. 387–399). Dordrecht, Netherlands: D. Reidel.

Loo, C., Tong, B., & True, R. (1989). A bitter bean: Mental health status and attitudes in Chinatown. *Journal of Community Psychology, 17,* 283–296.

Lowe, E. D. (2003). Identity, activity, and the well-being of adolescents and youth: Lessons from young people in a Micronesian society. *Culture, Medicine and Psychiatry, 27*(2), 187–219.

Makini, G. K., Jr., Andrade, N. N., Nahulu, L. B., Yuen, N., Yate, A., McDermott, J. F., Jr., et al. (1996). Psychiatric symptoms of Hawaiian adolescents. *Cultural Diversity and Mental Health, 2*(3), 183–191.

Marshall, M. (1979). *Weekend warriors: Alcohol in a Micronesian culture.* Palo Alto, CA: Mayfield Press.

Matsuoka, J. K., Breaux, C., & Ryujin, D. H. (1997). National utilization of mental health services by Asian Americans/Pacific Islanders. *Journal of Community Psychology, 25*(2), 141–145.

McCabe, K. M., Yeh, M., & Hough, R. L. (1999). Racial/ethnic variation across five public systems of care for youth. *Journal of Emotional and Behavioral Disorders, 7,* 72–82.

Muehlenkamp, J. J., Gutierrez, P. M., Osman, A., & Barrios, F. X. (2005). Validation of the Positive and Negative Suicide Ideation (PANSI) Inventory in a diverse sample of young adults. *Journal of Clinical Psychology, 61,* 431–445.

Mui, A. C. (1996). Geriatric depression scale as a community screening instrument for elderly Chinese immigrants. *International Psychogeriatrics, 8*(3), 445–458.

Mui, A. C. (2001). Stress, coping and depression among elderly Korean immigrants. *Journal of Human Behavior in the Social Environment, 3,* 281–299.

Mui, A. C., Kang, S. Y., Chen, L. M., & Domanski, M. D. (2003). Reliability of the Geriatric Depression Scale for use among elderly Asian immigrants in the USA. *International Psychogeriatrics, 15*(3), 253–271.

National Center for Health Statistics. (2004). *Health, United States, 2004, with chartbook on trends in the health of Americans* (Publication No. 2004–1232). Hyattsville, MD: U.S. Government Printing Office.

Oh, Y., Koeske, G. F., & Sales, E. (2002). Acculturation, stress, and depressive symptoms among Korean immigrants in the United States. *Journal of Social Psychology, 142*(4), 511–526.

Okazaki, S. (1997). Sources of ethnic differences between Asian-American and White American college students on measures of depression and social anxiety. *Journal of Abnormal Psychology, 106*(1), 52–60.

Okazaki, S. (2000). Asian American and White American differences on affective distress symptoms: Do symptom reports differ across reporting methods? *Journal of Cross-Cultural Psychology, 31*(5), 603–625.

Okazaki, S., Lui, J. F., Longworth, S. L., & Minn, J. Y. (2002). Asian American-White American differences in expressions of social anxiety: A replication and extension. *Cultural Diversity & Ethnic Minority Psychology, 8,* 234–247.

O'Sullivan, M. J., Peterson, P. D., Cox, G. B., & Kirkeby, J. (1989). Ethnic populations: Community mental health services ten years later. *American Journal of Community Psychology, 17*(1), 17–30.

Parker, G., Gladstone, G., & Chee, K. T. (2001). Depression in the planet's largest ethnic group: The Chinese. *American Journal of Psychiatry, 158,* 857–864.

Prescott, C. A., McArdle, J. J., Hishinuma, E. S., Johnson, R. C., Miyamoto, R. H., & Andrade, N. N. (1998). Prediction of major depression and dysthymia from CES-D scores among ethnic minority adolescents. *Journal of the American Academy of Child & Adolescent Psychiatry, 37,* 495–503.

Radloff, L. (1977). The CES-D scale: A self-report depression scale for research in the general population. *Applied Psychological Measurement, 1,* 385–401.

Raskin, A., Chien, C., & Lin, K. (1992). Elderly Chinese-Americans compared on measures of psychic distress, somatic complaints and social competence. *International Journal of Geriatric Psychiatry, 7,* 191–198.

Roberts, R. E., Roberts, C. R., & Chen, Y. R. (1997). Ethnocultural differences in prevalence of adolescent depression. *American Journal of Community Psychology, 25*(1), 95–110.

Robins, L. N., Helzer, J. E., Weissman, M. M., Orvaschel, H., Gruenberg, E., Burke, J. D., et al. (1984). Lifetime prevalence of specific psychiatric disorders in three sites. *Archives of General Psychiatry, 41,* 949–995.

Robins, L. N., & Regier, D. A. (1991). *Psychiatric disorders in America: The Epidemiologic Catchment Area Study.* New York: Free Press.

Rogers, T., & Izutsu, S. (1980). The Japanese. In J. J. F. McDermott, W. S. Tseng & T. W. Maretzki (Eds.), People and cultures of Hawaii: A psychocultural profile (pp. 73–99). Honolulu: John A. Burns School of Medicine and the University Press of Hawaii.

Rubinstein, D. H. (1995). Love and suffering: Adolescent socialization and suicide in Micronesia. *The Contemporary Pacific, 7,* 21–53.

Shiang, J., Blinn, R., Bongar, B., Stephens, B., Allison, D., & Schatzberg, A. (1997). Suicide in San Francisco, CA: A comparison of Caucasian and Asian groups, 1987–1994. *Suicide & Life-Threatening Behavior, 27*(1), 80–91.

Shibusawa, T., & Mui, A. C. (2001). Stress, coping and depression among Japanese-American elders. *Journal of Gerontological Social Work, 36,* 63–81.

Shin, S. K., & Lukens, E. P. (2002). Effects of psychoeducation for Korean-Americans with chronic mental illness. *Psychiatric Services, 53*(9), 1125–1131.

Siegel, J. M., Aneshensel, C. S., Taub, B., Cantwell, D. P., & Driscoll, A. K. (1998). Adolescent depressed mood in a multiethnic sample. *Journal of Youth and Adolescence, 27,* 413–427.

Simon, G. E., Goldberg, D. P., Von Korff, M., & Ustun, T. B. (2002). Understanding cross-national differences in depression prevalence. *Psychological Medicine, 32,* 585–594.

Snowden, L. R., & Cheung, F. K. (1990). Use of inpatient mental health services by members of ethnic minority groups. *American Psychologist, 45*(3), 347–355.

Sue, D., Ino, S., & Sue, D. M. (1983). Nonassertiveness of Asian-Americans: An inaccurate assumption? *Journal of Counseling Psychology, 30,* 581–588.

Sue, D., & Sue, S. (1987). Cultural factors in the clinical assessment of Asian Americans. *Journal of Consulting and Clinical Psychology, 55*(4), 479–487.

Sue, S. (1977). Community mental health services to minority groups. Some optimism, some pessimism. *American Psychologist, 32*(8), 616–624.

Sue, S. (2002). Asian American mental health: What we know and what we don't know. In W. J. Lonner, D. L. Dinnel, S. A. Hayes, & D. N. Sattler (Eds.), *Online readings in psychology and culture* (unit 3, chap. 4). Bellingham: Western Washington University, Center for Cross-Cultural Research. Retrieved February 27, 2006, from http://www.ac.wwu.edu/~culture/SueS.htm

Sue, S., Fujino, D. C., Hu, L. T., Takeuchi, D. T., & Zane, N. W. (1991). Community mental health services for ethnic minority groups: A test of the cultural responsiveness hypothesis. *Journal of Consulting and Clinical Psychology, 59*(4), 533–540.

Sue, S., Sue, D. W., Sue, L., & Takeuchi, D. T. (1995). Psychopathology among Asian Americans: A model minority? *Cultural Diversity and Mental Health, 1*(1), 39–51.

Suen, L. W., & Tusaie, K. (2004). Is somatization a significant depressive symptom in older Taiwanese Americans? *Geriatric Nursing, 25*(3), 157–163.

Takeuchi, D. T., Chung, R. C., Lin, K. M., Shen, H., Kurasaki, K., Chun, C. A., et al. (1998). Lifetime and twelve-month prevalence rates of major depressive episodes and dysthymia among Chinese Americans in Los Angeles. *American Journal of Psychiatry, 155*(10), 1407–1414.

U.S. Department of Health and Human Services. (2001). Mental health: Culture, race, and ethnicity—A supplement to mental health: A report of the Surgeon General. Rockville, MD: U.S. Department of Health and Human Services, Substance Abuse and Mental Health Services Administration, Center for Mental Health Services.

Virnig, B., Huang, Z., Lurie, N., Musgrave, D., McBean, M., & Dowd, B. (2004). Does Medicare managed care provide equal treatment for mental illness across races? *Archives of General Psychiatry, 61,* 201–205.

Weissman, M. M., Bland, R. C., Canino, G. J., Faravelli, C., Greenwald, S., Hwu, H. G., et al. (1996). Cross-national epidemiology of major depression and bipolar disorder. *Journal of the American Medical Association, 276,* 293–299.

Weissman, M. M., Bland, R. C., Canino, G. J., Faravelli, C., Greenwald, S., Hwu, H. G., et al. (1997). Cross-national epidemiology of panic disorder. *Archives of General Psychiatry, 54,* 305–309.

World Mental Health Survey Consortium. (2004). Prevalence, severity and unmet need for treatment of mental disorders in the World Health Organization World Mental Health Surveys. *Journal of the American Medical Association, 291*(21), 2581–2590.

Yamamoto, J., Machizawa, S., Araki, F., Reece, S., Steinburg, A., Leung, J., et al. (1985). Mental health of Elderly Asian Americans in Los Angeles. *American Journal of Social Psychiatry, 5,* 37–46.

Yamamoto, J., Rhee, S., & Chang, D. S. (1994). Psychiatric disorders among elderly Koreans in the United States. *Community Mental Health Journal, 30,* 17–27.

Yang, L. H. (2003a). Causal attributions, expressed emotion, and patient relapse: Recent findings and application to Chinese societies. *Hong Kong Journal of Psychiatry, 13*(2), 16–25.

Yang, L. H. (2003b). *Chinese-American attitudes towards Western vs. traditional Chinese medicine for mental disorders.* Paper presented at Columbia University's Psychiatric Epidemiology Training Program Seminar, New York.

Yang, L. H. (in review). Application of stigma theory to Chinese-Americans with mental illness. *Journal of Immigrant and Minority Health.*

Yang, L. H., & Pearson, V. (2002). Understanding families in their own context: Schizophrenia and structural family therapy in Beijing. *Journal of Family Therapy, 24,* 233–257.

Yang, L. H., Phillips, M. R., Licht, D. M., & Hooley, J. M. (2004). Causal attributions and their relation to expressed emotion, stigma, and relapse in patients with schizophrenia in China. *Journal of Abnormal Psychology, 113,* 592–602.

Yeh, M., McCabe, K., Hurlburt, M., Hough, R., Hazen, A., Culver, S., et al. (2002). Referral sources, diagnoses, and service types of youth in public outpatient mental health care: A focus on ethnic minorities. *Journal of Behavioral Health Services and Research, 29*(1), 45–60.

Yen, S., Robins, C. J., & Lin, N. (2000). A cross-cultural comparison of depressive symptom manifestation: China and the United States. *Journal of Consulting and Clinical Psychology, 68*(6), 993–999.

Yeung, A., Chang, D., Gresham, R. L., Jr., Nierenberg, A. A., & Fava, M. (2004). Illness beliefs of depressed Chinese American patients in primary care. *Journal of Nervous and Mental Disease, 192*(4), 324–327.

Yeung, A., Howarth, S., Chan, R., Sonawalla, S., Nierenberg, A. A., & Fava, M. (2002). Use of the Chinese version of the Beck Depression Inventory for screening depression in primary care. *Journal of Nervous and Mental Disease, 190*, 94–99.

Yeung, A., Neault, N., Sonawalla, S., Howarth, S., Fava, M., & Nierenberg, A. A. (2002). Screening for major depression in Asian-Americans: A comparison of the Beck and the Chinese Depression Inventory. *Acta Psychiatrica Scandinavica, 105*(4), 252–257.

Ying, Y. W. (1988). Depressive symptomatology among Chinese-Americans as measured by the CES-D. *Journal of Clinical Psychology, 44*(5), 739–746.

Ying, Y. W., & Hu, L. T. (1994). Public outpatient mental health services: Use and outcome among Asian Americans. *American Journal of Orthopsychiatry, 64*(3), 448–455.

Ying, Y. W., Lee, P. A., Tsai, J. L., Yeh, Y. Y., & Huang, J. S. (2000). The conception of depression in Chinese American college students. *Cultural Diversity & Ethnic Minority Psychology, 6*(2), 183–195.

Young, D. (1989). Neurasthenia and related problems. *Culture, Medicine and Psychiatry, 13*(2), 131–138.

Young, D., Zhang, Y., Li, L. J., Lin, K. M., & Zheng, Y. P. (1997). *Diagnosis and cultural meaning of neurasthenia in China.* Paper presented at the 150th annual meeting of the American Psychiatric Association, San Diego, CA.

Yuen, N. Y., Nahulu, L. B., Hishinuma, E. S., & Miyamoto, R. H. (2000). Cultural identification and attempted suicide in Native Hawaiian adolescents. *Journal of the American Academy of Child & Adolescent Psychiatry, 39*(3), 360–367.

Zhang, A. Y., & Snowden, L. R. (1999). Ethnic characteristics of mental disorders in five U.S. communities. *Cultural Diversity & Ethnic Minority Psychology, 5*(2), 134–146.

Zhang, A. Y., Snowden, L. R., & Sue, S. (1998). Differences between Asian- and White-Americans' help-seeking and utilization patterns in the Los Angeles area. *Journal of Community Psychology, 26*, 317–326.

Zheng, Y. P., Lin, K. M., Takeuchi, D., Kurasaki, K. S., Wang, Y., & Cheung, F. (1997). An epidemiological study of neurasthenia in Chinese-Americans in Los Angeles. *Comprehensive Psychiatry, 38*(5), 249–259.

PART V

Assessment and Interventions

23

ASSESSMENT OF ASIAN AMERICANS: FUNDAMENTAL ISSUES AND CLINICAL APPLICATIONS

LISA M. KINOSHITA

JEANETTE HSU

You are a research psychologist in an academically affiliated medical center developing a private practice in a college town in a Western state. In one month, you encounter the following situations:

1. A 22-year-old, Vietnamese American, male student comes into the clinic to talk about his family relationships and a new romantic relationship.

2. A recently divorced, 49-year-old, Filipino nurse complaining of low energy and headaches is referred to you by her general physician.

3. A research colleague is deciding whether or not she should use an adapted assessment instrument with her Chinese American client who may suffer from generalized anxiety. She asks you for consultation about psychometric issues she should consider before administering the adapted measure to this client.

Will you be ready to address these different situations? If needed, will you know how to respond to the assessment needs in each scenario? Reading this chapter will be one step in a continuous process of developing cultural competence in assessment with Asian Americans. Specifically, we discuss clinical issues related to the formal assessment process with a focus on promoting culturally competent practices in Asian American assessment. This discussion is followed by a review of the issues related to use of standardized and adapted assessment measures. We conclude the chapter with a discussion of the elements of a thorough assessment, including the clinical interview and specific self-report measures used with Asian Americans.

The Asian American population is very diverse, with the largest groups being Chinese, Filipino, Asian Indian, Korean, Vietnamese, and Japanese (Barnes & Bennett, 2002). Other chapters in this volume address the difficulty in examining and describing a "psychology of Asian Americans" with such a heterogeneous population from distinct regions and ethnicities, speaking many different languages, and adhering to various religions. The pan-ethnic use of the socially constructed term *Asian American* presupposes a commonality among ethnic minorities in the United States, as they face similar impacts of acculturation and assimilation, stereotyping, prejudice, discrimination, and subtle, as well as overt, racism. Despite the great number of groups under the "Asian American" umbrella, there are also some common cultural influences in East and South Asia. Rather than describing and reifying these commonalities, however, we intend to propose approaches that will guide psychologists in exploring and understanding the multilayered and distinctive lived experiences of their Asian American therapy clients and research subjects.

Due to the rapidly changing demographics in the United States population, psychologists will need to adapt their existing skills to work with individuals from increasingly diverse communities and backgrounds where culturally sensitive interventions and assessment techniques may be more effective in enhancing human functioning and reducing suffering. In an effort to promote cultural competence in psychology, the American Psychological Association (APA) published *Guidelines on Multicultural Education, Training, Research, Practice, and Organizational Change* (APA, 2002b). In these guidelines, APA presents the rationale for understanding individuals and their behaviors within their social contexts, and for culturally competent assessment of individuals from diverse backgrounds in research and practice. Moreover, the APA *Code of Ethics* (APA, 2002a) also contains an ethical principle which upholds that psychologists respect cultural diversity, as well as standards related to cultural diversity, as it applies to assessment and research. Specifically, Principle E states, in part,

> Psychologists are aware of and respect cultural, individual, and role differences, including those based on age, gender, gender identity, race, ethnicity, culture, national origin, religion, sexual orientation, disability, language, and socioeconomic status and consider these factors when working with members of such groups. (APA, 2002a, p. 4)

Further, an emerging literature addresses cultural factors in psychological assessment in response to the increasing cultural, ethnic, and linguistic diversity in the U.S. population. Because the Asian American population is one of the fastest-growing racial groups in the United States, comprising approximately 13.5 million individuals (U.S. Census, 2005) and representing at least 40 different subgroups, it is imperative that psychologists have the ability to utilize culturally competent assessment approaches and techniques with this population. This chapter intends to serve as a practical guide for implementing culturally competent assessment with Asian Americans.

Steps to culturally competent assessment include the following:

1. Self-awareness and self-assessment

2. Building and establishing rapport

3. Multidimensional interview assessment

4. Collateral input from family and/or community members

5. Culturally appropriate choice and use of assessment instruments

6. Culturally appropriate analysis, interpretation, and generalizability of assessment results

SELF-AWARENESS AND SELF-ASSESSMENT

It is now well established that "cultural competence" is a necessary aspiration for psychologists to practice ethically and effectively. The literature on cultural competence describes many attempts to define cultural competence in assessment over the past 30 years (e.g., Hansen, Pepitone-Arreola-Rockwell, & Greene, 2000; Hays, 2001; Herrick & Brown, 1998; Huang, 1994; Padilla & Medina, 1996; S. Sue & Chang, 2003; Wong & Fujii, 2004), with varying results. However, most of the literature affirms that self-awareness is a first step in working toward cultural competence and forms one element of a triad of awareness, knowledge, and skills (Hansen et al., 2000). Self-assessment of cultural competence is part of the process of continuous self-development and lifelong learning. As stated by Hansen et al. (2000), "development of multicultural competencies is not a static task. It requires an open, flexible commitment to ongoing introspection, education, and involvement" (p. 658).

What do self-awareness and self-assessment involve? Researchers and scholars in multicultural psychology have called on their psychology colleagues to reflect on and understand their own cultural heritage and other dimensions of personal history (Hansen et al., 2000; Hays, 2001), such as racial-ethnic identity, gender, sexual orientation, religious preference, ability status, and age, all of which may influence personal values, assumptions, and biases. Hays (2001) has provided a useful acronym to organize one's own self-assessment, which can then be applied to assessment of diverse individuals who may represent multiple dimensions of identity. The ADDRESSING framework includes Age and generational influences, Developmental and acquired Disabilities, Religion, Ethnicity, Social status, Sexual orientation, Indigenous heritage (i.e., claiming heritage from Native or aboriginal peoples of particular regions, such as Native Americans, Alaska Natives, Native Hawaiians), National origin, and Gender (Table 23.1).

Notably, Hays (2001) does not include *race* in this framework, discussing the problematic use of the concept of race while recognizing the importance of its meaning to individuals and their lived experiences. We contend that race is a socially constructed concept based on phenotypic characteristics rather than distinct racial or genotypic classifications. At the same time, race has psychological importance in how individuals perceive and identify themselves (e.g., racial identity) and how they are perceived by others. Moreover, race has implications for how individuals are treated by society and what opportunities and privileges are available to them. Therefore, in clinical practice, it continues to be meaningful and essential to consider race and racial identity in assessment and therapy. We suggest that psychologists using the ADDRESSING framework can add Race to the Ethnicity line (i.e., Ethnicity and Race), as we have done in Table 23.1, in order to obtain the most information about an individual's self-identification

and relationship to majority and minority cultures.

Hays (2001) also recommends a useful exercise in which therapists assess themselves on their ability to do the following:

1. Understand the influence of culture on one's own belief system and worldview

2. Make personal the kind of exploration we may later repeat with clients

3. Acknowledge that our experiences are drawn from multiple dimensions of identity and multiple sociocultural contexts

4. Become more aware of the role of privilege in one's experiences

She suggests that, after assessing ourselves using the ADDRESSING framework, we label the dimensions on which we hold a dominant cultural identity, or privilege (e.g., gender if we are male, social status if we are from a middle- or upper-class background, sexual orientation if we are heterosexual, ethnicity if we are European American). According to Hays (2001), the dimensions on which we hold privilege are the ones in which we have likely developed less awareness and knowledge; these are areas in which we can benefit from further self-exploration and education.

This self-knowledge provides a basis for understanding one's own views of health and illness, beliefs about what constitutes adaptive behavior or functioning, clinical judgments, approaches and interventions, and goals in assessment or treatment. In addition, awareness of the dimensions on which one holds privilege and social status may increase insight into one's degree of power in society and how social power, biases, and assumptions may play out in therapy or assessment relationships. With this foundation, psychologists can proceed with the cross-cultural encounter with clients or research participants.

GENERAL SKILLS AND CONSIDERATIONS IN THE CROSS-CULTURAL ENCOUNTER

The question "What should I do?" is the most common one asked by students of multicultural

Table 23.1   Cultural Self-Assessment Exercise Using the ADDRESSING Framework

Cultural Influences	Therapist's Self-Assessment
Age and Generational Influences	
Disabilities (Developmental)	
Disabilities (Acquired)	
Religion and Spiritual Influences	
Ethnicity and Race	
Socioeconomic Status	
Sexual Orientation	
Indigenous Heritage	
National Origin	
Gender	

Place an asterisk (*) next to categories in which you hold privilege (i.e., have a dominant cultural identity).
    Age – between 30-60 years old; Disability – if you do not have a disability; Religion – if you grew up in secular or Christian home; Ethnicity – if you are of European American heritage; Socioeconomic status – if you were brought up in a middle- to upper-middle class family or are currently of this status; Sexual orientation – if you are heterosexual; Indigenous heritage – if you are not of indigenous/Native heritage; National origin – if you are living in the country in which you were born and grew up; and Gender – if you are male.

Source: Adapted from Hays (2001).

psychology. One answer, that therapy is as much art as science, is not sufficient, although clinical judgment, thoughtful phrasing, and sensitive timing are unquestionably critical to any therapeutic encounter. So what tools can help both the seasoned clinician and the student learn and improve clinical skills when engaging with individuals from diverse cultural backgrounds and, in particular, of Asian American cultural heritage?

First of all, it is important to increase one's specific knowledge and understanding of historical and sociocultural factors impacting Asian American groups and their experiences in the United States. These factors include the history of immigration of different ethnic subgroups; patterns of prejudice and discrimination; common cultural values and beliefs; acculturation and its differential impact on Asian American individuals by age, gender, and cohort, family systems and structures; and the range of diversity within the heterogeneous Asian American "umbrella." There are numerous references, texts (including this volume), and articles that can educate psychologists wishing to learn more about these areas.

With these factors in mind, S. Sue (1998) suggests that clinicians approach Asian American clients and others with "scientific mindedness," meaning that culture-specific knowledge should inform the development of hypotheses, or potential cultural explanations, for the presenting problem or referral question. Further inquiry or data gathering can confirm or disconfirm these hypotheses, which can eventually lead to more accurate cultural case conceptualizations. For example, two different Asian American clients can present with very different levels of ethnic identification, acculturation, and adherence to traditional Asian cultural values, which may lead to quite divergent case conceptualizations and treatment plans. This general approach avoids the pitfalls of stereotyping, encourages the clinician to flexibly move between individual and group characteristics, and conveys respect for the individual's experiences within his or her larger sociocultural context.

In addition, many multicultural and Asian American psychologists point to the importance

of several initial considerations in the assessment of Asian American populations. Some of the following are general considerations when working with diverse populations, whereas others are more specific recommendations with regard to Asian American populations.

- Increased and early self-disclosure in the service of making a personal, contextualized, and meaningful connection with the client
- Acknowledgment of cultural factors that may influence the client's presenting problem or referral question
- Attention to nonverbal behaviors and different communication styles
- Focusing on client strengths and cultural assets, not deficits
- Understanding the importance of the family in Asian American culture
- Avoiding psychological jargon and terminology
- Conveying respect and compassion for the client's lived experiences
- Gaining further culture-specific knowledge and utilizing culturally sensitive interventions
- Seeking consultation from cultural "experts" whenever needed
- Staying humble and as open to being changed by the cross-cultural encounter as the client

Finally, psychologists working with Asian Americans must increase their awareness of the impact of prejudice, discrimination, and racism in society and how these factors do or do not manifest in their clients' lives. The clinical encounter is an inherently unequal one, with the psychologist typically holding more social power than an Asian American client. Therefore, psychologists who continue the process of self-assessment and self-examination (as described in an earlier section) should monitor whether these unequal social power dynamics are played out in the clinical encounter, such as in dominating the therapeutic relationship, perpetuating or confirming stereotypes of Asian Americans, or otherwise marginalizing or pathologizing an Asian American client's experiences.

BUILDING AND ESTABLISHING RAPPORT

Underutilization of mental health services is a problem for many ethnic minority groups, not just Asian Americans. However, the framing of the problem as "underutilization" directs attention to individuals either seeking or not seeking services rather than to the system of mental health care, which still, overall, does not provide culturally responsive or culturally competent treatment. Asian American psychotherapy clients typically do not seek services from Western practitioners; when they do, they typically discontinue services sooner compared to their counterparts from other American ethnic minority and majority groups despite being significantly more symptomatic at the time of seeking services. Researchers of this early termination phenomenon (e.g., D. W. Sue & Sue, 2003; S. Sue, 1977) attribute these higher dropout rates to lack of ethnic or cultural "match" between therapist and client, particularly for clients who have recently immigrated and are less acculturated and/or for those who speak a primary language other than English. The more acculturated the Asian American client is, the less important is the degree of ethnic or cultural match and the more important is the degree of cognitive match (or congruence of therapeutic approaches and goals). Other researchers suggest that the more proximal factor in determining whether an Asian American client continues with treatment is not degree of ethnic match, per se, but the extent to which a therapist attends to essential cultural issues and the subsequent development of the therapeutic alliance on which the effectiveness of treatment is based (Hays, 1996; Tsui & Schultz, 1985).

We suggest that, in primary therapy settings such as community mental health clinics, therapists be aware of cultural differences between themselves and the client and, with this awareness, begin their interview assessment with obtaining a clear sense of the client's goals in seeking treatment, understanding the circumstances of the referral, and making a meaningful connection with the client. Because Asian American clients are less likely to view Western mental health services as their first source of help, it also is useful to inquire of the client what other sources of help they have accessed,

what worked, and what did not. Also, it is important to find out whether the client had requested a therapist or tester from any particular ethnic background, which may give you more information about their ethnic identification and possible issues. A frank discussion of the process of therapy, the therapist's role and the client's role in therapy, and the limits of confidentiality is imperative in the first session with Asian American clients.

In primary assessment settings such as research labs or neuropsychological assessment clinics, in which the purpose of assessment is not therapy but rather different forms of testing for research or other purposes, the establishment of rapport also facilitates the process of accurate assessment. Most Asian American individuals are not familiar with formal testing and will need a thorough explanation of the process and goals of assessment, limits of confidentiality, and ways in which the results will be reported and used.

In either setting, attention to initial considerations outlined previously will lend greater credibility to the psychologist, especially the considerations of judicious self-disclosure to facilitate making a meaningful connection with the client and acknowledgment of cultural issues that may play a role in the presenting problem or referral question. Moreover, approaching Asian American clients with respect for their individual and cultural strengths, appreciation for their lived experiences, and an empirical hypothesis-testing approach to assessment and case conceptualization will provide the basis for an effective therapeutic alliance (S. Sue, 1998).

LANGUAGE AND RECOMMENDATIONS FOR SELECTION AND USE OF INTERPRETERS

One additional area of assessment that deserves special attention in this chapter is the determination of English language proficiency and language preference by the client. The extent to which a client is able to communicate in the language of the monolingual English-speaking therapist or assessor, or prefers to communicate in his/her own language, are important factors in determining whether the individual should be referred to a bilingual provider, or if an interpreter can be used. Current recommendations for selection of appropriate interpreters include the following guidelines (Hays, 2001):

1. Plan for extra time for the assessment.

2. Use a certified interpreter whenever possible.

3. Discuss expectations with the interpreter before an assessment meeting (e.g., limits of confidentiality, importance of verbatim translation) and ensure that she or he understands the process of assessment and therapy.

4. Allow time for the interpreter and client to talk together before the initial session to establish rapport.

5. Do not use an interpreter with a prior personal or social relationship with the client (e.g., the client's child, spouse, sibling, or social acquaintance) who may distort or omit the client's self-report or contribute to problems with confidentiality.

If the use of a socially connected interpreter is unavoidable, such as in a crisis situation with no appropriate interpreter available, it is important to carefully weigh the disadvantages of using the available interpreter with the possible immediate therapeutic benefits to the client (e.g., refill of psychiatric medications, need for psychiatric hospitalization for safety). Strongly consider the possibility of biases or distortions that may be introduced by the interpreter, and obtain appropriate interpreter services as soon as possible to confirm or disconfirm information previously obtained from the socially connected interpreter.

MULTIDIMENSIONAL ASSESSMENT

Let us return to the cross-cultural encounter with the psychotherapy or assessment client. After gaining an initial understanding of the presenting problem or referral question in the client's own words, discussing how the client chose to come for therapy or assessment, and clarifying the structure, process, and goals of the therapy or assessment, the therapist should explain to the client that he or she will ask some questions designed to help understand the problem in the context of the client's whole person. Some questions to begin with include the following:

- What is your main ethnic and/or racial identification?
- Are there other cultural groups you identify with?
- Are there other important aspects of your identity?
- How might your upbringing/what you were taught within your family influence the difficulty you are currently experiencing?
- Are there ways in which your ethnic identity is related to (the presenting problem)?

Additional questions can flow from use of the ADDRESSING framework (Hays, 2001) described previously. Take the case of a 22-year-old, Vietnamese American, male student who comes into the clinic asking to talk about his family relationships and a new romantic relationship. Examples of questions using the ADDRESSING framework include the following:

- What are the age-related and generational influences on this young man? What are his level of ethnic identity development as a young adult, his immigration status (e.g., refugee vs. voluntary immigrant, possible history of Vietnam War trauma), and his level of acculturation? Are there cultural conflicts with his parents or other significant family members? What is his primary cultural peer group (i.e., with which cultural age-peers does he identify)?
- What is this young man's experience with disability? Does he have a visible disability or one that is not readily apparent? Does he have family members with disabilities, and what is his role in relation to these family members?
- What is his religious upbringing? Many older Vietnamese have a Catholic upbringing but also have Buddhist ties or practices. Does this young man adhere to more traditional religious practices, other practices, or none?
- What is the meaning of his ethnic and/or racial identity in a college town without a

visible Vietnamese community? Did he grow up in this area or one with a larger ethnic community? With which different cultural groups might he or his family identify (e.g., Chinese Vietnamese, French cultural influences)?

- What is his current socioeconomic status as defined by his student status, individual and family income, marital status, and family name and reputation? How does his family's current socioeconomic status compare to their status prior to immigrating to the United States, and how might his future socioeconomic status be different from that of his immigrant parents?

- What is the client's sexual orientation? He reported a "new romantic relationship" without a specified gender or ethnic identity. If he is not heterosexual, how comfortable is he with his sexual orientation? What is his degree of "outness" (i.e., disclosure to self, friends, family members, other students or coworkers)? How might his choice of romantic/sexual partner(s) be perceived by his parents and family, who traditionally would expect him to date and marry a Vietnamese American woman?

- Does he or his family have indigenous heritage (i.e., from an indigenous or aboriginal cultural or ethnic group in Vietnam)?

- What is his national identity (Vietnamese, American, both, or some other)? What is his primary language? Is there need for an interpreter or translator?

- Finally, what gender-related information would be important, especially regarding roles and expectations for him as the only son in a Vietnamese family?

A FAMILY SYSTEMS APPROACH TO ASSESSMENT

When assessing Asian American clients, collateral sources such as family members as well as community members and/or leaders can provide important perspectives and information on the presenting problem or target of assessment, such as the nature, frequency, and onset of the target behaviors. Information from such sources also helps to establish the sociocultural context in which the individual lives. In addition, family strengths and resources can be harnessed in the service of assessment and treatment if family members can participate productively in the process. Bringing in partners/spouses, valued elders, and other community members can also increase credibility for interventions once a treatment plan is determined. In such treatment situations, family members should be offered information about the process of therapy, including that they are valued in helping the client get better and yet, for the client's benefit in therapy, some information must remain confidential between the psychologist and the client in order for treatment to be effective.

Furthermore, even if family or community members are not present, the individual must be understood in the context of his or her family and the cultural beliefs and values as carried by the family and community. In assessing the individual, assessment must be "family oriented," even if the family members are not actually present. For example, in the case of the recently divorced, 49-year-old, Filipino nurse complaining of low energy and headaches, she may have difficulty accepting mental health treatment and thus may not initially wish to let family members know she is seeing a mental health professional, let alone invite her family to a session. Nevertheless, the following questions may be useful to ask regarding her family and cultural context:

- How does her family view her presenting problem (e.g., low energy and headaches)? What do they think is causing the problem?

- Who else in the family has had this problem? How did they cope with the problem?

- How does this problem affect other family members? How are they reacting to the problem (both positively and negatively)?

- What have they suggested would help the problem? What have they done to help the client with the problem? Who is most helpful to the client regarding this problem?

- What are family members' attitudes toward mental health treatment? Do they feel the client will benefit from seeing a mental health provider?

- How do people in the cultural community typically cope with this kind of problem?

These example questions will help the therapist/assessor and the client arrive at a richer understanding of the presenting problem in the context of the family system and cultural values, beliefs, and practices. This line of inquiry can elucidate cultural beliefs about health and illness, cultural practices regarding this type of problem, family and cultural strengths, and how the problem impacts the family system and vice versa. One may find that the problem is reinforced by family dynamics and that there are interpersonal, behavioral, and emotional effects on the individual and other family members as a consequence of the problem. The resulting enriched understanding of the presenting problem then informs a culturally sensitive case conceptualization and opens new possibilities for intervention and treatment.

USING STANDARDIZED ASSESSMENT MEASURES WITH ASIAN AMERICANS

Culturally competent mental health care professionals recognize that differences exist between Asian Americans and non–Asian Americans with regard to assessment process, procedure, and methods. In recent years, a growing body of literature has emerged that illustrates the use of standardized assessment measures with Asian and Asian American individuals (e.g., Cheung, Leong, & Ben-Porath, 2003; Okazaki, 1998; S. Sue & Chang, 2003). As additional measures become more widely available, it is important for culturally competent mental health practitioners to recognize the inherent methodological issues related to assessment of Asian American individuals, as there are inherent problems when using standardized measures with culturally diverse populations. Next, we review the current state of culturally sensitive assessment practices with Asian American individuals and discuss standardized assessment measures, test development involving adapted assessment measures, and application of specific assessment measures with Asian American individuals.

Assessment Considerations: Language and Education

Nearly two-thirds of the Asian American population residing in the United States were born in Asian countries; therefore, English may not be their first language (Ong & Hee, 1993). If a mental health professional has difficulty communicating with his or her client, the validity of test administration and interpretation of the results become problematic. Furthermore, some Asian American elderly completed only a few years of formal education in their native country before moving to the United States. Data from original normative samples may be grouped by age and educational level, which poses a problem for interpreting assessment results with individuals who have few years of formal education. Two potential problems exist. First, the education norms are likely not equivalent from one country to another. Second, the original normative data may not include the lower end of the educational level. Therefore, assessors often have difficulty deciding how to interpret the assessment results when using a mainstream standardized measure with these subgroups of Asian Americans.

Furthermore, the majority of available standardized tests do not include an Asian American normative sample. On the rare occasion in which Asian American groups are included in the standardization, problems arise because most of the tests were developed without consideration of the values, beliefs, ethnic identity, or acculturation status of the Asian American sample or the heterogeneity among Asian American groups. Often, clinicians and researchers do not know whether a test is valid for specific Asian American groups. Therefore, one cannot assume that the measure is standardized to the values and beliefs of Asian American individuals, even with Asian American normative data, but skewed to those of the normative sample. Careful examination of the measures prior to administering them to Asian American clients is important so that misleading assessment information and misdiagnosis can be minimized.

Measurement Selection

When a measure has been designed and validated on a European American population, interpreting the results can be problematic. The results seen may actually reflect differences of the Asian American individual from the mainstream cultural norm rather than true psychiatric maladjustment. Research conducted on Asian American assessment using standardized measures (e.g., Minnesota Multiphasic Personality Inventory [MMPI], Center for Epidemiological Studies Depression [CES-D]) suggest that Asian Americans evidence more severe psychopathology symptoms compared to non–Asian American comparison groups (S. Sue & Sue, 1974; Ying, 1988). The question arises: Are these differences due to true psychiatric maladjustment or due to nonpathological cultural factors? It is the responsibility of culturally competent mental health professionals to distinguish true psychopathology from cultural differences based on the individual's socioethnocultural context and to choose assessment methods that are appropriate for the specific Asian American individual.

It is important for mental health professionals to understand the test development of the measures they use with Asian American clients. Mental health professionals have the responsibility of being cautious when selecting specific standardized measures and using caution when interpreting and generalizing the assessment results to their patients and other Asian American individuals, especially when the measures were not originally normed on Asian American samples.

Given the complexities involved in measurement selection and interpretation, how does one know which standardized measures to use with Asian American clients? When deciding on the appropriateness of an assessment measure for a specific Asian American individual, it is important to consider the following questions:

- On what population was this measure originally normed? Was an Asian American standardization group included in the normative sample? If so, what were the characteristics of the sample (e.g., what was the educational level, language fluency, and socioeconomic status of the Asian American normative population)?
- What is the acculturation level of my client? What is the ethnic identity of my client? What is the language proficiency/literacy level of my client? What is the educational level of my client?
- Does my client understand the purpose of the assessment? Has he or she been exposed to standardized measures in the past?

In sum, before administering and interpreting standardized measures to Asian American clients, culturally competent mental health care providers have a responsibility to evaluate the characteristics of the normative sample from the standardized measure and assess the match between the normative sample and the individual's characteristics (e.g., acculturation level, educational level, and English proficiency).

USING ADAPTED MEASURES WITH ASIAN AMERICANS

When working with monolingual and bilingual clients with limited English proficiency, it may be necessary to use a translated or adapted version of an assessment measure that was originally developed and used in the mainstream culture. Ideally, a translated measure with established psychometric properties would be administered to an Asian American client in his or her native language. However, often this is not the case because clinicians have limited access to adapted assessment measures that are psychometrically established, and they also lack access to bicultural, bilingual translators. In recent years, researchers have attempted to adapt mainstream measures for use with Asian and Asian American groups and have proposed guidelines for adapting an assessment measure from the mainstream culture to diverse cultures (Geisinger, 1994).

Let us now explore a scenario. Your research colleague would like to consult with you regarding whether or not she should use an adapted assessment instrument with her Chinese American client who she believes is suffering from generalized anxiety. She wonders what psychometric issues she should consider before administering the adapted measure to her client. Researchers have explored the area of adapted measures and have proposed suggestions for use of such measures with Asian Americans.

When using measures that have been adapted from mainstream culture for cross-cultural use with Asian American individuals, several questions are likely to arise:

- Should I use assessment measures that have been translated into my client's native language? What should I consider before administering these adapted measures to my Asian American clients?

- Were the psychometrics of the translated measure assessed? Are the test items valid for specific Asian American populations (e.g., does the psychiatric construct exist in my client's native culture)?
- What are the acculturation level, generational level, ethnic identity, and educational level of my client?

The Standards for Educational and Psychological Testing (American Educational Research Association, American Psychological Association, & National Council on Measurement in Education, 1999) emphasize evaluating the reliability and validity of a translated measure and establishing sound psychometrics of the instrument for the intended ethnic minority group. S. Sue and Chang (2003) highlight psychometric issues to consider when choosing to use an adapted assessment measure; such issues include linguistic equivalence, content equivalence, procedural and normative equivalence, conceptual equivalence, functional equivalence, and metric equivalence. The different forms of equivalence are important to consider before choosing an adapted assessment instrument for use with Asian and Asian American clients.

First, when using an instrument that was adapted from English and translated into another language, it is important to assess the linguistic equivalence of the measure. Linguistic equivalence occurs when translated items are similar in meaning to the original items (S. Sue & Chang, 2003). Often, this type of equivalence is accomplished by employing translation back-translation methodology or, as Geisinger (1994) suggests, by using a group of individuals who meet the same criteria as the original translator to review the quality of the translation. Difficulties arise when no single translation standard has been employed across studies and when multiple translations of measures exist (Leong, Okazaki, & Tak, 2003; S. Sue & Chang, 2003). Furthermore, sound linguistic equivalence does not guarantee cross-cultural equivalence, as linguistic nuances may not be represented in the translated language.

Content equivalence of a measure is obtained when the items from the mainstream instrument are readily represented in the diverse culture. Problems arise when original items have a mainstream culture–specific meaning that does not equate to the same meaning in another culture. Furthermore, specific test items may not lend themselves well to cultural adaptation. More specifically, according to S. Sue and Chang (2003), a measure may not have content equivalence due to "differences in the familiarity of words or concepts, culture-specific words or phrases, level of difficulty or skill required on items, [and] emotional value of the items" (p. 308).

Procedural and normative equivalence involves the generalizability of the test-taking procedures to diverse cultures. Test results may be altered due to the simple fact that an individual from another culture is not familiar with how to complete a self-report measure, for example. Similarly, revised or new norms may need to be developed before an adapted measure can be used with confidence with individuals from diverse cultures (Butcher, Cheung, & Lim, 2003).

Conceptual equivalence occurs when the main aspects of the factor structure are the same for both the original and the adapted measure. When assessing conceptual equivalence, clinicians and researchers may ask, "Does the client's native culture have a clear meaning for the construct of interest?" To be conceptually equivalent, the construct that describes the specific behavior or characteristic must exist and have similar meanings in both cultures.

Functional equivalence is related to the comparability of the outcomes from specific behaviors in mainstream and diverse cultures. If an instrument has sound functional equivalence, the adapted measure should be able to predict behavioral outcomes in the diverse culture in the same manner as the original measure. Finally, metric equivalence answers the question of whether measurements (e.g., scaled scores) are in the same scale from one culture to the next (S. Sue & Chang, 2003).

In addition to evaluating the various types of measurement equivalence, Geisinger (1994) notes the importance of ensuring that the adapted instrument is both pilot tested and later field tested with specific ethnic minority groups before using the measure with individuals from the target population. Extensive psychometric and statistical analyses are conducted during and after field testing, and scores are standardized as appropriate with the original measure. After thorough analyses (as outlined earlier in the chapter), the mental health professional can have more confidence in the interpretation of the testing results.

THE CASE OF MRS. Y

Let us now review the case of Mrs. Y to illustrate the problems that may arise if forethought is not instituted before selecting an adapted assessment measure. Mrs. Y is an 82-year-old, Chinese American woman who is currently caring for her husband who has dementia. She was referred to you by her primary care physician because she complains of stomach problems and headaches that have lasted for the past month. After numerous medical tests, her doctor could not determine a medical reason for her physical complaints. You hypothesize that Mrs. Y may be suffering from caregiver stress.

Mrs. Y immigrated to the United States when she was 34 years old, has lived in Chinatown since arriving in the United States, and speaks limited English. You would like to assess her degree of caregiver stress to aid in case formulation and treatment planning. However, after a careful literature review, you find there are no published psychometric articles that contain translated measures of this type. Your Chinese American colleague has a translated measure of caregiver stress with limited psychometric validation that she is currently using in a research study, so you decide to administer the measure to Mrs. Y., thinking that "something is better than nothing." While Mrs. Y was completing the measure, she looked confused and didn't answer some of the items. When looking at the test results, you find that she endorses extensive caregiver stress, and you conclude that she is experiencing severe caregiver stress. After the first few therapy sessions with Mrs. Y, you realize that she does not understand the concept of caregiver stress, and, thus, you return to the results of the adapted instrument to determine if the outcome may be suspect.

There are a number of issues to carefully review, in the case of Mrs. Y, that were not considered before administering the translated measure to the client, including the following questions:

- Does the concept of caregiver stress exist in Chinese culture?
- How was the adapted measure translated?
- Are the psychometric properties of the translated measure established?
- Does Mrs. Y feel comfortable sharing private information regarding her husband and their relationship?
- What are Mrs. Y's acculturation level, ethnic identity, educational level, and English language proficiency?

To avoid misdiagnosing or incorrectly assessing Asian American clients, it is important to carefully choose adapted measures using forethought and empirical evidence. Furthermore, it behooves culturally competent mental health providers to consult closely with knowledgeable colleagues whenever questions arise regarding measurement selection and interpretation of test results.

CULTURALLY APPROPRIATE INTERPRETATION AND GENERALIZABILITY OF ADAPTED MEASURES

Even after following the guidelines suggested in the previous section, interpretation of cross-culturally adapted instruments still can be problematic. When researchers develop a standardized assessment measure with sound psychometric properties in European American culture, such an endeavor often takes a number of years. When adapting that measure for use with Asian Americans and ensuring that it has equally sound psychometrics, this is often a costly and time-consuming process. By the time a measure is adapted and tested for sound psychometrics, another revised version of the mainstream test may be published with more current normative data. Interpretive and ethical considerations arise when using norms that are outdated, as the client's scores may not be comparable to the older normative data (Okazaki & Sue, 2000). Similar to interpretive considerations when using standardized measures, culturally competent clinicians are responsible for ensuring that the interpretation and generalizability of the adapted instruments are accurate. When accuracy of the results is suspect, clinicians are expected to note such limitations of interpretive accuracy.

ASSESSMENT PROCEDURES AND SPECIFIC ASSESSMENT MEASURES

Culturally biased assessment measures exist (Dana, 1993; Paniagua, 1998), and it is the responsibility of culturally competent mental health professionals to exercise forethought when assessing their Asian American clients. Assessment methodologies are noted here from least to most biased: physiological measures, behavioral observation, self-monitoring, self-report rating scales, clinical interview, trait measures, self-report psychopathology measures (e.g., MMPI), and projective tests. Researchers suggest that mental health professionals initially consider using assessment methodologies that minimize subjective interpretation and speculation to decrease bias that may affect the accuracy of the diagnosis and subsequent treatment plan.

Clinical Interview

The psychiatric assessment process usually begins with a thorough clinical interview. As previously discussed in detail, mental health professionals assume an important role, that is, to interpret their Asian American clients' information using a culturally competent and culturally sensitive approach. It is important for the clinician to recognize his or her knowledge of Asian American cultural norms and to clarify Asian American clients' responses carefully.

Self-Report Measures

Psychiatric assessment with Asian American clients often will involve not only a culturally sensitive clinical interview, collateral information gathering, and careful behavioral observation but also administration of standardized tests. One type of standardized test—self-report measures—aims to assess specific, clearly defined psychiatric constructs. Self-report measures have been utilized and researched

extensively with Asian Americans. Although the outward stereotype of Asian Americans has been of the "model minority," self-report measures of psychological distress tend to report otherwise, especially with foreign-born Asian Americans who recently immigrated to the United States (Uba, 1994). Similarly, other researchers have found that the results of personality assessments that measure such constructs as self-esteem, anxiety, and assertiveness suggest that Asian American individuals evidence psychological maladjustment (Okazaki & Sue, 1995; Uba, 1994). Questions arise when choosing specific assessment methodologies:

- Do Asian Americans exhibit psychiatric distress in the same way as non–Asian Americans?
- If differences are detected when using specific measures with Asian Americans and non–Asian Americans, how does one know if the difference is due to true maladjustment or to nonpathological cultural factors?

As discussed previously, culturally competent mental health professionals are responsible for carefully choosing culturally appropriate measures to use with their specific Asian American clients. In this section, we review a number of self-report measures that have been used with Asian and Asian American individuals and discuss available empirical research findings. It must be noted, however, that the following is not intended to serve as a comprehensive review of all available self-report instruments used with Asian Americans but as a discussion of some commonly used assessment measures. Table 23.2 summarizes the measures that we review.

Acculturation and ethnic identity. As discussed previously, an integral component of the assessment process when conducting a thorough psychiatric evaluation involves consideration of the Asian American client's acculturation status. When acculturation is assessed early in the process, it guides the general approach and thought process of the clinician. A number of measures of acculturation have been developed for various ethnic groups as well as for specific Asian populations. The Suinn-Lew Asian

Table 23.2   Assessment Measures Used With Asian and Asian American Groups

Instrument	Construct	Reference
Suinn-Lew Asian Self-Identity Acculturation Scale	Acculturation	Suinn, Rickard-Figueroa, Lew, and Vigil (1987)
Taiwan Aboriginal Acculturation Scale	Acculturation	Cheng and Hsu (1995)
The Acculturation Scale for Southeast Asians	Acculturation	Anderson, Moeschberger, Chen, and Kunn (1993)
The Hawaiian Acculturation Scale	Acculturation	Rezentes (1993)
Fear of Negative Evaluation	Anxiety	Watson and Friend (1969)
Social Avoidance and Distress	Anxiety	Watson and Friend (1969)
Korean version of the Consortium to Establish a Registry for Alzheimer's Disease Assessment Battery	Dementia battery	Lee et al. (2002)
Cognitive Abilities Screening Instrument	Dementia/Mental Status	Teng et al. (1994)
Beck Depression Inventory	Depression	Beck, Rush, Shaw, and Emery (1979)
Center for Epidemiological Studies Depression	Depression	Radloff (1977)
Geriatric Depression Scale	Geriatric Depression	Yesavage et al. (1983)
Multigroup Ethnic Identity Measure	Ethnic Identity	Phinney (1992)
Japanese Weschler Adult Intelligence Scale–Revised	Intelligence	Shinagawa, Kobayashi, Fujita, and Maekawa (1990)
Wechsler Adult Intelligence Scale–Revised for China	Intelligence	Gong (1982)
Chinese Minnesota Multiphasic Personality Inventory	Personality/Psychopathology	Cheung, 1995
Chinese Minnesota Multiphasic Personality Inventory for Adolescents	Personality/Psychopathology	Cheung and Ho, 1997
Japanese Minnesota Multiphasic Personality Inventory–2	Personality/Psychopathology	Shiota, Krauss, and Clark, 1996
Vietnamese Minnesota Multiphasic Personality Inventory–2	Personality/Psychopathology	Dong and Church, 2003

Self-Identity Acculturation Scale (SL-ASIA; Suinn, Rickard-Figueroa, Lew, & Vigil, 1987) is a widely used instrument for this purpose with sound psychometric properties (Ponterotto, Baluch, & Carielli, 1998; Suinn, Ahuna, & Khoo, 1992). Additional Asian culture–specific acculturation scales include the Taiwan Aboriginal Acculturation Scale (Cheng & Hsu, 1995), the Acculturation Scale for Southeast Asians (Anderson, Moeschberger, Chen, & Kunn, 1993), and the Hawaiian Acculturation Scale (Rezentes, 1993). Such acculturation measures typically include questions (e.g., food preferences, socialization experiences, contact with one's native country) that place the individual on an acculturation continuum between the individual's native culture and the mainstream culture.

Criticisms of acculturation measures include the unidirectional conceptualization of movement from the native culture to the mainstream culture. Critics argue that the actual process of acculturation is more bidirectional and/or multi-directional and multidimensional (Sciarra, 2001; also see Chapter 9, this volume). Furthermore, Marin (1992) notes that some acculturation scales lack extensive psychometric investigation, rely on English language ability, and do not consider variables such as cognitive style, personality, and attitudes. Therefore, culturally competent clinicians are responsible for keeping these limitations in mind when selecting acculturation scales to use with specific Asian American clients.

In the area of ethnic identity assessment, self-report measures have been used extensively in recent years (Phinney, 1990). The Multigroup Ethnic Identity Measure (MEIM; Phinney, 1992) is a widely used instrument that was developed to assess the ethnic identity of adolescents and adults from diverse ethnic groups. The overall psychometric properties of the MEIM are fairly sound (Ponterotto, Gretchen, Utsey, Stracuzzi, & Saya, 2003). Specifically, the psychometrics has been studied with Asian Americans and results are promising (Lee & Yoo, 2004; Phinney, 1992). Although the MEIM has been used widely in research, the measure can be used clinically to assess the ethnic identity of Asian American clients in conjunction with a thorough clinical interview (described previously in this chapter).

Personality and psychopathology inventories. Normative studies that focus on personality and psychopathology inventories with Asian Americans began in the 1970s. At that time, personality assessment researchers began to study measures like the MMPI with Japanese and Chinese Americans. Specific differences between Asian Americans and European Americans clearly emerged. The MMPI results suggested that Asian American subjects experienced more psychopathology compared to their non-Asian counterparts (S. Sue & Sue, 1974). More recent research on the MMPI and MMPI-2 indicate that compared to European Americans, Asian Americans report more depression, somatic problems, anxiety, and social isolation (Kwan, 1999; Tsai & Pike, 2000). Severity of psychopathology reported on the MMPI appears to be moderated by acculturation level (Tsai & Pike, 2000). It is

unclear, however, whether MMPI scale elevations suggest cultural differences or true psychopathology in these individuals. In an attempt to improve on the potential biases of the MMPI, in recent years, a Chinese version of both the MMPI (Cheung, 1995) and the MMPI for Adolescents (MMPI-A; Cheung & Ho, 1997) have been developed that appear to have sound psychometric properties, good equivalence, and usefulness in clinical practice (Cheung & Ho, 1997; Cheung, Song, & Zhang, 1996). Furthermore, a Japanese MMPI-2 (Shiota, Krauss, & Clark, 1996) and a Vietnamese translation of the MMPI-2 (Dong & Church, 2003) have been developed and validated.

Depression. The assessment of depression in Asian Americans has been widely studied (Kuo, 1984; Okazaki, 1998). Measures such as the CES-D (Radloff, 1977) and the Beck Depression Inventory (BDI; Beck, Rush, Shaw, & Emery, 1979) have been used in studies to assess depression in such Asian American groups as Chinese, Japanese, Korean, and Vietnamese individuals (Kuo, 1984; Lam, Pepper, & Ryabchenko, 2004; Ying, 1988). The results from these studies suggest that Asian Americans tend to report higher levels of depressive symptoms as measure by the CES-D and the BDI compared to their non-Asian counterparts. However, it is difficult to conclude whether these results reflect a possible bias in these standardized measures of depression or true psychiatric maladjustment.

Similarly, the Geriatric Depression Scale (GDS; Yesavage et al., 1983) has been used with Asian American older adults, including Chinese, Japanese, Korean, Vietnamese, Filipino, and Asian Indian individuals (Mui, Kang, Chen, & Domanski, 2003). Roughly 40% of this elderly sample of Asian immigrants were found to be depressed, suggesting higher depression rates than in previous studies of other Asian elderly samples in the United States and in Asia. Moreover, the GDS has been translated into Asian languages, including Chinese, Japanese, Korean, Vietnamese, Thai, and Malay. However, psychometric research focusing on these translated measures is lacking; therefore, further research needs to be done on these translated versions of the GDS.

Anxiety. While the majority of available research focuses on psychological distress, specifically depression, in Asian Americans, a handful of studies have examined anxiety, namely social anxiety (Okazaki, 1997; D. Sue, Ino, & Sue, 1983). The measurement of anxiety is difficult because of the narrow range of anxiety symptoms that are assessed and the limited applicable age range of some measures (Casey, 2001). However, the Social Avoidance and Distress Scale (Watson & Friend, 1969) and the Fear of Negative Evaluation Questionnaire (Watson & Friend, 1969) have been used with Chinese, Japanese, and Korean Americans in the past (Okazaki, 1997; D. Sue et al., 1983). Similar to the results found in depression studies, Asian Americans tend to report more anxiety compared to European Americans. Specifically, Chinese Americans were more likely to report anxiety in social situations and greater apprehension in evaluative situations as measured by the Social Avoidance and Distress Scale and the Fear of Negative Evaluation Questionnaire compared to their European American counterparts (D. Sue et al., 1983). On further study, ethnicity and self-construal appear to implicate symptoms of social anxiety (Okazaki, 1997). Anxiety in Asian Americans can also be assessed using a personality and psychopathology inventory such as the MMPI/MMPI-2.

Assessment of intelligence. Adapted versions of intelligence tests have been developed and standardized for use with Asian individuals. For example, a Japanese version of the Wechsler Adult Intelligence Scale–Revised (WAIS-R; Wechsler, 1981; Shinagawa, Kobayashi, Fujita, & Maekawa, 1990); a Chinese version (mainland Chinese) of the original Wechsler Adult Intelligence Scale (WAIS; Wechsler, 1955), called the Wechsler Adult Intelligence Scale–Revised for China (WAIS-RC; Gong, 1982); and an old Korean version of the Wechsler-Bellevue Intelligence Scale (WBIS; Wechsler, 1939; Koh, 1954) are in existence. Although there are several studies that focus on the validity and reliability of the original mainstream versions of these tests, limited psychometric information is available regarding these adapted intelligence batteries for Asian and Asian American individuals. It is important to interpret the results of these adapted intelligence batteries carefully and clearly report limitations in interpretive accuracy.

Neuropsychological Measures

Research suggests that ethnicity and culture play important roles in brain function (Adams, Boake, & Crain, 1982; Thompson & Heaton, 1990). Neuropsychological assessment is the method clinicians use to assess a client's cognitive functioning and brain-behavior interaction. In order to conduct a comprehensive neuropsychological evaluation, clinicians focus on client variables such as affect, mood, perceptions, and attitudes and administer specific neuropsychological measures. However, the research on neuropsychological assessment and instruments used with Asian American individuals is fairly nonexistent (Horton, Carrington, & Lewis-Jack, 2001); this forces clinicians to make important diagnostic decisions with little supporting empirical data.

Like other assessment measures, neuropsychological instruments were normed on European Americans with minimal inclusion of ethnic minority normative samples. These measures were developed to reflect European American culture, traditions, values, and ideals. Therefore, biases have emerged when using these instruments with Asian Americans, which affect the conclusions that can be drawn from the measures. For example, in the Honolulu-Asia Aging Study, the Consortium to Establish a Registry for Alzheimer's Disease (CERAD) Neuropsychological Assessment Battery, a widely used dementia battery, was used to assess the participants' cognitive functioning (Ross et al., 1997). A large proportion of the Japanese American sample, roughly 60%, was suspected of having dementia based on the results of the CERAD battery. Some critics argue that such results may actually reflect a fundamental bias within the battery and suggest that additional psychometric research be conducted on the CERAD battery. Recently, the CERAD battery has been adapted for use with Korean individuals (Lee et al., 2002). Preliminary research suggests that the adapted battery is equal in reliability and validity to the English version and has sound psychometric properties

(Lee et al., 2002). To reduce cultural bias, Horton and colleagues (2001) recommend that clinicians use a multiple levels of inference model in which the assessor focuses on pathognomonic signs, pattern of performance, and right-left comparisons rather than a level-of-performance model which is concerned with how high or low a specific test score is.

In addition to the CERAD battery, the Cognitive Abilities Screening Instrument (CASI; Teng et al., 1994) was developed to assess global cognitive functioning and mental status with Asian Americans, measuring nine cognitive domains. The CASI is similar to the Mini Mental Status Examination (Folstein, Folstein, & McHugh, 1975) and can be used to screen for dementia in Asian Americans. Moreover, the CASI has been translated into different Asian languages. However, currently, psychometric data are available for the Japanese (Teng et al., 1994) and Chinese versions of the measure (see Lu, Luo, & Liu, 2000), which demonstrate excellent reliability and validity of these forms of the CASI.

Furthermore, neuropsychological assessment with Asian Americans can be challenging because of the wide range of measures that require English fluency. Therefore, when an Asian American client has limited fluency in English, it may be necessary to assess the individual's English language proficiency before administering a full neuropsychological battery. To estimate English comprehension, clinicians can use the Peabody Picture Vocabulary Test–Revised (Dunn & Dunn, 1981), which will provide an estimated age-level score, before administering the neuropsychological battery (Wong & Fujii, 2004).

In conclusion, additional adapted measures with sound psychometrics and culture-specific normative data need to be developed and studied for use with Asian Americans. Moreover, clinicians are encouraged to be sensitive to potential sources of cultural bias inherent in the psychiatric and neuropsychological measures they choose.

CONCLUSION

When assessing Asian American clients, it is clear that specific assessment procedures should be exercised with regard to the assessment process and the use of standardized and adapted assessment measures. The issues related to multicultural assessment with Asian Americans are complex because of the demographic and cultural diversity that exists among various Asian American groups. Moreover, problems exist within the mental health community with regard to multicultural assessment and the standards set forth within the practice of professional psychology. For example, there is no official central body to help guide professionals or to set forth standards or guidelines for assessment procedures and measurement development. It would benefit the mental health community to develop a governing group of experts who would make recommendations regarding future directions in multicultural assessment. Furthermore, because of the lack of normative data collected using Asian American samples, it is equally important to make funding of normative studies a priority at a national level (i.e., mandating the inclusion of nationally representative Asian American samples as part of validation studies for new or newly revised instruments). Without adequate assessment development and expansion, it is possible that Asian American patients will be misdiagnosed and provided with improper mental health treatment. In the meantime, clinicians are encouraged to carefully select assessment methods and instruments before using them with Asian American clients as well as interpret the results of assessment measures with forethought and special care.

REFERENCES

Adams, R., Boake, C., & Crain, C. (1982). Bias in a neuropsychological test classification related to education, age, and ethnicity. *Journal of Consulting and Clinical Psychology, 50,* 143–145.

American Educational Research Association, American Psychological Association, & National Council on Measurement in Education. (1999). *The standards for educational and psychological testing* (2nd ed.). Washington, DC: American Psychological Association.

American Psychological Association. (2002a). *Ethical principles of psychologists and code of conduct.* Washington, DC: Author.

American Psychological Association. (2002b). *Guidelines on multicultural education, training, research, practice, and organizational change for psychologists.* Washington, DC: Author.

Anderson, J., Moeschberger, M., Chen, M. S., & Kunn, P. (1993). An acculturation scale for Southeast Asians. *Social Psychiatry and Psychiatric Epidemiology, 8,* 134–141.

Barnes, J. S., & Bennett, C. E. (2002). *The Asian population: 2000* (Census 2000 Brief No. C2KBR/01-16). Retrieved February 20, 2006, from http://www.census.gov/prod/2002pubs/c2kbr01-16.pdf

Beck, A. T., Rush, A. J., Shaw, B. F., & Emery, G. (1979). *Cognitive therapy of depression.* New York: Guilford Press.

Butcher, J. N., Cheung, F. M., & Lim, J. (2003). Use of the MMSI-2 with Asian populations. *Psychological Assessment, 15,* 248–256.

Casey, R. J. (2001). Social and emotional assessment. In L. A. Suzuki, J. G. Ponterotto, & P. J. Meller (Eds.), *Handbook of multicultural assessment: Clinical, psychological, and educational applications* (2nd ed., pp. 383–404). San Francisco: Jossey-Bass.

Cheng, A. T., & Hsu, M. (1995). Development of a new scale for measuring acculturation: The Taiwan Aboriginal Acculturation Scale (TAAS). *Psychological Medicine, 25,* 1281–1287.

Cheung, F. M. (1995). *The Chinese Minnesota Multiphasic Personality Inventory manual.* Shatin, Hong Kong: Chinese University Press.

Cheung, F. M., & Ho, R. M. (1997). Standardization of the Chinese MMPI-A in Hong Kong: A preliminary study. *Psychological Assessment, 9,* 499–502.

Cheung, F. M., Leong, F. T. L., & Ben-Porath, Y. S. (2003). Psychological assessment in Asia: Introduction to the special section. *Psychological Assessment, 15,* 243–247.

Cheung, F. M., Song, W., & Zhang, J. (1996). The Chinese MMPI-2: Research and applications in Hong Kong and the People's Republic of China. In J. B. Butcher (Ed.), *International adaptations of the MMPI-2* (pp. 137–161). Minneapolis: University of Minnesota Press.

Dana, R. H. (1993). *Multicultural assessment perspectives for professional psychology.* Boston: Allyn & Bacon.

Dong, Y. T., & Church, A. T. (2003). Cross-cultural equivalence and validity of the Vietnamese MMPI-2: Assessing psychological adjustment of Vietnamese refugees. *Psychological Assessment, 15,* 370–377.

Dunn, L. M., & Dunn, L. M. (1981). *Peabody Picture Vocabulary Test—Revised.* Circle Pines, MN: American Guidance Services.

Folstein, M. F., Folstein, S. E., & McHugh, P. R. (1975). Mini-mental state: A practical method for grading the mental status of patients for the clinician. *Journal of Psychiatric Research, 12,* 189–198.

Geisinger, K. F. (1994). Cross-cultural normative assessment: Translation and adaptation issues influencing the normative interpretation of assessment instruments. *Psychological Assessment, 6,* 304–312.

Gong, Y. X. (1982). *Manual for the Wechsler Adult Intelligence Scale: Chinese Revision.* Changsha, Hunan, China: Hunan Medical College.

Hansen, N. D., Pepitone-Arreola-Rockwell, F., & Greene, A. F. (2000). Multicultural competence: Criteria and case examples. *Professional Psychology: Research and Practice, 31,* 652–660.

Hays, P. A. (1996). Culturally responsive assessment with diverse older clients. *Professional Psychology: Research and Practice, 27,* 188–193.

Hays, P. A. (2001). *Addressing cultural complexities in practice: A framework for clinicians.* Washington, DC: American Psychological Association.

Herrick, C. A., & Brown, H. N. (1998). Underutilization of mental health services by Asian-Americans residing in the United States. *Issues in Mental Health Nursing, 19,* 225–240.

Horton, A. M., Carrington, C. H., & Lewis-Jack, O. (2001). In L. A. Suzuki, J. G. Ponterotto, & P. J. Meller (Eds.), *Handbook of multicultural assessment: Clinical, psychological, and educational applications* (2nd ed., pp. 433–460). San Francisco: Jossey-Bass.

Huang, L. N. (1994). An integrative approach to clinical assessment and intervention with Asian-American adolescents. *Journal of Clinical Child Psychology, 23,* 21–31.

Koh, S. (1954). A statistical evaluation of the Korean conversion of the Wechsler-Bellevue Intelligence Scale. *Studies in Psychology, Ewha Woman's University, 1,* 26–53.

Kuo, W. H. (1984). Prevalence of depression among Asian-Americans. *Journal of Nervous and Mental Disease, 172,* 449–457.

Kwan, K. K. (1999). MMPI and MMPI-2 performance of the Chinese: Cross-cultural applicability. *Professional Psychology: Research and Practice, 30,* 260–268.

Lam, C. Y., Pepper, C. M., & Ryabchenko, K. A. (2004). Case identification of mood disorders in Asian American and Caucasian American college students. *Psychiatric Quarterly, 75*(4), 361–373.

Lee, J. H., Lee, K. U., Lee, D. Y., Kim, K. W., Jhoo, J. H., Kim, J. H., et al. (2002). Development of the Korean version of the Consortium to Establish a Registry for Alzheimer's Disease Assessment Packet (CERAD-K): Clinical and neuropsychological assessment batteries. *Journals of Gerontology: Series B: Psychological Sciences & Social Sciences, 57B,* P47–P53.

Lee, R. M., & Yoo H. C. (2004). Structure and measurement of ethnic identity for Asian American college students. *Journal of Counseling Psychology, 51,* 263–269.

Leong, F. T. L., Okazaki, S., & Tak, J. (2003). Assessment of depression and anxiety in East Asia. *Psychological Assessment, 15,* 290–305.

Lu, R., Luo, Z., & Liu, X. (2000). Reliability and validity of the Cognitive Abilities Screening Instrument C-2.0 (CASI) used in elderly people in Chengdu, China. *Chinese Journal of Clinical Psychology, 8,* 69–71.

Marin, G. (1992). Issues in the measurement of acculturation among Hispanics. In K. F. Geisinger (Ed.), *Psychological testing of Hispanics* (pp. 235–251). Washington, DC: American Psychological Association.

Mui, A. C., Kang, S., Chen, L. M., & Domanski, M. D. (2003). Reliability of the Geriatric Depression Scale for use among elderly Asian immigrants in the USA. *International Psychogeriatrics, 15,* 253–271.

Okazaki, S. (1997). Sources of ethnic differences between Asian American and White American college students on measures of depression and social anxiety. *Journal of Abnormal Psychology, 106,* 52–60.

Okazaki, S. (1998). Psychological assessment of Asian Americans: Research agenda for cultural competency. *Journal of Personality Assessment, 70,* 54–70.

Okazaki, S., & Sue, S. (1995). Cultural considerations in psychological assessment of Asian Americans. In J. N. Butcher (Ed.), *Clinical personality assessment: Practical approaches* (pp. 107–119). New York: Oxford University Press.

Okazaki, S., & Sue, S. (2000). Implications of test revisions for assessment with Asian Americans. *Psychological Assessment, 12*(3), 272–280.

Ong, P, & Hee, S. J. (1993). The growth of the Asian Pacific American population: Twenty million in 2020. In *The State of Asian Pacific America: Policy issues to the year 2020* (pp. 11–23). Los Angeles, CA: LEAP Asian Pacific American Public Policy Institute and UCLA Asian American Studies Center.

Padilla, A. M., & Medina, A. (1996). Cross-cultural sensitivity in assessment: Using tests in culturally appropriate ways. In L. A. Suzuki, P. J. Meller, & J. G. Ponterotto (Eds.), *Handbook of multicultural assessment: Clinical, psychological, and educational applications* (pp. 3–28). San Francisco: Jossey-Bass.

Paniagua, F. A. (1998). *Assessing and treating culturally diverse clients: A practical guide* (2nd ed.). Thousand Oaks: Sage.

Phinney, J. S. (1990). Ethnic identity in adolescents and adults: Review of research. *Psychological Bulletin, 108,* 499–514.

Phinney, J. S. (1992). The multigroup ethnic identity measure: A new scale for use with diverse groups. *Journal of Adolescent Research, 7,* 156–176.

Ponterotto, J. G., Baluch, S., & Carielli, D. (1998). The Suinn-Lew Asian Self-Identity Acculturation Scale (SL-ASIA): Critique and research recommendations. *Measurement and Evaluation in Counseling and Development, 31,* 109–124.

Ponterotto, J. G., Gretchen, D., Utsey, S. O., Stracuzzi, T., & Saya, R. (2003). The Multigroup Ethnic Identity Measure (MEIM): Psychometric review and further validity testing. *Educational and Psychological Measurement, 63,* 502–515.

Radloff, L. (1977). The CES-D scale: A self-report depression scale for research in the general population. *Applied Psychological Measurement, 1,* 385–401.

Rezentes, W. C. (1993). Na Mea Hawai'i: A Hawaiian acculturation scale. *Psychological Reports, 73,* 383–393.

Ross, G. W., Abbott, R. D., Petrovitch, H., Masaki, K. H., Murdaugh, C., Trockman, C., et al. (1997). Frequency and characteristics of silent dementia among elderly Japanese-American men: The

Honolulu-Asia Aging Study. *Journal of the American Medical Association, 277,* 800–805.

Sciarra, D. T. (2001). Assessment of diverse family systems. In L. A. Suzuki, J. G. Ponterotto, & P. J. Meller (Eds.), *Handbook of multicultural assessment: Clinical, psychological, and educational applications* (2nd ed., pp. 135–168). San Francisco: Jossey-Bass.

Shinagawa, F., Kobayashi, S., Fujita, K., & Maekawa, H. (1990). *Japanese Weschler Adult Intelligence Scale–Revised.* Tokyo: Nihon Bunka Kagakusha.

Shiota, N., Krauss, S., & Clark, L. (1996). Adaptation and validation of the Japanese MMPI-2. In J. Butcher (Ed.), *International adaptations of the MMPI-2* (pp. 67–87). Minneapolis: University of Minnesota Press.

Sue, D., Ino, S, & Sue, D. M. (1983). Nonassertiveness of Asian Americans: An accurate assumption? *Journal of Counseling Psychology, 30,* 581–588.

Sue, D. W., & Sue, D. (2003). *Counseling the culturally diverse: Theory and practice* (4th ed.). New York: Wiley.

Sue, S. (1977). Community mental health services to minority groups: Some optimism, some pessimism. *American Psychologist, 32,* 616–624.

Sue, S. (1998). In search of cultural competence in psychotherapy and counseling. *American Psychologist, 53,* 440–448.

Sue, S., & Chang, J. (2003). The state of psychological assessment in Asia. *Psychological Assessment, 15,* 306–310.

Sue, S., & Sue, D. W. (1974). MMPI comparisons between Asian American and non-Asian students utilizing a student health psychiatric clinic. *Journal of Counseling Psychology, 32,* 570–579.

Suinn, R. M., Ahuna, C., & Khoo, G. (1992). The Suinn-Lew Asian Self-Identity Acculturation Scale: Concurrent and factorial validation. *Educational and Psychological Measurement, 52,* 1041–1046.

Suinn, R. M., Rickard-Figueroa, K., Lew, S., and Vigil, P. (1987). The Suinn-Lew Asian Self-Identity Acculturation Scale: An initial report. *Educational and Psychological Measurement, 47,* 401–407.

Teng, E. L., Hasegawa, K., Homma, A., Imai, Y., Larson, E., Graves, A., et al. (1994). The Cognitive Abilities Screening Instrument (CASI): A practical test for cross-cultural epidemiological studies of dementia. *International Psychogeriatrics, 6,* 45–58.

Thompson, L., & Heaton, R. (1990). Use of demographic information in neuropsychological assessment. In D. Tupper & K. Cicerone (Eds.), *The neuropsychology of everyday life: Assessment and basic competencies* (pp. 234–256). Norwell, MA: Kluwer.

Tsai, D. C., & Pike, P. L. (2000). Effects of acculturation on the MMPI-2 scores of Asian American students. *Journal of Personality Assessment, 74,* 216–230.

Tsui, P., & Schultz, G. L. (1985). Failure of rapport: Why psychotherapeutic engagement fails in the treatment of Asian clients. *American Journal of Orthopsychiatry, 55,* 561–569.

Uba, L. (1994). *Asian Americans: Personality patterns, identity, and mental health.* New York: Guilford Press.

U.S. Census Bureau. (2005, April 29). *Facts for features: Asian/Pacific American Heritage Month.* Retrieved May 4, 2005, from www.census.gov/Press-Release/www/releases/archives/facts_for_features_special_editions/004522.html

Watson, D., & Friend, R. (1969). Measurement of social-evaluative anxiety. *Journal of Consulting and Clinical Psychology, 33,* 448–457.

Wechsler, D. (1939). *Wechsler-Bellevue Intelligence Scale.* New York: The Psychological Corporation.

Wechsler, D. (1955). *WAIS manual: Wechsler Adult Intelligence Scale.* New York: The Psychological Corporation.

Wechsler, D. (1981). *Wechsler Adult Intelligence Scale–Revised.* San Antonio, TX: The Psychological Corporation.

Wong, T. M., & Fujii, D.E. (2004). Neuropsychological assessment of Asian Americans: Demographic factors, cultural diversity, and practical guidelines. *Applied Neuropsychology, 11,* 23–36.

Yesavage J. A., Brink, T. L., Rose, T. L., Lum, O., Huang, V., Adey, M. B., et al. (1983). Development and validation of a geriatric depression screening scale: A preliminary report. *Journal of Psychiatric Research, 17,* 37–49.

Ying, Y. (1988). Depressive symptomatology among Chinese-Americans as measured by the CES-D. *Journal of Clinical Psychology, 44,* 739–774.

24

COUNSELING AND PSYCHOTHERAPY WITH ASIAN AMERICANS: PROCESS AND OUTCOMES

FREDERICK T. L. LEONG

DORIS F. CHANG

SZU-HUI LEE

More than three decades ago, articles began appearing that addressed the issue of how to provide effective psychotherapy for Asian Americans (e.g., Sue & Sue, 1972; Yamamoto, 1978). Since that time, articles dealing with that topic that are either clinical, theoretical, or empirical have continued to appear, and scholars have periodically provided state-of-art reviews of that literature. One of those reviews (Leong, 1986) serves as the foundation for this chapter. In an effort to update that critical review, we review the literature on psychotherapy process and outcome with Asian Americans published since 1985. Space limitations do not allow us to review, in addition, the extensive new literature on client and therapist variables. These latter topics are reviewed in a separate paper (Leong, Lee, & Chang, in press). Our chapter is organized into four main categories: empirical studies, culture-specific treatment models, general treatment strategies and recommendations, and clinical case studies.

EMPIRICAL STUDIES OF COUNSELING PROCESS AND OUTCOME

Leong's (1986) review pointed out the need for more empirical research investigating psychotherapy process and outcome as they pertain to Asian Americans. Since that time, the question of which factors contribute to therapy effectiveness among diverse Asian American and Pacific Islander (AA/PI) populations has been examined using two different methodological approaches. First, a number of investigations have examined the impact of culturally responsive mental health services (i.e., parallel services and ethnic/language matching between client and therapist) on indirect measures of outcome such as service utilization. A second group of studies have examined how factors such as client values and counseling preferences, therapist counseling style, and cultural competence influence the therapy process. With few exceptions, these two lines of research have failed to converge, largely because of differences in level of analysis and sample characteristics. For example, psychotherapy process research with Asian Americans has typically taken the form of smaller-scale analogue studies involving international students or more acculturated college student samples. These studies tend to be theoretically grounded and hypothesis driven, examining specific cultural variables that may predict ratings of therapeutic alliance and session outcome. However, the restricted sampling frame raises questions about the generalizability of findings to clinical populations and less acculturated Asian American groups.

In contrast, studies assessing outcomes of culturally responsive services typically draw from large public mental health databases involving large samples of more demographically diverse Asian Americans. These studies, however, are limited by their reliance on more distal measures of cultural responsiveness (e.g., ethnic and language matching) and indirect measures of therapy outcome (e.g., dropout rates, number of sessions, and Global Assessment Scale [GAS] scores). Even though more studies are needed to link the more theoretically developed studies of therapy process to the more generalizable studies of service utilization and outcome, the extant empirical literature has yielded a number of important insights that have brought the field a step closer to improving the cultural fit of psychotherapy for Asian Americans. Our discussion of the empirical literature is divided into five sections: (a) indirect measures of treatment outcome (i.e., service utilization, rates of premature treatment termination, and length of treatment), (b) direct measures of psychotherapy outcomes, (c) factors contributing to underutilization and poor treatment outcomes, (d) empirical evaluations of culturally responsive services programs and interventions designed to address these barriers to care, and (e) psychotherapy process research.

Indirect Measures of Treatment Outcome: Studies of Mental Health Service

Utilization. A number of studies have tracked Asian American service utilization patterns since the 1970s. Research conducted in the 1970s generally indicated higher dropout rates after one session and shorter length of treatment for Asian Americans, with some studies finding equal treatment conditions (i.e., Kinzie & Tseng, 1978; Sue, 1977; Sue & McKinney, 1975) and other studies finding objective differences in the treatments received (i.e., Yamamoto, James, & Palley, 1968). Ten years after Sue and McKinney's (1975) landmark study of the Seattle–King County mental health care system, O'Sullivan, Peterson, Cox, and Kirkeby (1989) reevaluated the service utilization patterns of ethnic minorities in the region. Using the same information database, O'Sullivan et al. found that the situation had dramatically improved. Asian Americans were no longer underutilizing services; they comprised 4.6% of the county population and 5.4% of county mental health clients. Dropout rates had declined and were comparable to those for Whites and there was no significant difference in the severity of illness between Asian American and White clients. These findings were interpreted as evidence that efforts to implement more culturally responsive programs and policies, such as creating ethnic-specific service programs and hiring more bilingual/bicultural staff, had been successful in addressing the needs of these underserved populations. Maynard, Ehreth, Cox, Peterson, and McGann's (1997) analysis study of four regional mental health networks in Washington State also found levels of representation by Asian Americans that matched their proportion in the local population.

Unfortunately, these signs of improvement in the delivery of services to Asian Americans have not been fully replicated in other regions of the country. Four large-scale studies conducted in the 1980s and 1990s demonstrate the continued underutilization of mental health services by Asian Americans. S. Sue, Fujino, Hu, Takeuchi, and Zane (1991) analyzed data supplied by the Automated Information System (AIS) maintained by the Los Angeles County Department of Mental Health. Only clients entering the outpatient system during the years 1983 to 1988 were examined. Results showed that Asian Americans constituted only 3.1% of outpatients but 8.7% of the county population, according to 1985 Census estimates. However, they were associated with the lowest dropout rates of all the ethnic groups (10.7%) and attended, on average, a greater number of treatment sessions compared to Whites. In a second AIS study that included both inpatients and outpatients seen in all Los Angeles County mental health facilities, Asian Americans were significantly more likely than Whites to receive outpatient services and to receive treatment that included medication (Flaskerud & Hu, 1992). These differences in service delivery are likely related to the finding that Asian clients tended to present with more severe disturbances; 63.8% of Asian clients were diagnosed with psychotic disorders versus 55.1% for Whites.

S. Chen, Sullivan, Lu, and Shibusawa (2003) analyzed 97,212 total admissions representing 45,774 individuals utilizing public mental health services in San Diego County between 1991 and 1994. Results show that Asian Americans accounted for only 3.96% of clients but 9.1% of the general population. Those Asian Americans who utilized services presented with more severe mental health symptoms, were more likely to use outpatient and day treatment programs, and tended to stay longer in treatment compared to other ethnic groups. They were also associated with the lowest dropout rates for the first three admissions compared to other groups. In another study, national utilization rates for a broad range of mental health services were examined using data provided by the National Institute of Mental Health (Matsuoka, Breaux, & Ryujin, 1997). Results indicated that Asian American and Pacific Islanders (AA/PIs) were three times less likely than their White counterparts to use available mental health services. With the exception of Colorado, this national pattern of underutilization by AA/PIs was supported in state-level analyses conducted for the 16 states with the highest populations of AA/PIs.

Two large-scale studies reveal a similar pattern of underrepresentation of Asian American youth in the public mental health system. In another analysis of Los Angeles County AIS data (1983–1988), Bui and Takeuchi (1992) found that Asian American adolescents accounted for only 2.7% percent of the treated population while representing 10.19% of the general population. After controlling for sociodemographic factors and diagnosis, no ethnic differences in dropout rates were found. Compared to Whites, however, Asian American

adolescents tended to stay longer in treatment. McCabe et al. (1999) examined service use patterns of four ethnic groups (aged 0 to 18 years old) across five public youth service sectors in San Diego County during a six-month period in the 1996–1997 fiscal year. To examine differences in rates of representation when socioeconomic status was or was not taken into account, utilization rates were compared to three population groups drawn from the 1996 Census and 1997 San Diego County public school enrollment records. For all comparison groups, AA/PIs were significantly underrepresented in the child welfare and mental health sectors and among services for children with serious emotional disturbance in the public schools. However, they were present in expected rates in the alcohol and drug treatment sector for all three comparison groups and the juvenile justice sectors, when compared to the full group census, and among households where income was at or below 200% of the poverty level.

In summary, with the exception of O'Sullivan et al. (1989) and Maynard et al. (1997), studies conducted in the 1980s and 1990s provide strong evidence of the continued underutilization of mental health services by AA/PI adults and youth. Among treated AA/PI populations, however, dropout rates appear to have declined and relative treatment length appears to have increased since the 1970s. These findings and others suggest that relative to Whites, AA/PIs experience more complex pathways to care or are delaying help-seeking until symptoms are more severe, thus necessitating a longer stay in treatment (Commander, Cochrane, Sashidharan, Akilu, & Wildsmith, 1999; Lam & Kavanagh, 1996).

As S. Chen et al. (2003) point out, the worsening of the general situation of mental health service delivery to AA/PI populations since the 1970s must be interpreted in light of the sociodemographic changes that have occurred in the past few decades. The influx of Southeast Asian refugees and other new immigrant groups has increased the need for social work and mental health services among Asian communities while also posing significant challenges to effective service delivery. More fine-grained analyses of specific AA/PI ethnic groups may reveal important subgroup differences in risk factors, treatment-seeking behaviors, and pathways to care (Flaskerud, 1986a).

Direct Measures of Treatment Outcome: Client and Therapist Ratings

Whereas the studies reviewed in this section so far have emphasized service use as an indirect measure of treatment outcome, a few studies have examined direct measures of psychotherapy outcomes for Asian American clients. In one of the first studies to examine how Asian Americans fare in mental health treatment, Zane, Enomoto, and Chun (1994) evaluated the short-term outcomes of individual therapy provided in the context of a community-based, culturally responsive outpatient clinic in San Francisco. Approximately 85% of the therapists reported using primarily psychodynamic-oriented, short-term treatment approaches, with the remainder using primarily cognitive-behavioral treatments. Therapy outcomes of both Asian and White clients were assessed at the first and fourth sessions using both client self-report (Symptom Check List, SCL-30) and therapist ratings (Brief Rating Scale). Compared to White American clients, Asian American clients reported feeling more depressed, more hostile, and more anxious after four sessions of treatment and were less satisfied with treatment. However, there were no ethnic differences found on the therapist-rated outcomes, indicating a discrepancy between clients and therapists in their experiences of treatment.

This discrepancy between client and therapist ratings of outcome may help to explain why some studies of Asian Americans report therapy effectiveness, whereas others do not. For example, community-based studies that rely on another therapist measure of outcome, the GAS, also report no ethnic differences in post-treatment GAS scores, after controlling for pretreatment GAS (S. Sue et al., 1991; Zane, Hatanaka, Park, & Akutsu, 1994). In contrast, in a study by Lee and Mixon (1995) that used client ratings to assess perceptions of helpfulness, Asian students rated the counseling they received as less helpful for their personal-social-emotional concerns and rated their counselors as less competent than did White students, despite their similarity in the number of presenting problems.

As Zane et al. (2004) point out, any conclusions about the effectiveness of psychotherapy for Asians are premature given the limited data that are available. However, a number of trends are worth noting here. First, the few large-scale studies that have been conducted suggest that Asian groups do benefit from psychotherapy; however, methodological confounds make it difficult to determine whether those findings are simply an artifact of the global measure of outcome used. Second, evidence suggests that Asian clients and their therapists may hold different perceptions of the therapy experience, which may reflect different expectations of treatment or different modes of communication and emotional expression. Finally, there is some evidence that Asian Americans are less satisfied with the services received, which may explain, in part, their reluctance as a group to seek help, particularly for mental health problems.

PROBLEMS IN THE DELIVERY OF MENTAL HEALTH SERVICES

Research seeking to explain the underrepresentation of Asians in mainstream mental health facilities has focused on the sociocultural factors and structural barriers believed to influence individuals' help-seeking attitudes and behaviors (Leong & Lau, 2001; Takeuchi, Leaf, & Kuo, 1988). A growing body of evidence supports the notion that cultural differences in mental health concepts, idioms of distress, stigmatization of the mentally ill and mental health service use, and preference for alternate coping strategies may contribute to the underutilization of psychological services by diverse Asian American populations (e.g., Edman & Johnson, 1999; Kagawa Singer & Chung, 2002; M. Y. Lee, Law, & Eo, 2003; Nguyen & Anderson, 2005; Ying & Miller, 1992).

For example, a focus group study of Korean Americans suffering from depression revealed that Korean values of self-reliance and emotional self-restraint led many to engage in solitary coping responses rather than reaching out to others for help (Shin, 2002). The major reason cited for delay in seeking professional mental health care was the strong reluctance by participants to accept their problem as depression, due to the strong stigmatization of the mentally ill and mental health service use. Similarly, Narikiyo and Kameoka (1992) found that Japanese American college students were much more likely than White American college students to attribute mental illness to interpersonal difficulties, to prefer to resolve problems on their own, and to seek help from informal sources of support such as family and friends. They were much less likely than their White counterparts to perceive mental health professionals as personally helpful for psychological problems (15% vs. 26%) and to have received mental health services in the past (5.6% vs. 25.0%). Additional evidence for the role of cultural factors in help-seeking behavior is provided by studies indicating that acculturation is related to positive help-seeking attitudes (Atkinson & Gim, 1989; B. S. K. Kim & Omizo, 2003; Tata & Leong, 1994) and help-seeking behavior for personal or emotional problems (Cachelin, Veisel, Barzegarnazari, & Striegel Moore, 2000; Kung, 2004). However, Ying and Miller (1992) noted that acculturation is a more distal predictor that exerts less influence on help-seeking when illness severity and service needs are high.

Underutilization may also stem from problems in the delivery of services, including perceptions that mainstream mental health services are not accessible or culturally responsive to the needs of Asian communities (Balabil & Dolan, 1992; Takeuchi et al., 1988). Other structural barriers may include not knowing where to locate a credible source of professional help, time constraints, distance, cost of treatment and lack of financial resources, access to transportation, and English-language proficiency (Mau & Jepsen, 1988; Takeuchi et al., 1988; Ying & Miller, 1992). An example of cultural incongruence between mainstream practices and characteristics of minority clients is provided by Bhui, Chandran, and Sathyamoorthy (2002). Their ethnographic study of eight South Asian men using mental health services found that cultural beliefs and religious issues were considered by their informants to be important but were rarely assessed by their mental health service providers. Communication and therapeutic engagement were judged to be poor, with some of the men experiencing their treatment as authoritarian and disrespectful. Surprisingly, the practitioners felt that the majority of clients were adequately managed with existing services, whereas, in fact, many of the men did not have a clear understanding of the nature of their diagnosis or the rationale for treatment.

Practical barriers such as cost, time, and language accessibility have been shown to pose more of a problem for less acculturated individuals, who must learn to navigate an entirely new health care system while also adjusting to life in a new culture. Drawing on a sample of 1,747 from the Chinese American Psychiatric Epidemiological Study, Kung (2004) examined the relationships among perceived barriers to mental health treatment, mental health need, and mental health service use. Cultural barriers, such as credibility of treatment and loss of face, were not as important as more practical concerns. Specifically, cost of treatment was rated as the single greatest barrier to mental health treatment (endorsed by 77.1% of respondents), followed by language (64.1%), time (64.0%), and knowledge of available services (48.0%). Only these practical barriers significantly reduced the likelihood of mental health service use, even after controlling for sociodemographic variables and level of mental distress. Comparative research shows that, in general, Asian Americans perceive greater barriers to mental health treatment compared to Caucasian populations and that the importance of specific barriers varies by the nature of the problem (Takeuchi et al., 1988).

Culturally Responsive Services: Client and Therapist Match, Ethnic-Specific Services, and Culturally Tailored Interventions

To address the significant sociocultural and structural barriers to effective service delivery, Sue (1977) proposed a number of solutions, including (a) augmenting existing services by, for example, hiring more ethnic specialists or improving the cultural competence of existing staff; (b) establishing parallel or ethnic-specific services programs; and (c) creating nonparallel programs that are culturally tailored to a particular group. Since then, great strides have been made to implement these suggestions in ethnically dense communities; however, empirical evaluations of such programs are few in number.

The available literature suggests that, within the public mental health system, client and therapist matching results in increased service utilization by Asian American clients (Flaskerud, 1986b; Takeuchi, Sue, & Yeh, 1995). In the AIS analysis performed by S. Sue et al. (1991), ethnic and/or language match was particularly important for Asians who did not speak English as a primary language. For these clients, ethnic match alone, language match alone, and a combination of ethnic and language match were all significantly associated with lower odds of premature termination and a greater number of sessions, when controlling for other demographic and clinical variables. In fact, when matched with a therapist of the same ethnicity, they were five times less likely to prematurely terminate from treatment than when they were not matched. Although matching was not associated with improvements in treatment outcome, these findings suggest that matching may have important effects in increasing the utilization of mental health services by Asian Americans.

Whereas ethnic and language matches may be conducted within mainstream service systems, parallel or ethnic-specific mental health services (ESS) involve systematic modifications designed to improve the cultural fit of mainstream service offerings. The assumption is that organizational improvements in cultural match or fit will lead to increased service use and improved therapeutic outcomes over time. ESS programs frequently are located within ethnic enclaves; extend service hours to accommodate clients' work schedules; work cooperatively with family members, indigenous healers, and community elders; and provide extensive case management services to address immigrants' social service needs (Ito & Maramba, 2002; Takeuchi, Mokuau, & Chun, 1992). Mental health services may also be integrated with primary care to capitalize on the preference for integrating health and mental health treatments.

Four studies analyzing data provided by the Los Angeles County Department of Mental Health provide evidence that ESS programs increase utilization by Asian American children and adults (Flaskerud & Hu, 1992; Lau & Zane, 2000; Takeuchi et al., 1995; Yeh, Takeuchi, & Sue, 1994). Takeuchi et al. (1995) studied 4,710 ethnic minority adults who entered an outpatient

setting that served either a predominantly ethnic population (ESS) or a predominantly White (mainstream) clientele. Compared to those attending mainstream programs, Asian Americans attending ESS programs had a higher rate of return after the first session and attended a greater number of treatment sessions, whether or not they were ethnically matched with their therapists. Asian Americans who were receiving mainstream services, but were ethnically matched with their therapist, also returned more often than their unmatched counterparts. However, type of program was not associated with treatment outcomes for Asian Americans.

Lau and Zane (2000) examined the cost utilization and outcomes of Asian Americans of all ages who used outpatient mental health services during 1993–1994. Their sample included 1,981 individuals who received services at ESS agencies and 1,197 who received services at mainstream agencies. Cost utilization for Asian clients in ESS programs was higher than in mainstream programs. However, better treatment outcomes were found for ESS clients, after controlling for demographic variables, pretreatment symptom severity, diagnosis, and type of reimbursement. There was also a significant relationship between level of care and outcome for ESS clients, whereas this was not the case for mainstream service users.

Although much of the evidence on the effects of ESS programs comes from studies of the Los Angeles County mental health care system, similar findings have been reported in case studies of specific ESS outpatient (Zane, Hatanaka, et al., 1994) and inpatient programs (Mathews, Glidden, Murray, Forster, & Hargreaves, 2002). In their investigation of 885 clients at an ESS community mental health center in central Los Angeles, Zane, Hatanaka, et al. (1994) reported that few ethnic differences in service effectiveness (i.e., premature termination, treatment duration, clinical outcomes) were observed when comparing White with Asian clients. These findings suggest that ESS programs can provide effective outpatient services to minority populations without producing service inequities between minority and majority clients. Matthews et al. (2002) assessed whether assigning minority patients to ethnically focused psychiatric inpatient units would affect treatment outcome. The sample consisted of 5,938 inpatients at San Francisco General Hospital between 1989 and 1996. Results indicated that matching to ethnically focused psychiatric inpatient units resulted in longer treatment stays and improved referral to follow-up treatment after discharge. Moreover, the inpatients were more willing to accept outpatient or residential treatment referrals and were less likely to be sent to locked facilities or refuse follow-up treatment, after controlling for primary language, diagnosis, sex, and number of admissions in the previous year. Although there was no association between ESS status of patients and the time of hospitalization, these results suggest that placement of minority patients in ethnically focused inpatient units may be important for improving patients' participation in ongoing treatment.

As shown, the research findings provide preliminary evidence that ESS programs are more effective than mainstream programs at reducing premature termination and increasing length of treatment, independent of ethnic and language match. However, ESS programs do not demonstrate a consistent benefit with regard to treatment outcome. Whereas some studies report better treatment outcomes (i.e., Lau & Zane, 2000; Yeh et al., 1994), others failed to find improved outcomes as a result of ESS utilization (Matthews et al., 2002; Takeuchi et al., 1995).

Besides ethnic/language matching and the development of ESS programs, a third strategy for addressing ethnic disparities in service utilization is to create nonparallel programs that are culturally tailored to a particular group (Sue, 1977). Although many of these programs are grounded in mainstream approaches to mental health treatment, they also incorporate indigenous healing practices and/or address the specific cultural concerns and social contexts of a particular ethnic group. As Takeuchi et al. (1992) pointed out, such programs are relatively rare, in part, because of difficulties acquiring funding for such innovative programs (including reimbursement by insurance companies). In addition, the evolving nature of such programs often makes it difficult to conduct a standard evaluation of effectiveness. Nevertheless, there is some preliminary evidence that such programs may play an increasingly important role in meeting the service needs of specific populations.

Choi et al. (1996) examined the efficacy of a brief skills training group aimed at reducing HIV risk among homosexual AA/PI men. In addition to providing psychoeducation modules on eroticizing and negotiating safer sex, the curriculum also included structured discussions aimed at fostering a positive ethnic and sexual identity. Although the study did not include a control group, Choi et al. found significant reductions in numbers of sexual partners and, for Chinese and Filipino men, a reduction in unprotected anal intercourse at three-month follow-up. T. Chang, Yeh, and Krumboltz (2001) found that an online support group for Asian American male college students was successful in addressing concerns about shame and stigma while retaining components considered essential to group process. Takeuchi et al. (2002) also described a community program designed for native Hawaiians, Hale Ola Ho'opakolea, which incorporates indigenous Native Hawaiian therapies to assist clients in the resolution of individual problems. The program has led to increased mental health service use and has received high client satisfaction ratings (Nishigaya, 1988). Although our discussion here is limited to those interventions that have been empirically evaluated, later in the chapter we briefly review other promising clinical approaches that have been described in the literature.

Psychotherapy Process Research

In contrast to the large-scale studies of psychotherapy outcome, empirical studies of psychotherapy process have tended to rely on small samples of convenience, with most adopting an analogue design and focusing on college student populations. Despite these methodological limitations, these small, focused studies have investigated some of the cultural and structural factors that may underlie the patterns of underutilization, help-seeking delay, and premature dropout described earlier. The literature in this area can be divided into three categories: client characteristics and preferences that may influence psychotherapy process, specific interventions or behavioral adaptations to improve the therapeutic alliance, and studies that examine the clinical encounter as an intercultural interaction.

First, a few studies have examined preferences of Asian international and Asian American students with regard to counseling style and counselor characteristics as a function of acculturation. For example, a survey of graduate students from Taiwan and the United States attending the same midwestern university found that Taiwanese students preferred that the counselor be older than themselves and of the same ethnic background, whereas the same was not true of the American students (Mau & Jepsen, 1988). These results were consistent with Kim and Atkinson's (2002) finding that students with high Asian value orientation rated their counselors as more empathic and credible than those with low Asian value orientation when the counselors were Asian. However, students with low adherence to Asian values rated counselors to be more empathetic when they were ethnically dissimilar. Despite the fact that these studies did not involve actual therapy clients seeking help for a mental health problem, the findings suggest that among non-native or less acculturated Asian Americans, ethnic match may contribute to the development of a positive working relationship.

Additional studies suggest that Asian clients may also possess different role expectations and treatment preferences (Exum & Lau, 1988). In Mau and Jepsen's (1988) study, the Taiwanese international students were much less likely than American students to view the counselor's role as that of a listener (31% vs. 77%, respectively). Rather, they were more likely to view the counselor as a friend (75%) or expert (62%) and endorse statements such as "When I seek counseling, I prefer a direct, concrete answer to my concerns" and "I like the counselor to make decisions for me." Lee and Mixon (1995) found that compared to White students, Asian students seeking help at a university counseling center were more likely to come in for career/vocational concerns than for personal, social, and emotional concerns; in addition, they had significantly fewer sessions. However, like the findings for ethnic match, there is some evidence that the preference for directive or structured approaches to counseling may be related to level of identification with the dominant culture. In a study conducted by Wong, Kim, Zane, Kim, and Huang (2003), Asian American college students rated the credibility of cognitive therapy and time-limited psychodynamic therapy as presented in written descriptions of their theoretical approach. Results indicated that cultural identity and self-construals moderated credibility ratings. Individuals with low levels of White identity (i.e., more culturally identified) rated cognitive therapy as more credible than psychodynamic therapy, whereas those with high White identity did not rate the two treatments differently. Contrary to expectation, those with *high* independent self-construals found cognitive therapy to be more credible than psychodynamic therapy, with no differences in credibility shown for those with low independent self-construals.

Second, a few studies have examined specific interventions that may improve the therapy process. One promising intervention focuses on concrete behaviors that can be used to establish rapport with Asian international students early in the therapeutic relationship with a White counselor. In a study by Zhang and Dixon (2001), White counselors conducted a participatory counseling analogue interview with 60 Asian international students. Students in the multiculturally responsive counseling condition were interviewed in a room decorated in an Asian style and were met with a traditional greeting in their native language. The counselor also expressed interest in the student's home country and engaged him or her in a discussion of cross-cultural differences in communication norms (e.g., nonverbal behavior). Clients in the culturally neutral position were interviewed in a room without Asian decorations, were greeted in English, and were not explicitly asked about their countries of origin or cross-cultural variants in communication style. Relative to clients in the control condition, clients in the culturally responsive condition rated their counselors as significantly more expert, attractive, and trustworthy. In addition, they rated their counselors higher in (a) ability to help people from different cultures with academic, social, and personal problems; (b) openness to different cultures; and (c) ability to relate to people from different cultures.

Lambert and Lambert (1984) tested a pretherapy intervention that aimed to address Asian immigrants' misconceptions about therapy and align clients' therapy expectations with actual therapy procedures. Clients in the intervention condition listened to a recorded message that explained such issues as role expectations for therapy, expectations for verbal disclosure, therapy processes, and the importance of regular attendance. Clients in the control condition listened to a recorded message about why people have trouble coping with problems and life demands. Results showed that clients in the intervention condition had lower dropout rates, were more satisfied with therapy, rated themselves as more changed, and became less dependent on the therapist for support, advice, and direction. These findings suggest that in working with Asian clients, therapists can improve the therapy process by implementing culturally focused rapport building and psychoeducational procedures. However, additional studies are needed to determine the generalizability of these findings.

A third group of studies examine therapy process as a function of the interaction between client and therapist variables. Building on the work of Atkinson and others, Kim and colleagues (B. S. K. Kim, Li, & Liang, 2002; B. S. K. Kim, Ng, & Ahn, 2005; Li & Kim, 2004) have initiated a program of research to study predictors of counseling process and outcome in Asian American college student volunteers. In a series of quasi-intervention analogue studies, the authors tested specific cultural hypotheses regarding interaction effects of client and therapist ethnicity and cultural value orientation, therapist counseling style, and session goal on ratings of therapy process. These studies report significant main effects of therapist self-disclosure of coping strategies (B. S. K. Kim et al., 2003), use of a directive counseling style (Li & Kim, 2004), and problem-focused interventions (B. S. K. Kim et al., 2002) on measures such as therapist empathy, credibility, and competence. However, the complex ways in which therapist and client variables interact across therapy situations have proven more difficult to tease apart. Despite the complicated and often conflicting findings from this body of work, the move toward transactional models of therapy process marks a significant advancement in the field. Additional studies are needed, however, to determine the generalizability of resulting models to actual community and university clients who represent greater diversity

with regard to variables such as age, social class, problem severity, and illness experience.

CULTURE-SPECIFIC TREATMENT MODELS

Although only a few empirical evaluations of culture-specific treatment models have been conducted, a number of descriptive papers have detailed innovative community- and clinic-based models of service delivery to specific Asian American subgroups. In particular, a number of therapeutic approaches have been developed to improve the cultural fit of mental health interventions for Southeast Asian refugees. In particular, Kinzie and his colleagues (Kinzie, 1985, 1989; Kinzie et al., 1988) have written extensively about their experiences providing group therapy, individual therapy, and psychiatric treatment at the Oregon Health Sciences University psychiatric clinic for Indochinese refugees. Martin and Zweben (1993) described a culture-specific pretherapy intervention for Southeast Asian Mien opium users in California, and Weiss and Parish (1989) reported on a culturally appropriate model of crisis counseling based on their work at the Indochinese Mental Health Project (IMHP). Finally, Canda (1989) described the therapeutic use of writing, artistic design, and other communication media in independent social work with Southeast Asian refugees.

In addition to special programs targeting Southeast Asian refugees because of their high service needs, a few programs have been described for other API populations, including Asian international students (Carr, Koyama, & Thiagarajan, 2003; Hom & Amada, 1985), psychiatric inpatients (Gee, Du, Akiyama, & Lu, 1999), and outpatients. With regard to the latter group, H. Chen, Kramer, and Chen (2003) presented the Charles B. Wang Community Health Center's Primary Care and Mental Health Services Bridge Program in New York City. This program addresses the stigma surrounding mental illness and mental health service use by integrating mental health services into primary care. Informal indicators of the success of the program include an increase in the numbers of identified mental health patients, an increase in the number of mental health encounters involving primary care physicians, positive patient ratings, and improvements in the rate of successful referrals to off-site specialty mental health treatments. Morelli, Fong, and Oliveira (2001) conducted an ethnographic study of a culture-based, woman-centered community residential treatment program for API clients with substance abuse problems in rural Hawaii. On the basis of 21 in-depth interviews with clients, Morelli et al. identified factors that were reported to be vital to the clients' experience of treatment, such as the inclusion of indigenous healing practices.

GENERAL TREATMENT STRATEGIES AND RECOMMENDATIONS

Even though empirical studies and descriptions of culture-specific treatment programs represent a small percentage of the literature published since the 1980s, there has been tremendous growth in the number of journal articles, books, and book chapters that offer general treatment guidelines and recommendations for working with Asian Americans. Atkinson, Morten, and Sue's (1998) landmark book, *Counseling American Minorities* (first published in 1983 and now in its fifth revised edition), called attention to the ways in which the counseling profession has failed to meet the mental health needs of racial and ethnic minority groups. Yet, a major thesis of their book was, and continues to be, that by increasing cultural sensitivity, knowledge, and skills, counselors can establish the necessary and sufficient conditions of a helping relationship with clients who come from cultural backgrounds different from their own.

Today, the expanding multicultural counseling literature includes strategies for applying and adapting mainstream approaches to therapy in order to better meet the needs of Asian clients. These approaches include solution-focused therapy (Berg & Miller, 1992), career counseling (Leong, 1993), feminist therapies (True, 1990), relational counseling (D. Y. F. Ho, 1999), crisis intervention (Bromley, 1987), group therapy (M. Chen & Han, 2001), psycho-analysis (Babcock & Gehrie, 1986; Mass, 2003; Tung, 1991), and play therapy (Kao & Landreth, 2001). Reflecting the centrality of the family in Asian constructions of the self (Kitano, 1989),

there are a large number of articles that address cultural considerations in conducting family therapy with Asian American families in general (T. H. H. Chang & Yeh, 1999; J. M. Kim, 2003; E. Lee, 1996; Wilson, Phillip, Kohn, & Curry El, 1995) as well as specific Asian subgroups, including Southeast Asians (Bemak, 1989; E. Lee, 1990; McKenzie Pollock, 1996), Pilipinos (Rita, 1996), Japanese (Tamura & Lau, 1992), and Chinese (E. Lee, 1989). Treatment models have also been presented for addressing specific mental health issues, such as post-traumatic stress disorder among interned Japanese Americans (Loo, 1993) and Southeast Asian refugees (Boehnlein, 1987b; Ying, 2001), ethnic and sexual identity among API gay and lesbian populations (Chung & Katayama, 1999), and substance abuse (Amodeo, Robb, Peou, & Tran, 1996; Varma & Siris, 1996), domestic violence (Futa, Hsu, & Hansen, 2001; C. K. Ho, 1990; Tatara, 1999); and suicidality (Takahashi, 1989) among Asian American clients.

Although the literature on working with Asian American clients is too great to review in depth here, there are a number of general treatment strategies and recommendations that consistently appear across publications. First, contained in the majority of texts is an explicit recommendation that providers acknowledge their own cultural biases and learn about the cultures, histories, and values of their Asian clients in order to determine the appropriateness of their therapeutic approaches and goals (e.g., Casas, 1995; Cerhan, 1990; Moy, 1992; S. Sue & Zane, 1987). Cultural differences in social roles and expression of emotion critically shape the initial phases of therapy and form intricate parts of an individual's dynamic, internal life. By attending to these implicit cultural factors and to one's own cultural attitudes, the therapist may improve the chances of developing a solid working alliance, which ultimately will allow for meaningful change to take place. For example, Tsui and Schultz (1985) outline specific guidelines for engaging unassimilated Asian clients into therapy that include some degree of therapist self-disclosure and explicit education about the purpose of questions regarding clinical history, family background, and psychosocial stressors.

A second general recommendation in the literature is that counselors recognize the tremendous heterogeneity within Asian American groups. Within-group differences with regard to ethnic identity, cultural background, degree of acculturation, experiences within the majority culture, circumstances of immigration, family structure, values, social class, and religion are highlighted as essential for understanding individual clients' adaptation efforts, help-seeking behaviors, and therapy process and outcome (Aponte & Barnes, 1995; Chin, 1998). Indeed, numerous publications address special issues in working with specific population subgroups, such as the elderly (Sakauye, 1992; Yamamoto, Silva, & Chang, 1998) and men (D. Sue, 1990, 2001). While much of the literature discusses Asian Americans in the aggregate, more articles are being written about specific ethnic subgroups, such as Southeast Asian Americans, Chinese Americans, and Japanese Americans, with relatively fewer written about South Asian, Korean, Filipino, and Pacific Islander Americans (e.g., Cimmarusti, 1996; Henkin, 1985; Huff & Kline, 1999; Inman & Tewari, 2003; E. Y. K. Kim, Bean, & Harper, 2004; Wenhao, Salomon, & Chay, 1999).

A third common suggestion in the literature is that highly structured therapeutic interventions are more effective, particularly for more traditional Asian American clients (e.g., Lin & Cheung, 1999; Takahashi, 1989). In their discussion of how non-Asian family therapists can work more successfully with Asian families, Berg and Jaya (1993) stress that pragmatic solutions, not exploration of feelings, tend to be valued by Asian clients. According to Berg and Jaya, when Asian families contact service providers, the contact tends to be crisis oriented, brief, and solution oriented; thus, they do not recommend insight and growth-oriented approaches. Whereas there are almost no data to suggest that there is differential effectiveness for different therapy approaches with Asian Americans, there is evidence that some Asian Americans prefer more structured, directive approaches, such as cognitive-behavior therapy and problem-focused approaches (Ito & Maramba, 2002; B. S. K. Kim et al., 2002; Wong et al., 2003). Fulfilling clients' expectations that the therapist assume the role of the expert helper is thought to facilitate client engagement and the development of the therapeutic alliance.

A final treatment recommendation commonly mentioned in the literature involves working collaboratively with clients' families, support networks, and other treatment providers (Atkinson et al., 1998) and integrating alternative belief systems that may be more culturally congruent with clients' perceptions of cause and cure (Chua, 2003; Martin & Zweben, 1993).

CLINICAL CASE STUDIES

Finally, clinical case studies provide a wealth of information for examining psychotherapy process and outcome with Asian American clients (Chin, Liem, Ham, & Hong, 1993). These detailed accounts illustrate important treatment issues such as psychodiagnosis of Asian culture-bound syndromes, cross-cultural counseling techniques, transference and countertransference issues, psychotherapeutic process, culturally grounded case conceptualization, and factors related to language and the use of interpreters.

Many of the case studies published since the 1980s describe the treatment of trauma reactions among Southeast Asian refugees (e.g., Boehnlein, 1987a, 1987b; Freimer, Lu, & Chen, 1989; Kinzie, 1989, 2001). Frances and Kroll (1989) described the treatment of a 57-year-old Hmong widow to illustrate the cultural shaping of depressive symptomatology and the principle of working collaboratively to address multiple dimensions of the client's illness experience. A team-based treatment approach was applied, involving individual, family, and group counseling through supervised indigenous workers; psychoeducation; and pharmacological treatment.

Case studies involving therapy conducted with other Asian American elderly (Berg & Jaya, 1993), couples (Hanson Kahn & L'Abate, 1998), and families (Ganesan, Fine, & Lin, 1989; Yeung & Chang, 2002) also have been published in recent years. Yeung and Chang (2002) described a family therapy case that involved severe intergenerational conflicts resulting from different acculturation attitudes held across three generations in the same Chinese immigrant family. A common theme appearing in many of these case studies is the conflict arising from differing Asian and American cultural constructions of the self and self-object, as exemplified by Babcock and Gehrie's (1986) longitudinal presentation of a Japanese immigrant at age 25 and at age 54. A number of case studies have also addressed adolescent conflicts and issues related to ethnic identity development among Asian American youth (Agbayani Siewert & Enrile, 2003; Cooper, 1988; M. K. Ho, 1992; Holt, Phillips, Shapiro, & Becker, 2003).

SUMMARY AND CONCLUDING COMMENTS

Leong (1986) concluded his review by observing that there was a definite lack of empirical studies in the counseling process and outcome literature as it pertained to Asian Americans. That observation is no longer true, and there has been a small but growing literature on psychotherapy process and outcome with Asian Americans; however, this progress is not without its attendant limitations. As pointed out earlier, there have been two lines of research: (a) examinations of the impact of culturally responsive mental health services on indirect measures of outcome such as service utilization, and (b) studies that examined how factors such as client values and counseling preferences, therapist counseling style, and cultural competence influence the therapy process. Unfortunately, these two lines of research have failed to converge. Future studies need to place greater emphasis on linking the more theoretically developed studies of therapy process to the more generalizable studies of service utilization and outcome reviewed in this chapter.

Furthermore, although Leong's (1986) call for more research on those Asian Americans who do not come in for treatment has been heeded, underutilization of mental health services by Asian Americans remains a major problem in need of further exploration, as noted by other reviews (e.g., U.S. Department of Health and Human Services, 2001). Within this area of service utilization research, the inconsistent findings of expected levels of utilization of mental health services in some regions and continued underutilization in other regions remain an unresolved puzzle. Regional variations are to be expected, but more theoretically driven research is needed to tease out the contributing

factors to these variations. In other words, researchers need to identify the internal (to the individual and the cultural group) and external (social, systems, and institutional) barriers that are contributing to underutilization of services in some regions and not others. A special issue of *Mental Health Services Research* (Leong, 2001) focused on barriers to providing effective mental health services to racial and ethnic minority groups, may serve as a good source of hypotheses to be tested. In the Asian American article in that special issue, Leong and Lau (2001) delineated the cognitive, affective, value-oriented, and physical barriers to help-seeking as well as specific barriers for Asian American subpopulations.

Similarly, further research is needed to explore the possible factors that explain why ESS are associated with higher service utilization and improved mental health outcomes for Asian Americans in some situations but not others. In addition, ESS for Asian Americans can only be provided in certain communities with sufficient numbers of Asian American mental health professionals. For many Asian Americans living in other urban or rural areas without such a concentration of Asian American mental health professionals, the only alternative solution is to ensure that culturally responsive services are provided by mainstream or majority group professionals. Recently, in response to this problem, Leong and his colleagues (see Leong & Serafica, 2001; Leong & Tang, 2002) have begun to develop a cultural accommodation model for providing more culturally relevant and effective psychotherapy for racial and ethnic minority groups. The proposed cultural accommodation approach involves three steps: (a) identifying the cultural gaps or cultural blindspots in an existing theory that restricts the cultural validity of the theory, (b) selecting current culture-specific concepts and models from cross-cultural and ethnic minority psychology to fill in the cultural gaps and accommodate the theory to racial and ethnic minorities, and (c) testing the culturally accommodated theory to determine if it has incremental validity above and beyond the culturally unaccommodated theory.

Finally, in terms of understanding the counseling process with Asian Americans, there has been a significant and important shift from the use of static and unidimensional models to more dynamic, transactional, and interactional models to guide research in this area. The previous unidimensional models of research tended to focus mainly on client characteristics as if the therapist were a static, uniform, and insignificant variable in the process. This new approach to counseling research with Asian Americans is best represented by the work of Bryan Kim and his colleagues in explicating the interaction effects of acculturation, cultural values, and preferences for counseling styles. While this type of research is difficult to undertake, it is also very consistent with the model of cross-cultural counseling research advocated by Helms (1990) whereby regressive, progressive, and parallel relationships between therapists and clients, in terms of their racial identity, are proposed to have a significant impact on the counseling process and outcome. Furthermore, these transactional and interactional models are much more ecologically valid and more closely represent the realities of cross-cultural counseling encounters.

REFERENCES

Agbayani Siewert, P., & Enrile, A. V. (2003). Filipino American children and adolescents. In L. N. Huang & J. T. Gibbs (Eds.), *Children of color: Psychological interventions with culturally diverse youth* (pp. 229–264). San Francisco: Jossey-Bass.

Amodeo, M., Robb, N., Peou, S., & Tran, H. (1996). Adapting mainstream substance-abuse interventions for Southeast Asian clients. *Families in Society, 77*(7), 403–413.

Aponte, J. F., & Barnes, J. M. (1995). Impact of acculturation and moderator variables on the intervention and treatment of ethnic groups. In R. Y. Rivers & J. F. Aponte (Eds.), *Psychological interventions and cultural diversity* (pp. 19–39). Needham Heights, MA: Allyn & Bacon.

Atkinson, D. R., & Gim, R. H. (1989). Asian-American cultural identity and attitudes towards mental health services. *Journal of Counseling Psychology, 36*(2), 209–212.

Atkinson, D. R., Morten, G., & Sue, D. W. (Eds.). (1998). *Counseling American minorities* (5th ed.). New York: McGraw-Hill.

Babcock, C. G., & Gehrie, M. J. (1986). The Japanese American experience: An approach through psychoanalysis and follow-up. *Journal of Psychoanalytic Anthropology, 9*(3), 373–390.

Balabil, S., & Dolan, B. (1992). A cross-cultural evaluation of expectations about psychological counselling. *British Journal of Medical Psychology, 65*(4), 305–308.

Bemak, F. (1989). Cross-cultural family therapy with Southeast Asian refugees. *Journal of Strategic and Systemic Therapies, 8,* 22–27.

Berg, I. K., & Jaya, A. (1993). Different and same: Family therapy with Asian-American families. *Journal of Marital & Family Therapy, 19*(1), 31–38.

Berg, I. K., & Miller, S. D. (1992). Working with Asian American clients: One person at a time. *Families in Society, 73*(6), 356–363.

Bhui, K., Chandran, M., & Sathyamoorthy, G. (2002). Mental health assessment and south Asian men. *International Review of Psychiatry, 14*(1), 52–59.

Boehnlein, J. K. (1987a). Clinical relevance of grief and mourning among Cambodian refugees. *Social Science & Medicine, 25*(7), 765–772.

Boehnlein, J. K. (1987b). Culture and society in post-traumatic stress disorder: Implications for psychotherapy. *American Journal of Psychotherapy, 41*(4), 519–530.

Bromley, M. A. (1987). New beginnings for Cambodian refugees: Or further disruptions? *Social Work, 32*(3), 236–239.

Bui, K. V. T., & Takeuchi, D. T. (1992). Ethnic minority adolescents and the use of community mental health care services. *American Journal of Community Psychology, 20*(4), 403–417.

Cachelin, F. M., Veisel, C., Barzegarnazari, E., & Striegel Moore, R. H. (2000). Disordered eating, acculturation, and treatment-seeking in a community sample of Hispanic, Asian, black, and white women. *Psychology of Women Quarterly, 24*(3), 233–244.

Canda, E. R. (1989). Therapeutic use of writing and other media with Southeast Asian refugees. *Journal of Independent Social Work, 4*(2), 47–60.

Carr, J. L., Koyama, M., & Thiagarajan, M. (2003). A women's support group for Asian international students. *Journal of American College Health, 52*(3), 131–134.

Casas, J. (1995). Counseling and psychotherapy with racial/ethnic minority groups in theory and practice. In L. E. Beutler & B. M. Bongar (Eds.),

Comprehensive textbook of psychotherapy: Theory and practice (pp. 311–335). London: Oxford University Press.

Cerhan, J. U. (1990). The Hmong in the United States: An overview for mental health professionals. *Journal of Counseling & Development, 69*(1), 88–92.

Chang, T., Yeh, C. J., & Krumboltz, J. D. (2001). Process and outcome evaluation of an on-line support group for Asian American male college students. *Journal of Counseling Psychology, 48*(3), 319–329.

Chang, T. H. H., & Yeh, R. L. (1999). Theoretical framework for therapy with Asian families. In K. S. Ng (Ed.), *Counseling Asian families from a systems perspective* (pp. 3–13). Alexandria, VA: American Counseling Association.

Chen, H., Kramer, E. J., & Chen, T. (2003). The Bridge Program: A model for reaching Asian Americans. *Psychiatric Services, 54*(10), 1411–1412.

Chen, M., & Han, Y. S. (2001). Cross-cultural group counseling with Asians: A stage-specific interactive approach. *Journal for Specialists in Group Work, 26*(2), 111–128.

Chen, S., Sullivan, N. Y., Lu, Y. E., & Shibusawa, T. (2003). Asian Americans and mental health services: A study of utilization patterns in the 1990s. *Journal of Ethnic & Cultural Diversity in Social Work, 12*(2), 19–42.

Chin, J. L. (1998). Mental health services and treatment. In N. W. S. Zane & L. C. Lee (Eds.), *Handbook of Asian American psychology* (pp. 485–504). Thousand Oaks, CA: Sage.

Chin, J. L., Liem, J. H., Ham, M. D. C., & Hong, G. K. (1993). *Transference and empathy in Asian American psychotherapy: Cultural values and treatment needs:* Westport, CT: Praeger.

Choi, K. H., Lew, S., Vittinghoff, E., Catania, J. A., Barrett, D. C., & Coates, T. J. (1996). The efficacy of brief group counseling in HIV risk reduction among homosexual Asian and Pacific Islander men. *AIDS, 10*(1), 81–87.

Chua, E. L. M. (2003). A return to spirituality: When eastern philosophy meets western practice. *Journal of Family Psychotherapy, 14*(1), 23–35.

Chung, Y., & Katayama, M. (1999). Ethnic and sexual identity development of Asian American lesbian and gay adolescents. In K. S. Ng (Ed.), *Counseling Asian families from a systems perspective* (pp. 159–169). Alexandria, VA: American Counseling Association.

Cimmarusti, R. A. (1996). Exploring aspects of Filipino-American families. *Journal of Marital & Family Therapy, 22*(2), 205–217.

Commander, M. J., Cochrane, R., Sashidharan, S. P., Akilu, F., & Wildsmith, E. (1999). Mental health care for Asian, black and white patients with non-affective psychoses: Pathways to the psychiatric hospital, in-patient and after-care. *Social Psychiatry and Psychiatric Epidemiology, 34*(9), 484–491.

Cooper, S. (1988). David: The first hour in the assessment and treatment of an adolescent. *Child and Adolescent Social Work Journal, 5*(3), 218–228.

Edman, J. L., & Johnson, R. C. (1999). Filipino American and Caucasian American beliefs about the causes and treatment of mental problems. *Cultural Diversity & Ethnic Minority Psychology, 5*(4), 380–386.

Exum, H. A., & Lau, E. Y. (1988). Counseling style preference of Chinese college students. *Journal of Multicultural Counseling and Development, 16*(2), 84–92.

Flaskerud, J. H. (1986a). Diagnostic and treatment differences among five ethnic groups. *Psychological Reports, 58*(1), 219–235.

Flaskerud, J. H. (1986b). The effects of culture-compatible intervention on the utilization of mental health services by minority clients. *Community Mental Health Journal, 22*(2), 127–141.

Flaskerud, J. H., & Hu, L. T. (1992). Racial/ethnic identity and amount and type of psychiatric treatment. *American Journal of Psychiatry, 149*(3), 379–384.

Frances, A., & Kroll, J. (1989). Ongoing treatment of a Hmong widow who suffers from pain and depression. *Hospital and Community Psychiatry, 40*(7), 691–693.

Freimer, N., Lu, F., & Chen, J. (1989). Posttraumatic stress and conversion disorders in a Laotian refugee veteran: Use of amobarbital interviews. *Journal of Nervous and Mental Disease, 177*(7), 432–433.

Futa, K. T., Hsu, E., & Hansen, D. J. (2001). Child sexual abuse in Asian American families: An examination of cultural factors that influence prevalence, identification, and treatment. *Clinical Psychology: Science and Practice, 8*(2), 189–209.

Ganesan, S., Fine, S., & Lin, T. Y. (1989). Psychiatric symptoms in refugee families from South East Asia: Therapeutic challenges. *American Journal of Psychotherapy, 43*(2), 218–228.

Gee, K. K., Du, N., Akiyama, K., & Lu, F. (1999). The Asian focus unit at UCSF: An 18-year perspective. In W. B. Lawson & J. M. Herrera (Eds.), *Cross cultural psychiatry* (pp. 275–285). New York: Wiley.

Hanson Kahn, P., & L'Abate, L. (1998). Cross-cultural couple therapy. In F. M. Dattilio (Ed.), *Case studies in couple and family therapy: Systemic and cognitive perspectives* (pp. 278–302). New York: Guilford Press.

Henkin, W. A. (1985). Toward counseling the Japanese in America: A cross-cultural primer. *Journal of Counseling & Development, 63*(8), 500–503.

Ho, C. K. (1990). An analysis of domestic violence in Asian American communities: A multicultural approach to counseling. *Women & Therapy, 9*(1–2), 129–150.

Ho, D. Y. F. (1999). Relational counseling: An Asian perspective on therapeutic intervention. *Psychologische Beitrage, 41*(1–2), 98–112.

Ho, M. K. (1992). Differential application of treatment modalities with Asian American youth. In J. D. Koss Chioino & L. A. Vargas (Eds.), *Working with culture: Psychotherapeutic interventions with ethnic minority children and adolescents* (pp. 182–203). San Francisco: Jossey-Bass.

Holt, D. J., Phillips, K. A., Shapiro, E. R., & Becker, A. E. (2003). "My face is my fate": Biological and psychosocial approaches to the treatment of a woman with obsessions and delusions. *Harvard Review of Psychiatry, 11*(3), 142–154.

Hom, A., & Amada, G. (1985). Overcoming the problem of face-saving: Outreach services to Chinese students. In G. Amada (Ed.), *Mental health on the community college campus* (2nd ed., pp. 83–91). Lanham, MD: University Press of America.

Huff, R. M., & Kline, M. V. (1999). Tips for working with Pacific Islander populations. In M. V. Kline & R. M. Huff (Eds.), *Promoting health in multicultural populations: A handbook for practitioners* (pp. 471–478). Thousand Oaks, CA: Sage.

Inman, A. G., & Tewari, N. (2003). The power of context: Counseling South Asians within a family context. In G. Roysircar, D. S. Sandhu, & V. B. Bibbins (Eds.), *Multicultural competencies: A guidebook of practices* (pp. 97–107). Alexandria, VA: American Counseling Association.

Ito, K. L., & Maramba, G. G. (2002). Therapeutic beliefs of Asian American therapists: Views from an ethnic-specific clinic. *Transcultural Psychiatry, 39*(1), 33–73.

Kagawa Singer, M., & Chung, R. C. Y. (2002). Toward a new paradigm: A cultural systems approach. In S. Okazaki & K. S. Kurasaki (Eds.), *Asian American mental health: Assessment theories and methods* (pp. 47–66). New York: Kluwer Academic/Plenum.

Kao, S. C., & Landreth, G. L. (2001). Play therapy with Chinese children: Needed modifications. In G. L. Landreth (Ed.), *Innovations in play therapy: Issues, process, and special populations* (pp. 43–49). New York: Brunner/Routledge.

Kim, B. S. K., Hill, C. E., Gelso, C. J., Goates, M. K., Asay, P. A., & Harbin, J. M. (2003). Counselor self-disclosure, East Asian American client adherence to Asian cultural values, and counseling process. *Journal of Counseling Psychology, 50*(3), 324–332.

Kim, B. S. K., Li, L. C., & Liang, T. H. (2002). Effects of Asian American client adherence to Asian cultural values, session goal, and counselor emphasis of client expression on career counseling process. *Journal of Counseling Psychology, 49*(3), 342–354.

Kim, B. S. K., Ng, G. F., & Ahn, A. J. (2005). Effects of client expectation for counseling success, client-counselor worldview match, and client adherence to Asian and European American cultural values on counseling process with Asian Americans. *Journal of Counseling Psychology, 52*(1), 67–76.

Kim, B. S. K., & Omizo, M. M. (2003). Asian cultural values, attitudes toward seeking professional psychological help, and willingness to see a counselor. *The Counseling Psychologist, 31*(3), 343–361.

Kim, B. K. S., & Atkinson, D. R. (2002). Asian American client adherence to Asian cultural values, counselor expression of cultural values, counselor ethnicity, and career counseling process. *Journal of Counseling Psychology, 49*(1), 3–13.

Kim, E. Y. K., Bean, R. A., & Harper, J. M. (2004). Do general treatment guidelines for Asian American families have applications to specific ethnic groups? The case of culturally-competent therapy with Korean Americans. *Journal of Marital & Family Therapy, 30*(3), 359–372.

Kim, J. M. (2003). Structural family therapy and its implications for the Asian American family. *Family Journal: Counseling and Therapy for Couples and Families, 11*(4), 388–392.

Kinzie, J. (1985). Cultural aspects of psychiatric treatment with Indochinese refugees. *American Journal of Social Psychiatry, 5*(1), 47–53.

Kinzie, J. (1989). Therapeutic approaches to traumatized Cambodian refugees. *Journal of Traumatic Stress, 2*(1), 75–91.

Kinzie, J. (2001). The Southeast Asian refugee: The legacy of severe trauma. In J. Streltzer & W. S. Tseng (Eds.), *Culture and psychotherapy: A guide to clinical practice* (pp. 173–191). Washington, DC: American Psychiatric Press.

Kinzie, J., Leung, P., Bui, A., Ben, R., Keopraseuth, K., Riley, C., et al. (1988). Group therapy with Southeast Asian refugees. *Community Mental Health Journal, 24*(2), 157–166.

Kinzie, J. D., & Tseng, W. S. (1978). Cultural aspects of psychiatric clinic utilization: A cross-cultural study in Hawaii. *International Journal of Social Psychiatry, 24*(3), 177–188.

Kitano, H. H. L. (1989). A model for counseling Asian Americans. In J. G. Draguns P. B. Pedersen, W. J. Lonner, & J. E. Trimble (Eds.), *Counseling across cultures* (3rd ed., pp. 139–151). Honolulu: University of Hawaii Press.

Kung, W. W. (2004). Cultural and practical barriers to seeking mental health treatment for Chinese Americans. *Journal of Community Psychology, 32*(1), 27–43.

Lam, A. P., & Kavanagh, D. J. (1996). Help seeking by immigrant Indochinese psychiatric patients in Sydney, Australia. *Psychiatric Services, 47*(9), 993–995.

Lambert, R. G., & Lambert, M. J. (1984). The effects of role preparation for psychotherapy on immigrant clients seeking mental health services in Hawaii. *Journal of Community Psychology, 12*(3), 263–275.

Lau, A., & Zane, N. (2000). Examining the effects of ethnic-specific services: An analysis of cost-utilization and treatment outcome for Asian American clients. *Journal of Community Psychology, 28*(1), 63–77.

Lee, E. (1989). Assessment and treatment of Chinese-American immigrant families. *Journal of Psychotherapy and the Family, 6*(1–2), 99–122.

Lee, E. (1990). Family therapy with Southeast Asian families. In M. P. Mirkin (Ed.), *The social and political contexts of family therapy* (pp. 331–354). Needham Heights, MA: Allyn & Bacon.

Lee, E. (1996). Asian American families: An overview. In J. Giordano & M. McGoldrick (Eds.), *Ethnicity and family therapy* (2nd ed., pp. 227–248). New York: Guilford Press.

Lee, M. Y., Law, P. F. M., & Eo, E. (2003). Perception of substance use problems in Asian American communities by Chinese, Indian, Korean, and Vietnamese populations. *Journal of Ethnicity in Substance Abuse, 2*(3), 1–29.

Lee, W. M. L., & Mixson, R. J. (1995). Asian and Caucasian client perceptions of the effectiveness of counseling. *Journal of Multicultural Counseling and Development, 23*, 48–56.

Leong, F. T. L. (1993). The career counseling process with racial-ethnic minorities: The case of Asian Americans. *Career Development Quarterly, 42*(1), 26–40.

Leong, F. T. L. (2001). Guest editor's introduction to a special issue: Barriers to providing effective mental health services to racial and ethnic minorities in the United States. *Mental Health Services Research, 3*(4), 179–180.

Leong, F. T. L., & Lau, A. S. L. (2001). Barriers to providing effective mental health services to Asian Americans. *Mental Health Services Research, 3*(4), 210–214.

Leong, F. T. L., Lee, S. H., & Chang, D. F. (in press). Counseling and psychotherapy with Asian Americans: Client and therapist variables. In P. Pedersen, J. Draguns, W. Lonner, & J. Trimble (Eds.), *Counseling across cultures* (6th ed.). Thousand Oaks, CA: Sage.

Leong, F. T. L., & Serafica, F. C. (2001). Cross-cultural perspective on Super's career development theory: Career maturity and cultural accommodation. In. F. T. L. Leong & A. Barak (Eds.), *Contemporary models in vocational psychology: A volume in honor of Samuel H. Osipow* (pp. 167–205). Mahwah, NJ: Lawrence Erlbaum.

Leong, F. T. L., & Tang, M. (2002). A cultural accommodation approach to career assessment with Asian Americans (2002). In K. S. Kurasaki, S. Okazaki, & S. Sue (Eds.), Asian American mental health: Assessment theories and methods (pp. 265–279). New York: Kluwer Academic/ Plenum.

Li, L. C., & Kim, B. S. K. (2004). Effects of counseling style and client adherence to Asian cultural values on counseling process with Asian American college students. *Journal of Counseling Psychology, 51*(2), 158–167.

Lin, K. M., & Cheung, F. (1999). Mental health issues for Asian Americans. *Psychiatric Services, 50*(6), 774–780.

Loo, C. M. (1993). An integrative-sequential treatment model for posttraumatic stress disorder: A case study of the Japanese American internment and redress. *Clinical Psychology Review, 13*(2), 89–117.

Martin, J., & Zweben, J. E. (1993). Addressing treatment needs of Southeast Asian Mien opium users in California. *Journal of Psychoactive Drugs, 25*(1), 73–76.

Mass, A. I. (2003). Asian-American women: Issues for clinical practice. In E. B. Ruderman & J. B. Sanville (Eds.), *Therapies with women in transition: Toward relational perspectives with today's women* (pp. 119–131). Madison, CT: International Universities Press.

Mathews, C. A., Glidden, D., Murray, S., Forster, P., & Hargreaves, W. A. (2002). The effect on treatment outcomes of assigning patients to ethnically focused inpatient psychiatric units. *Psychiatric Services, 53*(7), 830–835.

Matsuoka, J. K., Breaux, C., & Ryujin, D. H. (1997). National utilization of mental health services by Asian Americans/Pacific Islanders. *Journal of Community Psychology, 25*(2), 141–145.

Mau, W.-C., & Jepsen, D. A. (1988). Attitudes toward counselors and counseling processes: A comparison of Chinese and American graduate students. *Journal of Counseling & Development, 67*(3), 189–192.

Maynard, C., Ehreth, J., Cox, G. B., Peterson, P. D., & McGann, M. E. (1997). Racial differences in the utilization of public mental health services in Washington State. *Administration and Policy in Mental Health, 24*(5), 411–424.

McCabe, K., Yeh, M., Hough, R. L., Landsverk, J., Hurlburt, M. S., Culver, S. W., et al. (1999). Racial/ethnic representation across five public sectors of care for youth. *Journal of Emotional and Behavioral Disorders, 7*(2), 72–82.

McKenzie Pollock, L. (1996). Cambodian families. In J. Giordano & M. McGoldrick (Eds.), *Ethnicity and family therapy* (2nd ed., pp. 307–315). New York: Guilford Press.

Morelli, P. T., Fong, R., & Oliveira, J. (2001). Culturally competent substance abuse treatment for Asian/Pacific Islander women. *Journal of Human Behavior in the Social Environment, 3*(3–4), 263–280.

Moy, S. (1992). A culturally sensitive, psychoeducational model for understanding and treating Asian-American clients. *Journal of Psychology and Christianity, 11*(4), 358–367.

Narikiyo, T. A., & Kameoka, V. A. (1992). Attributions of mental illness and judgments about help seeking among Japanese-American and White American students. *Journal of Counseling Psychology, 39*(3), 363–369.

Nguyen, Q. C. X., & Anderson, L. P. (2005). Vietnamese Americans' attitudes toward seeking mental health services: Relation to cultural variables. *Journal of Community Psychology, 33*(2), 213–231.

Nishigaya, L. (1988). *Waianae coast children and youth mental health services* (Executive summary). Honolulu, HI: Hale Ola Ho'opakolea.

O'Sullivan, M. J., Peterson, P. D., Cox, G. B., & Kirkeby, J. (1989). Ethnic populations: Community mental health services ten years later. *American Journal of Community Psychology, 17,* 17–30.

Rita, E. S. (1996). Pilipino families. In M. McGoldrick, J. Giordano, & J. K. Pearce (Eds.), *Ethnicity and family therapy* (2nd ed., pp. 324–330). New York: Guilford Press.

Sakauye, K. (1992). The elderly Asian patient. *Journal of Geriatric Psychiatry, 25*(1), 85–104.

Shin, J. K. (2002). Help-seeking behaviors by Korean immigrants for depression. *Issues in Mental Health Nursing, 23*(5), 461–476.

Sue, D. (1990). Culture in transition: Counseling Asian-American men. In F. Leafgren & D. Moore (Eds.), *Problem solving strategies and interventions for men in conflict* (pp. 153–165). Alexandria, VA: American Association for Counseling.

Sue, D. (2001). Asian American masculinity and therapy: The concept of masculinity in Asian American males. In G. E. Good, & G. R. Brooks (Eds.), *The new handbook of psychotherapy and counseling with men: A comprehensive guide to settings, problems, and treatment approaches* (Vol. 2, pp. 780–795). San Francisco: Jossey-Bass.

Sue, D. W., & Sue, S. (1972). Counseling Chinese-Americans. *Personnel & Guidance Journal, 50,* 637–644.

Sue, S. (1977) Psychological theory and implications for Asian Americans. *Personnel & Guidance Journal, 55*(7), 381–389.

Sue, S., Fujino, D. C., Hu, L. T., Takeuchi, D. T., & Zane, N. W. S. (1991). Community mental health services for ethnic minority groups: A test of the cultural responsiveness hypothesis. *Journal of Counseling Psychology, 59,* 533–540.

Sue, S., & McKinney, H. (1975). Asian-Americans in the community health care system. *American Journal of Orthopsychiatry, 45,* 111–118.

Sue, S., & Zane, N. (1987). The role of culture and cultural techniques in psychotherapy: A critique and reformulation. *American Psychologist, 42,* 37–45.

Takahashi, Y. (1989). Suicidal Asian patients: Recommendations for treatment. *Suicide and Life Threatening Behavior, 19*(3), 305–313.

Takeuchi, D. T., Leaf, P. J., & Kuo, H.-S. (1988). Ethnic differences in the perception of barriers to help-seeking. *Social Psychiatry and Psychiatric Epidemiology, 23*(4), 273–280.

Takeuchi, D. T., Mokuau, N., & Chun, C. A. (1992). Mental health services for Asian Americans and Pacific Islanders. *Journal of Mental Health Administration, 19*(3), 237–245.

Takeuchi, D. T., Sue, S., & Yeh, M. (1995). Return rates and outcomes from ethnicity-specific mental health programs in Los Angeles. *American Journal of Public Health, 85*(5), 638–643.

Tamura, T., & Lau, A. (1992). Connectedness versus separateness: Applicability of family therapy to Japanese families. *Family Process, 31*(4), 319–340.

Tata, S. P., & Leong, F. T. (1994). Individualism-collectivism, social-network orientation, and acculturation as predictors of attitudes toward seeking professional psychological help among Chinese Americans. *Journal of Counseling Psychology, 41*(3), 280–287.

Tatara, T. (Ed.). (1999). *Understanding elder abuse in minority populations.* Philadelphia: Brunner/Mazel.

True, R. H. (1990). Psychotherapeutic issues with Asian American women. *Sex Roles, 22*(7–8), 477–486.

Tsui, P., & Schultz, G. L. (1985). Failure of rapport: Why psychotherapeutic engagement fails in the treatment of Asian American clients. *Journal of Orthopsychiatry, 55*(4), 561–569.

Tung, M. (1991). Insight-oriented psychotherapy and the Chinese patient. *American Journal of Orthopsychiatry, 61*(2), 186–194.

U.S. Department of Health and Human Services (2001). *Mental Health: Culture, Race, and Ethnicity—A Supplement to Mental Health: A Report of the Surgeon General.* Rockville, MD: U.S. Department of Health and Human Services, Public Health Service, Office of the Surgeon General.

Varma, S. C., & Siris, S. G. (1996). Alcohol abuse in Asian Americans: Epidemiological and treatment issues. *American Journal on Addictions, 5*(2), 136–143.

Weiss, B. S., & Parish, B. (1989). Culturally appropriate crisis counseling: Adapting an American method for use with Indochinese refugees. *Social Work, 34*(3), 252–254.

Wenhao, J., Salomon, H. B., & Chay, D. M. (1999). Transcultural counseling and people of Asian origin: A developmental and therapeutic perspective. In J. McFadden (Ed.), *Transcultural counseling* (2nd ed., pp. 259–281). Alexandria, VA: American Counseling Association.

Wilson, M. N., Phillip, D. A. G., Kohn, L. P., & Curry El, J. A. (1995). Cultural relativistic approach toward ethnic minorities in family therapy. In J. F. Aponte, R. Y. Rivers, & J. Wohl (Eds.), *Psychological interventions and cultural diversity* (pp. 92–108). Needham Heights, MA: Allyn & Bacon.

Wong, E. C., Kim, B. S. K., Zane, N. W. S., Kim, I. J., & Huang, J. S. (2003). Examining culturally based variables associated with ethnicity: Influences on credibility perceptions of empirically supported interventions. *Cultural Diversity & Ethnic Minority Psychology, 9*(1), 88–96.

Yamamoto, J. (1978). Research priorities in Asian-American mental health delivery. *American Journal of Psychiatry, 135*(4), 457–458.

Yamamoto, J., James, Q. C., & Palley, N. (1968). Cultural problems in psychiatric therapy. *Archives of General Psychiatry, 19*(1), 45–49.

Yamamoto, J., Silva, J., & Chang, C. Y. (1998). Transitions in Asian-American elderly. In S. I. Greenspan & G. H. Pollock (Eds.), *The course of life. Vol. 7: Completing the journey* (pp. 135–159). Madison, CT: International Universities Press.

Yeh, M., Takeuchi, D. T., & Sue, S. (1994). Asian American children treated in mental health system: A comparison of parallel and mainstream outpatient service centers. *Journal of Clinical Child Psychology, 23,* 5–12.

Yeung, A., & Chang, D. (2002). Cultural formulation of psychiatric diagnosis. Adjustment disorder: Intergenerational conflicts in a Chinese immigrant family. *Culture, Medicine and Psychiatry, 26,* 509–525.

Ying, Y.-W. (2001). Psychotherapy with traumatized Southeast Asian refugees. *Clinical Social Work Journal, 29*(1), 65–78.

Ying, Y.-W., & Miller, L. S. (1992). Help-seeking behavior and attitude of Chinese Americans regarding psychological problems. *American Journal of Community Psychology, 20*(4), 549–556.

Zane, N., Enomoto, K., & Chun, C. (1994). Treatment outcomes of Asian and White American clients in outpatient therapy. *Journal of Community Psychology, 22,* 177–191.

Zane, N., Hall, G. N., Sue, S., Young, K., & Nunez, J. (2004). Research on psychotherapy with culturally diverse populations. In M. J. Lambert (Ed.), *Bergin and Garfield's Handbook of psychotherapy and behavior change* (5th ed., pp. 767–804). New York: Wiley.

Zane, N., Hatanaka, H., Park, S. S., & Akutsu, P. (1994). Ethnic-specific mental health services: Evaluation of the parallel approach for Asian-American clients. *Journal of Community Psychology, 22,* 68–81.

Zhang, N., & Dixon, D. N. (2001). Multiculturally responsive counseling: Effects on Asian students' ratings of counselors. *Journal of Multicultural Counseling and Development, 29*(4), 253–262.

25

EMPIRICALLY SUPPORTED THERAPIES FOR ASIAN AMERICANS

GORDON C. NAGAYAMA HALL

SOPAGNA EAP

There is a growing body of evidence of the general effectiveness of treatments for psychological disorders, but evidence of the effectiveness of such treatment is limited for ethnic minorities. The demand that practices be based on evidence has influenced psychology, as well as medicine, education, and public policy (Levant, 2005). Evidence-based practice involves the integration of research evidence, clinical expertise, and patient values (Institute of Medicine, 2001). This chapter focuses on treatment research with Asian Americans and how Asian American patients' cultural values may moderate treatment outcomes.

The relative merits of research evidence and clinical expertise with respect to treatment have been debated (Beutler, 2004; Levant, 2004). However, research need not be pitted against clinical expertise, as one can inform the other

(Beutler, 2004; Westen, Novotny, & Thompson-Brenner, 2004). There are elegant conceptual models of psychotherapy with ethnic minority groups based on clinical expertise (Lee, 1997). Hall (2001) recommended that such conceptual models can both guide research and be evaluated with existing methods that have been established for empirically supported therapies.

Asian Americans are a relevant population to study with respect to treatment outcome research because (a) Asian Americans are the fastest-growing ethnic group in the United States and have poorer mental health outcomes relative to other groups, (b) there is less empirical support for treatments of psychological disorders for Asian Americans than for most other ethnic groups, and (c) there are cultural variables specific to Asian Americans that may influence the effectiveness of treatments (Zane,

---

Authors' Note: Work on this chapter was supported by National Institute of Mental Health grants R01 MH58726 and R25 MH62575. We thank Melissa Foynes, Jessica Murakami, Sharon Tang, and Lauren Visconte for their comments on an earlier draft of this chapter. We are also grateful to good cooks in Japanese restaurants.

Hall, Sue, Young, & Nunez, 2004). Relative to non-Hispanic Whites, Asian Americans under-utilize mental health services, and when they do utilize mental health services, they benefit less from them (Zane et al., 2004). It is possible that this failure to use services, as well as the failure to benefit from services, is associated with cultural variables.

EMPIRICALLY SUPPORTED THERAPIES

Empirically supported therapies are those that have been demonstrated to be superior in efficacy to a placebo or another treatment (Chambless & Hollon, 1998). Efficacy involves clinical research in controlled laboratory settings, whereas effectiveness involves the applications of efficacious treatments in actual clinical settings where there is much less experimental control. There is less research on treatment effectiveness than on treatment efficacy. Treatment effectiveness research is relevant to Asian Americans and other ethnic minority groups who most commonly are treated in clinical settings and less commonly participate in clinical research.

One criterion for well-established, empirically supported treatments is at least two good between-group design experiments, by at least two different investigators, demonstrating superiority to pill or psychological placebo or to another treatment, or equivalence to an already established treatment (Chambless & Hollon, 1998). An alternative criterion for well-established treatments is 10 or more single-case design experiments by at least two different investigators demonstrating consistent results. Treatment manuals are required in these experiments, and patient characteristics (e.g., diagnosis) must be clearly specified. The criteria for probably efficacious treatments are two experiments showing the treatment is more effective than a waiting list control group, one or more experiments meeting the well-established treatment criteria, or four or more single-case design experiments.

A meta-analytic review of studies, in which the efficacy of a psychotherapy was compared to a waiting-list control condition, an alternative psychotherapy, a pharmacotherapy, or some combination of these conditions, revealed efficacious psychotherapies for depression, panic, and generalized anxiety disorder, at least on a short-term basis (Westen & Morrison, 2001). Most of these efficacious psychotherapies are behavioral or cognitive-behavioral. Multiple placebo-controlled or comparative pharmacological studies have identified the efficaciousness of pharmacotherapy in treating major depression, panic disorder, generalized anxiety disorder, and social phobia (Boerner & Moller, 1999; Thase, 2000). Nevertheless, the previous studies did not identify the effects of treatment for ethnic minorities, and the general evidence for the effectiveness of psychotherapy or pharmacotherapy for psychological disorders among ethnically diverse populations is limited (Hall, 2001; Miranda et al., 2005; Zane et al., 2004).

The methods that have been used to establish empirically supported therapies have been criticized (Westen et al., 2004). Most of these criticisms involve the disconnect between the controlled conditions of clinical trials (e.g., patients having a single diagnosis, short-term study) and the relatively uncontrolled conditions in actual clinical settings (e.g., polysymptomatic patients, long-term relapse). Thus, there is a need for clinical effectiveness research. There is also a need to determine the effectiveness of empirically supported therapies with groups that have not been adequately represented in clinical trials, including Asian Americans.

IS PSYCHOTHERAPY RELEVANT FOR ASIAN AMERICANS?

Which Asian Americans are likely to perceive psychotherapy as relevant to their needs? Who is likely to seek help from methods other than psychotherapy? For those who do seek psychotherapy, which therapists would be perceived as most helpful? In some ways, selecting a treatment intervention and therapist is similar to selecting a restaurant. The treatment intervention is analogous to the food, the therapist is analogous to the cook, and the mental health center is analogous to the restaurant. The characteristics of the treatment intervention, therapist, and mental health center may attract or deter potential patients.

I (GCNH) am a Japanese American and I like to eat authentic Japanese food. If I visit a Japanese restaurant in the United States, I want to know that the cook is Japanese. It is also reassuring to see Japanese people eating in the restaurant, which attests to its authenticity. Although a Japanese cook and Japanese customers do not guarantee good Japanese food, they are an inviting presence that may attract me toward trying the restaurant's food.

The Japanese cook/customers proxy for good Japanese food has failed me when the cook has adapted the cuisine to local tastes, and most of the restaurant's clientele are not Japanese. Such adaptations are a disappointment when I am seeking authentic Japanese food. The explanation of the Japanese customers at a nonauthentic restaurant may be that their tastes have adjusted to local norms (or they are paid by the restaurant management to pose as customers to attest to the authenticity of the restaurant!).

I also like to eat American food. Once, while in Japan, I wanted a breakfast that was familiar to my American tastes. I cannot read Japanese, so I went to an American fast food restaurant and ordered from the breakfast menu what appeared from the photo depiction to be an egg sandwich. To my surprise, I discovered that I had ordered a fish sandwich. Fish was not something I expected on an American breakfast menu. Perhaps I should not have been surprised, as I was the only American in this American fast food restaurant. Fish may be an acceptable breakfast item for Japanese tastes.

Occasionally, I want to try cuisine that is a fusion of cultures. I have eaten at some excellent Asian fusion restaurants in Hawai'i, where Asian and Western flavors were tastefully combined. The cooks and many customers in these restaurants were Asian Americans, which also may have had some bearing on my satisfaction.

In one community where I lived, there were no good Japanese, or any good Asian, restaurants. I was able to find good food, but none of it was Asian. Although the food was good, I did yearn for and missed the satisfaction of good Japanese food.

Let us emphasize that there are real differences between choosing a restaurant and choosing a therapist. We do not intend to trivialize the process by which people in distress seek help.

Perhaps a better analogy would be experiences with Asian American health professionals. Nevertheless, food is an important part of culture, and the restaurant analogy illustrates some cultural match/mismatch issues. In the above examples, my dining experiences were a function of my expectations. When the food matched my expectations, I was satisfied. When it did not, I was disappointed.

Expectancy theory posits that treatment effects are mediated by the patient's conscious expectancies (Stewart-Williams & Podd, 2004). If the therapy context is compatible with the patient's expectancies, then therapy is likely to be successful. The role of expectancies in psychotherapy outcome has been discussed for at least 30 years (Frank, 1973). Expectancies also have been demonstrated across studies to have a major role in the effects of drugs for psychological disorders (Kirsch & Sapirstein, 1999).

Incompatibility between patients and therapists or therapies has been conceptualized as resistance. Resistance need not be unconscious in the classic psychoanalytic sense, but may involve conscious behaviors, including the patient's countertherapeutic beliefs (Beutler, Moleiro, & Talebi, 2002). Across studies, resistance has been demonstrated to be a strong indicator of a poor treatment prognosis (Beutler, Clarkin, & Bongar, 2000). Resistance would be expected to be less likely when patients are in treatments that they believe to be effective than when they are in treatments that they believe to be ineffective. Indeed, there is evidence from the National Institute of Mental Health Treatment of Depression Collaborative Research Program (TDCRP) that patients who were assigned to a treatment that they believed to be relevant to the cause of their problems were more engaged in initial therapy sessions than were patients in treatments incongruent with their etiological beliefs (Elkin et al., 1999). Patients in the TDCRP who expected a treatment to be effective also improved more than those who did not expect treatment effectiveness (Meyer et al., 2002). Individual differences, including cultural background, may also shape a person's expectancies concerning effective treatment (Stewart-Williams & Podd, 2004).

My experiences with restaurant food may mirror to some degree the process by which

Table 25.1   Optimal Therapies and Therapists for Asian American Patients

Therapy	Therapist Ethnicity	Patient
Eastern methods (e.g., acupuncture)	Asian	Unacculturated
Western methods (e.g., cognitive therapy, antidepressant drugs)	European American	Acculturated
Culturally adapted Western methods	Asian American or European American	Bicultural

Asian Americans select interventions for their problems. Desirable treatment interventions may vary as a function of acculturation. Unacculturated Asian Americans may prefer Eastern methods of treatment. Acculturated Asian Americans may prefer Western methods. Bicultural Asian Americans may prefer an integration of Eastern and Western methods. Optimal therapies and therapists for Asian American patients are summarized in Table 25.1.

Some Asian Americans may expect that their problems will be best addressed by Asian traditional forms of healing, such as acupuncture or meditation. It is also probable that they may perceive Asian healers as more helpful than non-Asians based on the assumption that Asians would be more knowledgeable than non-Asians about traditional healing methods. Knowing that other Asian Americans seek help from these traditional sources would legitimize the traditional methods. These Asian Americans would be unlikely to seek help in the form of Western psychotherapy. Those who seek traditional forms of healing are also likely to be the least acculturated to Western values. Sixty-nine percent of Asian Americans were born outside the United States (Reeves & Bennett, 2004). Although not all Asian Americans born outside the United States adhere to traditional Asian values, it is likely that many do, particularly recent immigrants.

Other Asian Americans may prefer psychotherapy or antidepressant drugs as an intervention for their problems. These Asian Americans are likely to be the most acculturated. Moreover, they may perceive Western approaches as more useful than Asian approaches. They also may perceive Western therapists as having more expertise than Asians in Western methods. The use of Western approaches by other Asian Americans is likely to be inconsequential in these Asian

Americans' perceptions of the legitimacy of the Western methods. Asian cultural considerations are probably of less consequence to acculturated Asian Americans than to other Asian Americans. Indeed, there is evidence that acculturated Asian Americans have more favorable views and positive expectations of Western psychotherapy than do less acculturated Asian Americans (Kim, Ng, & Ahn, 2005; Tata & Leong, 1994), although one study found no differences (Wong, Kim, Zane, Kim, & Huang, 2003). Acculturated Asian Americans are most likely to participate in psychotherapy research and most likely to benefit from Western psychotherapy. Among college students, who are likely to be more acculturated than young adults who are not in college, those who consider themselves to be acculturated to the United States range from 16% to 56% (Abe-Kim, Okazaki, & Goto, 2001; Chung, 2001). Evidence of psychotherapy effectiveness with acculturated Asian Americans does not necessarily imply effectiveness with less acculturated Asian Americans.

Asian Americans having a bicultural identity may value Western psychotherapy but may also expect cultural context to be considered. The most effective therapist might be one who understands both Asian American and European American cultures, regardless of the therapist's ethnicity. For example, a biculturally competent therapist would consider the effects of assertiveness, a behavior valued in Western psychotherapy, in the context of Asian American concerns about maintaining group harmony. Assertive behavior might be more culturally appropriate on behalf of a group's concerns (e.g., the boss is insensitive to us) than on behalf of individual concerns (e.g., the boss is insensitive to me). Support for bicultural treatment approaches among other bicultural Asian Americans is likely to be important in determining the legitimacy of such approaches. Bicultural Asian Americans range from 18% to 67% of college students (Abe-Kim et al., 2001; Chung, 2001). The percentage of bicultural Asian Americans in noncollege community settings is unknown.

Similar to my experience in the community where there were no good Asian restaurants, some Asian Americans may seek Western psychotherapy because resources in the Asian American community are unavailable. The unavailability of Asian American resources may be a function of accessibility. Asian Americans having limited economic resources may be unable to access culturally sensitive resources unless they are located in their own community. However, poor Asian Americans are unlikely to be acculturated and may be less likely to benefit from Western psychotherapy than more acculturated Asian Americans. Similarly, some unacculturated Asian Americans may be mandated to receive treatment (e.g., child abuse or neglect) that may not be culturally responsive. Nevertheless, it could be contended that Western psychotherapy is better than no intervention because of the limited resources and options for poor Asian Americans. Alternatively, Western psychotherapy could be iatrogenic for poor Asian Americans if it is unresponsive to their practical and cultural needs.

In summary, the relevance of psychotherapy for Asian Americans is likely to be a function of acculturation. Asian Americans who are least acculturated are least likely to seek psychotherapy and may be least likely to benefit from it. Unacculturated Asian Americans may also be least likely to participate in psychotherapy research. Acculturated Asian Americans may be most likely to seek and benefit from standard Western forms of psychotherapy. Bicultural Asian Americans may expect and benefit from cultural adaptation of standard Western psychotherapy.

LIMITED EMPIRICAL SUPPORT FOR TREATMENTS AMONG ASIAN AMERICANS

Most well-established empirically supported treatments are behavioral or cognitive-behavioral (Chambless & Hollon, 1998). Behavioral and cognitive-behavioral intervention studies tend to include control or comparison groups, which are requirements for establishing empirical support. The following review of treatments for Asians and Asian Americans includes only those studies that described a specific treatment intervention and included a control or comparison group. Not surprisingly, almost all the studies included a cognitive-behavioral intervention. As discussed above, Asian Americans who participate in treatment research are not necessarily representative of the population of Asian Americans. In this section, we review treatment outcome studies on cognitive-behavioral interventions, pharmacotherapy, play therapy, acupuncture, and meditation.

Cognitive-Behavioral Interventions

Cognitive therapy (CT) has been demonstrated to be efficacious in treating depression for non-Asian groups (Chambless & Hollon, 1998). CT is based on a cognitive model of depression in which cognitive vulnerabilities to depression such as core beliefs and dysfunctional beliefs are hypothesized to interact with stressful life events to produce the characteristic skewed information processing, negative automatic thoughts, and emotional and behavioral symptoms of depression (Beck, Rush, Shaw, & Emery, 1979). CT is a psychoeducational approach in which the risk of relapse is reduced by having patients systematically evaluate their beliefs and information-processing tendencies (Beck et al., 1979). Through a process of "collaborative empiricism," therapists and patients work together to help patients learn a number of behavioral and cognitive skills (Greenberger & Padesky, 1995). These include increasing activity level, developing relationship and problem-solving skills, as well as identifying, testing, and modifying assumptions and schemas that may be maintaining the depression.

CT has much promise as an intervention for Asian Americans. The rational aspects of CT and the emphasis on perceptions of situations as determining one's reaction more than the situations themselves are consistent with Asian cultural norms (Chen & Davenport, 2005). Relative to non-Asians, Asian Americans tend to have less tolerance for ambiguity and prefer structured counseling involving practical solutions (Leong, 1986). CT therapists often are in active roles as teachers, a role that has long been respected in Asian societies (Chen & Davenport, 2005). Asian Americans may perceive the directive and structured nature of CT as helpful. Indeed, there is evidence that Asian Americans view the rationale for CT as credible for treating depression (Wong et al., 2003). Moreover, there was not a significant difference in the perceived credibility for treating depression with CT among Asian Americans who were highly identified with mainstream American culture vs. those whose identification was low.

CT is one of the psychosocial interventions having the most empirical support in randomized clinical trials, and there is evidence that CT can be effectively implemented in community mental health center settings (Merrill, Tolber, & Wade, 2003). An analysis of four large randomized clinical trials indicates that CT is as efficacious as antidepressant medications in reducing depression (DeRubeis, Gelfand, Tang, & Simons, 1999) and a recent report suggests that CBT may be as effective as medication even in severely depressed individuals (DeRubeis et al., 2005).

There are few controlled outcome studies of CT among Asians or Asian Americans, and their methodology has been highly criticized. CT in combination with health education over six weeks was found to decrease depression among 41 depressed older adults in China relative to 41 depressed older adults who did not receive the intervention (Zhao et al., 1992). However, the participants were not randomly assigned to conditions, and the diagnostic system and assessment measures were specific to China. Moreover, a standard form of manual-based CT was not included in the study.

There is only one published controlled outcome study of cognitive behavioral therapy for depression among Asian Americans (Dai et al., 1999). Viewing eight 25-minute videotapes of cognitive-behavioral and muscular relaxation interventions was found to reduce depression, anxiety, and somatization among 23 elderly Chinese American participants recruited from a Chinese-speaking church relative to a control group of 7 elderly Chinese American participants recruited from an apartment housing Asian seniors. Limitations of this study were the small sample size and nonrandom assignment to conditions.

One other controlled outcome study that included Asian Americans examined the effects of cognitive-behavioral interventions on parenting skill. Parent training (strengthening parent competencies, fostering parents' involvement with school, decreasing children's problem behavior, and strengthening children's academic and social competencies) for mothers with children in Head Start was compared with participation in the Head Start program without the parent training (Reid, Webster-Stratton, & Beauchaine, 2001). Although the training program was generic, it was contended that cultural sensitivity was fostered by parents identifying their own individual goals for their children and by respecting diverse viewpoints and goals. However, cultural sensitivity was not operationally defined in the study with the level of rigor that characterized the other aspects of the intervention. Seventy-three of the 634 families in the project were Asian. The intervention involved 8 to 12 weeks of parenting classes. After one year, mothers in the intervention group were observed to be more competent in their parenting than control mothers, and children of intervention mothers were observed to exhibit fewer behavior problems than children of mothers in the control condition. There were no ethnic differences in treatment effects.

Pharmacotherapy

Pharmacotherapy has been found in clinical trials as efficacious in treating depression as CT in non-Asian groups (DeRubeis et al., 1999; Otto, Smits, & Reese, 2005). Combined pharmacotherapy and CT tend to have only subtle benefits over either treatment alone for most depressed patients (Otto et al., 2005). Pharmacotherapy has also been found to be an effective treatment for depression among Asian populations. Both venlafaxine and paroxetine were found to significantly reduce self-reported depression in an elderly sample of 99 inpatients in China (Hwang, Yang, & Tsai, 2004). In a meta-analytic review, fluoxetine was found to reduce depression or dysthymia among 460 patients in seven Asian countries (Kwong, Fung, Wu, Plewes, & Judge, 1999).

Three outcome studies that included Asians compared CT and pharmacotherapy (Miranda et al., 2004; Otto et al., 2003; Zhang et al., 2002). In a pilot study of 10 Khmer women psychiatric outpatients in the United States, sertraline combined with 10 sessions of group CT, as well as sertraline alone, reduced post-traumatic stress symptoms (PTSD), anxiety, and depression (Otto et al., 2003). Sertraline combined with CT was more effective than sertraline alone in reducing PTSD symptoms and anxiety.

The largest combined CT and pharmacotherapy outcome study involving Asians was conducted in China, in which 143 psychiatric patients diagnosed with generalized anxiety disorder (GAD) were randomly assigned to one of three treatment groups: (1) 14 sessions of CT that was modified to incorporate Taoist philosophy, (2) benzodiazepine treatment, or (3) 14 sessions of CT + benzodiazepines (Zhang et al., 2002). Benzodiazepines were found to have immediate, short-term effects in reducing GAD symptoms. These effects subsided after six months. Conversely, the effects of CT in reducing GAD symptoms occurred more slowly, but at six months, GAD symptoms were significantly lower among CT patients than among benzodiazepine patients. The combined treatment was associated both with short-term and six-month symptom reduction. Although it ultimately may be important to modify CT for it to become culturally responsive, a first step would be to determine if existing forms of CT that have received empirical support with other populations are effective with Asian Americans.

Cognitive-behavioral therapy (CBT) and antidepressant medication interventions, both of which involved provider and patient education about depression, were found to reduce depression relative to treatment as usual (TAU), which did not involve the education component, among 1,356 depressed adults including Asians (Miranda et al., 2004). CBT treatments were from 8 to 12 sessions. After six months, 24% of minority patients who received CBT or antidepressants were diagnosed as depressed versus 71% in TAU. Although a small number of English-speaking Asian Americans was included in this sample, the actual number is unclear ("24 Asian or Native American patients"), and there were no separate analyses for Asian Americans.

Play Therapy

Group play therapy was evaluated among 30 elementary school children in Taiwan who had experienced a major earthquake and were at risk for maladjustment (Shen, 2002). Children were randomly assigned to ten 40-minute sessions of play group or no treatment. It was not specified whether the treatment directly addressed issues of anxiety, but the treatment group exhibited less anxiety than the control group following treatment. The viability of play therapy with Chinese children may be questionable, as the author observed that play is not encouraged among Chinese children. The actual mechanism of how play therapy reduced anxiety is also unclear.

Acupuncture and Meditation

Acupuncture and meditation have origins in Asia. There is some evidence that acupuncture and meditation reduce psychopathology more than control conditions do. Literature reviews have suggested that acupuncture reduces depression in women (Manber, Allen, & Morris, 2002) and reduces chronic pain (Ezzo et al., 2000). A meta-analysis suggests that meditation reduces psychopathology (e.g., depression, anxiety) and psychosomatic conditions (e.g., pain) (Grossman, Niemann, Schmidt, & Walach, 2004). However, Asians or Asian Americans generally were not included in these studies. Moreover, these studies did not compare acupuncture or meditation with Western psychotherapy.

Conclusions

The limited available evidence consistently suggests treatment effects of both CT and pharmacotherapy among Asians and Asian Americans. However, the effectiveness of CT or pharmacotherapy for Asian Americans has yet to be adequately evaluated. There is some evidence of the efficacy of these treatments for anxiety and depression among Asian Americans, but this evidence is based on relatively few patients. Play therapy was found in a single study to reduce anxiety in Asian children, but the mechanisms by which play therapy reduces depression are unknown. Acupuncture and meditation, which might be desirable for Asian Americans desiring Eastern interventions, have been found to be effective in reducing psychopathology, but Asian Americans have not been included in the research on these interventions. Moreover, the moderators of treatment effects among Asian Americans are unknown.

THERAPIST-PATIENT ETHNIC MATCH

Not all patients respond to treatment interventions. Patient treatment response may be a function of individual differences, but individual differences that may affect treatment response are poorly understood (Hollon, DeRubeis, Shelton, & Weiss, 2002). Nevertheless, randomized clinical trials have largely ignored individual differences and have treated them as a source of error. Rather than considering individual differences to be a source of error, it may be possible to capitalize on the effects of individual differences. Individual differences may offer clues to what might constitute the most effective treatments for particular persons. An important individual difference is patient ethnicity.

Sue and Zane (1987) have proposed that patients who work with therapists having similar characteristics (e.g., ethnicity, gender, language), and thus are matched, will fare better in psychotherapy than patients who work with therapists having dissimilar characteristics and thus are mismatched. One of the most salient aspects of match with ethnic minority patients in general, and with Asian American patients in particular, is ethnic match. Similar to my restaurant experiences with cooks, having a therapist of one's own ethnicity may provide some initial reassurance that the therapist understands a person.

Sue, Fujino, Hu, Takeuchi, and Zane (1991) reported on a large-scale study of the effects of ethnic match on the length of treatment and on outcomes of outpatients seen in the Los Angeles County Mental Health System. Ethnic match between the patient and therapist was associated with a greater number of therapy sessions attended and a lower likelihood of dropout after one session for Asian American patients. In addition, for those Asian Americans for whom English was not a primary language, ethnic match, language match, and gender match were associated with a decrease in the likelihood of premature termination and an increase in the number of therapy sessions attended. Thus, at least in terms of indirect indices of treatment

effectiveness, ethnic match exerted a significant influence for Asian American patients. Moreover, non-English-speaking Asian Americans were found to have better outcomes, as measured by Global Assessment Scale (GAS) change, when matched with a therapist of similar ethnicity and language. The Sue et al. (1991) findings that ethnic match facilitated patient outcomes have generally been replicated in analyses of the Los Angeles County Mental Health System since 1991 (e.g., Gamst, Dana, Der-Karabetian, & Kramer, 2000, 2001; Lau & Zane, 2000; Yeh, Takeuchi, & Sue, 1994). In addition to benefiting from therapist-patient ethnic match, Asian Americans had better outcomes at mental health centers that primarily served ethnic minority patients versus those that primarily served European Americans (Lau & Zane, 2000). In keeping with the cook/customer analogy, both the therapist and the therapy environment affected treatment outcomes for Asian Americans.

A meta-analysis of these and other therapist-patient ethnic match studies suggests that the statistically significant effects of ethnic match may be a function of the large sample sizes in these studies (Maramba & Hall, 2002). The effect sizes for the associations between ethnic match and dropout following a single treatment session, length of treatment, and GAS scores are all small. Similarly, language match has statistically significant but small effects on mental health services utilization and outcome among Asian Americans (Maramba & Hall, 2002). These small effect sizes suggest that there may be moderators of treatment effects in addition to ethnic match.

CULTURAL MODERATORS OF TREATMENT EFFECTS

Returning to the Japanese restaurant analogy, certain cultural factors can influence the quality of the dining experience. About half of persons of Chinese, Japanese, and Korean heritage have a genetically defined deficiency in the aldehyde dehydrogenase gene (ALDH2) that leads to slower removal of acetaldehyde during alcohol metabolism (Luczak, Wall, Cook, Shea, & Carr, 2004). The ALDH2 deficiency is rare among persons of European heritage. For persons having the ALDH2 deficiency, drinking alcohol leads to skin flushing, increased pulse rate, subjective feelings of being drunk, and severe hangovers (Luczak, Elvine-Kreis, Shea, Carr, & Wall, 2002; Wall et al., 2000). Persons who are aware of these somatic reactions may choose to avoid alcohol ingestion, or expect such reactions when ingesting alcohol and learn how to cope with them (e.g., drink less). However, such somatic reactions to alcohol could interfere with a dining experience in a Japanese restaurant if one, or those with whom one is dining, is unaware of these somatic reactions.

Another culturally based factor that could influence a dining experience is concern about saving face. In order to save face, a person from an East Asian background may not express his or her actual desires for food. It is often customary for East Asians to share food entrees at restaurants. However, when food is initially offered, many persons of East Asian backgrounds may refuse to accept the food even if they want it. To accept the food might result in loss of face because expressing one's own hunger may deprive someone else of having the food. Only when the person offering the food insists repeatedly (usually three times) that the other person have the food, and the other person is assured that accepting the food will not result in loss of face, does that person accept the food. Although it is unspoken, the other person is expected to reciprocate by offering his or her food. Those who are unaware of these cultural customs might (a) not offer to share food, (b) not offer food more than once if they do offer food, or (c) fail to reciprocate if they are offered food. Unawareness of these cultural customs could have a negative effect on a person who adheres to these customs.

Similar to the somatic and face issues in this restaurant analogy, somatic and face issues may affect psychotherapy process and outcome. Across studies, Asian American patients tend to somatize more than European American patients do, and loss of face is generally more prominent among Asian Americans than among European Americans. Somatization is consistent with Asian traditions that have regarded the mind and body as unitary and contrasts with Western mind-body dualism that has its roots in Greek philosophies (K. Lin & Cheung, 1999).

Loss of face is consistent with strong traditions in Asian societies of social interdependence. Somatization and loss of face may interfere with some Asian Americans seeking Western psychotherapy and may moderate the effects of psychotherapy and pharmacotherapy on depression when Asian Americans do participate in psychotherapy.

Somatization

Many Asian Americans are influenced by a unitary model of health, which may result in psychological distress being expressed in somatic symptoms. A review of the literature on Chinese persons worldwide suggests that depression is likely to be expressed somatically, and that somatic expression of depression is culturally sanctioned (Parker, Gladstone, & Tsee Chee, 2001). Moreover, affective expression of depression often carries social stigma in Asian communities because of its potential to upset interpersonal harmony (Yen, Robins, & Lin, 2000). *Shenjing shuairuo* in China and *hwabyung* in Korea are culture-bound syndromes that involve both depressive and somatic symptoms. Shenjing shuairuo, or neurasthenia, has been found to occur as commonly as major depression, without somatic symptoms, among Chinese Americans (Takeuchi et al., 1998).

Among Asian Americans, somatic symptoms may be more likely to be expressed than depressive symptoms. In a sample of 40 Chinese Americans in a primary care setting, 76% complained to their physicians of somatic symptoms, but none of these patients spontaneously complained of depressed mood. Conversely, 93% endorsed depressed mood when privately completing the self-report Beck Depression Inventory (Yeung, Chang, Gresham, Nierenberg, & Fava, 2004). However, it is possible that the primary care setting created demand characteristics for patients to seek help for somatic symptoms.

Somatic symptoms are common in Asian and Asian American psychiatric patients. In a sample of 70 Mien and 30 Lao outpatients, 53% reported unexplained pain or paresthesias (Moore et al., 2001). In a community sample of 1,747 Chinese Americans, 57% indicated that they had experienced at least one of 12 somatic symptoms on the Symptom Checklist 90–Revised (Kessler et al., 1994), and 12.9% met the Somatic Symptom Index 5 (Escobar & Canino, 1989) criteria of five endorsed items on the SL-90-R for a somatization disorder (Mak & Zane, 2004). The most common somatic symptoms were headaches, muscle soreness, and lower back pain. Somatization and depression are commonly concurrent. In the Chinese American community sample, major depression was the most common comorbid disorder with somatization, with 29.5% of those meeting the diagnostic criteria for somatization also meeting the diagnostic criteria for a depressive disorder (Mak & Zane, 2004).

Available evidence suggests that Asians somatize at least as much as non-Asians. In a cross-cultural study of 50 depressed Chinese patients in Malaysia and 50 Caucasian patients in Australia, the Chinese were distinctly more likely to nominate a somatic symptom as their presenting complaint, while the Caucasians were more likely to nominate depressed mood, cognitive, and anxiety items (Parker, Cheah, & Roy, 2001). Somatization was more common among 85 Chinese American than among 85 European American psychiatric patients (Hsu & Folstein, 1997). Chinese American somatizers complained predominantly of cardiopulmonary and vestibular symptoms, whereas European American somatizers complained primarily of abnormal motor functions. In a study of 112 Chinese outpatients, 112 Chinese nonpatients, 98 Chinese college students, 99 Chinese American college students, and 99 European American college students, the outpatients endorsed the greatest number of somatic symptoms (Yen et al., 2000). However, Chinese college students endorsed fewer somatic symptoms than either Chinese American or European American college students, who did not differ from one another in somatic symptom expression. Thus, ethnic differences in somatization may be more pronounced in patient than in nonpatient populations. The high endorsement of somatic symptoms among Asian patients may be consistent with the stigma of admitting depression among Asians in mental health settings (Parker, Cheah et al., 2001).

It might be expected that acculturation influences symptom expression among Asian Americans. Less acculturated Asian Americans would be expected to express psychological distress with somatic symptoms, which would be consistent with Asian cultural conceptualizations, whereas more acculturated Asian Americans would be expected to express psychological distress with psychological symptoms, which would be consistent with Western conceptualizations. However, the evidence of an association between acculturation and symptom expression suggests that acculturation is only significantly positively associated with psychological expressions of depression (e.g., feeling blue, feeling lonely, crying easily) but is not significantly associated with the expression of somatic symptoms (e.g., chronic fatigue) (Mak & Zane, 2004; Takeuchi et al., 1998).

One theory related to Asian American somatization is that it occurs because Asian cultures discourage the expression of emotion (K. Lin & Cheung, 1999). Difficulty in identifying emotions and distinguishing them from bodily sensations, in combination with difficulty in communicating emotions to others, has been conceptualized as alexithymia (Taylor, 1984). Yet, the lack of distinction between mind and body in Asian cultural traditions could be interpreted as alexithymia. There exists empirical evidence that both Malaysians and Asian Americans report greater levels of alexithymia than do European Americans (Le, Berenbaum, & Raghavan, 2002). Acculturation among Asian Americans was not associated with alexithymia (Le et al., 2002). Moreover, alexithymia was more strongly associated with somatization in the Asian groups than among European Americans.

Although alexithymia literally means an inability to read one's feelings, somatization in apparently alexithymic Asian Americans may simply be an alternate form of expressing distress rather than an inability to do so (Kleinman, 1977). Asian Americans seeking mental health services for depression may present with culturally acceptable somatic symptoms, but this does not imply that they are unable to read or experience emotion. When directly asked, Chinese patients and nonpatients endorsed affective symptoms at levels comparable to Chinese Americans and European Americans (Yen et al., 2000). Evidence suggests that alexithymia is negatively associated with improvement during psychotherapy (McCallum, Piper, Ogrodniczuk, & Joyce, 2003). Therefore, because alexithymia and somatization are strongly associated among Asian Americans, it can be inferred that Asian Americans who somatize may not expect psychotherapy to be effective.

Asian American culturally based tendencies toward somatization might result in expectations of treatments that directly address somatic symptoms, such as pharmacotherapy, to be the most effective. Although CT has been found to reduce somatic symptoms across studies (Nezu, Nezu, & Lombardo, 2001), it is unknown whether CT is effective in reducing somatic symptoms among Asian Americans. Moreover, somatic symptom reduction occurs when the focus of CT is on mind-body connections rather than on depression.

Loss of Face

Loss of face in Asian cultures occurs when one fails to fulfill one's social role in a manner and so upsets interpersonal harmony (Zane & Mak, 2003). Loss of face is more similar to shame, which involves public exposure of a transgression, than to guilt, which involves private feelings of remorse or self-blame for wrongdoings that are not necessarily known to others (Smith, Webster, Parrott, & Eyre, 2002). Similar to shame, loss of face involves concern about the interpersonal impact of one's behavior. Indeed, loss of face is more strongly correlated with public self-consciousness than with private self-consciousness (Zane & Yeh, 2002). Moreover, Asian Americans have been found to experience more shame than other American ethnic groups but an equal amount of guilt relative to the other ethnic groups (Lutwak, Razzino, & Ferrari, 1998). However, unlike shame and similar to guilt, public exposure is not necessary to induce loss of face.

Interpersonal harmony is critical in interdependent cultures, in which the unit of identity is the group rather than the individual. Asian Americans are more interdependent and less independent than other American ethnic groups (Oyserman, Coon, & Kemmelmeier, 2002). European Americans tend to be more independent and less interdependent than Asian Americans, and there is also consistent evidence that Asian Americans are more concerned about loss of face than are European Americans (Zane & Yeh, 2002).

It might be expected that less-acculturated Asian Americans would be more concerned about loss of face. In a sample of 355 Asian American undergraduates, those who were born in Asia, as well as those who were more Asian-oriented, tended to be more concerned about loss of face (Abe-Kim, Okazaki, & Goto, 2001). Nevertheless, the differences between the Asian groups were small. Thus, loss of face may be influential even among Asian Americans who are born in the United States and are acculturated.

Loss of face may be an important moderator of treatment effectiveness, particularly in approaches that involve self-disclosure (Zane & Yeh, 2002). Disclosures in psychotherapy could result in perceived loss of face not only for the individual but also for significant others. Among Asian Americans, loss of face has been found to be significantly negatively associated with disclosing aspects about one's personality, negative aspects about self, and aspects about one's intimate relationships (Zane & Mak, 2003).

Expression of depressive symptoms may be a function of perceived cultural norms among Asian Americans. In a study of 100 Asian American and 100 European American college women, Asian Americans who viewed depression as culturally normative (e.g., more common for Asian Americans, more favorable for Asian Americans, of less concern for Asian Americans) were more likely to endorse depression on the Beck Depression Inventory-II than were Asian Americans who viewed depression as culturally nonnormative (Okazaki & Kallivayalil, 2002). In contrast, cultural norms did not influence the expression of depression among European Americans, even though there were no overall differences between European Americans and Asian Americans on how culturally normative depression was perceived. Thus, Asian Americans who view depression as culturally nonnormative may lose face by disclosing depression in psychotherapy.

ADAPTING TREATMENTS TO PATIENT EXPECTANCIES

How should cultural moderators of treatment effects be addressed in psychotherapy? One approach is to attempt to reduce the influence of these moderators by reconceptualizing the patient's problems in terms that are compatible with psychotherapy approaches. It has been proposed that the basis of effective psychotherapy involves the therapist changing the patient's beliefs (Beck, 1976; Kirsch, 1990). Thus, if the patient's beliefs are at odds with those of the therapist or the treatment approach, the patient's beliefs need to be changed. The therapist's task is to persuade the patient of the validity of the therapeutic approach (Frank, 1973). However, efforts to change a patient's beliefs are not always effective. Such a directive approach may be contraindicated with patients who are resistant to treatment (Beutler, Clarkin, & Bongar, 2000).

With ethnic minority patients, therapists' efforts to change patient beliefs may at times be coercive. Power disparities exist between all therapists and patients, and such power disparities may be particularly prominent with ethnic minority patients. When a therapist and patient do not share the same cultural worldview, the therapist's attempts to change the patient's beliefs may amount to cultural control (Hall & Malony, 1983). The patient is being acculturated, sometimes involuntarily, to the therapist's worldview (cf. Hall, Lopez, & Bansal, 2001).

Therapists do not necessarily know what is best for all patients, particularly when they do not share the patient's cultural worldview. A recent meta-analysis indicates that majority groups are less accurate in perceiving emotions of minority groups than of other majority group members (Elfenbein & Ambady, 2002). European Americans are particularly poor in detecting depression and anxiety among Asian Americans (Okazaki, 2002). Moreover, the ethnic and cultural match literature discussed above suggests poorer outcomes when therapists and patients are mismatched. Even when therapists and patients are ethnically and culturally matched, this does not ensure that they share the same worldview or beliefs about the causes and solutions of mental health problems.

Rather than uniformly attempting to change patient etiological beliefs, therapists may face less resistance if they assess these beliefs and then attempt to modify treatments to become compatible with patient beliefs. In this case, cultural competence involves respecting the patient's beliefs about etiology. Of course, some changes in maladaptive patient beliefs may be necessary during the course of treatment.

Cultural adaptations of treatments may attract Asian Americans who have a cultural identification and may be unfamiliar with or skeptical of Western treatment methods. These include unacculturated Asian Americans and those who are bicultural. Moreover, word of mouth in Asian American communities may enhance the credibility of therapists who culturally adapt treatments.

Therapy Content

An important issue that has not been evaluated is whether cultural modifications of CT will be more effective than existing forms of CT. Consistent with the research on matching etiological beliefs and treatments, it is possible that Asian Americans who are strongly identified with Asian American cultures will benefit most from a therapy approach that is culturally isomorphic. Various recommendations have been offered to modify CT to become more culturally sensitive.

One culturally relevant modification of standard CT for depression might be a greater emphasis on mind-body connections. Reframing somatic symptoms as problems having a behavioral solution may be useful (Iwamasa, Hsia, & Hinton, in press). Standard CT conceptualizes somatic symptoms in cognitive terms. However, CT that focuses on mind-body connections has been found to reduce somatic symptoms (Nezu et al., 2001). CT for somatization involves educating patients about how psychological problems, such as stress, can affect physical symptoms.

Somatization is conceptualized in CT as a result of learning factors (Nezu et al., 2001). Social learning factors involve learning behaviors through observing others in one's family or sociocultural environment. In Asian American contexts, much social learning involving the observation of somatization among family and community members is likely to occur. Respondent conditioning may also occur when people associate physical symptoms with stressful stimuli. Finally, somatization may be operantly conditioned when a person's somatic symptoms result in positive (e.g., medical attention, sympathy) or negative conditioning (e.g., avoidance of responsibility). The focus of CT for somatization is on helping patients better cope with stress and other psychological problems that may be associated with physical symptoms.

Another method of addressing somatization among Asian Americans would be to augment psychotherapy with pharmacotherapy. Psychotherapy combined with pharmacotherapy, however, does not appear to have any incremental effects over either approach alone (Otto et al., 2005). Moreover, the use of medication could undermine psychological explanations of somatic symptoms that are central to CT.

Concerns about losing face may be a deterrent to Asian Americans' self-disclosure in psychotherapy (Zane & Mak, 2003). Self-disclosure in psychotherapy could result not only in the individual losing face but also in the individual's significant others losing face, as well. One method to address face issues in CT would be to conceptualize self-disclosure as a means of saving face. The temporary shame that one may experience in self-disclosure during psychotherapy could be reframed as a method of solving problems that could result in the individual, the individual's family, and other significant others losing face if the problems are not addressed (Iwamasa et al., in press). Although it might be expected that a skilled cognitive therapist would instinctively attend to such issues, loss of face issues could easily be overlooked by a therapist who is not attuned to them. Because of concerns about self-disclosure, Asian American patients are unlikely to attempt to explain loss of face to a therapist. Moreover, they may be unaware of or be unable to convincingly explain to the therapist the influence of loss of face in their lives.

It could be contended that one of the goals of psychotherapy would be to reduce Asian Americans' concerns about loss of face. Reducing such concerns could result in more self-disclosure that would facilitate the psychotherapy process and outcome. However, such an analysis is overly simplistic. Loss of face appears to be a trait-like variable that persists among Asian Americans across generations and independently of acculturation (Zane & Mak, 2003). Loss of face may have protective effects that may be diminished if it is reduced

(Hall et al., in press). Acculturation may create acculturative stress, such as conflicts with one's family or ethnic group. Acculturative stress has been found to be associated with depression among Asian Americans and other ethnic minority groups (Constantine, Okazaki, & Utsey, 2004; Hwang et al., 2005). Thus, it may be adaptive to modify CT to incorporate face concerns rather than to attempt to modify Asian Americans' concerns about face.

Chang (1996) has found that depression among Asian Americans may be more a function of a lack of optimism than of pessimism, in that optimism was associated with subsequent depressive symptoms but pessimism was not. Thus, CT for Asian Americans might focus more on increasing optimism than on decreasing pessimism (Chang, 2001). Another emphasis in CT that might be useful for Asian American patients would be the individual's adjustment to external realities, in contrast to modifying circumstances to fit an individual's needs (Wong et al., 2003). Such an emphasis on external norms is compatible with emphases in Asian cultures on being an interdependent member of a group, as opposed to being independent from others (Y. Lin, 2001). Thus, behaviors, such as assertiveness, that may be consistent with CT principles but may upset group harmony may be incongruent with Asian cultural values.

Mindfulness, which borrows components of Eastern meditation, has been incorporated into cognitive-behavioral therapy (Hayes, Follette, & Linehan, 2004). The incorporation of meditation into a Western approach could be beneficial to those Asian Americans who seek an integration of Eastern and Western interventions. Moreover, meditation has been found to be effective with somatic symptoms (Grossman et al., 2004), which may moderate treatment effectiveness among Asian Americans. However, Western approaches to meditation tend to focus on the individual and extract meditation from its interdependent context in Asian cultures. Whereas the goal of Western versions of meditation may be individual fulfillment, the goal of meditation in Asian contexts may be better adjustment to one's reference group. As with other aspects of cognitive-behavioral therapy, this emphasis on individual goals may not be compatible with Asian American values with respect to interdependence.

There is some literature on Asian Americans' preferences regarding existing treatments (Edman & Johnson, 1999; Wong et al., 2003), but Asian Americans' preferences regarding optimal treatments for mental disorders are unknown. In designing culturally sensitive treatments, it would be important to solicit the input of actual and potential Asian American patients. This input could be gathered via focus groups, surveys based on focus groups, and expert recommendations.

FUTURE DIRECTIONS

This chapter underscores the limited empirical support for psychotherapy with Asian Americans. There is a strong need for the demonstration of the effectiveness of empirically supported therapies with Asian American populations. There is also a need to determine if cultural characteristics, such as somatization and loss of face, moderate treatment effects. If cultural moderators of treatment effects exist, therapies that address these cultural moderators should be developed, and it should be determined if these culturally modified forms of therapy are more effective than standard forms of therapy or pharmacotherapies. Cultural adaptations of therapy may attract a broader group of Asian Americans than those who currently use Western treatment services and who are likely to be the most acculturated.

In 2001, Hall recommended that additional research be conducted on the effectiveness of empirically supported therapies with ethnic minorities. Although there has been some progress with African American and Latino American populations, such effectiveness research with Asian Americans has been sparse (Miranda et al., 2005). Why has there been so little progress with Asian Americans?

Much of the recent empirical research on psychotherapy with Asian Americans has involved college populations (e.g., Kim et al., 2005; Wong et al., 2003). Research on college populations is informative, as it often allows more experimental control over variables than is possible in community studies of clinical

populations. Nevertheless, Asian American college students are more acculturated than other Asian Americans.

Most of the recent empirical research involving Asian American community and clinical populations has relied on data gathered in the 1990s by the National Research Center on Asian American Mental Health (NRCAAMH) (Abe-Kim, Takeuchi, & Hwang, 2002; Akutsu, Tsuru, & Chu, 2004; Kung, 2004; Mak & Zane, 2004). The relative absence of empirical research on Asian American clinical populations and the absence of a large-scale randomized clinical trial with Asian Americans are associated with federal funding priorities. There has been a hiatus in federal funding of NRCAAMH, despite multiple applications for renewal of funding. Moreover, two separate proposals to evaluate the effectiveness of psychotherapy with Asian Americans have been part of these unfunded applications to support NRCAAMH. Clinical research with Asian Americans is expensive, and it is unlikely that this research will be conducted without federal support.

It is imperative that treatment studies be specifically devoted to the study of Asian Americans. All too often, Asian Americans are an afterthought in research. When Asian Americans comprise a small proportion of a sample, examination of means for the whole sample or for the whole ethnic minority sample obscure any effects that may be specific to Asian Americans. Although there are some commonalities across Asian American groups that make them different from other groups, such as somatization and concern about loss of face, there also is much variability within Asian American groups. Thus, there is complexity in studying Asian Americans, and research combining Asian Americans with other ethnic groups will miss important culture-specific phenomena.

The mid-2000s is a time of tight federal budgets for mental health research. Nevertheless, Asian Americans are the fastest-growing ethnic group in the United States and represent ethnic groups that are part of a worldwide majority. Thus, funding for mental health research on Asian Americans must become a federal priority if effective treatments for this population are to be developed.

REFERENCES

Abe-Kim, J., Okazaki, S., & Goto, S. G. (2001). Unidimensional versus multidimensional approaches to the assessment of acculturation for Asian American populations. *Cultural Diversity & Ethnic Minority Psychology, 7,* 232–246.

Abe-Kim, J., Takeuchi, D., & Hwang, W. (2002). Predictors of help seeking for emotional distress among Chinese Americans: Family matters. *Journal of Consulting and Clinical Psychology, 70,* 1186–1190.

Akutsu, P. D., Tsuru, G. K., & Chu, J. P. (2004). Predictors of nonattendance of intake appointments among five Asian American client groups. *Journal of Consulting and Clinical Psychology, 72,* 891–896.

Beck, A. T. (1976). *Cognitive therapy and the emotional disorders.* New York: International Universities Press.

Beck, A. T., Rush, A. J., Shaw, B. F., & Emery, G. (1979). *Cognitive therapy of depression.* New York: Guilford Press.

Beutler, L. E. (2004). The empirically supported treatments movement: A scientist-practitioner's response. *Clinical Psychology: Science and Practice, 11,* 225–229.

Beutler, L. E., Clarkin, J. F., & Bongar, B. (2000). *Guidelines for the systematic treatment of the depressed patient.* Washington, DC: American Psychological Association.

Beutler, L. E., Moleiro, C., & Talebi, H. (2002). Resistance in psychotherapy: What conclusions are supported by research? *Journal of Clinical Psychology, 58,* 207–217.

Boerner, R. J., & Moeller, H. J. (1999). The importance of new antidepressants in the treatment of anxiety/depressive disorders. *Pharmacopsychiatry, 32,* 119–126.

Chambless, D. L., & Hollon, S. D. (1998). Defining empirically supported therapies. *Journal of Consulting and Clinical Psychology, 66,* 7–18.

Chang, E. C. (1996). Cultural differences in optimism, pessimism, and coping: Predictors of subsequent adjustment in Asian American and Caucasian American college students. *Journal of Counseling Psychology, 43,* 113–123.

Chang, E. C. (2001). Cultural influences on optimism and pessimism: Differences in Western and Eastern construals of the self. In E. C. Chang (Ed.), *Optimism and pessimism: Implications for theory, research, and practice* (pp. 257–280). Washington, DC: American Psychological Association.

Chen, S. W., & Davenport, D. S. (2005). Cognitive-behavioral therapy with Chinese American clients: Cautions and modifications. *Psychotherapy: Theory, Research, Practice, Training, 42,* 101–110.

Chung, R. H. G. (2001). Gender, ethnicity, and acculturation in intergenerational conflict of Asian American college students. *Cultural Diversity & Ethnic Minority Psychology, 7,* 376–386.

Constantine, M. G., Okazaki, S., & Utsey, S. O. (2004). Self-concealment, social self-efficacy, acculturative stress, and depression in African, Asian, and Latin American international college students. *American Journal of Orthopsychiatry, 74,* 230–241.

Dai, Y., Zhang, S., Yamamoto, J., Ao, M., Belin, T. R., Cheung, F., et al. (1999). Cognitive behavioral therapy of minor depressive symptoms in elderly Chinese Americans: A pilot study. *Community Mental Health Journal, 35,* 537–542.

DeRubeis, R. J., Gelfand, L. A., Tang, T. Z., & Simons, A. D. (1999). Medications versus cognitive behavior therapy for severely depressed outpatients: Mega-analysis of four randomized comparisons. *American Journal of Psychiatry, 156,* 1007–1013.

DeRubeis, R., Hollon, S., Amsterdam, J., Shelton, R., Young, P., Salomon, R., et al. (2005). Cognitive therapy vs. medications in the treatment of moderate to severe depression. *Archives of General Psychiatry, 2,* 409–416.

Edman, J. L., & Johnson, R. C. (1999). Filipino American and Caucasian American beliefs about the causes and treatment of mental problems. *Cultural Diversity & Ethnic Minority Psychology, 5,* 380–386.

Elfenbein, H. A., & Ambady, N. (2002). Is there an in-group advantage in emotion recognition? *Psychological Bulletin, 128,* 243–249.

Elkin, I., Yamaguchi, J. L., Arnkoff, D. B., Glass, C. R., Sotsky, S. M., & Krupnick, J. L. (1999). "Patient-treatment fit" and early engagement in therapy. *Psychotherapy Research, 9,* 437–451.

Escobar, J. I., & Canino, G. (1989). Unexplained physical complaints: Psychopathology and epidemiological correlates. *British Journal of Psychiatry, 154,* 24–27.

Ezzo, J., Berman, B., Hadhazy, V. A., Jadad, A. R., Lao, L., & Singh, B. B. (2000). Is acupuncture effective for the treatment of chronic pain? A systematic review. *Pain, 86,* 217–225.

Frank, J. D. (1973). *Persuasion and healing.* Baltimore: Johns Hopkins University Press.

Gamst, G., Dana, R. H., Der-Karabetian, A., & Kramer, T. (2000). Ethnic match and client ethnicity effects on global assessment and visitation. *Journal of Community Psychology, 28,* 547–564.

Gamst, G., Dana, R. H., Der-Karabetian, A., & Kramer, T. (2001). Asian American mental health clients: Effects of ethnic match and age on global assessment and visitation. *Journal of Mental Health Counseling, 23,* 57–71.

Greenberger, D., & Padesky, C. A. (1995). *Mind over mood: A cognitive therapy treatment manual for clients.* New York: Guilford Press.

Grossman, P., Niemann, L., Schmidt, S., & Walach, H. (2004). Mindfulness-based stress reduction and health benefits: A meta-analysis. *Journal of Psychosomatic Research, 57,* 35–43.

Hall, G. C. N. (2001). Psychotherapy research with ethnic minorities: Empirical, ethical, and conceptual issues. *Journal of Consulting and Clinical Psychology, 69,* 502–510.

Hall, G. C. N., Lopez, I. R., & Bansal, A. (2001). Academic acculturation: Race, gender, and class issues. In D. Pope-Davis & H. Coleman (Eds.), *The intersection of race, gender, and class: Implications for counselor training* (pp. 171–188). Thousand Oaks, CA: Sage.

Hall, G. C. N., & Malony, H. N. (1983). Cultural control in psychotherapy with minority patients. *Psychotherapy: Theory, Research and Practice, 20,* 131–142.

Hall, G. C. N., Teten, A. L., DeGarmo, D. S., Sue, S., & Stephens, K. A. (2005). Ethnicity, culture, and sexual aggression: Risk and protective factors. *Journal of Consulting and Clinical Psychology, 73,* 830–840.

Hayes, S. C., Follette, V. M., & Linehan, M. M. (2004). *Mindfulness and acceptance: Expanding the cognitive-behavioral tradition.* New York: Guilford.

Hollon, S. D., DeRubeis, R. J., Shelton, R. C., & Weiss, B. (2002). The emperor's new drugs: Effect size and moderation effects. *Prevention and Treatment, 5.*

Hsu, L. K. G., & Folstein, M. F. (1997). Somatoform disorders in Caucasian and Chinese Americans. *Journal of Nervous and Mental Disease, 185,* 382–387.

Hwang, J., Yang, C., & Tsai, S. (2004). Comparison study of venlafaxine and paroxetine for the treatment of depression in elderly Chinese inpatients. *International Journal of Geriatric Psychiatry, 19,* 189–190.

Institute of Medicine. (2001). *Crossing the quality chasm: A new health system for the 21st century.* Washington, DC: Author.

Iwamasa, G. Y., Hsia, C., & Hinton, D. (2006). Cognitive-behavior therapy with Asians and Asian Americans. In P. A. Hays & G. Y. Iwamasa (Eds.), *Cognitive-behavior therapy with diverse people* (pp. 117–140). Washington, DC: American Psychological Association.

Kessler, R. C., McGonagle, K. A., Zhao, S., Nelson, C. B., Hughes, M., Eshleman, S., et al. (1994). Lifetime and 12-month prevalence of DSM-III–R psychiatric disorders in the United States: Results from the national comorbidity study. *Archives of General Psychiatry, 51,* 8–19.

Kim, B. S. K., Ng, G. F., & Ahn, A. J. (2005). Effects of client expectation for counseling success, client-counselor worldview match, and client adherence to Asian and European American cultural values on counseling process with Asian Americans. *Journal of Counseling Psychology, 52,* 67–76.

Kirsch, I. (1990). *Changing expectations: A key to effective psychotherapy.* Pacific Grove, CA: Brooks/Cole.

Kirsch, I., & Sapirstein, G. (1999). Listening to Prozac but hearing placebo: A meta-analysis of antidepressant medications. In I. Kirsch (Ed.), *How expectancies shape experience* (pp. 303–320). Washington, DC: American Psychological Association.

Kleinman, A. M. (1977). Depression, somatization, and the new cross-cultural psychiatry. *Social Science and Medicine, 11,* 3–10.

Kung, W. V. (2004). Cultural and practical barriers to seeking mental health treatment for Chinese Americans. *Journal of Community Psychology, 32,* 27–43.

Kwong, K., Fung, M. C., Wu, H., Plewes, J., & Judge, R. (1999). Meta-analysis of safety of fluoxetine in Asian patients. In J. M. Herrera & W. B. Lawson (Eds.), *Cross cultural psychiatry* (pp. 221–238). New York: Wiley.

Lau, A., & Zane, N. (2000). Examining the effects of ethnic-specific services: An analysis of cost-utilization and treatment outcome for Asian American patients. *Journal of Community Psychology, 28,* 63–77.

Le, H., Berenbaum, H., & Raghavan, C. (2002). Culture and alexithymia: Mean levels, correlates and the role of parental socialization of emotions. *Emotion, 2,* 341–360.

Lee, E. (1997). *Working with Asian Americans: A guide for clinicians.* New York: Guilford Press.

Leong, F. T. (1986). Counseling and psychotherapy with Asian-Americans: Review of the literature. *Journal of Counseling Psychology, 33,* 196–206.

Levant, R. F. (2004). The empirically validated treatments movement: A practitioner/educator perspective. *Clinical Psychology: Science and Practice, 11,* 219–224.

Levant, R. F. (2005). Evidence-based practice in psychology. *Monitor on Psychology, 36*(2), 5.

Lin, K., & Cheung, F. (1999). Mental health issues for Asian Americans. *Psychiatric Services, 50,* 774–780.

Lin, Y. (2001). The application of cognitive-behavioral therapy to counseling Chinese. *American Journal of Psychotherapy, 55,* 46–58.

Luczak, S. E., Elvine-Kreis, B., Shea, S. H., Carr, L. G., & Wall, T. L. (2002). Genetic risk for alcoholism relates to level of response to alcohol in Asian American men and women. *Journal of Studies on Alcohol, 63,* 74–82.

Luczak, S. E., Wall, T. L., Cook, T. A. R., Shea, S. H., & Carr, L. G. (2004). ALDH2 status and conduct disorder mediate the relationship between ethnicity and alcohol dependence in Chinese, Korean, and White American college students. *Journal of Abnormal Psychology, 113,* 271–278.

Lutwak, N., Razzino, B. E., & Ferrari, J. R. (1998). Self-perceptions and moral affect: An exploratory analysis of subcultural diversity in guilt and shame emotions. *Journal of Social Behavior and Personality, 13,* 333–348.

Mak, W. W. S., & Zane, N. W. S. (2004). The phenomenon of somatization among community Chinese Americans. *Social Psychiatry and Psychiatric Epidemiology, 39,* 967–974.

Manber, R., Allen, J. J. B., & Morris, M. M. (2002). Alternate treatments for depression: Empirical support and relevance to women. *Journal of Clinical Psychiatry, 63,* 628–640.

Maramba, G. G., & Hall, G. C. N. (2002). Meta-analysis of ethnic match as a predictor of

drop-out, utilization, and outcome. *Cultural Diversity & Ethnic Minority Psychology, 8,* 290–297.

McCallum, M., Piper, W. E., Ogrodniczuk, J. S., & Joyce, A. S. (2003). Relationships among psychological mindedness, alexithymia, and outcome in four forms of short-term psychotherapy. *Psychology and Psychotherapy: Theory, Research, and Practice, 76,* 133–144.

Merrill, K. A., Tolbert, V. E., & Wade, W. A. (2003). Effectiveness of cognitive therapy for depression in a community mental health center: A benchmarking study. *Journal of Consulting and Clinical Psychology, 71,* 404–409.

Meyer, B., Pilkonis, P. A., Krupnick, J. L., Egan, M. K., Simmens, S. J., & Sotsky, S. M. (2002). Treatment expectancies, patient alliance, and outcome: Further analyses from the National Institute of Mental Health treatment of depression collaborative research program. *Journal of Consulting and Clinical Psychology, 70,* 1051–1055.

Miranda, J., Bernal, G., Lau, A., Kohn, L., Hwang, W., & LaFromboise, T. (2005). State of the science on psychosocial interventions for ethnic minorities. *Annual Review of Clinical Psychology, 1,* 113–142.

Miranda, J., Schoenbaum, M., Sherbourne, C., Duan, N., & Wells, K. (2004). Effects of primary care depression treatment on minority patients' clinical status and employment. *Archives of General Psychiatry, 61,* 827–835.

Moore, L. J., Sager, D., Keopraseuth, K., Chao, L. H., Riley, C., & Robinson, E. (2001). Rheumatological disorders and somatization in U.S. Mien and Lao refugees with depression and post-traumatic stress disorder: A cross-cultural comparison. *Transcultural Psychiatry, 38,* 481–505.

Nezu, A. M., Nezu, C. M., & Lombardo, E. R. (2001). Cognitive-behavior therapy for medically unexplained symptoms: A critical review of the treatment literature. *Behavior Therapy, 32,* 537–583.

Okazaki, S. (2002). Self-other agreement on affective distress scales in Asian Americans and White Americans. *Journal of Counseling Psychology, 49,* 428–437.

Okazaki, S., & Kallivayalil, D. (2002). Cultural norms and subjective disability as predictors of symptom reports among Asian Americans and White Americans. *Journal of Cross-Cultural Psychology, 33,* 482–491.

Otto, M. W., & Hinton, D., Korbly, N. B., Chea, A., Ba, P., Gershuny, B. S., et al. (2003). Treatment of pharmacotherapy-refractory post-traumatic stress disorder among Cambodian refugees: A pilot study of combination treatment with cognitive-behavior therapy vs. sertraline alone. *Behaviour Research and Therapy, 41,* 1271–1276.

Otto, M. W., Smits, J. A. J., & Reese, H. E. (2005). Combined psychotherapy and pharmacotherapy for mood and anxiety disorders in adults: Review and analysis. *Clinical Psychology: Science and Practice, 12,* 72–86.

Oyserman, D., Coon, H. M., & Kemmelmeier, M. (2002). Rethinking individualism and collectivism: Evaluation of theoretical assumptions and meta-analyses. *Psychological Bulletin, 128,* 3–72.

Parker, G., Cheah, Y., & Roy, K. (2001). Do the Chinese somatize depression? A cross-cultural study. *Social Psychiatry and Psychiatric Epidemiology, 36,* 287–293.

Parker, G., Gladstone, G., & Tsee Chee, K. (2001). Depression in the planet's largest ethnic group: The Chinese. *American Journal of Psychiatry, 158,* 857–864.

Reeves, T. J., & Bennett, C. E. (2004, December). *We the people: Asians in the United States* (Census 2000 Special Report No. CENSR–17). Washington, DC: U.S. Department of Commerce, U.S. Census Bureau.

Reid, M. J., Webster-Stratton, C., & Beauchaine, T. R. (2001). Parent training in Head Start: A comparison of program response among African American, Asian American, Caucasian, and Hispanic mothers. *Prevention Science, 2,* 209–227.

Shen, Y. (2002). Short-term group play therapy with Chinese earthquake victims: effects on anxiety, depression, and adjustment. *International Journal of Play Therapy, 11,* 43–63.

Smith, R. H., Webster, J. M., Parrott, W. G., & Eyre, H. L. (2002). The role of public exposure in moral and nonmoral shame and guilt. *Journal of Personality and Social Psychology, 83,* 138–159.

Stewart-Williams, S., & Podd, J. (2004). The placebo effect: Dissolving the expectancy versus conditioning debate. *Psychological Bulletin, 130,* 324–340.

Sue, S., Fujino, D. C., Hu, L. T., Takeuchi, D. T., & Zane, N. W. S. (1991). Community mental health services for ethnic minority groups: A test of the cultural responsiveness hypothesis. *Journal of Consulting and Clinical Psychology, 59,* 533–540.

Sue, S., & Zane, N. (1987). The role of culture and cultural techniques in psychotherapy: A critique and reformulation. *American Psychologist, 42,* 37–45.

Takeuchi, D. T., Chung, R. C., Lin, K., Shen, H., Kurasaki, K., Chun, C., et al. (1998). Lifetime and twelve-month prevalence rates of major depressive episodes and dysthymia among Chinese Americans in Los Angeles. *American Journal of Psychiatry, 155,* 1407–1414.

Tata, S. P., & Leong, F. T. L. (1994). Individualism-collectivism, social-network orientation, and acculturation as predictors of attitudes toward seeking professional psychological help among Chinese Americans. *Journal of Counseling Psychology, 41,* 280–287.

Taylor, G. J. (1984). Alexithymia: Concept, measurement, and implications for treatment. *American Journal of Psychiatry, 141,* 725–732.

Thase, M. E. (2000). Relapse and recurrence of depression: An updated practical approach for prevention. In K. J. Palmer (Ed.), *Drug treatment issues in depression* (pp. 35–52). Auckland, New Zealand: Adis International.

Wall, T. L., Horn, S. M., Johnson, M. L., Smith, T. L., & Carr, L. G. (2000). Hangover symptoms in Asian Americans with variations in the aldehyde dehydrogenase (ALDH2) gene. *Journal of Studies on Alcohol, 61,* 13–17.

Westen, D., & Morrison, K. (2001). A multidimensional meta-analysis of treatments for depression, panic, and generalized anxiety disorder: An empirical examination of the status of empirically supported therapies. *Journal of Consulting and Clinical Psychology, 69,* 875–899.

Westen, D., Novotny, C. M., & Thompson-Brenner, H. (2004). The empirical status of empirically supported psychotherapies: Assumptions, findings, and reporting in controlled clinical trials. *Psychological Bulletin, 130,* 631–663.

Wong, E. C., Kim, B. S. K., Zane, N. W. S., Kim, I. J., & Huang, J. S. (2003). Examining culturally based variables associated with ethnicity: Influences on credibility perceptions of empirically supported interventions. *Cultural Diversity & Ethnic Minority Psychology, 9,* 88–96.

Yeh, M., Takeuchi, D. T., & Sue, S. (1994). Asian-American children treated in the mental health system: A comparison of parallel and mainstream outpatient service centers. *Journal of Clinical Child Psychology, 23,* 5–12.

Yen, S., Robins, C. J., & Lin, N. (2000). A cross-cultural comparison of depressive symptom manifestation: China and the United States. *Journal of Consulting and Clinical Psychology, 68,* 993–999.

Yeung, A., Chang, D., Gresham, R. L., Nierenberg, A. A., & Fava, M. (2004). Illness beliefs of depressed Chinese American patients in primary care. *Journal of Nervous and Mental Disease, 192,* 324–327.

Zane, N., Hall, G. C. N., Sue, S., Young, K., & Nunez, J. (2004). Research on psychotherapy with culturally diverse populations. In M. J. Lambert (Ed.), *Handbook of psychotherapy and behavior change* (5th ed., pp. 767–804). New York: Wiley.

Zane, N., & Mak, W. (2003). Major approaches to the measurement of acculturation among ethnic minority populations: A content analysis and an alternative empirical strategy. In K. M. Chun, P. B. Organista, & G. Marin (Eds.), *Acculturation: Advances in theory, measurement, and applied research* (pp. 39–60). Washington, DC: American Psychological Association.

Zane, N., & Yeh, M. (2002). The use of culturally-based variables in assessment: Studies on loss of face. In K. S. Kurasaki, S. Okazaki, & S. Sue (Eds.), *Asian American mental health: Assessment theories and methods* (pp. 123–138). New York: Kluwer Academic/Plenum.

Zhang, Y., Young, D., Lee, S., Li, L., Zhang, H., Xiao, Z., et al. (2002). Chinese Taoist cognitive psychotherapy in the treatment of generalized anxiety disorder in contemporary China. *Transcultural Psychiatry, 39,* 115–129.

Zhao, J., Chen, Z., Yan, W., Chen, K., Dai, & Chen, Y. (2002). Intervention on depression of the elderly in the community. *Chinese Mental Health Journal, 16,* 179–180.

AUTHOR INDEX

Abbott, R. D., 219, 424
Abe, J., 72, 112, 113
Abe, J. S., 285
Abe-Kim, J., 145, 452, 453, 459, 462
Abeles, N., 221
Abelmann, N., 36
Abraham, M., 189, 367, 368
Abramson, P. R., 271
Abreu, J. M., 143, 146, 147
Acevedo-Garcia, D., 91
Adams, L. J., 33
Adams, R., 269 (tab), 424
Adey, M., 217
Adey, M. B., 422 (tab), 423
Adler, N., 372
Adler, N. E., 303, 304, 305, 306, 312
Adler, P. S., 253
Agbayani Siewert, P., 440
Agretsi, A., 61
Aguirre, B. E., 74
Ahmad, F., 365, 367, 368
Ahmed, I., 217, 309
Ahn, A. J., 153, 155, 437, 452, 462
Ahn Toupin, E. S. W., 112, 113
Ahuna, C., 145, 175, 253, 422
Aikman, G., 270
Akan, G. E., 187
Akilu, F., 431
Akimoto, S. A., 293
Akiyama, H., 80
Akiyama, K., 437
Akutsu, P., 432, 434
Akutsu, P. D., 462
Al-Sharideh, K. A., 250
Al-Timimi, N. R., 332
Aldeguer, C. M. R., 272
Alden, L. E., 33, 145, 253
Aldwin, C., 285, 394 (tab)
Alegria, M., 368, 372, 384
Alexander, A. A., 248, 255
Alexitch, L. R., 248, 251
Alibhai, N., 187, 251

Alipuria, L. L., 127
Allan, R., 304
Allen, C., 311
Allen, F. C. L., 247, 248
Allen, J. J. B., 455
Allik, J., 274, 291
Allis, S., 207
Allison, D., 398
Almeida, D., 127
Almeida, R. V., 373
Almirol, E. B., 367
Althen, G., 248, 249, 250, 255
Altman, A., 74
Alvarez, A., 353
Alvarez, A. N., 33, 131, 133, 327
Amada, G., 437
Ambady, N., 134, 185, 290, 460
American Association of Retired Persons AARP, 72
American Association of Retired Persons AARP Minority Affairs, 220
American Educational Research Association American Psychological Association, National Council on Measurement in Education, 419
American Heart Association, 304
American Psychiatric Association, 218
American Psychological Association, 221, 410
Amkoff, D. B., 451
Amodeo, M., 438
Amow, B., 369
Amsterdam, J., 454
Anda, R. F., 369
Andal, J., 49
Andersen, B. L., 268 (tab), 271
Anderson, J., 422, 422 (tab)
Anderson, L. E., 247, 248, 250, 251, 252, 254
Anderson, L. P., 432

Anderson, N. B., 305–306
Anderson, W. W., 38
Andrade, N. N., 127, 389, 390 (tab), 391 (tab)
Aneshensel, C. S., 389, 390 (tab)
Angleitner, A., 266, 293
Anh, N. T., 170
Ani, C., 95
Anis, R. C., 234
Anna, C., 245
Annis, R. C., 144, 327
Ansak, M. L., 220
Anthony, J. C., 330
Antonucci, T. C., 80, 216
Ao, M., 221, 454
Aoki, B., 50
Aponte, J. F., 439
Appelbaum, M., 368
Apprey, M., 229
Araki, F., 217, 387
Aranalde, M. A., 144, 146
Archer, D., 366
Archus, D., 94
Arganza, G., 232, 235
Armenian, H. K., 308
Armstead, C. A., 306
Armstrong, K. L., 331
Armstrong, M. A., 310, 311, 312
Arnold, B., 146, 147
Arnone, M., 247
Aroian, K. J., 220
Aronson, J., 237
Arora, A. K., 131, 327, 331, 332
Arps, K., 269 (tab), 272
Arredondo, P., 255
Arroyo, W., 91
Arseneault, L., 364
Arthur, N., 247, 248, 249, 250, 255, 256, 257
Asakawa, K., 270
Asamen, J. K., 330
Asay, P. A., 154, 333, 437
Ascherio, A., 309
Aseltine, R. H., Jr., 390 (tab)

469

Asian American Legal Defense and Education Fund, 91, 350, 352
Asian Americans for Community Involvement, 285
Asian and Pacific Islander Child Care Task Force, 93
Asian/Pacific Islander Task Force on Youth, 92
Asian Pacific Islander Youth Violence Prevention Center, 115
Asrabadi, B., 253
Atchley, R. C., 215
Atkinson, D. R., 142, 143, 146, 147–148, 149, 152, 154, 189, 203, 249, 256, 275, 328, 433, 436, 438, 439
Atkinson, P., 51, 54
Attra, S. L., 394 (tab)
Audas, M. C., 251, 252
Aufseeser, D., 94
Avia, M. D., 293
Avis, N., 392, 393 (tab)
Avolio, B. J., 288
Avrushin, M. F., 49
Awakuni, G. I., 341, 342
Ayyub, R., 188, 368
Azada, J., 49
Azuma, H., 97

Ba, P., 454
Babcock, C. G., 438, 440
Bachman, R., 364
Bacon, S. F., 274
Baden, A. L., 254
Bagley, S., 94
Bakan, D., 283
Baker, E., 311
Baker, F. M., 398
Balabil, S., 433
Balsink Krieg, D., 109
Baluch, S., 145, 422
Baluja, K. F., 126, 134, 310
Banaji, M. R., 128, 129, 198
Bandura, A., 269 (tab)
Bankston, C., 92
Bankston, C. L., 115
Bankston, C. L., III, 201
Bansal, A., 460
Barata, P., 365, 367, 368
Barnes, E. J., 92
Barnes, J. M., 439
Barnes, J. S., 73, 342, 409
Barnett, E., 308
Barón, A., 248, 255
Barrett, D. C., 435
Barrett, M. E., 370
Barrett-Connor, E., 311
Barringer, H. R., 72, 328–329
Barrios, F. X., 398
Bartels, S. J., 217

Barudy, J. A., 231
Barzegamazari, E., 433
Baskin, D., 187
Bass, B. M., 284, 287, 288, 293
Bassett, M. E., 394 (tab)
Bastani, R., 310
Bates, J. E., 369
Bates, S. R., 311
Batson, C. D., 269 (tab), 272
Batson, J. G., 269 (tab), 272
Baumeister, R. F., 268 (tab), 295
Baumgartner, H., 59
Baumrind, D., 96
Beaman, A. L., 269 (tab), 272
Bean, R. A., 439
Beauchaine, T. R., 454
Beaumont, R., 185, 323, 325, 326, 327
Beck, A. T., 422 (tab), 423, 453, 460
Becker, A. E., 440
Bedford, O., 371
Beehr, T. A., 252
Behar-Mitrani, V., 270
Beiser, M., 127, 231, 234, 238, 330
Belin, T. R., 221, 454
Bell, R. M., 271
Bellas, M. L., 185
Belsky, J., 371
Bemak, F., 228, 229, 230, 231, 234, 235, 236, 237, 238, 239, 438
Bemal, G., 450, 462
Bemporad, J. R., 369
Ben, R., 238, 437
Ben-Ari, A., 332
Ben-Porath, Y. S., 417
Benavage, A., 187
Benet-Martínez, V., 133, 134
Bennan, B., 455
Bennett, C., ix, 87
Bennett, C. E., 73, 77, 78, 114, 115, 227, 231, 232, 342, 409, 452
Bennett, L. W., 366
Benson, M. J., 75
Bentler, P. M., 59
Berenbaum, H., 458
Berg, I. K., 438, 439
Berglund, P., 396
Berkel, L. A., 247, 249, 255
Berkman, L. F., 309
Bernat, J. A., 188
Berndt, T. J., 76
Berry, G. L., 330
Berry, J. W., 33, 131, 142, 143, 144, 146, 150, 234, 250, 253, 323, 325, 327, 366, 372
Berry, J. W., 33
Betancourt, H., 30, 184
Beutler, L. E., 449, 451, 460

Bhadha, B. R., 72, 372
Bhatia, S., 34
Bhopal, R., 311
Bhui, K., 433
Bialystok, E., 97
Bianchi, F. T., 292
Biermeier, C., 267, 271
Biggs, D. A., 249, 251, 252
Bingham, R. P., 30
Bingi, R., 247
Bishop, G. D., 309
Bjorck, J. P., 330
Black, S. A., 216
Blackburn, T. C., 274, 330
Blaine, B., 126, 127
Blair, S. L., 111
Blanchard, L., 267, 268 (tab)
Bland, R. C., 382
Bland, S. H., 309
Blankenship, E. S., 247, 248
Blazer, D., 369
Blinn, R., 398
Bluestone, H., 187
Blumenthal, J. A., 309
Boake, C., 424
Bobo, L., 288, 289
Bobrowitz, T., 394 (tab), 395 (tab), 396
Bochner, S., 248, 250, 251
Bodenhausen, G. V., 33, 134
Boehnlein, J. K., 438, 439
Boemer, R. J., 450
Bogardus, E. S., 173
Bohannon, A. S., 312
Bojczyk, K. E., 91, 95
Bond, G. E., 218
Bond, M. H., 274
Bongar, B., 398, 451, 460
Bono, J. E., 271, 272
Bontempo, R., 283
Borenstein, A. R., 218
Borkovec, T., 218
Bottorff, J. L., 324
Bourne, P. G., 398
Bowker, J., 324
Bowlby, J., 88
Bowman, P. J., 99
Boyce, T., 312
Boyle, M. H., 370
Bracero, W., 190
Bradley, L., 247
Bradshaw, C. K., 35, 181, 182, 185, 186, 189, 190, 191
Braham, V. E., 308
Bramlette, J., 187
Brand, D., 105, 119
Brandt, J. R., 269 (tab), 272
Brannon, R., 203
Branscombe, N. R., 132, 250
Brassington, G. S., 187
Braun, K., 74

Braun, K. L., 81
Breaux, C., 328, 385 (tab), 431
Brennan, J. M., 276
Brenner, B. R., 333
Brenner, M., 315
Bright, C. M., 171
Brillon, L., 93
Bringle, J. R., 81
Brink, T. L., 217, 422 (tab), 423
Brinson, J. A., 250
Brintnall, R., 310
Brislin, R., 251, 257
Broadnax, S., 126, 127
Brodbeck, C., 218
Brody, C. M., 189
Broh, B. A., 110, 111
Bromberger, J. T., 392, 393 (tab)
Bromley, M. A., 438
Bronfenbrenner, U., 88, 90
Brook, J., 186, 187
Brooks, W., 314
Brown, B., 94
Brown, C., 253, 254
Brown, C. V., 74
Brown, D., 159, 167
Brown, H. N., 410
Brown, J., 369, 370
Brown, J. D., 295
Brown, K., 312
Brown, L. G., 218
Brown, M. J., 95
Brown, M. T., 170, 174
Brown, R. D., 153, 255
Brown, S. D., 160, 163, 166, 173
Brown, T., 312, 352
Brown-Collins, A., 191
Browne, A., 364
Browne, M. W., 59
Brownson, R. C., 311
Bruce, J. C., 346
Brummett, B. H., 272
Bryk, A. S., 57
Buchwald, D., 230
Buck, R., 97
Bui, A., 238, 437
Bui, H. N., 366, 368
Bui, K. V., 384, 385 (tab), 386, 431
Burchfiel, C., 310, 311
Burgess, D., 290
Buriel, R., 88, 93, 99, 324,
    325, 329
Burke, J. D., 398
Burke, P. M., 268 (tab)
Burkham, D. T., 108
Burlew, A. K., 50
Burr, R., 218
Burton, D., 219, 221
Burts, D. C., 370, 371
Butcher, J. N., 419
Bybee, D., 133
Byrne, B., 58

Byrne, B. M., 58
Byrnes, J. P., 267, 268 (tab)
Bzostek, S., 94

Cabezas, A., 284, 285
Cachelin, F. M., 433
California Department
    of Justice, 237
Callao, M. J., 285, 291
Cambra, R., 291
Cambra, R. E., 285
Camic, P. M., 51, 53, 55
Camilli, G., 60
Camp, P., 392, 393 (tab),
    395 (tab), 396
Campbell, J. C., 368
Canda, E. R., 437
Canino, G., 368, 382, 384, 458
Cantu, C. L., 206
Cantwell, D. P., 389, 390 (tab)
Capps, R., 227
Carey, J. C., 326, 329
Carielli, D., 145, 422
Carmichael, S., 343
Carney, R. M., 309
Carr, J. L., 437
Carr, L. G., 456, 457
Carrington, C. H., 424, 425
Carroll, S. J., 172
Carter, J. S., 311
Carter, R. T., 255
Carter, W. B., 237
Carter-Pokras, O., 313
Carver, C. S., 270
Casa, J. M., 255
Casas, J., 438
Casey, M. A., 51
Casey, R. J., 424
Casper, M. L., 308
Caspi, A., 364, 369
Caspi, Y., 230, 237
Cassidy, J., 96
Cassuto, N., 267, 268 (tab)
Castelino, P., 79
Castellanos, J., 153
Castellazzo, G., 372
Castelli, W. P., 309
Castellino, D., 88
Castro, J. R., 112
Catania, J. A., 435
Cauce, A. M., 75, 90, 133
Caughy, M. O., 99
Celentano, E., 203
Cen, G., 94
Centers for Disease Control and
    Prevention, 310
Cerhan, J. U., 438
Chaiyasit, W., 332
Chambless, D. L., 450, 453
Chan, C. C. H., 314
Chan, C. S., 184, 188, 197

Chan, D., 58
Chan, D. W., 271
Chan, E., 97, 289
Chan, F., 315
Chan, G., 134
Chan, J. C., 133
Chan, J. W., 199
Chan, K. S., 128, 131, 132, 328
Chan, N., 388
Chan, R., 217, 218, 392, 394 (tab),
    395 (tab)
Chan, S., 38, 117, 118, 198, 199,
    207, 329, 367, 371
Chan, S. Q., 88, 93
Chand, A., 369
Chandran, M., 433
Chang, C., 312
Chang, C. F., 310
Chang, C. Y., 168, 214, 439
Chang, D., 381, 439, 457
Chang, D. F., 368, 429
Chang, D. S., 396, 397 (tab), 398
Chang, E., 394 (tab)
Chang, E. C., 270, 295, 324,
    330, 461
Chang, I., 232
Chang, J., 52, 410, 417, 419
Chang, J. Y., 127
Chang, L., 389, 390 (tab)
Chang, M., 106, 117
Chang, T., 197, 206, 332, 435
Chang, T. H. H., 438
Chang, W. C., 330
Chao, C., 236
Chao, L. H., 457
Chao, R., 72, 75, 76, 78, 79
Chao, R. K., 30, 31, 96, 107, 108,
    111, 114, 371
Chapdelaine, R. F., 248, 251
Chapman, D. W., 249, 251, 252
Charles, H., 249
Charmaz, K., 55
Chasnoflf, I. J., 369–370
Chavira, V., 99
Chavous, T. M., 125
Chay, D. M., 439
Chea, A., 454
Cheah, Y., 458
Chee, K. T., 381, 382, 386
Chen, A. S., 197, 199, 205, 206
Chen, C., 78, 79, 95, 267, 271, 332
Chen, C. P., 249
Chen, E. H., 310
Chen, H., 94, 217, 437
Chen, H.-J., 252
Chen, J., 439
Chen, L., 99
Chen, L. M., 396, 397 (tab), 423
Chen, M., 314, 438
Chen, M. S., 422, 422 (tab)
Chen, R., 217, 309

Chen, S., 431
Chen, S. W., 453, 454
Chen, T., 437
Chen, X., 94
Chen, Y. R., 206, 389, 390 (tab), 398
Cheng, A. T., 422, 422 (tab)
Cheng, C., 167, 168
Cheng, S. K., 324
Chentsova-Dutton, Y., 33, 35, 98, 125, 126, 132, 135n1, 291, 292
Chepesiuk, R., 250
Cherry, D., 314
Cheryan, S., 33, 129–130, 131, 134
Chesla, C. A., 52, 55
Chesney, M., 230, 231
Chesney, M. A., 312
Cheung, A., 290
Cheung, F., 221, 380, 386, 387, 439, 454, 458
Cheung, F. H., 152, 237
Cheung, F. K., 216, 220, 385 (tab)
Cheung, F. M., 273, 275, 276, 383, 417, 419, 422 (tab), 423
Cheung, L., 311
Cheung, P. C., 76
Cheung, R. T. F., 314
Cheung, S. F., 273, 383
Chew, T., 310
Chi, I., 367
Chiang, F., 314
Chiang, L., 330, 331
Chien, C., 396, 397 (tab)
Chien, K., 314
Chin, J. L., 189, 342, 439
Chin, K., 201
Chin, P., 344
Chin, R., 16, 327
Chin-Hansen, J., 220
Ching, W., 109
Chiocca, E. M., 97
Chiriboga, D. A., 81
Chiu, C., 134
Chiu, C. Y., 96
Chiu, H. F., 309
Cho, S., 315
Choe, J., 81, 325, 326, 372
Choi, G., 252
Choi, H., 383, 389, 390 (tab)
Choi, K. H., 332, 435
Chou, E. L., 247, 248, 255, 256, 257, 258
Chow, C. S., 200
Chow, E. N., 182, 183
Chow, E. O. W., 314
Christiansen, N. D., 252
Chrosniak, L. D., 268 (tab), 270
Chu, J., 184
Chu, J. P., 462
Chua, E. L. M., 439

Chua, P., 197, 200
Chua, W. L., 330
Chun, 107
Chun, C., 330, 432, 457, 458
Chun, C. A., 382, 384, 389, 391 (tab), 392, 394 (tab), 396, 398, 399, 400, 434, 435
Chun, C.-A., 276
Chun, K. M., 33, 52, 53, 55
Chun, K. T., 171, 172
Chun, M. B. J., 31
Chung, C., 221
Chung, H., 394 (tab), 395 (tab), 396
Chung, R. C., 384, 392, 394 (tab), 396, 398, 399, 457, 458
Chung, R. C.-Y., 228, 229, 230, 231, 234, 235, 236, 237, 238, 239, 432
Chung, R. H., 171, 174
Chung, R. H. G., 77, 146, 151, 452, 453
Chung, Y., 438
Church, A. T., 247, 248, 249, 250, 255, 256, 257, 422 (tab), 423
Chyou, P., 310
Cialdini, R. B., 269 (tab), 272
Cicirelli, V. G., 76
Cimmarusti, R. A., 367, 439
Clark, L., 422 (tab), 423
Clarke, H., 324
Clarkin, J. F., 451, 460
Clement, W., 79
Cleveland, B., 94
Close, N., 311
Cloud, N., 77
Clum, G. A., 249, 252
Coakley, E., 217
Coalition for Asian American Children and Families, 91
Coates, T. J., 435
Cobb, J. L., 309
Cochran, S. D., 188, 268 (tab), 271
Cochrane, R., 431
Coffey, C., 188, 190
Cohen, J. B., 309
Cohen, P., 369, 370
Cohen, R., 40
Cohen, S., 312
Coldits, G. A., 311
Colditz, G. A., 309
Cole, J. B., 247, 248
Coleman, H. L., 5, 34, 98, 130, 131
Coleman, H. L. K., 150, 297
Coleman, J., 134
Coleman, J. S., 272
Coll, C. G., 324, 326, 328
College Board National Report, 286
Collins, C., 312

Collins, L. M., 57
Comas-Diaz, L., 184, 185, 191
Commander, M. J., 431
Commission on Wartime Relocation and Internment of Civilians, 349, 350
Conger, J. A., 287
Conger, R. D., 267, 268 (tab)
Constantine, M. G., 81, 185, 254, 326, 327, 328, 461
Constantino, G., 217
Conway, M. M., 132, 133
Cook, E. P., 184
Cook, T. A. R., 456
Coombs, M., 132, 133
Coombs, W. T., 288
Coon, D. W., 220
Coon, H. M., 32, 459
Cooper, S., 440
Corbie Smith, G., 172
Corbin, J., 56
Cordal, A., 392, 393 (tab)
Cort, K. A., 326
Cortina, J. M., 268 (tab), 270
Costa, P. T. J., 293
Costa, P. T., Jr., 266
Costanzo, J. M., 126, 134
Cottington, E. M., 309
Cottington, F., 285
Council of National Psychological Association for the Advancement of Ethnic Minority Interests, 18
Cox, G. B., 384, 385 (tab), 430, 431
Coyne, J. C., 399
Cozza, T., 203
Crago, M., 187
Crain, C., 424
Cram, J. R., 21
Crandall, R. C., 216
Crane, D. R., 72
Crites, J. O., 162, 163
Crnic, K., 3, 88, 89 (fig), 90, 92
Crocker, J., 126, 127, 206
Crombie, G., 58
Cromer, L., 311
Cross, S. E., 253
Cross, W. E. J., 127
Croughan, J., 218
Crouter, A. C., 90
Crow, T., 220
Crum, R. M., 308
Csikszentmihalyi, M., 269 (tab), 272, 274
Cuellar, I., 145–146, 147
Culver, S., 386
Culver, S. W., 431
Cummins, R. A., 314
Cunningham, C. V., 220
Curb, J. D., 310, 311

Curran, P. J., 58
Curry, E. J. A., 438
Cushner, K., 257
Cuthbertson, W., 330
Cutting, M. L., 35–36
Cyranowski, J. C., 268 (tab), 271
Czajkowski, S. M., 309

D'Agostino, R. B., 309
Dahlstrom, W. G., 58, 59
Dai, Y., 221, 454
Daiger, D. C., 163
Dalaker, J., 94
Dalton, M. A., 95
Dana, R. H., 421, 456
D'Andrea, M., 49
Dang, T., 117
Danico, M. Y., 344
Daniels, J., 49
Daniels, R., 345–346, 348, 349
Danko, G. P., 389, 390 (tab)
Das, A. K., 352
Dasen, P. R., 142, 143, 150
Dasgupta, S., 184, 189, 326
Dasgupta, S. D., 184, 188, 189,
    326, 364, 365, 367, 368, 373
Dash-Scheuer, A., 330
Davenport, D. S., 453, 454
David, D., 203
David, L., 202
Davies, C. A., 239
Davis, A. J., 80
Davis, C., 187
Davis, C. J., 126, 134
Davis, J. A., 126
Davis, M. H., 269 (tab), 272
Davis, P., 130
De Jong, G. F., 167
de Lima, M. P., 266
De Ment, T., 324, 325, 329
De Vos, G. A., 295
de Wolf, A., 36
Dean, B. L., 41
Deaux, K., 134
DeBaryshe, B. D., 72, 76
Deci, E. L., 56
DeGanno, D. S., 461
Del Pilar, G. H., 293
DeLisi, M., 269 (tab), 273
Dell, D. M., 127
DeMent, T., 99
Demo, D. H., 329
DeNavas-Walt, C., 94
Denton, K., 108
Denzin, N. K., 51, 55, 56
Der, H., 284
Der-Karabetian, A., 456
Der-McLeod, D., 81
Dernier, O., 396
DeRubeis, R. J., 454, 456
DesJardins, K., 365, 373, 374n2

Desmond, B., 81
Devereux, E., 289
Devos, T., 128, 129, 198
Dhingra, P., 133
Di Minno, M., 219
Diaz, R. M., 97
Dickason, D., 231
Dickson, G. L., 215
Dickson, W., 97
Diener, C., 295
Diener, E., 31, 32, 295
DiJiosia, M., 109
DiNicola, V., 187
DiNoia, J., 367
Dion, K. K., 330
Dion, K. L., 77, 330
Dishion, T. J., 127
Dixon, D. N., 152, 436
Dodge, K. A., 369
Doh, H.-S., 40
Doi, T. C. E., 274
Dolan, B., 187, 433
Dolan, L. M., 306
Dolan-Delvecchio, K., 373
Domanski, M. D., 396,
    397 (tab), 423
Donatelle, R. J., 311
Dong, Y. T., 422 (tab), 423
Dopkins, S. C., 270
Dorham, C. L., 127
Dornbusch, S. M., 75, 76, 112
Doshi, S. J., 132
Doss, B. D., 200
Dovidio, J. F., 130
Dowd, B., 385 (tab)
Drantz, D. S., 304
Driscoll, A. K., 389, 390 (tab)
Du, N., 437
Du Bois, B., 363
Du Bois, W. E. B., 131
Duan, C., 253, 272
Duan, N., 368, 384, 454, 455
Dubanoski, J. P., 269 (tab), 273
Duefield, C. A., 171
DuFour, M. C., 218
Dunagan, M. S., 332
Dunahoo, C. L., 330
Dunn, L. M., 425
Dunn, R., 268 (tab), 270
Duong, D. A., 312
Duong Tran, Q., 171
Durvasula, R., 386
Durvasula, R. S., 328
Dyck, J. L., 269 (tab), 272
Dye, J. L., 74
Dyregov, A., 231

Eaker, E. D., 309
Eastman, K., 332
Eaton, W. W., 308
Ebbin, A. J., 247, 248

Ebreo, A., 35, 48
Eccles, J. S., 125
Edgerly, E., 220
Edman, J. L., 332, 389, 390 (tab),
    432, 462
Edwards, V., 369
Egan, J., 202
Egan, M. K., 451
Eggebeen, D. J., 73
Egusa, G., 310
Ehreth, J., 430, 431
Eichenfield, G. A., 251, 252
Eisenberg, L., 216
Eisenberg, M., 93
Eisenberg, N., 272
Eisler, R. M., 204, 205
Ekman, P., 292
Elfenbein, H. A., 460
Elkin, I., 451
Elliott, K. S., 219
Ellis, M. V., 249
Elmes, G. A., 308
Elon, L., 172
Else, R. N., 127
Elvine-Kreis, B., 457
Embretson, S. E., 60
Emerson, R. M., 53, 54, 55, 56
Emery, G., 422 (tab), 423, 453
Endler, N. S., 330
Endo, R., 20
Enomoto, K., 276, 330, 432
Enrile, A. V., 440
Enriquez, V. G., 72
Eo, E., 432
Epel, E., 372
Epstein, N., 269 (tab), 272
Erez, A., 271, 272
Erickson, C. D., 332
Erikson, E., 88, 98, 215
Escobar, J. I., 383, 458
Eshlemaii, S., 382, 383, 384, 387
Eshleman, S., 458
Esperat, M. C., 308, 310
Espiritu, Y. L., 77, 79, 107, 117,
    132, 133, 134, 198, 342
Estes, L. S., 187
Eth, S., 238
Ethier, K. A., 134
Evanoski, P. O., 171
Everson, H. T., 58
Everson-Rose, S. A., 304, 305, 309
Ewen, R. B., 265
Ewing, N. J., 268 (tab), 270
Exum, H. A., 255, 436
Eyler, A. A., 311
Eyre, H. L., 459
Ezzo, J., 455

Fahs, M., 219, 221
Fairbank, J. A., 33
Fairchild, H. H., 30, 32

Fals-Stewart, W., 267, 268 (tab)
Fan, R. M., 275, 383
Faravelli, C., 382
Farley, T. H., 315
Farver, J. A. M., 72, 372
Fava, M., 218, 381, 383, 392, 394
    (tab), 395 (tab), 457
Fawzi, M. C. S., 231
Federal Bureau of
    Investigation, 128
Feinleib, M., 309
Feldman, C. M., 367
Feliciano, C., 98
Felitti, V. J., 369
Feng, D., 308, 310
Feng, W. Y., 94
Fenton, R. E., 99
Feren, D. B., 172
Fernandez, M., 172
Fernandez, T., 144, 145
Ferrari, J. R., 288, 459
Ferrari, M., 91–92
Feshbach, S., 126
Feurer, I. D., 368
Fierro-Cobas, V., 97
Fillmore, L. W., 78
Fine, S., 439
Finkelhor, D., 370
Finn, J., 367
Fischbacher, C., 311
Fischer, J., 197, 203, 205
Fischer, S. R., 348
Fisher, C. B., 99
Fisher, S., 269 (tab), 272
Fiske, S. T., 127, 290, 330, 333
Fitzgibbon, M., 248, 255
Flannery, W. P., 33
Flaskerud, J. H., 431, 432, 434
Fleming, J. E., 370
Flisher, A. J., 369
Flores, L. Y., 247, 249, 255
Foley, D. J., 217, 309
Folkman, S., 312, 323
Follette, V. M., 461
Folstein, M. F., 381, 425, 458
Folstein, S. E., 425
Folts, E., 220
Foltz, K., 344
Fong, G., 72, 76
Fong, K. M., 183
Fong, R., 438
Fong, T. P., 344
Ford, D., 330
Ford, D. E., 308
Ford, T. E., 199
Forman, B. D., 144, 206, 327
Forster, P., 434, 435
Fortenbach, V. A., 272
Foster, J., 389, 390 (tab)
Fouad, N. A., 79, 151, 160, 161,
    163, 164, 171, 255

Fountain, H., 32
Fox, D., 38
Fraleigh, M., 76
Frances, A., 439
Frank, A. C., 161, 166, 276
Frank, E., 172
Frank, J. D., 451, 460
Frankel, M., 230, 237
Frasure-Smith, N., 308
Freedland, K. E., 309
Freedman, D. G., 94
Freedman, N., 94
Freeley, R., 310
Freeman, J. L., 95
Freimer, N., 439
Freire-Bebeau, L., 291, 292
French, S., 267, 268 (tab)
Frensch, P. A., 95
Fretz, R. I., 53, 54, 55, 56
Freud, S., 88, 266
Frey, L. L., 332
Fried, S. B., 213, 215, 220
Friedlander, M. L., 35–36
Friend, R., 422 (tab), 424
Frisch, M. B., 291
Froggett, L., 324, 328
Fromm, S., 369
Fu, M., 185, 190
Fu, V., 326
Fu, V. R., 96, 371
Fuchs, L., 346, 348
Fuentes-Afflick, E., 95
Fuertes, J., 197
Fugita, S., 72
Fugita, S. S., 93
Fujii, D. E., 410, 425
Fujii, J. S., 168
Fujila, K., 327
Fujimoto, W., 311
Fujimoto, W. Y., 311
Fujino, D., 74, 238
Fujino, D. C., 52, 189, 190, 197,
    200, 289, 384, 385 (tab), 430,
    432, 434, 456
Fujita, K., 422 (tab), 424
Fujitomi, I., 184
Fukushima, S. N., 168
Fukuyama, M. A., 291, 293
Fula, K. T., 438
Fuligni, A. J., 111, 112, 127,
    133, 134
Fultz, J., 269 (tab), 272
Fung, H. H., 131
Fung, M. C., 454
Fung, X.-S., 315
Furnham, A., 187, 248,
    250, 251
Furoto, S. M., 75
Furukawa, T., 252
Furutani, W., 350
Furuto, S. M., 237

Gable, R. K., 202
Gaertner, S. L., 130
Gainor, K. A., 254
Galanis, D. J., 218
Galea'i, K. E., 315
Gallagher-Thompson, D., 217, 219
Gallo, J. J., 308, 330, 396
Gamst, G., 456
Ganellen, R. J., 270
Ganesan, S., 439
Gangestad, S. W., 271
Gannon, M., 133
Gara, M. A., 383
Garcia, C., 272
Garcia, E. E., 131
Garcia, H. V., 88, 89 (fig), 90, 92
Garcia Coll, C. T., 3, 88, 89 (fig),
    90, 92, 93
Gardner, D., 246, 247
Gardner, R. W., 72
Gardner, W. L., 288
Garfinkel, P. E., 187
Garland, A. F., 369, 370
Garner, D. M., 187
Gartner, R., 366
Gatz, M., 80, 219, 221
Gee, E., 184
Gee, G. C., 91, 329
Gee, K. K., 437
Gehrie, M. J., 438, 440
Geisinger, K. F., 418, 419
Gelfand, L. A., 454
Gelfand, M. J., 127
Gelles, R. J., 364, 370, 374n2
Gelso, C. J., 154, 204, 437
Gemake, J., 268 (tab), 270
Genes, R. J., 364, 365
Genesee, F., 77
George, L. K., 215
George, M., 117
Germino-Hausken, E., 108
Gerrard, M., 58
Gershuny, B. S., 454
Gerton, J., 5, 34, 98, 130, 131,
    150, 297
Gessner, T. L., 268 (tab), 270
Ghatak, R., 112
Gibbs, J. T., 91, 92
Gibson, M. A., 77, 116, 117, 118
Gibson, R. C., 216
Gilbert, L. A., 191
Gilbody, S., 309
Gilligan, C., 133
Gim, R. H., 152, 433
Ginges, N. G., 230
Giovannucci, E., 309
Gladstone, G., 381, 382, 386, 457
Glass, C. R., 451
Glass, R., 306
Glassman, A. H., 308
Glater, J. D., 284

Glenn, P. A., 188
Glick, J. E., 74
Glick, P., 290
Glidden, C., 167
Glidden, D., 434, 435
Glipa, J., 389, 390 (tab)
Gloria, A. M., 153
Glutting, J. J., 60–61
Goates, M. K., 154, 437
Goe, W. R., 250
Goebert, D. A., 127
Goldberg, D. P., 382
Goldfried, A. P., 291
Goldfried, M. R., 291
Gong, Y. X., 422 (tab), 424
Gonzales, E. W., 308, 310
Gonzales, N., 75
Gonzales, N. A., 133
Good, B., 216, 237
Good, G. E., 191, 202, 205
Goodman, E., 306
Goodwin, R. D., 369
Gordon, P., 217
Gore, S., 390 (tab)
Gorman, J. C., 371
Gortmaker, S. L., 311
Gorzalka, B. B., 268 (tab), 271
Goto, S. G., 97, 145, 329, 452,
    453, 459
Gottman, J. M., 74
Gould, L. J., 247
Goyette, K., 108, 112, 114
Graham, S., 114
Grantham-MacGregor, S., 95
Gratch, L. V., 394 (tab)
Graves, A., 422 (tab), 425
Graves, A. B., 218
Graves, T. D., 142
Gray, H., 311
Greenberg, B., 238
Greenberger, A., 389, 390 (tab),
    394 (tab)
Greenberger, D., 453
Greenberger, E., 267, 271, 285,
    332, 394 (tab)
Greene, A. F., 410, 411
Greene, B., 184, 191
Greene, P., 131, 327
Greene, S., 94
Greenfield, P. M., 53
Greenfield, T. K., 291, 293
Greenhalgh, A., 127
Greenwald, A. G., 274
Greenwald, S., 369, 382
Greer Sullivan, J., 392, 393 (tab),
    395 (tab), 396
Gresham, R. L., Jr., 381, 457
Gretchen, D., 423
Grewal, S., 324
Grieco, E. M., 73
Grigorenko, E. L., 270

Grills, S., 55, 56
Grilo, C. M., 187
Grossman, P., 455, 461
Grove, K., 75
Groves, K. S., 287
Gruenberg, E., 398
Guamaccia, P., 394 (tab),
    395 (tab), 396
Guerrero, J. L., 315
Guijarro, M. L., 309
Guillermo, T., 186, 187, 188,
    189, 191
Guimares, B. L., 283
Gullahorn, J. E., 251
Gullahorn, J. T., 251
Guo, Z., 219
Gupta, M. D., 77
Gupta, S., 198, 329
Gutierrez, P. M., 398
Gutkin, T. B., 49
Gutmann, D., 214

Hackett, G., 160, 163, 166, 173
Hadhazy, V. A., 455
Haera, H., 219
Hafen, M., 72
Haidar, S., 354
Haines, D. W., 169
Hall, A. E., 311
Hall, C. C. I., 184, 187
Hall, G. C. N., 21, 30, 31, 188,
    190, 332, 449, 450, 456,
    460, 461
Hall, G. N., 52, 432
Hallet, A. J., 309
Halverson, J. A., 308
Ham, M. D. C., 342, 439
Hamayan, E., 77
Hambleton, R. K., 60
Hamby, S. L., 370
Hamilton, C. V., 343
Hamm, J. V., 97
Hammer, L. D., 187
Hammersley, M., 51, 54
Han, M., 133
Han, Y. S., 438
Hanassab, S., 249, 251
Hance, M., 309
Hankin, J. H., 310
Hanna, S. E., 270
Hansen, A. A., 350
Hansen, D., 239
Hansen, D. I, 438
Hansen, I. G., 134
Hansen, N. D., 410, 411
Hanson Kahn, P., 439
Happersett, C. J., 80
Harbin, J. M., 154, 437
Hardin, E., 30, 31, 79, 107, 108
Hardin, E. E., 151, 163, 165, 174
Harford, T. C., 218

Hargreaves, W. A., 434, 435
Haritatos, J., 38
Harland, J., 311
Harlow, S., 392, 393 (tab)
Harnish, R., 134
Harper, J. M., 439
Harren, V., 163
Harris, C. I., 198
Harris, L. C., 145
Harris, P. M., 73, 77, 78
Harrison, A. A., 151, 161, 162,
    165, 166, 174
Harrison, A. O., 88, 93
Harrison, K., 133
Hartle, T., 250
Haruki, G., 80
Hasegawa, K., 422 (tab), 425
Haslam, N., 187
Hastings, P. D., 94
Hastings, S. O., 324
Hatanaka, H., 432, 434
Hau, K., 76
Haudek, C., 187
Hauff, E., 231
Havas, S., 311
Haydel, K. F., 187
Hayden, D., 255
Hayes, L., 311
Hayes, R. L., 252
Hayes, S. C., 461
Hayes, T. J., 171, 172
Haynes, S. B., 309
Haynes, S. G., 309
Hays, C. L., 237
Hays, P. A., 410, 411, 412 (tab),
    414, 415
Hazen, A., 386
Healy, C. C., 170
Heath, A. E., 141, 155
Heaton, R., 424
Hechanova-Alampay, R., 252
Heck, R., 49
Hedden, T., 215
Hee, S. J., 417
Hee-Soon, J., 219
Heejung, S., 332
Heiby, E. M., 269 (tab), 273
Hein, J., 329
Heine, S. J., 270, 283, 295, 296
Helms, B. J., 202
Helms, J. E., 30, 32, 33, 131, 133,
    203, 206, 327
Helms, L., 257
Helstrom, A. W., 188, 190
Helzer, J. E., 218, 398
Hender, J., 94
Henderson, B. E., 310
Henker, B., 187
Henkin, W. A., 439
Henry, P. J., 289
Henwood, K., 56

Heppner, M. J., 257
Hermans, H. J. M., 32
Hernandez, J., 203
Herr, E. L., 249
Herrick, C. A., 410
Hershberger, S. L., 57, 60
Herskovits, M. J., 142
Herzog, D. B., 311
Hess, D., 128
Hess, R., 97
Hessol, N. A., 95
Hezel, F. X., 398
Hickey, G. G., 238
Hicks, M. H., 395 (tab), 396
Hicks, R. A., 187
Hickson, J., 270
Higgins, R. L., 291
Higham, J., 346
Higuchi, S., 218
Hill, C. E., 154, 272, 437
Hill, L., 311
Hill, P. C., 274
Hill, P. T., 115
Hill, S., 203
Hilliard, K. M., 52, 217, 218, 387,
    396, 397 (tab)
Hillygus, J., 219
Hilton, B. A., 324
Him, C., 231
Himes, C. L., 73
Hines, D. A., 74
Hines, R M., , 324
Hinton, D., 454, 460, 461
Hinton, L., 219
Hinton, W. L., 230, 231
Hiraga,Y., 75
Hirayama, H., 186, 188
Hirayama, K. K., 186, 188
Hirsch, L., 203
Hishinuma, E. S., 127,
    391 (tab), 398
Ho, C. K., 188, 367, 368, 373, 438
Ho, D., 96
Ho, D. Y. F., 371, 438
Ho, M. K., 167, 440
Ho, R. M., 422 (tab), 423
Hobbs, F., 1
Hobfoll, S. E., 330
Hodge, C. N., 134
Hoffman, C. M., 113
Hofstede, G., 71, 142
Hogan, D. P., 73
Hohm, C. F., 371
Holladay, S. J., 288
Holland, J. L., 161, 163
Hollon, S. D., 450, 453, 454, 456
Holmes, D., 394 (tab),
    395 (tab), 396
Holmes, J. G., 270
Holmes, S., 202, 205
Holt, D. J., 440

Holtzworth-Munroe, A., 364
Hom, A., 437
Homma, A., 422 (tab), 425
Homma-True, R., 332
Homung, C. A., 366
Hong, E., 268 (tab), 270
Hong, G. K., 315, 342, 370,
    371, 439
Hong, L. K., 370, 371
Hong, S., 59, 148, 149
Hong, S. H., 59
Hong, Y., 134
Hong, Z. G., 311
Hook, J. V., 74
Hooley, J. M., 400
Hooyman, N. R., 216
Hopkins, J. R., 200
Horenczyk, G., 130, 131, 134
Horn, J. L., 58
Horn, S. M., 457
Horton, A. M., 424, 425
Horwitz, R. I., 309
Hosoda, M., 314
Hotaling, G. T., 367
Hotaling, M., 35–36
Hou, F., 127, 234, 330
Hough, R., 386
Hough, R. L., 369, 370,
    385 (tab), 431
Houlihan, D., 269 (tab), 272
Hoven, C. W., 369
Howard, A., 75
Howard, C., 99
Howard, E. E., 185, 323, 325,
    326, 327
Howard-Hamilton, M. F., 127
Howarth, S., 218, 383, 392, 394
    (tab), 395 (tab)
Hoyos Nervi, C., 383
Hrebícková, M., 293
Hsia, C., 460, 461
Hsia, J., 164–165, 166, 171,
    172, 311
Hsu, E., 239, 438
Hsu, J., 72, 74
Hsu, L. K., 381
Hsu, L. K. G., 458
Hsu, M., 422, 422 (tab)
Hsu, R. T., 314
Hu, L., 52, 59, 190, 238, 285, 288,
    292, 293
Hu, L. T., 383, 384, 385 (tab),
    400n2, 430, 431, 432,
    434, 456
Hu, T. W., 385 (tab)
Huang, B., 306, 310
Huang, J., 52
Huang, J. S., 154, 190, 381, 436,
    439, 452, 454, 461, 462
Huang, K., 50, 232
Huang, L., 52

Huang, L. N., 69, 74, 82, 91, 92,
    98, 232, 235, 236, 410
Huang, P., 314
Huang, V., 217, 422 (tab), 423
Huang, Z., 385 (tab)
Hubinette, T., 41
Huff, R. M., 439
Hughes, D., 99
Hughes, M., 329, 382, 383,
    384, 387, 458
Hui, C. H., 251
Hui, K. K., 312
Hui, M. K., 125, 135n1
Huisman, K. A., 368, 373
Hull, W. F., 246, 248, 251, 252
Hulsizer, M. R., 330
Humes, K., 197, 198
Hune, S., 38, 128, 131, 132, 328
Hung, Y., 33, 112
Hunter, C. D., 327, 330, 331
Huntsinger, C. S., 109, 371
Huntsinger, P. R., 371
Huo, Y. J., 130
Hurh, W. M., 167, 285, 296, 392,
    393 (tab)
Hurlburt, M. S., 386, 431
Hurtado, A., 131
Hussong, A. M., 58
Huston, A. C., 75
Hwang, J., , 454, 461
Hwang, L. J., 311
Hwang, M., 257, 331, 333
Hwang, S., 74
Hwang, W., 450, 462
Hwang, W. C., 382, 398, 399, 400
Hwu, H. G., 382
Hyde, J. S., 271

Ibrahim, E., 351
Ickovics, J., 372
Ida, D. J., 91, 98
Ignatiev, N., 133
Igra, I., 310, 312
Ikels, C., 80
Ima, K., 117, 236, 371
Imai, Y., 422 (tab), 425
Inman, A. G., 74, 81, 185, 186,
    188, 323, 324, 325–326, 327,
    328, 329, 330, 331, 332, 333,
    342, 352, 353, 439
Ino, S., 285, 291, 293, 387, 424
Inose, M., 131, 252, 253, 327,
    330, 332
Inouye, J., 308, 310
Institute of Medicine, 308, 449
Inui, T. S., 235, 386
Ishibashi, K., 78
Iso, H., 309
Itai, G., 221, 222
Ito, C., 310
Ito, K. L., 72, 434, 439

Ivey, A. E., 255
Ivey, D., 160, 161, 165, 166
Iwamasa, G. Y., 52, 214, 215, 217,
    218, 221, 342, 387, 396, 397
    (tab), 460, 461
Iwamoto, D., 200, 203
Iwamoto, D. K., 203
Iwasaki, M., 310
Iyengar, S. S., 131
Iyer, D. S., 187
Izutsu, S., 398

Ja, D. Y., 291, 366
Jackson, J. S., 216, 312, 372
Jackson, L. A., 134
Jackson, P. B., 91
Jackson-Triche, M. E., 392, 393
    (tab), 395 (tab), 396
Jacob, E. J., 251
Jacobson, M. F., 198
Jadad, A. R., 455
Jaeger, E., 90
Jaffee, S. R., 364, 369
Jai, P. R., 219
Jalali, F., 268 (tab), 270
Jalbert, R. R., 228, 229, 230, 234
Jambunathan, S., 370, 371
James, D. C. S., 96, 98
James, Q. C., 430
Jarama, S. L., 292
Jarcho, J., 332
Jasinskaja-Lahti, I., 135n1
Jasinski, J. L., 364
Jasso, R., 145
Jaya, A., 439
Jayadev, R., 352, 353
Jenkins, R., 3, 88, 89 (fig), 90, 92
Jensen, A. R., 95
Jensen, M., 255
Jensen, R. H., 284
Jepsen, D. A., 159, 167, 255, 332,
    433, 436
Jernigan, M., 32
Jerrell, J. M., 385 (tab)
Jetten, J., 132
Jhoo, J. H., 422 (tab), 424, 425
Ji, L., 131
Jin, R., 396
Joe, H., 61
Johnson, C. A., 310
Johnson, D. J., 90, 92
Johnson, D. L., 77, 185
Johnson, F. A., 291
Johnson, J. G., 369, 370
Johnson, J. L., 324
Johnson, K. R., 289
Johnson, M. L., 457
Johnson, R. C., 330, 332, 391
    (tab), 432, 462
Johnson, V. E., 271
Johnson-Powell, G., 91

Jolly, A., 332
Jones, D. F., 311
Jones, J. M., 343
Jones, N. A., 73, 77, 78
Jöreskog, K. G., 58
Jorgannathon, P., 188, 190
Jose, P. E., 109, 371
Joseph, C., 218
Josephs, R. A., 268 (tab)
Jost, J. T., 290
Joyce, A. S., 458
Juang, L. P., 72
Judge, R., 454
Judge, T. A., 271, 272
Jue, S., 220
Julian, T. W., 269 (tab), 273
Jung, S., 327
Junkin, D., 344
Juvonen, J., 114

Kado, S., 310
Kaduvettoor, A., 74
Kagan, J., 94
Kagawa-Singer, M., 229, 230, 231,
    234, 237, 238, 432
Kai, N., 314
Kakar, S., 323
Kallivayalil, D., 185, 459
Kalmuss, D. S., 364
Kameoka, V. A., 216, 217, 269
    (tab), 273, 276, 433
Kan, S. H., 310
Kana'iapuni, S. M., 78
Kanatsu, A., 111
Kang, G. E., 216, 220, 221
Kang, S., 423
Kang, S. Y., 396, 397 (tab)
Kang, T. S., 216, 220, 221
Kannel, W. B., 309
Kanouse, D. E., 271
Kanungo, R. N., 287
Kao, G., 78–79, 109, 110, 111,
    112, 116, 289
Kao, S. C., 438
Kaplan, H. S., 271
Kaplan, J., 309
Kaplan, M. S., 312
Kaprio, J., 309
Karasek, R. A., 309
Kashima, Y., 131
Kashiwagi, K., 97, 295
Kashubeck, S., 187
Kasindorf, M., 344
Kasper, V., 127, 330
Kaste, M., 348
Katayama, M., 438
Katon, W., 396
Katzman, M. A., 187
Kaufman Kantor, G. F., 364
Kaur, K. P., 352
Kavanagh, D. J., 431

Kavanaugh, M., 94
Kaw, E., 187
Kawachi, I., 306, 309
Kawahara, D. M., 183
Kay, R., 309
Keane, E. M., 230
Kearsley, R. B., 94
Keller, J., 311
Kelley, M. L., 370, 371
Kemmelmeier, M., 32, 459
Kemp, S. E., 352
Kempen, H. J. G., 32
Kennedy, B. P., 306
Kennedy, M. A., 268 (tab), 271
Keopraseuth, K. O., 238, 437, 457
Kessler, R. C., 185, 330, 368, 382,
    383, 384, 387, 396, 458
Khoi, S., 171
Khoo, G., 145, 175, 253, 422
Khoun, F., 229, 230
Kibria, N., 77, 79, 132, 133, 134,
    200, 325
Killen, J. D., 187
Kim, A., 327, 328
Kim, A. B., 188, 323, 328, 330,
    331, 332, 333
Kim, B. S., 190, 275
Kim, B. S. K., 31, 33, 143, 146,
    147–148, 149, 150, 152, 153,
    154, 155, 198, 203, 249, 256,
    275, 333, 433, 436, 437, 439,
    452, 454, 461, 462
Kim, C., 125, 135n1
Kim, C. J., 41
Kim, D., 153
Kim, E. H., 199
Kim, E. J., 197, 202
Kim, E. Y., K., 439
Kim, G., 81, 325, 326, 372
Kim, H. H., 152
Kim, H. S., 131
Kim, I. J., 154, 190, 367, 436, 439,
    452, 454, 461, 462
Kim, J., 133, 310
Kim, J. G. S., 330
Kim, J. H., 221, 422 (tab),
    424, 425
Kim, J. I., 215
Kim, J. M., 438
Kim, J. Y., 365, 368, 374n3
Kim, K., 80, 220
Kim, K. C., 167, 285, 296, 392,
    393 (tab)
Kim, K. K., 310
Kim, K. W., 422 (tab), 424, 425
Kim, L. S., 389, 391 (tab)
Kim, M. T., 384
Kim, S., 167, 392, 394 (tab)
Kim, S. C., 190
Kim, S. S., 127
Kim, S. Y., 91, 97

Kim, T. E., 97
Kim, U., 31, 327
Kim-Ju, G. M., 134
Kimmel, M., 198
Kincaid, D. L., 168
Kindaichi, M., 254
Kinder, D. R., 288
King, A. C., 311
King, D. W., 33
King, L. A., 274
Kinoshita, L., 217
Kinzie, D., 230
Kinzie, J., 217, 437, 439
Kinzie, J. D., 229, 238, 239,
    285, 430
Kirk, B. A., 160, 161, 165, 166,
    172, 276
Kirkeby, J., 384, 385 (tab),
    430, 431
Kirmayer, L. J., 380, 400n1
Kirsch, I., 451, 460
Kishimoto, Y., 257
Kitano, H. H. L., 345–346, 348,
    367, 438
Kitano, M. K., 109
Kitayama, S., 31, 32, 72, 97,
    272, 274, 283, 292, 295,
    323, 330, 331
Kiyak, H., 216
Klatsky, A. L., 310, 311, 312
Klein, M. H., 248, 255
Kleinman, A., 216, 221, 237, 380
Kleinman, A. M., 235, 237, 381,
    386, 458
Kleinman, J., 237
Klessig, J., 80
Kline, M. V., 439
Klineberg, O., 246, 248, 251, 252
Klonoff, E. A., 191
Klopf, D. W., 285, 291
Knutson, B., 131
Kobayashi, R., 314
Kobayashi, S., 422 (tab), 424
Kobori, A., 332
Koenig, B. A., 80
Koeske, G. F., 252, 254, 392,
    394 (tab)
Koff, E., 187
Koh, S., 424
Kohn, L., 450, 462
Kohn, L. P., 438
Koibly, N. B., 454
Kolonel, L. N., 310
Kong, D., 250
Konrad, A. M., 127
Koplewicz, H. S., 389, 390 (tab)
Korbin, J. E., 75
Koretz, D., 396
Korn/Ferry International, 284
Kost, C., 217, 387, 396, 397 (tab)
Kottler, J., 250

Koyama, M., 437
Kramer, E. J., 437
Kramer, R. A., 369
Kramer, T., 456
Krantz, D. S., 303
Krauss, S., 422 (tab), 423
Kravitz, H. M., 392, 393 (tab)
Kreiger, N., 312
Kristal, A. R., 310
Krogh, V., 309
Kroll, J., 439
Krueger, R. A., 51
Krumboltz, J. D., 162, 197, 435
Krupnick, J. L., 451
Krysan, M., 288
Kuga, D., 311
Kukull, W. A., 218
Kulig, J. C., 271
Kuller, L. H., 309
Kumantika, S., 310, 311
Kung, W. V., 462
Kung, W. W., 433
Kunn, P., 422, 422 (tab)
Kuo, H.-S., 432, 433
Kuo, W. H., 217, 285, 381, 392,
    393 (tab), 423
Kurasaki, K., 384, 392, 394 (tab),
    396, 398, 399, 457, 458
Kurasaki, K. S., 21, 386, 387
Kurien, P., 133
Kurtines, W., 144, 146
Kurtines, W. M., 144, 145, 372
Kurtz, D. A., 206
Kwak, J. C., 161
Kwak, K., 72
Kwan, K. K., 423
Kwan, V. S. Y., 290
Kwon, J., 190, 285, 288, 292, 293
Kwong, A., 330, 331
Kwong, K., 454

L'Abate, L., 439
Laberty, G., 3
LaCroix, A. Z., 309
Ladany, N., 81, 185, 326, 327, 328
LaFromboise, L., 297
LaFromboise, T., 5, 34, 98, 130,
    131, 150, 450, 462
Lai, C. F., 164
Lai, E. W. M., 324, 326, 327
Lai, L., 314
Lai, V., 351
Lam, A. G., 330
Lam, A. P., 431
Lam, C. S., 315
Lam, C. Y., 388, 393 (tab), 423
Lam, D., 219
Lam, D. H., 388
Lam, D. J., 324, 325
Lambert, M. J., 436
Lambert, R. G., 436

Lamberty, G., 88, 89 (fig), 90, 92
Lamborn, S. D., 75
Lan, W. Y., 247
Land, A. J., 270
Landress, H. J., 369–370
Landreth, G. L., 438
Landrine, H., 191
Landsford, J. E., 80
Landsverk, J., 369, 370, 431
Lao, L., 455
Larney, L. C., 35–36
Laroche, M., 125, 135n1
Larson, E., 422 (tab), 425
Larson, E. B., 218
Larson, J. H., 72
Larson, S. L., 109
Lattuca, L. R., 42
Lau, A., 313, 434, 435, 438, 450,
    456, 462
Lau, A. L. D., 314
Lau, A. S., 369, 370, 372
Lau, A. S. L., 432, 440
Lau, E. Y., 255, 436
Lau, J. T. F., 370
Lau, S., 76
Laursen, B., 269 (tab)
Lauver, P. J., 252
Lavee, Y., 332
Lavelle, J., 228, 229, 230, 231
Law, P. F. M., 432
Lawson, W. E., 311
Lay, C., 126
Lazarus, R. S., 323
Le, H., 458
Leaf, P. J., 432, 433
Lebowitz, B. D., 396
Lebra, T. S., 74
LeCompte, M. D., 53, 55, 56
Lee, A. M., 187
Lee, C. C., 331
Lee, D. B., 197
Lee, D. Y., 422 (tab), 424, 425
Lee, E., 21, 52, 345, 367, 368,
    438, 449
Lee, F., 133, 134
Lee, J., 252
Lee, J. H., 422 (tab), 424, 425
Lee, J. J., 119
Lee, K. U., 422 (tab), 424, 425
Lee, L. C., 1, 21, 92, 237, 351–352
Lee, M. K., 59
Lee, M. Y., 432
Lee, P. A., 30, 33, 34, 112, 126,
    127, 130, 131, 132, 133, 197,
    330, 381
Lee, R., 326, 330, 332
Lee, R. G., 38
Lee, R. M., 40, 41, 81, 127, 325,
    326, 330, 372, 423
Lee, S., 171, 187, 190, 380, 384,
    454, 455

Lee, S. H., 429
Lee, S. J., 114, 116, 117, 118, 119, 200, 201
Lee, S. M., 233
Lee, V. E., 108
Lee, W. H., 128, 345
Lee, W. M. L., , 432, 436
Lee, Y., 116, 314
Lee, Y. S., 330
Leff, J., 388
Lehman, D. R., 270, 283, 295, 324
Leiderman, P., 76
Lent, R. W., 160, 163, 166, 173
Leo-Summers, L., 309
Leon, J. J., 133
Leonard, A., 310, 312
Leonard, K. I., 351
Leong, C. W., 367
Leong, F. T. L., 6, 11, 12, 13, 19, 20, 21, 30, 31, 42, 79, 107, 108, 151, 152, 153, 159, 160, 161, 162, 163, 165, 166, 167, 170, 171, 172, 173, 174, 175, 185, 191, 247, 248, 249, 252, 255, 256, 257, 258, 274, 285, 290–291, 385 (tab), 417, 419, 429, 432, 433, 438, 440, 452 453
Leong, R. C., 351
Leor, J., 309
Lepper, M. R., 131
Lerner, J. V., 72
Lerner, R., 88
Lesperance, F., 308
Leu, J., 133, 134
Leung, C. M., 187
Leung, J., 217, 387
Leung, K., 275, 383
Leung, L., 115, 188, 268 (tab), 271
Leung, L.-S., 73
Leung, P., 229, 238, 315, 437
Leung, S., 160, 161, 165, 166
Leung, T., 187
Levant, R. F., 197, 201, 202, 203, 205, 449
Levenson, H. M., 271, 272
Levin, M. J., 72
Levin, S., 126, 127, 134
Levkoff, S., 219
Lew, A., 69, 74, 82
Lew, S., 30, 33, 126, 145, 202, 276, 422, 422 (tab), 435
Lew, W. J., 76
Lewis, T. T., 304, 305, 309
Lewis-Jack, O., 424, 425
Li, L., 454, 455
Li, L. C., 31, 33, 148, 154, 198, 275, 437, 439
Li, L. J., 387
Li, R., 327

Li, R. H., 131
Li, Y. Q., 309
Li, Z., 395 (tab), 396
Liang, C. T., 333
Liang, C. T. H., 33, 154, 198
Liang, T. H., 437, 439
Liang, W., 51
Liaw, F., 109
Liaw, F.-R., 371
Licht, D. M., 400
Lie, J., 36
Liebkind, K., 130, 131, 134, 135n1, 234
Liem, J. H., 439
Liem, R., 134, 288
Lien, P., 132, 133
Liese, L. H., 258
Lim, J., 419
Lin, C. C., 96
Lin, C. Y., 326
Lin, C.-Y. C., 371
Lin, E. H., 237
Lin, H., 252
Lin, J. C. G., 255, 256, 257
Lin, K., 396, 397 (tab), 457, 458
Lin, K. M., 229, 234, 235, 237, 238, 384, 386, 387, 388, 392, 394 (tab), 396, 398, 399, 439
Lin, L., 231
Lin, M., 33, 112
Lin, M. C., 388
Lin, M. H., 290
Lin, N., 381, 385 (tab), 457, 458
Lin, P.-Y., 327
Lin, T., 164
Lin, T. Y., 439
Lin, Y., 461
Lin-Fu, J. S., 184, 191
Lincoln, Y. S., 51, 55, 56
Lind, E. A., 130
Lindholm, K. J., 272
Linehan, M. M., 291, 461
Ling, H., 185
Ling, J., 199
Linn, N., 35, 48
Linnehan, F., 127
Linstone, H. A., 21
Linton, R., 142
Litt, I. F., 187
Liu, J. F., 293
Liu, J. L. Y., 370
Liu, M., 315
Liu, W., 197
Liu, W. M., 30, 185, 197, 199, 200, 201, 202–203
Liu, W. T., 80, 220, 310, 332
Liu, X., 57, 425
Liu, Y., 220
Lochner, B. T., 98
Lochner, K. A., 91
Locke, B. D., 203, 204

Lombardo, E. R., 459, 460
Lommel, J., 354
Lon, W., 219
London, M., 127
Long, J. M., 237
Long, P. D. P., 201
Longworth, S. L., 293, 387
Loo, C., 385 (tab), 392, 393 (tab)
Loo, C. M., 33, 438
Lopez, I. R., 460
Lopez, S. R., 30, 184
Lopez-Garcia, J. J., 274
Lotz, S., 127
Lowe, B. M., 285
Lowe, E. D., 398
Lowe, L., 38
Lowe, S., 52, 328
Lowe, S. M., 152
Lu, F., 437
Lu, R., 425, 439
Lu, Y. E., 431
Lu, Z. Z., 185
Lubben, J. E., 367
Lucas, M. S., 247, 249, 255
Lucero, K., 187
Luczak, S. E., 456, 457
Luhtanen, R., 126, 127, 206
Lui, H. T., 326, 330, 332
Lui, J. E., 387
Lukens, E. P., 388
Lum, J. L., 200, 365
Lum, O., 217, 422 (tab), 423
Luo, Z., 425
Lurie, N., 385 (tab)
Luthar, S. S., 70
Lutwak, N., 288, 459
Lutz, C., 292
Luu, V., 235
Lye, C., 284
Lyons, A. C., 332
Lysgaard, S., 250

Ma, G., 310
Ma, P.-W., 326, 327
MacCallum, R. C., 59
Maccoby, E., 75
MacEachern, M., 203
Machizawa, S., 217, 387
Mackay, J., 304
MacMillan, H. L., 370
Madamba, A. B., 167
Madan, A., 327
Madan-Bahel, A., 324, 328, 329, 330, 331, 332, 333, 353
Madden, T., 72, 326
Maddock, J. W., 271
Maden-Bahel, A., 326
Madriz, E., 52
Maejima, H., 314
Maekawa, H., 422 (tab), 424
Maestas, M. V., 147

Magnuson, K., 324, 326, 328
Mahalik, J. R., 200, 203, 204
Mahalingam, R., 38
Majeed, Z. A., 308
Mak, W., 34, 35, 459, 461
Mak, W. S., 98
Mak, W. W. S., 458, 462
Makini, G. K., Jr., 389
Maldonado, R., 146, 147
Malik, M. L., 59
Malley-Morison, K., 74
Mallinckrodt, B., 72, 145, 252
Malone, N., 126, 134
Malone, N, J., 78
Malony, H. N., 460
Manalansan, M. F., 49
Manaster, G. J., 133
Manber, R., 455
Mandelblatt, J. S., 51
Manson, S. M., 230, 366
Maramba, G. G., 52, 188, 190,
    434, 439, 456
Marcus, E. B., 311
Marcus, M. B., 133
Marecek, J., 50
Marín, G., 33, 423
Marino, S., 330
Markides, K. S., 216
Markovitz, J. H., 309
Markus, H., 97
Markus, H. R., 31, 32, 72, 131,
    268 (tab), 272, 274, 283,
    283.292, 295, 323, 330, 331
Marmot, M. G., 309
Marsden, P. V., 126
Marsella, A. J., 217, 276, 291, 330
Marshall, M., 398
Marshall, S., 99
Martens, R., 296
Martin, J., 75, 437, 439
Martinez, G. A., 289
Masaki, K. H., 217, 218, 219,
    309, 424
Mascher, J., 32
Mason, C. A., 75
Mason, R., 58
Mass, A. I., 189, 350, 438
Masse, L. C., 206
Masters, W. H., 271
Masuda, M., 229, 235
Matheny, K. B., 234
Mathews, C. A., 434, 435
Mathews, K., 303, 304
Matsumoto, D., 32, 216, 292
Matsumoto, V., 350
Matsumoto, Y., 310
Matsuoka, J. K., 169, 328,
    385 (tab), 431
Matthews, K. A., 309
Matthews, L., 152, 328
Mau, W., 79, 111, 255

Mau, W.-C., 332, 433, 436
Maume, D. J., 185
Maxwell, A., 310
Maydeu-Olivares, A., 61
Maykovitch, M. K., 350
Maynard, C., 430, 431
Mays, V. M., 188, 268 (tab), 271
Mazel, R., 392, 393 (tab), 395
    (tab), 396
Mazumdar, S., 182
McAdoo, H. P., 3
McArdle, J. J., 58, 391 (tab)
McBean, M., 385 (tab)
McCabe, K. M., 369, 370, 385
    (tab), 386, 431
McCallum, M., 458
McCarter, R., 311
McCarthy, P. M., 272
McCarty, C. A., 332
McCauley, E., 268 (tab)
McCeney, M. K., 303
McCourt, J., 187
McCracken, L. M., 215
McCrae, R. R., 266, 274, 291, 293
McCubbin, H., 70, 74
McCubbin, L., 74
McCubbin, M. A., 70
McCullough, B. C., 366
McCurry, S. M., 218
McDavis, R. J., 255
McDermott, J. F., 285
McDermott, J. F., Jr., 389
McDonald, R. P., 59
McDonnell, L. M., 115
McEwen, B. S., 306
McFarland, B. H., 312
McFarlane, F. R., 315
McGann, M. E., 430, 431
McGonagle, K. A., 382, 383, 384,
    387, 458
McHugh, P., 425
McKelvey, M. W., 269 (tab), 273
McKenna, K., 313, 314
McKenry, P. C., 269 (tab), 273
McKenzie Pollock, L., 438
McKinney, H., 430
McKinney, J. P., 72
McKinnon, J., 197, 198
McLaughlin, C. S., 267, 271
McLaughlin, L. A., 81
McLeod, J. D., 306
McLoyd, V. C., 75
McMaster, M. R., 269 (tab), 272
McQuillan, J., 78
McRae, C., 221, 222
Medina, A., 410
Mehrabian, A., 269 (tab), 272
Mehrota, C. M., 213, 215, 220
Meininger, J. C., 383, 389,
    390 (tab)
Mendis, G., 304

Meng, X., 384
Meng, X.-L., 368
Meredith, G. M., 269 (tab),
    272, 276
Meredith, W., 58–59
Merikangas, K. R., 396
Merrill, K. A., 454
Merta, R. J., 153, 255
Mesquita, B., 292
Meston, C. M., 268 (tab), 271
Metcalfe, J., 269 (tab), 273
Metzger, R., 218
Meyer, B., 451
Meyer, E. C., 93
Meyer, T., 218
Meyers, B., 394 (tab),
    395 (tab), 396
Mikelson, K. D., 330
Miller, D. C., 267, 268 (tab)
Miller, L. S., 432, 433
Miller, M., 218
Miller, M. H., 248, 255
Miller, P. A., 272
Miller, S. D., 438
Miller, T. Q., 309
Millsap, R. E., 58
Min, J. W., 220
Minami, D., 284
Minde, T., 327
Minematsu, A., 314
Minn, J. Y., 293, 387
Minor, C. W., 159, 167
Mintz, L. B., 187, 189
Mio, J. S., 341, 342
Miranda, A. O., 234
Miranda, J., 450, 454, 455, 462
Mischel, H. N., 273
Mischel, W., 269 (tab), 273, 293
Mischoulon, D., 217
Mistry, R. S., 75
Mitchell, J. R., 268 (tab)
Mitchell, L. K., 162
Mitchell, S. L., 127
Mitson, B. E., 350
Miyake, K., 96
Miyamoto, R. H., 391 (tab), 398
Miyazaki, H., 310
Miyong, K., 219
Miyoshi, N., 350
Mobley, M., 252
Modarres, A., 115
Moeller, H. J., 450
Moeschberger, M., 422, 422 (tab)
Moffitt, T. E., 364, 369
Moghaddam, F. M., 38
Mohr, J. J., 201
Mok, D., 327
Mok, T. A., 197, 286
Mokuau, N., 74, 434, 435
Moleiro, C., 451
Molgaard, C. A., 80

Mollica, R. F., 228, 229, 230, 231, 234, 237
Molnar, B. E., 368
Moneta, G. B., 269 (tab), 272
Moniier, J., 330
Monin, B. M., 129–130, 131, 134
Monterrosa, A., 311
Montes, L., 220
Moon, A., 80
Moon, J. H., 217
Moore, L. J., 457
Morano, C. K., 81, 185, 326, 327, 328
Morash, M., 366, 368
Morelli, G., 96
Morelli, P. T., 438
Morera, O. F., 35, 48
Mori, L., 188
Mori, S., 247, 248, 249, 252
Morishima, J., 16, 20, 21, 350
Morishima, J. K., 21
Morling, B., 330, 333
Morris, M. M., 455
Morris, M. W., 133, 134
Morrison, A. M., 329
Morrison, K., 450
Morrissey, M., 328
Morrissey, R. F., 389, 390 (tab)
Morstensen, H., 128
Morten, G., 438, 439
Morton, D. J., 80
Mosher, D. L., 201
Moskowitz, D. S., 57
Moss, S. J., 268 (tab)
Mossakowski, K. N., 126, 127
Mosso, C. O., 290
Mouanoutoua, V. L., 218
Mountcastle, A. R., 331
Mounts, N. S., 75
Mouw, T., 111
Moy, S., 438
Moyerman, D. R., 144, 206, 327
Mrazek, D. A., 271
Mrazek, P. B., 271
Muecke, M. A., 238
Muehlenkamp, J. J., 398
Mui, A. C., 396, 397 (tab), 423
Mullatti, L., 324
Mullen, M., 35
Muller, J. H., 81
Mura, D., 350
Murakami, F., 310
Murase, K., 237
Murdaugh, C., 219, 424
Murphy, E., 231
Murphy, H. B., 227
Murphy, R., 98
Murray, S., 434, 435
Murry, V. M., 202
Musgrave, D., 385 (tab)
Muthén, B., 58

Myburgh, C. P. H., 254
Myers, D., 310
Myers, D. G., 342
Myers, H. F., 382, 305, 306, 307 (fig), 316, 398, 399, 400
Myles, J., 79
Mylvaganam, G. A., 328

Nagasawa, R., 164
Nagata, D. K., 32–33, 186, 200, 229, 346, 350
Nahulu, L. B., 389, 398
Nakagawa, K., 92
Nakajima, G. A., 271
Nakamura, D., 199
Nakamura, L. N., 72, 76
Nakanishi, D., 107
Nakanishi, D. T., 351
Nakano, C., 220
Nandakumar, R., 60–61
Narang, S. K., 72, 372
Narikiyo, T. A., 216, 217, 433
Nash, D., 251
Nath, S., 324, 328, 329, 330, 331, 332, 333, 353
National Asian Pacific American Legal Consortium, 237, 329, 353
National Asian Women's Health Organization, 80
National Center for Education, , 287
National Center for Education Statistics, 108, 109, 110
National Center for Health Statistics, 304, 311, 398
National Heart, Lung, and Blood Institute, 304
National Research Council, 364, 371
National Science Foundation NSF, 161, 164, 166, 172, 173
Neault, N., 383
Neighbors, H., 372
Neighbors, H. W., 185, 312
Neilands, T., 30
Neimeyer, G. J., 141, 155
Nelson, C. B., 382, 383, 384, 387, 458
Nelson, M., 187
Nemoto, T., 50
Neumark-Sztainer, D., 267, 268 (tab)
Nevitt, J., 185, 197
Nevo, S., 187
New York Judicial Commission on Minorities, 285
Newsom, J. T., 312
Nezu, A. M., 459, 460
Nezu, C. M., 459, 460
Ng, F., 344

Ng, G. F., 31, 148, 153, 155, 275, 437, 452, 462
Ng, K. M., 161
Ng, M., 167–168
Ngai, S. W., 72
Nghe, L. T., 200
Ngo, D., 231
Ngo, V., 81, 325, 326, 372
Nguyen, D. L., 238
Nguyen, L. H., 238
Nguyen, N. A., 72, 326
Nguyen, P. H., 238
Nguyen, Q. C. X., 432
Nguyen, S., 229
Nguyen, T. D., 385 (tab)
Nguyen, T. V., 231
Nicassio, P. M., 169, 217
Nicholson, B. F., 229, 231
Nickens, H. W., 172
Nickerson, K., 99
Niemann, L., 455, 461
Nierenberg, A. A., 217, 218, 381, 383, 392, 394 (tab), 395 (tab), 457
Nightingale, D., 30
Nihaus, L., 254
Nilsson, J. E., 247, 249, 255
Nisbett, R., 215
Nisbett, R. E., 131
Nishigaya, L., 435
Nishimura, M., 81
Nishina, A., 114
Nitz, K., 80
Noh, C.-Y., 40
Noh, S., 127, 330
Nomura, A. M. Y., 310
Nomura, G. M., 181
Nordenberg, D., 369
Nordvik, H., 161
Norenzayan, A., 296
Norton, I. M., 366
Novotny, C. M., 449, 450
Nukariya, K., 91–92, 221
Nunez, J., 432, 450

Oakland, T., 60–61
Oberg, K., 250
Oberman, A., 311
O'Brien, D. J., 93
O'Brien, T. P., 169, 170
O'Campo, P. J., 99
O'Donohue, W., 269 (tab), 272
Office of Analysis and Information Management, 112–113
Office of Juvenile Justice and Delinquency Prevention, U.S. Department of Justice, 87
Office of Refugee Resettlement, 229
Office of Student Research, 113
Ogawa, Y., 309

Ogbu, J. V., 88
Oggins, J., 188
Ogrodniczuk, J. S., 458
Oh, M. Y., 331
Oh, Y., 254, 392, 394 (tab)
Ohira, T., 309
Ohnishi, H., 351
Oishi, S., 31, 32
Okagaki, L., 91, 95
Okamura, M., 310
Okazaki, S., 21, 30, 31, 48, 78, 95,
    108, 114, 145, 163, 165, 189,
    190, 228, 229, 234, 238, 254,
    271, 273, 285, 293, 387, 388,
    417, 419, 420, 421, 423, 424,
    452, 453, 459, 460, 461
Okazaki, S., & Sue, S. (2000).
    [NIT chapter 16]
Okihiro, G., 198
Okihiro, G. Y., 38
Okubo, Y., 131, 188, 323, 326,
    327, 328, 330, 331, 332, 333
Olemedo, E. L., 366
Olian, J. D., 172
Oliveira, J., 438
Oliver, M. B., 271
Olmedo, E. L., 186, 191
Omatsu, G., 119
Omi, M., 289, 342
Omizo, M. M., 150, 152,
    153, 433
Omoto, A. M., 269 (tab), 272
O'Neil, J. M., 189, 197, 202, 205
Ong, A., 38, 40, 72, 326
Ong, P., 115, 132, 133, 417
Ong, P. M., 73
Organista, P. B., 33
Ormrod, R., 370
Orona, C. J., 80
Oropeza, B. A. C., 248, 255
Orozco, C., 257
Orvaschel, H., 398
Ory, M. G., 220
Osato, S. S., 217, 218
Osipow, S. H., 151, 163, 174
Oslin, D., 217
Osman, A., 398
Ostendorf, F., 266, 293
Ostrove, J. M., 305
O'Sullivan, M. J., 384, 385 (tab),
    430, 431
Osvold, L. L., 187
Osypuk, T. L., 91
Otani, T., 310
Otto, M. W., 454, 461
Owen, D. C., 308, 310
Owen, S. V., 197, 202
Owyoung, B. H., 330
Oxman, T. E., 217
Oyserman, D., 32, 33, 133, 134,
    290, 459

Padesky, C. A., 453
Padgett, D., 220
Padilla, A. M., 272, 410
Pak, A., 330
Pallak, M. S., 12
Palley, N., 430
Palsane, M. N., 324, 325
Pan, E., 199
Pang, V. O., 200
Paniagua, F. A., 421
Panter, A. T., 58, 59
Paris, M. J., 315
Parish, B., 437
Park, D. C., 215
Park, J., 310
Park, M. S., 371, 372
Park, S. E., 151, 161, 162, 165,
    166, 174
Park, S. S., 432, 434
Park, Y. S., 153
Parker, G., 381, 382, 386, 457, 458
Parker, J. D. A., 330
Parker, J. S., 75
Parker, W. D., 293
Parr, G., 247
Parreñas, R. S., 40
Parrish, K. M., 218
Parron, D. L., 186, 191
Parrott, W. G., 459
Pasic, J., 312
Pasick, R. J., 51
Passel, J. S., 227
Pate, J. K., 169, 217
Patel, N. R., 330
Patterson, R. E., 310
Paulhus, D. L., 33, 145, 165, 253
Peake, P. K., 273
Pearl, J. H., 217
Pearson, V., 388
Peck, C. P., 267
Pedersen, P., 235, 237, 238, 239
Pederson, P. B., 141, 155, 248,
    249, 250, 251, 253, 255, 256,
    257, 258
Penaranda- Ortega, M., 274
Peng, K., 131
Peng, S. S., 79, 109, 110–111
Peou, S., 438
Pepitone-Arreola-Rockwell, F.,
    410, 411
Pepper, C. M., 388, 393 (tab), 423
Pernice, R., 186, 187
Perry, S. I., 314
Petersen, W., 106–107, 344
Peterson, C., 274
Peterson, P. D., 384, 385 (tab),
    430, 431
Peterson, W., 328
Petrovitch, H., 218, 219, 424
Pettengill, S. M., 76
Petticrew, M., 309

Pettit, G. S., 369
Pham, T., 231
Phillip, D. A. G., 438
Phillips, K. A., 440
Phillips, M. R., 400
Phinney, J. S., 30, 32, 72, 98,
    99, 126, 127, 130, 131, 133,
    134, 175, 206, 326, 371,
    422 (tab), 423
Pidgeon, N., 56
Pierce, G. R., 332
Pierce, S., 370, 371
Pike, M. C., 310
Pike, P. L., 423
Pilkonis, P. A., 451
Pine, C. J., 88, 93
Pinsky, J., 309
Piper, W. E., 458
Pittinsky, T. L., 134, 185, 290
Plake, B. S., 253
Plant, E. A., 369
Pleck, J. H., 201, 202, 203, 205
Plemons, G., 59
Plewes, J., 454
Pluralism Project, 352, 353
Podd, J., 451
Poggenpoel, M., 254
Ponterotto, J. G., 145, 153, 255,
    422, 423
Poole, C., 230, 237
Poortinga, Y. H., 142, 143, 150
Popatia, N., 324
Pope-Davis, D. B., 30, 185, 197
Porche-Burke, L., 30
Porter, J. R., 206
Porter, O. F., 113
Porter, R. Y., 185, 186, 187, 190
Portes, A., 110, 114, 115
Portman, T. A. A., 257
Pott, M., 96
Poulos, G., 112
Powell, A. L., 269 (tab), 272
Power, P. G., 163
Prathikanti, S., 324
Pratt, L. A., 308
Pratto, F., 126, 289
Prescott, C. A., 391 (tab)
Pressier, A. B., 189
Price, G., 97
Prilleltensky, I., 38
Proctor, B. D., 94
Przymus, D. E., 291, 292
Pugh, J. A., 311
Pugh, R. H., 58
Pulkkinen, L., 269 (tab)
Pyke, K., 76, 77, 117
Pyke, K. D., 185
Pynoos, R., 238

Qian, Z., 111
Qing Li, Y., 217

Qu, J., 219, 221
Qualls, S. H., 221
Quick, C., 257
Quinn, P., 268 (tab), 270
Quinones-Vidal, E., 274

Racine, Y., 370
Radloff, L., 381, 422 (tab), 423
Raghavan, C., 458
Rahman, O., 253, 330
Rai, S., 354
Ramirez, M. III, 145
Ramisetty-Mikler, S., 325, 329
Randolph, S. M., 99
Rao, R. N., 351
Rappaport, J., 38
Rasch, G., 148, 149
Raskin, A., 396, 397 (tab)
Ratcliff, K., 218
Rathbun, A., 108
Raudenbush, S. W., 57
Ray, D., 161
Razzino, B. E., 288, 459
Reaney, L. M., 108
Recce, S., 217
Redd, D., 220
Redding, S. G., 167–168
Redfield, R., 142
Reece, S., 387
Reed, D., 309
Reese, H. E., 454, 461
Reeves, T., ix, 87
Reeves, T. J., 73, 77, 78, 114, 115,
    227, 231, 232, 452
Refugee Women in
    Development, 230
Regier, D. A., 383
Rehm, L. P., 269 (tab)
Reid, M. J., 454
Reid, P. T., 185
Reise, S. P., 33, 58, 60
Reitman, F., 127
Repetti, R. L., 303, 312
Rew, L., 392, 394 (tab)
Reynolds, K., 310
Rezentes, W. C., 422, 422 (tab)
Rhee, S., 367, 396, 397 (tab), 398
Rhoads, R. A., 119
Rhodes, C., 133
Rhodes, J. E., 51, 53, 55
Rhys Davids, T. W., 324
Riaz, S., 365, 367, 368
Rice, K. G., 112
Rice, M. M., 218
Richman, S., 355
Rickard-Figueroa, K., 30, 33, 126,
    145, 202, 276, 422, 422 (tab)
Ridley, C. A., 367
Riggio, R. E., 287, 288
Riggs, F. W., 346
Riley, C., 238, 437, 457

Rimm, E. B., 309
Rimonte, N., 200
Riskind, J. H., 268 (tab), 270
Rita, E. S., 438
Ritenbaugh, C., 187
Ritsma, S., 332
Ritter, P. L., 76, 112
Rivlin, G., 352
Robb, N., 438
Roberts, C. R., 206, 389,
    390 (tab), 398
Roberts, D., 76
Roberts, K., 257
Roberts, R. E., 206, 383, 389,
    390 (tab), 398
Robins, C. J., 381, 385 (tab),
    457, 458
Robins, L. N., 218, 383, 398
Robins, R. W., 292
Robinson, E., 457
Robinson, G., 309
Robinson, T., 184
Robinson, T. N., 187
Rochlen, A., 201
Rodriguez, B., 310
Rodriguez, B. L., 311
Rogers, H. J., 60
Rogers, T., 398
Rogers, W., 392, 393 (tab),
    395 (tab), 396
Rohner, R. P., 76
Rokeach, M., 173
Rolland, J., 293
Rollock, D., 253, 330
Romano, S. J., 369
Romero, A., 206
Root, M. P. P., 30, 35, 182, 183,
    184, 186, 187, 189, 234
Rorty, M., 187
Rose, T. L., 217, 422 (tab), 423
Rosenberg, M., 162
Rosenberg, M. S., 364
Rosenbloom, S. R., 116, 117,
    118, 119
Ross, G., 218, 219
Ross, G. W., 424
Ross, M. C., 312
Rossman, B. B. R., 364
Rothbaum, F., 96
Rothbaum, F. M., 274, 330
Rotheram-Borus, M. J., 270
Rotherman, M. J., 127
Rotter, J. B., 269 (tab), 271
Rowley, S. J., 125
Roy, K., 458
Roysircar-Sodowsky, G., 332
Rozanski, A., 309
Rozée, P. D., 186, 190, 229
Rubin, K. H., 94
Rubinstein, D. H., 398
Ruch, L. O., 33

Rucker, T., 306, 312, 313
Rudmin, F. W., 33, 34
Rumbaut, R., 98, 110, 114, 115,
    217, 236, 326, 328
Rumberger, R. W., 112
Rummen, J., 330
Rummens, J., 127
Rush, A. J., 422 (tab), 423, 453
Rushton, J. P., 95
Russel, D. W., 72
Ryabchenko, K. A., 388,
    393 (tab), 423
Ryals, J., 285
Ryan, A. S., 216
Ryan, J., 185, 186
Ryan, R. M., 56
Ryder, A. G., 33, 145, 253
Ryujin, D. H., 169, 328,
    385 (tab), 431

Sachs-Ericsson, N., 369
Sack, W. H., 231
Saenz, R., 74
Sager, D., 457
Saito, A., 219
Sakamoto, I., 33, 134, 290
Sakauye, K., 439
Salcido, R. M., 220
Sales, E., 252, 254, 392, 394 (tab)
Sales, S. M., 296
Salomon, H. B., 439
Salomon, R., 454
Saltzman, L. E., 364
Sameroff, A., 125
Sanbonmatsu, D. M., 293
Sanborn, K. O., 276
Sandage, S. J., 274
Sanders, L. M., 288
Sandhu, D. S., 186, 253, 326, 342,
    351, 352
Sandin, E., 364
Sands, D. J., 69
Sankai, T., 309
Sapirstein, G., 451
Sarason, B. R., 332
Sarason, I. G., 332
Sargent, J. D., 95
Sasaki, H., 314
Sashidharan, S. P., 431
Sathyamoorthy, G., 433
Satia-Abouta, J., 310
Satoh, S., 309
Saul, T. T., 197
Saya, R., 423
Sayer, A. G., 57
Scaramella, L. V., 267, 268 (tab)
Scarr, S., 93
Schafer, J., 267, 268 (tab)
Schafer, W. D., 267, 268 (tab)
Schaller, M., 269 (tab), 272
Schatzberg, A., 398

Scheidt, S., 304
Scheinmann, R., 219, 221
Schelling, T. C., 294
Schensul, J. J., 53, 55, 56
Scher, M., 191
Schewe, P. A., 269 (tab), 272
Schimmack, U., 32
Schmidley, A. D., 114, 115
Schmidt, S., 455, 461
Schmitt, M. T., 132, 250
Schneider, B., 109, 110, 112, 116,
    269 (tab), 272
Schnittker, J., 306
Schoenbaum, M., 454, 455
Schram, J. L., 252
Schulberg, H., 396
Schultz, G. L., 414, 438
Schulz, R., 220
Schuman, H., 288
Schuster, M. A., 271
Schwam, M., 35–36
Schwartz, D., 187
Sciarra, D. T., 423
Scopetta, M. A., 144, 146
Scott, R. P. J., 203, 204
Scurfield, R. M., 33
Seale, W., 251
Sears, D. O., 288, 289
Sedlacek, W., 197, 249, 255
Sedlacek, W. E., 96, 197
Seeman, T., 303, 312
Segall, M. H., 142, 143, 150
Seiffge-Krenke, I., 330
Seligman, M. E. P., 269 (tab),
    272, 274
Selle, L. L., 188
Sellers, R. M., 125, 127
Sellers, S., 312
Sellers, S. L., 312
Serafica, F., 94, 162, 174, 175
Serafica, F. C., 440
Services and Advocacy for Asian
    Youth Consortium, 115
Seymour, S., 76
Shah, H., 289
Shakib, S., 310
Shaligram, C., 109
Shapiro, D., 344
Shapiro, E. R., 440
Shapiro, P. A., 308
Sharp, A., 270
Sharp, D. S., 311
Shavelson, R. J., 58
Shaver, P. R., 96
Shaw, B. F., 422 (tab), 423
Shaw, B. R., 453
Shaw, L. L., 53, 54, 55, 56, 272
Shaw, R. L., 272
Shea, J. M.-Y., 327
Shea, M., 326
Shea, S. H., 456, 457

Sheldon, K. M., 274
Sheldon, T. A., 309
Shelley, D., 219, 221
Shelton, J. N., 125, 127
Shelton, R., 454
Shelton, R. C., 456
Shen, B. J., 368
Shen, H., 384, 392, 394 (tab), 396,
    398, 399, 457, 458
Shen, Y., 455
Shen, Y.-J., 249
Shepard, L. A., 60
Sherboume, C., 454, 455
Sherman, D. K., 332
Sherwin, R., 311
Sheth, M., 351, 352
Shiang, J., 398
Shibata, K., 215
Shibusawa, T., 396, 397 (tab), 431
Shigeoka, S., 145
Shih, F., 314
Shih, M., 134, 185, 290
Shih, S., 314
Shih, S. F., 253, 254
Shim, S., 127
Shimada, E., 131
Shin, J. K., 432
Shin, S. K., 388
Shinagawa, R., 422 (tab), 424
Shiota, N., 422 (tab), 423
Shisslak, C. M., 187
Shizuru, L. S., 276
Shoda, Y., 273
Shon, S. P., 291, 366
Shook, E. V., 75
Shrout, P., 368, 384
Shrout, P. E., 270
Shum, L. M., 185, 186
Shumaker, S. A., 309
Shuraydi, M., 74
Shweder, R. A., 293
Sidanius, J., 126, 127, 134, 289
Siddarth, P., 382, 398, 399, 400
Siegel, J. M., 389, 390 (tab)
Silva, J., 91–92, 214, 439
Simmons, T., 74
Simões, A., 266
Simon, G. E., 382
Simons, A. D., 454
Simons, R. L., 267, 268 (tab)
Simpson, J. A., 271
Sinclair, S., 127, 134
Singer, E., 204
Singer, G. H. S., 315
Singh, B. B., 455
Sins, S. G., 438
Siramens, S. J., 451
Skala, J., 309
Skau, M., 35–36
Slaughter-Defoe, D. T., 92
Sluzki, C., 232, 325

Smailes, E. M., 369, 370
Smart, D. W., 144, 327
Smart, J. F., 144, 327
Smedley, A., 30, 32
Smedley, B. D., 30, 32
Smith, D., 291
Smith, D. P., 383, 389, 390 (tab)
Smith, H. J., 130
Smith, J. A., 56
Smith, M. A., 125
Smith, M. B., 12, 13, 27n1
Smith, P. L., 79, 151, 160, 161,
    163, 164, 171
Smith, R. H., 459
Smith, T. A., 126
Smith, T. L., 457
Smith, T. W., 309
Smits, J. A. J., 454, 461
Smutzler, N., 364
Snadomsky, A., 133
Snidman, N., 94
Snowden, L. R., 152, 216, 220,
    381, 385 (tab), 387–389, 395
    (tab), 396
Snyder, M., 269 (tab), 272
Snyder, T. D., 113
Social Science Data Analysis
    Network, ix
Sodowsky, G. R., 49, 147, 187,
    253, 324, 326, 327, 329
Solberg, V. S., 332
Solheim, E., 135n1
Solomon, L. J., 215
Son, L., 112, 113
Sonawalla, S., 217, 218, 383, 392,
    394 (tab), 395 (tab)
Song, W., 275, 423
Song, W. Z., 383
Song, Y. I., 365, 366, 367, 368
Sorocco, K. H., 52, 214, 215, 217
Sorrentino, R. M., 270
Sotsky, S. M., 451
Spears, R., 132, 250
Spencer-Rodgers, J., 250
Spiridakis, J., 268 (tab), 270
Spitz, A. M., 369
Spruiji-Metz, D., 310
Stafford, L., 383, 389, 390 (tab)
Stamfer, J. J., 309
Stanford, E. P., 80
Stangor, C., 199
Stavig, G., 310, 312
Steeh, C., 288
Steele, C. M., 99, 237, 289, 290,
    293, 295
Steenkamp, J., 59
Stein, B. N., 230
Stein, M. B., 369
Steinberg, A., 217
Steinberg, L., 58, 75
Steinburg, A., 387

Stem, M., 330
Stephens, B., 398
Stephens, K. A., 461
Stern, I. R., 72, 76
Sternberg, R. J., 270
Stevenson, H. W., 72, 78, 79, 95
Stewart, A. L., 51
Stewart, D., 365, 367, 368
Stewart, E., 38
Stewart, M. A., 249
Stewart, S. L., 94
Stewart-Williams, S., 451
Stigler, J. W., 72
Stinchfield, R., 267
Stipek, D. J., 56, 69
Stokes, S. C., 220
Stone, V. A., 171
Stoops, N., 1
Story, M., 267, 268 (tab)
Stracuzzi, T., 423
Straus, M. A., 364, 365, 370, 374n2, 374n3
Strauss, A., 56
Striegel Moore, R. H., 433
Strunin, L., 267
Studer, C., 38
Stukel, T. A., 95
Stürmer, S., 269 (tab), 272
Suarez-Orozco, C., 115
Suarez-Orozco, M., 115
Subramanian, S. V., 91
Suchday, S., 304
Sue, D., 14, 30, 34, 35, 52, 98, 183, 197, 220, 247, 248, 255, 285, 289, 291, 293, 323, 328, 331, 383, 387, 414, 424, 439
Sue, D. M., 165, 285, 291, 293, 387, 424
Sue, D. W., 14, 30, 34, 35, 38, 42n1, 48–49, 52, 98, 160, 161, 165, 166, 172, 183, 220, 247, 248, 255, 276, 323, 328, 329, 331, 332, 387, 414, 418, 423, 429, 438, 439
Sue, L., 49, 387
Sue, S., 14, 16, 20, 21, 30, 34, 37, 38, 42n1, 49, 51, 52, 78, 95, 108, 112, 113, 114, 163, 165, 190, 221, 238, 273, 276, 283, 285, 288, 289, 292, 293, 327, 330, 381, 383, 384, 385 (tab), 386, 387, 410, 413, 414, 417, 418, 419, 420, 421, 423, 429, 430, 432, 433, 434, 435, 438, 450, 456, 461
Suen, H. K., 60
Suen, L. J., 217
Suen, L. W., 397 (tab)
Suen, S., 310
Sugarman, D. B., 367
Sugawara, H. M., 59

Sugimoto, T., 366
Suh, B. K., 268 (tab), 270
Suh, E. M., 292, 293, 294
Suinn, R. M., 30, 33, 126, 145–146, 175, 202, 253, 276, 422, 422 (tab)
Sullivan, L. A., 134, 199
Sullivan, N. Y., 431
Sun, C., 51
Sun, P., 310
Sunaga, R., 310
Sung, B. L., 327
Sung, K., 220, 365, 368, 374n3
Super, D. E., 162
Suwanlert, S., 332
Suzanne, S. M., 90
Suzuki, B. H., 106, 107, 108, 118, 119, 344
Suzuki, L., 160, 161, 165, 166
Suzuki, L. A., 145
Swagler, M. A., 249
Swain, S., 219, 221
Swaminathan, H., 60
Swygert, K. A., 58, 59
Szapocznik, J., 144, 145, 146, 372
Sze, K. H., 309

Tafarodi, R. W., 268 (tab)
Taffe, R. C., 49
Tajfel, H., 127, 134, 205, 206, 207
Tajima, R. E., 183
Tak, J., 419
Takagi, K., 332
Takahashi, Y., 438, 439
Takaki, R., 38, 107, 199, 207, 232, 329
Takaki, R. T., 351, 352
Takamura, J. C., 80
Takanishi, R., 92
Takeshita, J., 217, 309
Takeuchi, D., 238, 368, 384, 386, 387, 462
Takeuchi, D. T., 21, 52, 72, 214, 236, 328–329, 344, 345, 352, 368, 372, 382, 384, 385 (tab), 386, 387, 392, 394 (tab), 396, 398, 399, 400, 430, 431, 432, 433, 434, 435, 456, 457, 458
Talajic, M., 308
Talbott, E., 309
Talebi, H., 451
Talmadge, W. T., 203, 204
Tam, C. F., 310
Tam, T. M., 285
Tamura, T., 438
Tan, A. G., 113
Tan, D. L., 112
Tan, Y., 310
Tanaka, J. S., 35, 48, 58, 59
Tang, C. S.-K., 371
Tang, J., 164, 166, 169, 170, 284

Tang, M., 79, 151, 160, 161, 163, 164, 171, 174, 175, 440
Tang, N. M., 200
Tang, T. N., 77
Tang, T. S., 215
Tang, T. Z., 454
Tang, W. K., 309
Tanigawa, T., 309
Tanjasiri, S. P., 215
Tanter, R., 294
Tata, S. P., 151, 152, 153, 161, 174, 433, 452
Tatara, T., 438
Taub, B., 389, 390 (tab)
Taylor, A., 364
Taylor, A C., 369
Taylor, C. M., 127
Taylor, G. J., 458
Taylor, S. E., 127, 295, 303, 312, 332
Tazuma, L., 229, 235
Teh, C., 310
Tekawa, I. S., 310, 311
Tempo, P. M., 219
Teng, E. L., 422 (tab), 425
Teng, L. N., 21
Teng, N. L., 221
Teraoka, M., 251, 252
Teresi, J., 394 (tab), 395 (tab), 396
Terracciano, A., 274
Tesser, A., 295
Teten, A. L., 461
Tewari, N., 186, 324, 326, 327, 328, 342, 352, 353, 439
Texeira, E., 105, 114, 115
Thase, M. E., 450
Theorell, T. G., 309
Thiagarajan, M., 437
Thissen, D., 58
Thoennes, N., 364
Thomas, K., 248, 249, 250, 255
Thomas, P., 310
Thompson, A. I., 70
Thompson, E. A., 70
Thompson, E. H., Jr., 203, 205
Thompson, J. S., 60, 78, 79, 110, 111, 112
Thompson, L., 424
Thompson, M., 187
Thompson-Brenner, H., 449, 450
Thomson, G., 113
Thongthiraj, R., 115
Thoresen, C. J., 271, 272
Thorstensson, L., 249
Thurman, J. W., 330
Tidwell, R., 249, 251
Tien, L., 186
Tienda, M., 78–79, 109, 110, 112
Tiet, Q., 230, 231
Timm, J., 238
Ting-Toomey, S., 133, 294–295

Tjaden, P., 364
Todd, R. M., 272
Toh, Y., 330
Tolbert, V. E., 454
Tolman, R. M., 366
Tomiuk, M. A., 125, 135n1
Tompkins, S. S., 201
Tong, B., 385 (tab), 392, 393 (tab)
Toporek, R. L., 185, 197
Torrens, J., 311
Torres, M., 312
Torres-Schow, R. M., 310
Tortosa-Gil, G., 274
Toshima, M. T., 133
Toupin, E. S. W. A., 189, 191
Towle, L. H., 218
Tracey, T. J., 167
Tracy, J. L., 292
Tran, C. G., 230, 231, 365, 366, 367, 368, 373, 374n2
Tran, H., 438
Tran, T. V., 215, 220, 326
Trapnell, P. D., 268 (tab), 271
Trautman, P. D., 270
Treharne, G. J., 332
Trevisan, M., 309
Triandis, H. C., 31, 131, 142, 251, 283, 292, 293, 294, 332
Trimble, J. E., 366
Trockman, C., 424
Trocme, N., 370
True, R., 385 (tab), 392, 393 (tab)
True, R. H., 184, 185, 186, 187, 188, 189, 190, 191, 438
Truss, C., 372
Trusty, J., 161
Tsai, D. C., 423
Tsai, J. L., 30, 33, 34, 35, 98, 112, 125, 126, 127, 128, 130, 131, 132, 133, 135n1, 197, 291, 292, 330, 381
Tsai, M., 221
Tse, F. W., 171
Tse, L., 78
Tsee Chee, K., 457
Tseng, H.-M., 370, 371
Tseng, V., 72, 75, 76, 78, 79, 108, 112
Tseng, W. S., 430
Tseng, W.-S., 72, 74
Tsui, A. M., 190
Tsui, P., 414, 438
Tsuru, G. K., 462
Tu, A. M., 219
Tu, S. P., 310
Tuan, M., 117
Tucker, D. L., 304
Tung, M., 438
Tupling, R. E., 332
Turner, C. W., 309
Turner, H., 370

Turner, J. C., 205, 206, 207
Turner, K. O., 285
Turoff, M., 21
Tusaie, K., 217, 397 (tab)
Tweed, R. G., 324
Tyler, T. R., 130

Uba, L., 21, 36–37, 72, 75, 96, 188, 216, 220, 273, 275, 325, 326, 327–328, 329, 330, 331, 351, 367, 421
UCLA Center for Health Policy Research, 311
Uhl, N. P., 272
Ui, S., 79
Ullah, K., 367
Umemoto, D., 143, 249, 256
Unger, J. B., 310
Ungvari, G. S., 309
United Nations Office at Vienna, Centre for Social Development and Humanitarian Affairs, 363, 373, 374
University of Hawai'i, Institutional Research Office, 78
Unwin, N., 311
U.S. Census Bureau, 1, 73, 77, 94, 97, 181, 213, 286, 410
U.S. Commission on Civil Rights, 91, 172, 236, 284
U.S. Department of Education, National Center for Education Statistics, 77, 78
U.S. Department of Health and Human Services, 234, 310, 379, 440
U.S. Department of Health and Human Services, Administration on Children, Youth, and Families, 369
U.S. General Accounting Office, 284
U.S. Surgeon General, 191
Ushijima, S., 221
Ustun, T. B., 382
Utsey, S. O., 423, 461

Vaglum, P., 231
Van Boemel, G., 186, 190, 229
van Horn, R. K., 252
Van Kirk, J. J., 183
Van Laar, C., 127, 134
Van Steenberg, C., 220
Vance, S., 310
Vandewater, E. A., 75
Vang, H. C., 274
Varma, S. C., 438
Varney, L. L., 272
Vasquez, M., 30
Vedder, P., 130, 131, 134
Veisel, C., 433

Verkuyten, M., 36, 126
Vida, P., 310
Vigil, J. D., 237
Vigil, P., 30, 33, 126, 145, 202, 276, 422, 422 (tab)
Villareal, M., 131
Villareal, M. J., 283
Virnig, B., 385 (tab)
Vittinghoff, E., 435
Vo, L. T., 49
von Eye, A., 72
von Glinow, M. A., 329
Von Korff, M., 382

Wada, S., 273
Wade, J. C., 204, 205
Wade, W. A., 454
Wagatsuma, Y., 272
Wagner, N. N., 20
Wagner, N. S., 152, 153
Walach, H., 455, 461
Walker, J. A., 185, 323, 325, 326, 327
Walker, L. E., 367
Wall, T. L., 456, 457
Wallace, S. A., 99
Wallace, S. P., 215
Waller, G., 187
Waller, N. G., 60
Wan, C. T., 33, 112
Wan, T., 249, 251, 252
Wang, C.-H. C., 371
Wang, L. L.-C., 106
Wang, N., 310
Wang, Y., 96, 386, 387
Wang, Y. W., 330, 331, 332
Wanitromanee, K., 332
Ward, C., 251
Ward, J., 90
Warda, U., 310
Warner, S., 364, 367, 368
Washington, R. E., 206
Wasik, B. H., 3, 88, 89 (fig), 90, 92
Watari, K., 218, 219, 221
Watari, K. F., 80
Watson, D., 422 (tab), 424
Way, N., 116, 117, 118, 119
Weathers, D., 344
Weaver, C. N., 162
Weber, M., 287
Webster, B. H., 94
Webster, J. M., 459
Webster, M. D., 219
Webster-Stratton, C., 454
Wechsler, D., 424
Wehrly, B., 255, 256
Wehrmeyer, M. L., 69
Wei, M., 72
Weisman, S., 133
Weiss, B., 456
Weiss, B. S., 437

Weiss, M. S., 285
Weisskirch, R. S., 78
Weissman, M. M., 382, 398
Weisz, J., 96
Weisz, J. R., 274, 330, 332
Weitzman, M., 94
Weizmann, F., 30, 32
Wells, K., 454, 455
Wells, K. B., 392, 393 (tab),
    395 (tab), 396
Welter, M. G., 187
Wenhao, J., 439
Wenk, E., 60
West, J., 108
Westbrook, F. D., 96
Westen, D., 449, 450
Westermeyer, J., 238
Westkott, M., 184
Whitbeck, L. B., 267, 268 (tab)
Whitborne, S. K., 81
White, K., 324
White, L., 218
White, M., 311
White, P. T., 229
White, W. G., 289
Whiteley, S., 152
Whitfield, J. R., 19, 20, 21, 42
Whitfield, K., 81
Widaman, K. F., 58, 59
Widamin, K. F., 58
Widom, C. S., 369
Wilcox, S., 311
Wildsmith, E., 431
Wilkens, L. R., 310
Wilkinson, S., 51
William, C. L., 253
William, D. R., 330
Williams, C. L., 372
Williams, D., 312
Williams, D. R., 91, 306, 312,
    313, 372
Williams, H. L., 72, 326
Williams, J. K. Y., 127
Williams, M., 79
Williams, N. L., 268 (tab), 270
Williams, O., 80
Williams, T. K., 35
Williamson, D. F., 369
Wilson, D. M., 187
Wilson, M. N., 88, 93, 438
Wing, L. C., 115
Winkelman, M., 251
Winkelstein, W., 309
Wise, S. L., 49
Wisocki, P., 218
Witherell, S., 246, 247
Witkow, M., 111
Wolf, A. M., 311
Wolfe, M. M., 148, 149
Wollenberg, C. M., 106, 107, 119
Wolmi, H., 219

Wolpe, J., 286
Womack, W., 235
Womack, W. M., 386
Wondover, A. K., 188, 190
Wong, A., 285
Wong, B., 187
Wong, C. A., 125
Wong, C. K., 370
Wong, D., 184, 315
Wong, E., 154, 217
Wong, E. C., 149, 190, 436, 439,
    452, 454, 461, 462
Wong, J., 132, 133
Wong, J. K., 249
Wong, M., 370
Wong, P., 164
Wong, P. T. P., 332
Wong, R. Y. M., 134
Wong, S., 231, 235
Wong, S. C., 80, 220, 257
Wong, S. L. C., 199
Wong, S. S., 269 (tab), 273
Wong, S. T., 51
Wong, T. M., 410, 425
Wong, V. Y., 91, 97
Wong, Y., 33, 35, 98, 125, 126,
    128, 135n1
Woo, J., 309
Woo, V., 313
Wooden, W. S., 133
Workneh, F., 248, 255
World Mental Health Survey
    Consortium, 382
Wright, D., 79, 109, 110–111
Wrightsman, L. S., 202
Wu, B., 220
Wu, F. H., 237, 329
Wu, H., 454
Wu, K. A., 331, 332
Wu, L., 311
Wu, R., 197, 203
Wu, S., 167
Wu, Y. Y., 311
Wu, Z. S., 311
Wyatt, G., 91
Wyatt, G. E., 30, 32
Wyshak, G., 228, 231

Xenos, P., 329
Xiao, L., 310
Xiao, Z., 454, 455
Xie, Y., 108, 111, 112, 114
Xin, K. R., 287
Xu, J., 127
Xu, X. M., 311

Yamada, M., 119
Yamaguchi, J. L., 451
Yamamoto, J., 91–92, 214, 217,
    221, 387, 396, 397 (tab), 398,
    429, 430, 439, 454

Yamaoka, K., 270
Yanagida, E. H., 190
Yang, B., 249, 251, 252
Yang, E., 257
Yang, K., 274
Yang, K. S., 330
Yang, L. H., 381, 388, 400
Yang, P., 91
Yang, P. H., 146, 147–148, 149,
    203, 275
Yankelovich Partners, 128
Yano, K., 310
Yao, C. H., 311
Yao, E. L., 144, 145
Yardley, L., 51, 53, 55
Yasuda, T., 253
Yasui, M., 127
Yate, A., 389
Yates, A., 389, 390 (tab)
Yau, E., 220
Yau, T. Y., 255
Yeatts, D. E., 220
Yee, A. H., 30, 32, 324
Yee, B. W., 230
Yee, B. W. K., 69, 74, 81, 82, 216
Yee, D., 214
Yeh, C. J., 131, 188, 197, 206,
    252, 253, 323, 324, 326,
    327, 328, 329, 330, 331,
    332, 333, 353, 435
Yeh, I., 310
Yeh, K. H., 371
Yeh, M., 149, 276, 369, 370,
    385 (tab), 386, 431, 434,
    435, 456, 459
Yeh, R. L., 438
Yeh, T. L., 133
Yeh, Y. Y., 381
Yen, S., 381, 385 (tab), 457, 458
Yeo, G., 81, 219
Yesavage, J. A., 217, 422 (tab), 423
Yeung, A., 217, 218, 381, 383,
    392, 394 (tab), 395 (tab),
    439, 457
Yi, J., 256, 257
Yick, A. G., 188, 190, 366
Yim, S. B., 368
Ying, Y., 30, 33, 34, 112, 126,
    127, 130, 131, 132, 133,
    236, 418, 423
Ying, Y. W., 189, 191, 197, 220,
    330, 381, 383, 392, 393 (tab),
    400n2
Ying, Y.-W., 232, 235, 258, 432,
    433, 438
Yip, T., 127, 133, 134
Yong, F. L., 268 (tab), 270, 272
Yoo, G. J., 51
Yoo, H. C., 40, 423
Yoon, E., 257
Yoshihama, M., 365

Yoshioka, M. R., 367
Young, A., 380, 400n1
Young, D., 386, 387, 454, 455
Young, K., 189, 190, 236,
    329, 344, 345, 352,
    432, 450
Young, K. N. J., 21, 214
Young, P., 454
Yu, A., 370
Yu, E., 310
Yu, E. S., 80
Yu, E. S. H., 220, 310
Yu, H., 187
Yu, J., 33
Yu, L. C., 167
Yuan, E., 51
Yuan, S. C., 72, 76
Yuen, N., 389
Yuen, N. Y., 398
Yuen, S., 72, 76
Yule, W., 231

Yum, J. O., 168
Yun, S., 237

Zaidi, A. U., 74
Zajonc, R. B., 296
Zakalik, R. A., 72
Zakaria, F., 247
Zane, N., 30, 52, 238, 285, 432,
    434, 435, 438, 449–450, 456,
    459, 461
Zane, N. W., 285, 288, 292, 293,
    384, 385 (tab)
Zane, N. W. S., 1, 21, 52, 149, 154,
    190, 276, 285, 330, 367, 430,
    432, 434, 436, 439, 452, 454,
    456, 458, 461, 462
Zarate, M. G., 188
Zavon, M. O., 330
Zea, M. C., 292
Zelazo, L. B., 70
Zelazo, P. R., 94

Zenhausern, R., 268 (tab), 270
Zhan, G., 92, 237
Zhan, L., 219
Zhang, A. Y., 381, 385 (tab),
    387–388, 395 (tab), 396
Zhang, H., 454, 455
Zhang, J., 273, 275, 383, 423
Zhang, J. P., 383
Zhang, J. X., 383
Zhang, L., 273
Zhang, M., 311
Zhang, N., 152, 436
Zhang, S., 59, 221, 454
Zhang, Y., 111, 387, 454, 455
Zhao, S., 382, 383, 384, 387, 458
Zheng, Y. P., 386, 387
Zhou, M., 41, 114, 115, 201
Zhou, Z., 200
Zia, H., 273
Zuckerman, M., 32
Zweben, J. E., 437, 439

SUBJECT INDEX

AAPA Executive Committee, 18
Academic achievement, Asian
    American, 107–111
    bullying/violence/teasing effect
        on, 117–118
    college entrance exam, 112–113
    college grades, 112
    college persistence/graduation,
        113–114
    environment influence on, 92
    future research on, 113–114, 118
    in elementary school, 108–109
    in high school, 110–111
    in middle school, 109–110
    outcomes, 111–113
    racism/intergroup relations
        effect, 114–115
    social/economic context of
        school, 115–116
    sociohistorical context, 106–107
    teacher/peer experience, 116–117
Acculturation
    bidimensional model, 33, 34
    bidirectional model, 33
    Chinese American, 35, 53,
        144–145
    Chinese Canadian, 33
    culture-learning model, 251,
        252–253
    defining, 66, 142–143, 333
    ethnic identity, 421–422
    four-fold theory of, 33
    gender role conflict, 202
    international students from Asia
        and, 253–254
    job satisfaction and, 290–291
    Mexican American, 145
    psychological, 142
    relation to hypertension, 312
    See also Acculturation process
Acculturation process
Acculturation Scale for Chinese
    Americans, 144–145
    attitudes toward mental health
        services, 151–153

bilinear measurement, 145–146
bilinear measurement/single
    construct dimension,
    146–150
construct definitions used in
    theory, 142–143
identity development
    acculturation model,
    253–254
psychological effects,
    143–144, 150
research recommendations, 155
therapy process, 153–155
unilinear measurement, 144–145
upward mobility, 41
vocational functioning, 151
See also Acculturation
Acculturation Rating Scale for
    Mexican Americans, 145
Acculturation Scale for Chinese
    Americans (ASCA), 144–145
Acculturation Scale for Southeast
    Asians, 422
Acculturative stress, 144, 366, 372
Action-oriented coping, 330
Activated gender identity, 290
ADDRESSING framework, 411,
    412 (tab), 415
adjustment, psychosocial, 234–237
    changing family dynamics, 235
    child-rearing practices, 235–236
    English language proficiency/
        employment, 234–235
    gangs, 237
    racism, 236–237
Adjustment theory, 250–255
Adoptees, 35–36, 41
Adult-persistent attention deficit
    and affective hyperactivity
    disorder (ADHD), 382
African Americans
    academic achievement, 107, 108,
        110, 112, 113
    career interests, 159
    hypertension, 311, 312

intergroup tension with Korean
    Americans, 109
    teacher/peer relationships of, 116
    underemployment, 167
Age-related roles, culturally
    prescribed, 52
Aging. See Asian American older
    adults
Alcohol use, 218–219, 367
Alexithymia, 458–459
Alzheimer's disease, 217
Amae (loving indulgence), 96
American Values Scale for Asian
    Americans (EAVS-AA), 149
American Values Scale for Asian
    Americans-Revised (EAVS-
    AA-R), 149–150
Analysis
    deductive, 55
    group/societal level, 170–173
    individual level, 160–170
    inductive, 55
    power, 59
Anglo Americans
    depression in older, 396–397
    See also European Americans;
        White Americans
Anxiety
    Asian American older adults, 218
    Asian American women,
        186–187
    Chinese Americans, 165
    correlates of, 387
    European Americans vs. Asian
        Americans, 165
    generalized anxiety disorder, 455
    Japanese Americans, 165
APA Council of Representatives,
    12, 13
APA Minority Fellowship
    Program, 12
Arab Americans, 351
Asian, as category, 232–233
Asian American
    as classification, 383

as culture, 30–32
as race, 32–33
Asian American and Pacific
    Islander families
  conceptual framework for
      studying, 70–71
  cultural values effect on
      interdependence, 71–72
  demographics, 73–74
  education/occupational
      pathways, 78–80
  family life cycle issues, 74–81
  language acquisition, 77–78
  marriage/marital satisfaction,
      74–75
  older adults, 80–81
  parenting styles/practices, 75–76
  research opportunities/policy
      challenges, 81–82
  risk/protective factors for
      resilience, 70–71
  sibling relationships, 76–77
  socialization of identity/gender
      roles, 77
Asian American and Pacific
    Islander Mental Health
    Summit, 16–17
Asian American Legal Defense and
    Education Fund, 114–115
Asian American masculinities
  cultural notions of masculinity,
      200–201
  historical constructions of,
      197–200
  social identity theory, 205–207
  theories of masculinity, 201–205
Asian American mental
    health conference
    (San Francisco), 16
Asian American Multidimensional
    Acculturation Scale
    (AAMAS), 146, 147, 150
Asian American Multidimensional
    Acculturation Scale–Culture
    of Origin (AAMAS-CO),
    146, 150
Asian American Multidimensional
    Acculturation Scale–European
    American Culture (AAMAS-
    EA), 146
Asian American Multidimensional
    Acculturation Scale–Other
    Asian American Cultures
    (AAMAS-AA), 146
Asian American older adults
  aging process and, 215–216
  alcohol/tobacco use, 218–219
  anxiety, 218
  caregiving issues, 220–222
  dementia, 219
  depression, 217–218

discrimination issues, 216
  family life cycle issues, 80–81
  mental health risk factors,
      219–220
  psychological research on,
      214–215
  views on mental health, 216–217
  See also individual subgroup
Asian American Psychological
    Association (AAPA)
  advocacy/alliance building,
      12–13
  advocacy through scholarship,
      13–14
  awards, 14, 15 (tab), 17, 18
  Council of Past Presidents,
      18–19
  Digital History Project, 19
  Division on Women, 19
  founding, 11–12
  future of field, 21–27, 24 (tab),
      25 (tab), 26 (tab)–27 (tab)
  key people, 11–12, 13–14
  leading researchers, 20
  newsletter, 16, 18
  presidents, 14 (tab), 17–18
  publications, 14, 16
  recent developments, 17–19
  significant conferences, 16–17
  substantive research areas, 19–21
  Web site, 18
Asian American Psychologist,
    16, 18
Asian American Race-Related
    Stress Inventory, 33
Asian American Social Workers
    Organization, 16
Asian American Studies, 38
Asian American Values Scale, 31
Asian American Values Scale-
    Multidimensional (AVS–M),
    147–148, 275
Asian American women
  body image, 187
  clinical issues, 184–189
  depression/anxiety, 186–187
  domestic violence, 188–189
  help-seeking patterns/
      behaviors, 189
  historical/political background,
      181–184
  immigration patterns, 182
  interracial issues, 186
  multiple minority statuses,
      184–185
  multiple roles, 185–186
  research recommendations,
      191–192
  sexuality, 188
  stereotypes, 182–183
  therapy, 190–191

trauma, 186
  woman/therapist dyad, 189
  women's movement, 183–184
  work adjustment by, 168
Asian Americans
  career development and,
      162–163
  effect of classification on
      psychopathology, 383
  occupational status, 164
  underemployment of, 167
  work values of, 161–162, 162
Asian/Asian American women's
    movement, 183–184
Asian Canadians , acculturation/
    enculturation, 145
Asian Exclusion Act of 1924, 341
Asian/Pacific Island Americans
    category, 342–343
Asian Pacific Islanders
  academic achievement, 107,
      109–110
  underemployment, 167
  See also Asian Pacific Islanders,
      cardiovascular disease;
      individual subgroup
Asian Pacific Islanders,
    cardiovascular disease
  disability from cardiovascular
      disease, 313–314
  influences on health, 305–308,
      307 (fig)
  integrative biopsychosocial
      model of, 306, 308
  race/ethnicity, 305–306
  modifiable behavioral
      risk/lifestyle factors and,
      310–312
  diabetes management/
      prevention, 311
  dietary factors, 310–311
  hypertension prevention/
      management, 311–312
  inadequate physical
      activity, 311
  tobacco use, 310
  mortality rate/prevalence, 304
  patient quality of life, 313–315
  psychosocial aspects of
      disabilities, 314–315
  psychosocial factors for,
      308–310
  social-environmental risk factors,
      312–313
  stress/biological pathways link,
      204–305
Asian Values Scale (AVS),
    147–148, 153, 203
Asian Values Scale-Revised
    (AVS-R), 147–148
Assertive behavior, 291–292

Assessment, issues/applications
adapted measures, 418–420
ADDRESSING framework,
412 (tab)
building/establishing
rapport, 414
case to illustrate research
problems, 420
culturally appropriate adapted
measures, 420–421
family systems approach to,
416–417
general skills/considerations in
cross-cultural encounter,
411–413
interpreter selection/use, 414–415
multidimensional assessment,
415–416
procedures/specific assessment
measures, 421–425
clinical interview, 421
neuropsychological measures,
424–425
overview, 422 (tab)
self-report measures, 421–424
researcher self-awareness/-
assessment, 410–411
standardized assessment
measures, 417–418
language/education issues, 417
measurement selection,
417–418
Standards for Educational
Psychological Testing,
419–420
Assessment instrument
Acculturation Rating Scale for
Mexican Americans, 145
Acculturation Scale for Chinese
Americans, 144–145
Acculturation Scale for
Southeast Asians, 422
American Values Scale for Asian
Americans, 149
American Values Scale for Asian
Americans-Revised,
149–150
Asian American
Multidimensional
Acculturation Scale, 146,
147, 150
Asian American
Multidimensional
Acculturation
Scale–Culture of Origin,
146, 150
Asian American
Multidimensional
Acculturation
Scale–European American
Culture, 146

Asian American
Multidimensional
Acculturation Scale–Other
Asian American
Cultures, 146
Asian American Values
Scale-Multidimensional,
147–148, 275
Asian Values Scale, 147–148,
153, 203
Asian Values Scale-Revised,
147–148
Assessment of Career Decision-
Making Style Subscale, 163
Beck Depression Inventory,
218, 423
Brief Rating Scale, 432
Brief Symptom Inventory, 145
Career Maturity Inventory, 163
Center for Epidemiologic
Studies-Depression,
480–481
Chinese Personality Assessment
Inventory, 275, 383
Cognitive Abilities Screening
Instrument, 218, 425
Conformity to Masculine Role
Norms Inventory, 204
Consortium to Establish a
Registry for Alzheimer's
Disease, 424–425
Diagnostic Interview Schedule,
217–218
European American Values Scale
for Asian Americans, 149
European American Values Scale
for Asian Americans-
Revised, 149–150
Fear of Negative Evaluation
Questionnaire, 424
Gender Role Conflict Scale, 203
Geriatric Depression Scale,
217, 423
Global Assessment Scale,
430, 456
Hamilton Anxiety Scale, 221
Hamilton Depression Scale, 221
Hawaiian Acculturation
Scale, 422
Hopkins Symptom
checklist-25, 218
Loss of Face, 149, 276
Male Role Norms Inventory, 203
Minnesota Multiphasic
Personality Inventory, 59,
165, 275–276, 383, 423
Multigroup Ethnic Identity
Measure, 165
My Vocational Situation, 163
Occupational Values Scale, 162
Ohio Work Values Inventory, 161

Omnibus Personality Inventory,
160, 165, 276
Peabody Picture Vocabulary
Test-Revised, 425
Penn State Worry
Questionnaire, 218
People of Color Racial Identity
Attitudes Scale, 203
Rasch model, 148
Reference Group Identity
Dependency Scale, 204
School and College Ability
Test, 160
Social Avoidance and Distress
Scale, 424
Social Cognitive Career Theory,
148, 163
Spheres of Control Scale, 165
Strong Vocational Interest
Blank, 160
Suinn-Lew Asian Self-Identity
Acculturation Scale,
145–146, 147, 151, 152,
161, 421–422
Symptom Check List, 432
Symptom Check List 90-
Revised, 458
Taiwan Aboriginal Acculturation
Scale, 422
Traditional Culture Identification
index, 145
Wechsler Adult Intelligence
Scale-Revised, 424
Wechsler Adult Intelligence
Scale-Revised for
China, 424
Wechsler-Bellevue Intelligence
Scale, 424
Western Cultural Identification
index, 145
World Mental Health-Composite
International Diagnostic
Interview, 382
Worry Scale-Revised, 218
Assessment of Career
Decision-Making
Style Subscale, 163
Assimilation, as acculturation
attitude, 143
Association of Asian American
Psychologists. *See* Asian
American Psychological
Association
Association of Black
Psychologists, 12
Attachment theory, 96
Attention deficit and affective
hyperactivity disorder
(ADHD), 382
Authoritative/authoritarian
parenting, 31, 75–76, 96

Bachelor's degrees, 73, 113, 171, 233
Barred Zone Act of 1917, 341
Beck Depression Inventory (BDI), 218, 423
Behavioral biculturalism, 150
Bicultural competence, 143–144
Bicultural identity, 326, 452–453
Bicultural Identity Integration (BII), 133
Biculturalism, 145, 150, 452
Bidimensional model of acculturation, 33, 34
Bidirectional model of acculturation, 33
Bilingual education, 106, 289
Biracial Asian Americans, 36
Black Students' Psychological Association, 12
Blacks. *See* African Americans
Board of Minority Affairs (BEMA), 13
Board on Social and Ethical Responsibility for Psychology (BSERP), 12, 13
Body image, 184, 187
BPS: 96/01, 113
Brief Rating Scale, 432
Brief Symptom Inventory, 145
Buddhism, 238, 324
Bullying/violence/teasing, in schools, 117–118

Cambodian Americans
    academic achievement, 109
    family demographics of, 73
Cambodian immigrants
    education, 73, 114
    percentage of Asian American population, 113
    socioeconomic status, 115
Cambodian refugees, school safety, 115
Cambodians
beliefs, 238
tobacco use among, 310
Cardiovascular disease, Asian Pacific Islanders. *See* Asian Pacific Islanders, cardiovascular disease in
Career. *See* Career development/vocational behaviors, Asian Americans; Leadership/career advancement/social competence
Career development/vocational behaviors, Asian Americans
    current status of research on, 173–174
    future research directions, 174

group/societal level of analysis, 170–173
    family influences, 171
    occupational discrimination, 171
    occupational segregation, 172–173
    occupational stereotyping, 171–172
individual level of analysis, 160–170
    career choices, 163–164
    career development, 162–163
    career interests, 160–161
    occupational values, 161–162
    personality variables in career development, 165–166
    professions, 164–165
    work adjustment/vocational problems, 166–170
Career Maturity Inventory, 163
Caregiving, Asian American older adults, 220–222
Carter, Jimmy, 13
Center for Epidemiologic Studies-Depression (CES-D) Scale, 380–361
Center for Mental Health Services (CMHS), 16
Central American immigrants, school safety and, 115
Chang, Alice, 19
Change shock, 248
Chi-square difference test, 59
Chiao shun, 31
Child care, 93
Child development
    social ecological frameworks for, 88–90, 89 (fig)
    See also Garcia Coll's Integrative Conceptual Model
Child physical abuse, 369–373, 370–372
    context in Asian American communities
    child rearing, 370–371
    immigrant family, 371–372
    emerging research on, 372–373
    implications on research for practice, 373
    scope/significance in general population, 369
    victimization rates, 369–370
Child-rearing practice
    Asian immigrants/refugees and, 235–236
    authoritative/authoritarian parenting, 31, 75–76, 96
Children of Immigrants Longitudinal Study (CILS), 109, 110

Chin, Robert, 12, 13
Chin, Vincent, 352
China
    child rearing in, 75–76
    older adults in, 80
Chinese
    depression in, 457
    traditional healing among, 238
Chinese adoptees, 41
Chinese-American Psychiatric Epidemiology Study (CAPES), 386, 433
Chinese Americans
    academic achievement, 106, 109–110, 110, 111, 113
    acculturation among, 35, 53, 144–145
    analyzing group interviews of, 55
    as hate crime victims, 330
    bicultural identity, 133
    career development, 165
    career interests, 160–161
    characteristics of infants, 94
    depression, 381, 386, 392, 393, 454
    English language proficiency, 234
    ethnic identity development, 34
    family affect on career development, 171
    group interviewing, 52–53
    hegemonic masculinity, 206
    occupational values, 161
    occupational values among students, 151
    older adults, 80, 215, 217, 219, 220, 221, 454
    parenting, 371
    participant observation and youth, 53–55
    partner violence, 368
    percentage of Asian American population, 73
    personality variables, 165
    psychological service use among, 152
    racial self-hatred in men, 289
    social anxiety, 165
    somatization, 381, 457–458
    values enculturation, 148–149
    work adjustment, 167
Chinese Canadians, 33, 288
Chinese Exclusion Act of 1882, 128, 345, 351
Chinese family, affect on career development, 171
Chinese immigrants
    academic achievement, 110, 113, 114, 115
    alienation felt by students, 116

immigration patterns, 232
percentage of Asian American
population, 232
school safety, 115
socioeconomic status, 115, 116
Chinese men
cardiovascular disease, 309
face, 167–168
masculine ideology, 203
Chinese Personality Assessment
Inventory (CPAI), 275, 383
Chinese Vietnamese refugees, 220
Chinese women, immigration
patterns of, 182
Clark, Kenneth B., 12
Clinical interview, 421
Coding, 55–56
Cognitive Abilities Screening
Instrument (CASI), 218, 425
Cognitive behavioral therapy
(CBT), 221, 454, 455
Cognitive therapy (CT), 153–154,
453–454, 459, 460–461
Collective self-esteem, 126, 150
Collectivism, 1, 41, 52, 71,
147–150, 162–163, 191, 235,
274–275, 283, 292, 293, 294,
295, 315, 330–333, 331, 371
Collectivism/individualism,
31–32, 148, 168, 174, 185,
222, 330, 427
Columbians, academic
achievement, 110
Commission on Wartime
Relocation and Internment of
Civilians (CWRIC), 349–351
Committee on Cultural and Ethnic
Affairs, 13
Committee on Equal Opportunity in
Psychology (CEOP), 13
Committee on Social and Ethical
Responsibility, 12
Comparative paradigm, 37
Conceptual approach, in Asian
American psychology
Asian Americanist
perspective, 38–42
internal processes, 41–42
major characteristics of,
39 (tab)
migration histories, 40
population trends, 40–42
critical discourses within
psychology, 37–38
critical psychology, 37–38
postmodernism, 37
scientific psychology, 37
reasons to reformulate, 36–37
Conformity to Masculine Role
Norms Inventory (CMNI), 204
Confucian cultures, 31, 97

Consortium to Establish a Registry
for Alzheimer's Disease
(CERAD), 424–425
Coping. *See* Stress/coping
Council of National Psychological
Association for the
Advancement of Ethnic
Minority Interests, 18
Council of Past Presidents (COPP;
AAPA), 18–19
Counseling
international students, 255–257
peer, 153–154, 255
Counseling/psychotherapy
clinical case studies, 439–440
counseling process/outcome
empirical studies, 429–432
direct measures of treatment
outcome, 432
general treatment, 438–439
indirect measures of treatment
outcome, 430–432
See also Empirically supported
therapies, for Asian
Americans;
Mental health services
Cross-cultural psychology,
30–31, 32, 33
Cubans, academic achievement,
100
Cultural Context Model, 373
Cultural frame switching, 134
Cultural identity, defining, 147
Cultural maintenance,
142–143, 253
Cultural translators, 235
Cultural values
adherence to, gender role
conflict, 203
effect on interdependence, 71–72
Japanese Americans, 92
of Nisei, 31–32
Culturally competent research
team, building, 48–49
Culture
defining, 142
hybrid, 31
Culture distance, 250
Culture-learning model, 251,
252–253
Culture shock, 247, 248

Deductive analysis, 55
Dementia, in Asian American older
adults, 219
Depression
Anglo American elder, 396–397
Asian American elder, 217–218
Asian American women,
186–187
Chinese, 457

Chinese Americans, 381, 386,
392, 393, 454
Korean Americans, 396–397
Developmental theory, 88
Diabetes management/
prevention, 311
Diagnostic Interview Schedule,
217–218
Diaspora, 40
Dietary factors, in cardiovascular
disease, 310–311
Digital History Project
(DHP; AAPA), 19
Disability
cardiovascular disease as,
313–314
defining, 313–314
psychosocial aspects, 314–315
Discrimination issues
as stressful, 329–330
career advancement, 288–291
categorization, 342–344
defining, 343
elder adults, 216
"model minority" stereotype, 344
occupational, 171
Disney theme park, 32
Diversity, of Asian American
population, 87–88, 141, 174,
409–410
Division on Women (AAPA), 19
Divorce, 367
Domestic violence, 74–75, 188–189
See also Intimate partner
violence
Double jeopardy, 216
Dragon Lady stereotype, 183, 289
Dulles Conference, 13

East Asia, child rearing in, 75–76
East Asian Americans
academic achievement, 112
education/occupational status, 73
East Indian immigrants, 113, 341
East Indian men, cardiovascular
disease, 309
Eating disorders, 187, 382
ECLS-K, 108
Economic segregation, 91
Education. *See* Academic
achievement, Asian American;
International students
Education/occupational pathways,
78–80
Elder Asian Americans. *See* Asian
American older adults
Emergency Quota Act, 182
Empirically supported therapies, for
Asian Americans
adapting treatments to patient
expectancies, 459–462

cultural moderators of treatment effects, 456–457
  loss of face, 459
  somatization, 457–459
defining, 450
future research directions, 462
limited empirical support for treatments, 453–456
  acupuncture/meditation, 455
  cognitive-behavioral interventions, 453–454
  conclusions, 455–456
  pharmacotherapy, 454–455
  play therapy, 45
relevance of psychotherapy for Asian Americans, 450–453
optimal theory overview, 452 (tab)
therapist-patient ethnic match, 456
Enculturation, defining, 142, 143
English language proficiency, 98, 170, 234–235, 253
English Only initiative, 289
ESS program, 434–435
Ethnic identity, 34–36, 126–127
  acculturation and, 421–422
  across individuals/situations, 132–134
  American identity, 128–130
  Asian American identity, 131–132
  Asian ethnic identity, 126–130
  relationships between Asian/American identities, 130–131
Ethnicity, influence on health, 305–306
European American Values Scale for Asian Americans (EAVS-AA), 149
European American Values Scale for Asian Americans-Revised (EAVS-AA-R), 149–150
European Americans
  academic achievement, 109–110, 111, 113
  alexithymia in, 458–459
European Americans vs. Asian Americans
  academic achievement, 113, 114
  career choice, influences on, 163–164
  career development and, 163–166
  occupational status, 164
  personality variables, 165
  social anxiety, 165
  work adjustment/vocational problems, 166–167
  work values, 161–162, 162

Evaluating measurement invariance, 58–61
Executive Order 9066, 346
Expectancy theory, 451
Exploratory factor analysis, 145

Face, loss of, 31, 167–168, 294–295, 457, 459
Face-giving, 294
Familism, 72
Family adaptation process, 71
Family interdependence, 71–72, 72, 235
Family life cycle issues, 74–81
  education/occupational pathways, 78–80
  language acquisition, 77–78
  marriage/marital satisfaction, 74–75
  older adults, 80–81
  parenting styles/practices, 75–76
  sibling relationships, 76–77
  socialization of identity/gender roles, 77
Family obligation, 72
Family resistance resources, 71
Family type, 71
Family violence
  child physical abuse, 369–373, 370–372
    context in Asian American communities
    child rearing, 370–371
    immigrant family, 371–372
    emerging research on, 372–373
    implications on research for practice, 373
    scope/significance in general population, 369
    victimization rates, 369–370
  future research directions, 373–374
  intimate partner violence, 364–369
    among Asian Americans, 364–366
    context in Asian American communities, 366–367
    immigration/acculturative stress, 366–367
    patriarchal ideology, 367–368
    emerging research, 368–369
    scope/significance in general population, 364
Fear of Negative Evaluation Questionnaire, 424
Fellows Committee, of AAPA
Female standard of beauty, 187

Filial piety, 21, 40, 72, 80, 148, 167, 169, 200, 220, 235, 249, 275, 324, 327, 371
Filipino Americans
  academic achievement, 109.110, 109–110, 111, 112, 113
  as study participants, 50
  hypertension, 311–312
  partner violence, 368
  percentage of Asian American population, 73
  values enculturation and, 148–149
Filipino immigrants
  alienation felt by students, 116
  as study participants, 50
  education, 113
  gender inequality, 77
  immigration patterns, 232
  percentage of Asian American population, 113
  school safety, 115
  work adjustment, 168
Filipino independence, 346
Filipino women, immigration patterns, 182
Fit indices, 59
FOB (fresh-off-the-boat), 117
Focus group ethnography, 50–56
Foreign student syndrome, 247
Four-fold theory of acculturation, 33

Gangs
  gender roles, 201
  immigrants/refugees, 237
  racism effects, 91
Garcia Coll's Integrative Conceptual Model, 89 (fig), 90–99
  adaptive culture creation, 93
  child characteristics effects, 94–95
  developmental competencies, 95–99
    biculturalism, 98
    cognitive development, 95
    coping with racism, 98–99
    emotional development, 97
    linguistic development, 97–98
    social development, 96–97
  family effects, 93–94
  promoting vs. inhibiting environment, 92–93
  social stratification effects, 91–92
Gender issues
  acculturation/gender roles, 202
  activated gender identity, 290
  career interests, 160
  ethnic identity, 133

gender identity, 290
gender role conflict paradigm, 202–203
health effects, 309–311, 310, 312
inequality among immigrants, 77
mental health services use, 364
risk taking, 267
roles, 52, 77, 200, 201, 275, 367
stereotype, 182–183, 185, 289
suicide rates, 398
wages, 73
work adjustment, 168
See also Asian American masculinities
Gender Role Conflict Scale (GRCS), 203
Generalized Anxiety Disorder and Major Depressive Disorder (DSM-IV), 218, 455
Generalized anxiety disorder (GAD), 455
Generation status, 40, 127, 131, 133, 141, 145
"Gentleman's Agreement," 182, 345
Geriatric Depression Scale (GDS), 217, 423
Gifted and talented education (GATE), 109
Global Assessment Scale (GAS), 430, 456
Global functioning, 386, 425
Globalization, 40, 182, 354–355
GPA, 110, 111, 112, 113
Grounded theory, 55, 56
Growth curve model, 57–58
Guamaniam American students, academic achievement, 109
Guan, 31
Guidelines for Research with Ethnic Minority Communities, 18

Haitians, academic achievement, 110
Hale Ola Ho'opakolea, 435
Hall, Christine, 14, 17–18
Hamilton Anxiety Scale, 221
Hamilton Depression Scale, 221
Harassment
interracial, 117–118
within group, 117
See also Violence
Hart Cellar Act of 1965, 107
Hawaii
parenting style of Native Hawaiians, 75
under US control, 346, 348
Hawaiian Acculturation Scale, 422
Hawaiian Americans, academic achievement, 109
Head Start, 454

Health psychology. *See* Asian Pacific Islanders, cardiovascular disease in
Hegemonic bargain, 206
Hegemonic masculinities, 205
Help-seeking, 386
Hinduism, 324
Hispanics
career interests, 159
underemployment, 167
See also Latinos
HIV, 435
Hmong Americans
academic achievement, 109
English language proficiency, 234
family demographics of, 73
Hmong immigrants
academic achievement, 73, 114
racism against students, 117
socioeconomic status of, 115
Ho, Tiffany, 16
Holocaust, Nazi, 33
Honolulu-Asia Aging Study, 219, 424
Honolulu Heart Program, 309
Hopkins Symptom checklist-25, 218
Hybrid culture, 31
Hypertension prevention/ management, 311–312

Ida, D. J., 17
Identity, 12, 34–36
acculturation process, 253–254
activated gender, 290
adoptee, 35–36
Asian American, 34–36
bicultural, 326, 452–453
Chinese American, 133
cultural, 147
gender, 77, 202–203
group, 206
international students from Asia and, 253–254
Japanese American, 127
male reference group, 204–205
multiracial, 35, 41
social identity, 205–207
third-culture, 41
White, 436
See also Ethnic identity
Identity development acculturation model, 253–254
Immigrants/refugees
cultural belief systems/mental illness, 237–238
barriers to mainstream services, 238
treatment preferences, 237–238

cultural responsive techniques for, 238–239
English proficiency, 98
immigrants *vs.* refugees, 227–228
intimate partner violence, 366–367
New Wavers, 117
overview of immigrants, 231–234
current demographics, 232–233
history, 232
intergroup/intragroup differences, 233–234
migration process, 232
premigration trauma/psychosocial adjustment, 229–231
psychopathy, 382–383
psychosocial adjustment, 234–237
changing family dynamics, 235
child-rearing practices, 235–236
English language proficiency/employment, 234–235
gangs, 237
racism, 236–237
school, 236
Southeast Asian refugees, 228–229
student alienation, 116
Immigration Act of 1924, 345–346
Immigration Act of 1965, 346
Immigration patterns, 182, 232
Immigration Regional Restriction Act, 351
Indian Americans, Asian
academic achievement, 109, 113
gender inequality, 77
occupational discrimination, 171
percentage of Asian American population, 73, 232
racism, 352–353
Indian Regional Exclusion Act, 351
Indigenous healers, 331
Individual mobility, 206–207
Individualism/collectivism, 31–32, 148, 168, 174, 185, 222, 330, 427
Indochinese Mental Health Project (IMHP), 437
Inductive analysis, 55
Inouye, Daniel, 13, 16
Institutional racism, 343
Integration, as acculturation attitude, 143
Integration strategy, 34

Integrative biopsychosocial model, 306, 308
Intergenerational conflict, 98, 141, 325–326, 332, 372, 439–440
Intergenerational living, 72, 74
International Classification of Disease, 10th Edition (ICD-10), 386
International students
  adjustment theory/research, 250–255
  culture-learning model, 251, 252–253
  identity development/ acculturation model, 253–254
  recuperation model, 250–251
  social support model, 251–253
  sociopsychological adjustment/coping model, 254–255
  common stressors for, 248–250
  academic difficulties, 249
  personal/vocational concerns, 249
  sociocultural issues, 249–250
  counseling, 255–257
  culture shock, 247, 248
  defining population, 246
  foreign student syndrome, 247
  further research, 257–258
  profile, 246–247
  Internment, 33, 329
Interracial marriage, 186, 283, 341, 351
Intimate partner violence
  Asian American, 364–366
  community context of, 366–367
  immigration/acculturative stress, 366–367
  patriarchal ideology, 367–368
  emerging research on, 368–369
  scope/significance in general population, 364
Item response function (IRF), 60
Item response theory (IRT), 59–61
Iwamasa, Gayle, 18

Ja, Davis, 12
Japan bashing, 350–351
Japanese, child emotional maturity expectations, 97
Japanese Americans
  academic achievement, 109–110, 111, 113
  as hate crime victims, 330
  cardiovascular disease in men, 309
  career interests, 160–161
  cultural values, 92
  identity, 127

internment during WWII, 348–351, 359–361
mental illness, 433–434
older adults, 217, 218, 219, 221, 222
psychological service use among, 152
self-efficacy, 293–294
sexuality, 188
social anxiety, 165
values enculturation, 148–149
Japanese immigrants
  academic achievement, 113
  immigration patterns, 232
  percentage of Asian American population, 113, 232
Japanese women immigrants
  family violence, 365
  immigration patterns, 182
Journal of Social Issues, 14
Journal of the Asian American Psychological Association, 14, 16

Kazama, Rod, 12
Khmer, underachievement by, 92
Kim, Irene, 19
Kinsey, David, 20
Kitanao, Harry, 14
Korea, child rearing in, 75–76
Korean adoptees, 41
Korean Americans
  academic achievement, 109–110, 111, 113
  depression in, 396–397
  education, and 109
  English language proficiency, 234
  family affect on career development, 171
  intergroup tension with African Americans, 109
  mental illness, 76–77, 433–434
  occupational status, 164
  older adults, 73, 215, 217
  percentage of Asian American population, 73
  psychological service use, 152, 153
  sibling relationships, 76–77
  tobacco use among men, 219
  values enculturation, 148–149
Korean immigrants
  education, 113
  immigration patterns, 232
  parenting, 371, 372
  percentage of Asian American population, 113
  work adjustment, 168
Korean women immigrants
  family violence, 365, 366, 367
  immigration patterns, 182

Language acquisition, 77–78,
language proficiency, English, 98, 170, 234–235, 253
Latino immigrant students, 116
Latinos
  academic achievement, 107, 113
  See also Mexican Americans; Mexican immigrants
Lau v. Nichols, 106
Leadership/career advancement/social competence
  career advancement difficulties, 284–285
  defining leader, 287–288
  leadership paradox, 286–287
  racism/discrimination effects, 288–291
  skill deficits in interpersonal qualities, 291–292
  social skills/behaviors related to agency, 285–286
  underrepresentation, 284–285
  Western-based social competence, 292–295
  conflict negotiation/loss of face, 294–295
  emotional expressivity/moderation/ constraint, 292
  extraversion/assertiveness and face concerns, 292–294
  self-enhancement/ -criticism, 295
Leadership coercion, 294
Leadership paradox, 286–287
Legislation, anti-Asian, 345–346
  Chinese Exclusion Act of 1882, 345
  early years, 345
  Executive Order 9066, 346
  Filipino independence, 346
  "Gentleman's Agreement," 345
  Immigration Act, 1965
  Immigration Act of 1924, 345–346
  Magnuson Act, 346
  McCarran-Walter act, 346
  Refugee Act of 1953
  timeline for, 347 (fig)
  Truman's proclamation, 346
Leong, Frederick, 16, 18, 19, 20
Lin, J.-C. Gisela, 18
Loatian Americans
  academic achievement, 109
  English language proficiency, 234
  family demographics, 73
Loatian immigrants

percentage of Asian American population, 113
socioeconomic status, 115
underachievement by, 92
Loatian refugees, school safety, 115
Loatians, beliefs, 238
Loss of Face (LOF), 149, 276
Lowland Laotians refugees, older adults, 220

Magnuson Act, 346
Male reference group identity, 204–205
Male Reference Group Identity Dependence (MRGID) theory, 204–205
Male Role Norms Inventory (MRNI), 203
Marginalization, as acculturation attitude, 143
Marriage, interracial, 186, 283, 351
Marriage/marital satisfaction, 74–75
Marsella, Anthony, 20
Masculine ideology theory, 203–204
Matsunaga, Spark, 16
McCarran-Walter Act, 346
Means and covariance structure analysis, 58–59
Measurement invariance, 58–61
Men
    face issues, 167–168
    racial self-hatred, 289
    tobacco use among, 219
    See also Asian American masculinities
Mental health. *See* Psychopathology, among Asian Americans
Mental health services
    Anglo/Asian American use, 384–385
    culturally responsive, 428–429, 433–435
    culture-specific treatment models, 437–438
    gender difference in use, 364
    immigrants, 238
    service delivery, 432–437
    underuse, 328, 330, 384, 386, 430–431
    underuse by ethnic minority, 414
    use of public, 431
    See also Counseling/ psychotherapy
Mexican Americans
    academic achievement, 111–112, 114, 115, 130
    acculturation, 145
Mexican immigrants

acculturation, 145
illegal, 353
immigrant paradox, 383
political climate toward, 353
school safety, 115
Minnesota Multiphasic Personality Inventory (MMPI), 59, 165, 275–276, 383, 423
Model minority stereotype, 33, 106, 107, 118–119, 328–329, 344
Modesty/shame, 33
Morishima, James, 20–21
Morita therapy, 221
Multidimensional assessment, 415–416
Multigroup Ethnic Identity Measure (MEIM), 165
Multiple migration pattern, 40
Multiple minority, 184–185
Multiracial Asian Americans, 23, 36, 41, 356
Multiracial/multiethnic Asian Americans, 41
Muslims, 351
Mutual aid organization, 92
My Vocational Situation, 163
Myers, Lewis, Parker-Dominguez model, 306, 308

NAEP, 78, 108–109, 110
National Asian American Pacific Islander Mental Health Association (NAAPIMHA), 17
National Asian American Psychology Training Conference, 16
National Conference for Increasing Roles of Culturally Diverse People in Psychology, 13
National Crime Victimization Survey, 364
National Institute of Mental Health (NIMH), 12, 13, 16, 21
National Latino and Asian American Study (NLAAS), 368, 384
National Multicultural Summit and Conference, 18
National Violence Against Women Survey, 364
Native Americans, academic achievement, 107, 108, 110, 111, 112, 113
Native Hawaiians
    educational attainment, 78
    traditional therapies, 435
NELS:88, 109–110, 116
Neurasthenia, 237, 386–387
Neuropsychological measures, 424–425

New Wavers, 117
Nicaraguans, academic achievement, 110
Nisei, cultural values of, 31–32

Occupational Values Scale, 162
Ohio Work Values Inventory (OWVI), 161
Okura, K. Patrick, 16, 17
Okura, Lily, 17
Okura Mental Health Leadership Foundation, 17
Older adults. *See* Asian American older adults
Omnibus Personality Inventory (OPI), 160, 165, 276
Operation Mango, 49–50
Outmarriage, 41
    See also Interracial marriage
Outsourcing, racism and, 354–355

Pacific Islander families. *See* Asian American and Pacific Islander families
Pacific Islander older adults, family life cycle issues, 80–81
Pakistani immigrants, academic achievement, 113, 114
Parent-child relationship, 96
Parenting, authoritative/ authoritarian, 31, 75–76, 96
Parsimony, 59
Participant-observation, 53–54
Patriarchal ideology, 200, 367–368
Peabody Picture Vocabulary Test-Revised, 425
Peer counselors, authoritative/collaborative, 153–154, 255
Peer harassment, 115
Peer relations, 96–97
Penn State Worry Questionnaire (PSWQ), 218
People of Color Racial Identity Attitudes Scale (POCRIAS), 203
Personality structure hypothesis, 165
Personality traits, Asian Americans
    cultural values/practices, 275–276
    defining personality, 265–266
    Eastern culture affect on, 274–275
    key traits, 267–273
    cognitive style, 270
    empathy, 272
    locus of control, 271–272
    risk taking, 267–270
    self-control, 272–273
    sexuality, 271

summary, 268 (tab)–269 (tab)
research needs, 273–274
research sources, 275–276
research trends, 266 (fig)
*Personnel and Guidance
    Journal,* 14
Physical activity, inadequate, 311
Physical aging, 215
Physical control, 370, 371
    See also Family violence
Population, Asian American
    overall, 1
    youth, 87–88
Population, immigrants,
    232–233
Post-traumatic stress disorder
    (PTSD), 186, 455
Power analysis, 59
Prejudice, defining, 343
President's Commission on Mental
    Health, 13
Primary Care and Mental Health
    Services Bridge Program,
    437–438
Psychological acculturation, 142
Psychological aging, 215–216
Psychological segregation, 91
Psychopathology
    cultural effects on, 380
    culture effects on somatization,
        380–381
    See also Psychopathology,
        among Asian Americans
Psychopathology, among Asian
    Americans
    future research directions,
        399–400
    prevalence/correlates, 386
    adult depressive disorders
    MDD diagnosis of,
        392, 394–396,
        394(tab)–395 (tab)
    symptoms of, 392,
        393 (tab)–394 (tab)
    anxiety disorders, 387
    conclusions about depressive
        disorders, 398–399
    elderly depressive disorders,
        397–397
    MDD diagnosis, 396, 397 (tab)
    symptoms of, 396, 397 (tab)
    major depressive disorders,
        388–399
    neurasthenia, 386–387
    schizophrenia-spectrum
        disorders, 387–388
    suicide, 398
    youth depressive disorders,
        389–392
    MDD diagnosis of, 389, 391
        (tab)–392

symptoms of, 388–389, 390 (tab)
    prevalence/manifestation
    "Asian American" classification
        effect on, 383
    diagnostic measures effects on, 383
    immigration effects on, 382–383
    in Asian countries, 382
    mental health service utilization
        studies and, 384–386,
        385 (tab)
Psychotherapy. *See*
    Counseling/psychotherapy
Psychotherapy process research,
    435–437
Puerto Ricans, academic
    achievement, 111
Punjabi students, racism
    against, 117

Qualitative research, defining,
    50–51
Qualitative research, focus group
    ethnography, 50–56
    analyzing qualitative data, 54–55
    defining ethnography, 53
    focus groups, 51–53
    observation, 54
    researcher levels
        of immersion, 53–54
    writing field notes, 54–66
Quantitative research, 56–61
    evaluating measurement
        invariance, 58–61
    growth curve models, 57–58
    item response theory, 59–61
    means and covariance structure
        analysis, 58–59
    random effects regression
        models, 56–57

Race
    as scientific concept, 37
    Asian as, 30
    influence on health, 305–306,
        312–313
Race-Related Stressor Scale, 33
Racial/Cultural Identity
    Development (R/CID)
    model, 34–35
Racial profiling, 115
Racial socialization, 94, 99
Racial triangulation theory, 41–42
Racism
    against Asian immigrants/
        refugees, 236–237
    against South Asians/South
        Asian Americans, 351–355
    as stressful, 329–330
    careers, 288–291
    defining, 343
    future research, 355–356

gang involvement and, 91
    institutional, 343
    intergroup relations and, 118
    internalized, 343
    symbolic, 288–289
    See also Racism, against
        Asian/Pacific Island
        Americans
Racism, against Asian/Pacific
    Island Americans, 344–351
    anti-Asian law, 345–346
    Chinese Exclusion Act
        of 1882, 345
    early years, 345
    Executive Order 9066, 346
    Filipino independence, 346
    "Gentleman's Agreement," 345
    Immigration Act of 1924,
        345–346
    Immigration Act of 1965, 346
    Magnuson Act, 346
    McCarran-Walter Act, 346
    Refugee Act of 1953
    timeline for, 347 (fig)
    Truman's proclamation, 346
    Hawaii under US control,
        346, 348
    Japanese American internment
        during WWII, 348–351,
        359–361
Ralph, James, 16
Random effects regression models,
    56–57
Rasch model, 148
Reagan, Ronald, 289
Recuperation model, 250–251
Recuperation models, 250–251
Reductionism, 38
Reference Group Identity
    Dependency Scale
    (RGIDS), 204
Refugee Act of 1953
Refugees. *See* Immigrants/refugees
Rejection-identification model, 41
Relational orientation, 71–72
Research, AAPA survey for
    forecasting future of, 21–27
    method, 21–22
    results/discussion, 22–23
    social/organizational issues,
        23–24, 26 (tab)–27 (tab)
    theory/research/practice issues,
        23, 24 (tab)
    training/preparation issues, 23,
        25 (tab)
Residential segregation, 91
Resilience, risk/protective factors
    for, 70–71
Resiliency Model of Family Stress,
    Adjustment, and Adaptation,
    70–71

Samoan Americans, academic achievement, 109
Samoan immigrants, work adjustment, 168
Scholastic Aptitude Test (SAT) 159
School and College Ability Test (SCAT), 160
Segregation
  economic, 91
  occupational, 172–173
  psychological, 91
  residential, 91
  social/psychological, 91
Self-criticism, 295
Self-enhancement, 295
Self-report measures, 421–424
Separation, as acculturation attitude, 143
Sex-role behaviors, 328
Sexuality, 188, 271
Shame, 23, 31, 33, 80–82, 168, 188–189, 190, 191, 211, 221, 235, 276, 294, 315, 328, 332, 350, 367, 371, 373, 381, 435, 459, 461
Sibling relationships, 76–77
Sikh community, 353
Smith, Brewster, 13
Social Avoidance and Distress Scale, 424
Social Cognitive Career Theory (SCCT), 148, 163, 166
Social competence. See Leadership/career advancement/social competence
Social competition, 207
Social creativity, 207
Social Group Identity Theory, 205–206
Social identity theory, 41, 205–207, 207
  individual mobility, 206–207
  social competition, 207
  social creativity, 207
Social isolation, 366–367
Social segregation, 91
Social support, 251–253, 309–310
Society for the Psychological Study of Social Issues (SPSSI), 12
Socioeconomic status (SES), 73, 312
Sociopsychological adjustment/coping model, 254–255
South Asian American students, academic achievement, 109–110

South Asian immigrants
  educational and, 78, 115
  older adults, 80, 216
  socioeconomic status of, 115
  youth and racism, 98–99
South Asian women, immigration patterns, 182
Southeast Asian Americans
  academic achievement, 109–110, 111
  education/occupational status, 73
  older adults, 109
Southeast Asian immigrants/refugees, 228–229
  school safety, 115
  work adjustment, 168–170
Southeast Asian women, immigration patterns of, 182
Southeast Asians
  academic achievement, 78, 114
  cultural notions of masculinity, 200–201
  tobacco use among, 310
Spheres of Control Scale, 165
Standards for Educational Psychological Testing, 419–420
Status inconsistency theory, 366
Stereotype
  Asian American, 36
  defining, 342–343
  effect on workplace performance, 289–291
  gender, 182–183, 185, 289
  internalized, 117
  occupational, 167, 171–172
  stereotype threat, 289–290
Strain theory, masculinities and, 201–202
Strasburger, Fred, 14
Stress/coping
  acculturative, 144
  Asian American cultural values effect on stress, 324–325
  Asian Pacific Islanders, cardiovascular disease in, 309
  coping from Asian American perspective, 330–333
  familial support, 331–332
  indigenous healers, 331
  religious/spiritual support, 333
  social support and, 332
  cultural affects on stress, 324
  types of stressors, 325–330
  acculturative stress, 325
  cultural conflict/bicultural identity, 326
  familial/intergenerational, 325–326

model minority, 328–329
racism/discrimination, 329–330
Strong factorial invariance, 59
Strong Vocational Interest Blank (SVIB), 160
Substance Abuse and Mental Health Services Administration (SAMHSA), 16
Sue, David, 14
Sue, Derald W., 11–12, 13, 14, 20
Sue, Stanley, 11–12, 13–14, 16, 18, 20–21
Suicide, 398
Suinn, Richard, 145
Suinn-Lew Asian Self-Identity Acculturation Scale (SL-ASIA), 145–146, 147, 151, 152, 161, 421–422
Symbolic racism, 288–289
Symptom Check List 90-Revised, 458
Symptom Check List (SCL-30), 432

Taiwan Aboriginal Acculturation Scale, 422
Taiwanese American older adults, 217
Taiwanese international students, 436
Tanaka, Jeffrey S., 16
Taoism, 324
Tape v. Hurley, 106
Terrorist attacks, on U.S., 351, 353
Therapist-patient ethnic match, 456
Therapy. *See* Empirically supported therapies, for Asian Americans
Thick description, 54–55
Third-culture identification, 41
Time limited dynamic psychotherapy (TLDP), 153–154
Tobacco use, 218–219
Traditional Culture Identification (TCI) index, 145
Traditional healing, 238, 452
Trauma
  Asian American women and, 186
  post-traumatic stress disorder, 186, 455
Treatment of Depression Collaborative Research (TDCRP), 451
Triple stigma, 184–185
True, Reiko, 13, 18
Truman's proclamation, 346

U-Curve theory, 251
U.S. Civil Rights Commission, 18

Values
conflict between Asian/
Western, 12
work, 161–162
See also Collectivism;
Collectivism/Individualism;
Filial piety; Physical
control; Shame
Values enculturation, 148–149,
152–155
Vietnam War veterans, Asian
American, 33
Vietnamese, tobacco use
among, 310
Vietnamese Americans
academic achievement, 100, 109
English language
proficiency, 234
hypertension, 312
occupational status, 164
older adults, 215
partner violence, 368
percentage of Asian American
population, 73
sibling relationships, 76–77
Vietnamese immigrants
masculinity, cultural notions and
youth, 201
percentage of Asian American
population, 113, 232
school safety and, 115–116
Vietnamese refugees
English language
proficiency, 170
family stress, 325
older adults, 220

Vietnamese women, 325
Vietnamese women immigrants,
family violence and, 366
Violence
against Asian Americans, 352
See also Family violence, among
Asian Americans
Vocational behaviors, Asian
Americans. *See* Career
development/vocational
behaviors, Asian Americans

W-Curve theory, 251
Wagner, Ned, 14
Weak factorial invariance,
58–59
Wechsler Adult Intelligence
Scale-Revised for China
(WAIS-RC), 424
Wechsler Adult Intelligence
Scale-Revised (WAIS-R), 424
Wechsler-Bellevue Intelligence
Scale (WBIS), 424
West Indians, academic
achievement, 110
Western Asian students, academic
achievement, 109–110
Western Cultural Identification
(WCI) index, 145
White Americans
academic achievement, 107, 108,
111, 112, 113
career interests, 159, 161
masculine ideology, 203
student alienation, 116
teacher/peer relationships, 116

underemployment, 167
See also Anglo Americans;
European Americans
White flight, 115
White identity, 436
"White-washed," 117
Women. *See* Asian American
masculinities; Asian American
women
Wong, Herbert Z., 13, 17
Wong, Martin R., 16
World Mental Health-Composite
International Diagnostic
Interview, 382
Worry Scale-Revised (WSR), 218

Yee, Albert H., 16
Yellow hordes/yellow peril,
106, 107
Youth
acculturation and, 53–55
career interests of students, 159
cultural notions of masculinity
and, 200–201
depressive disorders, 389–392
growth in Asian American
population, 87–88
South Asian immigrants/racism,
98–99
underuse of mental health
services, 386, 431
See also Academic achievement;
International students

Zane, Nolan, 17
Zen Buddhism, 324

ABOUT THE EDITORS

Frederick T. L. Leong is Professor of Psychology at Michigan State University (MSU). Before coming to MSU, he was on the faculty at Southern Illinois University (1988–1991), The Ohio State University (1991–2003), and University of Tennessee (2003–2006). He obtained his Ph.D. from the University of Maryland with a double specialty in counseling and industrial/organizational psychology. He has authored or coauthored more than 100 articles in various counseling and psychology journals and 45 book chapters and has edited or coedited six books and two encyclopedias. Dr. Leong is a fellow of the American Psychological Association (APA) (Divisions 1, 2, 17, 45, and 52) and the American Psychological Society. He is the recipient of the 1998 Distinguished Contributions Award from the Asian American Psychological Association and the 1999 John Holland Award from the APA Division of Counseling Psychology. His major research interests are in cross-cultural psychology (particularly culture and mental health and cross-cultural psychotherapy), vocational psychology (career development of ethnic minorities), and organizational behavior. He is a past President of the Asian American Psychological Association and President of the Division of Counseling Psychology of the International Association of Applied Psychology. He is also President-Elect of the APA's Division 45 (Society for the Psychological Study of Ethnic Minority Issues). His latest project is the *Sage Encyclopedia of Counseling* for which he is the editor in chief.

Arpana G. Inman is Assistant Professor in the Counseling Psychology Program at Lehigh University, Pennsylvania. She received her Ph.D. in counseling psychology from Temple University. Her research interests are in the areas of Asian American–South Asian psychology and multicultural competencies. Specifically, these interests span several topics, including understanding acculturative experiences along generational lines, cultural conflicts and identity, the impact of culture on help-seeking behaviors, and supervision and training. She has presented nationally and internationally at several conferences and published in these different areas. Dr. Inman is also the recipient of the 2002 Jeffrey S. Tanaka Memorial Dissertation Award in Psychology, American Psychological Association Committee on Ethnic Minority Affairs. She cofounded a Listserv and a Web site for South Asian concerns called South Asian Psychological Networking Association (SAPNA). Dr. Inman was the cochair for the Division on Women (2002–2003) and Vice President (2003–2005) of the Asian American Psychological Association. She is currently Vice President of the Asian American Pacific Islander Special Interest Group in the Association for Multicultural Counseling and Development.

Angela Ebreo is Assistant Director for Research at the Institute for Research on Race and Public Policy, University of Illinois at Chicago (UIC), where she coordinates the institute's Asian American Initiatives and assists with several other research activities including the Race and Ethnic Disparities in Health Initiative. Before her appointment at UIC, she was a postdoctoral fellow in the Department of Behavioral Science, University of Kentucky College of Medicine. Dr. Ebreo received her Ph.D. in social psychology from the University of Illinois at Urbana-Champaign. Dr. Ebreo is a member of the American Psychological Association (Divisions 9, 27, 38, and 45) and the American Public Health Association. She served on the executive committee of the Asian American Psychological Association (2002–2004) and currently serves as the association's membership officer. Her research interests include cultural differences in social support and health maintenance, campus-community collaborative research, and culturally sensitive research methodology.

Lawrence Hsin Yang is Assistant Professor in the Department of Epidemiology at the School of Public Health at Columbia University. Dr. Yang received his B.A. in psychology from Wesleyan University (Middletown, CT) and graduated Phi Beta Kappa with high honors in psychology. He received his Ph.D. from Boston University with a specialization in clinical psychology, completing his clinical internship at Massachusetts Mental Health Center/Harvard Medical School. He has received multiple fellowships during his graduate career, including the American Psychological Association (APA) Clinical Minority Fellowship, the Presidential University Fellowship (Boston University), and the Rosenblum Fellowship (Massachusetts Psychological Association). Dr. Yang received the National Security Education Plan–Graduate International Fellowship to study schizophrenia in families in Beijing, China (1998–2000). He received two outstanding dissertation awards from the APA for this work and has published the major results in the *Journal of Abnormal Psychology*. He has authored or coauthored more than a dozen peer-reviewed articles in various psychology and psychiatry journals. He recently received a five-year mentored research scientist award (K-01) from the National Institute of Mental Health to examine how sociocultural factors—in particular, family environment and stigma—relate to course of schizophrenia in Chinese immigrant populations. He also served on the board of directors of the Asian American Psychological Association (2003–2005).

Lisa M. Kinoshita is Social Science Research Associate in the Department of Psychiatry and Behavioral Sciences at Stanford University School of Medicine. Her research focuses on risk factors related to memory impairment in older adults. Before her appointment at Stanford, Dr. Kinoshita received her Ph.D. in clinical psychology from Pacific Graduate School of Psychology and completed her clinical psychology internship at the Veterans Affairs (VA) Palo Alto Health Care System where she received extensive training in clinical geropsychology, neuropsychological assessment, and Asian American psychology. Dr. Kinoshita was the first postdoctoral fellow in dementia research with the Mental Illness Research, Education and Clinical Center (MIRECC) at the VA Palo Alto Health Care System. As a fellow, she pursued additional training in neuropsychological assessment with older adults and began conducting research on culture-fair memory assessments, in particular with Japanese and Chinese elders. Dr. Kinoshita has published a number of articles and book chapters that focus on cultural diversity within a clinical setting. She recently published an article on the influence of traditional Japanese cultural beliefs on Japanese American dementia caregiving. She also coauthored a book chapter on practicing cognitive-behavioral therapy with culturally diverse older adults. Dr. Kinoshita is the past Secretary-Historian (2001–2003) and a current board member of the Asian American Psychological Association.

Michi Fu is a licensed clinical psychologist in the states of Hawaii and California. She has a private practice and is a supervising psychologist at the Asian Pacific Family Center (APFC) of Pacific Clinics in Rosemead, California. Before joining APFC, she was a psychologist working at the Counseling and Student Development Center at the University of Hawaii (2000–2004) and the Sex Abuse Treatment Center at Kapiolani Medical Center for Women and Children (2002–2004). She received her Ph.D. from the California School of Professional Psychology at Alliant International University in Los Angeles, California, with an emphasis in multicultural community clinical psychology. She has authored a chapter on play therapy with Asian Americans, and her dissertation examined the relationship between acculturation, ethnic identity, and family conflict among Chinese Americans. She was an Okura Mental Health Leadership Fellow in 2002. Her research interests are ethnic identity, acculturation, interracial relationships, and women's issues among Asian Americans. She is a past board member of the Asian American Psychological Association (AAPA) (1998–2000, 2003–2005). She is currently serving on the AAPA's Executive Task Force for Social Justice and Advocacy and the Mentoring Committee of the American Psychological Association (Division 12, Section 6).

ABOUT THE CONTRIBUTORS

Jolynne D. Andal (Ph.D., Clinical Psychology, Illinois Institute of Psychology at the Illinois Institute of Technology, 2001) is a research scientist at the National Opinion Research Center (NORC) at the University of Chicago, where she is involved in policy research in the areas of education and substance abuse, mental health, and criminal justice. She has also been involved in child clinical psychology research, including in the areas of autism and Down syndrome, as well as community research work in the Chicago Filipino community. Her current interests are focused on meeting the educational needs of minority and underserved children and improving mental health services to minority communities.

Fred Bemak (Ed.D., University of Massachusetts at Amherst, 1975) is Professor of Counseling and Development and Director of the Diversity Research and Action Center at George Mason University. His research interests are in cross-cultural counseling, youth and families identified as being at-risk, refugee and immigrant mental health, group counseling, and social justice. He is coauthor of a number of books, including *Counseling Refugees: A Psychosocial Approach to Innovative Multicultural Interventions,* and has lectured, offered seminars, and provided consultation in more than 30 countries and throughout the United States.

Doris F. Chang (Ph.D., Clinical Psychology, University of California, Los Angeles, 2000) is Assistant Professor of Psychology at the New School for Social Research. Grounded in an interdisciplinary framework, her research and clinical interests include cross-cultural issues in diagnosis and mental health treatment, the cultural contexts of domestic violence and service delivery in Asian immigrant communities, and mental health care in the People's Republic of China. Dr. Chang completed postdoctoral training at the Department of Social Medicine, Harvard Medical School in clinically relevant medical anthropology.

Edward C. Chang (Ph.D., State University of New York at Stony Brook) is Associate Professor of Clinical Psychology and Faculty Associate in Asian/Pacific Islander American Studies at the University of Michigan, Ann Arbor. He received his B.A. in psychology and philosophy from the State University of New York at Buffalo and his M.A. from the State University of New York at Stony Brook. He completed his APA-accredited clinical internship at Bellevue Hospital Center–New York University Medical Center. He serves as an associate editor of the *Journal of Social and Clinical Psychology* and *Cognitive Therapy and Research* and is on the editorial boards of several leading journals, including the *Journal of Personality and Social Psychology* and the *Asian Journal of Social Psychology*. He has published numerous works on optimism and pessimism, perfectionism, social problem solving, and cultural influences on behavior. Dr. Chang is the editor of *Optimism and Pessimism: Implications for Theory, Research, and Practice* (2001) and *Self-Criticism and Self-Enhancement: Theory, Research, and Clinical Implications* (forthcoming) and is a coeditor of *Virtue, Vice, and Personality: The Complexity of Behavior* (2003), *Social Problem Solving: Theory, Research, and Training* (2004), and *Judgments Over Time: The Interplay of Thoughts, Feelings, and Behaviors* (2006). He is currently working on a book that takes a critical look at adaptive and maladaptive perfectionism (forthcoming, Oxford University Press) and an edited handbook that examines adult psychopathology in Asians (forthcoming, Oxford University Press).

Rita Chang is a student in the Graduate Program in Clinical Psychology at the University of Michigan, Ann Arbor. She received a B.A. in psychology and English from Northwestern University and is currently doing research on adaptive and maladaptive aspects of socially prescribed perfectionism and their relation to depressive symptoms in Asian American populations.

Tai Chang (Ph.D., Clinical/Community Psychology, University of Illinois at Urbana-Champaign, 1999) is Assistant Professor at the California School of Professional Psychology, San Francisco Bay, Alliant International University. He is interested in variations in acculturation and identity within individuals and across social contexts, particularly among Asian Americans. He also is interested in the interface of counseling and the Internet, including online support, mutual help, and self-help.

Ruth Chao (Ph.D., University of California, Los Angeles, 1992) is Associate Professor in the Department of Psychology at the University of California, Riverside. She received her B.A. from University of California, Irvine. Formerly, Dr. Chao was Assistant Professor in the Department of Child and Families Studies at Syracuse University. Her research interests include sociocultural perspectives of parenting and the family, focusing on Asian immigrants. She is currently conducting a five-year, longitudinal study, funded by the National Institutes of Health, examining the effects of parental control, warmth, and parental involvement in school on adolescents' school performance and behavioral adjustment. Her research also includes studies of the language acculturation of Asian immigrant families across time and its effects on adolescents' adjustment.

Sapna Cheryan is a graduate student in social psychology at Stanford University. She received her B.A. in psychology and American studies from Northwestern University. Her research examines the strategies people use when their sense of belonging to social groups is threatened. She has studied this phenomenon in Asian Americans, who are perceived as being less American than their peers, and she is currently examining the phenomenon in female engineers.

Joyce P. Chu (Ph.D., Clinical Psychology, University of Michigan, 2005) is a Clinical Psychology Fellow at the University of California, San Francisco. She received her B.A. and M.A. in psychology from Stanford University. Her research interests are in the areas of Asian American mental health with a focus on depression, coping, and service delivery. Broadly, her research examines the consequences of emotion inhibition—an influential cultural element for Asian Americans—on the mental illness experience and service delivery perspective. This work has spanned basic research examining coping strategies as differentially adaptive, to clinical research focusing on development of empirically supported psychotherapy treatment options for Asian Americans. Dr. Chu has received awards including the American Psychological Association (APA) Minority Fellowship and the Asian American Psychological Association (AAPA) Dissertation Award.

Kevin M. Chun (Ph.D., Clinical Psychology, University of California, Los Angeles) is Associate Professor of Psychology and Asian American Studies at the University of San Francisco. His research focuses on family acculturation processes and their relation to health and psychosocial adjustment. Currently, Dr. Chun is collaborating with a UCSF colleague on a study funded by the National Institutes of Health that examines cultural issues in disease management and acculturation for Chinese Americans with type 2 diabetes and their families. Dr. Chun's publications include *Acculturation: Advances in Theory, Measurement, and Applied Research* and the forthcoming textbook, *Psychology of Ethnic Groups in the U.S.,* with coauthors Professors Pamela Balls Organista and Gerardo Marín. He also is a contributing author to a number of scholarly publications, including *Handbook of Asian American Psychology* (1st ed.), *Handbook of Racial & Ethnic Minority Psychology,* and *Acculturation and Parent-Child Relationships: Measurement and Development.*

Rita Chi-Ying Chung (Ph.D., Victoria University of Wellington, New Zealand, 1989) is Associate Professor in the Counseling and Development Program in the College of Education and Human Development at George Mason University. Her research focuses on social justice and multiculturalism in the areas of psychosocial adjustment of Asian refugees and immigrants, interethnic group relations and racial stereotypes, trafficking of Asian girls, cross-cultural and multicultural issues in mental health, and cross-cultural achievement motivation and aspirations. She is coauthor of the book *Counseling Refugees: A Psychosocial Approach to Innovative Multicultural Interventions.* She has lived and worked in the Pacific Rim, Asia, and Latin America.

E. J. R. David is a doctoral student in the Clinical/Community Psychology Division at the University of Illinois at Urbana-Champaign. He received his B.A. in psychology from the University of Alaska Anchorage and his M.A. in psychology from the University of Illinois at Urbana-Champaign. His primary interest is in the psychological experiences of Filipino Americans and their mental health. Using survey and experimental methodologies, he studies the psychological processes and effects of colonization (e.g., colonial mentality) on historically colonized groups. Relatedly, he is interested in the worldwide growth of the indigenous psychology movement and postcolonial psychology. He is currently serving as a student editor of the journal *Cultural Diversity & Ethnic Minority Psychology.*

Barbara D. DeBaryshe (Ph.D., Developmental Psychology, State University of New York at Stony Brook, 1987) is a developmental psychologist and Associate Specialist at the University of Hawaii Center on the Family. Her work has a dual focus on original research and application/outreach. Her research interests include the relationship between parenting practices, culturally relevant values, family problem solving, and resilient outcomes in Asian American/Pacific Islander families living in poverty. Her current outreach work involves the implementation of a culturally responsive preschool literacy and mathematics curriculum for Head Start programs in Hawaii.

Sopagna Eap is a doctoral student in clinical psychology at the University of Oregon. She received her B.A. in psychology from the University of California, Davis, in 2003. Her research interests are in culture and mental health. She has worked as a research assistant at the Asian American Mental Health Research Center at UC Davis. She has also collaborated with Dr. Gordon Hall on several papers related to Asian American psychology. Currently, she is working with Dr. David DeGarmo at the Oregon Social Learning Center on investigating the cultural context of parenting and families.

Angela Ebreo (see entry in **About the Editors** section)

Michi Fu (see entry in **About the Editors** section)

Arpana Gupta is a doctoral student in the Counseling Psychology Program at the University of Tennessee, Knoxville. She received her B.S. degree in biology from Edinboro University of Pennsylvania and a nuclear medicine technology certification from George Washington University in 1998. She received an M.Ed. in counseling from Wake Forest University in 2003. Her primary research interests include Asian American psychology; acculturation, adjustment, racial identity, and mental health issues within the context of multicultural counseling; and public policy related to the Asian population. Currently, she is working on a meta-analysis study with Asian Americans and other projects related to culture, ethnicity, and minority issues within the same population. She is an active student member within the Asian American Psychological Association's Division 45 and Division 17's Student Affiliate Group and Section on Ethnic and Racial Diversity.

Gordon C. Nagayama Hall (Ph.D., Clinical Psychology, Fuller Theological Seminary, 1982) is Professor of Psychology at the University of Oregon. He is editor of the journal *Cultural Diversity & Ethnic Minority Psychology* and is associate editor of the *Journal of Consulting and Clinical Psychology*. He coedited (with Sumie Okazaki) the book, *Asian American Psychology: The Science of Lives in Context*. His research, which has been supported by the National Institute of Mental Health, is on the cultural context of psychopathology.

Jeanette Hsu (Ph.D., Clinical Psychology, University of California, Berkeley, 1995) is a staff psychologist at the Veterans Affairs Palo Alto Health Care System and Training Director for the psychology internship and postdoctoral training programs. Formerly, she was Visiting Graduate Faculty at San Jose State University, Stanford University, and the Pacific Graduate School of Psychology, where she taught courses in clinical supervision, multicultural psychology, and substance abuse assessment and treatment. She is active in numerous professional associations, including the Asian American Psychological Association and Association for Women in Psychology, and she is currently serving on the board of the Association of Psychology Postdoctoral and Internship Centers (APPIC).

Larke Nahme Huang (Ph.D., Yale University, 1980) is a licensed clinical-community psychologist who is currently on special appointment as the Senior Advisor on Children in the Office of the Administrator at the Substance Abuse and Mental Health Services Administration, U.S. Dept of Health and Human Services. For the past 25 years she has worked in the field of children's mental health as a researcher, a practitioner, and faculty member. She has provided technical assistance to states and communities on building systems of care for children and families, been involved in developing national policy in behavioral health care, and established programs and services for diverse racial and ethnic populations.

Arpana G. Inman (see entry in **About the Editors** section)

Gayle Y. Iwamasa (Ph.D., Clinical Psychology, Purdue University, 1992) is Associate Professor in the Clinical-Community Psychology Program at DePaul University. Her research interests are in multicultural mental health across the life span, and she received a grant from the National Institute of Mental Health for some of this work. She is a past President of the Asian American Psychological Association and has been active in the American Psychological Association and Association for Behavioral and Cognitive Therapies. She has published numerous chapters and articles on multicultural mental health issues and is coeditor of both *Culturally Diverse Mental Health: The Challenges of Research and Resistance* (with Jeff Mio) and *Cognitive Behavioral Therapy with Culturally Diverse Populations* (with Pamela Hays). Dr. Iwamasa serves on the editorial boards of several psychology journals and is a practicing psychologist.

Debra M. Kawahara (Ph.D., Clinical Psychology, California School of Professional Psychology, 1994) is Assistant Professor in the Clinical Psychology Program at the California School of Professional Psychology, Alliant International University. Her research and professional interests include multicultural and feminist psychology, Asian American mental health, women and leadership, and multicultural competencies in clinical/counseling work. Dr. Kawahara is currently coediting a special issue of *Women & Therapy,* focusing on integrating multicultural and feminist principles in psychotherapy when working with Asian and Asian American women.

Bryan S. K. Kim (Ph.D., Counseling, Clinical, and School Psychology with Counseling Psychology emphasis, University of California, Santa Barbara, 2000) is Associate Professor in the Department of Psychology at the University of Hawai'i at Hilo. Previous to this position, he was Associate Professor in the Department of Counseling, Clinical, and School Psychology at the University of California, Santa Barbara. His research focuses on multicultural counseling process and outcome, the measurement of cultural constructs, and counselor education and supervision. He currently serves on the editorial boards of the *Journal of Counseling Psychology; Cultural Diversity & Ethnic Minority Psychology; Psychotherapy Theory, Research, Practice, and Training;* and *Measurement and Evaluation in Counseling and Development.* In 2003, he received the Early Career Award for Distinguished Contributions from the Asian American Psychological Association. In 2005, he received the ACA Research Award from the American Counseling Association and the MECD (*Measurement and Evaluation in Counseling and Development*) Journal Editor's Award from the Association for Assessment in Counseling and Education. Most recently in 2006, Dr. Kim received the Fritz and Linn Kuder Early Career Scientist/Practitioner Award from the Society of Counseling Psychology (Division 17) of the American Psychological Association.

Irene J. Kim (Ph.D., Clinical Psychology, University of California, Santa Barbara, 2001) is Assistant Professor of Psychology at the University of Notre Dame. Her primary research interests focus on culture, family processes, and the development of psychopathology or psychological well-being in diverse contexts among underserved populations. She is especially interested in cultural influences on emotion regulation and developmental psychopathology among Asian American adolescents. Her other research interests include intimate partner violence and cultural influences on beliefs surrounding the etiology and treatment of mental illness.

Su Yeong Kim (Ph.D., Human Development, University of California, Davis, 2003) is Assistant Professor in the Department of Human Ecology at the University of Texas at Austin. She studies the development of adolescents in ethnic minority and immigrant families by examining the intersection of family and cultural contexts in shaping adolescent development. She is the recipient of the Tanaka Dissertation Award from the American Psychological Association for the most outstanding research on ethnic minority psychological issues and concerns. She is also the 2001 winner of the Newman Award from the American Psychological Association for the best graduate research paper in psychology.

Lisa Kinoshita (see entry in **About the Editors** section)

Anna S. Lau (Ph.D., University of California, Los Angeles, 2000) is Assistant Professor in the Department of Psychology at the University of California, Los Angeles. She is interested in how sociocultural contexts may influence the etiology and phenomenology of child maltreatment. A major objective of her research is to inform the delivery of effective interventions to ethnic minority families and children at risk of child maltreatment. Dr. Lau's research is supported by the National Institute of Mental Health.

Richard M. Lee (Ph.D., Psychology, Virginia Commonwealth University, 1996) is Associate Professor of Psychology at the University of Minnesota, Twin Cities. He also is a faculty member in the Asian American Studies Program in the Department of American Studies. His research interests focus on the process and outcome of cultural socialization, such as ethnic identity development and acculturation-enculturation, and its relevance to mental health and well-being in Asian immigrant, U.S-born, refugee, and adoptee individuals and families.

Szu-Hui Lee (Ph.D., Counseling Psychology, The Ohio State University, 2006) received a B.A. in psychology from the University of California, Irvine, and was a psychology intern at McLean Hospital, Harvard Medical School. It is her ambition to facilitate change and transmit knowledge on the individual, group, and community levels through the integration of practice, teaching, research, and service. Her interests include multidisciplinary mental health treatment and service delivery as well as issues of diagnoses, health-seeking disparities, education/prevention, and training within the cross-cultural context. Her research has focused on the correlates between culturally salient factors and psychological well-being of people of color broadly and Asian/Asian Americans specifically. Szu-Hui is actively involved with professional organizations such as the Asian American Psychological Association and American Psychological Association (Divisions 17 and 45).

Frederick T. L. Leong (see entry in **About the Editors** section)

Paul Leung (Ph.D., Counseling Psychology, Arizona State University, 1970) is Professor in and Chair of the Department of Rehabilitation, Social Work and Addictions at the University of North Texas. He has held administrative and academic appointments at Deakin University (Victoria, Australia), the University of Illinois at Urbana-Champaign, the University of North Carolina at Chapel Hill, and the University of Arizona. Dr. Leung's interest has been related to disability and rehabilitation of diverse and underserved racial/ethnic populations. He served as editor of the *Journal of Rehabilitation* from 1987 to 1996.

Jun-chih Gisela Lin (Ph.D., Counseling Psychology, University of Massachusetts, Amherst, 1993) is a board-certified counseling psychologist and coordinator of international students counseling programs and services at the Student Counseling Service, Texas A&M University. She is a past President of the Asian American Psychological Association (2001–2003). Her research interests include international students' utilization of counseling services, developing cultural specific outreach programs, and modifying traditional counseling approaches for the culturally different.

William Ming Liu (Ph.D., Counseling Psychology, University of Maryland, 2000) is Program Director for the Counseling Psychology Program at the University of Iowa. He is the coeditor of the *Handbook of Multicultural Competencies in Counseling and Psychology* (Sage, 2003). He has also served on the editorial boards for the journals *The Counseling Psychologist, Cultural Diversity & Ethnic Minority Psychology,* and *Psychology of Men and Masculinity*. His research interests are in men of color, social class and classism, and poverty.

Hamilton I. McCubbin (Ph.D., Family Studies and Child Welfare, University of Wisconsin–Madison, 1970) is Professor/Specialist at the Center on the Family, University of Hawaii at Manoa, and Chief Executive Officer (CEO) and President of the Pacific American Foundation. Formerly, he was Chancellor and CEO of a multibillion-dollar educational trust and education system for children of Hawaiian ancestry. He has retired from his position as Professor in the Department of Human Development and Family Studies, University of Wisconsin–Madison, where he also served as Dean of the School of Human Ecology for 14 years. Dr. McCubbin has authored or coedited 16 books on family stress, coping and resilience, along with more than 100 articles and book chapters. He has served as editor or associate editor of 10 family science and family social work journals and holds copyrights to 36 family measures, which have been translated into seven languages. His current research focuses on multiethnic families, stress, coping, resilience, and well-being.

Jeffery Scott Mio (Ph.D., Clinical Psychology, University of Illinois, Chicago, 1984) is Professor in the Psychology and Sociology Department at California State Polytechnic University, Pomona, where he also serves as Director of the Master of Science in Psychology Program. His interests are in the teaching of multicultural issues, the development of allies, and how metaphors are used in political persuasion. His recent books include *Culturally Diverse Mental Health: The Challenges of Research and Resistance* (2003), which he coedited with Gayle Y. Iwamasa, and *Multicultural Psychology: Understanding Our Diverse Communities* (2006), which he coauthored with Lori Barker-Hackett and Jaydee S. Tumambing.

Osvaldo F. Morera (Ph.D., Quantitative Psychology, University of Illinois at Urbana-Champaign, 1997) is Associate Professor in the Department of Psychology at the University of Texas at El Paso. He is co-guest editing (with Robyn Dawes) a special issue in the *Journal of Behavioral Decision Making* that is dedicated to Paul Meehl. He also serves on the editorial boards of *Cultural Diversity & Ethnic Minority Psychology* and *Medical Decision Making*. His research interests are in medical decision making, health psychology, and applied psychometrics. His current research projects include the evaluation of a decision aid for informed consent discussions regarding colorectal cancer screening among Latino patients and the development of a web-based smoking cessation intervention geared toward Mexican-American female college students at the University of Texas at El Paso. His research has been funded by the National Institutes of Health and the National Institute of Mental Health.

Donna K. Nagata (Ph.D., Clinical Psychology, University of Illinois at Urbana-Champaign, 1981) is Professor of Psychology at the University of Michigan, Ann Arbor. Her research interests include the psychosocial impacts of the World War II incarceration of Japanese Americans, historical trauma, Asian American mental health, intergenerational relationships, and Asian American grandparenting. Dr. Nagata is author of the book *Legacy of Injustice: Exploring the Cross-Generational Impact of the Japanese American Internment* (1993) and has published multiple book chapters and peer-reviewed articles on the long-term effects of wartime internment on Japanese Americans. She has served on the editorial board of *Women & Therapy* and is currently a consulting editor for the journal *Cultural Diversity & Ethnic Minority Psychology*.

Ly Nguyen (Ph.D., Clinical and Community Psychology, University of Maryland, 1999) is President of Nguyen Consulting, LLC, which provides research and consultation services on issues of minority mental health and related public policy matters. Dr. Nguyen is an alumna W. K. Kellogg Scholar in Health Disparities. She also served in the U.S. House of Representatives as Legislative Assistant to Congressman

Robert C. "Bobby" Scott, working to advance federal policy in the areas of health, mental health, and women's and children's issues.

Sumie Okazaki (Ph.D., Clinical Psychology, University of California, Los Angeles, 1994) is Associate Professor of Psychology at the University of Illinois at Urbana-Champaign. Her research interests revolve around the impact of immigration, community contexts, individual differences, and racial minority status on the mental health of Asian American individuals and families. She is currently serving as an associate editor of the journal *Cultural Diversity & Ethnic Minority Psychology*.

Inna Artati Padmawidjaja (Ph.D., University of Rochester, 1999) is a postdoctoral researcher in psychology at University of California, Riverside, where she is also Project Director of the Multicultural Families and Adolescents Study. She received her M.A. in Human Development and Family Studies at the University of California, Los Angeles. Dr. Padmawidjaja's research interest is in the area of motivational and emotional development in early childhood, school age, and early adulthood and how the developmental processes as well as mental and physical health are affected by contextual factors, including intervention programs, ethnic, gender, and cultural differences. More specifically, she is interested in how parental distal variables (culturally based belief and attitude systems) can exert a powerful influence on early childhood, adolescent, and early adulthood learning behavior by shaping the direction and effectiveness of parental proximal processes (parenting practices).

Lan-Sze Pang is a graduate student in the Counseling Psychology Program at Southern Illinois University at Carbondale (SIUC). She received her B.A. degree in psychology from SIUC in 2003. Her primary research interests include adjustment issues and career development of international students, as well as cross-cultural psychology.

Frances C. Shen is a graduate student in the Counseling Psychology Program at Southern Illinois University at Carbondale (SIUC). She received her M.A. degree in counseling psychology from SIUC in 2006 and her B.A. degree in psychology from Illinois Wesleyan University in 2003. Her primary research interests include Asian and Asian American psychology, multicultural counseling, religion and spirituality issues in counseling, and international student adjustment. Currently, she is involved in research related to sexual assault/abuse in cultural contexts and training in multicultural and religion/spirituality issues.

Yukiko Shiraishi (Ph.D., Counseling Psychology, Northwestern University, 2000) is Project Director for a study on chronic fatigue syndrome following mononucleosis in adolescents in the Department of Occupational Therapy, University of Illinois at Chicago. She completed her clinical internship at Tri-City Community Mental Health Center, East Chicago, Indiana. While at Northwestern University, she was the recipient of an American Psychological Association Minority Fellowship. Her dissertation research, conducted on a multiethnic sample of students, focused on the role of attributions in coping during the transition to college. Her current research interests are in the areas of stress and physical and mental health across racial/ethnic groups.

Monica C. Skewes is a doctoral candidate in health psychology at the University of Texas at El Paso. She received her M.A. in clinical psychology from the University of Texas at El Paso and her B.A. in psychology from the University of California, Davis. She conducts research in the areas of behavior change and addictions and is committed to solving problems related to minority health disparities.

Anna Song is an advanced doctoral student in personality and social psychology at the University of California, Davis, where she also received her M.A. She received her B.A. in psychology and political science from the University of Michigan, Ann Arbor, specializing in psychological factors in leadership and conflict negotiation. Her two primary interests are methodological techniques in measuring personality and leadership characteristics "at-a-distance" and investigating how personality and culturally specific factors influence the decision-making process and the expression of leadership skills. Her research experience includes work in the field of political psychology with the Summer Institute for Political Psychology at Stanford University, the study of the history of psychology as a Mountjoy Research Fellow at the Archives for the History of American Psychology, and work with autobiographical narratives of leaders in the field of community psychology.

Kristen H. Sorocco (Ph.D., Clinical Psychology, Oklahoma State University, 2001) is Assistant Professor of Research within the Donald W. Reynolds Department of Geriatric Medicine at University of Oklahoma Health Sciences Center and a licensed psychologist. She completed her clinical internship at the Palo Alto Veterans Affairs Health Care System, where she received specialized training in geropsychology. She also received a certificate in gerontology from Oklahoma State University. Her research interests include the influence of culture on the conceptualization of mental illness and the development of effective caregiver interventions. She has written several chapters and articles focusing on cultural diversity issues.

Stanley Sue (Ph.D., University of California, Los Angeles, 1971) is Distinguished Professor of Psychology and Asian American Studies at the University of California, Davis. His research has been devoted to the study of the adjustment of, and delivery of mental health services to, culturally diverse groups. His work documented the difficulties that ethnic minority groups experience in receiving adequate mental health services and offered directions for providing culturally appropriate forms of treatment. He was a member of the planning board for the *U.S. Surgeon General's Report on Mental Health* (1999) and science editor for the *U.S. Surgeon General's Report on Mental Health: Culture, Race, and Ethnicity* (2001). He has served as an associate editor of the *American Psychologist.*

Nita Tewari (Ph.D., Counseling Psychology, Southern Illinois University at Carbondale, 2000) is a staff psychologist in the Counseling Center and Adjunct Faculty in the School of Social Sciences at the University of California, Irvine (UCI). She teaches Asian American Psychology at UCI, provides clinical services to university students, and researches and publishes in the area of Indian/South Asian American and Asian American mental health. Dr. Tewari is currently coediting *Asian American Psychology: Current Perspectives* with Alvin Alvarez. Dr. Tewari also served as a cochair and board member (2000–2003) of the Division on Women for the Asian American Psychological Association. In 2002, Dr. Tewari cofounded the South Asian Psychological Networking Association (SAPNA) and received grant monies through the Committee on Ethnic Minority Affairs of the American Psychological Association to create a Listserv, Web site, and organization founded to connect individuals interested in South Asian American mental health concerns.

Amy H. Tsai is a graduate student at the University of Michigan, Ann Arbor. She received her M.A. in clinical psychology from University of Michigan in 2005. She researches and publishes in the area of Asian American families and mental health, teaches sections for introductory psychology courses, and provides clinical services as a psychology intern at the University Center for the Child and the Family.

Jeanne L. Tsai (Ph.D., Clinical Psychology, University of California, Berkeley, 1996) is Assistant Professor of Personality Psychology at Stanford University. Her research examines how cultural ideas and practices shape basic psychological and social processes related to emotion, emotional distress, acculturation, and ethnic identity. Her research is currently funded by the National Institute on Aging, the National Institute of Mental Health, and the National Alliance for Research on Schizophrenia and Depression.

Vivian Tseng (Ph.D., Community and Developmental Psychology, New York University, 2001) is a Postdoctoral Fellow and Program Associate at the William T. Grant Foundation. She conducts research to guide the foundation's grantmaking and is involved in program activities including the development of priorities, new initiatives, and requests for proposals; review of proposals; and ongoing contact with grantees. She was formerly Assistant Professor of Psychology and Asian American Studies at California State University, Northridge. She received her B.A. at the University of California, Los Angeles. Her empirical studies focus on the role of immigration, race, and culture in youths' and their families' experiences in U.S. society. This work has been published in *Child Development, Journal of Marriage and the Family,* and the *Handbook of Parenting.* In addition, she is interested in frameworks for promoting social change and improving social settings for youth and has published this work in the *American Journal of Community Psychology.*

Yu-Wei Wang (Ph.D., Counseling Psychology, University of Missouri–Columbia, 2004) is Assistant Professor of Psychology at Southern Illinois University at Carbondale. Her research and professional interests include stress, trauma, and coping/problem solving; sexual abuse/assault recovery; and multicultural counseling and training issues. Her research articles have appeared in the *Journal of Counseling Psychology, Journal of College Student Development, Career Development Quarterly,* and *Journal of Multilingual & Multicultural Development.* In addition, she has published several book chapters on qualitative research methodology.

Ahtoy J. WonPat-Borja is a graduate student at Columbia University's Mailman School of Public Health. She received her B.A. degree in biology at Barnard College and began her research endeavors in psychiatric epidemiology by evaluating the effectiveness of mental health screening programs for adolescents. Her primary research interests include evidence-based assessment and treatment strategies for Asian American and Pacific Islander youth.

Lawrence Hsin Yang (see entry in **About the Editors** section)

Barbara W. K. Yee (aka Bobbie) (Ph.D., Developmental Psychology, University of Denver, 1982) is Professor in and Chair of the Department of Family and Consumer Sciences at the University of Hawaii at Mânoa. Her research examines how gender, health literacy, and acculturation influence health beliefs and lifestyle practices among Asians and Pacific Islanders. Dr. Yee has served on the editorial boards of the *Journals of Gerontology: Psychological Sciences, Psychology and Aging,* and *Topics of Geriatric Rehabilitation* and was guest editor for *Health Psychology* Special Issue "Behavioral and Sociocultural Perspectives on Ethnicity and Health." Dr. Yee is a Fellow of the American Psychological Association and Gerontological Society of America and serves on the Advisory Committee for the Office of Research on Women's Health at the National Institutes of Health (2006–2010).

Christine J. Yeh (Ph.D., Counseling Psychology, Stanford University 1996) is Associate Professor of Psychology and Education, Department of Counseling Psychology, University of San Francisco. She has published in the areas of Asian American ethnic identity, self, coping, and mental health. She recently received a five-year grant from the National Institute of Mental Health to investigate Asian immigrant cultural adjustment. In 2001, she received the Asian American Psychological Association's Early Career Award for Distinguished Contributions. She has served on several editorial boards, including *Journal of Counseling Psychology* and *The Counseling Psychologist.*

Jenny Kisuk Yi (Ph.D., University of Massachusetts, School of Public Health, 1992) is Associate Professor in the Department of Health and Human Performance at the University of Houston. Her B.S. and M.Ph. degrees are from the University of Minnesota. Her research and scholarly activities have focused on the influence of socio-cultural factors on preventive health care among Asian Americans. Her current project is working with Asian American communities to involve them in the Breast and Cervical Cancer Early Detection Program. Her primary teaching areas are in minority health, women's health, program evaluation, and behavioral sciences as these relate to public health. In addition to her academic and scholarly activities, she is active in professional organizations and community service. She serves on multiple local, state, and national committees involved with issues of ethnicity and health care.

Sylvia Yuen (Ph.D., Social Psychology, University of Hawaii, 1975) is Director of the Center on the Family at the University of Hawaii. Her research and professional interests focus on development over the life span and family resiliency, with special attention to Hawaii's multicultural population. She has received several awards for excellence in teaching and outstanding community service, served on the Board of Directors of the National Council on Aging and National Asian Pacific Center on Aging, and is a Fellow of the Gerontological Society of America.

Nolan Zane (Ph.D., University of Washington) is Professor of Psychology and Asian American Studies at the University of California, Davis. He also is Director of the National Research Center on Asian American Mental Health. His research has focused on specific cultural variables that influence the processes and outcomes of psychological interventions. He is interested in the development and evaluation of culturally based treatments for ethnic minority clients, change mechanisms in mental health interventions, program evaluation of substance abuse and mental health programs, and the cultural determinants of addictive behaviors. His current research examines the role of loss of face and shame in interpersonal relationships with a special focus on client and care provider interactions.